TEXT, CASES AND MATERIALS ON EQUITY AND TRUSTS

Fourth Edition

Mohamed Ramjohn

Routledge·Cavendish
Taylor & Francis Group
LONDON AND NEW YORK

First published in Great Britain in 1995 by Cavendish Publishing Limited,
The Glass House, Wharton Street, London WC1X 9PX

Fourth edition published 2008 by Routledge-Cavendish
2 Park Square, Milton Park, Abingdon, Oxon OX14 4RN

Simultaneously published in the USA and Canada
by Routledge
270 Madison Ave, New York, NY 10016

Routledge is an imprint of the Taylor & Francis Group, an informa business

© 1995, 1998, 2004, 2008 Mohamed Ramjohn

Typeset in Palatino and Gill Sans by
RefineCatch Limited, Bungay, Suffolk
Printed and bound in Great Britain by
TJ International Ltd, Padstow, Cornwall

British Library Cataloguing in Publication Data
A catalogue record for this book is available from the British Library

Library of Congress Cataloging in Publication Data
Ramjohn, Mohamed.
Cases and materials on equity and trusts / Mohamed Ramjohn.—4th ed.
p. cm.
Simultaneously published in the USA and Canada.
Includes bibliographical references and index.
1. Equity—England—Cases.   2. Trusts and trustees—England—Cases.
3. Equity—Wales—Cases.   4. Trusts and trustees—Wales—Cases.
I. Title.   II. Title: Equity and trusts.
KD1480.A7R36   2008
346.4205′9—dc22
2007047166

ISBN13: 978–0–415–44293–0 (hbk)
ISBN10: 0–415–44293–1
ISBN13: 978–0–415–44294–7 (pbk)
ISBN10: 0–415–44294–X

TEXT, CASES AND MATERIALS ON EQUITY AND TRUSTS

Fourth Edition

Text, Cases and Materials on Equity and Trusts has been considerably revised to broaden the focus of the text in line with most LLB core courses to encompass equity, remedies and injunctions and to take account of recent major statutory and case law developments.

The new edition features increased pedagogical support to outline key points and principles and improve navigation; 'notes' to encourage students to reflect on areas of complexity or controversy; and self-test questions to consolidate learning at the end of each chapter.

New to this edition:

* Detailed examination of The Civil Partnership Act 2004 and the Charities Act 2006.
* Important case law developments such as *Stack v Dowden* (constructive trusts and family assets), *Oxley v Hiscock* (quantification of family assets), *Barlow Clowes v Eurotrust* (review of the test for dishonesty), *Abou-Ramah v Abacha* (dishonest assistance and change of position defence), *AG for Zambia v Meer Care & Desai* (review of the test for dishonesty), *Re Horley Town Football Club* (gifts to unincorporated association), *Re Loftus* (defences of limitation, estoppel and laches), *Templeton Insurance v Penningtons Solicitors* (*Quistclose* trust and damages), *Sempra Metals Ltd v HM Comm of Inland Revenue* (compound interest on restitution claims) and many more.
* New chapters on the equitable remedies of specific performance, injunctions, rectification, rescission and account.
* Now incorporates extracts from the Law Commission's Reports and consultation papers on 'Sharing Homes' and 'Trustee Exemption Clauses' as well as key academic literature and debates.

The structure and style of previous editions have been retained, with an emphasis on introductory text and case extracts of sufficient length to allow students to develop analytical and critical skills in reading legal judgments. Substantial author commentary helps the text give the flow, coherence and direction of a textbook while providing the reader with a wide range of primary and secondary material from a variety of sources. A supporting companion website provides biannual updates to the cases and legislation discussed within the text; answers to the questions contained within the text; and sample essay questions.

Mr Mohamed Ramjohn LLB, LLM, CIOT, JP is a Principal Lecturer in Law at Thames Valley University and a Justice of the Peace at Brent Magistrates' Court. He has served as external examiner for the Bar Council and Coventry University. He is the author of nine student books on The Law of Trusts and Revenue Law and has published a wide selection of articles on Equity and Evidence.

CONTENTS

PREFACE TO FOURTH EDITION

The three years that have elapsed since the publication of the last edition of this book have been a period of rapid development in the law of trusts. This has necessitated extensive revision of the text including commentary on the Civil Partnership Act 2004 and the Charities Act 2006. I have incorporated a few valuable extracts from the Law Commission's Reports and consultation papers on 'Sharing Homes' and 'Trustee Exemption Clauses' as well as the views of many academics on various aspects of trusts law.

It is in the field of case law that there has been a steady accumulation in the volume of significant decisions in the field of trusts. Some of these include the seminal decisions in *Stack v Dowden* [2007] UKHL 17 (constructive trusts and family assets), *Oxley v Hiscock* [2004] EWCA 546 (quantification of family assets). Other significant decisions include *Lightfoot v Light-Brown* [2005] All ER (D) 115 (no agreement as to a beneficial interest in family assets), *Barlow Clowes v Eurotrust* [2005] UKPC 37 (review of the test for dishonesty), *Abou-Ramah v Abacha* [2006] EWCA 1492 (dishonest assistance and change of position defence), *AG for Zambia v Meer Care & Desai* [2007] EWHC 952 (review of the test for dishonesty), *Horley Town Football Club* [2006] EWHC 2386 (gifts to unincorporated association), *Cattley v Pollard* [2006] EWHC 3130 (breach of fiduciary duties and the limitation period), *Halton v Guernroy* [2006] EWCA 801 (fiduciary duties and constructive trusts), *Patel v Shah* [2005] All ER (D) 214 (defence of laches), *Re Loftus* [2006] EWCA 1124 (defences of limitation, estoppel and laches), *Templeton Insurance v Penningtons Solicitors* [2006] All ER (D) 191 (*Quistclose* trust and damages), *Baker v Clark* [2006] All ER (D) 337 (trustee exemption clauses), *Bonham v Blake Lapthorn Linell* [2006] EWHC 2513 (the *Beddoe* test and recovery of litigation costs), *Fea v Roberts* [2005] All ER (D) 69 (defences of limitation and change of circumstances), *Credit Suisse v Attar* [2004] EWHC 374 (change of position defence), *Charter plc v City Index Ltd* [2006] EWHC 2508 (contribution under the Civil Liability Act 1978), *Re Harding* [2007] EWHC 3 (charitable bequest), *Chirkinian v Arnfield* [2006] EWHC 1917 (breach of trust), *Land v Land* [2006] All ER (D) 71 (manslaughter of the deceased and the Forfeiture Act 1982), *Daraydan v Solland International Ltd* [2004] EWHC 622 (bribes and constructive trusts), *Crown Dilmun and another v Sutton* [2004] EWHC 52 (breach of fiduciary duties and knowingly receiving trust property), *Kilcarne Holdings Ltd v Targetfollow* [2005] EWCA Civ 1355 (*Pallant v Morgan* constructive trust), *Commerzbank Aktiengesellschaft v IMB Morgan* [2004] EWHC 2771 (tracing).

The principal objectives of writing the fourth edition of this book remain the same as those stated in previous editions namely, to present the relevant principles of trusts law in an intelligible and simplified form and, at the same time, to provide easy access to a collection of source materials in order to facilitate an understanding of the law and stimulate critical thought. I have followed the structure and style of previous editions with emphasis on introductory text and case extracts of sufficient length to allow students to develop important skills in reading legal judgments. I have, however, made some changes, or additions, by including new chapters on the equitable remedies of specific performance, injunctions, rectification, rescission and account.

I would like to thank the members of staff at Routledge-Cavendish who have assisted me in the preparation of this book. I am especially grateful to Kate Murphy, Fiona Kinnear and Sonny Leong, without whose support and encouragement this work would not have been possible.

ACKNOWLEDGMENTS

The author and publishers are most grateful and would like to thank the following for permission to reproduce copyright material:

Blackwell Publishers: extracts from the *Modern Law Review*;

Butterworths: extracts from the *All England Law Reports*;

HMSO for permission to reproduce Crown Copyright material. Reproduced under the terms of PSI Licence C2007000258;

The Incorporated Council for Law Reporting for England and Wales: extracts from the *Law Reports* and *Weekly Law Reports*;

Jordan: extracts from the *Family Law Reports*;

Oxford University Press: extracts from the *Web Journal of Current Legal Issues*;

Sweet & Maxwell: extracts from the *Property, Planning and Compensation Reports, The Conveyancer* and the *Law Quarterly Review*;

Tolley Publishing: extracts from *Trust Law International*.

TABLE OF CASES

TABLE OF STATUTES

TABLES OF STATUTORY INSTRUMENTS & EUROPEAN LEGISLATION

HISTORICAL OUTLINES OF EQUITY

INTRODUCTION

Equity, unlike the common law, was never intended to be an independent system of law. It presupposed the existence of the common law, which it supplemented and modified. The history of equity is intimately connected with the common law writ system, the rigidity of the common law, the Lord Chancellor and the Court of Chancery. Petitions to the King in Council to do justice were made as a consequence of the inflexibility of the common law system of justice. Originally, an action in the King's Courts commenced only with a writ, but this was only available in a limited number of cases. In addition, changing social conditions gave rise to novel disputes, including the 'use' (the forerunner to the trust). The effect was that aggrieved parties petitioned the King in Council to do justice. These petitions were transferred to the Lord Chancellor who, after a period of reflection, made his decision. Ultimately, the Court of Chancery was set up to deal with such cases. The rulings by the Court of Chancery formed a body of law called equity.

Before the Judicature Acts 1873 and 1875, there were in effect two systems of law: rules of law applied in the common law courts; and rules of equity created in the Chancery Court. One of the policies of the Judicature Acts was to fuse the administration of law and equity. Thus, today, rules of equity are recognised and may be applied in any court of law.

CONTRIBUTIONS OF EQUITY

The contributions of equity in the development of the law may be classified into three categories:

(a) Exclusive jurisdiction (new rights). This category refers to the rights that the Court of Chancery had created and which the common law courts had failed to enforce, for example trusts, mortgages, partnerships, administration of estates, bankruptcy, company law, etc.

(b) Concurrent jurisdiction (new remedies). Equity developed a wide range of remedies for the enforcement of rights both at law and in equity. They are all discretionary. Examples are:

(i) specific performance – an order to force the defendant to fulfil his bargain;

(ii) injunctions – an order to restrain a party from committing a wrong;

(iii) rectification – an order requiring the defendant to modify a document to reflect the agreement made with the claimant;

(iv) account – an order requiring a party who has control of money belonging to the claimant to report on the way in which the funds have been spent.

(c) Auxiliary jurisdiction (new procedures). Procedural rules created by the Court of Chancery were discovery of documents, testimony on oath, subpoena of witnesses and interrogatories (now 'disclosure'; witness summons; requests for further information).

Court of Appeal in Chancery

The eighteenth and nineteenth centuries witnessed great strides forward in the development of equity. However, the personnel of the Court of Chancery proved to be corrupt. Frequently, such personnel were bribed in order to issue the common injunction. In addition, the court became overloaded with petitions, which resulted in delays. Until 1813, there were only two judges in the Court of Chancery, namely, the Lord Chancellor and the Master of the Rolls. They were unhurried in arriving at their decisions.

In 1813, a Vice-Chancellor was appointed. In 1841, two more Vice-Chancellors were appointed. In 1851, two Lord Justices of Appeal in Chancery were appointed. By the early nineteenth century, the Lord Chancellor had ceased to hear petitions at first instance. In 1851, the Court of Appeal in Chancery was created to hear appeals from decisions of Vice-Chancellors and the Master of the Rolls. This court consisted of the Lord Chancellor and two Lord Justices of Appeal. There was a further appeal to the House of Lords.

Question
How would you classify the major contributions of equity in the development of the law?

Nineteenth century reforms

Before Parliament intervened, the Court of Chancery was capable of granting only equitable remedies. Likewise, common law courts could have granted only the legal remedy of damages. This inconvenience was overcome by two statutory provisions:

(a) the Common Law Procedure Act 1854. This Act permitted the common law courts to grant equitable remedies;

(b) the Chancery Procedure Amendment Act 1858 (Lord Cairns' Act). This Act gave the Court of Chancery power to award damages in addition to or in substitution for an injunction or specific performance.

However, what was needed was a more radical change, which fused the administration of law and equity. It was an unnecessary waste of time and resources to require claimants entitled to common law and equitable rights or remedies to go to the respective court to redress their wrongs.

This change was effected by the Judicature Acts 1873 and 1875, which adopted the following policies:

(a) the abolition of the separate courts of Queen's Bench, Exchequer, Common Pleas, Chancery, Probate, the Divorce Court and the Court of Admiralty. Instead, the Supreme Court of the Judicature was created. The High Court was divided into divisions known as the Queen's Bench, Chancery, and Probate, Divorce and Admiralty (the last was renamed the Family Division, the admiralty jurisdiction being transferred to the Queen's Bench Division and the probate business transferred to the Chancery Division under the Administration of Justice Act 1970);

(b) each division of the High Court exercises both legal and equitable jurisdiction. Thus, any point of law or equity may be raised in and determined by any division;

(c) it was foreseen that a court which applied rules of common law and equity would face a conflict where the common law rules produce one result and equity rules another; for example, s 4 of the Statute of Frauds 1677 (now repealed) enacted that contracts for the sale or other disposition of land must be evidenced in writing. The strict common law rule was rigidly adhered to whether this produced unjust results or not. Equity adopted a notion of part performance which entitled the court to intervene in order to prevent fraud even though all the terms of the contract were not in writing.

Judicature Act 1873, s 25(11)

Generally, in all matters not hereinbefore mentioned in which there is any conflict or variance between the rules of equity and the rules of common law with reference to the same matter, the rules of equity shall prevail.

The effect of the Acts is therefore procedural in the sense that the administration of law and equity, as distinct from the rules of law and equity, has been fused.

MCC Proceeds Inc v Lehman Bros International [1998] 4 All ER 675, CA

Mummery LJ: The position is that an equitable owner had no title at common law to sue in conversion, unless he could also show that he had actual possession or an immediate right to possession of the goods claimed; this substantive rule of law was not altered by the Supreme Court of Judicature Acts, which were intended to achieve procedural improvements in the administration of law and equity in all courts, not to transform equitable interests into legal titles or to sweep away altogether the rules of the common law . . .

Maxims of equity

The intervention of the court of equity over the centuries may be reduced into a number of maxims. The importance of the maxims ought not to be overstated. They are far from being rigid principles, but exist as terse sentences which only illustrate the policy underlying specific principles.

Equity will not suffer a wrong to be without a remedy

This maxim illustrates the intervention of the Court of Chancery to provide a remedy if none was obtainable at common law. At the same time it must not be supposed that every infringement of a right was capable of being remedied. The 'wrongs' which equity was prepared to invent new remedies to redress were those subject to judicial enforcement in the first place.

Equity follows the law

The view originally taken by the court of equity was that deliberate and carefully considered rules of common law would be followed. Equity intervened only when some important factor became ignored by the law.

Where there is equal equity, the law prevails

Equity did not intervene when, according to equitable principles, no injustice resulted in adopting the solution imposed by law.

Thus, the bona fide purchaser of the legal estate for value without notice is capable of acquiring an equitable interest both at law and in equity.

Where the equities are equal, the first in time prevails

Where two persons have conflicting interests in the same property, the rule is that the first in time has priority at law and in equity: *qui prior est tempore potior est jure.*

He who seeks equity must do equity

A party who claims equitable relief is required to act fairly towards his opponent, for example, a tracing order would not be obtained in equity if the effect would be to promote injustice.

He who comes to equity must come with clean hands

The assumption here is that the claimant or party claiming an equitable relief must demonstrate that he has not acted with impropriety in respect of the claim.

Delay defeats equity (equity aids the vigilant and not the indolent)

Where a party has slept on his rights and has given the defendant the impression that he has waived his rights, a court of equity may refuse its assistance to the claimant. This is known as the doctrine of laches.

Equality is equity

Where two or more parties have an interest in the same property but their respective interests have not been quantified, equity as a last resort may divide the interest equally.

Equity looks at the intent rather than the form

The court looks at the substance of an arrangement rather than its appearance in order to ascertain the intention of the parties, for example a deed is not treated in equity as a substitute for consideration.

Equity imputes an intention to fulfil an obligation

The principle here is based on the premise that if a party is under an obligation to perform an act and he performs an alternative but similar act, equity assumes that the second act was done with the intention of fulfilling the obligation.

Equity regards as done that which ought to be done

If a person is under an obligation to perform an act that is specifically enforceable, the parties acquire the same rights and liabilities in equity as though the act had been performed.

Equity acts in personam

Originally, equitable orders were enforced against the person of the defendant with the ultimate sanction of imprisonment. A later equitable invention permitted an order to be attached to the defendant's property, that is, *in rem*. Today this maxim has lost much of its importance.

Question
What is the significance today of the maxims of equity?

FURTHER READING

Gardner, S, 'Two maxims of equity' (1995) 54 CLJ 60.

Martin, J, 'Fusion, fallacy and confusion' [1994] Conv 13.

Mason, A, 'The place of equity and equitable remedies in contemporary society' (1994) 110 LQR 238.

Pettit, P, 'He who comes into equity must come with clean hands' [1990] Conv 416.

Winder, W, 'Precedent in equity' (1941) 57 LQR 245.

INTRODUCTION

One of the fundamental features of a trust concerns the division of ownership of property into legal and equitable interests. The trust concept creates a special duty, which attaches to the trust property and to the trustees. The beneficiaries acquire proprietary interests in the trust property, which are inviolable except against bona fide transferees of the legal estate for value without notice. The duties imposed on trustees are personal fiduciary obligations, which are enforceable at the instance of the beneficiaries by way of equitable remedies.

DEFINITION

There are a variety of definitions of trusts that have been used from time to time. It is not an easy task to offer a precise definition of a trust, for the concept has been developed piecemeal over a number of centuries.

Underhill's definition

A trust is an equitable obligation binding a person (called a trustee) to deal with property over which he has control (called the trust property) for the benefit of persons (called beneficiaries or *cestui que trust*) of whom he himself may be one and any of whom may enforce the obligation [Underhill, A and Hayton, D, *Law of Trusts and Trustees*, 14th edn, 1987, London: Butterworths, p 1].

It should be noted that, although this is a fairly comprehensive definition, charitable trusts such as the RSPCA and the NSPCC (enforceable by the Attorney-General) and, exceptionally, valid private purpose trusts (not enforceable by the beneficiaries) are excluded from the definition. However, Underhill's definition highlights a number of features inherent in trust law such as the obligatory nature of trusts, the notion that control is vested in the trustees on behalf of beneficiaries who are entitled to protect their interests and enforce the trust duties.

In essence, the mechanism of the trust is an equitable device by which property is controlled by trustees for the benefit of others, called beneficiaries. For a variety of reasons, it may be prudent to prevent the entire ownership of property (both legal and equitable) being vested in and enjoyed by one person. A trust may be set up in order to advance such an objective.

By origin, the trust was the exclusive product of the now defunct Court of Chancery but, since the Judicature Acts 1873 and 1875, trusts may be enforced in any court of law.

Section 1 of the Recognition of Trusts Act 1987

Enacting the terms of Art 2 of the Hague Convention on the Recognition of Trusts:

1(1) The provisions of the Convention set out in the Schedule to this Act shall have the force of law in the United Kingdom ...

Schedule

For the purposes of this Convention, the term 'trust' refers to the legal relationship created – *inter vivos* or on death – by a person, the settlor, when assets have been placed under the control of a trustee for the benefit of a beneficiary or for a specified purpose.

A trust has the following characteristics:

(a) the assets constitute a separate fund and are not a part of the trustee's own estate;

(b) title to the trust assets stands in the name of the trustee or in the name of another person on behalf of the trustee;

(c) the trustee has the power and the duty, in respect of which he is accountable, to manage, employ or dispose of the assets in accordance with the terms of the trust and the special duties imposed upon him by law.

The reservation by the settlor of certain rights and powers and the fact that the trustee may himself have rights as a beneficiary, are not necessarily inconsistent with the existence of a trust.

This definition has been formulated by reference to the characteristics of a trust.

CHARACTERISTICS OF A TRUST

The following sections set out some of the main features of a trust.

Mandatory

A trust (unlike a power of distribution) is obligatory. The trustees have no choice as to whether or not they may fulfil the intention of the settlor. The trustees are required to fulfil the terms of the trust as stipulated in the trust instrument and implied by rules of law. The trustees have a number of duties imposed on them in order to maintain a balance between the trustees and the beneficiaries, for example, trustees are not allowed to derive a benefit from acting as trustees unless authorised. The beneficiaries are given a *locus standi* to ensure that the trustees carry out their duties. (But note the anomalous nature of private purpose trusts: see Chapter 13 below.)

Separation of the legal and equitable titles

The legal title to property is a representation to the world that the legal owner has the right to retain and control the property. The equitable title is the right to enjoy the property. Such right may be enforced against anyone interfering with the interest except a bona fide transferee of the legal estate for value without notice. The equitable owner under a 'bare trust' (that is, a trust under which the trustees have no active duties to perform) is incapable of asserting his rights to the assets as against a bona fide purchaser of the legal interest from the trustee.

When the two titles are united in the hands of one person to such an extent that there is no separation of interest (not even a nominal separation), no trust exists. It would follow that such a person, with both legal and equitable interests, has not only the right to control the property but also the right to benefit from and enjoy the same.

For example, A buys a computer from his own funds for his sole use. A has both the legal and equitable interests (referred to as the 'absolute entitlement' or 'title to the property'). No trust exists. However, if A and B purchase the computer for their joint benefit so that the legal and equitable interests are divided, a trust is created even though the same persons are both trustees and beneficiaries.

One of the key issues in understanding trust law is to appreciate that the two titles (legal and equitable) may be separated. When this is the case, a trust is created. The legal title is acquired by the trustee, but the beneficial interest or equitable title is acquired by the equitable owner.

The settlor's position

The settlor is the creator of an express trust. He decides the form that the trust property may take, the interests of the beneficiaries, the identity of the beneficiaries and the persons who will be appointed trustees. Indeed, he may appoint himself one of the trustees or the sole trustee. In short, the settlor is the author of the trust.

For example, S, a settlor, purchases land which is conveyed in the names of T and T(1) (the trustees) on trust for the sole benefit of B (the beneficiary). An express trust is created. Indeed, in this example, S is capable of being one of the trustees and at the same time one of the beneficiaries. S may even be the sole beneficiary under the trust. Once there is a separation of the legal interest from the equitable title (which may be established through more than one owner), a trust is created.

Once the trust is created, the settlor *qua* settlor loses all control or interest in the trust property. Unless he has reserved an interest for himself, he is not entitled to derive a benefit from the trust property nor is he allowed to control the conduct of the trustees. In other words, following the creation of a trust, the settlor in his capacity as settlor is treated as a stranger in respect of the trust: see *Re Bowden*.

Re Bowden [1936] Ch 71, HC

Facts

The settlor, before becoming a nun and in order to undertake the vows of poverty, chastity and obedience, transferred property to trustees on trust for specified beneficiaries. Later, she changed her mind when she left the convent and attempted to reclaim the property for her benefit.

Held

A valid trust was created and the claimant, as a settlor, lost all interest in the property and therefore could not recover the property:

> **Bennett J:** . . . the persons appointed trustees under the settlement received the settlor's interest . . . and, immediately after it had been received by them, as a result of her own act and her own declaration . . . it became impressed with the trusts contained in the settlement.

The trustees' position

The trustees bear the responsibility of controlling and managing the trust property solely for the benefit of the beneficiaries.

The trustees are the representatives of the trust. Owing to the opportunities to take advantage of their position as controllers of the property, rules of equity were formulated to impose a collection of strict and rigorous duties on the trustees. Indeed, the trustees' duties are so onerous that (subject to authority in the trust instrument) the trustees are not even entitled to invest trust moneys as they might do with their own funds, but are required to invest in authorised investments.

Trustees are liable in their personal capacity for mismanaging the trust funds and in extreme cases may be made bankrupt, should they neglect their duties.

The beneficiary's position

The beneficiaries (as the owners of the equitable interest) are given the power to compel the due administration of the trust. They are entitled to sue the trustees and any third party for damages (joining the trustees in the proceedings as co-defendants) for breach of trust. In addition, the beneficiaries may trace the trust property in the hands of third parties with the exception of bona fide transferees of the legal estate for value without notice. The beneficiaries are given an interest in the trust property (i.e., a proprietary interest) and are entitled to assign the whole or part of such interest to others. The beneficiaries are entitled to terminate the trust by directing the trustees to transfer the legal title to them, provided that they have attained the age of majority and are *compos mentis* and absolutely entitled to the trust property: see *Saunders v Vautier* (1841) 4 Beav 115, Chapter 20 below.

Trust property

Any property that is capable of being transferred may be the subject matter of the trust. Thus, land (real property), chattels (tangible moveable property such as computers), chattels real (leases) and intangible personal property (such as shares in a company, intellectual property, loans, etc) may be the subject matter of a trust.

Inter vivos or by will

Trusts may be created either *inter vivos* (during the lifetime of the settlor) or on death, by will or on an intestacy (under the Administration of Estates Act 1925, as amended).

Four essential features of a trust

Lord Browne-Wilkinson in *Westdeutsche Landesbank Girozentrale v Islington BC* identified four fundamental principles of trusts law that he considered as uncontroversial.

Westdeutsche Landesbank Girozentrale v Islington BC [1996] AC 669, HL Lord Browne-Wilkinson:

(i) Equity operates on the conscience of the owner of the legal interest. In the case of a trust, the conscience of the legal owner requires him to carry out the purposes for which the property was vested in him (express or implied trust) or which the law imposes on him by reason of his unconscionable conduct (constructive trust).

(ii) Since the equitable jurisdiction to enforce trusts depends upon the conscience of the holder of the legal interest being affected, he cannot be a trustee of the property if and so long as he is ignorant of the facts alleged to affect his conscience, ie until he is aware that he is intended to hold the property for the benefit of others in the case of an express or implied trust, or, in the case of a constructive trust, of the factors which are alleged to affect his conscience.

(iii) In order to establish a trust there must be identifiable trust property. The only apparent exception to this rule is a constructive trust imposed on a person who dishonestly assists in a breach of trust who may come under fiduciary duties even if he does not receive identifiable trust property.

(iv) Once a trust is established, as from the date of its establishment the beneficiary has, in equity, a proprietary interest in the trust property, which proprietary interest will be enforceable in equity against any subsequent holder of the property (whether the original property or substituted property into which it can be traced) other than a purchaser for value of the legal estate without notice.

These propositions are fundamental to the law of trusts and I would have thought uncontroversial.

Question
List four essential characteristics of a trust.

CLASSIFICATION OF TRUSTS

There are many ways of classifying trusts. The simplest classification is into express, implied and statutory trusts.

Express trusts

An express trust is one created in accordance with the express intention of the settlor. The settlor is required to transfer the relevant property to third party trustees subject to the terms of the trust manifested in favour of the beneficiaries: see *Re Bowden* (p 7 above). Alternatively, the settlor may expressly declare himself a trustee for the benefit of the objects (that is, self-declaration of trust).

For example, S, the holder of 900 shares in British Gas plc, declares that the shares are held on trust for his son, B, absolutely. S will become the trustee for the benefit of his son.

Private/public (charitable) trusts

Express trusts may be sub-classified into 'private' and 'charitable' trusts.

Private trusts exist for the benefit of persons or benefit a narrow section of the public. For example, a gift on trust for the education of the children of the settlor. There are a number of anomalous trusts in respect of which the beneficiaries are private purposes. These beneficiaries are obviously incapable of enforcing such trusts, for example, a trust for the benefit of the testator's pets or a trust for the execution and maintenance of a monument in memory of the testator. These are called 'hybrid' trusts or trusts for imperfect obligations.

Charitable trusts are public trusts that benefit the public as a whole in a number of specified ways such as the relief of poverty, the advancement of education, the propagation of religion and other purposes that are beneficial to society within the spirit and intendment of the preamble to the Charitable Uses Act 1601. The Charities Act 2006 introduces a statutory definition of charities by reference to a list of charitable purposes.

Fixed/discretionary trusts

Express trusts may also be classified into 'fixed' and 'discretionary' trusts.

A fixed trust is one where the beneficiaries and their interests are identified by the settlor. The trustees have no duty to select the beneficiaries or to quantify their interest. The settlor has declared the interests that may be enjoyed by the beneficiaries.

For example, on trust for A for life remainder to B absolutely. A enjoys the interest or income for as long as he lives, whereas B has a vested interest in the capital or the entire property subject to A's interest.

A discretionary trust is one whereby the trustees are given a duty to exercise their discretion in order to distribute the property in favour of a selected group of persons. The objects, individually considered, do not have an interest in the property but have only a hope (*spes*) of acquiring an interest in the property, prior to the exercise of the discretion by the trustees.

For example, £50,000 is transferred to T and T(1) as trustees in order to distribute the property to such of the settlor's relations as the trustees may decide in their absolute discretion. All the settlor's relations are not beneficiaries *simpliciter*, but form a class from whom the trustees are required to select and distribute to the appropriate beneficiaries.

For example, for a period of 21 years from the date of the transfer to hold on trust to apply the income to such of the settlor's children as the trustees may decide in their absolute discretion.

Discretionary trusts may be 'exhaustive' or 'non-exhaustive'.

An 'exhaustive' discretionary trust is one where the trustees are required to distribute the income and/or capital to the objects. The trustees are given a discretion as to which objects may benefit and the 'quantum' of the benefit.

A 'non-exhaustive' discretionary trust is one where the trustees are not required to distribute the entirety of the income and/or capital but may retain or accumulate the relevant property at their discretion.

Question
How would you classify express trusts?

Implied trusts

There are two types of implied trusts, namely, 'resulting' and 'constructive' trusts.

Resulting trusts

These are trusts that spring back in favour of the settlor/transferor in accordance with his implied intention. The trust is a default mechanism and may be created in order to fill a gap in ownership, or in respect of a surplus of trust funds left over after the trust purpose has been fulfilled. For example S, a settlor, transfers the legal title to property to T, a trustee, on trust. But S fails to declare the terms of the trust. Thus, the intended express trust fails and T holds the property on resulting trust for S: see *Vandervell v IRC* [1967] 2 AC 291.

Similarly, a resulting trust will be set up when a transfer of property is subject to a condition precedent which fails. For example L, a lender, loans B, a borrower, £50,000 to be used *solely* to pay a dividend to B's shareholders. Before the dividend is paid, B goes into liquidation. B's liquidator is required to hold the fund on resulting trust for L: see *Barclays Bank v Quistclose* [1970] AC 567.

In addition, a 'resulting trust' may be created by the courts in accordance with the presumed intention of the settlor. The settlor or his estate is presumed to be the equitable owner. An occasion giving rise to this presumption is the purchase of property in the name of another.

For example, B purchases shares and directs the vendor to transfer the legal title to the shares in the name of T. T is presumed to hold the shares on trust for B.

Question
What are resulting trusts?

Constructive trusts

A constructive trust is created whenever the court decides that it would be unconscionable for the legal owner of property to deny the claimant an equitable interest in the property. On occasions when a trustee abuses the confidence reposed in him by realising an unauthorised profit derived from the trust property, or becomes unjustly enriched at another's expense, the court may impose a constructive trust on the party who acted with impropriety. These are occasions when the courts feel that it is inequitable for a person to retain the equitable interest for his own benefit. Accordingly, where an express trustee purchases the trust property without the consent of all the beneficiaries, the sale is voidable and the profits are held on constructive trust for the beneficiaries: see *Keech v Sandford* (1726) Sel Cas Ch 437.

Question
The occasions when a constructive trust may be created have been deliberately left vague by the courts. Why?

Statutory trusts

Statutory trusts are trusts created by Parliament. There are a vast number of statutory provisions that create trusts in a wide variety of circumstances.

Section 33 of the Administration of Estates Act 1925 declares that the personal representatives of an intestate are required to hold all the deceased's property on trust with power to postpone the sale.

Administration of Estates Act 1925, s 33(1) (as amended by Trusts of Land and Appointment of Trustees Act 1996)

On the death of a person intestate as to any real or personal estate, that estate shall be held by his personal representatives with a power to sell it.

Section 34(2) of the Law of Property Act 1925 enacts that where land is conveyed to persons in undivided shares it will vest in the first four named persons on trust for all the grantees beneficially as tenants in common.

Law of Property Act 1925, s 34(2) (as amended by Trusts of Land and Appointment of Trustees Act 1996)

Where . . . land is expressed to be conveyed to any persons in undivided shares and those persons are of full age, the conveyance shall (notwithstanding anything to the contrary in this Act) operate as if the land had been expressed to be conveyed to the grantees, or if there are more than four grantees, to the four first named in the conveyance, as joint tenants in trust for the persons interested in the land.

Section 36(1) of the Law of Property Act 1925 provides that where land is conveyed to joint tenants, it vests in the first four named persons on trust for sale for all the grantees as joint tenants.

Law of Property Act 1925, s 36(1) (as amended by Trusts of Land and Appointment of Trustees Act 1996)

Where a legal estate (not being settled land) is beneficially limited to or held in trust for any persons as joint tenants, the same shall be held in trust, in like manner as if the persons beneficially entitled were tenants in common, but not so as to sever their joint tenancy in equity.

REASONS FOR THE CREATION OF EXPRESS TRUSTS

The trust concept is a flexible institution, which may be created for a variety of reasons.

Tax avoidance

One of the most popular reasons for the creation of a trust is to avoid or mitigate the settlor's liability to tax. There are many ways in which this objective may be achieved. Subject to statutory provisions to the contrary, the settlor, having exhausted his personal relief from income tax, may alienate his income by way of a trust in favour of another who may use his relief to reduce the amount of tax payable, for example, a settlor may transfer 50,000 shares in Moneybags Ltd to trustees for the benefit of his impecunious nephew, N. Trustees pay income tax at the basic rate of tax. On distributing the income, the beneficiary, N, is entitled to set off his personal relief against the income liable to income tax.

To protect spendthrift beneficiaries

The settlor may believe that an outright transfer of property to a donee may result in the dissipation of the fund by the donee. To avoid this, the settlor may create a protective trust under s 33 of the Trustee Act 1925 in favour of the beneficiary. The protective trust is a determinable life interest in favour of the nominated beneficiary, which terminates on the happening of any course of events that is capable of prejudicing the interest of the beneficiary. On the termination of the life interest, a discretionary trust is set up and the life tenant becomes an object of the discretionary trust. The terms of the trust laid out in s 33 may be adapted to suit the needs of any settlor.

To avoid adverse publicity from a published will

On death, a testator's will is published and transfers, as well as the identity of the beneficiaries, may become public. In order to avoid adverse publicity, a testator may create a fully secret trust by transferring property under his will to a person (say, a legatee) whose identity is not a source of embarrassment. Before his death, the testator is required to make a bargain with the legatee to the effect that, following the receipt of the legacy, he will be required to hold the property on trust for the secret beneficiary (say, the testator's illegitimate child). Thus, the existence of the trust and the identity of the beneficiary will be concealed on the face of the will.

To protect purchasers before entering into commercial transactions

A customer who makes an advance payment for goods may be entitled to utilise the trust concept in order to secure the return of the purchase money in the event of the company going into liquidation: see *Re Kayford*.

Re Kayford [1975] I WLR 279, HC

Facts
Customers made advance payments to a mail order company when ordering goods. Following advice, the company paid these sums into a separate account. The company treated funds in this account as belonging to customers until the goods were delivered in accordance with the order. On the liquidation of the company, the issue arose as to ownership of the funds in the bank account.

Held
The funds were impressed with a trust in favour of the customers who failed to receive their goods.

Clubs and unincorporated associations

Unincorporated associations have no separate legal existence. Such bodies are not entitled to own funds separately for their members. The funds are owned by the members and the club is treated as the collective 'alter ego' of the members. The members may elect or appoint officers of the club. The officers may hold the club's assets and income as trustees for the purposes declared in the constitution of the association.

Commercial objectives

The trust may be used as a vehicle to promote a variety of commercial objectives such as unit trust investments and pension funds. Unit trusts exist as a machinery for members of the public to participate in investments in the stock market with the assistance of specialist fund managers. These managers undertake the investment decisions and manage the funds on a daily basis. The investor buys units (in a trust), the price of which is determined by the value of the underlying securities in which the trust invests. The money invested by a new investor is used to buy further securities and so more units are created for sale by the managers. The fund is divided between the investors who thereby acquire an interest therein.

Question
Why may an individual be prompted to create an express trust?

FURTHER READING

Bartlett, R, 'When is a trust not a trust? The National Health Service' [1996] Conv 186.

Goodhart, W, 'Trust law for the 21st century' (1996) 10(2) Tru LI 38.

Hayton, D, 'Developing the law of trusts for the 21st century' (1990) 106 LQR 87.

Hayton, D, 'Trust law and occupational pension schemes' [1993] Conv 283.

Matthews, P, 'The black hole trusts uses, abuses and possible reforms: Pt 1' [2002] PCB 42.

Matthews, P, 'The black hole trusts uses, abuses and possible reforms: Pt 2' [2002] PCB 103.

Millett, P, 'Equity – the road ahead' (1995) 9(2) Tru LI 35.

Lord Millett, 'Pension schemes and the law of trusts: the tail wagging the dog' (2000) 14(2) Tru LI 2.

Milner, M, 'Pension trust: a new trust forum' [1997] Conv 89.

Moffatt, G, 'Pension funds: a fragmentation of trust law' (1993) 56 MLR 471.

Nobles, R, 'Pensions Act 1995' (1996) 59 MLR 241.

Waters, D, 'The future of trust: Part 1' (2006) ITCP Vol 13, Issue 4, 179.

EXPRESS PRIVATE TRUSTS AND FORMALITIES

INTRODUCTION

A settlor who wishes to create an express trust is required to comply with the *Milroy v Lord* principle. This test stipulates that the subject matter of the trust is required to be transferred to the trustees, subject to a valid declaration of trust. This is known as the transfer and declaration mode. Alternatively, the settlor may declare himself a trustee of the property for the respective beneficiaries. This is referred to as a self-declaration of trust. In both cases, the settlor is required to declare the terms of the trust. The three certainties test exists as a principle to determine whether a valid declaration of trust has been created by the settlor. The three certainties are certainty of intention, subject matter (including beneficial interests) and objects. As an additional requirement, the settlor is required to comply with such statutory formalities, if any, in respect of the transfer of the property to the trustees and the declaration of trust.

MODES OF CREATING AN EXPRESS TRUST

A trust is perfectly created when the trust property is 'at home', that is, the trustees have acquired the property subject to the terms of the trust as declared by the settlor. There are two modes of creating an express trust. First, a transfer of property to the trustees, subject to a declaration of trust by the settlor. This is the transfer and declaration mode. Second, there is a mode of creation that requires the settlor to declare himself a trustee for the beneficiaries. This is a self-declaration of trust.

Transfer and declaration

The settlor may transfer property to third party trustees subject to the terms of the trust as declared by the settlor. Thus, the settlor will be required to effect the trust in two stages. One stage imposes on the settlor the obligation to transfer the property to the trustees and the settlor fulfils his obligation. The other stage requires the settlor to declare the terms of the trust, that is, to comply with the three certainties test (see p 39 below). The settlor may be one of the trustees and/or one of the beneficiaries. As the author of the trust, he is required to identify the trustees and beneficiaries. It must follow that both these requirements or stages are complementary. A transfer of property to another without a declaration of trust will be construed as nothing more than a gift in favour of the transferee, and a declaration of trust executed with the intention of making a third party a trustee for another will be of no effect if the third party has not acquired the property.

For example, S, the legal and equitable owner of land, wishes to make T1 and T2 trustees of the property for the benefit of B, his nephew. S will have to transfer the legal title to T1 and T2 and declare the terms of the trust in favour of B. On completion of these requirements, B will acquire an equitable interest in the land.

Self-declaration

The other mode of creating an express trust requires the settlor to declare that the relevant property retained by him is held as a trustee subject to the terms of the trust, that is, a self-declaration of trust. This mode has the advantage of requiring the settlor to execute one transaction, namely, the declaration of trust. No third party trustee is involved in the arrangement. The settlor's interest will be converted from absolute entitlement to partial ownership as trustee for the beneficiaries as declared.

For example, S, the legal and equitable owner of shares, wishes to make a self-declaration of trust in favour of B, absolutely. S is required to declare himself a trustee for B absolutely. On completion of this requirement, S will become the bare legal owner and B will become the sole equitable owner.

Once a trust is perfectly created, the beneficiaries acquire equitable interests in the property, which they may protect, even though they are 'volunteers' (that is, they have not provided consideration). Conversely, an imperfect trust is one where the settlor has not fully complied with either of these two modes of creation. An imperfect trust exists as an agreement to create a trust that is enforceable only by those who have furnished consideration. Two equitable maxims summarise the general rule: 'equity will not assist a volunteer' and 'equity will not perfect an imperfect gift'.

The classical statement concerning the various modes of creating a trust was enunciated by Turner LJ in *Milroy v Lord*.

Milroy v Lord (1862) 31 LJ Ch 798, HC Turner LJ:

. . . in order to render a voluntary settlement valid and effectual, the settlor must have done everything which, according to the nature of the property comprised in the settlement, was necessary to be done in order to transfer the property and render the settlement binding upon him. He may, of course, do this . . . if he transfers the property to a trustee for the purposes of the settlement, or declares that he himself holds it in trust for those purposes . . . but, in order to render the settlement binding, one or other of these modes must . . . be resorted to, for there is no equity in this court to perfect an imperfect gift. The cases go further to this extent, that if the settlement is intended to be effectuated by one of the modes to which I have referred, the court will not give effect to it by applying another of those modes. If it is intended to take effect by transfer, the court will not hold the intended transfer to operate as a declaration of trust, for then every imperfect instrument would be made effectual by being converted into a perfect trust.

Thus, in order to create an express trust, the settlor is required to fulfil two conditions, namely:

(a) transfer the property to the trustees; and

(b) declare the terms of the trust.

The transfer of the property to the trustees may be effected by way of a gift or a contract. The correct mode of transfer is required to be followed in order to vest the property in the hands of the trustees. The requirements concerning the mode of transfer of the property vary with the nature of the property and the type of interest (whether legal or equitable) that the settlor intends to transfer. Thus, the transfer of the legal title to land requires a conveyance. Tangible moveable property (a chattel) requires delivery with the intention of transferring the property. The assignment of a legal chose in action (for example, a debt) requires writing and notice to the debtor. The transfer of the legal title to shares requires an appropriate entry in the company's register made in pursuance of a proper instrument of transfer.

Transfer effective in equity by operation of law

In appropriate circumstances, the transfer of the property may be effective in equity, despite the failure of the transferor to complete the transfer of the legal title. This would be the position when the settlor has done all in his power to give the trustee the legal title and the only hurdle for the complete transfer of the legal title lies outside the settlor's control. This difficulty is frequently experienced in respect of shares where the transfer is required to be executed in accordance with the company's articles of association followed by registration in the company's share register (see Companies Act 2006). The articles of association of most private companies give the directors an absolute discretion to refuse to register a transfer of shares without stating reasons (notification of refusal is required to be made within two months of the instrument of transfer being lodged with the company – the Companies Act 2006). A transferor who has executed the appropriate documents of transfer of shares and has delivered the same to the company in the expectation that the transfer of the legal title will be complete will have done everything that is required of him to transfer the shares. At this time the transfer of the equitable title to the shares will be complete. The directors may or may not refuse to register the shares. This is a matter that is beyond the transferor's control. The transferor will hold the legal title to the shares on constructive trust for the transferee. This is known as the principle in *Re Rose*. The effect of this principle is that voting powers are required to be exercised by the legal owner in favour of the beneficiaries. Likewise, dividends declared are held in trust for the beneficiaries. A transfer, for estate duty (and inheritance tax) purposes, will be recognised on the earlier date of the transfer of the equitable interest.

Re Rose [1952] Ch 499, CA

Facts

On 30 March 1943, the settlor executed a transfer of 20,000 shares to his wife. The transfers were in the form required by the company's articles of association. The transfers were registered in the company's books on 30 June 1943. On the date of death of the settlor, it was necessary to know the precise date of the transfer for estate duty purposes. If the transfer had taken place before 10 April 1943, no estate duty was payable. The Revenue claimed that duty was payable on the ground that the transfer was not complete until 30 June 1943.

Held

Estate duty was not payable for the transfer of the equitable title was complete on 30 March 1943. On this date, the settlor had done everything in his power to transfer the shares. The transfer of the legal title did not become complete until 30 June 1943:

> **Lord Evershed MR:** If a man executes a document transferring all his equitable interest, say, in shares, that document, operating and intended to operate as a transfer, will give rise to and take effect as a trust, for the assignor will then be a trustee of the legal estate in the shares for the person in whose favour he has made an assignment of his beneficial interest. And for my part I do not think that *Milroy v Lord* (1862) 31 LJ Ch 798, is an authority which compels this court to hold that in this case, where, in the terms of Turner LJ's judgment, the settlor did everything which, according to the nature of the property comprised in the settlement, was necessary to be done by him in order to transfer the property, the result necessarily negatives the conclusion that, pending registration, the settlor was a trustee of the legal interest for the transferee.
>
> I think the matter might be put, perhaps, in a somewhat different fashion though it reaches the same end. Whatever might be the position during the period between the execution of this document and the registration of the shares, the transfers were, on 30 June 1943, registered. After registration, the title of Mrs Rose was beyond doubt complete in every respect, and if Mr Rose had received a dividend between execution and registration and Mrs Rose had claimed to have that dividend handed to her, what would Mr Rose's answer have been? It could no longer be that the purported gift was imperfect; it had been made perfect.

Question

What is the justification for the *Re Rose* principle?

In *Pennington v Waine*, the court decided that where the settlor manifests an immediate and irrevocable intention to transfer shares to an individual, and executes the appropriate forms regarding such transfer, the *Re Rose* principle will be satisfied. Thus, the equitable interest will be acquired by the transferee.

Pennington v Waine and Others [2002] All ER (D) 24, CA

Facts

Ada Crampton (A) was the beneficial owner of 75% of the issued share capital of a company of which she was one of two directors. In September 1998, she informed Mr Pennington (P), a partner in the form of the company's auditors, that she wished to transfer immediately 400 of her shares to her nephew, Harold (H). P prepared a share transfer form for the 400 shares and A signed and returned it to P. It was placed on the company's file. A indicated to H that she wanted to give him some of her shares and for him to become a director of the company. In October 1998, P wrote to H stating that he had been appointed as a director on 1 September 1998 and that A had instructed him to arrange the transfer to H of 400 shares. He added that no action was required on H's part to effect the transfer. H signed the form appointing him as a director and A countersigned the same. No further action was taken in relation to the transfer. On 10 November 1998, A executed a will in which she made no specific mention of the 400 shares. A died in November 1998. If the shares were transferred to H, he would become a 51% majority shareholder. In an action brought to determine whether the 400 shares formed part of A's residual estate or whether they were held in trust for H absolutely, it was contended in the Court of Appeal that A intended an immediate gift of the shares which was incomplete, and had not intended to constitute herself a trustee for the benefit of H.

Held

The disposition of the equitable interest to the transferee was complete on the following grounds:

(a) it was not necessary for the donor to have done all that was necessary to be done, short of registration, to complete the gift. It was sufficient if the donor had done all that was *necessary for him or her to do*;

(b) it is not always necessary that there should be delivery of the share certificates in order to transfer the equitable interest in the shares;

(c) on the facts there was clear evidence that A had intended to make an immediate and irrevocable gift of the shares to H. In the circumstances, there was an equitable assignment of the equitable interest in the shares to H.

Arden LJ: The equitable assignment [of the 400 shares] clearly occurs at some stage before the shares are registered. But does it occur when the share transfer is executed, or when the share transfer is delivered to the transferee, or when the transfer is lodged for registration . . .? The principle [in *Milroy v Lord* (1862) 31 LJ Ch 798] that, where a gift is imperfectly constituted, the court will not hold it to operate as a declaration of trust, does not prevent the court from construing it to be a trust if that interpretation is permissible as a matter of construction, which may be a benevolent construction. The same must apply to words of gift. [On this basis] a donor will not be permitted to change his or her mind if it would be unconscionable, in the eyes of equity, vis à vis the donee to do so, what is the position here? There can be no comprehensive list of factors which makes it unconscionable for the donor to change his or her mind: it must depend on the court's evaluation of all the relevant considerations. What then are the relevant factors here? Ada made the gift of her own free will: there is no finding that she was not competent to do this. She not only told Harold about the gift and signed a form of transfer which she delivered to Mr Pennington for him to secure registration: her agent also told Harold that he need take no action. In addition Harold agreed to become a director of the Company without limit of time, which he could not do without the shares being transferred to him. If Ada had changed her mind on (say) 10 November 1998, in my judgment the court could properly have concluded that it was too late for her to do this as by that date Harold signed the form, the last of the events identified above, to occur.

There was a clear finding that Ada intended to make an immediate gift. It follows that it would also have been unconscionable for Ada to recall the gift. It follows that it would also have been unconscionable for her personal representatives to refuse to hand over the share transfer to Harold after her death. In those circumstances, in my judgment, delivery of the share transfer before her death was unnecessary so far as perfection of the gift was concerned.

It is not necessary to decide the case simply on that basis. After the share transfers were executed Mr Pennington wrote to Harold on Ada's instructions informing him of the gift and stating that there was no action that he needed to take. I would also decide this appeal in favour of the respondent on this further basis. If I am wrong in the view that delivery of the share transfers to the company or the donee is required and is not dispensed with by reason of the fact that it would be unconscionable for Ada's personal representatives to refuse to hand the transfers over to Harold, the words used by Mr Pennington should be construed as meaning that Ada and, through her, Mr Pennington became agents for Harold for the purpose of submitting the share transfer to the Company. This is an application of the principle of benevolent construction to give effect to Ada's clear wishes. Only in that way could the result 'This requires no action on your part' and an effective gift be achieved. Harold did not question this assurance and must be taken to have proceeded to act on the basis that it would be honoured.

In *Milroy v Lord*, the settlor had not done everything in his power to transfer the shares to the transferee. Thus, the gift was incomplete and the intended donee as a volunteer was incapable of enforcing the intended settlement.

Milroy v Lord (1862) 31 LJ Ch 798, HC

Facts

A settlor attempted to transfer to Lord 50 shares in the Louisiana Bank upon trust for the benefit of the plaintiffs. The legal title to the shares was transferable by entry on the books of the bank. Lord held a power of attorney, executed by the settlor, entitling him to transfer the shares. The settlor gave the share certificates to Lord. The settlor also paid dividends to the plaintiffs during his lifetime. On the settlor's death, Lord gave the share certificates to the settlor's executors and the question arose whether the shares were held upon trust for the plaintiffs.

Held

There was no gift of the shares to the objects nor was there a transfer to the intended trustee. Having failed to transfer the shares to the trustee, the court will not infer that the settlor is a trustee for the plaintiffs:

> **Turner LJ:** The question is, whether the defendant Samuel Lord did not become a trustee of these shares? Upon this question I have felt considerable doubt; but in the result, I have come to the conclusion that no perfect trust was ever created in him. The shares, it is clear, were never legally vested in him; and the only ground on which he can be held to have become a trustee of them is that he held a power of attorney under which he might have transferred them into his own name; but he held that power of attorney as the agent of the settlor; and if he had been sued by the plaintiffs as trustee of the settlement for an account under the trust, and to compel him to transfer the shares into his own name as trustee, I think he might well have said: 'These shares are not vested in me; I have no power over them except as the agent of the settlor, and without his express directions I cannot be justified in making the proposed transfer, in converting an intended into an actual settlement.' A court of equity could not, I think, decree the agent of the settlor to make the transfer, unless it could decree the settlor himself to do so, and it is plain that no such decree could have been made against the settlor. In my opinion, therefore, this decree cannot be maintained as to the fifty Louisiana Bank shares . . .

Note

In *Milroy v Lord*, in order to transfer the equitable interest in the shares, the settlor was required to instruct Mr Lord (his power of attorney) to transfer the shares to himself (Lord). Alternatively, the settlor could have effected a direct transfer of the shares to Lord by executing the appropriate documents. He did neither of these, but merely executed a power of attorney in favour of Lord and delivered the share certificates to him. This was treated as insufficient conduct on the settlor's part.

In *Re Fry*, the transferor also failed to fulfil all his duties. The transfer of the equitable interest became a nullity.

Re Fry, Chase National Executors and Trustees Corp Ltd v Fry and Others [1946] Ch 312, HC

Facts

In 1940, the testator, who was resident in the USA, intended to make an *inter vivos* gift to his son, Sydney Fry. The subject matter of the intended transfer was shares held in an English company. Such transfers were subject to the Defence (Finance) Regulations 1939, which prohibited the transfer of any securities by a person resident outside the sterling area, unless Treasury permission and licence were obtained. The testator executed a transfer and sent it to the company for registration. The company notified the testator of the need to complete Treasury licence forms. After such forms were completed, but before the licence was granted, the testator died. The question in issue was whether Sydney Fry was entitled to force the testator's personal representatives to complete the transfer.

Held

The gift was incomplete and the son was not entitled to call on the personal representatives to obtain for him the legal and beneficial interests in the shares:

> **Romer J:** Sydney Fry and the Cavendish Trust clearly had not acquired, at the date of the testator's death, the legal title to the shares which they now claim, because the transfers had not been registered by Liverpool Borax Ltd. Had they, however, arrived at the position which entitled them, as against that company, to be put on the register of members? Had everything been done which was necessary to put the transferees into the position of the transferor? If these questions, could be answered affirmatively, the transferees would have had more than an inchoate title; they would have had it in their own hands to require registration of the transfers. Having regard, however, to the Defence (Finance) Regulations, 1939, it is impossible, in my judgment, to answer the questions other than in the negative. The requisite consent of the Treasury to the transactions had not been obtained, and, in the absence of it, the company was prohibited from registering the transfers. In my opinion, accordingly, it is not possible to hold that, at the date of the testator's death, the transferees had either acquired a legal title to the shares in question, or the right, as against all other persons (including Liverpool Borax Ltd) to be clothed with such legal title.
>
> Moreover, the Treasury might in any case have required further information of the kind referred to in the questionnaire which was submitted to him, or answers supplemental to those which he had given in reply to it; and, if so approached, he might have refused to concern himself with the matter further, in which case I do not know how anyone could have compelled him to do so. Apart, however, from considerations of this kind, it appears to me that the Defence (Finance) Regulations, 1939, reg 3A, prevents me from giving effect to the argument, however formulated, that at the time of the testator's death a complete equitable assignment had been effected.

Note

In *Re Fry*, the testator had not done everything that was required of him before sending the transfer documents to the company. He was required to obtain Treasury consent. This was a pre-condition in the sense that the company was prohibited from considering registration of the shares, unless and until a valid certificate of Treasury approval was received. Therefore, the documents delivered to the company were incomplete.

Question

How would you reconcile *Re Rose* with *Re Fry*?

The principle in *Re Rose* applies to registered land following the execution of the relevant documents and pending registration of the transferee: see *Mascall v Mascall* (1985) 49 P & CR 119.

Likewise, if the settlor's property consists solely of an equitable interest, he (the settlor) is required to do everything in his power to effect the transfer or assignment. An omission on the part of the intended transferor to fulfil one or more of his duties concerning the assignment of the interest will result in an ineffective transfer: see *Re McCardle* [1951] Ch 668.

FORMALITIES AND s 53(1)(C) OF THE LAW OF PROPERTY ACT 1925

In addition, if the settlor (transferor) owns the equitable interest in property subsisting under a trust and wishes to transfer this interest to another as trustee or beneficiary, he is required to transfer the interest in writing in order to comply with s 53(1)(c) of the Law of Property Act 1925. In other words, a beneficiary under a trust who wishes to assign his equitable interest may only accomplish his aim by reducing the transfer into writing. If T1 and T2 hold the legal title concerning property upon trust for B, a beneficiary, a transfer of B's equitable title must be in writing. It makes no difference whether the equitable interest exists in realty or personalty.

Law of Property Act 1925, s 53(1)(c)

A disposition of an equitable interest or trust subsisting at the time of the disposition, must be in writing signed by the person disposing of the same, or by his agent thereunto lawfully authorised in writing or by will.

The policy of enacting this sub-section was to prevent fraud by nullifying oral 'hidden' transfers in respect of either real or personal properties. In addition, the requirement of writing enables the trustee to chart the movement or destination of the equitable interest. The effect of the provision is that writing, executed by the intended transferor of the equitable interest, is mandatory. A purported oral disposition is void. The signature of the transferor or his agent lawfully appointed in writing will be sufficient compliance with the requirements of the sub-section.

Disposition

The various modes of disposing of a subsisting equitable interest were summarised by Romer LJ in *Timpson's Executors v Yerbury*.

Timpson's Executors v Yerbury (HM Inspector of Taxes) [1936] 1 KB 645, CA

Facts

Mrs Timpson was a beneficiary under a New York trust which gave the beneficiary a right to resort to the English Court of Equity in order to compel the trustees to discharge their duties. Mrs Timpson, from time to time, wrote letters to the trustees requesting them to pay certain sums to her children. These sums were remitted to England and paid to or on behalf of the children. On Mrs Timpson's death, the question arose whether her estate was liable to income tax in respect of the sums paid to the children. In other words, the issue was whether Mrs Timpson had alienated such part of her interest in favour of her children.

Held

Mrs Timpson's estate was correctly assessed to income tax. The letters of request did not create irrevocable mandates alienating part of her property for the benefit of the children.

> **Romer LJ:** The only question, therefore, that falls to be determined on this appeal is whether the sums paid to each of the children of Mrs Timpson in pursuance of the requests made by her to the American trustees were paid out of her income, or whether they were paid out of the income of that child.
>
> Now the equitable interest in property in the hands of a trustee can be disposed of by the person entitled to it in favour of a third party in any one of four different ways. The person entitled to it:
>
> (1) can assign it to the third party directly;
>
> (2) can direct the trustees to hold the property in trust for the third party;
>
> (3) can contract for valuable consideration to assign the equitable interest to him; or
>
> (4) can declare himself to be a trustee for him of such interest [emphasis added].
>
> Unless, therefore, the letters constituted an assignment to the children respectively of the equitable interest of Mrs Timpson in the net income to the extent therein mentioned, by one of the first two methods to which I have referred, no equitable interest in the income ever passed to them.
>
> I regard the letters as no more than revocable mandates given to the trustees, and conferring no rights whatsoever upon Mrs Timpson's children. There was no valuable consideration given by the children nor were the letters ever communicated to them by anybody. The mandates were, therefore, revocable at all times material to the present case.

Note

Section 53(1)(c) of the 1925 Act has no application to the original creation of a trust. The sub-section is applicable only when a beneficiary (under a subsisting trust) wishes to dispose of his equitable interest to another. Thus, s 53(1)(c) is not applicable where S, the settlor, with both legal and equitable interests in property, wishes to transfer the equitable interest to B, a beneficiary.

Question
What is the meaning of the expression 'disposition' within s 53(1)(c) of the Law of Property Act 1925?

Direction to trustees

The sub-section is applicable where the equitable owner under a subsisting trust directs the trustees to hold the property on trust for another beneficiary. This transfer must be in writing, otherwise the purported transfer is void. This mode of transfer falls within category 2 of Romer LJ's classification in *Timpson's Executors v Yerbury*. In *Grey v IRC* the issue was whether the owner of an equitable interest in personalty, subsisting under a trust, succeeded in disposing of his interest. The method adopted by the intended transferor, which proved unsuccessful, was to issue a verbal direction to the trustees to hold the property upon trust for a third party, despite the clear wording of s 53(1)(c) of the Law of Property Act 1925.

Grey v Inland Revenue Commissioners [1960] AC 1, HL

Facts
In 1949, Mr Hunter (the settlor) transferred shares of a nominal sum to trustees upon trust for his six grandchildren. In 1955, the settlor transferred 18,000 £1 shares to the same trustees upon trust for himself. In an attempt to avoid *ad valorem* stamp duty (payable on instruments which transfer any property or interest in property), the settlor orally instructed the trustees to hold the shares upon trust for the grandchildren. The trustees subsequently executed confirmatory documents affirming the oral instructions. The Revenue assessed the documents to *ad valorem* stamp duty.

Held
The oral instructions were ineffective for non-compliance with s 53(1)(c), but the documents executed subsequently had the effect of transferring the equitable interest and were stampable:

> **Lord Radcliffe:** My Lords, there is nothing more in this appeal than the short question whether the oral direction that Mr Hunter gave to his trustees on 18 February 1955, amounted in any ordinary sense of the words to a 'disposition of an equitable interest or trust subsisting at the time of the disposition'. I do not feel any doubt as to my answer. I think that it did [and was void for non-compliance with s 53(1)(c)]. Whether we describe what happened in technical or in more general terms, the full equitable interest in the eighteen thousand shares concerned, which at that time was his, was (subject to any statutory invalidity) diverted by his direction from this ownership into the beneficial ownership of the various equitable owners, present and future, entitled under his six existing settlements.
>
> Moreover, there is warrant for saying that a direction to his trustee by the equitable owner of trust property prescribing new trusts of that property was a declaration of trust. But it does not necessarily follow from that that such a direction, if the effect of it was to determine completely or *pro tanto* the subsisting equitable interest of the maker of the direction, was not also a grant or assignment for the purposes of s 9 [of the Statute of Frauds 1677] and therefore required writing for its validity. Something had to happen to that equitable interest in order to displace it in favour of the new interests created by the direction: and it would be at any rate logical to treat the direction as being an assignment of the subsisting interest to the new beneficiary or beneficiaries or, in other cases, a release or surrender of it to the trustee.
>
> I do not think, however, that that question has to be answered for the purposes of this appeal. It can only be relevant if s 53(1) of the Law of Property Act 1925 is treated as a true consolidation of the three sections of the Statute of Frauds concerned and as governed, therefore, by the general principle, with which I am entirely in agreement, that a consolidating Act is not to be read as effecting changes in the existing law unless the words it employs are too clear in their effect to admit of any other construction. But, in my opinion, it is impossible to regard s 53 of the Law of Property Act 1925 as a consolidating enactment in this sense.
>
> The Law of Property Act 1925 itself was, no doubt, strictly a consolidating statute. But what it consolidated was

not merely the Law of Property Act 1922, a statute which had itself effected massive changes in the law relating to real property and conveyancing, but also the later Law of Property (Amendment) Act 1924. The Statute of Frauds sections had not been touched by the Act of 1922, but they were, in effect, repealed and re-enacted in altered form by the operation of s 3 of the Act of 1924. This new wording is what is carried into s 53 of the Act of 1925.

For these reasons I think that there is no direct link between s 53(1)(c) of the Act of 1925 and s 9 of the Statute of Frauds. The link was broken by the changes introduced by the amendment Act of 1924, and it was those changes that s 53 must be taken as consolidating. If so, it is inadmissible to allow the construction of the word 'disposition' in the new Act to be limited or controlled by any meaning attributed to the words 'grant' or 'assignment' in s 9 of the old Act.

Appeal dismissed.

Note

The settlor could have avoided s 53(1)(c) and stamp duty had he declared himself a trustee of his equitable interest in 18,000 shares in the first place, instead of transferring the shares to the trustees upon trust for himself in 1955.

Disposition of the legal and equitable interests to a third party

Section 53(1)(c) has no application where the equitable owner effectively terminates the trust by directing the trustees to transfer their legal title to a third party and, in the same transaction, assigns the equitable interest to that third party. The rationale behind this principle, as stated by Lord Upjohn in *Vandervell v Inland Revenue Commissioners*, is that the unification of the legal and equitable interests is outside of the mischief of s 53(1)(c). It is unnecessary for the legal owner to chart the movement of the equitable interest simply because the trust no longer exists. Thus, the beneficiary under a subsisting trust may avoid the rigour of s 53(1)(c) by effecting the transfer of both the legal (including such formalities as appropriate) and equitable interests to a third party: see *Vandervell v Inland Revenue Commissioners*.

Vandervell v Inland Revenue Commissioners [1967] 2 AC 291, HL

Facts

In 1958, Mr Vandervell decided to donate £150,000 to the Royal College of Surgeons to found a chair of pharmacology. He decided to achieve this purpose by transferring 100,000 ordinary shares in Vandervell Products Limited (a private company controlled by Mr Vandervell) to the college subject to an option (vested in a separate company, Vandervell Trustee Company) to re-purchase the shares for £5,000. In pursuance of this scheme, Mr Vandervell orally directed the National Provincial Bank (which held the legal title to the shares on behalf of Mr Vandervell) to transfer the shares to the college, subject to the option exercisable by the trustee company. The bank complied with the directions. During the tax years 1958–59 and 1959–60, dividends on the shares amounting to £162,500 and £87,500, respectively, were paid to the college. In October 1961, the trustee company exercised the option and paid the college £5,000 and recovered the shares. The Inland Revenue assessed Mr Vandervell to surtax in respect of the dividends on the grounds that Mr Vandervell had not absolutely divested himself from the shares so that the dividends fell to be treated as his income within s 415 of the Income Tax Act 1952. In addition, the Revenue asserted that Mr Vandervell had not transferred his equitable interest in the shares to the college for failure to comply with s 53(1)(c) of the Law of Property Act 1925.

Held

(a) The assessment to surtax was valid on the ground that Mr Vandervell had retained an equit-able interest in the shares by way of a resulting trust. This trust had been created by reference to the incomplete disposal of the equitable interest in the *option* (Lords Reid and Donovan dissenting).

(b) In favour of Mr Vandervell on the ground that s 53(1)(c) was inapplicable when the equitable owner, in a composite transaction, transfers the equitable interest to a third party and directs the trustees to transfer the legal title to the same third party, namely the college:

Lord Upjohn: The question is whether notwithstanding the plainly expressed intention of the appellant by himself or his agents the absence of writing prevented any equitable or beneficial interest in the shares passing to the college so that contrary to his wishes and understanding they remained bare trustees for him. This depends entirely upon the true construction of s 53(1)(c) of the Law of Property Act 1925, which the Crown maintain makes writing necessary to pass the beneficial interest. This section was generally thought to re-enact s 9 of the Statute of Frauds and that section had never been applied to a trust of an equitable interest of pure personalty. Before the cases of *Grey v IRC* [1960] AC 1 and *Oughtred v IRC* [1960] AC 206, both in your Lordships' House, this argument would have been quite untenable.

It was shown in those cases that the Law of Property Act 1925 was not re-enacting s 9 but that it had been amended by the Law of Property Act 1924. The relevant words of s 53 are:

> . . . a disposition of an equitable interest or trust subsisting at the time of the disposition, must be in writing signed by the person disposing of the same . . .

Those words were applied in *Grey* and *Oughtred* to cases where the legal estate remained outstanding in a trustee and the beneficial owner was dealing and dealing only with the equitable estate. That is understandable; *the object of the section, as was the object of the old Statute of Frauds, is to prevent hidden oral transactions in equitable interests in fraud of those truly entitled, and making it difficult, if not impossible, for the trustees to ascertain who are in truth his beneficiaries. But when the beneficial owner owns the whole beneficial estate and is in a position to give directions to his bare trustee with regard to the legal as well as the equitable estate there can be no possible ground for invoking the section where the beneficial owner wants to deal with the legal estate as well as the equitable estate* [emphasis added].

As I have said, that section [s 53(1)(c)] is, in my opinion, directed to cases where dealings with the equitable estate are divorced from the legal estate and I do not think any of their Lordships in *Grey* and *Oughtred* had in mind the case before your Lordships. To hold the contrary would make assignments unnecessarily complicated; if there had to be assignments in express terms of both legal and equitable interests that would make the section more productive of injustice than the supposed evils it was intended to prevent.

I turn, then, to the second point.

Where A transfers, or directs a trustee for him to transfer, the legal estate in property to B otherwise than for valuable consideration it is a question of the intention of A in making the transfer whether B was to take beneficially or on trust and, if the latter, on what trusts. If, as a matter of construction of the document transferring the legal estate, it is possible to discern A's intentions, that is an end of the matter and no extraneous evidence is admissible to correct and qualify his intentions so ascertained.

But if, as in this case (a common form share transfer), the document is silent, then there is said to arise a resulting trust in favour of A. But this is only a presumption and is easily rebutted. All the relevant facts and circumstances can be considered in order to ascertain A's intentions with a view to rebutting this presumption.

As Lindley LJ said in *Standing v Bowring* (1885) 31 Ch D 282:

> Trusts are neither created nor implied by law to defeat the intentions of donors or settlors; they are created or implied or are held to result in favour of donors or settlors in order to carry out and give effect to their true intentions, expressed or implied.

But the doctrine of resulting trust plays another very important part in our law and, in my opinion, is decisive of this case.

If A intends to give away all his beneficial interest in a piece of property and thinks he has done so but, by some mistake or accident or failure to comply with the requirements of the law, he has failed to do so, either wholly or partially, there will, by operation of law, be a resulting trust for him of the beneficial interest of which he had failed effectually to dispose. If the beneficial interest was in A and he fails to give it away effectively to another or others or on charitable trusts it must remain in him. Early references to equity, like nature, abhorring a vacuum, are delightful but unnecessary. Let me give an example close to this case.

A, the beneficial owner, informs his trustees that he wants forthwith to get rid of his interest in the property and instructs them to hold the property forthwith upon such trusts as he will hereafter direct; that beneficial interest, notwithstanding the expressed intention and belief of A that he has thereby parted with his whole beneficial interest in the property, will inevitably remain in him for he has not given the property away effectively to or for the benefit of others. As Plowman J [at first instance] said: 'As I see it, a man does not cease to own property simply by saying "I don't want it". If he tries to give it away the question must always be, has he succeeded in doing so or not?'

While the Court of Appeal assumed that there was a resulting trust of the option for the appellant – they did not decide it upon that ground alone. Diplock LJ said: 'It is next contended that the trustee company took the option beneficially. This also seems to me to fly in the face of the evidence' – which he then examined in some detail.

Wilmer LJ in the next judgment said: 'Later – prompted, I suspect, by certain observations made by members of this court – the argument was developed that the trustee company should be regarded as taking the option beneficially.'

He also examined the evidence and came to the conclusion that there was no intention to give any beneficial interest to the trustee company. Harman LJ came to the same conclusion.

My Lords, this question is really one of inference from primary facts, but having regard to the way in which the matter has developed I should be reluctant to differ from the courts below, and I do not think that the question whether the doctrine of resulting trust applies to options, on the facts of this case in the least degree invalidates the reasoning of the Court of Appeal or its conclusions upon this point.

I agree with the conclusions of the Court of Appeal and Plowman J that the intention was that the trustee company should hold on such trusts as might thereafter be declared by the trustee company or the appellant and so in the event for the appellant.

Lord Donovan: . . . If, owning the entire estate, legal and beneficial, in a piece of property, and desiring to transfer that entire estate to another, I do so by means of a disposition which *ex facie* deals only with the legal estate, it would be ridiculous to argue that s 53(1)(c) has not been complied with, and that therefore the legal estate alone had passed. The present case, it is true, is different in its facts in that the legal and equitable estates in the shares were in separate ownership; but when the taxpayer, being competent to do so, instructed the bank to transfer the shares to the college, and made it abundantly clear that he wanted to pass, by means of that transfer, his own beneficial or equitable interest, plus the bank's legal interest, he achieved the same result as if there had been no separation of the interests. The transfer thus made, pursuant to his intentions and instructions, was a disposition, not of the equitable interest alone, but of the entire estate in the shares. In such a case, I see no room for the operation of s 53(1)(c) . . .

Declaration of trust by equitable owner of part of his interest

A controversial issue, which has yet to be resolved, is whether a declaration of trust by an equitable owner of a *part* of his interest under a subsisting trust is required to be in writing. The view seems to be that if the equitable owner declares a trust in respect of his entire interest so that he drops out of the picture, writing is required. But if he declares a trust in respect of a part of his interest so that a *new trust* is created in respect of a part of his original interest, imposing active duties on him to perform, writing is not essential. For example, if T1 and T2 hold the legal title on trust for B, a beneficiary, absolutely, and B declares himself a trustee of the shares for B for life with remainder to C absolutely, this declaration may not be within s 53(1)(c). The transfer of the remainder interest to C concerns a new trust and s 53(1)(c) is not applicable to the creation of trusts: see *Re Lashmar* [1891] 1 Ch 258. This view has been challenged by Brian Green: see p 33 below.

The importance of resulting and constructive trusts

Law of Property Act 1925, s 53(2)

This section does not affect the creation or operation of resulting, implied or constructive trusts.

The effect of s 53(2) is to dispense with writing in respect of implied, resulting and constructive trusts. Controversy surrounds the extent to which s 53(1)(c) may be restricted by the operation of the constructive and resulting trusts. On the one hand, a number of Law Lords have declined to recognise the constructive trust as relieving the transferor from the full rigour of s 53(1)(c) (see the opinions of Lords Cohen and Denning in *Oughtred v Inland Revenue Commissioners* [1960] AC 206). On the other hand, a constructive trust exception to an all pervasive s 53(1)(c) would appear to be consistent with policy and common sense. After all, a constructive trust is created by the courts in order to satisfy the demands of justice and conscience. If the circumstances surrounding a transaction demand the imposition of a constructive trust by the courts in order to maintain a balance between the trustees and the beneficiaries, the requirement of writing under s 53(1)(c) ought not to impede this process (see the opinion of Lord Radcliffe in *Oughtred v Inland Revenue Commissioners*, Megarry VC in *Re Holt's Settlement* [1969] Ch 100, Nourse LJ in *Neville v Wilson* [1996] 3 WLR 460 and the compromise adopted by Lord Denning MR in *Re Vandervell's Trusts (No 2)* [1974] Ch 269).

Oughtred v Inland Revenue Commissioners [1960] AC 206, HL (Lords Jenkins, Keith and Denning; Lords Radcliffe and Cohen dissenting)

Facts
Mrs Oughtred was the tenant for life under a settlement which comprised 200,000 shares in a company. The remainder interest in the shares was held on trust for her son, Peter, absolutely. Mrs Oughtred was also the absolute owner of 72,700 shares in the same company. As part of an estate duty avoidance scheme, Mrs Oughtred and Peter orally agreed on 18 June 1956 to transfer her absolute interest in 72,700 shares to Peter in exchange for Peter's remainder interest in 200,000 shares. The oral agreement was followed by the execution of three documents, all dated 26 June 1956:

(1) Mrs Oughtred executed a simple transfer to nominees for Peter of her 72,700 shares 'in consideration of 10 s'.

(2) By a deed of release expressed to be made between Mrs Oughtred of the first part, Peter of the second part and the trustees of the settlement of the third part, the parties confirmed that the trustees held the 200,000 shares upon trust for Mrs Oughtred absolutely.

(3) By a simple transfer, the trustees transferred the 200,000 shares to Mrs Oughtred 'in consideration of 10 s'.

The Inland Revenue claimed that the transfer of the 200,000 shares attracted *ad valorem* stamp duty on 'the amount or value of the consideration for the sale'. Section 54 of the Stamp Act 1891 declares that 'a conveyance on sale includes every instrument . . . whereby any property, or any estate or interest is transferred to or vested in a purchaser upon the sale thereof'. The Commissioners of Inland Revenue upheld the claim, but on appeal to the High Court, Upjohn J allowed the appeal and dismissed the claim. His decision was reversed by the Court of Appeal on the grounds that the transfer of the legal interest was 'a conveyance on sale'. The constructive trust doctrine did not replace the transfer for there still remained something which could be conveyed as part of the bargain, namely Peter's reversionary interest. The transfer of this reversionary interest attracted *ad valorem* stamp duty. On appeal to the House of Lords.

Held
Ad valorem stamp duty was payable on the transfer of Peter's reversionary interest in 200,000 shares. Only three Law Lords (Lords Radcliffe, Cohen and Denning) considered the relationship between ss 53(1)(c) and 53(2):

> **Lord Radcliffe (dissenting):** The whole point of the present appeal seems to me to turn on the question whether it is open to a court of law to deduce from the documents of this case that Mrs Oughtred's title to her son's equitable reversionary interest rested upon anything more than the oral agreement which admittedly took place.
>
> My Lords, on this short point my opinion is that such a deduction is not open to a court of law. The materials that

would support it are simply not there. I think that the judgment of Upjohn J in the High Court, which was in favour of Mrs Oughtred, was correct, and I agree with his reasons. I am afraid that I do not agree with the judgment of the Court of Appeal, which was in favour of the commissioners, or with the conclusion which, as I understand, commends itself to a majority of your Lordships.

The reasoning of the whole matter, as I see it, is as follows: On 18 June 1956, the son owned an equitable reversionary interest in the settled shares: by his oral agreement of that date he created in his mother an equitable interest in her reversion, since the subject matter of the agreement was property of which specific performance would normally be decreed by the court. He thus became a trustee for her of that interest *sub modo*: having regard to sub-s (2) of s 53 of the Law of Property Act, 1925, sub-s (1) of that section did not operate to prevent that trusteeship arising by operation of law. On 26 June, Mrs Oughtred transferred to her son the shares which were the consideration for her acquisition of his equitable interest: upon this transfer he became in a full sense and without more a trustee of his interest for her. She was the effective owner of all outstanding equitable interests. It was thus correct to recite in the deed of release to the trustees of the settlement, which was to wind up their trust, that the trust fund was by then held upon trust for her absolutely. There was, in fact, no equity to the shares that could be asserted against her, and it was open to her, if she so wished, to let the matter rest without calling for a written assignment from her son. Given that the trustees were apprised of the making of the oral agreement and of Mrs Oughtred's satisfaction of the consideration to be given by her, the trustees had no more to do than to transfer their legal title to her or as she might direct. This and no more is what they did.

It follows that, in my view, this transfer cannot be treated as a conveyance of the son's equitable reversion at all. The trustees had not got it: he never transferred or released it to them: how then could they convey it? With all respect to those who think otherwise, it is incorrect to say that the trustees' transfer was made either with his authority or at his direction. If the recital as to Mrs Oughtred's rights was correct, as I think that it was, he had no remaining authority to give or direction to issue. A release is, after all, the normal instrument for winding up a trust when all the equitable rights are vested and the legal estate is called for from the trustees who hold it. What the release gave the trustees from him was acquittance for the trust administration and accounts to date, and the fact that he gave it in consideration of the legal interest in the shares being vested in his mother adds nothing on this point. Nor does it, with respect, advance the matter to say, correctly, that at the end of the day Mrs Oughtred was the absolute owner of the shares, legal and equitable.

Lastly, I ought perhaps to say that I do not myself see any analogy between the operations embraced by the oral agreement and documents and the common case of a sale of shares by an owner for whom they are held by a nominee or bare trustee. What is sold there is the shares themselves, not the owner's equitable interest. What is passed by the transfer executed by his nominee is the shares, according to the contract, without any incumbrance on the title, equitable or legal.

Lord Cohen (dissenting): Before your Lordships Mr Wilberforce was prepared to agree that on the making of the oral agreement Peter became a constructive trustee of his equitable reversionary interest in the settled funds for the appellant, but he submitted that nonetheless s 53(1)(c) applied and accordingly Peter could not assign that equitable interest to the appellant except by a disposition in writing. My Lords, with that I agree, but it does not follow that the transfer was a conveyance of that equitable interest on which *ad valorem* stamp duty was payable under the Stamp Act 1891. It might well be that there has been no document transferring the equitable interest. The appellant may have been content to rely on getting in the legal interest by the transfer and on the fact that it would be impossible for Peter to put forward successfully a claim to an equitable interest in the settled shares once the consideration shares had been transferred to him or his nominees by the appellant.

Lord Denning: Was this transfer 'a conveyance or transfer on sale, of any property' such as to attract stamp duty on the value of the consideration? I have no doubt it was. Peter had agreed to sell his reversionary interest in the 200,000 shares to his mother for a stated consideration (the 72,700 shares). He did not convey this reversionary interest direct to her, nor did he convey it to the trustees of the settlement. But he authorised the trustees to convey it to her – not in the shape of a reversionary interest as such – but by way of enlarging her life interest into absolute ownership. It is clear to me that, by the transfer so made by his authority, she acquired his reversionary interest as effectively as if he had conveyed it direct to her. And that is quite enough to attract stamp duty.

I do not think it necessary to embark upon a disquisition on constructive trusts: because I take the view that, even if the oral agreement of 18 June 1956, was effective to transfer Peter's reversionary interest to his mother, nevertheless, when that oral agreement was subsequently implemented by the transfer, then the transfer became liable to stamp duty. But I may say that I do not think the oral agreement was effective to transfer Peter's reversionary interest to his mother. I should have thought that the wording of s 53(1)(c) of the Law of Property Act 1925, clearly made a writing necessary to effect a transfer: and s 53(2) does not do away with that necessity.

Lord Jenkins (with whom Lord Keith concurred): *I find it unnecessary to decide whether s 53(2) has the effect of excluding the present transaction from the operation of s 53(1)(c),* for, assuming in the appellant's favour that the oral contract did have the effect in equity of raising a constructive trust of the settled shares for her untouched by s 53(1)(c), I am unable to accept the conclusion that the disputed transfer was prevented from being a transfer of the shares to the appellant on sale because the entire beneficial interest in the settled shares was already vested in the appellant under the constructive trust, and there was accordingly nothing left for the disputed transfer to pass to the appellant except the bare legal estate. The constructive trust in favour of a purchaser which arises on the conclusion of a contract for sale is founded upon the purchaser's right to enforce the contract in proceedings for specific performance. In other words, he is treated in equity as entitled by virtue of the contract to the property which the vendor is bound under the contract to convey to him. This interest under the contract is no doubt a proprietary interest of a sort, which arises, so to speak, in anticipation of the execution of the transfer for which the purchaser is entitled to call. But its existence has never (so far as I know) been held to prevent a subsequent transfer, in performance of the contract, of the property contracted to be sold from constituting for stamp duty purposes a transfer on sale of the property in question. Take the simple case of a contract for the sale of land. In such a case a constructive trust in favour of the purchaser arises on the conclusion of the contract for sale, but (so far as I know) it has never been held on this account that a conveyance subsequently executed in performance of the contract is not stampable *ad valorem* as a transfer on sale. Similarly, in a case like the present one, but uncomplicated by the existence of successive interests, a transfer to a purchaser of the investments comprised in a trust fund could not, in my judgment, be prevented from constituting a transfer on sale for the purposes of stamp duty by reason of the fact that the actual transfer had been preceded by an oral agreement for sale [emphasis added].

In truth, the title secured by a purchaser by means of an actual transfer is different in kind from, and may well be far superior to, the special form of proprietary interest which equity confers on a purchaser in anticipation of such transfer.

This difference is of particular importance in the case of property such as shares in a limited company. Under the contract the purchaser is no doubt entitled in equity as between himself and the vendor to the beneficial interest in the shares, and (subject to due payment of the purchase consideration) to call for a transfer of them from the vendor as trustee for him. But it is only on the execution of the actual transfer that he becomes entitled to be registered as a member, to attend and vote at meetings, to effect transfers on the register, or to receive dividends otherwise than through the vendor as his trustee.

The parties to a transaction of sale and purchase may no doubt choose to let the matter rest in contract. But if the subject matter of a sale is such that the full title to it can only be transferred by an instrument, then any instrument they execute by way of transfer of the property sold ranks for stamp duty purposes as a conveyance on sale notwithstanding the constructive trust in favour of the purchaser which arose on the conclusion of the contract.

In the context of a variation of the terms of a trust under the Variation of Trusts Act 1958 (see Chapter 20), Megarry VC, in *Re Holt's Settlement*, adopted Lord Radcliffe's reasoning in *Oughtred v Inland Revenue Commissioners*, despite the fact that the latter's judgment was a minority opinion.

Re Holt's Settlement [1969] I Ch 100, HC

Megarry VC: Mr Millett for the tenant for life, provided . . . [a] means of escape from s 53(1)(c) in his helpful reply: 'Where, as here, the arrangement consists of an agreement made for valuable consideration, and that agreement is specifically enforceable, then the beneficial interests pass to the respective purchasers on the making of the agreement. Those interests pass by virtue of the species of constructive trust made familiar by contracts for the sale of land, whereunder the vendor becomes a constructive trustee for the purchaser as soon as the contract is made . . .' Section 53(2), he continued, provides that: 'This section does not affect the creation or operation of resulting, implied or constructive trusts.'

Accordingly, because the trust was constructive, s 53(1)(c) was excluded. He supported this contention by the House of Lords' decision in *Oughtred v IRC*. He relied in particular upon passages in the speeches of Lord

Radcliffe and Lord Cohen, albeit that they were dissenting on the main point for decision. He pointed out that although Lord Jenkins (with whom Lord Keith concurred) had not decided the point, he had assumed for the purposes of his speech that it was correct, and that the rejection of the contention by Lord Denning was in a very brief passage. 'Mr Millett accepts that if there were to be some subsequent deed of family arrangement which would carry out the bargain, then this deed might well be caught by s 53(1)(c); but that, he said, cannot affect the "arrangement" and the parties might well be willing to let matters rest on that.' It seems to me that there is considerable force in this argument in cases where the agreement is specifically enforceable, and in its essentials I accept it . . . For this and the other reasons I have given, though with some hesitation, I accordingly hold this to be the case.

Notes

In *Oughtred v Inland Revenue Commissioners*, three Law Lords (Lords Denning, Cohen and Radcliffe) considered the relationship between the two sub-sections of the Law of Property Act. Lord Denning sided with the majority opinions (on the issue of stamp duty) delivered by Lord Jenkins, with whom Lord Keith concurred. Lord Denning, in an uncharacteristically short speech, decided that the wording of s 53(2) was not intended to limit s 53(1)(c). This view was delivered without explanation. Lord Cohen dissented on the question of the imposition of stamp duty, but to a large extent agreed with Lord Denning on the relationship between the two sub-sections. Lord Cohen expressed the view that the transferor became a constructive trustee of his equitable interest for the transferee, but that, nonetheless, s 53(1)(c) applied. At the same time, the transferor could not rely on the non-compliance with s 53(1)(c) in order to defeat the transferee's interest, for he is treated as a constructive trustee. This view appears to be synonymous with an estoppel. Lord Radcliffe was the only Law Lord who gave a sound rational analysis of the relationship between the two sub-sections. His view was that the constructive trust (and, likewise, the resulting trust) was exempt from the formal requirements of s 53(1)(c). This was consistent with the wording of s 53(2) and settled principles. Thus, comparing the above three opinions of the Law Lords, it would appear that Lord Radcliffe's view represented, in more than one sense, a minority view incorporating a more realistic and rational analysis of the relationship between the two sub-sections. Above all, a constructive trust is created by the courts to satisfy the demands of justice and conscience. If the circumstances surrounding a transaction demand the imposition of a constructive trust by the courts in order to maintain a balance between the trustees and the beneficiaries, the formal requirement of writing under s 53(1)(c) ought not impede this process. It was against this background that Megarry VC in *Re Holt* decided to endorse Lord Radcliffe's opinion.

Lord Denning in *Re Vandervell's Trusts (No 2)* [1974] Ch 269 (see p 31 below) proceeded on a different platform when he decided that equitable estoppel prevented Mr Vandervell – and, after his death, his executors – from relying on the formal requirements of s 53(1)(c).

The case of *Neville v Wilson* is a landmark decision, representing the first decision since the High Court case of *Re Holt's Settlement* to consider rationally the relationship between ss 53(1)(c) and 53(2) of the Law of Property Act 1925.

In *Neville v Wilson*, Nourse LJ, after analysing the speeches of the Law Lords, decided that the effect of the agreement in 1969 constituted each shareholder a constructive trustee for the other shareholders. On this basis, there was no convincing reason to restrict the effect of the general words enacted in s 53(2).

Neville v Wilson [1996] 3 WLR 460, CA

Facts

JE Neville Ltd (J Ltd), a small family company, was the registered owner of all the issued share capital in another company, Universal Engineering Co Ltd (U Ltd), save for 120 ordinary shares, which were registered in the names of two directors of U Ltd as nominees for J Ltd. In 1965, the directors of U Ltd resolved that U Ltd shares, registered in the name of J Ltd, be transferred to the shareholders of J Ltd in proportions corresponding to their shareholdings in J Ltd. The transfers were executed within two weeks of the resolution. Neither the resolution of the directors nor the subsequent transfers extended to the 120 shares registered in the names of the directors of U Ltd. By 1970, J Ltd, although not formally liquidated, was treated by all concerned as being defunct. In July 1970, it was struck off the register and dissolved with the consequence that any assets owned beneficially by J Ltd passed to the Crown as *bona vacantia*. The question in issue concerned the beneficial ownership of the remaining 120 shares registered in the names of U Ltd directors. The plaintiffs claimed that J Ltd intended to distribute all its shares in U Ltd including the 120 shares in dispute. Thus, the plaintiffs argued that the shares were held on constructive trust for the shareholders in J Ltd. This, the plaintiffs claimed, was a true interpretation of the 1965 resolution. The judge dismissed the plaintiffs' claim and decided that no such distribution was intended. The plaintiffs appealed and raised an alternative argument to the effect that an agreement was entered into between the shareholders of J Ltd for the informal liquidation of J Ltd, which had the effect of disposing not only the assets but also its equitable interest in the remaining 120 shares in U Ltd. In other words, the shareholders of J Ltd agreed to a process whereby J Ltd's debts and liabilities were discharged and the balance of its assets, whether ascertained or not, were distributed to its shareholders rateably according to their shareholdings, *in specie* or in cash. The questions in issue were:

(a) whether there was an oral agreement for the informal liquidation of the company and, if so;

(b) whether it had the effect of disposing of the company's equitable interest in the shares of another company within s 53(1)(c) of the Law of Property Act 1925.

Held

It was an undisputed fact that after 1969 J Ltd was treated by all concerned as being defunct. From that it was reasonable to infer that its shareholders, in making their agreement, intended that it should not be left with any assets. In other words, it was reasonable to infer that the shareholders intended their agreement to apply to all assets, whether known or unknown.

The effect of the agreement was to create a constructive trust within s 53(2) of the Law of Property Act 1925 which dispensed with the requirement for writing under s 53(1)(c):

> **Nourse LJ:** This is a dispute between the shareholders of a small family company. The substantial questions now in issue are whether there was an agreement for the informal liquidation of the company and, if so, whether it had the effect of disposing of the company's equitable interest in the shares of another company. The latter question involves a consideration of s 53(1)(c) and (2) of the Law of Property Act 1925 and a point left open by the House of Lords in *Oughtred v IRC* [1960] AC 206.
>
> The simple view of the present case is that the effect of each individual agreement was to constitute the shareholder an implied or constructive trustee for the other shareholders, so that the requirement for writing contained in sub-s (1)(c) of s 53 was dispensed with by sub-s (2). That was the view taken by Upjohn J [1958] Ch 383 at first instance and by Lord Radcliffe in the House of Lords in *Oughtred v IRC* [1960] AC 206.
>
> [His Lordship considered the views of the Law Lords in *Oughtred's* case and continued:] The views of their Lordships as to the effect of s 53 can be summarised as follows: Lord Radcliffe, agreeing with Upjohn J, thought that sub-s (2) applied. He gave reasons for that view. Lord Cohen and Lord Denning thought that it did not. Although neither of them gave reasons, they may be taken to have accepted the submissions of Mr Wilberforce at pp 220–22. Lord Keith and Lord Jenkins expressed no view either way.
>
> We do not think that there is anything in the speeches in the House of Lords which prevents us from holding that the effect of each individual agreement was to constitute the shareholder an implied or constructive trustee for the other shareholders. In this respect we are of the opinion that the analysis of Lord Radcliffe, based on the proposition that a specifically enforceable agreement to assign an interest in property creates an equitable interest in the assignee, was unquestionably correct; cf *London and South Western Railway Co v Gomm* (1882) 20 Ch D 562, p 581, *per* Sir George Jessel MR. A greater difficulty is caused by Lord Denning's outright rejection of the application of s 53(2), with which Lord Cohen appears to have agreed.
>
> So far as it is material to the present case, what sub-s (2) says is that sub-s (1)(c) does not affect the creation or operation of implied or constructive trusts. Just as in *Oughtred v IRC* [1960] AC 206, the son's oral agreement

created a constructive trust in favour of the mother, so here each shareholder's oral or implied agreement created an implied or constructive trust in favour of the other shareholders. Why then should sub-s (2) not apply? No convincing reason was suggested in argument and none has occurred to us since. Moreover, to deny its application in this case would be to restrict the effect of general words when no restriction is called for, and to lay the ground for fine distinctions in the future. With all the respect which is due to those who have thought to the contrary, we hold that sub-s (2) applies to an agreement such as we have in this case.

For these reasons we have come to the conclusion that the agreement entered into by the shareholders of JEN in about April 1969 was not rendered ineffectual by s 53 of the Act of 1925.

Promissory estoppel

In *Re Vandervell's Trusts (No 2)*, Lord Denning MR in the Court of Appeal conceded that equitable estoppel provides an exception to the rigid requirements enacted in s 53(1)(c). He also decided that the resulting trust for Mr Vandervell ended when the option was exercised, following Mr Vandervell's oral direction, and the registration of the shares in the name of the trustee company. He classified the trust as express, but glossed over the requirements of writing under s 53(1)(c). Stephenson LJ (in the same case), although expressing some hesitation about the decision, supported the other Lord Justices of Appeal.

Re Vandervell's Trusts (No 2) [1974] Ch 269, CA

Facts

This was a sequel to *Vandervell v IRC* (see p 29 above). In October 1961, V orally directed the Vandervell Trustee Company to exercise the option. The trustee company complied with this instruction, taking £5,000 from the Vandervell Trustee Company's children's settlement in order to repurchase the shares from the college. In 1965, V received a surtax assessment from the Revenue in respect of the dividends from the shares. Such dividends were paid to the trustee company. The assessment was made on the basis that the equitable title to the shares, like the option, was held on resulting trust for V. Following this assessment, V executed a deed, dated 19 January 1965, which transferred all interest, if any, which he may have retained in the shares in favour of the children's settlement. In 1967, V died. V's executors claimed the dividends from the trustee company.

Held

V's estate was not liable to surtax on the ground that the resulting trust of the option in favour of V terminated on the date of the exercise of the option by the trustee company. A declaration of trust in favour of the children's settlement was effectively made by reference to three items of evidence. First, the exercise of the option was funded from the children's settlement. Secondly, the dividends were paid to the trustee company for the benefit of the children's settlement. Thirdly, the trustee company had informed the Revenue that the option was exercised and the shares were held upon the trusts of the children's settlement.

Lord Denning MR: [after summarising the history of the litigation, his Lordship continued] The executors admit that from 19 January 1965, Mr Vandervell had no interest whatsoever in the shares. The deed of that date operated so as to transfer all his interest thenceforward to the trustee company to be held by them on trust for the children. I asked counsel for the executors: what is the difference between the events of October and November 1961 and the event of 19 January 1965? He said that it lay in the writing. In 1965 Mr Vandervell disposed of his equitable interest in writing, whereas in 1961 there was no writing. There was only conduct or word of mouth. That was insufficient. And, therefore, his executors were not bound by it.

The answer to this argument is [that] Mr Vandervell did not dispose in 1961 of any equitable interest. All that happened was that his resulting trust came to an end – because there was created a new valid trust of the shares for the children's settlement.

Estoppel

Even if counsel for the executors were right in saying that Mr Vandervell retained an equitable interest in the shares, after the exercise of the option, the question arises whether Mr Vandervell can in the circumstances be heard to assert the claim against his children. Just see what happened. He himself arranged for the option to be exercised. He himself agreed to the shares being transferred to the trustee company. He himself procured his products company to declare dividends on the shares and to pay them to the trustee company for the benefit of the children. Thenceforward, the trustee company invested the money and treated it as part of the children's settlement. If he himself had lived, and not died, he could not have claimed it back. He could not be heard to say that he did not intend the children's trust to have it. Even a court of equity would not allow him to do anything so inequitable and unjust. Now that he has died, his executors are in no better position. If authority were needed, it is to be found in *Milroy v Lord* (1862) 31 LJ Ch 798. [After referring to the facts in *Milroy v Lord*, his Lordship continued]: Knight-Bruce and Turner LJJ held that the executors were entitled to the bank shares, because 'there is no equity in this court to perfect an imperfect gift'. But the executors were not entitled to the fire insurance shares. Turner LJ said:

> ... the settlor made a perfect gift to [the niece] of the dividends upon these shares, so far as they were handed over or treated by him as belonging to her, and these insurance shares were purchased with dividends which were so handed over or treated.

So here Mr Vandervell made a perfect gift to the trustee company of the dividends on the shares, so far as they were handed over or treated by him as belonging to the trustee company for the benefit of the children. Alternatively, there was an equitable estoppel. His conduct was such that it would be quite inequitable for him to be allowed to enforce his strict rights (under a resulting trust) having regard to the dealings which had taken place between the parties (see *Hughes v Metropolitan Railway Co* (1877) 2 App Cas 439).

I would allow the appeal and dismiss the claim of the executors.

Stephenson LJ: Lord Denning MR and Lawton LJ are able to hold that no disposition is needed because: (1) the option was held on such trusts as might thereafter be declared by the trustee company or Mr Vandervell himself; and (2) the trustee company has declared that it holds the shares in the children's settlement. I do not doubt the first, because it was apparently the view of the majority of the House of Lords in *Vandervell v IRC* [1967] 2 AC 291. I should be more confident of the second if it had been pleaded or argued either here or below and we had had the benefit of the learned judge's views on it. I see, as perhaps did counsel, difficulties in the way of a limited company declaring a trust by parol or conduct and without a resolution of the board of directors, and difficulties also in the way of finding any declaration of trust by Mr Vandervell himself in October or November 1961, or any conduct then or later which would in law or equity estop him from denying that he made one.

However, Lord Denning MR and Lawton LJ are of the opinion that these difficulties, if not imaginary, are not insuperable and that these shares went into the children's settlement in 1961 in accordance with the intention of Mr Vandervell and the trustee company – a result with which I am happy to agree as it seems to me to be in accordance with the justice and the reality of the case.

Lawton LJ began with the point that it was the late Mr Vandervell's intention that the trustee company should hold the option on such trusts as might thereafter be declared by the trustee company or Mr Vandervell himself and held that the trustee company declared trusts for the children in 1961. He also held that Mr Vandervell was estopped from denying the existence of a beneficial interest for his children.

He went on to create a most unlawyerlike distinction between the option held on a resulting trust and the shares acquired upon exercising the option: he took the view that after the option had been exercised it had been extinguished, so no old equitable interest existed to be capable of assignment, so that only new equitable interests could be created! However, the option is not distinct from the shares but merely a limited right created out of the larger bundle of rights inherent in the ownership of the shares. For this very reason the House of Lords in *Vandervell v IRC* had held that Vandervell, the original beneficial owner of the shares, who had remained beneficial owner under a resulting trust of the option relating to the shares, had failed to divest himself absolutely of the shares which the option governed. If the right to the shares under the option was held by the trustee company under a resulting trust for Vandervell then any shares actually acquired by exercising the right should surely be similarly held under a resulting trust.

Disclaimers

Although a conscious and intentional transfer of a subsisting equitable interest must be in writing, it seems that when an equitable owner intends to disclaim an equitable interest, the disclaimer is not required to be in writing. The reason being that no one may be compelled to retain an equitable interest. The manifestation of an intention to disown an interest will be sufficient to disclaim that interest. The effect is that on a disclaimer by an equitable owner, a resulting trust will be created in favour of the settlor or his estate in the absence of provisions to the contrary.

In *Re Paradise Motor Co*, one of the questions in issue was whether a disclaimer of an equitable interest in shares operated by way of a 'disposition' within s 53(1)(c). The court decided that a disclaimer is outside s 53(1)(c).

Re Paradise Motor Co [1968] 1 WLR 1125, CA

Dankwerts LJ: We think that the short answer to this is that a disclaimer operates by way of avoidance and not by way of disposition. For the general aspects of disclaimer we refer briefly to the discussion in *Re Stratton's Disclaimer* [1958] Ch 42.

Nominations

In addition, nominations by pension fund holders of the persons who will become entitled to benefits under a pension fund after the deaths of the pension fund holders are not 'dispositions' within s 53(1)(c) of the 1925 Act. Accordingly, such nominations are not required to be in writing: see *Re Danish Bacon Co Staff Pension Fund*.

Re Danish Bacon Co Staff Pension Fund [1971] 1 WLR 248, HC

Megarry J: What I am concerned with is a transaction whereby the deceased dealt with something which *ex hypothesi* could never be his. He was not disposing of his pension, nor of his right to the contributions and interest if he left the company's service. He was dealing merely with a state of affairs that would arise if he died while in the company's pensionable service, or after he had left it without becoming entitled to a pension. If he did this, then the contributions and interest would, by force of the rules, go either to his nominee, if he had made a valid nomination, or to his personal representatives, if he had not. If he made a nomination, it was revocable at any time before his death.

The question is thus whether an instrument with this elective, contingent and defeasible quality, which takes effect only on the death of the person signing it, can fairly be said to be a 'a disposition of an equitable interest or trust subsisting at the time of the disposition'. Mr Ferris put much emphasis on the word 'subsisting': however wide the word 'disposition' might be in its meaning, there was no disposition of a subsisting equity, he said. I should hesitate to describe an instrument which has a mere possibility of becoming a 'disposition' as being in itself a disposition *ab initio*; and I agree that the word, 'subsisting' also seems to point against the nomination falling within s 53(1)(c) ... I very much doubt whether the nomination falls within s 53(1)(c); but as I have indicated, I do not have to decide that point, and I do not do so.

Question
What judicial limitations have been imposed on the meaning of the term 'disposition' within s 53(1)(c) of the Law of Property Act 1925?

Green, B, 'Grey, Oughtred and Vandervell: a contextual reappraisal' (1984) 47 MLR 385

Green subjected the four decisions (including *Re Vandervell's Trusts (No 2)*) to a searching analysis. The focus of attention was to ascertain the ambit of s 53(1)(c) of the Law of Property Act 1925. He asserts that the policy of enacting s 53(1)(c), like s 9 of the Statute of Frauds 1677, was: '(i) to prevent hidden oral transactions in equitable interests in fraud of those truly entitled; and (ii) to enable trustees to know where the equitable interests behind their trusts reside at any particular time.' Moreover, the subsection draws no distinction between dealings with equitable interests carrying beneficial rights on the one hand and, on the other hand, dealings with equitable interests shorn of beneficial rights, that is, valuable and valueless equitable interests. Green contends that both types of interests fall within the ambit of s 53(1)(c):

> ... it is said that a declaration of trust over a subsisting equitable interest, with beneficial entitlement annexed thereto, is not within the sub-section since it merely entails a disposition of beneficial interest, and not of the subsisting equitable interest itself, which continues to exist in its original proprietor despite the declaration having taken place. If this is right then s 53(1)(c) is seen to operate in a somewhat arbitrary fashion, permitting the oral declaration of trust which shifts the valuable beneficial rights out of a subsisting equitable interest, but requiring written assignment if, at a later stage, the declarant decided to part with the valueless equitable interest retained by him ... at most, a declaration of trust over a subsisting equitable interest involves a disposition 'out of' that interest, not a disposition of the interest itself – and it is to dispositions of subsisting equitable interests, not to dispositions 'out of' such interests, that the literal words of s 53(1)(c) are addressed.

> [Professor Hayton] expressed the view that, in deciding whether a 'declaration of trust' over a subsisting equitable interest falls within s 53(1)(c), it is necessary to distinguish between declarations under which the declarant purports to reserve to himself an active role as trustee of the derivative equitable interest established by him, and declarations whereby the declarant renders himself a bare trustee for others. The former case is said to fall outside s 53(1)(c), whilst the latter is said to be within it on the basis that the declarant having no further role to play simply 'drops out of the picture' from the moment of declaration onwards. Three 19th century cases are cited in support of this view, *Onslow v Wallis* (1849) 1 Mac & G 506; *Re Lashmar* [1891] 1 Ch 258; *Grainge v Wilberforce* (1889) 5 TLR 436.

Mr Green examines these cases and concludes:

> ... this somewhat inelegant distinction between declarations within s 53(1)(c) and declarations outside it, whatever its intuitive appeal, is certainly not justified by the 19th century authorities marshalled in its support, and is inconsistent with the view adopted by the House of Lords in *Oughtred v IRC* (1960) in relation to a constructive bare trustee of an equitable interest who most definitely remained 'in the picture' until the execution of a 'completion document' deliberately removed him from it.

Battersby examined in detail five important cases concerning s 53(1)(c) of the Law of Property Act 1925. These cases are: *Grey v Inland Revenue Commissioners* [1960] AC 1; *Oughtred v Inland Revenue Commissioners* [1960] AC 206; *Vandervell v Inland Revenue Commissioners* [1967] 2 AC 291; *Re Holt's Settlement* [1969] 1 Ch 100; and *Re Vandervell's Trusts (No 2)* [1974] Ch 269. He concluded with the principles derived from these decisions.

Battersby, G, 'Formalities for the disposition of equitable interests under a trust' [1979] Conv 17

Battersby tabulated his conclusion as follows:

(1) the beneficiary (B) assigns his beneficial interest directly to a third party (X). This is clearly within s 53(1)(c) and must be in writing;

(2) B assigns his interest to new trustees to hold on trust for X. The assignment to the trustees must be in writing, but there is also a declaration of trust, which requires written evidence if the trust property is land. The assignment itself need not contain any particulars of the new trusts, see *Re Tyler's Fund Trusts* [1967] 3 All ER 389;

(3) B directs the original trustees to hold his interest for X. This is a disposition within s 53(1)(c), see *Grey v IRC* [1960] AC 1, but, it is submitted, is not at the same time a declaration of trust;

(4) B, the absolute beneficial owner, directs the trustees to convey the legal title to X, with the intention that X shall hold beneficially, and the trustees execute the conveyance. X takes beneficially, and there is no need for any separate written assignment by X, see *Vandervell v IRC* [1967] 2 AC 291;

(5) B contracts for value to assign to X. If the contract is specifically enforceable it creates a constructive trust in favour of X. The original trustees will hold directly for X, so that the transaction resembles an assignment by B to X; nevertheless, it is submitted that, as a constructive trust, the transaction is exempted by s 53(2) from

the requirements of writing, see *Oughtred v IRC* [1960] AC 206; *Re Holt* [1969] 1 Ch 100; *per* Lord Wilberforce in *Vandervell v IRC* [1967] 2 AC 291;

(6) B contracts for value to assign to new trustees to hold on trust for X. The result is the same as in transaction (5) above, but in addition there is an express declaration of trust which, if it relates to land, must be evidenced in writing;

(7) B declares himself a trustee in favour of X. It is submitted that B will drop out of the picture, unless he has active duties to perform as a trustee. In the latter case, the transaction is a declaration of trust, and must be evidenced in writing if it relates to land. In the former case, the original trustees hold for X directly, the transaction is in truth an assignment and must be in writing, see *Grainge v Wilberforce* (1889) 5 TLR 436; *Re Lashmar* [1891] 1 Ch 258;

(8) B, the absolute beneficial owner, declares himself a trustee in favour of X for life, then for Y absolutely. B has active duties to perform as a trustee, since otherwise the duties of the original trustees would be enlarged; the transaction is therefore a declaration of trust, and must be evidenced in writing if it relates to land. B can call for the legal title, see *Onslow v Wallis* (1849) 1 Mac & G 506;

(9) B is the legal and beneficial owner of personal property which he conveys to persons as trustees but without declaring any beneficial interests. B therefore is beneficially entitled under a resulting trust. B then declares that the trustees shall hold for X. Despite the exemption of a resulting trust from the requirement of writing, it is submitted that B's declaration is a disposition to X which must be in writing, unless the declaration is made by a person other than B under a power reserved to that person by the original conveyance to the trustees, and therefore having priority to the resulting trust, see *Re Vandervell's Trusts (No 2)* [1974] Ch 269.

THE DECLARATION OF TRUSTS AND FORMALITIES

The additional requirement imposed on the settlor in order to perfect a trust is the declaration of the terms of the trust. In other words, the identity of the trustees and beneficiaries, the ascertainment of the trust property and the nature of the beneficial interest are required to be sufficiently clear so that the court may enforce the trust. The expression 'declaration of trust' is a phrase that reflects the settlor's intention to create a trust including the terms of the trust. The three certainties test determines whether a valid declaration of trust has been created. A settlor may even declare himself a trustee. This is known as a self-declaration of trust. The question here is whether the retention of the property by the settlor is as trustee or not. If the self-declaration is valid, it is treated as effective as transferring the property to a third party, subject to a declaration of trust.

Generally, no formalities are required to be complied with for 'equity looks at the intent rather than the form'. Thus, the declaration of trust may be made orally, or by conduct or in writing. Exceptionally, Parliament may impose formal requirements for the creation of a trust.

Law of Property Act 1925, s 53(1)(b)

. . . a declaration of trust respecting any land or any interest therein must be manifested and proved by some writing signed by some person who is able to declare such trust or by his will.

The predecessor to this sub-section was enacted in the Statute of Frauds 1677 which was passed for the purpose of preventing fraud by requiring evidence of the terms of the trust in writing.

Under Sched 1 to the Interpretation Act 1978, ' "land" includes buildings and other structures, land covered with water, and any estate, interest, easement, servitude or right in or over land'.

Law of Property Act 1925, s 205(1)(ix), (x)

(ix) 'land' includes land of any tenure, and mines and minerals, whether or not held apart from the surface, buildings or parts of buildings (whether the division is horizontal, vertical or made in any other way) and other corporeal hereditaments; also a manor, an advowson, and a rent and other incorporeal hereditaments, and an easement, right, privilege, or benefit in, over, or derived from land; and 'mines and minerals' include any strata or seam of minerals or substances in or under the land, and powers of working and getting the same; and 'manor' includes a lordship, and reputed manor or lordship; and 'hereditament' means any real property which on an intestacy occurring before the commencement of this Act might have devolved upon an heir;

(x) 'legal estates' mean the estates, interests and charges, in or over land (subsisting or created in law) which are by this Act authorised to subsist or to be created as legal estates; 'equitable interests' mean all the other interests and charges in or over land; and equitable interest 'capable of subsisting as a legal estate' means such as could validly subsist or be created as a legal estate under this Act.

Under the Trusts of Land and Appointment of Trustees Act 1996, an all-pervasive concept known as a 'trust of land' was created. This term is applicable to all trusts – express, resulting, construct-ive or statutory – which include land (s 1). The dual concepts of strict settlements and trusts for sale, which existed prior to the introduction of the 1996 Act, are now treated as trusts of land. Express trusts for sale may still be created after the 1996 Act, but these take effect as trusts of land. A power to postpone the sale is implied into every trust for sale, which is capable of being postponed indefinitely in the exercise of the discretion of the trustees. This power to postpone the sale is incapable of being excluded by the settlor.

Section 3 of the 1996 Act abolishes the doctrine of conversion. The effect is that a trust of land is treated as realty and the interests of the beneficiaries under the trust are treated as interests in land. For example, if S, a settlor, transfers land to trustees, T1 and T2, to hold upon trust for A and B equally, the beneficiaries are treated as enjoying interests in land. A declaration of trust by A and/or B of his (or their) interest falls within s 53(1)(b) of the Law of Property Act 1925.

Writing for these purposes may be taken to mean any permanent form of representation. In this respect, regard may be had the Civil Evidence Act 1995. A document is defined in s 13.

Civil Evidence Act 1995, s 13

[A document is] anything in which information of any description is recorded ... a statement means any representation of fact or opinion, however made.

The document is required to incorporate all the terms of the trust, signed by the person declaring the trust (settlor). If, however, there is a series of documents, each incorporating a material term of the trust, each document may be joined together to form a complete memorandum, provided that a subsequent document is referred to in the earlier document, and each document or one of the composite documents is signed by the settlor. The signature of agents of the settlor is not permit-ted. The settlor's signature may constitute any form of endorsement of the terms of the document, such as initials, thumbprint, etc. Reference may be made to the expression 'sign' in s 1(4) of the Law of Property (Miscellaneous Provisions) Act 1989, which states that, for the purposes of s 1 of the Act, ' "sign", in relation to an instrument, includes making one's mark on the instrument and "signature" is to be construed accordingly'.

Effect of non-compliance with s 53(1)(b) of the Law of Property Act 1925

The effect of s 53(1)(b) of the Law of Property Act 1925 is that a declaration of trust in respect of real property is required to be evidenced in writing. Non-compliance with this formal require-ment renders the declaration of trust *unenforceable*. In other words, the trust is not rendered void, but, instead, no one is entitled to enforce the trust for failure to satisfy s 53(1)(b). If evidence in writing of the terms of the trust is adduced subsequent to the declaration, the trust will be enforced, not from the date of the execution of the document, but from the earlier date of the parol declaration of trust. For example, on day one, S, a settlor, orally declares himself a trustee of his real property, Blackacre, in favour of B, a beneficiary. This trust is unenforceable for non-compliance with s 53(1)(b). On day two, S executes a signed document containing the terms of the trust. The trust is now enforceable retrospectively from day one.

Law of Property Act 1925, s 53(2)

This section shall not affect the creation or operation of implied, resulting and constructive trusts.

In other words, a person who claims an equitable interest in land without being able to establish the terms of the trust in writing is entitled to prove that his interest arises by way of a resulting or constructive trust. (These are implied trusts created by the courts: see Chapters 8 and 9.) In *Hodgson v Marks*, the court decided that a resulting trust of land was created and this institution relieved the declarant from the requirements of s 53(1)(b) of the Law of Property Act 1925.

Hodgson v Marks [1971] Ch 892, CA

Facts

Mrs H transferred the legal title to her house in favour of her lodger (Evans) on the oral understanding that the property would continue to be hers. Evans then attempted to sell the house to Marks who had notice of the agreement but claimed that Mrs H's interest was unenforceable. Mrs H relied on s 53(2).

Held

Mrs H retained her equitable interest by way of a resulting trust which exempted her from the formal requirements under s 53(1)(b).

> **Russell LJ:** ... the evidence is clear that transfer [to Mr Evans] was not intended to operate as a gift, and, in those circumstances, I do not see why there was not a resulting trust of the beneficial interest to the plaintiff, which would not, of course, be affected by s 53(1). It was argued that a resulting trust is based upon implied intention, and that where there is an express trust for the transferor intended and declared – albeit ineffectively – there is no room for such an implication. I do not accept that. If an attempted express trust fails, that seems to me just the occasion for implication of a resulting trust, whether the failure be due to uncertainty, or perpetuity, or lack of form. It would be a strange outcome if the plaintiff were to lose her beneficial interest because her evidence had not been confined to negativing a gift but had additionally moved into a field forbidden by s 53(1) for lack of writing. I remark in this connection that we are not concerned with the debatable question whether on a voluntary transfer of land by A to stranger B there is a presumption of a resulting trust. The accepted evidence is that this was not intended as a gift, notwithstanding the reference to love and affection in the transfer, and s 53(1) does not exclude that evidence.

Note

The same result could have been achieved by Mrs H contending that a constructive trust had been created in her favour. The maxim, 'equity will not allow a statute to be used as an engine for fraud', could have been adopted by the court to prevent Mr Marks relying on the non-compliance with s 53(1)(b) in order to support his claim. It would have been ironic if a section originally introduced by the Statute of Frauds 1677 in order to prevent fraud could be used to perpetrate a fraud.

Law of Property (Miscellaneous Provisions) Act 1989, s 2

(1) A contract for the sale or other disposition of an interest in land can only be made in writing and only by incorporating all the terms which the parties have expressly agreed in one document or, where contracts are exchanged, in each.

(2) The terms may be incorporated in a document either by being set out in it or by reference to some other document.

(3) The document incorporating the terms or, where contracts are exchanged, one of the documents incorporating them (but not necessarily the same one) must be signed by or on behalf of each party to the contract.

(4) ...

(5) This section does not apply in relation to:

    (a) ...

    (b) ...

    (c) ...

and nothing in this section affects the creation or operation of resulting, implied or constructive trusts.

(6) In this section:

'disposition' has the same meaning as in the Law of Property Act 1925;

'interest in land' means any estate, interest or charge in or over land or in or over the proceeds of sale of land.

Unlike s 53(1)(b) of the Law of Property Act 1925, non-compliance with the 1989 Act renders the purported transfer void. But both provisions are subject to the existence of a resulting or constructive trust.

The declaration of trust may take two forms. Either:

(a) a direction to the trustees to hold the property subject to the terms set out by the settlor (a third party declaration); or

(b) an acknowledgment by the settlor as to his new status as trustee in respect of property retained by him (a self-declaration).

Accordingly, the settlor, as the original owner of both the legal and equitable interests in property, may transfer the legal title to a trustee subject to the terms of the trust, or the settlor may retain the legal title but declare himself a trustee of the property for the benefit of another or others. In either case, the test is whether the settlor intended to impose a trust in respect of the relevant property and whether he had incorporated the minimum set of terms. This is a question that varies with the facts of each case.

In *Singla v Bashir*, the court compared the effects of non-compliance with s 2 of the Law of Property (Miscellaneous Provisions) Act 1989 and s 53(1)(b) of the Law of Property Act 1925. Under the 1989 Act, the contract is void, subject to exceptions, whereas non-compliance with the 1925 Act makes the declaration of trust unenforceable but not void, subject to the same exceptions.

Singla v Bashir [2002] All ER (D) 176, HC

Facts

The defendant had been a tenant of a council property for a number of years. He was entitled to purchase the property at a discount under the 'right to buy' scheme under the Housing Act 1985, but could not afford to do so. A third party introduced the defendant to the claimant who professed an interest in acquiring the property as an investment. The defendant was 66 years old, had a very poor grasp of English and because of ill health had not worked for some 20 years. By an oral agreement, the claimant undertook to provide the amount required for the defendant to purchase the property. The claimant alleged that under the agreement the defendant was to remain in the property for three years, but after that period he would transfer it to the claimant. A transfer before three years would have resulted in the defendant having to repay the discount to the local authority. The defendant executed a written declaration of trust to the effect that he held the property on trust for the claimant. At the end of the three-year period, the defendant remained in occupation of the property and refused to transfer the legal title to the claimant. The claimant commenced proceedings to enforce his rights under the declaration of trust and claimed an order requiring the defendant to transfer the legal title to him. The defendant sought to have the declaration of trust set aside on the ground of undue influence and an allegation of unconscionable bargain. In addition, the defendant claimed that the oral agreement was void under s 2(1) of the Law of Property (Miscellaneous Provisions) Act 1989.

Held

A valid trust of land had been created in favour of the claimant on the following grounds:

(a) By reference to the evidence and surrounding circumstances, it was clear that there had been an agreement between the parties under which the defendant would hold the legal title to the property upon trust for the claimant. Setting aside the agreement on the ground of undue influence required a pre-existing relationship between the parties. There had been no prior relationship between the parties when the transaction was made. Thus, the equitable doctrine of undue influence was not made out.

(b) The court was not prepared to set aside the transaction on the ground that it was an unconscionable bargain. The claimant benefited greatly from the agreement. He was a medical doctor and was far more educated than the defendant, but there was not sufficient evidence that he behaved in a morally reprehensible manner. There was no evidence that the defendant could have done significantly better elsewhere and that the claimant was aware of that.

(c) The claimant was not seeking to enforce the oral contract which was void under s 2(1) of the Law of Property (Miscellaneous Provisions) Act 1989 (subject to the existence of a constructive trust). Instead, the claimant was suing to enforce the declaration of trust which was executed by the defendant in writing.

THE THREE CERTAINTIES TEST

The 'three certainties' test exists as a means of ascertaining whether the settlor has validly declared the terms of the trust. This test was laid down by Lord Langdale MR in *Knight v Knight* as:

(a) certainty of intention;

(b) certainty of subject matter; and

(c) certainty of objects.

Knight v Knight (1840) 3 Beav 148

Lord Langdale MR: . . . the recommendation, entreaty, or wish shall be held to create a trust.

First, if the words were so used, that upon the whole, they ought to be construed as imperative; secondly, if the subject of the recommendation or wish be certain; and thirdly, if the objects or persons intended to have the benefit of the recommendation or wish be also certain.

On the other hand, if the giver (donor) accompanies his expression of wish, or request by other words, from which it is to be collected, that he did not intend the wish to be imperative; or if it appears from the context that the first taker was intended to have a discretionary power to withdraw any part of the subject from the object of the wish or request; or if the objects are not such as may be ascertained with sufficient certainty, it has been held that no trust is created.

Certainty of intention

This test requires the court to consider the words used by the settlor and all the surrounding circumstances, including the settlor's conduct, in order to ascertain whether he intended to impose the obligations of trusteeship in respect of property for the benefit of the beneficiaries. This narrow requirement is materially different from an intention merely to benefit another. There are many different ways of benefiting another, but the narrow issue here is whether the settlor has gone further and *declared his intention to impose an equitable obligation on the trustees in respect of the property*. The question is simply whether the settlor manifested an intention to create a trust. This is a question of fact and degree. Although desirable, the settlor need not use the expression 'trust', but substitute expressions used by the settlor must have this effect in order to create a trust, for 'equity looks at the intent rather than the form'.

In *Jones v Lock*, it was decided that an imperfect gift was made by the intended donor and such an imperfect gift will not be construed as a valid self-declaration of trust.

Jones v Lock (1865) LR I Ch App 25, CA

Facts

Robert Jones placed a cheque for £900 into the hand of his nine-month-old baby, saying 'I give this to baby and I am going to put it away for him'. He then took the cheque from the child and told his nanny: 'I am going to put this away for my son.' He put the cheque in his safe. A few days later, he told his solicitor: 'I shall come to your office on Monday to alter my will, that I may take care of my son.' He died the same day. The question in issue was whether the cheque funds belonged to the child or to the residuary legatees under Robert Jones's will.

Held

The fund belonged to the residuary legatees. The delivery of the cheque to the child did not transfer the relevant funds and Jones had not declared a trust of the cheque:

> **Lord Cranworth LC:** I cannot bring myself to think that, either on principle or on authority, there has been any gift or any valid declaration of trust. No doubt a gift may be made by any person *sui juris* and *compos mentis*, by conveyance of a real estate or by delivery of a chattel; and there is no doubt also that, by some decisions, unfortunate I must think them, a parol declaration of trust of personalty may be perfectly valid even when voluntary. If I give any chattel that, of course, passes by delivery, and if I say, expressly or impliedly, that I constitute myself a trustee of personalty, that is a trust executed, and capable of being enforced without consideration. I do not think it necessary to go into any of the authorities cited before me; they all turn upon the question, whether what has been said was a declaration of trust or an imperfect gift. In the latter case the parties would receive no aid from a court of equity if they claimed as volunteers. But when there has been a declaration of trust, then it will be enforced, whether there has been consideration or not. Therefore, the question in each case is one of fact; has there been a gift or not, or has there been a declaration of trust or not? I should have every inclination to sustain this gift, but unfortunately I am unable to do; the case turns on the very short question whether Jones intended to make a declaration that he held the property in trust for the child; and I cannot come to any other conclusion than that he did not. I think it would be a very dangerous example if loose conversations of this sort, in important transactions of this kind, should have the effect of declarations of trust.

In *Paul v Constance*, the court decided that having regard to the statements and conduct of the parties a valid trust had been created.

Paul v Constance [1977] I WLR 527, CA

Facts

Ms Paul and Mr Constance lived together as man and wife. Mr C received £950 compensation for an industrial injury and both parties agreed to put the money in a deposit account in Mr C's name. On numerous occasions, both before and after the opening of the account, Mr C told Ms P that the money was as much hers as his. After Mr C's death, Ms P claimed the fund from Mrs C, the administratrix.

Held

Mr C, by his words and deeds, declared himself a trustee for himself and Ms P of the damages. Accordingly, 50% of the fund was held upon trust for Ms P:

> **Scarman LJ:** There is no suggestion of a gift by transfer in this case. [Counsel for the defendant argued] that there must be a clear declaration of trust, and that means there must be clear evidence from what is said or done of an intention to create a trust, or as counsel for the defendant put it, 'an intention to dispose of a property or a fund so that somebody else to the exclusion of the disponent acquires the beneficial interest in it'. He submitted that there was no such evidence.
>
> When one looks to the detailed evidence to see whether it goes as far as that – and I think that the evidence does have to go as far as that – one finds that from the time that Mr Constance received his damages right up to his death he was saying, on occasions, that the money was as much the plaintiff's as his. When they discussed the damages, how to invest them or what to do with them, when they discussed the bank account, he would say to her: 'The money is as much yours as mine.' The judge, rightly treating the basic problem in the case as a question of fact, reached this conclusion. He said:

I have read through my notes, and I am quite satisfied that it was the intention of [the plaintiff] and Mr Constance to create a trust in which both of them were interested.

In this court the issue becomes: was there sufficient evidence to justify the judge reaching that conclusion of fact? In submitting that there was, counsel for the plaintiff draws attention first and foremost to the words used. When one bears in mind the unsophisticated character of Mr Constance and his relationship with the plaintiff during the last few years of his life, counsel for the plaintiff submits that the words that he did use on more than one occasion namely: 'This money is as much yours as mine,' convey clearly a present declaration that the existing fund was as much the plaintiff's as his own. The judge accepted that conclusion. I think he was well justified in doing so and, indeed, I think he was right to do. There are, as counsel for the plaintiff reminded us, other features in the history of the relationship between the plaintiff and Mr Constance which support the interpretation of those words as an express declaration of trust. I have already described the interview with the bank manager when the account was opened. I have mentioned also the putting of the 'bingo' winnings into the account, and the one withdrawal for the benefit of both of them.

It might, however, be thought that this was a borderline case, since it is not easy to pinpoint a specific moment of declaration, and one must exclude from one's mind any case built on the existence of an implied or constructive trust; for this case was put forward at the trial and is now argued by the plaintiff as one of express declaration of trust. It was so pleaded, and it is only as such that it may be considered in this court. The question, therefore, is whether in all the circumstances the use of those words on numerous occasions as between Mr Constance and the plaintiff constituted an express declaration of trust. The judge found that they did. For myself, I think he was right so to find. I therefore would dismiss the appeal.

In *Re Kayford*, a mail order company intended to create a trust of deposited sums for its customers.

Re Kayford Ltd [1975] I All ER 604, HC

Facts

A mail order company received advice from accountants as to the method of protecting advance payments of the purchase price or deposits for goods ordered by customers. The company was advised to open a separate bank account to be called 'Customer Trust Deposit Account' into which future sums of money received for goods not yet delivered to customers were to be paid. The company accepted the advice and its managing director gave oral instructions to the company's bank, but instead of opening a new account, a dormant deposit account in the company's name was used for this purpose. A few weeks later, the company was put into liquidation. The question in issue was whether the sums paid into the bank account were held upon trust for customers who had paid wholly or partly for goods which were not delivered, or whether they formed part of the general assets of the company.

Held

A valid trust had been created in favour of the relevant customers in accordance with the intention of the company and the arrangements effected. The position remained the same even though payment was not made into a separate banking account:

Megarry J: I feel no doubt that the intention was that there should be a trust. There are no formal difficulties. The property concerned is pure personalty, and so writing, though desirable, is not an essential. There is no doubt about the so called 'three certainties' of a trust. The subject matter to be held on trust is clear, and so are the beneficial interests therein, as well as the beneficiaries. As for the requisite certainty of words, it is well settled that a trust can be created without using the words 'trust' or 'confidence' or the like: the question is whether in substance a sufficient intention to create a trust has been manifested.

In *Re Nanwa Gold Mines Ltd* [1955] I WLR 1080 the money was sent on the faith of a promise to keep it in a separate account, but there is nothing in that case or in any other authority that I know of to suggest that this is essential. I feel no doubt that here a trust was created. From the outset the advice (which was accepted) was to establish a trust account at the bank. The whole purpose of what was done was to ensure that the moneys remained in the beneficial ownership of those who sent them, and a trust is the obvious means of achieving this. No doubt the general rule is that if you send money to a company for goods which are not delivered, you are merely a creditor of the company unless a trust has been created. The sender may create a trust by using appropriate words when he sends the money (though I wonder how many do this, even if they are equity lawyers), or the company may do it by taking suitable steps on or before receiving the money. If either is done, the obligations in respect of the money are transformed from contract to property, from debt to trust. Payment into a separate bank account is useful (though by no means conclusive) indication of an intention to create a trust, but of course there is nothing to prevent the company from binding itself by a trust even if there are no effective banking arrangements.

Accordingly, of the alternative declarations sought by the summons, the second, to the effect that the money is held in trust for those who paid it, is in my judgment the declaration that should be made.

I should, however, add one thing. Different considerations may perhaps arise in relation to trade creditors; but here I am concerned only with members of the public, some of whom can ill afford to exchange their money for a claim to a dividend in the liquidation, and all of whom are likely to be anxious to avoid this. In cases concerning the public, it seems to me that where money in advance is being paid to a company in return for the future supply of goods or services, it is an entirely proper and honourable thing for a company to do what this company did, on skilled advice, namely, to start to pay the money into a trust account as soon as there begin to be doubts as to the company's ability to fulfil its obligations to deliver the goods or provide the services. I wish that, sitting in this court, I had heard of this occurring more frequently; and I can only hope that I shall hear more of it in the future.

Question

What evidence would the court take into consideration in deciding whether a person intended to create a trust?

Trusts of choses in action

A chose in action is a right to intangible personal property and is capable of being the subject matter of a trust. The settlor is required to manifest a clear intention to create a trust of the chose in action, for the right is obviously incapable of delivery. In *Don King Productions Inc v Warren*, the court decided that where an attempted assignment of rights under a contract was ineffective in law, it is still open to the parties to create a trust of the benefit of the obligations under the contract. Whether the terms of the contract prohibit such a declaration of trust depends on the facts of each case. But a contractual term prohibiting an assignment of rights *prima facie* does not extend to declarations of trust of the benefits of the contract. Accordingly, the parties retained their freedom to create a trust of benefits under the contract.

Don King Productions Inc v Warren and Others [1998] 2 All ER 608, HC

Facts

The plaintiff was Don King Productions Inc (DKP), a company owned by Mr Don King, a leading boxing promoter in the USA. The first defendant was Mr Frank Warren (W), a leading boxing promoter in the UK. The other defendants were Mr Warren's business associates. In 1994, the plaintiff and defendants agreed to extend their business relationship and entered into two part-nership agreements for the purpose of the promotion and management of boxing in Europe. In the first agreement, W purported to assign to the partnership all benefits and burdens of his existing promotion and management agreements with boxers. In the second agreement, it was provided that the partners would hold all promotion and management agreements for the benefit of the partnership absolutely. It transpired that some of the promotion agreements and all of the management agreements contained express provisions prohibiting assignments. Thereafter, W entered into fresh agreements, including a 'multi-fight agreement' for the broadcasting of certain fights in the USA. A dispute arose between the parties as to W's entitlement to enter into the 'multi-fight agreement' and the partnership was terminated. The plaintiff commenced proceedings against the defendants.

The issue before the court was whether the benefit of the promotion and management agree-ments was capable of being the subject matter of a trust, despite the express clause prohibiting the assignment of rights.

Held

A valid trust of a chose in action was created in favour of the plaintiff. This was created in accordance with the intention of the parties. Accordingly, W's entry into the 'multifight agreement' intended for his benefit was in breach of the duties owed to the plaintiff:

Lightman J:

Non-assignable contracts

[Counsel for the defendant] submitted that, where a contract contains a provision prohibiting assignment, a party cannot, by a declaration of trust or otherwise, make himself the trustee of the benefit of that contract, because this would defeat the whole purpose of the non-assignment obligation which is to ensure that the other contracting party alone, and no one else, can enforce the obligations contained in the contract against him; and that if a trust is created and if the trustee refuses to enforce an obligation, the beneficiary may sue for enforcement, joining the trustee as a defendant: see *Vandepitte v Preferred Accident Insurance Corp of New York* [1932] All ER 527, p 532.

This contention likewise fails for (amongst others) the following reasons: (a) if one party wishes to protect himself against the other party declaring himself a trustee, and not merely against an assignment, he should expressly so provide. That has not been done in this case; (b) the applicable principles of trusts law in this situation are the basic principles and those (and only those) whose rationale have application in this commercial context (see *Target Holdings Ltd v Redferns (A Firm)* [1995] 3 All ER 785, pp 795–96). The courts will accordingly be astute to disallow use of the procedural shortcut sanctioned in *Vandepitte's* case in a commercial context where it has no proper place. A beneficiary cannot be allowed to abrogate the fullest protection that the parties to the contract have secured for themselves, under the terms of the contract, from intrusion into their contractual relations by third parties; (c) a declaration of trust cannot prejudice the rights of the obligor. If the contract requires any judgment to be exercised, whether by the obligor or the obligee, an assignment cannot alter who is to exercise it, or how that judgment is to be exercised, or vest the right to make that judgment in the court; (d) the rule in *Saunders v Vautier* [1835–42] All ER 58 (which enables the sole beneficiary or beneficiaries to give directions to the trustee) only applies if the beneficiary is entitled to wind up the trust and require the trustee to assign to him the subject matter of the trust. If the trust cannot be determined because the trustee has, under the contract, held as a trust asset outstanding obligations and has no power to transfer the trust asset to the beneficiary or his order, the rule does not apply: see *Re Brockbank (Decd), Ward v Baker* [1948] 1 All ER 287. Accordingly, in a case where the subject matter of the trust is a non-assignable contract and there are outstanding obligations to be performed by the trustee, the beneficiary under the trust cannot interfere.

Accordingly, in principle, I can see no objection to a party to contracts involving skill and confidence or containing non-assignment provisions from becoming trustee of the benefit of being the contracting party as well as the benefit of the rights conferred. I can see no reason why the law should limit the parties' freedom of contract to creating trusts of the fruits of such contracts received by the assignor or to creating an accounting relationship between the parties in respect of the fruits. The broader approach, which I favour, appears to be in accord with the authorities, so far as they go. The leading authority is *Re Turcan* (1888) 40 Ch D 5. The Vice Chancellor of the County Palatine of Lancaster (Bristowe VC) in that case held that an agreement to assign a non-assignable policy constituted the assignor a trustee of the policy for the assignee. The Court of Appeal upheld the validity of the trusteeship of these assets, and Lord Browne-Wilkinson in *Linden Gardens Trust Ltd v Lenesta Sludge Disposals Ltd* [1993] 3 All ER 417, p 428; referred to *Re Turcan* as authority for the proposition that a party to a contract may agree with a third party to account for him for the fruits he receives from the other contracting party. No doubt was cast by the Court of Appeal in *Re Turcan* or by the House of Lords in the *Linden Gardens* case on the decision of Bristowe VC. As Lord Browne-Wilkinson said in the *Linden Gardens* case [1993] 3 All ER 417, pp 430–31; the House of Lords only had to consider the validity of the restriction of an assignment which would have the effect of bringing the assignee into direct contractual relations with the other party to the contract. The view of Bristowe VC finds some support in *Devefi Pty Ltd v Mateffy Pearl Nagy Pty Ltd* [1993] RPC 493, pp 555–56 and *Williams v Commissioner of Inland Revenue* [1965] NZLR 395, p 401. But most importantly this view accords with common sense and justice and achieves the commercial objective of the parties.

Result

I accordingly hold that the clear intent of the parties, manifested in the first and second agreements, was that the PM & A agreements should be held by the partnership or by the partners for the benefit of the partnership absolutely, and that this intent should be given fullest possible effect. The agreements have accordingly at all times been held by the partners as trustees for the partnership. Accordingly, the ordinary equitable principles apply (including the rule in *Keech v Sandford* (1726) Sd Cas ch 437) and the partnership assets include all renewal and replacement agreements obtained by any partner during the partnership and over the period between dissolution and the completion of winding up.

It was found in *Burton v FX Music and Taube* that a contract between two parties directing that royalty payments be made to a third party may, on construction, create a trust in favour of the third party.

Burton v FX Music and Taube (1999) *The Times*, 8 May, HC

Facts

The claims related to royalties in respect of a successful song called, 'Ooh Aah Just a Little Bit' sung by Gina G. Mr Taube, a barrister, composed the song. Mr Burton and another (trading as the Next Room) were the producers of the original demo version of the song. By contracts made in 1995, FX Music (FX) became the main producers of the song for commercial distribution, although the Next Room made significant contributions. In March 1996, FX entered into an agreement with Warner concerning the making and distribution of discs of the song. In a letter, FX notified Warner that royalties were payable directly to the Next Room and Mr Taube. A further letter by FX authorised Warner to deduct and pay the royalties directly to the Next Room and Mr Taube. A dispute arose between FX on the one hand and Mr Taube and the Next Room on the other hand. Warner failed to distribute the royalties and retained them in an interest bearing account pending a resolution. FX went into a creditors' voluntary liquidation. The claimants sought accounts and payment of the royalties due under the agreements with FX.

Held

A trust of a chose in action was created in favour of the claimants. The letters sent by FX to Warner were intended to have contractual effect and were sufficient to give the claimants proprietary rights in the royalties by way of a trust. The subject matter of the trust was Warner's contractual obligation to FX to make royalties payments directly to the claimants. The same result could be achieved under a *Quistclose* trust (see *Barclays Bank v Quistclose Investments* [1970] AC 567, p 158) in respect of moneys currently held by Warner. The moneys ought to have been paid to FX and the claimants. Instead, they were retained pending resolution of the dispute.

In *Duggan v Governor of Full Sutton Prison* an interesting point was raised concerning the status of a prisoner's right to his money, which he was obliged to transfer to the prison authorities on arrival. The issue was whether the governor became merely a debtor for the prisoner or was a trustee of such property.

Duggan v Governor of Full Sutton Prison (2004) *The Times*, 13 February, CA

Facts

The claimant was a prisoner serving a life sentence imposed on him in or about 1984. The claim raised the question whether: (i) cash of which he was deprived when arriving at the prison; or (ii) cash or securities for money which had subsequently been sent to him while in prison; or (iii) money which he had earned while in prison was held by one or other of the defendants (respectively the Home Office and the prison governor) on trust for him. Rule 43(3) of the Prison Rules 1999 provides:

> any cash which a prisoner has at a prison shall be paid into an account under the control of the governor and the prisoner shall be credited with the amount in the books of the prison.

The claimant contended that r 43 imposed a trust that obliged the governor to pay those moneys or assets representing the same to the prisoner upon his release from prison, and in the meantime to invest the same in an interest bearing account.

Held

The High Court rejected the claim.

The Court of Appeal dismissed the appeal on the following grounds:

- It was impossible to find any clear intention in r 43 to create a trust by reference to the language used.

- The wording of the rule ('account' and 'credited') was consistent with a creditor/debtor relationship.

- There was no reason to construe r 43 so as to imply a trust which had not been expressed. The construction contended by the claimant would have brought him little, if any, practical benefit, while imposing a disproportionate administrative burden on the prison authorities.

- If the rule-maker had intended to impose a trust obligation in respect of prisoners' funds, he might have been expected to say so.

Precatory words

The same principles concerning an intention to create a trust apply to testamentary dispositions. Precatory words, such as words of entreaty, prayer, confidence, expectation or hope, may or may not create a trust. Such ambiguous words are required to be construed by the courts, in the context of the will and surrounding circumstances, in order to ascertain the intention of the testator.

In *Re Adams and Kensington Vestry*, the will and surrounding circumstances were so unclear that no trust could have been intended by the precatory words used by the testator.

Re Adams and the Kensington Vestry (1884) 27 Ch D 394, CA

Facts

A testator left property, by his will, subject to the following clause: 'unto and to the absolute use of my wife, Harriet, in full confidence that she will do what is right as to the disposal thereof between my children either in her lifetime or by will after her decease.' The question in issue was whether a trust in favour of the children was created.

Held

No trust was created and the wife acquired the property beneficially:

Cotton LJ: Undoubtedly, to my mind, in the later cases, especially *Lambe v Eames* (1871) 6 Ch App 597 and *Re Hutchinson and Tenant* (1878) 8 Ch D 540, both the Court of Appeal and the late Master of the Rolls shewed a desire really to find out what, upon the true construction, was the meaning of the testator, rather than to lay hold of certain words which in other wills had been held to create a trust, although on the will before them they were satisfied that that was not the intention. I have no hesitation in saying myself, that I think some of the older authorities went a great deal too far in holding that some particular words appearing in a will were sufficient to create a trust. Undoubtedly confidence, if the rest of the context shews that a trust is intended, may make a trust, but what we have to look at is the whole of the will which we have to construe, and if the confidence is that she will do what is right as regards the disposal of the property, I cannot say that that is, on the true construction of the will, a trust imposed upon her. Having regard to the later decisions, we must not extend the old cases in any way, or rely upon the mere use of any particular words, but, considering all the words which are used, we have to see what is their true effect, and what was the intention of the testator as expressed in his will. In my opinion, here he has expressed his will in such a way as not to shew an intention of imposing a trust on the wife, but on the contrary, in my opinion, he has shewn an intention to leave the property, as he says he does, to her absolutely.

In contrast, in *Comiskey and Others v Bowring-Hanbury*, the will and surrounding circumstances were sufficiently clear for the court to conclude that a trust was intended by the testator.

Comiskey and Others v Bowring-Hanbury and Another [1905] AC 84, HL

Facts

Mr Hanbury, the testator, transferred his property by his will to his widow:

> ... in full confidence that she will make such use of it as I should have made myself and that at her death she will devise it to such one or more of my nieces as she may think fit and in default of any disposition by her thereof by her will or testament. I hereby direct that all my estate and property acquired by her under this my will shall at her death be equally divided among the surviving said nieces.

The widow having acquired the property took out an originating summons to determine whether, on construction of the will, she took the property absolutely or subject to a trust in favour of the nieces.

Held

On construction of the will, the intention of the testator was to transfer the property absolutely to his widow for life and, after her death, one or more of his nieces was or were entitled to benefit subject to a selection by his widow. Failing such selection, the nieces were entitled equally:

> **Lord Davey:** My Lords, in my opinion the question really is this: do those words, 'in default of any disposition by her thereof by her will or testament', mean any disposition in favour either of the nieces or anybody else, or are they, as Mr Warmington contended, to be construed as relating to such a disposition as that which he has expressed his confidence that his wife would make? I come to the conclusion that the testator is speaking only of a default of any such disposition as he had expressed his confidence that his wife would make, and, if so, I am of opinion that there is a good executory limitation.
>
> Therefore, even if you treat the words 'in confidence' as only expressing a hope or belief, the will would run thus: 'I hope and believe that she will give the estate to one or more of my nieces, but if she does not do so, then I direct that it shall be equally divided between them.' I think that is a perfectly good limitation. The true antithesis I think is between the words 'such one or more of my nieces as she may think fit' and the words 'equally divided between my surviving said nieces'.

Likewise, in *Re Steele's Will Trusts*, a trust was intended by the testatrix where her will was drafted in similar terms to a precedent that created a trust.

Re Steele's Will Trusts, National Provincial Bank Ltd v Steele [1948] Ch 603, HCM

Facts

The testatrix, Mrs Adelaide Steele, who died on 19 November 1929, by her will provided as follows:

> I give my diamond necklace to my son, Charles, to go and be held as an heirloom by him and by his eldest son on his decease and to go and descend to the eldest son of such eldest son and so to the eldest son of his descendants as far as the rules of law and equity will permit (and I request my said son to do all in his power by his will or otherwise to give effect to this my wish).

Charles died in April 1945 having made a will declaring: 'I give my diamond necklace to my trustees upon trust for my son, Ronald, during his life and after his death for his eldest son absolutely.'

It was clear that the provision in Adelaide's will bore a striking similarity to a clause included in the testatrix's will in *Shelley v Shelley* (1868) LR 6 Eq 540. In that case, the court decided that a trust was imposed on the eldest son of the settlor for life with remainder to his eldest son for life and continuing, subject to the perpetuities rule, in trust for the eldest son.

The question in issue was whether Charles took the necklace absolutely or whether there was a trust for a succession of the eldest sons of eldest sons, subject to the perpetuity rule.

Held

On construction of the will, a trust was created in accordance with the intention of the testatrix.

> **Wynn-Parry J:** With the exception of the latter words, 'as to these things so directed to go as heirlooms as

aforesaid', the relevant provision in the will which I have to construe in terms *mutatis mutandis* exactly corresponds with those in the will which fell to be construed in *Shelley v Shelley* (1868) LR 6 Eq 540. In that case it was held that on the true construction of that provision a valid executory trust was created for John Shelley for life with remainder to his eldest son for his life and on the death of that eldest son in trust for his eldest son to be a vested interest in him when he should attain 21, but if he should die in his father's lifetime or after his death without having attained 21, leaving an eldest son born before his father's death, in trust for such last mentioned eldest son to be a vested interest when he should attain 21, and, subject to these limitations, the jewels vested in John Shelley absolutely and passed by his will. The basis of the decision was this. Sir W Page Wood VC, held that the words of the gift to John Shelley 'to go and be held as heirlooms by him and by his eldest son on his decease' if they stood alone, would have been a gift to the first taker for life and on his death would have gone to the next taker absolutely.

It is, therefore, clear that, if *Shelley v Shelley* governs the present case, there is complete machinery for working out the trust on which this necklace ought to be held. The attack is made on the basis that, in view of the modern trend of decisions as regards precatory trusts, *Shelley v Shelley* should not be followed. I do not propose to embark on a detailed review of the authorities, but will content myself with observing that it appears to me from a review of the later authorities to which I was referred – *Re Hamilton (Decd)* [1895] 2 Ch 370, *Re Williams (Decd)* [1897] 2 Ch 12 and *Re Hill (Decd)* [1897] 1 QB 483 – that there is no ground for regarding the authority of *Shelley v Shelley* as being no longer binding.

Shelley v Shelley has stood for eighty years and I have before me a will which, as I have already observed, is, as regards the relevant passage, couched in the same language *mutatis mutandis* as that which was considered by Wood VC, in *Shelley v Shelley*. That appears to me to afford the strongest indication that the testatrix by this will, which appears clearly on the face of it to have been prepared with professional aid, intended that the diamond necklace in question should devolve in the same manner as the jewellery in *Shelley v Shelley* was directed to devolve by the order made therein. Having regard to the nature of this indication of intention and to the circumstances, I cannot see any good reason why, notwithstanding the admitted trend of modern decisions, I should treat *Shelley v Shelley* as wrongly decided, and, therefore, a case which I ought not to follow.

I come to the conclusion that I must declare that, on the true construction of the will of the testatrix, the diamond necklace should have been held on trust for Charles Steele for his life, and after his death for the second plaintiff, Charles Ronald Steele, for his life, and after his death for David Steele, the third plaintiff, for his life, and after the death of the survivor of them on trust for the eldest son or grandson of the third plaintiff, David Steele, and otherwise in the manner decided in *Shelley v Shelley* including the ultimate trust (in default of any male issue of David Steele who take an absolutely vested interest) in favour of Charles Steele absolutely and that the order in this case will follow *mutatis mutandis* the minutes which appear in the case of *Shelley v Shelley*. If the courts decide that the transferor did not manifest an intention to create a trust, the assignee or transferee takes the property beneficially. This is treated as a gift to the assignee.

Note

Despite Wynn-Parry J's ruling that he was obliged to come to the same conclusion as Wood VC in *Shelley v Shelley*, the issue of intention is one of fact that is not subject to binding precedent.

On construction of the will the donor may create a general gift in favour of A, subject to a specific intended gift in favour of B. If the specific gift fails, the court may treat the gift to A as absolute or unconditional, unhindered by any limitation in favour of B. In the case of wills, A's estate is entitled to retain the property: see *Hancock v Watson* [1902] AC 14. This principle is sometimes referred to as the rule in *Lassence v Tierney* (1849) 1 Mac & G 551.

Hancock v Watson [1902] AC 14, HL

Facts

A testator gave his residuary estate to trustees on trust for his widow for life and after her death to be divided into five portions. Two portions were donated to a friend, Susan Drake, for life and after her death upon trust for her children, but in default of issue in favour of the children of the testator's brother, Charles, on condition that they attain the age of 21 or earlier marriage. Susan died without issue. At the time of her death, Charles's children had attained the age of 21 or married. The questions in issue were: (a) whether Charles's children took the property in accordance with the testator's will; or alternatively (b) on Susan's death, whether her estate became entitled to the property absolutely.

Held

The intended gift in favour of Charles's children was void for infringing the perpetuity rule. On construction, the testator created an absolute gift in favour of Susan, subject to trusts which failed. In these circumstances, the absolute gift took effect to the exclusion of the resulting trust. Thus, Susan was entitled to dispose of the property in any way she liked:

> **Lord Davey:** The appellant's second point is that the two fifths allotted to Susan Drake on failure of the gift over goes to the next of kin of the testator, and not to Susan's representatives. I confess to some surprise at hearing this point treated as arguable. For, in my opinion, it is settled law that if you find an absolute gift to a legatee in the first instance, and trusts are engrafted or imposed on that absolute interest which fail, either from lapse or invalidity or any other reason, then the absolute gift takes effect so far as the trusts have failed to the exclusion of the residuary legatee or next of kin (of the original testator) as the case may be. Of course, as Lord Cottenham pointed out in *Lassence v Tierney* (1849) I Mac & G 551, if the terms of the gift are ambiguous, you may seek assistance in construing it – in saying whether it is expressed as an absolute gift or not – from the other parts of the will, including the language of the engrafted trusts. But when the court has once determined that the first gift is in terms absolute, then if it is a share of the residue (as in the present case) the next of kin are excluded in any event.

Certainty of subject matter

The subject matter may take a variety of forms such as land, shares, chattels, etc, but whatever form it takes the trust property is required to be specified with sufficient clarity to enable the court to identify the same.

Uncertainty of trust property

When the property, subject to an intended trust (as distinct from the beneficial interest), is uncertain, the intended express trust fails. This is because it is unclear which property is allegedly subject to the trust and the transferee may take the property beneficially, unburdened by a trust. In effect, this issue is interconnected with certainty of intention.

In *Sprange v Barnard*, the intended express trust failed because the trust property was incapable of ascertainment.

Sprange v Barnard (1789) 2 Bro CC 585, CA

Facts

A testatrix provided as follows:

> This is my last will and testament at my death, for my husband Thomas Sprange, to bewill to him the sum of £300, which is now in the joint stock annuities, for his sole use; and, at his death, *the remaining part of what is left, that he does not want for his own wants and use*, to be divided between my brother John Crapps, my sister Wickenden, and my sister Bauden, to be equally divided between them [emphasis added].

The stock became vested in the trustees and Thomas Sprange applied to them for payment, but they refused, whereupon he filed this bill.

Held

No trust was created and Thomas Sprange was entitled to the absolute beneficial interest:

> **Lord Arden MR:** It is contended, for the persons to whom it is given in remainder, that he shall only have it for his life, and that the words are strictly mandatory on him to dispose of it in a certain way; but it is only to dispose of what he has no occasion for: therefore the question is whether he may not call for the whole; and it seems to be perfectly clear on all the authorities that he may. I agree with the doctrine in *Pierson v Garnet* (1787) 2 Bas CC 226 following the cases *Harland v Trigg* (1782) I Bas CC 142 and *Wynne v Hawkins* (1782) I Bas CC 179 that the *property, and the person to whom it is to be given, must be certain* in order to raise a trust. Now here the property is

wasting, as it is only what shall remain at this death . . . It is contended that the court ought to impound the property; but it appears to me to be a trust which would be impossible to be executed. I must, therefore, declare him to be absolutely entitled to the £300, and decree it to be transferred to him [emphasis added].

Likewise, in *Palmer v Simmonds* the trust failed because the means of identifying the trust property was hopelessly vague.

Palmer v Simmonds (1854) 2 Drew 221, HC

Facts

A testatrix by her will disposed of the residue of her estate to Thomas Harrison subject to the following stipulation: 'that if he should die without lawful issue he will, after providing for his widow during her life, leave the bulk of my said residuary estate unto [four named persons equally].'

Held

No trust was intended for there was no identifiable property capable of being subject to a trust. Thus, Thomas Harrison's estate was entitled to the property beneficially:

> **Kindersley VC:** What is the meaning then of bulk? The appropriate meaning, according to its derivation, is something which bulges out. [His Honour referred to *Todd's Johnson and Richardson's Dictionary* for the different meanings and etymology of the word.] Its popular meaning we all know. When a person is said to have given the bulk of his property, what is meant is not the whole but the greater part, and that is in fact consistent with its classical meaning. When, therefore, the testatrix uses that term, can I say she has used a term expressing a definite, clear, certain part of her estate, or the whole of her estate? I am bound to say she has not designated the subject as to which she expresses her confidence; and I am therefore of the opinion that there is no trust created; that Harrison took absolutely, and those claiming under him now take.

The test is whether the subject matter of the trust is identified or capable of being identified with sufficient precision to enable a court to attach an order to such property.

The purchase of a specific quantity of goods from a supplier, who fails to identify and appropriate stock in pursuance of the sale, will not transfer *property* in the goods to the purchaser. Moreover, the supplier will not, without more, be treated as a trustee for the purchaser. The property may be too imprecise for the court to attach an order.

In *Re London Wine Co*, property from within a bulk did not pass to purchasers under the Sale of Goods Act 1979 because the customers' goods were not segregated, and thus no express trust of the goods arose in favour of the customers.

Re London Wine Co (Shippers) Ltd [1986] PCC 121, HC

Facts

The company had substantial stocks of wine in a number of warehouses. Large quantities were sold but in many instances remained warehoused with the company. There was no appropriation from the bulk of any wine to answer particular contracts, but the customer received from the company a 'certificate of title' describing the wine for which he had paid. He was charged storage and insurance periodically.

When receivers were appointed, there were sufficient stocks to satisfy all claims. The court considered three types of transaction: (a) a single purchaser of the total stock of a particular wine; (b) a number of purchasers whose combined purchases exhausted the total stock of a particular wine; (c) a number of purchasers whose combined purchases did not exhaust the relevant stock.

Held

The legal title had not passed to the customers under the contracts of sale. There was no ascertainment or appropriation of the property sold. Orders could have been fulfilled from any source, not necessarily existing stocks. There was no undivided interest.

In addition, no express trust was created for the customers for there was no certainty of subject matter. No proprietary rights arose from the payments of purchase moneys. The existence of a right to specific performance does not necessarily imply a proprietary interest in the subject matter. Hence, the claims wholly failed:

> **Oliver J:** Mr Wright said that a trust may be constituted not merely by direct and express declaration but also by the consequences flowing from the acts of the persons themselves to which consequences the law attaches the label 'trust'. A trust, to put it another way, is the technical description of a legal situation; and where you find (i) an intention to create a beneficial interest in someone else, (ii) an acknowledgement of that intention and (iii) property in the ownership of the person making the acknowledgement which answers the description in the acknowledgement, then there is, at the date of the acknowledgement, an effective and completed trust of all the property of the acknowledger answering to that description. This is, in essence, the same submission as that made by Mr Stamler – he submits that where one is dealing with a homogeneous mass there is no problem about certainty. So long as the mass can be identified and there is no uncertainty about the quantitative interest of the beneficiary the court will find no difficulty in administering the trust if it once finds the necessary intention to create an equitable interest in property of the type comprised in the mass. I think that if the case is to be made out at all, it must be put in this way, for the submission itself is based on the premise that there are no specific or ascertained goods in which the beneficiary is interested. Were it otherwise there would be no need to invoke the concept of trust for the title would have passed under the Sale of Goods Act. If trust there be, then it must be a trust of the homogeneous whole and the terms of the trust must be that the trustee is to hold that whole upon trust to give effect thereout to the proportionate interest of the beneficiary. Thus if we postulate the case of the company having in its warehouse 1,000 cases of a particular wine and selling 100 cases to X the circumstances of this case indicate, it is submitted, that the company created an equitable tenancy in common between itself and X in the whole 1,000 cases in the proportions of 9/10ths and 1/10th.
>
> It is with regret that I feel compelled to reject these submissions, for I feel great sympathy with those who paid for their wine and received an assurance that they had title to it. But I find it impossible to spell either out of the acknowledgements signed by the company or out of the circumstances any such trust as is now sought to be set up. It seems to me any such trust must fail on the ground of uncertainty of subject matter. It seems to me that in order to create a trust it must be possible to ascertain with certainty not only what the interest of the beneficiary is to be but to what property it is to attach.
>
> A farmer could, by appropriate words, declare himself to be a trustee of a specified proportion of his whole flock and thus create an equitable tenancy in common between himself and the named beneficiary, so that a proprietary interest would arise in the beneficiary in an undivided share of all the flock and its produce. But the mere declaration that a given number of animals would be held upon trust could not, I should have thought, without very clear words pointing to such an intention, result in the creation of an interest in common in the proportion which that number bears to the number of the whole at the time of the declaration. And where the mass from which the numerical interest is to take effect is not itself ascertainable at the date of the declaration, such a conclusion becomes impossible.
>
> In the instant case, even if I were satisfied on the evidence that the mass was itself identifiable at the date of the various letters of confirmation I should find the very greatest difficulty in construing the assertion that 'you are the sole and beneficial owner of 10 cases of such and such a wine as meaning or being intended to mean 'you are the owner of such proportion of the total stock of such and such a wine now held by me as 10 bears to the total number of cases comprised in such stock'.

The Sale of Goods (Amendment) Act 1995 introduced a significant change in the law. Today, multiple purchasers of goods are deemed to acquire interests in the subject matter as tenants in common.

In *Re Staplyton*, the court decided that, notwithstanding that property in the goods passed to the purchasers, the suppliers who retained possession of the goods were not automatically treated as trustees for the purchasers.

Re Staplyton [1994] 1 WLR 1181, HC

Facts

Wines kept by companies in warehouses for customers but not marked with customers' names were treated as 'ascertained' for the purpose of s 16 of the Sale of Goods Act 1979.

Held

Such contracts for the sale of goods did not *per se* create equitable interests in favour of customers:

> **Judge Baker QC:** We next come to the decision of the Court of Appeal in *Re Wait* [1927] 1 Ch 606. W bought 1,000 tons of wheat to be shipped from Oregon. He sub-sold 500 tons to the claimants, who paid in full. It was shipped but before it arrived W went bankrupt. His trustee claimed to receive the whole of the 1,000 tons, leaving the claimants to their rights in damages. The majority held that the 500 tons due to the claimants had not been appropriated and so this was not specific or ascertained goods in respect of which specific performance could be ordered under s 52 of the [Sale of Goods] Act of 1893. The interest of the case lies in the acute division of opinion in the court. Sargant LJ would have held that the claimants had an equitable assignment of part enforceable against the whole. The view of the majority can best be taken from the following passages in the judgment of Atkin LJ, at pp 629–30, 636:
>
>> In any case, however, I am of opinion that the claimants fail, and that to grant the relief claimed would violate well established principles of common law and equity. It would also appear to embarrass to a most serious degree the ordinary operations of buying and selling goods, and the banking operations which attend them . . . The rules for transfer of property as between seller and buyer, performance of the contract, rights of the unpaid seller against the goods, unpaid seller's lien, remedies of the seller, remedies of the buyer, appear to be complete and exclusive statements of the legal relations both in law and equity. They have, of course, no relevance when one is considering rights, legal or equitable, which may come into existence dehors the contract for sale. A seller or a purchaser may, of course, create any equity he pleases by way of charge, equitable assignment or any other dealing with, or disposition of, goods, the subject matter of sale; and he may, of course, create such an equity as one of the terms expressed in the contract of sale. But the mere sale or agreement to sell, or the acts in pursuance of such a contract mentioned in the code, will only produce the legal effects which the code states.
>
> This landmark decision demonstrates that, normally, a contract for the sale of goods takes effect at law, and gives rise to no equitable interest in favour of the buyer.
>
> In the present case we are concerned with the buying and selling of consumables. I am bound by the decision in *Re Wait* [1927] 1 Ch 606 to hold that a contract for the sale of goods does not, of itself, create equitable rights. Furthermore, as Gault J himself commented in *Liggett v Kensington* [1993] 1 NZLR 257, p 279: 'A contractual obligation to store the goods of another does not give rise to a trust.' The respective rights and obligations of the parties are governed exclusively by the terms of the two contracts.

Specific property may be delineated as trust property, such as a pecuniary legacy or identified paintings, etc. But equally effective would be property that is subject to a clear criterion for identifying the property from a group of assets, such as the residue of the testator's estate. In respect of a declaration of trust of part of a holding of shares, the court decided in *Hunter v Moss* that it is unnecessary to identify the trust shares by reference to the numbers stated in the certificates. It would be sufficient if the settlor quantifies the shares to such an extent that the court is entitled to ascertain the shares that are subject to the trust.

Hunter v Moss [1994] 1 WLR 452, CA

Facts

The defendant declared himself a trustee for the benefit of the plaintiff in respect of a 5% holding in the issued share capital of a company (1,000 issued shares). The defendant was the registered holder of 950 shares. The judge held that a trust was created in respect of 50 of the defendant's 950 shares. The defendant applied by motion to set aside the judgment on the ground that the purported trust failed for uncertainty of subject matter. The defendant argued that his failure to appropriate the relevant shares resulted in the subject matter of the intended trust being unascertainable.

Held

A trust was created in favour of the plaintiff, on the ground that the test for certainty of subject matter did not necessarily require segregation or appropriation of the trust property. The test is satisfied if immediately after the declaration of trust the court could have made an order for the execution of the trust. Since the shares were of the same category and thus equally capable of fulfilling the trust obligation, the quantification of the intended trust holding was sufficient to satisfy the test for certainty of subject matter:

> **Dillon LJ:** All these shares were identical in one class: 5 per cent was 50 shares and the defendant held personally more than 50 shares. It is well known that a trust of personalty can be created orally.
>
> [The learned judge then referred to the test laid down by Turner LJ in *Milroy v Lord* and continued:] In the present case there was no question of an imperfect transfer. What is relied on is an oral declaration of trust. Again, it would not be good enough for a settlor to say, 'I declare that I hold 50 of my shares on trust for B,' without indicating the company he had in mind of the various companies in which he held shares. There would be no sufficient certainty as to the subject matter of the trust. But here the discussion is solely about the shares of one class in the one company.
>
> It is plain that a bequest by the defendant to the plaintiff of 50 of his ordinary shares in MEL would be a valid bequest on the defendant's death which his executors or administrators would be bound to carry into effect. Mr Hartman sought to dispute that and to say that if, for instance, a shareholder had 200 ordinary shares in ICI and wanted to give them to A, B, C and D equally he could do it by giving 200 shares to A, B, C and D as tenants in common, but he could not validly do it by giving 50 shares to A, 50 shares to B, 50 shares to C and 50 shares to D, because he has not indicated which of the identical shares A is to have and which B is to have. I do not accept that. That such a testamentary bequest is valid, appears sufficiently from *In Re Clifford* [1912] 1 Ch 29 and *In Re Cheadle* [1900] 2 Ch 620. It seems to me, again, that if a person holds, say, 200 ordinary shares in ICI and he executes a transfer of 50 ordinary shares in ICI either to an individual donee or to trustees, and hands over the certificate for his 200 shares and the transfer to the transferees or to brokers to give effect to the transfer, there is a valid gift to the individual or trustees/transferees of 50 of the shares without any further identification of their numbers. It would be a completed gift without waiting for registration of the transfer: see *In Re Rose* [1952] Ch 499. In the ordinary way a new certificate would be issued for the 50 shares to the transferee and the transferor would receive a balance certificate in respect of the rest of his holding. I see no uncertainty at all in those circumstances.
>
> [Dillon LJ referred to the case of *Re London Wine* [1986] PCC 121 and distinguished it thus:] It seems to me that that case is a long way from the present. It is concerned with the appropriation of chattels and when the property in chattels passes. We are concerned with a declaration of trust, accepting that the legal title remained in the defendant and was not intended, at the time the trust was declared, to pass immediately to the plaintiff. The defendant was to retain the shares as trustee for the plaintiff.
>
> [On the subject of a possible creation of an equitable charge over a mixed fund rather than a trust, Dillon LJ continued:] As I see it, however, we are not concerned in this case with a mere equitable charge over a mixed fund. Just as a person can give, by will, a specified number of his shares of a certain class in a certain company, so equally, in my judgment, he can declare himself trustee of 50 of his ordinary shares in MEL or whatever the company may be and that is effective to give a beneficial proprietary interest to the beneficiary under the trust. No question of a blended fund thereafter arises and we are not in the field of equitable charge.

Note

In *Hunter v Moss*, the court was concerned with the status of the declaration by the employer as to whether he had declared himself a trustee or not. In *Re London Wine Co* and *Re Staplyton*, on the other hand, the aggrieved customers were attempting to use the trust institution in order to side step the rules enacted by the Sale of Goods Act 1979 for the passing of property. Thus, the courts drew a distinction between the nature of the subject matter, i.e., a contract to transfer fungibles on the one hand, and goods on the other hand. In addition, the effect of the trust in *Hunter v Moss* was to prevent the employer benefiting from his breach.

Question

How would you reconcile *Re London Wine Co* with *Hunter v Moss*?

In *Re Harvard Securities Ltd (In Liquidation), Holland v Newbury*, the High Court decided that although there could not, in English law, be a valid equitable assignment of an unappropriated interest in chattels, there could be such an equitable assignment of shares.

Re Harvard Securities Ltd (In Liquidation), Holland v Newbury (1997) The Times, 18 July, HC

Facts

Harvard, a licensed dealer in securities, had acquired and sold to clients various registered Australian and US shares. The clients were told in writing that their non-numbered shares were held by nominees on their behalf. The question in issue was whether there was certainty of subject matter in order to create an express trust.

Held

The holders of rights to shares acquired beneficial interests in them by way of trusts.

Note

In *Re Goldcorp Exchange Ltd* [1995] 1 AC 74 (see p 591 below), customers who bought gold bullion but allowed the vendors to retain possession of the goods did not create express trusts in their favour. The Privy Council followed the principles laid down in *Re London Wine Co* and *Re Staplyton*.

In *Re Golay*, the court decided that in respect of a direction concerning 'reasonable income' the test for subject matter was satisfied. The court is only too familiar with the objective standard of reasonableness.

Re Golay Morris v Bridgewater and Others [1965] 2 All ER 660, HC

Facts

A testator by his will directed his executors to let Tossy enjoy one of his flats during her lifetime and 'to receive a reasonable income from my other properties'. The question in issue was whether the direction was void for uncertainty.

Held

The direction was valid. The words 'reasonable income' imported an objective enquiry as to the amount of income:

> **Ungoed-Thomas J:** In this case, however, the yardstick indicated by the testator is not what he or any other specified person subjectively considers to be reasonable but what he identifies objectively as 'reasonable income'. The court is constantly involved in making such objective assessments of what is reasonable and it is not to be deterred from doing so because subjective influences can never be wholly excluded. In my view the testator intended by 'reasonable income' the yardstick which the court could and would apply in quantifying the amount so that the direction in the will is not in my view defeated by uncertainty.

In *Re Kolb*, the expression 'blue chips', used in a will, was not sufficiently precise to be considered valid.

Re Kolb's Will Trusts, Lloyds Bank Ltd v Ullmann and Others [1961] 3 All ER 811, HC

Facts

By his will, a testator who died in May 1959 directed his trustees, *inter alia*, to invest the proceeds of sale of trust property in such stocks, shares and/or convertible debentures in the 'blue chip' category as his trustees should think fit. The question in issue was whether the expression 'blue chip' category was void for uncertainty.

Held

The direction was void for uncertainty. On construction of the will, the testator had not empowered the trustees to decide independently the issue but the testator intended to adopt a purely subjective standard (which was unclear) for identifying the type of investments:

> **Cross J:** Mr John Arnold Ellert, who has been a member of the Stock Exchange, London, for nearly thirty years, has made an affidavit in which he deals with the meaning of the expression 'blue chip'. He says that this term is commonly applied by members of the Stock Exchange and financial journalists to the ordinary stocks and shares of industrial or commercial companies of the highest standing from an investor's point of view, but that there is no strict definition of the term and the opinions of different stockbrokers and others differ as to what stocks and shares can properly be called 'blue chips' at any given time.

The conclusion which I draw is that, while there are, no doubt, many investments which all persons competent to judge of such matters would call 'blue chips' and many others which no person competent to judge would call 'blue chips', there are a number of investments which some stockbrokers would class as 'blue chips' but which other stockbrokers equally competent would not class as 'blue chips'.

In this case I feel no doubt on which side of the line the phrase in question falls. Whether or not an investment is 'first class' or 'blue chip' depends essentially on the standards applied by the speaker and cannot be regarded as an objective quality of the investment. The testator might have made his trustees the judges; but, as he has not done so, that part of the clause is, in my judgment, void for uncertainty.

Uncertainty of beneficial interest

If the trust property is certain but the interest intended for the beneficiary is uncertain then, although the purported express trust fails, a resulting trust may be set up for the benefit of the settlor or his estate. This was the effect of *Boyce v Boyce*.

Boyce v Boyce (1849) 16 Sim 476

Facts

The trust property consisted of two houses to be taken by each of two beneficiaries. One of the named beneficiaries was required to make a selection from the two houses and the house not selected was required to be held on trust for the other named beneficiary. The beneficiary failed to make the selection.

Held

The omission to make the selection resulted in the failure of the express trust for uncertainty of beneficial interest, and both houses were held on resulting trust for the testator's estate.

Note

It must be stressed that *Boyce v Boyce* was an exceptional case and the harshness of the result stemmed from the preliminary ruling by the judge. This ruling was to the effect that a personal obligation was imposed on the named beneficiary to select in order to identify the beneficial interest. The court came to a different conclusion in *Re Knapton* [1941] 2 All ER 573.

Certainty of objects (beneficiaries)

It is obvious that no express trust may stand when it is unclear in whose favour the trust has been created. The settlor has a duty to identify the beneficiaries with a sufficient degree of precision. The effect of uncertainty of objects (assuming certainty of intention and property) is that the intended express trust fails and a resulting trust is set up for the benefit of the settlor or his estate. The test for certainty of objects varies with the type of trust intended. The courts have drawn a distinction between 'fixed' (non-discretionary) and discretionary trusts.

Fixed trusts

These are trusts in which the number of beneficiaries and the extent of their interests are specified in the trust instrument. The test for certainty of objects is whether the objects are ascertained or capable of being ascertained. In other words, at the time of the creation of the trust, the trustees are required to draw up a comprehensive list of all the beneficiaries. Failure to achieve this would result in the failure of the express trust. For example, '£50,000 is transferred to trustees T1 and T2 to distribute equally between all my friends'. If all of the settlor's friends cannot be identified or listed, the intended express trust fails and a resulting trust for the settlor is created. See *Inland Revenue Commissioners v Broadway Cottages Trust* [1955] Ch 20 (see p 107 below).

In the recent decision of *OT Computers Ltd v First National Tricity Finance Ltd and Others*, the

High Court considered whether the formula adopted by the settlor for identifying the beneficiaries satisfied the test for certainty of objects for fixed trusts.

OT Computers Ltd v First National Tricity Finance Ltd and Others [2003] EWHC 1010, HC

Facts

The claimant (company) traded as 'Tiny Computers' and was a retailer of computer products and accessories. In 2000, it started making substantial losses. On 23 January 2002, the company instructed its bank to open two separate trust accounts for the payment of customer deposits and of moneys due to 'urgent suppliers'. The company transferred sums from its current account into each of the trust accounts. The bank acknowledged that the sums in the two trust accounts were not available to be set off against any accounts held by the bank in the company's name. The company created two schedules, one contained the names of customers and the other reflected some of the names of its suppliers, who were potential beneficiaries. The company was subsequently put into receivership. The bank later demanded repayment of a loan from the company. One of the defendants was an unpaid supplier whose name did not appear on the company's schedule.

The question in issue was whether valid trusts had been created for customers and 'urgent suppliers'.

Held

The court held that a valid trust had been created for the customers. The intended express trust in favour of 'urgent suppliers' was void for uncertainty of objects. It was not possible to identify each member of the class of 'urgent suppliers'. The expression, 'urgent' was too vague in order to define a class and identify each beneficiary. Accordingly, a resulting trust for the company was created:

> **Pumfrey J:** The trusts alleged to have been created are necessarily express trusts, and for such trusts to be created there must be certainty of words, certainty of subject matter, and certainty of objects. Certainty of words requires that the words used are sufficient to demonstrate an intention to create a trust, and, so far as necessary, the terms of that trust. Second, the property to be comprised within the trust must itself be identified with sufficient clarity. Finally, the class of persons who are beneficiaries of the trust have to be sufficiently ascertained. When I use the word 'sufficiently' I refer to the underlying requirement that the Court be in as good a position as the trustee to ascertain the nature of the trust, the property comprised within it and the class of objects. It is suggested by Mr Mann QC that the trust of suppliers in the present case is insufficiently certain in respects of certainty of objects.
>
> The question immediately arises what can be meant by 'urgent suppliers'. Mr Mann submits with considerable justification that the term 'urgent' is simply too vague to define any class of beneficiary. He observes that no evidence is forthcoming from the two directors most particularly involved . . . it is important to remember that the trust which is proposed is a fixed trust. Accordingly, it must be possible to identify each member of the class of beneficiaries.
>
> In my judgment it is essential to distinguish clearly between the Suppliers Trust on the one hand and the Customers Trust on the other. So far as the Customers Trust is concerned, there is no such difficulty about identification of the beneficiaries as is presented by the suppliers trust. In my judgment, the requirement for certainty of beneficiaries for the latter is plainly not met. It follows that the suppliers trust was imperfectly constituted.

Discretionary trusts

A discretionary trust is one whereby the objects are not given an interest in the property but the trustees are invested with a duty to select, in their discretion, the beneficiaries and/or their interests from amongst a class of objects. In short, the trustees are required to decide on the identity of the beneficiaries from a class of objects and the corresponding interests that they may acquire.

For example, 'on trust, for 21 years, to distribute the dividends from my shareholding in Marks & Spencer plc to such of my dependants and relatives as my trustees will decide in their absolute discretion'. The trustees are required to decide not only who will benefit, but also the quantum of the interest of the beneficiaries from within the class of objects, namely, the settlor's dependants and relatives.

The test for certainty of objects is whether the trustees may say with certainty that any given postulant (individual) is or is not a member of a class of objects. Thus, the test is whether the qualifying class or classes of objects is or are capable of being legally defined and it is unnecessary to draw up a list of all the objects. See *McPhail v Doulton* [1971] AC 424 (see p 108 below).

FURTHER READING

Baldry, R and Shipwright, A, 'Writing and other formalities for trusts' (2005) Tax Journal Issue 818, 19.

Battersby, G, 'A reconsideration of property and title in the Sale of Goods Act' [2001] JBL 1.

Clarke, P, 'Mr Vandervell again' [1974] 38 Conv 405.

Goodhart, W and Jones, G, 'The infiltration of equitable doctrine into English commercial law' (1980) 43 MLR 489.

Grubb, A, ' Powers, trusts and classes of objects' [1982] Conv 432.

Harpum, C, 'Administrative unworkability and purpose trusts' [1986] CLJ 391.

Hayton, D, 'Certainty of objects – what is heresy?' [1984] Conv 307.

Hayton, D, 'Uncertainty of subject-matter of trusts' (1994) 110 LQR 335.

Hill, G, 'Section 2 of the Law of Property (Miscellaneous Provisions) Act 1989' (1990) 106 LQR 396.

Howell, J, 'Informal conveyances and s 2 of the Law of Property (Miscellaneous Provisions) Act 1989' [1990] Conv 441.

Jones, A, 'Creating a trust over an unascertained part of a homogeneous whole' [1993] Conv 466.

Lowrie, S and Todd, P, '*Re Rose* Revisited' (1998) 57 CLJ 46.

Martin, J, 'Certainty of objects – what is heresy?' [1984] Conv 304.

Martin, J, 'Validity of trust of unidentified shares' [1996] Conv 223.

Nolan, R, 'The triumph of technicalities' (1996) 55 CLJ 436.

Pettit, P, 'Farewell s 40' [1989] Conv 431.

Reid, K, 'Privity of contract: third parties' (2000) 21 Co Law 207.

Thompson, M, 'Disposition of equitable interests' [1996] Conv 368.

Worthington, S, 'Sorting out ownership interests in a bulk: gifts, sales and trusts' [1999] JBL 1.

Youdan, T, 'Formalities for trusts of land and the doctrine in *Rochefoucauld v Boustead*' [1984] CLJ 306.

CONSTITUTION AND EFFECT OF AN EXPRESS TRUST

INTRODUCTION

An express trust is completely constituted in accordance with the test laid down *Milroy v Lord* (1862) 31 LJ Ch 798 (see Chapter 3) if:

(a) the settlor transfers the property (or has done everything in his power to transfer the legal title) to the trustees, subject to a valid declaration of trust; or

(b) the settlor declares himself a trustee for the beneficiaries.

The consequences of creating a perfect trust are that:

(a) the settlor is not entitled to change his mind;

(b) the trustees are required to hold the property in accordance with the terms of the trust;

(c) the beneficiaries acquire a proprietary interest in the property and may enforce the trust against the trustees or anyone, with the exception of the bona fide transferee of the legal estate for value without notice.

If the trust is imperfect, the promise to benefit another is treated as an agreement to create a trust and is enforceable: (i) at law or in equity by non-volunteers; or (ii) at law by the parties to the contract, if they are volunteers; and (iii) at law by those who are treated as parties to the contract under the Contracts (Rights of Third Parties) Act 1999, if they are volunteers. The remedy that is available to the claimant will vary with his status, in particular, whether he is a volunteer or a non-volunteer.

CONSTITUTION OF A TRUST

It was stated earlier (see Chapter 3) that an express trust may be created in one of two ways, namely: by a transfer of the property to third party trustees subject to a declaration of trust (transfer and declaration of trust); or the retention of the property by the settlor subject to the terms of the trust (self-declaration of trust): see *Milroy v Lord* (1862) 31 LJ Ch 798. If either mode of creation has been fully implemented by the settlor, the trust is treated as perfect or completely constituted. The issue discussed below examines the scope of these two requirements.

If the settlor adopts an improper mode of creating a trust, the intention of the settlor will not be construed as sufficient to create a perfect trust by implying a different mode of creation, for otherwise all imperfect gifts will be construed as perfect. Likewise, as in *Richards v Delbridge*, an ineffectual gift will not be sufficient to imply an intention to make the intended donor a trustee for the intended donee. Since the gift is imperfect, trust principles will not be implied to perfect the imperfect gift: 'Equity will not perfect an imperfect gift.'

Richards v Delbridge (1874) LR 18 Eq 11, CA

Facts

A settlor attempted to assign a lease of business premises to his grandson by endorsing the lease and signing a memorandum: 'This deed and all thereto I give to R from this time henceforth with all stock in trade.' He gave the lease certificate to R's mother to hold on his behalf. On the death of the settlor, it was ascertained that his will made no reference to the business premises. The question in issue was whether the lease belonged to the grandson or to the residuary beneficiaries under the testator's will.

Held

The lease was subject to a resulting trust for the residuary beneficiaries. There was an imperfect gift *inter vivos* to the grandson as the assignment, not being under seal, was ineffectual to transfer the lease. Further, no trust had been created for the grandson, as the grandfather did not declare himself a trustee of the lease for him. The court will not construe an ineffectual transfer as a valid declaration of trust:

> **Sir George Jessel MR:** The principle is a very simple one. A man may transfer his property, without valuable consideration, in one of two ways: he may either do such acts as amount in law to a conveyance or assignment of the property, and thus completely divest himself of the legal ownership, in which case the person who by those acts acquires the property takes it beneficially, or on trust, as the case may be; or the legal owner of the property may, by one or other of the modes recognised as amounting to a valid declaration of trust, constitute himself a trustee, and, without an actual transfer of the legal title, may so deal with the property as to deprive himself of its beneficial ownership, and declare that he will hold it from that time forward on trust for the other person. It is true he need not use the words, 'I declare myself a trustee', but he must do something which is equivalent to it, and use expressions which have that meaning; for, however anxious the court may be to carry out a man's intention, it is not at liberty to construe words otherwise than according to their proper meaning . . .

> The true distinction appears to me to be plain, and beyond dispute: for a man to make himself a trustee there must be an expression of intention to become a trustee, whereas words of present gift show an intention to give over property to another, and not retain it in the donor's own hands for any purpose, fiduciary or otherwise.

> In *Milroy v Lord* (1862) 31 LJ Ch 798, Turner LJ, after referring to the two modes of making a voluntary settlement valid and effectual, added these words:

>> The cases, I think, go further, to this extent, that if the settlement is intended to be effectuated by one of the modes to which I have referred, the Court will not give effect to it by applying another of those modes. If it is intended to take effect by transfer, the Court will not hold the intended transfer to operate as a declaration of trust, for then every imperfect instrument would be made effectual by being converted into a perfect trust.

Self-declaration of trust as one of several trustees

Alternatively, the settlor, as the sole owner of property, may declare himself one of several trustees. If, on construction, the settlor has irrevocably and unconditionally declared himself a trustee, the trust will be fully constituted, despite his failure to transfer the relevant property to the other intended trustees. In other words, if there is a valid self-declaration of trust, it ought to make no difference whether the settlor intended to create a trust with himself as the sole trustee, or intended to set up a trust with multiple trustees, *including himself*. In both cases, the trust will be perfect even though the other trustees have not acquired the trust property. The beneficiaries will acquire an equitable interest and, as against the settlor/trustee, will be entitled to insist on a transfer to the other trustees. This was the approach adopted by the Privy Council in *T Choithram International v Pagarani*.

T Choithram International SA and Others v Pagarani and Others [2001] I WLR I, PC

Facts

The settlor, Mr Choithram Pagarani (CP), a successful businessman, controlled a number of companies. After providing for his family, CP intended to leave the remainder of his wealth for charitable purposes. He hoped to achieve this by setting up a foundation to serve as an umbrella organisation for four charitable bodies that he had already established. CP and the other trustees executed the foundation trust deed on 17 February 1992, despite CP's rapidly failing health. The trust deed was made between CP, as settlor, and CP and seven other named individuals as trustees. CP transferred £1,000 to the trustees as the initial subject matter of the trust, with further property to be placed under the control of the trustees. The deed also set out the terms of the trust. Immediately after signing the documents, CP said words to the effect that, 'I have given all my wealth to the trust'. He then told his accountant, who was present at the time of signing, to transfer all his balances with the companies and his shares to the foundation trust. At a subsequent meeting of the trustees, CP reported that the foundation had been established and all his wealth had been given to the trust. The relevant documents were prepared but CP refused to sign. Evidence was adduced that CP had an aversion to signing such documents and had been advised that it was not necessary to do so. However, CP repeatedly declared that he had done his 'bit'; he had given all his wealth to the foundation and that there was nothing more for him to do. In the end, CP had failed to execute the forms that were necessary to carry out the formal transfer of the further assets. CP died on 19 March 1992. On 20 June 1992, the companies registered the trustees of the foundation as shareholders, cancelled CP's certificates and issued new share certificates.

The claimants, CP's first wife and her children, commenced proceedings in the British Virgin Islands for a part of CP's estate. The claim was made on the ground that the intended gifts to the foundation were ineffective because CP had failed to transfer the relevant properties, namely CP's shares and deposit balances in the companies, to the foundation. The trial judge found that CP intended to make immediate gifts of the relevant properties on 17 February, but his intention was not irrevocable. In addition, the judge found that, despite CP's intention to make immediate gifts to the foundation, he had failed to vest the properties in the hands of all the trustees of the foundation. This decision was affirmed by the Caribbean Court of Appeal. The defendants (executors of CP) appealed to the Privy Council.

Held

Effective transfers *inter vivos* had been made to the trustees subject to the trusts, on the following grounds:

(a) CP's intention was to make a present, immediate, unconditional and irrevocable gift to the foundation. This was manifested by the execution of the foundation deed on 17 February, verbally declaring his intention upon signing the document and instructing his accountant to transfer all his balances with the companies and his shares to the foundation trust.

(b) Although the words used by CP were appropriate to an outright gift, 'I give to X', on construction, those words were intended to create a gift to the trustees of the foundation on trust for the foundation. This is partly attributed to the fact that the foundation had no legal existence apart from the trust declared by the foundation trust deed. Accordingly, the *Milroy v Lord* principle for the creation of an express trust had been satisfied.

(c) Since the property was vested in one of the trustees, namely CP himself, the express trust was constituted. Accordingly, there was a duty to transfer the property to all of the trustees of the foundation trust. In principle, there is no distinction between a case where a settlor declares himself to be a sole trustee for a beneficiary and the case where he declares himself to be one of the trustees for that beneficiary. In both cases, the trust is perfect and the beneficiary acquires an equitable proprietary interest in the property.

(d) The subject matter of the trust comprised all of CP's wealth in the British Virgin Islands, namely, CP's deposit balances and shares in the four companies. This was in accordance with CP's statements and conduct.

Lord Browne-Wilkinson: [His Lordship took the view that, by reference to the surrounding circumstances, the settlor had manifested an irrevocable and unconditional intention to create a trust, and continued.] The judge and the Court of Appeal understandably took the view that a perfect gift could only be made in one of two ways, viz (a) by a transfer of the gifted asset to the donee, accompanied by an intention in the donor to make a gift; or (b) by the donor declaring himself to be a trustee of the gifted property for the donee. In case (a), the donor has to have done everything necessary to be done which is within his own power to do in order to transfer the gifted asset to the donee. If the donor has not done so, the gift is incomplete since the donee has no equity to perfect an imperfect gift (see *Milroy v Lord* (1862) 31 LJ Ch 798; *Richards v Delbridge* (1874) LR 18 Eq 11; *Re Rose (decd), Midland Bank Executor and Trustee Co Ltd v Rose* [1948] 2 All ER 971; and *Re Rose, Rose v IRC* [1952] 1 All ER 1217). Moreover, the court will not give a benevolent construction so as to treat ineffective words of outright gift as taking effect as if the donor had declared himself a trustee for the donee (see *Milroy v Lord* (1862) 31 LJ Ch 798). So, it is said, in this case TCP used words of gift to the foundation (not words declaring himself a trustee): unless he transferred the shares and deposits so as to vest title in all the trustees, he had not done all that he could in order to effect the gift. It therefore fails. Further it is said that it is not possible to treat TCP's words of gift as a declaration of trust because they make no reference to trusts. Therefore the case does not fall within either of the possible methods by which a complete gift can be made and the gift fails.

Though it is understandable that the courts below should have reached this conclusion since the case does not fall squarely within either of the methods normally stated as being the only possible ways of making a gift, their Lordships do not agree with that conclusion. The facts of this case are novel and raise a new point. It is necessary to make an analysis of the rules of equity as to complete gifts. Although equity will not aid a volunteer, it will not strive officiously to defeat a gift. This case falls between the two common-form situations mentioned above. Although the words used by TCP are those normally appropriate to an outright gift – 'I give to X' – in the present context there is no breach of the principle in *Milroy v Lord* if the words of TCP's gift (ie to the foundation) are given their only possible meaning in this context. The foundation has no legal existence apart from the trust declared by the foundation trust deed. Therefore the words 'I give to the foundation' can only mean 'I give to the trustees of the foundation trust deed to be held by them on the trusts of the foundation trust deed'. Although the words are apparently words of outright gift they are essentially words of gift on trust.

But, it is said, TCP vested the properties not in *all* the trustees of the foundation but only in one, ie TCP. Since equity will not aid a volunteer, how can a court order be obtained vesting the gifted property in the whole body of trustees on the trusts of the foundation? Again, this represents an over-simplified view of the rules of equity. Until comparatively recently the great majority of trusts were voluntary settlements under which beneficiaries were volunteers having given no value. Yet beneficiaries under a trust, although volunteers, can enforce the trust against the trustees. Once a trust relationship is established between trustee and beneficiary, the fact that a beneficiary has given no value is irrelevant. It is for this reason that the type of perfected gift referred to in class (b) above is effective since the donor has constituted himself a trustee for the donee who can as a matter of trust law enforce that trust.

What then is the position here where the trust property is vested in one of the body of trustees, viz TCP? In their Lordships' view there should be no question. TCP has, in the most solemn circumstances, declared that he is giving (and later that he has given) property to a trust which he himself has established and of which he has appointed himself to be a trustee. All this occurs at one composite transaction taking place on 17 February. There can in principle be no distinction between the case where the donor declares himself to be sole trustee for a donee or a purpose and the case where he declares himself to be one of the trustees for that donee or purpose. In both cases his conscience is affected and it would be unconscionable and contrary to the principles of equity to allow such a donor to resile from his gift. Say, in the present case, that TCP had survived and tried to change his mind by denying the gift. In their Lordships' view it is impossible to believe that he could validly deny that he was a trustee for the purposes of the foundation in the light of all the steps that he had taken to assert that position and to assert his trusteeship. In their Lordships' judgment in the absence of special factors where one out of a larger body of trustees has the trust property vested in him he is bound by the trust and must give effect to it by transferring the trust property into the name of all the trustees.

The plaintiffs relied on the decision of Romilly MR in *Bridge v Bridge* (1852) 16 Beav 315 at 324, as showing that the vesting of the trust property in one trustee, the donor, out of many is not sufficient to constitute the trust. Their Lordships have some doubt whether that case was correctly decided on this point, the judge giving no reasons for his view. But in any event it is plainly distinguishable from the present case since the judge considered that the trust could not be fully constituted unless the legal estate in the gifted property was vested in the trustees and in that case the legal estate was vested neither in the donor nor in any of the other trustees.

Therefore in their Lordships' view the assets, if any, validly included in TCP's gift to the foundation are properly vested in the trustees and are held on the trusts of the foundation trust deed.

What then are the gifted assets? It will be recalled that TCP referred to the subject matter of the gift in a number of different ways: 'all my wealth', 'everything', 'all my wealth, all my shares, to the trust', 'all his balances . . . with the company . . . and his shares as well', 'all my wealth with the companies'. The judge found that TCP made a gift of all his wealth with the companies, ie the deposit balances and the shares in the four defendant companies which together constitutes his whole wealth in the British Virgin Islands and are the only assets at issue in these proceedings. It was submitted that a gift of 'all my wealth' was void for uncertainty. Their Lordships express no view on that point since there can be no question but that the deposit balances and the shares in the four companies were identified by TCP as being included in the gift and the gift of them is *pro tanto* valid.

Question

How would you reconcile *T Choithram International v Pagarani* with *Milroy v Lord*?

Express incorporation of both modes of creation

In *Re Ralli's Will Trusts*, it was held that the settlor may expressly incorporate both modes of creating an express trust, namely, declaring that he will retain the property as trustee pending the transfer to third party trustees. Once the trustees (third parties) ultimately acquire the relevant property during the lifetime of the settlor, the trust becomes perfect. It is immaterial how the trustees acquire the property, provided that their acquisition was not improper. It is essential that the settlor expressly declares himself a trustee pending the transfer, for the court will not imply this requirement.

Re Ralli's Will Trusts [1964] Ch 288, HC

Facts

In 1899, a testator died leaving the residue of his estate upon trust for his wife for life with remainder to his two children, Helen and Irene, absolutely. In 1924, Helen covenanted in her marriage settlement and under clause 7 to settle all her 'existing and after acquired property' upon trusts which failed and ultimately on trust for the children of Irene. The settlement declared that all the property comprised within the terms of the covenant will under clause 8 'become subject in equity to the settlement hereby covenanted to be made'. Irene's husband was appointed one of the trustees of the settlement. In 1946, Irene's husband was also appointed a trustee of the 1899 settlement. In 1956, Helen died and, in 1961, the widow died. Irene's husband became the sole surviving trustee of both the 1899 settlement and Helen's settlement. The question in issue was whether Helen's property from the 1899 settlement was held upon trust for Irene's children, as stipulated in Helen's marriage settlement, or subject to Helen's personal estate.

Held

Helen's property was subject to a trust for Irene's children. Following the declaration in Helen's settlement in 1924, Helen and, since her death, her personal representative (Irene's husband) held her share of the 1899 settlement subject to the trust of Helen's settlement. This was the position even though the vesting of the property in Irene's husband came to him in his other capacity as trustee of the 1899 settlement. The same result was reached by virtue of the principle in *Strong v Bird* (1874) LR 18 Eq 315 (see p 77 below).

> **Buckley J:** [held that the vested reversionary interest was existing property of Helen pending assignment to the trustees of her marriage settlement. He then continued:] In my judgment the circumstances that the plaintiff holds the fund because he was appointed a trustee of the will is irrelevant. He is at law the owner of the fund and the means by which he became so have no effect on the quality of his legal ownership. The question is: for whom, if any one, does he hold the fund in equity? In other words, who can successfully assert an equity against him disentitling him to stand on his legal right? It seems to me to be indisputable that Helen, if she were alive, could not do so, for she has solemnly covenanted under seal to assign the fund to the plaintiff and the defendants can stand in no better position. It is, of course, true that the object of the covenant was not that the plaintiff should retain the property for his own benefit, but that he should hold it on the trusts of the settlement.
>
> Had someone other than the plaintiff been the trustee of the will and held the fund, the result of this part of the case would, in my judgment, have been different; and it may seem strange that the rights of the parties should depend on the appointment of the plaintiff as a trustee of the will in 1946, which for present purposes may have been a quite fortuitous event.
>
> In the circumstances of the present case it is not unconscientious in the plaintiff to withhold from Helen's estate the fund which Helen covenanted that he should receive: on the contrary, it would have been unconscientious in

Helen to seek to deprive the plaintiff of that fund, and her personal representatives can be in no better position. The inadequacy of the volunteers' equity against Helen and her estate consequently is irrelevant, for that equity does not come into play; but they have a good equity as against the plaintiff, because it would be unconscientious of him to retain as against them any property which he holds in consequence of the provisions of the settlement.

Question
How would you reconcile *Re Ralli* with *Milroy v Lord*?

No trust of an expectancy

A trust may be created only in respect of existing property. Accordingly, in *Re Ellenborough*, it was decided that a trust cannot be created in respect of an expectancy or future property, such as an anticipated interest under a will during the lifetime of the testator. The reason being that there is no property which is capable of being subject to the protection of equity.

Re Ellenborough [1903] 1 Ch 697, HC

Facts
Emily Law was entitled to property under the will of her brother, Lord Ellenborough. Before his death, Emily voluntarily covenanted to convey her anticipated inheritance to trustees upon trust. On his death, the covenantor changed her mind and declined to transfer the property to the covenantees, who brought an action claiming a declaration as to whether Emily might be forced to perform the agreement.

Held
No trust was created by the covenant for the subject matter involved future property. In addition, the agreement was not enforceable for lack of consideration:

Buckley J: The question is whether a volunteer can enforce a contract made by deed to dispose of an expectancy. It cannot be and is not disputed that if the deed had been for value the trustees could have enforced it. If value be given, it is immaterial what is the form of assurance by which the disposition is made, or whether the subject of the disposition is capable of being thereby disposed of or not. An assignment for value binds the conscience of the assignor. A court of equity against him will compel him to do that which *ex hypothesi* he has not yet effectually done. Future property, possibilities, and expectancies are all assignable in equity for value: *Tailby v Official Receiver* (1888) 13 App Cas 523. But when the assurance is not for value, a court of equity will not assist a volunteer. In *Meek v Kettlewell* (1842) 1 Hare 464, affirmed by Lord Lyndhurst (1843) 1 Ph 342, the exact point arose which I have here to decide, and it was held that a voluntary assignment of an expectancy, even though under seal, would not be enforced by a court of equity. 'The assignment of an expectancy,' says Lord Lyndhurst, 'such as this is, cannot be supported unless made for a valuable consideration'.

In my judgment the interest of the plaintiff as sole heiress-at-law and next of kin of the late Lord Ellenborough was not effectually assigned to the trustees by the deed, and the trustees cannot call upon her to grant, assign, transfer, or pay over to them his residuary real and personal estate.

Similarly, members of a class of objects subject to a power of appointment are not treated as having an interest in the subject matter of the discretion but merely an expectancy. Thus, in *Re Brooks' Settlement Trusts*, the purported assignment of an expectancy by a member of a class of objects was treated as of no effect.

Re Brooks' Settlement Trusts [1939] 1 Ch 993, HC

Facts
Under a marriage settlement, the income of the settled fund was payable to the wife for life with remainder to such of her issue as she might by deed or will appoint and, in default of appointment, on trust in favour of all of her children in equal shares. In 1929, T, one of her sons, executed a voluntary settlement whereby he assigned his share, whether vested or contingent, in the trust property to Lloyds Bank Ltd as trustees. In 1939, his mother exercised the power of appointment

in his favour in respect of £3,517. Thereupon, Lloyds Bank Ltd applied to the court to determine whether it should pay T the £3,517.

Held

The sum ought to be paid to T for, prior to an appointment by his mother, T had an interest that was subject to defeasance and was defeasible by a valid appointment executed by his mother. T, therefore, was only entitled to assign this defeasible interest in 1929. The mother's appointment in 1939 defeated the original interest enjoyed by T (as an object entitled in default of appointment) and, at the same time, transferred an interest in the sum of £3,517 to T:

> **Farwell J:** The legal position in the case of a special power of appointment is not in any doubt at all. Referring to *Farwell on Powers,* 3rd edn, 1916, p 310, 'The exercise of a power of appointment divests (either wholly or partially according to the terms of the appointment) the estates limited in default of appointment and creates a new estate, and that, too, whether the property be real or personal' . . . That being so, it is, in my judgment, impossible to say that until an appointment has been made in favour of this son, that son had any interest under his mother's settlement, other than an interest as one of the people entitled in default of appointment; he had an interest in that; but that interest was liable to be divested, and, if an appointment was made (as in fact it was made) in favour of the son, then to that extent the persons entitled in default were defeated and he was given an interest in the funds which he had never had before and which came into being for the first time when the power was exercised. No doubt it is quite true to say that the appointment has to be read into the marriage settlement, but, in my judgment, that it is not sufficient ground for saying that at the time when this voluntary settlement was made the son had any interest at all in the fund other than this vested interest in default of appointment; for the rest, he had nothing more than a mere expectancy, the hope that at some date his mother might think fit to exercise the power of appointment in his favour, but, until she did so choose, he had nothing other than his interest in default of appointment to which he could point and say: 'that is a fund to which I shall become entitled in future or to which I am contingently entitled'. Apart from this he was not contingently entitled at all; he had no interest whatever in the fund until the appointment had been executed.

> If that be the true view, as I believe it to be, the result must be that, whatever the language of the settlement may be, the settlor under the voluntary settlement was purporting to assign to the trustees something to which he might in certain circumstances become entitled in the future, but to which he was not then entitled in any sense at all, and if that be so, then it is plain on the authorities that the son cannot be compelled to hand over or to permit the trustees to retain this sum that he is himself entitled to call upon them to pay it over to him.

> . . . I feel compelled by the principles to which I have referred to hold that the answer to the summons must be that the trustees ought to pay to the defendant the sum in question on the footing that that settlement does not operate as a valid assignment or declaration of trust in respect thereof. I make that declaration accordingly.

Trusts of the benefit of covenants (choses in action)

A chose in action is capable of being the subject matter of a trust. A chose in action is a right to intangible personal property, such as the creditor's right to have a loan repaid, or the rights in shares or intellectual property. In accordance with this principle, a settlor may create a trust of the benefit of a deed, provided that the property is in existence at the time of the creation. The approach adopted in *Fletcher v Fletcher* is based on the notion that the trust property may take the form of the benefit under a deed to transfer money (that is, a chose in action). Such benefit may be assigned to the trustees. On the date of the execution of the deed, the covenantees (trustees) will acquire the benefit of the deed. The declaration of trust will have the effect of transferring the equitable interest to the beneficiaries. In short, the deed will have the effect of:

(a) creating the trust property (chose in action);

(b) assigning the benefit of the chose in action to the beneficiaries; and

(c) declaring the terms of the trust.

For example, S, a settlor, and T, a trustee, execute a deed whereby S agrees to transfer the right to £20,000 to T on trust for B absolutely. S fails to transfer the sum to T. Nevertheless, the trust may be perfect, for the benefit of the deed may have been transferred to T in accordance with S's intention on the date of the execution of the deed.

Fletcher v Fletcher (1844) 4 Hare 67, HC

Facts

Ellis Fletcher covenanted (for himself, his heirs, executors and administrators) with trustees (their heirs, executors, administrators and assignees) to the effect that if either or both of his natural issue, Jacob and John, survived him and attained the age of 21, his executors would pay to the covenantees (or heirs, etc) £60,000 within 12 months of his death to be held on trust for the relevant natural issue. In the circumstances, Jacob alone survived the settlor and attained the age of 21. The surviving trustees declined to act in respect of the trust unless the court ordered otherwise. Jacob brought an action directly against the executors claiming that he became solely entitled to the property beneficially under a trust.

Held

A trust of the rights under the covenant was created in favour of Jacob, who was entitled to enforce it as a beneficiary:

> **Wigram VC:** The first proposition relied upon against the claim in equity was, that equity will not interfere in favour of a volunteer. A court of equity, for example, will not, in favour of a volunteer, enforce the performance of a contract *in specie*. That it will, however, sometimes act in favour of a volunteer is proved by the common case of a volunteer on a bond who may prove his bond against the assets. Again, where the relation of trustee and *cestui que trust* is constituted, as where property is transferred from the author of the trust into the name of a trustee, so that he has lost all power of disposition over it, and the transaction is complete as regards him, the trustee, having accepted the trust, cannot say he holds it, except for the purposes of the trust, if it is not already perfect. This covenant, however, is already perfect. The covenantor is liable at law, and the court is not called upon to do any act to perfect it. One question made in argument has been whether there can be a trust of a covenant the benefit of which shall belong to a third party; but I cannot think there is any difficulty in that. Suppose, in a case of a personal covenant to pay a certain annual sum for the benefit of a third person, the trustee were to bring an action against the covenantor; would he be afterwards allowed to say he was not a trustee? If he cannot do so after once acknowledging the trust, then there is a case in which there is a trust of a covenant for another . . . The proposition, therefore, that in no case can there be a trust of a covenant is clearly too large, and the real question is whether the relation of trustee and *cestui que trust* is established in the present case.
>
> I think the proposition insisted upon, that because the covenant was voluntary therefore the plaintiff could not recover in equity, was too broadly stated. I referred to the case of a volunteer by specialty claiming payment out of assets, and to the case of one claiming under a voluntary trust, where a third has been transferred. The rule against relief to volunteers cannot, I conceive, in a case like that before me, be stated higher than this, that a court of equity will not, in favour of a volunteer, give to a deed any effect beyond what the law will give to it. But if the author of the deed has subjected himself to a liability at law, and the legal liability comes regularly to be enforced in equity . . . the observation that the claimant is a volunteer is of no value in favour of those who represent the author of the deed. If, therefore, the plaintiff himself were the covenantee so that he could bring the action in his own name, it follows, from what I have said, that in my opinion he might enforce payment out of the assets of the covenantor in this case. Then, does the interposition of the trustee of this covenant make any difference? I think it does not.
>
> The testator has bound himself absolutely. There is a debt created and existing. I give no assistance against the testator. I only deal with him as he has dealt by himself, and, if in such a case the trustee will not sue without the sanction of the court, I think it is right to allow the *cestui que trust* to sue for himself, in the name of the trustee, either at law, or in this court, as the case may require. The rights of the parties cannot depend upon mere accident and caprice.

Questions

1   To what extent is the rule in *Fletcher v Fletcher* consistent with the principle in *Milroy v Lord*?

2   When was the trust in *Fletcher v Fletcher* created?

3   In *Fletcher v Fletcher*, had the settlor done everything in his power to transfer the subject matter of the trust to the trustees?

Debts enforceable at law

The *Fletcher v Fletcher* principle, by its nature, is restricted to debts enforceable at law, which are in existence at the time of the declaration. Thus, the *Fletcher* rule is restricted to covenants to transfer money (and no other type of chose in action) that exist at the time of the declaration. This limitation on the *Fletcher* rule was imposed by the High Court in *Re Cook's Settlement Trust*.

Re Cook's Settlement Trust [1965] Ch 902, HC

Facts

Settled property in the nature of paintings were transferred to Sir Francis Cook by his father. At the same time, Sir Francis covenanted with the trustees to the effect that if any of the paintings were sold during his lifetime, the net proceeds of sale would be paid to the trustees to be held by them upon trusts in favour of Sir Francis' children. Sir Francis gave one of the paintings to his wife who wished to sell it. The trustees issued a summons to ascertain whether, on the sale of the painting, the trustees would be obliged to enforce the covenant for the benefit of the children.

Held

The trustees were directed not to enforce the covenant. The intended trust was not perfect within the *Fletcher v Fletcher* principle, because on the date of the declaration of trust the property did not exist. It was an expectancy. Moreover, Sir Francis' children were volunteers and could not enforce the covenant. Likewise, the volunteers were not entitled to have the covenant enforced on their behalf:

> **Buckley J:** The covenant with which I am concerned did not, in my opinion, create a debt enforceable at law, that is to say, a property right, which, although to bear fruit only in the future and on a contingency, was capable of being made the subject of an immediate trust, as was held to be the case in *Fletcher v Fletcher* (1844) 4 Hare 67. Nor is this covenant associated with property which was the subject of an immediate trust, as in *Williamson v Codrington* (1750) 1 Ves Sen 511. Nor did the covenant relate to property which then belonged to the covenantor, as in *Re Cavendish Browne's Settlement Trusts* (1916) 61 SJ 27. In contrast to all these cases, this covenant on its true construction is, in my opinion, an executory contract to settle a particular fund or particular funds of money which at the date of the covenant did not exist and which might never come into existence. It is analogous to a covenant to settle an expectation or to settle after acquired property. The case, in my judgment, involves the law of contract, not the law of trusts . . .
>
> Accordingly, the second and third defendants are not in my judgment entitled to require the trustees to take proceedings to enforce the covenant, even if it is capable of being construed in a manner favourable to them.

EFFECT OF A PERFECT TRUST

Once the trust is constituted, the beneficiaries are given a recognisable interest in the property. They are entitled to protect their interest against anyone, with the exception of a bona fide transferee of the legal estate for value without notice: see *MCC Proceeds Inc v Lehman* [1998] 4 All ER 675, CA (see p 3 above). The beneficiaries are entitled to sue directly for either a common law remedy or, in appropriate cases, an equitable remedy irrespective of whether or not they have provided consideration (*Fletcher v Fletcher* (1844) 4 Hare 67). In any event, the trustees (as representatives of the trust) are entitled to sue or be sued on behalf of the trust. This is the position even though the beneficiaries are volunteers, as illustrated in *Paul v Paul*.

Paul v Paul (1882) 20 Ch D 742, CA

Facts

Under a marriage settlement, property was settled on the wife for life, with remainder to the husband for life if he should survive her, with remainder to the issue of the marriage and, failing issue, on trust for the next of kin (the wife's father). There were no children from the marriage. The husband and wife sought to have the fund paid to them absolutely, claiming that the next of kin was a volunteer and unable to enforce the trust.

Held

The trust was completely constituted and the beneficiaries, including the next of kin, were entitled to enforce it. It was therefore immaterial that the next of kin was a volunteer.

Volunteers and non-volunteers

A volunteer is one who has not provided valuable consideration. Valuable consideration is treated as either common law consideration in money or money's worth, or marriage consideration. Common law consideration is the price promised by each party to an agreement. Marriage consideration has been judicially described as 'the most valuable consideration imaginable'. It takes the form of a settlement made before and in consideration of marriage, i.e., an antenuptial settlement. In addition, a post-nuptial settlement made in pursuance of an antenuptial agreement is treated as a marriage settlement.

An antenuptial agreement is one made before or at the time of the marriage and:

(a) on condition that the marriage takes place; and

(b) on the occasion of the marriage; and

(c) for the purpose of facilitating the marriage: see *Re Park (Decd) (No 2)* [1972] Ch 385.

The persons who are treated as providing marriage consideration are the parties to the marriage and the issue of the marriage, including remoter issue. Any other children connected with the parties to the marriage are volunteers. Thus, illegitimate, legitimated and adopted children, as well as children of a subsequent marriage, are volunteers. But exceptionally, the interest of such volunteer children may be intertwined with the interest of the non-volunteers to such an extent that the non-volunteers are required to acknowledge the interest of the volunteers. In this event, the volunteers may obtain incidental benefits ancillary to the interest of the non-volunteer: see *AG v Jacob-Smith* [1895] 2 QB 341.

Question

What is meant by valuable consideration?

EFFECT OF AN IMPERFECT TRUST

The significance of identifying volunteers is that, unless they are beneficiaries under an express trust, they are not entitled to equitable assistance under an imperfect trust. In other words, the imperfect trust operates as an agreement to create a trust and, in accordance with contractual principles, a party is entitled to sue for a breach of contract only if he has provided valuable consideration for the promise, subject to the principles laid down in the Contracts (Rights of Third Parties) Act 1999: 'Equity will not assist a volunteer' and 'equity will not perfect an imperfect gift'. Accordingly, a non-volunteer may compel the covenantee (intended trustee) to bring a claim in law for damages for breach of a contract to create a trust, or the non-volunteer may claim an equitable remedy of specific performance forcing the covenantor to transfer the property to the intended trustee. The effect is equivalent to the imperfect trust being treated as perfect at the behest of the non-volunteer. In other words, the claimant (non-volunteer) in respect of an imperfect trust is placed in the same position as a beneficiary under a perfect trust and is entitled to such equitable assistance as is appropriate in the circumstances. *Jefferys v Jefferys* is an authority that illustrates both propositions: the enforcement of a perfect trust of freehold property by a volunteer/beneficiary, and the non-enforcement of an imperfect trust of copyhold property by, or on behalf of, a volunteer.

Jefferys v Jefferys (1841) Cr & Ph 138, HC

Facts

A father voluntarily conveyed freehold property to the trustees upon trust for the benefit of his daughters. He also covenanted with the trustees to surrender copyhold properties to the trustees subject to the same trust. He died without surrendering the copyholds and by his will devised parts of both the freehold and copyhold to his widow. After his death, the daughters sought to have the trusts of the deed carried into effect and to compel the widow to surrender the copyhold property.

Held

In respect of the freehold, the trust was completely constituted and the daughters' interest was complete. However, in respect of the copyhold, the trust was incompletely constituted and, since the daughters were volunteers, they had no right to compel the widow to part with the legal interest, which she had legitimately acquired.

In *Pullan v Koe*, non-volunteers were entitled to enforce (or perfect) an imperfect trust for their own benefit. The result from the point of view of the non-volunteer is equivalent to the trust being perfectly created.

Pullan v Koe [1913] 1 Ch 9, HC

Facts

By a marriage settlement made in 1859, a wife covenanted to settle after-acquired property of £100 and over. In 1879, she received a gift of £285 but did not transfer the relevant sum to the trustees. Instead, the money was paid into her husband's bank account and he later invested it in bonds that remained in his estate at the time of his death in 1909. The trustees of the marriage settlement claimed the securities from the husband's executors on behalf of the children of the marriage. The executors pleaded the Statute of Limitations as a defence.

Held

In favour of the trustees, who were entitled to trace the intended trust assets in favour of the non-volunteers. The claim was treated as equivalent to an action brought in respect of a perfectly created trust:

> **Swinfen Eady J:** It was contended that the bonds never in fact became trust property, as both the wife and husband were only liable in damages for breach of covenant, and that the case was different from cases where property which has once admittedly become subject to the trusts of an instrument has been improperly dealt with, and is sought to be recovered. In my opinion as soon as the £285 was paid to the wife it became in equity bound by and subject to the trusts of the settlement. The trustees could have claimed that particular sum, could have obtained at once the appointment of a receiver of it, if they could have shewn a case of jeopardy, and, if it had been invested and the investment could be traced, could have followed the money and claimed the investment [emphasis added].

> This point was dealt with by Jessel MR in *Smith v Lucas* (1881) 18 Ch D 531 at 543, where he said:

>> What is the effect of such a covenant in equity? It has been said that the effect in equity of the covenant of the wife, as far as she is concerned, is that it does not affect her personally, but that it binds the property: that is to say, it binds the property under the doctrine of equity that that is to be considered as done which ought to be done. That is in the nature of specific performance of the contract no doubt. If, therefore, this is a covenant to settle the future-acquired property of the wife, and nothing more is done by her, the covenant will bind the property.

Again in *Collyer v Issacs* (1881) 19 Ch D 342 at 351 Jessel MR said:

> A man can contract to assign property which is to come into existence in the future, and when it has come
> into existence, equity, treating as done that which ought to be done, fastens upon that property, and the
> contract to assign thus becomes a complete assignment. If a person contracts for value, for example, in his
> marriage settlement, to settle all such real estate as his father shall leave him by will, or purports actually to
> convey by the deed all such real estate the effect is the same. It is a contract for value which will bind the
> property if the father leaves any property to his son.

*The property being thus bound, these bonds became trust property, and can be followed by the trustees and claimed from
a volunteer* [emphasis added].

Again the trustees are entitled to come into a court of equity to enforce a contract to create a trust, contained
in a marriage settlement, for the benefit of the wife and the issue of the marriage, all of whom are within the
marriage consideration. The husband covenanted that he and his heirs, executors, and administrators, should, as
soon as circumstances would admit, convey, assign, and surrender to the trustees the real or personal property
to which his wife should become beneficially entitled. The trustees are entitled to have the covenant specifically
enforced by a court of equity. In *Re D'Angibau* (1880) 15 Ch D 228 and *In Re Plumptre's Marriage Settlement* [1910]
1 Ch 609 it was held that the court would not interfere in favour of volunteers, not within the marriage
consideration, but here the plaintiffs are the contracting parties and the object of the proceeding is to benefit the
wife and issue of the marriage.

In effect, a completely constituted trust, in terms of enforcement, is similar to an incompletely
constituted trust in favour of someone who has furnished consideration.

On the other hand, a volunteer is not entitled to maintain a claim in equity, directly or
indirectly, in order to force the settlor to perfect an imperfect gift. In *Re Plumptre*, a volunteer, or
anyone acting on his behalf, had no *locus standi* to bring an action to enforce an imperfect trust, in
the absence of statutory provisions to the contrary.

In Re Plumptre's Marriage Settlement, Underhill v Plumptre [1910] 1 Ch 609, HC

Facts

A marriage settlement, dated 7 October 1878, made between Alice of the first part (the wife),
Reginald of the second part (the husband) and the trustees of the third part, contained a covenant
to settle the wife's after-acquired property which exceeded £500 upon trust to pay the income to
the wife during the joint lives of herself and husband, and following the death of either of them to
the survivor for life with remainder as to capital and income for the issue of the marriage and, in
default of issue, upon trust for the wife's statutory next of kin. In August 1884, the husband
bought stock in the wife's name for £1,018. In May 1887, she sold this stock for £1,125 and
purchased Grand Trunk Railway of Canada stock, which remained in her name at the date of her
death intestate and without issue on 2 February 1909. The husband took out letters of administration to her estate on 21 August 1909. In November 1909, the trustees issued an originating summons requiring the determination of the court as to whether they were bound to take any steps on
behalf of the next of kin (volunteers) to enforce the covenant.

Held

The claim was statute-barred but, in any event, the next of kin, as volunteers and strangers to the
marriage consideration, were not entitled to enforce (or seek the enforcement of) the covenant:

> **Eve J:** Now what is their position here? They are not in my opinion *cestuis que trust* under the settlement, for
> nothing therein amounts to a declaration of trust, or to anything more than an executory contract on the part of
> the husband and wife; it is, so far as the next of kin are concerned, what Cotton J calls a voluntary contract to
> create a trust as distinguished from a complete voluntary trust such as existed in the case of *Fletcher v Fletcher*
> (1844) 4 Hare 67, on which Mr Clayton so strongly relied. The collaterals are not parties to the contract; they are
> not within the marriage consideration and cannot be considered otherwise than as volunteers, and in these
> respects it makes no difference that the covenant sought to be enforced is the husband's and that the property
> sought to be brought within it comes from the wife. For each of the foregoing propositions authority is to be
> found in the judgment of the Court of Appeal in *Re D'Angibau* (1880) 15 Ch D 228; and in the same judgment is

to be found this further statement – that where, as in this case, the husband has acquired a legal title as administrator of his wife to property which was subject to the contract to settle, volunteers are not entitled to enforce against that legal title the contract to create a trust contained in the settlement. I think that judgment really disposes of the second question upon this summons, but before answering it, as I propose to do, in the negative, I ought perhaps to add that the argument founded on the rule that equity looks on that as done which ought to be done is, in my opinion, met and disposed of by what Lindley LJ says in *Re Anstis* (1886) 31 Ch D 596. After stating the rule he adds:

> But this rule, although usually expressed in general terms, is by no means universally true. Where the obligation to do what ought to be done is not an absolute duty, but only an obligation arising from contract, that which ought to be done is only treated as done in favour of some person entitled to enforce the contract as against the person liable to perform it.

I therefore answer the second question by saying that the applicants are not bound to take any steps.

The court came to a similar conclusion in *Re McCardle* in respect of an imperfect assignment of a sum of money in favour of a volunteer.

Re McCardle [1951] 1 All ER 905, CA

Facts

A testator (who died in 1935) left his residuary estate upon trust for his widow for life with remainder to his five children equally. Part of the estate consisted of a bungalow that was occupied in 1943 by M (one of the testator's sons) and his wife. During their occupation, certain repairs, valued at £488, were carried out to the bungalow and were paid for by Mrs M. Two years later (1945), the five children signed a document declaring: 'In consideration of your carrying out certain alterations to the property ... we, the beneficiaries under the will hereby agree that the executors shall repay you from the said estate when so distributed the said sum of £488 in settlement of such improvements.' In 1948, the widow died. In 1950, Mrs M claimed payment of £488 from the executors. The children (other than M) objected to the sum being paid.

Held

The court found in favour of the defendants on the following grounds:

(a) The document, on construction, did not constitute an immediate assignment by the beneficiaries of their equitable interest to Mrs M but, instead, purported to create a contract whereby the executors shall, at a future date (when the estate was distributed), pay £488.

(b) Since the repairs and agreement to remunerate constituted two separate transactions, the consideration was not treated as valuable but past.

IMPERFECT TRUSTS BY DEEDS

Section 1 of the Law of Property (Miscellaneous Provisions) Act 1989 abolished the requirement of affixing a seal on a document in order to create a deed (originally called a covenant or specialty contract).

Law of Property (Miscellaneous Provisions) Act 1989, s 1

(1) Any rule of law which:

    (a) restricts the substances on which a deed may be written;

    (b) requires a seal for the valid execution of an instrument as a deed by an individual; or

    (c) requires authority by one person to another to deliver an instrument as a deed on his behalf to be given by deed,

    is abolished.

A deed is any document intended and executed as a deed that is signed and delivered by the parties in the presence of attesting witnesses:

(2) An instrument shall not be a deed unless:

    (a) it makes it clear on its face that it is intended to be a deed by the person making it or, as the case may be, by the parties to it (whether by describing itself as a deed or expressing itself to be or signed as a deed or otherwise); and

    (b) it is validly executed as a deed by that person or, as the case may be, one or more of those parties.

(3) An instrument is validly executed as a deed by an individual if, and only if:

    (a) it is signed:

        (i) by him in the presence of a witness who attests the signature; or

        (ii) at his discretion and in his presence and the presence of two witnesses who each attest the signature; and

    (b) it is delivered as a deed by him or a person authorised to do so on his behalf.

Before the Contracts (Rights of Third Parties) Act 1999

The consequence of executing a deed is that it constitutes an agreement enforceable at common law, notwithstanding the absence of consideration. A claim may exist for damages for breach of contract, at common law, even though the claimant (party to the deed) did not furnish consideration for the promise.

Equity, on the other hand, adopts a different approach to deeds and refuses to recognise the special nature of such agreements. Courts of equity require the claimants to establish the existence of consideration before becoming entitled to their assistance by claiming the equitable remedy of specific performance or any other equitable remedy: 'Equity would not assist a volunteer.' See *In Re Plumptre's Marriage Settlement* (see p 68 above).

Moreover, a party to a deed (the covenantee or intended trustee) may not be compelled by a volunteer to bring a claim for damages against the covenantor for breach of a deed to create a trust. The volunteer, not being a party to the deed, requires equitable assistance to claim an interest under the deed. But the court will not assist the volunteer by such circuitous device. The reason being that a volunteer should not be placed in a position where he may obtain, by indirect means, a remedy which he may not enjoy by direct procedure.

For example, S, by deed, agrees with T, an intended trustee, that future property to be acquired by S will be transferred to T to hold on trust for B, a beneficiary (volunteer), absolutely. S acquires property but fails to transfer the same to T. It is clear that B may not directly claim damages for he is not a party to the contract. B may not directly claim an equitable remedy for he is a volunteer. In addition, B may not force T to sue S for damages on his behalf because he is a volunteer. Hence, B may not obtain a remedy indirectly by enlisting equitable support.

In *Re Pryce* the intended beneficiary (volunteer and third party) under an imperfect trust, e.g., a covenant to transfer future property, applied to the court for directions seeking to force the intended trustees (covenantees) to sue the settlor/covenantor for damages for breach of contract. Eve J dismissed the application on the ground that the volunteer third party might not obtain a remedy indirectly when the same remedy was not available to him directly. The effect of this decision is that a court of equity will not grant assistance to a volunteer when he cannot obtain assistance directly for 'equity will not assist a volunteer'. The court assumed that if the directions were granted, the intended trustees would be allowed to exercise their common law right to bring an action for damages. If substantial damages were awarded to the intended trustees, the imperfect trust might be converted into a perfect trust.

Re Pryce, Nevill v Pryce [1917] 1 Ch 234, HC

Facts

In 1887, a marriage settlement contained a covenant to settle the wife's after-acquired property upon trust as to income for the wife for life with remainder to her husband for life if he should survive her, with an ultimate remainder as to capital and income on trust for the issue of the marriage, but failing issue on trust for the wife's next of kin. In 1906, the husband gave his wife £4,700. The husband died in 1907 and there was no issue of the marriage. The trustees issued a summons for the court to determine whether they ought to take any steps to enforce the covenant.

Held

The trustees ought not to take any steps to enforce the covenant. The trust was imperfect. The wife's next of kin were volunteers who could not maintain an action to enforce the covenant. Likewise, the next of kin might not obtain a remedy indirectly, namely damages, through the directions of the court requiring the trustees to enforce the covenant:

> **Eve J:** Seeing that the next of kin could neither maintain an action to enforce the covenant nor for damages for breach of it, and that the settlement is not a declaration of trust constituting the relationship of trustee and *cestui que trust* between the defendant and the next of kin, in which case effect could be given to the trusts even in favour of volunteers, but is a mere voluntary contract to create a trust, ought the court now for the sole benefit of these volunteers to direct the trustees to take proceedings to enforce the defendant's covenant? I think it ought not; to do so would be to give the next of kin by indirect means relief they cannot obtain by any direct procedure, and would in effect be enforcing the settlement as against the defendant's legal right to payment and transfer from the trustees of the parents' marriage settlement. The circumstances are not unlike those which existed in the case of *Re D'Angibau* (1880) 15 Ch D 228, and I think the position here is covered by the judgments of the Lords Justices in that case [emphasis added].

> Accordingly, I declare that the trustees ought not to take any steps to compel the transfer or payment to them of the premises assured to the wife by the deed of 12 December 1904.

This principle has been extended even further in *Re Kay's Settlement* in order to prevent T, by his own volition, from pursuing his common law remedy for damages for breach of contract. The assumption is that the damages which would have been awarded to the claimant (T) may be held on trust for the volunteer (B), thus allowing the volunteer indirect access to the courts.

In *Re Kay's Settlement* [1939] Ch 329, the intended trustee under the imperfect trust brought an action for damages for breach of contract, of his own accord, against the intended settlor. The court dismissed the claim for the same reasons as stated in *Re Pryce*.

Note

The decision in *Re Kay* involved an extension of the principle in *Re Pryce*, in the sense that the court was actively prepared to prevent the intended trustees/covenantees pursuing their common law right to sue for damages for breach of contract. The underlying assumption was that substantial damages would otherwise have been held on trust for the volunteer third party.

In *Re Cavendish Browne's Settlement Trusts*, the court allowed the intended trustees' claim for damages for breach of contract and awarded substantial damages to the claimant. The second issue, namely, whether these damages were to be held on trust for the volunteer beneficiary, was not considered by the court.

Re Cavendish Browne's Settlement Trusts, Horner v Rawle [1916] WN 341, HC

Facts

By a voluntary covenant, dated 19 September 1911, made between the settlor and the trustees, the settlor covenanted that she would transfer to the trustees property to which she was entitled under the will of two others. The transfer was expressed to be subject to the terms of a trust. The covenant included a power of revocation.

The settlor died on 24 December 1914 intestate without having exercised the power of revocation. Her administrators applied by summons to determine whether damages were payable for breach of the covenant.

Held

The trustees were entitled to recover substantial damages from the administrators for breach of covenant. The measure of such damages was the value of the property that would have come into the hands of the trustees if the covenant had been duly performed.

Note

A possible reconciliation of this case with *Re Pryce* and *Re Kay* is that in *Re Cavendish Browne's Settlement Trusts*, the property covenanted to be transferred was in existence on the date of the covenant. This, however, is a rather precarious means of reconciling the decisions.

If the volunteer is a party to the deed, he will be entitled to bring a claim at law for damages for breach of the agreement, and equity will not interfere with his power to bring such a claim. In this situation, as illustrated in *Cannon v Hartley*, the claimant will be seeking to give effect directly to his common law rights by bringing a claim for damages. His rights will not be dependent on a third party taking proceedings to represent his interest.

Cannon v Hartley [1949] Ch 213, HC

Facts

By a deed of separation executed on 23 January 1941 between the defendant (H) of the first part, his wife (W) of the second part and the plaintiff, their daughter, of the third part, H covenanted, *inter alia*, as follows:

> If and whenever during the lifetime of W or daughter, H shall become entitled to any money or property exceeding £1,000 he will forthwith settle one half of such money upon trust for himself for life, then to W for life with remainder to the daughter absolutely.

In 1944, H became entitled to £12,500. W died in 1946. H refused to execute the settlement in accordance with the covenant. The daughter brought an action claiming damages for breach of covenant.

Held

In favour of the claimant on the ground that she was a party to the deed and was seeking a common law remedy to enforce her claim for breach of covenant:

> **Romer J:** [The learned judge considered the judgments of Eve J in *Re Pryce* [1917] Ch 329 and Simonds J in *Re Kay* [1939] Ch 329 and continued:] Now it appears to me that neither *Re Pryce* nor *Re Kay's Settlement* is any authority for the proposition which has been submitted to me on behalf of the defendant. In neither case were the claimants parties to the settlement in question, nor were they within the consideration of the deed. When volunteers were referred to in *Re Pryce* it seems to me that what Eve J intended to say was that they were not within the class of non-parties, if I may use that expression, to whom Cotton LJ recognised in *Re D'Angibau* (1880) 15 Ch D 228 that the court would afford assistance. In the present case the plaintiff, although a volunteer, is not only a party to the deed of separation but is also a direct covenantee under the very covenant upon which she is suing. She does not require the assistance of the court to enforce the covenant for she has a legal right herself to enforce it. She is not asking for equitable relief for damages at common law for breach of covenant.

Furthermore, a non-volunteer may bring a claim at law or in equity against the other party to the deed. This claim may be brought for his own benefit (see *Pullan v Koe*, p 67 above) or apparently for the benefit of others, including volunteers. This appears to represent the view taken by the Law Lords in *Beswick v Beswick*.

Beswick v Beswick [1968] AC 58, HL

Facts

Peter Beswick was assisted in his business as a coal merchant by his nephew, the defendant. Peter entered into a contract, by deed, with the defendant for the transfer of the business. The material terms were that Peter would assign the business to the defendant in consideration of the defendant employing him as a consultant for the remainder of his life at £6, 10s a week and paying an annuity of £5 a week to his widow after his death. Peter subsequently died. The defendant paid the widow the first £5 but thereafter refused to pay any more. The widow sued the defendant as administratrix of her husband's estate and in her personal capacity for arrears of the annuity and for specific performance of the agreement. The High Court dismissed the action. The Court of Appeal allowed her appeal on the ground that, as administratrix, the plaintiff was entitled to specific performance. The defendant appealed to the House of Lords. It was not argued that the plaintiff was entitled to pursue her claim in her personal capacity. The question in issue was whether the plaintiff was entitled to claim specific performance of the agreement.

Held

The plaintiff was entitled, as administratrix of her husband's estate, to specific performance of the agreement. In short, her deceased husband could have enforced the agreement on behalf of his volunteer wife and, since an award of damages was an inadequate remedy, the rights under the agreement were adequately protected by an order of specific performance:

> **Lord Pearce:** In the present case I think that the damages, if assessed, must be substantial. It is not necessary, however, to consider the amount of damages more closely since this is a case in which, as the Court of Appeal rightly decided, the more appropriate remedy is that of specific performance.
>
> What, then, is the obstacle to granting specific performance? It is argued that since the widow personally had no rights which she personally could enforce the court will not make an order which will have the effect of enforcing those rights. I can find no principle to this effect. The condition as to payment of an annuity to the widow personally was valid. The estate (though not the widow personally) can enforce it. Why should the estate be barred from exercising its full contractual rights merely because in doing so it secures justice for the widow who, by a mechanical defect of our law, is unable to assert her own rights? Such a principle would be repugnant to justice and fulfil no other object than that of aiding the wrongdoer. I can find no ground on which such a principle should exist.
>
> In my opinion, the plaintiff as administratrix is entitled to a decree of specific performance.

Note

On the question of whether parties to a contract may succeed in claims for damages on behalf of third parties, see also *Coulls v Bagot's Executor and Trustee Co Ltd* (1967) ALR 385; *Jackson v Horizon Holidays Ltd* [1975] 1 WLR 1468, CA; *Jarvis v Swan Tours Ltd* [1973] QB 233.

The Contracts (Rights of Third Parties) Act 1999

The Contracts (Rights of Third Parties) Act 1999 introduced a long overdue reform of the law. Its purpose, as stated in the House of Commons Explanatory Note to the Bill, was 'to reform the rule of privity of contract under which a person can only enforce a contract if he is a party to it'.

Entitlement to sue

Section 1(1) of the Contracts (Rights of Third Parties) Act 1999 sets out the circumstances when a third party to a contract will have a right to enforce the agreement. These are that the contract was made expressly or impliedly for the benefit of the third party (s 1(1) and(2)). The third party is required to be identified by name or description, although he need not be in existence at the time the contract was made (s 1(3)).

This provision will be satisfied if A covenants (or makes a simple agreement) with B to transfer property to him upon trust for C. Assuming that A has not transferred the property to B and that C is a 'volunteer' then, as a third party, the requirements above will be satisfied. The effect is that the third party (C) is entitled 'in his own right to enforce' the contract (s 1(1)). This is the typical case with regard to an incompletely constituted trust.

The remedy

Section 1(5) of the 1999 Act declares the remedy that will be available to the third party (C in the above example).

Contracts (Rights of Third Parties) Act 1999, s 1(5)

For the purpose of exercising his right to enforce a term of the contract, there shall be available to the third party *any remedy that would have been available to him in an action for breach of contract if he had been a party to the contract* (and the *rules* relating to damages, injunctions, specific performance and other relief shall apply accordingly) [emphasis added].

The effect of the provision is to treat C, the volunteer and third party, as if he is a party to the agreement and to grant him such remedies as would be available to him as a party to the agreement. There is no doubt that s 1(5) gives C a claim for damages, but subject to the rules regarding the quantification of the damages. Under the Act, C's position is treated as similar to that of the claimant in *Cannon v Hartley* [1949] Ch 213. Alternatively, if C has provided consideration for the promise but is not a party to the agreement (i.e., he has provided marriage consideration), he would be entitled to damages if this remedy were appropriate (as declared by the Act). But if the remedy of damages is not appropriate, the third party non-volunteer would be entitled to an equitable remedy such as specific performance as in *Pullan v Koe* [1913] 1 Ch 9. This principle has not been changed by the Act but is simply confirmed by the provision.

Is the volunteer entitled to an equitable remedy?

The contentious issue is what remedy would C, a volunteer and third party to the contract, be entitled to in a claim against A for breach of contract? The remedy that C (the claimant) is entitled to, save for damages, has not been altered by the Act. It is submitted that C, as a volunteer, will only be entitled to damages for four reasons.

First, the policy of the Act was to reform the privity rule and treat the third party in the circumstances laid down in the Act as if he is a party to the contract.

House of Commons Explanatory Note, para 3

The Bill reforms the rule of privity of contract under which a person can only enforce a contract if he is a party to it.

On this basis, the third party (who is now treated under the Act as though he is a party) is entitled to bring a claim against the party in breach *in his own right*, i.e., the claim is not dependent on the means of another. In our example, C may sue A directly without joining B as a co-claimant or a co-defendant.

Secondly, the reformation of the privity rule does not automatically change the law with regard to equitable remedies. These remain discretionary, but damages are obtainable as of right, subject to the rules regarding the quantification of damages.

Thirdly, s 1(5) confirms that the *rules* regarding damages and specific performance shall apply. The rules regarding damages are well known, in particular, the rules concerning remoteness of damage and the duty to mitigate the loss. These rules remain the same after the Act. In addition, the equitable concept that 'equity will not assist a volunteer' is applicable with equal force after the Act. Since C is a volunteer, he should not expect an equitable remedy such as specific performance for he was not entitled to such a remedy prior to the passing of the Act and the Act has not changed this rule. Support for this view may be gained by reference to the Explanatory Note accompanying the Bill. It states that 'subsection (5) makes it clear that all remedies which are available to a person bringing a claim for breach of contract are available to a third party seeking to enforce his rights under subsection (1). The normal rules of law applicable to those remedies, including the rules relating to causation, remoteness and the duty to mitigate one's loss, apply to the third party's claim'. Thus, it follows that since the volunteer non-covenantee (i.e., C) is now treated as though he is a party to the covenant, his status remains a volunteer and as such he will not gain any equitable assistance.

Fourthly, a volunteer in the eyes of equity is treated as not having lost anything under the contract and, without more, is not entitled in his own right to gain any benefits under the contract. The position is not the same at common law with regard to damages, which are obtainable as of right. Thus, it makes no difference whether the subject matter of the contract to transfer property to B for the benefit of C involves land, shares in a private company or cash. Under a voluntary contract as opposed to a trust, C has no justifiable basis in the eyes of equity to pursue a claim for breach of contract.

In conclusion, the 1999 Act has effected the following changes:

(a) A reversal of *Re Pryce* – where a volunteer non-covenantee (C) was not able to force the covenantee (B) to bring an action for damages.

(b) A reversal of *Re Kay* – where a covenantee (B) was prevented from bringing an action for damages on behalf of a volunteer non-covenantee (C).

(c) An endorsement of *Re Cavendish-Browne* – where a covenantee (B) successfully brought an action for damages on behalf of a non-covenantee (C).

(d) An approval of the *Cannon v Hartley* principle – the volunteer covenantee is entitled to claim substantial damages for breach of covenant, but is not entitled to the equitable remedy of specific performance.

(e) An endorsement of *Beswick v Beswick* – where in substance a covenantee (non-volunteer) (B) was able to bring an action in equity on behalf of a volunteer non-covenantee (C).

Question
How far has the Contracts (Rights of Third Parties) Act 1999 improved the position of volunteers under an imperfect trust?

FURTHER READING

Barton, J, 'Trusts and covenants' (1975) 91 LQR 236.
Friend, M, 'Trusts of voluntary covenants: an alternative approach' [1982] Conv 280.
Goddard, D, 'Equity, volunteers and ducks' [1988] Conv 19.
Halliwell, M, 'Perfecting imperfect gifts and trusts: have we reached the end of the Chancellor's foot?' [2003] Conv 192.
Hornby, J, 'Covenants in favour of volunteers' (1962) 78 LQR 228.
Jaconelli, J, 'Privity: the trust exception examined' [1998] Conv 88.
Jones, G, 'The enforcement of settlements in equity by volunteers' [1965] CLJ 46.
Matheson, D, 'The enforceability of a covenant to create a trust' (1966) 29 MLR 397.
Meagher, R and Lehane, L, 'Trusts of voluntary covenants' (1976) 92 LQR 425.
Rickett, C, 'Completely constituting an inter vivos trust: property rules' [2001] Conv 515.
Roe, T, 'Contractual intention under s 1(1)(b) and s 1(2) of the Contracts (Rights of Third Parties) Act 1999' (2000) 63 MLR 887.
Williams, G, 'Contracts for the benefit of third parties' (1943) 7 MLR 123.

EXCEPTIONS TO THE RULE THAT EQUITY WILL NOT PERFECT AN IMPERFECT GIFT

INTRODUCTION

An incomplete transfer of property to the donee (or trustee) will be regarded as complete in a number of exceptional circumstances. The consequences of these principles are that the intended transferees are entitled to enlist the support of equity in order to perfect imperfect gifts. The claims may be brought even at the instance of volunteers. These are exceptions to the rule that 'equity will not assist a volunteer' or 'equity will not perfect an imperfect gift'.

The exceptional principles are:

(a) The rule in *Strong v Bird* (1874) LR 18 Eq 315. Where an *inter vivos* gift (or transfer) is imperfect because the transferor has failed to transfer the relevant property to the transferee, the imperfect transfer will become perfect on the death of the transferor. This will be the case if the transferee becomes the executor of the transferor's estate and the donor manifests a present, continuing intention to make an *inter vivos* gift.

(b) *Donatio mortis causa* (DMC). A DMC is an *inter vivos* delivery of property by a person contemplating death, subject to the condition that the gift will take effect only on the donor's death. The effect is that on the date of death of the donor the conditional transfer becomes complete. The donee (volunteer) automatically becomes entitled to retain the property or, if the transfer is incomplete, he may compel the personal representatives of the deceased to transfer the property to him.

(c) Proprietary estoppel. This is a right given to a volunteer whenever a landowner stands by and permits a volunteer to incur expenditure in order to improve his (the landowner's) property on the promise or assumption that there will be a transfer of an interest to him. The principle may be used as a cause of action entitling the volunteer to acquire an interest in land. The landowner, and his successors in title, will be estopped from denying the interest in land acquired by the volunteer. The court will decide the nature of the interest that may be acquired by the volunteer.

THE RULE IN *STRONG v BIRD*

A perfect gift of property requires the donor to transfer the property to the donee with the intention of gifting the property to the donee. The rule in *Strong v Bird* is that if an *inter vivos* gift is imperfect by reason only of the transfer to the donee being incomplete, the gift will become perfect when the donee acquires the property in the capacity of executor of the donor's estate. In probate law, the deceased's estate devolves on his executor, who, after payment of all the debts of the testator, is required to distribute the estate in accordance with the testator's will. The donee/executor will take the property beneficially in accordance with the intention of the donor, even though he acquires the asset in the capacity of executor of the donor's estate.

Strong v Bird (1874) LR 18 Eq 315, CA

Facts

The defendant's stepmother lived with him and his wife, paying for board and lodging. He had borrowed £1,000 from her and it was agreed that the debt should be repaid by deductions of £100 from each quarter's rent. Deductions were made for two quarters and on the third quarter the stepmother refused to hold the defendant to the agreement and paid the full rent until her death. This arrangement by conduct did not discharge the debt at law since there was no consideration for the release. The defendant became the sole executor of his stepmother's estate. The issue was whether the loan was repayable by the defendant. The next of kin (plaintiff) attempted to recover the money from the defendant.

Held

The transfer of the relevant sum had been perfected and the debt extinguished by the appointment of the defendant as executor. The stepmother's donative intention had continued until her death:

> **Sir George Jessel MR:** When a testator makes his debtor executor, and thereby releases the debt at law, he is no longer liable at law. It is said that he would be liable in this court: and so he would, unless he could shew some reason for not being made liable. Then what does he shew here? Where he proves to the satisfaction of the court a continuing intention to give; and it appears to me that there being the continuing intention to give, and there being a legal act which transferred the ownership or released the obligation – for it is the same thing – the transaction is perfected, and he does not want the aid of a court of equity to carry it out, or to make it complete, because it is complete already, and there is no equity against him to take the property away from him. On that ground I shall hold that this gentleman had a perfect title to the £900.

Question
How would you reconcile the rule in *Strong v Bird* with testamentary dispositions?

Donor's intention

The donor's intention is of paramount importance. It is the donor's intention that entitles the court to perfect the gift at the instance of the volunteer executor. The donor is required to manifest a present, continuous intention to make an *inter vivos* gift. Thus, the rule will not be satisfied if the donor declares an intention to transfer a car to the donee in the future: see *Re Freeland* [1952] Ch 110.

Continuous intention

Similarly, it must be established that the testator's intention to gift the asset to his executor was unbroken, in the sense that, from the time of the declaration of intention to the date of his death, the donor had not changed his mind. Accordingly, in *Re Wale* [1956] 1 WLR 1346, it was held that the rule would not be satisfied if the donor once had the relevant intention to give away the asset, but had forgotten about the declaration, and treated the property as his own up to the date of his death.

Note
The rule has been extended to perfect an imperfect trust where the trustee/executor acquires the property under the will of the donor. In other words, the capacity in which the property is acquired is immaterial for the purpose of ascertaining whether the trust is perfect, provided that the transferee/executor was appointed a trustee. Thus, in *Re Ralli* (see p 61 above), when Irene's husband became a trustee of the 1899 settlement, he acquired, *inter alia*, Helen's property as executor, and since he was also appointed a trustee of Helen's intended marriage settlement in 1924, he had therefore acquired the trust property and was required to hold the same on trust for the beneficiaries under the 1924 settlement.

Question
Is *Re Ralli* an unwarranted extension of the rule in *Strong v Bird*?

Intestacies

The simple rule in *Strong v Bird* was unjustifiably extended in *Re James* [1935] 1 Ch 449 to transfers made to the administrator on an intestacy. However, Walton J, in *Re Gonin*, severely criticised this unwarranted extension and expressed serious doubts as to the validity of the decision.

Re Gonin (Decd) [1979] Ch 16, HC

Facts

A mother who wanted to make a gift of her house to her daughter erroneously believed that she could not do so because the daughter was illegitimate. As an alternative, the mother wrote out a cheque for £33,000 in her daughter's favour. This cheque was found after her mother's death. At this point, the cheque could not be cashed because on the mother's death the funds in her account became frozen. The daughter became administratrix of her mother's estate and claimed the house under the *Strong v Bird* rule.

Held

The *Strong v Bird* principle was not applicable for there was no continuing intention to give the house to the daughter:

> **Walton J:** . . . by appointing the executor, the testator has by his own act made it impossible for the debtor to sue himself. And, indeed, so far has the rule been taken, that although it will no longer apply if the person appointed executor has renounced probate, yet it will still apply if power to prove has been reserved to him.
>
> The appointment of an administrator is not the act of the deceased but of law. It is often a matter of pure chance which of many persons equally entitled to a grant of letters of administration finally takes them out. Why, then, should any special tenderness be shown to a person so selected by law and not the will of the testator. It would seem an astonishing doctrine of equity that if the person who wishes to take the benefit of the rule in *Strong v Bird* manages to be the person to obtain a grant then he will be able to do so, but if a person equally entitled manages to obtain a prior grant, then he will not be able to do so. This appears to treat what ought to be a simple rule of equity as something in the nature of a lottery.

Question

In your view, should the rule in *Strong v Bird* be extended to intestacies?

Kodilinye, G, 'A fresh look at the rule in *Strong v Bird*' [1982] Conv 14

Kodilinye examined the basis of the rule in *Strong v Bird*. He concluded that the criticisms by Walton J in *Re Gonin* of the principle in *Re James* were unfounded. The administrator of the deceased's estate was in the same position as the executor for the purposes of the *Strong v Bird* rule. Both fiduciaries acquired the deceased's property. As an administrator, the deceased's property is acquired by the next of kin by operation of law, whereas the executor obtains the testator's estate by the conscious and positive act of naming the executor in his will. For the purpose of the rule, it is immaterial how the legal estate vests in the personal representative. There is no requirement that the vesting of the estate in the donee must come about through the voluntary act of the donor.

In addition, Kodilinye contends that the application of the *Strong v Bird* rule to *Re Ralli* marks an unjustified extension of the principle for the following reasons:

(i) the plaintiff [in *Re Ralli*] was trustee of a third party's, not the donor's, will;

(ii) [in *Re Ralli*] there was no attempted immediate gift of any property but only a promise to settle property in the future;

(iii) it is doubtful whether *Strong v Bird* applies where the executor appointed is not the intended donee of the beneficial interest but a trustee of such interest for the donee;

(iv) it was central to Buckley J's reasoning in *Re Ralli* that the settlor had bound herself by covenant to assign the property to the trustees of the marriage settlement, and he expressly limited his decision to such a case;

(v) Buckley J did not expressly base his decision on *Strong v Bird*.

DONATIO MORTIS CAUSA (DEATHBED GIFTS)

A *donatio mortis causa* (DMC) is the *inter vivos* delivery of property by a person contemplating death, subject to the intention that the gift shall take effect only on the donor's death. The effect is that on the donor's death the gift becomes unconditional and the donee is entitled to retain the property or, if the gift is still imperfect, the donee (volunteer) may compel the personal representatives to perfect the transfer of the property to him. The donee under a DMC takes the asset in preference to beneficiaries under the will or an intestacy.

For example, T made his will disposing of all his property to A and on his deathbed delivered to B his watch and building society passbook showing a credit balance of £100. On T's death, the gift of the watch becomes complete. The transfer of the building society funds is incomplete but B will be entitled to compel T's personal representatives to perfect the gift.

A DMC is distinct from an absolute *inter vivos* gift because the transfer of the asset is conditional on death and during the lifetime of the donor the transfer of the property is incomplete. On the other hand, a DMC is different from a testamentary gift because the conditional transfer of property *inter vivos* is not made by will. Thus, the formalities under the Wills Act 1837 are not required to be complied with.

The nature of a DMC was declared by Buckley J in *Re Beaumont* and Farwell J in *Re Craven's Estate (No 1)* in the following two judicial pronouncements.

Re Beaumont [1902] 1 Ch 889, CA

Buckley J: A *donatio mortis causa* is a singular form of gift. It may be said to be of an amphibious nature, being a gift which is neither entirely *inter vivos* nor testamentary. It is an act *inter vivos* by which the donee is to have absolute title to the gift not at once but if the donor dies. If the donor dies the title becomes absolute not under the will but as against the executor. In order to make the gift valid it must be made so as to take complete effect on the donor's death.

Re Craven's Estate (No 1) [1937] 1 Ch 423, HC

Farwell J: Generally speaking, it is not permissible by the law of this country for a person to dispose of his or her property after his or her death except by an instrument executed in accordance with the provisions of the Wills Act 1837. One exception to the general rule is the case of a *donatio mortis causa*, but in order that it may be valid certain conditions must be exactly complied with; otherwise the attempted *donatio* is not effected and the property remains part of the property of the testatrix at her death passing under her will. The conditions which are essential to a *donatio mortis causa* are firstly, a clear intention to give, but to give only if the donor dies, whereas if the donor does not die then the gift is not to take effect and the donor is to have back the subject matter of the gift. Secondly, the gift must be made in contemplation of death, by which is meant not the possibility of death at some time or other, but death within the near future, what may be called death for some reason believed to be impending. Thirdly, the donor must part with dominion over the subject matter of the *donatio* . . .

Question
How would you reconcile DMCs with testamentary dispositions?

There are three conditions to be satisfied in order to create a valid DMC:

(1) the transfer of the property is required to be made *inter vivos* and in contemplation of death;

(2) the transfer is required to be made conditional on death; and

(3) dominion over the property is transferred to the donee.

Transfer made in contemplation of death

It is necessary for the donor to contemplate death more specifically than by reflecting that we must all die some day. The test here is subjective and the court may decide this question by having regard to the surrounding circumstances such as the injuries or illness of the donor, or the fact that the donor was a patient in a hospital, etc. In *Wilkes v Allington* [1931] 2 Ch 104, the condition was satisfied where the donor contemplated death from one cause but died from another cause.

In exceptional circumstances where the donor specifies death from a special condition, then death only from that condition will satisfy this requirement.

Transfer *inter vivos* but conditional on death

This requirement distinguishes a DMC from an absolute *inter vivos* gift. The intention must be that the gift will automatically become complete on death, but subject to the condition that it may be revoked by the donor expressly and will be revoked automatically if he recovers from his illness within a reasonable period of time. The court is required to consider all the circumstances in deciding whether this requirement is satisfied.

Express revocation may take the form of the donor resuming dominion over the property. This would depend on the intention of the donor. Recovery of the property for safe custody will not have this effect. It is impossible for the donor to revoke a DMC by will, for the will takes effect after death, and on death the gift becomes perfect. It follows that if the donee pre-deceases the donor the gift will fail, for the donee's title is conditional on the death of the donor, and on the donee's death title reverts back to the donor.

Parting with dominion

This definitive condition requires the transferor, during his lifetime, to dispose of the property in favour of the transferee and surrender control over the property. In *Re Craven's Estate (No 1)*, Farwell J considered the reasons for imposing this requirement, in particular, the need to identify the subject matter of the DMC and to ascertain whether the donor has transferred control over the property to the donee.

Re Craven's Estate (No 1) [1937] Ch 423, HC

Farwell J: I have considered what was the reason for imposing as a condition of a valid *donatio* that the donor must part with dominion over the subject matter thereof and the answer seems to me to be that the subject matter of the *donatio* must be some *definite property*, and, to ensure that, the donor must put it out of his power between the date of the donation and the date of the death to alter the subject matter of the gift and substitute other chattels. Otherwise, so long as the subject-matter of the gift remained in the dominion of the donor, the donor might at any time between the *donatio* and the gift deal with it as he or she pleased. Take for instance the case of a box. The donor says to the donee: 'This box contains certain valuables which are to be yours in the event of my death from the operation which I am going to undergo in a few days, but I propose to retain the box and the key of the box.' If that was the position it would be open to the donor at any time to take out of the box whatever was in it replacing it with other valuables, and in my view it is in order that that should be parted with dominion so that whatever the original subject matter of the *donatio* was it should remain the subject matter in the event of the death of the donor. In the case of the box it is not necessary to hand over the box if the key is handed over because it is assumed that the key which unlocks the box being in the possession of the donee the donor cannot have access to the contents so as to deal with them in any way [emphasis added].

Chattels

The basic rule is that the property to be disposed of must be actually handed over to the donee, or to someone else as trustee for the donee. This transfer must be accompanied by the necessary intent to part with dominion or control over the property during the lifetime of the donor. No difficulty arises with small articles in respect of which possession may be transferred by the physical delivery to the donee, for example, jewellery, books, paintings, etc. But it is a question of degree as to whether the intention to transfer dominion over the property has been manifested. In *Reddell v Dobree* (1839) 10 Sim 244, delivery of a cash box for safe custody did not satisfy this test.

Symbolic delivery

When the article is too bulky to be physically handed over, it is sufficient for the donor to hand over the means whereby the donee may take possession and control, provided that at the same time the donor is deprived of the power of dealing with the property. For example, delivery of a key to a trunk or safe has been regarded as an effective delivery (constructive delivery) of the property in the trunk or safe.

In *Re Craven's Estate (No 1)*, Farwell J declared that the retention of a duplicate set of keys by the donor may be construed as evidence of the retention of dominion over the chattel, provided that there was a conscious decision on the part of the donor to retain control.

Re Craven's Estate (No 1) [1937] 1 Ch 423, HC

Farwell J: I know of no decided cases in which the question has arisen whether the handing over of a box and one key, it being proved that there was another key retained by the donor, would be sufficient [to transfer dominion] . . . it would probably be held not to be sufficient parting with dominion because the donor would have retained dominion over the box and the contents of the box by retaining the power to open it although it might be in the possession of the donee.

More recently, in *Woodard v Woodard*, the Court of Appeal considered that the effect of the retention of a spare set of keys by the donor would vary with the facts of each case. The reason for the retention will be considered by the courts. If the purpose of the retention of the keys is to retain control over the property then, obviously, dominion would not be transferred. On the other hand, if the retention of the key is not a deliberate and conscious decision taken by the donor this, in itself, may not be inconsistent with the transfer of dominion. The question is determined by having regard to the donor's intention.

Woodard v Woodard (1991) The Times, 18 March, CA

Facts
The plaintiff, sole beneficiary and personal representative of her late husband's estate, brought an action against her son claiming the proceeds of sale of a car which was sold by the defendant shortly after his father's death. The defendant claimed that the car was the subject matter of an outright gift in accordance with his father's intention. Possession of the car was obtained or retained during the period of his father's hospitalisation while suffering from leukaemia (from which he failed to recover). Witnesses testified that the donor said, at various times a few days before his death, that the defendant might keep the car ('You may keep the key'). The trial judge decided that there was an outright gift of the car to the defendant.

Held
The circumstances did not create an outright gift but a valid DMC was constituted. An inference could be drawn that the father's intention was conditional on death. On the question of the transfer of dominion over the car, the court adopted a common sense approach and decided that since the defendant already had possession of the car, the declaration of intention by the father was sufficient to transfer dominion over the car. It was unnecessary for the father to re-acquire possession of the car from the son as a preliminary to transferring dominion or control to the defendant. The significance of the retention of a spare set of keys was dependent on the donor's motive or purpose. If the purpose of retention of the keys by the donor was to retain control over the property, then a DMC would not be established. However, if the evidence showed that the retention of the additional key was not a deliberate and conscious effort by the donor, control or dominion might be transferred.

Note

In *Woodard v Woodard*, reliance was placed on the judgment of Lawrence J in *Re Stoneham* [1919] 1 Ch 149, to the effect that it was unnecessary for the claimant to release possession of the chattels to the donor and re-acquire the same in order to constitute delivery.

Choses in action

Choses in action (such as bank accounts, etc) are incapable of physical delivery. The question in issue is whether the donee can adduce sufficient evidence to compel the personal representatives to complete the gift by transferring the legal title to the chose. The test is whether the donor has delivered a document of title to the donee, that is, a document which is essential evidence of title to the chose. In *Birch v Treasury Solicitor*, Lord Evershed declared the test that is applicable to this type of property:

> The real test is whether the instrument amounts to a transfer as being the essential *indicia* or evidence of title, possession or production of which entitles the possessor to the money or property purported to be given.

Birch v Treasury Solicitor [1951] 1 Ch 298, CA

Facts

Mrs Birch, shortly before her death in hospital on 29 March 1948, expressed her wish that the plaintiffs [her nephew and his wife] be paid the funds within three joint stock bank accounts and a Post Office savings account in the event of her death. Mrs Birch delivered to the plaintiffs the passbooks to the various bank accounts and the Post Office Savings book, reiterating her wish. On the death of Mrs Birch, the Treasury Solicitor took out letters of administration. The plaintiffs commenced proceedings claiming the funds in the various accounts by way of *donationes mortis causa*.

Held

The circumstances established valid *donationes mortis causa*. The bank and Post Office savings books were *indicia* or evidence of title as the books contained a stipulation that they were required to be produced in order to withdraw funds:

> **Lord Evershed MR:** The question then is where actual transfer does not or cannot take place, what will 'amount to that' [a transfer of dominion]? As a matter of principle the *indicia* of title, as distinct from mere evidence of title, the document or thing the possession or production of which entitles the possessor to the money or property purported to be given, should satisfy [the] condition. On this ground, in our judgment, the validity of a donation of money standing to the donor's credit in a Post Office Savings Bank deposit, or a mortgage debt, should be sustained; and it appears to us irrelevant in such cases whether all the terms of the contract out of which a chose in action arises are stated in the document of title.
>
> In our judgment, Byrne J, in *Re Weston* [1902] 1 Ch 680, and Luxmoore LJ, in *Delgoffe v Fader* [1939] Ch 922, went further than was necessary in stating that a record of all the essential terms of the contract in the document handed over was a condition or test of the validity of the donation. For reasons which we have attempted to give, we think that the real test is whether the instrument 'amounts to a transfer' as being the essential *indicia* or evidence of title, possession or production of which entitles the possessor to the money or property purported to be given.
>
> What, then, is the evidence here? In the case of the London Trustee Savings Bank, Mr Buckley did not, and could not, press the point far; for, according to the local actuary: 'Really, we always insist on the production of the passbook except in exceptional circumstances where hardship may be caused, for instance, with a lost passbook.' The requirements of the two joint stock banks, Barclays and Westminster, are no doubt no less stringent.
>
> We think, accordingly, that in the case of both banks the condition stated on the face of the deposit books must be taken to have remained operative, ie, that the book was, and is, the essential *indicia* of title and that delivery of the book 'amounted to transfer' of the chose in action.
>
> The result is that, in our judgment, the plaintiffs are entitled to succeed as to the deposits in all three cases, the London Savings Bank, Barclays Bank and Westminster Bank. And we think the result satisfactory, for it avoids, as

it seems to us desirable to avoid, fine distinctions between moneys on deposit with the Post Office Savings Bank on the one hand and with trustee savings banks and joint stock banks on the other, where in the latter cases the deposit account is a true deposit account as distinct from an ordinary current account.

Question
How is dominion in choses in action transferred?

Unregistered land

The title deeds to unregistered land are essential *indicia* or evidence of title. In *Sen v Headley*, it was decided that the transfer of the title deeds, accompanied by the relevant donative intent, is capable of constituting a DMC.

Sen v Headley [1991] 2 WLR 1308, CA

Facts

The plaintiff and the deceased (Mr Hewett) lived together as man and wife for many years. In hospital on his deathbed, Mr Hewett told the plaintiff that the house and contents were hers. The deeds to the house were in a steel box and the sole key was given to her. The plaintiff also had a set of keys to the house. Mr Hewett had retained his own set of house keys. After his death, intestate, the plaintiff claimed the house as a DMC. No claim had been made in respect of the contents. The next of kin, a sister, nephew and a niece of Mr Hewett, defended the claim. The trial judge (Mummery J) held in favour of the next of kin, applying the principle in *Duffield v Elwes* to the effect that land could not be the subject matter of a DMC. In addition, he decided that Mr Hewett had retained dominion over the house. The plaintiff appealed to the Court of Appeal.

Held

The court found in favour of the plaintiff on the ground that the transfer of the title deeds to unregistered land was sufficient to transfer (and did transfer) dominion over the house. The court acknowledged that a DMC is capable of giving rise to a constructive trust. The retention of the house keys by Mr Hewett was, in the circumstances, insufficient evidence of retention of ownership:

> **Nourse LJ:** It cannot be doubted that title deeds are the essential *indicia* of title to unregistered land. Moreover, on the facts found by the judge, there was here a constructive delivery of the title deeds of 56 Gordon Road equivalent to an actual handing of them by Mr Hewett to Mrs Sen. And it could not be suggested that Mr Hewett did not part with dominion over the deeds. The two questions which remain to be decided are: first, whether Mr Hewett parted with dominion over the house; secondly, if he did, whether land is capable of passing by way of a *donatio mortis causa*.
>
> It is true that in the eyes of the law Mr Hewett, by keeping his own set of keys to the house, retained possession of it. But the benefits which thereby accrued to him were wholly theoretical. He uttered the words of gift, without reservation, two days after his readmission to hospital, when he knew that he did not have long to live and when there could have been no practical possibility of his ever returning home. He had parted with dominion over the title deeds. Mrs Sen had her own set of keys to the house and was in effective control of it. In all the circumstances of the case, we do not believe that the law requires us to hold that Mr Hewett did not part with dominion over the house. We hold that he did.
>
> Having now decided that the third of the general requirements for a *donatio mortis causa* was satisfied in this case [ie, parting with dominion over the property], we come to the more general question whether land is capable of passing by way of such a gift. For this purpose we must return to *Duffield v Elwes* (1827) Cr & Ph 138. While that decision was supported by pronouncements from both Lord Hardwicke and Lord Mansfield, we believe that it was, for its times, creative, if not quite revolutionary.
>
> Let it be agreed that the doctrine is anomalous. Anomalies do not justify anomalous exceptions. If due account is taken of the present state of the law in regard to mortgages and choses in action, it is apparent that to make a distinction in the case of land would be to make just such an exception. A *donatio mortis causa* of land is neither more nor less anomalous than any other. Every such gift is a circumvention of the Wills Act 1837. Why should

the additional statutory formalities (such as the requirements of s 53(1)(b) of the Law of Property Act 1925 and s 2 of the Law of Property (Miscellaneous Provisions) Act 1989, for the creation and transmission of interests in land be regarded as some larger obstacle. The only step which has to be taken is to extend the application of the implied or constructive trust arising on the donor's death from the conditional to the absolute estate. Admittedly, that is a step which the House of Lords would not have taken in *Duffield v Elwes*, and, if the point had been a subject of decision, we would have loyally followed it in this court. But we cannot decide a case in 1991 as the House of Lords would have decided it, but did not decide it, in 1827. We must decide it according to the law as it stands today. Has any sound reason been advanced for not making the necessary extension? Having carefully considered the reasons put forward by Mummery J as elaborated in the argument of Mr Leeming for the defendant, we do not think that there has. While we fully understand the judge's view that there was a special need for judicial caution at this level of decision, it is notable that the two previous authorities in this court, *Re Dillon* (1880) 44 Ch D 76 and *Birch v Treasury Solicitor* [1951] 1 Ch 298, have extended rather than restricted the application of the doctrine. Indeed, we think that the latter decision may have put others of the earlier authorities on choses in action in some doubt. Moreover, certainty of precedent, while in general most desirable, is not of as great an importance in relation to a doctrine which is as infrequently invoked as this. Finally, while we certainly agree that the policy of the law in regard to the formalities for the creation and transmission of interests in land should be upheld, we have to acknowledge that that policy has been substantially modified by the development to which we have referred.

We hold that land is capable of passing by way of a *donatio mortis causa* and that the three general requirements for such a gift were satisfied in this case. We therefore allow Mrs Sen's appeal.

Types of property that are incapable of being the subject matter of a DMC

There are certain types of property that, owing to their nature, are incapable of being the subject matter of a DMC. The primary reason being that it cannot be established that the intended transferor has deprived himself of control of the property during his lifetime.

Cheques

The donor's cheque is a revocable order to the bank to pay the person in whose favour the cheque is drawn and, in *Re Beaumont* [1902] 1 Ch 889, it was decided that a cheque is incapable of being the subject matter of a DMC. Payment of the cheque may be revoked during the lifetime of the donor and is revoked on death. Alternatively, if the cheque is cashed during the donor's lifetime, the transfer becomes perfect, and there is no need to rely on a DMC to perfect the gift.

Land

At one stage, it was perceived that land was incapable of being the subject matter of a DMC. In *Duffield v Elwes* (1827) 1 Bli (NS) 497, Lord Eldon, in an *obiter* pronouncement, laid down this rule. However, in *Sen v Headley* (see p 84 above), the Court of Appeal decided that delivery of the title deeds to unregistered land was capable of constituting a valid DMC. It would appear that the *Duffield v Elwes* principle is restricted to interests in registered land.

Shares

In *Staniland v Willot* (1852) 3 Mac & G 664, it was decided that shares in a public company were capable of being the subject matter of a DMC, whereas in *Moore v Moore* (1874) LR 18 Eq 474 and *Re Weston* [1902] 1 Ch 680, it was decided that railway stock and building society shares were not capable of being comprised in a DMC. The position today remains far from clear. It is submitted that the better view is the approach adopted in *Re Weston*, for share certificates are not documents of title.

Question
Are shares capable of being the subject matter of a DMC?

PROPRIETARY ESTOPPEL

Proprietary estoppel is a right given to a volunteer whenever a landowner stands by and permits the volunteer to improve his property by incurring expenditure on the assumption that there will be a transfer of an interest to him. The landowner and his successors in title will be estopped from denying the estate acquired by the volunteer. In *Dillwyn v Llewellyn*, a volunteer obtained the freehold interest in land because the landowner was estopped from denying his promise to transfer such an estate.

Dillwyn v Llewellyn (1862) 4 De GF & J 517

Facts
A father, wishing his son to live nearby, offered him a farm so that he could build a house on the land. The son accepted the offer and spent £14,000 building a house on the land with the know-ledge and approval of the father. No conveyance of the legal estate was ever made. After the father's death, the son claimed that the land ought to be conveyed to him.

Held
The father's actions entitled the son to claim the legal estate from him. Likewise, the father's personal representatives were obliged to convey the fee simple to the claimant:

> **Lord Westbury:** A voluntary agreement will not be completed or assisted by a court of equity, in cases of mere gift. If anything be wanting to complete the title of the donee, a court of equity will not assist him in obtaining it; for a mere donee can have no right to claim more than he has received. But the subsequent acts of the donor may give the donee the right or ground of claim which he did not acquire from the original gift. If A puts B in possession of a piece of land and tells him 'I give it to you that you may build a house on it', and B, on the strength of that promise, with the knowledge of A expends a large sum of money in building a house, I cannot doubt that the donee acquires a right from the subsequent transaction to call on the donor to perform that contract and complete the imperfect donation which was made.
>
> The equity of the donee and the estate to be claimed by virtue of it depends on the transaction, that is, on the acts done, and not on the language of the memorandum, except as that shows the purpose and intent of the gift. The estate was given as the site of a dwelling to be erected by the son. The ownership of the dwelling house and the ownership of the estate must be considered as intended to be co-extensive and co-equal. No one builds a house for his own life only, and it is absurd to suppose that it was intended by either party that the house, at the death of the son, should become the property of the father.

In *Ramsden v Dyson*, the rationale for this principle was stated in the dissenting judgment of Lord Kingsdon.

Ramsden v Dyson (1866) LR 1 HL 129

Facts
A tenant at will built on the land in the belief that he would be entitled to demand a long lease. The tenant claimed for an interest in the land.

Held
The majority in the House of Lords decided that he would not succeed in the claim. Lord Kingsdon dissented on the facts and stated the principle of law thus:

> **Lord Kingsdon:** The rule of law applicable to the case appears to me to be this: if a man, under a verbal agreement with a landlord for a certain interest in the land, or, what amounts to the same thing, under an expectation, created or encouraged by the landlord, that he shall have a certain interest, takes possession of such land, with the consent of the landlord, and upon the faith of such promise or expectation, with the knowledge of the landlord, and without objection by him, lays out money upon the land, a court of equity will compel the landlord to give effect to such promise or expectation.

Since this decision, the ingredients of the claim were set out in more detail by Fry J in *Willmot v Barber*. These were called the five probanda.

Willmot v Barber (1880) 15 Ch D 96

Fry J: A man is not to be deprived of his legal rights unless he has acted in such a way as would make it fraudulent for him to set up those rights. What then are the elements necessary to constitute fraud? In the first place, the plaintiff must have made a mistake as to his legal rights. Secondly, the plaintiff must have expended some money or must have done some act (not necessarily upon the defendant's land) on the faith of his mistaken belief. Thirdly, the defendant, the possessor of the legal right must know of the existence of his own right which is inconsistent with the right claimed by the plaintiff. Fourthly, the defendant must know of the plaintiff's mistaken belief of his rights . . . Lastly, the defendant must have encouraged the plaintiff in his expenditure of money or in the other acts which he has done, either directly or by abstaining from asserting his legal right. Where all these elements exists, there is fraud of such a nature as will entitle the court to restrain the possessor of the legal right from exercising it, but nothing short of this will do.

Further refinements of the principle of law indicate that if the landowner makes assurances to the promisee which were relied on by the latter, the volunteer promisee may acquire an interest in the land which the court considers just and equitable. In this respect, a presumption will arise that the volunteer promisee has relied on the promise and although a significant number of cases of proprietary estoppel involve expenditure or a detriment undertaken by the promisee, this appears to be unnecessary. This extremely broad basis of proprietary estoppel was laid down by the Court of Appeal in *Greasley and Others v Cooke*.

Greasley and Others v Cooke [1980] 3 All ER 710, CA

Facts
The plaintiff had given assurances to the defendant, a maid, to the effect that she was entitled to remain in the house for as long as she wished. The defendant remained in the house, caring for the family (including a mentally retarded child), without payment. Possession proceedings were brought against her.

Held
An equity in the defendant's favour was raised and an order was made entitling her to occupy the house rent free for as long as she wished to stay there:

Lord Denning MR: The statements to the defendant were calculated to influence her, so as to put her mind at rest, so that she should not worry about being turned out . . . There is a presumption that [she remained in the house] relying on assurances given to her . . . The burden is not on her but on them to prove that she did not rely on their assurances. They did not prove it, nor did their representatives. So she is presumed to have relied on them . . . It so happens that in many of these cases of proprietary estoppel there has been expenditure of money. But that is not a necessary element. I see that in *Snell's on Equity* it is said that A must have incurred expenditure or otherwise have prejudiced himself. But I do not think that that is necessary. It is sufficient if the party, to whom the assurance is given, acts on the faith of it, in such circumstances that it would be unjust and inequitable for the party making the assurance to go back on it.

More recently, the principle was restated on a much more flexible basis. The test laid down in *Taylor Fashions v Liverpool Victoria Trustees* is whether it would be unconscionable for the defendant to deny the interest of the claimant volunteer and promisee. In other words, the equity in favour of the promisee arises if, having regard to all the circumstances of the case, it would be unconscionable to deny the promisee an interest or right in the land.

In recent years the emphasis in cases of proprietary estoppel has been away from a concentration on set criteria and the courts have instead emphasised that the central question is whether it would in all the circumstances be unconscionable for the maker of the representation to be allowed to go back on what he has promised. Whereas nineteenth century cases such as *Ramsden v Dyson* (1866) LR 1 HL 129 contained references to the need to show an expenditure created or encouraged by the representor, more modern authorities take a broader approach. This is illustrated by Oliver J's judgment in the *Taylor Fashions Ltd* case:

Taylor Fashions Ltd v Liverpool Victoria Trustees [1981] 1 All ER 897 (HC)

Oliver J: The more recent cases indicate that the application of the *Ramsden v Dyson* principle (1866) LR 1 HL 129 ... requires a very much broader approach which is directed rather at ascertaining whether it would be unconscionable for a party to be permitted to deny that which, knowingly or unknowingly, he has allowed or encouraged another to assume to his detriment than to inquiring whether the circumstances can be fitted within the confines of some preconceived formula serving as a universal yardstick for every form of unconscionable behaviour. So regarded, knowledge of the true position by the party alleged to be estopped becomes merely one of the relevant factors (it may even be a determining factor in certain cases) in the overall inquiry. This approach, so it seems to me, appears very clearly from the authorities.

This new approach was endorsed by Oliver LJ in the Court of Appeal in *Habib Bank Ltd v Habib Bank AG* who said:

Habib Bank Ltd v Habib Bank AG [1981] 1 WLR 1263

Oliver LJ: For myself I believe that the law as it has developed over the past twenty years has now evolved a far broader approach to the problem than that suggested by Mr Aldous and one which is in no way dependent upon the historical accident of whether any particular right was first recognised by the common law or was invented by the Court of Chancery. It is an approach exemplified in such cases as *Inwards v Baker* [1965] 2 QB 29 and *Crabb v Arun DC* [1976] Ch 179. We have been referred ... to a recent judgment of my own in *Taylor Fashions Ltd v Liverpool Victoria Trustees Co Ltd*, [1981] 1 All ER 897 in which I ventured to collect and review the authorities.

In *Jennings v Rice* [2002] EWCA Civ 159 the Court of Appeal emphasised that an important aspect of this branch of equity was the need for the remedy granted to be proportionate to the justice of the case. This may not be the same as the expectations of the claimant.

Aldous LJ in Jennings v Rice [2002] EWCA Civ 159

There is a clear line of authority from at least *Crabb's* case [1976] Ch 179, to the present day which establishes that once the elements of proprietary estoppel are established an equity arises. The value of that equity will depend upon all the circumstances including the expectation and the detriment. The task of the court is to do justice. The most essential requirement is that there must be proportionality between the expectation and the detriment.

Likewise in the same case Robert Walker LJ said:

It is no coincidence that these statements of principle refer to satisfying the equity (rather than satisfying, or vindicating, the claimant's expectations). The equity arises not from the claimant's expectations alone, but from the combination of expectations, detrimental reliance, and the unconscionableness of allowing the benefactor (or the deceased benefactor's estate) to go back on the assurances.

Question

What is the test today in order to establish a claim under proprietary estoppel?

Nature of the estate

The precise nature of the estate that may be acquired by the volunteer is left to the discretion of the court and varies with the circumstances of the case. In *Voyce v Voyce*, it was decided that the interest that may be acquired would depend on the nature of the promise made, the degree of expenditure incurred, if any, the events which have taken place since the promise was made and the appropriate method of granting relief, for example, the plaintiff may acquire the freehold estate, a licence, a life interest, etc.

Voyce v Voyce (1991) 62 P & R 290, CA

Nicholls LJ: The extent to which the landowner is precluded or estopped depends on all the circumstances. Regard must be had to the subject matter of the dispute, what was said and done by the parties at the time and what has happened since.

Facts

The defendant, shortly after his marriage in 1958, was allowed to move into a cottage known as Coles Cottage, which was part of the Coles Farm property owned by the defendant's mother. The mother told the defendant that he would be entitled to take the cottage provided that it was renovated to her satisfaction. It was agreed that this condition was satisfied at great expense to the defendant. No deed of gift was executed in favour of the defendant. In 1964, the mother made a gift of the farm and the cottage, duly executed by deed of gift, to the plaintiff (her younger son). The plaintiff was aware that the defendant was living in the cottage. The mother subsequently died. In 1984, the plaintiff claimed an order requiring the defendant to vacate the cottage. The judge held in favour of the defendant and made an order requiring the freehold of the cottage and specified garden to be transferred to the defendant absolutely. The plaintiff appealed against that decision on the ground that the judge had wrongly exercised his discretion since the defendant's equity could have been satisfied by a narrower order granting the defendant, at best, a right of occupation during his life.

Held

The defendant was entitled to the conveyance of the freehold cottage and garden on the basis of the promise made by the mother, the substantial expenditure incurred by the defendant, and the knowledge and status of the plaintiff.

In *Inwards v Baker*, the circumstances were such that an order permitting the defendant to remain in the house for as long as he wished was sufficient to satisfy the defendant's equity.

Inwards v Baker [1965] 2 QB 29, CA

Facts

A father suggested to his son, who was interested in a plot of land on which to build a bungalow, that he (the son) should build the bungalow on a portion of his (the father's) land. The son acceded to the father's request, looked no further for a site and built a bungalow on the father's land. The father made no contractual arrangement or promise as to the terms on which the son should occupy the land or for how long he should remain in occupation, but the son believed that he would be allowed to remain there for his lifetime or for so long as he wished. The father died 20 years later and by his will, made nearly 10 years before his original promise to his son, vested the property in trustees for the benefit of persons other than the son. The trustees now claimed possession of the bungalow.

Held

An equity was created in favour of the son, since he expended money on the land to the knowledge of his father and in the expectation that he would be allowed to remain in occupation for as long as he wished. An order was made permitting the son to remain in the bungalow for as long as he wished:

Lord Denning MR: Even though there is no binding contract to grant any particular interest to the licensee, nevertheless, the court can look at the circumstances and see whether there is an equity arising out of the expenditure of money. All that is necessary is that the licensee should, at the request or with the encouragement of the landlord, have spent the money in the expectation of being allowed to stay there. If so, the court will not allow that expectation to be defeated where it would be inequitable to do so.

In *Pascoe v Turner*, the Court of Appeal decided that, in view of the special facts of this case, a conveyance of the legal estate was an appropriate remedy to give effect to the equity which was created in favour of the defendant.

Pascoe v Turner [1979] 1 WLR 431, CA

Facts
The plaintiff, having lived with the defendant as man and wife in the plaintiff's house, had told the defendant repeatedly that the house was hers to keep. In reliance on this promise, the defendant used her own money to effect repairs and improvements to the house. The plaintiff left the defendant for another woman and moved out of the house. The defendant stayed in the house but was served with a notice to determine her licence.

Held
A licence to live in the house for her lifetime would not have offered her sufficient protection; instead, the court awarded a conveyance of the house:

> **Cummings-Bruce LJ:** The court must grant a remedy effective to protect her against future manifestations of his ruthlessness. It was conceded that if she is granted a licence, such a licence cannot be registered as a land charge, so that she may find herself ousted by a purchaser for value without notice. If she has in the future to do further and more expensive repairs she may only be able to finance them by a loan, but as a licensee she cannot charge the house. The plaintiff as legal owner may well find excuse for entry in order to do what may plausibly represent as necessary works and so contrive to derogate from her enjoyment of the licence in ways that make it difficult or impossible for the court to give her effective protection. Weighing such considerations, this court concludes that the equity to which the facts in this case give rise can only be satisfied by compelling the plaintiff to give effect to his promise and her expectations. He has so acted that he must now perfect the gift.

In *Griffiths v Williams* a lease was sufficient to satisfy the volunteer's equity on the facts of this case.

Griffiths v Williams (1977) 248 EG 947, CA

Facts
A daughter looked after her mother in her latter years and expended her own money on repairs and improvements to the house. She did so for two reasons, primarily for the care of the mother but also in the belief that she would be entitled to the house for the remainder of her life. The mother left the house by will to another relative.

Held
That the most appropriate way to give effect to her equity in the house was to grant her a non-assignable lease, at a nominal rent, determinable on death.

Question
What estate is acquired by a successful claimant under proprietary estoppel?

FURTHER READING

Baker, P, 'Land as a *donatio mortis causa*' (1993) 109 LQR 19.
Barlow, A, 'Gifts *inter vivos* of a chose in possession by delivery of a key' (1956) 19 MLR 394.
Davis, C, 'Proprietary estoppel: future interests and future property' [1996] Conv 193.
Martin, J, 'Casenotes on *Sen v Headley* and *Woodard v Woodard*' [1992] Conv 53.
Moore, I, 'Proprietary estoppel, constructive trust and s 2 of the Law of Property (Miscellaneous Provisions) Act 1989' (2000) 63 MLR 912.
Milne, P, 'Proprietary estoppel in a procrustean bed' (1995) 58 MLR 413.
Pawlowski, M, 'Death bed gifts' (1994) 144 NLJ 48.
Samuels, A, 'Donatio mortis causa of a share certificate' [1966] 30 Conv 189.
Thompson, M, 'From representation to explanation – estoppel as a cause of action' [1983] CLJ 257.
Thompson, M, 'The widow's plight – *Lloyds Bank plc v Carrick*' [1996] Conv 295.
Thompson, M, 'Emasculating estoppel – *Taylor v Dickens*' [1998] Conv 210.

DISCRETIONARY TRUSTS

INTRODUCTION

A 'power of appointment' is an authority to distribute property belonging to another. The appointor (or donee of the power) is not obliged to distribute the property. In the event of a failure to distribute the property, the beneficiary entitled on an express gift over in default of appointment will acquire the property. Alternatively, a resulting trust may arise in favour of the settlor (or donor of the power). A power may be 'personal', i.e. no fiduciary duties are imposed on the donee of the power, 'fiduciary', i.e. imposing fiduciary duties on the donee of the power (see *Re Hay's Settlement Trusts*), or a 'fiduciary power in the full sense'. This last type of power is incapable of being released: see *Mettoy Pension Trustees v Evans* [1990] 1 WLR 1587, HC (see p 97 below).

A 'discretionary trust' involves an obligation to distribute property in favour of members of a class of objects. Although the trustees are required to distribute the trust property within the trust period or a reasonable period of time, they have a discretion as to whom they may distribute from within a class. A discretionary trust may be 'exhaustive', i.e. the trustees have no power to withhold the property such as the income from the fund, or 'non-exhaustive'. In the latter case, the trustees have a power to accumulate the income.

In respect of both powers of appointment and discretionary trusts, the test for certainty of objects is broadly the same, namely, whether the trustees may say with certainty that any given postulant is or is not a member of a class of objects: see *Re Gestetner* [1953] 1 Ch 672, HC; *Re Gulbenkian* [1970] AC 508, HL and *McPhail v Doulton* [1971] AC 424, HL (see p 108 *et seq* below). There have been a variety of judicial approaches to this test. An additional similarity between the two concepts is that, prior to the exercise of the discretion, the objects do not have an interest in the property but merely a hope of acquiring an interest: see *Gartside v Inland Revenue Commissioners* [1968] AC 553, HL (see p 122 below).

DISCRETIONARY TRUSTS AND MERE POWERS

The concept of a 'discretionary trust' in trusts law is a generic description of duties and powers of trustees in respect of a class of objects and the property subject to a trust. In tax law, 'trusts without an interest in possession' is adopted as a substitute. In its broadest sense, a discretionary trust is a trust in respect of which the trustees are given a discretion to pay or apply the income, or capital or both to or for the benefit of all or any one of a group or class of objects on such terms and conditions as the trustees may see fit.

For example, S, a settlor, transfers a cash fund of £100,000 to trustees on trust to pay or apply the income and capital (including accumulations of income) to or for the benefit of any or all of the settlor's children, A, B and C, as the trustees may decide in their absolute discretion. In this example, a discretionary trust is created in respect of both income and capital.

Fixed/discretionary trusts

The antithesis of a discretionary trust is a 'fixed' trust or trust with an interest in possession, that is, on the date of the creation of the trust the settlor has defined the interest acquired by each beneficiary with relative precision and ownership of such interest is vested in each beneficiary. Since the income and capital are acquired by each beneficiary, he or she is entitled to sell, exchange or gift away his or her interest, subject to provisions to the contrary as detailed in the trust instrument. Under a discretionary trust, however, the individual members of the class of objects have only a hope or *spes* of acquiring a benefit under the trust. In other words, under a discretionary trust, the members of the class of objects, prior to the exercise of the trustees' discretion, do not enjoy an interest in the trust property but are treated as potential beneficiaries and are incapable of disposing of their potential interests by way of a trust.

For example, trustees hold on trust for the children of the settlor, D, E and F, in equal shares absolutely. This is a fixed trust, for the trustees have no discretion to decide the extent of the beneficial interest which the objects may enjoy. The settlor has quantified their interest. On the date of the creation of the trust, each beneficiary has a fixed one-third share of the fund which he may sell, exchange or give away as he likes.

Combination of fixed and discretionary trusts

Moreover, the settlor may create a combination of discretionary and fixed trusts. In this event, it would be necessary to know the precise scope of the discretionary trust, that is, whether the trustees' discretion extends to income only or to capital including accumulations of income. The fixed trust will take effect in respect of property not subject to the discretionary trust.

For example, property is held for a period not exceeding 21 years from the date of creation on trust to apply the income as it arises to or for the benefit of any or all of the settlor's children, G, H and I, as the trustees may decide in their absolute discretion and, subject thereto, to apply the capital on trust for the survivors of the said children in equal shares. The discretionary trust exists for 21 years in respect of the income of the trust fund, but the capital is held on fixed trust for the surviving children in equal shares at the end of the period of the discretionary trust.

A discretionary trust may be either 'exhaustive' or 'non-exhaustive' in accordance with the intention of the settlor.

Exhaustive discretionary trusts

An exhaustive discretionary trust is one where, during the trust period, the trustees are required to distribute the income, or capital or both, but retain a discretion as to the mode of distribution and the persons to whom the distribution may be made. Thus, in the above example, an exhaustive discretionary trust of the income from the trust is created in favour of the class of objects, G, H and I. The trustees are required to distribute the income each year as it arises but have a discretion as to the persons who may actually benefit.

Non-exhaustive discretionary trusts

A non-exhaustive discretionary trust is one where the trustees are given a discretion as to whether or not to distribute the property (either income or capital). A non-exhaustive discretionary trust of income exists where the trustees may legitimately decide not to distribute the income and the settlor has specified the effect of nondistribution, for example, the undistributed income will be accumulated or paid to another. In short, a non-exhaustive discretionary trust of the income is a trust for distribution of the income coupled with a power to accumulate or otherwise dispose of the undistributed income.

For example, on trust to apply the income to the settlor's children, J, K and L, as the trustees may decide in their absolute discretion and subject thereto to distribute the capital and any accumulated income in favour of X, Y and Z equally.

Similarly, a non-exhaustive discretionary trust of capital exists where the trustees are not obliged to distribute all the capital during the trust period. In this event, the settlor will normally specify in whose favour the undistributed capital shall be taken, otherwise it is held on resulting trust for the settlor.

It is not possible to create a non-exhaustive discretionary trust of both income and capital for this would lack an obligation to distribute income or capital, which is the hallmark of a trust. In such a case, if the trustees are given a discretion as to whether to distribute both the income and capital, the settlor would have created a mere power of appointment in favour of a fiduciary.

It follows that the distinction between an exhaustive and non-exhaustive discretionary trust is based on the ability of the trustees legitimately to omit to distribute the property that is subject to the discretion. In the ordinary course of events, the trustees will be required to accumulate the income that has not been distributed. In *Inland Revenue Commissioners v Blackwell Minor's Trustees*, it was decided that the accumulated income is treated as capitalised income or capital in both trusts law and tax law.

Inland Revenue Commissioners v Blackwell Minor's Trustees (1925) 10 TC 235, HC

Facts

A testator, by his will, gave property on trust for his eldest son on attaining the age of majority, with gifts over. He also gave the trustees the power to apply any part of the income to which the child should become absolutely or contingently entitled towards his maintenance and education, and any unapplied income was directed to be accumulated and added to capital. The question in issue was whether income which was accumulated by the trustees during the child's minority formed part of the child's income for income tax purposes.

Held

The accumulated income did not form part of the child's income but became converted into capital:

> **Rowlatt J:** The first point which Mr Latter makes is this. He says it does not matter whether the interest of the eldest son under the will is vested or contingent, because even assuming that this specific request is vested in the eldest son . . . the part of the income which is accumulated is not income of the infant. It is a very important point, but I have come to the conclusion that he is right. It is perfectly true to say, as Mr Harman did, that in a case of that kind the income must come to the infant in the end if his interest is vested; but in my judgment it does not come to him as income; it comes to him in the future in the form of capital. The trustees are directed to accumulate it, and accumulate it they must. It is income which is in trust for him in the sense that he will ultimately get it, but it is not in trust for him in the sense that the trustees have to pay the income to him year by year while he is an infant; all he can get while he is an infant is such amount as they allow for his maintenance. I think it is quite different if the infant has the right to the money now. I think in that case it would be his income now, although he could not touch it and he could not give a receipt for it. But where the will expressly provides that the surplus income shall be accumulated and only lets the trustees spend a certain amount on his maintenance, it seems to me that it is not the income of the minor yet.

Question

What is the difference between an 'exhaustive' and a 'non-exhaustive' discretionary trust?

Period of accumulation

Where the trustees are entitled to accumulate the income from the trust, the Law of Property Act 1925 and the Perpetuities and Accumulations Act 1964 have specified the maximum periods during which the power of accumulation may be exercised.

Law of Property Act 1925, s 164 (as amended by Perpetuities and Accumulations Act 1964, s 13)

(1) No person may by any instrument or otherwise settle or dispose of any property in such manner that the income thereof shall, save as hereinafter mentioned, be wholly or partially accumulated for any longer period

than one of the following, namely:

(a) the life of the grantor or settlor; or

(b) a term of 21 years from the death of the grantor, settlor or testator; or

(c) the duration of the minority or respective minorities only of any person or persons who under the limitations of the instrument directing the accumulations would, for the time being, if of full age, be entitled to the income directed to be accumulated.

In every case where any accumulation is directed otherwise than as aforesaid, the direction shall (save as hereinafter mentioned) be void; and the income of the property directed to be accumulated shall, so long as the same is directed to be accumulated contrary to this section, go to and be received by the person or persons who would have been entitled thereto if such accumulation had not been directed.

(2) This section does not extend to any provision:

(i) for payment of the debts of any grantor, settlor, testator or other person;

(ii) for raising portions for:

(a) any child, children or remoter issue of any grantor, settlor or testator; or

(b) any child, children or remoter issue of a person taking any interest under any settlement or other disposition directing the accumulations or to whom any interest is thereby limited;

(iii) . . .

(3) . . .

Perpetuities and Accumulations Act 1964, s 13

(1) The periods for which accumulations of income under a settlement or other disposition are permitted by s 164 of the Law of Property Act 1925 shall include:

(a) a term of 21 years from the date of the making of the disposition; and

(b) the duration of the minority or respective minorities of any person or persons in being at that date.

(2) It is hereby declared that the restrictions imposed by the said s 164 apply in relation to a power to accumulate income whether or not there is a duty to exercise that power, and that they apply whether or not the power to accumulate extends to income produced by the investment of income previously accumulated.

The combined effect of s 164 of the Law of Property Act 1925 and s 13 of the Perpetuities and Accumulations Act 1964 is that the settlor is entitled to select any one (but only one) of the following periods as the maximum period during which the trustees may accumulate the income. These periods are:

(a) the life of the settlor;

(b) a term of 21 years from the death of the settlor or testator;

(c) the minority or respective minorities of any person or persons living or *en ventre sa mère* at the death of the settlor or testator;

(d) the minority or respective minorities only of any person or persons who, under the limitations of the instrument directing the accumulations, would for the time being, if of full age, be entitled to the income directed to be accumulated;

(e) a term of 21 years from the date of the making of the disposition;

(f) the minority or respective minorities of any person or persons in being at that date.

A direction to accumulate which exceeds the periods mentioned above, but which is otherwise valid, will be void only in so far as it exceeds the appropriate statutory period. In short, the excess period alone is void, for example, if the accumulation is ordered for the life of a person other than the settlor (which is not one of the stated periods) the power to accumulate will be valid for 21 years.

Reasons for creating discretionary trusts

Flexibility

Where the settlor is uncertain as to future events and wishes the trustees to react to changed circumstances and the needs of the potential beneficiaries, he may create a discretionary trust. This would require the trustees to take into consideration the circumstances, including fiscal factors, surrounding individual members of the class of objects. The trustees may well take into account that the distribution of income will be more tax efficient if paid to objects with lower income and transfers of capital may be more beneficial to those with larger incomes. The effect is that the discretionary trust has the advantage of flexibility. Indeed, the settlor may be one of the trustees and, even if he is not, he may still be entitled to exercise some influence over the trustees. On the creation of a fixed trust, the beneficiaries acquire a quantified or quantifiable interest in the trust property. Such interest may be varied only in exceptional circumstances.

Protection of objects from creditors

Since an object under a discretionary trust is not entitled to an interest in the trust property prior to the exercise of the discretion in his favour, but is merely entitled to a hope of acquiring a benefit, the bankruptcy of such an object does not entitle the trustee in bankruptcy to a share of the trust fund. The trustee in bankruptcy is only entitled to funds paid to the object in the exercise of the discretion of the trustees. Moreover, the trustee in bankruptcy is not entitled to claim funds paid to third parties (such as tradesmen and hoteliers) in discharge of obligations *bona fide* undertaken by the potential beneficiaries.

Question
Why may a settlor wish to create a discretionary trust?

Administrative discretion

Virtually all trusts (fixed and discretionary) involve the exercise of powers and discretions on the part of trustees. Thus, the trustees may have a power or discretion over the type of investments which may be made by the trust, whether to appoint agents on behalf of the trust, whether to apply income for the maintenance of infant beneficiaries, whether to make an advancement on behalf of a beneficiary, whether to appoint additional trustees, etc. But these powers and discretions are of an administrative nature, and do not affect the beneficial entitlement of the objects. Accordingly, the existence of such administrative powers do not create discretionary trusts but are consistent with both fixed and discretionary trusts.

Mere powers and trust powers

Mere powers

The settlor may authorise another or others to distribute property to a class of objects but without imposing an obligation to distribute the same. This is called a mere power of appointment (or bare power or power collateral).

For example, S may transfer property by will to his widow, W, for life with the remainder to such of his children A, B and C as W may appoint by will. W is referred to as a donee of the power (or appointor) and A, B and C are identified as the objects of the power. They are not beneficiaries but, like the objects of a discretionary trust, are potential beneficiaries or have a *spes* of enjoying a benefit prior to the exercise of the power in their favour. If W makes a valid appointment in favour of the objects, they become beneficiaries in respect of the amount of property distributed in their favour. On the other hand, if the donee of the power fails to make an appointment, the property may be held on resulting trust for the settlor or his estate.

In order to dispense with the resulting trust, it is customary for the settlor to insert an 'express gift over in default of appointment' in the trust instrument. If this clause is inserted, the objects under the 'gift over' take the property unless the donee of the power validly exercises the power. Indeed, *prima facie* the individuals entitled on a gift over in default of appointment are entitled to the property subject to such interest being defeated on a valid exercise of the power.

The donee of the power may be granted a 'personal' or a 'fiduciary' power of appointment in favour of the objects.

Personal powers

A 'personal' or non-fiduciary power is a power of appointment granted to a donee of the power in his capacity as an individual, such as the testator's widow in the above example. There is no duty to consider exercising the authority, nor is there a duty to distribute the property in favour of the objects. In short, the donee of the power is given almost complete freedom in exercising his discretion. Indeed, the donee of the power may release the power even if this would mean that he will benefit from the release. On the assumption that the donee of the power wishes to exercise the authority, the only obligation imposed on him is to distribute the property *bona fide* in favour of the specified objects.

In *Re Hay's Settlement*, Megarry VC described the scope of the authority given to a non-fiduciary donee of the power thus:

Re Hay's Settlement Trusts [1982] 1 WLR 202, HC

Megarry VC: If he does exercise the power, he must, of course confine himself to what is authorised, and not go beyond it . . . A person who is not in a fiduciary position is free to exercise the power in any way he wishes unhampered by any fiduciary duties . . .

Fiduciary powers

A 'fiduciary' power, unlike a personal power, is a power of appointment granted to an individual *virtute officio*, such as a trustee. The fiduciary power is similar to a personal power in only one respect in that there is no obligation to distribute the property. But unlike a personal power, the trustees are required to deal with the discretion in a responsible manner. Accordingly, a number of duties are imposed on the trustees which have been summarised by Megarry VC in *Re Hay's Settlement Trusts*.

Re Hay's Settlement Trusts [1982] 1 WLR 202, HC

Megarry VC: The duties of a trustee which are specific to a mere power seem to be threefold. Apart from the obvious duty of obeying the trust instrument, and in particular of making no appointment that is not authorised by it, the trustee must, first, consider periodically whether or not he should exercise the power; second, consider the range of objects of the power; and third, consider the appropriateness of individual appointments. I do not assert that this list is exhaustive; but as the authorities stand it seems to me to include the essentials, so far as relevant to the case before me.

In *Re Manisty*, Templeman J outlined the rights available to the objects who wish to challenge the exercise of the power.

Re Manisty's Settlement [1973] 3 WLR 341, HC

Templeman J: If a person within the ambit of the power is aware of its existence he can require the trustees to consider exercising the power and in particular to consider a request on his part for the power to be exercised in his favour. The trustees must consider this request, and if they decline to do so or can be proved to have omitted to do so, then the aggrieved person may apply to the court which may remove the trustees and appoint others in their place. This, as I understand it, is the only right and only remedy of any object of the power . . . The court may also be persuaded to intervene by removing the trustees if the trustees act 'capriciously', that is to say, act for reasons which I apprehend could be said to be irrational, perverse or irrelevant to any sensible expectation of the settlor; for example, if they chose a beneficiary by height or complexion or by the irrelevant fact that he was a resident of Greater London.

Question
What duties are imposed on donees of powers of appointment?

Fiduciary powers in the full sense

In *Mettoy Pensions Trustees Ltd v Evans*, the High Court created a third type of power, namely, 'a fiduciary power in the full sense'. This is a power that cannot be released by the trustees. The courts will not compel the trustees to exercise their discretion, for the gift remains a fiduciary power and is not treated as a trust. But if the trustees fail to exercise the power, the court may adopt a scheme that has the effect of exercising the power in accordance with the aims of the gift and the surrounding circumstances. This unique type of power is exercisable in respect of pension funds.

Mettoy Pension Trustees Ltd v Evans [1990] I WLR 1587, HC

Facts

Mettoy Co plc launched an occupational pension scheme on 1 January 1968. The plaintiff, a wholly owned subsidiary of Mettoy, became the sole trustee of the scheme. In 1980, with the introduction of new legislation, new scheme rules were made. Rule 13(5) provided as follows:

> Any surplus of the trust fund remaining after securing all the aforesaid liabilities in full may, at the absolute discretion of the employer be applied to secure further benefits within the limits stated in the rules, and any further balance thereafter remaining shall be properly apportioned amongst the principal employer and each participating employer.

Mettoy experienced financial difficulties and receivers were appointed in 1983. The company was wound up in 1984. As a consequence, the scheme was required to be liquidated. The plaintiff asked the court for directions in respect of a surplus of funds.

Held

Warner J held that r 13(5) created a fiduciary power that could not be released or exercised by a receiver or liquidator. Accordingly, the court was required to decide what method of exercise of the power would be appropriate as if a trust had been created:

> **Warner J:** The beneficiaries under a pension scheme such as this are not volunteers. Their rights have contractual and commercial origins. They are derived from the contracts of employment of the members. The benefits provided under the scheme have been earned by the service of the members under those contracts and, where the scheme is contributory, *pro tanto* by their contributions.
>
> It would be inappropriate and indeed perverse to construe such documents so strictly as to undermine their effectiveness or their effectiveness for their purpose. I do not think that, in saying that, I am saying anything different from, what was said by Lord Upjohn when in *In Re Gulbenkian's Settlements* [1970] AC 508, he referred, in the context of a private settlement, to 'the duty of the court by the exercise of its judicial knowledge and experience in the relevant matter, innate common sense and desire to make sense of the settlor's or parties' expressed intentions, however obscure and ambiguous the language that may have been used, to give a reasonable meaning to that language it if can do so without doing complete violence to it'.
>
> What the court has to do here is to perform that duty in the comparatively novel and different context of pension scheme trusts. The most important and difficult, though by no means the only, question in this case is as to the validity of the conferment on the employer, by the last paragraph of r 13(5) of the 1983 rules, of the discretion to augment benefits out of surplus.

The first of those questions is whether that discretion is a fiduciary power. As Mr Walker pointed out, so to express the question is, in a way, to oversimplify it, because there are different kinds of fiduciary power. Mr Walker, in an impartial and helpful way, afforded me a wide-ranging and illuminating discussion of the law about fiduciary powers as it has so far been developed in the context of trusts.

I am attracted by counsel's submission that the classification of powers into powers simply collateral, powers in gross, and powers appendant or appurtenant, which was set out by Sir George Jessel MR in *Re D'Angibau* (1880) 15 Ch D 228, is now of antiquarian interest only. That seems to be the view also of the authors of Megarry and Wade on *The Law of Real Property* 5th ed, 1984, p 489. I accept at all events that that classification is of no assistance in deciding the present case. Mr Walker suggested a more pertinent classification, which I accept, of fiduciary discretions into four categories. In this classification, category 1 comprises any power given to a person to determine the destination of trust property without that person being under any obligation to exercise the power or to preserve it. Typical of powers in this category is a special power of appointment given to an individual where there is a trust in default of appointment. In such a case the donee of the power owes a duty to the beneficiaries under that trust not to misuse the power, but he owes no duty to the objects of the power. He may therefore release the power but he may not enter into any transaction that would amount to a fraud on the power, a fraud on the power being a wrong committed against the beneficiaries under the trust in default of appointment: see *Re Mills* [1930] 1 Ch 654 and *Re Greaves* [1954] Ch 434. It seems to me to follow that, where the donee of the power is the only person entitled under the trust in default of appointment, the power is not a fiduciary power at all, because then the donee owes no duty to anyone. That was the position in *Re Mills* [1930] 1 Ch 654 and will be the position here if the discretion in the last paragraph of r 13(5) of the 1983 rules is in category 1.

Category 2 comprises any power conferred on the trustees of the property or on any other person as a trustee of the power itself: *per* Romer LJ, at p 669. I will, as Chitty J did in *Re Somes* [1896] 1 Ch 250 at p 255, call a power in this category 'a fiduciary power in the full sense'. Mr Walker suggested as an example of such powers vested in persons other than the trustees of the property the powers of the managers of a unit trust. *A power in this category cannot be released; the donee of it owes a duty to the objects of the power to consider, as and when may be appropriate, whether and if so how he ought to exercise it; and he is to some extent subject to the control of the courts in relation to its exercise:* see, for instance, *Re Abrahams' Will Trust* [1969] 1 Ch 463 at p 474, *per* Cross J; *Re Manisty's Settlement* [1974] Ch 17 at p 24 *per* Templeman J; and *Re Hay's Settlement Trusts* [1982] 1 WLR 202 at p 210 *per* Sir Robert Megarry VC [emphasis added].

Category 3 comprises any discretion which is really a duty to form a judgment as to the existence or otherwise of particular circumstances giving rise to particular consequences. Into this category fall the discretions that were in question in such cases as *Weller v Ker* (1866) LR 1 Sc & Div 11; *Dundee General Hospitals Board of Management v Walker* [1952] 1 All ER 896 and the two cases reported by LEXIS that I have already mentioned, namely, *Kerr v British Leyland (Staff) Trustees Ltd* [1989] IRLR 522 and *Mihlenstedt v Barclays Bank International Ltd* (1989) The Times, 18 August; Court of Appeal (Civil Div) Transcript No 817 of 1989.

Category 4 comprises discretionary trusts, that is to say, cases where someone, usually but not necessarily the trustees, is under a duty to select from among a class of beneficiaries those who are to receive, and the proportions in which they are to receive, income or capital of the trust property. Mr Walker urged me to eschew the phrases 'trust power', 'power coupled with a duty', 'power coupled with a trust' and 'power in the nature of a trust', which, as he demonstrated by means of an impressive survey of reported cases, have been variously used to describe discretions in categories 2, 3 and 4.

In the present case the question is whether the discretion given to the employer by the last paragraph of r 13(5) of the 1983 rules is in category 1 or category 2. That depends on whether the words by which that discretion is expressed to be conferred on the employer mean in effect no more than that the employer is free to make gifts out of property of which it is the absolute beneficial owner or whether those words import that the employer is under a duty to the objects of the discretion to consider whether and if so how the discretion ought to be exercised. That is a question of construction of the deed of 1983 in the light of the surrounding circumstances.

I have come to the conclusion that the discretion conferred on the employer by the last paragraph of r 13(5) of the 1983 rules is a fiduciary power in the full sense. The considerations that have led me to that conclusion are these. If that discretion is not such a fiduciary power it is, from the point of view of the beneficiaries under the scheme, illusory. As I have pointed out, the words conferring the power mean no more, on that construction of them, than that the employer is free to make gifts to those beneficiaries out of property of which it is the absolute beneficial owner.

The exercise of a fiduciary power in the full sense vested in the company cannot be necessary for distributing its assets. Whether it may be necessary for winding up the affairs of the company is less clear. However the liquidator in this case would, as Mr Inglis-Jones submitted, be precluded from exercising the power because, if he did so, he would be in a position where his duties conflicted. As trustee of the power he would be under a duty to hold the balance between the interests of the beneficiaries under the pension scheme and the interests of the persons entitled to share in the assets of the company, namely its creditors and possibly its contributories. As liquidator his duty would be to have regard primarily, if not exclusively, to the interests of the creditors and contributories. His position in that respect would differ from that of the directors of the company while it was a going concern, for they would be able to pay proper regard to the interests of the beneficiaries under the pension scheme and would be concerned to do so if only for the sake of the company's reputation as an employer.

The question then arises, if the discretion is a fiduciary power which cannot be exercised either by the receivers or by the liquidator, who is to exercise it? I heard submissions on that point. The discretion cannot be exercised by the directors of the company, because on the appointment of the liquidator all the powers of the directors ceased. Mr Inglis-Jones and Mr Walker urged me to say that in this case the court should step in by giving directions to the trustees as to the distribution of the surplus in the pension fund. They relied in particular on the passage in *Re Baden's Deed Trusts* [1971] AC 424, pp 456, 457, where Lord Wilberforce said:

> As to powers, I agree with my noble and learned friend Lord Upjohn in *Re Gulbenkian's Settlements* [1970] AC 508 that although the trustees may, and normally will, be under a fiduciary duty to consider whether or in what way they should exercise their power, the court will not normally compel its exercise. It will intervene if the trustees exceed their powers, and possibly if they are proved to have exercised it capriciously. But in the case of a trust power, if the trustees do not exercise it, the court will: I respectfully adopt as to this, the statement in Lord Upjohn's opinion (p 525). I would venture to amplify this by saying that the court, if called upon to execute the trust power, will do so in the manner best calculated to give effect to the settlor's or testator's intentions. It may do so by appointing new trustees, or by authorising or directing representative persons of the classes of beneficiaries to prepare a scheme of distribution, or even, should the proper basis for distribution appear by itself directing the trustees so to distribute. The books give many instances where this has been done, and I see no reason in principle why they should not do so in the modern field of discretionary trust.

Clearly, in the first two sentences of that passage, Lord Wilberforce was referring to a discretion in category 2 and in the following part of it to a discretion in category 4. In that latter part he was indicating how the court might give effect to a discretionary trust when called on to execute it. It seems to me, however, that the methods he indicated could be equally appropriate in a case where the court was called on to intervene in the exercise of a discretion in category 2. In saying that, I do not overlook that, in *Re Manisty's Settlement* [1974] Ch 17, p 25, Templeman J expressed the view that the only right and the only remedy of an object of the power who was aggrieved by the trustees' conduct would be to apply to the court to remove the trustees and appoint others in their place. However, the earlier authorities to which I was referred, such as *Re Hodges* (1878) 7 Ch D 754 and *Klug v Klug* [1918] 2 Ch 67, had not been cited to Templeman J. I conclude that, in a situation such as this, it is open to the court to adopt whichever of the methods indicated by Lord Wilberforce appears most appropriate in the circumstances.

Question

How many types of powers of appointment exist?

Trust powers

By way of contrast, the settlor may create a 'trust power' or a 'power in the nature of a trust'. This gift is like a chameleon. On the face of the trust instrument the gift looks like a mere power, but on a true construction of the instrument the courts decide that a trust is imposed on the trustees to distribute the relevant property amongst the objects. In substance, a trust power is a discretionary trust in that the trustees are required to distribute the subject matter of their discretion, whether this be income or capital. Thus, the trustees may not release their discretion and if they refuse to exercise their discretion the court will intervene. If the wording of the settlement is unclear, the court will be called on to decide whether a power or a trust power was intended by the settlor. This type of discretion was introduced by the court in *Brown v Higgs*. Thus, in form, the discretion appears to resemble a power, but in substance the gift is construed as creating a trust.

Brown v Higgs (1803) 8 Ves 561

Lord Eldon: There are not only a mere trust and a mere power, but there is also known to this court a power, which the party to whom it is given, is entrusted and required to execute; and with regard to that species of power the court considers it as partaking so much of the nature and qualities of a trust, that if the person who has that duty imposed on him does not discharge it, the court will, to a certain extent, discharge the duty in his room and place . . .

The effect is that whether a mere power of appointment (albeit a fiduciary power) or a trust power is created is a highly speculative question. The court is required to place itself in the position of the testator or settlor and consider whether the author of the will or trust intended to 'authorise' (mere power) or 'compel' (trust power) the trustees to distribute the fund. This is a question of degree. In *Burrough v Philcox*, on construction of the will and surrounding circumstances, the court decided that a trust was intended.

Burrough v Philcox (1840) 5 My & Gr 72

Facts

The testator transferred property on trust for his two children for life, with remainder to their issue and declared that if they should die without issue, the survivor should have the power to dispose by will 'among my nieces and nephews, or their children, either all to one or to as many of them as my surviving child shall think fit'. The testator's children died without issue and without any appointment having been made by the survivor.

Held

A trust was created in favour of the testator's nieces and nephews and their children. The trust was subject to a power of selection in the surviving child:

Lord Cottenham: Where there appears a general intention in favour of a class, and a particular intention in favour of individuals of a class to be selected by another person, and the particular intention fails from that selection not having been made, the court will carry into effect the general intention in favour of the class.

In contrast, in *Re Weekes*, the court concluded that the will created a power of appointment in accordance with the intention of the testatrix.

Re Weekes' Settlement [1897] 1 Ch 289, HC

Facts

By her will, a testatrix transferred property to her husband for life with a 'power to dispose of all such property by will amongst our children'. There was no express gift over in default of appointment. The husband died intestate without exercising the power in favour of the children. The surviving children claimed that an implied gift over in default of appointment was created in their favour and thus they were entitled in equal shares.

Held

On construction of the instrument, a mere power of appointment was created by the testatrix which was merely authoritative. There was no clear indication in the will that the testatrix intended the power to be regarded in the nature of a trust. The property was held on resulting trust for the heir of the testatrix:

Romer J: . . . The husband did not exercise the power of appointment, and the question is whether the children take in default of appointment.

Now, apart from the authorities, I should gather from the terms of the will that it was a mere power that was conferred on the husband, and not one coupled with a trust that he was bound to exercise. I see no words in the will to justify me in holding that the testatrix intended that the children should take if her husband did not execute the power.

A brief survey of the cases illustrates how unpredictable the question is likely to be whether a 'mere power of appointment' or a 'trust power' is created. However, there are two pieces of evidence that determine the issue conclusively in favour of a mere power of appointment, as follows.

Express gift over in default of appointment

The existence of an express gift over in default of appointment is inconsistent with a trust. An express gift over in default of appointment is an express alternative gift in the event of the donee of the power failing to exercise the power. The testator or settlor has implicitly condoned the non-exercise of the power by declaring in whose favour the beneficial interest will be transferred, for example, 'upon trust to distribute in favour of such of the objects, A, B and C as the trustees may decide in their discretion, but failing to distribute the property, I hereby declare that D shall be entitled to the property'. In this example, D is the object entitled on the gift over and is treated as the primary object with an interest subject to defeasance. In *Re Mills*, the donee of the power was motivated to release the power of appointment in order to benefit the donee entitled on a gift over in default of appointment. This is only possible on the creation of a power of appointment.

Re Mills, Mills v Lawrence [1930] 1 Ch 654, CA

Facts

A testator by his will set up a trust and directed that all statutory accumulations of income were to be held upon such trusts for the benefit of all or any of the children and remoter issue of the testator's father who, in the opinion of the testator's brother, one of the trustees of the will, should evidence an ability and desire to maintain the family fortune by replacing the sums of which it had been depleted by death duties and other taxation, as the testator's brother should by deed revocable or irrevocable appoint, and in default of such appoint in trust for such brother absolutely. The brother entitled in default of appointment (one of the trustees) wanted to release the power in order to trigger off the gift over in favour of himself. This was possible only if the will created a mere power of appointment as opposed to a trust power.

Held

The will created a power of appointment and not a power coupled with a trust. Accordingly, the power could be released:

> **Lord Hanworth MR:** If there is a fiduciary duty connected with the power, the power, being in the nature of a trust, cannot be released, because a breach of trust must not be committed . . . I find it impossible to treat the power in this case as so connected with a duty that it is a power in the nature of a trust, which cannot be released by the donee. There is a gift over to the donee himself, and this takes the case out of the rule in *Farwell on Powers*, 3rd edn, 1916, p 528 . . .
>
> If there is a power to appoint, among certain objects, but no express gift to those objects, and no gift over in default of appointment, the court implies a trust for or a gift to those objects equally, if the power be not exercised. Here there is a gift over to the donee in default of appointment and a gift to him until appointment, and, therefore, it is not, to my mind, possible to construe this clause as one in which there is a gift to the possible objects of the power – namely, the children or remoter issue of the first Lord Hillingdon. It follows that it is not a power which is coupled with or embedded in a trust.

General and hybrid powers of appointment

A general power of appointment is by definition incapable of being a trust power for the courts are incapable of exercising such power. A general power of appointment is one that entitles the donee of the power to appoint in favour of anyone, including himself. Thus, there are no limits to the objects of such a power of appointment. Anyone is a potential beneficiary. But owing to the principle that all property is required to be owned, the donee of the power is treated as being entitled to the property until he disposes of it in favour of another.

Similarly, a hybrid or intermediate power of appointment is incapable of being a trust power. A hybrid power is similar in appearance to a general power, save for the disqualification from benefiting an excluded class of objects, for example, 'on trust for X to appoint in favour of anyone except the settlor and his spouse'. In *Re Manisty* the court decided that, on the facts of the case, a hybrid power was created.

Re Manisty's Settlement [1973] 3 WLR 341, HC

Facts
The trustees were given a power to add objects to a class of potential beneficiaries, which excluded the settlor, his wife and certain named persons.

Held
A valid hybrid power of appointment was created and no duty to distribute the property was imposed on the donees of the power:

> **Templeman J:** The power to add beneficiaries and to benefit the persons so added is exercisable in favour of anyone in the world except the settlor, his wife, the other members of the excepted class for the time being and the trustees . . . This is not a general power exercisable in favour of a class, but an intermediate power exercisable in favour of anyone, with certain exceptions . . . The argument based on the principle of non-delegation stems from the proposition that a testator must not delegate to other persons the right to make a will for him. It is however, established by authority that a testator and *a fortiori* a settlor, may create powers of disposition exercisable by individuals or by trustees without thereby infringing any rule against delegation . . . In *Re Park* [1932] I Ch 580, Clauson J held valid an intermediate power conferred by a testator on an individual to appoint to anyone in the world, except the donee of the power . . . in *Re Abrahams' Will Trust* [1969] I Ch 463, Cross J held valid an intermediate power conferred by a testator on trustees to appoint to anyone in the world except the trustees, and he expressly rejected the argument based on the principle of non-delegation. I conclude that the settlor in the present case was not precluded by the doctrine of non-delegation from conferring an intermediate power on his trustees.

Note
A similar decision was reached in *Blausten v Inland Revenue Commissioners* [1972] Ch 256.

Moreover, a testator may create a hybrid power of appointment by will, authorising his executors or trustees to distribute the property after his death. In *Re Beatty*, the court reasoned that if the power would have been valid had it been created *inter vivos*, the mere fact that it was created by will does not invalidate it. Such disposition does not amount to a delegation of testamentary freedom and does not contravene the Wills Act 1837.

Re Beatty (Decd), Hinves and Others v Brooke and Others [1990] I WLR 1503, HC

Facts
The testatrix died in 1986, leaving an estate valued at £32m, and by will made the following dispositions:

Clause 3(a):
> I bequeath all my personal chattels . . . to my trustees who shall at any time or times (but nevertheless within the period of two years following my death or such shorter period as they my trustees in writing decide) allocate divide or make over all or any such personal chattels to or among such person or persons (whether individual or corporate) as they think fit and any of my said personal chattels not so allocated divided or made over shall fall into and become part of my residuary estate . . .

Clause 4(a):
> I bequeath a legacy of £1.5 m to my trustees' subject to similar terms as included in clause 3(a) above.

Subject to these gifts, Mrs Beatty left the residue of her estate in three equal shares, subject to certain trusts and gifts over to her daughter and grandchildren. The executors and trustees applied to the court to determine the validity of clauses 3 and 4 of the will.

Held

Both clauses were valid. The clauses created hybrid powers of appointment which conferred fiduciary duties on the executors and trustees:

> **Hoffman J:** The powers, being fiduciary, are not general powers in the sense of the traditional classification which equates such a power with an outright beneficial disposition to the donee himself. Nor are they special powers in the traditional sense. The objects of the powers can hardly be described as a class. They are intermediate or hybrid powers of the kind considered in *Re Park* [1932] 1 Ch 580.
>
> Mr Price (counsel for the residuary beneficiaries) conceded that if clauses 3 and 4 had appeared in a settlement (*inter vivos*), they would have been valid powers. But he said that as part of a will they were invalidated by the rule that a testator cannot delegate the making of his will. In support of the existence of such a rule, Mr Price [referred to a statement by Lord Simonds in] *Chichester Diocesan Fund and Board of Finance (Incorporated) v Simpson* [1944] AC 341. Lord Simonds said, at p 371:
>
>> It is a cardinal rule, common to English and to Scots law, that a man may not delegate his testamentary power. To him the law gives the right to dispose of his estate in favour of ascertained or ascertainable persons. He does not exercise that right if in effect he empowers his executors to say what person or objects are to be his beneficiaries. To this salutary rule there is a single exception. A testator may validly leave it to his executors to determine what charitable objects shall benefit, so long as charitable and no other objects may benefit.
>
> But Lord Simonds must also have known that for centuries testators had been creating special powers of appointment. Furthermore, they had also been creating general powers of appointment.
>
> The execution of an otherwise valid general, special, or intermediate power is giving effect to the testator's will and not making a will for a testator who has failed to do so himself. The reason why Lord Simonds said that charitable gifts were the only exception to this rule was because they are, indeed, the only case in which the courts will uphold a gift in terms which would otherwise be regarded as too vague. Thus, it seems to me that Lord Simonds, like other judges in earlier cases concerning gifts void for uncertainty, was intending to do no more than to state in forceful and dramatic terms the rule that a gift which is expressed in language too vague to be enforced cannot be rescued by giving the executor a power of choice. Lord Simonds would, I think, have been astonished to learn that he had just outlawed the use of widely expressed powers, or perhaps even any powers at all, in wills.
>
> The result is that once it is conceded that clauses 3 and 4 qualify as powers which would be valid if created by deed, there is in my judgment no rule of law to invalidate them because they happen to be in a will. Nor can I think of any good reason why such a distinction should exist. I shall accordingly declare that clauses 3 and 4 of the will are valid.

Special powers

However, a special power of appointment may or may not create a trust power. A special power of appointment confers on the trustee an authority or a duty to distribute the fund in favour of a specific class of objects, such as the children of the settlor. If there is no express gift over in default of appointment, it is extremely difficult to predict whether a special power of appointment creates a trust power or a mere power. The court ultimately decides this question in accordance with the intention of the testator or settlor. There is, however, no rule of construction to the effect that the absence of a gift over in default of appointment automatically interprets the settlor's intention as pointing in the direction of a trust power. Indeed, in *Re Weekes*, the court decided that the absence of an express gift over in default of appointment is nothing more than an argument that the settlor intended to create a trust. The weight of such an argument will vary with the facts of each case.

Re Weekes' Settlement [1897] 1 Ch 289, HC

Romer J: The authorities do not show, in my opinion, that there is a hard-and-fast rule that a gift to A for life with a power to A to appoint among a class and nothing more must, if there is no gift over in the will, be held a gift by implication to the class in default of the power being exercised. In my opinion the cases show . . . that you must find in the will an indication that the testatrix did intend the class or some of the class to take – intended in fact that the power should be regarded in the nature of a trust, only a power of selection being given, as, for example, a gift to A for life with a gift over to such of a class as A shall appoint.

Note

In *Re Gestetner's Settlement* [1953] 1 Ch 672 (see p 105 below), Harman J categorised the various types of powers in the following summary:

It seems to be law, at any rate in this court, that a power may be a general power (which has often been called the equivalent of property because the donee can exercise it in his own favour), or it can be a special power, namely, a power to benefit a known and defined class of persons, or it can be something betwixt and between.

Fiduciary duties

The duties imposed on the trustees in respect of a *fiduciary power* are similar to the duties imposed on *discretionary trustees*. The main difference between the two gifts is that, in the former, there is no obligation imposed on the trustees to exercise their discretion but, in the context of a discretionary trust, the trustees are obliged to exercise their discretion. This distinction was pointed out in *Re Gulbenkian*.

Re Gulbenkian [1970] AC 508

Lord Upjohn: The basic difference between a mere power and a trust power is that in the first case trustees owe no duty to exercise it and the relevant fund or income falls to be dealt with in accordance with the trusts in default of its exercise, whereas in the second case the trustees must exercise the trust and in default the court will.

If the trustees exercise their discretion under a fiduciary power of appointment, the trustees are required to comply with the same duties imposed on discretionary trustees. Thus, the distinction between the fiduciary power and the trust would lack any significance, but this would be the case only in the event of an exercise of the discretion.

Trustees exercising a fiduciary power or discretionary trust are under a duty to refrain from acting capriciously and are under a duty to act in a responsible manner, surveying the range of objects both in terms of the categories of objects and the qualifications of individual objects with a view to distribution. The nature of a fiduciary duty was declared by Lord Wilberforce in *McPhail v Doulton*.

McPhail v Doulton [1971] AC 424

Lord Wilberforce: A trustee with a duty to distribute, particularly among a potentially very large class, would surely never require the preparation of a complete list of names, which anyhow would tell him little that he needs to know. He would examine the field, by class and category; might indeed make diligent and careful enquiries, depending on how much money he had to give away and the means at his disposal, as to the composition and needs of particular categories and of individuals within them; decide on certain priorities or proportions and then select individuals according to their needs and qualifications.

Question
What are the differences between powers of appointment and discretionary trusts?

THE GIVEN POSTULANT TEST

Test for certainty of objects

The test for certainty of objects varies with the nature of the transfer effected by the settlor. The position today is that if the settlor creates, on the one hand, a mere power of appointment or trust power, the test for certainty of objects is the 'given postulant' criterion. On the other hand, if the settlor creates a fixed trust, the test for certainty of objects is the 'list test'.

Mere powers

The test for powers has always been whether the donee of the power may say with certainty that a given individual (postulant) is or is not a member of a class of objects. This test was laid down by Harman J in *Re Gestetner's Settlement*:

> The trustees as I see it, have a duty to consider whether or not they are to distribute any and, if so, what part of the fund and if so, to whom they should distribute it . . . if therefore, there be no duty to distribute, but only a duty to consider, there is no difficulty in ascertaining whether any given postulant is a member of the specified class. Of course, it can be easily postulated whether John Doe or Richard Roe is or is not eligible to receive the settlor's bounty. It is not necessary that the trustees worry their heads to survey the world from China to Peru when there are perfectly good objects of the class in England.

In essence, the 'given postulant test' will be satisfied if the boundaries concerning the identification of the classes of objects are clearly drawn and it is unnecessary to name each member of the class of objects, for example, if a power of distribution is given in favour of the relatives of the settlor. The gift will be valid if the expression 'relatives' is capable of a legal definition so that the trustees may be able to distinguish between objects and non-objects. It is unnecessary for the trustees to identify each object. In *Re Gestetner*, the issue involved the status of the gift created, in particular, whether a power of appointment or a trust for distribution was created.

Re Gestetner's Settlement, Barnett and Others v Blumka and Others [1953] 1 Ch 672, HC
Facts

By an *inter vivos* settlement, a capital fund was held upon trust for members of a specified class of objects as the trustees might appoint, with a gift over in default of appointment. The specified class included:

(a) four named individuals;

(b) descendants of the settlor's father, David Gestetner, or his uncle, Jacob;

(c) any spouse, widow or widower of any such person as aforesaid;

(d) five specified charitable bodies;

(e) any former employees of the settlor or his wife.

The settlor, his spouse and the trustees were excluded from the class. The Inland Revenue claimed that an express trust was created and was void, and that a resulting trust was set up in favour of the settlor. The trustees applied to the court for directions.

Held

A valid power of appointment was created. Although the trustees did not have a duty to select the beneficiaries from the class of objects, there was a duty to consider distributing the fund:

> Harman J: . . . If a power be a power collateral, or a power appurtenant, or any of those powers which do not impose a trust upon the conscience of the donee, then I do not think that it can be the law that it is necessary to know of all the objects in order to appoint to one of them. If that were so, many appointments which are made every day would be bad. It must often be uncertain whether there will be further objects coming into existence. It may often be uncertain what objects are in existence; but, in an ordinary family settlement, the fact that a father

did not know whether one of his sons had married and had children or not could not possibly invalidate the exercise by him of a power of appointment in favour of those grandchildren of whom he did not know . . .

The document on its face shows that there is no obligation on the trustees to do more than consider – from time to time, I suppose – the merits of such persons of the specified class as are known to them and, if they think fit, to give them something . . .

If, therefore, there be no duty to distribute, but only a duty to consider, it does not seem to me that there is any authority binding on me to say that this whole trust is bad. In fact, there is no difficulty, as has been admitted, in ascertaining whether any given postulant is a member of the specified class. Of course, if that could not be ascertained the matter would be quite different, but of John Doe or Richard Roe it can be postulated easily enough whether he is or is not eligible to receive the settlor's bounty. There being no uncertainty in that sense, I am reluctant to introduce a notion of uncertainty in the other sense, by saying that the trustees must worry their heads to survey the world from China to Peru, when there are perfectly good objects of the class in England . . . There is no uncertainty in so far as it is quite certain whether particular individuals are objects of the power. What is not certain is how many objects there are; and it does not seem to me that such an uncertainty will invalidate a trust worded in this way.

Abolition of the diluted approach

Prior to the House of Lords' decision in *Re Gulbenkian's Settlement*, the courts adopted a diluted approach to the given postulant test, namely, whether at least *one person clearly fell within the class of objects*, even though it might not be possible to say whether others came within the class or fell outside of it. The House of Lords in *Re Gulbenkian's Settlement* overruled this approach and reiterated the strict given postulant test.

Re Gulbenkian's Settlement [1970] AC 508, HL

Facts

A special power of appointment was granted to trustees to appoint in favour of Nubar Gulbenkian, 'any wife and his children or remoter issue . . . and any person . . . in whose house or apartment or in whose company or under whose care and control or by or with whom he may from time to time be employed or residing' subject to a gift over in default of appointment. The issue was whether the test for certainty of objects applicable to powers was satisfied.

Held

The gift created a valid power of appointment within the *Gestetner* test and the court overruled the diluted approach to the test adopted by the Court of Appeal:

Lord Upjohn: My Lords . . . Lord Denning MR [in the Court of Appeal] propounded a test in the case of powers collateral, namely that if you can say of one particular person meaning thereby, apparently, any one person only that he is clearly within the category the whole power is good though it may be difficult to say in other cases whether a person is or is not within the category, and he supported that view by reference to authority. Moreover, Lord Denning MR expressed the view that the different doctrine with regard to trust powers should be brought into line with the rule with regard to conditions precedent and powers collateral. So I propose to make some general observations on this matter.

The principle is, in my opinion, that the donor must make his intentions sufficiently plain as to the object of his trust and the court cannot give effect to it by misinterpreting his intentions by dividing the fund merely among those present. Secondly, and perhaps it is the most hallowed principle, the Court of Chancery, which acts in default of trustees, must know with sufficient certainty the objects of the beneficence of the donor so as to execute the trust. Then, suppose the donor does not direct an equal division of his property among the class but gives a power of selection to his trustees among the class; exactly the same principles must apply. The trustees have a duty to select the donees of the donor's bounty from among the class designated by the donor; he has not entrusted them with any power to select the donees merely from among known claimants who are within the class, for that is constituting a narrower class and the donor has given them no power to do this.

So if the class is insufficiently defined the donor's intentions must in such cases fail for uncertainty. Perhaps I should mention here that it is clear that the question of certainty must be determined as of the date of the document declaring the donor's intention (in the case of a will, his death). Normally the question of certainty will arise because of the ambiguity of definition of the class by reason of the language employed by the donor, but occasionally owing to some of the curious settlements executed in recent years it may be quite impossible to construct even with all the available evidence anything like a class capable of definition (Re Sayer's Trust [1957] Ch 423), though difficulty in doing so will not defeat the donor's intentions (Re Hain's Settlement [1961] 1 WLR 440). But I should add this: if the class is sufficiently defined by the donor the fact that it may be difficult to ascertain the whereabouts or continued existence of some of its members at the relevant time matters not. The trustees can apply to the court for directions to pay a share into court.

But when mere or bare powers are conferred on donees of the power (whether trustees or others) the matter is quite different. As I have already pointed out, the trustees have no duty to exercise it in the sense that they cannot be controlled in any way. If they fail to exercise it then those entitled in default of its exercise are entitled to the fund. Perhaps the contrast may be put forcibly in this way: in the first case it is a mere power to distribute with a gift over in default; in the second case it is a trust to distribute among the class defined by the donor with merely a power of selection within that class. The result is in the first case even if the class of appointees among whom the donees of the power may appoint is clear and ascertained and they are all of full age and *sui juris*, nevertheless they cannot compel the donees of the power to exercise it in their collective favour. If, however, it is a trust power, then those entitled are entitled (if they are of full age and *sui juris*) to compel the trustees to pay the fund over to them, unless the fund is income and the trustees have power to accumulate for the future.

Again, the basic difference between a mere power and a trust power is that in the first case trustees owe no duty to exercise it and the relevant fund or income falls to be dealt with in accordance with the trusts in default of its exercise whereas in the second case the trustees must exercise the power and in default the court will.

So, with all respect to the contrary view, I cannot myself see how consistently with principle, it is possible to apply to the execution of a trust power the principles applicable to the permissible exercise by the donees, even if the trustees of mere powers; that would defeat the intention of donors completely.

But with respect to mere powers, while the court cannot compel the trustees to exercise their powers, yet those entitled to the fund in default must clearly be entitled to restrain the trustees from exercising it save among those within the power. So the trustees, or the court, must be able to say with certainty who is within and who is without the power. It is for this reason that I find myself unable to accept the broader position advanced by Lord Denning MR and Winn LJ, mentioned earlier, and agree with the proposition as enunciated in Re Gestetner [1953] 1 Ch 672 and the later cases.

Fixed and discretionary trusts

Prior to the House of Lords' decision in *McPhail v Doulton (sub nom Re Baden)* (below), the test for certainty of objects, applicable to all express private trusts, was whether the beneficiaries (or objects) were ascertained or ascertainable, ie, whether the trustees were capable of drawing up a comprehensive list of all the beneficiaries (or objects). This was known as the 'list test' or the 'Broadway Cottages test', associated with the case *Inland Revenue Commissioners v Broadway Cottages*. If the trustees were unable to draw up such a list, the trust was void for uncertainty of objects. This test was applicable to both fixed and discretionary trusts but was considered too restrictive only in respect of discretionary trusts.

Inland Revenue Commissioners v Broadway Cottages Trust [1955] Ch 20

Facts

A settlement was created whereby trustees held property upon trust to apply the income for the benefit of all or any of a class of objects including, *inter alia*, the settlor's wife, specific relations of the settlor and the Broadway Cottages Trust, a charitable institution. The trustees paid income to the Broadway Cottages Trust and claimed exemption from income tax in respect of this. It was not possible to ascertain all the objects who might fall within the class of objects, but it was possible to determine with certainty whether a particular person was a member of the class. The question in issue was whether the trust was valid or void.

Held
The trust was void for uncertainty of objects and the claim for a repayment of income tax failed.

The test continues to be applicable to fixed trusts, but in respect of discretionary trusts what was needed was a much broader test than the list test. This change in the test concerning objects was adopted by the House of Lords in *McPhail v Doulton*.

McPhail v Doulton [1971] AC 424, HL

Facts
Mr Bertram Baden executed a settlement and under clause 9(a) empowered the trustees to apply the net income in their absolute discretion 'to or for the benefit of any of the officers and employees or ex-officers or ex-employees of the company or to any relatives or dependants of any such persons in such amounts at such times and on such conditions (if any) as they think fit . . .'. The trustees were under no obligation to exhaust the income in any one year. They were also entitled to realise capital if the income was insufficient. The issue was whether a mere power or a trust power was created and whether the gift was valid. The High Court and the Court of Appeal decided that a mere power of appointment was created which was valid as satisfying the *Gulbenkian* test. Had a trust power been created, this would have been void as not satisfying the restrictive *Broadway Cottages* test.

Held
A trust power was intended by the settlor. The Law Lords rejected the *Broadway Cottages* test in respect of discretionary trusts, and extended the *Gulbenkian* test to discretionary trusts:

> **Lord Wilberforce:** It is striking how narrow and in a sense artificial is the distinction, in cases such as the present, between trusts or as the particular type of trust is called, trust powers, and powers. It is only necessary to read the learned judgments in the Court of Appeal to see that what to one mind may appear as a power of distribution coupled with a trust to dispose of the undistributed surplus, by accumulation or otherwise, may to another appear as a trust for distribution coupled with a power to withhold a portion and accumulate or otherwise dispose of it. A layman and, I suspect, also a logician, would find it hard to understand what difference there is.
>
> It does not seem satisfactory that the entire validity of a disposition should depend on such delicate shading.
>
> Differences there certainly are between trusts (trust powers) and powers, but as regards validity should they be so great as that in one case complete, or practically complete ascertainment is needed, but not in the other? Such distinction as there is would seem to lie in the extent of the survey which the trustee is required to carry out; if he has to distribute the whole of a fund's income, he must necessarily make a wider and more systematic survey than if his duty is expressed in terms of a power to make grants. But just as, in the case of a power, it is possible to underestimate the fiduciary obligation of the trustee to whom it is given, so, in the case of a trust (trust power), the danger lies in overstating what the trustee requires to know or to enquire into before he can properly execute his trust. The difference may be one of degree rather than of principle; in the well known words of Sir George Farwell (*Farwell on Powers* (3rd ed, 1916)) trusts and powers are often blended, and the mixture may vary in its ingredients.
>
> With this background I now consider whether the provisions of clause 9(a) constitute a trust or a power. Naturally read, the intention of the deed seems to me clear: clause 9(a), whose language is mandatory ('shall'), creates, together with a power of selection, a trust for distribution of the income . . . I therefore agree with Russell LJ [in the Court of Appeal] and would . . . allow the appeal, declare that the provisions of clause 9(a) constitute a trust and remit the case to the Chancery Division for determination whether on this basis clause 9 is (subject to the effects of s 164 of the Law of Property Act 1925) valid or void for uncertainty.
>
> This makes it necessary to consider whether, in so doing, the court should proceed on the basis that the relevant test is that laid down in the *Broadway Cottages* case [1955] Ch 20 or some other test. That decision gave the authority of the Court of Appeal to the distinction between cases where trustees are given a power of selection and those where they are bound by a trust for selection. In the former case the position, as decided by this House, is that the power is valid if it can be said with certainty whether any given individual is or is not a member of the class and does not fail simply because it is impossible to ascertain every member of the class (the

Gulbenkian case [1970] AC 508). But in the latter case it is said to be necessary, for the trust to be valid, that the whole range of objects (I use the language of the Court of Appeal) should be ascertained or capable of ascertainment.

The conclusion which I would reach, implicit in the previous discussion, is that the wide distinction between the validity test for powers and that for trust powers, is unfortunate and wrong, that the rule recently fastened on the courts by the *Broadway Cottages* case [1955] Ch 20 ought to be discarded, and that the test for the validity of trust powers ought to be similar to that accepted by this House in *Re Gulbenkian's Settlement Trusts* [1970] AC 508 for powers, namely that *the trust is valid if it can be said with certainty that any given individual is or is not a member of the class* [emphasis added].

Assimilation of the validity test does not involve the complete assimilation of trust powers with powers. As to powers, I agree with my noble and learned friend Lord Upjohn in *Re Gulbenkian's Settlement* [1970] AC 508 that although the trustees may, and normally will, be under a fiduciary duty to consider whether or in what way they should exercise their power, the court will not normally compel its exercise. It will intervene if the trustees exceed their powers, and possibly if they are proved to have exercised it capriciously. But in the case of a trust power, if the trustees do not exercise it, the court will; I respectfully adopt as to this the statement in Lord Upjohn's opinion. I would venture to amplify this by saying that the court, if called on to execute the trust power, will do so in the manner best calculated to give effect to the settlor's or testator's intentions. It may do so by appointing new trustees, or authorising or directing representative persons of the classes of beneficiaries to prepare a scheme of distribution, or even, should the proper basis for distribution appear, by itself directing the trustees so to distribute . . . Then, as to the trustees' duty of enquiry or ascertainment, in each case the trustees ought to make such a survey of the range of objects or possible beneficiaries as will enable them to carry out their fiduciary duty (cf *Liley v Hey* (1842) 1 Hare 580). A wider and more comprehensive range of enquiry is called for in the case of trust powers than in the case of powers.

Three limitations on the given postulant test

In extending the test for certainty of objects regarding powers to discretionary trusts, Lord Wilberforce laid down three limitations to the 'any given postulant test'.

McPhail v Doulton [1971] AC 424

Lord Wilberforce: Two final points: first, as to the question of certainty, I desire to emphasise the distinction clearly made and explained by Lord Upjohn (in *Re Gulbenkian* [1970] AC 508) between linguistic or semantic uncertainty which, if unresolved by the court, renders the gift void, and the difficulty of ascertaining the existence or whereabouts of members of the class, a matter with which the court can appropriately deal on an application for directions. There may be a third case where the meaning of the words used is clear but the definition of beneficiaries is so hopelessly wide as not to form 'anything like a class' so that the trust is administratively unworkable or in Lord Eldon LC's words one that cannot be executed (*Morice v Bishop of Durham* (1805) 10 Ves 522). I hesitate to give examples for they may prejudice future cases, but perhaps 'all the residents of Greater London' will serve. I do not think that a discretionary trust for 'relatives' even of a living person falls within this category . . .

Semantic or linguistic uncertainty (conceptual uncertainty)

This proviso is applicable to both powers and discretionary trusts. If the gift suffers from such uncertainty, it is void. This involves uncertainty or vagueness in defining the class or classes of individuals in respect of whom the trustees are entitled or required to exercise their discretion, for example, a distribution by the trustees in their discretion in favour of anyone who the trustees may consider to have a moral claim on the settlor.

Evidential uncertainty

This principle applies to both powers and discretionary trusts but does not invalidate either. This limitation concerns uncertainty in ascertaining the existence or whereabouts of objects. In this event, the trustees may apply to the courts for directions and the courts may make such order as is appropriate in the circumstances.

Administrative unworkability

This involves situations where the testator or settlor expressed the class of objects so broadly that it becomes difficult for the court to ascertain any sensible exercise of the discretion. In the event of the trustees failing to exercise their discretion, the court may find it difficult to exercise it in a rational manner, for example, a duty to distribute a fund in favour of such of the residents of Greater London as the trustees may decide in their absolute discretion. This type of uncertainty does not affect the validity of powers of appointment (see *Re Manisty*) but has the effect of invalidating trusts.

Re Manisty's Settlement [1973] 3 WLR 341, HC

Templeman J: It is said that if a power is too wide the trustees cannot perform the duty reiterated in *Gulbenkian* [1970] AC 508 and *McPhail v Doulton* [1971] AC 424 of considering from time to time whether and how to exercise the power and the court cannot determine whether or not the trustees are in breach of their duty. In my judgment, however, the mere width of a power cannot make it impossible for trustees to perform their duty nor prevent the court from determining whether the trustees are in breach ... I conclude from *Gestetner* [1953] 1 Ch 672; *Gulbenkian* [1970] AC 508; *McPhail v Doulton* [1971] AC 424 and *Baden (No 2)* [1973] Ch 9, that a power cannot be uncertain merely because it is wide in ambit.

The effect of vagueness of objects in respect of a trust power was considered in *R v District Auditor ex p West Yorkshire CC.*

R v District Auditor ex p West Yorkshire Metropolitan CC (1986) 26 RVR 24, DC

Facts

The council, threatened with abolition by the Government, settled £400,000 on trust to spend the capital and income within two years from the transfer for the purposes of benefiting 'any or all or some of the inhabitants' of West Yorkshire (about 2.5 million) by:

(a) assisting their economic development within the county;

(b) providing assistance for youth, ethnic and minority groups; and

(c) informing interested persons or bodies of the consequences of the proposed abolition of the Metropolitan County Councils.

The question in issue was whether the gift was valid or void for uncertainty.

Held

The purported gift was void because, on construction, a trust was intended which was administratively unworkable:

Lloyd LJ: A trust with as many as two and a half million potential beneficiaries is, in my judgment, quite simply unworkable. The class is far too large. In *Re Gulbenkian's Settlements* [1970] AC 508 Lord Reid said at p 518:

It may be that there is a class of case where, although the description of a class of beneficiaries is clear enough, any attempt to apply it to the facts would lead to such administrative difficulties that it would for that reason be held to be invalid.

My conclusion is that the *dictum* of Lord Wilberforce [in *McPhail v Doulton* [1971] AC 424] remains of high persuasive authority, despite *Re Manisty* [1973] 3 WLR 341. *Manisty's* case was concerned with a power, where a function of the court is more restricted. In the case of a trust, the court may have to execute the trust. Not so in the case of a power. That there may still be a distinction between trusts and powers in this connection was recognised by Templeman J himself in the sentence immediately following his quotation of Lord Wilberforce's *dictum*, when he said: In these guarded terms, Lord Wilberforce appears to refer to trusts which may have to be executed and administered by the court and not to powers where the court has a very much more limited function.

There can be no doubt that the declaration of trust in the present case created a trust and not a power. Following Lord Wilberforce's *dictum*, I would hold that the definition of the beneficiaries of the trust is 'so hopelessly wide', as to be incapable of forming 'anything like a class'. I would therefore reject counsel for the County Council's argument that the declaration of trust can take effect as an express private trust.

Question

In *McPhail v Doulton* what does Lord Wilberforce mean by 'administrative unworkability'?

Hardcastle, IM, 'Administrative unworkability: a reassessment of an abiding problem' [1990] Conv 24

Hardcastle reviews the arguments advanced for and against the workability criterion. The author examines the basis of the 'unworkability' criterion, propounded by Lord Wilberforce in *McPhail v Doulton*, as a method of invalidating a discretionary trust and suggests that it is an extension of the 'evidential uncertainty' criterion. He questions whether the mere size of a class of objects alone is sufficient to invalidate a trust and submits that the idea is based on a potentially innumerable class of beneficiaries coupled with a lack of provable definitional criteria. Unlike Emery (see (1982) 98 LQR 551), Hardcastle takes the view that administrative unworkability is extended to fixed trusts. He also considers whether the same notion is extended to powers of appointment:

> A trust must be one which the courts can control. Where judicial execution has been undertaken, there have normally been 'metes and bounds' within which the trusts have been defined; parameters that act as 'pointers or guides' to enable the court to substitute its own discretion for that of the trustees. In the course of so doing, the paramount objective of the court has been to execute the trust in a practical way; one best calculated to realise the settlor's intentions. The court has several options at its disposal, and the problem lies in determining when barriers to judicial execution are such that all such options are otiose.

> The incertitude stemming from immeasurably wide classes makes a nonsense of judicial supervision of the trustees' duties, since who is to say that a given selection of a beneficiary is wrong, and according to what criteria? . . . Perhaps the unworkability criteria should only be employed where the trustees are unable to devise even a preliminary strategy, and where the court is similarly 'none the wiser'.

Controversy in applying the given postulant test

Following the decision of the House of Lords in *McPhail v Doulton*, the case was remitted to the High Court to decide whether the new test for certainty of objects in respect of trust powers was satisfied. The High Court decided in favour of validity. This decision was affirmed by the Court of Appeal in *Re Baden's Deed Trusts (No 2)* [1973] Ch 9. The question in issue was whether the expressions 'relatives' and 'dependants' were linguistically certain.

The Court of Appeal held that the test was satisfied (although Stamp LJ was prepared to give a narrower definition of 'relatives' than the other Lord Justices of Appeal). The expression 'relatives' was taken to mean anyone who may establish a common ancestry with the settlor, and the term 'dependants' was defined as a person who is wholly or partly dependent on the means of another.

Each Lord Justice of Appeal adopted a different approach to the *Gestetner* test. Some judges expressed a lax approach to the test, while others adhered to the strict test. There seem to be at least five approaches to the test.

The question of fact approach

This approach is based on the assumption that the gift is conceptually certain (that is, linguistically certain). It then becomes a question of evidence or fact as to whether an individual proves to be within the class. Failure to discharge this burden of proof means that he is outside the class. In this respect, it makes no difference whether the class is small or large. It is submitted that this approach concerns the practicalities of exercising the discretion as opposed to a test of validity of the gift. This mode of applying the test was laid down by Sachs LJ in *Re Baden (No 2)* thus:

> Once the class of persons to be benefited is conceptually certain it then becomes a question of fact to be determined on evidence whether any postulant has on enquiry been proved to be within it; if he is not so proved then he is not in it. That position remains the same whether the class to be benefited happens to be small (such as 'first cousins') or large (such as 'members of the X Trade Union' or 'those who have served in the Royal Navy'). The suggestion that such trusts could be invalid because it might be impossible to prove of a given individual that he was not in the relevant class is wholly fallacious.

Applying this approach to the facts in *Re Baden (No 2)*, it would appear that it would be for the trustees to be convinced that a given individual is a relative or dependant of an officer or ex-officer, etc, of the specified company. Failure to convince the trustees means that the individual is not within the class.

The substantial number approach

This approach advocated by Megaw LJ in *Re Baden (No 2)* is to the effect that, in terms of validity of the gift, the test for certainty of objects is whether a substantial number of objects are within the class of objects and it is immaterial whether it is not possible to say with certainty that other objects are within or outside the class of objects. What is a substantial number of objects is for the courts to decide. Accordingly, the given postulant test is diluted to a substantial number of objects test:

> **Megaw LJ:** To my mind, the test is satisfied if, as regards at least a substantial number of objects, it can be said with certainty that they fall within the trust; even though, as regards a substantial number of other persons, if they ever for some fanciful reason fell to be considered, the answer would have to be, not 'they are outside the trusts', but 'it is not proven whether they are in or out'. What is a 'substantial number' may well be a question of common sense and of degree in relation to the particular trust: particularly where, as here, it would be fantasy, to use a mild word, to suggest that any practical difficulty would arise in the fair, proper and sensible administration of this trust in respect of relatives and dependants.

Note

The advantage of this approach is that the gift remains valid despite the fact that the classes of objects are incapable of definition. To a limited extent, the broad objective of the settlor will be fulfilled but this approach attracts a number of objections such as the striking similarity with the now defunct 'one person approach', which had been overruled by the House of Lords in *Re Gulbenkian*. The substantial number test seems to be a variant of the outdated approach. In addition, this diluted approach to the given postulant test creates a class within a class. The class as laid down by the settlor is varied to include only a substantial number of objects. It is questionable whether such an approach accords with the intention of the settlor. According to Lord Upjohn in *Re Gulbenkian*:

> The trustees have a duty to select the donees from among the class designated by the donor; he has not entrusted them with any power to select the donees merely from among known claimants who are within the class, for that is constituting a narrower class and the donor has given them no power to do this.

The strict approach

Stamp LJ subscribed to the view that the 'any given postulant test' requires the trustees to say of any individual that he either is clearly within or outside the class of objects. Accordingly, everyone is classified as being within or outside the class of objects. This requires clarity and precision in defining the qualifying class or classes of objects without listing the objects who fall within the class or classes. If such precise definitions are not forthcoming, the gift is void.

Re Baden's Deed Trusts (No 2) [1973] Ch 9

Stamp LJ: Validity or invalidity is to depend on whether you can say of *any* individual and the accent must be on that word 'any', for it is not simply the individual whose claim you are considering who is spoken of – that he 'is or is not a member of the class', for only thus can you make a survey of the range of objects or possible beneficiaries.

If the matter rested there, it would in my judgment follow that, treating the word 'relatives' as meaning descendants from a common ancestor, a trust for distribution such as is here in question would not be valid. Any 'survey of the range of objects or possible beneficiaries' would certainly be incomplete, and I am able to discern no principle on which such a survey could be conducted or where it should start or finish. The most you could do, so far as regards relatives, would be to find individuals who are clearly members of the class – the test which was accepted in the Court of Appeal, but rejected in the House of Lords, in the *Gulbenkian* case [1970] AC 508. The matter does not however, rest there . . . *Harding v Glyn* (1739) 1 Atk 469 is authority endorsed by the decision of the House that a discretionary trust for 'relations' was a valid trust to be executed by the court by distribution to the next of kin. The class of beneficiaries thus becomes a clearly defined class and there is no difficulty in determining whether a given individual is within it or without it.

Does it then make any difference that here the discretionary trust for relations was a reference not to the relations of a deceased person but of one who was living? I think not. The next of kin of a living person are as readily ascertainable at any given time as the next of kin of one who is dead.

The dictionary approach

The dictionary approach is based on the notion that the settlor may adopt a definition of the class or classes of objects specifically in a clause in the trust instrument. The effect is that there is likely to be little doubt as to the category of objects intended to benefit, for example, the settlor may give the trustees a discretion to distribute in favour of such of my 'old friends' as they may decide. He may then define the expression 'old friends' in any way he considers appropriate. In this way, the class of objects which would otherwise have failed may be rescued by the settlor. A variation on this theme entitles the settlor to appoint a third person (or trustee) as sole arbiter of the definition of the class of objects and perhaps all issues incidental to the exercise or non-exercise of the discretion. This approach was sanctioned by the Court of Appeal in *Re Tuck's Settlement Trusts*.

Re Tuck's Settlement Trusts [1978] Ch 49, HC

Facts

Sir Adolf Tuck, the first baronet, made a settlement in 1912 with the intention of ensuring that each baronet in succession would marry an 'approved wife'. The settlement provided for the payment of income to the baronet for the time being so long as he should be of the Jewish faith and married and living with an 'approved wife'. An 'approved wife' was identified in the settlement as 'a wife of Jewish blood by one or both of her parents and who has been brought up in and has never departed from and at the date of her marriage continues to worship according to the Jewish faith'. The settlor then added an arbitration clause to the effect that '. . . the decision of Chief Rabbi in London . . . shall be conclusive'. Sir Adolf died in 1926. He was succeeded by his eldest son, Sir William Tuck, who married an approved wife. Sir William died 1954 and was succeeded by his eldest son, Sir Bruce Tuck. Sir Bruce first married an approved wife but was divorced in 1964. In 1968, he married a lady who was not an approved wife. The question in issue was whether the limitation was valid or void.

Held

The limitation was not void on the grounds that the restriction created a condition precedent which was not wholly uncertain, and the Chief Rabbi clause constituted a valid delegation of decision making power on the relevant questions of fact in the event of a dispute. The clause was similar to an arbitration clause in contract law:

Lord Denning MR: The dichotomy between 'conceptual' and 'evidential' uncertainty was adumbrated by Jenkins J in *Re Coxen* [1948] Ch 747. It is implicit in Lord Upjohn's speech in *Re Gulbenkian's Settlement* [1970] AC 508 and accepted by Lord Wilberforce in *Re Baden's Deed Trusts (McPhail v Doulton)* [1971] AC 424. I must confess that I find the dichotomy most unfortunate. It has led the courts to discordant decisions. I will give some relevant instances. On the one hand, a condition that a person shall 'not be of Jewish parentage' has been held by the House of Lords to be void for conceptual uncertainty, at any rate in a condition subsequent: see *Clayton v Ramsden* [1943] AC 320, and a condition that a person shall be 'of the Jewish race' was held by Danckwerts J to be void for conceptual uncertainty, even in a condition precedent: see *Re Tarnpolsk* [1958] 3 All ER 479. The reason in each case being that the testator had given no information or clue as to what percentage or proportion of Jewish blood would satisfy the requirement. Is it to be 100%, or will 75%, or 50% be sufficient? The words do not enable any definite answer to be given.

On this reasoning the condition in the Tuck settlement that an 'approved wife' should be of 'Jewish blood' would seem to be afflicted with conceptual uncertainty.

There is another distinction to be found in the cases. It is between conditions precedent and conditions subsequent. Conceptual uncertainty may avoid a condition subsequent, but not a condition precedent. I fail to see the logic of this distinction. Treating the problem as one of construction of words, there is no sense in it. If the words are conceptually uncertain – so as to avoid a condition subsequent – they are just as conceptually uncertain in a condition precedent – and should avoid it also. But it is a distinction authorised by this court in *Re Allen* [1953] Ch 810 and acknowledged by Lord Wilberforce in *Blathwayt v Baron Cawley* [1976] AC 397 [emphasis added].

I deplore both these dichotomies, for a simple reason and a good reason. They serve in every case to defeat the intention of the testator or settlor. The courts say: 'We are not going to give effect to his intentions – because he has not expressed himself with sufficient distinctness or clearness.'

How is any testator or settlor to overcome these legal difficulties? Sir Adolf Tuck in this settlement said: 'Let any dispute or doubt be decided by the Chief Rabbi.' That seemed to him a good solution, and it seems a good solution. The Chief Rabbi should be able to decide – better than anyone else – whether a wife was 'of Jewish blood' and had been brought up 'according to the Jewish faith' . . . I see no reason why a testator or settlor should not provide that any dispute or doubt should be resolved by his executors or trustees, or even a third person. To prove this, I will first state the law in regard to contracts. *Here the general principle is that whenever persons agree together to refer a matter to a third person for decision, and further agree that his decision is to be final and binding upon them, then, so long as he arrives at his decision honestly and in good faith, the two parties are bound by it.* They cannot reopen it for mistakes or errors on his part, either in fact or law, or for any reason other than fraud or collusion . . . *Such an agreement (to abide by the decision of a third person) does not oust the jurisdiction of the courts.* It only offends when the parties go further and seek by their agreement to take the law out of the hands of the courts and put it into the hands of a private tribunal without recourse to the courts in case of error of law . . . If the appointed person should find difficulty in the actual wording of the will or settlement, the executors or trustees can always apply to the court for directions so as to assist in the interpretation of it. But if the appointed person is ready and willing to resolve the doubt or difficulty, I see no reason why he should not do so. *So long as he does not misconduct himself or come to a decision which is wholly unreasonable, I think his decision should stand* . . . But still the testator may even today think that the courts of law are not really the most suitable means of deciding the dispute or doubt. He would be quite right. As this very case shows, the courts may get bogged down in distinctions between conceptual uncertainty and evidential uncertainty: and between conditions subsequent and conditions precedent. The testator may want to cut out all that cackle, and let someone decide it who really will understand what the testator is talking about: and thus save an expensive journey to the lawyers and the courts. For my part, I would not blame him. I would give effect to his intentions . . . So it comes to this: if there is any conceptual uncertainty in the provisions of this settlement, it is cured by the Chief Rabbi clause [emphasis added].

Note

This approach is objectionable on the ground that the relevant clause is arbitrary in effect. There is a limit to the extent to which a settlor or testator may 'rescue' a class of objects. If the class of objects is incapable of definition, no arbitrator would be capable of applying a rational definition of the class. Moreover, it was declared in *Re Coxen* that it is not open to the testator or settlor to adopt the trustees' opinion as the criterion to determine the objects of the mere power or trust power without clear guidance in the first place as to the class or classes of objects.

Re Coxen, McCallum v Coxen [1948] 1 Ch 747, HC

Facts

A testator devised a dwelling house to his trustees subject to a direction to permit his widow to 'reside therein during her life, or so long as she shall desire to reside therein' and specified that 'if in the opinion of the trustees she permanently ceases to reside therein' the house would form part of the residuary estate. The question in issue was whether the limitation was valid or void.

Held

The restriction was clear and valid:

> **Jenkins J:** It seems to me that so far as definition goes the double event involved in the condition ... is prescribed with sufficient certainty and precision. I see no reason why a judge of fact should not on any given state of facts be perfectly capable of deciding whether it has or has not happened ... The circumstance that it may be difficult in this or that state of facts to determine whether the double event has happened or not does not, in my judgment, make the condition bad ...

> I have so far treated the condition as if it was simply in the terms 'if she shall have ceased permanently to reside' whereas its actual terms are 'if in the opinion of my trustees she shall have ceased permanently to reside'. That I think makes a material difference. The opinion of the trustees that the double event has happened, and not simply the happening of the double event, is what brings about the cesser of Lady Coxen's interest. *If the testator had insufficiently defined the state of affairs on which the trustees were to form their opinion, he would not I think have saved the condition from invalidity on the ground of uncertainty merely by making their opinion the criterion ...* but as I have already indicated, I think the relevant double event is sufficiently defined to make it perfectly possible for the trustees (as the judges of fact for this purpose) to decide whether it has happened or not, and in my view the testator by making the trustees' opinion the criterion has removed the difficulties which might otherwise have ensued [emphasis added].

Note

In addition, a dictionary clause has the tendency to oust the jurisdiction of the courts except in cases where the arbitrator has acted in bad faith. Generally, 'ouster clauses' are void on public policy grounds: see *Re Raven*.

Re Raven [1915] 1 Ch 673, HC

Facts

The testator by his will dated 29 September 1911 bequeathed a charitable legacy of £1,000 to the 'National Association for the Prevention of Consumption' and directed in his will that 'if any doubt shall arise in any case as to the identity of the institution intended to benefit, the question shall be decided by my trustees whose decision shall be final and binding on the parties'. There was no society of that name but there was a society incorporated in 1899 whose full name was 'The National Association for the Prevention of Consumption and other Forms of Tuberculosis'. This association had power to constitute branches, and amongst other branches there was an unincorporated branch whose full name was 'The Leicester Branch of the National Association for the Prevention of Consumption and other Forms of Tuberculosis'. The testator had been a subscriber to the Leicester branch for some years prior to his death, but had not subscribed to the National Association itself. The legacy was claimed by each of the charities which for this purpose were independent institutions. The trustees of the will and the Leicester branch were keen to allow the trustees to decide the question of the identity of the beneficiary. The National Association, on the other hand, insisted that the court should decide the question.

Held

The arbitration clause in the will was void on grounds of repugnancy and public policy, for it purported to oust the jurisdiction of the courts. In addition, the legacy was payable to the National Association for extrinsic evidence was not admissible in the circumstances:

> **Warrington J:** In my opinion it is not competent for a testator to confer certain legal rights by giving legacies and at the same time to say that the question whether that legal right is or is not to be enjoyed is not to be determined by the ordinary tribunal – in other words, it is not competent for him to deprive the person to whom that legal right is given of one of the incidents of that legal right; and if necessary I should be prepared to rest my decision upon the ground that the attempt to do so is an attempt to do two inconsistent things. In my opinion the gift of a legacy to a legatee, even if it be of doubtful construction, is in fact a gift to the person who shall be determined to be the legatee according to legal principles, and to give effect to a provision such as the provision which the testator has inserted in his will in the present case is in fact to assert the direct contrary and to say that the gift is not to the person who shall be determined to be the legatee by the courts which administer the legal principles to which I have referred, but to the person who shall be decided to be the legatee by the trustees, who by the will are unfettered and may make their decision upon such grounds as they think fit . . . I think therefore that I can safely decide the point on that ground alone; but I also think that I may and ought to decide it on wider grounds, namely, *that it is contrary to public policy to attempt to deprive persons of their right of resorting to ordinary tribunals for the purpose of establishing their legal rights* . . . In the present case, certain rights are claimed, namely, the right to be treated as a legatee, the existence of which does not depend upon the fulfilment of any condition precedent or upon anything to be ascertained by a prescribed method. It has been attempted to say that the gift is equivalent to a gift to such institution as the trustees shall select. In my opinion that is not the effect of this gift. The gift of this legacy is to a particular institution, and that institution, if it proves its right, is entitled to the legacy and is not in the position of having to fulfil any condition precedent; nor does the right depend on ascertainment by any prescribed method; the right is ascertained by the gift itself. That being so, it seems to me impossible for the testator to qualify that gift by providing that the right to the legacy, the subject of the gift, shall be determined by some tribunal other than that of the country [emphasis added] . . .

Gifts subject to conditions precedent and subsequent

The approach here is based on the property law distinction between gifts subject to conditions precedent and subsequent, as illustrated in *Re Allen*. In the case of gifts subject to conditions precedent, the requirement of certainty is less strict as opposed to gifts subject to conditions subsequent (see *Blathwayt v Baron Cawley* [1976] AC 397). A gift subject to a condition precedent is one where the donee does not acquire an interest in the property until he satisfies the relevant condition, for example, a gift of £500 to A provided that he passes his year one LLB examinations. A does not obtain the property until he passes the relevant examination. On the other hand, a gift subject to a condition subsequent is one which vests in the donee but terminates on the occasion when the relevant condition is satisfied, for example, an endowment to B until he passes his year one LLB examinations. Here, B obtains a vested interest, which is determined when he passes the relevant examinations.

Re Allen (Decd), Faith v Allen [1953] I Ch 810, CA

Facts

A testator devised his dwelling house and another property, subject to life interests, to the eldest son of his nephew, Francis, subject to the qualification that he shall be 'a member of the Church of England and an adherent to the doctrine of that Church'. The question in issue was whether the qualification was valid or void.

Held

The qualification was valid. The limitation created a condition precedent and, to satisfy it, it was not necessary that the condition be capable of exact definition. The claimant was required to prove that he, at least, satisfied the limitation.

> **Sir Raymond Evershed MR:** The judge was, in my opinion, plainly right in his view that the formula here in question is not a condition subsequent. In my judgment the effect of such a formula as part of a condition subsequent differs from its effect in a condition precedent or as part of a qualification or limitation . . .

A condition subsequent operates to divest or determine a gift or estate previously or otherwise vested; so that if the condition be void the gift or estate remains. It has long been established that the courts (which are inclined against the divesting of gifts or estates already vested) will hold a condition subsequent void if its terms are such that (apart from mere difficulties of construction of the language or of the ascertainment of the facts) it cannot clearly be known in advance or from the beginning what are the circumstances the happening of which will cause the divesting or determination of the gift or estate. The strictness of the special rule as to conditions subsequent was the basis of all the opinions of the noble Lords in *Clayton v Ramsden* [1943] AC 320 [Lord Evershed then referred to the judgment of Lord Russell of Killowen]. I feel therefore, no doubt that if the present formula constituted a condition subsequent it would . . . be held to be void – its second part falls clearly, I think, within the reasoning and language of Lord Russell and Lord Romer in *Clayton v Ramsden* to which I shall later again refer . . .

. . . In the present case, if the formula constitutes a condition precedent, I will assume that failure to satisfy the condition will involve failure to take the benefit of the devise. And the same result is equally (if not more) clear if the formula is not a condition at all but part of the description of the devisee (as though it were to the eldest son who should have red hair); in other words, is a limitation or qualification, as I think it is . . .

I am not persuaded that where a formula constitutes a condition precedent or a qualification it is right for the court to declare the condition or qualification void for uncertainty so as thereby to defeat all possible claimants to the gift unless the terms of the condition or qualification are such that it is impossible to give them any meaning at all, or such that they involve repugnancies or inconsistencies in the possible tests which they postulate, as distinct, for example, from mere problems of degree.

On the evidence so far before the court it does not seem to me that the words are shown to involve any insoluble inconsistency, or that they are incapable of any reasonably clear meaning or any sensible definition at all.

A gift subject to a condition subsequent is construed strictly and if the meaning of the condition cannot be resolved by the court, the condition fails and the transferee takes the property without the restriction: see *Clayton v Ramsden*.

Clayton v Ramsden [1943] AC 320, HL (Lords Atkin, Thankerton, Russell of Killowen and Romer; Lord Wright dissenting)

Facts

By his will, a testator bequeathed a legacy and a share of the residue of his estate upon trust for his daughter, Edna, for life with remainder on trust for her issue equally. The gift was subject to forfeiture (expressly inserted by the testator) if she should marry a person 'not of Jewish parentage and of the Jewish faith'. Edna married the appellant, Harold Clayton, who was an English Wesleyan who was admittedly not of Jewish parentage. The question in issue was whether the forfeiture clause was valid or void.

Held

The clause created a composite set of conditions subsequent, which were void for uncertainty. The majority decided that both limbs of the disqualification clause were void:

Lord Russell of Killowen: My Lords, for the reasons which I will indicate I am of the opinion that your Lordships should hold this condition of defeasance to be void, and allow this appeal. The courts have always insisted that conditions of defeasance, in order to be valid, should be so framed that the persons affected (or the court, if they seek its guidance) can from the outset know with certainty the exact event on the happening of which their interests are to be divested. The principle was enunciated many years ago by Lord Cranworth in *Clavering v Ellison* (1859) 7 HL Cas 707 in the following words: 'Where a vested estate is to be defeated by a condition on a contingency that is to happen afterwards, that condition must be such that the court can see from the beginning, precisely and distinctly, upon the happening of what event it was that the preceding vested estate was to determine.' In all such cases that is the test which has to be applied to the particular condition which the testator has chosen to impose . . .

Let me now apply the principle to this condition. The crucial words are 'who is not of Jewish parentage and of the Jewish faith'. A preliminary question was raised. Is this one condition, or do the words impose alternative conditions on the happening of either of which a forfeiture occurs. This is a question of construction, separate from the main question. The testator has insisted on his daughter's husband having both the qualifications which he has mentioned. It was suggested that, if there was no uncertainty as to one of the qualifications, and the husband did not possess it, the forfeiture clause would operate. I cannot agree with this view, for its corollary would be that marriage with a husband not of Jewish parentage (whatever those words mean) but who before the wedding became a convert to the Jewish faith (whatever those words mean) would not bring about a forfeiture, a result quite inconsistent with the intention of the testator as disclosed by the language which he has used. I am of the opinion that there is here only one condition of forfeiture, and that the whole of the contingency on the happening of which the forfeiture is to take place must be certain.

In my opinion, on construction, the words 'of Jewish parentage' refer to race. Other elements of doubt surrounds the words. Must both parents be of the Jewish race, or would one alone, and which, suffice? I confess myself unable to find any context which provides an answer, but the answer may well be that, in the absence of a context to the contrary, the true construction is that both parents must be of the Jewish race. But at this point the real difficulty begins, namely, the question of degree. The testator has given no information or clue as to what percentage or proportion of Jewish blood in the husband will satisfy the requirement that he should be of Jewish parentage. The daughter could never, before marrying the man of her choice, be certain that he came up to requisite standard of Jewish parentage, nor could a court enlighten her beforehand. The standard is unknown, and incapable of ascertainment. It is this uncertainty of degree which prevents the divesting event from being seen precisely and distinctly from the beginning, and uncertainty attaching to the requirement of Jewish parentage avoids the whole condition subsequent, with the result that no defeasance takes place.

In these circumstances it is unnecessary to express an opinion on the certainty of the words 'of Jewish faith', but, had it been necessary, I should have felt a difficulty in holding that their meaning was clear or certain. It seems to me that . . . the testator has given no indication of the degree of attachment or adherence to the faith which he requires on the part of his daughter's husband. The requirement that a person shall be of Jewish faith seems to me too vague to enable it to be said with certainty that a particular individual complies with the requirement.

The approach adopted by the High Court in *Re Barlow's Will Trusts* was, more or less, a practical approach striving for the validity of the gift. This approach was based on two assumptions, first, that the quantum of the gift did not vary with the extent of the class of objects. In other words, the property and paintings were to be acquired at an undervalue. This privilege did not vary with the extent of the class of objects as opposed to a gift of £1,000 to be divided equally between 'my old friends'. Secondly, the gift was subject to a condition precedent, or subject to a description, which permitted the court to adopt a more liberal application of the test of certainty.

Re Barlow's Will Trusts [1979] I All ER 296, HC

Facts
A testatrix died in 1975 leaving a valuable collection of paintings. Her immediate survivors were eight nephews and nieces, 24 great nephews and nieces and 14 great great nephews and nieces.

By her will, the testatrix directed her executor to sell the remainder of her collection subject to the provision that 'any member of my family and any friends of mine' be allowed to purchase any of the paintings at a catalogue price compiled in 1970 which was substantially below their market value on the date of death.

The executors applied to the court to ascertain whether the direction was void for uncertainty and guidance as to the appropriate method for identifying members of the testatrix's family.

Held
The direction as to 'friends' was valid, for the properties were to be distributed *in specie* to persons answering the description 'friend'. The court also gave guidelines on the identification of friends namely:

(a) the relationship with the testatrix was of long standing;

(b) the relationship must have been social as opposed to a business or professional relationship;

(c) when circumstances permitted they met frequently. The expression 'family' meant a blood relationship with the testatrix.

Browne-Wilkinson J: The main questions which arise for my decision are:

(a) whether the direction to allow members of the family and friends to purchase the pictures is void for uncertainty since the meaning of the word 'friends' is too vague to be given legal effect; and

(b) what persons are to be treated as being members of the testatrix's family.

I will deal first with the question of uncertainty.

Those arguing against the validity of the gift in favour of the friends contend that, in the absence of any guidance from the testatrix, the question, 'who were her friends?', is incapable of being answered. The word is said to be 'conceptually uncertain' since there are so many different degrees of friendship and it is impossible to say which degree the testatrix had in mind. In support of this argument they rely on Lord Upjohn's remarks in *Re Gulbenkian's Settlement Trusts (Whishaw v Stephens)* [1970] AC 508 and the decision of the House of Lords in *McPhail v Doulton* [1971] AC 424 (on appeal from *Re Baden's Deed Trusts*) to the effect that it must be possible to say who is within and who is without the class of friends. They say that since the testatrix intended all her friends to have the opportunity to acquire a picture it is necessary to be able to ascertain with certainty all the members of that class.

Counsel for the fourth defendant, who argued in favour of the validity of the gift, contended that the tests laid down in the *Gulbenkian* case, and *McPhail v Doulton* were not applicable in this case. The test, he says, is that laid down by the Court of Appeal in *Re Allen* [1953] Ch 810 as appropriate in cases where the validity of a condition precedent or description is in issue, namely that the gift is valid if it is possible to say of one or more persons that he or they undoubtedly qualify even though it may be difficult to say of others whether or not they qualify.

The distinction between the *Gulbenkian* test and the *Re Allen* test is, in my judgment, well exemplified by the word 'friends'. The word has a great range of meanings; indeed, its exact meaning probably varies slightly from person to person. Some would include only those with whom they had been on intimate terms over a long period; others would include acquaintances whom they liked. Some would include people with whom their relationship was primarily business; others would not. Indeed, many people, if asked to draw up a complete list of their friends, would probably have some difficulty in deciding whether certain of the people they knew were really 'friends' as opposed to 'acquaintances'. Therefore, if the nature of the gift was such that it was legally necessary to draw up a complete list of 'friends' of the testatrix or to be able to say of any person that 'he is not a friend', the whole gift would probably fail even as to those who, by any conceivable test, were friends. But in the case of a gift of a kind which does not require one to establish all the members of the class (for example, 'a gift of £10 to each of my friends'), it may be possible to say of some people that, on any test, they qualify. Thus, in *Re Allen* [1953] Ch 810 at 817 Evershed MR took the example of a gift to X 'if he is a tall man'; a man 6 ft 6 inches tall could be said on any reasonable basis to satisfy the test, although it might be impossible to say whether a man, say 5 ft 10 inches high satisfied the requirement.

So in this case, in my judgment, there are acquaintances of a kind so close that, on any reasonable basis, anyone would treat them as being 'friends'. Therefore, by allowing the disposition to take effect in their favour, one would certainly be giving effect to part of the testatrix's intention even though as the others it is impossible to say whether or not they satisfy the test.

In my judgment, it is clear that Lord Upjohn in *Re Gulbenkian* was considering only cases where it was necessary to establish all the members of the class. He made it clear that the reason for the rule is that in a gift which requires one to establish all the members of the class (for example, 'a gift to my friends in equal shares') you cannot hold the gift good in part, since the quantum of each friend's share depends on how many friends there are. So all persons intended to benefit by the donor must be ascertained if any effect is to be given to the gift. In my judgment, the adoption of Lord Upjohn's test by the House of Lords in *McPhail v Doulton* is based on the same reasoning, even though in that case the House of Lords held that it was only necessary to be able to survey the class of objects of a power of appointment and not to establish who all the members were. But such reasoning has no application to a case where there is a condition or description attached to one or more individual gifts; in such cases, uncertainty as to some other persons who may have been intended to take does not in any way affect the quantum of the gift to persons who undoubtedly possess the qualification. Hence, in my judgment, the different test laid down in *Re Allen*. The recent decision of the Court of Appeal in *Re Tuck's Settlement Trust* [1978] Ch 49 establishes that the test in *Re Allen* is still the appropriate test in considering such gifts, notwithstanding the *Gulbenkian* and *McPhail v Doulton* decisions.

Accordingly, in my judgment, the proper result in this case depends on whether the disposition in clause 5(a) is properly to be regarded as a series of individual gifts to persons answering the description 'friend' (in which case it will be valid), or a gift which requires the whole class of friends to be established (in which case it will probably fail).

The effect of clause 5(a) is to confer on friends of the testatrix a series of options to purchase. Although it is obviously desirable as a practical matter that steps should be taken to inform those entitled to the options of their rights, it is common ground that there is no legal necessity to do so. Therefore, each person coming forward to exercise the option has to prove that he is a friend; it is not legally necessary, in my judgment, to discover who all the friends are. In order to decide whether an individual is entitled to purchase, all that is required is that the executors should be able to say of that individual whether he has proved that he is a friend. The word 'friend' therefore is description or qualification of the option holder.

It was suggested that by allowing undoubted friends to take I would be altering the testatrix's intentions. It is said that she intended all her friends to have a chance to buy any given picture, and since some people she might have regarded as friends will not be able to apply, the number of competitors for that picture will be reduced. This may be so, but I cannot regard this factor making it legally necessary to establish the whole class of friends. The testatrix's intention was that a friend should acquire a picture. My decision gives effect to that intention.

I therefore hold, that the disposition does not fail for uncertainty, but that anyone who can prove that by any reasonable test he or she must have been a friend of the testatrix is entitled to exercise the option. Without seeking to lay down any exhaustive definition of such test, it may be helpful if I indicate certain minimum requirements:

(a) the relationship must have been a long standing one;

(b) the relationship must have been a social relationship as opposed to a business or professional relationship;

(c) although there may have been long periods when circumstances prevented the testatrix and applicant from meeting, when circumstances did permit they must have met frequently. If in any case the executors entertain any real doubt whether an applicant qualifies, they can apply to the court to decide the issue.

In *Re Tepper's Will Trusts*, the court admitted extrinsic evidence in order to clarify the definition of the class of objects in the context of a gift subject to a condition subsequent.

Re Tepper's Will Trusts, Kramer and Another v Ruda and Others [1987] Ch 358, HC

Facts

By his will made in 1953, a testator (a devout Jew), who died in 1959, left his residuary estate upon trust, *inter alia*, for his grandchildren living at the date of his death 'provided that they attain the age of 25 years and shall not marry outside the Jewish faith'. The testator had six grandchildren, four of whom married persons of the Jewish faith and two married persons outside the Jewish faith. The question in issue was whether the restrictive clause was valid or void.

Held

The clause created a condition subsequent which was *prima facie* void for uncertainty, but extrinsic evidence, if available, was admissible to clarify the meaning of the expression 'of Jewish faith' in a way which was consistent with the notion that the testator had in mind. The proceedings were adjourned pending inquiries concerning the availability of such evidence:

> **Scott J:** The question is what the testator, sitting in his armchair, meant by 'the Jewish faith'. Direct evidence of his intention is not admissible; but I would have regarded as admissible extrinsic of the Jewish faith as practised by the testator and his family. It would, in my view, be well arguable that when the testator in his will referred to 'the Jewish faith' he meant the Jewish faith in accordance with which he practised his religion. I would have regarded it as possible and, indeed, likely that objective evidence might be available as to what was the Jewish faith in accordance with which he practised his religion. If evidence of that character were adduced it might well, in my view, be possible to attribute to the expression 'the Jewish faith' a meaning sufficiently certain to enable the *Clayton v Ramsden* [1943] AC 320 test to be satisfied. This approach to construction is, in my view, supported by that of the Court of Appeal in *Re Tuck's Settlement Trusts* [1978] Ch 49 . . .
>
> A question of construction of a will depends on the language of the particular will construed with the aid of admissible evidence of relevant surrounding circumstances. A decision by another court, even a court as august as the House of Lords, is not binding on the question whether in Nathan Tepper's will a sufficiently certain

meaning can be attributed to the expression 'the Jewish faith' so as to enable the conditions of defeasance to be upheld. Counsel for the defendants, in the event that I should decide against them on the condition precedent or condition of defeasance point, and I have done so, have asked for the opportunity to adduce extrinsic evidence of surrounding circumstances in order to elucidate the meaning of the expression 'the Jewish faith' as used by the testator in his will. I think I should give them an opportunity to do so.

Question
What judicial approaches to the 'any given postulant test' exist?

McKay, L, 'Re Barlow and the certainty of objects rule' [1980] Conv 263

McKay examined the validity of the test laid down in *Re Barlow* and suggested that it is an unjustified extension of the test overruled by the House of Lords in *Re Gulbenkian*. McKay contends:

A variety of conflicting tests were proffered by lower courts as being the 'proper' criteria by which certainty issues were to be resolved. One which surfaced briefly is the Court of Appeal decision in *Re Gulbenkian* [1968] Ch 126, in respect of trust powers, [which] was a test adopted by an earlier Court of Appeal [*Re Allen* [1953] 1 Ch 810] in relation to conditions precedent, namely, whether it could be said of any *one* individual that he satisfied the beneficiary-defining words. Without discussing its propriety as the test of certainty of conditions precedent, the House of Lords [in *Re Gulbenkian*] at once rejected it in the context of both trust powers and discretionary trusts. It did not surface in the *Baden* litigation.

The decision of Browne-Wilkinson J in *Re Barlow's Will Trusts* [1979] 1 All ER 296 has, however, brought the test into contention once again. The thrust of that decision is that the test is not limited to issues of certainty of conditions precedent but is in some circumstances the appropriate criterion for assessing the validity of the beneficiary-defining language of a broader class of settlement. This approach invites an analysis of the propriety of the extension of the test beyond the area of conditions precedent. But it does more than that. It also raises the broader issue, not resolved in *Re Gulbenkian*, of whether even in that narrow context the test can be regarded as good law following the *Baden* and *Gulbenkian* decisions.

. . . the test of certainty laid down in *Re Allen* [1953] Ch 810 is inadequate . . . it is defined, seemingly deliberately, in such a way as to ensure compliance with it in virtually every case. It is indeed difficult to conceive of any language in respect of which it will not be satisfied, other than that which would be capricious in any event. Certainly, those trusts most frequently used as illustrations of post-*McPhail v Doulton* [1971] AC 424 'semantic uncertainty' – trusts for 'those with a moral claim upon me' for instance – will have no difficulty in satisfying it. That its avoiding potential is virtually non-existent is, of course, no bad thing in itself. But what is objectionable, in terms of the policy considerations, is that it provides no basis for filtering out those trusts which are manifestly inadequate in terms of the control and supervision to which the trustee will be subject.

At first glance there seems little in common between either the fact situation of *Re Allen* and that of *McPhail v Doulton* or the respective issues of certainty thrown up by those fact situations. Nor, also at the superficial level, does the test of certainty articulated by Lord Wilberforce in the latter decision seem broadly appropriate to a resolution of issues such as that before the Court of Appeal in the earlier case. On an impressionistic basis, the indications point the other way. The *McPhail v Doulton* test was laid down in respect of discretionary trusts. In condition precedent cases, such as that in *Re Allen*, there is seldom a discretion in the trustee. It is usually only a matter of determining whether the applicant before the trustees with an (otherwise) unqualified entitlement to the fund fulfils the last remaining condition. On this basis the emphasis in *Re Allen* on an individual claimant rather than upon each and every potential beneficiary might seem 'proper'. In respect of discretionary trusts on the other hand, the prevailing fact situation is quite different. No individual has a fixed entitlement. The exercise of a discretion, rather than the fulfilment of a qualifying condition, stands between each potential beneficiary and payment. There is typically a range of persons among whom the discretion is to be exercised. Most significantly, the trustees have obligations to survey and consider the range of possible beneficiaries prior to making any payment. In these circumstances, the *McPhail v Doulton* emphasis upon an ability to determine of *any* individual whether he is or is not a member of the class might seem, again impressionistically, a 'proper' emphasis. Browne-Wilkinson J may have had this general distinction in mind in *Re Barlow* [1979] 1 All ER 296, when he refused to categorise the trust before him as one for 'a class' but rather as one conferring a series of individual gifts to persons answering the description 'friend'.

McKay concludes by saying:

> The view forwarded in this note is that the test [laid down in *Re Allen*] is both wrong in principle and must be regarded as being inconsistent with those later decisions [*Re Gulbenkian* and *McPhail v Doulton*], that it should not have been adopted by Browne-Wilkinson J, and that the decision in *Re Barlow* is on that account incorrect.

INTERESTS OF OBJECTS UNDER DISCRETIONARY TRUSTS

A discretionary trust is mandatory in nature. The question that arises is what interest, if any, do objects (individually or collectively) enjoy under a discretionary trust.

Individual interests

In respect of a discretionary trust, the trustees are given a discretion to decide what interest, if any, may be distributed to the objects. The objects are dependent on the trustees exercising their discretion in their favour. No object is entitled to a quantifiable interest in the property. Prior to the exercise of the discretion, the objects, individually considered, have an expectation or hope of acquiring a benefit. Each object does not have a right to the income of the fund but merely a right to require the trustees to consider whether they will distribute any property to the object. If the trustees decide to distribute property to an object, he gets it not by reason of having the right to have his case considered, but only because the trustees have decided to distribute the property to him: see *Gartside v Inland Revenue Commissioners*. This is the position whether the discretionary trust is exhaustive or non-exhaustive.

Gartside and Another v Inland Revenue Commissioners [1968] AC 553, HL

Facts
By his will, the testator, who died in January 1941, transferred one-quarter share of his estate upon trust for the benefit of his son, John, and John's family. The settlement provided that during John's lifetime the trustees were given an unfettered discretion to provide the income from the trust fund 'for or towards the maintenance, support or otherwise for the benefit of John or his wife or children (if any) ... and shall accumulate the surplus of the said income ...' (non-exhaustive discretionary trust). The accumulations of income were to be added to the trust fund and the trustees were given a discretion to apply the same for the maintenance, support and benefit of the same class of discretionary objects during John's lifetime, and after his death the capital was to be held on trust for such of his children as should attain 21 or, if daughters, marry. John married in 1942 and had twin sons born in 1945. The trustees accumulated all of the income until 1960. In 1961, they paid out income of £786 to John and £50 to his wife and accumulated the balance. In 1962, the trustees advanced accumulated income to the twins. John died in 1963. It was conceded that estate duty was payable on the remainder of the trust funds by virtue of John's death, but in addition, the Revenue claimed duty on the sums advanced to the twins in 1962 on the ground that the advancement amounted to a termination of an interest in possession.

Held
In favour of the trustees on the ground that the class of discretionary beneficiaries did not have, individually or collectively, an interest in possession prior to the exercise of the trustees' discretion in their favour. Accordingly, the advancement in 1962 did not amount to a termination of an interest in possession:

> **Lord Reid:** In my judgment an examination of the relevant provisions of this legislation leads to the clear conclusion that objects of a discretionary trust do not have interests extending to the whole or any part of the income of the trust fund ... *a fortiori* they do not have interests in possession ... To have an interest in possession does not merely mean that you possess the interest. You also possess an interest in expectancy for you may be able to assign it and you can rely on it to prevent the trustees from dissipating the trust fund. 'In

possession' must mean that your interest enables you to claim now whatever may be the subject of the interest. For instance, if it is the current income from a certain fund your claim may yield nothing if there is no income, but your claim is a valid claim, and if there is any income you are entitled to get it; but a right to require trustees to consider whether they will pay you something does not enable you to claim anything. If the trustees do decide to pay you something, you do not get it by reason of having the right to have your case considered: you get it only because the trustees have decided to give it to you. Even if I had thought that objects of discretionary trusts have interests, I would not find any good reason for holding that they have interests in possession.

Lord Wilberforce: The obligation to distribute the whole income does not entitle any object to the whole or any definable part of the income, and, therefore, the object cannot have a quantifiable interest in the fund. The only right which any object has in an exhaustive, as in a non-exhaustive, trust is to have the trustees exercise their discretion and to be protected by the court in that right.

Note

Indeed, a sole member of a class of discretionary objects is not entitled as of right to claim the income from the trust while there remains a possibility that other members might come into existence: see *Re Trafford's Settlement* [1984] 1 All ER 1108.

Where an object assigns his rights under a discretionary trust to a third party or becomes bankrupt, the assignee or trustee-in-bankruptcy can be in no better position than the object. Accordingly, the assignee or trustee-in-bankruptcy obtains property at the discretion of the trustees and has no right to demand the income as it arises: see *Re Coleman*.

Re Coleman, Henry v Strong (1888) 39 Ch D 443, CA

Facts

A testator by his will directed his trustees to pay the income, after the death of his widow, for the maintenance, education and advancement of his children 'in such manner as they shall deem most expedient until the youngest of the children attains the age of 21 years'. At the time of the death of the widow there were four children, two of whom had attained the age of 21 but the youngest was aged seven years. The trustees shortly afterwards paid each of the adult children one quarter of the income. The eldest son made an absolute assignment for consideration of all his interest under the will to Henry. The trustees declined to pay any funds to Henry who applied to the court for an order requiring the trustees to pay him. He argued that the assignor acquired an interest in possession.

Held

Henry was entitled to no interest in the income except such sums as were paid to the beneficiary and reduced into possession.

Cotton LJ: I am of the opinion that no child has a right to any share of the income. The trustees have a discretion to apply the income for the maintenance of the children in such manner as they think fit. This excludes the notion of the children being entitled to aliquot shares . . . Here no property is given to JS Coleman, but only a discretion to the trustees to apply such part as they think fit of the income for his benefit . . .

However, following an assignment of rights to third parties, any income actually paid to the assignor may be claimed by the assignee or trustee-in-bankruptcy in the capacity as a representative of the assignor vis-à-vis the trust. However, a payment in a non-traceable form by the trustees to another, on behalf of the object of the trust, may not be claimed by the assignee or trustee-in-bankruptcy. This was stated *obiter* by Cotton LJ in *Re Coleman*.

Re Coleman, Henry v Strong (1888) 39 Ch D 443, CA

Cotton LJ: Does the assignment include every benefit which the trustees give to JS Coleman out of income? I think not. If the trustees were to pay an hotel-keeper to give him a dinner he would get nothing but the right to eat a dinner, and that is not property which could pass by assignment or bankruptcy, but if they pay or deliver money or goods to him, or appropriate money or goods to be paid or delivered to him, the money or goods would pass by the assignment.

Group interests

In respect of the collective interest of the totality of objects under a discretionary trust, there seems to exist a discrepancy regarding their interest in trust law and estate duty law (inheritance tax law). In trusts law, if all the objects entitled to both income and capital act in unison and if they are of full age and sound mind, they are entitled to terminate the discretionary trust and acquire the property for their own benefit. This principle is applicable to both exhaustive and non-exhaustive trusts. For example, if trustees hold property on discretionary trust to distribute the income in favour of all or any of a closed group of persons, A, B and C for 21 years and, subject thereto, the capital is held on trust for D. Provided A, B, C and D are of full age and sound mind and are in agreement, they may terminate the trust.

Similarly, it was decided in *Re Smith* that the objects collectively are entitled to assign their interests to a third party. In these circumstances, the third party is entitled to demand the fund from the trustee.

Re Smith, Public Trustee v Aspinall [1928] Ch 915, HC

Facts

In this case, a testator gave one quarter of the residue of his estate to trustees on trust to pay, at their absolute discretion, the income for the maintenance of Mrs Aspinall for life and/or all or any of her children. On the death of Mrs Aspinall, the trustees were required to pay both income and capital, including capitalised income, to the children in equal shares. Mrs Aspinall joined with her two surviving children and the personal representative of her deceased child in executing an assignment of their interest in favour of Legal and General Assurance Company in order to secure a mortgage. The question in issue was whether the trustees were required to pay the income as it arose to the company until the discharge of the mortgage, or whether they were at liberty to pay the income at their discretion to Mrs Aspinall.

Held

The income was payable to the company because the sole objects of the trust were entitled to dispose of the entire income and had disposed of the same to the company:

> **Romer J:** What is to happen where the trustees have a discretion whether they will apply the whole or only a portion of the fund for the benefit of one person, but are obliged to apply the rest of the fund, so far as not applied for the benefit of the first named person, to or for the benefit of a second named person? There, two people together are the sole objects of the discretionary trust and, between them, are entitled to have the whole fund applied to them or for their benefit . . . you treat all the people put together just as though they formed one person, for whose benefit the trustees were directed to apply the whole of a particular fund.

In estate duty law (the same applies in inheritance tax law), all the objects acting collectively are not treated as owning the trust property. Indeed, the objects are treated as owning individual rights that are in competition with each other as distinct from property rights held jointly or in common. This was declared in an *obiter* pronouncement by Lord Reid in *Gartside v Inland Revenue Commissioners*.

Gartside v Inland Revenue Commissioners [1968] AC 553

> **Lord Reid:** Two or more persons cannot have a single right unless they hold it jointly or in common. But clearly objects of a discretionary trust do not have that: they each have individual rights: they are in competition with each other and what the trustees give to one is his alone.

Question

What is the status of objects that are subject to powers of appointment and discretionary trusts?

FURTHER READING

Emery, C, 'The most hallowed principle – certainty of beneficiaries in trusts and powers of appointment' (1982) 98 LQR 551.

Gardner, S, 'Fiduciary powers in Toytown' (1991) 107 LQR 214.

Grbich, Y, '*Baden*: awakening the conceptually moribund trust' (1974) 37 MLR 643.

Grubb, A, 'Powers, trusts and classes of objects – *Re Hay's Settlement*' [1982] Conv 432.

Harris, J, 'Trust, power and duty' (1971) 87 LQR 31.

McKay, L, '*Re Baden* and the third class of certainty' [1974] 38 Conv 269.

Martin, J, 'Casenote on *Mettoy v Pension Trustees Ltd*' [1991] Conv 364.

Sheridan, L, 'Discretionary trusts' (1957) 21 Conv 55.

PROTECTIVE TRUSTS

INTRODUCTION

The settlor may be concerned about protecting the trust property from claims by third parties. He may feel that the beneficiary is, or may become, financially insecure. The settlor may be apprehensive that the beneficiary may surrender the trust funds if he is given control of the equitable interest, or that the trust property may become subject to the claims of his creditors.

In order to avoid such adverse claims the settlor may create:

(a) a discretionary trust with the intended beneficiary as an object of the trust; or

(b) a determinable life interest for the beneficiary, specifying the occasions when the interest will determine. However, in drafting the determining event, the settlor is required to be careful to avoid a conditional interest, ie, an interest subject to a condition subsequent. There is a fine distinction in form between a determinable and conditional interest; or

(c) a protective trust. A standard form protective trust may be created under s 33 of the Trustee Act 1925, but the settlor is entitled to modify the terms of this statutory trust.

There are special limitations enacted under the Insolvency Act 1986 which restrict the power of the settlor to create trusts. If the settlor acts in contravention of these provisions, the trust will be treated as voidable.

DISCRETIONARY TRUSTS

This topic was examined earlier (see Chapter 6 above), but pertinent issues in this context are the nature of the interest of an object under a discretionary trust, the fiduciary nature of the trustees' discretion, the creation of a non-exhaustive discretionary trust, the effect of an assignment of rights under a discretionary trust and the consequence of being a sole object of a discretionary trust.

DETERMINABLE INTERESTS

A determinable interest exists in respect of an estate that *prima facie* is treated as an estate less than an absolute interest in property and denotes the event or events that will determine the interest. On the occurrence of the determining event, the interest ceases or becomes void automatically. There is no need for the settlor or any other person to take steps to enforce the limitation. If no gift over is specified by the draftsman, the settlor could become entitled to the interest by way of a resulting trust, but it is customary for the settlor to indicate in whose favour the gift over will take effect.

For example, S may settle a fund on B for life until he attempts to alienate the interest or becomes bankrupt, with remainder to C absolutely. In this case, a determinable life interest is created in favour of B with a gift over for the benefit of C. If B attempts to alienate his interest, his right of enjoyment terminates automatically and C acquires the absolute interest. Likewise, if B becomes bankrupt, his trustees in bankruptcy acquire nothing in respect of the trust property because B's interest terminates immediately and the gift over takes effect.

Conditional interests

The settlor ought to be wary about creating an interest subject to a condition subsequent as opposed to a determinable interest. The distinction is subtle but significant. A conditional interest is *prima facie* an absolute interest, which is reduced by an event (or events) that has (or have) the effect of terminating the interest. When the relevant condition(s) is (are) satisfied, the interest becomes voidable (as opposed to a determinable interest) and positive steps are required to avoid the interest. Another distinction between a conditional and a determinable interest is that, if the limitation specified in a conditional interest is void (such as being contrary to public policy), the interest takes effect as if the limitation had not been imposed. Thus, the beneficiary may acquire an absolute life interest. Conversely, if the limitation imposed on a determinable interest is treated as void, the interest or estate fails altogether. The intended beneficiary would not acquire an interest. Expressions such as 'on condition that' and 'provided that' have been construed as creating a conditional interest, but words like 'until', 'so long as', 'whilst' or 'during' create determinable interests.

Lord Eldon in *Brandon v Robinson* sought to clarify the distinction between a determinable and conditional interest.

Brandon v Robinson (1811) 18 Ves 429, HL

Lord Eldon: There is no doubt that property may be given to a man until he shall become bankrupt. It is equally clear, generally speaking, that if property is given to a man for his life, the donor cannot take away the incidents to a life estate; and as I have observed, a disposition to a man, until he shall become bankrupt, and after his bankruptcy over, is quite different from an attempt to give to him for his life, with a proviso that he shall not sell or alienate it. If that condition is so expressed as to amount to a limitation, reducing the interest short of a life interest, neither the man nor his assignees can have it beyond the period limited.

Facts

A testator transferred property by will on trust for sale for his children in equal shares. He directed that the share of his son, Thomas, be invested and the income paid to him 'provided that' the income shall not be grantable, assignable or otherwise transferable with a remainder on such occasion. Thomas subsequently became bankrupt. The assignee in bankruptcy claimed the interest on the grounds that a conditional interest was created and the condition was void as against the trustee-in-bankruptcy. The effect was that the interest became absolute and the creditors were entitled.

Held

In favour of the trustee-in-bankruptcy on the ground that the avoidance of the restriction imposed on the interest created an absolute interest. Thus, the creditors of the bankrupt were entitled to the property.

On the other hand, a determinable interest was created in *Rochford v Hackman* which terminated the beneficiary's interest automatically on the occurrence of the event.

Rochford v Hackman (1852) 21 LJ Ch 511, HC

Facts

A testator bequeathed property to trustees to pay the income to the testator's wife for life, with remainder on trust to pay a fourth share of the income to his eldest son for life with remainder to that son's children subject to the direction 'that in case my said wife or any of my said children shall in any manner sell, assign or transfer his or their share in the said dividends, the bequest shall cease as if the same had not been mentioned and as if such person or persons were dead'. After the testator's wife's death, the eldest son became bankrupt. The trustee-in-bankruptcy claimed the son's share.

Held

A determinable interest was created with a valid gift over. The direction in the will operated to determine the son's life interest automatically on his insolvency. The gift over took effect with the result that the trustee-in-bankruptcy became entitled to nothing because the eldest son's share was transferred to his two children:

> **Turner VC:** The court has to collect the intention of the testator from the whole will, looking at the primary disposition for the purpose of seeing to what extent the interest is given and to the ulterior disposition for the purpose of seeing to what extent and in what events the primary disposition is defeated. If there is a limitation over and it meets the events which have occurred, it is plain that the testator did not intend the life interest to continue in that event and it ceases accordingly, but if the limitation over does not meet the events which have occurred, the life interest continues in that event. I am of the opinion that the testator has been made a valid gift over on a determinable event.

Question

How does a determinable interest differ from a conditional interest?

Note

Although a determinable limitation may be imposed in the event of a beneficiary becoming bankrupt, a settlor is not entitled to create a determinable interest for himself for life until bankruptcy *simpliciter* with a remainder over on such occasion. Such a clause is not void *ab initio* but is voidable against the trustee-in-bankruptcy. Accordingly, in *Re Burroughs-Fowler* [1916] 2 Ch 251, where the settlor purported to create a determinable life interest until his bankruptcy and he subsequently became bankrupt, the settlor's interest became vested in his trustee-in-bankruptcy and accrued for the benefit of his creditors.

PROTECTIVE TRUSTS UNDER s 33 OF THE TRUSTEE ACT 1925

A protective trust under s 33(1) of the Trustee Act 1925 involves a determinable life interest in favour of the principal beneficiary and, in the event of a termination or forfeiture of the interest taking place, the establishment of a discretionary trust of the income in favour of a class of objects, including the principal beneficiary, his or her spouse and issue. But if the principal beneficiary has no spouse or issue, the capital and income will be held on discretionary trust in favour of the principal beneficiary and his or her next of kin. This 'ready made' protective trust exists as a device to obviate the risk to the settlor of inadvertently creating a conditional interest instead of a determinable interest.

Trustee Act 1925, s 33(1)

Where any income . . . is directed to be held on protective trusts for the benefit of any person (in this section called 'the principal beneficiary') for the period of his life or for any less period, then, during that period (in this section called the 'trust period') the said income shall . . . be held [on the trusts laid down in s 33(1)(i) and (ii)].

In *Re Wittke* [1944] Ch 166, it was decided that it is unnecessary for the settlor to set out the details of the trust. All that is required is that the settlor manifest an intention to create a protective trust. The model trust under s 33 will be adopted.

In any event, the settlor is entitled to set up his special express protective trust incorporating as much detail as he considers appropriate. Furthermore, s 33(2) entitles the settlor to adopt any variation of the structure of the protective trust as laid down in s 33(1).

For example, the settlor may incorporate the s 33 trust but exclude the discretionary trust that arises when the forfeiture event takes place and substitute a remainder interest of both capital and income in favour of the principal beneficiary's issue or, failing issue, his next of kin.

Trustee Act 1925, s 33(2)

This section . . . has effect subject to any variation of the implied trusts aforesaid contained in the instrument creating the trust.

Section 33(3) enacts what would have been implied in any event, namely, that s 33 does not validate any provision which would be liable to be set aside. Accordingly, a determinable life interest in favour of the settlor is void as against his trustee-in-bankruptcy.

Trustee Act 1925, s 33(3)

Nothing in this section operates to validate any trust which would, if contained in the instrument creating the trust, be liable to be set aside.

Question
What is the effect of creating a protective trust under s 33 of the Trustee Act 1925?

Determining events (forfeiture)

Section 33(1)(i) adopts a broad formula for ascertaining the occasions when the life interest will be determined.

Trustee Act 1925, s 33(1)(i)

. . . when the principal beneficiary does or attempts to do or suffers any act or thing, or until any event happens, other than an advance under any statutory or express power, whereby, if the said income were payable during the trust period to the principal beneficiary . . . he would be deprived of the right to receive the same on any part thereof . . .

It is to be noted that an advancement under an express or statutory power (such as s 32 of the Trustee Act 1925) is excluded from the forfeiting events. An advancement involves the provision of an enduring benefit on behalf of a beneficiary such as the provision of a house or the setting up of a business.

The burden of proving a forfeiture lies on any party who claims that a determining event has taken place. In this respect, the principal beneficiary may rely on a presumption that the forfeiting event has not taken place, until the contrary is proved to the satisfaction of the court.

The determining event formula under s 33 of the Trustee Act 1925 not only includes the acts or omissions of the principal beneficiary, but also circumstances outside his control which deprive him of the right to receive the income under the trust. In *Re Gourju* [1943] Ch 24, the principal beneficiary, an English national, became marooned in German-occupied Nice. The effect was that the income from the trust became payable to the Custodian of Enemy Property under the Trading with the Enemy Act 1939. It was decided that this event triggered a forfeiture of the beneficiary's interest. In *Re Hall* [1944] Ch 46, however, in similar circumstances, there was no forfeiture in respect of a French national who lived in France and was regarded as an 'enemy' under the 1939 Act. It appears that, subject to an express provision to the contrary, a positive act on the part of the beneficiary which is outside the ordinary course of events is required to be done in order to trigger a forfeiture.

Accordingly, the purported sale, gift or other disposition by the principal beneficiary of his interest, as well as his bankruptcy, have the effect of activating the determining event.

Other examples of forfeiting events are:

- *Re Balfour's Settlement* [1938] Ch 928 – the impounding by trustees of part of the income of the principal beneficiary in order to repair a breach of trust instigated by the beneficiary prior to the date of bankruptcy of the beneficiary.
- *Re Baring's Settlement Trust* [1940] Ch 737 – a sequestration order against the beneficiary

following her failure to obey a court order to return her infant children to the jurisdiction of the court.

- *Re Dennis's Settlement Trusts* [1942] Ch 283 – the execution of a deed of variation releasing the principal beneficiary's right to part of the income.

It seems that there is no forfeiture if a representative of the principal beneficiary is appointed in order to look after the beneficiary's interests, as opposed to a transfer of property to a representative for the benefit of another: see *Re Oppenheim's Will Trusts* [1950] Ch 633 – the appointment of a receiver to handle the affairs of the beneficiary, who was certified as a person of unsound mind, did not cause a forfeiture. Likewise, in *Re Westby's Settlement* [1950] Ch 296, fees paid to the receiver, who was appointed in order to represent the interests of a person of unsound mind, did not cause a forfeiture.

Question
What events are capable of triggering a determinable event under s 33 of the Trustee Act 1925?

Section 57 of the Trustee Act 1925 and forfeiture

Section 57 of the Trustee Act 1925 empowers the court to authorise the trustees to perform any act connected with the management and administration of the trust which is not authorised by the trust instrument (such as any sale, lease, mortgage, surrender, release or other disposition, or any purchase, investment, acquisition, expenditure or other transaction) if the court considers it expedient to do so. In the exercise of its power, the court is required to have regard to the interests of all the beneficiaries under the trust, as opposed to any individual beneficiary.

The section had been considered by the court in *Re Mair* as though it had been inserted into every trust with the effect that if the court ordered the trustees to mortgage the principal beneficiary's interest in order to discharge certain pressing liabilities, this event by itself would not cause a forfeiture.

Re Mair [1935] Ch 562, HC

Farwell J: If and when the court sanctions an arrangement or transaction under s 57, it must be taken to have done it as though the power which is being put into operation had been inserted in the trust instrument as an overriding power . . . the forfeiture clause remains attached to the income which is payable to the tenant for life from time to time.

On the other hand, if a scheme is sanctioned by the court and the principal beneficiary fails to comply with the scheme, this omission, by itself, will amount to a forfeiture of the life tenant's interest: see *Re Salting* [1932] 2 Ch 57.

Series of protective trusts

It is possible to create a series of protective trusts at various stages in the beneficiary's life in order to avoid condemning him to a discretionary class of objects for the rest of his life because of an indiscretion during his youth. For example, one protective trust until the beneficiary is 25, another from 25 to 35, a third from 35 to 45 and another for the rest of his life. The effect would be that an indiscretion would not irretrievably condemn the beneficiary to an expectation under a discretionary trust for the rest of his life, but would give him a fresh start on the date of the next protective trust. This policy was adopted in *Re Richardson's Will Trusts*.

Re Richardson's Will Trusts [1958] Ch 504, HC

Facts
A testator bequeathed £2,000 to trustees to hold the income on a s 33 protective trust for the benefit of his grandson, Douglas William Evans, until he reached the age of 35. If, on attaining that age,

the grandson had not attempted to do or suffer any act or thing whereby he became deprived of the right to receive all or part of the income or capital, he would become entitled to the capital absolutely. If, on the other hand, he had made such attempt or sufferance or such event had happened, then he was to receive the income on protective trusts for the rest of his life. Before the grandson attained 35, he became divorced from his wife and an order was made by the court charging his interest with an annual payment of £50 for the benefit of his ex-wife. The grandson reached the age of 35 and 10 months later was adjudicated bankrupt. The trustee-in-bankruptcy claimed the income from the trust fund.

Held

(a) the maintenance order caused a forfeiture of the beneficiary's interest;

(b) as a consequence of the forfeiture, the trustees held the income on the second set of protective trusts.

Accordingly, the act of bankruptcy created a second forfeiture of the income with the result that the discretionary trust was set up. The trustee-in-bankruptcy received nothing from the trust:

> **Danckwerts J:** It seems to me that the effect of the order was to create, or attempt to create, an equitable charge on his interest under the testator's will. When this order was made, if he had been absolutely entitled, he would have been deprived of the right to receive part of the income, because part of the income was to be payable to his former wife to the extent of £50 a year. Consequently, it seems to me that there was a forfeiture at that date; but in any case under the express terms of the will he never succeeded in attaining his absolute interest, and the protective trusts which were to take effect during the rest of his life in accordance with s 33 Trustee Act 1925 came into effect because the direction was, if such event had happened, that the protective trusts were to come into effect. Consequently, I have come to the conclusion that, in the events which have happened in this case, by the time that Douglas William Evans became bankrupt his interest under the will had been forfeited, and a discretionary trust had come into effect. Consequently, the trustee-in-bankruptcy cannot take anything under the testator's will.

However, in the subsequent case, *General Accident Fire and Life Assurance Corp v Inland Revenue Commissioners* [1963] 1 WLR 1207, the Court of Appeal decided that a matrimonial order diverting part of the income belonging to the principal beneficiary in favour of his divorced wife did not cause a forfeiture, because such trusts are deemed to be subject to the order of the court. Although the *General Accident* case has cast some doubt on the *ratio* of *Re Richardson*, it seems that the technique adopted in the latter case is sound and may be explored by draftsmen.

Consequences of forfeiture

Under s 33 of the Trustee Act 1925, on the occasion of the forfeiture of the principal beneficiary's interest a discretionary trust is set up in favour of the principal beneficiary and spouse and issue. If there is no spouse or issue, the class will include the beneficiary's next of kin. It appears that the discretionary trust is of an exhaustive nature, that is, the trustees are required to distribute the income in favour of the objects. Thus, the trustees have no power to accumulate the income: see *Re Gourju's Will Trust* [1943] Ch 24. But the trustees are not required to distribute the income in favour of the principal beneficiary, although they may in the exercise of their discretion distribute to any one or more of the objects. If the trustees distribute income in favour of the principal beneficiary, such funds (*Re Coleman* (1888) 39 Ch D 433, p 123 above) or the surplus, beyond that which is needed for his support (*Re Ashby* [1892] 1 QB 872), may be claimed by the trustee-in-bankruptcy.

Moreover, all the objects of the discretionary trust, if they are *sui juris* and absolutely entitled to the trust property, may get together and terminate the trust or assign the trust property to another: see *Re Smith, Public Trustee v Aspinall* [1928] Ch 915, p 124 above.

VOIDABLE TRUSTS

A voidable trust is one that may be set aside in limited circumstances. In this context, a number of provisions have been enacted which have the effect of upsetting trusts, that is, frustrating the attempts of settlors transferring property beyond the reach of claimants.

But for special provisions to the contrary, a settlor who was about to undertake some hazardous venture would have been entitled to transfer property to his wife and/or children in order to prevent his property being claimed by creditors. There are a number of provisions which have the effect of making such trusts voidable.

Bankruptcy provisions: ss 339–42 of the Insolvency Act 1986

The policy of these provisions is to empower the trustee-in-bankruptcy of a settlor to recover trust property on behalf of the creditors.

Transactions at an undervalue

Section 339 of the Insolvency Act 1986 enables the trustee-in-bankruptcy to apply to the court for relief where a person is adjudicated bankrupt but, during the five years before the presentation of the petition, he had entered into a transaction at an undervalue.

A transaction is at an undervalue if:

(a) it is a gift by the bankrupt;

(b) the bankrupt received no consideration;

(c) the bankrupt entered into the transaction in consideration of marriage; or

(d) the bankrupt received consideration which, in money or money's worth, was significantly less in value than that provided by the bankrupt.

Thus, the creation of a trust (by way of a gratuitous transfer of property to trustees) in favour of the settlor's children within one year prior to the presentation of a petition of bankruptcy may be set aside by the trustee-in-bankruptcy.

The mental state of the bankrupt need not be proved.

Preference of creditors: s 340 of the Insolvency Act 1986

Where an individual is adjudicated bankrupt, but has given a preference to a creditor, surety or guarantor within specified time limits, the trustee-in-bankruptcy may apply to the court for relief.

A transaction is a preference if a debtor:

(a) does anything or suffers anything to be done that has the effect of putting a creditor, surety or guarantor for any of the debts or liabilities into a position which, in the event of his (debtor's) bankruptcy, will be better than if that thing had not been done or suffered; and

(b) was insolvent at the time; and

(c) was influenced by a desire to produce the effect of putting such creditor, etc, into a better position.

A person is insolvent if he cannot from his own resources meet his debts and liabilities as they fall due, or if the value of his assets is less than the amount of his liabilities taking into account protective and contingent liabilities (s 341(3)).

A preferential transaction in favour of an associate of the bankrupt is presumed to be influenced by a desire of putting such creditor into a better position until the contrary is proved (s 340(5)).

An associate is exhaustively defined in s 435 and includes relatives of the bankrupt or spouse, as well as partners, employers, employees and related companies.

The time limits are defined in s 341. In the case of a preference with a non-associate and not at an undervalue, the period is six months. In the case of a preference in favour of an associate, the period is two years before the petition of bankruptcy.

In respect of proceedings under ss 339 and 340, the court may make such order as it thinks fit for restoring the position to what it would have been if the bankrupt had not entered the transaction. However, the court's power of redress does not affect two categories of third parties, namely:

(a) any bona fide transferee for value without notice of the relevant circumstances who acquires the property from another but who in turn acquired such property as a party to the undervalue or preference; and

(b) any person receiving a benefit in good faith for value without notice of the relevant circumstances.

Transactions defrauding creditors: ss 423–25 of the Insolvency Act 1986

The policy of these sections is designed to upset transactions at an undervalue for the purpose:

(a) of putting assets beyond the reach of a person who is making, or may at some time make, a claim against him (the transferor); or

(b) of otherwise prejudicing the interests of such a person in relation to the claim which he is making or may make.

The section is wider than s 339 in the sense that there is no time limit (such as five years before the presentation of the bankruptcy petition) attaching to the transactions which may be upset. In addition, the claim for relief is not dependent on the solvency of the party entering into the impugned transaction. But s 423 is subject to the limitation that the transaction entered into must have been at an undervalue. Thus, the court has no jurisdiction if the transaction was entered into for valuable and adequate consideration even if the transferee is aware that it was entered into with the intention of prejudicing the interest of creditors.

The court is entitled to make such order as it thinks fit for:

(a) restoring the position to what it would have been if the transaction had not been entered into; and

(b) protecting the interests of persons who are victims of the transaction.

Insolvency Act 1986, s 423

(1) This section relates to transactions entered into at an undervalue; and a person enters into such a transaction with another person if –

    (a) he makes a gift to the other person or he otherwise enters into a transaction with the other on terms that provide for him to receive no consideration;

    (b) he enters into a transaction with the other in consideration of marriage; or

    (c) he enters into a transaction with the other for a consideration the value of which, in money or money's worth, is significantly less than the value, in money or money's worth, of the consideration provided by himself.

(2) Where a person has entered into such transaction, the court may . . . make such order as it thinks fit for:

    (a) restoring the position to what it would have been if the transaction had not been entered into; and

    (b) protecting the interests of persons who are victims of the transaction.

(3) In the case of a person entering into such a transaction, an order shall only be made if the court is satisfied that it was entered into by him for the purpose:

(a) of putting assets beyond the reach of a person who is making, or may at some time make, a claim against him; or

(b) of otherwise prejudicing the interests of such a person in relation to the claim which he is making or may make.

Section 436 defines a 'transaction' as 'including a gift, agreement or arrangement ...'. In *Agricultural Mortgage Corp plc v Woodward* (1994) *The Times*, 30 May, it was decided that the creation of a tenancy of a farm in favour of the wife of the transferor in order to defeat the claims of creditors would be set aside at the instance of the creditors.

Question
What is the policy of enacting ss 339–42 and 423–25 of the Insolvency Act 1986?

FURTHER READING

Furey, N, 'Bankruptcy and the family – the effect of the Insolvency Act 1986' [1987] 17 Family Law 316.

Potterton, R and Cullen, S, 'Transactions at an undervalue' (1994) 138 SJ 710.

Williams, G, 'The doctrine of repugnancy – conditions in gifts' (1943) 59 LQR 343.

RESULTING TRUSTS

INTRODUCTION

A resulting trust is created by the court in favour of the settlor or transferor. This trust arises whenever the location of the equitable interest in property is so unclear that no other person is capable of making out a successful claim to the property. The occasions that give rise to the resulting trust may be classified into two broad categories:

(a) automatic; and

(b) presumed.

An automatic resulting trust springs back in favour of the settlor/transferor simply because it cannot be acquired by anyone else. Thus, a transfer to a trustee subject to a condition precedent which fails to materialise gives rise to a resulting trust.

A presumed resulting trust arises whenever property is purchased, or a voluntary transfer of the legal title is made, in the name of another, or others. If the purchase or transfer is silent as to the location of the equitable title, a presumed resulting trust arises. In exceptional circumstances, an alternative presumption arises in favour of the transferee, called a presumption of advancement. These are occasions when a specially defined relationship exists between the transferor and transferee. The legal owner is presumed to be the equitable owner. Both presumptions – resulting trusts and advancements – may be rebutted by evidence as to the real intention of the purchaser or transferor. This is the position even if the evidence takes the form of an intention to pursue an unlawful transaction that was not carried out.

AXIOMATIC

An express trust arises out of the settlor's or testator's express intention. As we have seen, subject to any formalities imposed by statute, this intention may be expressed wholly or partly, orally or by conduct, or in writing. In order to ascertain the terms of the trust (such as the beneficiaries and their interests, the trust property and the trustees), the court is required to construe the evidence which manifests the intention of the creator of the trust.

By way of contrast, a resulting trust is implied by equity in favour of the settlor, or his estate if he is dead. Such trust arises by virtue of the unexpressed or implied intention of the settlor or testator. The settlor or his estate becomes the beneficial owner under the resulting trust. It is as though the settlor had retained a residual interest in the property, albeit implied or created by the courts. The expression, 'resulting trust', derives from the Latin verb, *resultare*, meaning to spring back (in effect, to the original owner). Examples are the transfer of property subject to a condition precedent which cannot be achieved, or the creation of an express trust which becomes void. In these circumstances, the legal owner or transferee holds the property on trust for the settlor or his estate: see *Vandervell v Inland Revenue Commissioners* (see p 23 above).

In *Re Vandervell's Trusts (No 2)*, Megarry J classified resulting trusts into two categories, namely, 'automatic' and 'presumed' (although his decision was reversed by the Court of Appeal). Automatic resulting trusts arise where the beneficial interest under an express trust remains undisposed of. Such trusts arise in order to fill a gap of ownership. The equitable or beneficial interest cannot exist in the air and ought to remain with the settlor. The 'presumed' resulting trust arises, in the absence of evidence to the contrary, when property is purchased in the name of another, or property is voluntarily transferred to another, for example, A purchases property which is conveyed in the name of B, or A transfers property to B. In these circumstances, B *prima facie* holds the property on trust for A.

Re Vandervell's Trusts (No 2) [1974] 1 All ER 47, HC

Megarry J: It seems to me that the relevant points on resulting trusts may be put in a series of propositions . . . The propositions are the broadest generalisations, and do not purport to cover the exceptions and qualifications that doubtless exist. Nevertheless, these generalisations at least provide a starting point for the classification of a corner of equity which might benefit from some attempt at classification. The propositions are as follows:

(1) if a transaction fails to make any effective disposition of any interest it does nothing. This is so at law and in equity, and has nothing to do with resulting trusts;

(2) normally the mere existence of some unexpressed intention in the breast of the owner of the property does nothing: there must at least be some expression of that intention before it can effect any result. To yearn is not to transfer;

(3) before any doctrine of resulting trust can come into play, there must at least be some effective transaction which transfers or creates some interest in property;

(4) where A effectually transfers to B (or creates in his favour) any interest in any property, whether legal or equitable, a resulting trust for A may arise in two distinct classes of case. For simplicity, I shall confine my statement to cases in which the transfer or creation is made without B providing any valuable consideration, and where no presumption of advancement can arise; and I shall state the position for transfers without specific mention of new interests:

   (a) the first class of case is where the transfer to B is not made on any trust. If, of course, it appears from the transfer that B is intended to hold on certain trusts, that will be decisive, and the case is not within this category; and similarly if it appears that B is intended to take beneficially. But in other cases there is a rebuttable presumption that B holds on a resulting for A. The question is not one of the automatic consequences of a dispositive failure by A, but one of presumption: the property has been carried to B, and from the absence of consideration and any presumption of advancement, B is presumed not only to hold the entire interest on trust, but also to hold the beneficial interest for A absolutely. The presumption thus establishes both that B is to take on trust and also what that trust is. Such resulting trust may be called 'presumed resulting trusts';

   (b) the second class of case is where the transfer to B is made on trusts which some or all of the beneficial interest undisposed of. Here B automatically holds on resulting trust for A to the extent that the beneficial interest has not been carried to him or others. The resulting trust here does not depend on any intentions or presumptions, but is the automatic consequence of A's failure to dispose of what is vested in him. Since *ex hypothesi* the transfer is on trust, the resulting trust does not establish the trust but merely carries back to A the beneficial interest that has not been disposed of. Such resulting trusts may be called 'automatic resulting trusts';

(5) where trustees hold property in trust for A, and it is they who, at A's direction, make the transfer to B, similar principles apply, even though on the face of the transaction the transferor appears to be the trustee and not A. If the transfer to B is on trust, B will hold any beneficial interest that has not been effectually disposed of on an automatic resulting trust for the true transferor, A. If the transfer to B is not on trust, there will be a rebuttable presumption that B holds on a resulting trust for A.

Note

This classification was doubted by Lord Browne-Wilkinson in *Westdeutsche Landesbank v Islington BC* (see p 177 below).

AUTOMATIC RESULTING TRUSTS

The policy which underpins this type of resulting trust involves the destination of the beneficial interest when the instrument creating the trust is silent as to the application of the equitable interest. The resulting trust arises in a variety of situations such as the failure of an express trust, or the transfer of property to trustees without specifying the terms of the trust, or where the transfer of property is made subject to a condition precedent which is incapable of being fulfilled, or where the trust exhausts only some of the trust property. Indeed, it may be possible to classify the occasions which give rise to an automatic resulting trust into two categories, namely:

(a) transfers subject to conditions precedent that have failed to occur; and

(b) the destination of a surplus of trust funds.

Transfers subject to conditions precedent

Where the transfer of property is made subject to a condition precedent which has not been achieved, the transferee is required to re-transfer the property back to the original owner. This result is based on the assumption that the foundation on which the transfer or trust was made did not materialise. The transferee is treated as a trustee on behalf of the original transferor or his estate. This is illustrated by *Re Ames*.

Re Ames' Settlement [1946] Ch 217, HC

Facts

A settlor transferred £10,000 to trustees in consideration of the marriage of his son on trust for the parties to the marriage for life, with remainder to the issue of the marriage absolutely. The marriage ceremony was a nullity for the son was already validly married.

Held

A resulting trust for the settlor's estate had arisen owing to the failure of the condition precedent:

> **Vaisey J:** It seems to me that the claim of the executors of the settlor must succeed. I think that the case is, having regard to the wording of the settlement, a simple case of money paid on a consideration which failed. I do not think that that hypothetical class of next of kin (who were only brought in, so to speak, and given an interest in the fund on the basis and footing that there was going to be a valid marriage between John Ames and Miss Hamilton) have really any merits in equity, and I do not see how they can claim under the express terms of a document which, so far as regards the persons with whom the marriage consideration was concerned, has utterly and completely failed. If their claim be good, it is difficult to see at what precise period of time their interest became an interest in possession. But I hold that their claim is not good, and that they have not been able to establish it.

Specific loan transactions

Similarly, where funds are paid to a borrower in order to advance a specific purpose, to such an extent that the funds do not become the general property of the borrower, and the purpose of the loan has not been achieved, the funds become subject to a resulting trust in favour of the lender. Accordingly, the borrower's trustee-in-bankruptcy or assignee of the debtor, with notice of the stipulated purpose, takes the property subject to the trust: see *Barclays Bank v Quistclose*.

Barclays Bank Ltd v Quistclose Investments Ltd [1970] AC 567, HL

Facts

The defendant, Quistclose Ltd (Q Ltd), loaned £209,719 to Rolls Razors Ltd (R Ltd) on the agreed condition that the latter would use the money to pay a dividend to its shareholders. Q Ltd's cheque for the relevant sum was sent to R Ltd with a covering letter dated 15 July 1964 which reiterated the purpose of the loan thus, 'We would like to confirm the agreement reached with you this morning that this amount will only be used to meet the dividend due'. Q Ltd's cheque was paid into a separate account opened specifically for this purpose with Barclays Bank Ltd which knew of the purpose of the loan.

Before the dividend was paid, R Ltd went into voluntary liquidation and Barclays Bank Ltd claimed the amount to set off against the overdrafts on R Ltd's other account at the bank.

Held

The terms of the loan were such as to impress on the money a trust in favour of Q Ltd, in the event of the dividend remaining unpaid. Further, Barclays had notice of the nature of the loan and it was not entitled to set off the amount against R Ltd's overdraft:

Lord Wilberforce: Two questions arise, both of which must be answered favourably to the respondents if they are to recover the money from the appellants. The first is whether, as between the respondents and Rolls Razor Ltd, the terms on which the loan was made were such as to impress on the sum of £209,719 a trust in their favour in the event of the dividend not being paid. The second is whether, in that event, the appellants had such notice of the trust or of the circumstances giving rise to it as to make the trust binding on them.

It is not difficult to establish precisely on what terms the money was advanced by the respondents to Rolls Razor Ltd. There is no doubt that the loan was made specifically in order to enable Rolls Razor Ltd to pay the dividend. There is equally, in my opinion, no doubt that the loan was made only so as to enable Rolls Razor Ltd to pay the dividend and for no other purpose. This follows quite clearly from the terms of the letter of Rolls Razor Ltd to the appellants of 15 July 1964, which letter, before transmission to the appellants, was sent to the respondents under open cover in order that the cheque might be (as it was) enclosed in it. The mutual intention of the respondents and of Rolls Razor Ltd and the essence of the bargain, was that the sum advanced should not become part of the assets of Rolls Razor Ltd but should be used exclusively for payment of a particular class of its creditors, namely, those entitled to the dividend. A necessary consequence from this, by process simply of interpretation, must be that if, for any reason, the dividend could not be paid, the money was to be returned to the respondents: the word 'only' or 'exclusively' can have no other meaning or effect.

That arrangements of this character for the payment of a person's creditors by a third person, give rise to a relationship of a fiduciary character or trust, in favour, as a primary trust, of the creditors, and secondarily, if the primary trust fails, of the third person, has been recognised in a series of decisions over some 150 years.

[His Lordship then reviewed some of the authorities on the point such as *Toovey v Milne* (1819) 2 B & Ald 683; *Edwards v Glynn* (1859) 2 E & E 29; *Re Rogers ex p Holland and Hannen* (1891) 8 Morr 243; *Re Drucker (No 1) ex p Basden* [1902] 2 KB 237; and *Re Hooley ex p Trustees* (1915) 84 LJKB 181; and continued:] These cases have the support of longevity, authority, consistency and, I would add, good sense. But they are not binding on your Lordships and it is necessary to consider such arguments as have been put why they should be departed from or distinguished.

It is said, first, that the line of authorities mentioned above stands on its own and is consistent with other, more modern, decisions. Those are cases in which money has been paid to a company for the purpose of obtaining an allotment of shares (see *Moseley v Cressey's Co* (1865) LR 1 Eq 405; *Stewart v Austin* (1866) LR 3 Eq 299; *Re Nanwa Gold Mines Ltd, Ballantyne v Nanwa Gold Mines Ltd* [1955] 3 All ER 219). I do not think it necessary to examine these cases in detail, nor to comment on them, for I am satisfied that they do not affect the principle on which this appeal should be decided. They are merely examples which show that, in the absence of some special arrangement creating a trust (as was shown to exist in *Re Nanwa Gold Mines Ltd*), payments of this kind are made on the basis that they are to be included in the company's assets. They do not negative the proposition that a trust may exist where the mutual intention is that they should not be included.

The second, and main, argument for the appellants was of a more sophisticated character. The transaction, it was said, between the respondents and Rolls Razor Ltd, was one of loan, giving rise to a legal action of debt. This necessarily excluded the implication of any trust, enforceable in equity, in the respondents' favour: a transaction may attract one action or the other, it could not admit of both.

My Lords, I must say that I find this argument unattractive. Let us see what it involves. It means that the law does not permit an arrangement to be made by which one person agrees to advance money to another, on terms that the money is to be used exclusively to pay debts of the latter, and if, and so far as not so used, rather than becoming a general asset of the latter available to his creditors at large, is to be returned to the lender. The lender is obliged, in such a case, because he is a lender, to accept, whatever the mutual wishes of lender and borrower may be, that the money he was willing to make available for one purpose only shall be freely available for others of the borrower's creditors for whom he has not the slightest desire to provide.

There is surely no difficulty in recognising the co-existence in one transaction of legal and equitable rights and remedies: when the money is advanced, the lender acquires an equitable right to see that it is applied for the primary designated purpose ... when the purpose has been carried out (ie, the debt paid) the lender has his remedy against the borrower in debt: if the primary purpose cannot be carried out, the question arises if a secondary purpose (ie, repayment to the lender) has been agreed, expressly or by implication: if it has, the remedies of equity may be invoked to give effect to it, if it has not (and the money is intended to fall within the general fund of the debtor's assets) then there is the appropriate remedy for recovery of the loan. I can appreciate no reason why the flexible interplay of law and equity cannot let these practical arrangements, and other variations if desired: it would be to the discredit of both systems if they could not. In the present case *the intention to create a secondary trust for the benefit of the lender, to arise if the primary trust, to pay the dividend, could not be carried out, is clear* and I can find no reason why the law should not give effect to it [emphasis added] ...

I pass to the second question, that of notice ... It is common ground, and I think right, that a mere request to put the money into a separate account is not sufficient to constitute notice. But on 15 July 1964, the appellants, when they received the cheque, also received the covering letter of that date ... Previously there had been a telephone conversation between Mr Goldbart and Mr Parker, to which I have also referred. From these there is no doubt that the appellants were told that the money had been provided on loan by a third person and was to be used only for the purpose of paying the dividend. This was sufficient to give them notice that it was trust money and not assets of Rolls Razor Ltd: the fact, if it be so, that they were unaware of the lenders' identity (though the respondents' name as drawers was on the cheque) is of no significance.

Note

Lord Wilberforce in *Barclays Bank v Quistclose* reasoned that the specific loan created a primary trust to pay a dividend. Is this an express or implied trust? If it is an intended express trust, is it a purpose trust? See Millett, P, 'The Quistclose trust: who can enforce it?' (1985) 101 LQR 269. See also Lord Millett's analysis of the *Quistclose* trust in *Twinsectra v Yardley* [2002] UKHL 12 (see p 143 et sec below).

Similarly, in *R v Common Professional Examination Board ex p Mealing-McCleod*, the Court of Appeal decided that a *Quistclose* trust was created where a specific loan from Lloyds Bank was made to the borrower for the purpose of security for costs and subject thereto, to be held on trust for the lender.

R v Common Professional Examination Board ex p Mealing-McCleod (2000) The Times, 2 May

Facts

The career of Sally Mealing-McCleod (the applicant), as a student at the Bar, had been dogged by disputes and litigation involving educational institutions and the Common Professional Board (the Board). The first proceedings were against Wolseley Hall and Oxford and Middlesex Universities in which the Board was joined as a third party. The cause of action was breach of contract. In those proceedings, a number of orders for costs were made against her. The applicant sought judicial review of two decisions of the Board made between 8 April 1997 and 15 July 1997. The effect of these decisions was that the applicant had not qualified for, or was not eligible for, the Bar Vocational Course. The Board declared that it would decline to give the applicant a certificate if she obtained the diploma for which she was studying. Sedley J refused the application. The Court of Appeal granted leave to appeal provided that the applicant gave security for costs in the sum of £6,000. The applicant complied with the order by borrowing £6,000 from Lloyds Bank. The loan agreement with the bank provided in clause 2(c) that: 'You must use the cash loan for the purpose specified ... You will hold that loan, or any part of it, on trust for us until you have used it for this purpose.' The money was paid into court on 21 December 1998. On 18 February 1999, the appeal was withdrawn because the Board conceded that the applicant was entitled to apply for a place on the Bar Vocational Course. The applicant sought to recover the sum paid into court on the ground that the money was subject to a trust in favour of the bank. Hidden J refused the application and ordered that the £6,000 and interest should be paid to the Board. The applicant appealed.

Held

Allowing the appeal, the court ordered that the relevant sum be paid to the bank. The nature of the loan and the surrounding circumstances created a *Quistclose* trust in respect of the purpose of the loan. The effect was that since the primary purpose of the loan was not carried out, a resulting trust for the lender was created.

In *Carreras Rothmans Ltd*, Peter Gibson J reasoned that where there is a common intention between the lender and borrower to make a loan for a specific purpose, to such an extent that the *conscience of the borrower* is affected by the loan, the *Quistclose* principle becomes operative.

Carreras Rothmans Ltd v Freeman Matthews Treasure Ltd [1984] 3 WLR 1016, HC

Facts

Carreras Rothmans Ltd (CR), a cigarettes and tobacco manufacturer, contracted with Freeman Matthews Treasure Ltd (FMT), an advertising agency, to manage the advertising side of its business. CR paid FMT on a monthly basis. Such fees were paid not only in respect of FMT's services but also in discharge of FMT's liabilities to media creditors. In 1983, FMT found itself in financial difficulties. CR, fearing the adverse implications on its business dealings if FMT were to collapse, made a special agreement with FMT to pay the latter's monthly invoices. In July 1983, CR agreed with FMT that a special bank account should be established in FMT's name, to be used 'only for the purposes of meeting the accounts of the media and production fees of third parties directly attributable to CR's involvement with the agency'. The bank was aware of this agreement. On 26 July 1983, CR paid £597,128 into the special account. On 3 August 1983, FMT went into liquidation. The media creditors called upon CR to meet FMT's liabilities in full. CR complied with their demands and took assignments from the media creditors of their rights against FMT. The liquidator of FMT refused to pay any moneys out of the special account. CR claimed a declaration that the moneys in the special account were held on trust for the sole purpose of paying FMT's fees and media creditors, and ought to be repaid to CR.

Held

The moneys in the special account were subject to a trust in favour of CR:

Peter Gibson J: The objective [of the plaintiff] was accurately described by Mr Higgs in his informal letter of 19 July as to protect the interests of the plaintiff and the third parties. For this purpose a special account was to be set up with a special designation. The moneys payable by the plaintiff were to be paid not to the defendant beneficially but directly into that account so that the defendant was never free to deal as it pleased with the moneys so paid. The moneys were to be used only for the specific purpose of paying the third parties and as the cheque letter indicated, the amount paid matched the specific invoices presented by the defendant to the plaintiff. The account was intended to be little more than a conduit pipe, but the intention was plain that whilst in the conduit pipe the moneys should be protected. There was even a provision covering the possibility (though what actual situation it was intended to meet it is hard to conceive) that there might be a balance left after payment and in that event the balance was to be paid to the plaintiff and not kept by the defendant. It was thus clearly intended that the moneys once paid would never become the property of the defendant. That was the last thing the plaintiff wanted in view of its concern about the defendant's financial position. As a further precaution the bank was to be put on notice of the conditions and purpose of the account. I infer that this was to prevent the bank attempting to exercise any rights of set off against the moneys in the account.

In my judgment the principle . . . is that *equity fastens on the conscience of the person who receives from another property transferred for a specific purpose only and not therefore for the recipient's own purposes, so that such person will not be permitted to treat the property as his own or to use it for other than the stated purpose.* Most of the cases in this line are cases where there has been an agreement for consideration so that in one sense each party has contributed to providing the property. But if the common intention is that property is transferred for a specific purpose and not so as to become the property of the transferee, the transferee cannot keep the property if for any reason that purpose cannot be fulfilled. I am left in no doubt that the provider of the moneys in the present case was the plaintiff. True it is that its own witnesses said that if the defendant had not agreed to the terms of the contract letter, the plaintiff would not have broken its contract but would have paid its debt to the defendant, but the fact remains that the plaintiff made its payment on the terms of that letter and the defendant received the moneys only for the stipulated purpose. That purpose was expressed to relate only to the moneys in the account. In my judgment therefore the plaintiff can be equated with the lender in *Quistclose* as having an enforceable right to compel the carrying out of the primary trust [emphasis added].

Note

Peter Gibson J's analysis in *Carreras Rothmans* of the rights of the lender appears to be based on a much broader footing than Lord Wilberforce's analysis in the *Quistclose* case. Peter Gibson's reasoning appears to be consistent with a constructive trust. This has the advantage of avoiding the difficulties posed by the express trust analysis and the limitations concerning the beneficiary principle.

In *Re EVTR*, the court decided that a loan made for a specific purpose imposed a constructive trust on the borrower. However, if only part of the sum borrowed was used for the stated purpose the remaining part of the fund, not so applied, was required to be held on resulting trust for the lender.

Re EVTR [1987] BCLC 646, CA

Facts

The claimant won £240,000 on premium bonds. He decided to assist the company that employed him by purchasing new equipment. He deposited £60,000 with the company's solicitors to be released to the company 'for the sole purpose of buying new equipment'. The sum was paid into the company's general funds. The new equipment was ordered but before it was delivered the company went into receivership. £48,536 of the £60,000 was returned to the company. The claimant alleged that this sum was repayable to him.

Held

The claim was allowed under the *Quistclose* principles and the sum was held on resulting trust:

Dillon LJ: [After reviewing the *Quistclose* principle declared:] . . . I have no doubt, in the light of *Quistclose*, that if the company had gone into liquidation, or the receivers had been appointed, and the scheme had become abortive before the £60,000 had been disbursed by the company, the appellant would have been entitled to recover his full £60,000, as between himself and the company, on the footing that it was impliedly held by the company as a resulting trust for him as the particular of the loan had failed.

At the other end of the spectrum, if after the £60,000 had been expended by the company . . . there could be no doubt that the appellant's only right would have been as an unsecured creditor of the company for the £60,000 . . .

The present case lies on its facts between those two extremes of the spectrum . . .

On *Quistclose* principles, a resulting trust in favour of the provider of the money arises when money is provided for a particular purpose only, and that purpose fails . . . It is a long established principle of Equity that, if a person who is a trustee receives money or property because of, or in respect of, trust property, *he will hold what he receives as a constructive trustee on the trusts of the original trust property.* It follows, in my judgment, that the repayments made to the receivers are subject to the *same trusts as the original £60,000* in the hands of the company. There is now, of course, no question of the £48,536 being applied in the purchase of new equipment for the company, and accordingly, in my judgment, *it is now held on a resulting trust for the [claimant]* [emphasis added]

Question

To what extent has Dillon LJ in *Re EVTR* clarified the status of the *Quistclose* trust?

Analysis of a Quistclose trust in Twinsectra Ltd v Yardley

Twinsectra v Yardley [2002] 2 All ER 377, HL

Lord Millett reviewed Lord Wilberforce's speech in the *Quistclose* case and affirmed that the circumstances gave rise to a trust. The lender had impressed the sum loaned with a trust by depriving the borrower of the right to use the funds as it wished. However, a general loan of money does not create the relationship of trustee and beneficiary. Likewise, payments in advance for goods do not create a trust relationship:

> **Lord Millett:** A *Quistclose* trust does not necessarily arise merely because money is paid for a particular purpose. A lender will often inquire into the purpose for which a loan is sought in order to decide whether he would be justified in making it. He may be said to lend the money for the purpose in question, but this is not enough to create a trust; once lent the money is at the free disposal of the borrower. Similarly payments in advance for goods or services are paid for a particular purpose, but such payments do not ordinarily create a trust. The money is intended to be at the free disposal of the supplier and may be used as part of his cash flow. Commercial life would be impossible if this were not the case.
>
> The question in every case is whether the parties intended the money to be at the free disposal of the recipient: *In Re Goldcorp Exchange Ltd* [1995] 1 AC 74, 100 *per* Lord Mustill. His freedom to dispose of the money is necessarily excluded by an arrangement that the money shall be used exclusively for the stated purpose.

Fiduciary relationship between borrower and lender

Lord Millett in *Twinsectra* decided that the borrower's duties in *Quistclose* were fiduciary and not merely contractual. The lender, by specifying the obligation to use the funds for a specific purpose, created a relationship of confidence.

Twinsectra v Yardley [2002] 2 All ER 377, HL

> **Lord Millett:** It is unconscionable for a man to obtain money on terms as to its application and then disregard the terms on which he received it. Such conduct goes beyond a mere breach of contract. As North J explained in *Gibert v Gonard* (1884) 54 LJ Ch 439, 440:
>
> > It is very well known law that if one person makes a payment to another for a certain purpose, and that person takes the money knowing that it is for that purpose, he must apply it to the purpose for which it was given. He may decline to take it if he likes; but if he chooses to accept the money tendered for a particular purpose, it is his duty, and there is a legal obligation on him, to apply it for that purpose.
>
> The duty is not contractual but fiduciary. It may exist despite the absence of any contract at all between the parties, as in *Rose v Rose* (1986) 7 NSWLR 679; and it binds third parties as in the *Quistclose* case itself. The duty is fiduciary in character because a person who makes money available on terms that it is to be used for a particular purpose only and not for any other purpose thereby places his trust and confidence in the recipient to ensure that it is properly applied. This is a classic situation in which a fiduciary relationship arises, and since it arises in respect of a specific fund it gives rise to a trust.

Resulting trust for lender

Lord Wiberforce in *Quistclose* decided that two successive trusts were created on the facts – a 'primary trust' for the shareholders and a 'secondary trust' for the lender arising on the failure of the primary trust. Lord Millett in *Twinsectra* considered the location of the beneficial interest pending the application of the funds for the stated purpose, or the failure of the purpose. He considered that there were four possibilities regarding the destination of the equitable interest. These are: (i) in the lender; (ii) in the borrower; (iii) in the contemplated beneficiary; or (iv) in suspense. After considering the merits of each case, he decided that, on balance, the equitable interest ought to belong to the lender by way of a resulting trust.

Twinsectra v Yardley [2002] 2 All ER 377, HL

> **Lord Millett:** (i). The lender: In 'The Quistclose Trust: Who Can Enforce It?' (1985) 101 LQR, 269, I argued that the beneficial interest remained throughout in the lender. This analysis has received considerable though not universal academic support: see for example Priestley J 'The Romalpa Clause and the Quistclose Trust' in *Equity and Commercial Transactions*, ed Finn (1987) 217, 237; and Professor M Bridge 'The Quistclose Trust in a World of

Secured Transactions' (1992) 12 OJLS 333, 352; and others. It was adopted by the New Zealand Court of Appeal in *General Communications Ltd v Development Finance Corporation of New Zealand Ltd* [1990] 3 NZLR 406 and referred to with apparent approval by Gummow J in *In re Australian Elizabethan Theatre Trust* (1991) 102 ALR 681. Gummow J saw nothing special in the *Quistclose* trust, regarding it as essentially a security device to protect the lender against other creditors of the borrower pending the application of the money for the sated purpose.

On this analysis, the *Quistclose* trust is a simple commercial arrangement akin (as Professor Bridge observes) to a retention of title clause (though with a different object) which enables the borrower to have recourse to the lender's money for a particular purpose without entrenching on the lender's property rights more than necessary to enable the purpose to be achieved. The money remains the property of the lender unless and until it is applied in accordance with his directions, and insofar as it is not so applied it must be returned to him. I am disposed, perhaps pre-disposed, to think that this is the only analysis which is consistent both with orthodox trust law and with commercial reality. Before reaching a concluded view that it should be adopted, however, I must consider the alternatives.

(ii). *The borrower.* It is plain that the beneficial interest is not vested unconditionally in the borrower so as to leave the money at his free disposal. That would defeat the whole purpose of the arrangements, which is to prevent the money from passing to the borrower's trustee-in-bankruptcy in the event of his insolvency.

(iii). *In the contemplated beneficiary.* In the *Quistclose* case itself [1970] AC 567, as in all the reported cases which preceded it, either the primary purpose had been carried out and the contest was between the borrower's trustee-in bankruptcy or liquidator and the person or persons to whom the borrower had paid the money; or it was treated as having failed, and the contest was between the borrower's trustee-in-bankruptcy and the lender. It was not necessary to explore the position while the primary purpose was still capable of being carried out and Lord Wilberforce's observations must be read in that light.

The question whether the primary trust is accurately described as a trust for the creditors first arose in *In re Northern Developments Holdings Ltd* (unreported) 6 October 1978, where the contest was between the lender and the creditors. The borrower, which was not in liquidation and made no claim to the money, was the parent company of a group one of whose subsidiaries was in financial difficulty. There was a danger that if it were wound up or ceased trading it would bring down the whole group. A consortium of the group's banks agreed to put up a fund of more than £500,000 in an attempt to rescue the subsidiary. They paid the money into a special account in the name of the parent company for the express purpose of 'providing money for the subsidiary's unsecured creditors over the ensuing weeks' and for no other purpose. The banks' object was to enable the subsidiary to continue trading, though on a reduced scale; it failed when the subsidiary was put into receivership at a time when some £350,000 remained unexpended. Relying on Lord Wilberforce's observations in the passages cited above, Sir Robert Megarry V-C held that the primary trust was a purpose trust enforceable (*inter alia*) by the subsidiaries' creditors as the persons for whose benefit the trust was created.

There are several difficulties with this analysis. In the first place, Lord Wilberforce's reference to *In re Rogers* (1891) 8 Morr 243 makes it plain that *the equitable right he had in mind was not a mandatory order to compel performance, but a negative injunction to restrain improper application of the money;* for neither Lindley LJ nor Kay LJ recognised more than this. In the second place, the object of the arrangements was to enable the subsidiary to continue trading, and this would necessarily involve it in incurring further liabilities to trade creditors. Accordingly the application of the fund was not confined to existing creditors at the date when the fund was established. The company secretary was given to understand that the purpose of the arrangements was to keep the subsidiary trading, and that the fund was 'as good as share capital'. Thus the purpose of the arrangements was not, as in other cases, to enable the debtor to avoid bankruptcy by paying off existing creditors, but to enable the debtor to continue trading by providing it with working capital with which to incur fresh liabilities. There is a powerful argument for saying that the result of the arrangements was to vest a beneficial interest in the subsidiary from the start. If so, then this was not a *Quistclose* trust at all [emphasis added].

In the third place, it seems unlikely that the banks' object was to benefit the creditors (who included the Inland Revenue) except indirectly. The banks had their own commercial interests to protect by enabling the subsidiary to trade out of its difficulties. If so, then the primary trust cannot be supported as a valid non-charitable purpose trust: see *In re Grant's Will Trusts* [1980] 1 WLR 360 and cf *In Re Denley's Trust Deed* [1969] 1 Ch 373.

The most serious objection to this approach is exemplified by the facts of the present case. In several of the cases the primary trust was for an abstract purpose with no one but the lender to enforce performance or restrain misapplication of the money. In *Edwards v Glyn* (1859) 2 E & E the money was advanced to a bank to enable the bank to meet a run. In *In Re EVTR, Gilbert v Barber* [1987] BCLC 646 it was advanced 'for the sole purpose of buying new equipment'. In *General Communications Ltd v Development Finance Corporation of New Zealand Ltd* [1990] 3 NZLR 406 the money was paid to the borrower's solicitors for the express purpose of purchasing new equipment. The present case is another example. *It is simply not possible to hold money on trust to acquire unspecified property from an unspecified vendor at an unspecified time.* There is no reason to make an arbitrary distinction between money paid for an abstract purpose and money paid for a purpose which can be said to benefit an ascertained class of beneficiaries, and the cases rightly draw no such distinction. Any analysis of the *Quistclose* trust must be able to accommodate gifts and loans for an abstract purpose [emphasis added].

(iv). In suspense. As Peter Gibson J pointed out in *Carreras Rothmans Ltd v Freeman Matthews Treasure Ltd* [1985] Ch 207, 223 the effect of adopting Sir Robert Megarry V-C's analysis is to leave the beneficial interest in suspense until the stated purpose is carried out or fails. The difficulty with this (apart from its unorthodoxy) is that it fails to have regard to the role which the resulting trust plays in equity's scheme of things, or to explain why the money is not simply held on a resulting trust for the lender.

The central thesis of Dr Chambers' book is that a resulting trust arises whenever there is a transfer of property in circumstances in which the transferor (or more accurately the person at whose expense the property was provided) did not intend to benefit the recipient. It responds to the absence of an intention on the part of the transferor to pass the entire beneficial interest, not to a positive intention to retain it. Insofar as the transfer does not exhaust the entire beneficial interest, the resulting trust is a default trust which fills the gap and leaves no room for any part to be in suspense. An analysis of the *Quistclose* trust as a resulting trust for the transferor with a mandate to the transferee to apply the money for the stated purpose sits comfortably with Dr Chambers' thesis, and it might be thought surprising that he does not adopt it.

Note
Swadling in an article entitled, 'Quistclose Trusts and Orthodoxy' (2004) ITCP Vol 11 issue 3, p 121, subjects the *Quistclose* decision to rigorous critical analysis. He identifies contra-indications to any trust being intended, including the fact that the money was transferred pursuant to a contract of loan involving an obligation to repay, no obligation was expressly imposed on the borrower to segregate the money from its own assets and the transaction was in an arm's length commercial bargain and inappropriate for the imposition of a fiduciary relationship. He concludes that the House of Lords' decision was incorrect in giving priority to the lender and finding the trust on the facts of the case. In his view the funds should have been held as part of Rolls Razor's general assets.

Question
What is meant by a *Quistclose* trust and how would you classify it?

Failure of an express trust

In addition, an automatic resulting trust will arise where an intended express trust fails *ab initio* for any reason whatsoever. In this event, the trustees have no option but to hold the property on resulting trust for the settlor.

In *Chichester Diocesan Fund v Simpson* [1944] AC 341, the House of Lords decided that a bequest for 'charitable or benevolent objects' failed as a charitable gift. The funds, which were unlawfully distributed to various charities and were identifiable, were held on resulting trust for the testator's next of kin.

Likewise, where the settlor earmarks trust property and transfers the same to trustees, but fails to declare the terms of the trust, the trustees hold on resulting trust for the settlor. The trust is created in order to fill a vacuum in respect of ownership. This is so, even though the retention of an interest may not accord with the intention of the settlor: see *Vandervell v Inland Revenue Commissioners* (for the facts, see p 23).

Vandervell v Inland Revenue Commissioners [1967] 2 AC 291, HL

Lord Upjohn: If A intends to give away all his beneficial interest in a piece of property and thinks that he has done so, but by some mistake or accident or failure to comply with the requirements of the law he has failed to do so ... there will, by operation of law, be a resulting trust of the beneficial interest which he has failed effectively to dispose of. If the beneficial interest was in A and he fails to give it away, it remains in him.

Lord Wilberforce: ... The conclusion, on the facts found, is simply that the option was vested in the trustee company as a trustee on trusts, not defined at the time, possibly to be defined later. But the equitable, or beneficial interest, cannot remain in the air: the consequence in law must be that it remains in the settlor ... he (Mr Vandervell) had, as a direct result of the option and of the failure to place the beneficial interest in it securely away from him, not divested himself absolutely of the shares which it controlled.

Note

Following *Vandervell v Inland Revenue Commissioners*, a resulting trust may arise in favour of the transferor even though he does not intend to receive such interest, and may not expect or wish the resulting trust to arise in his favour.

Acceleration as opposed to resulting trust

The doctrine of acceleration of a postponed interest is based on the notion that if a prior interest under a trust fails so that the reason for postponement disappears, a subsequent interest may be brought forward and be enjoyed immediately. The gap in ownership may be filled by an acceleration of a subsequent interest. There is no room for a resulting trust in order to delay the enjoyment of the subsequent interest, for instance, the life tenant who disclaims his life interest may accelerate the remainder interest. Such complications often happen where a draftsperson of a trust or will fails to foresee a contingency which has in fact taken place. The court will construe the trust instrument or will in order to ascertain whether there is a gap in ownership and whether the doctrine of acceleration is capable of filling that gap. This will vary with the facts of each case. An example where there was no room for an acceleration of an interest is *Re Cochrane*.

Re Cochrane's Settlement Trusts, Shaw v Cochrane and Others [1955] 1 All ER 222, HC

Facts

By a post-nuptial settlement dated 17 August 1898, assets were vested in trustees on trust to pay the income to the wife for life, 'so long as she shall continue to reside with the said, WJB Cochrane' and after her death or prior determination of the trust in her favour, to the husband for life and, after the death of the survivor, on trust for their issue in equal shares. The survivor of the husband and wife was given a power of appointment to distribute the fund to the issue of the marriage and in default of such appointment in favour of the children equally. The wife, during the subsistence of the marriage, ceased to reside with her husband. Her interest therefore ceased. The husband enjoyed a life interest in the fund until his death in January 1953; his wife survived him. The question in issue was whether the children's interest could be accelerated on the death of their father.

Held

Despite the clear omission by the draftsman, there was no room to read into the settlement a term accelerating the interests of the children. The wife continued to retain a power of appointment in favour of the children. Accordingly, during the remainder of her life a resulting trust was set up:

Harman J: The question I have to determine is, what happens to the trust fund, or the income thereof on the death of the husband? The settlement is silent on income thereof on the death of the husband?

Is it clear here not only that something has been left out but also what it is that ought to be supplied? The second is much the more difficult matter to decide. One can see that the limitations over do not marry with the prior trusts, and that it should have been obvious to the draftsman that the event which in fact has happened might happen. But is it clear that the gift over should, so to speak, be accelerated? I do not think it is clear on this particular settlement, and I base my decision on this, that I cannot see clearly what it is that would have been written in. There is a power for the spouses jointly to appoint to issue and there is a power for the survivor to appoint. That power clearly did not cease with the cesser of her interest, so that she could alter the beneficial interests by appointing not to the children but in favour of grandchildren or by making an unequal division between her daughters, and it seems to me in the face of that that it is impossible to say that the interest vested in the children at the date of the cesser of the husband's interest. The result is that there is a resulting trust of the income of the fund until the death of the survivor of the spouses. The income will be divisible according to the proportion one part bears to the other or if the parts have become intermixed then in proportion to their respective values as recited in the settlement.

Surplus of trust funds

Where express trusts or specific gifts of property have utilised only a part of the funds so that there remains a surplus of assets, the destination of this unused part of the funds varies with the surrounding circumstances of each case. The following solutions have been adopted by the courts.

Resulting trust

The surplus funds are held on resulting trust for the settlor or the donor on the ground that he had parted with the funds for a specific purpose and by implication had retained an interest in the remainder where the specific purpose remained unfulfilled; see *Re Abbott*.

Re The Trusts of the Abbott Fund [1900] 2 Ch 326, HC

Facts

Funds were collected for the relief of two sisters who were dumb and deaf. In 1891, an appeal was made to invite subscriptions to enable the ladies to reside in lodgings in Cambridge and to provide for their 'very moderate wants'. Considerable sums were received leaving a large surplus outstanding on the death of the ladies in 1899. The question in issue was whether the personal representatives of the ladies or the subscribers to the fund were entitled to the surplus.

Held

Since there was no intention that the fund would ever be the absolute property of the ladies, but merely that the trustees should have a discretion as to the method of making payments for the ladies' benefit, there was a resulting trust for the subscribers:

> **Stirling J:** The ladies are both dead, and the question is whether so far as this fund has not been applied for their benefit, there is a resulting trust of it for the subscribers. I cannot believe that it was ever intended to become the absolute property of the ladies so that they should be in a position to demand a transfer of it to themselves, or so that if they became bankrupt the trustee in the bankruptcy should be able to claim it. I believe it was intended that it should be administered by Mr Smith, or the trustees who had been nominated in pursuance of the circular. I do not think the ladies ever became absolute owners of this fund. I think that the trustee or trustees were intended to have a wide discretion as to whether any, and if any what, part of the fund should be applied for the benefit of the ladies and how the application should be made.

The same solution was adopted where a collection was raised by means of *anonymous donors* in the case of *Re Gillingham Bus Disaster Fund*.

Re Gillingham Bus Disaster Fund [1958] Ch 300, HC

Facts

Funds were raised by means of collecting boxes following a disaster where marine cadets were maimed or killed by a bus. The collection was to be used for funeral expenses, caring for the disabled and 'for worthy causes' in memory of the dead boys (non-charitable purposes). A surplus of funds remained after the bus company admitted liability and paid substantial sums for similar purposes. The court was asked to determine the destination of the surplus.

Held

On construction of the circumstances, the donors did not part 'out and out' with their contributions but only for the specific purposes as stated in the appeal. In this respect, it was immaterial that the donors contributed anonymously. Accordingly, the surplus amount was held on resulting trust for the donors. The sum would be paid into court to await claimants. Failing claimants, the fund would be taken by the Crown on a *bona vacantia*:

> **Harman J:** In my judgment the Crown has failed to show that this case should not follow the ordinary rule merely because there was a number of donors who, I will assume, are unascertainable. I see no reason myself to suppose that the small giver who is anonymous has any wider intention than the large giver who can be named. They all give for the one object. If they can be found by inquiry the resulting trust can be executed in their favour. If they cannot I do not see how the money could then . . . change its destination and become *bona vacantia*. It will be merely money held upon a trust for which no beneficiary can be found. Such cases are common and where it is known that there are beneficiaries the fact that they cannot be ascertained does not entitle the Crown to come in and claim. The trustees must pay the money into court like any other trustee who cannot find his beneficiary. I conclude, therefore, that there must be an inquiry for the subscribers to this fund.

Note

This case was heavily criticised in *Re West Sussex Constabulary's Widows Children and Benevolent Fund Trusts* [1971] Ch 1, HC: see p 153 below.

Retention beneficially

The surplus is retained by the transferee or beneficiary. On construction of the circumstances, the court may decide that the ulterior purpose of the settlor may be fulfilled by permitting the transferee or beneficiary to retain the property even though the specific or primary intention of the settlor or donor has become frustrated. This solution may be adopted when the donee or beneficiary is still capable of deriving a benefit from the property. In this event, there is no room for the resulting trust solution for, in a sense, the overriding objective is still capable of being achieved: see *Re Andrew's Trust*.

Re Andrew's Trust, Carter v Andrew [1905] 2 Ch 48, HC

Facts

In 1881, money was donated 'for or towards' the education of the infant children of a deceased clergyman. By 1899, the children had completed their formal education with only part of the fund. The court was asked to determine the destination of the fund.

Held

The surplus was taken by the children in equal shares (distinguishing *Re Abbott* on the ground that, in the present case, the beneficiaries were still alive, whereas in the earlier case the ladies had died). There was no resulting trust for, in the circumstances, the intentions of the subscribers were to benefit the children and education was merely one method of providing that benefit:

> **Kekewich J:** Here the only specified object was the education of the children. But I deem myself to *construe 'education' in the broadest possible sense*, and not to consider the purpose exhausted because the children have attained such ages that education in the vulgar sense is no longer necessary. Even if it be construed in the narrower sense *it is merely the motive of the gift*, and the intention must be taken to have been to provide for the children in the manner (they all being then infants) most useful [emphasis added].
>
> Therefore . . . I am prepared to hold that the shares and accumulated dividends belong to the children, and the only remaining question is in what proportions do they take. The letter states that the fund was not subscribed for equal division, but was intended to defray the expenses of all as deemed necessary, and apparently the trustees of the fund exercised their discretion in dividing the money so far as it was divided at all. But there is no

longer room for discretion, and I think the only safe course is to hold that the children are entitled to what remains in equal shares.

A similar result was reached by the Court of Appeal in *Re Osoba*. The court construed the will as providing absolute gifts to the testator's wife and daughter as joint tenants. The declaration concerning the daughter's education was merely the motive for the gift.

Re Osoba [1979] 1 WLR 247, CA

Facts

A gift was made by will to the testator's widow 'for her maintenance and for the training of my daughter up to university grade'. The widow died and the daughter completed her formal education.

Held

The widow and daughter took as joint tenants and, on the death of the widow, the daughter succeeded to the entire fund. The references to maintenance and education in the will were merely declarations of the testator's motive for the gift:

> **Buckley LJ:** If a testator has given the whole of a fund, whether of capital or income, to a beneficiary . . . he is regarded, in the absence of any contraindication, as having manifested an intention to benefit that person to the full extent of the subject matter . . . This is because the testator has given the whole fund; he has not given so much of the fund as the trustee or anyone else should determine, but the whole fund. This must be reconciled with the testator having specified the purpose for which the gift is made. This reconciliation is achieved by treating the reference to the purpose as merely a statement of the testator's motive in making the gift. Any other interpretation of the gift would frustrate the testator's expressed intention that the whole subject matter should be applied for the benefit of the beneficiary. These considerations have, I think, added force where the subject matter is the testator's residue, so that any failure of the gift would result in intestacy. The specified purpose is regarded as of less significance than the dispositive act of the testator.

DISSOLUTION OF UNINCORPORATED ASSOCIATIONS

An unincorporated association is a group of individuals joined together to promote a common purpose or purposes, such as cricket, or golf or trade union activities. Such associations vary in size and objectives; some may be long-standing or exist with a view to making profits and have open or restricted membership. They differ from incorporated associations in that they lack a legal personality – separate and distinct from their members. The association is regulated by its rules, which have the effect of imposing an implied contract between all the members *inter se*. Thus, all the members are collectively joined together by the rules of the association. Its affairs are normally handled by a committee and its assets may be held on trust for the association in order to ensure that the association's property is kept separate from its members.

The rules of the association usually provide the procedure for enforcing rights and ownership interests in respect of a distribution of the assets of the society on a dissolution.

In *Conservative and Unionist Central Office v Burrell*, Lawton LJ laid down the following definition of an unincorporated association for the purposes of the Taxes Act 1988 and general law.

Conservative and Unionist Central Office v Burrell [1982] 1 WLR 522, CA

> **Lawton LJ:** I infer that by 'unincorporated association' in this context Parliament meant two or more persons bound together for one or more common purposes, not being business purposes, by mutual undertakings, each having mutual duties and obligations, in an organisation which has rules which identify in whom control of it and its funds rests and upon what terms and which can be joined or left at will. The bond of union between the members of an unincorporated association has to be contractual.

In *Re Bucks Constabulary*, Walton J explored the significance of the rules of the association.

Re Bucks Constabulary Widows' and Orphans' Fund Society (No 2)
[1979] 1 WLR 936

Walton J: It is I think desirable to view the question of the property of unincorporated associations in the round. If a number of persons associate together, for whatever purpose, if that purpose is one which involves the acquisition of cash or property of any magnitude, then, for practical purposes, some one or more persons have to act in the capacity of treasurers or holders of the property. In any sophisticated association there will accordingly be one or more trustees in whom the property which is acquired by the association will be vested. These trustees will of course not hold such property on their own behalf. Usually there will be a committee of some description which will run the affairs of the association; though, of course, in a small association the committee may well comprise all the members; and the normal course of events will be that the trustee, if there is a formal trustee, will declare that he holds the property of the association in his hands on trust to deal with it as directed by the committee. If the trust deed is a shade more sophisticated it may add that the trustee holds the assets on trust for the members in accordance with the rules of the association. Now in all such cases it appears to me quite clear that, unless under the rules governing the association the property thereof has been wholly devoted to charity, or unless and to the extent to which the other trusts have validly been declared of such property, the persons, and the only persons, interested therein are the members. Save by way of a valid declaration of trust in their favour, there is no scope for any other person acquiring any rights in the property of the association, although of course it may well be that third parties may obtain contractual or proprietary rights, such as a mortgage, over those assets as the result of a valid contract with the trustees or members of the committee as representing the association.

The issue to be considered in this context concerns the occasions when the rules are silent as to the destination of assets following a dissolution of an unincorporated association. In effect, there are a number of issues involved, namely, whether the members of the association (and, if so, whether only members on the date of dissolution or all members, past and present) are entitled to the assets on a distribution, or whether the Crown should be entitled as *bona vacantia*. If the members are entitled, how much ought they to claim? In short, the question is on what basis should a distribution of assets of a society be made?

So far the courts have adopted the following three approaches to this question.

The resulting trust

The resulting trust was the original remedy adopted and represents, in theory, a solution to the problem, although the more recent cases have considered this basis of distribution with disfavour. This approach was adopted in *Re Printers and Transferrers Society*.

Re Printers and Transferrers Society [1899] 2 Ch 84, HC

Facts

A trade union society was founded by weekly subscriptions to raise funds for strikes and other benefits for its members. The scale of benefits varied with the duration of membership. The rules of the society were silent as to the mode of distribution of assets on a dissolution. There were assets of £1,000 and the society consisted of 201 subsisting members.

Held

A resulting trust was set up in favour of subsisting members on the date of dissolution and the assets were divisible in proportion to their contributions over the years (for example, a member of 10 years' standing received 10 times more of the funds than a member for one year only) irrespective of benefits received over the years:

Byrne J: Now, a careful reading of the judgment of the Court of Appeal in *Cunnack v Edwards* [1895] 1 Ch 489, points to this as the leading ground of the decision: that, on the true construction of the rules in that case, it was held that each member on making a payment had finally and forever parted with the whole of his interest in the money he so subscribed in favour of third parties. That does not exist in the present case. *The funds provided here are for the benefit of members for the time being*; it is true they would not all necessarily take the same amount – some of them might and perhaps did get nothing, some did get a good deal under the rules; but they were all alike entitled to a contingent benefit on the happening of certain events, though the different classes on becoming entitled would receive at different rates [emphasis added].

Now, the true principle I think is to be found in this – that there is a resulting trust in favour of those who have contributed to these funds, and I think that the proper and legitimate way of dividing therefore, will be in accordance with the amounts contributed by the existing members at the time of the passing of the resolution.

This approach was followed with some variations in *Re Hobourn Aero Components Air Raid Distress Fund*.

Re Hobourn Aero Components Ltd's Air Raid Distress Fund, Ryan v Forrest [1946] Ch 194, HC

Facts

During the war years from 1940 to the end of 1944, collections were made weekly from the employees of a company operating three munitions factories. The moneys were initially expended on comforts or money payments for servicemen abroad or on leave, who were ex-employees or dependants of employees of the company. After September 1940, the collected funds were also used to relieve cases of employees who had suffered damage and distress from air raids. On the closing down of the fund, a claim was made for the determination of the surplus moneys.

Held

The surplus funds were held on resulting trust for every contributor, past and present, in proportion to their contributions, but with a reduction for any benefits received from the fund:

> **Cohen J:** [Having decided that the gift failed as a charity, the learned judge continued:] I therefore turn to the second question raised by the summons. The Crown does not claim the fund as *bona vacantia*, and the question is as to how it ought to be distributed amongst the contributories thereto. In my opinion, since the basis on which the contributions are returned is that each donor retained an interest in the amount of his contributions except so far as they are applied for the purposes for which they were subscribed. Accordingly, I propose to declare that the fund now available for distribution ought to be distributed amongst all the persons who during their employment by Hobourn Aero Components Ltd, contributed to the fund at any time after 12 December 1940, in proportion to the total amount contributed by them respectively to the fund, each such person bringing into hotchpot any amount received by him by way of benefit out of the fund.

The courts have repeatedly stressed that the resulting trust is unsuitable in this context for the members paid their subscriptions on a contractual basis. The distribution of assets ought to be *effected on a contractual basis*.

Bona vacantia

A second solution adopted by the courts is that the members of a society who make their contributions have received, or are receiving, or expect to receive benefits from the funds of the society during its continuance. On the date of liquidation, such members do not expect the return of their subscriptions or assets of the society, for the members had parted 'out and out' with their subscriptions. Accordingly, the assets of the society may be taken by the Crown as *bona vacantia*. This doctrine means that where property has no apparent owner, it will pass to the Crown. This solution is adopted only as a last resort when neither the settlor nor the beneficiary nor anyone else is entitled to claim the property. The property being ownerless, the Crown steps in to fill the gap: see *Cunnack v Edwards*.

Cunnack v Edwards [1896] 2 Ch 679, CA

Facts

A society was formed to raise funds by subscriptions, fines, etc, from its members in order to provide annuities for the widows of deceased members. By 1879, all the members had died and by 1892 the last widow died. There was a surplus of funds of £1,250. The personal representatives of the last widow claimed the fund.

Held

The Crown took the fund as *bona vacantia*. There was no room for a resulting trust in favour of past members for each member on paying his contribution parted with all interest in his subscription subject to one reservation, that if he left a widow she was to be provided for during widowhood:

> **Smith LJ:** As the member paid his money to the society, so he divested himself of all interest in this money for ever, with this one reservation, that if the member left a widow she was to be provided for during her widowhood. Except as to this he abandoned and gave up the money forever.

A similar result was achieved in *Re West Sussex Constabulary's Widows, Children and Benevolent Fund Trusts*, on the basis that the members of the association and others contributed not for their benefit, but for the benefit of third parties.

Re West Sussex Constabulary's Widows, Children and Benevolent Fund Trusts [1971] Ch 1, HC

Facts

A fund was established for providing payments to widows of deceased members of the West Sussex Constabulary. Clause (10) of the rules provided that, with exceptions, a member who resigned would forfeit all claims to the fund. Receipts were derived from four classes of contributors, namely:

(a) identifiable donations and legacies;

(b) members' subscriptions;

(c) collecting boxes; and

(d) proceeds of entertainment, sweepstakes and raffles.

On 1 January 1968, the Constabulary was amalgamated with other police forces and the fund came to an end. The question in issue concerned the distribution of the fund.

Held

With the exception of contributors in category (a) (such donations were made for a specific purpose which failed, hence a resulting trust was set up for these contributors), the balance of the fund passed to the Crown as *bona vacantia*. The contributors within category (b) had got what they bargained for, following *Cunnack v Edwards* (see p 152 above). The members' contributions were for their widows (third parties) and not for themselves. In any event, members' contributions were received by way of contract and not trust.

The contributors in category (c) were treated as parting with their moneys 'out and out'. The court refused to follow *Re Gillingham* (see p 148 above) on the ground that that solution was 'absurd and inconceivable'. In respect of contributors in category (d), they received what they were contractually entitled to; indeed, it was conceivable that they did not contribute directly to the fund:

> **Goff J:** In my judgment the doctrine of resulting trust is clearly inapplicable to the contributions of both classes. Those persons who remained members until their deaths are in any event excluded because they have had all they contracted for, either because their widows and dependants have received or are in receipt of the prescribed benefits, or because they did not have a widow or dependants. In my view that is inherent in all the speeches in the Court of Appeal in *Cunnack v Edwards* [1896] 2 Ch 679. Further, whatever the effect of the fund's rule 10 may be upon the contributions of those members who left prematurely, they and the surviving members alike are also in my judgment unable to claim under a resulting trust because they put up their money on a contractual basis and not one of trust: see *per* Harman J in *Re Gillingham Bus Disaster Fund* [1958] Ch 300, p 314. The only case which has given me difficulty on this aspect of the matter is *Re Hobourn Aero Components Ltd's Air Raid Distress Fund* [1946] Ch 86 where in somewhat similar circumstances it was held there was a resulting trust. The argument postulated, I think, the distinction between contract and trust but in another connection, namely, whether the fund was charitable. There was in that case a resolution to wind up but that was not, at all events as expressed, the *ratio decidendi*: see *per* Cohen J at p 97, but, as Cohen J observed, there was no argument for *bona vacantia*. Moreover, no rules or regulations were ever made and although in fact £1 per month was paid or saved for each member serving with the forces, there were no prescribed contractual benefits. In my judgment that case is therefore distinguishable.

Accordingly, in my judgment all the contributions of both classes are *bona vacantia*, but I must make a reservation with respect to possible contractual rights. In *Cunnack v Edwards* [1895] 1 Ch 489 and *Braithwaite v AG* [1909] 1 Ch 510 all the members had received, or provision had been made for, all the contractual benefits. Here the matter has been cut short. Those persons who died whilst still in membership cannot, I conceive, have any rights because in their case the contract has been fully worked out, and on a contractual basis I would think that members who retired would be precluded from making any claim by rule 10, although that is perhaps more arguable. The surviving members, on the other hand, may well have a right in contract on the ground of frustration or total failure of consideration, and that right may embrace contributions made by past members, though I do not see how it could apply to moneys raised from outside sources. I have not, however, heard any argument based on contract and therefore the declarations I propose to make will be subject to the reservation which I will later formulate. This will not prevent those parts of the fund which are *bona vacantia* from being paid over to the Crown as it has offered to give a full indemnity to the trustees.

I must now turn to the moneys raised from outside sources. Counsel divided the outside moneys into three categories, first, the proceeds of entertainments, raffles and sweepstakes; secondly, the proceeds of collecting boxes; and, thirdly, donations, including legacies if any, and he took particular objections to each.

I agree that there cannot be any resulting trust with respect to the first category. I am not certain whether Harman J in *Re Gillingham Bus Disaster Fund* [1958] Ch 300, meant to decide otherwise. It appears to me to be impossible to apply the doctrine of resulting trust to the proceeds of entertainments and sweepstakes and such-like money raising operations for two reasons: first, the relationship is one of contract and not of trust; the purchaser of a ticket may have the motive of aiding the cause or he may not; he may purchase a ticket merely because he wishes to attend the particular entertainment or to try for the prize, but whichever it be, he pays his money as the price of what is offered and what he receives; secondly, there is in such cases no direct contribution to the fund at all; it is only the profit, if any, which is ultimately received and there may even be none.

In any event, the first category cannot be any more susceptible to the doctrine than the second to which I now turn. Here one starts with the well known *dictum* of PO Lawrence J in *Re Welsh Hospital (Netley) Fund* [1921] 1 Ch 655, at p 660 where he said:

> So far as regards the contributors to entertainments, street collections, etc, I have no hesitation in holding that they must be taken to have parted with their money out and out. It is inconceivable that any person paying for a concert ticket or placing a coin in a collecting box presented to him in the street should have intended that any part of the money so contributed should be returned to him when the immediate object for which the concert was given or the collection made had come to an end. To draw such an inference would be absurd on the face of it.

This was adopted by Upjohn J in *Re Hillier's Trusts* [1954] 1 WLR 9, where the point was actually decided.

The analysis of Upjohn J was approved by Denning LJ in the Court of Appeal [1954] 1 WLR 700, although it is true he went on to say that the law makes a presumption of charity. I quote from p 714:

> Let me first state the law as I understand it in regard to money collected for a specific charity by means of a church collection, a flag day, a whist drive, a dance, or some such activity. When a man gives money on such an occasion, he gives it, I think, beyond recall. He parts with the money out and out . . .

In *Re Ulverston and District New Hospital Building Trusts* [1956] Ch 622, at p 633, Jenkins LJ threw out a suggestion that there might be a distinction in the case of a person who could prove that he put a specified sum in a collecting box, and, in the *Gillingham* case [1958] Ch 300, Harman J after noting this, decided that there was a resulting trust with respect to the proceeds of collections.

It will be observed that Harman J considered that *Re Welsh Hospital (Netley) Fund* [1921] 1 Ch 655, *Re Hillier's Trusts* [1954] 1 WLR 9, and *Re Ulverston and District New Hospitality Building Trusts* did not help him greatly because they were charity cases. It is true that they were, and, as will presently appear, that is in my view very significant in relation to the third category, but I do not think it was a valid objection with respect to the second, and for my part I cannot reconcile the decision of Upjohn J in *Re Hillier's Trusts* with that of Harman J in the *Gillingham* case. As I see it, therefore, I have to choose between them. On the one hand it may be said that Harman J had the advantage, which Upjohn J had not, of considering the suggestion made by Jenkins LJ. On the other hand, that suggestion with all respect, seems to me somewhat fanciful and unreal. I agree that all who put their money into collecting boxes should be taken to have the same intention, but why should they not all be regarded as intending to part with their money out and out absolutely in all circumstances? I observe that PO Lawrence J in *Re Welsh*

Hospital ibid, p 661 used very strong words. He said any other view was inconceivable and absurd on the face of it. That commends itself to my humble judgment, and I therefore prefer and follow the judgment of Upjohn J in *Re Hillier's Trusts* . . . Therefore, where, as in the present case, the object was neither equivocal nor charitable, I can see no justification for infecting the third category with the weaknesses of the first and second, and I cannot distinguish this part of the case from *Re Abbott Fund Trusts* [1900] 2 Ch 326.

> And I make the following declarations: first, that the portion attributable to donations and legacies is held on a resulting trust for the donors or their estates of the respective testators; secondly, that the remainder of the fund is *bona vacantia*.

Question

How would you reconcile *Re Gillingham Bus Disaster Fund* with *Re West Sussex Constabulary Fund*?

Contractual basis

The courts in *Cunnack v Edwards* and *Re West Sussex* adopted the notion that members contributed to the society on a contractual basis, but decided on the facts that such contributions were taken by the Crown as *bona vacantia*. In more recent cases, the courts have decided that subsisting members of the association are entitled to participate in the distribution of the society's funds. Their contributions were made as an accretion to the funds of the association by reference to the contract made *inter se* in accordance with the rules of the society. The members control the association subject to the constitution of the society. Equally, the subsisting members alone ought to be entitled to the surplus funds on a dissolution, in the absence of any agreement between members to the contrary. In *Re Sick and Funeral Society of St John's Sunday School, Golcar*, the court decided that since the rules of the society differentiated between the two categories of members, the distribution of the assets to the subsisting members would likewise be conducted on the basis of this inequality. Subject to this qualification, all the subsisting members were treated alike.

Re Sick and Funeral Society of St John's Sunday School, Golcar [1973] Ch 51, HC

Facts

In 1866, a society was formed at a Sunday school to provide for sickness and death benefits for its members. Teachers and children were entitled to join and subscriptions were based on a sliding scale according to age, those under 13 paying half of one old penny per week (rule 9) and those over 12 paying one old penny. The benefits for those paying the full subscription were twice those of the smaller subscribers (rules 12 and 14).

On 12 December 1966, a meeting unanimously decided to wind up the Society as from 31 December. No further subscriptions were paid. There was some £4,000 of surplus assets.

Before the assets were distributed among the current members, four ex-members, who had been excluded from membership for failure to pay subscriptions since 1963 (rules 9 and 17), claimed to pay up their arrears and to participate. A further meeting was held in September 1968 in which it was again resolved to wind up the Society and to distribute the assets among the persons who were members on 31 December 1966 and the personal representatives of such members who had subsequently died.

Held

The distribution would be made with full shares for full members and half shares for the children. The ex-members were excluded:

> **Megarry J:** [After reviewing the authorities which the learned judge concluded was in a state of confusion, he continued:] It seems to me, with all respect, that much of the difficulty arises from confusing property with contract. A resulting trust is essentially a property concept: any property that a man does not effectually dispose of remains his own. If, then, there is a true resulting trust in respect of an unexpended balance of payments made to some club or association, there will be a resulting trust in respect of that unexpended balance, and the beneficiaries under that trust will be those who made the payments. If any are dead, the trusts will be for their

estates; death does not deprive a man of his beneficial interest. Yet, in what I may call 'the resulting trust cases', the beneficiaries who were held to be entitled were the members living at the time of the dissolution to the exclusion of those who had died or otherwise ceased to be members. If, then, there was any resulting trust, it must be a trust modified in some way, perhaps by some unexplained implied term, that distinguishes between the quick and the dead. It cannot be merely an ordinary resulting trust.

On the other hand, membership of a club or association is primarily a matter of contract. The members make their payments, and in return they become entitled to the benefits of membership in accordance with the rules. *The sums they pay cease to be their individual property, and so cease to be subject to any concept of resulting trust. Instead, they become the property, through the trustees of the club or association, of all the members for the time being, including themselves.* A member who, by death or otherwise, ceases to be a member thereby ceases to be the part owner of any of the club's property: those who remain continue owners. If, then, dissolution ensues, there must be a division of the property of the club or association among those alone who are owners of that property, to the exclusion of former members [emphasis added].

On the footing that the rules of a club or association form the basis of the contract between all the members, *I must look at the rules of the society to see whether they indicate any basis other than that of equality.* It seems to me that they do. Those aged from five to 12 years old pay contributions at half the rate (rule 9), and correspondingly their allowances (rule 12) and death benefit (rule 14) are also paid at half the rate. Where the rules have written into them the basis of inequality this ought also to be applied to the surplus property of the society [emphasis added].

The court came to a similar conclusion (ie, excluding any claim of the Crown as *bona vacantia*) in *Re Bucks Constabulary Widows' and Orphans' Fund Friendly Society (No 2)*.

Re Bucks Constabulary Widows' and Orphans' Fund Friendly Society (No 2) [1979] I WLR 936, HC

Facts

The objects of a friendly society included the relief of widows and orphans of deceased members of Bucks Constabulary. In April 1968, the Bucks Constabulary was amalgamated with others to form the Thames Valley Constabulary. The question in issue concerned whether the assets should be distributed among the subsisting members on the date of dissolution, or whether they would pass to the Crown as *bona vacantia*.

Held

The fund belonged to the subsisting members on the date of dissolution and they took the fund in equal shares (per capita):

Walton J: Now, in the present case, I am dealing with a society which was registered under the Friendly Societies Act 1896. This does not have any effect at all on the unincorporated nature of the society. The fact is made very explicit by the provisions of s 49(1) of the 1896 Act which reads as follows:

All property belonging to a registered society, whether acquired before or after the society is registered, shall vest in the trustees for the time being of the society, for the use and benefit of the society and the members thereof, and of all persons claiming through the members according to the rules of the society.

There can be no doubt, therefore, that in the present case the whole of the property of the society is vested in the trustees for the use and benefit of the society and the members thereof and of all persons claiming through the members according to the rules of the society. Members paid a contribution in exchange for which in the event of their deaths their widows and children would receive various benefits. There is indeed no rule which says what is to happen to surplus assets of the society on a dissolution. But in view of s 49(1) there is no need. The assets must continue to be held, the society having been dissolved, and the widows and orphans being out of the way, simply for the use and benefit of the members of the society, albeit they will all now be former members.

Before I turn to a consideration of the authorities, *it is I think pertinent to observe that all unincorporated societies rest in contract to this extent, that there is an implied contract between all of the members inter se governed by the rules of the society.* In default of any rule to the contrary, and it will seldom if ever be that there is such a rule, when a member ceases to be a member of the association he *ipso facto* ceases to have any interest in its funds. Once again, so far as friendly societies are concerned, this is made very clear by s 49(1), that it is the members, the present members, who, alone, have any right in the assets. As membership always ceases on death, past members or the estates of deceased members therefore have no interest in the assets. Further, unless expressly so provided by the rules, unincorporated societies are not really tontine societies, intended to provide benefits for the longest liver of the members. Therefore, although it is difficult to say in any given case precisely when a society becomes moribund, it is quite clear that if a society is reduced to a single member neither he, still less his personal representatives on his behalf, can say he is or was the society and therefore entitled solely to its fund. It may be that it will be sufficient for the society's continued existence if there are two members, but if there is only one the society as such must cease to exist. There is no association, since one can hardly associate with oneself or enjoy one's own society. And so indeed the assets have become ownerless [emphasis added].

Finally, there comes a case which gives me great concern, Re West Sussex Constabulary's Widows, Children and Benevolent (1930) Fund Trusts [1971] Ch 1. The case is indeed easily distinguishable from the present case in that what was there under consideration was a simple unincorporated association and not a friendly society, so that the provisions of s 49(1) of the 1896 Act do not apply. Otherwise the facts in that case present remarkable parallels to the facts in the present case.

[The learned judge, after referring to Goff J's judgment in Re West Sussex Constabulary Fund, continued:] It will be observed that the first reason given by the judge for his decision is that he could not accept the principle of the members' clubs as applicable. This is a very interesting reason, because it is flatly contrary to the successful argument of Mr Ingle Joyce who appeared for the Attorney General in the case. Goff J purported to follow Cunnack v Edwards. If all that Goff J meant was that the purposes of the fund before him were totally different from those of a members' club then of course one must agree, but if he meant to imply that there was some totally different principle of law applicable one must ask why that should be. His second reason is that in all the cases where the surviving members had taken, the organisation existed for the benefit of the members for the time being exclusively. This may be so, so far as actual decisions go, but what is the principle? Why are the members not in control, complete control, save as to any existing contractual rights, of the assets belonging to their organisation? One could understand the position being different if valid trusts had been declared of the assets in favour of third parties, for example charities, but that this was emphatically not the case was demonstrated by the fact that Goff J recognised that the members could have altered the rules prior to dissolution and put the assets into their own pockets. If there was no obstacle to their doing this, it shows in my judgment quite clearly that the money was theirs all the time. Finally, he purports to follow Cunnack v Edwards and it will be seen from the analysis which I have already made of that case that it was extremely special in its facts, resting on a curious provision of the 1829 Act which is no longer applicable. As I have already indicated, in the light of s 49(1) of the 1896 Act the case before Goff J is readily distinguishable, but I regret that, quite apart from that, I am wholly unable to square it with the relevant principles of law applicable [emphasis added].

The conclusion therefore is that, as on dissolution there were members of the society here in question in existence, its assets are held on trust for such members to the total exclusion of any claim on behalf of the Crown. The remaining question under this head which falls now to be argued is, of course, whether they are simply held per capita, or, as suggested in some of the cases, in proportion to the contributions made by each.

That being the case, prima facie there can be no doubt at all but that the distribution is on the basis of equality, because, as between a number of people contractually interested in a fund, there is no other method of distribution if no other method is provided by the terms of the contract.

The courts apply similar principles as above in respect of the surplus funds on the winding up of pension schemes. The terms of the scheme are required to be construed and are treated as of paramount importance. The contractual basis of creating rights under the scheme is treated as highly relevant to, but not conclusive of, the question whether the resulting trust ought to be imposed. Thus, in *Davis v Richards and Wallington Industries Ltd*, the court decided that in respect of a pension fund surplus, the employer's contributions were subject to a resulting trust, but the employees' contributions were payable to the Crown as *bona vacantia*.

Davis v Richards and Wallington Industries Ltd [1990] 1 WLR 1511, HC

Facts

In 1975, a group of companies established, by way of trust, a pension scheme to replace a previous scheme originally set up in 1968. The contributions were derived from three sources, namely, employers' contributions, employees' contributions and the transferred funds. In 1982, the companies terminated the scheme due to financial difficulties. The question in issue was, *inter alia*, whether the surplus funds (£3m) were held on resulting trust for the contributors or were taken by the Crown as *bona vacantia*.

Held

The employers' contributions were held on resulting trust. The employees' contributions were taken by the Crown. The portion of the surplus attributable to the transferred funds was taken by the Crown as *bona vacantia*:

> **Scott J:** The question is whether a resulting trust applies to the surplus, or to so much of the surplus as was derived from each of the three sources. As to the surplus derived from the employers' contributions, I can see no basis on which the resulting trust can be excluded. Equity demands, in my judgment, the conclusion that the trustees hold the surplus derived from the employers' contributions upon trust for the employers. There is no express provision excluding a resulting trust and no circumstances from which, in my opinion, an implication to that effect could be drawn. On the other hand, in my judgment, the circumstances of the case seem to me to point firmly and clearly to the conclusion that a resulting trust in favour of the employees is excluded.

> Each employee paid his or her contributions in return for specific financial benefits from the fund. The value of these benefits would be different for each employee, depending on how long he had served, how old he was when he joined and how old he was when he left. Two employees might have paid identical sums in contributions but have become entitled to benefits of a very different value. The point is particularly striking in respect of the employees (and there were several of them) who exercised their option to a refund of contributions. How can a resulting trust work as between the various employees *inter se*? I do not think it can and I do not see why equity should impute to them an intention that would lead to an unworkable result.

> Finally, there are the transferred funds. The intention, in my judgment, appears sufficiently clear from the documents by which the transfers were effected and from the surrounding circumstances that the trustees of the transferred schemes were divesting themselves once and for all of the transferred funds. Some of the transferor schemes expressly excluded any refund of assets to the employer contributors. Those employers could not, therefore, assert any resulting trust. As to the others, it is possible to regard the transferred funds as being subject to some contingent resulting trust of surplus in favour of employer contributors. But, as I understand the evidence, it would be virtually impossible now to identify the part of the £3m odd surplus that represented the surplus (if there was one) inherent in any of the transferred funds.

> Accordingly, in my judgment, if any part of the surplus has derived from employees' contributions or from the funds transferred from the pension schemes of other companies, that part of the surplus devolves as *bona vacantia*. Subject thereto, the surplus is, in my judgment, held upon trust for the employer contributors.

Date of dissolution

In the ordinary course of events, the date of the dissolution of an association will not be in dispute. This will be the date when a formal resolution is passed to wind up the association. But, exceptionally, an association may become inactive for a very long period of time; the formal resolution to wind up the body may not, in itself, reflect the true state of affairs concerning the date of termination. In these circumstances, the extraordinarily prolonged period of inactivity may offer strong evidence of spontaneous dissolution. The court will decide, on the facts, the precise date of dissolution. The subsisting members of the association will then be entitled to participate in the distribution of the assets. In *Re GKN Bolts & Nuts*, the court decided that mere inactivity, by itself, is insufficient to constitute spontaneous dissolution. The association may be treated as going through a dormant period.

In Re GKN Bolts & Nuts Ltd (Automotive Division), Birmingham Works Sports and Social Club, Leek v Donkersley [1982] 1 WLR 774, HC

Facts

In 1946, the trustees of a social club established for the benefit of company employees bought a sports ground. By 1969, the club was in financial difficulties and the sports ground was no longer in use. In January 1975, membership cards ceased to be issued. In February 1975, the last general meeting was held. No further annual accounts were prepared. In April 1975, the club ceased to be registered for VAT. In September 1975, the stocks of the club were sold. On 18 December 1975, a special meeting of the club was convened to consider an offer which was made to buy the sports ground and the members voted unanimously to sell the property. The sale did not take place but, in May 1978, planning permission was granted for development of the site. On 21 July 1978, the trustees entered into a conditional contract to sell the club. This sale became unconditional on 4 August 1978 and completion of the sale took place on 18 August 1978. The issues before the court were:

(a) whether the club ceased to exist and, if so, when?

(b) as from which date were the assets distributable to the members?

Held

(a) The club ceased to exist on 18 December 1975, the date of the resolution to sell the sports ground. On this date, it was clear that the club accepted formally that it could no longer carry out its objects.

(b) Applying the principle in the *Golcar* and *Re Bucks Constabulary* cases, the distribution of the assets would be on the basis of equality among members (ordinary or full) irrespective of the length of membership or amount of subscriptions paid:

Megarry VC: As a matter of principle I would hold that it is perfectly possible for a club to be dissolved spontaneously. I do not think that mere inactivity is enough: a club may do little or nothing for a long period, and yet continue in existence. A cataleptic trance may look like death without being death. But inactivity may be so prolonged or so circumstanced that the only reasonable inference is that the club has become dissolved. In such cases there may be difficulty in determining the *punctum temporis* of dissolution: the less activity there is, the greater the difficulty of fastening upon one date rather than another as the moment of dissolution. In such cases the court must do the best it can by picking a reasonable date somewhere between the time when the club could still be said to exist, and the time when its existence had clearly come to an end.

In *Re William Denby & Sons Ltd Sick and Benevolent Fund* [1971] 1 WLR 973, Brightman J classified four categories of cases in which an unregistered friendly society or benevolent fund should be regarded as having been dissolved or terminated so that its assets became distributable. The first three categories of dissolution or termination were: (1) in accordance with the rules; (2) by agreement of all persons interested; and (3) by order of the court in the exercise of its inherent jurisdiction. The fourth category was when the substratum on which the society or fund was founded had gone, so that the society or fund no longer had any effective purpose, and the assets became distributable without any order of the court. On the facts of the case, it was held that the substratum had not gone, so that the fund was not distributable; but the judgment considered a number of the authorities, and plainly supports the view that there may be a spontaneous dissolution of a society. The judgment does not mention the *Abbatt* case [1969] 1 WLR 561, though it was cited in argument; but I think the two cases have much in common as supporting a doctrine of spontaneous dissolution. Brightman J [1971] 1 WLR 973, at pp 981–82 expressed grave doubts whether mere inactivity of the officers of the society or the fund would suffice and in this I would respectfully concur. Mere inactivity is equivocal: suspended animation may be continued life, not death; and the mere cessation of function that was mentioned in the *Abbatt* case would not, I think, suffice *per se*. But inactivity coupled with other circumstances may demonstrate that all concerned regard the society as having ceased to have any purpose or function, and so as no longer existing. The question is whether on the facts of the present case the society ceased to exist on 18 December 1975. On that date, the position was that the club had ceased to operate as a club for several months. The picture was not one of mere inactivity alone; there were positive acts towards the winding up of the club. The sale of the club's stock of drinks was one instance, and others were the ending of the registration for VAT, and the dismissal of the steward. The cessation of any club activities, the ending of the use of the sports ground and the abandonment of preparing accounts or issuing membership cards were all in one sense examples of inactivity; but I think that there was in all probability some element of deliberation in these matters, and not a mere inertia. In Mr Sher's phrase, there was a systematic dismantling of the club and its activities.

However that may be, the resolution to sell the sports ground seems to me to conclude the matter. Having taken all steps, active or passive, required to terminate the activities of the club, short of passing a formal resolution to wind it up or dissolve it, the general meeting of the club resolved to sell the club's last asset.

Question
What is an unincorporated association? What principles are applied in order to identify the ownership of surplus funds on a dissolution of an unincorporated association?

Green, G, 'The dissolution of unincorporated non-profit associations' (1980) 45 MLR 626
Green examines the modes of dissolution of unincorporated associations and the judicial methods of distributing the funds. On the latter issue, he highlights four solutions, namely, equal division, tenancy in common, proportionate division based on a resulting trust and *bona vacantia*.

The equal division of the funds appears to be the court's prima facie response, save when the society's rules indicate that a different method of distribution is appropriate: see *Re Sick and Funeral Society, Golcar* [1973] Ch 51:

> As a conclusion of last resort, the maxim, 'Equality is equity' produces certainty and fairness between parties, and was the context in which it was adopted in the early cases: *Brown v Dale* (1878) 9 Ch 51 and *Feeny and Shannon v MacManus* [1937] IR 23. The more modern cases represent an unnecessary and illegitimate departure from the past authorities by elevating a maxim of last resort to the status of a *prima facie* presumption.

Megarry J in *Golcar* decided that past contributions of present members did not entitle them to join in the distribution of the society's assets because they had enjoyed the benefits of membership. Green attacks this reasoning as false logic:

> The initial claim is a narrow contractual one, the alleged conclusion is a quite separate proposition of property law. The question, 'Who is entitled to share in the benefits which the society exists to provide?', does not even provide an automatic answer to the question, 'Who is entitled to share in the society's property when it is dissolved?' let alone to the further question: 'How should the property be divided between those who are entitled to share it?

Green contends that the tenancy in common provides the guiding principle which should be adopted by the courts on a distribution on dissolution. In the majority of cases the surplus assets of a society may comprise contributions from a variety of sources – the abandoned property of past members, donations from non-members and members. Green submits: 'this property should be divided on the same proportionate basis . . .'

The resulting trust solution is appropriate where a member's subscription is construed as having been handed over on a primary trust which fails when the association is dissolved. The existence of the primary trust would depend on all the circumstances surrounding membership of a society, and it may be that the association's charter would be thought particularly important in this context. This solution was adopted in *Re Printers and Transferrers Society* [1899] 2 Ch 84, but the decision was criticised on the ground that resulting trust principles could not account for the exclusion of the rights of past members.

Green lists five reasons why the co-ownership principles ought to be given preference over the resulting trust solution. First, the co-ownership rule is applicable to all cases, whereas the resulting trust rule is applicable where a primary purpose can be ascertained. Secondly, the common ownership rule will be exhaustive of the society's surplus assets but the resulting trust is strictly limited to returning members' contributions. Thirdly, the tenancy in common solution will not lead to priority of members over the society's general creditors in the event of a liquidation or bankruptcy. Fourthly, the primary trust attendant on the resulting trust solution requires someone in whose favour the court may decree performance in the event of default by the trustees of the society's purposes. Fifthly, a resulting trust claim may be void if it fails to vest within the perpetuity period.

Finally, Green, after examining the cases that adopted the *bona vacantia* solution, concludes that:

> . . . members will only be unable to claim an interest in their association's funds in the rare case where an express or externally imposed regulation prevents them doing so. Aside of these limited occasions, *bona vacantia* is an improper conclusion in these cases.

PRESUMED RESULTING TRUST

On the creation of an express trust, the declaration of the settlor's intention would be decisive as to the ownership of the beneficial interest. Similarly, on the creation of a gift, the donor transfers the beneficial interest to the donee. However, in a presumed resulting trust, the destination of the beneficial interest is unclear on the face of the instrument effecting the transfer. In an effort to reduce the element of doubt concerning the beneficial interest, the court implies or presumes a trust in favour of the transferor. The rationale behind this principle is that equity is inclined to lean against a gift.

A presumed resulting trust is a *prima facie* rule of evidence which is capable of being rebutted. When there is no definitive evidence in the first place concerning the transferor's real intention, but merely a purchase of property or the voluntary transfer of property in the name of another, equity prima facie considers the transferee as a trustee for the transferor. In short, the transferor is presumed to have retained the equitable title. The transferee is presumed to obtain a nominal interest in the property. The rule is arbitrary but the presumption has the advantage of determining the ownership of the beneficial interest, subject to evidence to the contrary.

There are two occasions when the presumption arises, namely:

(a) a purchase of property in the name of another; and

(b) a voluntary conveyance of property in the name of another.

Purchase in the name of another

The rule is that where a purchaser contracts with a vendor to acquire real or personal property, but directs the vendor to transfer the property in the name of another, the transferee is presumed to hold the property on trust for the purchaser. Parol evidence is admissible in order to identify the purchaser.

Thus, if A purchases shares in the name of B (that is, B becomes the legal owner), the latter is presumed to hold the shares on trust for A. Accordingly, A is presumed to retain an equitable interest. B is a mere nominee for A until he rebuts the presumption.

Similarly, where A and B jointly purchase a house and have it conveyed in the name of B so that B becomes the legal owner of the house, B is presumed to hold the house on trust for both A and B in proportion to the contribution made by each of them. If A provides four-fifths and B one-fifth of the purchase money, B is presumed to hold the house for himself beneficially as to one-fifth and the remainder on trust for A: see *Bull v Bull*.

Bull v Bull [1955] 1 QB 234, CA

Facts

In 1949, the plaintiff and his mother, the defendant, jointly purchased a freehold house. The plaintiff contributed a greater part of the purchase price than the defendant. The house was conveyed in the sole name of the plaintiff. The plaintiff and defendant lived together in the house. In April 1953, on the marriage of the plaintiff, it was agreed that the defendant should occupy two rooms and the plaintiff and his wife should occupy the rest of the house. Differences arose between the parties and the plaintiff brought an action for possession of the house.

Held

The plaintiff was not allowed to recover possession of the house. The intention of the parties at the time of the purchase was that they became tenants in common. The plaintiff held the property as trustee on trust for sale for both of them. The defendant, as a tenant in common, was entitled to remain in the house until it was sold:

Denning LJ: My conclusion, therefore, is that when there are two equitable tenants in common, then, until the place is sold, each of them is entitled concurrently with the other to the possession of the land and to the use and enjoyment of it in a proper manner: and that neither of them is entitled to turn out the other.

The permutations of circumstances giving rise to the presumption are abundant. If the subject matter of the purchase is not vested in the name(s) of the purchaser(s), the *prima facie* rule referred to in *Dyer v Dyer* is that the person(s) in whose name(s) the property is conveyed is (are) presumed to hold on trust in favour of the individual(s) who provided the purchase moneys. Accordingly, the burden of rebutting the presumption lies on the party against whom the presumption operates.

Dyer v Dyer (1788) 2 Cox Eq 92, HC

Eyre CB: The clear result of all the cases, without a single exception is that the trust of a legal estate, whether taken in the names of the purchasers and others jointly, or in the names of others without that of the purchaser, whether in one name or several; whether jointly or successive – results to the man who advances the purchase money. It is the established doctrine of a court of equity that this resulting trust may be rebutted by circumstances in evidence.

In this respect, rent payable under a flat sharing arrangement is not treated as a purchase, for the tenants merely acquire the right to occupy the premises. Accordingly, such an arrangement does not involve the presumption. Hence, if A and B share a flat as tenants which is taken in A's name and the parties contribute to the outgoings, this arrangement does not involve a resulting trust. Following *Savage v Dunningham* [1973] 3 WLR 471, where A purchased a flat from his own resources and had it conveyed in his name, B was not entitled to claim an interest in the property.

Likewise, following *Hoare v Hoare* (1982) *The Times*, 9 November, where a general loan (whether secured or not) is used to purchase property, but is treated as a transaction separate from the purchase so that the borrower is entitled to use the funds as he wishes, this does not give rise to the presumption of a resulting trust. The lender, undoubtedly, retains his right to have the loan repaid but enjoys no beneficial interest in the property purchased.

In *Abrahams v Abrahams*, members of a syndicate who purchased lottery tickets acquired property rights in the lottery winnings by way of resulting trusts.

Abrahams v Trustee in Bankruptcy of Abrahams (1999) The Times, 26 July, HC

Facts

In February 1996, Mr and Mrs Abrahams joined a National Lottery syndicate at their local public house. Each person became a member and each member's weekly contribution was £1. Membership was restricted to 15 in total. There were no written rules of the syndicate, nor any formal meetings of the members. On 13 October 1996, Mrs A left her husband. At the early stage after their parting, Mrs A continued to pay £1 a week as her membership of the syndicate and a further £1 per week for her husband. The effect was that Mr A's name remained on the list of members. Occasionally Mrs A was able to recover arrears of contributions paid by her on behalf of her husband. Subsequently, after a row with Mrs A, Mr A refused to repay Mrs A for subscriptions paid on his behalf. Nevertheless, Mrs A continued to make £2 per week contributions for herself and her husband. There was no secrecy about the amount and extent of her contribution and no syndicate member objected. Mrs A intended that if there should be any substantial wins, she would be entitled to two shares rather than one.

Mr A was declared bankrupt on 25 March 1997. On 10 May 1997, the syndicate won £3,632,327. Each one-fifteenth share was worth £242,155. Mrs A claimed two one-fifteenth shares and Mr A's trustee-in-bankruptcy claimed a one-fifteenth share of the winnings. A one-fifteenth share was paid to Mrs A, but on legal advice the syndicate held back the additional one-fifteenth share.

Counsel for Mrs A argued that since she contributed the additional one-fifteenth share in the name of Mr A (a nominee), she should be entitled to that share. In addition, counsel contended that Mrs A was entitled to rely on the unrebutted presumption of resulting trust.

Held

In favour of Mrs A on the following grounds:

(a) Each weekly contribution by her constituted a present right to have any winnings received by the syndicate duly administered in accordance with its rules; *Re Campbell* [1996] 2 All ER 537 was distinguishable. This right of Mrs A was property which was capable of being held on resulting trust.

(b) On the facts, the presumption of resulting trust had arisen. Indeed, its consequence was supported by the evidence. The court decided that Mrs A had purchased a property right in the name of her husband. The right was to have winnings, if any, received by the appropriate person on the syndicate's behalf, duly administered in accordance with the rules of the syndicate, and in the absence of clear rules as the court may direct.

(c) The court was prepared to go further and decide that even before a win, a syndicate member would have been entitled to a declaration that a ticket holder would hold winnings upon trust to apply in accordance with the rules of the syndicate. The purchase of the ticket in the circumstances was treated as an existing property right that might bear fruit in the future. In contrast, in *Re Campbell* [1996] 2 All ER 537, a claim to compensation from the Criminal Injuries Compensation Board was not treated as a property right before the award was made. The applicant had a hope that his or her claim might be successful. The applicant did not have a right, but only a power, to claim an award from the Compensation Board.

(d) The court also decided that there was little or no evidence to rebut the presumption of resulting trust in favour of Mrs A.

Voluntary transfer in the name of another

Another state of affairs that gives rise to a presumed resulting trust is the occasion of a voluntary transfer of personal property in the name of another. No consideration is provided by the person in whose favour the transfer is made. Following *Re Vinogradoff*, where A transferred the legal title to shares in the name of B for no consideration, a resulting trust was presumed in favour of A.

Re Vinogradoff [1935] WN 68, HC

Facts

A grandmother voluntarily transferred £800 worth of War Loan stock into the joint names of herself and granddaughter, then aged four. By her will, the grandmother transferred her interest in the stock to another. Following the grandmother's death, the executors brought an action to determine what interest, if any, the granddaughter held in the stock.

Held

A resulting trust in favour of the grandmother was created by the transfer. Accordingly, the granddaughter was required to hold the stock on trust for her grandmother's estate.

Realty conveyed in the name of another

Where real property is voluntarily conveyed in the name of another, a presumption of resulting trust does not automatically arise under s 60(3) of the Law of Property Act 1925.

Law of Property Act 1925, s 60(3)

In a voluntary conveyance a resulting trust for the grantor shall not be implied merely by reason that the property is not expressed to be conveyed for the use or benefit of the grantee.

However, a resulting trust may still arise in accordance with the intention of the grantor, despite a voluntary conveyance in the name of the grantee: see *Hodgson v Marks* [1971] Ch 892, p 37 above.

It is unclear whether s 60(3) is applicable if the property is voluntarily conveyed in the joint names of the grantor and grantee. A case could be made out that s 60(3) is not applicable and a resulting trust will be presumed in favour of the grantor in accordance with the general rule.

Presumption of advancement

A presumption of advancement, unlike a presumption of a resulting trust, is a presumption of a gift in favour of the transferee. Where there is a special relationship between the transferor and transferee, a purchase of property in the name of another or the voluntary transfer of real or personal property in another's name gives rise to a presumption of a gift. Thus, the transferor is presumed to lose his beneficial interest in the property. This presumption, like the presumption of a resulting trust, may be rebutted by evidence of the intention of the transferor.

In *Bennet v Bennet*, Jessel MR explained the nature of the presumption of advancement.

Bennet v Bennet (1879) 10 Ch D 474, CA

Sir George Jessel MR: The doctrine of equity as regards presumption of gifts is this, that where one person stands in such a relation to another that there is an obligation on that person to make a provision for the other, and we find either a purchase or investment in the name of the other, or in the joint names of the person and the other, of an amount which could constitute a provision for the other, the presumption arises of an intention on the part of the person to discharge the obligation to the other; and therefore, in the absence of evidence to the contrary, that purchase or investment is held to be in itself evidence of a gift. In other words, the presumption of gift arises from the moral obligation to give.

That reconciles all the cases upon the subject but one, because nothing is better established than this, that as regards a child, a person, not the father of the child, may put himself in the position of one *in loco parentis* to the child, and so incur the obligation to make provision for the child . . .

But the father is under that obligation from the mere fact of his being the father, and therefore no evidence is necessary to show the obligation to provide for his child, because that is part of his duty. In the case of a father, you have only to prove the fact that he is the father, and when you have done that the obligation at once arises; but in the case of a person *in loco parentis* you must prove that he took upon himself the obligation.

The special relationships with the transferees which give rise to the presumptions of advancement are occasions which the courts have recognised in the past as involving moral obligations on the part of the transferors to benefit the transferees. These are:

(a) the transferor is the husband of the transferee;

(b) the transferor is the father of the transferee (legitimate child);

(c) the transferor stands *in loco parentis patris* (surrogate male parent) to the child.

Husband and wife

The strength of this presumption as a means of ascertaining ownership of family assets has been reduced since the mid-1940s: see *Pettitt v Pettitt* [1970] AC 777, p 226 below. The principle applicable to the family home will be discussed later under constructive trusts.

The presumption operates when the husband transfers property in the name of his wife. The rationale for the rule was the husband's natural obligation to provide for his wife. The rule was stated in *Re Eykyn's*.

Re Eykyns's Trusts (1877) 6 Ch D 115

Malins VC: The law of this court is perfectly settled that when a husband transfers money or other property into the name of his wife only, then the presumption is, that it is intended as a gift or advancement to the wife absolutely at once . . . And if the husband invests in money, stocks or otherwise, in the names of himself and his wife, then also it is an advancement for the benefit of the wife absolutely if she survives the husband.

However, the presumption of resulting trust applies if the wife transfers property in the name of the husband. The essential point is that the wife (transferee) is required to be the lawful wife of the transferor so that the presumption of advancement will not, of course, arise in favour of a mistress or person via similar relationships.

Note

Sarah Greer in an article entitled, 'A last resort' (2007) 157 NLJ 696, questions whether the presumption of advancement concerning transfers from a husband to his wife serves any useful purpose today and whether it contravenes Art 5 of the Seventh Protocol to the European Convention on Human Rights by maintaining a gender bias?

Father and child

'Child' refers to the legitimate child of the transferor. If the father transfers property or purchases property in the name of his legitimate child, the presumption of a gift arises. This presumption is not displaced by slight evidence: see *Shephard v Cartwright* [1955] AC 431.

On the other hand, if the mother transfers property in the name of her legitimate child, the presumption of a resulting trust arises (see the summary of the principle stated by Jessel MR in *Bennet v Bennet*, above).

Persons standing in loco parentis patris

This category of presumed gifts is applicable to persons who undertake the duties of fatherhood in respect of the child; see *Bennet v Bennet*. These duties, apparently, cannot be undertaken by a female donor.

Bennet v Bennet (1879) 10 Ch D 474, CA

Jessel MR: A person *in loco parentis* means a person taking upon himself the duty of a father of a child to make provision for that child. It is clear that the presumption can only arise from that obligation, and therefore the doctrine can only have reference to the obligation of a father to provide for his child, and nothing else.

Whether the donor stands *in loco parentis* to the donee is a question of degree. The essential issue is whether the male donor has placed himself in the position of a father to that child, that is, treating the child as his own, maintaining and providing care and attention for the child. *Re Paradise Motor Co* illustrates this proposition.

Re Paradise Motor Co [1968] I WLR 1125, CA

Facts

In 1948, F, the stepfather of S, executed a transfer of 350 shares in favour of S, whom he treated in the same way as his three other sons. S's name appeared in the company's register of members. In 1954, F, having fallen out with S, wished to claim back 300 of the shares. In pursuance of this objective, F procured a transfer to himself of 300 shares which appeared to bear S's signature (this was not authorised). The company's register of members was accordingly altered. In 1964, the company was wound up and £12,000 was available for distribution. The liquidator informed S that he was the registered holder of 50 shares only. S told his half brother and the liquidator that he laid no claim to the shares. Later, he changed his mind and claimed to be entitled to 350 shares in the company.

Held

In favour of F, on the following grounds:

(a) The relationship between F and S was such as to give rise to the presumption of advancement in favour of S. *Prima facie*, in 1948, F was treated as having made a gift of 350 shares to S.

(b) S's statement to his half brother and the liquidator manifested an intention to disclaim his interest in the holding of 350 shares.

(c) This disclaimer *inter vivos* (which was outside the province of s 53(1)(c) of the Law of Property Act 1925 because it operated by way of 'avoidance' rather than 'disposition') could not, in the circumstances, be withdrawn and amounted to a rebuttal of the presumption of advancement. F was therefore entitled to claim the benefit of 350 shares.

Question

What role do the presumptions of resulting trust and advancement play in the law of trusts?

Rebuttal of the presumptions

The presumptions of resulting trust and advancement are, in a sense, artificial rules for deciding the intention of the transferor or purchaser and may give way to the real intention of the parties.

Although the weight of the presumptions will vary with the circumstances of each case, the courts will consider all the surrounding facts and decide whether the presumption has been rebutted or not: see *Fowkes v Pascoe*. The quality of the rebutting evidence varies from case to case.

Fowkes v Pascoe (1875) LR 10 Ch App 343, CA

Mellish LJ: . . . the presumption must . . . be of very different weight in different cases. In some cases it would be very strong indeed. If, for instance, a man invested a sum of stock in the name of himself and his solicitor, the inference would be very strong indeed that it was intended solely for the purpose of a trust, and the court would require very strong evidence on the part of the solicitor to prove that it was intended as a gift; and certainly his own evidence would not be sufficient. On the other hand, a man may make an investment of stock in the name of himself and some person, although not a child or wife, yet in such a position to him as to make it extremely probable that the investment was intended as a gift. In such a case, although the rule of law, if there is no evidence at all, would compel the court to say that the presumption of trust must prevail, even if the court might not believe that the fact was in accordance with the presumption, yet, if there is evidence to rebut the presumption, then the court must go into the actual facts.

Facts

Mrs Baker purchased stock in the joint names of herself and John Pascoe, the son of Mrs Baker's daughter-in-law. By her will, Mrs Baker gave her residuary estate to her daughter-in-law for life with remainder to John Pascoe and his sister in equal shares. After Mrs Baker's death, John Pascoe claimed to be entitled to the dividends due before and after her death as well as the stock capital after her death.

Held

The claimant was entitled to the dividends and the stock capital after Mrs Baker's death. The resulting trust in favour of Mrs Baker which arose on the date of purchase was rebutted, but only after her death. Thus, she was entitled to the income during her lifetime.

In *Lord Grey v Lady Grey* (1677) 2 Swan 594, the court held that a conveyance of real property from a father to his adult son created the presumption of advancement. This presumption was not rebutted when the son allowed the father to receive the rents from the land. Such conduct was treated as an 'act of reverence and good manners'.

In *Shephard v Cartwright*, it was decided that where an infant acts in accordance with the directions of his father, this evidence may be insufficient to rebut the presumption of advancement. The infant may not have been capable of exercising an independent judgment.

Shephard v Cartwright [1955] AC 431, HL

Viscount Simonds: It appears to me to be an indispensable condition of such conduct being admissible that it should be performed with knowledge of the material facts. In the present case, the undisputed fact that the appellants under their father's guidance did what they were told without inquiry or knowledge precludes the admission in evidence of their conduct and, if it were admitted, would deprive it of all probative value.

In this case, the court laid down the test of admissibility of evidence, namely, evidence of matters arising after the transaction, so as to be independent from the purchase, may only be admissible against the party who performed the act or made the declaration; whereas acts and declarations occurring before such transaction are admissible for or against the party.

Facts

In 1929, the plaintiffs' father promoted several private companies and had the shares allotted to his three children. In a series of subsequent transactions, these shares were sold and a large portion of the proceeds of sale dissipated. In 1934, the children signed documents at the request of their father without understanding the effect of what they were doing. The result was that the shares were sold by the father and the proceeds of sale paid into their accounts. In 1935, the father obtained the children's signatures to documents authorising him to withdraw moneys from their accounts. By 1936, the father had withdrawn all the money from the accounts, some of it used for the benefit of the children but a large part of it remaining unaccounted for at the time of his death in 1949.

The children brought an action against their father's executors claiming an account of the money due to them.

Held

It was found in favour of the children, on the following grounds:

(a) The registration of the shares in the children's names created a presumption of advancement.

(b) The events which took place after the allotment (signatures of the children) were capable of being evidence against the children in that the evidence could be construed as 'admissions' against their interest. However, such evidence was not admissible against the children because they signed the documents under the guidance and control of their father. They did what they were told without inquiry or knowledge.

(c) Accordingly, the presumption of advancement was not rebutted:

Viscount Simonds: [Having decided that the transfer of shares to the children created a presumption of advancement, he continued:] It must be asked by what evidence can the presumption be rebutted, and it would, I think, be very unfortunate if any doubt were cast (as I think it has been by certain passages in the judgments under review) upon the well settled law on this subject. It is, I think, correctly stated in substantially the same terms in every textbook that I have consulted and supported by authority extending over a long period of time. I will take, as an example, a passage from *Snell's Equity*, 24th edn, 1954, p 153, which is as follows:

> The acts and declarations of the parties before or at the time of the purchase, or so immediately after it as to constitute a part of the transaction, are admissible in evidence either for or against the party who did the act or made the declaration ... But subsequent declarations are admissible as evidence only against the party who made them, and not in his favour.

But although the applicable law is not in doubt, the application of it is not always easy. There must often be room for argument whether a subsequent act is part of the same transaction as the original purchase of transfer, and equally whether subsequent acts which it is sought to adduce in evidence ought to be regarded as admissions by the party so acting, and if they are so admitted, further facts should be admitted by way of qualification of those admissions ...

I conceive it possible, and this view is supported by authority, that there might be such a course of conduct by a child after a presumed advancement as to constitute an admission by him of his parent's original intention, though such evidence should be regarded jealousy. But it appears to me to be an indispensable condition of such conduct being admissible that it should be performed with knowledge of the material facts. *In the present case the undisputed fact that the appellants under their father's guidance did what they were told without inquiry or knowledge precludes the admission in evidence of their conduct and, if it were admitted, would deprive it of all probative value.* I do not hesitate to say that the only conclusion which I can form about the deceased's original intention is that he meant the provision he then made for his children to be for their permanent advancement [emphasis added].

In *Re Gooch* (1890) 62 LT 384, the presumption of advancement was rebutted. In this case, a father bought shares in the name of his son to enable him (the son) to qualify as a director of a company. The son consistently paid the dividends over to his father and later delivered the share certificates to him.

In *Re Paradise Motor Co*, the presumption of advancement was rebutted by a disclaimer on the part of the equitable owner.

Re Paradise Motor Co Ltd [1968] 1 WLR 1125, CA

Facts

A stepfather, who stood *in loco parentis* to his stepson, transferred a block of shares in his name. After an argument with his stepfather, the stepson told his half brother and the liquidator of the company that he was no longer interested in the relevant shares. The question in issue was whether the presumption of advancement was rebutted.

Held

The conduct of the stepson had the effect of disclaiming his interest and rebutting the presumption of advancement.

In *Warren v Guerney*, the presumption of advancement was also rebutted. The conduct of the father and his statement at the time of the transfer were sufficient evidence to rebut the presumption of advancement.

Warren v Guerney [1944] 2 All ER 472, CA

Facts

A father purchased a house for £300 in 1929 and had it conveyed in the name of his daughter. At the same time, he declared orally that his wish after his death was that the house should be used for the benefit of his three daughters equally. The father retained the title deeds. In 1943, the father signed a document headed 'my wish' in which he repeated his earlier oral declaration. He died in 1944; the title deeds were still in his possession at the time of his death. The executors of the father's will contended that the daughter became a trustee of the property for her father's estate.

Held

The court found in favour of the executors, on the following grounds:

(a) The document headed 'my wish' was not admissible in evidence as it was a subsequent declaration by the donor, and did not operate against the donor's interest.

(b) However, the retention of the title deeds by the father coupled with his contemporaneous declaration at the time of the purchase were sufficient evidence in rebuttal of the presumption.

Thus, the daughter held the house as trustee for her father's estate:

> **Morton LJ:** It is well established that when a parent buys a property and has it conveyed into the name of his child, there arises a presumption that the parent intended to make a gift or advancement to the child of that property. Of course, that is a presumption which can be rebutted by evidence that that was not the father's intention. The father retained the title deeds of the property and he still had them in his possession when he died in the year 1944.
>
> Three points were taken by counsel for the appellant. First of all, he contended that the judge was wrong in admitting as evidence a document headed 'my wish', which he held was signed by Elijah Gurney, which was dated 6 September 1943. In my view counsel's contention under that heading was quite correct. The document headed 'my wish' was not admissible in evidence. It was in the nature of a subsequent declaration by the alleged donor, which was not against his own interest, and it is clearly established that subsequent declarations by the alleged donor are only admissible if they are against his interest. The reason for that is quite obvious. If the rule were otherwise, it would be extremely easy for persons to manufacture evidence, even although at the time when they made the purchase they in fact intended the child to have the gift of the property.

The second contention put forward by counsel for the appellants was that, on the admissible evidence, the judge was not justified in coming to the conclusion that the defendants had rebutted the presumption of advancement. In my view, there was ample evidence to justify that conclusion of the judge. In the first place, there is the fact that the father retained the title deeds from the time of purchase to the time of his death. I think that is a very significant fact, because title deeds, as it was said in *Coke on Littleton*, are 'sinews of the land'. One would have expected the father to have handed them over, either to the plaintiff or her husband, if he had intended the gift. It is to be noted that the judge accepted the evidence given by the plaintiff's mother, Mary Ann Gurney, and by her brother, Meyrick George Gurney, and rejected the evidence of Denis Warren, the plaintiff's husband, where it conflicted with that given by those two witnesses.

It is quite clear that contemporaneous declarations by the alleged donor are admissible in evidence. I am satisfied that there was ample evidence upon which the judge could found his conclusion, and, indeed, it is difficult to see how, on the evidence which he believed, he could have reached any other conclusion.

[The third contention raised by counsel for the appellants was not related to the beneficial ownership of the house.]

In *McGrath v Wallis*, the Court of Appeal decided that a house acquired for joint occupation by a father and son, but conveyed in the sole name of the son, gave rise to the equitable presumption of advancement, which was rebutted by comparatively slight evidence. The court reiterated Lord Upjohn's view in *Pettitt v Pettitt* [1970] AC 777, to the effect that the presumptions of advancement and resulting trust, when properly understood and applied to circumstances of today, remained as useful as ever in solving questions of title, but are readily rebutted by comparatively slight evidence. Although *Pettitt v Pettitt* was a case between husband and wife, the same principle applies to transactions between father and child.

McGrath v Wallis [1995] 2 FLR 114, CA

Facts

In 1959, the father of the plaintiff (daughter) and the defendant (the plaintiff's brother) acquired a house in Luton which was placed in the sole name of the father and remained the family home for many years. The plaintiff lived there until she married in 1974. The defendant lived there until his mother died in 1985. In 1986, the father decided to sell the house and move elsewhere. To acquire the second house (Talbot Road), an additional amount was required to be raised by way of a mortgage. The father was not employed at the time, but a mortgage offer was made by a building society to the defendant and, in due course, the house was conveyed into his sole name. The father instructed his solicitors to draw up a deed which was intended to have been a declaration of trust. The deed declared that the Talbot Road house was to be held by the defendant upon trust for his father and himself in unequal shares of 80% and 20% respectively. The deed was never sent by the solicitors to the father but was found unsigned in their files. The father died intestate in 1990 and the plaintiff claimed to be entitled to a share of the Talbot Road property. The defendant denied that she had any such interest. The trial judge decided in favour of the defendant on the ground that the presumption of advancement arose in favour of the defendant and the plaintiff had failed to discharge the burden of proof cast on her. The plaintiff appealed to the Court of Appeal.

Held

The appeal was allowed. In the circumstances, the presumption of advancement was rebutted by evidence in accordance with the intention of the parties. This was reflected in the sharing of the beneficial interest between the father and son on an 80:20 basis. The decisive factors were:

(a) the defendant alone was acceptable as a mortgagor of the property;

(b) the father had never told the defendant that he had instructed the solicitors not to proceed with the declaration of trust;

(c) no reason had been suggested for the father wishing to divest himself of all interest in the house.

It would appear that this rule concerning the admissibility of evidence has been overtaken by the Civil Evidence Act 1995 which admits the relevant evidence, even evidence of subsequent acts or declarations, either for or against the actor or declarant. Section 2 is an extremely broad provision which admits both hearsay and narrative assertions made orally, or in a document or otherwise and irrespective of whether the maker of the statement is a witness or not. In this context, no cases have been decided. The document which was excluded in *Warren v Guerney* (see p 168 above) would now be admissible under s 1 of the 1995 Act. The weight to be attached to the evidence will vary with the facts of each case. Section 4 of the Act declares that in evaluating the weight to be attached to hearsay statements, the court is required to consider all the circumstances in which the statement was made, including the question whether the statement was made contemporaneously with the occurrence of the event or not.

Civil Evidence Act 1995, s 1: admissibility of hearsay evidence

(1) In civil proceedings evidence shall not be excluded on the ground that it is hearsay.

Civil Evidence Act 1995, s 4: considerations relevant to weighing of hearsay evidence

(1) In estimating the weight (if any) to be given to hearsay evidence in civil proceedings the court shall have regard to any circumstances from which any inference can reasonably be drawn as to the reliability or otherwise of the evidence.

(2) Regard may be had, in particular, to the following:

(a) whether it would have been reasonable and practicable for the party to whom the evidence was adduced to have produced the maker of the original statement as a witness;

(b) whether the original statement was made contemporaneously with the occurrence or existence of the matters stated;

(c) whether the evidence involves multiple hearsay;

(d) whether any person involved had any motive to conceal or misrepresent matters;

(e) whether the original statement was an edited account, or was made in collaboration with another or for a particular purpose;

(f) whether the circumstances in which the evidence is adduced as hearsay are such as to suggest an attempt to prevent proper evaluation of its weight.

Rebuttal evidence and intended illegality

Originally, the court did not allow a party to rebut the presumption of advancement by adducing evidence of his own attempted illegality or fraudulent purpose on public policy grounds (but see *Tribe v Tribe* [1995] 3 WLR 913, CA, p 175 below). If the transfer is made in order to avoid creditors and the transferor becomes insolvent then, by virtue of the Insolvency Act 1986, the conveyance may be set aside by the court. The situation that we are now considering is in respect of a transfer in an attempt to put the property out of reach of the creditors. The precaution taken by the transferor has become unnecessary because he (the transferor) does not become insolvent, but he wishes to put the clock back to what it was before the transfer. In short, the claim is made by the transferor to recover the property from the transferee. The court originally applied the following maxim indiscriminately, 'He who comes to Equity, must come with clean hands': see *Gascoigne v Gascoigne*.

Gascoigne v Gascoigne [1918] 1 KB 223, DC

Facts

A husband, who was heavily in debt, took a lease of land. In order to protect his property from his creditors, he arranged for the lease to be taken in his wife's name. The wife was also aware of the purpose behind the husband's action. He then built a bungalow on the land with his own money.

Later, when the marriage had broken down, the husband claimed that the wife held the lease as trustee for him and called on her to assign it to him. The wife contended that the presumption of advancement existed in her favour and this presumption could not be rebutted by evidence of her husband's impropriety.

Held

The decision of the county court judge was reversed. The presumption of advancement could not be rebutted by evidence of the husband's fraudulent conduct, despite the wife being a party to the transaction:

> **Lush LJ:** Now, assuming that there was evidence to support the finding that the defendant was a party to the scheme which the plaintiff admitted, but without deciding it, what the learned judge has done is this: he has permitted the plaintiff to rebut the presumption which the law raises by setting up his own illegality and fraud, and to obtain relief in equity because he has succeeded in proving it. The plaintiff cannot do this; and, whether the point was taken or not in the county court this court cannot allow a judgment to stand which has given relief under such circumstances as that.

Note

The court came to a similar conclusion in *Re Emery's Investment* [1959] Ch 410. A husband, who transferred shares in the name of his wife in order to evade the tax laws of a foreign country, was not allowed to adduce evidence of the purpose of the transfer.

The principle applied in *Gascoigne v Gascoigne* and *Re Emery* was approved by the Court of Appeal in *Tinker v Tinker*. The transferor (husband) was not allowed to adduce evidence of his improper motives regarding the conveyance.

Tinker v Tinker [1970] 1 All ER 540, CA

Facts

In 1967, the husband bought a garage business near Bodmin in his own name. He also entered into negotiations to purchase a residence for himself and his family. At first he thought of having the residence put into his own name but on consulting his solicitor, he decided that it should be put into his wife's name so that, if his garage business was not a success, his creditors would not be able to take it. The legal title to the house was conveyed in his wife's name. Subsequently, the marriage broke up. The wife claimed the house as hers. The registrar dismissed her claim to it. He found that the husband was an honest businessman intending and able to honour his financial commitments; that he intended this house to belong to him beneficially; and accordingly that the wife held the house in trust for her husband absolutely. The wife appealed to the Court of Appeal.

Held

The wife's appeal was allowed. The husband was not allowed to adduce evidence to the effect that the conveyance to the wife was as nominee for him:

> **Lord Denning MR:** Accepting that in the present case the husband was honest – he acted, he said, on the advice of his solicitor – nevertheless, I do not think that he can claim that the house belongs to him. The solicitor did not give evidence. But the only proper advice that he could give was: 'In order to avoid the house being taken by your creditors, you can put it into your wife's name; but remember that, if you do, it is your wife's and you cannot go back on it.'
>
> But, whether the solicitor gave that advice or not, I am quite clear that the husband cannot have it both ways. So he is on the horns of a dilemma. He cannot say that the house is his own and, at one and the same time, say that it is his wife's. As against his wife, he wants to say that it belongs to him. As against his creditors, that it belongs to her. That simply will not do. Either it was conveyed to her for her own use absolutely; or it was conveyed to her as trustee for her husband. It must be one or other. The presumption is that it was conveyed to her as trustee for her husband. It must be one or other. The presumption is that it was conveyed to her for her own use; and he does not rebut that presumption by saying that he only did it to defeat his creditors. I think that it belongs to her.

In *Rowan v Dann* (1992) 64 P & CR 202, the Court of Appeal adopted a different approach to the issue. If the transfer creates a resulting trust in favour of the transferor so that *prima facie* he retains the equitable interest and he does not rely on his own improper conduct in order to recover the property, the court may allow him to do so. It is immaterial that the defendant raises the issue that the transferor does not have 'clean hands'.

Rowan v Dann (1992) 64 P & CR 202, CA

Facts

Rowan was the owner of farmland. He granted tenancies to Dann in order to prevent the assets falling into the hands of his creditors should he become bankrupt, and also in pursuance of an intended joint business venture. No rent was actually paid although such payment was stipulated in the agreement. Rowan claimed that the land should revert to him under a resulting trust as the purpose of the transfer (a joint business venture) had failed to materialise. Dann claimed that Rowan could not rely on the resulting trust as he did not have 'clean hands', having created sham tenancies in order to defeat his creditors.

Held

A resulting trust existed in favour of Rowan by reason of the failure of the joint business venture, and this presumption was not rebutted. The improper, underlying purpose of the transfer was common to both sides. The creditors were not disadvantaged and Rowan did not have to rely on the unlawful purpose to support his claim:

> **Mellish LJ:** . . . if the illegal transaction had been carried out, the plaintiff himself, in my judgment, could not afterwards have recovered the goods. But the illegal transaction was not carried out; it wholly came to an end. To hold that the plaintiff is enabled to recover does not carry out the illegal transaction, but the effect is to put everybody in the same situation as they were before the illegal transaction was determined upon, and before the parties took any steps to carry it out. That, I apprehend, is the true distinction in point of law. If money is paid or goods delivered for an illegal purpose, the person who had so paid the money or delivered the goods may recover them back before the illegal purpose is carried out; but if he waits till the illegal purpose is carried out, or if he seeks to enforce the illegal transaction, in neither case can he maintain an action; the law will not allow that to be done.
>
> In the present case, there is no evidence that the scheme to defeat creditors was put into effect. There is no evidence that any creditor was persuaded to hold his hand in the belief that Mr Rowan's land was encumbered by the tenancies and the option. In my opinion, the present case is on its facts covered by the principle expressed in *Taylor v Bowers* [1876] 1 QBD 291.

In *Tinsley v Milligan*, the House of Lords reviewed the authorities and adopted the approach laid down in *Rowan v Dann*. There is no inflexible or rigid rule to the effect that evidence of a fraudulent or unlawful purpose for a conveyance is sufficient to prevent an equitable owner recovering his property if he does not rely on this purpose to support his claim.

Tinsley v Milligan [1993] 3 WLR 126, HL (Lords Jauncey of Tullichettle, Lowry and Browne-Wilkinson; Lords Keith of Kinkel and Goff of Chieveley dissenting)

Facts

The plaintiff and defendant jointly purchased a house which was conveyed in the name of the plaintiff. Over a period of years, the defendant, with the knowledge and assent of the plaintiff, made false claims on the Department of Social Security. Having the property in the sole name of the plaintiff assisted in the fraud. A very small amount of the proceeds of fraud was put into the house by the defendant. The plaintiff also made fraudulent claims on the DSS but was convicted, fined and ordered to make repayments. The parties had an argument. This led to the plaintiff serving a notice to quit on the defendant. The defendant counterclaimed for a declaration that the property was held on trust for sale for both parties in equal shares.

Held

In favour of the defendant and affirming the decision of the Court of Appeal, but on different grounds. *Prima facie*, the claimant had an equitable interest in the property equivalent to the contribution she made to its purchase. Since she was not relying on her own illegality in order to maintain her interest, the court would not prevent her establishing her claim:

Lord Browne-Wilkinson: Neither at law nor in equity will the court enforce an illegal contract which has been partially, but not fully, performed. However, it does not follow that all acts done under a partially performed contract are of no effect. In particular it is now clearly established that at law (as opposed to in equity), property in goods or land can pass under, or pursuant to, such a contract. *If so, the rights of the owner of the legal title thereby acquired will be enforced, provided that the plaintiff can establish such title without pleading or leading evidence of the illegality.* It is said that the property lies where it falls, even though legal title to the property was acquired as a result of the property passing under the illegal contract itself [emphasis added].

In the present case, Miss Milligan claims under a resulting or implied trust. The court below have found, and it is not now disputed, that apart from the question of illegality Miss Milligan would have been entitled in equity to a half share in the house in accordance with the principles exemplified in *Gissing v Gissing* [1971] 1 AC 886; *Grant v Edwards* [1986] Ch 638 and *Lloyds Bank plc v Rosset* [1991] AC 107. The creation of such an equitable interest does not depend upon a contractual obligation but on a common intention acted upon by the parties to their detriment. It is a development of the old law of resulting trust under which, where two parties have provided the purchase money to buy a property which is conveyed into the name of one of them alone, the latter is presumed to hold the property on a resulting trust for both parties in shares proportionate to their contributions to the purchase price. In arguments, no distinction was drawn between strict resulting trusts and a *Gissing v Gissing* type of trust.

The presumption of a resulting trust is, in my view, crucial in considering the authorities. On that presumption (and on the contrary presumption of advancement) hinges the answer to the crucial question 'does a plaintiff claiming under a resulting trust have to rely on the underlying illegality?' Where the presumption of resulting trust applies, the plaintiff does not have to rely on the illegality. If he proves that the property is vested in the defendant alone but that the plaintiff provided part of the purchase money, or voluntarily transferred the property to the defendant, the plaintiff establishes his claim under a resulting trust unless either the contrary presumption of advancement displaces the presumption of resulting trust or the defendant leads evidence to rebut the presumption of resulting trust. *Therefore, in cases where the presumption of advancement does not apply, a plaintiff can establish his equitable interest in the property without relying in any way on the underlying illegal transaction.* In this case Miss Milligan as defendant simply pleaded the common intention that the property should belong to both of them and that she contributed to the purchase price: she claimed that in consequence the property belonged to them equally. To the same effect was her evidence in chief. Therefore, Miss Milligan was not forced to rely on the illegality to prove her equitable interest. Only in the reply and the course of Miss Milligan's cross-examination did such illegality emerge: it was Miss Tinsley who had to rely on that illegality [emphasis added].

Although the presumption of advancement does not directly arise for consideration in this case, it is important when considering the decided cases to understand its operation. On a transfer from a man to his wife, children or others to whom he stands *in loco parentis*, equity presumes an intention to make a gift. Therefore, in such a case, unlike the case where the presumption of resulting trust applies, in order to establish any claim the plaintiff has himself to lead evidence sufficient to rebut the presumption of gift and in so doing will normally have to plead, and give evidence of, the underlying illegal purpose.

A party to an illegality can recover by virtue of a legal or equitable property interest if, but only if, he can establish his title without relying on his own illegality. *In cases where the presumption of advancement applies, the plaintiff is faced with the presumption of gift and therefore cannot claim under a resulting trust unless and until he has rebutted that presumption of gift: for those purposes the plaintiff does have to rely on the underlying illegality and therefore fails* [emphasis added].

In my judgment the time has come to decide clearly that the rule is the same whether a plaintiff founds himself on a legal or equitable title: he is entitled to recover if he is not forced to plead or rely on the illegality, even if it emerges that the title on which he relied was acquired in the course of carrying through an illegal transaction.

As applied in the present case, that principle would operate as follows. Miss Milligan established a resulting trust by showing that she had contributed to the purchase price of the house and that there was common understanding between her and Miss Tinsley that they owned the house equally. She had no need to allege or prove why the house was conveyed into the name of Miss Tinsley alone, since that fact was irrelevant to her claim: it was enough to show that the house was in fact vested in Miss Tinsley alone. The illegality only emerged at all because Miss Tinsley sought to raise it. Having proved these facts, Miss Milligan had raised a presumption of resulting trust. There was no evidence to rebut that presumption. Therefore Miss Milligan should succeed. This is exactly the process of reasoning adopted by the Ontario Court of Appeal in *Gorog v Kiss* (1977) 78 DLR (3rd ed) 690 which in my judgment was rightly decided.

Likewise, in *Silverwood v Silverwood*, despite the unlawful nature of the transaction, the plaintiff did not have to rely on evidence of illegality in order to establish a claim based on a resulting trust. This was presumed in his favour. Moreover, in order to rebut a defence that the transfer was intended as a gift, the plaintiff was entitled to lead evidence of the unlawful nature of the transaction. It would be 'absurd as well as unjust' to prevent the plaintiff adducing such evidence.

Silverwood v Silverwood (1997) 74 P & CR 453, CA

Facts

The plaintiff (Geoffrey) was appointed sole executor of the will of his mother, Daisy. In February 1991, when Daisy was aged 88, the sum of £21,278 was withdrawn from her account and deposited in equal shares in the names of her two grandchildren, Gillian and Andrew. An application was made on Daisy's behalf for Income Support. On the application form, no reference was made to the moneys transferred to the grandchildren. The DSS commenced paying Income Support to, or on behalf of, Daisy. Under Daisy's will, Geoffrey and another brother, Arnold, were made the only beneficiaries. After Daisy's death, the plaintiff obtained probate of the will and commenced proceedings against the defendants, seeking recovery of the moneys paid in 1991. The defendants contended that the moneys paid to them were by way of a gift. The judge decided in favour of the plaintiff, applying the principle in *Tinsley v Milligan*. The defendants appealed.

Facts

The resulting trust in favour of the plaintiff had not been rebutted. The defence, that the donor intended to make a gift, was rejected. The plaintiff was entitled to lead rebutting evidence of the unlawful nature of the transaction to show that no gift was intended:

Peter Gibson LJ: [referred to Lord Browne-Wilkinson's judgment in *Tinsley v Milligan* [1993] 3 WLR 126 and continued:] The test is whether, of necessity, reliance is placed by the claimant on the illegality in proving his claim. Whether there is reliance such as would disentitle the claimant to succeed depends on the particular circumstances of the particular case, and it is of importance in this regard to look at the pleadings. Thus, as Lord Browne-Wilkinson pointed out in *Tinsley v Milligan*, Miss Milligan as defendant simply pleaded the common intention that the property should belong to both her and Miss Tinsley and that she, Miss Milligan, contributed to the purchase price, and she claimed that, in consequence, the property belonged to them equally. Lord Browne-Wilkinson went on to say that to the same effect was Miss Milligan's evidence-in-chief, and only in the reply of Miss Tinsley and, in the course of the cross-examination of Miss Milligan, did such illegality emerge.

There is, therefore, a factual difference between *Tinsley v Milligan* and the present case, in that in our case *the defendants did not plead the illegality and some evidence of the illegality was led by Geoffrey.* Mr Carswell (counsel for the defendants) said that Geoffrey led in-chief, enthusiastically and at length, evidence by witness statements which were supplemented by live testimony, asserting that the transfer of money out of Mrs Silverwood's account was made in fraud of the DSS, so that Mrs Silverwood would qualify for income support. In this regard, Mr Carswell referred to the witness statements of Geoffrey and of two of his witnesses, Mr Ellis and Gillian's ex-husband, Mr Whiteley, and to parts of their oral evidence. Having read all the evidence, I think Mr Carswell's description of what Geoffrey did is somewhat overstated. But the only relevance of that evidence was to rebut the defence that the transfer to Andrew and Gillian was a gift, a defence which the judge found to have been concocted [emphasis added].

It would be absurd as well as unjust if a claimant, claiming a resulting trust, could not lead evidence of fraud in order to disprove a spurious defence. Consistently with the statement of principle by Lord Browne-Wilkinson, I do not regard the leading of that evidence as of crucial importance. To claim title under the resulting trust, Geoffrey had no need to allege or prove why the money was transferred to Andrew and Gillian, and for that purpose he did not rely on the illegality, which did not, of necessity, form part of Geoffrey's case. He did not plead the illegality: he simply pleaded the transfer to Andrew and Gillian and the consequent resulting trust.

Accordingly, the test laid down by the majority in *Tinsley v Milligan*, namely, whether, of necessity, reliance is placed by the claimant on the illegality in pursuing his claim, is not satisfied.

The Court of Appeal in *Tribe v Tribe* decided that where the presumption of advancement is created by a transfer of property intended to promote an unlawful purpose, but which has not been carried into effect, the transferor is entitled to adduce evidence of the unlawful purpose in order to rebut the presumption of advancement. *Gascoigne v Gascoigne* was distinguished on the ground that, in that case, there was sufficient evidence that the husband intended to transfer the beneficial interest in the house to his wife. Moreover, *Tinker v Tinker* was regarded as a case where the husband's evidence confirmed the presumption of advancement as distinct from rebutting it.

Tribe v Tribe [1995] 3 WLR 913, CA

Facts

A father voluntarily transferred shares to his son. The purpose of the transfer was to deceive creditors by creating the appearance that the father no longer owned the shares in the company. The father never carried the illegal purpose into effect, in that he had no cause to rely on the transfer as against any creditor. The father now claimed the return of the shares from the son. The judge at first instance allowed the father to lead evidence of the illegal purpose in order to rebut the presumption of advancement on the ground that the illegal purpose had not been carried into effect. Having admitted the evidence, the judge held that the father's claim succeeded. The son appealed to the Court of Appeal.

Held

The appeal was dismissed. The court ruled that the prohibition against a claimant founding his action on an illegal act had led to seemingly unjust results. The courts had made exceptions to this rule. In *Tinsley v Milligan*, the House of Lords decided that where the legal interest in property is transferred to another in order to promote an illegal purpose and the presumption of a resulting trust operated in favour of the transferor, the latter is entitled to recover the property on the ground that he was not forced to rely on the illegality but only on the resulting trust that arose in his favour on the transfer. In this case, the Court of Appeal expressed the view that the Law Lords in *Tinsley v Milligan* did not decide that a claimant was not entitled to restitution where the illegal purpose had not been carried into effect. In order to rebut the presumption of advancement in respect of a transfer for an intended illegal purpose, it was necessary for the claimant to show:

(a) that the illegal purpose had not been carried out;

(b) that he intended to retain a beneficial interest in the property based on compelling circumstantial evidence; and

(c) that he concealed this interest from his creditors.

Millett LJ: The question in the present case is the converse: whether the transferor can rebut the presumption of advancement by giving evidence of his illegal purpose so long as the illegal purpose has not been carried into effect. The leading cases on illegality and the presumption of advancement are *Childers v Childers* (1857) 3 K & J 310; *Crichton v Crichton* (1895) 13 R 770; *Perpetual Executors and Trustees Association of Australia Ltd v Wright* (1917) 23 CLR 185; *Gascoigne v Gascoigne* [1918] 1 KB 223; *McEvoy v Belfast Banking Co Ltd* [1935] AC 24; *Re Emery's Investments Trusts* [1959] Ch 410; *Palaniappa Chettiar v Arunasalam Chettiar* [1962] AC 294; and *Tinker v Tinker* [1970] P 136.

[His Lordship considered these authorities and continued:] The question whether a transferor can repudiate his fraudulent scheme before it is carried into effect and then give evidence of his dishonest intention in order to rebut the presumption of advancement did not fall for consideration in either of those cases. It was not considered in *Gascoigne v Gascoigne*, where it was arguably too late for him to do so; and it did not arise in *Tinker v Tinker*, where he was found to have had no dishonest intention.

In my opinion, the weight of the authorities supports the view that a person who seeks to recover property transferred by him for an illegal purpose can lead evidence of his dishonest intention whenever it is necessary for him to do so provided that he has withdrawn from the transaction before the illegal purpose has been carried out. It is not necessary, if he can rely on an express or resulting trust in his favour; but it is necessary (i) if he brings an action at law, and (ii) if he brings proceedings in equity and needs to rebut the presumption of advancement. The availability of the *locus poenitentiae* is well documented in the former case. I would not willingly adopt a rule which differentiated between the rule of the common law and that of equity in a restitutionary context [emphasis added].

In my opinion the following propositions represent the present state of the law:

(1) title to property passes both at law and in equity even if the transfer is made for an illegal purpose. The fact that title has passed to the transferee does not preclude the transferor from bringing an action for restitution;

(2) the transferor's action will fail if it would be illegal for him to retain any interest in the property;

(3) subject to (2), the transferor can recover the property if he can do so without relying on the illegal purpose. This will normally be the case where the property was transferred without consideration in circumstances where the transferor can rely on an express declaration of trust or a resulting trust in his favour;

(4) it will almost invariably be so where the illegal purpose has not been carried out. It may be otherwise where the illegal purpose has been carried out and the transferee can rely on the transferor's conduct as inconsistent with his retention of a beneficial interest;

(5) the transferor can lead evidence of the illegal purpose whenever it is necessary for him to do so provided that he has withdrawn from the transaction before the illegal purpose has been wholly or partly carried into effect. It will be necessary for him to do so:

(i) if he brings an action at law; or

(ii) if he brings proceedings in equity and needs to rebut the presumption of advancement;

(6) the only way in which a man can protect his property from his creditors is by divesting himself of all beneficial interest in it. Evidence that he transferred the property in order to protect it from his creditors, therefore, does nothing by itself to rebut the presumption of advancement; it reinforces it. To rebut the presumption it is necessary to show that he intended to retain a beneficial interest and conceal it from his creditors;

(7) the court should not conclude that this was his intention without compelling circumstantial evidence to this effect. The identity of the transferee and the circumstances in which the transfer was made would be highly relevant. It is unlikely that the court would reach such a conclusion where the transfer was made in the absence of an imminent and perceived threat from known creditors.

I would dismiss this appeal.

Question

In what circumstances may a person enlist equitable assistance if he transfers property to another in pursuance of an intended unlawful transaction and subsequently claims to recover the property?

Theories concerning resulting trusts

Professor Birks's thesis on resulting trusts ('Restitution and Resulting Trusts', 1992) is that both types of resulting trusts – automatic and presumed – are based on the intention of the settlor/transferor and to prevent unjust enrichment. If the settlor/transferor does not intend to transfer a beneficial interest to the legal owner, the court will create a resulting trust in order to prevent the unjust enrichment of the transferee. The same principle applies where the transferor disposes of his interest to the transferee by virtue of a mistake or on a total failure of consideration. The transferee does not acquire a proprietary interest in the subject matter of the transfer but is under an obligation to hold the property on trust for the transferor. On the other hand, William Swadling ((1996) 16 LS 110) has argued that the resulting trust is displaced by evidence of intention which is contrary to the intention to create a trust. If the transferor intended the transferee to have the equitable interest, the existence of a mistake on the part of the transferor does not change things and does not give rise to a resulting trust. The transferor will be able to recover the mistaken payment at common law on a total failure of consideration. Swadling's theory was endorsed by Lord Browne-Wilkinson in the *Westdeutsche* case, see below.

Megarry J's classification of resulting trusts in *Re Vandervell's Trust (No 2)* (see p 138 above) has been the subject of some refinement. Lord Browne-Wilkinson, in the *Westdeutsche* case, did not fully agree with Megarry VC's classification and declared that resulting trusts arise on two occasions.

Westdeutsche Landesbank Girozentrale v Islington BC [1996] AC 669

Lord Browne-Wilkinson: A resulting trust arises in two sets of circumstances: (A) where A makes a voluntary payment to B or pays (wholly or in part) for the purchase of property which is vested either in B alone or in the joint names of A and B, there is a presumption that A did not intend to make a gift to B: the money or property is held on trust for A (if he is the sole provider of the money) or in the case of a joint purchase by A and B in shares proportionate to their contributions. It is important to stress that this is only a presumption, which presumption is easily rebutted either by the counter-presumption of advancement or by direct evidence of A's intention to make an outright transfer: (B) Where A transfers property to B on express trusts, but the trusts declared do not exhaust the whole beneficial interest: *ibid* and *Quistclose Investments Ltd v Rolls Razor Ltd (In Liquidation)* [1970] AC 567. Both types of resulting trust are traditionally regarded as examples of trusts giving effect to the common intention of the parties. A resulting trust is not imposed by law against the intentions of the trustee (as is a constructive trust) but gives effect to his presumed intention. Megarry J. in *In re Vandervell's Trusts (No 2)* [1974] Ch 269 suggests that a resulting trust of type (B) does not depend on intention but operates automatically. I am not convinced that this is right. If the settlor has expressly, or by necessary implication, abandoned any beneficial interest in the trust property, there is in my view no resulting trust: the undisposed-of equitable interest vests in the Crown as *bona vacantia*: see *In Re West Sussex Constabulary's Widows, Children and Benevolent (1930) Fund Trusts* [1971] Ch 1.

Question

How does Megarry J's classification of resulting trusts in *Re Vandervell's Trust (No 2)* differ from Lord Browne-Wilkinson's classification in *Westdeutsche Landesbank v Islington BC*?

Note

It may be observed that, in comparison with Megarry J's classification of resulting trusts, the points of difference lie with the 'automatic' resulting trust and whether the basis of imposition of the trust is the common intention of the parties (as Lord Browne-Wilkinson suggested). Classification B of Lord Browne-Wilkinson's categorisation of resulting trusts refers only to a surplus of trust funds left over after the purpose of an express trust has been fulfilled. It is submitted that this classification is incomplete for there is no acknowledgment of a resulting trust that arises to fill a gap in ownership (see *Vandervell v Inland Revenue Commissioners*) or an occasion where a transfer to a fiduciary fails *ab initio* (see *Re Ames*). In addition, Lord Browne-Wilkinson opines that both types of resulting trusts (categories A and B) arise by reference to the common intention of the parties.

The notion of a common intention resulting trust was also expressed by Peter Gibson J in *Carreras Rothmans Ltd v Freeman*.

Carreras Rothmans Ltd v Freeman [1984] 3 WLR 1016

Peter Gibson J: Equity fastens on the conscience of the person who receives from another property transferred for a specific purpose only and not therefore for the recipient's own purposes, so that such person will not be permitted to treat the property as his own or to use it for other than the stated purpose. If the common intention is that property is transferred for a specific purpose and not so as to become the property of the transferee, the transferee cannot keep the property if for any reason that purpose cannot be fulfilled.

Note

The idea in *Carreras Rothmans* is that if property is transferred to the trustee for a specific purpose, so that property remains in the transferor until the specified purpose is carried out, it would be unconscionable for the trustee to deny the existence of a resulting trust. This resulting trust will arise in accordance with the intention of the settlor and the knowledge of the trustee.

The difficulty with this rationale for the creation of a resulting trust is that the boundaries between resulting and constructive trusts become blurred. It is true that in both cases the courts create the trust. In the case of constructive trusts, the courts have deliberately left open the boundaries for the imposition of such trusts. The objective here is to prevent the trustee abusing his position. The court retains the power to monitor the transaction and to impose an order that will redress the imbalance. It is unnecessary for the resulting trust to perform the same task but with the added restriction of restoring the property to the settlor or transferror. See also Dillon LJ's reasoning in *Re EVTR*, at p 143 above.

In *Air Jamaica v Charlton*, Lord Millett emphasised the relevance of intention in the context of a resulting trust. But he also added that the resulting trust will arise whether or not the settlor/ transferor intended to retain a beneficial interest.

Air Jamaica v Charlton [1999] 1 WLR 1399

Facts

Air Jamaica had set up a pension trust. Clause 4 of the deed declared that: 'No moneys which have been contributed by the company under the terms hereof shall, in any circumstances, be repayable to the company.' The company lawfully discontinued the scheme and, after providing for the existing beneficiaries, a surplus of $400 million dollars was left over.

Held

The surplus was divisible between the company and its members equally. Clause 4 did not oust the resulting trust for the company, for the clause was not intended to cover events outside the scheme as was the case here. The Jamaican Government's claim to be entitled to the members' share on a *bona vacantia* was rejected on the ground that the members had not received what they had bargained for:

> **Lord Millett:** Like a constructive trust, a resulting trust arises by operation of law, though unlike a constructive trust it gives effect to intention. But it arises whether or not the transferor intended to retain a beneficial interest – he almost always does not – since it responds to the absence of any intention on his part to pass a beneficial interest to the recipient. It may arise even where the transferor positively wished to part with the beneficial interest, as in *Vandervell v Inland Revenue Commissioners* [1967] 2 AC 291. In that case the retention of a beneficial interest by the transferor destroyed the effectiveness of a tax avoidance scheme which the transferor was seeking to implement. The House of Lords affirmed the principle that a resulting trust is not defeated by evidence that the transferor intended to part with the beneficial interest if he has not in fact succeeded in doing so. As Plowman J had said in the same case at first instance [1966] Ch 261, 275: 'As I see it, a man does not cease to own property simply by saying "I don't want it." If he tries to give it away the question must always be, has he succeeded in doing so or not?' Lord Upjohn [in the same case] expressly approved this.

Note

Essentially, a resulting trust arises as a default mechanism that returns the property to the transferor, in accordance with his presumed (or implied) intention, as determined by the courts. Very often the transferor may not have contemplated the possibility of a return of the property (see *Vandervell v Inland Revenue Commissioners*), but this may be regarded as immaterial if, in the discretion of the court, the circumstances trigger a return of the property to the transferor.

Question

What are the underlying theories concerning resulting trusts?

FURTHER READING

Cotterill, I, 'Property and impropriety – the *Tinsley v Milligan* problem again' (1999) LMCLQ 465.

Creighton, P, 'The recovery of property transferred for illegal purposes' (1997) 60 MLR 102.

Cullity, M, 'Joint bank accounts with volunteers' (1969) 84 LQR 530.

Dowling, A, 'The presumption of advancement between mother and child' [1996] Conv 274.

Euonchong, N, 'Title clauses and illegal transactions' (1995) 111 LQR 135.

Greer, S, 'A last resort' (2007) 157 NLJ 696.

Hayton, D, 'Note on *Hussey v Palmer*' [1973] 37 Conv 65.

Ho, L and Smart, P, 'Reinterpreting the *Quistclose* trust: a critique of Chambers' analysis' (2001) 210 JLS 267.

Kenny, A, 'Trust clauses for lawyers and their clients' (1995) 139 SJ 826.

Kodilinye, G, 'Resulting trusts, advancements and fraudulent transfers – *Sekhon v Alissa*' [1990] Conv 213.

Millett, P, 'The *Quistclose* trust: who can enforce it?' (1985) 101 LQR 269.

Pettit, P, 'Illegality and repentance' (1996) 10 Tru LI 51.

Rickett, C, 'Unincorporated associations and their dissolution' [1980] CLJ 88.

Rimmer, J, 'Resulting trusts and the presumption of advancement – another piece in the jigsaw' [1999] PCB 181.

Rose, F, 'Gratuitous transfers and illegal purposes' (1996) 112 LQR 386.

Smart, P, 'Holding property for non-charitable purposes: mandates, conditions and estoppels' [1987] Conv 415.

Swadling, W, 'A new role for resulting trusts' (1996) 16 LS 110.

Swadling, W, 'Quistclose trusts and orthodoxy' (2004) ITCP vol 11, issue 3, 121.

CONSTRUCTIVE TRUSTS: CONFLICT OF DUTY AND INTEREST

INTRODUCTION

A constructive trust, as distinct from an express or resulting trust, is not created in accordance with the express or implied intention of the settlor. It is a device created by the courts in the interests of justice and good conscience. The rationale for the creation of such a trust is the prevention of unjust enrichment at the expense of an innocent party. The constructive trust forms a residual category of trust which is called into play whenever the court desires to impose a trust and no other category of trust is suitable. The court reserves to itself the power to interpret a transaction as giving rise to a constructive trust. It will have regard to all the circumstances surrounding a transaction and, in particular, the conduct of the relevant parties in order to decide whether in the interests of justice a trust ought to be imposed.

For example, T1 and T2 hold property on trust but, in breach of trust, purport to sell the property to X, a third party, who has knowledge of the breach of trust. Although T1 and T2 are already express trustees and liable for breach of trust, they will become accountable as constructive trustees for any unauthorised profit made from their office as trustees, such as the proceeds of sale received from X. By virtue of X's participation in the breach with knowledge of the facts, he will be treated as a constructive trustee of the property in favour of the innocent beneficiary.

The constructive trust may be imposed on express trustees and other fiduciaries in respect of any unauthorised benefits received by them. In addition, strangers or third parties who have misconducted themselves with knowledge that their actions constitute an unwarranted interference with the interest of the beneficiary will become constructive trustees.

The effect of a constructive trust is similar in many ways to any other type of trust in that the beneficiary retains a proprietary interest in the subject matter of the trust. In the event of the constructive trustee becoming bankrupt, the trust property is granted priority over his creditors in favour of the beneficiaries. If the trustee has disposed of the property, the beneficiary is entitled to 'trace' his funds in the hands of a third party, not being a *bona fide* transferee of the legal estate for value without notice. However, an express trust differs from a constructive trust in that the settlor is the creator of an express trust, whereas a constructive trust is created by the court. In addition, the express trust is more likely to continue for a duration determined by the settlor, but the constructive trust may take the form of a court order requiring a fiduciary or third party to transfer property to a beneficiary and will end when this event is achieved. Moreover, an express trustee may be entitled to exercise a variety of powers, such as the power to appoint agents and other trustees, the power to maintain infant beneficiaries, the power to make advancements of capital, the power to invest trust funds, etc. A constructive trustee has no such powers but is only required to comply with the order of the court.

CATEGORIES OF CONSTRUCTIVE TRUSTS

A constructive trust arises from circumstances in which equity considers it unconscionable for the holder of property to deny the claimant an interest in the same. It is difficult to state exactly when the defendant's conduct may give rise to a constructive trust. In English law, the boundaries surrounding a constructive trust have not been precisely drawn, for the circumstances that may give rise to such a trust are inexhaustible. In the *Carl Zeiss Stiftung* case, Edmund-Davies LJ declared the reasons why the boundaries of a constructive trust have been deliberately left vague by the courts and stated that the basis for imposing a constructive trust is to satisfy the demands of justice and good conscience.

Carl Zeiss Stiftung v Herbert Smith and Co (No 2) [1969] 2 Ch 276, CA

Edmund-Davies LJ: English law provides no clear and all-embracing definition of a constructive trust. Its boundaries have been left perhaps deliberately vague, so as not to restrict the court by technicalities in deciding what the justice of a particular case may demand. But it appears that in this country unjust enrichment or other personal advantage is not a *sine qua non*. Thus, in *Nelson v Larholt* [1948] 1 KB 339, it was not suggested that the defendant was himself one penny better off by changing an executor's cheques; yet, as he ought to have known of the executor's want of authority to draw them, he was held liable to refund the estate, both on the basis that he was a constructive trustee for the beneficiaries and on a claim for money had and received to their use. Nevertheless, the concept of unjust enrichment has its value as providing one example among many of what, for lack of a better phrase, I would call 'want of probity', a feature which recurs through and seems to connect all those cases drawn to the court's attention where a constructive trust has been held to exist. *Snell's Principles of Equity* expresses the same idea by saying 26th ed, 1966, p 201 that:

> A possible definition is that a constructive trust is a trust which is imposed by equity in order to satisfy the demands of justice and good conscience, without reference to any express or presumed intention of the parties.

It may be objected that, even assuming the correctness of the foregoing, it provides no assistance, inasmuch as reference to 'unjust enrichment', 'want of probity' and 'the demands of justice and good conscience' merely introduces vague concepts which are in turn incapable of definition and which therefore provide no yardstick. I do not agree. Concepts may defy definition and yet the presence in or absence from a situation of that which they denote may be beyond doubt. The concept of 'want of probity' appears to provide a useful touchstone in considering circumstances said to give rise to constructive trusts, and I have not found it misleading when applying it to the many authorities cited to this court. It is because of such a concept that evidence as to 'good faith', 'knowledge' and 'notice' plays so important a part in the reported decisions.

However, a number of general categories may be posited as to when the trust may be imposed. These are:

(a) occasions when a trustee or fiduciary makes unauthorised profits;

(b) contracts for the sale of land;

(c) the operation of the maxim, 'Equity will not allow a statute to be used as an engine for fraud'; and

(d) occasions when it would be unconscionable for the legal owner of property to deny an interest in property in favour of another.

On the other hand, in the USA, the constructive trust is defined in a relatively precise manner from the point of view of 'unjust enrichment': a constructive trust arises 'where a person holding title to property is subject to an equitable duty to convey it to another on the ground that he would be unjustly enriched if he were permitted to retain it' (American Restatement on Restitution). In other words, in the USA, the constructive trust device is used as a remedy to rectify certain wrongs.

Institutional/remedial constructive trusts

The distinction between an 'institutional' and a 'remedial' constructive trust was considered by Lord Browne-Wilkinson in the *Westdeutsche* case.

Westdeutsche Landesbank Girozentrale v Islington BC [1996] AC 669

Lord Browne-Wilkinson: Under the institutional constructive trust, the trust arises by operation of law as from the date when the circumstances give rise to it. The function of the court is merely to declare that such trust has arisen in the past. The consequences which flow from such trust having arisen (including the possibly unfair consequences to third parties who in the interim receive trust property) are also determined by rules of law, not under discretion. A remedial constructive trust is different. It is a judicial remedy giving rise to an enforceable equitable obligation; the extent to which it operates retrospectively to the prejudice of third parties lies in the discretion of the courts [emphasis added].

In the UK, remedies exist in quasi-contract which are based on unjust enrichment. It is arguable that the use of the constructive trust to provide a remedy is not justifiable. Moreover, it is equally unwarranted to equate a constructive trust with a resulting trust. In *Hussey v Palmer*, Lord Denning MR declared that a constructive trust exists as a remedy.

Hussey v Palmer [1972] 1 WLR 1286, CA

Lord Denning MR: Although the plaintiff alleged that there was a resulting trust, I should have thought that the trust in this case, if there was one, was more in the nature of a constructive trust: but this is more a matter of words than anything else. The two run together. By whatever name it is described, it is a trust imposed by law whenever justice and good conscience require it. It is a liberal process, founded upon large principles of equity, to be applied in cases where the legal owner cannot conscientiously keep the property for himself alone, but ought to allow another to have the property or the benefit of it or a share in it. The trust may arise at the outset when the property is acquired, or later on, as the circumstances may require. *It is an equitable remedy by which the court can enable an aggrieved party to obtain restitution.* It is comparable to the legal remedy of money had and received which, as Lord Mansfield said, is 'very beneficial and therefore much encouraged' in *Moses v Macferlan* (1760) 2 Burr 1005, p 1012 [emphasis added].

Facts
The plaintiff paid £607 in providing an extension to the house of her daughter and son-in-law. The extension was built to accommodate the plaintiff who, at that time, was living with the defendants. A dispute arose between the parties and the plaintiff left the house. She now claimed an interest in the house.

Held
The Court of Appeal decided by a majority that a trust was created in her favour in respect of her contribution in providing the extension (Lord Denning MR decided that a constructive trust was created in favour of the plaintiff, Phillimore LJ decided the case on the basis of a resulting trust in favour of the plaintiff and Cairns LJ decided that no trust was created but that the plaintiff loaned the amount to the defendants):

Lord Denning MR: If, during her [Mrs Hussey's] lifetime, he [Mr Palmer] had sold the house, together with the extension, she would be entitled to be repaid the £607 out of the proceeds. He admits this himself. But he has not sold the house. She has left, and the son in law has the extension for his own benefit and could sell the whole if he so desired. It seems to me to be entirely against conscience that he should retain the whole house and not allow Mrs Hussey any interest in it, or any charge upon it. The court should, and will, impose or impute a trust by which Mr Palmer is to hold the property on terms under which, in the circumstances that have happened, she has an interest in the property proportionate to the £607 which she put into it. She is quite content if he repays her the £607. If he does not repay the £607, she can apply for an order for sale, so that the sum can be paid to her. But the simplest way for him would be to raise the £607 on mortgage and pay it to her. But, on the legal point raised, I have no doubt there was a resulting trust, or more accurately, a constructive trust, for her, and I would so declare. I would allow the appeal accordingly.

Phillimore LJ: This mother in law advanced money to improve the property of her son in law. She did not intend to make a gift of the money. She could not afford to do that. No terms of repayment were agreed except perhaps in the event of the house being sold at an early date. She has described it as a loan, and that might be true. I do not for myself think that it would be inconsistent with the transaction also being or involving a resulting trust. In all the circumstances here, in the absence of clear arrangements for repayment and in circumstances where repayment on demand might be very difficult for the son in law, I should have thought it was more appropriate to regard it as an example of a resulting trust; and I would accordingly entirely agree with Lord Denning MR that she has an interest in this house proportionate to the £607 which she paid. It follows that this appeal should be allowed.

Cairns LJ (dissenting): It must be a common thing indeed for a parent or a parent in law to make a loan of money to a son or daughter or a son in law which both of them know is a loan, as to which it is obvious that there is no immediate prospect of repayment, but which in law is a loan repayable on demand. In my view that is the position here. As it was a loan, I think it is quite inconsistent with that to say that it could create a resulting trust at the same time.

It ought to be pointed out that Lord Denning's view that the constructive trust is an equitable remedy does not represent the traditional view of the English courts. In *Re Sharpe*, Browne-Wilkinson J declared that the constructive trust creates a property right in favour of the claimant on the date of the transaction, as opposed to the date of the court order. The claimant then adopts the most appropriate remedy in order to give effect to such right.

Re Sharpe [1980] 1 All ER 198, HC

Browne-Wilkinson J: Even if it be right to say that the courts can impose a constructive trust as a remedy in certain cases (which to my mind is a novel concept in English law), in order to provide a remedy the court must first find a right which has been infringed ... The introduction of an interest under a constructive trust is an essential ingredient if the plaintiff has any right at all. Therefore ... it cannot be that the interest in property arises for the first time when the court declares it to exist. The right must have arisen at the time of the transaction in order for the plaintiff to have any right the breach of which can be remedied ...

Note

In *Halifax Building Society v Thomas*, Peter Gibson LJ echoed the view that in English law the constructive trust does not exist as a remedy.

Halifax Building Society v Thomas [1996] 2 WLR 63, CA

Peter Gibson LJ: English law has not followed other jurisdictions where the constructive trust has become a remedy for unjust enrichment. As is said in *Snell's Equity*, 29th edn, 1990, p 197:

> In England the constructive trust has in general remained essentially a substantive institution; ownership must not be confused with obligation, nor must the relationship of debtor and creditor be converted into one of trustee and *cestui que* trust.

Question

Do remedial constructive trusts exist in English law?

Liability to account distinct from the constructive trust

Should the liability to account, owing to a dishonest transaction on the part of a stranger to a trust, be treated as falling within the confines of a constructive trust, even though the defendant does not receive the trust property?

One of the features of a trust is that the trustees have control of the trust property. With regard to a liability to account, such as accessory liability (see p 281 below), the defendant (alleged constructive trustee) does not acquire control of the property but merely assists in a breach of trust. It is arguable that such defendants should not be treated as constructive trustees; indeed it is suggested that liability in this context is personal and not *in rem*. Provided that the defendant is solvent, there are no difficulties. However, if the defendant is insolvent, the classification of his status will have important consequences. A proprietary remedy (tracing process) may subsist even though the defendant is insolvent. This remedy is based on the assumption that the property wrongly acquired by the defendant belongs to the innocent claimant. The aggrieved party may assert his interest in the property, subject to the *bona fide* transferee for value without notice exception. This claim may succeed irrespective of transformations in the nature of the property. Thus, third party rights may be affected by this remedy. Judges have sometimes used the language of constructive trusts and all that entails when in reality they have been considering the personal duty of the defendant to account (see Millett LJ's judgment in *Paragon Finance plc v Thakerar* [1999] 1 All ER 410, p 282 below).

Question
Why is it important to distinguish the duty to account from the constructive trust?

CONFLICT OF DUTY AND INTEREST

Trustee or fiduciary making an unauthorised profit

The rule is that a person occupying a position of confidence (such as a trustee or fiduciary) is prohibited from deriving any personal benefit by availing himself of his position, in the absence of authority from the beneficiaries, trust instrument or the court. In other words, the trustee or fiduciary should not place himself in position where his duty may conflict with his personal interest. If such a conflict occurs and the trustee obtains a benefit or profit, the advantage is held on constructive trust for the beneficiary. This is generally known as the rule in *Keech v Sandford*.

Keech v Sandford [1726] Sel Cas Ch 437, HL

Facts
The defendant, a trustee, held the profits of a lease of Romford market on trust for a minor. Before the expiration of the lease, the defendant requested a renewal of the lease in favour of the beneficiary personally, but this was refused. The trustee then attempted to renew the lease in his capacity as trustee for the infant, but this was also refused. The lessor agreed to renew the lease in favour of the trustee personally and this was done. A claim was brought on behalf of the beneficiary.

Held
The profits of the renewed lease were held on constructive trust in favour of the beneficiary:

> **Lord King LC:** I must consider this as a trust for the infant, for I very well see, if a trustee, on the refusal to renew, might have a lease to himself, few trust estates would be renewed to the *cestui que use*. Though I do not say there is fraud in this case, yet he should rather have let it run out than to have had the lease to himself. It may seem hard that the trustee is the only person of all mankind who might not have the benefit of the lease; but it is very proper that the rule should be strictly pursued and not in the least relaxed; for it is very obvious what would be the consequences of letting trustees have the lease, on refusal to renew to the *cestui que trust*.

Note
Perhaps the reason for this harsh rule is that the courts are reluctant to run the risk of finding it difficult in many cases to ascertain accurately whether or not an unfair advantage has been taken by the trustee or not. Unfairness to the trustee is not the major concern; the primary consideration of the courts is to ensure that there is no possibility of injustice to the beneficiaries.

The rationale for the harsh rule in *Keech v Sandford* was stated by Lord Herschell in *Bray v Ford*.

Bray v Ford [1896] AC 44, HL

> **Lord Herschell:** It is an inflexible rule of a court of equity that a person in a fiduciary position . . . is not, unless otherwise expressly provided, entitled to make a profit; he is not allowed to put himself in a position where his interest and his duty conflict. It does not appear to me that this rule is . . . founded upon principles of morality. I regard it rather as based on the consideration that human nature being what it is, there is a danger, in such circumstances, of the person holding a fiduciary interest being swayed by interest rather than duty, and thus prejudicing those he is bound to protect. It has, therefore, been deemed expedient to lay down this positive rule.

The doctrine in *Keech v Sandford* (as it is sometimes called) has been extended to other fiduciary relationships including agents on behalf of principals; directors in favour of companies; partners vis à vis co-partners; solicitors in respect of clients.

Fiduciaries

A fiduciary is an individual who is aware that his judgment and confidence are relied on, and have been relied on, by the claimant.

A definition of a fiduciary was offered by Millett LJ in *Bristol and West Building Society v Mothew*.

Bristol and West Building Society v Mothew [1996] 4 All ER 698, CA

Millett LJ: A fiduciary is someone who has undertaken to act for or on behalf of another in a particular matter in circumstances which give rise to a relationship of trust and confidence. The distinguishing obligation of a fiduciary is the obligation of loyalty. The principal is entitled to the single minded loyalty of his fiduciary. This core liability has several facets. A fiduciary must act in good faith; he must not make a profit of his trust; he must not place himself in a position where his duty and interest may conflict; he may not act for his own benefit or the benefit of a third person without the informed consent of his principal. This is not intended to be an exhaustive list but it is sufficient to indicate the nature of fiduciary obligations. They are defining characteristics of the fiduciary.

Note

In this case, the Court of Appeal decided that a breach of the duty of care by a firm of solicitors did not constitute a breach of the fiduciary duties of loyalty and fidelity to their client.

Apart from the traditional categories of fiduciaries, the existence of such relationship is a question for the court to decide.

Essentials of liability

In claims concerning breaches of fiduciary duties, the claimant is required to establish the following three propositions:

(a) the defendant holds a fiduciary position towards the claimant; and

(b) the defendant obtained a benefit; and

(c) there is a causal connection between the relationship and the benefit.

Failure to establish any or all of these conditions would lead to a failure in the proceedings.

In *Re Biss*, the claimant failed to establish that the defendant was a fiduciary.

Re Biss [1903] Ch 40, CA

Facts

The lessee of a house in Westminster carried on a profitable business as a lodgings-housekeeper, but died intestate. His widow took out letters of administration and with her two adult children continued to carry on the business under the existing lease. On the expiration of the original lease, the widow applied to the lessor for a new lease for the benefit of the estate. The lessor refused, but granted a new lease to one of the sons personally. The widow applied to the court to have the new lease treated as held on behalf of the estate.

Held

The son was entitled to the lease beneficially on the ground that he did not stand in a fiduciary relationship to the others interested in the estate:

Lord Collins MR: The appellant (son) is simply one of the next of kin of the former tenant and had, as such, a possible interest in the term. He is not, as such, trustee for the others interested, nor is he in possession. The administratrix represented the estate and alone had the right to renew incident thereon, and unquestionably could renew only for the benefit of the estate. But is the appellant in the same category? Or is he entitled to go into the facts to shew that he had not, in point of fact, abused his position, or in any sense intercepted an advantage coming by way of accretion to the estate. He did not take under a will or a settlement with interests coming after his own, but simply got a possible share upon an intestacy in case there was a surplus of assets over debts. It seems to me that this obligation cannot be put higher than that of any other tenant in common against whom it would have to be established, not as a presumption of law but as an inference of fact, that he had abused his position. If he is not under a personal incapacity to take a benefit, he is entitled to shew that the renewal was not in fact an accretion to the original term, and that it was not until there had been an absolute refusal on the part of the lessor and after full opportunity to the administratrix to procure it for the estate if she could, that he accepted a proposal of renewal made to him by the lessor. These questions cannot be considered or discussed when the party is by his position debarred from keeping a personal advantage derived directly or indirectly out of his fiduciary or quasi-fiduciary position, but when he is not so debarred I think it becomes a question of fact whether that which he has received was in his hands an accretion to the interest of the deceased, or whether the connection between the estate and the renewal had not been wholly severed by the action of the lessor before the appellant accepted a new lease. This consideration seems to get rid of any difficulty that one of the next of kin was an infant. The right or hope of renewal incident to the estate was determined before the appellant intervened.

Note
In *Re Biss*, the application by the widow was under the rule against 'self-dealing' (a phrase coined by Megarry VC in *Tito v Waddell (No 2)* [1977] Ch 106). This rule is a derivative of the *Keech v Sandford* principle: see *Ex p Lacey* (1802) 6 Ves 625 and *Ex p James* (1803) 8 Ves 337 (p 188 below).

An impugned purchase by the trustee or trustees of trust property is treated as a voidable transaction at the instance of the beneficiaries, even though the purchase may have the appearance of being fair. This rule cannot be evaded by transfers to nominees with the ultimate aim of benefiting the trustee (or trustees), for such nominees, with knowledge of the circumstances, cannot acquire a better title than the trustee. Alternatively, if the trustee has resold the property and realised a profit, the beneficiaries may adopt the sale and require the trustee to account for the profit.

The rule against 'self-dealing' is applicable to executors (as fiduciaries) but, on the special facts in *Holder v Holder*, the Court of Appeal decided that the sale to the defendant was not invalid because the defendant was not a fiduciary.

Holder v Holder [1968] Ch 353, CA

Facts
The testator appointed his widow, daughter and one of his sons, Victor, to be his executors and trustees. Victor at first took a few minor steps in connection with the administration of the estate (signing cheques, etc) but then abstained from taking any further part in the administration. One of the assets of the estate included a farm. Victor had acquired no special knowledge of the farm in his capacity as executor and all the knowledge about the farm was acquired as a tenant of that farm. The farm was then offered for sale at an auction subject to Victor's tenancy. At the auction, Victor made a successful bid for the farm. Another son applied to the court for the sale to be set aside.

Held
The sale ought not be set aside for the following reasons:

(a) Victor had not instructed the valuer nor had he arranged the auction.

(b) Victor had never assumed the duties of executor, for he had done virtually nothing in the administration of the estate, nor had Victor any influence on the two other executors in respect of the sale.

(c) In any case, Victor had made no secret of his intention to buy the farm and had paid a good price for the property.

(d) Victor was not relied upon by other beneficiaries to protect their interests.

Harman LJ: It was admitted at the bar in the court below that the acts of Victor were enough to constitute intermeddling with the estate and that his renunciation was ineffective. On this footing, he remained a personal representative, even after probate had been granted to his co-executors, and could have been obliged by the creditor or a beneficiary to re-assume the duties of the executor. The judge decided in favour of the plaintiff on this point because Victor at the time of the sale was himself still in a fiduciary position and like any other trustee could not purchase the trust property. I feel the force of this argument, but doubt its validity in the very special circumstances of this case. The reason for this rule is that a man may not be both vendor and purchaser; but Victor was never in that position here. He took no part in instructing the valuer who fixed the reserves or in the preparations for the auction. Everyone in the family knew that he was not a seller but a buyer. In this case Victor never assumed the duties of an executor. It is true that he concurred in signing a few cheques for trivial sums and endorsing a few insurance policies, but he never, so far as appears, interfered in any way with the administration of the estate. It is true he managed the farms, but he did that as tenant and not as executor. He acquired no special knowledge as executor. What he knew he knew as tenant of the farms.

Another reason lying behind the rule is that there must never be a conflict of duty and interest, but in fact there was none here in the case of Victor, who made no secret throughout that he intended to buy. There is of course ample authority that a trustee cannot purchase [the trust property]. The leading cases are decisions of Lord Eldon – *Ex p Lacey* (1802) 6 Ves 625 and *Ex p James* (1803) 8 Ves 337. In the former case the Lord Chancellor expressed himself thus:

> The rule I take to be this; not, that a trustee cannot buy from his *cestui que* trust, but, that he shall not buy from himself. If a trustee will so deal with his *cestui que* trust, that the amount of the transaction shakes off the obligation, that attaches upon him as trustee, then he may buy. If that case is rightly understood, it cannot lead to much mistake. The true interpretation of what is there reported does not break in upon the law as to trustees. The rule is this. A trustee, who is entrusted to sell and manage for others, undertakes in the same moment in which he becomes a trustee, not to manage for the benefit and advantage of himself.

In *Ex p James*, the same Lord Chancellor said:

> This doctrine as to purchases by trustees, assignees and persons having a confidential character, stands much more upon general principle than upon the circumstances of any individual case. It rests upon this; that the purchase is not permitted in any case, however honest the circumstances; the general interests of justice requiring it to be destroyed in every instance.

These are no doubt strong words, but it is to be observed that Lord Eldon was dealing with cases where the purchaser was at the time of sale acting for the vendors. In this case Victor was not so acting; his interference with the administration of the estate was of a minimal character and the last cheque he signed was in August before he executed the deed of renunciation. He took no part in the instructions for probate, nor in the valuations or fixing of the reserves. Everyone concerned knew of the renunciation and of the reason for it, namely, that he wished to be a purchaser.

I hold, therefore, that the rule does not apply in order to disentitle Victor to bid at the auction, as he did . . .

In *Ward v Brunt*, the claimant failed to prove that the profit obtained by the defendant was in the capacity of a fiduciary.

Ward v Brunt [2000] All ER (D) 586, HC

Facts

The claimant, John, was the younger brother of Susan and Helen, the defendants. The claim concerned a farm which was owned by four partners, Norman, the grandfather, John, Susan and Helen, his grandchildren. A tenancy of the farm was held in partnership. Susan was a full-time manager of the farm and was paid an annual salary. John took little part in the running of the business. Norman was eager that the farm should remain in the family. This led to a considerable rift between Norman and John.

Helen sold her interest in the partnership to Susan. In 1992, Norman died. In 1993, Susan exercised an option to purchase the freehold to the farm granted under Norman's will, but subject to the tenancy of the farm. On 11 November 1994, by consent, a declaration was made to dissolve the partnership tenancy. In 1996, Susan served notice to quit the farm which had the effect of terminating the partnership tenancy of the farm.

John claimed that Susan was in breach of fiduciary duties on the following grounds:

(a) Susan profited from her position as a fiduciary when, pursuant to the option granted by Norman's will, she acquired the freehold reversion to the farm by reason of the partnership tenancy; and

(b) the service of the notice to quit was a breach of her fiduciary duty.

Held

Peter Leaver QC decided in favour of the defendants on the following grounds:

(a) Susan did not profit from her position as a fiduciary when she acquired the freehold reversion to the farm. The freehold was acquired by her as a beneficiary under Norman's will and not as a partner of the farm tenancy. Thus, she owed no duty to account to the partners when she acquired the freehold.

(b) The partnership tenancy agreement was a partnership asset which had no value to the partnership.

(c) The service of the notice to quit had the effect of bringing to an end Susan's liability, and this did not amount to a breach of fiduciary duty. In the alternative, even if this amounted to a breach, the 'breach' mitigated the loss which the partnership was sustaining, rather than causing damage.

> **Peter Leaver QC:** The real issue ... which has to be decided in this case is whether Susan obtained her opportunity to serve the notice to quit, and thereby to obtain the merger of the freehold and leasehold interests, by reason and in the course of her position as a partner. If she did, and profited thereby, she will have to account to her partners for that profit.
>
> ... it is important to identify precisely the capacity in which the activity of which complaint is made was carried out, and that it is not necessarily every conflict of interest, whether actual or potential, which will inevitably lead to a finding that there has been a breach of fiduciary obligation. In my judgment, therefore, in deciding this issue, it is necessary to consider, in the light of the authorities, the rights and obligations of the partners as partners, and Susan's rights and obligations as a beneficiary under Norman's Will. It will be remembered that on the 11th November 1994, by consent, it had been declared that the partnership was dissolved as from that date, and it was ordered that an account should be taken of the assets and liabilities of the partnership. One of the assets was the tenancy of the farm. However, that asset could not be assigned, charged or underlet without the previous licence in writing of the landlord: nor could the partners part with the possession of that asset without such licence. It was inevitable that, on the taking of the account, the tenancy would have to be terminated so that the asset could be realised (if it had a value) and so that (in any event) the liability to pay rent could be terminated. Under the agricultural tenancy agreement, notice to terminate could have been given either by the landlords, who at the date of the Order were Norman's Executors, if they had grounds upon which to do so, or by the partners, or, as they were joint tenants, by any of the partners. Until such notice was given, and had expired, the tenancy was an asset of the partnership, and the rent was a liability of the partnership. As one year's notice to terminate the tenancy had to be given, it was clearly in the interests of the partnership to give that notice sooner rather than later, unless the surrender value of the tenancy to the landlord was greater than the rent that was payable. If the tenancy was an asset of the partnership but had no value, it was in the interests of the partners to bring to an end the liability to pay rent at the earliest possible time, and to co-operate with each other in doing so.

Note

In *Meara v Fox* [2001] All ER (D) 68, the claimant failed to establish that the defendant, who was a professional adviser, had owed him fiduciary duties.

In *English v Dedham Vale*, a purchaser who abused his position became a fiduciary in respect of the vendor.

English v Dedham Vale Properties [1978] I WLR 93, HC

Facts

During negotiations for the purchase of land, the purchasers, in the name of and purportedly acting for the vendors, sought and obtained planning permission for the land. The vendors did not consent to this application and, had they been aware, this would have influenced the purchase price.

Held

A fiduciary relationship had been established between the parties. The purchasers were liable to account to the vendors for the profits which accrued as a result of the grant of planning permission:

Slade J: I do not think that the categories of fiduciary relationships which give rise to a constructive trusteeship should be regarded as falling into a limited number of straitjackets or as being necessarily closed. They are, after all, no more than formulae for equitable relief. As Ungoed-Thomas J said in *Selangor United Rubber Estates Ltd v Cradock (No 3)* [1968] I WLR 1555, p 1582:

The court of equity says that the defendant shall be liable in equity, as though he were a trustee. He is made liable in equity as trustee by the imposition or construction of the court of equity. This is done because in accordance with equitable principles applied by the court of equity it is equitable that he should be held liable as though he were a trustee. Trusteeship and constructive trusteeship are equitable conceptions.

My reasons may be put in the form of two general propositions:

(1) where during the course of negotiations for a contract for the sale and purchase of property, the proposed purchaser, in the name of and purportedly as agent on behalf of the vendor, but without the consent or authority of the vendor, takes some action in regard to the property (whether it be the making of a planning application, a contract for the sale of the property, or anything else) which, if disclosed to the vendor, might reasonably be supposed to be likely to influence him in deciding whether or not to conclude the contract, a fiduciary relationship in my judgment arises between the two parties;

(2) such fiduciary relationship gives rise to the consequences that there is a duty on the proposed purchaser to disclose to the vendor before the conclusion of the contract what he has done as the vendor's purported agent, and correspondingly, in the event of non-disclosure, there is a duty on him to account to him for any profit made in the course of the purported agency, unless the vendor consents to his retaining it. In such circumstances, the person who, for his own private purposes, uses the vendor's name and purports to act as his agent cannot reasonably complain if the law subjects him to the same consequences vis à vis his alleged principal as if he had actually had the authority which he purported to have.

On my analysis of the facts of the present case, the plaintiffs never consented to the defendant or Mr Harrington, or Mr Mead purporting to make the planning application as their agent before contract; the fact that this had been done was never disclosed to them before the exchange of contracts; and they never consented to the defendant's retaining the profit ultimately received by it as a result of the making of the planning application. In these circumstances, the defendant is in my judgment accountable for such profit.

Similarly, an individual becomes a fiduciary if he purports to act on behalf of a trust without authority, and obtains confidential information as a result of being an apparent representative of the trust. In this event, any profits obtained by the fiduciary in connection with the use of such confidential information are subject to the trust. Indeed, in *Boardman v Phipps*, it was decided that the confidential information obtained in such circumstances may be treated as trust property.

Boardman and Another v Phipps [1967] 2 AC 46, HL (Lords Cohen, Hodson and Guest; Viscount Dilhorne and Lord Upjohn dissenting)

Facts

The trust property consisted of shares in a company. One of the beneficiaries and Mr Boardman, the solicitor to the trust, were dissatisfied with the way the company's business was organised and obtained control of the company on behalf of the trust by acting on privileged information available only to the trust. The company was reorganised and substantial profits accrued to the trust. Mr Boardman at all material times had acted honestly but wrongly believed that he had the full approval of the trustees and beneficiaries. John Phipps, a beneficiary, claimed that Mr Boardman and his accomplice were required to account to the trust for their profits as constructive trustees.

Held

The appellants were fiduciaries and were liable to account for their profits but the court awarded them generous remuneration for their efforts:

> **Lord Hodson:** The proposition of law involved in this case is that no person standing in a fiduciary position, when a demand is made upon him by the person to whom he stands in the fiduciary relationship to account for profits acquired by him by reason of the opportunity and the knowledge, or either, resulting from it, is entitled to defeat the claim upon any ground save that he made profits with the knowledge and assent of the other person.
>
> It is obviously of importance to maintain the proposition in all cases and to do nothing to whittle away its scope or the absolute responsibility which it imposes.
>
> So far as Mr Tom Phipps is concerned, he was not placed in a fiduciary position by reason of his being a beneficiary under his father's will. He was acting as agent for trustees with Mr Boardman before any question of acting with him for his own benefit arose. He has not, however, sought to be treated in a different way from Mr Boardman upon whom the conduct of the whole matter depended and with whom he has acted throughout as a co-adventurer; he does not claim that he should succeed in this appeal if Mr Boardman fails.
>
> Mr Boardman's fiduciary position arose from the fact that he was at all material times solicitor to the trustees of the will of Mr Phipps senior. This is admitted, although counsel for the appellants has argued, and argued correctly, that there is no such post as solicitor to trustees. The trustees either employ a solicitor or they do not in a particular case and there is no suggestion that they were under any contractual or other duty to employ Mr Boardman or his firm. Nevertheless, as an historical fact they did employ him and look to him for advice at all material times and this is admitted. It was as solicitor to the trustees that he obtained the information . . . This information enabled him to acquire knowledge of a most extensive and valuable character which was the foundation upon which a decision could, and was taken to buy the shares in Lester & Harris Ltd.
>
> As to this it is said on behalf of the appellants that information as such is not necessarily property and it is only trust property which is relevant. I agree, but it is nothing to the point to say that in these times corporate trustees, for example, the public trustee and others, necessarily acquire a mass of information in their capacity of trustees for a particular trust and cannot be held liable to account if knowledge so acquired enables them to operate to their own advantage, or to that of other trusts. Each case must depend on its own facts and I dissent from the view that information is of its nature something which is not properly to be described as property. We are aware that what is called 'know how' in the commercial sense is property which may be very valuable as an asset. *I agree with the learned judge and with the Court of Appeal that the confidential information acquired in this case which was capable of being and was turned to account can be properly regarded as the property of the trust.* It was obtained by Mr Boardman by reason of the opportunity which he was given as solicitor acting for the trustee in the negotiations with the chairman of the company, as the correspondence demonstrates. The end result was that out of the special position in which they were standing in the course of the negotiations the appellants got the opportunity to make a profit and the knowledge that it was there to be made [emphasis added].
>
> The relevant information is not any information but special information which I think must include that confidential information given to the appellants which is so fully detailed in the judgment of Wilberforce J. There is a passage in *Aas v Benham* [1891] 2 Ch 244 in the judgment of Bowen LJ which I think is of assistance, although the learned Lord Justice was dealing with partnership, not trusteeship: he was explaining some observation of Cotton LJ in *Dean v MacDowell* (1877) 8 Ch D 345. These were:
>
> > Again, if he [that is, a partner] makes any profit by the use of any property of the partnership, including, I may say, information which the partnership is entitled to, there the profit is made out of the partnership property.
>
> Bowen LJ commented:
>
> > He is speaking of information which a partnership is entitled to in such a sense that it is information which is the property, or is to be included in the property of the partnership – that is to say, information the use of

which is valuable to them as a partnership, and to the use of which they have a vested interest. But you cannot bring the information obtained in this case within that definition.

Aas v Benham is an important case as showing that a partner may make a profit from information obtained in the course of the partnership business where he does so in another firm which is outside the scope of the partnership business. In that case the partnership business was shipbroking and the profit made was in a business which had no connection with that of the partnership.

The appellants obtained knowledge by reason of their fiduciary position and they cannot escape liability by saying that they were acting for themselves and not as agents of the trustees. Whether or not the trust or the beneficiaries in their stead could have taken advantage of the information is immaterial, as the authorities clearly show. No doubt it was but a remote possibility that Mr Boardman would ever be asked by the trustees to advise on the desirability of an application to the court in order that the trustees might avail themselves of the information obtained. Nevertheless, even if the possibility of conflict is present between personal interest and the fiduciary position the rule of equity must be applied. This appears from the observation of Lord Cranworth LC in *Aberdeen Railway Co v Blaikie* (1854) 1 Macq 461.

The question whether or not there was a fiduciary relationship at the relevant time must be a question of law and the question of conflict of interest directly emerges from the facts pleaded, otherwise no question of entitlement to a profit would fall to be considered. No positive wrongdoing is proved or alleged against the appellants but they cannot escape from the consequence of the acts involving liability to the respondent unless they can prove consent. This they endeavoured without success to do, for, although they gave the respondent some information, that which they gave was held by the learned judge to be insufficient and there is no appeal against his decision on this point.

I agree with the decision of the learned judge and with that of the Court of Appeal which, in my opinion, involves a finding that there was a potential conflict between Boardman's position as solicitor to the trustees and his own interest in applying for the shares. He was in a fiduciary position vis à vis the trustees and through them vis à vis the beneficiaries. For these reasons in my opinion the appeal should be dismissed; but I should add that I am in agreement with the learned judge that payment should be allowed on a liberal scale in respect of the work and skill employed in obtaining the shares and the profits therefrom.

Likewise, in *Crown Dilmun v Sutton* the claimant was successful in establishing that the defendant was under a duty to account in breach of his fiduciary relationship. The claimant contended that the defendant owed fiduciary duties by virtue of his capacity as a managing director and the existence of a restraint of trade clause. Thus, the defendant owed the claimant a duty to make full and frank disclosure of profit making opportunities concerning the claimant's land.

Crown Dilmun Ltd v Sutton and another [2004] EWHC 52, HC

Facts

The claimant co. was a property developer. The first defendant, Mr Sutton (Mr S), was a director of the claimant co. He was employed under a written service agreement that contained a restraint of trade clause to the effect that Mr S was obliged to keep confidential information secret during his employment and after its termination. In the course of his employment Mr S received a brochure detailing a development opportunity for Fulham Football Stadium at Craven Cottage, which he rejected on behalf of the claimant. However, he later entered into negotiations in respect of the same property. Mr S incorporated a company, Fulham River Projects, (FRP), the second defendant, and appointed Ms Hamilton (Ms H), a solicitor, its sole director. The second defendant then entered into an agreement to develop the stadium. The opportunity, negotiations and subsequent agreement were not disclosed to the claimant, nor was there a disclosure of Mr S's involvement with the second defendant. Mr S's employment was terminated when the claimant became aware of the circumstances. The claimant brought proceedings against Mr S seeking damages for breach of contract or an account for any profits made from the agreement. In respect of the second defendant, the claimant instituted proceedings for an account on the basis of dishonest assistance and/or knowing receipt.

Held

Smith J decided that both defendants were liable to account to the claimant on the following grounds:

- Mr S could not have had a genuine bona fide belief that the claimant would not have been interested in the development scheme;

- Mr S's decision was dishonest and in breach of his fiduciary duties;

- in respect of the second defendant's liability to account, Mr S's knowledge was attributable to it because he was the 'directing mind and will' of this company. In addition, Ms H was aware that Mr S was a director of the claimant co., and had been reckless in addressing the consequences of him acting in breach of his fiduciary duties. Her knowledge was attributable to the second defendant and, in the circumstances, it was unconscionable for the second defendant to retain the benefit.

Peter Smith J: For a fiduciary to escape liability to account because of breach of his fiduciary duty he must show that full informed consent has been given by the beneficiaries after a full and proper disclosure has been made. The burden is therefore upon Mr Sutton to show that he made full disclosure, frank disclosure, and that, in the light of that full and frank disclosure, informed consent has been given. I do not see how, when the minute of 19th February 2002 has been obtained by deception, it can be said that he has made full disclosure and that any consent that has been given is fully informed. It is also a significant point to observe that he failed in any event to disclose his interest in Max Hotels (Ludgate Hill) Limited. If he obtains a consent by serious misrepresentation no consent is established.

Given my decision that Mr Sutton had no right to make any decision to take opportunities which came his way whilst he was a Director of the Claimants, the parties all agree that he came under a duty not to take opportunities which arose that might put him in conflict with his duties to the Claimants. As a director of the Claimants, he had a duty to exploit every opportunity that he became aware of for the benefit of the Claimants. The only exception is if they permit him to take such opportunities after he has made full and frank disclosure and they have given full and informed consent. I have already found that none of that happened.

180. The acceptance of those duties was inevitable given the line of authorities starting with *Keech -v- Sandford* [1726] Sel. Cas. 1. King 61 through to *Boardman -v- Phipps* [1967] 2 AC 46 and *Island Export Finance -v- Umunna* [1986] BCLC 460.

In addition, for what it is worth, I am of the view that as a fiduciary he had a positive duty to disclose his own misconduct: see the cases summarised by me in *Tesco Stores -v- Pook* [2003] EWHC 823 (Ch).

It is essential to appreciate two restrictions which apply to a fiduciary in the position of Mr Sutton. First, he is not allowed to set up for business in competition with a business carried on by CD. That is self evident from the express wording of his contract of employment. The second prohibition is, where he obtains an opportunity to purchase or otherwise acquire property from a third party, or obtains special knowledge or information which indicates such a purchase or acquisition might be worthwhile, then he is disabled from taking any benefit resulting from the purchase. In order to found liability, it is not necessary to establish that the fiduciary was unable to purchase the property as a result of an opportunity or special knowledge or information required by him by reason of the fiduciary relationship. It is not all knowledge or information which counts, and in general terms a fiduciary is allowed to use knowledge or information acquired during the course of his fiduciary relationship for his own purposes.

There are two instances where a fiduciary might be liable. The first is where a fiduciary obtains knowledge or information which is not available to the general public and is obtained by him as confidential information in the course of his fiduciary relationship and had a special value, in that it enables him to assess the commercial feasibility of a purchase by him and the appropriate terms of a purchase offer and thereby substantially contributes to the successful purchase by him. In that situation, liability attaches whether or not matters such as the skill of the fiduciary contribute to the purchase, even though the purchase involved risk-taking despite the knowledge and information gained by him. The second situation is where a fiduciary obtains confidential information in the course of his fiduciary relationship and then enters into a purchase for his own benefit in circumstances where his personal interest conflict or may conflict with his fiduciary duties, for example his duty to consider a purchase on behalf of the trust or even an application to the court for authority to purchase.

PROFIT OBTAINED BY A THIRD PARTY

There is limited English authority providing guidance about the rules applicable in a case where profit is obtained by a third party who is not in a fiduciary relationship with the beneficiary. That is potentially the position of the Second Defendant. A claim against a third party may be based on (i) a connection between the third party and the trustee, (ii) breach of confidence or (iii) participation in breach of fiduciary duty.

In this context, it is essential to analyse what matters are attributable to the Second Defendant. I have already found that Ms Hamilton was aware of all the circumstances as to Mr Sutton's breach of fiduciary duty and was reckless in considering them. That knowledge is admittedly attributable to the Second Defendant. The Second Defendant therefore comes to this claim with an attitude of being reckless as to whether or not Mr Sutton was in breach of fiduciary duty.

I am firmly of the view that the formation of the Second Defendant and the appointment of Ms Hamilton as the sole Director and the registration of the shares in a Forsters nominee company was, amongst other things, to hide Mr Sutton's interests in it. I accordingly conclude that the Second Defendant was both reckless as to whether or not Mr Sutton was committing a breach of duty in bringing the Opportunity and the Agreement to the Second Defendant and, further, knew of Mr Sutton's dishonesty in that regard.

Question
To what extent may confidential information be treated as trust property?

Pallant v Morgan Equity

A 'Pallant v Morgan equity' derives from the case *Pallant v Morgan* [1953] Ch 43, to the effect that if A and B agree that A will acquire some specific property for the joint benefit of A and B on terms yet to be agreed, and B, in reliance on A's agreement, is thereby induced to refrain from attempting to acquire the property, equity will not permit A, when he acquires the property, to insist on retaining the whole of the benefit for himself to the exclusion of B. Unlike a proprietary estoppel, the claimant (B) has not suffered a detriment as a consequence of the defendant (A) acquiring the property. However, the defendant has obtained an advantage by keeping the claimant out of the market. In these circumstances equity may intervene and, in its discretion, prevent A from claiming the entire property beneficially. The nature of the interest acquired by B will vary with the circumstances of each case. The fact that the terms of the agreement are too vague to be specifically enforceable does not affect B's interest in the property.

Pallant v Morgan [1953] Ch 43

Facts
An agreement was entered between the claimant's and defendant's respective agents that they would not compete against each other in bidding for a property at an auction. It was agreed that the defendant's agent alone should bid and if he was successful the property was to be divided between them. The basis of the division was to be subsequently agreed. Thus, the bidding by the defendant at the auction was on behalf of both parties. The defendant's bid was successful and he attempted to deny the claimant an interest in the property.

Held
The High Court decided that, although the agreement for division was too uncertain to be specifically enforceable, the defendant was not entitled to keep the property for his sole benefit, but was required to hold the property upon trust for the parties jointly.

Harman J: Can, then, the plaintiff have specific performance of the agreement so reached? In my judgment, he cannot, for there is too much left undecided. There is the margin between £3 and £5 an acre, there is the exact method of valuing the timber, and there is the question of what part if any of "A" affects the defendant's water rights. Is the result, then, that the plaintiff must fail? In my judgment, not so. To allow the defendant to retain lot 16 in these circumstances would be tantamount to sanctioning a fraud on his part, and I find the following in *Fry On Specific Performance*, 6th ed, p 184, para 386, where the author is dealing with what he styles the uncertainty of the contract:

The same certainty will not be required in cases where there is any element of fraud, as in simple cases of specific performance of a contract. Thus where A agreed with B in effect that if B would not try to buy a certain estate, A would try to buy, and in case of success would cede a portion of the estate to B at a certain price: and B acted on his bargain and allowed A to purchase: and A having purchased refused to perform his part and set up the uncertainty of the part to be ceded: the court held that the defence could not avail, and directed an inquiry to ascertain the portion to be given up and the price. It seems that if this could not have been ascertained, B might have claimed the whole estate.

In my judgment, the proper inference from the facts is that the defendant's agent, when he bid for lot 16, was bidding for both parties on an agreement that there should be an arrangement between the parties on the division of the lot if he were successful. The plaintiff and the defendant have failed to reach such an agreement, and the court cannot compel them to one. The best it can do is to decree that the property is held by the defendant for himself and the plaintiff jointly, and, if they fail to agree on a division, the property must be re-sold, either party being at liberty to bid, and the proceeds of sale being divided equally after repaying to the defendant the £1,000 which he paid with interest at 4 per cent. It is true that the suggested agreement would have involved the transfer to the plaintiff of a portion of lot 15, but, in default of an agreement, he cannot obtain that, for his agent had no instructions to bid for that lot in any event.

Pallant v Morgan was reviewed by the Court of Appeal in *Banner Homes plc v Luff Developments Ltd* and the principle approved.

In *Banner Homes v Luff*, a constructive trust (or a duty to account) arose where two rival bidders made an arrangement concerning the purchase of property, and the defendant conducted itself in a way inconsistent with the agreement and in an inequitable manner.

Banner Homes Group v Luff Development Ltd [2000] 2 WLR 772, CA

Facts

In March 1995, Peter Luff of Luff Development Ltd (L) was interested in the joint development of a 6.8 acre site. L was keen to acquire the site but was eager to share the risks of the acquisition. Banner Group (B) had known of and was interested in the site in 1994, but its interest was not pursued at that time. By 14 July 1995, B and L had reached an agreement in principle for the purchase and development of the site through the medium of a single enterprise company which was to be jointly owned. In pursuance of this understanding, Stowhelm Ltd, an 'off the shelf' company, was acquired by L. By mid-October 1995, L began to have second thoughts over the wisdom of having B as a joint venture partner. These reservations were never revealed to B. Indeed, B was kept 'on board' to avoid the risk of a rival bid for the site. By about 27 October 1995 (shortly before the exchange of contracts with the vendors of the site), L led B to believe that the joint venture proposal was proceeding, subject to a formal agreement to be drawn up in the future setting out the terms of their relationship. No such agreement was concluded owing to delays on both sides. The purchase of the site was completed on 22 November 1995. The purchase moneys were made available by L. On 15 December 1995, B was informed that L was no longer willing to continue the joint venture arrangement.

B, the claimant, brought an action for breach of contract or, in the alternative, for an order that L held half the shares in Stowhelm as constructive trustee for the claimant. The trial judge dismissed both claims. He decided that no contract was concluded between the parties. The claim in equity was unfounded because the understanding between the parties was revocable, and could not be converted into an unqualified undertaking by way of a trust. In addition, B had failed to establish that it acted to its detriment in reliance on the arrangement. The claimant appealed.

Held

The appeal was allowed. L became a constructive trustee of half the shares in Stowhelm for the benefit of B. L acquired an advantage by eliminating a rival bid from B, in reliance on an arrangement which made it inequitable to allow L to retain the property for itself. It was not necessary for B to prove a detriment in reliance on the arrangement. An advantage to L or a detriment to B was sufficient to found the claim in equity. Moreover, the arrangement concerning a joint venture was not required to be contractually enforceable:

Chadwick LJ: [The Court of Appeal endorsed the rules laid down in the following principal first instance decisions: *Chattock v Muller* (1878) 8 ChD 177; *Pallant v Morgan* [1953] Ch 43; *Holiday Inns Inc v Broadhead* (1974) 232 EG 951; *Time Products Ltd v Combined English Stores Group Ltd* (1974) unreported, 2 December 1974; and *Island Holdings Ltd v Birchington Engineering Ltd* (1981) unreported, 7 July.]

The Pallant v Morgan equity

It is important to identify the features which give rise to a *Pallant v Morgan* equity and to define its scope.

(1) A *Pallant v Morgan* equity may arise where the arrangement or understanding on which it is based precedes the acquisition of the relevant property by one of those parties to that arrangement. It is the pre-acquisition arrangement which colours the subsequent acquisition by the defendant and leads to his being treated as a trustee if he seeks to act inconsistently with it. Where the arrangement or understanding is reached in relation to property already owned by one of the parties, he may (if the arrangement is of sufficient certainty to be enforced specifically) thereby constitute himself trustee on the basis that 'equity looks on that as done which ought to be done'; or an equity may arise under the principles developed in the proprietary estoppel cases. As I have sought to point out, the concepts of constructive trust and proprietary estoppel have much in common in this area. *Holiday Inns Inc v Broadhead* (1974) 232 EG 951, may, perhaps, best be regarded as a proprietary estoppel case; although it might be said that the arrangement or understanding, made at the time when only the five acre site was owned by the defendant, did, in fact, precede the defendant's acquisition of the option over the fifteen acre site.

(2) It is unnecessary that the arrangement or understanding should be contractually enforceable. Indeed, if there is an agreement which is enforceable as a contract, there is unlikely to be any need to invoke the *Pallant v Morgan* equity; equity can act through the remedy of specific performance and will recognise the existence of a corresponding trust. On its facts *Chattock v Muller* (1878) 8 Ch D 177 is, perhaps, best regarded as a specific performance case. In particular, it is no bar to a *Pallant v Morgan* equity that the pre-acquisition arrangement is too uncertain to be enforced as a contract – see *Pallant v Morgan* itself and the *Time Products* case – nor that it is plainly not intended to have contractual effect – see *Island Holdings Ltd v Birchington Engineering Co Ltd*.

(3) It is necessary that the pre-acquisition arrangement or understanding should contemplate that one party ('the acquiring party') will take steps to acquire the relevant property; and that, if he does so, the other party ('the non-acquiring party') will obtain some interest in that property. Further it is necessary, that (whatever private reservations the acquiring party may have) he has not informed the non-acquiring party before the acquisition (or, at the least, before it is too late for the parties to be restored to a position of no advantage/ no detriment) that he no longer intends to honour the arrangement or understanding.

(4) It is necessary that, in reliance on the arrangement or understanding, the non-acquiring party should do (or omit to do) something which confers an advantage on the acquiring party in relation to the acquisition of the property; or is detrimental to the ability of the non-acquiring party to acquire the property on equal terms. It is the existence of the advantage to the one, or detriment to the other, gained or suffered as a consequence of the arrangement or understanding, which leads to the conclusion that it would be inequitable or unconscionable to allow the acquiring party to retain the property for himself, in a manner inconsistent with the arrangement or understanding which enabled him to acquire it. *Pallant v Morgan* itself provides an illustration of this principle. There was nothing inequitable in allowing the defendant to retain for himself the lot (lot 15) in respect to which the plaintiff's agent had no instructions to bid. In many cases the advantage/detriment will be found in the agreement of the non-acquiring party to keep out of the market. That will usually be both to the advantage of the acquiring party – in that he can bid without competition from the non-acquiring party – and to the detriment of the non-acquiring party – in that he loses the opportunity to acquire the property for himself. But there may be advantage to the one without corresponding detriment to the other. Again, *Pallant v Morgan* provides an illustration. The plaintiff's agreement (through his agent) to keep out of the bidding gave an advantage to the defendant – in that he was able to obtain the property for a lower price than would otherwise have been possible; but the failure of the plaintiff's agent to bid did not, in fact, cause detriment to the plaintiff – because, on the facts, the agent's instructions would not have permitted him to outbid the defendant. Nevertheless, the equity was invoked.

(5) That leads, I think, to the further conclusions: (i) that, although, in many cases, the advantage/detriment will be found in the agreement of the non-acquiring party to keep out of the market, that is not a necessary feature; and (ii) that, although there will usually be advantage to the one and co-relative disadvantage to the other, the existence of both advantage and detriment is not essential – either will do. What is essential is that the circumstances make it inequitable for the acquiring party to retain the property for himself in a manner inconsistent with the arrangement or understanding on which the non-acquiring party has acted. Those circumstances may arise where the non-acquiring party was never 'in the market' for the whole of the property to be acquired; but (on the faith of an arrangement or understanding that he shall have a part of that property) provides support in relation to the acquisition of the whole which is of advantage to the acquiring party. They may arise where the assistance provided to the acquiring party (in pursuance of the arrangement or understanding) involves no detriment to the non-acquiring party; or where the non-acquiring party acts to his detriment (in pursuance of the arrangement or understanding) without the acquiring party obtaining any advantage therefrom.

The present appeal

The judge summarised the findings in two passages in his judgment:

> Banner's belief, encouraged by Luff's conduct and representations leading up to and in the days following exchange of contracts for the White Waltham site on 1 November, that the joint venture proposal was proceeding and that there *would* be a formal agreement setting out the terms of their relationship . . .

Secondly, at page 74, lines 17–19, he said this:

> . . . from 14 July until 16 November (if not later) Luff gave Banner to understand that there would be a joint venture and that it intended to enter into a shareholder agreement to regulate their relationship . . .

In my view the judge misunderstood the principles upon which equity intervenes in cases of this nature. The *Pallant v Morgan* equity does not seek to give effect to the parties' bargain, still less to make for them some bargain which they have not themselves made, as the cases to which I have referred make clear. The equity is invoked where the defendant has acquired property in circumstances where it would be inequitable to allow him to treat it as his own; and where, because it would be inequitable to allow him to treat the property as his own, it is necessary to impose on him the obligations of a trustee in relation to it. It is invoked because there is no bargain which is capable of being enforced; if there were an enforceable bargain there would have been no need for equity to intervene in the way that it has done in the cases to which I have referred.

I am satisfied, also, that the judge was wrong to reject the constructive trust claim on the grounds that Banner had failed to show that it had acted to its detriment in reliance on the arrangement agreed on 14 July 1995.

As I have sought to show, the *Pallant v Morgan* equity is invoked where it would be inequitable to allow the defendant to treat the property acquired in furtherance of the arrangement or understanding as his own. It may be just as inequitable to allow the defendant to treat the property as his own when it has been acquired by the use of some advantage which he has obtained under the arrangement or understanding as it is to allow him to treat the property as his own when the plaintiff has suffered some detriment under the arrangement or understanding. That, as it seems to me, is this case.

For those reasons I would allow this appeal.

In order to attract the jurisdiction of equity to require the defendant to account for unauthorised profits, the claimant is obliged to establish that it would be inequitable to allow the defendant to retain the benefit or profit with impunity. Thus, the exact nature of the transaction or relationship entered into between the parties will be considered by the courts. Loan agreements on their own, created between independent commercial entities, may be insufficient to impose a duty to account or constructive trust on the defendant if there is no evidence of a joint commercial venture between the parties. In *Kilcarne Holdings Ltd v Targetfollow Ltd* the court decided that the claim failed because there was no evidence of a joint venture between the parties.

Kilcarne Holdings Ltd v Targetfollow Ltd [2005] All ER (D) 203, CA

Facts

The subject matter of the claim involved a 250 year lease of Baskerville House, Centenary Square, Birmingham. The defendant company (TBL) was set up specifically to acquire the lease of the property. On 5 February 2002 completion took place of an agreement by Birmingham City Council to grant the lease to TBL. The amount required to complete the transaction was £2.5m of which £1m was loaned by Kilcarne Ltd in exchange for loan notes of the same value. The loan was secured with a first charge on the property. As part of a composite transaction Kilcarne and an associated company called, Rosedale Ltd, together lent £2.5m to TBL. There was evidence of some discussion concerning financial arrangements between the principal shareholder of TBL and the managing director of another company, Sitac Ltd (which acted on behalf of the claimant companies). The claimants contended that, in addition to the secured loans, a legally enforceable oral agreement was created between the claimants and the defendant for a joint venture for the development of the property. The judge considered the circumstances, including the minutes of the meetings held by the various companies, and decided that there was no evidence of a joint venture between the parties. The claimants further alleged that constructive trusts had been created in their favour based on the *Gissing v Gissing* and *Pallant v Morgan* principles. The judge rejected these claims and decided that the intentions of the parties were reflected in the formal legal contracts creating loan agreements between the parties. The claimants appealed to the Court of Appeal.

Held

The appeal would be dismissed. There was ample evidence to support the judge's decision. On 5 February 2002 the parties did not share a common intention to create equitable interests in relation to the lease. Such a common intention was necessary in order to establish a *Gissing v Gissing* constructive trust (see later). There was some evidence of discussions and negotiations between the parties but no concluded agreement as to a joint venture had been reached. In addition, the *Pallant v Morgan* constructive trust claim failed because the parties did not commit themselves to a joint venture or a venture whereby the claimants would obtain some interest in the property.

> **Sir Martin Nourse:** In summary, it is apparent that there was ample evidence on which it was open to the judge to come to the conclusion that TBL and Kilcarne did not, at or before the completion of the transaction on 5th February 2002, share the common intention necessary to establish a *Gissing v Gissing* constructive trust in relation to the lease of Baskerville House. On that footing, it is unnecessary to go into the question of reliance I turn to the *Pallant v Morgan* constructive trust, as to which the judge said:
>
> > Essentially the principle is that (i) if A and B agree that A will acquire some specific property for the joint benefit of A and B and (ii) B, in reliance on A's agreement, refrains from attempting to acquire the property, then equity will not permit A, when he acquires the property, to keep it for his own benefit, to the exclusion of B.
>
> That formulation does not fit the facts of the present case because Kilcarne never intended to acquire the lease itself and cannot therefore be said to have refrained from attempting to do so. But it has not been suggested that that in itself is an objection to the application of the principle. Mr Nugee submitted that, when applied to this case, the principle required, first, that there be an arrangement or understanding between the parties that A will acquire the property and that if he does so B will obtain some interest in it; and, secondly, that B must act in reliance on that arrangement or understanding. I agree with that submission.
>
> It follows that, however it is put, the case for a *Pallant v Morgan* constructive trust also fails at the first hurdle. There was never any agreement, arrangement or understanding between TBL and Kilcarne that the lease should be acquired for their joint benefit or that Kilcarne would obtain some interest in it.
>
> It is unnecessary to go further. On the facts of this case it is difficult, if not impossible, to discern any material difference between the application of the *Gissing v Gissing* and *Pallant v Morgan* principles. For myself, I would have thought that it was the former that fitted the case better than the latter. But whether that be right or wrong it is clear that, if the case is not covered by the former, it will not be covered by the latter.

Unauthorised remuneration

In accordance with the rule in *Keech v Sandford*, a trustee is not entitled to receive any remuneration or benefit for his services as trustee, except that he may be reimbursed in respect of expenditure properly incurred in connection with his trusteeship (s 31 of the Trustee Act 2000 (replacing s 30(2) of the Trustee Act 1925)).

In *Williams v Barton*, a trustee received unauthorised remuneration and was therefore accountable to the trust.

Williams v Barton [1927] 2 Ch 9, HC

Facts

Barton, one of two trustees under a will, was employed as a stockbroker's clerk and in this capacity was entitled to commission on business introduced to his firm. He persuaded his co-trustee to use his firm to value the trust property. Barton took no part in the work of valuation. The trustees paid the fees charged by the firm and Barton received his commission. The co-trustee now claimed to recover the commission on behalf of the trust.

Held

Despite the fact that the valuation was quite proper in the circumstances, Barton was required to account for the commission because the opportunity to earn the reward derived from his position as trustee:

> **Russell J:** It is a well established and salutary rule of equity that a trustee may not make a profit out of his trust. A person who has the management of property as a trustee is not permitted to gain any profit by availing himself of his position, and will be a constructive trustee of any such profit for the benefit of the persons equitably entitled to the property.
>
> It was argued on behalf of the defendant that the case was altogether outside that rule of equity, because the sums received by the defendant were merely parts of his salary paid to him by his employers under the contract of service and were not of a character for which he is liable to account.
>
> The case is clearly one where his duty as trustee and his interest in an increased remuneration are in direct conflict. As a trustee, it is his duty to give the estate the benefit of his unfettered advice in choosing the stockbrokers to act for the estate; as the recipient of half the fees to be earned by George Burnand & Co on work introduced by him his obvious interest is to choose or recommend them for the job.
>
> The services rendered remain unchanged, but the remuneration for them has been increased. He has increased his remuneration by virtue of his trusteeship. In my opinion this increase of remuneration is profit made by the defendant out of and by reason of his trusteeship, which he would not have made but for his position as trustee.

The logical effect of this rule is that if a trustee legitimately appoints an agent to do trust work that agent may be paid, but if the trustee himself performs the relevant duties he may not be paid.

In *Box v Barclays Bank*, the High Court refused to impose a constructive trust on the defendant, despite the unlawful receipt of funds by an unlicensed deposit-taking business conducted by a party which banked with the defendant. The court decided that under the Banking Act 1987, the claimant's contractual remedies were expressly preserved. It was therefore unnecessary and inappropriate to provide an alternative remedy based in equity.

Box v Barclays Bank [1998] 1 All ER 108, HC

Facts

Each of the three plaintiffs, Mrs Box, Mrs Brown and Mrs Jacobs, invested funds with a deposit-taking business run by Sylcon Finance Ltd (Sylcon). Sylcon paid the funds into an account at Barclays Bank plc (the defendant). At all material times, the account was overdrawn, although none of the plaintiffs was aware of this. In October 1992, the Bank of England commenced proceedings against Sylcon, on the ground that the latter company was carrying on a deposit-taking business without being authorised under Pt 1 of the Banking Act 1987. Section 3(1) of the Banking

Act 1987 states: '. . . no person shall . . . accept a deposit in the course of carrying on a deposit-taking business unless that person . . . is authorised by the Bank . . .' Section 3(3) of the Act provides as follows: 'The fact that a deposit has been taken in contravention of this section shall not affect any civil liability arising in respect of the deposit.' An order was made freezing the assets of Sylcon and subsequently the business was liquidated. The plaintiffs proved as creditors and received a distribution of only 12 p in the pound in respect of the amounts claimed. The plaintiffs claimed to recover their losses on the ground that the business of Sylcon was tainted by illegality under s 3(1) of the Banking Act 1987, and therefore the deposits were held on constructive trust and could be recovered from the defendant.

Held

The unlicensed deposit-taking business of Sylcon constituted a special form of illegality in respect of which s 3(3) of the 1987 Act preserved the ordinary contractual remedies of the depositors. Thus, it was unnecessary to create an alternative remedy in equity. Indeed, to do so would have been contrary to the express provisions of s 3(3) of the Act:

> **Ferris J:** Mr Browne-Wilkinson [counsel for the plaintiffs] argued that the contracts of deposit were affected by illegality, and that, on authority, equity would impose a constructive trust so as to enable the plaintiffs to recover their money. He said that there is a principle under which, where money passes under an illegal transaction in relation to which the recipient of the money is at fault to a greater degree than the payer, equity will give the payer a right to recover his money. This right, being equitable, will bind successors in title to the original recipient unless they take in good faith and for value and without notice of it.
>
> I cannot accept this argument. In my view illegality consisting of the taking of deposits by a person who conducts an unlicensed deposit-taking business constitutes a special form of illegality which does not bring in its train the ordinary consequences of illegality at common law. This is achieved by means of s 3(3). That sub-section leaves the ordinary contractual remedies of the depositor intact. It is unnecessary in these circumstances to seek an alternative remedy in equity. Indeed, to do so would go against the very terms of s 3(3). It is not suggested that there would be a remedy in equity were it not for the illegality consisting of the contravention of s 3(1). But if that contravention gives rise to an equitable remedy where none would otherwise exist this would 'affect' the civil liability arising in respect of the deposit by giving the new remedy. Section 3(3) expressly negatives this.

In *AG v Blake*, the House of Lords decided that a member of the secret service who unlawfully disclosed information for reward, in breach of his duty of confidentiality, was liable to disgorge the profits.

AG v Blake [2000] 3 WLR 625, HL

Facts

The defendant, George Blake, was a member of the Secret Intelligence Service (SIS) who disclosed secret information and documents to the Soviet Union. He was convicted for an offence under the Official Secrets Act 1911 and was sentenced to 42 years' imprisonment but escaped and made his way to Moscow, where he lived. In 1989, Mr Blake wrote his autobiography detailing his activities as a member of the SIS. The book, entitled *No Other Choice*, was published in 1990. Jonathan Cape Ltd (the publishers) had paid him about £60,000 under the publishing agreement. For all practical purposes this amount was not recoverable, but Mr Blake was entitled to receive royalties from future sales of the book. The Attorney General, representing the Crown, claimed the financial benefits accrued from the publication of the book, in addition to future royalties. The claim was based on the ground that in writing the book, the defendant acted in breach of his duty of confidentiality owed to the Crown as an ex-member of the SIS. It was alleged that the Crown was the beneficial owner of the copyright in the book and the defendant was accountable to the Crown for all sums received in respect of the publication. It was not contended that in writing the book the defendant had committed any breach of his duty of confidence. Moreover, it was conceded by the Crown that the information contained in the book relating to the SIS was no longer confidential. The High Court dismissed the claim on the ground that an ex-member of the SIS did not owe the Crown a continuing duty not to use any information imparted to him in that capacity in order to generate a profit or benefit himself. The Court of Appeal allowed the appeal. Mr Blake appealed to the House of Lords. The Attorney General raised an additional argument, namely, a claim for an account of Mr Blake's profits even though the Crown could not establish that it had suffered loss. This claim is sometimes referred to as 'restitutionary damages'.

Held

The appeal was dismissed by a 4:1 majority (Lord Hobhouse dissenting), but the order made by the Court of Appeal was varied on the following grounds:

(a) As a result of his breach of contract, practical justice demanded that Mr Blake be disentitled to the profits that he would otherwise have received.

(b) The decision of the Court of Appeal on the public law claim was reversed. The court has no power at common law to make a confiscation order. Parliament created such a power within clearly defined limits under the Criminal Justice Act 1988, which did not exist on these facts:

> **Lord Nicholls:** The law is now sufficiently mature to recognise a restitutionary claim for profits made from a breach of contract in appropriate situations. These include cases of 'skimped' performance, and cases where the defendant obtained his profit by doing 'the very thing' he contracted not to do.
>
> The present case fell into the latter category: Blake earned his profit by doing the very thing he had promised not to do.
>
> This is a subject on which there is a surprising dearth of judicial decision. By way of contrast, over the last 20 years there has been no lack of academic writing. Most writers have favoured the view that in some circumstances the innocent party to a breach of contract should be able to compel the defendant to disgorge the profits he obtained from his breach of contract. However, there is a noticeable absence of any consensus on what are the circumstances in which this remedy should be available. Professor Burrows has described this as a devilishly difficult topic (see 'No restitutionary damages for breach of contract' [1993] LMCLQ 453). The broad proposition that a wrongdoer should not be allowed to profit from his wrong has an obvious attraction. The corollary is that the person wronged may recover the amount of this profit when he has suffered no financially measurable loss. As Glidewell LJ observed in *Halifax Building Society v Thomas* [1995] 4 All ER 673 at 682, [1996] Ch 217 at 229, the corollary is not so obviously persuasive. In these choppy waters the common law and equity steered different courses. The effects of this are still being felt.

> **Interference with rights of property**
>
> So I turn to established, basic principles. As with breaches of contract, so with tort, the general principle regarding assessment of damages is that they are compensatory for loss or injury. The general rule is that, in the oft-quoted words of Lord Blackburn, the measure of damages is to be, as far as possible, that amount of money which will put the injured party in the same position he would have been in had he not sustained the wrong (see *Livingstone v Rawyards Coal Co* (1880) 5 App Cas 25 at 39). Damages are measured by the plaintiff's loss, not the defendant's gain. But the common law, pragmatic as ever, has long recognised that there are many commonplace situations where a strict application of this principle would not do justice between the parties. Then compensation for the wrong done to the plaintiff is measured by a different yardstick. A trespasser who enters another's land may cause the landowner no financial loss. In such a case damages are measured by the benefit received by the trespasser, namely, by his use of the land. The same principle is applied where the wrong consists of use of another's land for depositing waste, or by using a path across the land or using passages in an underground mine. The same principle is applied to the wrongful detention of goods.
>
> Courts of equity went further than the common law courts. In some cases equity required the wrongdoer to yield up all his gains. In respect of certain wrongs which originally or ordinarily were the subject of proceedings in the Court of Chancery, the standard remedies were injunction and, incidental thereto, an account of profits. These wrongs included passing off, infringement of trade marks, copyrights and patents, and breach of confidence. Some of these subjects are now embodied in statutory codes. In these cases the courts of equity appear to have regarded an injunction and account of profits as more appropriate remedies than damages because of the difficulty of assessing the extent of the loss. In these types of case equity considered that the appropriate response to the violation of the plaintiff's right was that the defendant should surrender all his gains, and that he should do so irrespective of whether the violation had caused the plaintiff any financially measurable loss. Gains were to be disgorged even though they could not be shown to correspond with any disadvantage suffered by the

other party. This lack of correspondence was openly acknowledged. In *Lever v Goodwin* (1887) 36 Ch D 1 at 7, [1886–90] All ER Rep 427 at 429, Cotton LJ stated it was 'well known' that in trade mark and patent cases the plaintiff was entitled, if he succeeded in getting an injunction, to take either of two forms of relief: he might claim from the defendant either the damage he had sustained from the defendant's wrongful act or the profit made by the defendant from the defendant's wrongful act. The question under discussion is whether the court will award substantial damages for an infringement when no financial loss flows from the infringement and, moreover, in a suitable case will assess the damages by reference to the defendant's profit obtained from the infringement. The cases mentioned above show that the courts habitually do that very thing.

My conclusion is that there seems to be no reason, in principle, why the court must in all circumstances rule out an account of profits as a remedy for breach of contract. I prefer to avoid the unhappy expression 'restitutionary damages'. Remedies are the law's response to a wrong (or, more precisely, to a cause of action). When, exceptionally, a just response to a breach of contract so requires, the court should be able to grant the discretionary remedy of requiring a defendant to account to the plaintiff for the benefits he has received from his breach of contract.

The court will have regard to all the circumstances, including the subject matter of the contract, the purpose of the contractual provision which has been breached, the circumstances in which the breach occurred, the consequences of the breach and the circumstances in which relief is being sought. A useful general guide, although not exhaustive, is whether the plaintiff had a legitimate interest in preventing the defendant's profit-making activity and, hence, in depriving him of his profit.

The present case

The present case is exceptional. The context is employment as a member of the security and intelligence services. Secret information is the lifeblood of these services. Blake deliberately committed repeated breaches of his undertaking not to divulge official information gained as a result of his employment. He caused untold and immeasurable damage to the public interest he had committed himself to serve. In the ordinary course of commercial dealings the disclosure of non-confidential information might be regarded as venial. In the present case disclosure was also a criminal offence under the Official Secrets Acts, even though the information was no longer confidential. An absolute rule against disclosure, visible to all, makes good sense. In considering what would be a just response to a breach of Blake's undertaking the court has to take these considerations into account. The undertaking, if not a fiduciary obligation, was closely akin to a fiduciary obligation, where an account of profits is a standard remedy in the event of breach. Had the information which Blake has now disclosed still been confidential, an account of profits would have been ordered, almost as a matter of course. In the special circumstances of the intelligence services, the same conclusion should follow even though the information is no longer confidential. That would be a just response to the breach.

The public law claim

In Pt VI of the Criminal Justice Act 1988, as amended by the Proceeds of Crime Act 1995, Parliament has carefully marked out when these orders may be made. The common law has no power to remedy any perceived deficiencies in this statutory code. An attempt to do so would offend the established general principle, of high constitutional importance, that there is no common law power to take or confiscate property without compensation. (See *AG v De Keyser's Royal Hotel Ltd* [1920] AC 508, [1920] All ER 80, *Burmah Oil Co (Burmah Trading) Ltd v Lord Advocate* [1964] 2 All ER 348, [1965] AC 75 and, in this context, *Malone v Comr of Police of the Metropolis* [1979] 1 All ER 256 at 264–265, [1980] QB 49 at 61–63, per Stephenson LJ.)

Bribes or unlawful sums received by fiduciaries

In accordance with the general rule, where a fiduciary accepts a bribe in breach of his fiduciary duty, the bribe, including property representing the unauthorised profit, is held upon trust for the persons to whom the duty is owed. On receipt of the bribe, the fiduciary becomes a trustee of the sum for the benefit of the innocent party and is liable to account for this property and any derivative profits. If the bribe is used to purchase other property which decreases in value, the fiduciary is required to account for the difference between the bribe and the undervalue. Alternatively, if the property has increased in value, the innocent party is entitled to claim the surplus, for the fiduciary is not entitled to profit from a breach of his duties. The alternative solution adopted in *Lister v Stubbs* to the effect that the recipient of the bribe becomes merely a debtor for the payer has been severely criticized and is now of doubtful authority.

AG for Hong Kong v Reid and Others [1993] 3 WLR 1143, PC

Facts

The Attorney General for Hong Kong brought an action for an account in respect of bribes received by Mr Reid, the former acting DPP for Hong Kong. The bribes, amounting to NZ$2.5 million, were paid to him as inducements to exploit his official position by obstructing the prosecution of certain prisoners. Mr Reid used the bribes in order to purchase three freehold properties in New Zealand valued in excess of NZ$2.4m. Two of the properties were vested in the joint names of Mr Reid and his wife and the other was conveyed to his solicitor. The Attorney General lodged a caution in respect of each of the properties in order to prevent any dealings pending a full hearing.

The question in issue concerned the status of a fiduciary who received a bribe, in particular, whether such a fiduciary became a mere debtor for the innocent party or alternatively a trustee for the aggrieved party. The defendants mounted an argument claiming that the fiduciary became a debtor for the innocent party and had no equitable interest in the properties, relying on *Lister v Stubbs*. The plaintiff asserted that the decision in *Lister v Stubbs* (1890) 45 Ch D should not be followed as it was inconsistent with basic equitable principles as illustrated in *Keech v Sandford* and *Boardman v Phipps*. The fiduciary, on receipt of the bribe, became a constructive trustee of the benefit on behalf of the person injured. Accordingly, the fiduciary became accountable to the plaintiff not only in respect of the bribe, but also for any property derived from the bribe (provided that this did not lead to double compensation).

Held

In favour of the plaintiff on the ground that the bribe and representative property acquired by the fiduciary were subject to the claims of the injured party. Since the representative property had decreased in value, the fiduciary was liable to account for the difference between the bribe and the undervalue:

> **Lord Templeman:** When a bribe is offered and accepted in money or in kind, the money or property constituting the bribe belongs in law to the recipient. *Money paid to the false fiduciary belongs to him. The legal estate in freehold property conveyed to the false fiduciary by way of bribe vests in him. Equity, however, which acts in personam,* insists that it is unconscionable for a fiduciary to obtain and retain a benefit in breach of duty. The provider of a bribe cannot recover it because he committed a criminal offence when he paid the bribe. The false fiduciary who received the bribe in breach of duty must pay and account for the bribe to the person to whom that duty was owed. In the present case, as soon as the first respondent received a bribe in breach of the duties he owed to the Government of Hong Kong, he became a debtor in equity to the Crown for the amount of that bribe. So much is admitted. But if the bribe consists of property which increases in value or if a cash bribe is invested advantageously, the false fiduciary will receive a benefit from his breach of duty unless he is accountable not only for the original amount or value of the bribe but also for the increased value of the property representing the bribe. As soon as the bribe was received it should have been paid or transferred instantly to the person who suffered from the breach of duty. *Equity considers as done that which ought to have been done. As soon as the bribe was received, whether in cash or in kind, the false fiduciary held the bribe on a constructive trust for the person injured.* Two objections have been raised to this analysis. First, it is said that if the fiduciary is in equity a debtor to the person injured, he cannot also be a trustee of the bribe. But there is no reason why equity should not provide two remedies, so long as they do not result in double recovery. If the property representing the bribe exceeds the original bribe in value, the fiduciary cannot retain the benefit of the increase in value which he obtained solely as a result of his breach of duty. Secondly, it is said that if the false fiduciary holds property representing the bribe in trust for the person injured, and if the false fiduciary is or becomes insolvent, the unsecured creditors of the false fiduciary will be deprived of their right to share in the proceeds of that property. But the unsecured creditors cannot be in a better position than their debtor. The authorities show that property acquired by a trustee innocently but in breach of trust and the property from time to time representing the same belong in equity to the *cestui que trust* and not to the trustee personally whether he is solvent or insolvent. Property

acquired by a trustee as a result of a criminal breach of trust and the property from time to time representing the same must also belong in equity to his *cestui que* trust and not to the trustee whether he is solvent or insolvent [emphasis added].

When a bribe is accepted by a fiduciary in breach of his duty then he holds that bribe in trust for the person to whom the duty was owed. If the property representing the bribe decreases in value the fiduciary must pay the difference between that value and the initial amount of the bribe because he should not have accepted the bribe or incurred the risk of loss. If the property increases in value, the fiduciary is not entitled to any surplus in excess of the initial value of the bribe because he is not allowed by any means to make a profit out of a breach of duty.

This case is of importance because it disposes succinctly of the argument which appears in later cases and which was put forward by counsel in the present case that there is a distinction between a profit which a trustee takes out of a trust and a profit such as a bribe which a trustee receives from a third party. If in law a trustee, who in breach of trust invests trust moneys in his own name, holds the investment as trust property, it is difficult to see why a trustee who in breach of trust receives and invests a bribe in his own name does not hold those investments also as trust property.

It has always been assumed and asserted that the law on the subject of bribes was definitively settled by the decision of the Court of Appeal in *Lister & Co v Stubbs* (1890) 45 Ch D 1. In that case the plaintiffs, Lister & Co, employed the defendant, Stubbs, as their servant to purchase goods for the firm. Stubbs, on behalf of the firm, bought goods from Varley & Co and received from Varley & Co bribes amounting to £5,541. The bribes were invested by Stubbs in freehold properties and investments. His masters, the firm Lister & Co, sought and failed to obtain an interlocutory injunction restraining Stubbs from disposing of these assets pending the trial of the action in which they sought, *inter alia*, £5,541 and damages. In the Court of Appeal, the first judgment was given by Cotton LJ, who had been party to the decision in *Metropolitan Bank v Heiron* (1880) 5 Ex D 319. He was powerfully supported by the judgment of Lindley LJ and by the equally powerful concurrence of Bowen LJ. Cotton LJ said, at p 12, that the bribe could not be said to be the money of the plaintiffs. He seemed to be reluctant to grant an interlocutory judgment which would provide security for a debt before that debt had been established. Lindley LJ said, at p 15, that the relationship between the plaintiffs, Lister & Co, as masters and the defendant, Stubbs, as servant who had betrayed his trust and received a bribe:

> . . . is that of debtor and creditor; it is not that of trustee and *cestui que* trust. We are asked to hold that it is – which would involve consequences which, I confess, startle me. One consequence, of course, would be that, if Stubbs were to become bankrupt, this property acquired by him with the money paid to him by Messrs Varley would be withdrawn from the mass of his creditors and be handed over bodily to Lister & Co. Can that be right? Another consequence would be that, if the appellants are right, Lister & Co could compel Stubbs to account to them, not only for the money with interest, but for all the profits which he might have made by embarking in trade with it. Can that be right?

For the reasons which have already been advanced their Lordships would respectfully answer both these questions in the affirmative. If a trustee mistakenly invests moneys which he ought to pay over to his *cestui que* trust and then becomes bankrupt, the moneys together with any profit which has accrued from the investment are withdrawn from the unsecured creditors as soon as the mistake is discovered. A *fortiori* if a trustee commits a crime by accepting a bribe which he ought to pay over to his *cestui que* trust, the bribe and any profit made therefrom should be withdrawn from the unsecured creditors as soon as the crime is discovered.

The decision in *Lister & Co v Stubbs* is not consistent with the principles that a fiduciary must not be allowed to benefit from his own breach of duty, that the fiduciary should account for the bribe as soon as he receives it and that equity regards as done that which ought to be done. From these principles it would appear to follow *that the bribe and the property from time to time representing the bribe are held on a constructive trust for the person injured.* A fiduciary remains personally liable for the amount of the bribe if, in the event, the value of the property then recovered by the injured person proved to be less than that amount [emphasis added].

Their Lordships are also much indebted for the fruits of research and the careful discussion of the present topic in the address entitled 'Bribes and secret commissions' (1993) RLR 7, delivered by Sir Peter Millett to a meeting of the Society of Public Teachers of Law at Oxford in 1993. The following passage, at p 20, elegantly sums up the views of Sir Peter Millett:

> [The fiduciary] must not place himself in a position where his interest may conflict with his duty. If he has done so, equity insists on treating him as having acted in accordance with his duty; he will not be allowed to say that he preferred his own interest to that of his principal. He must not obtain a profit for himself out of

his fiduciary position. If he has done so, equity insists on treating him as having obtained it for his principal; he will not be allowed to say that he obtained it for himself. He must not accept a bribe. If he has done so, equity insists on treating it as a legitimate payment intended for the benefit of the principal; he will not be allowed to say that it was a bribe.

For the reasons indicated their Lordships consider that the three properties so far as they represent bribes accepted by the first respondent are held in trust for the Crown.

Endorsing the decision in *Reid*, the High Court in *Daraydan Holdings Ltd v Solland Interiors Ltd* decided that a fiduciary who receives a bribe or a secret commission becomes a constructive trustee. Such a fiduciary or agent who makes a secret profit is accountable to his trustee or principal. The agent should not put himself in a position where his duty and interest may conflict, for such bribes deprive the principal of objective advice from the agent to which the principal is entitled. The agent and the third party who pays the bribe are jointly and severally liable to account for the bribe and each may be liable in damages to the principal for fraud or deceit or conspiracy to deceive.

Further, in proceedings against the third party who pays the bribe, it is unnecessary for the principal to prove:

- that the third party acted with a corrupt motive,
- that the agent's mind was affected by the bribe,
- that the third party knew or suspected that the agent would conceal the payment from the principal,
- that the principal suffered any loss or that the transaction was in some way unfair.

Daraydan Holdings Ltd and Others v Solland Interiors Ltd and Others
[2004] EWHC 622 (HC)

Facts

The claimants were a Middle Eastern consortium that purchased residential properties in London. One of the defendants, Mr Khalid was relied on by the claimants to identify and obtain quotations from contractors for the refurbishment of the properties and make recommendations to the claimants who made the final decision. Mr and Mrs Solland, who carried on business through a design and refurbishment company, Solland Interiors Ltd., was introduced to the claimants through Mr Khalid. Ultimately Solland Interiors was contracted to refurbish the properties of the claimants. However, Solland Interiors Ltd procured the discreet payment to Mr Khalid of 10% of the sums paid by the claimants to Solland Interiors Ltd in the expectation of receiving additional contracts. This additional amount was surreptitiously written into the quotations provided by Solland Interiors Ltd. to the claimants. A dispute arose between the claimants and Solland Interiors Ltd and the claimants became aware of the secret commissions paid to Mr Khalid. The claimants commenced proceedings against Solland Interiors Ltd and Mr Khalid. The claim against Solland Interiors Ltd was eventually settled. The claims against Mr Khalid were for an account of all secret commissions, an order for restitution of the secret profits and a declaration that they were received on resulting or constructive trust.

Held

(1) Mr Khalid was a fiduciary who extracted substantial payments from the Sollands and their companies in return for his influence in obtaining contracts from the claimants.

(2) The bribes or secret commissions received by Mr Khalid were in breach of his fiduciary duties owed to the claimants.

(3) Following the Privy Council decision in *AG for Hong Kong v Reid* [1994] 1 AC 324, Mr Khalid became a constructive trustee for the claimants.

Collins J: The claimants seek against Mr Khalid: (a) an account of all secret commissions, monies and other benefits received by him in connection with the Contracts; (b) an order for restitution as money had and received of all secret commissions, monies and other benefits received in connection with the Contracts; (c) a declaration that all such secret commissions, monies and benefits were received by him on resulting or constructive trust for the relevant claimant and that the relevant claimant is entitled to trace into such commissions, monies and other benefits all assets acquired by or representing such monies; and an order for delivery up of all such monies or assets; and (d) damages for deceit or conspiracy to defraud by reason of his corrupt agreement with the first to fourth defendants that he would be paid a secret commission on all sums paid under the Contracts. The claimants seek restitutionary remedies against Mr Khalid because they wish to trace the proceeds of the bribes in the hands of recipients.

Legal principles

An agent or other fiduciary who makes a secret profit is accountable to his or her principal or *cestui que trust*. There have been many cases in the development of the rules for civil liability for bribery of which perhaps the most important are *Panama & South Pacific Telegraph Co v India Rubber, etc Works Co* (1875) LR 10 Ch App 515; *Hovenden & Sons v Millhoff* (1900) 83 LT 41; *Reading v R* [1949] 2 KB 232, [1949] 2 All ER 68, affd [1951] AC 507, [1951] 1 All ER 617; *Mahesan v Malaysia Government Officers' Co-operative Housing Society* [1979] AC 374, [1978] 2 All ER 405; *Logicrose Ltd v Southend United Football Club Ltd* [1988] 1 WLR 1256; and *AG for Hong Kong v Reid* [1994] 1 AC 324. The following principles can be distilled from the cases.

An agent should not put himself in a position where his duty and interest may conflict, and if bribes are taken by an agent, the principal is deprived of the disinterested advice of the agent, to which the principal is entitled. Any surreptitious dealing between one principal to a transaction and the agent of the other is a fraud on the other principal. For this purpose sub-agents owe the same duty not to take bribes as agents, despite the absence of privity of contract between them and the principal: see *Bowstead and Reynolds on Agency* (17th ed Reynolds, 2001), para 6-085 and *Powell & Thomas v Evans Jones & Co* [1905] 1 KB 11, at 18 (CA).

In proceedings against the payer of the bribe there is no need for the principal to prove (a) that the payer of the bribe acted with a corrupt motive; (c) that the agent's mind was actually affected by the bribe; (d) that the payer knew or suspected that the agent would conceal the payment from the principal; (d) that the principal suffered any loss or that the transaction was in some way unfair: the law is intended to operate as a deterrent against the giving of bribes, and it will be assumed that the true price of any goods bought by the principal was increased by at least the amount of the bribe, but any loss beyond the amount of the bribe itself must be proved; (e) that the bribe was given specifically in connection with a particular contract, since a bribe may also be given to an agent to influence his mind in favour of the payer generally (eg in connection with the granting of future contracts).

The agent and the third party are jointly and severally liable to account for the bribe, and each may also be liable in damages to the principal for fraud or deceit or conspiracy to injury by unlawful means. Consequently, the agent and the maker of the payment are jointly and severally liable to the principal (1) to account for the amount of the bribe as money had and received and (2) for damages for any actual loss. But the principal must now elect between the two remedies prior to final judgment being entered: *Mahesan v Malaysia Government Officers' Co-operative Housing Society* [1979] AC 374, at 383. The third party may also be liable on the basis of accessory liability in respect of breach of fiduciary duty: *Bowstead and Reynolds*, para 8-221. The principal is also able to rescind the contract with the payer of the bribe.

In the normal case it is not difficult to determine whether the relationship is such as to give rise to a duty to account. In the present case the Sollands and Mr Khalid have denied that he was an agent or fiduciary. It is not always easy to delimit the scope of fiduciary relationships from arm's length relationships not involving a fiduciary duty: see, eg Oakley, *Constructive Trusts*, 3rd ed. 1997, pp 85–99; Meagher, Gummow and Lehane, *Equity Doctrines and Remedies*, 4th ed 2002, pp 156–167. Very often the definitions are circular: eg *Ex p Dale & Co* (1879) 11 Ch D 772, at 778: a fiduciary relationship "is one in respect of which if a wrong arise, the same remedy exists against the wrongdoer on behalf of the principal as would exist against a trustee on behalf of the *cestui que trust*." In *Bristol and West Building Society v Mothew* [1998] Ch 1, [1996] 4 All ER 698, at 18, Millett LJ said:

> A fiduciary is someone who has undertaken to act for or on behalf of another in a particular matter in circumstances which give rise to a relationship of trust and confidence. The distinguishing obligation of a fiduciary is the obligation of loyalty. The principal is entitled to the single-minded loyalty of his fiduciary. This core liability has several facets. A fiduciary must act in good faith; he must not make a profit out of his trust; he must not place himself in a position where his duty and interest may conflict; he may not act for his own benefit or the benefit of a third person without the informed consent of his principal. This is not intended to

be an exhaustive list, but it is sufficient to indicate the nature of fiduciary obligations. They are the defining characteristics of the fiduciary.

In *Reading v R* [1949] 2 KB 232, at 236, Asquith LJ said that there is a fiduciary relationship whenever the plaintiff entrusts a job to be performed, for instance the negotiation of a contract, and relies on the defendant to procure for the plaintiff the best terms available (approved by Lord Porter [1951] AC 507, at 516).

I am wholly satisfied that, on any application of the concept of fiduciary, Mr Khalid was a fiduciary who extracted very substantial payments from the Sollands and their companies in return for his influence in obtaining and carrying out the Contracts. This is demonstrated by his own admissions; by statements made by the Sollands in these proceedings and in the adjudication proceedings; and by numerous documents. It is also confirmed by the evidence of Sheikh Sultan and Mr Dajani in these proceedings, and also by the evidence of Mr Meisterhans. Although it would make no difference to his liability whether it was he who solicited the payments, or Mrs Solland who offered them, there is no reason to doubt Mrs Solland's account that it was Mr Khalid who requested the payments, and no reason whatever to think that (as he contended) that it was Mrs Solland who volunteered to make the payments.

In *Daraydan* the court expressed a preference for the decision of the Privy Council in *Reid* but, in any event, was able to distinguish *Lister v Stubbs* on two grounds. In *Daraydan* the bribe received by Mr Khalid derived directly from the claimants' property owing to the deception practised by the former. This amounted to restitution of money extracted from the claimants. Secondly, the portion representing the bribe was paid as a result of a fraudulent representation of the Sollands to which Mr Khalid was a party, giving the appearance that the invoice price was the true costs when in fact the costs had been inflated to pay the bribes.

> **Collins J** continued: Those who have supported *Lister & Co v Stubbs* rely on the policy that proprietary restitution is only justified where there has been a subtraction from the claimant's ownership or where the claimant has a proprietary basis for the claim. The general creditors have given value, and there is no reason why the agent's principal should have a preferred position. The policy against bribery is sufficiently vindicated through a personal remedy. Thus, according to Professor Goode, proprietary remedies should only be available where the defendant receives gains which derive from the claimant's property, or where they stem from activity which the defendant was under an equitable obligation to undertake (if at all) for the plaintiff: the decision in *Lister & Co v Stubbs* was correct, because the bribe resulted from conduct in which the defendant should not have engaged at all: Goode, *Property and Unjust Enrichment*, in *Essays on the Law of Restitution*, ed. Burrows 1991, 215 at 230–231; *Proprietary Restitutionary Claims*, in *Restitution: Past, Present and Future*, ed Cornish et al, 1998, 63, at 69. So also Professor Birks considers that proprietary restitution is only justified where the claimant has a proprietary base to his claim, ie where the defendant's breach of duty consists of misapplication of property belonging to the claimant; but in the case of bribery, the money paid to the agent comes from the third party, and not from the principal: Birks, *Introduction to the Law of Restitution*, 1989, at 386. See also Virgo, *Principles of the Law of Restitution*, 1999, p 543; Burrows, *Law of Restitution*, 2nd ed 2002, p 500; Tettenborn, *Law of Restitution in England and Ireland*, 2nd ed. 1996, pp 231–233.
>
> . . . if this case were not distinguishable from *Lister & Co v Stubbs*, I would have applied *AG for Hong Kong v Reid*. There are powerful policy reasons for ensuring that a fiduciary does not retain gains acquired in violation of fiduciary duty, and I do not consider that it should make any difference whether the fiduciary is insolvent. There is no injustice to the creditors in their not sharing in an asset for which the fiduciary has not given value, and which the fiduciary should not have had.
>
> But even if I were bound by *Lister & Co v Stubbs*, in my judgment there are two very significant differences between this case and that decision which in any event justify the restitutionary remedy. First, the facts of this case make it a case where there is a proprietary basis for the claim and where the bribe derives directly from the claimants' property. This is not a case where the price is presumed (for the purposes of the personal remedy) to have been increased by the amount of the bribe. Rather it is a case where the evidence is that the price was actually increased by the amount of the bribe, and where the bribe was paid out of the money paid by the claimants for what they thought was the price. These factors make the claim one for the restitution of money extracted from the claimants.
>
> Secondly (and independently), the portion representing the bribe was paid as a result of a fraudulent mis-representation of the Sollands, to which Mr Khalid was a party, that the true price was the invoice price, when in

fact the price had been inflated to pay the bribes. I do not consider that *Halifax Building Society v Thomas* [1996] Ch 217 rules out a proprietary claim to the proceeds of fraud. In that case the defendant fraudulently obtained a loan from the building society, and it sought a declaration that it could keep the proceeds of sale as against the Crown's competing claim to confiscate the surplus in execution of a criminal confiscation order. The Court of Appeal refused to make the declaration on the grounds that the fraudster was not a fiduciary, that there was no universal principle that wherever there was a personal fraud the fraudster would become a trustee for the defrauded party, and that the building society had, with knowledge of the fraud, affirmed the mortgage, and was therefore only a secured creditor. The decision is controversial: see eg Goff & Jones, para 36-017; Burrows, p 476; Virgo, pp 494–6. But in the present case Mr Khalid was a fiduciary, and the claimants had not affirmed any of the Contracts, and had rescinded the only contracts still to be performed.

Question
Should the recipient of a bribe, who is accountable for the profit, be treated as a constructive trustee?

In *Halifax Building Society v Thomas*, it was decided that a borrower who fraudulently induced a building society to execute a mortgage on a flat was entitled to the surplus proceeds of sale from the flat. This surplus was not held on resulting trust for the building society. Moreover, the building society had no restitutionary remedy against the borrower, whose unjust enrichment was not gained at the expense of the building society. Accordingly, the borrower was not a constructive trustee of the surplus funds for the society. On conviction of the borrower, the Crown Prosecution Service was entitled to a charging order as against the society.

Halifax Building Society v Thomas and Another [1996] 2 WLR 63, CA

Facts
Mr Thomas obtained a 100% mortgage advance from the Halifax Building Society (the society) to finance the purchase of a flat. The purchase was completed in February 1986. In order to obtain the advance, Mr Thomas fraudulently misrepresented himself as Mr Robb. During 1986, Mr Thomas made a number of payments of interest but then defaulted. The society commenced proceedings against Mr Thomas in his assumed name and obtained an order for possession. In 1988, the society learnt from the police of the true identity of the mortgagor. Nevertheless, the society proceeded with the sale of the property. In 1989, the flat was sold and after the society recouped what was due to it under the mortgage, a surplus of £10,504 remained which was placed into a suspense account. Mr Thomas pleaded guilty in respect of criminal proceedings brought against him. A confiscation order in favour of the CPS was made in respect of the funds in the suspense account. The society commenced proceedings for a declaration that it was entitled to the surplus funds. The trial judge held against the society and decided that the CPS stood in the shoes of Mr Thomas and was entitled to the surplus. The society appealed to the Court of Appeal.

Held
The appeal was dismissed. The surplus funds were held on trust for Mr Thomas:

> **Peter Gibson LJ:** Mr Waters accepts, as he must, that the surplus does not represent property which the society has lost. Accordingly it cannot rely on the principle of subtractive unjust enrichment, to use the language of Professor Peter Birks QC, in his influential work, *An Introduction to the Law of Restitution* (1985). Instead it relies on the broad principle of restitution for wrongs: Mr Thomas has been enriched at the society's expense, in the sense that he has gained by committing a wrong against the society. Thereby the society seeks a remedy enabling it 'to obtain restitution of a benefit gained by the tortfeasor from a tortious act in circumstances where he has suffered little or no loss': Goff and Jones, *The Law of Restitution*, 4th edn, 1993, p 715. I accept that the starting point must be Mr Thomas' position before the confiscation order. Indeed the charging order only applied to Mr Thomas' interest in the suspense account. *Prima facie*, that is governed by s 105 of the Law of Property Act 1925, dealing with the application of the proceeds of sale following the exercise by a mortgagee of his power of sale:
>
> > The money which is received by the mortgagee, arising from the sale, after discharge of prior incumbrances to which the sale is not made subject, if any, or after payment into court under this Act of a sum to meet any

prior incumbrance, shall be held by him in trust to be applied by him: first, in payment of all costs, charges, and expenses properly incurred by him as incident to the sale or any attempted sale, or otherwise; and secondly, in discharge of the mortgage money, interest, and costs, and other money, if any, due under the mortgage; and the residue of the money so received shall be paid to the person entitled to the mortgaged property, or authorised to give receipts for the proceeds of the sale thereof.

In my judgment on the sale of the mortgaged property by the society, in 1989 Mr Thomas became entitled under s 105 to the surplus and the society could not have claimed the surplus on the ground of a further liability to account being established against him in subsequent proceedings.

On the facts of the present case, in my judgment, the fraud is not in itself a sufficient factor to allow the society to require Mr Thomas to account to it.

I would add that, in so far as the society relies on the submission that to allow a fraudster to take a profit derived from his fraud would be offensive to concepts of justice, the House of Lords in *Tinsley v Milligan* [1994] 1 AC 340, although divided in their decision, were unanimous in rejecting the 'public conscience' test as determinative of the extent to which rights created by illegal transactions should be recognised. It is not appropriate to ask whether the allowance of a claim would be an affront to the public conscience. The correct test is whether a claimant to an interest in property must plead or rely on an illegality. If so, he will not be entitled to recover. That question does not arise in the present case where it is the society which is claiming a declaration.

For these reasons I conclude that s 105 required the society to hold the surplus in trust for Mr Thomas.

Question

How would you reconcile *AG for Hong Kong v Reid* with *Halifax Building Society v Thomas*?

Remuneration of trustees

The general rule illustrated in *Williams v Barton* (see p 199 above) is subject to the following seven exceptions:

(1) Authority in the trust instrument

The settlor may authorise the trustees to be paid from the trust funds, but such power is required to be expressed in the trust instrument. The court will not imply such charging clauses. Professional trustees normally insist on an adequate charging clause before they undertake the duties of trusteeship. It would be prudent for non-professional trustees to insist on the insertion of such clauses even though they may wish to undertake such duties without reward, the reason being to facilitate the appointment of professional trustees should the need ever arise in the future.

However, charging clauses are strictly construed against the trustees in the event of any ambiguity: see Harman J in *Re Gee* [1948] Ch 284. Furthermore, trustees are not entitled to charge any sums as they wish but may only charge a reasonable amount which would vary with the circumstances of each case.

(2) Statutory provisions

The Trustee Act 2000 updates the law concerning the remuneration of trustees:

(a) Section 31 of the Trustee Act 2000 (which repeals and replaces s 30(2) of the Trustee Act 1925) entitles trustees to be reimbursed for expenses properly incurred when acting on behalf of the trust.

(b) Section 28 of the Trustee Act 2000 provides that, subject to provisions to the contrary in the trust instrument, a trust corporation or a professional trustee who is authorised to charge for services is entitled to remuneration even though the services may be provided by a lay trustee. In the case of a charitable trust, a trustee who is not a trust corporation may charge for such services only if he is not the sole trustee and a majority of the other trustees agree in writing.

(c) If the trust instrument is silent as to the remuneration of trustees, s 29 of the 2000 Act provides that a trustee who is either:

   (i)   a trust corporation; or

   (ii) a trustee acting in a professional capacity, but not a trustee of a charitable trust, may receive *reasonable remuneration* for services provided for or on behalf of the trust. In the case of a trustee acting in a professional capacity, who is not a sole trustee, each of the other trustees is required to agree in writing to authorise the trustee to be remunerated. The expression, 'reasonable remuneration', is defined in s 29(3) of the Trustee Act 2000.

Trustee Act 2000, s 29(3)

'Reasonable remuneration' means, in relation to the provision of services by a trustee, such remuneration as is reasonable in the circumstances for the provision of those services to or on behalf of that trust by that trustee and . . . includes, in relation to the provision of services by a trustee who is an authorised institution under the Banking Act 1987 and provides the services in that capacity, the institution's reasonable charges for the provision of such services.

Trustee Act 2000, s 29(4)

A trustee is entitled to remuneration . . . even if the services in question are capable of being provided by a lay trustee.

(3) Authority of the court

The court will only authorise reasonable remuneration for services performed by trustees which are of exceptional benefit to the trust.

See *Boardman v Phipps* [1967] 2 AC 46, where generous remuneration was awarded by the court for the efforts of the appellants.

Moreover, the court is entitled to increase the amount of the remuneration as laid down in the charging clause: see *Re Duke of Norfolk's Settlement Trusts* [1981] 3 All ER 220.

In *Foster v Spencer*, the court decided that, in the exercise of its inherent jurisdiction, trustees of a cricket club were entitled to remuneration for past services but not to future remuneration. In addition, the trustees were entitled to past expenses but not to interest thereon.

Foster and Others v Spencer (1995) *The Times*, 14 June, HC

Facts

The plaintiffs had been persuaded, in 1969, to become trustees of a five acre sportsfield at Elmers End, near Beckenham in Kent. The land was purchased in 1921 for £700 which was raised by subscriptions from the members at that time and well wishers. There was no remuneration clause in the trust instrument. The plaintiffs discovered, shortly after appointment, that the club was experiencing a financial crisis. Membership, and consequently income, was declining and there was no capital reserve. For some time football was played, but that eventually ceased and the only activity which remained centred round the bar in a ramshackle pavilion. At a meeting of contributors in April 1972, unanimous support was given to a proposal to sell the ground for development and to look for another site, but obstacles emerged in that the land was zoned as an open space, which would need to be altered, and planning permission would have to be sought if a reasonable price was to be obtained from a developer. In addition, there was considerable trouble in evicting gypsy squatters and securing the land against further invasions. The land was finally sold in 1992, the net proceeds amounting to £911,188. The expertise of Mr Foster as a chartered surveyor was particularly valuable in eventually marketing the site. Likewise, the contribution of Mr Sealy as a building contractor and one who lived near the site was substantial. The plaintiffs claimed:

(a) remuneration for their services:

    (i)   Mr Foster and Mr Sealy claimed remuneration in bringing about the successful sale; and

    (ii) the other three plaintiffs claimed remuneration in respect of the tasks still to be performed;

(b) reimbursement of their expenses;

(c) interest pursuant to s 35(A) of the Supreme Court Act 1981.

Held

Judge Paul Barker QC decided as follows:

(a) In the exercise of his inherent jurisdiction, Mr Foster and Mr Sealy were entitled to remuneration for their past services. The decisive factors were that:

    (i)   there were no funds out of which to pay remuneration at the time of their appointment;

    (ii) the refusal of the claim to remuneration would have resulted in the beneficiaries being unjustly enriched at the expense of the trustees;

    (iii) there was no true appreciation of the extent of the task at the time of appointment. Had Mr Foster and Mr Sealy realised what they were in for they would have declined to act unless remunerated in some way.

(b) The quantum of the remuneration, in the absence of guidance from the authorities, would be determined at 5% commission on the net proceeds, that is, £45,560 for Mr Foster and a fee of £5,000 per year for the period between 1982 and 1992.

(c) No remuneration for future services of the trustees would be allowed as this would be unnecessary for the good administration of the trusts.

(d) The trustees were entitled to be reimbursed their expenses under s 30(2) of the Trustee Act 1925 (see now s 31 of the Trustee Act 2000).

(e) The plaintiffs' claim for interest on their expenses would be refused. There was no jurisdiction to award interest in these circumstances.

(4) Agreement with all the beneficiaries

Where the beneficiaries are all '*sui juris*' and absolutely entitled to the trust property, they may make an agreement with the trustees for the latter to be remunerated. This is an application of the rule in *Saunders v Vautier* (1841) 4 Beav 115 (see p 519 below).

(5) The rule in Cradock v Piper

The rule is that where a trustee/solicitor acts as a solicitor for himself and his co-trustees in litigation concerning the trust then, provided the cost of acting for himself and the co-trustees is less than or equal to the expense of acting for his co-trustees alone, the solicitor/trustee is entitled to be paid his usual costs. In short, the solicitor/trustee may charge his usual fees for acting in litigation on behalf of his co-trustees, but is not permitted fees for representing himself.

Cradock v Piper (1850) 1 Mac & G 664

Facts

A trustee/solicitor who represented his co-trustees and the beneficiaries in proceedings brought by creditors of the testator claimed the costs of such representation and the costs for defending himself.

Held

The trustee was allowed to claim the costs of representing his co-trustees but was disallowed the costs of acting for himself:

Lord Cottenham: The rule has been supposed to be founded upon the well known principle that a trustee cannot be permitted to make a profit of his office, which he would do, if, being party to a cause as trustee, he were permitted, being also a solicitor, to derive professional profits from acting for himself. The rule is confined to cases in which the business or employment of the solicitor is the proper business of the trustee; but it is no part of the business or employment of a trustee to assist other parties in suits relative to the property. If, therefore, the trustee acts as solicitor for such other parties, such business or employment is not any business or employment of the trustee; and the rule as hitherto laid down does not apply. I am therefore of the opinion that the rule does not extend beyond costs of the trustee, where he acts as solicitor for himself.

Note

This rule is regarded as an anomaly and will not be extended to non-contentious work and to persons other than solicitor/trustees, such as barristers, accountants, etc.

(6) Section 42 of the Trustee Act 1925

Where the court appoints a trust corporation to act as trustee, the court is empowered to ensure that the corporation is paid for its services.

Trustee Act 1925, s 42

Where the court appoints a corporation, other than the Public Trustee, to be a trustee either solely or jointly with another person, the court may authorise the corporation to charge such remuneration for its services as trustee as the court may think fit.

(7) The rule in Re Northcote

The principle is that English executors and trustees, who are entitled to earn a commission under a foreign jurisdiction in which the trust assets are situated, are empowered to retain such remuneration for their own benefit.

Re Northcote's Will Trust [1949] 1 All ER 442, HC

Facts

A testator, domiciled in England, died leaving assets in England and the USA. His executors obtained a grant of probate in England. They also obtained a grant in New York in respect of the American assets. They collected the American assets and were entitled to agency commission under the law of that State. The question in issue was whether they were accountable.

Held

The executors were not accountable:

Harman J: Here these trustees were under an obligation to take out this American grant, and everything flows from that. The same remuneration would have been payable to any other person to whom they had given a power of attorney. The only question is whether there is an equity against these trustees to disgorge that which they have put in their pockets from an outside source, on the ground that their interest in the matter conflicted with their duty. I do not think that it did. *Qua* the American executors, they are not accountable for this sum. They have accounted fully in that capacity, and in my judgment, the English beneficiaries are not entitled to call them to account for a sum which accrued to them by reason of the obligation they undertook in order to obtain the English grant.

Question

In what circumstances may a trustee be entitled to remuneration for his services?

Trustee/director's remuneration

The articles of association of a private company may provide that a director must obtain a share qualification within a stated time, that is, in order to advance the interests of the company and shareholders, a person may be appointed a director if he holds the prescribed number of shares. The articles may provide that a director must hold the share qualification 'in his own right'. In *Pulbrook v Richmond*, it was decided that the requirement will be satisfied even though the shares are held by the individual as a trustee because, between the company and the trustee, he is the registered holder of the shares. Neither the company nor the court will look behind the share register to identify the beneficial owner.

Pulbrook v Richmond Consolidated Mining Co (1878) 9 Ch D 610, CA

Facts

Mr P, a director of a company, was excluded by his fellow directors from attending directors' meetings. He brought an action against his fellow directors for an injunction to restrain them from wrongfully excluding him from such meetings. Mr P was the registered holder of the relevant number of shares as stated in the company's articles of association, but it was alleged that shortly before his appointment he had executed a charge of his shares as security for a loan. One of the questions in issue was whether Mr P remained qualified as a director.

Held

The clause in the articles of association, 'no person shall be eligible unless he holds in his own right capital of the nominal value of £500', was to be construed by having regard only to the legal ownership of the shares as appeared on the register:

Sir George Jessel MR: The company cannot look behind the register as to beneficial interest, but must take the register as conclusive, and cannot inquire, either for this purpose, or indeed for any other, into the trusts affecting the shares. That being so, in my opinion, whether or not there was an absolute trust, or whether Mr Cuthbert was only the mortgagee, is not material; Mr Pulbrook was well elected . . .

If the trustee uses the shareholding of the trust in order to secure his appointment as a director, he may be accountable for the remuneration or profits as constructive trustee for the trust. In other words, if there is a causal link between the trust and the appointment as a director, the profits received as a director are subject to the trust. This is a question of fact: see *Re Macadam*.

Re Macadam [1946] Ch 73, HC

Facts

The articles of a company provided that the trustees of a will had a power to appoint two persons to directorships. The trustees appointed themselves directors and received remuneration.

Held

They were liable to account to the trust for the directors' fees received from the company:

Cohen J: Did he acquire the position in respect of which he drew the remuneration by virtue of his position as trustee? In the present case there can be no doubt that the only way in which the plaintiffs became directors was by the exercise of the powers vested in the trustees of the will under article 68 of the articles of association of the company. The principle is one which has always been regarded as of the greatest importance in these courts, and I do not think I ought to do anything to weaken it . . . although the remuneration was remuneration for services as director of the company, the opportunity to receive the remuneration was gained as a result of the exercise of a discretion vested in the trustees, and they had put themselves in a position where their interest and duty conflicted. In those circumstances, I do not think that this court can allow them to make a profit out of doing so, and I do not think the liability to account for a profit can be confined to cases where the profit is derived directly from the trust estate . . . the root of the matter really is: Did he acquire the position in respect of which he drew the remuneration by virtue of his position as trustee?

It follows that a director who secures his appointment as a director before he acquires the trust shares is not required to account to the trust for his remuneration as a director. In *Re Dover Coalfield Extension*, it was decided that the position remains the same if the trust shares are subsequently registered in his name in order to enable him to continue as a director.

Re Dover Coalfield Extension [1908] 1 Ch 65, HC

Facts

Dover Coalfield Extension Ltd (D Co) held shares in Consolidated Kent Collieries Corp (K Corp) with whom it conducted business. In order to protect the interests of D Co, a director of D Co was appointed a director of K Corp. The articles of K Corp required directors to acquire 1,000 shares within a month. D Co accordingly transferred 1,000 of its shares in K Corp to the director, which he held on trust for D Co. When D Co was wound up, the liquidator claimed the remuneration which the director received.

Held

The director was allowed to retain his remuneration. He was appointed a director by an independent board before he had acquired the shares on trust for D Co, even though he could not have continued in office without the shares. In other words, the director did not use his position as a trustee for the purpose of acquiring his directorship, for he had been appointed a director before he became a trustee of the shares.

Likewise in *Re Gee*, a trustee/director was not accountable to the trust for his remuneration where he secured his appointment as director by the use of shares or votes held in his personal capacity, provided that the use of the trust votes could not prevent his appointment as director. In this event, the trustee will be appointed independently of the trust votes.

Re Gee [1948] Ch 284, HC

Facts

The issued capital of a private company, Gee & Co Ltd, was 5,000 £1 shares. Immediately before his death, Alfred Gee (the testator) was the registered holder of 4,996 shares in Gee & Co. The remaining four shareholders, who held one share each, were: Miss Gee (the testator's sister); the testator's wife; his daughter, Mrs Hunter; and his son-in-law, Mr Staples. By his will, the testator appointed his wife, Mrs Hunter and Mr Staples to be his executors and trustees after his death. After the death of the testator and before his will was probated, Mr Staples was appointed managing director of the company by the unanimous agreement of the three executors and Miss Gee, who together constituted all the registered beneficial shareholders at that time. Mr Staples agreed to act as director of the company and received £15,721 as remuneration for the 10 years that he managed the company. The beneficiaries under the will now claimed that Mr Staples was liable to account for the profit.

Held

In favour of Mr Staples who was not accountable because he was appointed a director unanimously by the shareholders for qualities independent of the trust votes. The trust votes were not used to secure his appointment:

> **Harman J:** The principle that a trustee, in the absence of a special contract, can neither make a profit out of his trust, nor be paid for his time and trouble, is an old one . . . The difficulty of applying this principle arises where the payment is made not directly out of the trust estate, but by a third party or body, and in particular by a limited company.
>
> I conclude from this view that a trustee who either uses a power vested in him as such to obtain a benefit (as in *Re Macadam* [1946] Ch 73) or who (as in *Williams v Barton* [1927] 2 Ch 9) procures his co-trustees to give him, or those associated with him, remunerative employment must account for the benefit obtained. Further, it appears to me that a trustee who has the power, by the use of trust votes, to control his own appointment to a remunerative position, and refrains from using them with the result that he is elected to the position of profit, would also be accountable. On the other hand, it appears not to be the law that every man who becomes a trustee holding as such shares in a limited company is made *ipso facto* accountable for remuneration received from that company independently of any use by him of the trust holding, whether by voting or refraining from doing so. For instance, A who holds the majority of the shares in a limited company becomes the trustee of the estate of B, a holder of a minority interest; this cannot, I think, disentitle A to use his own shares to procure his appointment as an officer of the company, nor compel him to disgorge the remuneration he so receives, for he

cannot be disentitled to the use of his own voting powers, nor could the use of the trust votes in a contrary sense prevent the majority prevailing.

I turn now to an examination of the facts in this case to see what (if any) use was made of the trust shares in the appointment of Mr Staples. In my judgment, when the facts are examined, no such use was made. After the death of the testator, only four persons remained on the register of this company, and they alone could attend meetings of it. As I have said before, the meeting of 6 January 1938, was attended by all the corporators. Each of them held one share, and as the resolutions were passed unanimously, they must be supposed to have voted in favour by the use of that share. If the corporators, as I think, held their shares beneficially, they were entitled to vote as they chose. If, on the other hand, they were nominees of the testator, there were still three of them whose votes outweighed the vote of Mr Staples if it was his duty to vote against his own interest. In neither event did the trust shares come into the picture at all.

Competition

In conformity with the general rule of avoiding a conflict of duty and interest, a trustee who is required to continue a specialised business in his representative capacity, will not be permitted to start up a similar business in his personal capacity in competition with the trust. In *Re Thomson*, it was decided that an injunction may be obtained restraining the trustee from setting up a competing business.

Re Thomson, Thomson v Allen [1930] 1 Ch 203, HC

Facts

A testator, a yacht broker, by his will appointed three persons to act as his executors and trustees. After his death, the trustees continued to carry on the business. One of the trustees threatened to set up a yacht-broker business in the same town in competition with the trust. An injunction was sought to restrain the trustee.

Held

In view of the specialised nature of such a business, a conflict of duty and interest would have arisen if the trustee was permitted to set up his own competing business. Accordingly, the injunction was granted:

> **Clauson J:** The rule of universal application is that an executor and trustee having duties to discharge of a fiduciary nature towards the beneficiaries under the will – in this particular case the duty of a fiduciary nature was to carry on the business of the testator to the best advantage of the beneficiaries – he shall not be allowed to enter into the engagement in which he has or can have a personal interest conflicting, or which possibly may conflict, with the interests of those whom he is bound to protect. Having regard to the special nature of a yacht agent's business, it appears to me clear that by starting such a business and entering into such engagements, Mr Allen would have been entering into engagements which would conflict, or certainly possibly might conflict with the interest of the beneficiaries under the will, because he would be obtaining for himself chances of earning a commission which, but for such competition, might be obtained for the beneficiaries under the will.

Note

It ought to be emphasised that the decision in *Re Thomson* appears to be based on the wholly unusual nature of the yacht broking business. Had the business been of a more common nature, the injunction may not have been granted. Moreover, a trustee who, at the time of his appointment, was already in business in competition with the trust would not be required to terminate his business, although this might be a ground for his removal from the trust.

Purchase of trust property

A trustee, without specific authority to the contrary, is not entitled to purchase trust property for his own benefit: see *Keech v Sandford*, p 185 above. The position remains the same even if the purchase appears to be fair. Perhaps the purchase price might significantly exceed the market value of the property. In such a case, the transaction is treated as voidable, ie, valid until avoided. This is the rule against self-dealing. The objections to such transactions are that the trustee would be both vendor and purchaser and it would be difficult to ascertain whether an unfair advantage had been obtained by the trustee. In addition, the property may become virtually unmarketable since the title may indicate that the property was at one time trust property. Third parties may have notice of this fact and any disputes concerning the trust property may affect their interest.

Wright v Morgan [1926] AC 788, PC

Facts

A testator by his will gave his son, Harry Herbert, the option to purchase a plot of land provided that the price was fixed by an independent valuer. Harry was also a trustee under the will. Harry assigned the option to Douglas Wright, his co-trustee and brother, but Douglas was not authorised to purchase the property. Douglas retired from the trust and purported to exercise the option at a price fixed by the valuers. The beneficiaries under the will brought an action to set aside the sale.

Held

The sale ought to be set aside on the ground of a conflict of duty and interest.

> **Viscount Dunedin:** Their Lordships do not doubt that Harry Herbert's option might have been assigned to a third person. There is nothing in the nature of the interest itself which points to non-assignability, nor are there any words in the will which would seem to forbid assignation. When, however, it is found that the assignation is in favour of the person who is himself a trustee, quite another question arises. Equity will not allow a person, who is in a position of trust, to carry out a transaction where there is a conflict between his duty and his interest. Accordingly, the real test to be applied to the circumstances is, assuming that Harry Herbert's option was validly assigned, so far as power to assign was concerned, to Douglas, did a conflict of duty and interest arise which would prevent Douglas from entering into a binding contract with the trustee? It was argued that no such conflict would arise, because by the terms of the will, which was the wish of the testator, the whole conditions of sale are regulated; valuers are to be appointed, and their decision to be accepted as to the price to be payable. There was no possibility of the higgling of the market between vendor and purchaser. Nevertheless, a conflict of duty and interest may arise, although there is no direct association between the two parties as vendor and purchaser.

Note

The position in *Wright v Morgan* might have been different if Harry had exercised the option, acquired the land and then disposed of the property to Douglas. The property would have ceased to be trust property after the option was exercised in the authorised manner. Douglas would have then bought Harry's beneficial interest and not a trust asset. The rule of 'fair dealing' (referred to by Megarry VC in *Tito v Waddell (No 2)* [1977] Ch 106) concerns the trustee purchasing the beneficiary's interest. The approach of the courts in this context is less stringent as compared with the 'self dealing' rule. The issue regarding the fair dealing rule is whether the trustee can discharge the onus of proving that he has made full disclosure of the material facts to the beneficiary. The duty of disclosure is required to be of such a degree that the beneficiary is able to exercise an independent judgment as to the nature and extent of the sale. In *Coles v Trescothick*, Lord Eldon explained the rigour of this rule.

Coles v Trescothick (1804) 9 Ves 234

> **Lord Eldon:** . . . a trustee may buy from the *cestui que trust*, provided there is a distinct and clear contract, ascertained to be such after a jealous and scrupulous examination of all the circumstances, proving that the *cestui que trust* intended the trustee should buy; and there is no fraud, no concealment, no advantage taken, by the trustee of information, acquired by him in the character of trustee.

Question

What is the 'fair dealing' rule and how does this differ from the rule against 'selfdealing'?

Directors and fiduciaries

In *Belmont Finance v Williams*, Buckley LJ asserted that the connection between a director and his company may give rise to a fiduciary relationship, analagous to a trust relationship.

Belmont Finance Corp v Williams Furniture and Others (No 2) [1980] I All ER 393, CA

Buckley LJ: A limited company is of course not trustee of its own funds; but in consequence of the fiduciary character of their duties the directors of a limited company are trusted as if they were trustees of those funds of the company which are in their hands or under their control, and if they misapply them they commit a breach of trust.

Thus, company directors stand in a fiduciary relationship to the company and are subject to the rigours of the trust principle. Accordingly, if a director places himself in a position where his duty to the company conflicts with his personal interest, he may become accountable to the company for any benefits received. In *Regal (Hastings) v Gulliver*, the court decided that any unauthorised profit made by the director, which is connected with the company organisation, is claimable by the company.

Regal (Hastings) Ltd v Gulliver [1942] I All ER 378, HL

Facts

The profit arose through the application by four of the directors of Regal for shares in a subsidiary company. It had been the original intention of the board that the shares should be subscribed for by Regal. Regal did not have the requisite money available and the four directors took it on themselves personally to raise the necessary funds, purchase the shares and sell them for a profit. It was found as a fact that all the transactions were *bona fide*. Regal now claimed that the directors were accountable for their profit.

Held

The directors were accountable to the company for the unauthorised profit:

Lord Russell of Killowen: The rule of equity which insists on those, who by use of a fiduciary position make a profit, being liable to account for that profit, in no way depends on fraud, or absence of *bona fides*; or upon such questions or considerations as whether the profit would or should otherwise have gone to the plaintiff, or whether the profiteer was under a duty to obtain the source of the profit for the plaintiff, or whether he took a risk or acted as he did for the benefit of the plaintiff, or whether the plaintiff has in fact been damaged or benefited by his action. The liability arises from the mere fact of a profit having, in the stated circumstances, been made. The profiteer, however honest and well-intentioned, cannot escape the risk of being called upon to account.

It now remains to consider whether in acting as directors of Regal they stood in a fiduciary relationship to that company. Directors of a limited company are the creatures of statute and occupy a position peculiar to themselves. In some respects they resemble trustees, in others they do not. In some respect they resemble managing partners, in others they do not.

In the result, I am of opinion that the directors standing in a fiduciary relationship to Regal in regard to the exercise of their powers as directors, and having obtained these shares by reason and only by reason of the fact that they were directors of Regal and in the course of the execution of that office, are accountable for the profits which they have made out of them. The equitable rule laid down in *Keech v Sandford* (1726) Sel Cas Ch 437 and *Ex p James* (1803) 8 Ves 337, and similar authorities applies to them in full force. It was contended that these cases were distinguishable by reason of the fact that it was impossible for Regal to get the shares owing to lack of funds, and that the directors in taking the shares were really acting as members of the public. I cannot accept this argument. It was impossible for the *cestui que* trust in *Keech v Sandford* to obtain the lease, nevertheless the trustee was accountable. The suggestion that the directors were applying simply as members of the public is a travesty of the facts. They could, had they wished, have protected themselves by resolution (either antecedent or subsequent) of the Regal shareholders in general meeting. In default of such approval, the liability to account must remain.

Similarly, where a fiduciary (director) has obtained sensitive information in his capacity as a fiduciary, he is required to make full disclosure to the company or person to whom he owes such duty. In *Industrial Development Consultants v Cooley*, it was decided that where a director conceals such confidential information and makes a profit as a result of the non-disclosure, he is accountable for the profit.

Industrial Development Consultants v Cooley [1972] 1 WLR 443, HC

Facts

The defendant was the managing director of the plaintiff company. He was approached by the Chairman of the Eastern Gas Board to work for them, although at the time the plaintiff company was interested in a project for the Gas Board. In his capacity as managing director, he had obtained special knowledge which should have been passed on to the plaintiff company. Concealing this knowledge, he obtained his release from the service of the plaintiff basing his request on alleged ill health. The plaintiff would not have released him had it known the full facts. The plaintiff sued the director claiming that he was a trustee of profits of his new contract on behalf of the plaintiff.

Held

In view of the conflict of duty and interest in failing to pass on the information to the plaintiff, the defendant was accountable:

> **Roskill J:** A more recent statement of the highest authority will be found in the speech of Lord Upjohn in *Boardman v Phipps* [1967] 2 AC 46, pp 123 et seq .
>
> The relevant rule for the decision of this case is the fundamental rule of equity that a person in a fiduciary capacity must not make a profit out of his trust which is part of the wider rule that a trustee must not place himself in a position where his duty and his interest may conflict:
>
> (i) the facts and circumstances must be carefully examined to see whether in fact a purported agent and even a confidential agent is in a fiduciary relationship to his principal. It does not necessarily follow that he is in such a position;
>
> (ii) once it is established that there is such a relationship, that relationship must be examined to see what duties are thereby imposed upon the agent, to see what is the scope and ambit of the duties charged upon him;
>
> (iii) having defined the scope of those duties one must see whether he has committed some breach thereof and by placing himself within the scope and ambit of those duties in a position where his duty and interest may possibly conflict. It is only at this stage that any question of accountability arises;
>
> (iv) finally, having established accountability it only goes so far as to render the agent accountable for profits made within the scope and ambit of his duty.
>
> It seems to me plain that throughout the whole of May, June and July 1969 the defendant was in a fiduciary relationship with the plaintiffs. From the time he embarked upon his course of dealing with the Eastern Gas Board, irrespective of anything which he did or he said to Mr Hicks, he embarked upon a deliberate policy and course of conduct which put his personal interest as a potential contracting party with the Eastern Gas Board in direct conflict with his pre-existing and continuing duty as managing director of the plaintiffs. In *Parker v Mackenna* (1874) 10 Ch App 96, James LJ said, p 124:
>
>> I do not think it is necessary, but it appears to me very important, that we should concur in laying down again and again the general principle that in this court no agent in the course of his agency, in the matter of his agency, can be allowed to make any profit without the knowledge and consent of his principal; that that rule is an inflexible rule, and must be applied inexorably by this court, which is not entitled, in my judgment, to receive evidence, or suggestion, or argument as to whether the principal did or did not suffer any injury in fact by reason of the dealing of the agent; for the safety of mankind requires that no agent shall be able to put his principal to the danger of such an inquiry as that.
>
> Therefore, I feel impelled to the conclusion that when the defendant embarked on this course of conduct of getting information on 13 June using that information and preparing those documents over the weekend of 14/ 15 June and sending them off on on 17 June, he was guilty of putting himself into the position in which his duty to his employers, the plaintiffs, and his own private interests conflicted and conflicted grievously. There being the fiduciary relationship I have described, it seems to me plain that it was his duty once he got this information to pass it to his employers and not to guard it for his own personal purposes and profit. He put himself into the

position when his duty and his interests conflicted. As Lord Upjohn put it in *Boardman v Phipps* [1967] 2 AC 46, p 127 'It is only at this stage that any question of accountability arises'.

Does accountability arise? If the defendant is not required to account he will have made a large profit, as a result of having deliberately put himself into a position in which his duty to the plaintiffs who were employing him and his personal interests conflicted. I leave out of account the fact that he dishonestly tricked Mr Hicks into releasing him on 16 June although Mr Brown urged that that was another reason why equity must compel him to disgorge his profit.

In my judgment, therefore, an order for an account will be issued because the defendant has made and will make his profit as a result of having allowed his interests and his duty to conflict.

Likewise, in *Guinness plc v Saunders and Others* [1990] 2 WLR 324, it was decided that a failure by a director to disclose an unauthorised payment of £5.2 million in connection with the takeover of Distillers plc rendered him a constructive trustee for Guinness. In addition, a *quantum meruit* claim by one of the defendants for reasonable remuneration for services performed, based on an implied contract with the plaintiff, was dismissed:

Lord Templeman: The short answer to the claim for an equitable allowance is the equitable principle which forbids a trustee to make a profit out of his trust unless the trust instrument, in this case the articles of association of Guinness, so provides. The law cannot and equity will not amend the articles of Guinness. The court is not entitled to usurp the functions conferred on the board by the articles.

Public policy and the Forfeiture Act 1982

The courts have adopted a principle of public policy to the effect that a person convicted of the killing of another would be prevented from benefiting from the deceased person's estate. The convicted person's potential interest will be forfeited on an application to the court. In *Cleaver v Mutual Reserve Fund Life Association* [1892] 1 QB 147, Fry LJ stated, '... no system of jurisprudence can with reason include amongst the rights which it enforces rights directly resulting to the person asserting them from the crime of that person'. The precise rationale for the forfeiture rule is unclear. If the convicted killer does not acquire title to the property there is no need for the courts to impose a constructive trust. In *Re Crippen* [1911] P 108, C murdered his wife who died intestate. C was executed and, in his will, left property to his mistress, X. The court decided that X was not entitled to the wife's estate because C was never beneficially entitled to it. But if the killer acquires title to the property there is room for the imposition of the constructive trust in order to prevent unjust enrichment. The constructive trust principles entitle the courts to focus on the broader question whether the taking of the benefit by the wrongdoer would be so unconscionable as to attract the public policy rule. The forfeiture rule is applicable to those convicted of murder, manslaughter and other unlawful killing and accessories to such offences. In *Re DWS (deceased)* [2001] 1 All ER 97, the Court of Appeal extended the forfeiture principle to those claiming through the wrongdoer such as the issue of the killer.

The Forfeiture Act 1982, s 2(1) authorises the court to modify the forfeiture rule in the case of a person who has unlawfully killed (excluding convicted murderers s 5) another. Section 2(2) identifies the factors which the court is required to consider in order to exercise its discretion including, the 'conduct of the offender and the deceased and such other material circumstances of the case' and the 'justice of the case'. Section 2(3) enacts that proceedings for relief are required to be brought within a period of three months beginning with the date of the conviction. Section 3 excludes the forfeiture rule in respect of applications for financial provision made pursuant to a number of specified Acts of Parliament, including the Inheritance (Provision for Family and Dependants) Act 1975.

In *Land v Land* the High Court decided that the time period of three months laid down in s 2(3) of the Forfeiture Act 1982 was incapable of extension.

Land v Land [2006] All ER (D) 71, High Court

Facts

The claimant was the only son of the deceased and the sole executor and beneficiary under her will dated 2 April 1996. He lived with her throughout her life and cared for her in her latter years. In 2002 the deceased, aged 82, asked the claimant to give up his job and look after her. He agreed to do so. The claimant and the deceased never went out. The claimant rarely went out except to visit his father's grave. The deceased was a stubborn, domineering person, hugely independent and shunned officialdom including doctors and home help. In January 2004 the claimant summoned an ambulance and the deceased was admitted to hospital suffering from huge bedsores. She was unconscious and so remained until her death two days later. On 27 April 2004 the claimant was convicted of involuntary manslaughter of the deceased and sentenced to four years imprisonment. He made an application for a share of the deceased's estate on two grounds:

(1) Despite the application being made four working days out of time, the claimant argued that the judge ought to entertain the application.

(2) In the alternative the forfeiture rule did not disentitle the claimant from seeking reasonable financial provision from the deceased's estate under the Inheritance (Provision for Family and Dependants) Act 1975. The claimant relied on s 3 of the Forfeiture Act 1982, which provides, 'The forfeiture rule shall not be taken to preclude any person from making an application under [any provision of the Inheritance (Provision for Family and Dependants) Act 1975] or the making of an order on the application.'

Held

(a) The time limit imposed by s 2 of the Forfeiture Act 1982 was a form of limitation period and gave the court no discretion to extend the time for commencing proceedings.

(b) On a true construction of s 3 of the 1982 Act, the court had the power to deprive the wrongdoer of benefit from the estate when it was in the public interest to do so, but to confer a discretion to mitigate the harshness of the rule when it was in the public interest to do so. On the facts of this case, the forfeiture rule did not serve the public interest. In the circumstances the claimant's conduct did not disentitle him to the relief sought under the 1975 Act.

Norris J: The Forfeiture Act 1982 is concerned with the adjustment of property rights and confers upon an individual a right to apply to the Court within a defined period. It is a form of limitation period similar to that applying to applications for reasonable provision to be made out of the estate or for rectification of a will, but (unlike the statutes which confer those rights) the Act gives the Court no discretion to extend the time for commencement of the action.

The forfeiture rule is a principle of public policy, the application of which may produce unfair consequences in some cases. It is not the statement of a principle of justice designed to produce a fair result: per Mummery LJ in *Dunbar v Plant* [1998] Ch 412 at 422D–E. There is a justifiable dissatisfaction with its indiscriminate application in every case of unlawful killing: per Phillips LJ in *Dunbar* at 431G. Following *Dunbar* however it is no longer possible to discriminate in the application of the rule, only to mitigate its effects where the ends of justice require. The rule will accordingly be applied even where the public interest does not require it (and even where its application may be contrary to the public interest), but in some circumstances its effects may be mitigated. Is it necessary to construe section 3 of the 1982 Act in such a way that it is not available to mitigate the effects of the rule if justice requires (leaving the Claimant to suffer possibly unfair consequences from the indiscriminate application of a rule) or can the statutory words (that the forfeiture rule shall not be taken to preclude the making of any order on an application under the 1975 Act) be given full effect?

For two reasons in my judgement the words must now be given their full effect. First, on the approach to construction that must now be adopted. Second, upon a consideration of what section 3 was designed to achieve.

Section 3 of the Human Rights Act 1998 requires the Court, so far as it is possible to do so, to read and give effect to primary legislation in a way that is compatible with Convention rights. Article 8 of the First Protocol to the ECHR provides that "every natural . . . person is entitled to the peaceful enjoyment of his possessions" and that "no-one shall be deprived of his possessions except in the public interest and subject to the conditions provided for by law". The right to inherit property under a will is in my judgement a "possession" within the protocol. The Claimant is not to be deprived of it except in the public interest. Following Dunbar he will be deprived of it even where the public interest does not require unless (a) "the appropriate course" under section 2 of the 1982 Act can be taken or (b) (where that is not available) section 3 is read as meaning that the forfeiture rule does not preclude the making of an order under the 1975 Act. In my judgment section 3 of the 1982 Act must now be read (so far as the language permits) in a way that enables the Court to deprive the wrongdoer of benefit from the estate when it is in the public interest so to do, but to confer a discretion to mitigate the harshness of the absolute rule where it is not in the public interest to deprive the wrongdoer of all benefit from the estate: because that is the only way the Forfeiture Act 1982 can be given effect in a way that is compatible with Convention rights: (compare the approach adopted in Law Commission Consultation Paper No 172 "Forfeiture and the Law of Succession").

Secondly, I consider that the Court should seek to discern the policy to which the section was directed. It is possible that it was directed to giving relief to the small class of unlawful killers who were either: (a) wives, children or dependants of the deceased but for whom provision was not made in the deceased's will, or (b) dependants who were not entitled under the intestacy rules. Such people would take no direct interest in the estate (so the forfeiture rule would have no direct application to deprive them of succession rights) but they would have a potential claim under the 1975 Act. It is possible that the section was directed at this small class and was designed to make clear that their 1975 Act claim (the effect of the will or the intestacy rules being to make no provision for them) was not barred.

In my judgment the true construction of the section and the discernible policy of the section both point to a reading of section 3 that gives the fullest effect to the words "the forfeiture rule shall not be taken to preclude . . . . the making of any order on [an] application [under the 1975 Act . . .". I would accordingly hold that section 3 permits the Court to make an order under the 1975 Act even though it is the forfeiture rule (not the terms of the Will itself) that mean no provision is made for the Claimant. The exercise under section 3 of the 1982 Act and under the provisions of the 1975 Act is, of course, different from that which would be undertaken under section 2 of the 1982 Act, and it is undoubtedly more advantageous to a claimant to seek relief in time directly under the 1982 Act; the Claimant however is confined to the 1975 Act.

CONTRACTS FOR THE SALE OF LAND

On the date that a specifically enforceable contract for the sale of land is made, the purchaser becomes the equitable owner of the property. Thus, on the date of the exchange of contracts, the vendor becomes a constructive trustee for the purchaser until the date of the completion of the sale: see *Lysaght v Edwards*.

Lysaght v Edwards (1874) 2 Ch D 498, CA

Facts

Edwards agreed in writing to sell real property to the plaintiff but, before completion, Edwards died. By his will, he devised his real property to trustees on trust to sell and invest the proceeds of sale. The plaintiff claimed for an order requiring the executors to complete the sale.

Held

On the date of the creation of the contract, the equitable title to the property becomes transferred to the purchaser by operation of law:

Lord Jessel MR: The effect of a contract for sale has been settled for more than two centuries. It is that the moment you have a valid contract for sale, in equity, the vendor becomes the trustee for the purchaser of the real estate sold; the beneficial ownership passes to the purchaser of the estate, the vendor retaining a right to the purchase money . . .

Note

This rule illustrates the equitable maxim, 'Equity regards as done that which ought to be done'.

EQUITY WILL NOT ALLOW A STATUTE TO BE USED AS AN ENGINE FOR FRAUD

Acts of Parliament are binding on all courts, even a court of equity. However, courts of equity are entitled to adopt a pragmatic approach in considering the validity of claims in equity with an overriding objective to achieve justice. Accordingly, if strict compliance with a statutory provision (such as the formalities) has the incidental effect of perpetrating a fraud, the court is entitled to suspend such provision. This compromise solution has the effect of preventing unjust enrichment: see *Rochefoucauld v Boustead*.

Rochefoucauld v Boustead [1897] I Ch 196, CA

Facts
The plaintiff was the mortgagor of several estates but found himself in financial difficulty. The defendant purchased the properties from the mortgagee and orally agreed to hold them on trust for the plaintiff subject to the repayment to the defendant of the purchase price and expenses. The defendant sold the estates and later became bankrupt. The plaintiff sued the trustee-in-bankruptcy for an account. The trustee-in-bankruptcy claimed that the oral agreement was not enforceable as the predecessor to s 53(1)(b) of the Law of Property Act 1925 (namely, s 7 of the Statute of Frauds 1677) was not complied with and the plaintiff had no interest in the proceeds of sale.

Held
In favour of the plaintiff on the ground that equity would not allow s 7 of the Statute of Frauds 1677 to be used as an engine for fraud. It is a fraud for a person to whom land is conveyed on trust to deny the trust and claim the land as his own. Even if there was insufficient evidence to constitute a memorandum in order to satisfy s 7 of the 1677 Act, parol evidence was admissible to establish that the defendant bought the properties as trustee:

> **Lindley LJ:** It is necessary to prove by some writing or writings signed by the defendant, not only that the conveyance to him was subject to some trust, but also what that trust was. But it is not necessary that the trust should have been declared by such a writing in the first instance; it is sufficient if the trust can be proved by some writing signed by the defendant, and the date of the writing is immaterial. It is further established by a series of cases, the propriety of which cannot now be questioned, that the Statute of Frauds does not prevent the proof of a fraud; and that it is a fraud on the part of a person to whom land is conveyed as a trustee, and who knows it was so conveyed, to deny the trust and claim the land himself. Consequently, notwithstanding the statute, it is competent for a person claiming land conveyed to another to prove by parol evidence that it was so conveyed upon trust for the claimant, and that the grantee, knowing the facts, is denying the trust and relying upon the form of conveyance and the statute, in order to keep the land himself.

Likewise, where property has been obtained by the fraudulent conduct of the defendant, a constructive trust may be imposed on him requiring him to re-transfer the property to the claimant or person defrauded. The fraud may take the form of setting up the absolute nature of a conveyance in an attempt to deny the claimant an interest in the property. This principle was applied in *Bannister v Bannister*.

Bannister v Bannister [1948] 2 All ER 133, CA

Facts
The defendant sold a cottage to the plaintiff on the oral understanding that the defendant would be allowed to live rent free in the property for as long as she wished. The purchase price was deflated to take into account this arrangement. The conveyance made no mention of the undertaking. The plaintiff subsequently attempted to evict the defendant in order to sell the property with vacant possession and argued that the conveyance was not obtained fraudulently.

Held
The plaintiff was bound by the trust obligation to permit the vendor to occupy the premises. The absence of written evidence could not be used to support the plaintiff's case:

Scott LJ: It is, we think, clearly a mistake to suppose that the equitable principle on which a constructive trust is raised against a person who insists on the absolute character of a conveyance to himself for the purpose of defeating a beneficial interest, which, according to the true bargain, was to belong to another, is confined to cases in which the conveyance itself was fraudulently obtained. The fraud which brings the principle into play arises as soon as the absolute character of the conveyance is set up for the purpose of defeating the beneficial interest, and that is the fraud to cover which the Statute of Frauds or the corresponding provisions of the Law of Property Act 1925, cannot be called in aid in cases in which no written evidence of the real bargain is available. Nor is it, in our opinion, necessary that the bargain on which the absolute conveyance is made should include any express stipulation that the grantee is in so many words to hold as trustee. It is enough that the bargain should have included a stipulation under which some sufficiently defined beneficial interest in the property was to be taken by another.

Questions

Why are the boundaries of a constructive trust deliberately left vague by the courts? How would you distinguish a constructive trust from a resulting trust?

FURTHER READING

Beatson, J and Prentice, D, 'Restitutionary claims by company directors' (1990) 106 LQR 365.

Bhandari, S, 'The virtue of Paragon' (2002) 152 NLJ 304.

Braithwaite, W, 'Directors' liability, constructive trusts and limitation periods' [1980] Conv 200.

Chong, A, 'The common law choice of law rules for resulting and constructive trusts' (2005) ICLQ Vol 54, Issue 4, 855.

Gardner, S, 'Two maxims of equity: casenote on *AG for Hong Kong v Reid*' (1995) 54 CLJ 60.

Goulding, S, 'Director as constructive trustee: *Guinness plc v Saunders*' [1990] Conv 296.

Green, B, 'Restitution for services rendered in breach of trust' (1982) 45 MLR 211.

Hayton, D, 'Developing the law of trusts for the 21st century' (1990) 106 LQR 87.

Hill, J, 'The Settled Land Act 1925: unresolved problems' (1991) 107 LQR 596.

Hodkinson, K, 'Casenote on *Re Duke of Norfolk Settlement Trust*' [1982] Conv 231.

Hopkins, J, 'Fiduciary duty – receipt of company's property by director' [1990] CLJ 220.

Jackson, P, 'Further extensions of the rule in *Keech v Sandford*' (1975) 38 MLR 226.

Jackson, P, 'Estate contracts, trusts and registered land' [1983] Conv 64.

Jones, A, 'Bribing the DPP: should he profit from abusing his position? *AG for Hong Kong v Reid*' [1994] Conv 156.

Jones, G, 'Unjust enrichment and the fiduciary duty of loyalty' (1968) 84 LQR 472.

Kenny, P, 'Constructive trust of registered land' (1983) 46 MLR 96.

Matthews, P, 'Remuneration for professional trustees' (1995) 9 Tru LI 50.

Millett, P, 'Equity's place in the law of commerce' (1998) 114 LQR 214.

Millett, P, 'Restitution and constructive trusts' (1998) 114 LQR 399.

Ockleton, C, 'Keeping it in the family' [1981] CLJ 243.

Paling, D, 'The pleadings in *Keech v Sandford*' [1972] 36 Conv 159.

Parry, N, 'Remuneration of trustees' [1984] Conv 275.

Pawlowski, M, 'Forfeiture relief' (2007) 157 NLJ 318.

Rider, B, 'The fiduciary and the frying pan' [1978] Conv 114.

Shepherd, J, 'Towards a unified concept of fiduciary relationships' (1981) 97 LQR 51.

Sparkes, P, 'Beneficial interest or licence for life? *Ungurian v Lesnoff*' [1990] Conv 223.

Sullivan, G, 'Going it alone – *Queensland Mines v Hudson*' (1979) 42 MLR 711.

Tabbush, S, 'Forfeiting inheritance' (2005) 155 NLJ 1202.

Watts, P, 'Unjust enrichment and misdirected funds' (1991) 107 LQR 521.

Watts, P, 'Bribes and constructive trusts' (1994) 110 LQR 178.

CONSTRUCTIVE TRUSTS: THE FAMILY HOME

INTRODUCTION

Family members and other individuals frequently contribute to the joint purchase of property (such as the family home and other assets) with the legal title taken either in their joint names or in the name of one person. Sometimes the parties express their intention as to the ownership of the equitable interest and this will be conclusive in the absence of fraud or mistake. If the asset is land, this express declaration of trust is required to be evidenced in writing in order to satisfy the requirements of s 53(1)(b) of the Law of Property Act 1925. Where the parties do not express their intention (or do not comply with s 53(1)(b) of the 1925 Act) the courts have adopted settled principles of trusts law in order to ascertain their beneficial interests. These are: (i) the resulting trust concept, which is applicable where the parties have made substantial contributions to the acquisition of the property; and (ii) the constructive trust principle, based on reliance on a common intention between the parties to the claimant's detriment. In addition, the interests of the parties may be modified in limited circumstances by statute, such as ss 23–25 of the Matrimonial Causes Act 1973.

PROPRIETARY RIGHTS IN THE FAMILY HOME

This issue concerns the beneficial rights in the family home (probably the most valuable asset belonging to the family) and other family assets. Consider the following example: Mary went to live with Norman. A year later, a house was bought in Norman's name, the purchase money being raised from his savings and by way of a mortgage. Mary gave up her job when a child was born to them. Four years later, when the parties were experiencing financial difficulties, Mary went back to work and used her earnings to contribute towards the housekeeping expenses, the family holidays and to pay for decorations to the house, while Norman continued paying the mortgage instalments. Ten years later, Mary left Norman, taking the child with her. She wishes to claim a beneficial interest in the house on the ground that Norman held the legal title to the house on trust for each of them in equal shares, or some other proportion. Some of the questions that are related to this issue are as follows:

- Are the presumptions of resulting trusts and advancements suitable principles to apply for identifying interests in the family assets?
- What principles of trusts law are applicable to ascertain the extent of the beneficial interest in the family home?
- When should such interest be valued?
- How may the interest be realised?
- What difference, if any, would it make if the parties were married or same sex couples registered under the Civil Partnership Act 2004?

Note
The Civil Partnership Act 2004 came into force on 5 December 2005 and enables same-sex couples to obtain legal recognition of their relationships by forming civil partnerships. 'Partners' include a civil partnership registered under the Civil Partnership Act 2004. A civil partnership is required to be registered in England and Wales at a registered office or approved premise. Civil partners have equal treatment with married couples in a wide range of matters including property rights, taxation including inheritance tax, inheritance of tenancy agreements and recognition

under intestacy rules. Consequently, a registered civil partnership, to all intents and purposes, is treated as a marriage.

In *Cooke v Head* it was decided that trusts principles are applicable to contributions to family assets made by spouses, registered civil partners, unmarried couples and any other relationships contracted by the parties.

Cooke v Head [1972] I WLR 518, CA

Facts
The plaintiff, Miss Cooke (C), and Mr Head (H) met in 1962. C became H's mistress. A plot of land was bought and conveyed into H's name. Both parties provided the labour and built a bungalow. C did a great deal of heavy work, including mixing and carting cement. She also contributed some of her earnings towards paying the mortgage instalments. Later, C and H separated and H alone lived in the bungalow, repaying the mortgage instalments. The plaintiff claimed a declaration that the property was jointly owned by the parties.

Held
The plaintiff was entitled to a one third share in the property on the ground that the parties jointly acquired the property for their joint benefit. In these circumstances, the legal owner held the property on trust for both of them:

> **Lord Denning MR:** In the light of recent developments, I do not think it is right to approach this case by looking at the money contributions of each and dividing up the beneficial interest according to those contributions. The matter should be looked at more broadly, just as we do in husband and wife cases. Lord Diplock, in *Gissing v Gissing* [1971] AC 886, p 909, intimated that it is quite legitimate to infer that:
>
> > . . . the wife should be entitled to a share which was not to be quantified immediately upon the acquisition of the home but should be left to be determined when the mortgage was repaid or the property disposed of. Likewise with a mistress.
>
> Having discussed it with my brethren, we think that one 12th is far too small, and that the plaintiff's share should be one third of the net proceeds of sale. I would allow the appeal, accordingly.

In the two seminal cases, *Pettitt v Pettitt* and *Gissing v Gissing*, the House of Lords decided that the principles of resulting (other than the presumptions) and constructive trusts are applicable in this context. These expressions have been used interchangeably by the courts as if they involve the same concepts. The presumptions of resulting trusts and advancement between married couples have outlived their usefulness in view of the social changes in society and would not be adopted readily in these circumstances.

Pettitt v Pettitt [1970] AC 777, HL

> **Lord Diplock:** The consensus of opinion which gave rise to the presumptions of advancement and resulting trusts in transactions between husbands and wives is to be found in cases relating to the propertied class of the nineteenth century and the first quarter of the twentieth century among whom marriage settlements were common and it was unusual for the wife to contribute by her earnings to the family income. It was not until after World War II that the courts were required to consider the proprietary rights in family assets of a different social class . . . It would be an abuse of the legal technique for ascertaining or imputing intention to apply to transactions between the post war generation of married couples, 'presumptions' which are based upon inferences of fact which an entire generation of judges drew as to the most likely intentions of an earlier generation of spouses belonging to the propertied classes of a different social era.

Facts
Mrs Pettitt purchased a cottage with her own money and had the legal title conveyed in her name. Mr Pettitt from time to time redecorated the property expending a total of £725. On a breakdown of the marriage he claimed a proportionate interest in the house (£1,000 *pro rata* value).

Held

The House of Lords dismissed the claim on the ground that Mr Pettitt's expenditure was not related to the acquisition of the house. In the absence of an agreement or understanding, his expenditure was to be treated as a gift. The court decided that settled principles of property law were applicable in this context:

> **Lord Diplock:** Where the acquisition or improvement is made as a result of contributions in money or money's worth by both spouses acting in concert the proprietary interests in the family asset resulting from their respective contributions depend upon their common intention as to what those interests should be.
>
> How, then, does the court ascertain the 'common intention' of spouses as to their respective proprietary interests in a family asset when at the time that it was acquired or improved as a result of contributions in money or money's worth by each of them they failed to formulate it themselves? It may be possible to infer from their conduct that they did in fact form an actual common intention as to their respective proprietary interests and where this is possible the courts would give effect to it.
>
> Nevertheless *the court imputes to the parties a common intention which in fact they never formed and it does so by forming its own opinion as to what would have been the common intention of reasonable men as to the effect of that event upon their contractual rights and obligations if the possibility of the event happening had been present to their minds at the time of entering into the contract.* In *Davis Contractors Ltd v Fareham UDC* [1956] AC 696 Viscount Radcliffe analyses this technique as applied to cases of frustration. See also Professor Glanville Williams' analysis of the legal doctrine of implied terms in 'Language and the law' (1944) 61 LQR 401 [emphasis added].
>
> In applying the technique to contracts the court starts with the assumption that, *prima facie*, the parties intended that whatever may happen their legal rights and obligations under their contract should be confined to those which they have expressed. Consequentially, the court will not imply a term unless it is of opinion that no reasonable men could have failed to form the common intention to which effect will be given by the term which it implies. But such an assumption, viz, that *prima facie* the parties intended at the time of the transaction to express all the legal consequences as to proprietary rights which would flow from it, whatever might happen in the future, is, for the reasons already indicated, inappropriate to transactions between husband and wife in relation to family assets. In most cases they express none and form no actual common intention about proprietary rights in the family asset because neither spouse gave any thought to an event happening, viz, the cesser of their common use and enjoyment of the asset, which alone would give any practical importance to their respective proprietary interests in the asset. *Unless it is possible to infer from the conduct of the spouses at the time of their concerted action in relation to acquisition or improvement of the family asset that they did form an actual common intention as to the legal consequences of their acts upon the proprietary rights in the asset the court must impute to them a constructive common intention which is that which in the court's opinion would have been formed by reasonable spouses* [emphasis added].
>
> In the present case we are concerned not with the acquisition of a matrimonial home on mortgage, but with improvements to a previously acquired matrimonial home.
>
> It is common enough nowadays for husbands and wives to decorate and to make improvements in the family home themselves, with no other intention than to indulge in what is now a popular hobby, and to make the home pleasanter for their common use and enjoyment. If the husband likes to occupy his leisure by laying a new lawn in the garden or building a fitted wardrobe in the bedroom while the wife does the shopping, cooks the family dinner or bathes the children, I, for my part, find it quite impossible to impute to them as reasonable husband and wife any common intention that these domestic activities or any of them are to have any effect upon the existing proprietary rights in the family home on which they have undertaken. It is only in the bitterness engendered by the break-up of the marriage that so bizarre a notion would enter their heads.

In *Gissing v Gissing*, the Law Lords endorsed their views in *Pettitt v Pettitt* and attempted to add more details to these principles.

Gissing v Gissing [1971] AC 886, HL

Facts

The parties were married in 1935. W, the wife, worked throughout her married life. In 1951, the matrimonial home was purchased by H, the husband, out of his resources and the property was conveyed in his name. W paid £220 for furnishings and laying a lawn. There was no common understanding as to the beneficial interest in the house. On a breakdown of the marriage, the question arose as to the ownership of the house.

Held

W was not entitled to an interest in the house for she made no contributions to the purchase price:

> **Lord Diplock:** Any claim to a beneficial interest in land by a person, whether spouse or stranger, in whom the legal estate in the land is not vested must be based upon the proposition that the person in whom the legal estate is vested holds it as a trustee upon trust to give effect to the beneficial interest of the claimant as *cestui que trust*. The legal principles applicable to the claim are those of the English law of trusts and in particular, in the kind of dispute between the spouses that comes before the courts, the law relating to the creation and operation of 'resulting, implied or constructive trusts'.

> **[Express declaration in writing:]** Where the trust is expressly declared in the instrument by which the legal estate is transferred to the trustee or by a written declaration of trust by the trustee, the court must give effect to it. *But to constitute a valid declaration of trust by way of gift of a beneficial interest in land to a cestui que trust the declaration is required by s 53(1) of the Law of Property Act 1925, to be evidenced in writing.* If it is not in writing it can only take effect as a resulting, implied or constructive trust to which that section has no application [emphasis added].

> **[Resulting/constructive trust:]** A resulting, implied or constructive trust – and it is unnecessary for present purposes to distinguish between these three classes of trust – is created by a transaction between the trustee and the *cestui que* trust in connection with the acquisition by the trustee of a legal estate in land, *whenever the trustee has so conducted himself that it would be inequitable to allow him to deny to the cestui que trust a beneficial interest in the land acquired. And he will be held so to have conducted himself if by his words or conduct he has induced the cestui que trust to act to his own detriment in the reasonable belief that by so acting he was acquiring a beneficial interest in the land* [emphasis added].

> That is why it has been repeatedly said in the context of disputes between the spouses as to their respective beneficial interests in the matrimonial home, that if at the time of its acquisition and transfer of the legal estate into the name of one or other of them an express agreement has been made between them as to the way in which the beneficial interest shall be held, the court will give effect to it – notwithstanding the absence of any written declaration of trust. Strictly speaking this states the principle too widely, for if the agreement did not provide for anything to be done by the spouse in whom the legal estate was not to be vested, it would be merely a voluntary declaration of trust and unenforceable for want of writing. But in express oral agreements contemplated by these dicta it has to be assumed *sub silentio* that they provide for the spouse in whom the legal estate in the matrimonial home is not vested to do something to facilitate its acquisition, by contributing to the purchase price or to the deposit or the mortgage instalments when it is purchased upon mortgage or to make some other material sacrifice by way of contribution to or economy in the general family expenditure. *What the court gives effect to is the trust resulting or implied from the common intention expressed in the oral agreement between the spouses that if each acts in the manner provided for in the agreement the beneficial interests in the matrimonial home shall be held as they have agreed* [emphasis added].

> **[Express intention:]** An express agreement between spouses as to their respective beneficial interests in land conveyed into the name of one of them obviates the need for showing that the conduct of the spouse into whose name the land was conveyed was intended to induce the other spouse to act to his or her detriment upon the faith of the promise of a specified beneficial interest in the land and that the other spouse so acted with the intention of acquiring that beneficial interest. The agreement itself discloses the common intention required to create a resulting, implied or constructive trust.

> **[Implied intention:]** But the parties to a transaction in connection with the acquisition of land may well have formed a common intention that the beneficial interest in the land shall be vested in them jointly without having used express words to communicate this intention to one another; or their recollections of the words used may be imperfect or conflicting by the time any dispute arises. In such a case – a common one where the parties are spouses whose marriage has broken down – it may be possible to infer their common intention from their conduct.

> As in so many branches of English law in which legal rights and obligations depend upon the intentions of the parties to a transaction, the relevant intention of each party is the intention which was reasonably understood by the other party to be manifested by that party's words or conduct notwithstanding that he did not consciously

formulate that intention in his own mind or even acted with some different intention which he did not communicate to the other party. On the other hand, he is not bound by inference which the other party draws from his words or conduct. *It is in this sense that in the branch of English law relating to constructive, implied or resulting trusts effect is given to the intentions of the parties to a transaction which a reasonable man would draw from their words or conduct and not to any subjective intention or absence of intention which was not made manifest at the time of the transaction itself. It is for the court to determine what those inferences are* [emphasis added].

In drawing such an inference, what the spouse said and did which led up to the acquisition of a matrimonial home and what they said and did while the acquisition was being carried through is on a different footing from what they said and did after the acquisition was completed. Unless it is alleged that there was some subsequent fresh agreement, acted upon by the parties, to vary the original beneficial interests created when the matrimonial home was acquired, *what they said and did after the acquisition was completed is relevant if it is explicable only upon the basis of their having manifested to one another at the time of the acquisition some particular common intention as to how the beneficial interests should be held.* But it would in my view be unreasonably legalistic to treat the relevant transaction involved in the acquisition of a matrimonial home as restricted to the actual conveyance of the fee simple into the name of one or other spouse [emphasis added].

[Purchase without a mortgage:] Where a matrimonial home has been purchased outright without the aid of an advance on mortgage, it is not difficult to ascertain what part, if any, of the purchase price has been provided by each spouse. If the land is conveyed into the name of a spouse who has not provided the whole of the purchase price, the sum contributed by the other spouse may be explicable as having been intended by both of them either as a gift or as a loan of money to the spouse to whom the land is conveyed or as consideration for a share in the beneficial interest in the land.

[Purchase with a mortgage:] Similarly when a matrimonial home is not purchased outright but partly out of moneys advanced on mortgage repayable by instalments, and the land is conveyed into the name of the husband alone, the fact that the wife made a cash contribution to the deposit and legal charges not borrowed on mortgage gives rise, in the absence of evidence which makes some other explanation more probable, to the inference that their common intention that she should share in the beneficial interest in the land conveyed. But it would not be reasonable to infer a common intention as to what her share should be without taking account also of the sources from which the mortgage instalments were provided. If the wife also makes a substantial direct contribution to the mortgage instalments out of her own earnings or unearned income this would be *prima facie* inconsistent with a common intention that her share in the beneficial interest should be determined by the proportion which her original cash contribution bore either to the total amount of the deposit and legal charges or to the full purchase price. The more likely inference is that her contributions to the mortgage instalments were intended by the spouses to have some effect upon her share.

[Indirect contributions:] Where there has been an initial contribution by the wife to the cash deposit and legal charges which points to a common intention at the time of the conveyance that she should have a beneficial interest in the land conveyed to her husband, it would be unrealistic to regard the wife's subsequent contributions to the mortgage instalments as without significance unless she pays them directly herself. It may be no more than a matter of convenience which spouse pays particular household accounts, particularly when both are earning, and if the wife goes out to work and devotes part of her earnings or uses her private income to meet joint expenses of the household which would otherwise be met by the husband, so as to enable him to pay the mortgage instalments out of his moneys this would be consistent with and might be corroborative of an original common intention that she should share in the beneficial interest in the matrimonial home and that her payments of other household expenses were intended by both spouses to be treated as including a contribution by the wife to the purchase price of the matrimonial home.

I take it to be clear that if the court is satisfied that it was the common intention of both spouses that the contributing wife should have a share in the beneficial interest and that her contributions were made upon this understanding, the court in the exercise of its equitable jurisdiction would not permit the husband in whom the legal estate was vested and who had accepted the benefit of the contributions to take the whole beneficial interest merely because at the time the wife made her contributions there had been no express agreement as to how her share in it was to be quantified.

[Quantum of interest:] In such a case the court must first do its best to discover from the conduct of the spouses whether any inference can reasonably be drawn as to the probable common understanding about the amount of the share of the contributing spouse upon which each must have acted in doing what each did, *even* *though that understanding was never expressly stated by one spouse to the other or even consciously formulated in words by either of them independently.* It is only if no such inference can be drawn that the court is driven to apply as a rule of law, and not as an inference of fact, the maxim 'equality is equity,' and to hold that the beneficial interest belongs to the spouses in equal shares [emphasis added].

Where the wife has made no initial contribution to the cash deposit and legal charges and no direct contribution to the mortgage instalments nor any adjustment to her contribution to other expenses of the household which it can be inferred was referable to the acquisition of the house, there is in the absence of evidence of an express agreement between the parties no material to justify the court in inferring that it was the common intention of the parties that she should have any beneficial interest in a matrimonial home conveyed into the sole name of the husband, merely because she continued to contribute out of her own earnings or private income to other expenses of the household. For such conduct is no less consistent with a common intention to share the day to day expenses of the household, while each spouse retains a separate interest in capital assets acquired with their own moneys or obtained here to rebut the *prima facie* inference that a purchaser of land who pays the purchase price and takes a conveyance and grants a mortgage in his own name intends to acquire the sole beneficial interest as well as the legal estate: and the difficult question of the quantum of the wife's share does not arise.

Both Buckley J and Edmund Davies LJ in his dissenting judgment in the Court of Appeal felt unable on this evidence to draw an inference that there was any common intention that the wife should have a beneficial interest in the house. I think that they were right. Like them I, too, come to the conclusion with regret, because it may well be that had the husband and wife discussed the matter in 1951 when the house was bought he would have been willing for her to have a share in it if she wanted to. But this is speculation.

Question

Why have the courts moved away from the presumptions of resulting trusts and advancements as a means of identifying ownership in family assets?

Legal ownership in joint names

The parties to the purchase may have the legal title to the property transferred in their joint names, subject to an express trust for themselves as equitable joint tenants or tenants in common, or they may expressly declare the terms of the trust outside the conveyance. Provided that the declaration of trust is evidenced in writing (in compliance with s 53(1)(b) of the Law of Property Act 1925), it will be conclusive as to the beneficial interests of the parties, in the absence of fraud or mistake: see *Goodman v Gallant*.

Goodman v Gallant [1986] 2 WLR 236, CA

Facts

In 1978, the plaintiff and defendant purchased a house which was conveyed in their joint names 'upon trust to sell . . . and until sale upon trust for themselves as joint tenants'. After a dispute arose between the parties, the defendant left the house. The plaintiff gave written notice of severance of the joint tenancy and claimed a declaration to the effect that she was entitled to a three quarters share in the house.

Held

In the absence of any claim for rectification or rescission, the express declaration in the conveyance was conclusive as to the intentions of the parties. The notice of severance had the effect of terminating the joint tenancy and substituting a tenancy in common in respect of the beneficial interest:

Slade LJ: In a case where the legal estate in property is conveyed to two or more persons as joint tenants, but neither the conveyance nor any other written document contains any express declaration of trust concerning the beneficial interests in the property (as would be required for an express declaration of this nature by virtue of s 53(1)(b) of the Law of Property Act 1925), the way is open for persons claiming a beneficial interest in it or its proceeds of sale to rely on the doctrine of 'resulting, implied or constructive trusts': see s 53(2) of the Law of Property Act 1925. If, however, the relevant conveyance contains an express declaration of trust which comprehensively declares the beneficial interests in the property or its proceeds of sale, there is no room for the application of the doctrine of resulting implied or constructive trusts unless and until the conveyance is set aside or rectified; until that event the declaration contained in the document speaks for itself.

Lord Upjohn in *Pettitt v Pettitt* [1970] AC 777, at p 813, put the matter thus:

> In the first place, the beneficial ownership of the property in question must depend upon the agreement of the parties determined at the time of its acquisition. If the property in question is land there must be some lease or conveyance which shows how it was acquired. If that document declares not merely in whom the legal title is to vest but in whom the beneficial title is to vest that necessarily concludes the question of title as between the spouses for all time, and in the absence of fraud or mistake at the time of the transaction the parties cannot go behind it at any time thereafter even on death or the break-up of the marriage.

Lord Diplock in *Gissing v Gissing* [1971] AC 856, p 905, reaffirmed the general principle:

> . . . where the trust is expressly declared in the instrument by which the legal estate is transferred to the trustee or by a written declaration of trust by the trustee, the court must give effect to it.

However, the reference by Lord Upjohn in *Pettitt v Pettitt* to the possibility of 'fraud or mistake at the time of the transaction' illustrates that there is one (though we think only one) qualification to this principle. The declaration of trust will no longer be binding if the court is satisfied by appropriate evidence either that the relevant document ought to be rectified or that it ought to be rescinded on the grounds of fraud or mistake.

It seems to us that it is of the very nature of a joint tenancy that, upon a severance, each takes an equal aliquot share according to the number of joint tenants. *Halsbury's Laws of England*, 4th edn 1982, Vol 39, p 349, para 529 which is headed 'Nature of joint tenants' interests', begins with the words:

> Each joint tenant has an identical interest in the whole land and every part of it. The title of each arises by the same act. The interest of each is the same in extent, nature and duration.

Note 2 to this passage begins: Until severance, each has the whole, but upon severance each has an aliquot part (a half or less) according to the number of joint tenants . . .

The note then points out that severance can only now take effect in respect of the beneficial interests.

In *Goodman v Carlton*, the court decided that, despite the legal title to the house being taken in the joint names of the parties, there was no evidence that they intended to share the beneficial interest. One party alone contributed to the purchase of the property and its outgoings. Accordingly, a resulting trust was set up for the purchaser.

Goodman v Carlton [2002] All ER (D) 284, CA

Facts

The claimant was the son and next of kin of Mr Goodman (G), who died intestate. The defendant, Anita (A), was the surviving legal owner of real property situated at 13 Zenoria Street, East Dulwich, London (the house). The legal title to the house was acquired by G and A in 1994. The material facts, as found by the judge, were that in 1989 G became a sitting tenant in the house and in 1993 was given an opportunity to purchase the house. The purchase price was finalised at £50,000, which was considerably lower than the open market value. G's original intention was to purchase the house alone and register it in his sole name. This was evidenced by G's initial instructions to his conveyancing solicitors. Subsequently, he told his solicitor that he did not have sufficient income to finance a mortgage by himself and would be buying the property with A as co-mortgagee. There was no evidence of any discussion between G and A about their respective interests in the house prior to the purchase and no agreement was made about their interests. A signed the relevant documents, as she trusted G, and the legal title to the house was transferred into the joint names of G and A. She also testified to the effect that G told her that she would 'come off the mortgage' after one year. G alone instructed and paid the solicitors and made all the mortgage repayments. In 1997 G tentatively instructed his solicitors to transfer the house into his sole name but this was not followed up. Shortly afterwards G died. At all material times, although A was G's girlfriend, she did not live in the property. As surviving joint tenant, A acquired the legal title to the house and G's son commenced proceedings claiming that A held the house on trust for G's estate absolutely. The trial judge decided in favour of the claimant. A appealed to the Court of Appeal.

Held

Dismissing the appeal, the court decided that the property was held on resulting trust for the claimant, as administrator of G's estate. A failed to contribute to the purchase of the property and there was no evidence of any agreement, understanding or common intention to share the beneficial ownership with A, who therefore acquired no interest:

> **Mummery LJ:** The main question raised by Mr Grant Crawford's [counsel for the appellant] submissions is whether the execution of a joint mortgage on jointly held property acquired for the sole use and occupation of one of them constituted the making of a contribution to the purchase price of the property, so as to entitle each party in all the circumstances, to a corresponding beneficial interest under a resulting trust of the property. In order to answer that question I turn to the fundamental principles described from over 200 years of case law and apply them to the facts of this case.
>
> (i)   The consequence of the transfer of the House by Mrs Croft into the joint names of Mr Goodman and Anita was that the legal estate was vested in them as trustees.
>
> (ii)   As there was no express declaration of the trusts of the beneficial interests, either in the Transfer or in any other document, it is necessary to ascertain whether beneficial interests have been created in an informal way allowed by equity, such as a resulting, implied or constructive trust, which are expressly recognised in, and exempted from statutory formalities by, s 53(2) Law of Property Act 1925. The only claim now made by Anita is under a resulting trust.
>
> (iii) The beneficial interests under a resulting trust are ascertained by the process of identifying the person who provided the purchase money to acquire the property and, if more than one person is identified as having done so, by ascertaining the respective amounts provided. As held in *Dyer v Dyer* (1788) 2 Cox 92 at p 93, 'the trust of a legal estate results to the man who advances the purchase-money ... It is the established doctrine of a Court of equity, that this resulting trust may be rebutted by circumstances in evidence.' See also *Walker v Hall* (1984) 14 Fam Law 21.
>
> (iv)   There is no dispute that only Mr Goodman directly provided purchase money for the House in the form of the £2,500 deposit paid out of his own resources. It is not disputed that only he contributed added value to the acquisition of the House in the form of the discounted purchase price solely attributable to his personal status as a sitting tenant (see *Springette v Defoe* [1992] 2 FLR 388, (1992) 65 P & CR 1).
>
> (v)   Anita made no direct payment of the purchase price of the House. She claims contribution in the form of the liabilities undertaken by her in the Mortgage, which was jointly entered into in order to fund payment of a substantial part of the purchase price. In principle, I see no reason why such an arrangement cannot be treated as a contribution to the payment of the purchase price of property capable of giving rise to a resulting trust: see *Calverley v Green* (1984) 155 CLR 242 at 257–258 and 276–278.
>
> (vi)   However, as observed by Laws LJ in the course of argument, the role in fact played by Anita was a different and lesser one than that of a contributor to the purchase price. She facilitated the purchase of the House by lending her name in order to secure the advance from the Alliance & Leicester. She thereby assisted Mr Goodman in his purchase of the House. But that form of assistance was not, on the facts found by the judge, a contribution by her, or intended to be a contribution by her, to the purchase price of the House so as to give rise to a resulting trust in her favour.
>
> (vii) The fact is that Anita paid nothing towards the purchase price, and it was never intended, as between Mr Goodman and her, that she should pay anything at all. Her involvement in the purchase was so circumscribed and temporary that it cannot fairly be described as a contribution to the purchase price, entitling her to an enduring beneficial interest in the House. She only became involved after Mr Goodman found that he could not obtain a mortgage on his own in order to purchase the House as his home. On her own evidence the understanding was that she would 'come off' the mortgage after a year. The fact that she remained potentially liable to the Alliance & Leicester on the covenant in the mortgage does not assist her claim to a beneficial interest. What has to be considered is her contribution, as between Mr Goodman and her, to the purchase price in the circumstances at the date of acquisition of the House. If she made no contribution at that time, subsequent enforcement of the covenant against her by the Alliance & Leicester

would not be a contribution to the purchase price. It would be a contribution to the discharge of the mortgage liabilities.

(viii)   Nor could the making of such mortgage payments be relied on as a circumstance rebutting the resulting trust to Mr Goodman as sole contributor to the purchase price. The position is that, as a trustee, she would be entitled to be indemnified out of the trust property for any expenses, such as mortgage repayments, incurred by her in respect of the trust property. She would not acquire a beneficial interest in the trust property simply as a result of making mortgage repayments to the building society.

(ix)   There were no other circumstances rebutting the presumption of resulting trust in favour of Mr Good-man, such as purchasing the House as a family home for them both to live in, or discussions between the parties leading to an agreement, arrangement or understanding between them that the beneficial interests in the House were to be shared, or conduct from which an inference could be drawn that there was a common intention that Anita was to be given a beneficial interest in the House.

On the facts found by the Deputy Judge, Mr Goodman was the person at whose expense the House was provided. He paid all the deposit. The discount in the price was solely referable to him as sitting tenant. He was to pay (and did in fact pay) all the mortgage payments and all the premiums on the endowment policy. There was no intention that the transfer of the House into joint names should confer a beneficial interest on Anita. It was part of the arrangements undertaken to acquire the House for his sole use, occupation and benefit. Anita's participation was intended only to be a temporary involvement on the basis of the limited understanding between them. A resulting trust arose by operation of law for the sole benefit of Mr Goodman. I would dismiss the appeal.

In *Stack v Dowden* the House of Lords restated the principles concerning the occasion when a conveyance of the legal title to property is taken in the joint names of the parties, but without an express declaration of trust as to their respective beneficial interests. As a starting point, the maxims 'equity follows the law' and 'equality is equity' are applicable in order to identify the existence of the equitable interest, subject to evidence to the contrary. Thus, whether we are dealing with joint legal ownership (as in *Stack v Dowden*) or sole legal ownership (see later), the beneficial interest will *prima facie* be enjoyed by the party(ies) with the legal title. Until the contrary is proved, the extent of the beneficial interest will also follow the legal title. Thus, where the transfer of the legal title is in joint names then *prima facie* the beneficial interest will be enjoyed in equal shares until the contrary is proved. The onus of proof is therefore on the party seeking to establish that the beneficial interest is different from the legal title, such as the defendant in the present case.

The contrary may be established where the legal owner(s) expressly declare a trust. Such a declaration is conclusive of the interests of the parties in the absence of fraud, mistake or variation by subsequent agreement (see *Goodman v Gallant* (ante)). In *Stack v Dowden* the court decided that a declaration that the survivor of the two legal owners can give a valid receipt for capital moneys arising on a disposition of the land did not amount to an express declaration of a beneficial joint tenancy. In this respect the court followed *Huntingford v Hobbs* [1993] 1 FLR 736.

Likewise, on the issue of evidence to the contrary, Baroness Hale raised the question whether the starting point ought to be the presumption of a resulting trust, i.e. the beneficial ownership being held in the same proportions as the contributions to the purchase price or by looking at all the relevant circumstances in order to discern the parties' common intention (constructive trust). In Baroness Hale's view the emphasis in the domestic context has moved away from crude factors of money contribution (resulting trust) towards more subtle factors of intentional bargain (constructive trust). Accordingly, strict mathematical calculations as to who paid what at the time of the acquisition of the property may be less significant today.

Stack v Dowden [2007] UKHL 17 (House of Lords)

Facts

The family home (Chatsworth Rd) was transferred in 1993 in the joint names of Ms Dowden (defendant) and Mr Stack (claimant). The purchase of the property was for £190,000. This was funded by a mortgage advance of £65,000 for which both parties were liable, the proceeds of sale of £67,000 from the first property (Purves Rd, which was registered in the sole name of the defendant) and savings of £58,000 from a building society account in the defendant's name. The transfer contained no words of trust but included a declaration by the purchasers that the survivor of them was entitled to give a valid receipt for capital moneys. There was no discussion between the parties at the time of the purchase as to their respective share in the property. In 2002, owing to the deterioration of the relationship between the parties, the defendant served a notice of severance that had the effect of converting the joint tenancy into a tenancy in common. In April 2003, the parties agreed to a time-limited order in the Family Proceedings Court, which excluded Mr Stack from the house and required Ms Dowden to pay him £900 per month, which reflected in the cost of alternative accommodation. After that order expired Mr Stack effectively accepted Ms Dowden's decision to exclude him. The result was that Ms Dowden remained in exclusive occupation and Mr Stack continued to pay for alternative accommodation. The claimant petitioned the court for a declaration that the property was held upon trust for the parties as tenants in common in equal shares. The trial judge ruled that the claimant had an interest in the first property and the savings and made an order to the effect that the claimant had an equal share in the property. In addition the court ordered that the defendant pay the claimant £900 per month as occupation rent. The defendant appealed against the order on the ground that the judge had misdirected himself. The Court of Appeal allowed the appeal and decided that the beneficial interests in the house were held in the proportion of 65%/35% in her favour. Further, there was no basis for assessing the compensation to the claimant at £900 per month. The claimant appealed to the House of Lords contending that the trial judge's original order be restored.

Held

(i) The House of Lords unanimously dismissed Mr Stack's appeal on the ground that there was no basis for varying the split of beneficial ownership (65%/35%) in favour of the defendant, which arose in 1993 on the acquisition of the Chatsworth Rd house.

(ii) A declaration as to the receipt for capital moneys in the transfer document could not be construed as an express declaration of trust, following *Huntingford v Hobbs* [1993] 1 FLR 736.

(iii) Having regard to all the circumstances and wishes of the beneficiaries, as the court is obliged to do under s 15 of the Trusts of Land and Appointment of Trustees Act 1996, the court would not award rent to the defendant (Lord Neuberger dissenting).

Baroness Hale:

The applicable legal principles

The issue before us is the effect of a conveyance into the joint names of a cohabiting couple, but without an explicit declaration of their respective beneficial interests, of a dwelling house which was to become their home. This is, so far as I am aware, the first time that this issue has come before the House, whether the couple be married or, as in this case, unmarried. The principles of law are the same, whether or not the couple are married, although the inferences to be drawn from their conduct may be different: *Bernard v Joseph* [1982] 3 All ER 162, per Griffiths LJ.

Just as the starting point where there is sole ownership is sole beneficial ownership, the starting point where there is joint legal ownership is joint beneficial ownership. The onus is upon the person seeking to show that the beneficial ownership is different from the legal ownership. So in sole ownership cases it is upon the non-owner to show that he has an interest at all. In joint ownership cases, it is upon the joint owner who claims to have other than a joint beneficial interest.

The issue as it has been framed before us is whether a conveyance into joint names indicates only that each is intended to have some beneficial interest but says nothing about the nature and extent of the beneficial interest, or whether a conveyance into joint names establishes a *prima facie* case of joint and equal beneficial interests until the contrary is shown. For the reasons already stated, at least in the domestic consumer context, a conveyance into joint names indicates both legal and beneficial joint tenancy, unless and until the contrary is proved.

The question is, how, if at all, is the contrary to be proved? Is the starting point the presumption of resulting trust, under which shares are held in proportion to the parties' financial contributions to the acquisition of the property, unless the contributor or contributors can be shown to have had a contrary intention? Or is it that the contrary can be proved by looking at all the relevant circumstances in order to discern the parties' common intention?

The presumption of resulting trust is not a rule of law. According to Lord Diplock in *Pettitt v Pettitt* [1970] AC 777, the equitable presumptions of intention are:

> no more than a consensus of judicial opinion disclosed by reported cases as to the most likely inference of fact to be drawn in the absence of any evidence to the contrary.

... These days, the importance to be attached to who paid for what in a domestic context may be very different from its importance in other contexts or long ago. As K Gray and SF Gray, in *Elements of Land Law*, 4th edition 2005, point out at p 864, para 10.21:

> In recent decades a new pragmatism has become apparent in the law of trusts. English courts have eventually conceded that the classical theory of resulting trusts, with its fixation on intentions presumed to have been contemporaneously with the acquisition of title, has substantially broken down ... Simultaneously the balance of emphasis in the law of trusts has transferred from crude factors of money contribution (which are pre-eminent in the resulting trust) towards more subtle factors of intentional bargain (which are the foundational premise of the constructive trust) ... But the undoubted consequence is that the doctrine of resulting trust has conceded much of its field of application to the constructive trust, which is nowadays fast becoming the primary phenomenon in the area of implied trusts

... The law has indeed moved on in response to changing social and economic conditions. The search is to ascertain the parties' shared intentions, actual, inferred or imputed, with respect to the property in the light of their whole course of conduct in relation to it.

The approach to quantification in cases where the home is conveyed into joint names should certainly be no stricter than the approach to quantification in cases where it has been conveyed into the name of one only. To the extent that *Walker v Hall* [1984] FLR 126, *Springette v Defoe* (1992) 65 P & CR 1 and *Huntingford v Hobbs* [1993] 1 FLR 736, hold otherwise, they should not be followed.

The questions in a joint names case are not simply 'what is the extent of the parties' beneficial interests?' but 'did the parties intend their beneficial interests to be different from their legal interests?' and 'if they did, in what way and to what extent?' There are differences between sole and joint names cases when trying to divine the common intentions or understanding between the parties. I know of no case in which a sole legal owner (there being no declaration of trust) has been held to hold the property on a beneficial joint tenancy. But a court may well hold that joint legal owners (there being no declaration of trust) are also beneficial joint tenants. Another difference is that it will almost always have been a conscious decision to put the house into joint names. Even if the parties have not executed the transfer, they will usually, if not invariably, have executed the contract which precedes it. Committing oneself to spend large sums of money on a place to live is not normally done by accident or without giving it a moment's thought.

The burden will therefore be on the person seeking to show that the parties intend their beneficial interests to be different from their legal interests, and in what way. This is not a task to be lightly embarked upon. In family disputes, strong feelings are aroused when couples split up. These often lead the parties, honestly, but mistakenly, to reinterpret the past in self-exculpatory or vengeful terms. They also lead people to spend far more on the legal battle than is warranted by the sums actually at stake. A full examination of the facts is likely to involve disproportionate costs. In joint names cases it is also unlikely to lead to a different result unless the facts are very unusual. Nor may disputes be confined to the parties themselves. People with an interest in the deceased's estate may well wish to assert that he had a beneficial tenancy in common. It cannot be the case that all the hundreds of thousands, if not millions, of transfers into joint names using the old forms are vulnerable to challenge in the courts simply because it is likely that the owners contributed unequally to their purchase.

In law, "context is everything" and the domestic context is very different from the commercial world. Each case will turn on its own facts. Many more factors than financial contributions may be relevant to divining the parties' true intentions. These include: any advice or discussions at the time of the transfer which cast light upon their intentions then; the reasons why the home was acquired in their joint names; the reasons why (if it be the case) the survivor was authorised to give a receipt for the capital moneys; the purpose for which the home was acquired; the nature of the parties' relationship; whether they had children for whom they both had responsibility to provide a home; how the purchase was financed, both initially and subsequently; how the parties arranged their finances, whether separately or together or a bit of both; how they discharged the outgoings on the property and their other household expenses. When a couple are joint owners of the home and jointly liable for the mortgage, the inferences to be drawn from who pays for what may be very different from the inferences to be drawn when only one is the owner of the home. The arithmetical calculation of how much was paid by each is also likely to be less important. It will be easier to draw the inference that they intended that each should contribute as much to the household as they reasonably could and that they would share the eventual benefit or burden equally. The parties' individual characters and personalities may also be a factor in deciding where their true intentions lay . . . At the end of the day, having taken all this into account, cases in which the joint legal owners are to be taken to have intended that their beneficial interests should be different from their legal interests will be very unusual.

This is not an exhaustive list. There may also be reason to conclude that, whatever the parties' intentions at the outset, these have now changed. An example might be where one party has financed (or constructed himself) an extension or substantial improvement to the property, so that what they have now is significantly different from what they had then.

Applying the law to the facts
The starting point is that it is for Ms Dowden to show that the common intention, when taking a conveyance of the house into their joint names or thereafter, was that they should hold the property otherwise than as beneficial joint tenants.

In some, perhaps many, cases of real domestic partnership, there would be nothing to indicate that a contrary inference should be drawn. However, there are many factors to which Ms Dowden can point to indicate that these parties did have a different common intention. The first, of course, is that on any view she contributed far more to the acquisition of Chatsworth Road than did Mr Stack. There are many different ways of calculating this . . . The Court of Appeal rejected the judge's view . . . and held that the whole of the purchase price, other than the mortgage loan, had been contributed by Ms Dowden. She had also contributed more to the capital repayment of that loan, although Mr Stack had made all the payments necessary to keep it going. It is not surprising that the Court of Appeal reached the conclusion that Ms Dowden was entitled to at least the 65% she claimed.

On the other hand, there was some evidence that Mr Stack had made payments into the Halifax account before the Purves Road purchase and that he had made payments thereafter which would have enabled Ms Dowden to save more of her income than would otherwise be possible. This, together with his contributions towards the substantial improvements made to Purves Road, might suffice to give him some interest in the proceeds of sale, although quantifying that share would be very difficult.

. . . This is not a case in which it can be said that the parties pooled their separate resources, even notionally, for the common good. The only things they ever had in their joint names were Chatsworth Road and the associated endowment policy. Everything else was kept strictly separate. Each made separate savings and investments most of which it was accepted were their own property.

There are other aspects to their financial relationship which tell against joint ownership. Chatsworth Road was, of course, to be a home for the parties and their four children. But they undertook separate responsibility for that part of the expenditure which each had agreed to pay. The only regular expenditure to which it is clear that Mr Stack committed himself was the interest and premiums on Chatsworth Road. All other regular commitments in both houses were undertaken by Ms Dowden.

This is, therefore an unusual case. There cannot be many unmarried couples who have lived together for as long as this, who have four children together, and whose affairs have been kept as rigidly separate as this couple's affairs were kept. This is all strongly indicative that they did not intend their shares, even in the property which was put into both their names, to be equal (still less that they intended a beneficial joint tenancy with the right of survivorship should one of them die before it was severed). Before the Court of Appeal, Ms Dowden contended for a 65% share and in my view she has made good her case for that.

In *Stack v Dowden* Lord Neuberger arrived at the same conclusion, but by a different route. He adopted the same starting point by regarding the equitable interest(s) as following the legal title(s), subject to evidence to the contrary. However, with regard to rebutting evidence he followed the traditional approach by having regard to the resulting and constructive trusts. Where the parties contributed to the purchase price of the property (including mortgage repayments) the beneficial ownership will be held in the same proportions as the contributions to the purchase price. This is the resulting trust solution.

> **Lord Neuberger:** In the absence of any relevant evidence other than the parties' respective contributions, I would favour the resulting trust solution as at the date of acquisition . . . On a resulting trust basis, Mr Stack had no more than a 35% share of the beneficial interest at the date of acquisition.

Note

In *Goodman v Carlton*, the court decided that the mere fact that that the legal title to property was vested in joint names does not entitle the surviving legal owner to an equitable interest in the property, if this does not accord with the intention of the parties. Similarly, in *Ali v Khan* [2002] EWCA Civ 974, the Court of Appeal decided that a transfer of the legal title to real property to the claimant at an undervalue in order to secure a mortgage on the property did not deprive the transferor of the equitable interest in the property, in accordance with the intention of the parties. In *Stack v Dowden* two different approaches as to the interests of the parties were advocated by the Law Lords as manifested by Baroness Hale and Lord Neuberger. Both approaches led to the same result. The Law Commission (2001, Law Com No 274) in its review of the law relating to the property rights of those who share homes commented that:

> It is widely accepted that the present law is unduly complex, arbitrary and uncertain in its application. It is ill-suited to determining the property rights of those who, because of the informal nature of their relationship, may not have considered their respective entitlements.

In 2002, the Commission published *Sharing Homes, A Discussion Paper* (2002, Law Com No 278), but failed to recommend any proposals for reform. The Commission declared:

> It is simply not possible to devise a statutory scheme for the ascertainment and quantification of beneficial interests in the shared home which can operate fairly and evenly across the diversity of domestic circumstances which are now to be encountered.

[See conclusions later.]

Legal estate in the name of one party

Where the legal estate in the property is conveyed in the name of one spouse only (say the husband) and the other spouse wishes to claim a beneficial interest, the claimant will be required to establish a contribution to the purchase of the house at the time of the acquisition (which includes the mortgage repayments). In other words, in the absence of an express declaration of trust in writing, the claimant must show that the legal owner holds the legal estate on trust in order to give effect to the interest claimed.

In *Burns v Burns*, it was decided that domestic duties, such as staying at home for the purpose of looking after the house and children without more, would not give the claimant an interest in the house because the claimant would have failed to show that he or she had made a contribution to the acquisition of the house.

Burns v Burns [1984] 2 WLR 582, CA

Facts

The plaintiff, Mrs Burns, lived with the defendant for 19 years from 1961 without being married. She gave up her employment shortly after their first child was born. In 1963, when she was expecting her second child, the defendant bought a house in his sole name for £4,900 of which £4,500 was raised by way of a mortgage. The plaintiff made no direct contributions to the purchase. Until 1975, the plaintiff was unable to take up gainful employment because she performed the duties of bringing up the children. Although the defendant gave her a generous housekeeping allowance and did not ask her to contribute to household expenses, from 1975 she became employed and used her earnings for household expenses and to purchase fixtures and fittings. In 1980, the plaintiff left the defendant and claimed a beneficial interest in the house. The judge decided that the plaintiff did not have an interest in the house. The plaintiff appealed.

Held

The plaintiff had failed to prove that she had made a contribution, directly or indirectly, to the acquisition of the property, and therefore she did not have an interest in the property. A common intention that the plaintiff had acquired an interest in the property could not be imputed to the parties on the basis that the plaintiff lived with the defendant for 19 years, brought up the children and did a fair share of domestic duties. In respect of unmarried couples, the court had no jurisdiction equivalent to the Matrimonial Causes Act 1973 to make an order dividing up the property on the basis of what was fair and reasonable:

> **Fox LJ:** If the plaintiff is to establish that she has a beneficial interest in the property, she must establish that the defendant holds the legal estate upon trust to give effect to that interest. That follows from *Gissing v Gissing* [1971] AC 886. For present purposes I think that such a trust could only arise (a) by express declaration or agreement, or (b) by way of a resulting trust where the claimant has directly provided part of the purchase price, or (c) from the common intention of the parties.
>
> In the present case, (a) and (b) can be ruled out. There was no express trust of an interest in the property for the benefit of the plaintiff; and there was no express agreement to create such an interest. And the plaintiff made no direct contribution to the purchase price. Her case, therefore, must depend upon showing a common intention that she should have a beneficial interest in the property. Whether the trust which would arise in such circumstances is described as implied, constructive or resulting does not greatly matter. If the intention is inferred from the fact that some indirect contribution is made to the purchase price, the term 'resulting trust' is probably not inappropriate. Be that as it may, the basis of such a claim, in any case, is that it would be inequitable for the holder of the legal estate to deny the claimant's right to a beneficial interest.
>
> In determining whether such common intention exists it is, normally, the intention of the parties when the property was purchased that is important [emphasis added].
>
> Looking at the position at the time of the acquisition of the house in 1963, I see nothing at all to indicate any intention by the parties that the plaintiff should have an interest in it . . .
>
> I come then to the position in the year after the house was purchased. I will deal with them under three heads, namely financial contributions, work on the house and finally housekeeping. There is some overlapping in these categories.
>
> So far as financial contributions are concerned . . . The judge's findings as to expenditure by the plaintiff were as follows:
>
> (i)   she made gifts of clothing and other things to the defendant and the children;
>
> (ii) she paid for the housekeeping. The defendant allowed her, latterly, £60 per week for housekeeping. It seems to be accepted that the defendant was generous with money and the plaintiff was not kept short as regards housekeeping money;
>
> (iii) she paid the rates. The housekeeping payments made by the defendant were, however, fixed at an amount which took account of this;
>
> (iv) she paid the telephone bills. That was a matter of agreement between her and the defendant because she spent a lot of time on the telephone talking to her friends;
>
> (v)   she bought a number of chattels for domestic use: a dishwasher, a washing machine, a tumble dryer and either a drawing room suite or three armchairs and a bed for her separate room. The bed, the dishwasher and the chairs she took with her when she left in 1980;
>
> (vi) she provided some doorknobs and door furnishings of no great value.
>
> None of this expenditure, in my opinion, indicates the existence of the common intention which the plaintiff has to prove. What is needed, I think, is evidence of a payment or payments by the plaintiff which it can be inferred was referable to the acquisition of the house.
>
> There remains the question of housekeeping and domestic duties. So far as housekeeping expenses are concerned, I do not doubt that (the house being bought in the man's name) if the woman goes out to work in order

to provide money for the family expenses, as a result of which she spends her earnings on the housekeeping and the man is thus able to pay the mortgage instalments and other expenses out of his earnings, it can be inferred that there was a common intention that the woman should have an interest in the house – since she will have made an indirect financial contribution to the mortgage instalments. But that is not this case.

But, one asks, can the fact that the plaintiff performed domestic duties in the house and looked after the children be taken into account? The mere fact that parties live together and do the ordinary domestic tasks is, in my view, no indication at all that they thereby intended to alter the existing property rights of either of them. The assertion that they do alter property rights seems to me to be, in substance, reverting to the idea of the 'family asset' which was rejected by the House of Lords in *Pettitt v Pettitt* [1970] AC 777.

The result, in my opinion, is that the plaintiff fails to demonstrate the existence of any trust in her favour.

Direct contributions

In the absence of an express declaration of an equitable interest (which is required to be in writing), the claimant is required to establish an implied agreement with the legal owner as to beneficial entitlement. The evidence of such agreement may take the form of substantial contributions directly to the purchase of the property, such as the deposit and/or the mortgage repayments. The interest acquired will correspond to the *pro rata* value of the contributions. Accordingly, in *Re Rogers' Question* [1948] 1 All ER 328, a wife contributed 10% of the purchase price of a house that was conveyed in the name of her husband. She was entitled to a 10% share of the value of the house.

Note that if the courts cannot ascertain the exact contributions made by each party, the best solution may be equal division in accordance with the maxim, 'Equality is equity'.

Indirect contributions

The claimant may acquire an interest in the property by making a substantial indirect contribution to the acquisition of the property (including mortgage repayments). This arrangement may be achieved by an undertaking between the parties to the effect that the claimant agrees to pay the household expenses on condition that the legal owner pays the mortgage instalments. In short, a link between the mortgage payments and the expenses undertaken by the claimant is required to be established and the claimant's expenses are required to be of a substantial nature, *per* Lord Pearson in *Gissing v Gissing*.

Gissing v Gissing [1971] AC 886, HL

Lord Pearson: Contributions are not limited to those made directly in part payment of the price of the property or to those made at the time when the property is conveyed into the name of one of the spouses. For instance there can be a contribution if by arrangement between the spouses one of them by payment of the household expenses enables the other to pay the mortgage instalments.

The undertaking between the parties concerning indirect contributions to the acquisition of the property may take the form of an express agreement, albeit not in writing, following discussions between the parties. An agreement without writing, conveying an interest in land, may be treated as a declaration of trust and is unenforceable by virtue of s 53(1)(b) of the Law of Property Act 1925 (see p 36 above). Frequently, the courts are required to consider whether such agreements may be implied by interpreting the conduct of the parties. Such conduct, if related to the acquisition of the property, may form the basis of a constructive or resulting trust which is exempt from s 53(1)(b) by virtue of s 53(2) of the Law of Property Act 1925: see *Grant v Edwards*.

Grant v Edwards [1986] Ch 638, CA

Facts

The claimant, a woman who lived with the defendant, was given a false reason for not having the house put in their joint names. The woman made substantial contributions to the family expenses in the hope of acquiring an interest in the house. The expenses undertaken by the woman enabled the man to keep up the mortgage instalments. The plaintiff claimed an interest in the house.

Held

The plaintiff was entitled to a half share in the property. She would not have made the substantial contributions to the housekeeping expenses, which indirectly related to the mortgage instalments, unless she had an interest in the house. This was the inevitable inference from the plaintiff's conduct which established a common intention and reliance to her detriment:

> **Nourse LJ:** Where there has been no written declaration or agreement, nor any direct provision by the plaintiff of part of the purchase price so as to give rise to a resulting trust . . . She [the claimant] must establish a common intention between her and the defendant, acted on by her, that she should have a beneficial interest in the property. If she can do that, equity will not allow the defendant to deny that interest and will construct a trust to give effect to it . . . In this regard the court has to look at expenditure which is referable to the acquisition of the home.
>
> It is in my view an inevitable inference that the very substantial contribution which the plaintiff made out of her earnings after August 1972 to the housekeeping and to the feeding and to the bringing up of the children enabled the defendant to keep down the instalments payable under both mortgages out of his own income and, moreover, that he could not have done that if he had had to bear the whole of the other expenses as well.
>
> Was the conduct of the plaintiff in making substantial indirect contributions to the instalments payable under both mortgages conduct upon which she could not reasonably have been expected to embark unless she was to have an interest in the house? I answer that question in the affirmative. I cannot see upon what other basis she could reasonably have been expected to give the defendant such substantial assistance in paying off mortgages on his house. I therefore conclude that the plaintiff did act to her detriment on the faith of the common intention between her and the defendant that she was to have some sort of proprietary interest in the house.

In the same case, Sir Nicolas Browne-Wilkinson VC (as he then was) expressed the approach of the court exclusively in terms of a constructive trust similar to a proprietary estoppel. The claimant without the legal interest is required to establish a constructive trust or a proprietary estoppel by showing that it would be inequitable for the legal owner to claim sole beneficial ownership. This requires two matters to be demonstrated:

(a) that there was a common intention that both parties should have a beneficial interest; and

(b) that the claimant had acted to his detriment on the basis of that common intention.

Note

The differences, in this context, between constructive trusts and proprietary estoppel are:

(1) The common intention constructive trust results from a frustrated bargain between the parties, whereas proprietary estoppel is based on the notion of frustrated expectations.

(2) Where a claim under the constructive trust is made the courts will require proof of contributions by the claimant to the purchase price of the property. But where the claim is made in proprietary estoppel detrimental actions need not entail financial expenditure. The real test is whether the detriment suffered by the party is sufficiently substantial that it would be unconscionable to permit the assurance to be disregarded.

(3) A beneficial interest under a constructive trust arises as soon as the claimant acts to his detriment in reliance on a common understanding with the defendant. But in proprietary estoppel the interest arises from the date of the court order.

(4) The discretion retained by the court is wider in the context of an estoppel compared with the constructive trust.

The disputed intention may be established by direct evidence of an express agreement in writing between the parties, or may be an inferred common intention from the conduct of the parties. Direct or indirect substantial financial contributions to the acquisition of the house (including the mortgage instalments) will have this effect. Indeed, contributions may be relevant for four different purposes:

(a) in the absence of direct evidence of intention, as evidence from which the parties' intentions can be inferred;

(b) as corroboration evidence of the intention of the parties;

(c) to show that the claimant has acted to his detriment in reliance on the common intention;

(d) to quantify the extent of the beneficial interest.

Grant v Edwards [1986] Ch 638, CA

Sir Nicolas Browne-Wilkinson VC: In my judgment, there has been a tendency over the years to distort the principles as laid down in the speech of Lord Diplock in *Gissing v Gissing* [1971] AC 886 by concentrating on only part of his reasoning. For present purposes, his speech can be treated as falling into three sections: the first deals with the nature of the substantive right; the second with the proof of the existence of that right; the third with the quantification of that right.

The nature of the substantive right (*ibid*, pp 905B–05G)

If the legal estate in the joint home is vested in only one of the parties ('the legal owner') the other party ('the claimant'), in order to establish a beneficial interest, has to establish a constructive trust by showing that it would be inequitable for the legal owner to claim sole beneficial ownership. This requires two matters to be demonstrated: (a) that there was a common intention that both should have a beneficial interest; (b) that the claimant has acted to his or her detriment on the basis of that common intention.

The proof of the common intention

(a) Direct evidence: (*ibid*, p 905H) It is clear that mere agreement between the parties that both are to have beneficial interests is sufficient to prove the necessary common intention. Other passages in the speech point to the admissibility and relevance of other possible forms of direct evidence of such intention (*ibid*, pp 907C–08C).

(b) Inferred common intention: (*ibid*, pp 906A–08D) Lord Diplock points out that, even where parties have not used express words to communicate their intention (and therefore there is no direct evidence), the court can infer from their actions an intention that they shall both have an interest in the house. This part of his speech concentrates on the types of evidence from which the courts are most often asked to infer such intention, viz, contributions (direct and indirect) to the deposit, the mortgage instalments or general housekeeping expenses. In this section of the speech, he analyses what types of expenditure are capable of constituting evidence of such common intention: he does not say that if the intention is proved in some other way such contributions are essential to establish the trust.

The quantification of the right (pp 908D–09)

Once it has been established that the parties had a common intention that both should have a beneficial interest and that the claimant has acted to his detriment, the question may still remain: 'what is the extent of the claimant's beneficial interest?' This last section of Lord Diplock's speech shows that here again the direct and indirect contributions made by the parties to the cost of acquisition may be crucially important.

If this analysis is correct, contributions made by the claimant may be relevant for four different purposes, viz:
(1) in the absence of direct evidence of intention, as evidence from which the parties' intentions can be inferred;
(2) as corroboration of direct evidence of intention; (3) to show that the claimant has acted to his or her detriment in reliance on the common intention: Lord Diplock's speech does not deal directly with the nature of the detriment to be shown; (4) to quantify the extent of the beneficial interest.

Applying those principles to the present case, the representation made by the defendant to the plaintiff that the house would have been in the joint names but for the plaintiff's matrimonial disputes is clear direct evidence of a common intention that she was to have an interest in the house: *Eves v Eves* [1975] 1 WLR 1338. Such evidence was in my judgment sufficient by itself to establish the common intention: but in any event it is wholly consistent with the contributions made by the plaintiff to the joint household expenses and the fact that the surplus fire insurance moneys were put into a joint account.

But as Lord Diplock's speech in *Gissing v Gissing* [1971] AC 886, p 905D and the decision in *Midland Bank plc v Dobson* (unreported) make clear, mere common intention by itself is not enough: the claimant has also to prove that she has acted to her detriment in the reasonable belief by so acting she was acquiring a beneficial interest.

There is little guidance in the authorities on constructive trusts as to what is necessary to prove that the claimant so acted to her detriment. What 'link' has to be shown between the common intention and the actions relied on? Does there have to be positive evidence that the claimant did the acts in conscious reliance on the common intention? Does the court have to be satisfied that she would not have done the acts relied on but for the common intention, for example, would not the claimant have contributed to household expenses out of affection for the legal owner and as part of their joint life together even if she had no interest in the house? Do the acts relied on as a detriment have to be inherently referable to the house, for example, contribution to the purchase or physical labour on the house?

I do not think it is necessary to express any concluded view on these questions in order to decide this case. *Eves v Eves* [1975] 1 WLR 1338 indicates that there has to be some 'link' between the common intention and the acts relied on as a detriment . . . In my judgment where the claimant has made payments which, whether directly or indirectly, have been used to discharge the mortgage instalments, this is a sufficient link between the detriment suffered by the claimant and the common intention. The court can infer that she would not have made such payments were it not for her belief that she had an interest in the house. On this ground therefore I find that the plaintiff has acted to her detriment in reliance on the common intention that she had a beneficial interest in the house and accordingly that she has established such beneficial interest.

I suggest that, in other cases of this kind, useful guidance may in the future be obtained from the principles underlying the law of proprietary estoppel which in my judgment are closely akin to those laid down in *Gissing v Gissing* [1971] AC 886. In both, the claimant must to the knowledge of the legal owner have acted in the belief that the claimant has or will obtain an interest in the property. In both, the claimant must have acted to his or her detriment in reliance on such belief. In both, equity acts on the conscience of the legal owner to prevent him from acting in an unconscionable manner by defeating the common intention. The two principles have been developed separately without cross-fertilisation between them: but they rest on the same foundation and have on all other matters reached the same conclusions.

What then is the extent of the plaintiff's interest? It is clear from *Gissing v Gissing* [1971] AC 886 that, once the common intention and the actions to the claimant's detriment have been proved from direct or other evidence, in fixing the quantum of the claimant's beneficial interest the court can take into account indirect contributions by the plaintiff such as the plaintiff's contributions to joint household expenses: see *Gissing v Gissing ibid*, pp 909A and D–E. In my judgment, the passage in Lord Diplock's speech *ibid*, pp 909G–10A is dealing with a case where there is no evidence of the common intention other than contributions to joint expenditure: in such a case there is insufficient evidence to prove any beneficial interest and the question of the extent of that interest cannot arise.

Where, as in this case, the existence of some beneficial interest in the claimant has been shown, *prima facie* the interest of the claimant will be that which the parties intended: *Gissing v Gissing ibid*, p 908G.

In *Midland Bank v Dobson and Dobson* (1985) 139 NLJ 751, the Court of Appeal decided that a common intention without evidence of reliance was insufficient to create a constructive trust, and thus a beneficial interest in property. Moreover, in this case, there was no contribution by the claimant, direct or indirect, to the purchase of the property and therefore there was no trust.

Would the claimant's conduct other than by way of a financial contribution be capable of establishing a common intention between the claimant and the legal owner? The Court of Appeal in *Grant v Edwards* was not opposed to treating such conduct as capable of giving rise to a common intention. The court reviewed the earlier case of *Eves v Eves* and treated it as an illustration of the constructive trust (proprietary estoppel) principle.

Eves v Eves [1975] 1 WLR 1338, CA

Facts
An unmarried couple bought a house which was conveyed in the name of the man (defendant) instead of both parties on the ground that the plaintiff (as suggested by the defendant) was under 21. She bore him two children and did a lot of heavy work in the house and garden before he left her for another woman. The plaintiff applied to ascertain her share of the house.

Held

The court found in favour of the plaintiff and awarded her a quarter share of the house on the ground that the property was acquired and maintained by both parties for their joint benefit:

> **Lord Denning MR:** Although Janet did not make any financial contribution, it seems to me that this property was acquired and maintained by both by their joint efforts with the intention that it should be used for their joint benefit until they were married and thereafter as long as the marriage continued. At any rate, Stuart Eves cannot be heard to say the contrary. He told her that it was to be their home for them and their children. He gained her confidence by telling her that he intended to put it in their joint names (just as married couples often do) but that it was not possible until she was 21. The judge described this as a 'trick' and said that it 'did not do him much credit as a man of honour'. The man never intended to put it in joint names but always determined to have it in his own name. It seems to me that he should be judged by what he told her – by what he led her to believe – and not by his own intent which he kept to himself.

Note

During the 1970s and early 1980s the Court of Appeal, in a series of decisions, advocated its own peculiar solution to disputes involving the family home. Its approach was based on a liberal interpretation of justice and good conscience. The court attempted to do justice between the parties on a case by case basis, by declaring property rights based on fairness. This system of 'palm tree' justice, called the 'new model constructive trust', had the counterproductive effect of creating unpredictable property rights which might affect third parties. *Eves v Eves* is an illlustration of this approach.

In *Grant v Edwards*, the Court of Appeal reviewed *Eves v Eves* and considered the case as an illustration of conduct manifesting a common intention between the parties which was relied on by the claimant. Nourse LJ in *Grant v Edwards* made the following observations concerning *Eves v Eves*.

Grant v Edwards [1986] Ch 638, CA

> **Nourse LJ:** First, as Brightman J himself observed, if the work had not been done the common intention would not have been enough. Secondly, if the common intention had not been orally made plain, the work would not have been conduct from which it could be inferred. That, I think, is the effect of the actual decision in *Pettitt v Pettitt* [1970] AC 777. Thirdly, and on the other hand, the work was conduct which amounted to an acting upon the common intention by the woman. It seems therefore, on the authorities as they stand, that a distinction is to be made between conduct from which the common intention can be inferred on the one hand and conduct which amounts to an acting upon it on the other. There remains this difficult question: what is the quality of conduct required for the latter purpose? The difficulty is caused, I think because although the common intention has been made plain, everything else remains a matter of inference. Let me illustrate it in this way. It would be possible to take the view that the mere moving into the house by the woman amounted to an acting upon the common intention. But that was evidently not the view of the majority in *Eves v Eves* [1975] 1 WLR 1338. And the reason for that may be that, in the absence of evidence, the law is not so cynical as to infer that a woman will only go to live with a man to whom she is not married if she understands that she is to have an interest in their home. So what sort of conduct is required? In my judgment it must be conduct on which the woman could not reasonably have been expected to embark unless she was to have an interest in the house. If she was not to have such an interest, she could reasonably be expected to go and live with her lover, but not, for example, to wield a 14lb sledge hammer in the front garden. In adopting the latter kind of conduct she is seen to act to her detriment on the faith of the common intention.

Question

What are the 'settled principles of property law' laid down in *Pettitt v Pettitt* and *Gissing v Gissing*, and to what relationships are these principles applicable?

In *Lloyds Bank plc v Rosset*, the House of Lords (Lords Bridge of Harwich, Griffith, Ackner, Oliver of Aylmerton and Jauncey of Tullichettle) endorsed the approach of the Court of Appeal in *Grant v Edwards*, and laid down two types of evidence that are capable of establishing a beneficial interest. These are:

(a) an agreement, arrangement or understanding reached between the parties concerning the beneficial interest in the property (*Eves v Eves* and *Grant v Edwards* illustrate this proposition); and

(b) reliance on a common intention based on the conduct of the parties which gives rise to a constructive trust, such as direct contributions (including mortgage payments) to the acquisition of the home.

Lloyds Bank plc v Rosset [1990] I All ER I I I, HL

Facts

A semi-derelict farmhouse was conveyed in the name of the husband but the wife spent a great deal of time in the house supervising the work done by builders. She also did some decorating to the house. Unknown to the wife, her husband had taken out an overdraft with the bank. The couple later separated but the wife remained in the house. The husband was unable to repay the overdraft, with the result that the bank started proceedings for the sale of the property. The wife resisted the claim on the ground that she was entitled to a beneficial interest in the house under a constructive trust. The trial judge and the Court of Appeal decided that the husband held the property as constructive trustee for the wife and himself. The plaintiff appealed.

Held

In favour of the bank on the ground that the wife had no beneficial interest in the property. There was no understanding between the parties that the property was to be shared beneficially, coupled with detrimental action by the claimant, nor had there been direct contributions to the purchase price. In any event, the court decided that the monetary value of the wife's work was trifling compared with the cost of acquiring the house:

> **Lord Bridge of Harwich:** The first and fundamental question which must always be resolved is whether, independently of any inference to be drawn from the conduct of the parties in the course of sharing the house as their home and managing their joint affairs, *there has at any time prior to acquisition, or exceptionally at some later date, been any agreement, arrangement or understanding reached between them that the property is to be shared beneficially. The finding of an agreement or arrangement to share in this sense can only, I think, be based on evidence of express discussions between the partners,* however imperfectly remembered and however imprecise their terms may have been. Once a finding to this effect is made it will only be necessary for the partner asserting a claim to a beneficial interest against the partner entitled to the legal estate to show that he or she has acted to his or her detriment or significantly altered his or her position in reliance on the agreement in order to give rise to a constructive trust or a proprietary estoppel [emphasis added].

> In sharp contrast with this situation is the very different one where there is no evidence to support a finding of an agreement or arrangement to share, however reasonable it might have been for the parties to reach such an arrangement if they had applied their minds to the question, and *where the court must rely entirely on the conduct of the parties both as the basis from which to infer a common intention to share the property beneficially and as the conduct relied on to give rise to a constructive trust. In this situation direct contributions to the purchase price by the partner who is not the legal owner, whether initially or by payment of mortgage instalments, will readily justify the inference necessary to the creation of a constructive trust. But, as I read the authorities, it is at least extremely doubtful whether anything less will do* [emphasis added].

> The leading cases in your Lordships' House are *Pettitt v Pettitt* [1970] AC 777 and *Gissing v Gissing* [1971] AC 886. Both demonstrate situations in the second category to which I have referred and their Lordships discuss at great length the difficulties to which these situations give rise. The effect of these two decisions is very helpfully analysed in the judgment of Lord MacDermott LCJ in *McFarlane v McFarlane* [1972] NI 59.

> Outstanding examples on the other hand of cases giving rise to situations in the first category are *Eves v Eves* [1975] I WLR 1338 and *Grant v Edwards* [1986] Ch 638. In both these cases, where the parties who had co-habited were unmarried, the female partner had been clearly led by the male partner to believe, when they set up home together, that the property would belong to them jointly. In *Eves v Eves* the male partner had told the

female partner that the only reason why the property was to be acquired in his name alone was because she was under 21 and that, but for her age, he would have had the house put into their joint names. He admitted in evidence that this was simply an 'excuse'. Similarly in *Grant v Edwards* the female partner was told by the male partner that the only reason for not acquiring the property in joint names was because she was involved in divorce proceedings and that, if the property were acquired jointly, this might operate to her prejudice in those proceedings. As Nourse LJ put it, p 649:

> Just as in *Eves v Eves*, these facts appear to me to raise a clear inference that there was an understanding between the plaintiff and the defendant, or a common intention, that the plaintiff was to have some sort of proprietary interest in the house; otherwise no excuse for not putting her name on to the title would have been needed.

The subsequent conduct of the female partner in each of these cases, which the court rightly held sufficient to give rise to a constructive trust or proprietary estoppel supporting her claim to an interest in the property, fell far short of such conduct as would by itself have supported the claim in the absence of an express representation by the male partner that she was to have such an interest. It is significant to note that the share to which the female partners in *Eves v Eves* and *Grant v Edwards* were held entitled were one quarter and one half respectively. In no sense could these shares have been regarded as proportionate to what the judge in the instant case described as a 'qualifying contribution' in terms of the indirect contributions to the acquisition or enhancement of the value of the houses made by the female partners.

Difficulties concerning the *Rosset* analysis

Lord Bridge in *Lloyds Bank v Rosset*, in issuing guidelines as to the relevance of evidence necessary to create proprietary interests in family assets, classified the evidence into two categories:

(a) Evidence of an agreement based on express discussion between the parties:

> The claimant is required to show that 'there has at any time prior to the acquisition, or exceptionally at some later date, been an agreement, arrangement or understanding between the parties that the property is to be shared beneficially *based on evidence of express discussion between the parties*. The claimant will then be required to establish that he or she acted to his or her detriment in reliance on the agreement in order to give rise to a *constructive trust or proprietary estoppel* [emphasis added].

(b) Evidence of the conduct of the parties based on direct contributions to the purchase of the home:

> Where there is no evidence to support a finding of an agreement or arrangement to share . . . and where the court must rely entirely on the conduct of the parties both as the basis from which to infer a common intention to share the property beneficially and as the conduct relied on to give rise to a constructive trust. In this situation *direct contributions* to the purchase price . . . will readily justify the inference necessary to the creation of a *constructive trust*. But . . . it is at least extremely *doubtful whether anything less will do* [emphasis added].

Express discussion between the parties

Lord Bridge's first category of evidence suggests that the common intention/agreement may only be established by evidence of express discussion between the parties. This appears to be an unwarranted restriction on the adduction of evidence of an agreement as to a beneficial interest. An agreement or understanding is capable of being inferred from conduct. For the application of this rule, see *Hammond v Mitchell* and *Springette v Defoe* [1992] 2 FLR 388, CA, p 248 below. Glover and Todd, in 'Inferring share of interest in home: *Midland Bank v Cooke*' [1995] 4 Web JCLI, take the view that constructive trusts and proprietary estoppels are separate and alternative ways of acquiring beneficial interests. The explanation of the requirement for express discussion is akin to an express declaration of trust. To be effective, an express declaration of trust must be immediate and attach to an identifiable amount of property. Statements as to future intention are insufficient to amount to declarations of trust, but may be sufficient to found an estoppel. The writers take the view that 'estoppels differ from trusts in that they do not necessarily create full beneficial interests, the position of third parties is different, A's intention can be as to future and indeed, the property need not even be identified'.

Constructive trust/proprietary estoppel

Lord Bridge equates the constructive trust (first category evidence) with proprietary estoppel. Although proprietary estoppel is to some extent related to a constructive trust, an estoppel operates *inter partes*. Constructive trusts, on the other hand, are capable of enforcement against third parties.

Professor Hayton takes the view that the distinction between common intention constructive trusts and proprietary estoppel is illusory (see 'Equitable rights of cohabitees' [1990] Conv 370).

Constructive/resulting trusts

The second category of evidence appears to be consistent with a resulting trust, in that the trust is based on direct contributions to the acquisition of the property. However, Lord Bridge equates this trust with a constructive trust: see *Drake v Whipp* [1996] 1 FLR 826, CA, p 252 below).

Indirect financial contributions

Lord Bridge makes no mention of indirect financial contributions. It could not have been intended from this omission to treat such contributions as irrelevant under the second category of evidence. Indirect contributions to the acquisition of the home were acknowledged in *Gissing v Gissing* and *Burns v Burns*. Such contributions ought to be relevant in determining beneficial interests within both categories of evidence: see *Le Foe v Le Foe* [2001] All ER CD 325, HC, p 253 below.

The approach in Midland Bank v Cooke

It was intended by Lord Bridge that the value of the claimant's interest be determined by reference to the two categories of evidence as laid down in *Rosset*. But the courts have adopted a different approach, namely, once an interest has been established under at least one of the categories of evidence, the court has a general discretion to do what it considers to be just and fair in the circumstances: see *Midland Bank plc v Cooke and Another* [1995] 4 All ER 562, CA, p 251 below.

Question
How far has the decision in *Lloyds Bank v Rosset* clarified the law in respect of family assets?

Rosset principles extended to commercial arrangements

In *Lloyd v Pickering*, the High Court acknowledged that, typically, the majority of decided cases concern domestic issues involving ownership of the house in which the parties have made their home. In *Lloyd v Pickering*, by contrast, the subject matter of the dispute concerned a gym business – a collection of assets, a lease, the goodwill from the business and the income derived from subscriptions. There was no conceptual reason why, the same principles laid down in *Rosset* cannot be extended to the circumstances of the present case. In the result the conclusion was that the evidence justified the inference of a common intention on the part of both parties that ownership of the business was shared equally.

Lloyd v Pickering [2004] EWHC 1513 (Ch)

Facts

The claimant and defendant lived together as a gay couple. The claimant gave up full-time employment as a computer systems manager at Barings Investment Bank in June 1993 and assisted his 'live-in' partner in setting up a gym business in April 1993. The lease of the business premises was taken in the name of the defendant who was also the employer of all the staff employed in the business. The defendant was the sole registered proprietor of the business for VAT purposes. The claimant received state benefits and explained in court that, as a result, he could not appear to draw a regular salary and to be entitled to an equal share in the profits from the business. In any event, his contention (which was accepted by the court) was that he actively and continuously participated in the running of the business. In February 2002 there was a breakdown in the personal relationship between the parties. The claimant applied to the court for a declaration that the business was jointly owned and that the parties were each entitled to an equal share of the business. The question in issue was whether, as the defendant submitted, the claimant's involvement in the business was no more than by way of support as the defendant's 'partner in life'. Alternatively, as the claimant maintained, he participated in a joint venture in which both parties remained equal participants.

Held

In reliance on the test laid down in *Rosset*, the court decided in favour of the claimant on the ground that he gave his time and energy in the running of the business in the belief, shared by the defendant, that he would be entitled to a share in the business. Weighing up all the factors in the case the proper conclusion to be drawn was that the business was to be regarded as owned in equal shares. Accordingly, the defendant held the business on constructive trust for both parties.

> **Blackburne J:** There is no conceptual reason why, in the case of an unincorporated business such as this, a person should not, through participation in its running (and provided that the participation is sufficiently substantial and continuous) acquire an interest in it even though the business is (like the Business in the instant case) conducted exclusively in the name of another. See, for example, *Nixon v Nixon* [1969] 1 WLR 1676. The authorities (some of them, including *Nixon v Nixon* are referred to in Lewin on Trusts, 17th edn at paragraph 9–67, footnote 45) were not explored in argument before me. But I did not understand Mr McCue to contest the proposition.
>
> I have come to the conclusion that the evidence justifies the inference of a common intention on the part of the two of them that ownership of the Business was shared. In reaching this conclusion I am fully alive to the fact that, in legal structure, the Business appeared to belong exclusively to Mr Pickering and that this was reflected in some at least of the Business documentation.

Extent of the application of *Rosset* principles

The *Rosset* principles were analysed and applied in *Hammond v Mitchell*. The quality of the evidence of an understanding or agreement regarding beneficial entitlement varies significantly with each case.

Hammond v Mitchell [1991] 1 WLR 1127, HC

Facts

The parties, Mr Hammond (H) and Miss Mitchell (M), lived together from 1977 to 1988. After the birth of the first of their two children in 1979, the couple moved into a bungalow in Essex, which was bought in H's name with the assistance of a mortgage. H assured M that, as he was going through a divorce, it would be in their best interests if the house was put in his name. He then told her: 'Don't worry about the future because when we are married it will be half yours anyway . . .' In 1980, surrounding land was bought and the bungalow was extended. M assisted H in his business ventures. H purchased a house in Spain and for a short while they lived there, but never gave up possession of the Essex house. In 1988, the relationship was terminated and M brought an action claiming a beneficial interest in the properties and other assets.

Held

In relation to the bungalow, there was evidence of an express understanding that M should have a beneficial interest, quantified as one half. But in relation to the Spanish house, there was no evidence to justify an intention to share the beneficial interest:

> **Waite J:** The law requires me in determining beneficial title to apply the principles enunciated in *Lloyds Bank plc v Rosset* [1991] 1 AC 107 and *Grant v Edwards* [1986] Ch 638. It will involve asking this question first: is there any, and if so which, property which has been the subject of some agreement, arrangement or understanding reached between the parties on the basis of express discussion to the effect that such property is to be shared beneficially; and (if there is) has Miss Mitchell shown herself to have acted to her detriment or significantly altered her position in reliance on the agreement so as to give rise to a constructive trust or proprietary estoppel? The answer to that question should, in my judgment, in both its parts be 'Yes'.
>
> In relation to the bungalow there was express discussion which, although not directed with any precision as to proprietary interests, was sufficient to amount to an understanding at least that the bungalow was to be shared beneficially. I am satisfied in the present case that the parties intended the bungalow, as it became successively enlarged by addition to its own original structure and by the purchase of the adjoining parcels of land and barns, to be subject to the same understanding as governed the original property. Miss Mitchell, by her participation wholeheartedly in what may loosely be called the commercial activities based on the bungalow, not only acted consistently with that view of the situation but also acted to her detriment in that she gave her full support on two occasions to speculative ventures which, had they turned out unfavourably, might have involved the entire bungalow property being sold up to repay the bank an indebtedness to which the house and land were all committed up to the hilt.
>
> There remains the question in relation to the bungalow of what the proportion of Miss Mitchell's beneficial interest should be held to be. This is not an area where the maxim that 'equality is equity' falls to be applied unthinkingly. That is plain from the lesser proportions awarded in both *Grant v Edwards* [1986] Ch 638 and in *Eves v Eves* [1975] 1 WLR 1338. Nevertheless, when account is taken of the full circumstances of this unusual case, and when Miss Mitchell's contribution as mother/helper/unpaid assistant and at times financial supporter to the family prosperity generated by Mr Hammond's dealing activities is judged for its proper effect, it seems right to me that her beneficial interest in the bungalow should be held to be one half.
>
> The next question, arising under the *Lloyds Bank plc v Rosset* formula, is whether there is any property in regard to which an intention to share a beneficial ownership should be imputed to the parties in the absence of any express discussion leading to an agreement or understanding to that effect. Miss Mitchell asserts that there is such a property, namely, the Spanish house. She acknowledges that there was no previous discussion remotely touching upon the terms of its ownership. Useful at times though her activities may have been in Spain during the fulfilment of the Soriano venture, Miss Mitchell's activities generally fell a long way short of justifying any inference of intended proprietary interest.

If the parties purchase a joint interest in the asset without an express declaration of trust concerning their respective interest, the quantification of their interest is dependent on the proportion of their contributions, i.e., the resulting trust solution or the second category of evidence laid down in *Rosset*.

By way of exception, this resulting trust analysis regarding the quantum of interest in the property may be adjusted only if there is evidence of a common intention to share the asset in a different proportion. In order to establish this intention, there is required to be *express discussion* between the parties as to their respective beneficial interests. An uncommunicated intention to share the beneficial interest is insufficient to alter the interest acquired by way of a resulting trust. This was the view put forward by the Court of Appeal in *Springette v Defoe*.

Springette v Defoe [1992] 2 FLR 388, CA

Facts

The parties lived as man and wife in a council house. In 1982, they made a formal offer to purchase the house for £14,445, which represented a discount of 41% because the plaintiff, Miss

Springette (S), had been a council tenant for 11 years or more. They bought the house jointly with the aid of a mortgage of £12,000. By agreement, they each contributed 50% of the mortgage instalments. The balance of the purchase price was provided by S. The legal title was registered in their joint names, but there was no quantification of their interests registered in the Land Registry. During 1985, the relationship between the parties became strained and the defendant (D) left the home. S claimed that she was entitled to a 75% share of the proceeds of sale of the house as represented by her contribution to the purchase. The learned recorder decided that the beneficial interests were shared equally despite the lack of evidence of any discussion concerning this issue. S appealed to the Court of Appeal.

Held

The interests of the parties were determined by reference to the contributions made. There was no evidence which had the effect of varying the interest acquired by way of a resulting trust because there was no discussion between the parties to that effect. Accordingly, the interests were shared on a 75:25 proportion.

> **Dillon LJ:** The common intention must be founded on evidence such as would support a finding that there is an implied or constructive trust for the parties in proportions to the purchase price. The court does not as yet sit, as under a palm tree, to exercise a general discretion to do what the man in the street, on a general overview of the case, might regard as fair.

> [His Lordship then referred to Lord Bridge's judgment in *Rosset* [1990] 1 All ER 111, and continued:]

> It is not enough to establish a common intention which is sufficient to found an implied or constructive trust of land that each of them happened at the same time to have been thinking on the same lines in his or her uncommunicated thoughts, while neither had any knowledge of the thinking of the other.

> Since, therefore, it is clear in the present case that there never was any discussion between the parties about what their respective beneficial interests were to be, they cannot, in my judgment, have had . . . any common intention as to the beneficial ownership of the property. I cannot, therefore, support the conclusion of the recorder. The presumption of a resulting trust is not displaced.

> **Steyn LJ:** Given that no actual common intention to share the property in equal beneficial shares was established, one is driven back to the equitable principle that the shares are presumed to be in proportion 'to the contributions'. If the matter is approached in this way, it seems to me right in principle that the discount of 41% should be regarded as a direct contribution by the woman to the purchase. That is how Bush J, a most experienced judge, approached the matter in *Marsh v Von Sternberg* [1986] 1 FLR 526. And that is how I consider this court should approach the matter.

In *Lightfoot v Lightfoot–Brown* the court decided that the unilateral payment by one party of capital expenses connected with the house was insufficient to establish an interest by way of a constructive trust. There was no discussion to the effect that the payment was intended to represent an interest in the house and no such intention was implied.

Lightfoot v Lightfoot–Brown [2005] All ER (D) 115, (CA)

Facts

The claimant, H, bought out his first wife's share in the matrimonial home. He met the defendant, W, and they began to live together. They later had children and subsequently married. The relationship deteriorated and the parties divorced. The consent order provided that H was required to transfer his interest in the property to W and the latter would pay the mortgage instalments on the property. The parties were later reconciled and continued to live together in the property. H paid the mortgage instalments amounting to £24,000 and made a capital payment of £41,000 on the house. He also paid the cost of improvements to the property amounting to £10,000. The parties considered remarriage, but before this could take place they finally separated. H claimed a beneficial half-share in the property on the ground that there had been an agreement between the parties to transfer the property into their joint names. W denied that there had been any firm agreement to transfer the property in their joint names. They had discussed remarriage and W's belief was that in that event the property would be transferred in their joint names. W denied knowledge of the capital repayment of £41,000. The judge decided, on balance, that W's evidence was to be preferred. The transfer of the property in their joint names was conditional on remarriage that failed to materialise. Subject thereto, the court found that there was no discussion about ownership of the assets. Accordingly H's claim was dismissed. The claimant appealed to the CA.

Held

Dismissing the appeal, there was sufficient evidence to support the decision of the judge. There was no evidence of discussion of a shared interest in the property, except on condition of marriage that did not occur. On the facts the court could not infer an intention to share the ownership of the house.

> **Arden LJ:** In many cases, however, there is no evidence of express discussions, and the intent to share the beneficial interest has to be inferred from the parties' conduct. In this respect the expenditure has to be referrable to the acquisition of the house. See Lord Bridge in *Lloyds Bank v Rossett* [1990] 1 All ER 111.
>
> In addition, the person making the expenditure must show that he acted on the basis of the common intention and did so to his detriment. In the absence of a common intention, no common intention construct-ive trust will arise. Contributions made by the non-property holding party may be relevant for a number of purposes: first, as evidence from which an intention can be inferred; second, as corroboration of direct evidence of intention; third, as evidence that the Claimant has acted in reliance on the intention and, fourth, to quantify the size of the beneficial interest: see *Grant v Edwards* [1986] Ch 638, 655 per Sir Nicolas Browne-Wilkinson VC.
>
> It is in my judgment quite clear that Chadwick LJ in *Oxley v Hiscock* [2004] EWCA Civ 546 did not dispense with the requirement for communication of the common intention when determining whether a common intention constructive trust had arisen. Indeed, the concept of communication of common intention has much in common with the manifestation of intention. An intention to share a beneficial interest in property has to be manifested to give rise to a rival obligation, per Lord Diplock in *Gissing v Gissing* [1971] AC 886.
>
> [After considering the judgment in the High Court, Arden LJ continued] In my judgment it is clear . . . that the judge does not misdirect himself into thinking that he was not required to consider whether a common intention constructive trust could be inferred from the conduct of the parties or into thinking that communica-tion had to be by express words.

In contrast to the three decisions considered above, the Court of Appeal in *McHardy v Warren* decided that once the claimant has established an interest in the property by way of direct contri-butions, the court will take into account all relevant factors in determining the interests of the parties. The conduct of the parties, irrespective of whether discussions took place or not, may be considered as sufficient to create a common understanding of the respective share of each party. Contributions to the purchase price are factors which are taken into account, but they are not decisive as to the quantum of interest acquired by the parties.

McHardy v Warren [1994] 2 FLR 338, CA

Facts

Mr and Mrs Warren (W) purchased their first matrimonial home by a contribution partly financed by Mr W's parents. His parents paid the deposit (£650) on the house as a wedding gift. The house was registered in Mr W's sole name. Two subsequent homes successively purchased by the parties out of the net proceeds of sale of the former homes were likewise put in Mr W's sole name. Mr W then procured a charge on his current home to secure his indebtedness to the plaintiffs, trade creditors. In proceedings to enforce the charge against the Warrens, the plaintiffs claimed that Mrs W was entitled, at best, to an interest equivalent to 8.97% of the value of the house, representing the proportion that 50% of the initial deposit of £650 (the wedding gift) related to the total purchase price of the first home. The learned judge rejected the claim. The claimant appealed to the Court of Appeal.

Held

Upholding the decision of the trial judge, the Court of Appeal decided that Mrs W was entitled to an equal share with Mr W, because this represented the intentions of the parties as reflected by their conduct.

Dillon LJ: To my mind it is the irresistible conclusion that where a parent pays the deposit, either directly to the solicitors or to the bride and groom – it matters not which – on the purchase of their first matrimonial home, it is the intention of all three of them that the bride and groom should have *equal interests in the matrimonial home*, not interests measured by reference to the percentage half the deposit [bears] to the full price, and certainly not an intention that the wife should have no interest at all because the property was put into the sole name of the husband [emphasis added].

Similarly, in *Midland Bank v Cooke,* the Court of Appeal decided that if an intention to share an interest in the matrimonial home had been established by the claimant by reference to direct contributions (second category of evidence as established in *Rosset*), the court has the power to quantify the interests of the parties by reference to the express and implied intentions of the parties. The conduct of the parties relevant to ownership of the property may be given effect, even though there may have been no discussion as to the beneficial interests therein.

Midland Bank plc v Cooke and Another [1995] 4 All ER 562, CA

Facts

H and W married in 1971 and moved into a house which was purchased for £8,500 and conveyed into H's sole name. The purchase was financed by a mortgage of £6,450. The balance was provided from H's savings and a wedding gift of £1,100 from his parents. In 1978, the mortgage was replaced by a general mortgage in favour of the Midland Bank in order to secure H's business overdraft. In 1979, W signed a form agreeing to postpone any present or future right as against the bank. The property was subsequently transferred into the joint names of H and W. There was no discussion between the parties as to their beneficial interests. In 1987, the bank commenced proceedings against H and W for arrears of payments and possession of the property. W defended herself on the ground that her signature on the form was procured by H's undue influence and the bank had knowledge of H's misconduct. W counterclaimed for a declaration that she was entitled to a 50% share in the house. The judge held that the form was signed under undue influence and that W was entitled to a beneficial interest of 6.74% in the property, equivalent to a half share of the wedding gift of £1,100 from H's parents, which was contributed to the purchase price of £8,500. W appealed, claiming that she was entitled to 50% of the value of the house based on her conduct. The bank cross-appealed on the issue of undue influence.

Held

Allowing W's appeal and awarding her a 50% share in the value of the house, the court dismissed the bank's cross-appeal. In accordance with the principles in *Pettitt v Pettitt, Gissing v Gissing* and *Grant v Edwards,* since W had established an interest in the house through direct contributions, the court was entitled to look at all the circumstances in order to give effect to the true intentions of the parties. Accordingly, the court might attribute to the parties an interest in the property which was different from the resulting trust contributions to the purchase price:

Waite LJ [considered the divergent approaches of the Court of Appeal to this question in *Springette v Defoe* [1992] 2 FLR 388 and *McHardy v Warren* [1994] 2 FLR 338 and observed:] I confess that I find the differences of approach in those two cases mystifying. In the one, a strict resulting trust geared to mathematical calculation of the proportion of the purchase price provided by cash contribution is treated as virtually immutable in the absence of express agreement: in the other, a displacement of the cash-related trust by inferred agreement is not only permitted but treated as obligatory. Guidance out of this difficulty is to be found, fortunately, in the passage in the speech of Lord Diplock in *Gissing v Gissing* [1971] AC 886, pp 908–09, where he is dealing with the approach to be adopted by the court when evaluating the proportionate shares of the parties, once it had been established through the direct contributions of the party without legal title, that *some* beneficial interest was intended for both.

The general principle to be derived from *Gissing v Gissing* [1971] AC 886 and *Grant v Edwards* [1986] Ch 638 can, in my judgment, be summarised in this way. When the court is proceeding, in cases like the present, where the partner without legal title has successfully asserted an equitable interest through direct contribution, to determine (in the absence of express evidence of intention) what proportions the parties must be assumed to have intended for their beneficial ownership, the duty of the judge is to undertake a survey of the whole course of dealing between the parties relevant to their ownership and occupation of the property and their sharing of its burdens and advantages. That scrutiny will not confine itself to the limited range of acts of direct contribution of the sort that are needed to found a beneficial interest in the first place. It will take into consideration all conduct which throws light on the question what shares were intended. Only if that search proves inconclusive does the court fall back on the maxim 'equality is equity'.

The court is not bound to deal with the matter on the strict basis of the trust resulting from the cash contribution to the purchase price, and is free to attribute to the parties an intention to share the beneficial interest in some different proportions.

Equity has traditionally been a system which matches established principle to the demands of social change. The mass diffusion of home ownership has been one of the most striking social changes of our own time. There will inevitably be numerous couples, married or unmarried, who have no discussion about ownership and who, perhaps advisedly, make no agreement about it. It would be anomalous, against that background, to create a range of home buyers who were beyond the pale of equity's assistance in formulating a fair presumed basis for the sharing of beneficial title, simply because they had been honest enough to admit that they never gave ownership a thought or reached any agreement about it.

[After referring to the judgments of Dillon and Steyn LJJ in *Springette v Defoe*, Waite LJ distinguished that authority, thus:] . . . they are observations which need to be read in the context of the decision relating to the part-pooling of resources by a middle aged couple already established in life, whose house purchasing arrangements were clearly regarded by the court as having the same formality as if they had been the subject of a joint venture or commercial partnership. I cannot, for my part, believe that it was intended in that case to lay down a principle, applicable to all instances, that absence of express agreement precludes inference of presumed agreement. This impression is confirmed by the subsequent participation of Dillon LJ in the decision in the *McHardy* case [1994] 2 FLR 338.

I would therefore hold that positive evidence that the parties neither discussed nor intended any agreement as to the proportions of their beneficial interest does not preclude the court, on general equitable principles, from inferring one.

In *Drake v Whipp*, Peter Gibson LJ classified the trusts involved in this context into two categories, resulting and constructive trusts. A resulting trust is created by reference to the contributions made by the parties towards the acquisition of the home. The quantum of the beneficial interest is measured by reference to these contributions. The constructive trust, on the other hand, arises by reference to the conduct of the parties, in particular, whether evidence exists of a common understanding between the parties to share the beneficial interest and the claimant relies on such agreement to his or her detriment. The court decided that it is entitled to adopt a 'broad brush' approach in determining the parties' respective shares under the constructive trust. It is entitled to look at the parties' entire course of conduct in evaluating their respective shares. This may involve direct and indirect contributions in money or money's worth and any other evidence of intention of the parties. Accordingly, in the absence of evidence that the claimant intended his or her share to be limited by contributions (resulting trust), the court is entitled to consider the parties' conduct (constructive trust) and quantify their interests.

Drake v Whipp [1996] 1 FLR 826, CA

Facts

Mrs Drake and Mr Whipp purchased a barn for conversion into a dwelling house. Mrs Drake provided 40% of the total purchase price and Mr Whipp provided the remainder. Both parties contributed to the conversion work in labour and financially (although Mr Whipp provided the bulk of the financial resources to effect the conversion). Mrs Drake also contributed to the costs of running the house. Mr Whipp formed a new relationship and Mrs Drake brought an action for a declaration of her share in the matrimonial home. The judge decided that Mrs Drake's share stood at 19.4% of the value of the house by way of a resulting trust. This was based on her contributions to the initial purchase and conversion costs.

Held

The court allowed the appeal and awarded Mrs Drake a one-third share in the property by way of the constructive trust:

> **Peter Gibson LJ:** A potent source of confusion, to my mind, has been suggestions that it matters not whether the terminology used is that of the constructive trust, to which the intention, actual or imputed, of the parties is crucial, or that of the resulting trust, which operates as a presumed intention of the contributing party in the absence of rebutting evidence of actual intention. I, therefore, like Waite LJ in *Midland Bank v Cooke and Another* [1995] 2 FLR 915, p 916, welcome the announcement earlier this year that the Law Commission is to examine the property rights of home sharers (Item 8, Sixth Programme of Law Reform, Law Com No 234).
>
> In the present case the judge has found what was the common intention of the parties as to their beneficial shares, but the only direct evidence in support of that finding was Mr Whipp's evidence as to his own intention. The judge appears to have imputed the like intention to Mrs Drake although there is nothing in her evidence to support it. Further, the judge refused to take into account the contributions of the parties by way of their labour, being unquantified in monetary terms, and similarly Mrs Drake's other contributions to the household were ignored. No doubt this was because he was not invited to consider the matter on the basis of a constructive trust.
>
> In my judgment, the judge's finding on common intention cannot stand in the absence of any evidence that Mrs Drake intended her share to be limited to her direct contributions to the acquisition and conversion costs. I would approach the matter more broadly, looking at the parties' entire course of conduct together. I would take into account not only those direct contributions, but also the fact that Mr Whipp and Mrs Drake together purchased the property with the intention that it should be their home, that they both contributed their labour in 70:30% proportions, that they had a joint account out of which the costs of conversion were met, but that that account was largely fed by his earnings, and that she paid for the food and some other household expenses and took care of the housekeeping for them both. I note that, whilst it was open to Mrs Drake to argue at the trial for a constructive trust and for a 50% share, she opted to rely solely on a resulting trust and a 40.1% share. In all the circumstances I would hold that her fair share should be one third.

Note

In *Chan v Leung* [2002] EWCA Civ 1075, the Court of Appeal decided that the claimant had successfully made out the ingredients of a constructive trust claim, namely, common intention, reliance and detriment, and awarded the claimant a 51% interest in the house.

Question

To what extent have the courts clarified the species of trusts that are created in respect of family assets?

In *Le Foe v Le Foe*, the High Court analysed the lacuna in Lord Bridge's judgment in *Lloyds Bank v Rossett* (see p 244) concerning 'indirect contributions' and explained that, exceptionally, indirect contributions to the purchase price of the asset will entitle such a party to a share.

Le Foe v Le Foe [2001] All ER (D) 325, HC

Facts

H and W were married on 2 April 1959. They separated, over 40 years later, on 25 November 1999. During this time a number of properties were acquired in succession with the aid of mortgages in H's name. Both parties worked, although H earned more than W. The court found that the family economy depended for its function on W's earnings. Between 1995 and 1999 W made substantial contributions from her resources, including an inheritance, to pay, *inter alia*, mortgage arrears and future payments. In 1999, H embarked on a deceitful subterfuge to strip the majority of the equity out of the matrimonial home in order to leave W for a much younger woman. He borrowed, by way of a Woolwich mortgage, more than he could possibly repay. Subsequently, H fell into arrears with the repayments and a suspended possession order was obtained. W presented a petition for a judicial separation and ancillary relief. The Woolwich claimed, *inter alia*, possession of the property. One of the questions in issue concerned W's interest in the matrimonial home.

Held

The court decided that by virtue of W's indirect contributions to the mortgage, it was entitled to infer that the parties commonly intended that W should have a beneficial interest in the former matrimonial home. Taking into account the conduct of the parties and in particular the capital contributions made by W from 1995, the court decided that they commonly intended that W should have a 50% share in the property:

> **Nicholas Mostyn QC:** [Referred to the two guidelines laid down by Lord Bridge in *Lloyds Bank v Rossett*, and continued:] It is pertinent to note that in the final sentence of the passage I have quoted Lord Bridge does not state the proposition he advances in absolute terms. In my view what Lord Bridge is saying is that in the second class of case to which he is adverting, namely where there is no positive evidence of an express agreement between the parties as to how the equity is to be shared, and where the court has fallen back on inferring their common intention from the course of their conduct, *it will only be exceptionally that conduct other than direct contributions to the purchase price, either in cash to the deposit, or by contribution to the mortgage instalments, will suffice to draw the necessary inference of a common intention to share the equity.*

> The next question is whether an indirect contribution to the mortgage will suffice to draw the necessary inference. I do not believe that in using the words 'direct contributions' Lord Bridge meant to exclude the situation which obtains here. In *Gissing v Gissing* [1971] AC 886, Lord Diplock referred to just such a case. He said (at pp 910–11):

> There is no suggestion that the wife's efforts or her earnings made it possible for the husband to raise the initial loan or the mortgage or that the relieving of the husband from the expense of buying clothing for herself and for their son was undertaken in order to enable him the better to meet the mortgage instalments or to repay the loan . . .

> Mr Wilson argued that because Lord Diplock was not addressing the scenario there mentioned he could not draw any conclusions as to what his decision would have been if he had. But I believe that Lord Diplock is saying quite clearly that if that was the situation, which I find to be the case here, then such would suffice to draw the necessary inference.

> The same point was addressed by May LJ in *Burns v Burns* [1984] FLR 216. [The learned judge considered May LJ's judgment and continued:]

> Mr Wilson has pointed to the fact that May LJ addresses indirect contributions to the mortgage only in the context of the claimant having made an initial direct contribution to the deposit. He says that in the next scenario, where that party has made no such contribution, the reference is only to direct contributions to the mortgage. I agree that May LJ does not directly address the position that we have here; namely where there was no initial cash contribution but only an indirect contribution to the mortgage. But I believe that a fair reading of his judgment is that such a state of affairs should suffice to enable the necessary inference to be drawn. Otherwise these cases would be decided by reference to mere accidents of fortune, being the arbitrary allocation of financial responsibility as between the parties.

> I therefore conclude that by virtue of her indirect contributions to the mortgage I am entitled to infer that the parties commonly intended that W should have a beneficial interest in the former matrimonial home.

> I agree that absent that state of affairs I could not draw the necessary inference from the sole fact of W's role in enhancing the quantum of the cash money supplied. But when coupled with W's indirect contributions to the mortgage I am reinforced in my view that the parties plainly held the unexpressed common intention that W should have a beneficial interest in the former matrimonial home.

> Having decided the question as a matter of principle I now turn to the issue of quantification of the beneficial interest. When I survey the whole course of dealings between H and W between 1971 and 1999, having regard, in particular, to the capital contributions made by W since 1995, I have been left with no doubt at all that they commonly intended that she should have a 50% share in the property.

Dixon, M, 'A case too far' [1997] Conv 66

Dixon takes the view that the approach of Waite LJ in *Midland Bank v Cooke* allows quantification on the basis of a presumed, fictitious intention. The parties claiming an interest in the matrimonial home through payments may trigger an interest larger than the actual payments. This is justifiable on the basis that 'the payments are merely evidence of some real common intention which requires the abandonment of the strict resulting trust option'. In addition, the pronouncement by Waite LJ that the parties need not have actually agreed on the extent of the enlarged share suggests that the court may be tempted to manufacture an agreement as to the quantum of the interest in the home. Indeed, Dixon observes that the court may:

> ... find such an agreement (a 'phantom interest consensus') not only when there is no evidence of the parties' intentions, but even where there is positive evidence that they did not agree.

Moreover, the statutory discretion created by s 37 of the Matrimonial Proceedings and Property Act 1970 could have been used by the claimant to acquire a sizeable share in the property 'without any violence to the principles of resulting and constructive trusts'.

Dunn, A, 'Whipping up resulting and constructive trusts' [1997] Conv 467

Dunn supports the view adopted by Peter Gibson LJ in *Drake v Whipp*. The distinction between constructive and resulting trusts remains crucial when determining beneficial interests. Where the courts cannot detect a common intention as to beneficial ownership relied on by the claimant to his or her detriment (sufficient to found a constructive trust), a resulting trust may be inferred from financial contribution towards the acquisition of the property. However, the resulting trust will only apply where there is no finding of a common intention. The two types of trusts therefore involve the judge in examining different aspects of evidence. Further, under the constructive trust, the courts have a discretion to ascertain the extent of the beneficial share of the claimant. The resulting trust, on the other hand, is more formulaic, and the share of the claimant will be in direct proportion to the amount contributed to the acquisition of the property.

In the case of married couples (and those registered under the Civil Partnership Act 2004), the same principles as outlined above apply in order to ascertain the interests of the parties in family assets. In addition, under ss 23–25 of the Matrimonial Causes Act 1973, the court is given wide discretionary powers to declare or vary the interests of spouses (and civil partners) in family assets on a divorce, decree of nullity or judicial separation. An analysis of these provisions is beyond the scope of this book.

Other jurisdictions

Australia

In Australia the courts have adopted the test of 'unconscionability' as the basis of the constructive trust. This approach required the court to conduct an objective assessment of the parties' conduct rather than a search for their 'common intention'. The effect has been that the court is entitled to evaluate whether, as a joint venture, it would be unfair for the defendant to deny the claimant a share, or an enlarged share, in the property. However, this flexible concept is capable of leading to differing judicial interpretations and may lead to the increase of unpredictable outcomes.

Canada

The Canadian model is based on principles of 'unjust enrichment'. This is a species of the 'remedial constructive trust'. The claimant is required to establish that, but for a remedy, the defendant would be enriched without any legal justification to the prejudice of the claimant. 'Enrichment' has been interpreted broadly to include domestic duties, repairs and maintenance as well as direct and indirect financial contributions to the purchase of the property. The 'prejudice' or 'deprivation' by the claimant may be established by proving a link between the benefit acquired by the defendant and the contribution by the claimant. The 'injustice' may arise as a result of the claimant's reasonable expectation of receiving an interest in the property.

New Zealand

In New Zealand the approach involves focusing on the 'reasonable expectation' of the parties. The claimant is required to establish that the parties had a reasonable expectation that he (claimant) will acquire an interest in the property by virtue of his contributions. The contributions have been interpreted broadly as including domestic duties as well as direct and indirect financial and non-financial contributions to the acquisition or improvement of the property.

It may be apparent that the solution adopted in Australia, Canada and New Zealand is a variation on the English law notion of proprietary estoppel. However, the broader approaches in these jurisdictions give rise to a degree of uncertainty and unpredictability as to the outcome in individual cases.

Quantification of beneficial interest – a fair share?

The issue here is the extent of the parties' beneficial interest in the property. The solution is dependent on evidence of what the parties agreed at the time of the acquisition. Where there is no evidence of discussion between the parties as to the amount of the share that each may have in the property, the court is still required to determine the issue. In these circumstances the court is entitled to make a declaration as to what it considers to be fair, having regard to the whole course of dealing between the parties. On this issue the Court of Appeal in *Oxley v Hiscock* identified three judicial approaches to quantification.

(i)   The approach adopted by Lord Diplock in *Gissing v Gissing* [1971] AC 886 and Nourse LJ in *Stokes v Anderson* [1991] 1 FLR 391, the respective shares of the parties are not to be determined at the time of the acquisition of the property but are left to be determined when their relationship comes to an end or the property sold. Thus, a complete picture of the whole course of dealing is available to the court in order to determine what is fair.

(ii) The approach suggested by Waite LJ in *Midland Bank v Cooke* [1995] 2 FLR 915. The court undertakes a survey of the whole course of dealing between the parties in order to determine what proportions the parties must be assumed to have intended from the outset for their beneficial ownership. Thus evidence of what the parties intended at the time of the acquisition may be inferred from the conduct of the parties while they were living together.

(iii) The suggestion put forward by Browne-Wilkinson V.C. in *Grant v Edwards* [1986] 1 Ch 638 and approved by Walker LJ in *Yaxley v Gotts* [2000] Ch 162. The court in its discretion makes such an order as the circumstances require in order to give effect to the beneficial interest in the property of the one party, the existence of which the party with the legal title is estopped from denying.

In *Oxley* the Court expressed a preference for the third approach. The second approach was capable of leading to an artificial or fictional intention of the parties. Likewise, the same point could be made of the first approach, i.e. at the time of the acquisition the parties' intention was that their shares should be left for late determination.

Oxley v Hiscock [2004] EWCA Civ 546

Facts
The claimant and defendant had lived together as an unmarried couple. In April 1991, 35 Dickens Close was purchased as a home for the claimant, defendant and the claimant's children by a

former marriage. The property was purchased in the name of the defendant for £127,000. The purchase price was funded by (i) a building society advance of £30,000, (ii) the net proceeds of the claimant's former house amounting to £61,000 (of which £36,600 was provided by the claimant and £25,200 was contributed by the defendant) and (iii) the balance of £35,500 (approximately) by the defendant from his own savings. The relationship came to an end in 2001. At this time the mortgage had been paid off and the property was sold by the defendant for £232,000. The claimant brought proceedings against the defendant pursuant to s 14 of the Trusts of Land and Appointment of Trustees Act 1996 for a declaration that the proceeds of sale were held by the defendant upon trust for the claimant and defendant in equal shares. The judge found that there was no express discussion between the parties as to their respective share in the property, but decided that there was in effect a pooling of resources (although there was no joint bank account) to such an extent that the court may infer that the parties intended to share the asset equally. Accordingly, the judge ordered an equal division of the proceeds of sale. The defendant appealed to the Court of Appeal.

Held

Allowing the appeal on the ground that the judge had misdirected herself by failing to follow established law and had given insufficient weight to the contribution by the defendant. He had directly contributed £60,700 to the purchase price of the house, which was substantially greater than the claimant's contribution of £36,300. Accordingly, a fair division of the proceeds of sale would be 40% to the claimant and 60% to the defendant.

> **Chadwick LJ:** (After reviewing the leading authorities, declared) I have referred . . . to 'cases of this nature'. By that, I mean cases in which the common features are: (i) the property is bought as a home for a couple who, although not married, intend to live together as man and wife; (ii) each of them makes some financial contribution to the purchase; (iii) the property is purchased in the sole name of one of them; and (iv) there is no express declaration of trust. In those circumstances the first question is whether there is evidence from which to infer a common intention, communicated by each to the other, that each shall have a beneficial share in the property. In many such cases – of which the present is an example – there will have been some discussion between the parties at the time of the purchase which provides the answer to that question. Those are cases within the first of Lord Bridge's categories in *Rosset's* case [1990] 1 All ER 1111. In other cases – where the evidence is that the matter was not discussed at all – an affirmative answer will readily be inferred from the fact that each has made a financial contribution. Those are cases within Lord Bridge's second category. And, if the answer to the first question is that there was a common intention, communicated to each other, that each should have a beneficial share in the property, then the party who does not become the legal owner will be held to have acted to his or her detriment in making a financial contribution to the purchase in reliance on the common intention.
>
> In those circumstances, the second question to be answered in cases of this nature is 'what is the extent of the parties' respective beneficial interests in the property?' Again, in many such cases, the answer will be provided by evidence of what they said and did at the time of the acquisition. But, in a case where there is no evidence of any discussion between them as to the amount of the share which each was to have – and even in a case where the evidence is that there was no discussion on that point – the question still requires an answer. It must now be accepted that (at least in this court and below) the answer is that each is entitled to that share which the court considers fair having regard to the whole course of dealing between them in relation to the property. And, in that context, 'the whole course of dealing between them in relation to the property' includes the arrangements which they make from time to time in order to meet the outgoings (for example, mortgage contributions, council tax and utilities, repairs, insurance and housekeeping) which have to be met if they are to live in the property as their home.
>
> As the cases show, the courts have not found it easy to reconcile that final step with a traditional, property-based, approach. It was rejected, in unequivocal terms, by Dillon LJ in *Springette v Defoe* [1992] 2 FCR 561 at 567 when he said that: 'The court does not as yet sit, as under a palm tree, to exercise a general discretion to do what the man in the street, on a general overview of the case, might regard as fair.' Three strands of reasoning can be identified. (1) That suggested by Lord Diplock in *Gissing v Gissing* [1970] 2 All ER 780 at 793, [1971] AC 886 at 909 and adopted by Nourse LJ in *Stokes v Anderson* [1991] FCR 539 at 543. The parties are taken to have agreed at the time of the acquisition of the property that their respective shares are not to be quantified then, but are

left to be determined when their relationship comes to an end or the property is sold on the basis of what is then fair having regard to the whole course of dealing between them. The court steps in to determine what is fair because, when the time came for that determination, the parties were unable to agree. (2) That suggested by Waite LJ in *Midland Bank plc v Cooke* [1995] 4 All ER 562 at 574. The court undertakes a survey of the whole course of dealing between the parties 'relevant to their ownership and occupation of the property and their sharing of its burdens and advantages' in order to determine 'what proportions the parties must be assumed to have intended [from the outset] for their beneficial ownership'. On that basis the court treats what has taken place while the parties have been living together in the property as evidence of what they intended at the time of the acquisition. (3) That suggested by Browne-Wilkinson V-C, in *Grant v Edwards* [1986] 2 All ER 426 at 439, [1986] Ch 638 at 656, 657 and approved by Robert Walker LJ in *Yaxley v Gotts* [2000] 1 All ER 711 at 722, [2000] Ch 162 at 177. The court makes such order as the circumstances require in order to give effect to the beneficial interest in the property of the one party, the existence of which the other party (having the legal title) is estopped from denying. That, I think, is the analysis which underlies the decision of this court in *Drake v Whipp* (see [1996] 2 FCR 296 at 302).

For my part, I find the reasoning adopted by this court in *Cooke*'s case to be the least satisfactory of the three strands. It seems to me artificial – and an unnecessary fiction – to attribute to the parties a common intention that the extent of their respective beneficial interests in the property should be fixed as from the time of the acquisition, in circumstances in which all the evidence points to the conclusion that, at the time of the acquisition, they had given no thought to the matter. The same point can be made – although with less force – in relation to the reasoning that, at the time of the acquisition, their common intention was that the amount of the respective shares should be left for later determination. But it can be said that, if it were their common intention that each should have some beneficial interest in the property – which is the hypothesis upon which it becomes necessary to answer the second question – then, in the absence of evidence that they gave any thought to the amount of their respective shares, the necessary inference is that they must have intended that question would be answered later on the basis of what was then seen to be fair. But, as I have said, I think that the time has come to accept that there is no difference in outcome, in cases of this nature, whether the true analysis lies in constructive trust or in proprietary estoppel.

This must, I think, be seen as a case where there is no evidence of any discussion between the parties as to the amount of the share which each was to have. And, on that basis, the judge asked herself the wrong question. She should not have sought, by reference to the conduct of the parties while they were living together at 35 Dickens Close, to determine what intention both were then 'evincing' – unless, by that, she was able to find a common intention, communicated to each other, to determine, definitively, the shares which had been left undetermined at the time of acquisition.

In my view to declare that the parties were entitled in equal shares would be unfair to Mr Hiscock. It would give insufficient weight to the fact that his direct contribution to the purchase price (£60,700) was substantially greater than that of Mrs Oxley (£36,300). On the basis of the judge's finding that there was in this case 'a classic pooling of resources' and conduct consistent with an intention to share the burden of the property (by which she must, I think, have meant the outgoings referable to ownership and cohabitation), it would be fair to treat them as having made approximately equal contributions to the balance of the purchase price (£30,000). Taking that into account with their direct contributions at the time of the purchase, I would hold that a fair division of the proceeds of sale of the property would be 60% to Mr Hiscock and 40% to Mrs Oxley.

Law Commission

The Law Commission in its discussion paper, 'Sharing Homes' (2002), reviewed the current legal principles that are applicable in determining property rights in family assets namely, resulting trusts, constructive trusts and proprietary estoppel. It criticised the current law as 'not ideally suited to the typical informality of those sharing homes' and declared that:

- Much depends on what the court identifies to be the common intention of the parties. This can be a somewhat unrealistic exercise, as people do not tend to think about their home in such legalistic terms.

- Although certain contributions towards the acquisition of the home can give rise to an interest in it, it is not very clear where the line is drawn between contributions which count and contributions which do not. (For instance, it is accepted that payment of the mortgage instalments is normally sufficient to obtain an interest, but it remains doubtful whether regular payment of household bills which enables the owner to pay the mortgage will suffice.)

- It does not seem to be the case that extensive work in and around the home which may include looking after children of a relationship – will result in the acquisition of a share.

- Quantifying the share is extremely difficult – and has led to decisions which are inconsistent and difficult to reconcile.

- The uncertainty of the law can lead to lengthy and therefore costly litigation.

The Commission stated that it was not making specific proposals for legislation and concluded thus:

- We have concluded that it is not possible to devise a statutory scheme for the determination of shares in the shared home which can operate fairly and evenly across all the diverse circumstances which are now to be encountered.

- It is essential that all those who are living together are positively encouraged to investigate the legal consequences of doing so and to make express written arrangements setting out clearly what they intend their rights to be. This is best achieved by executing a declaration of trust.

- Where no express declaration of trust has been executed, we believe that the courts must continue to ask themselves what the parties' intentions were. There are some useful reforms which can be made by the courts themselves taking a broader view of the kinds of contributions from which they might infer 'common intention'. For instance, where a person who is living with the home owner has paid the household bills and thereby enabled the home owner to pay the instalments due under the mortgage, that should normally be sufficient to enable the courts to infer that the person was intended to obtain a share in the home. We also believe that it would be more just if courts adopted a broader approach to quantifying the value of the share.

- We accept that marriage [including registered civil partnerships] is a status deserving of special treatment. However, we have identified, in the course of this project, a wider need for the law to recognise and to respond to the increasing diversity of living arrangements in this country. We believe that further consideration should be given to the adoption – necessarily by legislation – of broader based approaches to personal relationships, such as . . . the imposition of legal rights and obligations on individuals who are or have been involved in a relationship outside marriage.

- It is not appropriate for the Law Commission to attempt to define a status which would lead to the vesting of rights and obligations. To do so would not only be well outside the remit of this project, it would also take it outside its function as a law reform body in requiring it to answer very difficult questions of social policy which are essentially matters for Government.

- The Law Commission would be prepared, if asked, to contribute to any further process of consideration of reform in this area in any way which is appropriate given its role as a body concerned with law reform.

Improvements under s 37 of the Matrimonial Proceedings and Property Act 1970

Under this section, spouses including registered civil partners under the Civil Partnership Act 2004 (but not unmarried couples), who contribute, in a substantial way, in money or money's worth to the improvement of real or personal property in which either or both of them have a beneficial interest may enjoy a share, or an enlarged share, in the asset. The court decides whether a contribution is substantial or not by having regard to all the circumstances of the case.

Matrimonial Proceedings and Property Act 1970, s 37

It is hereby declared that where a husband or wife [or registered civil partners] contributes in money or money's worth to the improvement of real or personal property in which or in the proceeds of sale of which either or both of them has or have a beneficial interest, the husband or wife so contributing shall, if the contribution is of a substantial nature and subject to any agreement between them to the contrary express or implied, be treated as having then acquired by virtue of his or her contribution a share or enlarged share, as the case may be, in that beneficial interest of such an extent as may have been then agreed or, in default of such agreement, as may seem in all the circumstances just to any court before which the question of the existence or extent of the beneficial interest of the husband or wife arises (whether in proceedings between them or in any other proceedings).

Note
Section 37 of the 1970 Act is applicable only to married persons or registered civil partners. Unmarried persons who make contributions in similar circumstances may only rely on the common law rules.

Question
How far has s 37 of the Matrimonial Proceedings and Property Act 1970 improved the position of married couples and registered civil partners in respect of claims to family assets?

Joint bank accounts

Where two or more individuals open a joint bank account, so that the legal title to the account is vested in their joint names, the question that often arises concerns the equitable ownership of the funds in the account. In the absence of any express intentions of the parties, the court will construe the surrounding circumstances in order to ascertain the intentions of the parties. If the funds are paid into the account by one party and the circumstances are such that the account was opened for the convenience of that party, a resulting trust of the funds in the account will arise in favour of that party. The same rule applies to sums withdrawn from the account. But if the account was treated as a 'joint enterprise' comprised of a pooling of the resources of all the parties, then a joint tenancy of the funds in the account in favour of all of parties might arise. The corollary to this principle is that a withdrawal of funds by one party remains the property of that party.

The general rule concerning ownership of funds in joint bank accounts was stated by Stamp J in *Re Bishop*.

Re Bishop [1965] Ch 450, HC

Stamp J: Where a husband and wife open a joint account at a bank on terms that cheques may be drawn on the account by either of them, then, in my judgment, in the absence of facts or circumstances which indicate that the account was intended, or was kept, for some specific or limited purpose, each spouse can draw upon it not only for the benefit of both spouses but for his or her own benefit. Each spouse, in drawing money out of the account, is to be treated as doing so with the authority of the other and, in my judgment, if one of the spouses purchases a chattel for his own benefit or an investment in his or her own name, that chattel or investment belongs to the person in whose name it is purchased or invested: for in such a case there is, in my judgment, no equity in the other spouse to displace the legal ownership of the one in whose name the investment is purchased. What is purchased is not to be regarded as purchased out of a fund belonging to the spouses in the proportions in which they contribute to the account or in equal proportions, but out of a pool or fund of which they were, at law and in equity, joint tenants. It also follows that if one of the spouses draws on the account to make a purchase in the joint names of the spouses, the property purchased, since it is purchased in joint names, is, *prima facie* joint property and there is no equity to displace the joint legal ownership. There is, in my judgment, no room for any presumption which would constitute the joint holders as trustees for the parties in equal or some other shares.

In *Steele v Steele*, the High Court recently affirmed the principle as stated by Stamp J in *Re Bishop*.

Steele v Steele [2001] All ER (D) 50, HC

Facts
The parties to the proceedings were formerly husband (defendant) and wife (claimant). After their marriage in 1988, the wife's bank account was transferred into their joint names. Either of the account holders was entitled to sign cheques, which did not need to be counter-signed by the other. In practice, the joint account was operated by the wife alone. The claimant alleged that in 1991 she had paid £50,440 out of her own money from the account for the benefit of her husband,

including the discharge of his liability to maintain and educate two children from his former marriage.

Held

The claimant was not entitled to recover the sum spent for the benefit of her husband. Where there had been a pooling of resources in a joint bank account to such an extent that withdrawals might be treated as done with the consent of the other, neither account holder had a right of recoupment from the other. In this case, the fact that the claimant made the withdrawal emphasised her express consent.

Question
What is the nature of the interest of a joint account holder?

DATE OF VALUATION

Having ascertained that the claimant has an interest in the house, the value of that interest is ascertained at the time the property is sold. Accordingly, any increases or decreases in the value of the property are taken into consideration. If a party remains in occupation paying the mortgage, rates and other outgoings, he or she is credited with these expenses. Conversely, the party in occupation is debited with occupation rent for using the premises partly owned by the other.

Gordon v Douce [1983] 1 WLR 563, CA

Facts

The claimant (female) and defendant (male) co-habited with each other between 1963 and 1980 and had two children. In 1977, a house was bought and conveyed in the sole name of the defendant. In 1980, the defendant left the home but the claimant continued to occupy the premises with the children. The defendant conceded that the house should remain the home of the claimant and the children and ought not be sold while the children still lived there. The claimant petitioned the court for a declaration that she was entitled to a half share in the house and an order that the defendant should convey the property in their joint names. The trial judge decided that the claimant was entitled to a one quarter share in the house, valued at the time of the separation in 1980, and ordered the defendant to convey the property in their joint names.

Held

There was no hard and fast rule that the interests of unmarried couples are to be valued at the time of the separation. Having regard to the reason for the acquisition of the home, the purpose had not come to an end. The claimant' s share ought to be valued at the time of the sale:

> **Fox LJ:** I now come to the second question, the date at which the shares are to be valued. *Prima facie* if persons are entitled to property in aliquot shares as tenants in common under a trust for sale, the value of their respective shares must be determined at the date when the property is sold, but that may have to give way to circumstances. For example, one of the parties may buy out the other, in which case the value of that party's share may have to be determined at a different date. Thus, in *Bernard v Josephs* [1982] Ch 391, to which I have referred, Lord Denning MR said, p 400:
>
>> After ascertaining the shares, the next problem arises when it is to be turned into money. Usually one of the parties stays in the house, paying the mortgage instalments and the rates and other outgoings. The house also increases in value greatly owing to inflation. None of that alters the shares of the parties in the house itself. But it does mean that when the house is sold – or the one buys the other out – there have to be many adjustments made.
>
> *Bernard v Josephs* was a mistress case in which the judge held that the parties were entitled in equal shares. The relationship broke up in 1976 and the woman left the house. The man stayed in the house and subsequently in 1978 he married. He was still living in the house with his wife at the hearing of the appeal in March 1982. The judge made an order for sale. The Court of Appeal upheld the judge's decision as to the shares of the parties. The court decided that it would be a hardship on Mr Josephs and his new wife if they were compelled to leave

the house to enable it to be sold, without an opportunity to buy the plaintiff out. Accordingly the court ordered that the property be sold but the order was not to be enforced if Mr Josephs paid £6,000 to Miss Bernard, the plaintiff, within four months, in return for which she should transfer all her share in the property to him. It is clear that £6,000 was calculated as being the value of Miss Bernard's share at the date of the hearing of the appeal: see the judgment of Griffiths LJ, p 406.

I see no reason, in the circumstances, why the valuation of the plaintiff's share should be at the date of separation. The plaintiff may make expenditure on the property to enable the children and herself to live there, which will have to be taken into account as between the plaintiff and the defendant at a later date. As a matter of law it seems to me that there is no rule which would have compelled the judge to decide that valuation must be at the date of separation. If he regarded himself as exercising discretion (and I doubt if he did), I see no reason to suppose that he took into account the very important circumstances that the purpose of the trust had not been determined. In my opinion there was no good reason in the present case for directing the valuation to be at the date of separation.

In *Turton v Turton*, the court endorsed the principle laid down in *Gordon v Douce*.

Turton v Turton [1987] 3 WLR 622, CA

Facts

The defendant and claimant lived together as man and wife. In 1972, a house was bought for £8,500 which was conveyed in the joint names of the parties as joint tenants, subject to an express trust for sale for themselves as joint tenants beneficially. The defendant paid £3,000 and the balance of the purchase price was raised by way of a mortgage. The claimant made no contributions to the acquisition of the house. The joint tenancy was subsequently severed. It was conceded that the express declaration of trust was definitive of the plaintiff's interest in the house. The parties separated in 1975, but the defendant remained in the house. The claimant sought a declaration that she held an equal share in the house and an order for sale. The county court judge made the declaration and ordered that the claimant's share be valued in 1975, the date of separation. The claimant appealed.

Held

The court allowed the appeal on the ground that the half share interest of the claimant might be valued only on the date of the realisation of the asset:

Kerr LJ: Unless there is some express declaration or agreement to the effect that the parties' respective beneficial shares are to be valued at the time of their separation if and when this should occur, there could never be any sufficient ground for attributing any such intention to them merely by implication from the circumstances. In the result, therefore, the parties' beneficial interests would always have to be regarded in the normal way under a trust for sale, with the effect that they would endure until such time as the property is sold, and that they will then attach to the proceeds of sale. I can see no basis in any event, by the exercise of any discretionary power, for cutting off the effect of the trust at some earlier point in time. The parties' separation will no doubt indicate that the purpose of the implied or constructive trust – to provide a joint home for them both – has failed. But this would merely trigger off a demand for a sale, as in *Bernard v Joseph* [1982] Ch 391. It would not give rise to any discretion, in subsequent proceedings to determine the parties' respective interests, to impose a valuation of these interests retrospectively by reference to the value of the property at that particular time.

Question

When may the interest of a party in family assets be valued?

REALISATION OF THE ASSET

Section 14 of the Trusts of Land and Appointment of Trustees Act 1996 enacted a means of resolving disputes concerning trusts of land. The dispute may be between the trustees themselves, or between the trustees and beneficiaries or, indeed, between third parties (such as creditors) and those interested under the trust. Section 14 of the 1996 Act repeals and replaces s 30 of the Law of Property Act 1925. The section declares that any person interested in the trust property (including the trustees of land) may apply to the court for an order relating to the exercise of the trustees' functions or declaring the extent of the beneficial interests. The application may relate to the exercise of the trustees' powers or duties, such as consultation or obtaining consents. The jurisdiction of the court, as enacted in s 14(a), is sufficiently wide so as to enable the court to authorise the trustees to carry out their duties in a manner which would otherwise constitute a breach of trust, for example, to relieve the trustees of any obligation to obtain the consent of, or to consult, any person. But the court has no power under this section to deal with the appointment and removal of trustees.

The court is directed in s 15 of the 1996 Act to have regard to a number of factors when deciding an application under s 14. These are:

(a) the intentions of the settlor;

(b) the purposes for which the property subject to the trust is held;

(c) the welfare of any minor who occupies or might reasonably be expected to occupy any land subject to the trust as his home;

(d) the interests of the mortgagee of any beneficiary;

(e) in the case of an application relating to the beneficiary's right to occupy under s 13, the circumstances and wishes of each of the beneficiaries entitled to occupy;

(f) in all other cases, except conveying the land to beneficiaries absolutely entitled, the circumstances and wishes of the adult beneficiaries entitled to possession.

(On an application by the trustee-in-bankruptcy of a co-owner, see p 265 below.)

Decisions made under the predecessor to s 14 may afford some guidance as to the interpretation of s 14. The starting point, under the now obsolete s 30 of the Law of Property Act 1925, was to see whether the object or underlying purpose of the trust had been fulfilled, and whether a sale would produce inequitable consequences.

In *Buchanan-Wollaston's Conveyance* [1939] Ch 738, a deed was executed by the co-owners which indicated the purpose of the purchase of the land, and they added that the land would not be dealt with except with the unanimous agreement of the trustees. This was sufficient to prevent a sale. In *Jones v Challenger* [1961] 1 QB 176, the house was bought as a matrimonial home and a sale was therefore ordered when the wife divorced her husband.

Before the 1996 Act was passed, the court was required to balance the interests of minors against the interests of the other parties interested in the land. In *Williams v Williams* [1976] Ch 278, the court refused to order a sale when a family home was bought and the wife remained in the home with her four children, despite a divorce from her husband.

The interests of the mortgagees are required to be balanced as against the interests of minors and co-owners. Under s 30 of the Law of Property Act 1925, the approach adopted by the courts was to regard the interests of the creditors as prevailing over the interests of others, except in 'exceptional circumstances'. In *Re Holliday* [1981] Ch 405, the court deferred a sale of a house for five years when an application for a sale was made at the instance of the trustee in bankruptcy of the husband. The husband became estranged from his wife, who was left to occupy the house with her three children. The husband subsequently became bankrupt. In many other cases the court has ordered a sale at the instance of the trustee in bankruptcy. In *Re Citro* [1991] Ch 142 (see p 265 below), the Court of Appeal stated that the fact that the wife, with young children, is faced with eviction on an application by the husband's trustee in bankruptcy is not to be considered an 'exceptional circumstance'. This issue is now dealt with under the Insolvency Act 1986 (see p 265 below). In *Abbey National v Moss* [1994] 1 FLR 307, the Court of Appeal decided that no distinction ought to be made, in the principles applicable in this context, between a trustee in bankruptcy and a chargee of the land. However, the court decided that the principle in *Citro* is that, since bankruptcy vested the share of the bankrupt's interest in the trustee in bankruptcy, this event has the effect of terminating the co-ownership which was the purpose of the purchase. In *Abbey National v Moss*, Mrs Moss transferred the matrimonial home, following the death of her husband, into the joint names of herself and daughter. The purpose of the transfer was to simplify the transfer arrangements to her daughter on the death of Mrs Moss. Mrs Moss had intended to spend the rest of her life in the house. The daughter forged Mrs Moss's signature and secured a mortgage on the house. The daughter later left the country. On an application by the mortgagees for an order of sale, the court decided that it would be grossly inequitable to order a sale, for Mrs Moss's purpose of living in the house for the rest of her life had not been destroyed and, in any event, the burden was on the mortgagee to ensure that the mortgage was properly executed by the parties.

In *Re Evers' Trust*, the Court of Appeal reviewed the leading authorities and declared the approach to an application for the sale of the asset under s 30 of the Law of Property Act 1925.

Re Evers' Trust [1980] 1 WLR 1327, CA

Facts

Mr Papps and Mrs Evers lived together as man and wife. In April 1978 the parties jointly acquired a cottage for £13,950, which was conveyed in their joint names as trustees for themselves as joint tenants. The purchase price was raised by a mortgage for £10,000, Mrs Evers made a direct contribution of £2,400 and Mr Papps contributed the balance. The cottage was purchased as a family home for the parties and their child as well as Mrs Evers' children from a former marriage. In 1979 the parties separated and Mr Papps applied for an order to sell the cottage under s 30 of the 1925 Act.

Held

The underlying purpose of the trust was to provide a home for the couple and the children and s 30 of the 1925 Act (now s 14 of the 1996 Act) would not be invoked to defeat this purpose:

> **Ormrod LJ:** The section gives the court a discretion to intervene to deal, *inter alia*, with the situation which arises when the trustees under a trust for sale are unable or unwilling to agree that the property should be sold. In such circumstances, the court can order a sale of the property, and if appropriate impose terms, or it can decline to make an order, leaving the property unsold unless and until the trustees reach agreement or the court makes an order at some future date.
>
> The usual practice in these cases has been to order a sale and a division of the proceeds of sale, thus giving effect to the express purpose of the trust. But the trust for sale has become a very convenient and much used conveyancing technique. Combined with the statutory power in the trustees to postpone the sale, it can be used to meet a variety of situations, in some of which an actual sale is far from the intentions of the parties at the time when the trust for sale comes into existence. So, when asked to exercise its discretionary powers under s 30 to execute the trust, the court must have regard to its underlying purpose.
>
> This approach to the exercise of the discretion given by s 30 has considerable advantages in these 'family' cases. It enables the court to deal with substance (that is reality) rather than form (that is, convenience of conveyancing); it brings the exercise of the discretion under this section, so far as possible into line with the exercise of the discretion given by s 24 of the Matrimonial Causes Act 1973 . . .
>
> [After considering the facts of this case, he continued:]
>
> The irresistible inference from these facts is that, as the judge found, the parties purchased this property as a family home for themselves and the three children. It is difficult to imagine that the mother, then wholly responsible for two children and partly for the third, would have invested nearly all her capital in the purchase of this property if it was not to be available to her as a home for the children for the indefinite future. It is inconceivable that the father, when he agreed to this joint venture, could have thought otherwise or contemplated the possibility of an early sale without the consent of the mother. The underlying purpose of the trust was, therefore, to provide a home for all five of them for the indefinite future.

Question

How may a party with an interest in family assets realise his share?

BANKRUPTCY

If one of the co-habiting partners (co-owners) becomes bankrupt, the beneficial interest in the matrimonial home of that partner vests in the trustee in bankruptcy, whose interest is the protection of the creditors. On a petition by the trustee in bankruptcy for an order of sale under s 14 of the Trusts of Land and Appointment of Trustees Act 1996, the court has a general discretion and may consider all the circumstances of the case (including the interests of the family and creditors and the contribution of either party towards the bankruptcy): see s 335A of the Insolvency Act 1986 (as amended by the Trusts of Land and Appointment of Trustees Act 1996).

Insolvency Act 1986, s 335A(2) (as amended by the Trusts of Land and Appointment of Trustees Act 1996)

On . . . an application . . . the court shall make such order . . . under s 14 of the Act of 1996 as it thinks just and reasonable having regard to:

(a) the interests of the bankrupt's creditors;

(b) where the application is made in respect of land which includes a dwelling house which is or has been the house of the bankrupt or the bankrupt's spouse or former spouse:

   (i) the conduct of the spouse or former spouse, so far as contributing to the bankruptcy;

   (ii) the needs and financial resources of the spouse or former spouse;

   (iii) the needs of any children; and

(c) all the circumstances of the case other than the needs of the bankrupt.

If, however, the application is made more than one year after the vesting of the property in the trustee in bankruptcy, the interests of the creditors will prevail, unless there are exceptional circumstances which compel the court to reach a different conclusion: s 335A(3) of the Insolvency Act 1986.

Insolvency Act 1986, s 335A(3)

Where such an application is made after the end of the period of one year beginning with the first vesting . . . of the bankrupt's estate in a trustee, the court shall assume, unless the circumstances of the case are exceptional, that the interests of the bankrupt's creditors outweigh all other considerations.

The significance of 'exceptional circumstances' under s 335A(3) of the 1986 Act was considered by the Court of Appeal in *Re Citro*.

Re Citro (A Bankrupt) [1991] Ch 142, CA

Facts

Two Citro brothers, D and C, ran a garage business. In 1985, they were declared bankrupt. They each had a half share of the beneficial interest in their separate matrimonial homes. The trustees in bankruptcy sought to sell their homes under s 30 of the Law of Property Act 1925. D was judicially separated from his wife, who lived in the house with their three children, the youngest of whom was 12 years old. C lived in his home with his wife. They also had three children, the youngest of whom was 10. Hoffman J made an order for possession and sale, but postponed the order until the youngest child in each case became 16. The trustee in bankruptcy appealed.

Held

The court allowed the appeal and varied the order to the extent that possession and sale were to be postponed for a period not exceeding six months:

Nourse LJ: [His Lordship examined the following authorities: *Jones v Challenger* [1961] 1 QB 176; *Re Mayo* [1943] Ch 302; *Re Buchanan-Wollaston's Conveyance* [1939] Ch 738; *Re Solomon* [1967] Ch 573; *Boydell v Gillespie* (1970) 216 EG 1505; *Re Hardy's Trust* (1970) The Times, 23 October; *Re Turner* [1974] 1 WLR 1556; *Re Densham* [1975] 1 WLR 1519; *Re Bailey* [1977] 1 WLR 278; *Re Holliday* [1981] Ch 405; *Re Lowrie* [1981] 3 All ER 353 and continued:] The broad effect of these authorities can be summarised as follows. Where a spouse who has a beneficial interest in the matrimonial home has become bankrupt under debts which cannot be paid without the realisation of that interest, the voice of the creditors will usually prevail over the voice of the other spouse and a sale of the property ordered within a short period. The voice of the other spouse will only prevail in exceptional circumstances. No distinction is to be made between a case where the property is still being enjoyed as the matrimonial home and one where it is not.

What, then, are exceptional circumstances? As the cases show, it is not uncommon for a wife with young children to be faced with eviction in circumstances where the realisation of her beneficial interest will not produce enough to buy a comparable home in the same neighbourhood, or indeed elsewhere. And, if she has to move elsewhere, there may be problems over schooling and so forth. Such circumstances, while engendering a natural sympathy in all who hear of them, cannot be described as exceptional.

In the husband and wife cases exemplified by *Jones v Challenger* [1961] 1 QB 176 it is held that neither spouse has a right to demand a sale of the property while the purpose of its enjoyment as a matrimonial home still exists. In order to be so enjoyed, it must be occupied by the spouses jointly. As a matter of property law, the basis of their joint occupation is their joint ownership of the beneficial interest in the home. Although the vesting of one of their interests in a trustee for creditors does not in itself destroy the secondary purpose of the trust, the basis for their joint occupation has gone. It must, I think, be implicit in the principle of *Jones v Challenger* that the secondary purpose can only exist while the spouses are not only joint occupiers of the home but joint owners of it as well.

Did Hoffmann J correctly apply it to the facts which were before him? I respectfully think that he did not. First, for the reasons already stated, the personal circumstances of the two wives and their children, although distressing, are not by themselves exceptional. Secondly, I think that the judge erred in fashioning his orders by reference to those which might have been made in the Family Division in a case where bankruptcy had not supervened. That approach, which tends towards treating the home as a source of provision for the children, was effectively disapproved by the earlier and uncontroversial part of the decision of this court in *Re Holliday*. Thirdly, and perhaps most significantly, he did not ask himself the critical question whether a further postponement of payment of their debts would cause hardship to the creditors. It is only necessary to look at the substantial deficiencies referred to earlier in this judgment in order to see that it would. Since then a further 18 months' interest has accrued and the trustee has incurred the costs of these proceedings as well.

I would allow both appeals by deleting the provisos for postponement from Hoffmann J's orders and substituting short periods of suspension.

FURTHER READING

Allison, D, 'All Change?' (2007) 157 NLJ 386.

Amin, S and Hicks, E, 'Shared intentions' (2007) 157 NLJ 922.

Clark, P, 'The family home: intention and agreement' [1992] Fam Law 73.

Cullity, M, 'Joint bank accounts with volunteers' (1969) 84 LQR 530.

Ferguson, P, 'Constructive trusts – a note of caution' (1993) 109 LQR 114.

Freeman, J, 'Equity's darlings or de facto couples?' (2006) 156 NLJ 1185.

Gardiner, S, 'A woman's work . . .' (1991) 54 MLR 126.

Gardiner, S, 'Rethinking family property' (1993) 109 LQR 114.

Gouriet, M, 'Til court do us part' (2006) 156 NLJ 170.

Harris, I, 'Pre-nuptial agreements, post *Miller*' (2006) 156 NLJ 1160.

Hayton, D, 'Equitable rights of co-habitees' [1990] Conv 370.

Hayton, D, 'Constructive trusts of homes – a bold approach' (1993) 109 LQR 485.

Law Commission Discussion Paper, *Sharing Homes*, www.law.go.uk.

Lawson, A, 'Acquiring a beneficial interest in the family home' [1992] Conv 218.

Lawson, A, 'The things we do for love: detrimental reliance in the family home' (1996) 16 LS 218.

Lawson, A, 'Working in a business and ownership of house' [1996] Conv 462.

Lord Millet, 'The husband, the wife and the bank' [2001] PCB 238.

Milne, P, 'The home: excuses and contributions' (1995) 145 NLJ 456.

Oldham, M, 'Quantification of beneficial interests in land' (1996) 55 CLJ 194.

Pascoe, S, 'Section 15 of the Trusts of Land and Appointment of Trustees Act 1996 – a change in law' [2000] Conv 315.

Pawlowski, M, 'Joint ownership and beneficial entitlement: Stack v Dowden' [2007] 37 Family Law 606.

Riniker, M, 'The fiction of common intention and detriment' [1998] Conv 202.

Townsend, P and Baker, A, 'Living together – the thorny issue' (1998) 148 NLJ 779.

Woods, U, 'Property disputes between co-owning cohabitees – Ireland and England compared' (2006) CLWR Vol 35 Issue 4, 297.

CONSTRUCTIVE TRUSTS: STRANGERS AS CONSTRUCTIVE TRUSTEES

INTRODUCTION

Strangers to a trust, or agents of the trustees who act in breach of their obligations, do not automatically become constructive trustees. They may be liable for breach of their duties in accordance with general principles of law. Strangers (or agents of the trustees) become construct-ive trustees or are accountable to the trust if they exceed their authority and intermeddle with the affairs of the trust. This is the case if:

(a) they act as trustees *de son tort* (the phrase literally means trustees of their own wrong); or

(b) they knowingly receive the trust property for their own benefit; or

(c) they dishonestly participate in a breach of trust without receiving the trust property. In this last event, the modern view is that such strangers are accountable for any profits made, but ought not to be treated as constructive trustees. The earlier decisions have not always drawn this distinction and have loosely declared that defendants within this category are constructive trustees.

LIABILITY OF STRANGERS

The general rule is that third parties or persons who have not been appointed trustees (such as agents of trustees, for example, accountants and solicitors) are not constructive trustees if they act in breach of their duties. They may be personally liable in damages for breach of contract or tort and are answerable to their principals, the trustees who appointed them. Provided that the agent acts within the course of his or her authority and does not receive the trust property for his or her own benefit and does not have knowledge that he or she is acting in a manner inconsistent with the terms of the trust, he or she does not become a constructive trustee. In other words, the agents of trustees do not become trustees *de son tort*, that is, do not perform acts characteristic of trustees, such as intermeddling with the trust property, they are not constructive trustees, although they may be personally liable if they act negligently. This general rule was declared in an *obiter* pronouncement by Bacon VC in *Lee v Sankey*.

Lee v Sankey (1872) LR 15 Eq 204, HC

Bacon VC: A mere agent of trustees is answerable only to his principal and not to *cestuis que trust* in respect of trust moneys coming into his hands merely in his character of agent. But it is also not less clearly established that a person who receives into his hands trust moneys, and deals with them in a manner inconsistent with the performance of the trusts of which he is cognisant, is personally liable for the consequences which may ensue upon his so dealing.

Facts
A firm of solicitors, acting with the authority of two trustees appointed under a will, and with full knowledge of the terms of the will, received the proceeds of sale of trust property and held it pending further instructions as to its investment. The solicitors were induced to transfer part of the proceeds of sale to one of the trustees who dissipated the moneys and died insolvent.

Held
The solicitors were liable in equity on two grounds: first, because the payment to one of two trustees did not discharge them from their duty to account to the principals; and, secondly,

because they had received the trust property pending instructions on investment and had acted inconsistently with such directions.

Note

In *Soar v Ashwell* [1893] 2 QB 390, Lord Esher expressed the view that an intermeddling stranger to the trust should be treated as though he was appointed a trustee:

> Where a person has assumed, either with or without consent, to act as a trustee of money or other property . . . a Court of Equity will impose upon him all the liabilities of an express trustee . . .

Other examples of agents becoming constructive trustees are *Boardman v Phipps* [1967] 2 AC 46, HL (see p 190 above) and *English v Dedham Vale Properties Ltd* [1978] 1 WLR 93, HC (see p 190 above). These are illustrations of trustees *de son tort*.

The principle governing the liability of an agent as a constructive trustee was summarised by Smith LJ in *Mara v Browne*.

Mara v Browne [1896] 1 Ch 199, CA

Facts

A solicitor acting on behalf of the trustees unlawfully invested trust funds on certain mortgages and the trust suffered loss.

Held

The solicitor was not liable as a constructive trustee, though he would have been liable in contract for his negligence had the action not become time barred:

> **Smith LJ:** It is said that the facts show that there should be imputed to Hugh Browne the character of a trustee, or, in other words, that he was a *trustee de son tort*, and upon this ground the learned judge has held him liable. It is not contended on behalf of the plaintiffs that Hugh Browne has been guilty of any fraudulent or dishonest conduct to the injury of the *cestuis que trust*, nor, to use Lord Langdale's words in *Fyler v Fyler* (1841) 3 Beav 560, did he, being a solicitor, 'take advantage of his position to acquire a benefit for himself at the hazard, if not to the prejudice, of the trust'; but it was said that he had made himself a constructive trustee, which, so far as I know, is the same thing as a trustee *de son tort*. Now, *what constitutes a trustee de son tort? It appears to me if one, not being a trustee and not having authority from a trustee, takes upon himself to intermeddle with trust matters or to do acts characteristic of the office of trustee, he may thereby make himself what is called in law a trustee of his own wrong, i.e. a trustee de son tort, or, as it is also termed, a constructive trustee* [emphasis added].
>
> [After referring to Lord Selborne's speech in *Barnes v Addy* (1874) LR 9 Ch App 244, he continued:] In my judgment it is incorrect to hold that he was acting as *trustee de son tort*; why is this to be assumed? The learned judge came to the conclusion that Arthur Reeves never acted under the deed of January 1884, and that it was abandoned; but why is it this to be so held? We find Arthur Reeves (a plaintiff) after its execution at once entering upon the business of the trust; and why is it to be assumed and held that he then acted as a trustee in his own wrong rather than as a properly appointed trustee? I can draw no such inference.

Some of the reasons put forward for limiting the liability of the agent as a constructive trustee are that, if the principle was otherwise, no agent would be prepared to act for the trust, or his services would be more expensive, or he might insist on an indemnity from the trustees. Another powerful reason for restricting the liability of agents concerns the difficult balancing act which agents are sometimes required to carry out in respect of honouring the contractual obligations to their principals and complying with their broader duty not to participate in a breach of trust.

One of the leading cases in this context is *Barnes v Addy*.

Barnes v Addy (1874) LR 9 Ch App 244, HL

Facts

An action was brought against a solicitor and the trustees of a trust settlement. The solicitor advised the settlement trustees against the appointment of a beneficiary as the sole trustee of a part of the trust funds, but nevertheless prepared the necessary documents. The sole trustee misapplied the property and became bankrupt.

Held

The solicitor was not liable for the loss for he did not receive the trust property but acted honestly and within the course of his authority. The settlement trustees were liable. Lord Selborne laid down the test of liability as follows:

> **Lord Selborne:** Those who create a trust clothe the trustee with a legal power and control over the trust property, imposing on him a corresponding responsibility. That responsibility may no doubt be extended in equity to others who are not properly trustees, if they are found either making themselves *trustees de son tort*, or actually participating in any fraudulent conduct of the trustee to the injury of the *cestui que trust* ... Strangers are not to be made constructive trustees merely because they act as agents of trustees in transactions within their legal powers, transactions, perhaps, of which a court of equity may disapprove, unless those agents:
>
> (a) receive and become chargeable with some part of the trust property; or
>
> (b) they assist with knowledge in a dishonest or fraudulent design on the part of the trustees [emphasis added].
>
> Those are the principles as it seems to me, which we must bear in mind in dealing with the facts of the case. If those principles were disregarded, I know not how anyone could, in transactions admitting of doubt, as to the view which a court of equity might take of them, safely discharge the office of solicitor, of banker, or of agent of any sort to trustees. But, on the other hand, if persons, dealing honestly as agents, are at liberty to rely on the legal power of the trustees, and are not to have the character of trustees constructively imposed upon them, then the transactions of mankind can safely be carried through; and I apprehend those who create trusts do expressly intend, in the absence of fraud and dishonesty, to exonerate such agents of all classes from the responsibilities which are expressly incumbent, by reason of the fiduciary relation upon the trustees.

Note

The above statement represents a summary of the law concerning the liability of a stranger to the trust as a constructive trustee. The two limbs of liability as stated by Lord Selborne have been construed by the courts as equivalent to a statutory provision. However, in *Royal Brunei v Tan* [1995] 3 WLR 64, the second limb of liability was modified by the Privy Council (see p 289 below).

Question

Would a stranger to a trust, who interferes with the management of the trust, be treated as a constructive trustee?

Rationale concerning the two heads of liability

The two limbs of liability as laid down by Lord Selborne in *Barnes v Addy* relate to strangers who:

(a) receive and become chargeable with some part of the trust property; or

(b) assist with knowledge in a dishonest or fraudulent design on the part of the trustees.

The rationale behind the trustee's liability under the first head is based on the premise that the stranger or agent has received the trust property with knowledge of the same before he or she acts, or fails to act, for his or her own benefit in a manner inconsistent with the trust. The stranger to the trust claims a proprietary interest in the subject matter of the trust and thus competes with the interests of the beneficiaries. Under the second limb, although the stranger does not receive the property for his or her own benefit, he or she becomes accountable by virtue of his or her participation in a dishonest scheme, with knowledge of the dishonest design. Some judges have loosely classified this liability as arising under a constructive trust. But strictly, it is a liability only to account. The dishonest stranger who participates in a fraudulent scheme does not receive the trust property and ought not to be treated as a constructive trustee (see Millett LJ's view in *Paragon Finance v Thakerar* [1999] 1 All ER 410, CA, p 282 below). Thus, the basis of liability under the two limbs is dissimilar. Equally, the extent of the knowledge of the stranger under each limb ought to be different. There has been a conflict of judicial views as to the types of knowledge which the stranger is required to possess under each head in order to found liability as a constructive trustee. Within the last two decades, there has been renewed judicial interest in this area of the law.

Categories of knowledge

Under both limbs of liability, the defendant is required to possess an element of knowledge of the circumstances. Peter Gibson J in *Baden Delvaux and Lecuit v Société Générale pour Favoriser le Développement de Commerce et de l'Industrie en France SA* enumerated the various kinds of knowledge which are relevant in this context.

Baden Delvaux and Lecuit v Société Générale pour Favoriser le Développement de Commerce et de l'Industrie en France SA [1983] BCLC 325, HC

Peter Gibson J: What types of knowledge are relevant for the purposes of constructive trusteeship? . . . knowledge can comprise any one of the five different mental states . . . as follows:

(i)   actual knowledge;

(ii) wilfully shutting one's eyes to the obvious;

(iii) wilfully and recklessly failing to make such inquiries as an honest and reasonable man would make;

(iv) knowledge of circumstances which would indicate the facts to an honest and reasonable man;

(v)   knowledge of circumstances which would put an honest and reasonable man on inquiry.

More accurately, apart from actual knowledge they are formulations of the circumstances which may lead the court to impute knowledge of the facts to the alleged constructive trustee even though he lacked actual knowledge of those facts . . .

The first three categories of knowledge involve a subjective or partly subjective inquiry, whereas categories (iv) and (v) require a purely objective assessment of the circumstances. Actual knowledge within category (i) concerns such facts of which the stranger is aware, positively and consciously. Wilfully shutting one's eyes to the obvious within category (ii) is a common law notion involving abstinence from making inquiries because the defendant knows what the result will entail. Similarly, knowledge within category (iii) embraces circumstances when the defendant foresees or suspects the likelihood of a serious risk of loss of the trust property if reasonable inquiries are not made, but is indifferent as to the consequences of failing to make such inquiries. Knowledge within categories (iv) and (v) involves a wholly objective inquiry in that the reasonable man would have made reasonable inquiries or would have been put on inquiry. The court adopts its own standard in fixing an individual with knowledge within categories (iv) and (v). The effect is that the degree of culpability that is required to make a stranger a constructive trustee within the last two categories borders on fraud and negligence. It is arguable that this test is divorced from dishonesty or want of probity, which ought to be the basis of the liability to account. In other words, an innocent failure to make reasonable inquiries is distinct from acting dishonestly, or consciously acting with impropriety.

In *Agip v Jackson*, Millett J declared that the real test in every case is whether the stranger conducted himself or herself with such impropriety as to make him or her accountable, or at any rate to prevent him or her relying on lack of actual knowledge as a defence to a claim brought on behalf of the trust.

Agip v Jackson [1990] Ch 265, HC

Millett J: The true distinction is between honesty and dishonesty. It is essentially a jury question. If a man does not draw the obvious inferences or make obvious inquiries, the question is: why not? If it is because, however foolishly, he did not suspect wrongdoing or, having suspected it, had his suspicions allayed, however unreasonably, that is one thing. But if he did suspect wrongdoing yet failed to make inquiries because 'he did not want to know' (category ii) or because he regarded it as 'none of his business' (category iii), that is quite another. Such conduct is dishonest and those who are guilty of it cannot complain if, for the purpose of civil liability, they are treated as if they had actual knowledge.

Note

The decision of Millett J was affirmed by the Court of Appeal.

KNOWINGLY RECEIVING TRUST PROPERTY

The basis of liability under this head is that a stranger, who knows that a fund is trust property transferred to him or her in breach of trust, cannot take possession of the property for his or her own benefit but is subject to the claims of the trust. He or she is not a *bona fide* transferee of the legal estate for value without notice. Thus, liability may arise where the stranger:

(a) receives trust property knowing that his or her possession is in breach of trust; or

(b) receives trust property initially without knowledge that his or her acquisition is in breach of trust, but subsequently becomes aware of the existence of the trust and acts in a manner inconsistent with the trust.

The elements of the cause of action were stated by Hoffmann LJ in *El Ajou v Dollar Land Holdings.*

El Ajou v Dollar Land Holdings [1994] 2 All ER 685, CA

Hoffmann LJ: the plaintiff must show, first, a disposal of his assets in breach of fiduciary duty; secondly, the beneficial receipt by the defendant of assets which are traceable as representing the assets of the plaintiff; and thirdly, knowledge on the part of the defendant that the assets he received are traceable to a breach of fiduciary duty.

The contest in this context is based on the assertion of proprietary rights. The trust sues the stranger claiming that it has better title to the property. Equity is entitled to adopt the most strenuous efforts in order to protect the beneficiary's interest under the trust and, in the majority of cases, has declared that any of the five types of knowledge would be sufficient to make the stranger liable. Thus, actual knowledge, wilful or reckless blindness, as well as constructive knowledge on the part of the stranger would make him or her liable to the trust under the first limb of liability laid down in *Barnes v Addy*. This is the approach advocated by Buckley LJ in *Belmont Finance v Williams*.

Belmont Finance Corp v Williams Furniture and Others (No 2) [1980] 1 All ER 393, CA

Facts

Williams Co owned the entire shareholding in City Industrial Ltd (City), which in turn owned all the shares in Belmont. A scheme was arranged whereby Belmont assisted in the unlawful purchase of its own shares in stages as follows: Belmont purchased all the shares in a fourth company called Maximum for £500,000 in cash (a price which was grossly in excess of the value of its assets); Maximum then bought from City the shares it held in Belmont for £489,000. Belmont was subsequently put into receivership – the receiver claimed damages for conspiracy and also sought to recover from City and its directors as constructive trustees the £489,000 which City received on the ground that this sum was received by the directors in breach of their fiduciary duties concerning the funds of the company.

Held

The court found in favour of the receiver on the ground that City was liable as a constructive trustee. Liability arose by the receipt of trust moneys and the fact that its directors knew all the circumstances, in particular, the unlawfulness of the transaction, and had knowledge or ought to have known that the sum received from the sale of Belmont's shares was trust money. There was no need to prove fraud:

> **Buckley LJ:** The directors of a limited company are treated as if they were trustees of those funds of the company which are in their hands or under their control, and if they misapply them they commit a breach of trust . . . So, if the directors of a company in breach of their fiduciary duties misapply the funds of their company so that they come into the hands of some stranger to the trust who receives them with the knowledge (actual or constructive) of the breach, he cannot conscientiously retain those funds against the company unless he has some better equity. He becomes a constructive trustee of the misapplied funds.

Similarly, in *International Sales and Agencies Ltd v Marcus*, Lawson J decided that, under this head of liability, the stranger will be a constructive trustee if he or she receives the trust property with knowledge (construed in the widest sense including constructive knowledge) of the breach.

International Sales and Agencies Ltd v Marcus [1982] 3 All ER 551

Facts

The defendant made a personal loan of £30,000 to a major shareholder of the plaintiff company. After the death of the debtor, a friend and director of the plaintiff company repaid the loan with the company's funds to the knowledge of the defendant. The plaintiff sought to make the defendant a constructive trustee of the funds.

Held

The defendant was liable to account for the company's funds as a constructive trustee:

> **Lawson J:** The knowing recipient of trust property for his own purposes will become a constructive trustee of what he receives if either he was in fact aware at the time that his receipt was affected by a breach of trust, or if he deliberately shut his eyes to the real nature of the transfer to him (this could be called imputed notice), or if an ordinary reasonable man in his position and with his attributes ought to have known of the relevant breach. This I equate with constructive notice. Such a position would arise where such a person would have been put on enquiry as to the probability of a breach of trust.

Where the claimant's interest in the property is seriously disputed by other parties, so that there is a reasonable doubt as to whether the claimant has an interest in the property, the defendant who receives the property cannot be made a constructive trustee. He or she could not really be treated as dealing with the claimant's property; see *Carl Zeiss Stiftung v Herbert Smith*.

Carl Zeiss Stiftung v Herbert Smith and Co (No 2) [1969] 2 Ch 276, CA

Facts

Following the partition of Germany, members of the East German firm of Carl Zeiss fled to the West and founded the West German firm of the same name. The East German firm claimed the assets of the West German firm. Solicitors of the West German firm were paid a sum of money for work done for their clients. The East German firm claimed this money from the solicitors contending that they had received the sum knowing that the same belonged to the plaintiff.

Held

The court found in favour of the defendants because the ownership of the assets of the plaintiff was seriously in dispute on reasonable grounds. The solicitors could have no knowledge that the funds belonged to the plaintiff. Furthermore, the defendants were under no duty to inquire. In short, the plaintiff had a 'doubtful equity':

> **Edmund-Davies LJ:** It is true that not every situation where probity is lacking gives rise to a constructive trust. Nevertheless, the authorities appear to show that nothing short of it will do. Not even gross negligence will suffice.
>
> Mr Kerr gave the court a helpful distillation of the numerous authorities to which reference has already been made by my Lords. Their effect, he rightly submits, may be thus stated: (A) a solicitor or other agent who receives money from his principal which belongs at law or in equity to a third party is not accountable as a constructive trustee to that third party unless he has been guilty of some wrongful act in relation to that money; (B) to act

'wrongfully' he must be guilty of (i) knowingly participating in a breach of trust by his principal; or (ii) intermeddling with the trust property otherwise than merely as an agent and thereby becomes a trustee *de son tort*; or (iii) receiving or dealing with the money knowing that his principal has no right to pay it over or to instruct him to deal with it in the manner indicated; or (iv) some dishonest act relating to the money. These are, indeed, but variants or illustrations of that 'want of probity' to which I have earlier referred.

Do the demands of justice and good conscience bring the present case within any of the foregoing categories? In my judgment, the question is one which demands a negative answer.

Alternative rationale for liability

Megarry VC, in *Re Montagu's Settlement*, reviewed the basis of liability under this head and concluded that:

> the constructive trust should not be imposed unless the conscience of the recipient is affected; this depends on knowledge, not 'notice'; want of probity includes actual knowledge, shutting one's eyes to the obvious, or wilfully and recklessly failing to make such inquiries as a reasonable and honest man would make; it does not include knowledge of circumstances which would indicate the facts to an honest and reasonable man or would put the latter on enquiry.

Thus, according to Megarry VC, cognisance within the first three categories of knowledge (subjective inquiry) as laid down by Gibson J in *Re Baden Delvaux* is relevant under this head; constructive knowledge including objective recklessness (categories (iv) and (v)) is unsuitable as a test of constructive trusteeship. In Megarry VC's view, the basis of liability under this head is 'want of probity' or 'dishonesty', which requires subjective knowledge of wrongdoing on the part of the defendant. Similarly, a stranger is not treated as having knowledge of a fact which he has genuinely forgotten.

Re Montagu's Settlement [1987] Ch 264, HC

Facts

Under a subsisting trust, the trustees, on advice from a firm of solicitors, settled chattels in favour of the beneficiary, the 10th Duke of Manchester, absolutely. The transfer was in breach of trust but as a result of an honest mistake on the part of the solicitors and the Duke. The Duke disposed of a number of chattels during his lifetime. After his death, the 11th Duke claimed that his predecessor had become a constructive trustee of the chattels and was liable to re-transfer the remaining assets (and traceable proceeds of sale of the disposed chattels), and was also personally liable in respect of the value of any assets disposed of and in respect of which the proceeds were not traceable.

Held

The Duke (or his estate) was not personally liable as a constructive trustee because he did not have subjective knowledge of the breach, but was liable to re-transfer to the settlement trustees undisposed trust assets and traceable proceeds as an innocent volunteer:

> **Megarry VC:** In the books and the authorities the word 'notice' is often used in place of the word 'knowledge', usually without any real explanation of its meaning. This seems to me to be a fertile source of confusion. The classification of 'notice' into actual notice, constructive notice and imputed notice has been developed in relation to the doctrine that a *bona fide* purchaser for value of a legal estate takes free from any equitable interests of which he has no notice. I need not discuss this classification beyond saying that I use the term 'imputed notice' as meaning any actual or constructive notice that a solicitor or other agent for the purchaser acquires in the course of the transaction in question, such notice being imputed to the purchaser. Some of the cases describe any constructive notice that a purchaser himself obtains as being 'imputed' to him; but I confine 'imputed' to notice obtained by another which equity imputes to the purchaser.
>
> In determining whether a constructive trust has been created, the fundamental question is whether the conscience of the recipient is bound in such a way as to justify equity in imposing a trust on him. The rules concerning a purchaser without notice seem to me to provide little guidance on this and to be liable to be

misleading. First, they are irrelevant unless there is a purchase. Second, although a purchaser normally employs solicitors, and so questions of imputed notice may arise, it is unusual for a volunteer to employ solicitors when about to receive bounty. Third, there seems to me to be a fundamental difference between the questions that arise in respect of the doctrine of purchaser without notice and constructive trusts.

If a person once has clear and distinct knowledge of some fact, is he to be treated as knowing that fact for the rest of his life, even after he has genuinely forgotten all about it? To me, such a question almost answers itself. It seems to me that a person should not be said to have knowledge of a fact that he once knew if at the time in question he has genuinely forgotten all about it, so that it could not be said to operate on his mind any longer. This is emphasised in relation to constructive trusts in that, in my view, it would be wrong to hold that a person's conscience is affected by something that he does not know about.

I shall attempt to summarise my conclusions. In doing this, I make no attempt to reconcile all the authorities and *dicta*, for such a task is beyond me; and in this I suspect I am not alone. Some of the difficulty seems to arise from judgments that have been given without all the relevant authorities having been put before the judges. All I need do is to find a path through the wood that will suffice for the determination of the case before me, and to assist those who have to read this judgment:

(1) The equitable doctrine of tracing and the imposition of a constructive trust by reason of the knowing receipt of trust property are governed by different rules and must be kept distinct. Tracing is primarily a means of determining the rights of property, whereas the imposition of a constructive trust creates personal obligations that go beyond mere property rights.

(2) In considering whether a constructive trust has arisen in a case of the knowing receipt of trust property, the basic question is whether the conscience of the recipient is sufficiently affected to justify the imposition of such a trust.

(3) Whether a constructive trust arises in such a case primarily depends on the knowledge of the recipient, and not on notice to him; and for clarity it is desirable to use the word 'knowledge' and avoid the word 'notice' in such cases.

(4) For this purpose, knowledge is not confined to actual knowledge, but includes at least knowledge of types (ii) and (iii) in the *Baden* case [1983] BCLC 325, p 407, i.e., actual knowledge that would have been acquired but for shutting one's eyes to the obvious, or wilfully and recklessly failing to make such inquiries as a reasonable and honest man would make; for in such cases there is a want of probity which justifies imposing a constructive trust.

(5) Whether knowledge of the *Baden* types (iv) and (v) suffices for this purpose is at best doubtful; in my view, it does not, for I cannot see that the carelessness involved will normally amount to a want of probity.

(6) For these purposes, a person is not to be taken to have knowledge of a fact that he once knew but has genuinely forgotten: the test (or a test) is whether the knowledge continues to operate on that person's mind at the time in question.

(7) (a) It is at least doubtful whether there is a general doctrine of 'imputed knowledge' that corresponds to 'imputed notice'.

(b) Even if there is such a doctrine, for the purposes of creating a constructive trust of the 'knowing receipt' type the doctrine will not apply so as to fix a donee or beneficiary with all the knowledge that his solicitor has, at all events if the donee or beneficiary has not employed the solicitor to investigate his right to the bounty, and has done nothing else that can be treated as accepting that the solicitor's knowledge should be treated as his own.

(c) Any such doctrine should be distinguished from the process whereby, under the name 'imputed knowledge', a company is treated as having the knowledge that its directors and secretary have.

(8) Where an alleged constructive trust is based not on 'knowing receipt' but on 'knowing assistance', some at least of these considerations probably apply; but I need not decide anything on that, and I do not do so.

From what I have said, it must be plain that in my judgment the Duke did not become a constructive trustee of any of the chattels. He was a layman, and he accepted and acted on what he was told by his solicitor and was acted on by the trustees and the solicitor to the trustees. I can see nothing that affected his conscience sufficiently to impose a constructive trust on him. Accordingly, I hold that the Duke never became a constructive trustee of any of the chattels.

Note

Similar views were expressed at first instance by Steyn J in *Barclays Bank v Quincecare Ltd* [1992] 4 All ER 363 and Alliott J in *Lipkin Gorman v Karpnale* [1992] 4 All ER 331.

Question

How does the rationale of liability for knowingly receiving trust property laid down by Buckley LJ in *Belmont Finance v Williams* differ from Megarry VC's reasoning in *Re Montagu*?

The court (Knox J) in *Cowan de Groot Properties Ltd v Eagle Trust plc* endorsed the decision of Megarry VC in *Re Montagu*. The court decided that a stranger to a trust cannot be made a constructive trustee unless he or she acts with 'knowledge' (categories (i) to (iii) in the *Baden* case) that his or her conduct is inconsistent with the trust. The basis of liability under this head, in Knox J's view, is dishonesty, or want of probity. Accordingly, on a counterclaim by the defendant, the court decided that the plaintiff was not a constructive trustee under the 'knowingly receiving' category.

Cowan de Groot Properties Ltd v Eagle Trust plc [1992] 4 All ER 700, HC

Facts

E plc agreed to sell three properties for a total of £900,000 to Pinepad Ltd (P Ltd) (a 100% subsidiary of C Ltd) and to grant an option to purchase two other properties to P Ltd. Prior to the completion of the sale, E sought to rescind the whole agreement. Shortly thereafter, P purported to exercise the option. In various stages, P sold on the three properties to C Ltd. C now brought an action against E, claiming a declaration that the notice exercising the option was valid and effective. E counterclaimed, maintaining that the agreement was defective and that P or C was liable as constructive trustee of the properties and proceeds of sale, on the ground of 'knowing receipt'. It was alleged by E that two of its directors acted fraudulently in bringing about the sale, and that C's managing director (Mr Samuelson) knew of the fraudulent breach. It was alleged that Mr Samuelson knew (subjectively within categories (i) to (iii) of *Baden*'s case) of the undervalue at which the properties were sold. In the alternative, it was alleged that P Ltd or C Ltd had objective knowledge (categories (iv) and (v) in *Baden*'s case) of the impropriety.

Held

The court found in favour of the plaintiff and rejected the constructive trust claim. C's managing director did not, on the facts, have subjective knowledge of any fraudulent conduct of E's directors. The duty of directors of a purchasing company was to purchase the property as economically as they possibly could. It was reasonable for C's managing director to assume that E was looking for a quick sale and had no time to market the property efficiently. Objective notice was not relevant to found a claim based on the 'knowingly receiving' category of constructive trust:

> **Knox J:** Mr Samuelson did not, in my judgment, have the knowledge in any of the categories (i), (ii) or (iii), of the *Baden* classification [1983] BCLC 325, of the facts that constituted the breach of fiduciary duty in the sale at the figure and on the terms on which it was affected. That is fatal to Eagle's claim on the basis of a sale at an undervalue, on the view which I take of the test to be applied to a purchase in a commercial transaction from a company vendor. If, contrary to my view, it is right to have regard to the categories (iv) and (v) of the *Baden* classification, I would still conclude that Mr Samuelson should not be treated as having the requisite knowledge.

In *Polly Peck International v Nadir (No 2)*, a contrary view was expressed by the Court of Appeal as to the basis of liability under the 'knowingly receiving' head. The approach here, which is supported by a wealth of authority, is that liability under this head is restitution based. The rationale for imposing liability on the defendant is based on the premise that he or she has acquired the plaintiff's property. Dishonesty or want of probity ought not to be the touchstones of liability. The issues in this context are: whether the defendant has acquired the plaintiff's property, and whether he or she knows that his or her acquisition was in breach of trust. The reverse situation, which will entitle the defendant to take free of the plaintiff's claim, depends on whether he or she is a *bona fide* purchaser for value without notice of the breach of trust. Accordingly, 'knowledge' within any of the five categories laid down in *Re Baden* will be sufficient to impose liability on the defendant.

Polly Peck International plc v Nadir and Others (No 2) [1992] 4 All ER 769, CA

Facts
The administrators of the plaintiff company (PPI) claimed that N and IBK (a bank controlled by N) had misapplied £142 million of PPI's funds. Part of that money had been transferred by the bank to the London account of the fourth defendant, the Central Bank of the Turkish Republic of Northern Cyprus. The Central Bank exercised the supervisory and regulatory role of a central bank in a sovereign State. The administrators claimed that a scheme whereby PPI's funds were transferred via IBK to Northern Cyprus was, at best, in breach of fiduciary duties owed by N to PPI and, at worst, a dishonest means of diverting PPI's funds for improper purposes. The plaintiff also contended that either the Central Bank had actual knowledge of the fraudulent scheme, or, at best, it was put on inquiry as to the impropriety of the scheme. Accordingly, the plaintiff claimed that the Central Bank was a constructive trustee, a tracing order in respect of some £8.9 million standing to the Central Bank's account at the London clearing bank, and a Mareva injunction against the Central Bank to protect the £8.9 million. The judge granted the injunction subject to a proviso to enable the Central Bank to carry on its banking business in the normal way. The bank appealed against the order.

Held
Allowing the appeal and discharging the order, the court decided that there was insufficient evidence for finding that the Central Bank had knowledge of the alleged impropriety perpetrated by N and IBK. The tracing claim failed for the same reason:

> **Scott LJ:** Receipt of trust money by a *bona fide* purchaser for value, without notice of the breach of trust, bars any equitable tracing remedy. It follows that actual or constructive knowledge on the part of the Central Bank of the trust character of the funds received from IBK and of the impropriety of the transfers is as much a requirement of the tracing claim as of the constructive trust claim.
>
> The real question, however, is whether the circumstances in which the transfers were made should have made the Central Bank suspicious of the propriety of what was being done. Millett J thought so. He thought so because of 'the sheer scale of the payments'.
>
> I find myself unimpressed by the 'sheer scale' argument in so far as it is put forward as a ground for contending that the Central Bank ought to have suspected impropriety. It is important in this regard to bear in mind that it is common ground, that at the relevant time Mr Nadir was a man of unblemished commercial reputation and integrity. He had achieved quite staggering commercial success over a relatively short period. He loomed in Northern Cyprus like a colossus over the local economy and over the commercial prospects and fortune of the country. Why should the Central Bank have suspected impropriety because of the scale of the funds being transferred into Northern Cyprus? . . . The question whether the bank did or did not have an honest belief only arises after the bank has become, or ought to have become, suspicious of possible impropriety. Unless ground had been given for suspicion, no one in the Central Bank would have any relevant belief at all. They would not address their minds to impropriety or to the legitimacy of the purpose for which the funds were being moved.
>
> In the present case the degree of knowledge on the part of the Central Bank that PPI must establish for the purposes of its constructive trust case is, in my judgment, requisite also for the purposes of its equitable tracing claim. It follows that the conclusions I have expressed on the constructive trust claim apply also to the tracing claim.

In *El Ajou v Dollar Land*, the issue was whether the knowledge of a non-executive director of the defendant company of a fraudulent dealing with the claimant's property was sufficient to impose liability as a constructive trustee on the defendant company.

El Ajou v Dollar Land Holdings plc and Another **[1994] 2 All ER 685, CA**

Facts

The plaintiff owned substantial funds and securities which were placed under the control of Mr Murad, his investment manager. Mr Murad was bribed in order to invest the plaintiff's money in fraudulent share selling schemes operated by three Canadians. The proceeds of these schemes were ultimately invested in a property company, Dollar Land Holdings plc (DLH), a company unconnected with the three Canadians. Mr Stern, the managing director of DLH, was introduced to the Canadians by Mr Ferdman (the chairman and non-executive director of DLH) through his Swiss company, Société d'Administration et de Financement SA (SAFI). SAFI acted as a fiduciary agent for the Canadians. Mr Stern approached Mr Ferdman for assistance in obtaining finance for DLH's property development project, and this led to the introduction to the Canadians. The plaintiff was able to trace his funds through the Canadians into DLH and sought to recover his funds from DLH on the ground that that company received his funds with knowledge that it represented the proceeds of fraud. Millett J, in the High Court, decided against the plaintiff, on the ground that there was insufficient evidence to establish that the defendant company had knowledge of the fraudulent scheme. The plaintiff appealed.

Held

Reversing the decision of the High Court, the Court of Appeal decided that DLH had knowledge of the relevant facts. Mr Ferdman, who played no active part in the management of the company but performed significant acts on behalf of DLH, was nevertheless the company's 'directing mind and will'. Accordingly, the director's knowledge that assets had been received by the company was sufficient to make the company a constructive trustee on behalf of the plaintiff.

However, on a separate ground, the court decided that Mr Ferdman's knowledge could not be imputed to DLH on agency principles. DLH was under no duty to inquire as to the source of the money and Mr Ferdman was under no duty to inform DLH of the origin of the money:

Hoffmann LJ: The phrase 'directing mind and will' comes from a well-known passage in the judgment of Viscount Haldane LC in *Lennards Carrying Co Ltd v Asiatic Petroleum Co Ltd* [1915] AC 705, [1914–15] All ER Rep 280 which distinguishes between someone who is 'merely a servant or agent' and someone whose action (or knowledge) is that of the company itself. Despite their familiarity, it is worth quoting the terms in which Viscount Haldane LC said that the directing mind could be identified ([1915] AC 705 at 713, [1914–15] All ER Rep 280 at 282):

> That person may be under the direction of the shareholders in general meetings; that person may be the board of directors itself, or it may be, and in some companies it is so, that that person has an authority co-ordinate with the board of directors given to him under the articles of association, and is appointed by the general meeting of the company, and can only be removed by the general meeting of the company . . .

The question in my judgment is whether in relation to the Yulara transaction, Mr Ferdman as an individual exercised powers on behalf of the company which so identified him. It seems to me that Mr Ferdman was clearly regarded as being in a different position from the other directors. They were associates of his who came and went. In my view, however, the most significant fact is that Mr Ferdman signed the agreement with Yulara on behalf of DLH. There was no board resolution authorising him to do so. Of course we know that in fact he signed at the request of Mr Stern, whom he knew to be clothed with authority from the Americans. But so far as the constitution of DLH was concerned, he committed the company to the transaction as an autonomous act which the company adopted by performing the agreement. I would therefore hold, respectfully differing from the judge, that this was sufficient to justify Mr Ferdman being treated, in relation to the Yulara transaction, as the company's directing mind and will. I do not think that DLH could have said that it received the money without imputed knowledge of the fraud. And in my judgment the subsequent acquisition of Yulara's interest was sufficiently connected with the original investment to be affected by the same knowledge.

I would therefore allow the appeal.

In *Bank of Credit and Commerce International (Overseas) Ltd and Another v Akindele*, Nourse LJ reviewed the law with regard to liability under the head of knowingly receiving trust property. He endorsed the approach adopted by Megarry VC in *Re Montagu*, which he considered a seminal judgment. The effect is that in his view liability under this head is based on actual or subjective knowledge on the part of the defendant that the assets received were linked to a breach of trust. He equated liability under this head with accessory liability and doubted the utility of the five categories of knowledge laid down by Peter Gibson J in *Re Baden Delvaux*. Nourse LJ identified the basis of liability under this head as involving the conscience of the defendant, i.e., 'whether the defendant's state of knowledge is such as to make it unconscionable for him to retain the property'.

Bank of Credit and Commerce International (Overseas) Ltd and Another v Akindele
[2000] 4 All ER 221, CA

Facts

International Credit and Investment Co (Overseas) Ltd (ICIC), whose affairs were managed by the BCCI group, needed money to give a false impression that dummy loans were performing normally. In 1985, in pursuance of this objective, it obtained $10 million from the defendant, a prominent Nigerian businessman, under an artificial loan agreement. In 1988, under the terms of the agreement, the defendant was paid $16.679 million by BCCI pursuant to a divestiture agreement. The claimants contended that the defendant was liable to account to them for $6.79 million as a constructive trustee. In pursuing this claim, the claimants relied on the defendant's knowledge of two factors from which they inferred his dishonesty: the artificial nature of the transaction and the abnormally high rate of return (15% compound interest) that he received. Two issues arose before the High Court judge: first, was the defendant liable for dishonestly assisting breaches of trust by bank employees (knowing assistance); and, secondly, was he liable for receiving the divestiture payment with knowledge of the breach (knowing receipt). The judge held that the defendant had not acted dishonestly and the claim under knowing assistance was bound to fail. The claim could only succeed, if at all, under the knowing receipt head.

On appeal to the Court of Appeal, the question involved the issue of whether the recipient was required to have actual knowledge, or the equivalent, that the assets received were traceable to a breach of trust, or whether constructive knowledge was sufficient.

Held

It was debatable whether the fivefold categorisation of knowledge laid down by Peter Gibson J in *Re Baden Delvaux* was of any use in knowing receipt cases. The test is whether a recipient could conscientiously retain the funds as against the company. Just as there is now a single test of dishonesty for knowing assistance, so ought there to be a single test of knowledge for knowing receipt cases. The material date for determining the defendant's state of knowledge was 1985, the date of the agreement. Additional knowledge that he acquired between 1985 and 1987, press rumours of irregularities involving BCCI, warnings to him from business figures in Nigeria and his becoming aware of the arrest of BCCI officials in connection with money laundering, did not make it unconscionable for him to retain the receipt. The additional knowledge went to the general reputation of BCCI. It was not sufficient to question the propriety of the 1985 transaction:

Nourse LJ: With the proliferation in the last 20 years or so of cases in which the misapplied assets of companies have come into the hands of third parties, there has been a sustained judicial and extra-judicial debate as to the knowledge on the part of the recipient which is required in order to found liability in knowing receipt. Expressed in its simplest terms, the question is whether the recipient must have actual knowledge (or the equivalent) that the assets received are traceable to a breach of trust or whether constructive knowledge is enough. The instinctive approach of most equity judges, especially in this court, has been to assume that constructive knowledge is enough. But there is now a series of decisions of eminent first instance judges who, after considering the question in greater depth, have come to the contrary conclusion, at all events when commercial transactions are in point. In the Commonwealth, on the other hand, the preponderance of authority has been in favour of the view that constructive knowledge is enough.

[His Lordship then reviewed the leading cases on the extent of the defendant's knowledge and continued:] Although my own view is that the categorisation [of knowledge laid down by Peter Gibson J in *Re Baden Delvaux*

[1983] BCLC 325] is often helpful in identifying different states of knowledge which may or may not result in a finding of dishonesty for the purposes of knowing assistance, I have grave doubts about its utility in cases of knowing receipt ... any categorisation is of little value unless the purpose it is to serve is adequately defined, whether it be fivefold, as in the *Baden* case, or twofold, as in the classical division between actual and constructive knowledge, a division which has itself become blurred in recent authorities.

What then, in the context of knowing receipt, is the purpose to be served by a categorisation of knowledge? It can only be to enable the court to determine whether, in the words of Buckley LJ in *Belmont (No 2)* [1980] 1 All ER 393 at 405, the recipient can 'conscientiously retain [the] funds against the company' or, in the words of Megarry V-C in *Re Montagu's Settlement Trusts* [1987] Ch 264, '[the recipient's] conscience is sufficiently affected for it to be right to bind him by the obligations of a constructive trustee'. But if that is the purpose, there is no need for categorisation. All that is necessary is that the recipient's state of knowledge should be such as to make it unconscionable for him to retain the benefit of the receipt.

For these reasons I have come to the view that, just as there is now a single test of dishonesty for knowing assistance, so ought there to be a single test of knowledge for knowing receipt. *The recipient's state of knowledge must be such as to make it unconscionable for him to retain the benefit of the receipt.* A test in that form, though it cannot, any more than any other, avoid difficulties of application, ought to avoid those of definition and allocation to which the previous categorisations have led. Moreover, it should better enable the courts to give commonsense decisions in the commercial context in which claims in knowing receipt are now frequently made [emphasis added].

There having been no evidence that the defendant was aware of the internal arrangements within BCCI which led to the payment to him of the $16.679 m pursuant to the divestiture agreement, did the additional knowledge which he acquired between July 1985 and December 1988 make it unconscionable for him to retain the benefit of the receipt? In my judgment it did not. The additional knowledge went to the general reputation of the BCCI group from late 1987 onwards. It was not a sufficient reason for questioning the propriety of a particular transaction entered into more than two years earlier, at a time when no one outside BCCI had reason to doubt the integrity of its management and in a form which the defendant had no reason to question.

Note

Lord Nicholls, in an essay entitled 'Knowing receipt: the need for a new landmark', in Cornish, WR, Nolan, R, O'Sullivan, J and Virgo, G (eds), *Restitution Past, Present and Future: Essays in Honour of Gareth Jones*, 1998, Oxford: Hart in reference to the decision of the House of Lords in *Lipkin Gorman (A Firm) v Karpnale Ltd* [1991] 2 AC 548; [1992] 4 All ER 512, said:

In this respect equity should now follow the law. *Restitutionary liability, applicable regardless of fault but subject to a defence of change of position,* would be a better-tailored response to the underlying mischief of misapplied property than personal liability which is exclusively fault-based. Personal liability would flow from having received the property of another, from having been unjustly enriched at the expense of another. It would be triggered by the mere fact of receipt, thus recognising the endurance of property rights. But fairness would be ensured by the need to identify a gain, and by making change of position available as a default in suitable cases when, for instance, the recipient had changed his position in reliance on the receipt [emphasis added].

Nourse LJ in *Akindele* doubted whether, in this context, strict liability coupled with the defence of change of position would be preferable to fault-based liability.

Question

Do the categories of knowledge laid down by Peter Gibson J in *Re Baden Delvaux* serve any useful purpose today?

ACCESSORY LIABILITY (DISHONEST ASSISTANCE)

Originally, this head of liability was known as 'knowing assistance in a dishonest and fraudulent design' (derived from Lord Selborne's judgment in *Barnes v Addy* (1874) LR 9 Ch App 244, p 270 above), but following the decision of the Privy Council in *Royal Brunei Airlines v Tan* [1995] 3 WLR 64 (see p 289 below), the leading authority on the subject, the expression 'accessory liability' was adopted. The alternative expression, 'dishonest assistance', is equally appropriate, but the original title, as stated by Lord Selborne in *Barnes v Addy*, is now viewed as misleading.

Liability to account

Under this head of liability, a stranger to a trust is accountable to the beneficiaries if he or she dishonestly assists in a breach of trust conducted by another (perhaps, but not necessarily, the settlement trustees). In *Tan*, it was decided that it is not necessary for the trustee to act dishonestly in order to fix liability on the third party. The trustee's state of mind is not important, because the liability of the stranger is dependent on his or her (the stranger's) state of mind and not that of the trustee. In short, the stranger acts as a dishonest accomplice in situations where there has been some wrongdoing. This is the position even though the stranger (third party) does not receive the trust property. In this respect, the liability of the third party is personal, not proprietary. One of the features of a trust is that the trustees have control of the trust property. Under the head of accessory liability, the defendant (alleged constructive trustee) does not acquire control of the property but merely assists in a dishonest breach of trust. He or she is under a duty to account and, strictly, he or she ought not to be labelled as a constructive trustee for liability is personal and not *in rem*: see Millett LJ in *Paragon Finance v Thakerar*. Provided that the defendant is solvent, there are no difficulties. But if the defendant is insolvent, the classification of his or her status will have important consequences. A proprietary remedy (tracing process) may subsist even though the defendant is insolvent. This remedy is based on the assumption that the property wrongly acquired by the defendant belongs to the innocent claimant. The aggrieved party may assert his or her interest in the property, subject to the *bona fide* transferee for value without notice exception. This claim may succeed irrespective of transformations in the nature of the property. Thus, third party rights may be affected by this remedy. But the dishonest accessory is not a constructive trustee in the strict sense of that expression.

Paragon Finance v Thakerar [1999] 1 All ER 410, CA

Millett LJ: The expressions 'constructive trust' and 'constructive trustee' have been used by equity lawyers to describe two entirely different situations. The first covers those cases where the defendant, though not expressly appointed as trustee, has assumed the duties of a trustee by a lawful transaction which was independent of and preceded the breach of trust and is not impeached by the plaintiff. The second covers those cases where the trust obligation arises as a direct consequence of the unlawful transaction which is impeached by the plaintiff.

A constructive trust arises by operation of law whenever the circumstances are such that it would be unconscionable for the owner of property (usually but not necessarily the legal estate) to assert his own beneficial interest in the property and deny the beneficial interest of another. In the first class of case, however, the constructive trustee really is a trustee. He does not receive the trust property in his own right but by a transaction by which both parties intend to create a trust from the outset and which is not impugned by the plaintiff. His possession of the property is coloured from the first by the trust and confidence by means of which he obtained it, and his subsequent appropriation of the property to his own use is a breach of that trust. Well known examples of such a constructive trust are *McCormick v Grogan* (1869) LR 4 HL 82 [a case of secret trust] and *Rochefoucald v Boustead* [1897] 1 Ch 196 [where the defendant agreed to buy property for the plaintiff but the trust was imperfectly recorded]. *Pallant v Morgan* [1952] 2 All ER 951 [where the defendant sought to keep for himself property which the plaintiff trusted him to buy for both parties] is another. In these cases the plaintiff does not impugn the transaction by which the defendant obtained control of the property. He alleges that the circumstances in which the defendant obtained control make it unconscionable for him thereafter to assert a beneficial interest in the property.

The second class of case is different [see *AG for Hong Kong v Reid* [1993] 3 WLR 1143]. It arises when the defendant is implicated in a fraud. Equity has always given relief against fraud by making any person sufficiently implicated in the fraud accountable in equity. In such a case he is traditionally, though I think unfortunately described, as a constructive trustee and said to be 'liable to account as a constructive trustee'. Such a person is not in fact a trustee at all, even though he may be liable to account as if he were. He never assumes the position of a trustee, and if he receives the trust property at all it is adversely to the plaintiff by an unlawful transaction which is impugned by the plaintiff. In such a case the expressions, 'constructive trust' and 'constructive trustee' are misleading, for there is no trust and usually no possibility of a proprietary remedy; they are nothing more than a formula of equitable relief.

In *Sinclair Investment Holdings v Versailles Trade Finance Ltd*, Rimer J after referring to Millett LJ's judgment in *Paragon* adopted the personal remedy for the dishonest accessory.

Sinclair Investment Holdings v Versailles Trade Finance Ltd [2007] EWHC 915

Rimer J: The importance of that passage [in *Paragon*] is, first, that it is concerned with a case such as the present in which Mr Cushnie was a dishonest party to a breach of a trust of which he was not a trustee. Secondly, it confirms that even though it has become traditional to describe such a wrongdoer as a 'constructive trustee', he is not in fact a trustee at all, and the formula is nothing more than one intended to indicate that equitable relief will or may be available against him by reason of his participation in the breach. It is not a formula which, once applied, has the effect of turning the wrongdoer into an actual trustee. The passage does not of course attempt a comprehensive explanation of the remedies that may be available against such a constructive trustee beyond recognising that he may be liable 'to account as if he were a trustee' and that, as against such a wrongdoer, there will 'usually [be no] possibility of a proprietary remedy'. [Emphasis added.]

However, the subject will be dealt with under the constructive trust umbrella because the majority of judges have treated the dishonest assistant as a constructive trustee when in reality he is only accountable as though he is a constructive trustee (a personal as opposed to a proprietary remedy is available to the aggrieved party).

According to Peter Gibson J, in *Re Baden Delvaux* [1983] BCLC 325, the following four elements are required to be established in order to attach liability to the stranger. They are:

(1) the existence of a trust [or a fiduciary relationship];

(2) the existence of a dishonest and fraudulent design [concerning the trust property];

(3) the assistance by the stranger in that design; and

(4) the knowledge of the stranger.

In relation to the first element, the trust need not be a formal trust. It is sufficient that the fiduciary relationship is created between the stranger and another person in respect of the latter's property. A fiduciary is one who is aware that his or her confidence and judgment are relied on (and they are, in fact, relied on) by another (see Millett LJ's definition in *Bristol and West Building Society v Mothew* [1996] 4 All ER 698, p 186 above). Thus, bankers, directors and agents stand in a fiduciary relationship to their customers, companies or principals.

With regard to the second element, no distinction is drawn between the words 'fraudulent' and 'dishonest'. They mean the same thing. But the words are to be construed in accordance with principles of equitable relief. Thus, conduct which is morally reprehensible can be said to be dishonest and fraudulent. Accordingly, not every breach of trust will satisfy this requirement, because a breach of trust falling short of dishonesty or fraud would be insufficient to impose a liability to account. Fraud, in this context, involves the taking of a risk which the stranger honestly knows that he or she has no right to take and which is prejudicial to another's right.

Lord Nicholls in *Royal Brunei Airlines v Tan* (see p 289 below) declared that, in order to decide whether a person is dishonest, the court is required to look at all the circumstances known to the defendant. This would require the court to have regard to the personal attributes of the defendant, such as his experience, intelligence and possible explanations for his or her actions (see also *Twinsectra v Yardley* [2002] UKHL 12 on the standard for dishonesty). In *Tan*, the court decided that a dishonest third party who assisted a trustee, or procured him or her to commit a breach of trust, was liable to the beneficiaries for the resulting loss. It was not necessary to prove, in addition, that the trustee's conduct was dishonest or fraudulent.

The third element involves assistance. This means any act (including an omission when there is a duty to act) effected by another which enables the defendant to commit a dishonest breach of trust. Whether this element is satisfied or not is a question of fact.

To render assistance as an accessory to a dishonest breach of trust, the defendant is required to lend assistance in the knowledge of, or belief in, the existence of the trust, and the knowledge that his or her assistance will facilitate the breach of trust.

In *Brinks v Abu-Saleh* the court decided that the defendant was not liable to account where he acted in ignorance of the fraudulent design of a third party.

Brinks Ltd v Abu-Saleh and Others (No 3) [1995] 1 WLR 1478, HC

Facts

Brinks Ltd suffered a bullion robbery in 1983 when gold and other valuables worth some £26 million were stolen from its warehouse at Heathrow. In order to recover the proceeds, it brought civil proceedings against 57 defendants who had allegedly been involved in the robbery and subsequent laundering operations. One of the defendants was Mrs Elcombe. It was alleged that, between August 1984 and February 1985, she *assisted* her husband, the 12th defendant, in the part he played in laundering part of the proceeds of the stolen gold by carrying approximately £3 million in cash to Mr Parry, one of the convicted robbers, from England to Zurich by car.

The learned judge found on the evidence that Mrs Elcombe and her husband believed the money to be derived from Mr Parry's business empire and was the subject of a tax evasion exercise. They were unaware of the true origin of the moneys.

Held

Dismissing the claim, Rimer J decided that:

(a) Mrs Elcombe went on the trips in the capacity of Mr Elcombe's wife. Her presence on such trips did not constitute 'assistance' in furtherance of a breach of trust;

(b) the claim based on accessory liability could only be brought against someone who knew of the existence of the trust, or at least of the facts giving rise to the trust, and dishonestly rendered assistance in pursuance of a design intended to defeat the trust.

The fourth element, 'knowledge', has provoked strong judicial disagreement. It is common ground that the stranger must know the three elements as mentioned above. The defendant is required to know that there was a trust in existence (although the details need not be known). He must know of the dishonest and fraudulent design of the trustee and that his act (or omission) will assist in the implementation of such design. The contentious issue involves the extent or scope of the knowledge of the stranger. The authorities are in a state of disarray. On the one hand, there is a series of decisions (the earlier cases) which suggest that any of the five categories of knowledge enumerated by Gibson J in *Re Baden Delvaux* would be sufficient to establish liability on the stranger (see *Selangor United Rubber Estates Ltd v Cradock (No 3)* [1968] 2 All ER 1073, *Karak Rubber Co Ltd v Burden (No 2)* [1972] 1 WLR 602 and *Re Baden Delvaux* [1983] BCLC 325). The more recent decisions have established that, since the defendant's conduct is tainted with the fraud of another, he (the defendant) ought not to be saddled with liability unless he participated in the breach with knowledge (subjective in categories (i) and (ii), or partly objective in category (iii)) of the fraudulent design of the other (see *Agip (Africa) Ltd v Jackson* [1992] 4 All ER 385; *Eagle Trust plc v SBC Securities Ltd* [1992] 4 All ER 488; *Polly Peck International plc v Nadir and Others (No 2)* [1992] 4 All ER 769; *Cowan de Groot Properties Ltd v Eagle Trust plc* [1992] 4 All ER 700).

In the case of *Selangor*, the liability of the bank to account was established even though it did not have subjective knowledge of the facts.

Selangor United Rubber Estates Ltd v Cradock (No 3) [1968] 2 All ER 1073, HC

Facts

Mr Cradock offered £188,000 for the plaintiff company which had liquid assets of some £232,500. His offer was accepted. He nominated directors who paid the company's money by several stages into Cradock's account, through the District Bank. Cradock was thereby entitled to fund the original offer. This amounted to an unlawful practice, namely, the company using its money to purchase its own shares. The liquidator of the company brought a claim against Mr Cradock, his nominee directors and the District Bank.

Held

In addition to the liability of Cradock and his nominee directors, the District Bank was liable as constructive trustee. The bank did not have subjective knowledge of the fraud, but it was held that it ought to have known (constructive knowledge) of the dishonest design.

In *Re Baden Delvaux*, Peter Gibson J accepted a concession made between counsel for the claimant and defendant to the effect that any of the five enumerated categories of knowledge would be sufficient to establish liability as a constructive trustee under either the 'knowingly receiving' or 'knowing assistance' head.

Re Baden Delvaux and Lecuit v Société Générale pour Favoriser le Développement du Commerce et de l'Industrie en France SA [1983] BCLC 325, HC

Facts

The plaintiff, a liquidator, claimed that the defendant, a bank, was liable to account as constructive trustee for over $4 million held in an account designated as a trust account by a trustee, a Bahamian bank (BCB). The trustee instructed the defendant to transfer the funds to a Panamanian bank in an account not designated as a trust account. The moneys were then dissipated. The defendant had relied on a Bahamian court order apparently releasing the moneys from the trust. The court order had been obtained by fraud and it was alleged that in all the circumstances the defendant ought to have known that the moneys were still trust property.

Held

The defendant, at the time of the transfer, did not have knowledge of the existence of the trust or the fraudulent design and was unaware that it was assisting in such a scheme. Accordingly, the defendant was not a constructive trustee:

Peter Gibson J: The 'knowing assistance' category as formulated by Lord Selborne LC appears to be directed to strangers who do not receive trust property and that is how it is described in *Snell*. Mr Price accepts that there are four elements which must be established if a case is to be brought within the category of 'knowing assistance'. They are: (1) the existence of a trust; (2) the existence of a dishonest and fraudulent design on the part of the trustee of the trust; (3) the assistance by the stranger in that design; and (4) the knowledge of the stranger. I would add that whilst it is of course helpful to isolate the relevant constituent elements of the 'knowing assistance' category in this way, it is important not to lose sight of the requirement that, taken together, those elements must leave the court satisfied that the alleged constructive trustee was a party or privy to dishonesty on the part of the trustee.

[Having outlined the extent of the defendant's knowledge, the learned judge continued:] What types of knowledge are relevant for the purposes of constructive trusteeship? Mr Price submits that knowledge can comprise any one of five different mental states which he described as follows:

(i) actual knowledge; (ii) wilfully shutting one's eyes to the obvious; (iii) wilfully and recklessly failing to make such inquiries as an honest and reasonable man would make; (iv) knowledge of circumstances which would indicate the facts to an honest and reasonable man; (v) knowledge of circumstances which would put an honest and reasonable man on inquiry. More accurately, apart from actual knowledge they are formulations of the circumstances which may lead the court to impute knowledge of the facts to the alleged constructive trustee even though he lacked actual knowledge of those facts. Thus the court will treat a person as having constructive knowledge of the facts if he wilfully shuts his eyes to the relevant facts which would be obvious if he opened his eyes, such constructive knowledge being usually termed (though by a metaphor of historical inaccuracy)

'Nelsonian knowledge'. Similarly the court may treat a person as having constructive knowledge of the facts – 'type (iv) knowledge' – if he has actual knowledge of circumstances which would indicate the facts to an honest and reasonable man.

Type (iii) knowledge imports in part an objective test in that the inquiries which were wilfully and recklessly omitted must be those which the honest and reasonable man would have made. There are other authorities which support the view that a wholly objective test is appropriate in determining whether knowledge is to be imputed to the alleged constructive trustee. Although the concept of the reasonable man is one of the common law, Megarry J said in *Coco v AN Clark (Engineers) Ltd* [1969] RPC 41, p 48, that he saw no reason why that hard worked creature should not labour in equity as well as at law. The *Selangor* case [1968] 1 WLR 1555, contains an extensive review by Ungoed-Thomas J of most of the relevant authorities. He reached this conclusion on the principles to be applied, at p 1590:

> The knowledge required to hold a stranger liable as constructive trustee in a dishonest and fraudulent design, is knowledge of circumstances which would indicate to an honest, reasonable man that such a design was being committed or would put him on inquiry, which the stranger failed to make, whether it was being committed.

I summarise therefore the principles of law that, in my judgment, I must apply in respect of the claim in equity as follows. (1) The plaintiffs must show (a) the existence of a trust affecting the $4 m deposited by BCB with SG; (b) the fraudulent and dishonest design on the part of the directors of BCB who gave instructions to SG to transfer the $4 m to Panama; (c) the assistance by SG in that design; (d) SG's knowledge of (a), (b) and (c). (2) The knowledge must be actual knowledge or knowledge which it would have obtained but for shutting its eyes to the obvious or wilfully and recklessly refraining from making such inquiries as the reasonable banker would have made from the circumstances known to SG or would have obtained from inquiries which the reasonable banker would have made, the onus being on the plaintiffs to establish that SG possessed that knowledge.

In my judgment the circumstances actually known to SG would not have indicated to the honest and reasonable banker the existence on 10 May of the trust or the existence of the fraudulent design and consequently they would not have indicated that SG by obeying its instructions was assisting in that design. Accordingly, I reject the plaintiff's submissions on type (iv) knowledge. For similar reasons the plaintiffs' submissions that SG wilfully shut its eyes to the obvious must fail. The facts of the trust, the fraud and the assistance were not obvious. Nor in any event can I accept that there was any wilfulness on SG's part in failing to recognise the trust, the fraud and the assistance.

In my judgment the reasonable banker would be entitled to assume, and would assume, that the order of a court of competent jurisdiction had been duly obtained and that the agreement which the court had directed to be executed was therefore a proper one.

Question

Should accessory liability be treated as an illustration of the constructive trust? In *Agip v Jackson*, the court decided that the defendants were accountable as constructive trustees because they had subjective knowledge of the fraudulent transactions.

Agip (Africa) Ltd v Jackson and Others [1991] 3 WLR 116, CA

Facts

The claimant company brought an action to recover £518,822 from the defendants, who were directors and shareholders of companies formed to 'launder' money in pursuance of a fraudulent scheme. The companies were formed in order to receive funds from Tunisia and pay the same to other companies in a series of transactions. Once the companies had fulfilled their roles, they were liquidated with the defendants acting as liquidators. One defendant, Mr Jackson, a chartered accountant, set up the arrangements to receive and pay out the funds. Another defendant, Mr Griffin, was employed to carry out the arrangements. The claimant also alleged that a third defendant, Mr Bowers, was vicariously liable for the acts of his partner, Mr Jackson.

Held

The defendants were liable to account as constructive trustees. At best, Messrs Jackson and Griffin were indifferent to the possibility of fraud. They had wilfully or recklessly failed to make inquiries after being put on enquiry:

> **Fox LJ:** The judge held, and it was not challenged, that Mr Bowers did not participate in the furtherance of the fraud at all; although he was a partner in Jackson & Co, he played no part in the movement of the money and gave no instructions about it. Mr Jackson and Mr Griffin were in quite a different position. Mr Jackson set up the company structures. Mr Jackson and Mr Griffin controlled the movement of the money from the time it reached Baker Oil to the time it was paid out of the account of Jackson & Co in the Isle of Man Bank. On the evidence, and in the absence of evidence from Mr Jackson and Mr Griffin themselves, I agree with the judge that both of them must be regarded as having assisted in the fraud. That, however, by no means concludes the matter. There remains the question of their state of mind. Did they have the necessary degree of knowledge?
>
> The first inquiry is what did they know. As to that: (1) they knew that a very large amount of money was involved: it was $10m in under two years. It had all come along the same track; (2) they knew the origin of the money and its destination. Its origin was Agip and the destination of most of it was Kinz; (3) Agip was an oil company with operations in Tunisia. Kinz were jewellers in France; (4) there is nothing to suggest that there was any commercial reason why Agip should be paying such sums to Kinz; (5) as the judge said, they must have realised that the only function of the payee companies or of Euro-Arabian was to act as 'cut-outs' in order to conceal the true destination of the moneys from Agip. And the purpose of having two cut-outs instead of one was to bar any connection between Agip and Kinz without reference to the records of Lloyds Bank.
>
> It is, of course, possible that Mr Jackson and Mr Griffin were honest men and that there were facts which we do not know which would demonstrate that. But, if so, they could have attended the trial and explained their position in the witness box. They did not do so. One can only infer that they were not prepared to submit their activities to critical examination. In the circumstances I think that the judge rightly came to the conclusion that they must have known they were laundering money, and were consequently helping their clients to make arrangements to conceal some dispositions of money which had such a degree of impropriety that neither they nor their clients could afford to have them disclosed.
>
> In the end, it seems to me that the most striking feature in the case is that in August 1984 Mr Jackson and Mr Griffin were being given advice on the possibility that a payment or payments might involve a fraud on Agip. Having got to that point it seems to me that persons acting honestly would have pursued the matter with a view to satisfying themselves that there was no fraud. But there is nothing to show that they did that. They made no inquiries of Agip at all. They let matters continue. In the circumstances, I conclude that Mr Jackson and Mr Griffin are liable as constructive trustees. Mr Bowers is liable for the acts of Mr Jackson, who was his partner, and of Mr Griffin, who was employed by the partnership. Accordingly, I think that the judge came to the right conclusion and I would dismiss the appeal.

In *Eagle Trust*, the claimant failed to establish that the defendant had subjective knowledge of the fraudulent transaction. Objective knowledge was not relevant.

Eagle Trust v SBC Securities Ltd **[1993] 1 WLR 484, HC**

Facts

The defendant company agreed with the claimant company to underwrite the terms of a take over offer. The defendant subsequently arranged to sub-underwrite its liability using a list of sub-underwriters introduced by the claimant's chief executive, Mr Ferriday (F). The list included F as underwriting £13.5 million. The defendant was able to discharge its obligation to the claimant on payment by F through a number of intermediary companies. It transpired that F had misappropriated the claimant's money to fund the payment of £13.5 million to the defendant. The claimant sued the defendant claiming that it was a constructive trustee of the funds misappropriated by F, on the ground that the defendant had knowingly participated in a fraudulent breach committed by F. The claimant alleged that the defendant should have been aware of the danger that F would have been tempted to discharge his liability by misappropriating the claimant's funds, but that the defendant made no inquiries as to the source of F's payments. The defendant applied to have the claim struck out as showing no reasonable cause of action.

Held

In favour of the defendant on the following grounds:

(a) the claimant's allegation failed to establish that the defendant knew that the moneys were misapplied trust funds. 'Knowledge' for these purposes means that the defendant has (i) actual knowledge of the breach of trust, or (ii) wilfully shut its eyes to the obvious, or (iii) wilfully and recklessly failed to make inquiries which an honest and reasonable man would have made. But constructive knowledge or purely objective knowledge (within categories (iv) and (v) of Peter Gibson's judgment in *Re Baden Delvaux*) would be insufficient to found liability in these circumstances;

(b) even if the defendant had entertained some suspicion concerning the source of F's funds, further inquiries from F would not necessarily have revealed the misappropriation of the claimant's funds;

(c) on the assumption that the alleged facts, as detailed in the claimant's statement of the case, were true and that the defendant adduced no evidence, the claim disclosed no cause of action.

> **Vinelott J:** [after referring to the principles laid down by the High Court in *Re Baden Delvaux* and the Court of Appeal in *Agip v Jackson*:] ... Actual or conscious knowledge gives rise to no difficulty and ... a defendant who wilfully closes his eyes to the obvious or who wilfully and recklessly fails to make such inquiries as an honest and reasonable man would make is disentitled to rely on the lack of actual knowledge.
>
> Knowledge may also be inferred, at least in civil cases, if the circumstances set out in paragraphs (iv) and (v) of Peter Gibson J's classification in the *Baden* case [1993] 1 WLR 509, pp 575H–576A, are established and if the defendant does not give evidence or offer any explanation of his conduct. If the circumstances are such that an honest and reasonable man would have appreciated that he was assisting in a dishonest breach of trust, the court may infer from the defendant's silence that he either appreciated the fact, or that he wilfully shut his eyes to the obvious, or wilfully and recklessly failed to make inquiries for fear of what he might learn.
>
> [After reviewing the leading authorities, the learned judge continued:] It can therefore, in my judgment, now be taken as settled law that, notwithstanding the wider language in which the test of liability as constructive trustee in a 'knowing assistance' case is stated in the *Selangor* case [1968] 1 WLR 1555, p 1590 and in the *Karak* case [1972] 1 WLR 602, p 639, and, notwithstanding the concession made by counsel and accepted by Peter Gibson J in the *Baden* case ... a stranger cannot be made liable for knowing assistance in a fraudulent breach of trust unless knowledge of the fraudulent design can be imputed to him on one of the grounds I have described. There must have been something amounting to want of probity on his part. Constructive notice is not enough, though, as I have said, knowledge may be inferred in the absence of evidence by the defendant if such knowledge would have been imputed to an honest and reasonable man.

Royal Brunei Airlines v Tan

Lord Nicholls' illuminating judgment, in *Royal Brunei Airlines v Tan*, reviewed the law concerning 'accessory liability'. He opined that the liability of a third party who assisted a trustee to commit a breach of trust is dependent on the state of mind of the third party and is fault based. Dishonesty on the part of the third party is an essential ingredient of liability, irrespective of the state of mind of the trustee who committed the breach of trust. The trustee will be liable in any event for breach of trust, even if he or she acted innocently, unless he or she is relieved by the court or is protected by an exclusion clause in the trust instrument. Dishonesty on the part of the trustee is, however, not a prerequisite in order to attach liability to the dishonest third party.

Lord Nicholls also rejected the following concepts as part of the dishonest assistance limb of liability:

(a) that no liability to the beneficiaries ought to attach to a third party who does not receive trust property but who procures a breach of trust;

(b) that a third party may be liable to the beneficiaries without being aware that he or she is acting contrary to the terms of the trust;

(c) that an honest third party may be liable if he or she procures a breach of trust by failing to make inquiries which a reasonable person would make;

(d) the expression 'unconscionable conduct' as a substitute for 'dishonesty'.

Royal Brunei Airlines v Tan [1995] 3 WLR 64, PC

Facts

In 1986, the claimant appointed a travel agent, Borneo Leisure Travel Sdn Bhd (BLT), to act in Sabah and Sarawak as its general travel agent for the sale of passenger and cargo transportation. BLT was required to account to the claimant for all amounts received from such sales. Thus, BLT became a trustee for the claimant of the money. Trust sums received were not paid into a separate account, but were paid into BLT's current account and used for its own purposes. The defendant was BLT's managing director and principal shareholder. He was effectively in charge and in control of BLT. BLT's payments fell into arrears and the claimant terminated the agreement. The company later became insolvent. The claimant commenced an action against the defendant claiming an account in respect of the unpaid money. The action was based under the second limb of Lord Selborne's *dictum* in *Barnes v Addy*: 'strangers are not to be made constructive trustees merely because they act as the agents of trustees in transactions . . . unless they assist with knowledge in a dishonest and fraudulent design on the part of the trustees.' The question in issue was whether the breach of trust, which was a prerequisite to liability, had to be a dishonest and fraudulent breach of trust by the trustee.

Held

Allowing the claim, the defendant was required to account to the claimant for the profits received. In equity, a stranger to the trust is liable to make good resulting loss if he or she dishonestly procured or assisted in a breach of trust or fiduciary obligation. It was not a prerequisite of that liability that, in addition, the trustee or fiduciary acted dishonestly:

> **Lord Nicholls of Birkenhead:** The issue on this appeal is whether the breach of trust which is a prerequisite to accessory liability must itself be a dishonest and fraudulent breach of trust by the trustee.
>
> What matters is the state of mind of the third party sought to be made liable, not the state of mind of the trustee. The trustee will be liable in any event for the breach of trust, even if he acted innocently, unless excused by an exemption clause in the trust instrument or relieved by the court. But his state of mind is, essentially, irrelevant to the question whether the third party should be made liable to the beneficiaries for the breach of trust. If the liability of the third party is fault-based, what matters is the nature of his fault, not that of the trustee. In this regard dishonesty on the part of the third party would seem to be a sufficient basis for his liability, irrespective of the state of mind of the trustee who is in breach of trust. It is difficult to see why, if the third party dishonestly assisted in a breach, there should be a further prerequisite to his liability, namely that the trustee also must have been acting dishonestly. The alternative view would mean that a dishonest third party is liable if the trustee is dishonest, but if the trustee did not act dishonestly that of itself would excuse a dishonest third party from liability. That would make no sense.
>
> There has been a tendency to cite and interpret and apply Lord Selborne LC's formulation in *Barnes v Addy* (1874) LR 9 Ch App 244, pp 251–52, as though it were a statute. This has particularly been so with the accessory limb of Lord Selborne LC's apothegm. This approach has been inimical to analysis of the underlying concept. Working within this constraint, the courts have found themselves wrestling with the interpretation of the individual ingredients, especially 'knowingly' but also 'dishonest and fraudulent design on the part of the trustees', without examining the underlying reason why a third party who has received no trust property is being made liable at all. One notable exception is the judgment of Thomas J in *Powell v Thompson* [1991] 1 NZLR 597, pp 610–15. On this point he observed, at p 613:
>
>> Once a breach of trust has been committed, the commission of which has involved a third party, the question which arises is one as between the beneficiary and that third party. If the third party's conduct has been unconscionable, then irrespective of the degree of impropriety in the trustee's conduct, the third party is liable to be held accountable to the beneficiary as if he or she were a trustee [emphasis added].
>
> To resolve this issue, it is necessary to take an overall look at the accessory liability principle. A conclusion

cannot be reached on the nature of the breach of trust which may trigger accessory liability without at the same time considering the other ingredients, including, in particular, the state of mind of the third party. It is not necessary, however, to look even more widely and consider the essential ingredients of recipient liability. The issue on this appeal concerns only the accessory liability principle. *Different considerations apply to the two heads of liability. Recipient liability is restitution-based; accessory liability is not* [emphasis added].

No liability

The starting point for any analysis must be to consider the extreme possibility: that a third party who does not receive trust property ought never to be liable directly to the beneficiaries merely because he assisted the trustee to commit a breach of trust or procured him to do so. This possibility can be dismissed summarily. On this, the position which the law has long adopted is clear and makes good sense. Stated in the simplest terms, a trust is a relationship which exists when one person holds property on behalf of another. If, for his own purposes, a third party deliberately interferes in that relationship by assisting the trustee in depriving the beneficiary of the property held for him by the trustee, the beneficiary should be able to look for recompense to the third party as well as the trustee. Affording the beneficiary a remedy against the third party serves the dual purpose of making good the beneficiary's loss should the trustee lack financial means and imposing a liability which will discourage others from behaving in a similar fashion.

The rationale is not far to seek. Beneficiaries are entitled to expect that those who become trustees will fulfil their obligations. They are also entitled to expect, and this is only a short step further, that those who become trustees will be permitted to fulfil their obligations without deliberate intervention from third parties. They are entitled to expect that third parties will refrain from intentionally intruding in the trustee-beneficiary relationship and thereby hindering a beneficiary from receiving his entitlement in accordance with the terms of the trust instrument. There is here a close analogy with breach of contract. A person who knowingly procures a breach of contract, or knowingly interferes with the due performance of a contract, is liable to the innocent party. The underlying rationale is the same.

Strict liability

The other extreme possibility can also be rejected out of hand. This is the case where a third party deals with a trustee without knowing, or having any reason to suspect, that he is a trustee. Or the case where a third party is aware that he is dealing with a trustee but has no reason to know or suspect that their transaction is inconsistent with the terms of the trust. The law has never gone so far as to give a beneficiary a remedy against a non-recipient third party in such circumstances. Within defined limits, proprietary rights, whether legal or equitable, endure against third parties who were unaware of their existence. But accessory liability is concerned with the liability of a person who has not received any property. His liability is not property-based. His only sin is that he interfered with the due performance by the trustee of the fiduciary obligations undertaken by the trustee. These are personal obligations.

Fault-based liability

Given, then, that in some circumstances a third party may be liable directly to a beneficiary, but given also that the liability is not so strict that there would be liability even when the third party was wholly unaware of the existence of the trust, *the next step is to seek to identify the touchstone of liability. By common accord, dishonesty fulfils this role*. Whether, in addition, negligence will suffice is an issue on which there has been a well known difference of judicial opinion [emphasis added].

Most, but not all, commentators prefer the test of dishonesty: see, among others, Birks, P, 'Misdirected funds: restitution from the recipient' (1989) LMCLQ 296; Brindle, MJ and Hooley, RJA, 'Does constructive knowledge make a constructive trustee?' (1987) 61 ALJ 281; Harpum, C, 'The stranger as constructive trustee' (1986) 102 LQR 114, p 267; Birks, P, *The Frontiers of Liability*, 1994, Vol 1, p 9; Loughlan, P, 'Liability for assistance in a breach of fiduciary duty' (1989) 9 OJLS 260; Parker, D and Mellows, A, *The Modern Law of Trusts*, 6th edn, 1994, p 253; Pettit, P, *Equity and the Law of Trusts*, 7th edn, 1993, p 172; Sales, P, 'The tort of conspiracy and civil secondary liability' (1990) 49 CLJ 491; *Snell's Equity*, 29th edn, 1990, p 194; and *Underhill's Law of Trusts and Trustees*, 14th edn, 1987, p 355 and noter-up.

Dishonesty

In the context of the accessory liability principle acting dishonestly, and with lack of probity, which is synonymous, means simply not acting as an honest person would in the circumstances. This is an objective standard. At first sight this may seem surprising. Honesty has a connotation of subjectivity, as distinct from the objectivity of negligence. Honesty, indeed, does have a strong subjective element in that it is a description of a type of conduct assessed in the light of what a person actually knew at the time, as distinct from what a reasonable person would have known or appreciated. Further, honesty and its counterpart dishonesty are mostly concerned with advertent conduct, not inadvertent conduct. Carelessness is not dishonesty. Thus, for the most part, dishonesty is to be equated with conscious impropriety. However, these subjective characteristics of honesty do not mean that individuals are free to set their own standards of honesty in particular circumstances. The standard of what constitutes honest conduct is not subjective. Honesty is not an optional scale, with higher or lower values according to the moral standards of each individual. If a person knowingly appropriates another's property, he will not escape a finding of dishonesty simply because he sees nothing wrong in such behaviour.

In most situations there is little difficulty in identifying how an honest person would behave. Honest people do not intentionally deceive others to their detriment. Honest people do not knowingly take others' property. Unless there is a very good and compelling reason, an honest person does not participate in a transaction if he knows it involves a misapplication of trust assets to the detriment of the beneficiaries. Nor does an honest person in such a case deliberately close his eyes and ears, or deliberately not ask questions, lest he learn something he would rather not know, and then proceed regardless. However, in the situations now under consideration the position is not always so straightforward. This can best be illustrated by considering one particular area: the taking of risks.

Taking risks

All investment involves risk. Imprudence is not dishonesty, although imprudence may be carried recklessly to lengths which call into question the honesty of the person making the decision. This is especially so if the transaction serves another purpose in which that person has an interest of his own.

This type of risk is to be sharply distinguished from the case where a trustee, with or without the benefit of advice, is aware that a particular investment or application of trust property is outside his powers, but nevertheless he decides to proceed in the belief or hope that this will be beneficial to the beneficiaries or, at least, not prejudicial to them. He takes a risk that a clearly unauthorised transaction will not cause loss.

A risk of this nature is for the account of those who take it. If the risk materialises and causes loss, those who knowingly took the risk will be accountable accordingly. This is the type of risk being addressed by Peter Gibson J in the *Baden* case [1993] 1 WLR 509, p 574, when he accepted that fraud includes taking 'a risk to the prejudice of another's rights, which risk is known to be one which there is no right to take'.

Acting in reckless disregard of others' rights or possible rights can be a tell-tale sign of dishonesty. An honest person would have regard to the circumstances known to him, including the nature and importance of the proposed transaction, the nature and importance of his role, the ordinary course of business, the degree of doubt, the practicability of the trustee or the third party proceeding otherwise and the seriousness of the adverse consequences to the beneficiaries. The circumstances will dictate which one or more of the possible courses should be taken by an honest person. He might, for instance, flatly decline to become involved. He might ask further questions. He might seek advice, or insist on further advice being obtained. He might advise the trustee of the risks but then proceed with his role in the transaction. He might do many things. Ultimately, in most cases, an honest person should have little difficulty in knowing whether a proposed transaction, or his participation in it, would offend the normally accepted standards of honest conduct.

Likewise, when called upon to decide whether a person was acting honestly, a court will look at all the circumstances known to the third party at the time. The court will also have regard to personal attributes of the third party, such as his experience and intelligence, and the reason why he acted as he did.

Before leaving cases where there is real doubt, one further point should be noted. To inquire, in such cases, whether a person dishonestly assisted in what is later held to be a breach of trust is to ask a meaningful question, which is capable of being given a meaningful answer. This is not always so if the question is posed in terms of 'knowingly' assisted. Framing the question in the latter form all too often leads one into tortuous convolutions about the 'sort' of knowledge required, when the truth is that 'knowingly' is inapt as a criterion when applied to the gradually darkening spectrum where the differences are of degree and not kind.

Negligence

It is against this background that the question of negligence is to be addressed. This question, it should be remembered, is directed at whether an honest third party who receives no trust property should be liable if he procures or assists in a breach of trust of which he would have become aware had he exercised reasonable diligence. Should he be liable to the beneficiaries for the loss they suffer from the breach of trust?

The majority of persons falling into this category will be the hosts of people who act for trustees in various ways: as advisers, consultants, bankers and agents of many kinds. This category also includes officers and employees of companies in respect of the application of company funds. All these people will be accountable to the trustees for their conduct. For the most part they will owe to the trustees a duty to exercise reasonable skill and care. When that is so, the rights flowing from that duty form part of the trust property. As such, they can be enforced by the beneficiaries in a suitable case if the trustees are unable or unwilling to do so. That being so, it is difficult to identify a compelling reason why, in addition to the duty of skill and care vis à vis the trustees which the third parties have accepted, or which the law has imposed upon them, third parties should also owe a duty of care directly to the beneficiaries.

There remains to be considered the position where third parties are acting for, or dealing with, dishonest trustees. In such cases the trustees would have no claims against the third party. The trustees would suffer no loss by reason of the third party's failure to discover what was going on. The question is whether in this type of situation the third party owes a duty of care to the beneficiaries to, in effect, check that a trustee is not misbehaving. The third party must act honestly. The question is whether that is enough. In agreement with the preponderant view, their Lordships consider that dishonesty is an essential ingredient here. There may be cases where, in the light of the particular facts, a third party will owe a duty of care to the beneficiaries. As a general proposition, however, beneficiaries cannot reasonably expect that all the world dealing with their trustees should owe them a duty to take care lest the trustees are behaving dishonestly.

Unconscionable conduct

Mention, finally, must be made of the suggestion that the test for liability is that of unconscionable conduct. Unconscionable is a word of immediate appeal to an equity lawyer. Equity is rooted historically in the concept of the Lord Chancellor, as the keeper of the Royal Conscience, concerning himself with conduct which was contrary to good conscience. It must be recognised, however, that unconscionable is not a word in everyday use by non-lawyers. If it is to be used in this context, and if it is to be the touchstone for liability as an accessory, it is essential to be clear on what, in this context, unconscionable means. If unconscionable means no more than dishonesty, then dishonesty is the preferable label. If unconscionable means something different, it must be said that it is not clear what that something different is. Either way, therefore, the term is better avoided in this context.

The accessory liability principle

Drawing the threads together, their Lordships' overall conclusion is that dishonesty is a necessary ingredient of accessory liability. It is also a sufficient ingredient. A liability in equity to make good resulting loss attaches to a person who dishonestly procures or assists in a breach of trust or fiduciary obligation. It is not necessary that, in addition, the trustee or fiduciary was acting dishonestly, although this will usually be so where the third party who is assisting him is acting dishonestly. 'Knowingly' is better avoided as a defining ingredient of the principle, and in the context of this principle the *Baden* . . . scale of knowledge is best forgotten.

Conclusion

From this statement of the principle it follows that this appeal succeeds. BLT committed a breach of trust by using the money instead of simply deducting its commission and holding the money intact until it paid the airline. The defendant accepted that he knowingly assisted in that breach of trust. In other words, he caused or permitted his company to apply the money in a way he knew was not authorised by the trust of which the company was trustee. Set out in these bald terms, the defendant's conduct was dishonest. By the same token, and for good measure, BLT also acted dishonestly. The defendant was the company, and his state of mind is to be imputed to the company.

Question

Lord Selborne in *Barnes v Addy* declares 'the knowingly assisting' test as, 'assisting with knowledge in a dishonest or fraudulent design on the part of the trustees'. Lord Nicholls in *Royal Brunei Airlines v Tan* refers to the same principle as, 'a person who dishonestly procures or assists in a breach of trust or fiduciary obligation'. How would you reconcile these two statements of liability?

Test for dishonesty

Recently, the House of Lords in *Twinsectra Ltd v Yardley* considered the standards that are required to be adopted in order to determine whether the defendant has acted dishonestly. The Law Lords treated the opinion of Lord Nicholls in *Royal Brunei Airlines v Tan* as definitive and subjected his speech to detailed analysis. The Law Lords considered that there are three possible standards by which a person's dishonesty may be judged – purely subjectively, purely objectively, and a combination of objectivity and subjectivity. The majority of the Law Lords (Lord Millett dissented) rejected the first two standards and decided in favour of the combined standard. The purely subjective standard was rejected for it would be impractical for the defendant to set his own standards of honesty. The purely objective standard was rejected by the majority of the Law Lords on the basis that dishonesty involves an element of subjectivity. The personal attributes of the defendant ought to be taken into account (although this standard appealed to Lord Millett). The majority of the Law Lords adopted the criminal law test for dishonesty (as laid down by Lord Lane CJ in *R v Ghosh* [1982] QB 1053), namely, the defendant's conduct is dishonest by reference to the ordinary standards of reasonable and honest people *and* he or she realised that his or her conduct was dishonest by those standards.

Twinsectra Ltd v Yardley [2002] UKHL 12, HL

Facts

Mr Leach (L) was a solicitor and the second defendant. He acted for an entrepreneur, Mr Yardley (Y), in a transaction which included the negotiation of a loan of £1m from Twinsectra Ltd. L did not deal directly with Twinsectra. Another firm of solicitors, Sims (S), represented themselves as acting on behalf of Y. S received the money in return for an undertaking to the effect that the fund would be applied solely in the acquisition of a specified property. Contrary to the undertaking, S did not retain the money. On being given an assurance by Y that the fund would be so applied, S paid it over to L. He in turn took no steps to ensure that it was utilised for the stated purpose but simply paid it out upon Y's instructions. The result was that £357,700 was used by Y for purposes other than the acquisition of property. The loan was not repaid. Twinsectra sued all the parties involved, including L. The claim against him was based on dishonestly assisting S in a breach of trust. The particulars of the claim were that the payment by S to L in breach of the undertaking was a breach of trust, and it was alleged that L was liable for dishonestly assisting S in that breach.

The trial judge did not accept that the moneys were subject to any form of trust in the hands of S and decided that, in any event, the terms of the undertaking were too vague to create a trust. He also held that L was not acting dishonestly (but was misguided) in receiving the money and paying it to Y without concerning himself about its application. The Court of Appeal reversed the decision of the judge and decided that the undertaking executed by S created a *Quistclose* trust (an express purpose trust) and that L had acted dishonestly in deliberately shutting his eyes to the implications of the undertaking. L appealed to the House of Lords.

Held

Allowing the appeal, the court decided that:

(a) Money held in a solicitor's client account was held on trust. The funds were paid to S, a firm of solicitors and were therefore subject to a trust. The only question was as to the terms of the trust. On these facts, the effect of the undertaking executed by S was that the fund remained Twinsectra's money until such time as it was applied for the stated purpose. It followed that S held the fund on trust for Twinsectra, but subject to a power to apply it by way of loan in accordance with the undertaking.

(b) The test for certainty of objects applicable to powers was satisfied. This test is whether the court can say that a given application of the money does or does not fall within its terms.

(c) (Lord Millett dissenting) In determining whether a defendant acted dishonestly under accessorial liability, a combined objective/subjective test was applicable. The test requires the claimant to prove that the defendant was (i) dishonest by the ordinary standards of reasonable and honest people (objective), and (ii) that he or she realised that his or her conduct was dishonest by those standards (subjective).

(d) A reversal of the decision of the trial judge on a question of fact may be done only in exceptional circumstances. It was not proper for the Court of Appeal to reverse the decision of the trial judge on the issue of dishonesty. On the facts, there was sufficient evidence to indicate that the trial judge had not misdirected himself as to the appropriate test for dishonesty.

Lord Hutton: Whilst in discussing the term 'dishonesty' the courts often draw a distinction between subjective dishonesty and objective dishonesty, there are three possible standards which can be applied to determine whether a person has acted dishonestly. There is a purely subjective standard, whereby a person is only regarded as dishonest if he transgresses his own standard of honesty, even if that standard is contrary to that of reasonable and honest people. This has been termed the 'Robin Hood test' and has been rejected by the courts. As Sir Christopher Slade stated in *Walker v Stones* [2000] Lloyds Rep PN 864, 877 para 164: 'A person may in some cases act dishonestly, according to the ordinary use of language, even though he genuinely believes that his action is morally justified. The penniless thief, for example, who picks the pocket of the multi-millionaire is dishonest even though he genuinely considers that theft is morally justified as a fair redistribution of wealth and that he is not therefore being dishonest.'

Secondly, there is a purely objective standard whereby a person acts dishonestly if his conduct is dishonest by the ordinary standards of reasonable and honest people, even if he does not realise this. Thirdly, there is a standard which combines an objective test and a subjective test, and which requires that before there can be a finding of dishonesty it must be established that the defendant's conduct was dishonest by the ordinary standards of reasonable and honest people and that he himself realised that by those standards his conduct was dishonest. I will term this 'the combined test'.

There is a passage in the earlier part of the judgment in *Royal Brunei* which suggests that Lord Nicholls considered that dishonesty has a subjective element. Thus in discussing the honest trustee and the dishonest third party, he stated:

> These examples suggest that what matters is the state of mind of the third party . . . But [the trustee's] state of mind is essentially irrelevant to the question whether the third party should be made liable to the beneficiaries for breach of trust.

However, after stating that the touchstone of liability is dishonesty, Lord Nicholls went on to discuss the meaning of dishonesty:

> Before considering this issue further it will be helpful to define the terms being used by looking more closely at what dishonesty means in this context. Whatever may be the position in some criminal or other contexts (see, for instance, *R v Ghosh* [1982] QB 1053), in the context of the accessory liability principle acting dishonestly, or with a lack of probity, which is synonymous, means simply not acting as an honest person would in the circumstances. This is an objective standard.

My noble and learned friend Lord Millett has subjected this passage and subsequent passages in the judgment to detailed analysis and is of the opinion that Lord Nicholls used the term 'dishonesty' in a purely objective sense so that in this area of the law a person can be held to be dishonest even though he does not realise that what he is doing is dishonest by the ordinary standards of honest people. This leads Lord Millett on to the conclusion that in determining the liability of an accessory dishonesty is not necessary and that liability depends on knowledge.

In *R v Ghosh* [1982] QB 1053 Lord Lane CJ held that in the law of theft dishonesty required that the defendant himself must have realised that what he was doing was dishonest by the ordinary standards of reasonable and honest people. The three sentences in Lord Nicholl's judgment which appear to draw a distinction between the position in criminal law and the position in equity, do give support to Lord Millett's view. But considering those sentences in the context of the remainder of the paragraph and taking account of other passages in the judgment, I think that in referring to an objective standard Lord Nicholls was contrasting it with the purely subjective standard whereby a man sets his own standard of honesty and does not regard as dishonest what upright and responsible people would regard as dishonest. Thus after stating that dishonesty is assessed on an objective standard he continued:

> At first sight this may seem surprising. Honesty has a connotation of subjectivity, as distinct from the objectivity of negligence. Honesty, indeed, does have a strong subjective element in that it is a description of a type of conduct assessed in the light of what a person actually knew at the time, as distinct from what a reasonable person would have known or appreciated. Further, honesty and its counterpart dishonesty are mostly concerned with advertent conduct, not inadvertent conduct. Carelessness is not dishonesty. Thus for the most part dishonesty is to be equated with conscious impropriety. However, these subjective characteristics of honesty do not mean that individuals are free to set their own standards of honesty in particular circumstances. The standard of what constitutes honest conduct is not subjective. Honesty is not an optional scale, with higher or lower values according to the moral standards of each individual. If a person knowingly appropriates another's property, he will not escape a finding of dishonesty simply because he sees nothing wrong in such behaviour.

Further, Lord Nicholls said:

> Ultimately, in most cases, an honest person should have little difficulty in knowing whether a proposed transaction, or his participation in it, would offend the normally accepted standards of honest conduct. Likewise, when called upon to decide whether a person was acting honestly, a court will look at all the circumstances known to the third party at the time. The court will also have regard to personal attributes of the third party, such as his experience and intelligence, and the reason why he acted as he did.

The use of the word 'knowing' in the first sentence would be superfluous if the defendant did not have to be aware that what he was doing would offend the normally accepted standards of honest conduct, and the need to look at the experience and intelligence of the defendant would also appear superfluous if all that was required was a purely objective standard of dishonesty. Therefore I do not think that Lord Nicholls was stating that in this sphere of equity a man can be dishonest even if he does not know that what he is doing would be regarded as dishonest by honest people.

Then Lord Nicholls stated the general principle that dishonesty is a necessary ingredient of accessory liability and that knowledge is not an appropriate test:

> There is, in my opinion, a further consideration which supports the view that for liability as an accessory to arise the defendant must himself appreciate that what he was doing was dishonest by the standards of honest and reasonable men. A finding by a judge that a defendant has been dishonest is a grave finding, and it is particularly grave against a professional man, such as a solicitor. Notwithstanding that the issue arises in equity law and not in a criminal context, I think that it would be less than just for the law to permit a finding that a defendant had been 'dishonest' in assisting in a breach of trust where he knew of the facts which created the trust and its breach but had not been aware that what he was doing would be regarded by honest men as being dishonest.

It would be open to your Lordships to depart from the principle stated by Lord Nicholls that dishonesty is a necessary ingredient of accessory liability and to hold that knowledge is a sufficient ingredient. But the statement of that principle by Lord Nicholls has been widely regarded as clarifying this area of the law and, as he observed, the tide of authority in England has flowed strongly in favour of the test of dishonesty. Therefore I consider that the courts should continue to apply that test and that your Lordships should state that dishonesty requires knowledge by the defendant that what he was doing would be regarded as dishonest by honest people, although he should not escape a finding of dishonesty because he sets his own standards of honesty and does not regard as dishonest what he knows would offend the normally accepted standards of honest conduct.

In cases subsequent to *Royal Brunei* there has been some further consideration of the test to be applied to determine dishonesty (the cases being helpfully discussed in an article by Mr Andrew Stafford QC on 'Solicitors' liability for knowing receipt and dishonest assistance in breach of trust' in (2001) 17 Professional Negligence 3). For the reasons which I have given I consider that in *Abbey National plc v Solicitors Indemnity Fund Ltd* [1997] PNLR 306 Steel J applied the correct test. In that case she referred to the test set out in *R v Ghosh* [1982] QB 1053 and to Lord Nicholl's judgment in *Royal Brunei* [1995] 2 AC 378 and observed that it was to the effect that honesty is to be judged objectively, and she continued:

> What in this case, did, Mr Fallon do, and was he acting as a reasonable and honest solicitor would do? In that

case it was laid down that individuals are not free to set their own standards. Mr Fenwick on behalf of the defendant says that if I find that by those standards Mr Fallon was dishonest that would be enough. I need to consider what he did and ask the question: Was he acting as an honest person should? Was what he did dishonest by the standards of a reasonable and honest man or a reasonable and honest solicitor? Having read that case, however, it seems to me that the judgment does not set down a wholly objective test for civil cases. Lord Nicholls particularly refers to a conscious impropriety. The test there, it seems, does embrace a subjective approach, and I have to look at the circumstances to see whether they were such that Mr Fallon must have known that what he did was by the standards of ordinary decent people dishonest. I accept totally that individuals should not be free to set their own standards, but there is in my view a subjective element both in civil and in criminal cases.

I agree with Lord Hoffmann that it is unfortunate that Carnwath J [the trial judge] referred to Mr Leach deliberately shutting his eyes to the problems and to the implications of the undertaking, but like Lord Hoffmann I do not think it probable that having cited the passage from the judgment of Lord Nicholls in the *Royal Brunei* case at [1995] 2 AC 378, 389 F, the judge then overlooked the issue of Nelsonian dishonesty in finding that Mr Leach was not dishonest. I also consider, as Lord Millett has observed, that this was not a case where Mr Leach deliberately closed his eyes and ears, or deliberately did not ask questions, lest he learned something he would rather not know – he already knew all the facts, but the judge concluded that nevertheless he had not been dishonest.

Lord Millett [dissenting on the standard of dishonesty]: In my opinion Lord Nicholls [in *Tan*] was adopting an objective standard of dishonesty by which the defendant is expected to attain the standard which would be observed by an honest person placed in similar circumstances. Account must be taken of subjective considerations such as the defendant's experience and intelligence and his actual state of knowledge at the relevant time. But it is not necessary that he should actually have appreciated that he was acting dishonestly; it is sufficient that he was.

The question for your Lordships is not whether Lord Nicholls was using the word dishonesty in a subjective or objective sense in *Royal Brunei Airlines Sdn Bhd v Tan* [1995] 2 AC 378. The question is whether a plaintiff should be required to establish that an accessory to a breach of trust had a dishonest state of mind (so that he was subjectively dishonest in the *R v Ghosh* sense); or whether it should be sufficient to establish that he acted with the requisite knowledge (so that his conduct was objectively dishonest). This question is at large for us, and we are free to resolve it either way. I would resolve it by adopting the objective approach. I would do so because:

(1) Consciousness of wrongdoing is an aspect of *mens rea* and an appropriate condition of criminal liability: it is not an appropriate condition of civil liability. This generally results from negligent or intentional conduct. For the purpose of civil liability, it should not be necessary that the defendant realised that his conduct was dishonest; it should be sufficient that it constituted intentional wrongdoing.

(2) The objective test is in accordance with Lord Selborne's statement in *Barnes v Addy* LR 9 Ch App 244 and traditional doctrine. This taught that a person who knowingly participates in the misdirection of money is liable to compensate the injured party. While negligence is not a sufficient condition of liability, intentional wrongdoing is. Such conduct is culpable and falls below the objective standards of honesty adopted by ordinary people.

(3) The claim for 'knowing assistance' is the equitable counterpart of the economic torts. These are intentional torts; negligence is not sufficient and dishonesty is not necessary. Liability depends on knowledge. A requirement of subjective dishonesty introduces an unnecessary and unjustified distinction between the elements of the equitable claim and those of the tort of wrongful interference with the performance of a contract.

Note

Slade LJ in *Walker v Stones* echoes Millett LJ's opinion (as he then was) in the earlier case, *Armitage v Nurse* [1997] 2 All ER 705. A flexible objective standard for dishonesty was adopted, ie, an objective test taking into account the characteristics of the defendant, such as his or her expertise and experience. Thus, following *Walker v Stones*, a solicitor–trustee who deliberately acts in breach of trust, but in good faith, may be treated as dishonest if no reasonable solicitor–trustee would have held such belief. This was expressed in the context of an exemption clause that did not exclude liability for dishonesty.

Walker v Stones [2000] 4 All ER 412, CA

Slade LJ: The clause in my judgment would not exempt the trustees from liability for breaches of trust, even if committed in the genuine belief that the course taken by them was in the interests of the beneficiaries, if such belief was so unreasonable that no reasonable solicitor–trustee could have held that belief.

Question
By what standard is dishonesty measured?

In *Brown v Bennett*, the court decided that a director of a company who was in breach of his managerial duties was not, without more, liable as a constructive trustee under the 'knowing assistance' head.

Brown v Bennett and Others (1998) The Times, 3 January, HC

Facts
The business of Pinecord Ltd was put into receivership and in February 1991 was purchased from the receiver by three defendants, Maurice and Michael Bennett and Vivian Scott. The purchase was effected through the medium of an off-the-shelf company, Oasis Ltd. The Bennetts and Mr Scott became directors of Oasis. A stock exchange flotation of Oasis followed in June 1995. The claimants' case against the defendants was that the Bennetts became *de facto* directors of Pinecord in February 1988 and shareholders of the company in August 1988. They allegedly followed a course of conduct in their management of Pinecord Ltd which was intended to put the company into financial difficulty in order to enable them to increase their share of its equity. The claimants alleged that the last step in their scheme was to put Pinecord Ltd into receivership with a view to buying the business from the receiver for their benefit. The claimants contended that Oasis had knowingly and dishonestly assisted the defendants so as to become a constructive trustee under the 'knowing assistance' limb of *Barnes v Addy*.

Held
The claimants failed to establish that the defendants were liable to account. It was impossible to contend that Oasis had any connection with the defendant directors' alleged breaches of trust. There was insufficient evidence to establish liability on the part of Oasis. The court also decided that where there had been no breach of trust affecting property, but merely a breach of directors' duties in relation to the management of a company's affairs, it would be an unwarranted extension of the *Barnes v Addy* principle to impose liability as constructive trustees on the directors.

Review of the test of dishonesty

In *Barlow Clowes International Ltd v Eurotrust International Ltd*, the Privy Council acknowledged that there was an element of ambiguity in the remarks of Lord Hutton in *Twinsectra*. This was sufficient to encourage some academics to suggest that the *Twinsectra* case had changed the law by inviting an inquiry not merely into the defendant's mental state about the nature of the transaction, but also into his views about generally acceptable standards of honesty. However their Lordships in the Privy Council did not consider that was what Lord Hutton meant. Their view of Lord Hutton's statement as to the test of dishonesty meant only that the defendant's knowledge of the transaction had to be such as to render his participation contrary to normally acceptable standards of honest conduct. It did not require that he should have had reflections about what those normally acceptable standards were.

Barlow Clowes International Ltd (in liquidation) v Eurotrust International Ltd and others
[2006] I All ER 333, Privy Council

Facts

The claimant, a Gibraltar company in liquidation, had previously operated a fraudulent offshore investment scheme purporting to offer high returns from investments in gilt-edged securities. It claimed that the first defendant, an Isle of Man company and its principal directors had dishonestly assisted in the misappropriation of investors' funds. The claimant brought proceedings in the High Court of the Isle of Man. The judge proceeded on the basis that liability for dishonest assistance required a dishonest state of mind on the part of the defendant. This involved a subjective mental state, but the standard set by law to measure the dishonesty was objective. In relation to the second defendant, Mr Henwood, one of the principal directors, the judge found that he had had a dishonest state of mind because he had strongly suspected that the funds passing through his hands were moneys that the claimant company had received from members of the public who thought they were investing in gilt-edged securities. If those suspicions were correct then no honest person could have assisted in the disposal of the funds. Further, the judge found that he had consciously decided not to make inquiries so as to avoid the risk of discovering the truth. Accordingly the judge found the defendants liable for dishonestly assisting in the misappropriation of the funds. On appeal, Mr Henwood's appeal was allowed on the basis that the evidence did not support the findings of the judge. The claimant appealed to the Privy Council. Mr Henwood argued that his state of mind could not have been dishonest unless he had been *aware* that his conduct was dishonest by the ordinary standards of society. It was argued on his behalf that an inquiry into the defendant's views about standards of honesty was required.

Held

Allowing the appeal, the court decided that an inquiry into the defendant's view about standards of honesty was not required. Consciousness of dishonesty required consciousness of those elements of the transaction which made participation transgress ordinary standards of honest behaviour. It did not also require the defendant to have thought about what those standards were. The Privy Council decided that there were sufficient evidence to justify the trial judge's findings. She found that Mr Henwood had solid grounds for suspicion, which he consciously ignored, that the disposals in which Mr Henwood participated involved dealings with misappropriated funds.

Lord Hoffman: [After referring to the judgment of Lord Hutton in *Twinsectra v Yardley* [2002] UKHL 12, his Lordship continued] In submitting that an inquiry into the defendant's views about standards of honesty is required, [counsel for Mr Henwood] relied upon a statement by Lord Hutton in *Twinsectra Ltd v Yardley* with which the majority of their Lordships agreed:

> There is, in my opinion, a further consideration which supports the view that for liability as an accessory to arise the defendant must himself appreciate that what he was doing was dishonest by the standards of honest and reasonable men. A finding by a judge that a defendant has been dishonest is a grave finding, and it is particularly grave against a professional man, such as a solicitor. Notwithstanding that the issue arises in equity law and not in a criminal context, I think that it would be less than just for the law to permit a finding that a defendant had been "dishonest" in assisting in a breach of trust where he knew of the facts which created the trust and its breach but had not been aware that what he was doing would be regarded by honest men as being dishonest.
>
> . . . I consider that the courts should continue to apply that test and that your Lordships should state that dishonesty requires knowledge by the defendant that what he was doing would be regarded as dishonest by honest people, although he should not escape a finding of dishonesty because he sets his own standards of honesty and does not regard as dishonest what he knows would offend the normally accepted standards of honest conduct.

Their Lordships accept that there is an element of ambiguity in these remarks which may have encouraged a belief, expressed in some academic writing, that the *Twinsectra* case had departed from the law as previously understood and invited inquiry not merely into the defendant's mental state about the nature of the transaction in which he was participating but also into his views about generally acceptable standards of honesty. But they do not consider that this is what Lord Hutton meant. The reference to 'what he knows would offend normally accepted standards of honest conduct' meant only that his knowledge of the transaction had to be such as to render his participation contrary to normally acceptable standards of honest conduct. It did not require that he should have had reflections about what those normally acceptable standards were.

Similarly in the speech of Lord Hoffmann [in *Twinsectra*], the statement that a dishonest state of mind meant 'consciousness that one is transgressing ordinary standards of honest behaviour' was in their Lordships' view intended to require consciousness of those elements of the transaction which make participation transgress ordinary standards of honest behaviour. It did not also require him to have thought about what those standards were.

In *Abou-Ramah v Abacha*, the Court observed that this was the first opportunity since the *Barlow Clowes* case for the Court of Appeal to consider the element of dishonesty for accessory liability. The Court decided that the test of dishonesty is predominantly objective but with a subjective element and the *Barlow Clowes* decision did not involve a departure from the *Twinsectra* case. Rather, the *Barlow Clowes* case gives guidance as to the proper interpretation of *Twinsectra* and demonstrates how *Royal Brunei* and *Twinsectra* could be read together to form a consistent corpus of law.

Abou-Ramah v Abacha [2006] All ER (D) 80, Court of Appeal

Facts

The claimants were a lawyer practising in Kuwait and a Kuwaiti trading company. They were the victims of a fraud practised by three of the defendants. The fraudsters contacted the claimants seeking the latter's assistance in investing about £65m in an Arab country on behalf of a trust. The claimants agreed to identify and manage suitable investments for the trust in return for 40% of the trust capital and 15% of its income. The fraudulent scheme involved the claimants being asked to make financial contributions to facilitate the transfer of sums from Benin to the claimants. They were told that bureaucratic conditions in Benin necessitated a contribution from the claimants and finally that £625,000 for VAT were payable on the alleged trust money. The claim concerned the payment of £625,000 paid by the claimants into the account of a Nigerian bank, City Express Bank (the bank) held at HSBC in London for onward transfer to a client described as Trusty International. The bank transferred the sum to its customer's account held at its branch in Nigeria. No trust money ever materialised, the sums paid into the account were withdrawn shortly after payment in and the fraudsters disappeared. The claimants commenced proceedings against the bank for knowing assistance and restitution of money had and received. The bank raised the defence of change of position. The trial judge dismissed the claims on the ground that there was no dishonesty on the part of the defendant bank and accepted the defendant's defence that there had been a change of position in that the bank was not conscious that the fraudulent transaction amounted to a money laundering scheme. The claimants appealed to the Court of Appeal.

Held

Dismissing the appeal. The court ruled as follows:

- since the trial judge decided that the bank did not act dishonestly it would be inappropriate to reverse this finding. The bank's general suspicion that the fraudsters (clients) were involved in money laundering at the instance of corrupt politicians was not sufficient to attribute dishonesty to the bank. The bank had no particular suspicions about the transactions in question. There were no grounds for the bank to raise additional inquiries of any person or to decline to act.

- The bank acted bona fide in changing its position to such an extent that it would be inequitable to require it to make restitution to the claimants (see later). The court decided that the requirement of good faith had to be construed not only by reference to the circumstances of the particular transactions in question, but by having regard to all the material circumstances of the case. The circumstance of the opening of the account was a suspicion that the bank's new customer might from time to time be engaged in money laundering. That put the bank on its guard and it was required to make further inquiries to remove any doubt attendant on the transactions in question. However, in reliance on the trial judge's findings the court (Rix LJ expressed some doubt without dissenting) decided that the bank had no particular suspicions that the transactions constituted money laundering. The bank had done all that it had to do by complying with the requirements of Nigerian law on money laundering and satisfied itself that there were no doubts about the transactions.

Arden LJ: In this appeal, there are two principal issues. The first is whether the respondent ("the bank") is liable for dishonest assistance in a breach of trust ("the dishonest assistance issue") and the second is whether the bank is entitled to rely on the defence of change of position in respect of the claim for money had and received ("the change of position issue"). In summary, my conclusions on these issues and reasons for those conclusions are as follows:

a. The dishonest assistance issue
I agree with Rix LJ that the appeal on this issue fails. In *Barlow Clowes International Ltd (in liquidation) v Eurotrust International Ltd* [2006] 1 All ER 333, the Privy Council considered the case law of England and Wales on the issue of the element of dishonesty necessary for liability under this head. Its interpretation of that case law was that it is unnecessary to show subjective dishonesty in the sense of consciousness that the transaction is dishonest. It is sufficient if the defendant knows of the elements of the transaction which make it dishonest according to normally accepted standards of behaviour. This is the first opportunity, so far as I am aware, that this Court has had an opportunity of considering the decision of the Privy Council, and in my judgment this court should follow the decision of the Privy Council. On the findings of the judge, the appellants' appeal on this dishonest assistance point must fail.

b. The change of position issue
In my judgment, the bank must show that, by making payments out of its HSBC account in response to the appellants' instructions, its position was so changed that it would be inequitable to require it to make restitution. The judge held that the bank was not conscious that these particular payments in issue in this case constituted a money laundering scheme. In those circumstances, in my judgment, the bank has established the requirements for change of position. I do not, with respect, agree with Rix LJ that this court should have regard to the fact that, when establishing the account, the bank suspected (in a general way) that Trusty International ("TI") might from time to time be involved in money laundering.

The decision of the House of Lords in *Twinsectra Ltd v Yardley* [2002] 2 AC 164 was widely interpreted as requiring both an objective and subjective test to be applied to the question of standard. In the case of the subjective test, that would mean that the defendant would not be guilty of dishonesty unless he was conscious that the transaction fell below normally acceptable standards of conduct. The Privy Council in the *Barlow Clowes* case has now clarified that this is a wrong interpretation of the *Twinsectra* decision. It is not a requirement of the standard of dishonesty that the defendant should be conscious of his wrongdoing. *Snell's Equity* now refers to this as the "better view" (31st ed, para.28–46 as updated).

66. On the basis of this interpretation, the test of dishonesty is predominantly objective: did the conduct of the defendant fall below the normally acceptable standard? But there are also subjective aspects of dishonesty. As Lord Nicholls said in the *Royal Brunei* case, honesty has "a strong subjective element in that it is a description of a type of conduct assessed in the light of what a person actually knew at the time, as distinct from what a reasonable person would have known or appreciated" (page 389 and see generally pp 389 to 391). In this case, the judge applied the *Barlow Clowes* decision without asking himself, on the basis that *Twinsectra* was binding on him under the doctrine of precedent and the *Barlow Clowes* case, as a decision of the Privy Council, was only persuasive authority.

Accordingly, in my judgment, before this court or the High Court decides to follow a decision of the Privy Council in place of a decision of the House of Lords the circumstances must be quite exceptional and the court must be satisfied that in practice the result would be a foregone conclusion. In my judgment, the circumstances of this case are also exceptional and justify the course which the judge took for the following reasons:

i.   The decision in *Twinsectra* is of course binding on this court and the judge. But the *Barlow Clowes* decision does not involve a departure from, or refusal to follow, the *Twinsectra* case. Rather, the *Barlow Clowes* case gives guidance as to the proper interpretation to be placed on it as a matter of English law. It shows how the *Royal Brunei* case and the the *Twinsectra* case can be read together to form a consistent corpus of law.

ii.   The meaning of dishonesty in the *Twinsectra* case appeared to involve an additional subjective element, namely an awareness on the part of the accessory that his conduct was dishonest. The decision under appeal in the *Barlow Clowes* case was an appeal from the Isle of Man but no distinction was drawn between the law of Isle of Man and the law of England and Wales. It would appear therefore that the Privy Council was also intending to clarify English law since that is the only logical implication from the methodology of interpretation of an English authority. That interpretation could hardly have been an interpretation which only applied in the Isle of Man but not in England and Wales. The approach of the Privy Council was both striking and bold: one writer has referred to it as taking judicial re-interpretation 'to new heights' (Virgo, *Mapping the Law, Essays in Memory of Peter Birks*, ed Burrows and Rodger (2006) (Oxford) ch 5 p 86). The decision in the *Barlow Clowes* case could probably have been reached without consideration of the *Twinsectra* decision for the purpose of English law, and it is significant that the Privy Council took another course.

iii. Furthermore, the members of the Privy Council in the *Barlow Clowes* case are (or were at the date of the hearing of the appeal) all members of the Appellate Committee of the House of Lords. Their number was five, and that does not represent a majority of the Appellate Committee as in *Holley*. But the approach in *Barlow Clowes* was to clarify the meaning of the speeches of Lord Hutton and Lord Hoffmann in the *Twinsectra* case. The view expressed by Lord Hutton represented the view of the majority. Two members of the constitution of the Appellate Committee which sat in *Twinsectra* (Lord Steyn and Lord Hoffmann) were parties to the decision in *Barlow Clowes*. It is difficult to see that another constitution of the Appellate Committee would itself come to a different view as to what the majority in *Twinsectra* had meant. Put another way, I do not see how in these particular circumstances this court could be criticised for adopting the interpretation of the *Twinsectra* decision unanimously adopted by the Privy Council, consisting of members of the Appellate Committee at least two of whom were parties to the *Twinsectra* decision, in preference to its own.

iv.   There is no overriding reason why in respect of dishonesty in the context of civil liability (as opposed to criminal responsibility) the law should take account of the defendant's views as to the morality of his actions.

In my judgment, the judge was right on this issue of dishonesty, on the findings he made. The court is entitled to take into account that the fact that these events occurred in a commercial setting which obliges banks to act on proper instructions. Mr Faronbi complied with the regulatory requirements for the reporting of large transactions. The evidence was that cash payments are commonly made legitimately in Nigeria. The highest that it can be put is that the bank had suspicions about TI's possible involvement in the money-laundering of money at the instance of corrupt politicians. But it had no knowledge of any specific act of dishonesty by TI and it had no grounds for believing that the appellants were, or were associates of, politicians and it had no particular suspicions about the transactions in question. There was no finding that in those circumstances a bank would normally raise additional inquiries of any person or decline to act. Thus, the lack of particular suspicions about the transactions in question in my judgment diminished Mr Faronbi's general suspicions for the purpose of those transactions to an extent that it was no longer commercially unacceptable for the bank to implement the instructions that the bank had received.

In the circumstances it is unnecessary for me to deal with the challenge to the judge's finding that the bank did not know about the existence of a situation giving rise to a fiduciary obligation or its breach. I would thus dismiss the appeal on the dishonest assistance issue. I do not consider that this is an appropriate case in which to order a retrial.

The change of position issue
As I have explained, the judge found that the bank's suspicions of the impropriety of the bank's customers did not relate to the two transactions in question, and therefore they did not disentitle the bank from relying on a defence of change of position. He also found that the failure to make further inquiries did not amount to commercially unacceptable conduct and therefore bad faith. Rix LJ considers that, in the light of the suspicions which the bank had when setting up the account and the importance in policy terms of creating a deterrent where a bank acts for a customer suspected of money-laundering, the bank is precluded from relying on a defence of change of position.

The defence of change of position was established in the *Lipkin Gorman* case [1991] AC 548. It was not comprehensively defined. Lord Goff, with whom Lord Bridge, Lord Ackner and Lord Griffith agreed, held:

    At present I do not wish to state the principle any less broadly than this: that the defence is available to a person whose position has so changed that it would be inequitable in all the circumstances to require him to make restitution, or alternatively, to make restitution in full.

To treat the defence of change position as unavailable in this situation is as I see it an insufficiently nuanced approach. Of course, once the bank had formed a suspicion about its customer, it had to be aware of that suspicion in all its dealings with the customer. But the bank had done all that it had to do to remove that suspicion by complying with the requirements of Nigerian law on money laundering and by being satisfied that it had no other residual doubts about the two payments. The imposition of liability in this case would serve to motivate banks not to act for customers in areas of business which gave rise to a general suspicion of money-laundering even where there was no information or suspicion that the customer was so involved. It seems to me that that is a road down which the court should not go, at any rate without fuller submissions than we have had. It would be different if as in the *Niru Battery* case there were further enquiries or steps which the bank should have made or taken, but that is not the appellants' case. In all the circumstances, I do not consider that the bank can be criticised for making the two payments, and accordingly in my judgment it is entitled to the defence of change of position.

With deference to the views of Rix LJ in this case, I do not consider that the bank here can be said to have acted otherwise than in good faith. Moreover, lack of good faith must in my judgment be related to the change of position, that is to say it must relate to the circumstances in which monies were received or in which they have been discharged, thus giving rise to the defence. Thus in this case, the fact that the bank opened an account when it had suspicions of possible money laundering does not amount to a lack of good faith when those suspicions did not extend to the payments under consideration in this case. It is not the function of the court in deciding whether a defence of change of position is made out to punish a defendant for conduct which is unrelated to the transactions on which the cause of action of the claimant is based. In addition, it is a relevant consideration that the bank did not receive any funds beneficially as its enrichment by the payments made by the appellants was of a lesser degree than where a party receives funds for its own use and benefit.

Rix LJ: It seems to me that once Mr Faronbi suspected Trusty International's directors of participating in money laundering, on the basis of the judge's clear findings of what Mr Faronbi was aware of, the distinction which the judge then drew between Mr Faronbi's suspicions of the business in general and his ignorance about the particular transactions in question in this case becomes a thin line whose value for the purposes of insulating Mr Faronbi and thus the Bank from the necessary complicity is highly uncertain. It is one thing to be negligent in failing to spot a possible money launderer, providing the negligence does not extend to shutting one's eyes to the truth. It is another thing, however, to have good grounds for suspecting money laundering and then to proceed as though one did not . . . I do not see why a bank which has, through its managers, a clear suspicion that a prospective client indulges in money laundering, can be said to lack that knowledge which is the first element in the tort.

Money had and received
I respectfully differ from Lady Justice Arden's and Lord Justice Pill's assessment of the facts. (1) There must of course be a relevant causal connection between the change of position and the circumstances in which payment is effected. In the present case, however, such a causal connection exists, because the loss would not have occurred, at any rate in the way in which it occurred, unless the bank had been willing to open an account for Messrs Ibrahim's and Saminu's company. (2) I do not agree that the bank did not receive the payments beneficially. It received them in the normal way in which banks receive moneys, that is to say, as the bank's own funds but subject of course to the rights of transferors and depositors. When the payments had been credited to Trusty International, the moneys remained the bank's funds. In the case of the first payment, because the bank had allowed Trusty International to make anticipatory withdrawals, the overdrawn moneys were recouped for the benefit of the bank out of the funds provided by the appellants. In the case of the second payment, the relevant change of position, that is to say, the withdrawal of those funds by Trusty International, had not yet occurred. Of course, it is highly relevant, as I have observed, that the appellants' instructions were to credit Trusty International, and it follows therefore that the appellants did not intend or contemplate that the bank would retain the value of the payments permanently for themselves: but they acted in ignorance of the bank's suspicions about its customer. The bank had those suspicions before it opened Trusty International's account and nevertheless wishes to rely on a defence of change of position. (3) The absence of a conviction for breach of Nigerian law is not a critical factor, given the finding of the judge concerning Mr Faronbi's suspicions about his prospective customers and the CBN's and the bank's own relevant guidelines referred to above. (4) For the same reason, namely the judge's finding of suspicions regarding Messrs Ibrahim's and Saminu's involvement in

money-laundering, this is not a case which turns on mere suspicion of an area of business. For these purposes, 'Know your customer' is the important and well recognised banking watchword. (5) The judge did not make a finding that the bank's opening of Trusty International's account was commercially acceptable: he only found, in relation to knowing assistance in a breach of trust, that the critical matter was that there were no suspicions and no dishonesty regarding the two actual transactions.

In sum, can it be said that a party who opens up an account for a prospective client who is suspected of lending himself to money laundering should have a defence of change of position just because he is unable to identify, and cannot be blamed for failing to identify as suspect, individual dishonest transactions? I think not.

Note

Lord Clarke MR in an article entitled, *'Claims Against Professionals: Negligence, Dishonesty and Fraud'* [2006] 22 Professional Negligence 70, tracks the development of the law in this area. He suggests that that the test of dishonesty is clearly an objective question but the breach involves a subjective assessment of the defendant in the light of what he knew at the time of the breach, as distinct from what a reasonable person would have known and appreciated. Carelessness is not dishonesty and dishonesty is to be equated with conscious impropriety. It is a jury question. Merely because a person says he did not believe what he did was dishonest does not mean the court has to accept that. Provided that the court is of the opinion that with his knowledge he consciously departed from the objective standards of propriety, he may be found to be dishonest. He observes that when Lord Nicholls's judgment in *Tan* is read fully he (Lord Nicholls) expressed the view that in testing an individual's honesty there is no question of what the defendant thought about his conduct. The court is required to assess honesty by taking account of the individual's experience, knowledge and reasons for acting the way he did. Lord Clarke MR concludes thus:

> . . . the simple fact of it seems to be that those who thought that the majority in *Twinsectra* interpreted the test for dishonesty as a combined test, had misunderstood the majority's decision. It might equally be said that the majority and minority in *Twinsectra* had also misunderstood what each other meant: Lord Hutton and Lord Hoffman misunderstood what Lord Millett held and vice versa. Everyone agreed that the test was an objective one i.e. the test did not require any inquiry into the defendant's subjective assessment of standards of honesty.

In *Barnes v Tomlinson* [2006] EWHC 3115 (Ch), Kitchin J stated that with regard to the test of dishonesty, (i) "It is for the court to determine what are normally acceptable standards of honest conduct. (ii) The fact that a defendant genuinely believes that he has not fallen below the normally acceptable standards of honest conduct is irrelevant." In *AG of Zambia v Meer Care & Desai* [2007] EWHC 952 (Ch), Peter Smith J declared:

> In my view the test propounded by Lord Clarke MR (in his article) is a better one. I do not think anything is gained by using potentially difficult words such as objective and subjective. I do not believe that there was anything other than a misunderstanding as between the effect of the various judgments in *Twinsectra* which spawned a huge unnecessary debate. This is what *Barlow Clowes* was intended to confirm and in my view it plainly did.

Standard of proof of dishonesty

In *Heinl and Others v Jyske Bank (Gibraltar) Ltd*, the Court of Appeal decided that the standard of proof on an accessory liability claim exceeds a balance of probabilities, but is not as high as the criminal standard of proof.

Heinl and Others v Jyske Bank (Gibraltar) Ltd (1999) The Times, 28 September, CA

Facts

Between 1989 and 1991, Mr Spjeldnaes (Mr S), the managing director of Jyske Bank (Gibraltar) Ltd (the bank), in fraudulent breach of his fiduciary duty to the bank, caused it to pay out £71.5

million to companies which were the creatures of Mr S and his associates, principally Mr Metcalf (Mr M). The payments were made from time to time in transactions which took the form of loans to the various companies. The claims were made against 17 defendants. The principal claims against those, other than Mr S, were made under the accessory liability head (formerly known as knowing assistance or knowing receipt). The basis of the bank's claim against Mr Heinl (Mr H), the appellant, was that Mr S had misappropriated more than £4.5m of the bank's moneys which were paid into accounts which Mr H controlled, and that the latter had knowingly assisted in the misapplication of these funds. The judge held, *inter alia*, that Mr H and a number of companies controlled by him were liable for knowingly assisting Mr S in the fraudulent extraction and money laundering operations of the bank's funds. Mr H conceded that the moneys had come under his control and that he had assisted Mr S in the frauds by dealing with the funds in accordance with instructions from Mr S and Mr M. He appealed against the judge's decision on the ground that that he (Mr H) did not act dishonestly, nor with the requisite degree of knowledge. Mr H claimed that he had been informed and believed that the moneys were profits made by Mr M from property dealings in Spain.

Held

On the facts, the claimant failed to prove that Mr H knew that the funds he was dealing with originated from frauds perpetrated by Mr S on the bank. Thus, Mr H did not act dishonestly:

(a) The court relied on the test of 'accessory liability' laid down by Lord Nicholls in *Royal Brunei Airlines v Tan* [1995] 2 AC 378. A defendant will be judged to have acted dishonestly if he or she rendered assistance when in all the circumstances an honest man, having the defendant's knowledge, would not have done so, either at all or without making further inquiry or taking some other steps to satisfy himself that there was no breach of trust. Dishonesty is to be equated with conscious impropriety.

(b) In analysing Mr H's state of knowledge so as to ascertain whether he rendered dishonest assistance, the test to be applied was not the objective principle of whether the defendant ought as a reasonable businessman to have appreciated that the funds had been fraudulently procured from the bank, but a subjective inquiry of whether the defendant had appreciated that the funds had been so procured. Carelessness is not dishonesty.

(c) In order to make a defendant accountable on the basis of accessory liability, the standard of proof of dishonesty involved a high level of probability, although not as high as the criminal standard of proof.

In *Satnam v Heywood*, the Court of Appeal decided that, in order to make a third party accountable as an accessory, a link has to be established between a profit made by the third party and confidential information obtained from a fiduciary.

Satnam v Dunlop Heywood Ltd [1999] 3 All ER 652, CA

Facts

Satnam Investments (S Ltd), a property development company, acquired an option to purchase a site with development potential. The site owners were entitled to terminate the option if S Ltd went into receivership. S Ltd was placed into receivership by its banks. Shortly afterwards, Dunlop Heywood Ltd (H Ltd), a company of surveyors which had acted for S Ltd in respect of the site, disclosed to Morbaine Ltd (M Ltd), a rival development company, that S Ltd had an interest in the site, administrative receivers had been appointed and that the local planning authority was well disposed towards development. This information was disclosed without S Ltd's authority. After receiving the information, M Ltd sought to acquire an interest in the site. The owners of the site terminated S Ltd's option and sold the site to M Ltd. After the discharge of the receivers, S Ltd brought proceedings against H Ltd and M Ltd contending that H Ltd had breached its fiduciary obligations by disclosing the information to M Ltd, and that M Ltd had been aware of the breach and became a constructive trustee of the site for S Ltd. The trial judge upheld the claim even though he made no finding that M Ltd had acted dishonestly or participated in H Ltd's breach of fiduciary duty. M Ltd appealed.

Held

The Court of Appeal allowed the appeal on the following grounds:

(a) H Ltd was a fiduciary and acted in breach of its duties to S Ltd in disclosing confidential information to M Ltd without S Ltd's authority.

(b) Some of the information disclosed to M Ltd was either available to M Ltd or would have been available on reasonable enquiry, once the news of S Ltd's receivership had become known.

(c) If the information could be treated as trust property, there was insufficient nexus between the information and the acquisition of the site in order to make M Ltd liable as a constructive trustee for knowingly receiving trust property.

(d) Since the judge made no finding that M Ltd acted dishonestly, M Ltd could not be liable as an accessory to a dishonest breach of trust by H Ltd.

> **Nourse LJ:** [After affirming the decision of the trial judge to the effect that H Ltd was in breach of fiduciary duties owed to S Ltd, and referring to the two categories of liability laid down in *Barnes v Addy* (1874) LR 9 Ch App 244, continued:] Before a case can fall into either category there must be trust property or traceable proceeds of trust property. Clearly, DH and Mr Murray can be regarded as trustees of the information and, clearly, Morbaine can be regarded as having been a knowing recipient of it. However, even assuming, first, that confidential information can be treated as property for this purpose and, secondly, that but for the disclosure of the information Morbaine would not have acquired the Brewery Street site, we find it impossible, in knowing receipt, to hold that there was a sufficient basis for subjecting the Brewery Street site to the constructive trust for which Satnam contends. The information cannot be traced into the site and there is no other sufficient nexus between the two. As for knowing assistance, of which dishonesty on the part of the accessory is a necessary ingredient, we would not have wanted to shut out the possibility of such a claim being successful if the judge had made a finding of dishonesty against Morbaine, dishonesty for this purpose having been equated, for the most part, with conscious impropriety; see *Royal Brunei Airlines Sdn Bhd v Tan* [1995] 3 All ER 97 at 106, [1995] 2 AC 378 at 389. No such finding having been made, a claim in knowing assistance also fails.
>
> While there are no doubt other cases in which someone who is not a trustee or does not owe a fiduciary duty to another will be held liable as a constructive trustee, we believe, and so hold, that in English law the liability depends on there having been dishonesty on the part of the person who is sought to be made liable. This question was fully considered by the Privy Council in *Royal Brunei Airlines Sdn Bhd v Tan*, where the same conclusion was reached in relation to the law of Brunei. After extensive reference to English and Commonwealth decisions and commentaries, Lord Nicholls said ([1995] 3 All ER 97 at 109, [1995] 2 AC 378 at 392):
>
> > Drawing the threads together, their Lordships' overall conclusion is that dishonesty is a necessary ingredient of accessory liability. It is also a sufficient ingredient. A liability in equity to make good resulting loss attaches to a person who dishonestly procures or assists in a breach of trust or fiduciary obligation.
>
> The essence of Satnam's complaint against Morbaine having been that Morbaine used the opportunity afforded to it by DH's and Mr Murray's breaches of fiduciary duty for its own purposes, Satnam's case is in the mould of those which were successful in *Regal (Hastings) Ltd v Gulliver* [1942] 1 All ER 378, [1967] 2 AC 134 and *Boardman v Phipps* [1966] 3 All ER 721, [1967] 2 AC 46. Chadwick J's reference to *Boardman v Phipps* at the end of the section of his judgment headed 'Equitable remedies: the law' suggests that he thought that the principle of those cases was applicable here. In each of them, however, the defendants owed fiduciary duties to the plaintiff, in the first as directors of the plaintiff company and in the second as persons who had placed themselves in a special position, of a fiduciary character, vis-à-vis the plaintiff beneficiary. In the absence of a fiduciary duty the principle of those cases cannot apply. Mere knowledge that the opportunity has been afforded in breach of someone else's fiduciary duty is not enough.

Gardner, S,'Knowing assistance and knowing receipt: taking stock' (1996) 112 LQR 56

Gardner reviews the authorities imposing liabilty on strangers under the 'knowing assistance' and 'receipt' heads. He comments on the rationale for liability under the knowing assistance head as laid down by Lord Nicholls in *Royal Brunei Airlines v Tan* [1995] 3 WLR 64:

Lord Nicholls' view appears to be that a liability for knowing assistance involving negligence is either unnecessary or inappropriate. He notes that many potential defendants under the knowing assistance head will be persons and entities such as banks – they may be loosely termed agents – who voluntarily enter into an engagement with the trustees, and consequently owe a duty of care which will normally be in contract but may perhaps, alternatively, be in tort. His Lordship believes that a defendant who has undertaken such a duty of care should be liable under it alone, and not be liable in knowing assistance as well. A defendant who has not undertaken such a duty of care, however, should, according to his Lordship, not find himself placed under such a duty by knowing assistance being allowed to operate in cases of negligence; only in cases of dishonesty.

Lord Nicholls offers an analysis of when a defendant will and will not be under such a negligence liability to the trust in contract or tort. His Lordship's view appears to be that the liability will start out in life as a duty which the agent owes to the trustees, to save them from breaching their trust. It will crystallise, if, failing in this duty, the agent allows the trustees to breach their trust, and thus to incur a loss by way of their own liability for breach. The agent's liability is to make good this loss. Then, says his Lordship, this liability of the agent to the trustees is held by the trustees for the trust. And that is how the agent comes to owe a liability for want of care to the trust. This analysis is in fact a little curious. On the one hand, whilst some agents will owe trustees a duty to save the latter from breach, and must indemnify them if they fail in this, any such duty will, by its nature, be owed to the trustees personally, and not held by them on their trust. This liability thus has no common ground with knowing assistance, which is indeed concerned with the defendant's liability to the trust. On the other hand, such an agent will normally owe the trust itself a duty of care in contract or tort. This is the main effect of an agent being engaged by trustees to provide services for the trust, the trustees in this case certainly holding the benefit of the engagement on the trust. It is this material, therefore, which is comparable with liability for knowing assistance. With the benefit of a duty of care arising thus, however, it should be noted that a defendant who breaks it will be liable to the trust not only where the trustees are innocent, as Lord Nicholls thought, but also where they are fraudulent.

Hudson, A, 'Liability for dishonest assistance in a breach of fiduciary duty' (2007) ITCP Vol 14 issue 1, p 23

Professor Hudson in an illuminating article entitled, 'Liability assistance in a breach of fiduciary duty' considers the secondary liability of a defendant who dishonestly assists another in breach of trust. He affirms the principle that such liability is fault based and if the claim is successful the defendant is required to account to the claimant for the loss that stems from the defendant's assistance in breach of trust. The author considers that the real test is not one of dishonesty as such, but rather in deciding what an honest person would have done in the circumstances. This is viewed from an objective standpoint, and furthermore, the requirement is whether the defendant did what an honest person would have done: 'A hermit living in a cave who is unaware of ordinary social conventions as to honesty will still be dishonest if she offends normal standards of behaviour: her liability is not dependent on any consciousness of those standards. It is an objective test.'

Professor Hudson analyses the leading cases that considered the issue, *Tan, Twinsectra, Dubai, Barlow Clowes* and *Abou-Ramah*, and concludes that in Lord Nicholls's judgment in *Tan* the question to be considered by the court is not 'what the defendant thought personally, but rather what an honest person would have done if he had been placed in the same circumstances as the defendant?' Lord Hutton in *Twinsectra* in purporting to follow *Tan* departed from the test in a significant way by introducing a subjective element to the test of dishonesty, i.e. the combined test laid down in the criminal case *R v Ghosh*. In *Barlow Clowes*, the Privy Council decided that the standard of measuring dishonesty is purely objective, per Lord Hoffman:

> Although a dishonest state of mind is a subjective mental state, the standard by which the law determines whether it is dishonest is objective. If, by ordinary standards, a defendant's mental state would be characterized as dishonest, it is irrelevant that the defendant judges by different standards.

In *Abou-Ramah* the approach of the Court of Appeal appeared to be closely aligned to Lord Hutton's view in *Twinsectra*. Arden LJ said that the Privy Council decision in *Barlow Clowes* was not a departure from *Twinsectra* but merely gave guidance as to the proper interpretation of the decision in *Twinsectra*. As a matter of precedent, a decision of the House of Lords (*Twinsectra*) should normally trump a decision of the Privy Council (*Barlow Clowes*) unless the circumstances were quite exceptional. She found the circumstances in *Abou-Ramah* to be exceptional and decided that, in the context of civil liability, it is unnecessary to show subjective dishonesty in the sense of consciousness that the transaction is dishonest. It is sufficient if the defendant has knowledge of the elements of the transaction, which makes it dishonest according to normally accepted standards of behaviour.

The author concludes that the effect of these decisions is that there is a great deal of uncertainty as to whether the court will require the defendant (in a claim under the head of accessory liability) to have understood that what he was doing was dishonest.

FURTHER READING

Baughen, S, '*Quistclose* trusts and knowing receipt' [2000] Conv 351.

Berg, A, 'Accessory liability for breach of trust' (1996) 59 MLR 443.

Birks, P, 'Misdirected funds: Casenote on *Lipkin Gorman v Karpnale*' (1989) 105 LQR 352.

Bryan, M, 'When does a bank receive money?' [1996] JBL 165.

Lord Clarke MR, 'Claims against professionals: Negligence, dishonesty and fraud' [2006] 22 Professional Negligence 70.

Fennell, S, 'Misdirected funds; problems of uncertainty and inconsistency: The bank's liability as a constructive trustee' (1994) 57 MLR 38.

Ferris, G, 'The advice of the Privy Council in *Royal Brunei Airlines v Tan*' (1996) 30 Law Teacher 111.

Gardner, S, 'Knowing assistance and knowing receipt: Taking stock' (1996) 112 LQR 56.

Harpum, C, 'The stranger as constructive trustee' (1986) 102 LQR 114.

Harpum, C, 'Casenote on *Re Montagu*' (1987) 50 MLR 217.

Harpum, C, 'Accessory liability for procuring or assisting a breach of trust' (1995) 111 LQR 545.

Hibbert, T, 'Dishonesty and knowledge of accessories and recipients' [2000] JIBL 138.

Howell, A, 'Caught up' (2007) 157 NLJ 239.

Hudson, A, 'Liability for dishonest assistance in a breach of fiduciary duty' (2007) ITCP Vol 14 issue 1, p 23.

Martin, J, 'Assisting in a breach of trust' (1996) 142 SJ 156.

McKendrick, E, 'Restitution, misdirected funds and change of position' (1992) 55 MLR 377.

Millett, P, 'Restitution and constructive trusts' (1998) 114 LQR 399.

Moss, G, 'Standard of liability for knowing receipt' (2003) 16 Insolv Int 35.

Nolan, R, 'From knowing assistance to dishonest facilitation' (1995) 54 CLJ 505.

Panesar, S, 'A loan subject to a trust and dishonest assistance by a third party' [2003] JIBL 9.

Speirs, A, 'The destination of an ill-gotten gain: *Halifax Building Society v Thomas*' [1996] Conv 387.

Speirs, A, 'Escape from the tangled web' [2002] 3 Web JCL 1.

Stevens, J, 'Delimiting the scope of accessory liability: *Brinks Ltd v Abu-Saleh (No 3)*' [1996] Conv 447.

Tijo, H, 'No stranger to unconscionability' [2001] JBL 299.

Vaswani, M, 'Bankers' liability for dishonesty – could you be caught? Part 1' (2007) 4 JIBFL 199.

Watts, P, 'Unjust enrichment and misdirected funds' (1991) 107 LQR 521.

Woodcock, A, 'Core breach' (2006) 156 NLJ 750

SECRET TRUSTS AND MUTUAL WILLS

INTRODUCTION

As a general rule of probate law, a testator who wishes to create trusts after his death is required to express his intention in his will. The relevant formalities, as enacted in s 9 of the Wills Act 1837 (as amended), are required to be complied with. The secret trust operates as an exception to this rule, whereby the will transfers the relevant property to the intended trustee (legatee/devisee) subject to the terms of the trust, which have been concealed on the face of the will.

There are two types of secret trusts. A fully secret trust is created where the existence and terms of the trust are fully concealed on the face of the will. The transferee under the will takes the property as an apparent beneficiary. A half secret trust is ostensibly set up where the existence of the trust, but not its terms, is acknowledged on the face of the will. In this case, the transferee takes the property as a trustee. In both cases, the testator, during his lifetime, is required to secure an agreement or understanding with the intended trustee as to the terms of the trust.

There are significant differences in the rules applicable to fully and half secret trusts, and it is therefore important to maintain the distinction between the two types of trusts.

Mutual wills arise out of an agreement between two (or more) persons to make substantially similar testamentary dispositions in favour of a particular beneficiary or beneficiaries. It is not enough that the wills are similar. There must be an agreement between the parties whereby each promises not to revoke his or her will in consideration of the other (or others) doing the same. A constructive trust may be created on the death of the first testator, for it would be inequitable for the survivor to renege on the promise.

SECRET TRUSTS

When a testator dies, his will becomes available for public inspection. Thus, any trusts created by his will will be open to public scrutiny. The testator may wish to make provision for some object concealed from the gaze of the public. Originally, the secret objects were mistresses and illegitimate children, but the object or objects which the testator may consider to be embarrassing is or are entirely dependent on his or her own sentiments.

In order to benefit such objects after his death, the testator may transfer relevant property to an 'acceptable' legatee or devisee under his will, subject to the understanding that the legatee or devisee will hold the property upon trust for the intended beneficiary. This is the secret trust device. The essence of a secret trust is an equitable obligation communicated to the intended trustee, during the testator's lifetime, but which is intended to attach to a gift arising under a will (or, exceptionally, a transfer created on an intestacy).

Two conditions are required to be satisfied by the testator, namely, a transfer of property by will to the legatee or devisee and an understanding between the testator and the trustee that, on the latter receiving the property, he will hold it on trust for the intended beneficiary.

In order to create a valid will, the testator is required to comply with the requirements of s 9 of the Wills Act 1837 (as amended).

Wills Act 1837, s 9 (as amended by the Administration of Justice Act 1982)
No will shall be valid unless:

(a) it is in writing, and signed by the testator, or by some other person in his presence and by his direction; and

(b) it appears that the testator intended by his signature to give effect to the will; and

(c) the signature is made or acknowledged by the testator in the presence of two or more witnesses present at the same time; and

(d) each witness either:

    (i) attests and signs the will; or

    (ii) acknowledges his signature, in the presence of the testator (but not necessarily in the presence of any other witness), but no form of attestation shall be necessary.

Fraud and the assumption of jurisdiction

The Chancery Court originally assumed jurisdiction to enforce secret trusts in order to prevent the legatee or devisee fraudulently reneging on his or her promise and attempting to take the property beneficially, or denying the existence of the promise to the testator. In other words, the court prevented the legatee or devisee using s 9 of the Wills Act 1837 (originally s 5 of the Statute of Frauds 1677) as a defence after the death of the testator, for 'equity will not allow a statute to be used as an engine for fraud'.

Thus, the 'fraud' which the courts historically prevented concerned the attempted denial of the obligation undertaken by the intended trustee. This was declared by Lord Westbury in *McCormick v Grogan*.

McCormick v Grogan (1869) LR 4 HL 82, HL

Lord Westbury: My Lords, the jurisdiction which is invoked here . . . is founded altogether on personal fraud. It is a jurisdiction by which a Court of Equity, proceeding on the ground of fraud, converts the party who has committed it into a trustee for the party who is injured by that fraud. Now, being a jurisdiction founded on personal fraud, it is incumbent on the Court to see that a fraud, a *malus animus*, is *proved by the clearest and most indisputable evidence.* The Court of Equity has, from a very early period, decided that even an Act of Parliament shall not be used as an instrument of fraud; and if in the machinery of perpetrating a fraud an Act of Parliament intervenes, the Court of Equity, it is true, does not set aside the Act of Parliament, *but it fastens on the individual who gets a title under that Act, and imposes upon him a personal obligation,* because he applies the Act as an instrument for accomplishing a fraud. In this way the Court of Equity has dealt with the Statute of Frauds, and in this manner, also, it deals with the Statute of Wills [emphasis added].

On the other hand, Lord Hathersley, in the same case, identified the 'fraud' as the improper inducement of the testator. The assumption that is made is that the intended trustee induced the testator to make a will in his or her favour on the faith of a promise, which the intended trustee now wishes to deny:

Lord Hatherley [*obiter*]: . . . this doctrine has been established, no doubt, a long time since upon a sound foundation with reference to the jurisdiction of courts of equity to interpose in all cases of fraud. But this doctrine evidently requires to be carefully restricted within proper limits. It is itself a doctrine which involves a wide departure from the policy which induced the legislature to pass the Statute of Frauds, and it is only in clear cases of fraud that this doctrine has been applied – *cases in which the court has been persuaded that there has been a fraudulent inducement held out on the part of the apparent beneficiary in order to lead the testator to confide to him the duty which he so undertook to perform* [emphasis added].

Facts

A testator, in 1851, left all his property by a three line will to his friend Mr Grogan. In 1854, the testator was struck down by cholera and had only a few hours to live. He sent for Mr Grogan and told him in effect that his will and a letter would be found in his desk. The letter named various intended beneficiaries and the intended gifts to them. The letter concluded with the words:

I do not wish you to act strictly to the foregoing instructions, but leave it entirely to your own good judgment to do as you think I would if living, and as the parties are deserving.

A disappointed plaintiff whom Mr Grogan thought it right to exclude sued Mr Grogan.

Held

No trust was created because the testator did not intend to impose a trust on the executor.

Declaration and transfer

An alternative basis for enforcing such trusts is simply to give effect to the intention of the testator which has been validly communicated to or acquiesced in by the intended trustee. Once the trustee has acquired the property subject to an undertaking given to the testator, the court will give effect to the arrangement. In so doing, the court does not infringe the requirements of s 9 of the 1837 Act, but merely compels the legatee or devisee to fulfil his or her undertaking. This theory was declared by Lord Sumner in *Blackwell v Blackwell*.

Blackwell v Blackwell [1929] AC 318, HL

Lord Sumner: The court of equity finds a man in the position of an absolute legal owner of a sum of money, which has been bequeathed to him under a valid will and it declares that, on proof of certain facts relating to the motives of the testator, it will not allow the legal owner to exercise his legal right to do what he wishes with the property. In other words *it lets him take what the will gives him and then makes him apply it as the Court of Conscience directs, and it does so in order to give effect to the wishes of the testator, which would not otherwise be effectual* [emphasis added].

Moreover, it is immaterial that one of the intended beneficiaries under the secret trust witnesses the will. In probate law (and in particular, s 15 of the Wills Act 1837), an attesting witness or spouse who receives an interest under a will loses that interest. The will may be attested by two or more witnesses.

Wills Act 1837, s 15 and Wills Act 1968, s 1(1) amendment

1837 Act: If any person shall attest the execution of any will to whom or to whose wife or husband any beneficial devise, legacy, estate, interest, gift, or appointment, of or affecting any real or personal estate . . . shall be thereby given or made, such devise, legacy, estate, interest, gift, or appointment shall, so far only as concerns such person attesting the execution of such will, or the wife or husband of such person, or any person claiming under such person or wife or husband, be utterly null and void, and such person so attesting shall be admitted as a witness to prove the execution of such will, or to prove the validity or invalidity thereof, notwithstanding such devise, legacy, estate, interest, gift, or appointment mentioned in such will.

1968 Act: For the purposes of s 15 of the Wills Act 1837 . . . the attestation of a will by a person to whom or to whose spouse there is given or made any such disposition as is described in that section shall be disregarded if the will is duly executed without his attestation and without that of any other such person.

Note

In short, the effect of the Wills Act 1968 is that where there are more than two attesting witnesses and only one of the witnesses (or spouse of such witness) takes an interest under the will, his attestation of the will, by itself, will not deprive him of an interest.

Dehors principle

As far as secret trusts are concerned, the interest of the beneficiary under the trust is enjoyed outside (*dehors*) the will and thus outside the Wills Act 1837. The trust is not created in the will but by the separate obligation undertaken by the legatee outside the will. The attestation of the will by the secret beneficiary (as opposed to the trustee) does not therefore attract the rigour of s 15 of the 1837 Act. This principle was applied in *Re Young*.

Re Young [1951] Ch 344, HC

Facts

A testator made a bequest to his wife subject to a direction that on her death she would leave the property for the purpose which he had communicated to her. One of the purposes was that she would leave a legacy of £2,000 to the testator's chauffeur, who witnessed the will.

The question in issue was whether the chauffeur had forfeited his interest.

Held

The trust in favour of the chauffeur was not contained in the will but was created separately outside the will:

> **Danckwerts J:** The whole theory of the formation of a secret trust is that the Wills Act 1837 has nothing to do with the matter because the forms required by the Wills Act are entirely disregarded, since the persons do not take by virtue of the gift in the will, but by virtue of the secret trusts imposed upon the beneficiary who does in fact take under the will.

Note

The modern basis for enforcing secret trusts is that the trust is declared *inter vivos* between the testator and the intended trustee, but the transfer of the property to the trustee takes effect on the death of the testator. The courts will enforce the obligation undertaken by the trustee by giving effect to the intention of the testator, when the trustee acquires the property. This is the declaration and transfer principle: see Lord Sterndale MR in *Re Gardner (No 1)* [1920] 2 Ch 523, CA (p 315 below) and Brightman J in *Ottaway v Norman* [1972] Ch 698, HC (p 315 below).

Question

To what extent is it possible to develop a coherent theory for the creation of secret trusts?

Two types of secret trusts

There are two types of secret trusts: a fully secret and a half secret trust.

A fully secret trust is one where the legatee or devisee takes the property beneficially on the face of the will. The *existence* of the trust, as well as its *terms*, is fully concealed by reference to the will.

For example, T, a testator, bequeaths a legacy of £5,000 to L absolutely. Before his death, T communicates the terms of a trust to L who agrees to abide by T's wishes after T's death. When L acquires the property, he will be required to hold the same, subject to the terms agreed.

A half secret trust is one where the legatee or devisee is named as a trustee on the face of the will but the terms are obviously concealed by the testator, eg, T, a testator, bequeaths a legacy of £5,000 to L 'on trust for purposes communicated to him'. Before executing his will, T communicates the purpose of the legacy to L who agrees to carry out T's wishes. L becomes a trustee when he acquires the relevant property.

Although the rules concerning the creation of fully and half secret trusts overlap, there are significant differences in respect of their constitution. Accordingly, it is necessary to distinguish between the two concepts.

FULLY SECRET TRUSTS

Communication and acceptance *inter vivos*

The court draws a distinction between a mere legacy or devise and a legacy or devise subject to a secret trust. The essence of the distinction is that in a legacy subject to a secret trust, the testator communicates the terms of the trust during his or her lifetime to the legatee. In this respect, it is immaterial that the communication of the terms is made before or after the execution of the will, provided that it is made before the testator's death.

Indeed, communication of the terms of the trust may even be made constructively by the testator delivering a sealed envelope to the intended trustee, subject to the direction, 'Not to be opened before my death'. This delivery may be treated as communication of the terms (contents) of the trust at the time of delivery, provided that (the intended trustee) is generally aware of the testator's wishes, even though the addressee becomes aware of the contents of the envelope only after the death of the testator. See *Re Keen* (p 319 below).

But if the legatee becomes aware of the terms of the trust only after the testator's death, and has given the testator no assurance to hold on trust during the testator's lifetime, he will be entitled to take the property beneficially. Having made no assurances to the testator to hold upon trust, he is entitled to retain the legacy beneficially as the will indicates. Section 9 of the Wills Act 1837 may be used by him as a defence: see *Wallgrave v Tebbs*.

Wallgrave v Tebbs (1855) 2 K & J 313, HC

Facts

A testator, T, bequeathed a legacy of £12,000 to Mr Tebbs and Mr Martin and also devised freehold properties 'unto and to the use of Tebbs and Martin as joint tenants'. T was contemplating whether or not to devote part of the properties to charitable objects. After the will was made, one of his executors, on request from T, prepared a draft letter from the testator to Messrs Tebbs and Martin setting out the charitable objects that T had in mind. The draft letter was not sent to Tebbs and Martin, nor did they become aware of it until after the testator's death. In addition, Tebbs and Martin had at no time given an undertaking to carry out T's wishes. The executor brought an action against Tebbs and Martin to have the money and other property applied for charitable purposes. They claimed that no trust was created and that they were entitled to the properties absolutely.

Held

The transfers amounted to mere gifts by will, not coupled with an obligation to hold upon trust:

> **Wood VC:** I am satisfied that I ought not overstep the clear line which separates 'mere trusts' from 'devises and bequests' ... Where a person, knowing that a testator in making a disposition in his favour intends it to be applied for purposes other than for his own benefit either expressly promises, or by silence implies, that he will carry out the testator's intention into effect, and the property is left to him upon the faith of an undertaking, it is in effect a case of trust and the court will not allow the devisee to set up the Statute of Frauds – or rather the Statute of Wills as a defence. But the question here is totally different. Here there has been no promise or undertaking on the part of the legatee. The latter knew nothing of the testator's intention until after his death. Upon the face of the will, the parties take indisputably for their own benefit.

Lord Sumner in *Blackwell v Blackwell* [1929] AC 318 said:

> The necessary elements, on which the question turns, are intention, communication and acquiescence. The testator intends his absolute gift to be employed as he and not as the donee desires; he tells the proposed donee of this intention and, either by express promise or by the tacit promise, which is satisfied by acquiescence, the proposed donee encourages him to bequeath the money on the faith that his intentions will be carried out.

Question

What is the effect of transferring property by will to a legatee without notifying him of the terms of the trust?

If the testator discloses the fact of the trust to the legatee, but fails to communicate the terms of the trust before his death, the secret trust will fail. However, the legatee will hold the property on resulting trust for the estate of the testator. In other words, the secret trust fails because there has been a failure to communicate the terms of the trust to the legatee during the lifetime of the testator. But, since the legatee is aware that he is required to hold on trust and acquires the property on the basis of this understanding, he holds the same on resulting trust for the testator. This principle was applied in *Re Boyes*.

Re Boyes, Boyes v Carritt (1884) 26 Ch D 531, HC

Facts

A testator in a will drawn up by his solicitor (Mr Carritt) gave his residuary estate to Carritt absolutely and appointed him the executor of his will. The testator had previously told Carritt that he wished him (Carritt) to hold the property according to directions which he would communicate by letter, and Carritt agreed. Such directions were not given by the testator during his lifetime, but, after his death, two unattested documents, both addressed to Carritt, were found in which the testator stated his wish that Mrs B was entitled to the property under the intended trust. The testator's next of kin sued Carritt claiming a declaration that they (next of kin) were entitled to the property because no valid secret trust was created. Carritt claimed to hold the property as trustee for Mrs B.

Held

No secret trust was created and the executor held the property for the benefit of the next of kin:

> **Kay J:** No case has ever yet decided that a testator can, by imposing a trust upon the devisee or legatee, the objects of which he does not communicate to him, enable himself to evade the Wills Act by declaring those objects in an unattested paper found after his death. I cannot help regretting that the testator's intention of bounty should fail by reason of an informality of this kind, but in my opinion it would be a serious innovation upon the law relating to testamentary instruments if this were to be established as a trust in her favour.
>
> If the trust was not declared when the will was made, it is essential, in order to make it binding, that it should be communicated to the devisee or legatee in the testator's lifetime and that he should accept that particular trust.

Once the legatee is aware of the terms of the trust, its acceptance may be communicated to the testator expressly or by the silence of the legatee amounting to an acquiescence (Wood VC in *Wallgrave v Tebbs* (see p 313 above) and Lord Sumner in *Blackwell v Blackwell* (see p 318 below)). The obligation is on the legatee. If the legatee does not wish to be bound by the trust, he is obliged to notify his refusal to the testator during his (the testator's) lifetime.

In *Moss v Cooper*, it was decided that a legatee's failure to communicate his intention to the testator during the latter's lifetime did not absolve the legatee from the liability known to him.

Moss v Cooper (1861) 1 J & H 352, HC

Facts

A testator transferred his residuary estate to Gawthorn, Sedman and Owen. At the time of the execution of the will, a memorandum, authorised by the testator, was prepared by Gawthorn to the effect that, after the residuary legatees had retained £25 each for their own use, the residue was to be divided between named charities. Gawthorn communicated the terms of the memorandum to Sedman and Owen. Sedman told the testator that he would abide by his wishes. Owen did not communicate his assent to the testator. Gawthorn predeceased the testator. The next of kin challenged the validity of the trust.

Held

A fully secret trust was created and Sedman and Owen held the property upon trust:

> **Wood VC:** If, immediately after making his will (for a bargain before the will is not essential), the testator had invited Gawthorn, Sedman and Owen to his house and had said to them, 'Here is my will, made in this form, because I am told that the property must be put entirely at your disposal; but I want a promise from you to dispose of it in a particular way': and if they, by their silence, led him to believe that they would so apply it, I apprehend it is quite clear that a trust would be created, and that it is altogether immaterial whether the promise is made before or after the execution of the will, that being a revocable instrument.

Here, there are sufficient grounds to infer that Gawthorn, in fact, and to the knowledge or belief of Owen, had authority to make the communication; and, in that case, Owen's silence is a sufficient acceptance of the trust to exclude him from any beneficial enjoyment of the property.

Note

Moreover, on general agency principles, the communication of the terms may be authorised by an agent of the testator. Likewise, express acceptance may be permitted through an agent of the legatee. For example, T, a testator, may appoint X, Y and Z as executors and trustees, and authorise X to communicate the terms of the trust to Y and Z.

Trust obligation to execute a will

Thus far, the examples of fully secret trusts are occasions where the trust obligation is accepted *inter vivos* and subsequently the property is transferred by the testator's will to the intended trustees upon trust for the secret objects. But a variation on this principle imposes an obligation on the intended trustee/beneficiary to make a will in favour of a second beneficiary. Thus, the primary donee (and trustee) becomes entitled to an interest for his or her life and the secondary donee becomes entitled to the relevant property under the will of the primary donee.

In *Re Gardner*, it was decided that the trust is created when the primary donee acquires the property under the donor's will.

Re Gardner, Huey v Cunnington (No 1) [1920] 2 Ch 523, CA

Facts

A testatrix had given all her estate to her husband for his use and benefit during his life, 'knowing that he will carry out my wishes'. Four days later, she signed a memorandum expressing the wish that what she described as 'the money I leave to my husband' should on his death be equally divided among certain named beneficiaries. She died in 1919 possessed of personal estate only, and her husband died four days later. After his death, his wife's will and the memorandum were found in his safe, and there was parol evidence that shortly after the execution of the will the testatrix had said in his presence that her property, after his death, was to be equally divided between the named beneficiaries, and that he assented thereto.

Held

After the death of his wife, the husband enjoyed a life interest in the relevant property but was required to transfer the same to the beneficiaries:

> **Lord Sterndale MR:** The obligation upon the husband and his next of kin seems to me to arise from this, that he takes the property in accordance with and upon an undertaking to abide by the wishes of the testatrix, and if he were to dispose of it in any other way he would be committing a breach of trust, or as it has been called in some of the cases, a fraud. I do not think it matters which you call it. The breach of trust or the fraud would arise when he attempted to deal with the money contrary to the terms on which he took it.

Following *Ottaway v Norman*, the approach of the courts is to affirm that the trust is created when the property is acquired by the primary donee but is kept in suspense during his lifetime and attaches to the estate of the trustee on his death. Of course, this principle is subject to the basic rule that the subject matter of the trust is required to be certain.

Ottaway v Norman [1972] Ch 698, HC

Facts

A testator, Harry Ottaway, by his will devised his bungalow (with fixtures, fittings and furniture) to his housekeeper, Miss Hodges, in fee simple and gave her a legacy of £1,500. It was alleged that Miss Hodges had orally agreed with the testator to leave by her will the bungalow and fittings, etc, and whatever 'money' was left over at the time of her death to the plaintiffs, Mr and Mrs William Ottaway (the testator's son and daughter-in-law). By her will, Miss Hodges left all her property to someone else. The plaintiffs sued Mr Norman (Miss Hodges' executor) for a declaration that the relevant parts of Miss Hodges' estate were held upon trust for the plaintiffs.

Held

There was clear evidence that a fully secret trust was created only in respect of the bungalow and fittings, etc, but not in respect of the 'money'. The intended trust of the money was uncertain and void. Mr Norman as her executor therefore held the bungalow on trust for Mr and Mrs William Ottaway:

> **Brightman J:** It will be convenient to call the person on whom such a trust is imposed the 'primary donee' and the beneficiary under that trust the 'secondary donee'. *The essential elements which must be proved to exist are: (i) the intention of the testator to subject the primary donee to an obligation in favour of the secondary donee; (ii) communication of that intention to the primary donee; and (iii) the acceptance of that obligation by the primary donee either expressly or by acquiescence.* It is immaterial whether these elements precede or succeed the will of the donor. I am informed that there is no recent reported case where the obligation imposed on the primary donee is an obligation to make a will in favour of the secondary donee as distinct from some form of *inter vivos* transfer. But it does not seem to me that that can really be a distinction which can validly be drawn on behalf of the defendant in the present case [emphasis added].
>
> The basis of the doctrine of a secret trust is the obligation imposed on the conscience of the primary donee and it does not seem to me that there is any materiality in the machinery by which the donor intends that that obligation shall be carried out.
>
> I believe that the suggestion of an express trust was not pursued because certainly Harry Ottaway, and I think also William Ottaway, had complete confidence that Miss Hodges would do what she had been told.
>
> I find as a fact that Harry Ottaway intended that Miss Hodges should be obliged to dispose of the bungalow in favour of the plaintiffs at her death, that he communicated that intention to Miss Hodges and that Miss Hodges accepted the obligation. I find the same facts in relation to the furniture, fixtures and fittings which passed to Miss Hodges under clause 4 of Harry Ottaway's will. I am not satisfied that any similar obligation was imposed and accepted as regards any contents of the bungalow which had not devolved on Miss Hodges under clause 4 of Harry Ottaway's will.
>
> I turn to the question of money. First as a matter of fact what did the parties intend should be comprised in Miss Hodges' obligation? All money which Miss Hodges had at her death, including money which she had acquired before Harry's death and money she acquired after his death from all sources? Or, only money acquired under Harry's will? Secondly, if such an obligation existed would it as a matter of law create a valid trust? *On the second question I am content to assume for present purposes but without so deciding that if property is given to the primary donee on the understanding that the primary donee will dispose by his will of such assets, if any, as he may have at his command at his death in favour of the secondary donee, a valid trust is created in favour of the secondary donee which is in suspense during the lifetime of the primary donee, but attaches to the estate of the primary donee at the moment of the latter's death.* There would seem to be at least some support for this proposition in an Australian case *Birmingham v Renfrew* (1937) 57 CLR 666 [emphasis added].
>
> I accept that the parties mentioned money on at least some occasions when they talked about Harry Ottaway's intentions for the future disposition of Ashcroft. I do not, however, find sufficient evidence that it was Harry Ottaway's intention that Miss Hodges should be compelled to leave all her money, from whatever source derived, to the plaintiffs. This would seem to preclude her giving even a small pecuniary legacy to any friend or relative. I do not think it is clear that Harry Ottaway intended to extract any such far-reaching undertaking from Miss Hodges or that she intended to accept such a wide obligation herself.
>
> Therefore, the obligation, if any, is in my view to be confined to money derived under Harry Ottaway's will. If the obligation is confined to money derived under Harry Ottaway's will, the obligation is meaningless and unworkable unless it includes the requirement that she shall keep such money separate and distinct from her own money. I am certain that no such requirement was ever discussed or intended.
>
> There is another difficulty. Does money in this context include only cash or cash and investment, or all moveable property of any description? The evidence is quite inconclusive. In my judgment the plaintiffs' claim succeeds in relation to the bungalow and in relation to the furniture, fixtures and fittings which devolved under clause 4 of Harry Ottaway's will subject, of course, to normal wastage and fair wear and tear, but not to any other assets.

Note

The explanation by Brightman J of the nature of the trust during the lifetime of the primary donee creates a number of difficulties, in particular, whether the primary donee becomes a trustee under the Trusts of Land and Appointment of Trustees Act 1996 (a tenant for life under the Settled Land Act 1925) with a power of sale over land and, if not, what level of protection is enjoyed by the secondary donees and purchasers of the property in good faith from the primary donee. See Burgess [1972] 36 Conv 113 (see below).

Revocation of the will on the strength of a promise by the trustee

The same principle, as stated above, applies with equal force where the testator revokes his or her will on the strength of a promise by the next of kin (trustees) to dispose of the property in a specified manner, in accordance with the intention of the settlor. Likewise, the secret trust principles will extend to intestacies. These are occasions where the settlor decides not to make a will on the faith of a promise by his or her next of kin to dispose of the property in accordance with the settlor's wishes as disclosed to him or her during the lifetime of the settlor. This was stated in an *obiter* pronouncement by Lord Hatherley in *McCormick v Grogan*.

McCormick v Grogan (1869) LR 4 HL 82, HL

Lord Hatherley LC: . . . if, for example, an heir said to a person who was competent to dispose of his property by will, 'Do not dispose of it by will, I undertake to carry into effect all such wishes as you may communicate to me'. And if the testator, acting on that representation, did not dispose of his property by will, and the heir has kept the property for himself, without carrying those instructions into effect, the court of equity has interposed on the ground of the fraud thus committed by the heir in inducing the testator to die intestate, upon the faith of the heir's representations that he would carry all such wishes as were confided to him into effect.

This principle was applied by the court in *Sellack v Harris*.

Sellack v Harris (1708) 5 Vin Ab 521

Facts

A father was induced by his heir presumptive (entitled to realty on an intestacy before 1925) not to make a will on the ground that the heir himself would make provision for the mother of the settlor. After the death of his father, the heir refused to make provision as promised.

Held

The heir was obliged to make the relevant provision for he had induced his father to refrain from making a will.

Burgess, R, 'Secret trust property' [1972] 36 Conv 113

Burgess considers the implications inherent in the decision of *Ottaway v Norman*. His concern was to examine when the secret trust commences and the extent of property capable of being affected by it. For these purposes, he posits four situations:

(1) Where specified property is left by will to X to be applied *inter vivos* in accordance with the terms of the secret trust [the normal secret trust situation].

(2) Where specified property is left by will to X to be left in X's will in accordance with the terms of the secret trust [the *Ottaway v Norman* [1972] Ch 698 scenario].

(3) Where specified property is left by will to X and where *all of X's property* is to be left by his will in accordance with the terms of the secret trust [*Re Green* [1951] Ch 148 (mutual wills)].

(4) Where specified property is left by will to X but where *other property belonging to X is to be left* by his will in accordance with the terms of the secret trust [a variation on (3) above].

Burgess then considers the two issues posed in each of the four situations. The common thread linking the four factual situations is the judgment of Brightman J in *Ottaway v Norman*, who applied a mutual wills solution in deciding when the secret trust is created and the extent of property subject to the trust. Burgess concludes that this innovation is regrettable.

HALF SECRET TRUSTS

As stated earlier, half secret trusts arise where the legatee (or devisee) takes as a trustee on the face of the will, but the terms are not specified in the will. Thus, the testator has represented to the public that the transferee under the will takes the property in a representative capacity as trustee for an object whose identity is concealed on the face of the will.

For example, the testator has transferred his property to L, a legatee, 'as trustee for purposes communicated to him'.

Rules for the creation of half secret trusts

The following rules are required to be complied with in order to create a valid half secret trust:

(1) It is clearly established that evidence cannot be adduced in order to contradict the terms of the will. The will is considered to be the last testament of the testator and is thus treated as sacrosanct. In accordance with probate rules, the will becomes irrevocable on the death of the testator. The validity of the secret trust is dependent on the will transferring the property to the trustee. To be allowed to contradict the will in order to prove the terms of the secret trust has the potential to perpetrate a fraud. Hence, a rigid principle has been developed by the courts which prohibits the adduction of such contradictory evidence even if this is in accordance with the intention of the testator.

   For example, if the will points to a past communication, evidence may not be adduced which points to a future communication (in any event, such evidence is incapable of being admitted in the first place: see *Blackwell v Blackwell*).

   Similarly, if the will refers to the legatee as a trustee, evidence may not be adduced to show that he or she is intended as a beneficiary (see *Re Rees* [1950] Ch 204, CA, p 321 below).

(2) Where the communication of the terms of the trust is made before or at the time of the execution of the will, evidence may be adduced in order to show the terms of the trust. The adduction of such evidence complements the intention of the testator and the will; see *Blackwell v Blackwell*.

Blackwell v Blackwell [1929] AC 318, HL

Facts

A testator by a codicil (the alteration of a will executed in accordance with the Wills Act 1837) bequeathed a legacy of £12,000 to five persons 'to apply for the purposes indicated by me to them'. Before the execution of the codicil, the terms of the trust were communicated to the legatees and the trust was accepted by them all. The beneficiaries were the testator's mistress and her illegitimate son. The plaintiff claimed a declaration that no valid trust in favour of the objects had been created on the ground that parol evidence was inadmissible to establish the trust.

Held

The trust was valid. Parol evidence was admissible to establish the terms of a half secret trust in order to prevent the testator's intention being fraudulently avoided:

> **Lord Sumner:** It seems to me that, apart from legislation, the application of the principle of equity in *Fleetwood's Case* (1880) 15 Ch D 594 ... was logical, and was justified by the same considerations as in cases of fraud and absolute gifts. Why should equity forbid an honest trustee to give effect to his promise, made to a deceased testator, and compel him to pay another legatee, about whom it is quite certain that the testator did not mean to make him the object of his bounty? In both cases the testator's wishes are incompletely expressed in his will.

Why should equity, over a mere matter of words, give effect to them in one case and frustrate them in the other? No doubt the words 'in trust' prevent the legatee from taking beneficially, whether they have simply been declared in conversation or written in the will, but the fraud, when the trustee, so called in the will, is also the residuary legatee, is the same as when he is only declared a trustee by word of mouth accepted by him.

Note

It appears that the justification for proving the terms of a half secret trust is similar to the rationale for the assumption of jurisdiction by the courts in order to enforce fully secret trusts, namely, the prevention of fraud. The fraud which is capable of being committed by a dishonest trustee in the context of a half secret trust is similar to the fraud vis à vis a fully secret trust, namely, reneging on the promise made to the testator. The consequences of a fraud intended by a dishonest trustee vary with the type of secret trust. In respect of a half secret trust, the trustee is not entitled to adduce evidence to show that he or she is beneficially entitled (compare the position under a fully secret trust), but a resulting trust for the benefit of the testator's estate would be set up.

(3) In respect of an intended half secret trust, communication of the terms of the intended trust after the execution of the will, but during the testator's lifetime, is not admissible (contrast a fully secret trust).

For example, the testator's will transfers property to L 'on trust for purposes to be communicated to him'. If, subsequent to the execution of the will, the testator makes an agreement with L as to the terms of the trust, this agreement will not be admissible to prove the terms of the trust.

The justification given by Lord Sumner in *Blackwell v Blackwell* for this prohibition of informal evidence is to prevent an infringement of the provisions of the Wills Act 1837. This is judicially considered to be the case if an unattested document or parol evidence is intended to be admitted to prove the terms of the trust when the testator makes provision in his or her will for a future communication of the terms of the trust.

Blackwell v Blackwell [1929] AC 318, HL

Lord Sumner: The limits beyond which the rules as to unspecified trusts must not be carried, have often been discussed. *A testator cannot reserve to himself a power of making future unwitnessed dispositions by merely naming a trustee and leaving the purposes of the trust to be supplied afterwards, nor can a legatee give testamentary validity to an unexecuted codicil by accepting an indefinite trust, never communicated to him in the testator's lifetime.* To hold otherwise would indeed be to enable the testator to 'give the go-by' to the requirements of the Wills Act, because he did not choose to comply with them. It is communication of the purpose to the legatee, coupled with acquiescence or promise on his part, that removes the matter from the provisions of the Wills Act and brings it within the law of trusts [emphasis added].

The rule applicable to half secret trusts concerning the date of the communication of the terms of the trust was applied in *Re Keen*.

Re Keen [1937] Ch 236, CA

Facts

Under clause 5 of the testator's will, a legacy was transferred to two legatees, Hazlehurst and Evershed, 'to be held upon trust and disposed of by them among such persons or charities as may be notified by me to them or either of them during my lifetime'. Prior to the execution of the will, Evershed had been given a sealed envelope subject to the directions, 'Not to be opened before my death'. Evershed considered himself bound to hold the legacy subject to the terms declared in the envelope. The envelope contained the name of the beneficiary under the intended trust. Subsequently, the testator revoked the original will and executed a new will which contained an identical clause 5. No fresh directions were issued to Evershed, who was still prepared to carry out the testator's wishes. After the testator's death, an originating summons was taken out by the executors to determine whether they were required to distribute the property to Evershed and Hazlehurst as trustees for the specified beneficiary, or for the residuary estate.

Held

The trust failed and the property fell into residue on the grounds that:

(a) the delivery of the envelope constituted communication of the terms of the trust at the time of delivery. Since this was made prior to the execution of the will and was inconsistent with the terms of the will, the letter was not admissible;

(b) the provision in the will contained a power to declare trusts in the future. This power was not enforceable and the terms of the intended trust were not admissible.

> **Lord Wright MR:** [In deciding that the date of the communication was the date of delivery of the envelope:] To take a parallel, a ship which sails under sealed orders is sailing under orders though the exact terms are not ascertained by the captain till later. I note that the case of a trust, put into writing, which is placed in the trustees' hands in a sealed envelope, was hypothetically treated by Kay J [in *Re Boyes* (1884) 26 Ch D 531] as possibly constituting a communication in a case of this nature. This, so far as it goes, seems to support my conclusion. The trustees had the means of knowledge available whenever it became necessary and proper to open the envelope. I think Mr Evershed was right in understanding that the giving of the sealed envelope was a notification within clause 5.
>
> There are two main questions: first, how far parol evidence is admissible to define the trust under such a clause as this and secondly, and in particular, how far such evidence, if admissible at all, would be excluded on the ground that it would be inconsistent with the true meaning of clause 5.
>
> It is first necessary to state what, in my opinion, is the true construction of the words of the clause.
>
> These words, in my opinion, can only be considered, as referring to a definition of trusts which have not yet, at the date of the will, been established and which, between that date and the testator's death, may or may not be established ... The words of the clause seem to me to refer only to something future and hypothetical, to something as to which the testator is reserving an option whether to do or not to do it.
>
> In my judgment, clause 5 should be considered as contemplating future dispositions, and as reserving to the testator the power of making such dispositions without a duly attested codicil, simply by notifying them during his lifetime, the principles laid down by Lord Sumner (*Blackwell v Blackwell*) must be fatal to the appellant's claim.
>
> In *Blackwell v Blackwell* [1929] AC 318, *Re Fleetwood* (1880) 15 Ch D 594, and *Re Huxtable* [1902] 2 Ch 793, the trusts had been specifically declared to some or all of the trustees, at or before the execution of the will, and the language of the will was consistent with that fact. There was, in these cases, no reservation of a future power to change the trusts, in whole or in part. Such a power would involve a power to change a testamentary disposition by an unexecuted codicil, and would violate s 9 of the Wills Act. This was so held in *Re Hetley* [1902] 2 Ch 866.
>
> But there is still a further objection which, in the present case, renders the appellant's claim unenforceable: the trusts which it is sought to establish by parol evidence would be inconsistent with the express terms of the will. That such an objection is fatal appears from the cases already cited, such as *Re Huxtable*. In that case, an undefined trust of money for charitable purposes was declared in the will, as in respect of the whole corpus and, accordingly, evidence was held inadmissible that the charitable trust was limited to the legatee's life, so that he was free to dispose of the corpus after his death. Similarly, in *Johnson v Ball* (1851) 2 De G & Son 85, the testator by the will left the property to trustees, upon the uses contained in a letter signed 'by them and myself': it was held that that evidence was not admissible to show that, though no such letter was in existence at the date of the will, the testator had made a subsequent declaration of trust; the court held that these trusts could not be enforced.
>
> In the present case, while clause 5 refers solely to a future definition, or to future definitions, of the trust, subsequent to the date of the will, the sealed letter relied on as notifying the trust was communicated before the date of the will. That it was communicated to one trustee only, and not to both, would not, I think, be an objection. But the objection remains that the notification sought to be put in evidence was anterior to the will, and hence not within the language of clause 5, and inadmissible simply on that ground, as being inconsistent with what the will prescribes.

This decision was followed by Pennycuick J in *Re Bateman's Will Trust*.

Re Bateman's Will Trust [1970] 1 WLR 1463, HC

Facts

A testator bequeathed £24,000 to his trustees and directed them to pay the income 'to such persons and in such proportions as shall be stated by me in a sealed letter'. After the execution of the will, the testator gave the trustees a sealed envelope, 'to be opened on my death', which contained the names of the beneficiaries. The residuary beneficiaries brought an action claiming the property.

Held

The intended secret trust failed and the property was held on resulting trust for the residuary beneficiaries:

> **Pennycuick J:** The direction clearly imports that the testator may, in the future after the date of the will, give a sealed letter to his trustees. It is impossible to confine the words to a sealed letter already so given. If that be the true construction of the wording it is not in dispute that the direction is invalid.

Note

It seems that this rule is firmly established by the courts, but it is submitted that the reasoning is open to challenge on principle. The enforceability of secret trusts (including half secret trusts) is based on the premise that they exist outside the will. The Wills Act 1837 is required to be complied with in order to transfer the property to the trustees; beyond this the formalities under the 1837 Act have nothing to do with the trust. To import the requirement that an attested document is required to be executed if the will points to a future communication but not if the will points to a contemporaneous or past communication seems to confuse the basis for enforcing such trusts. It is submitted that the courts have confused the probate doctrine of incorporation by reference to the enforceability of such trusts. Under the probate doctrine of incorporation by reference, it is possible to incorporate in a will a document which is not executed in accordance with the 1837 Act provided that the document is in existence on the date of the execution of the will and is specifically referred to in the will. When this principle is complied with, the incorporated, unattested document is admitted to probate and the advantage of secrecy, so crucial to secret trusts, is lost. Needless to say, the courts have not openly espoused this principle as the basis for prohibiting evidence of the terms of the agreement between the testator and the trustee, posterior to the execution of the will.

Question

What justifications are commonly provided for refusing to admit evidence of post-will communications in the context of intended half secret trusts?

(4) The persons named as trustees on the face of the will cannot, in any event, take the property beneficially even if this is in accordance with the intention of the testator. Such named trustees are prohibited from adducing evidence to this effect because to admit such evidence would contradict the terms of the trust: see *Re Rees*.

Re Rees [1950] Ch 204, CA

Facts

By his will, a testator appointed his friend H and his solicitor W to be executors and trustees, and he devised and bequeathed all his property to 'my trustees absolutely, they well knowing my wishes concerning the same'. The testator told the executors and trustees at the time of making the will that he wished them to make certain payments out of the estate and retain the remainder for their own use. After the payments were made, there was a substantial surplus remaining. The executors claimed that they were entitled to keep the surplus in that there was no secret trust but a conditional gift in their favour.

Held

The surplus funds passed on intestacy. The relevant clause in the will created a half secret trust and the trustees were not entitled to adduce evidence to show that they were entitled beneficially:

Sir Raymond Evershed MR: I agree with the judge that to admit evidence to the effect that the testator informed of the executors – or I will assume both of the executors – that he intended them to take beneficial interests, would be to conflict with the terms of the will as I have construed them; for the inevitable result of admitting that evidence and giving effect to it would be that the will would be regarded not as conferring a trust estate only upon the two trustees, but as giving them a conditional gift which on construction is the thing which, if I am right, it does not do.

In the public interest it is not to be forgotten that Parliament has laid down that *prima facie* a will disposing of the property of a deceased person must follow certain strict forms. The courts have also been very insistent on the importance of the principle that those who assume the office of trustees should not, so far as they fairly can prevent it, allow themselves to be in a position in which their interests and their duties conflict. In the general public interest it seems to me desirable that if a testator wishes his property to go to his solicitor and the solicitor prepares the will, that intention on the part of the testator should appear plainly on the will and should not be arrived at by the more oblique method of what is sometimes called a secret trust.

Note
There is no objection to benefiting the trustee by a separate clause in the will.

The principle preventing the named trustee from adducing evidence to show that he or she is entitled beneficially was applied in *Re Pugh's Will Trust*.

Re Pugh's Will Trust [1967] 1 WLR 1262, HC

Facts
The testator appointed his solicitor as executor and trustee, and left the residue of his estate to the solicitor 'to dispose in accordance with my letters or memoranda I may leave with this my will and otherwise in such manner as he may in his absolute discretion think fit'. The testator died without leaving any letters or memoranda with his will. The solicitor sought a declaration as to whether he was entitled to take the residue beneficially.

Held
The direction to apply the estate in accordance with the letters and memoranda created a fiduciary obligation on the solicitor. Since the letters, etc, did not exist, the trust had no defined objects and was void. Accordingly, the residuary estate was held on trust for the next of kin.

Note
It must be emphasised that the principle in *Re Rees* is applicable only to half secret trusts. It does not extend to fully secret trusts because, in such trusts, the intended trustee is not named as a trustee on the face of the will.

Question
Are the rules for the creation of fully secret trusts the same for half secret trusts?

ADDITIONS TO SECRET TRUSTS

If a testator wishes to add further property to an intended secret trust, he or she is required to take the trustees into his or her confidence and communicate the additional terms of the trust to them. Failure to inform the trustees of the additional property will result in the intended trust failing in respect of the additional property. In the context of a half secret trust, a resulting trust of the extra property will be created: see *Re Colin Cooper*.

Re Colin Cooper, Le Neve-Foster v National Provincial Bank [1939] Ch 811, CA

Facts
A testator bequeathed the sum of £5,000 to two trustees upon trust for purposes 'already communicated to them'. Shortly before his death, he executed a codicil giving the same trustees the sum of £10,000 declaring, 'they knowing my wishes regarding that sum'. The testator failed to

inform the trustees of this new bequest. The question concerned the validity of the trust of the additional bequest.

Held

The gift failed and a resulting trust of the additional £5,000 was created. In respect of £5,000 which the trustees agreed to hold upon trust, a valid secret trust was created:

> **Sir Wilfred Greene MR:** It seems to me that upon the facts of this case it is impossible to say that the acceptance by the trustees of the onus of trusteeship in relation to the first and earlier legacy is something which must be treated as having been repeated in reference to the second legacy or the increased legacy, which ever way one chooses to describe it . . . I cannot myself see that the arrangement between the testator and the trustees can be construed as though it had meant '£5,000 or whatever sum I may hereafter choose to bequeath'. That is not what was said and it was not with regard to any sum other than the £5,000 that the consciences of the trustees were burdened.

Note

If, on construction of the will and the circumstances of the case, the court had come to the preliminary conclusion that the intention of the trustees was to hold '£5,000 or whatever sum the testator may from time to time transfer', assuming the testator from time to time increased his bequest to the trustees beyond £5,000, it is arguable that the trustees would have been required to hold the final amount bequeathed to them. The trustees, having made a blanket agreement to hold an unlimited amount of property transferred to them, would have been hard pressed to show that they might, consistently without fraud, hold any additional property on resulting trust. The agreement simply is not restricted to a specific amount or a ceiling.

In principle, the rule in *Re Colin Cooper* ought to be extended to fully secret trusts. Thus if, on the facts, the court decides that the circumstances involve an agreement with the trustees to hold a specific amount of funds, say £5,000 upon trust for the beneficiaries, and the testator increases the legacy to £6,000 without informing the trustees, it is open to the court to decide that the extra amount of £1,000 is not subject to the trust. In this event, the legatees may take the additional sum beneficially (see *Wallgrave v Tebbs*, p 313 above). Alternatively, if the court considers the circumstances of the agreement and imposes a broad understanding to hold *any* property transferred to the trustees upon trust for the beneficiaries, then the changes in the amount of funds may be irrelevant.

CONTROVERSIAL ISSUES INVOLVING SECRET TRUSTS

There are a number of unresolved or inadequately resolved issues in the context of secret trusts. There follows a selection of these issues.

Communication of the terms to some of the trustees

Where a testator leaves property by will to two or more persons apparently beneficially, but informs one or some of the apparent legatees or devisees of the terms of the trust, the question has arisen whether the persons who were unaware of the trust are bound to hold upon trust or not. The solution adopted by the courts, which is far from adequate, depends on the status of the co-owners and the time when the communication was made to those who are aware of the trust.

If the informed legatee or devisee was told of the terms of the trust before or at the time of the execution of the will and the multiple owners take as joint tenants, then the uninformed legatee is bound by the terms of the trust communicated to the informed legatee. The reason commonly ascribed to this solution is that 'no one is allowed to claim property under a fraud committed by another' (*per* Farwell J in *Re Stead*, p 324 below). In other words, the court assumes that the reason why only one person has been informed of the trust is based on *a fraud committed by the informed legatee*. The testator is assumed to be induced to make his will by the promise of those who have been informed of the trust. Thus, the uninformed legatee ought not to be placed in an advantageous position of profiting from this fraud by being allowed to claim the property (or part thereof) beneficially. This approach was adopted in *Russell v Jackson*.

Russell v Jackson (1852) 10 Hare 204, HC

Facts

The testator transferred property by his will to joint tenants. Before making the will, he communicated the trust to some but not all of the intended trustees. The question concerned the extent of the secret trust.

Held

All the joint tenants were bound by the trust owing to the fraud of the informed beneficiary.

Alternatively, if the promise is made after the execution of the will to one (or some) of the co-owners but not to them all, and the will is left unrevoked, the informed legatee or devisee alone is bound to hold upon the terms of the secret trust. The uninformed co-owners are not bound to hold upon trust and may take the property (or part) beneficially. The status of the co-owners is immaterial. Thus, they may acquire the property as joint tenants or tenants in common. The legatees whose consciences are affected by the terms of the trust are those who made promises to the testator. The justification given for this solution is that the 'gift is not tainted by any fraud in procuring the execution of the will' (*per* Farwell J in *Re Stead*, see below).

In *Tee v Ferris*, the transfer of property by will was made to tenants in common, but since only one co-owner was informed of the terms, only he was bound to hold the property on trust.

Tee v Ferris (1856) 2 K & J 357, HC

Facts

The testator by his will gave the residue of his estate to Ferris and three other persons as tenants in common. By a contemporaneous memorandum, the testator expressed his confidence that the four persons would hold the property for 'charity objects'. Ferris alone was informed of the trust during the lifetime of the testator. The question concerned the validity of the secret trust.

Held

Ferris alone was bound to hold upon trust. Accordingly, the trust affected one quarter of the estate. The others were each entitled to take a quarter share of the property beneficially.

In *Re Stead*, Farwell J reviewed the authorities and concluded that there was no logic in the principle:

> I am unable to see any difference between a gift made on the faith of an antecedent promise and a gift left unrevoked on the faith of a subsequent promise to carry out the testator's wishes; but apparently a distinction has been made by the various judges who have had to consider the question. I am bound, therefore, to decide in accordance with these authorities.

Re Stead, Witham v Andrew [1900] 1 Ch 237, HC

Facts

A testatrix by her will gave her residuary estate to her executrices, Mrs Witham (W) and Mrs Andrews (A), absolutely. Following the death of the testatrix, W alleged that prior to the execution of the will the testatrix had informed her of the terms of a trust distribution. W further alleged that the testatrix executed her will on the faith of a promise by W to carry out the trust. A claimed that no communication had been made to her during the testatrix's lifetime and that she was entitled to half of the property beneficially.

Held

(a) Rejecting the evidence of W as to the time of the communication of the terms of the trust to her, the court decided that A therefore took half of the property beneficially.

(b) W was nevertheless bound by the terms of the trust communicated to her.

Farwell J: If A induces B either to make, or to leave unrevoked, a will leaving property to A and C as tenants in common, by expressly promising, or tacitly consenting, that he and C will carry out the testator's wishes, and C knows nothing of the matter until after A's death, A is bound, but C is not bound (*Tee v Ferris* (1856) 2 K & J 357); the reason stated being, that to hold otherwise would enable one beneficiary to deprive the rest of their benefits by setting up a secret trust. If, however, the gift were to A and C as joint tenants, the authorities have established a distinction between those cases in which the will is made on the faith of an antecedent promise by A and those in which the will is left unrevoked on the faith of a subsequent promise. In the former case, the trust binds both A and C (*Russell v Jackson* (1852) 10 Hare 204; *Jones v Badley* (1865) LR 3 Ch App 362), the reason stated being that no person can claim an interest under a fraud committed by another; in the latter case A and not C is bound (*Burney v MacDonald* (1845) 15 Sim 6 and *Moss v Cooper* (1861) 1 J & H 352), the reason stated being that the gift is not tainted with any fraud in procuring the execution of the will . . . I hold that the defendant Mrs Andrews is not bound by any trust.

Note

In respect of a fully secret trust, the authorities on the rule concerning the scope of the liability of multiple trustees where one or some of them has or have been informed of the terms of the trust are at best arbitrary. These cases tend to focus perhaps on the wrong issue. The central issue here ought to be the intention of the testator. If the testator was induced by the promise of A to transfer property to A and B for the benefit of another, and B was unaware of the trust, then A and B ought to be bound, for B should not be entitled to profit from the fraud of A. This ought to be the position irrespective of whether A and B are joint tenants or tenants in common. If, on the other hand, the testator would have given the property to B in any event, then there is no justification for subjecting B to the terms of a trust (see Perrins, B, 'Can you keep half a secret?' (1972) 88 LQR 225).

In respect of half secret trusts, the consequences concerning a failure to communicate the terms of the trust to all the trustees have been resolved piecemeal by the courts. It is the established practice of the courts that evidence of the terms of the trust is not admissible if made after the execution of the will. In such circumstances, the trustees hold upon resulting trust. Further, the justification (in the context of a fully secret trust) for imposing a trust on the uninformed trustees in respect of an antecedent communication to some of the trustees who are joint tenants (that is, 'no one is allowed to claim property beneficially under a fraud committed by another', *per* Farwell J in *Re Stead*) has no application to half secret trusts.

There have been a few occasions when the courts have considered the principle of incomplete communication to all the trustees of an intended half secret trust. The solution adopted by the courts in each case has been restricted to its own facts.

If the will permits communication to one of several trustees such as, 'to all or either of the trustees', the communication to one of the trustees before or at the time of the execution of the will bind all of them.

Per Lord Wright in *Re Keen* [1937] Ch 236:

. . . If the communication was made to one trustee only, and not to both, that would not, I think, be an objection to the secret trust.

Lord Wright did not indicate why he had no objection 'to the secret trust'. It is submitted that possible justifications of Lord Wright's decision are that the adduction of such evidence is consistent with the will and the trusteeship undertaken (as apparent on the face of the will) is a joint office.

If the will declares that the terms of the trust have been communicated to 'all of the trustees', evidence of the communication to one of the trustees is inadmissible in order to bind the conscience of the other trustees. The intended secret trust will fail for uncertainty of objects and a resulting trust will be set up: see *Re Spence*.

Re Spence [1949] WN 237, HC

Facts

A testator by his will, dated 11 August 1943, gave his estate to four trustees, A, B, C and D, 'to be dealt with in accordance with my wishes which I have made known to them'. At different times, between January 1941 and August 1943, he obtained promises from B, C and D to dispose of his property in accordance with memoranda to be drawn up at some unspecified future time and to be found among his papers at his death. In January 1943, he sent to A, his solicitor and fourth trustee, an envelope containing three sealed envelopes addressed to A, B and C, bearing a statement in the testator's handwriting that they were not to be opened until after his death. Each envelope subsequently turned out to contain a copy of a memorandum by the testator dated 6 and 9 December 1942 setting forth, *inter alia*, a series of dispositions of income and capital of his estate. (Copies of a further memorandum, dated 10 January 1944 and addressed to A, B, C and D, were deposited in the same way with A on 2 February 1944, eight days before the testator died on 10 February 1944.) A, B and C (the surviving trustees) asked the court to decide whether the memoranda dated 6 and 9 December 1942 constituted the terms of a valid secret trust, or whether there was a resulting trust in favour of the persons entitled to the testator's estate as on total intestacy.

Held

The intended secret trust failed for uncertainty on the following grounds:

(a) the promises obtained from B, C and D between January 1941 and August 1943 were ineffective as amounting to an irregular dispositive power;

(b) the delivery of the envelopes to A in January 1943 subject to the directions amounted to a constructive communication of the terms of the trust to A;

(c) it was not possible to substitute the communication to A for wishes communicated to other trustees (B, C and D) relating to unspecified memoranda to be drawn up in the future.

Classification of secret trusts

The classification of secret trusts is not entirely of academic importance. Express trusts concerning land are required to be 'manifested and proved by some writing' as enacted in s 53(1)(b) of the Law of Property Act 1925 (see p 36 above). On the other hand, constructive trusts in respect of land are exempt from the requirements of writing (see s 53(2) of the Law of Property Act 1925) (see p 36). The question considered here is whether a secret trust is an express or a constructive trust.

Half secret trusts

Half secret trusts are treated as express trusts because the existence of the trust is declared on the face of the will, although the objects are not specified in the will. Accordingly, in *Re Baillie*, the High Court decided that a half secret trust is an express trust and, if the agreement between the testator and the intended trustee is not evidenced in writing, the purported half secret trust is unenforceable.

Re Baillie (1886) 2 TLR 660, HC

Facts

A testator appointed Mrs Fitzgerald his executrix and gave her 'all his real and personal property upon trust to carry out my verbal wishes'. Prior to the execution of the will, the testator verbally informed the executrix that she might use the fund to educate and assist the children of the testator's deceased cousin if this was necessary, but subject to her doing so, the property was hers to enjoy beneficially. The trustee claimed to have exhausted the first purpose of the trust and sought to retain the surplus of property beneficially.

Held

The property was held on resulting trust. The intended secret trust in favour of the trustee failed because:

(a) the trustee was prohibited from adducing evidence that she was entitled beneficially;

(b) the trust of the realty was unenforceable because of failure to comply with s 9 of the Statute of Frauds 1677 (predecessor to s 53(1)(b) of the Law of Property Act 1925).

> **North J:** When an estate is given to a man in the character of a trustee, without anything to indicate that a beneficial interest is intended, then, if the trusts are exhausted there is a resulting trust ... The point raised by counsel for the defendant that the Statute of Frauds applied so far as the realty was concerned was a good one, because the trust was not indicated in writing.

Fully secret trusts

The classification of fully secret trusts has not been positively achieved.

Originally, secret trusts were enforced by the courts in order to prevent the intended trustee committing a fraud. As we have seen, a fully secret trustee takes the property apparently beneficially on the face of the will. It was the practice of the courts, in enforcing such trusts, to prevent the intended trustee using up s 9 of the Wills Act 1837 as a defence, to negate any attempt to take the property beneficially.

McCormick v Grogan (1869) LR 4 HL 82, HL

> **Lord Westbury:** The court of equity has, from a very early period, decided that even an Act of Parliament shall not be used as an instrument of fraud; and if in the machinery of perpetrating a fraud an Act of Parliament intervenes, the court of equity, it is true, does not set aside the Act of Parliament but it fastens on the individual who gets a title under that Act, and imposes upon him a personal obligation, because he applies the Act as an instrument for accomplishing a fraud.

This approach is consistent with the constructive trust jurisdiction. Accordingly, a fully secret trust concerning land may be declared orally and be effective under s 53(2) of the Law of Property Act 1925.

Alternatively, it is arguable that the trust is express, for the testator has declared the trust *inter vivos* and transferred the property to the trustees under his or her will. Thus, the requirements of *Milroy v Lord* (1862) 31 LJ Ch 798 (see p 19 above) are required to be complied with. Further, the modern basis for enforcing such trusts is to give effect to the intention of the testator, expressed outside the will (see Lord Sumner's judgment in *Blackwell v Blackwell*, p 318 above). If this is the case, it is arguable that s 53(1)(b) of the Law of Property Act 1925 is required to be complied with. However, the intended trustee is not entitled to raise the defence of non-compliance with the sub-section in order to take the property beneficially, for equity will not allow a statute to be used as an engine for fraud.

This issue was not raised in *Ottaway v Norman* (see p 315 above) and remains unresolved.

Question

Are secret trusts express or constructive trusts?

Proof of the secret trust

The earlier cases were consistent in applying the standard of proof in order to prove the terms of a secret trust, namely, 'clear evidence' of the terms of the trust analagous to the standard of proof required for rectification of an instrument. In short, the standard of proof was higher than the ordinary civil standard of a balance of probabilities.

McCormick v Grogan (1869) LR 4 HL 82, HL

Lord Westbury: It is incumbent on the court to see that a fraud, a *malus animus*, is proved by the clearest and most indisputable evidence.

Ottaway v Norman [1972] Ch 698, HC

Brightman J: . . . if a will contains a gift which is in terms absolute, clear evidence is needed before the court will assume that the testator did not mean what he said. It is perhaps analagous to the standard of proof which this court requires before it will rectify a written instrument, for there again a party is saying that neither meant what they have written.

Megarry VC in *Re Snowden* adopted a different approach to the standard of proof of a secret trust. There are two standards of proof in the context of a secret trust. The ordinary civil standard of proof (balance of probabilities) is required to be complied with in a way similar to proving the terms of an ordinary trust. The burden of proof lies on the party seeking to establish the trust. However, if there has been a *fraudulent denial of the trust or promise*, the standard of proof is higher.

Re Snowden, Smith v Spowage and Others [1979] Ch 528, HC

Facts

A testatrix, aged 86, made her will six days before she died. She had no children and her nearest relatives apart from her brother were five nephews and nieces, 13 great-nephews and great-nieces. She left her residuary estate to her brother, Bert (B), absolutely. B died six days after the testatrix, leaving all of his property to his son. Evidence was given by members of a firm of solicitors who had prepared and witnessed the will that the testatrix wished to be fair to everyone, including her nephews and nieces, and wanted B to look after the division for her. The question in issue was whether a secret trust was created.

Held

No secret trust was created and B's son took beneficially. B was subject only to a moral obligation to respect the wishes of the testatrix. In the absence of fraud or other special circumstances, the standard of proof that was required to establish a secret trust was merely the ordinary civil standard of proof required to establish an ordinary trust:

Megarry VC: I am not sure that it is right to assume that there is a single, uniform standard of proof for all secret trusts. The proposition of Lord Westbury in *McCormick v Grogan* (1869) LR 4 HL 82, with which Brightman J was pressed in *Ottaway v Norman* [1972] Ch 698 was that the jurisdiction in cases of secret trust was – 'founded altogether on personal fraud. It is a jurisdiction by which a Court of Equity, proceeding on the ground of fraud, converts the party who has committed it into a trustee for the party who is injured by that fraud. Now, being a jurisdiction founded on personal fraud, it is incumbent on the court to see that a fraud, *a malus animus*, is proved by the clearest and most indisputable evidence'.

Of that, it is right to say that the law on the subject has not stood still since 1869, and that it is now clear that secret trusts may be established in cases where there is no possibility of fraud.

McCormick v Grogan has to be read in the light both of earlier cases that were not cited, and also of subsequent cases, in particular *Blackwell v Blackwell* [1929] AC 318.

It seems to me that fraud comes into the matter in two ways. First, it provides an historical explanation of the doctrine of secret trusts: the doctrine was evolved as a means of preventing fraud. That, however, does not mean that fraud is an essential ingredient for the application of the doctrine: the reason for the rule is not part of the rule itself. Second, there are some cases within the doctrine where fraud is indeed involved. *There are cases where for the legatee to assert that he is a beneficial owner, free from any trust, would be a fraud on his part* [emphasis added].

It is to this latter aspect of fraud that it seems to me that Lord Westbury's words are applicable. If a secret trust can be held to exist in a particular case only by holding the legatee guilty of fraud, then no secret trust should be found unless the standard of proof suffices for fraud. On the other hand, if there is no question of fraud, why should so high a standard apply? In such a case, *I find it difficult to see why the mere fact that the historical origin of the* doctrine lay in the prevention of fraud should impose the high standard of proof for fraud in a case in which no issue of fraud arises. In accordance with the general rule of evidence, the standard of proof should vary with the nature of the issue and its gravity (see *Hornal v Neuberger Products Ltd* [1956] 3 All ER 970) [emphasis added].

Now in the present case there is no question of fraud. The will directed the residue to be held in trust for the brother absolutely, and the only question is whether or not the beneficial interest thus given to him has been subjected to a trust, and if so, what that trust is. The trust, if it is one, is plainly one which required the brother to carry it out: it was he who was to distribute the money and see that everything was dealt with properly, and not the trustees of the will. There was thus no attempt to cancel the testamentary trust of residue for the brother and require the trustees of the will to hold the residue on the secret trust instead. Accordingly, I cannot see that rectification provides any real analogy. The question is simply that of the ordinary standard of evidence required to establish a trust.

I therefore hold that in order to establish a secret trust where no question of fraud arises, the standard of proof is the ordinary civil standard of proof that is required to establish an ordinary trust.

Notes

(1) Professor Crane, in commenting on the decision in *Re Snowden* (see [1979] Conv 448), questions whether the rule requiring a higher standard of proof is necessary. Such a rule could be regarded as benefiting unscrupulous trustees. He suggests that it would be preferable to adopt the ordinary civil standard of proof throughout, bearing in mind that the court will have to weigh up the merits of the evidence on both sides.

(2) Megarry VC's justification in *Re Snowden* for imposing a higher standard of proof where there is an allegation of fraud appears to be based on the notion that the 'beneficial owner' under the will may otherwise be entitled to the property beneficially. This would be the case in the context of an intended fully secret trust, where the intended trustee denies the existence of a valid agreement between him or her and the testator. The higher standard of proof may not be imposed on an intended fully secret trustee who admits the agreement but disputes some of the details, or an intended half secret trustee, whether he or she denies the agreement or not. Moreover, the expression, 'fraud', in the context of secret trusts, has different shades of meanings.

Question
Who is required to prove the existence of a secret trust and to what standard?

Trustee predeceasing the testator

In probate law, the general rule (subject to the *per stirpes* rule and a number of other exceptions) is that, if the legatee or devisee predeceases the testator, the legacy or devise lapses and the interest falls into residue: see *Elliott v Davenport* (1705) 1 P Wms 83.

In the context of a fully secret trust, if the sole intended trustee predeceases the testator, his or her interest will lapse and the property, which would have been subject to the secret trust, will fall into residue. Accordingly, the intended secret trust will fail.

Although there is no direct authority that supports this analysis, Cozens Hardy LJ in *Re Maddock* in an *obiter* pronouncement hinted at this conclusion.

Re Maddock [1902] 2 Ch 220, CA

Facts

A testatrix by her will left her residuary estate 'absolutely' to X whom she appointed one of her executors. By a subsequent memorandum communicated to X during her lifetime, she directed X to hold part of the residue upon trust for named beneficiaries. There were insufficient assets to pay the debts of the estate. The question in issue was whether the secret beneficiaries took their interests subject to the payment of the debts or not.

Held

The part of the residuary estate that was bound by the trust must be treated as if it were specific-ally bequeathed and could not be used to pay the debts:

> **Cozens Hardy LJ:** . . . the so called trust does not affect property except by reason of a personal obligation binding the individual devisee or legatee. If he renounces and disclaims, or dies in the lifetime of the testator, the persons claiming under memorandum can take nothing against the heir at law or next of kin or residuary devisee or legatee.

On the other hand, in the context of a half secret trust, since the trustee takes as trustee on the face of the will, it could be argued that the trust ought not to fail, provided that the terms of the trust could be established.

Secret beneficiary predeceasing the testator

If the beneficiary under an intended secret trust dies before the testator, on general principles, the trust will fail. The trust is created when the property is transferred to the trustees subject to the trusts of the settlement. The beneficiary's interest may vest only at the time of the creation of the trust. At this point, of course, the beneficiary no longer exists and a trust cannot exist without a beneficiary. However, in *Re Gardner (No 2)*, the court decided that the deceased beneficiary's heirs were entitled to the trust funds.

Re Gardner (No 2) [1923] 2 Ch 230, HC

Facts

A testatrix by her will left her estate to her husband absolutely, 'knowing that he will carry out my wishes'. During her lifetime she informed her husband of the terms of the trust, namely, an equal distribution between her nephews and nieces after his death. The husband died five days after the testatrix and it was discovered that one of the nieces had died before the testatrix but after the communication of the terms to her husband. The question in issue was whether the personal representative of the niece was entitled to a share of the property.

Held

The personal representative was entitled to succeed on the ground that the trust was created at the time of the *inter vivos* communication by the testatrix:

> **Romer J:** Apart from authority I should, without hesitation, say that in the present case the husband held the corpus of the property upon trust for the two nieces and the nephew, notwithstanding the fact that the niece predeceased the testatrix. The rights of the parties appear to me to be exactly the same as though the husband, after the memorandum had been communicated to him by the testatrix . . . had executed a declaration of trust binding himself to hold any property that should come to him upon his wife's partial intestacy upon trust as specified in the memorandum.

Note

It is submitted that this conclusion cannot be supported in trusts law or probate law. In trusts law, as explained above, the trust may be created at the earliest moment on the death of the testatrix. During the testatrix's lifetime, a trust cannot exist because the trustees will not have acquired the intended trust property. At this time, the intended beneficiaries may enjoy only a *spes*. In any event, in probate law, a disposition by will takes effect on the death of the testator.

Question
When are secret trusts created?

Hodge, D, 'Secret trusts: the fraud theory revisited' [1980] Conv 341

Hodge examines the theoretical basis for the enforcement of secret trusts. His theory is that the prevention of fraud is the bedrock for enforcing secret trusts. Megarry VC, in *Re Snowden* [1979]

Ch 528, formulated the standard of proof needed to establish a secret trust by reference to the existence or non-existence of fraud. In this context, fraud has two meanings: the wider and narrower meaning. The wider view of fraud involves the secret trustee attempting to defeat the wishes of the testator by attempting to renege on the promise made to the testator during the latter's lifetime. Support for this view is to be found in the Court of Appeal's judgments, for example, Scott LJ in *Bannister v Bannister* [1948] 2 All ER 133. The narrower view of fraud is laid down by Lord Westbury in *McCormick v Grogan* (1869) LR 4 HL 82, and is based on the deceitful nature of the secret trustee's conduct considered by reference *to the time he made the undertaking*. Hodge submits that, of the two views, the wider view of fraud is preferable, 'for acceptance of the narrower view would not only impose upon a person seeking to establish a secret trust the heavy onus of showing at what point of time the secret trustee decided to resile from his promise, but would also make the validity of the secret trust dependent upon what is in fact an irrelevant consideration'.

Matthews, P, 'The true basis of the half secret trust' [1979] Conv 360

Mr Matthews subscribes to the view that 'the probate doctrine of incorporation by reference' represents the true basis of half secret trusts. Although there is a variety of objections to such a theory, this doctrine may explain the discrepancy concerning the admissibility of evidence as to the time of the communication of the terms of the trust: see *Blackwell v Blackwell* [1929] AC 318 and *Re Keen* [1937] Ch 236.

MUTUAL WILLS

Where two testators desire to make provision for the survivor and other ascertainable beneficiaries and conclude an *inter vivos* agreement to this effect, they may make separate wills (or joint wills) in substantially identical form in each other's favour, perhaps by giving the survivor a life interest in the deceased's estate with remainder to the ultimate beneficiary. Such arrangement attracts the mutual wills doctrine.

The motive of the testators may be to pool their resources together for the benefit of the ultimate beneficiary and to give the survivor a life interest in the property of the first testator to die.

For example, A and B decide that after their death their joint property will be transferred to Cancer Research. They may each make separate wills transferring their property to the named charity. This does not involve mutual wills. Assume, further, that the parties agree that the survivor ought to enjoy a life interest in the deceased's estate and then transfer their joint resources to the specified charity. Each testator makes a will in substantially identical terms transferring his estate to the survivor on the understanding that the *inter vivos* agreement is binding. Each testator's will may spell out the terms of the trust, that is, 'to the survivor for life with remainder to Cancer Research'. Alternatively, each testator may transfer his or her entire estate to the survivor. When the first testator dies (say A), his will will be probated, a trust will be created and B will enjoy a life interest in accordance with the agreement. When B dies, his entire estate (including the property taken under A's will) will be held upon trust for Cancer Research in accordance with the *inter vivos* agreement.

The above represents the intentions of the parties. Whether the intentions will be fulfilled depends on a mixture of rules of contract law, probate law and trust law.

Importance of the agreement

The agreement between the parties acts as the backbone of the trust. Every will is revocable by a testator before his death. If, therefore, the surviving testator revokes his will after the death of the other testator, the intended beneficiaries may not have a remedy against the surviving testator unless they can prove an agreement not to revoke his will.

There must be clear evidence of an agreement, proved on a balance of probabilities, to create irrevocable interests for the beneficiaries. The best evidence of an agreement to create mutual wills would be separate wills (or a joint will) which recite (or recites) the terms of the agreement made by the parties. However, there is no obligation to include the terms of the agreement in the will. Wherever the terms of the agreement are found, the requirement is whether the agreement creates irrevocable interests.

The fact that the parties have made substantially identical wills on the same date is not by itself proof of an irrevocable agreement, although it is a relevant factor to be taken into account along with the other evidence available: see *Re Oldham*.

Re Oldham [1925] Ch 75, HC

Facts
On 4 January 1907, a husband and wife made substantially identical wills. Each spouse left his or her property to the other absolutely, with identical alternatives in the event of the predecease of the other. There was no evidence of an agreement that the wills were irrevocable. The husband died in 1914 and the widow received his property under his will. The widow remarried and made a new will which was different from her 1907 will. She died in 1922. The plaintiff, who claimed to be entitled to an interest under the alleged mutual will trust, asserted that the wife's executors held her property on trust for him.

Held
The dispositions under the wife's second will must be upheld. The court will not presume the existence of a trust on the basis of the simultaneous execution of virtually identical wills:

> **Astbury J:** . . . the fact that two wills were made in identical terms does not necessarily connote any agreement beyond that of so making them. There is no evidence that there was an agreement that the trust should in all circumstances be irrevocable. In order to enforce the trust I must be satisfied that its terms are certain and unequivocal and such as in the circumstances I am bound to give effect. What is the evidence of that? Of course it is a strong thing that these two parties came together, agreed to make their wills in identical terms and in fact so made them, but that is not sufficient evidence of an irrevocable interest.

See also *Re Goodchild*, where the Court of Appeal decided that the execution of identical wills by a married couple did not import the inference that the wills were intended to be mutually binding.

Re Goodchild (Decd), Goodchild and Another v Goodchild [1997] 3 All ER 63, CA

Facts
On 11 February 1988, the testator (Dennis) and his first wife (Joan) executed wills in identical form in favour of the survivor of both of them and then to their adult son, Gary. On 14 April 1991, Joan died and Dennis received all of her estate. Dennis married the defendant, Enid, on 16 November 1992, and made a new will leaving his estate to Enid. On 1 January 1993, the testator died. Gary and his wife commenced proceedings against Enid claiming a declaration that Enid held Dennis's estate on trust for Gary and his wife in compliance with the wills executed in February 1988 or, alternatively, an order for reasonable financial provision payable out of Dennis's estate under s 2 of the Inheritance (Provision for Family and Dependants) Act 1975. The judge held that despite the identical nature of the wills of February 1988, there was no clear evidence of an agreement between Dennis and Enid not to revoke the wills. However, Joan's mistaken belief that the terms of the wills were binding imposed a moral obligation on Dennis, which was a special circumstance, exceptional enough to justify the claim under the 1975 Act. The defendant appealed.

Held
An essential ingredient of the doctrine of mutual wills is the existence of a contract between the two testators that both wills are irrevocable and will remain unaltered. There was no evidence of

an express agreement between Dennis and Joan and none could be implied on the facts, notwithstanding that the wills were not mutually binding. Joan's understanding of the effect of her will was such as to impose on Dennis a moral obligation to devote to Gary so much of Joan's estate as would have come to him if the mutual wills mechanism was effective:

> **Leggatt LJ:** Two wills may be in the same form as each other. Each testator may leave his or her estate to the other with a view to the survivor leaving both estates to their heir. But there is no presumption that a present plan will be immutable in future. A key feature of the concept of mutual wills is the irrevocability of the mutual intentions. Not only must they be binding when made, but the testators must have undertaken, and so must be bound, not to change their intentions after the death of the first testator. The test must always be: suppose that during the lifetime of the surviving testator the intended beneficiary did something which the survivor regarded as unpardonable, would he or she be free not to leave the combined estate to him? The answer must be that the survivor is so entitled unless the testators agreed otherwise when they executed their wills. Hence the need for a clear agreement. Dennis and Joy executed wills in the same terms, save that each left his or her estate to the other. Thus, the survivor was to have both estates. They wanted Gary to inherit the combined estates. But there was no express agreement not to revoke the wills. Nor could any such agreement be implied from the fact that the survivor was in a position to leave both estates to Gary. The fact that each expected that the other would leave them to him is not sufficient to impress the arrangement with a floating trust, binding in equity. A mutual desire that Gary should inherit could not of itself prevent the survivor from resiling from the arrangement. What is required is a mutual intention that both wills should remain unaltered and that the survivor should be bound to leave the combined estates to the son. That is what is missing here. The judge found that Joan regarded the arrangement as irrevocable, but that Dennis did not. No mutual intention was proven that the survivor should be bound to leave the joint estate to Gary. That is what they meant to achieve. It could not happen unless they first left their respective estates to the survivor of them. But the fact that each was able to leave the combined estate to Gary does not, without more, mean that both were bound to do so.

The agreement between the two testators to make irrevocable wills operates as a contract between the parties. This contract may be included in a deed, or may be proved by parol evidence, or may exist in the will of each testator. During the lifetime of each testator, if either party withdraws from the agreement and revokes his or her will, the other party to the agreement is entitled to sue the guilty party for breach of contract. The damages recoverable are likely to be nominal since the loss suffered is impossible to quantify (see *Robinson v Ommanney* (1883) 23 Ch D 285). If notice of a breach of contract is given to the other party during the lifetime of both parties, the innocent party will be discharged from the agreement and may revoke his or her will (see *Stone v Hoskins* [1905] P 194). Until recently the ultimate beneficiary under the intended trust, not being privy to the contract, had no *locus standi* regarding a claim for breach of contract. However, the Contracts (Rights of Third Parties) Act 1999 empowers the ultimate beneficiary to pursue a claim in his own right for breach of contract.

Wills Act 1837, s 18(1)

... a will shall be revoked by the testator's marriage.

It is arguable that revocation of a will by marriage *per se* will not have the effect of creating a breach of the agreement entitling the innocent party to claim damages for breach of contract (see *Re Marsland* and, also, the effect of an annulment of a marriage under s 18A of the Wills Act 1837).

In Re Marsland [1939] Ch 820

Facts

A husband executed a deed of separation and covenanted in the same deed not to revoke a will previously made. The husband later obtained a divorce and expressed his wishes to remarry. The wife brought an action against him claiming damages for breach of covenant.

Held

Remarriage does not have the effect of revoking the contract. To be actionable, a revocation of the agreement is required to be intentional.

Moreover, where two testators make mutual wills arrangements, a unilateral alteration of the will by the first testator to die has the effect of terminating the agreement. The second testator to die becomes free to dispose of his or her estate, during his or her lifetime, in whatever way he or she pleases: see *Re Hobley*.

Re Hobley (Decd) (1997) The Times, 16 June, HC

Facts
On 4 December 1975, Mr and Mrs Hobley executed mutual wills in favour of each other, whosoever might survive, with substitutionary gifts to common beneficiaries. The house at No 65 Russel Terrace was devised to Mr Blyth and there were 11 pecuniary legatees, eight of whom were entitled to the residue. Some time later, Mr Hobley executed a codicil revoking the devise of No 65 Russel Terrace to Mr Blyth and left it as part of the residuary estate. There was no evidence as to the reason for the change, or whether Mrs Hobley knew of or consented to it. Mr Hobley died on 13 January 1980 and Mrs Hobley inherited his entire estate, including No 65 Russel Terrace. On 13 March 1992, Mrs Hobley executed a will which was substantially different from the 1975 will. She died on 23 May 1993. The National Westminster Bank plc was appointed executor of Mrs Hobley's will and commenced the application to the court. The question in issue concerned the effect on the mutual will arrangement of the alteration of Mr Hobley's will. Counsel for the original beneficiaries, relying on *Hong Kong Fir Shipping Co v Kawasaki Kisen Kaisha Ltd* [1962] 2 QB 26, argued that Mr Hobley's codicil did not amount to a fundamental breach of the 1975 agreement so as to discharge Mrs Hobley from the agreement.

Held
The High Court decided that the principles on which the court acted in order to give effect to an agreement to make and not revoke mutual wills were not precisely the same as applied in the law of contract. The court could not evaluate the significance to the parties of any alteration in the terms of the will of the first testator, nor their subjective intentions. Moreover, it is irrelevant that the alteration did not personally disadvantage the survivor. Accordingly, the unilateral alteration of Mr Hobley's will had the effect of discharging Mrs Hobley from the agreement in 1975. She was, therefore, free to dispose of her estate as she wished.

Creation of the trust

The trust is created by the courts in favour of the beneficiaries and is imposed on the survivor when the first testator dies, leaving a will unrevoked which complies with the terms of the agreement. If the survivor alters or executes another will, as he is entitled to do in accordance with probate rules, this adjusted or new will will be admitted to probate but his personal representatives will hold his property upon trust to perform the agreement: see *Dufour v Pereira*.

Dufour v Pereira (1769) 1 Dick 419, HL

Facts
A joint will was made pursuant to an agreement between husband and wife whereby the residuary estate of each of them was to constitute a common fund to be held for the survivor for his or her life with remainders over. On the death of the husband, the wife, who was one of his executors, proved the will. She took possession of her husband's property and enjoyed the benefit of his residuary estate together with her separate property for many years, but on the death of the wife it was found that her last will disregarded the provisions of the joint will and left her estate to her daughter, the defendant, Mrs Pereira. The plaintiffs were the beneficiaries under the joint will and claimed that the wife's personal estate was held in trust for them.

Held
The House of Lords found in favour of the plaintiffs, upholding the mutual will in accordance with the agreement between the husband and wife:

Lord Camden LC: [The mutual wills doctrine creates] a contract between the parties which cannot be rescinded but by the consent of both. The first that dies carries his part of the contract into execution. Will the court afterwards permit the other to break the contract? Certainly not.

The defendant has taken the benefit of the bequest in her favour by the mutual will; and has proved it as such; she has thereby certainly confirmed it; and therefore I am of opinion, the last will of the wife, so far as it breaks in upon the mutual will, is void. And declare that [the defendant] having proved the mutual will, after her husband's death; and having possessed all his personal estate, and enjoyed the interest thereof during her life, has by those acts bound her assets to make good all her bequests in the said mutual will; and therefore let the necessary accounts be taken.

In *Re Hagger*, the court decided that the trust was created on the death of the first party under the mutual will arrangement.

Re Hagger [1930] 2 Ch 190, HC

Facts

A husband and wife made a joint will in 1902 in which it was stated that they agreed to dispose of their property by will and there was to be no alteration or revocation except by agreement. By their will, they gave the whole of their property to the survivor for life and on the death of the survivor to divide the proceeds of sale between nine beneficiaries, including Eleanor Palmer. The wife died in 1904 and the husband made another will in 1921 indicating that his property was to be divided between various persons of whom some were not mentioned in the joint will. The husband died in 1928 and Eleanor Palmer died in 1923. Her personal representatives claimed her portion of the estate under the joint will.

Held

From the time of the wife's death, the surviving husband held the property upon trust for those entitled in remainder under the joint will, subject to the husband's life interest:

Clauson J: To my mind, *Dufour v Pereira* (1769) 1 Dick 419, decides that where there is a joint will such as this, on the death of the first testator the position as regards that part of the property which belongs to the survivor is that the survivor will be treated in this court as holding the property on trust to apply it so as to carry out the effect of the joint will . . . it is clear that Lord Camden (in *Dufour v Pereira*) has decided that if the survivor takes a benefit conferred on him by the joint will he will be treated as a trustee in this court, and he will not be allowed to do anything inconsistent with the provisions of the joint will.

I am bound to hold that from the death of the wife the husband held the property, according to the tenor of the will, subject to the trusts thereby imposed upon it, at all events if he took advantage of the provisions of the will. In my view he did take advantage of those provisions.

Question

What type of trust is derived from the mutual wills doctrine and when is it created?

In *Re Cleaver*, the court decided that evidence of an enforceable agreement is required to be established on a balance of probabilities.

Re Cleaver [1981] 1 WLR 939, HC

Facts

In October 1967, the testator (H), aged 78, married the testatrix (W), then aged 74. H had three children by a previous marriage. W had no children, but she did have two nieces. H and W both simultaneously made wills in substantially identical terms. H gave each of his three children a legacy of £500, and his residuary estate to W absolutely, subject to her surviving him for one month with gifts over. The testatrix's will was in identical terms, save that, in lieu of the legacies of £500 to the testator's children, she gave legacies of £500 to each of her two nieces. H died in 1975, and W duly received the whole of H's net residue. On 23 June 1977, W made her last will, and in this she gave her net residuary estate to M and her husband. No provision was made either for the plaintiffs or for W's two nieces. W died on 30 May 1978. The plaintiffs sought a declaration that W's executors held W's estate on trust to give effect to the mutual will arrangement between H and W.

Held

The court found in favour of the plaintiffs on the ground that, on H's death, a trust was created in favour of the beneficiaries nominated by H and W during their lifetime:

> **Nourse J:** I would emphasise that the agreement or understanding must be such as to impose on the donee a legally binding obligation to deal with the property in the particular way and that the other two certainties, namely, those as to the subject matter of the trust and the persons intended to benefit under it, are as essential to this species of trust as they are to any other. The principal difficulty is always whether there was a legally binding obligation or merely what Lord Loughborough LC in *Lord Walpole v Lord Orford* (1797) 3 Ves Jun 402, p 419, described as an honourable engagement.
>
> It is clear from *Birmingham v Renfrew* (1937) 57 CLR 666, that an enforceable agreement to dispose of property in pursuance of mutual wills can be established only by clear and satisfactory evidence. That seems to me to be no more than a particular application of the general rule that all claims to the property of deceased persons must be scrutinised with very great care. However, that does not mean that there has to be a departure from the ordinary standard of proof required in civil proceedings. I have to be satisfied on a balance of probabilities that the alleged agreement was made, but before I can be satisfied of that I must find clear and satisfactory evidence to that effect.

The constructive trust created by the courts is imposed on the survivor irrespective of whether or not he or she takes an interest in accordance with the agreement made between the two testators: see *Re Dale*. The reason for this rule is to prevent the survivor committing a fraud on the beneficiaries by attempting to renege on the agreement.

Re Dale (Decd), Proctor v Dale [1993] 3 WLR 652, HC

Facts

On 5 September 1988, the father and mother of the plaintiff (daughter) and defendant (son) each made an identical will. Each will contained a clause revoking all former wills and transferring all real and personal property in favour of the plaintiff and defendant in equal shares. The father died on 9 November 1988 without altering his will. Probate of his will was granted to the plaintiff and defendant on 24 August 1990. On 14 July 1990 the mother made a new will revoking her former will and, after appointing the defendant to be her executor, modified the terms of her previous will. She bequeathed the sum of £300 to the plaintiff and gave the residue of her estate to her son. The mother died on 30 November 1990 and probate of her will was obtained on 13 June 1992. The value of her net estate was £19,000.

The plaintiff claimed that on her father's death, her mother became bound in equity to give effect to the agreement and dispose of her estate in accordance with the agreement. Thus, the defendant, as executor of his mother's estate, became bound in equity to distribute the estate to the plaintiff and defendant equally. The defendant argued that under the doctrine of mutual wills it was essential that the will of each testator should transfer to the other a direct, personal and financial benefit either absolutely or for life as the consideration for the agreement by each person not to revoke the will. Since this requirement was lacking, the defendant submitted that no trust was created on his father's death and his mother was free to modify her will as she pleased.

Held

The court found in favour of the plaintiff on the ground that the underlying theory of the mutual wills doctrine is the prevention of fraud. It would have been a fraud on the first testator to die (Mr Dale) and the beneficiaries entitled under the agreement (the children equally) to allow the survivor to change the terms of the agreement following the death of the first testator. The fraud remains the same whether the agreement benefits the surviving testatrix or persons other than the surviving testatrix. Accordingly, it is not essential that the surviving testatrix receive a benefit:

Morritt J: There is no doubt that for the doctrine to apply there must be a contract at law. It is apparent from all the cases to which I shall refer later, but in particular from *Gray v Perpetual Trustee Co Ltd* [1928] AC 391, that it is necessary to establish an agreement to make and not to revoke mutual wills, some understanding or arrangement being insufficient – 'without such a definite agreement there can no more be a trust in equity than a right to damages at law' (see *per* Viscount Haldane, at p 400).

It is to be assumed that the first testator and the second testator had agreed to make and not to revoke the mutual wills in question. The performance of that promise by the execution of the will by the first testator is in my judgment sufficient consideration by itself.

[After reviewing the leading authorities the learned judge concluded:] All the cases show the doctrine applies when the second testator benefits under the will of the first testator. But I am unable to see why it should be any the less a fraud on the first testator if the agreement was that each testator should leave his or her property to particular beneficiaries, for example, their children, rather than to each other.

I see no reason why the doctrine should be confined to cases where the second testator benefits when the aim of the principle is to prevent the first testator from being defrauded. A fraud on the first testator will include cases where the second testator benefits, but I see no reason why the principle should be confined to such cases. In my judgment so to hold is consistent with all the authorities, supported by some of them, and is in furtherance of equity's original jurisdiction to intervene in cases of fraud.

Question
When is a constructive trust created in accordance with the mutual wills doctrine?

Extent of the agreement

It is a question of construction to determine the scope and extent of the property subject to the agreement and thus the trust. If the agreement is expressed to bind the whole of the interest owned by each party, the trust will bind the entire property owned by each party and the surviving testator may be unable to deal with his own property during his lifetime. Each case is determined on its own facts: see *Re Green*.

Re Green [1951] Ch 148, HC

Facts
On 31 August 1940, a husband (H) and wife (W) executed separate mutual wills in identical form. They recited, in effect, that if H's first wife should not survive him, the house in its entirety would be transferred to a specified hospital and the remainder of his estate be divided into two equal parts – one moiety being his personal estate and the other moiety to be disposed of in accordance with the agreement. W died in April 1942 and, under the terms of her will, her residuary estate passed to H absolutely. In April 1945, H remarried and, in December 1946, he made a new will whereby, after giving certain pecuniary legacies, he gave the entire residuary estate to his second wife. H died in 1946. The court considered the question of the validity of the trust.

Held
H's second will operated to transfer only one half of his property, because the other half of his estate was subject to the trusts for named persons on his death. The house was also subject to the trust:

Vaisey J: In my view [the testator's will] can only operate as regards one moiety which was under the testator's control at his death, and, with regard to the other moiety, ie, the moiety which was notionally the property of his first wife, the pre-existing will must take effect, not as a will, but as evidence of a trust which is plainly to be discerned in the two wills, viz, the first will of the testator – which, of course, never became a will in the sense that it was a proved will – and the will of the first wife which was proved and under which the husband took an absolute interest in the residue.

In my judgment, one moiety of the estate must be held on the trusts declared by the first will. The other moiety passes under the provisions contained in the second will subject to this, that, before the moieties are ascertained, the first will is also operative so far as regards the property, 141 Billy Lows Lane, the entirety of which is to pass with the furniture therein to the successors in title, whoever they may be under the National Health Service Act 1946, of the Potters Bar Hospital absolutely.

Question
What is the significance of an agreement in the context of the law regarding mutual wills?

In *Birmingham v Renfrew*, Dixon J summarised the law with regard to mutual wills. This summary has been considered by courts in the United Kingdom as an authoritative statement of the rules.

Birmingham v Renfrew (1937) 57 CLR 666, HC

Dixon J: It has long been established that a contract between persons to make corresponding wills gives rise to equitable obligations when one acts on the faith of such an agreement and dies leaving his will unrevoked so that the other takes property under its dispositions. It operates to impose upon the survivor an obligation regarded as specifically enforceable. It is true that he cannot be compelled to make and leave unrevoked a testamentary document and if he dies leaving a last will containing provisions inconsistent with his agreement it is nevertheless valid as a testamentary act. But the doctrines of equity attach the obligation to the property. The effect is, I think, that the survivor becomes a constructive trustee and the terms of the trust are those of the will which he undertook would be his last will.

There is a third element which appears to me to be inherent in the nature of such a contract or agreement, although I do not think it has been expressly considered. The purpose of an arrangement for corresponding wills must often be, as in this case, to enable the survivor during his life to deal as absolute owner with the property passing under the will of the party first dying. That is to say, the object of the transaction is to put the survivor in a position to enjoy for his own benefit the full ownership so that, for instance, he may convert it and expend the proceeds if he chooses. But when he dies he is to bequeath what is left in the manner agreed upon. It is only by the special doctrines of equity that such a floating obligation, suspended, so to speak, during the lifetime of the survivor can descend upon the assets at his death and crystallise into a trust. No doubt gifts and settlements, *inter vivos*, if calculated to defeat the intention of the compact, could not be made by the survivor and his right of disposition, *inter vivos*, is, therefore, not unqualified. But, substantially, the purpose of the arrangement will often be to allow full enjoyment for the survivor's own benefit and advantage upon condition that at his death the residue shall pass as arranged.

FURTHER READING

Andrews, J, 'Creating secret trusts' [1963] 27 Conv 92.
Brierly, A, 'Mutual wills – Blackpool illuminations' (1995) 58 MLR 95.
Davis, C, 'Mutual wills; formalities; constructive trusts' [2003] Conv 238.
Gratton, S, 'Mutual wills and remarriage' [1997] Conv 153.
Kincaid, D, 'The tangled web: the relationship between a secret trust and the will' [2000] Conv 421.
Meager, R, 'Secret trusts – do they have a future?' [2003] Conv 203.
Mitchell, J, 'Some aspects of mutual wills' (1951) 14 MLR 136.
Perrins, B, 'Can you keep half a secret?' (1972) 88 LQR 225.
Richardson, N, 'Floating trusts and mutual wills' (1996) 10 Tru LI 88.
Rickett, C, 'Mutual wills and the law of restitution' (1989) 105 LQR 534.
Rickett, C, 'Mutual wills – the New Zealand approach: *Re Newey*' [1996] Conv 136.
Stevens, J, 'Avoiding disinheritance' (1996) 146 NLJ 961.
Sunnocks, F, 'Close relations of the secret trust' (1988) 138 NLJ 35.
Wilde, D, 'Secret and semi-secret trusts: justifying distinctions between the two' [1995] Conv 366.

PRIVATE PURPOSE TRUSTS

INTRODUCTION

An intended express trust for non-charitable purposes, as distinct from a trust to benefit persons, is void. Instead, a resulting trust will be created for the settlor or his estate. The justification for this rule is the absence of a person (a beneficiary) who has *locus standi* to enforce the trust. There are a number of exceptions to this rule. These are:

(a) trusts for the maintenance of specific animals;

(b) trusts for the erection and maintenance of monuments;

(c) the gift may *prima facie* appear to benefit purposes but, on construction, the court may decide that the gift benefits persons (see *Re Denley's Trust Deed* [1969] 1 Ch 673 at pp 346–47 below).

Gifts to unincorporated associations provide special difficulties in this context. Transfers to such bodies may be construed as creating gifts on trust for the purposes of the association and may be invalidated under the lack of beneficiary principle. In addition, such gifts may infringe the rule against perpetuities. However, there are a number of ways in which such gifts may be treated as valid. These are:

(a) the gift to the association may be construed as a gift to the present members of the association as joint tenants; or

(b) the gift to the association may be construed as an accretion to the funds of the association for the benefit of the members; or

(c) a transfer to the association may be treated as a gift for all the members of the association, both present and future. Provided that the gift does not infringe the perpetuity rule, it may be valid; or

(d) the transfer to the association may be construed as a gift on trust for the present members of the association. Provided that the rules concerning express trusts have been complied with, the trust may be valid.

PRIVATE PURPOSE TRUSTS

A purpose trust is designed to promote a purpose as an end in itself, for example, to discover an alphabet of 40 letters, to provide a cup for a yacht race or to provide for the boarding up of certain rooms in a house. The effect is that such intended trusts are void, for the court cannot give effect to a trust which it cannot supervise. There is no beneficiary with *locus standi* capable of enforcing such trust. In other words, a trust creates rights in favour of beneficiaries and imposes correlative duties on the trustees. If there are no persons with the power to enforce such rights, then equally there can be no duties imposed on trustees. In consequence, a resulting trust will be set up in favour of the donor or settlor on the failure of a non-charitable purpose trust. This general rule may be illustrated by *In Re Astor*.

In Re Astor's Settlement Trusts, Astor v Scholfield [1952] Ch 534, HC

Facts

Lord Astor purported to create a trust for, *inter alia*, 'the maintenance of good understanding between nations and the preservation of the independence and integrity of newspapers'. The question in issue involved the validity of this gift.

Held

The trust was void for uncertainty on the grounds: (a) that the means by which the trustees were to attain the stated aims were unspecified; and (b) of the absence of a person who was entitled, as of right, to enforce the trust:

> **Roxburgh J:** The typical case of a trust is one in which the legal owner of property is constrained by a court of equity so to deal with it as to give effect to the equitable rights of another. These equitable rights have been hammered out in the process of litigation in which a claimant on equitable grounds has successfully asserted rights against a legal owner or other person in control of property. *Prima facie*, therefore, a trustee would not be expected to be subject to an equitable obligation unless there was somebody who could enforce a correlative equitable right, and the nature and extent of that obligation would be worked out in proceedings for enforcement. Moreover . . . no officer has ever been constituted to take, in the case of non-charitable purposes, the position held by the Attorney General in connection with charitable purposes, and no case has been found in the reports in which the court has ever directly enforced a non-charitable purpose against a trustee. Indeed where, as in the present case, the only beneficiaries are purposes and at present unascertainable persons, it is difficult to see who could initiate such proceedings. If the purposes are valid trusts, the settlors have retained no beneficial interest and could not initiate them. It was suggested that the trustees might proceed *ex parte* to enforce the trusts against themselves. I doubt that, but at any rate nobody could enforce the trusts against them.
>
> What Sir William Grant had said as Master of the Rolls in *Morice v The Bishop of Durham* (1805) 10 Ves 522 as long ago as 1804: 'There must be somebody, in whose favour the court can decree performance.' The position was recently restated by Harman J in *In Re Wood* [1949] Ch 498: 'A gift on trust must have a *cestui que trust*,' and this seems to be in accord with principle. On the other side is a group of cases relating to horses and dogs, graves and monuments – matters arising under wills and intimately connected with the deceased – in which the courts have found means of escape from these general propositions and also *In Re Thompson* [1934] Ch 342. The rest may, I think, properly be regarded as anamolous and exceptional and in no way destructive of the proposition which traces descent from or through Sir William Grant through Lord Parker to Harman J. Perhaps the late Sir Arthur Underhill was right in suggesting that they may be concessions to human weakness or sentiment, see Underhill, A, Law of Trusts, 8th ed, p 79. They cannot, in my judgment, of themselves (and no other justification has been suggested to me) justify the conclusion that a court of equity will recognise as an equitable obligation affecting the income of large funds in the hands of trustees a direction to apply it in furtherance of enumerated non-charitable purposes in a manner which no court or department can control or enforce. I hold that the trusts here in question are void on the first of the grounds submitted by Mr Jennings and Mr Buckley.

Note

This general rule is subject to a number of exceptions to be considered later.

Question

What is the effect of attempting to create a private purpose trust?

REASONS FOR FAILURE

There are a number of common reasons why private purpose trusts fail. The list is not exhaustive, but pitfalls which a settlor should avoid are:

(a) the lack of a beneficiary;

(b) uncertainty of objects; and

(c) the infringement of the perpetuity rule.

Lack of beneficiaries

A trust is mandatory in nature. The courts have always jealously guarded the rights and interests of the beneficiaries under trusts. But such rights may be protected only if the beneficiary has *locus standi* to enforce the same. Purposes cannot initiate proceedings against the trustees because, as

Lord Grant MR said in *Morice v Bishop of Durham* (1805) 10 Ves 522, 'There must be somebody in whose favour the court can decree performance'.

On the other hand, with charitable purpose trusts (see Chapters 14–17 below), the Attorney General is charged with the duty of enforcing public trusts. No public official is charged with enforcing private trusts.

Uncertainty

As a corollary to the above-mentioned rule, it is obvious that the rights of the beneficiaries will be illusory unless the court is capable of ascertaining to whom those rights belong. Thus, as a second ground for the decision in *Re Astor*, the trust failed for uncertainty.

In Re Astor's Settlement Trusts, Astor v Scholfield [1952] Ch 534, HC

Roxburgh J: The second ground upon which the relevant trusts are challenged is uncertainty. If (contrary to my view) an enumeration of purposes outside the realm of charities can take the place of an enumeration of beneficiaries, the purposes must, in my judgment, be stated in phrases which embody definite concepts and the means by which the trustees are to try to attain them must also be prescribed with a sufficient degree of certainty. The test to be applied is stated by Lord Eldon in *Morice v Bishop of Durham* (1805) 10 Ves 522, as follows:

> As it is a maxim, that the execution of a trust shall be under the control of the court, it must be of such a nature, that it can be under that control; so that the administration of it can be reviewed by the court; or, if the trustee dies, the court itself can execute the trust.

Applying this test, I find many uncertain phrases in the enumeration of purposes, for example, 'different sections of people in any nation or community' in paragraph 1 of the third schedule, 'constructive policies' in paragraph 2, 'integrity of the press' in paragraph 3, 'combines' in paragraph 5, 'the restoration ... of the independence of ... writers in newspapers' in paragraph 6, and 'benevolent schemes' in paragraph 7. The purposes must be so defined that if the trustees surrendered their discretion, the court could carry out the purposes declared, not a selection of them arrived at by eliminating those that are too uncertain to be carried out.

Accordingly, in my judgment, the trusts for the application of income during 'the specified period' are also void for uncertainty.

A case that illustrates this principle is *In Re Endacott*.

In Re Endacott (Decd), Corpe v Endacott [1960] Ch 232, CA

Facts

A testator transferred his residuary estate to the Devon Parish Council 'for the purpose of providing some useful memorial to myself'. The question in issue was whether a trust had been created.

Held

No out-and-out gift to the council was created. The testator intended to impose an obligation in the nature of a trust on the council which failed for uncertainty of objects:

> **Lord Evershed MR:** I therefore, so far as this case is concerned, conclude that, though this trust is specific, in the sense that it indicates a purpose capable of expression, yet it is of far too wide and uncertain a nature to qualify within the class of cases cited. It would go far beyond any fair analogy to any of those decisions.
>
> I cannot myself see that the utility is confined to the inhabitants of North Tawton. It would be wrong to treat this formula as being merely synonymous with 'for the benefit of the inhabitants of North Tawton' and so construing it (but, I think, illogically) to give to this formula the inherent quality which would make it a charitable gift. It would be contrary to the tenor of the law, more particularly as it has been recently expounded, and it would be carrying this case beyond any limits which authority justifies.

Note

Charitable trusts, as we will see later, are subject to a special test for certainty of objects (see Chapter 14, p 360).

Perpetuity rule

English law views with disfavour an obligation to retain property within a group of persons (the family, an unincorporated association, etc) for a period longer than the perpetuity period.

At common law, this period is measured in terms of a life or lives in being plus 21 years. Only human lives may be chosen and not the lives of animals, some of which are noted for their longevity (such as tortoises and elephants). In this respect, an embryonic child (*en ventre sa mère*) constitutes a life in being if this is relevant in measuring the period. A life (or lives in being), whether connected with the gift or not, may be chosen expressly by the donor or settlor, or may be implied in the circumstances if the life (or lives) is (or are) so related to the gift or settlement that it is (or they are) capable of being used to measure the date of the vesting of the interest. If no lives are selected or are implied, the perpetuity period at common law is 21 years from the date that the instrument creating the gift takes effect (a will takes effect on the date of the death of the testator or testatrix; a deed takes effect on the date of execution).

For example, if S, a settlor, during his lifetime transfers a portfolio of shares to T1 and T2 as trustees, on trust contingently for his first child to marry, and S has unmarried children, the gift, before the introduction of the Perpetuities and Accumulations Act 1964, would be void. S would be treated impliedly as the life in being, and it was possible that none of his children might marry within 21 years after his death. Thus, the gift might not vest within the perpetuity period. The perpetuity period commences from the date the instrument takes effect and, at common law, the interest was void if there was any possibility, however remote, that the gift might vest outside the perpetuity period.

Moreover, the settlor may expressly select a life or lives in being in order to extend the perpetuity period. Any number of lives may be selected. The test is whether the group of lives selected is certain and identifiable to such an extent that it is possible to ascertain the date of death of the last survivor. This test was clearly incapable of being satisfied in *Re Moore*.

Re Moore [1901] 1 Ch 936, HC

Facts

The question in issue was whether a gift was valid or void where a testator attempted to define the perpetuity period as '21 years from the death of the last survivor of all persons who shall be living at my death'.

Held

The gift was void for uncertainty. It was impossible to identify the date of death of the last survivor:

> **Joyce J:** I think this gift is void for uncertainty. It is impossible to ascertain when the last life will be extinguished, and it is, therefore, impossible to say when the period of 21 years will commence. Under these circumstances it is not, I think, necessary for me to consider whether the gift is void as transgressing the rule against perpetuity.

Note

The settlor may select lives which have no connection with the trust. It became the practice to select royal lives, such as 'the lineal descendants of Queen Elizabeth II living at my death', with the objective of ascertaining the date of death of the last survivor of such descendants.

In substance, the perpetuity rule not only requires a future interest to vest within the perpetuity period, but also stipulates the maximum period of duration in which such interest may be enjoyed following the vesting of the interest.

On analysis, the rule may be classified into two categories, namely:

(a) the rule against remote vesting; and

(b) the rule against excessive duration.

The rule against remote vesting

This rule stipulates the maximum period of time in which the vesting of a future interest may be postponed. A future interest (such as a contingent interest) is one that has not vested in the beneficiary. An interest may be vested 'in possession' or 'in interest' and will not be subject to this rule. An interest is vested 'in possession' if the beneficiary has a 'present right of present enjoyment', such as a gift to 'A for life' or a gift to 'A absolutely'. A has an unrestricted right to enjoy the income as it arises, or an absolute right to the property respectively. An interest is vested 'in interest' if the beneficiary has a present right to future possession, for example, A for life, remainder to B absolutely. B has a present right to the capital, which he may sell, exchange or give away as he pleases while A is still alive. B obtains a right to possession when A dies, that is, B obtains the right to the income (in addition to his right to the capital) when A dies. A contingent interest, on the other hand, is not a vested interest while the contingency remains unperformed. A contingent interest is not an immediate right of enjoyment but a future right of enjoyment which may or may not accrue on the fulfilment of a condition, for example, 'to C (who is currently aged 10) if he attains the age of 18', or any other contingency.

The rule at common law was that an interest was void if it was possible to imagine a sequence of events rendering the possibility that the interest might vest outside the perpetuity period.

Before 1964, the common law judges, in their enthusiasm to avoid future interests, decided absurdly that there was no upper or lower age limit in respect of which a living person was capable of procreation. Thus, it was decided that an octogenarian on the one hand and a toddler at the other extreme were capable of reproducing.

This degree of volatility continued until the passing of the Perpetuities and Accumulations Act 1964. This Act introduced three major reforms to the law, namely, the 'wait and see' rule, the 'statutory life' period and a maximum statutory period. Under the Act, a future interest is no longer void on the ground that it 'may' vest outside the perpetuity period. It is void if, in the circumstances, the interest does not vest within the perpetuity period. In the meantime, the court will 'wait and see' whether or not the gift will vest. Moreover, s 3(5) of the 1964 Act introduced a comprehensive list ('statutory lives' – see below) to be used for measuring the 'wait and see' period. In addition, the Act introduced a certain and fixed specified period, namely, a period not exceeding 80 years. This period may be adopted by the settlor only if he or she specifically selects it. In short, the specified period will not be implied into a settlement. In such a case, the common law period will be adopted.

Statutory lives, under s 3(5) of the 1964 Act, include:

(a) the grantor;

(b) the beneficiary or potential beneficiary from a class of persons;

(c) the donee of a power, option or other right;

(d) parents and grandparents of persons in category (a);

(e) any person on the failure or determination of whose prior interest the disposition is to take effect.

Note

The 'statutory lives' are not identical to the 'lives in being' at common law. The position today is that if the disposition is void under the common law rule, using the common law lives plus 21 years or the specified period not exceeding 80 years (if so specified), the interest will be treated as valid (unless it is clear that the interest will not vest within the period) during a period measured by the 'statutory lives' plus 21 years. In short, if the disposition is void under the common law rule, there is a 'wait and see' period measured by the statutory lives plus 21 years. Thus, as a result of the Act, there are no fewer than three perpetuity periods – at common law, the specified period, and the statutory lives.

Rule against excessive duration

Closely related to the above rule is the rule against the inalienability of property. This rule renders void any trust or interest which is required to be enjoyed for longer than the perpetuity period. Charitable trusts are exempt from this principle. The issue here is not whether the property or interest is, in fact, tied up forever, but whether the owner is *capable of disposing* of the same within the perpetuity period. The question concerns merely the power of disposal, and not the actual disposal, of the capital. Thus, property may be owned perpetually by persons, companies or unincorporated associations if these bodies are entitled to dispose of the same at any time but have refrained from exercising the right of disposal. This principle may be illustrated by *Re Chardon*.

Re Chardon, Johnston v Davies [1928] Ch 464, HC

Facts

A testator gave a fund to a cemetery company subject to the income being used for the maintenance of two specified graves with a gift over. The question in issue was whether the gift was void for infringing the perpetuity rule.

Held

The gift which was valid for the company was capable of alienating the property:

> **Romer J:** The cemetery company and the persons interested in the legacy, subject to the interest of the cemetery company, could combine tomorrow and dispose of the whole legacy. The trust does not, therefore, offend the rule against inalienability. The interest of the cemetery company is a vested interest; the interest of the residuary legatee, it being agreed on all hands that, subject to the interest of the cemetery company, the legacy falls into residue, is also vested. All the interests therefore created in this £200, legal and equitable, are vested interests and, that being so, the trusts do not offend the rule against perpetuity. I know of no other rule which will enable me to come to the conclusion that this is an invalid gift.

Question

What is the perpetuity rule?

EXCEPTIONS TO THE *ASTOR* PRINCIPLE

There are a number of private purpose trusts which are exceptionally considered to be valid. Despite the objections to the validity of purpose trusts as stated above, a number of anomalous exceptions exist. These trusts are created as concessions to human weakness. However, it must be emphasised that the only concession granted by the courts is that it is unnecessary for the beneficiaries (purposes) to enforce the trust. The other rules applicable to trusts are equally applied to these anomalous trusts: see *In Re Endacott*, p 341 above, where the test for certainty of objects was not satisfied. These exceptionally valid private purpose trusts are not mandatory in effect but are merely 'directory', in the sense that the trustees are entitled to refuse to carry out the wishes of the settlor and the courts will not force them to do otherwise. At the same time, the courts will not forbid the trustees from carrying out the terms of the trust. These trusts are called 'hybrid trusts' or 'trusts for imperfect obligations'.

Trusts for the maintenance of animals

Gifts for the maintenance of animals generally are charitable (see Chapter 15 below), but trusts for the maintenance of specific animals, such as pets, are treated as private purpose trusts, as illustrated by *Pettingall v Pettingall*.

Pettingall v Pettingall (1842) 11 LJ Ch 176, HC

Facts

The testator's executor was given a fund to spend £50 per annum for the benefit of the testator's black mare. On her death, any surplus funds were to be taken by the executor. The question in issue was whether a valid trust in favour of the animal was created.

Held

In view of the willingness of the executor to carry out the testator's wishes, a valid trust in favour of the animal was created. The residuary legatees were entitled to supervise the performance of the trust.

This principle was unjustifiably extended by Clauson J in *Re Thompson*. The purpose of the gift was the promotion and furtherance of fox hunting. The court drew an analogy with *Pettingall v Pettingall* and decided that the gift was valid.

Re Thompson [1934] Ch 342, HC

Clauson J: In my judgment the object of the gift has been defined with sufficient clearness and is of a nature to which effect can be given. The proper way for me to deal with the matter will be, not to make, as it is asked by the summons, a general declaration, but, following the example of Knight-Bruce VC in *Pettingall v Pettingall* (1842) 11 LJ Ch 176, to order that, upon the defendant Mr Lloyd giving an undertaking (which I understand he is willing to give) to apply the legacy when received by him towards the object expressed in the testator's will, the plaintiffs do pay to the defendant Mr Lloyd the legacy of £1,000; and that, in case the legacy should be applied by him otherwise than towards the promotion and furthering of fox hunting, the residuary legatees are to be at liberty to apply.

Note

The courts take judicial notice of the lifetime of the animal and if this does not exceed the perpetuity period the gift may be valid. In *Re Haines* (1952) *The Times*, 7 November, the testator bequeathed property for the maintenance of specific cats. This gift was valid in view of the lifespan of cats. However, in *Re Dean* (1889) 41 Ch D 552 a gift to maintain the testator's horses and hounds for 50 years 'if they should so long live' was held to be valid, despite infringing the perpetuity rule.

Monument cases

A trust for the building of a memorial or monument for an individual is not charitable but may exist as a valid purpose trust if the trustees express a desire to perform the trust: see *Mussett v Bingle*.

Mussett v Bingle [1876] WN 170, HC

Facts

A testator bequeathed £300 to his executors to be used to erect a monument to the testator's wife's first husband.

Held

The gift was valid as the executors expressed a desire to carry out the testator's wishes.

Similarly, a gift for the maintenance of a specific grave or particular graves may be valid as a private purpose trust but, additionally, the donor is required to restrict the gift within the perpetuity period, otherwise the gift will be void: see *Re Hooper*.

Re Hooper [1932] 1 Ch 38, HC

Facts

A bequest was made to trustees on trust to provide 'so far as they can legally do so' for the care and upkeep of specified graves in a churchyard. The question in issue was whether this gift infringed the perpetuity rule.

Held

The perpetuity period was satisfied by the phrase, 'so far as they can legally do so':

> **Maugham J:** The conclusion at which I arrive is that this trust is valid for a period of 21 years from the testator's death so far as regards the three matters which involve the upkeep of graves or vaults or monuments in the churchyard or in the cemetery. As regards the tablet in St Matthias' Church and the window in the same church there is no question but that that is a good charitable gift, and, therefore, the rule against perpetuities does not apply.

Note

A gift for the maintenance of all the graves in a churchyard may be charitable (see p 359 below).

THE *DENLEY* APPROACH

The approach adopted by the courts is to ascertain whether a gift or trust is intended for the promotion of a purpose *simpliciter* (and thus falls within the *Astor* principle) that is void, or alternatively whether the trust is for the benefit of persons who are capable of enforcing the trust. This is a question of construction for the courts to decide. The promotion of virtually all purposes affects persons. The settlor may, in form, create what appears to be a purpose trust, but in substance the trust may be considered to be for the benefit of human beneficiaries.

In this respect, there is a distinction between a form of gift remotely in favour of individuals, to such an extent that those individuals do not have *locus standi* to enforce the trust, and a gift that may appear to propagate a purpose which is directly or indirectly for the benefit of individuals. In this event, if the beneficiaries satisfy the test for certainty of objects, the gift may be valid: see *Re Denley*. The courts are required to consider each gift before classification.

Re Denley's Trust Deed [1969] 1 Ch 373, HC

Facts

A plot of land was conveyed to trustees for use, subject to the perpetuity rule, as a sports ground primarily for the benefit of employees of a company and secondarily for the benefit of such other person or persons as the trustees might allow to use the same. The question in issue was whether the trust was void as a purpose trust.

Held

The trust was valid in favour of human beneficiaries:

> **Goff J:** I think there may be a purpose or object trust, the carrying out of which would benefit an individual or individuals, where that benefit is so indirect or intangible or which is otherwise so framed as not to give those persons any *locus standii* to apply to the court to enforce the trust, in which case the beneficiary principle would, as it seems to me, apply to invalidate the trust, quite apart from any question of uncertainty or perpetuity. Such cases can be considered if and when they arise. The present is not, in my judgment, of that character, and it will be seen that clause 2(d) of the trust deed expressly states that, subject to any rules and regulations made by the trustees, the employers of the company shall be entitled to the use and enjoyment of the land. Apart from this possible exception, in my judgment the beneficiary principle of *In Re Astor's Settlement Trusts* [1952] Ch 534, which was approved in *In Re Endacott (Decd)* [1960] Ch 232 – see particularly by Harman LJ – is confined to purpose or object trusts which are abstract or impersonal.
>
> Where, then, the trust, though expressed as a purpose, is directly or indirectly for the benefit of an individual or individuals, it seems to me that it is in general outside the mischief of the beneficiary principle. I am fortified in this conclusion by the *dicta* of Lord Evershed MR and Harman LJ in *In Re Harpur's Will Trusts* [1962] Ch 78.
>
> I also derive assistance from what was said by North J in *In Re Bowes* [1896] 1 Ch 507. That was a bequest of a sum of money upon trust to expend the same in planting trees for shelter on certain settled estates. It happened that there was a father and a son of full age, tenant for life in possession and tenant in tail in remainder respectively; so that, subject to the son disentailing, they were together absolutely entitled, and the actual

decision was that they could claim the money, but North J said: 'If it were necessary to uphold it, the trees can be planted upon the whole of it until the fund is exhausted. Therefore, there is nothing illegal in the gift itself' – and later – 'I think there clearly is a valid trust to lay out money for the benefit of the persons entitled to the estate'.

The trust in the present case is limited in point of time so as to avoid any infringement of the rule against perpetuities and, for the reasons I have given, it does not offend against the beneficiary principle; and unless, therefore, it be void for uncertainty, it is a valid trust.

Question
What is the *Denley* principle and when may it be adopted?

GIFTS TO UNINCORPORATED ASSOCIATIONS

There is some difficulty in deciding whether a gift to an unincorporated association creates a trust for a purpose which fails for want of a beneficiary to enforce the trust (under the *Astor* principle), or whether the gift will be construed in favour of human beneficiaries, the members of the association. This involves a question of construction of the circumstances surrounding the gift and the rules of the association.

For example, a gift to the National Anti-Vivisection Society (an unincorporated non-charitable body) may be construed as a gift on trust for the work or purpose of such association and not for the benefit of its members. Accordingly, the gift may be considered void under the *Astor* principle: see Viscount Simonds in *Leahy v AG for New South Wales*.

Leahy v AG for New South Wales [1959] AC 457, PC

Viscount Simonds: A gift can be made to persons (including a corporation) but it cannot be made to a purpose or to an object: so also, a trust may be created for the benefit of persons as *cestuis que trust* but not for a purpose or object unless the purpose or object be charitable. For a purpose or object cannot sue, but if it be charitable, the Attorney General can sue to enforce it.

An analysis of gifts to unincorporated associations was offered by Cross J in *Neville Estates Ltd v Madden*.

Neville Estates Ltd v Madden [1962] Ch 832, HC

Cross J: The question of the construction and effect of gifts to or in trust for unincorporated associations was recently considered by the Privy Council in *Leahy v AG for New South Wales* [1959] AC 457. The position, as I understand it, is as follows. Such a gift may take effect in one or other of three quite different ways. In the first place, it may, on its true construction, be a gift to the members of the association at the relevant date as joint tenants, so that any member can sever his share and claim it whether or not he continues to be a member of the association. Secondly, it may be a gift to the existing members not as joint tenants, but subject to their respective contractual rights and liabilities towards one another as members of the association. In such a case a member cannot sever his share. It will accrue to the other members on his death or resignation, even though such members include persons who became members after the gift took effect. If this is the effect of the gift, it will not be open to objection on the score of perpetuity or uncertainty unless there is something in its terms or circumstances or in the rules of the association which precludes the members at any given time from dividing the subject of the gift between them on the footing that they are solely entitled to it in equity. Thirdly, the terms or circumstances of the gift or the rules of the association may show that the property in question is not to be at the disposal of the members for the time being, but is to be held in trust for or applied for the purposes of the association as a quasi-corporate entity. In this case the gift will fail unless the association is a charitable body.

An unincorporated association is not a legal person but may take the form of a group of individuals joined together with common aims usually laid down in its constitution. The association was defined in *Conservative and Unionist Central Office v Burrell*.

Conservative and Unionist Central Office v Burrell [1982] 1 WLR 522, CA

Lawton LJ: Two or more persons bound together for one or more common purposes, not being business purposes, by mutual undertakings each having mutual duties and obligations, in an organisation which has rules which identify in whom control of it and its funds rests and on what terms and which can be joined or left at will.

The following solutions have been adopted from time to time by the courts in respect of gifts to unincorporated associations. Although the courts have a wide discretion in construing the intention of the donor or settlor and the function and purpose of the association, the adoption of any of the solutions will vary with the facts of each case.

Gifts to members as joint tenants

A settlor may make a gift to an unincorporated association which, on a true construction, is a gift to the members of that association who take as joint tenants free from any contractual fetter. Any member is entitled to sever his share. In these circumstances, the association is used as a label or definition of the class which is intended to take. For instance, a testator may give a legacy to a dining or social club of which he is a member, with the intention of giving an interest which is capable of being severed in favour of each of the members. Such cases are extremely uncommon.

Cocks v Manners (1871) LR 12 Eq 574, HC

Facts

A testatrix left part of her estate to the Dominican Convent at Carisbrooke 'payable to the supervisor for the time being'. The issue concerned the validity of the gift.

Held

The gift was not charitable but was valid in favour of the individual members of the stated community.

Gifts to members as an accretion to the funds of the society

More frequently, the gift to the association may be construed as a gift to the subsisting members of the association on the date of the gift, not beneficially, but as an accretion to the funds of the society which is regulated by the contract (evidenced by the rules of the association) made by the members *inter se*. A member who leaves the association by death or resignation will have no claim to the property, in the absence of any rules to the contrary. This approach was supported in an *obiter* pronouncement by Brightman J in *Re Recher's Will Trust*.

Re Recher's Will Trust [1972] Ch 526, HC

Brightman J: . . . it appears to me that the life members, the ordinary members and the associate members of the London Provincial Society were bound together by a contract *inter se*, with the result that the society represented an organisation of individuals bound together by a contract. Now just as two parties to a bi-partite bargain can vary or terminate their contract by mutual assent, so it must follow that the members of the society could, at any moment of time by agreement, authorised by its constitution, vary or terminate their multi-partite contract. There is no private trust or trust for charitable purposes or other trust to hinder the process. The funds of such an association may, of course, be derived not only from the subscriptions of contracting parties but also from donations from non-contracting parties and legacies from persons who have died. In the case of a donation and a legacy which are not accompanied by any words which purport to impose a trust, it seems that the gift takes effect in favour of the existing members of the association not as joint tenants or tenants-in-common so as to entitle each member to an immediate share, but as an accretion to the funds of the organisation.

Facts

A testatrix gave her residuary estate to the 'Anti-Vivisection Society, 76 Victoria Street, London SW1'. The London and Provincial Anti-Vivisection Society had carried on its activities at this address, but shortly before the will was made the society ceased to exist (it was amalgamated with other societies) and it gave up its premises in Victoria Street. The question in issue was whether the gift could be taken by the amalgamated society, or failed and was subject to a resulting trust.

Held

On construction of the will, the testator intended to benefit the Society at Victoria Street and not the larger body. Accordingly, the gift failed and a resulting trust was set up:

> **Brightman J:** A trust for non-charitable purposes, as distinct from a trust for individuals, is clearly void because there is no beneficiary. It does not, however, follow that persons cannot band themselves together as an association or society, pay subscriptions and validly devote their funds in pursuit of some lawful non-charitable purpose. An obvious example is a members' social club. But it is not essential that the members should only intend to secure direct personal advantages to themselves. The association may be one in which personal advantages to the members are combined with the pursuit of some outside purpose. Or the association may be one which offers no personal benefit at all to the members, the funds of the association being applied exclusively to the pursuit of some outside purpose. Such an association of persons is bound, I would think, to have some sort of constitution; that is to say, the rights and liabilities of the members of the association will inevitably depend on some form of contract *inter se*, usually evidenced by a set of rules. In the present case it appears to me clear that the life members, the ordinary members and the associate members of the London & Provincial society were bound together by a contract *inter se*. Any such member was entitled to the rights and subject to the liabilities defined by the rules. If the committee acted contrary to the rules, an individual member would be entitled to take proceedings in the courts to compel observance of the rules or to recover damages for any loss he had suffered as a result of the breach of contract. As and subjecting his money to the disposition and expenditure thereof laid down by the rules. That is to say, the members would be bound to permit, and entitled to require, the honorary trustees and other members of the society to deal with that subscription in accordance with the lawful direction of the committee. Those directions would include the expenditure of that subscription, as part of the general funds of the association.
>
> The funds of such an association may, of course, be derived not only from the subscription of the contracting parties but also from donations from non-contracting parties and legacies from persons who have died. In the case of a donation which is not accompanied by any words which purport to impose a trust, it seems to me that the gift takes effect in favour of the existing members of the association as an accretion to the funds which are the subject matter of the contract which such members have made *inter se*, and falls to be dealt with in precisely the same way as the funds which the members themselves have subscribed. So, in the case of a legacy. In the absence of words which purport to impose a trust, the legacy is a gift to the members beneficially, not as joint tenants or as tenants in common so as to entitle each member to an immediate distributive share, but as an accretion to the funds which are the subject matter of the contract which the members have made *inter se*.
>
> In my judgment the legacy in the present case to the London & Provincial society ought to be construed as a legacy of that type, that is to say, a legacy to the members beneficially as an accretion to the funds subject to the contract which they had made *inter se*. Of course, the testatrix did not intend the members of the society to divide her bounty between themselves, and doubtless she was ignorant of that remote but theoretical possibility. Her knowledge or absence of knowledge of the true legal analysis of the gift is irrelevant. The legacy is accordingly in my view valid, subject only to the effect of the events of 1 January 1957.
>
> [The learned judge referred to the judgment of Cross J in *Neville Estates v Madden* [1962] Ch 832, p 849, and continued:] In my judgment the London & Provincial society was dissolved on 1 January 1957, and the contract theretofore binding persons together, under the name and according to the rules of the London and Provincial Anti-Vivisection Society, was terminated. The position after 1956 was that all the members of the London & Provincial society lost their rights and shed their obligations under that contract, and some of such persons, namely, the life and ordinary members of the London & Provincial society (or those who wished) automatically acceded to another association of persons who were then bound together by another contract, namely, the National society, and assumed the rights and obligations attaching to members of that association. What I find in the will is a gift to the members of the London & Provincial society as an accretion to the funds subject to the contract between such members. In my judgment, I am not entitled to construe the gift as a gift to the members of a different association as an accretion to the funds subject to a different contract.
>
> At the end of the day, therefore, I feel bound to decide that the share or residue expressed to be given to 'The Anti-Vivisection Society, 76 Victoria Street, London SW1' has failed.

More recently the High Court in *Re Horley Town Football Club* endorsed the *Recher* approach and decided on the facts that the trust deed will be construed as a gift to the Club as a 'contract-holding' gift to the Club and its members. In addition, the beneficial ownership of the assets of the Club was vested in the current full members of the Club on a bare trust. Moreover, a clause will be implied into the rules of the Club to the effect that the surplus funds of the club on a dissolution will be divided amongst its members at the time of dissolution on a *per capita* basis, irrespective of the length of membership or subscriptions paid.

Re Horley Town Football Club; Hunt v McLaren [2006] All ER (D) 34, High Court

Facts

In 1948 Major Jennings, the president of Horley Football Club (the Club) settled land by deed on trust to secure a permanent sports ground for the Club. In May 2002 the land was sold to a developer for almost £4m. The trustees used the proceeds to purchase another site for £850,000 and to construct a Clubhouse and ancillary facilities amounting to approximately £2.2m. This new sports complex was subject to certain restrictive covenants which limited its use to sports and leisure. As a consequence the land was worth less than the amount spent on it. The rules of the Club made provisions for several varieties of membership ranging from the current full members to temporary and associate members. The claimants (trustees) applied to the Court for directions concerning the basis on which they held the assets of the Club and the proper construction of the rules of the Club.

Held

The High Court decided as follows:

(a) A gift to or in trust for an unincorporated association might take effect as a gift to the existing members, not as joint tenants, but subject to their respective contractual rights and liabilities towards each other as members of the association. In this event the member could not sever his share and it would accrue to the other members on his death or resignation. Such members included persons who became members, after the gift took effect.

(b) The deed of 1948 was construed as a gift to the members of the Club as a contract-holding gift to the Club and its members, including subsequent members.

(c) The beneficial ownership of the assets of the Club was in the subsisting full members, but not the temporary and associate members. The trustees of the Club held the assets on bare trust for the full members.

(d) The members acquired the assets of the Club subject to the current rules and could unanimously or by a general meeting call for the assets to be transferred.

Collins J: [after reviewing the leading cases on the subject continued] I am satisfied that the Deed should be construed as a gift to the Club, as a 'contract-holding' gift to the Club and its members for the time being within category (2) in *Neville Estates v Madden* [1962] Ch 832, per Cross J:

> Second, it may be a gift to the existing members, not as joint tenants, but subject to their respective contractual rights and liabilities towards one another as members of the association. In such a case the member cannot sever his share, and it will accrue to the other members on the death or resignation of an existing member, even though such members include persons who became members after the gift took effect.

The next question is the identity of the persons who hold the beneficial interest. I am satisfied that the beneficial ownership is in the current full members (and not the temporary or associate members), and is held on bare trust for them. The members hold subject to the current rules, and could unanimously or by AGM call for the assets to be transferred. Adult and senior members are entitled to share in distribution on per capita basis.

In *Re GKN Bolts & Nuts Ltd etc Works Sports and Social Club* [1982] 1 WLR 774 the question was whether a social club formed for the benefit of employees had ceased to exist in 1975 when, following financial difficulties, it resolved to sell the sports ground, and the basis on which there should be distribution of the assets.

Sir Robert Megarry V-C said (at 776):

> As is common in club cases, there are many obscurities and uncertainties, and some difficulty in the law. In such cases, the court usually has to take a broad sword to the problems, and eschew an unduly meticulous examination of the rules and regulations ... I think that the courts have to be ready to allow general concepts of reasonableness, fairness and common sense to be given more than their usual weight when confronted by claims to the contrary which appear to be based on any strict interpretation and rigid application of the letter of the rules.

He held that the club had ceased to exist ... In my judgment I should adopt the same approach as Sir Robert Megarry in taking a "broad sword" and applying fairness and common sense. The consequence would be that the beneficial ownership is held on bare trust for the members, who could either unanimously or at an AGM call for the assets to be transferred.

The members may agree to dissolve the Club and to distribute the assets amongst themselves or the association may be wound up by the court: *Re Lead Co.'s Workmen's Fund Society* [1904] 2 Ch 196; *Neville Estates v Madden* [1962] Ch 832, 849; *Re Recher* [1972] Ch 526, 538-539. The Rules do not specify how the Club's assets are to be distributed following dissolution. In the absence of any rule to the contrary, there is to be implied into the rules of the Club a rule to the effect that the surplus funds of the Club should be divided on a dissolution amongst the members of the Club, and this distribution will normally be per capita among the members (irrespective of length of membership or the amount of subscriptions paid) but may reflect different classes of membership: *Re Sick and Funeral Society of St John's Sunday School, Golcar* [1973] Ch 51, at 60; *Re Bucks Constabulary Widows' and Orphans' Fund Friendly Society (No. 2)* [1979] 1 WLR 936, at 952; *Re GKN Bolts & Nuts Ltd etc. Sports & Social Club* [1982] 1 WLR 774, at 778.

Note

The effect of the approach in *Re Recher* is that if a donor transfers property to the association for its general purposes, the gift may be construed as intended for the benefit of the members of an association to be enjoyed collectively subject to the constitution of the society. However, a gift to an association for a particular purpose may be construed as a gift to the members of the association for the time being for their own use, where the association exists solely for the benefit of its members. In this respect, the members of the association would be both trustees and beneficiaries: see *Re Turkington*.

Re Turkington [1937] 4 All ER 501, HC

Facts

A gift was made in favour of a masonic lodge 'as a fund to build a suitable temple in Stafford'. The members of the lodge were both the trustees and the beneficiaries. The question concerned the validity of the gift.

Held

The gift was absolute to the members of the lodge for the time being. The purpose stipulated was construed as '... simply an indication by the testator of the purpose for which he would like the money to be expended, without imposing any trust on the beneficiaries':

> **Luxmoore J:** The whole question is whether this is a trust or whether it is simply an indication by the testator of the purposes for which he would like the money to be expended, without imposing any trust on the beneficiary. It is to be observed that the gift is to the lodge, and that must mean to the members for the time being. There is no separate trustee of the fund constituted. The beneficial interest in the fund is in the persons who are the trustees – in the body which is said to be the trustee – and, in those circumstances, where one finds the legal and equitable estate equally and co-extensively united in the same person or entity, the equitable interest merges in the legal interest, on the footing that a person cannot be a trustee for himself.
>
> The decision of Farwell J, as he then was, in *Re Selous, Thomson v Selous* [1901] 1 Ch 921, seems to me to lay down the governing principle which is applicable to this case. I therefore hold that this gift is a gift to the masonic lodge for the purpose of the lodge, and that the members of the lodge for the time being are at liberty to deal with it in accordance with their constitution in the ordinary way, in the way they think fit; in other words, they have complete domination over the fund.

Gifts to present and future members

The court may construe a gift to an association as a gift for the benefit of the members of the association, both present and future. In coming to this conclusion, the courts are required to consider the rules of the association and its function, in addition to the intention of the donor. However, if the members of the society (in accordance with its constitution) are incapable of disposing of the assets of the society, or are incapable of altering the rules of the association, the gift may fail for infringing the perpetuity rule.

Re Drummond [1914] 2 Ch 90, HC

Facts

A testator transferred his residuary estate to the 'Old Bradfordians Club, London (being a club for old boys of the Bradford Grammar School), to be utilised as the Committee of the Club should think best in the interests of the Club'. The issue concerned the validity of the gift.

Held

The gift was valid and was for the benefit of the current and future members of the club. The rules of the club did not infringe the perpetuity rule since the committee was free to spend the capital in any manner it might consider fit.

Note

Eve J in *Re Drummond* said that he could not hold that the residuary gift of realty and personality for the Old Bradfordians Club was a gift to the members individually.

There was, in his opinion, a trust, and abundant authority for holding that it was not such a trust as would render the legacy void as tending to a perpetuity as in *In Re Clarke* [1901] 2 Ch 110. In the opinion of Eve J, the legacy was not subject to any trust which would prevent the committee of the club from spending it in any manner it might decide for the benefit of the class intended. In his opinion, therefore, there was a valid gift to the club for such purposes as the committee should determine for the benefit of the old boys or members of the club.

In *Re Grant's Will Trusts*, the court decided that, on construction of the rules of the association, the gift failed because the association did not have control of the funds.

Re Grant's Will Trusts [1980] I WLR 360, HC

Facts

A gift was made for the purposes of the Chertsey Labour Party Headquarters (a non-charitable unincorporated association). The issue concerned the validity of the gift.

Held

The gift failed. The members of the local association did not control the association's property, nor could they change the rules and obtain control because the rules were subject to the approval of the National Executive Committee. Accordingly, the members of the local Labour Party did not have the power to liquidate the association and distribute its assets amongst themselves. A resulting trust was set up:

> **Vinelott J:** [Having considered the pronouncement of Cross J in *Neville Estates Ltd v Madden* [1962] Ch 832, p 849, continued:] . . . the members of the Chertsey and Walton CLP do not control the property, given by subscription or otherwise, to the CLP. The rules which govern the CLP are capable of being altered by an outside body which could direct an alteration under which the general committee of the CLP would be bound to transfer any property for the time being held for the benefit of the CLP to the National Labour Party for national purposes. The members of the Chertsey and Walton CLP could not alter the rules so as to make the property bequeathed by the testator applicable for some purpose other than that provided by the rules; nor could they direct that property to be divided amongst themselves beneficially.

> Brightman J observed in *In Re Recher's Will Trusts* [1972] Ch 526:

>> It would astonish a layman to be told there was a difficulty in his giving a legacy to an unincorporated non-charitable society which he had, or could have, supported without trouble during his lifetime.

It is, in my judgment, impossible, in particular having regard to the gift over to the National Labour Party, to read the gift as a gift to the members of the National Labour Party at the testator's death, with a direction not amounting to a trust, for the National Party to permit it to be used by the Chertsey and Walton CLP for headquarters purposes.

That first ground is of itself conclusive, but there is another ground which reinforces this conclusion. The gift is not in terms a gift to the Chertsey and Walton CLP, but to the Labour Party property committee, who are to hold the property for the benefit of, that is in trust for, the Chertsey headquarters of the Chertsey and Walton CLP. The fact that a gift is a gift to trustees and not in terms to an unincorporated association, militates against construing it as a gift to the members of the association at the date when the gift takes effect, and against construing the words indicating the purposes for which the property is to be used as expressing the testator's intention or motive in making the gift and not as imposing any trust. This was, indeed, one of the considerations which led the Privy Council in *Leahy*'s case [1959] AC 457, to hold that the gift '. . . upon trust for such Order of Nuns of the Catholic Church or the Christian Brothers as my executors and trustees should select would . . . have been invalid'.

I am, therefore, compelled to the conclusion that the gift of the testator's estate fails, and that his estate accordingly devolves as on intestacy.

Intended trusts for purposes

If a settlor transfers property on trust for an association, it is possible for the court to decide that, on construction, the transfer is made on trust for the function or operation of the society and not for its members. If this construction is adopted, the court may decide that the trust fails under the *Astor* principle, owing to the intention to promote a purpose: see *Leahy v AG for New South Wales*. Such a construction would be exceptional. In addition, if the intention of the settlor is to set up an endowment in favour of the beneficiary (that is, the association), the gift may fail on the separate ground of the infringement of the perpetuity rule.

Leahy v AG for New South Wales [1959] AC 457, PC

Facts

A testator devised a plot of land of 730 acres on trust for 'such order of nuns of the Catholic church or the Christian brothers as my trustees shall select'. This transfer was not wholly charitable, as it permitted the trustees to select cloistered nuns. Under Australian law, the trust was capable of being saved as a charitable donation by confining the gift to non-cloistered orders. The trustees, however, wanted to retain the freedom to give to cloistered nuns if possible. The question in issue was whether the trust in its existing form was valid as a non-charitable trust.

Held

As a non-charitable gift the trust failed, because the testator's intention was clearly to create an endowment for the order of nuns (both present and future) and not for the benefit of individuals:

Viscount Simonds: In law a gift to such a society *simpliciter* (ie, where, to use the words of Lord Parker in *Bowman v Secular Society Ltd* [1917] AC 406, 437, neither the circumstances of the gift nor the directions given nor the objects expressed impose on the donee the character of a trustee) is nothing else than a gift to its members at the date of the gift as joint tenants or tenants in common. It is for this reason that the prudent conveyancer provides that a receipt by the treasurer or other proper officer of the recipient society for a legacy to the society shall be a sufficient discharge to executors. If it were not so, the executors could only get a valid discharge by obtaining a receipt from every member. This must be qualified by saying that by their rules the members might have authorised one of themselves to receive a gift on behalf of them all.

The question then appears to be whether, even if the gift to a selected Order of Nuns is *prima facie* a gift to the individual members of that Order, there are other considerations arising out of the terms of the will, or the nature of the society, its organisation and rules, or the subject matter of the gift which should lead the court to conclude that, though *prima facie* the gift is an absolute one (absolute both in quality of estate and in freedom from restriction) to individual nuns, yet it is invalid because it is in the nature of an endowment and tends to a perpetuity or for any other reason.

It must now be asked, then, whether in the present case there are sufficient indications to displace the *prima facie* conclusion that the gift made by clause 3 of the will is to the individual members of the selected Order of Nuns at the date of the testator's death so that they can together dispose of it as they think fit. It appears to their Lordships that such indications are ample.

In the first place, it is not altogether irrelevant that the gift is in terms upon trust for a selected Order. It is true that this can in law be regarded as a trust in favour of each and every member of the Order. But at least the form of the gift is not to the members, and it may be questioned whether the testator understood the niceties of the law. In the second place, the members of the selected Order may be numerous, very numerous perhaps, and they may be spread over the world. If the gift is to the individuals it is to all the members who were living at the death of the testator, but only to them. It is not easy to believe that the testator intended an 'immediate beneficial legacy' (to use the words of Lord Buckmaster) to such a body of beneficiaries.

In the third place, the subject matter of the gift cannot be ignored. It appears from the evidence filed in the suit that Elmslea is a grazing property of about 730 acres, with a furnished homestead containing 20 rooms and a number of outbuildings. With the greatest respect to those judges who have taken a different view, their Lordships do not find it possible to regard all the individual members of an Order as intended to become the beneficial owners of such a property. Little or no evidence has been given about the organisation and rules of the several Orders. But it is at least permissible to doubt whether it is a common feature of them, that all their members regard themselves or are to be regarded as having the capacity of (say) the Corps of Commissionaires (see *In Re Clarke* [1901] 2 Ch 110) to put an end to their association and distribute its assets. On the contrary, it seems reasonably clear that, however little the testator understood the effect in law of a gift to an unincorporated body of persons by their society name, his intention was to create a trust, not merely for the benefit of the existing members of the selected Order, but for its benefit as a continuing society and for the furtherance of its work.

Trusts for persons

Moreover, a transfer of property on trust for an association may be construed as a transfer on trust for the current members of the association and not on trust for purposes. In this event, provided that the rules of the association empower the members to liquidate and distribute the assets of the association, the perpetuity rule will not be infringed and the trust will be valid. The position remains the same even though the settlor may specify a purpose for which the fund may be used. Such stipulation may not be sufficient to prevent the members (beneficiaries) disposing of the property in any way they consider appropriate within the rules of the society: see *Re Lipinski*.

Re Lipinski's Will Trust [1977] 1 All ER 33, HC

Facts

A testator transferred one half of his residuary estate to the Hull Judeans (Maccabi) Association, an unincorporated, non-charitable association, 'in memory of my late wife to be used "solely" in the work of constructing new buildings for the association and/or improvements to the said buildings'. The question in issue was whether the trust was valid.

Held

The trust was for the benefit of ascertainable beneficiaries (the members at the date of the gift). On construction, the expression 'in memory of my late wife' was not intended as a permanent endowment but merely a tribute which the testator paid to his wife. The stipulation concerning the use of the funds was not intended to reduce the power of the members to dispose of the assets of the association in accordance with the rules of the association. For the same reason, the perpetuity rule was not infringed:

> **Oliver J:** [The learned judge referred to Cross J's construction of gifts into three categories in *Neville Estates v Madden* [1962] Ch 832, and said:] For my part, I think that very little turns on the testator's having expressed the gift as being in memory of his late wife. I see nothing in this expression which suggests any intention to create a permanent endowment. It indicates merely, I think, a tribute which the testator wished to pay. It does, however, seems to me that nothing is to be derived from these words beyond the fact that the testator wished the association to know that his bounty was a tribute to his late wife.

If the gift were to the association *simpliciter*, it would, I think, clearly fall within the second category of Cross J's categories. At first sight, however, there appears to be a difficulty in arguing that the gift is to members of the association subject to their contractual rights *inter se* when there is a specific direction or limitation sought to be imposed on those contractual rights as to the manner in which the subject matter of the gift is to be dealt with.

There would seem to me to be, as a matter of common sense, a clear distinction between the case where a purpose is prescribed which is clearly intended for the benefit of ascertained or ascertainable beneficiaries, particularly where those beneficiaries have the power to make the capital their own, and the case where no beneficiary at all is intended (for instance, a memorial to a favourite pet) or where the beneficiaries are unascertainable (as, for instance, in *Re Price* [1943] Ch 422). If a valid gift may be made to an unincorporated body as a simple accretion to the funds which are the subject matter of the contract which the members have made *inter se* and *Neville Estates v Madden* [1962] Ch 832 and *Re Recher's Will Trusts* [1971] 3 All ER 401 show that it may, I do not really see why such a gift, which specifies a purpose which is within the powers of the unincorporated body and of which the members of that body are the beneficiaries, should fail. Why are not the beneficiaries able to enforce the trust or, indeed, in the exercise of their contractual rights, to terminate the trust for their own benefit? Where the donee body is itself the beneficiary of the prescribed purpose, there seems to me to be the strongest argument in common sense for saying that the gift should be construed as an absolute one within the second category, the more so where, if the purpose is carried out, the members can by appropriate action vest the resulting property in themselves, for here the trustees and the beneficiaries are the same persons.

A striking case which seems to be not far from the present is *Re Turkington* [1937] 4 All ER 501, where the gift was to a masonic lodge 'as a fund to build a suitable temple in Stafford'. The members of the lodge being both the trustees and the beneficiaries of the temple, Luxmoore J construed the gift as an absolute one to the members of the lodge for the time being. Directly in point is the more recent decision of Goff J in *Re Denley's Trust Deed* [1968] 3 All ER 65, p 67, where the question arose as to the validity of a deed under which land was held by trustees as a sports ground:

> ... primarily for the benefit of the employees of [a particular] company and secondarily for the benefit of such other person or persons ... as the trustees may allow to use the same ...

The latter provision was construed by Goff J as a power and not a trust. The same deed conferred on the employees a right to use and enjoy the land subject to regulations made by the trustees. Goff J held that the rule against enforceability of non-charitable 'purpose or object' trusts was confined to those which were abstract or impersonal in nature where there was no beneficiary or *cestui que trust*. A trust which, though expressed as a purpose, was directly or indirectly for the benefit of an individual or individuals was valid provided that those individuals were ascertainable at any one time and the trust was not otherwise void for uncertainty. I am unable to conclude that the testator had any specific building in mind; and, in my judgment, the reference to 'the ... buildings for the Association' means no more than whatever buildings the association may have or may choose to erect or acquire. The reference to improvements reflects, I think, the testator's contemplation that the association might purchase or might, at his death, already have purchased an existing structure which might require improvement or conversion, or even that it might, as had at one time been suggested, expend money in improving the premises which it rented from the Jewish Institute. The association was to have the legacy to spend in this way for the benefit of its members.

I have already said that, in my judgment, no question of perpetuity arises here, and accordingly the case appears to me to be one of the specification of a particular purpose for the benefit of ascertained beneficiaries, the members of the association for the time being. There is an additional factor. This is a case in which, under the constitution of the association, the members could, by the appropriate majority, alter their constitution so as to provide, if they wished, for the division of the association's assets among themselves. This has, I think, a significance. I have considered whether anything turns in this case on the testator's direction that the legacy shall be used 'solely' for one or other of the specified purposes. Counsel for the association has referred me to a number of cases where legacies have been bequeathed for particular purposes and in which the beneficiaries have been held entitled to override the purpose, even though expressed in mandatory terms.

Perhaps the most striking in the present context is the case of *Re Bowes* [1896] 1 Ch 507, where money was directed to be laid out in the planting of trees on a settled estate. That was a 'purpose' trust, but there were ascertainable beneficiaries, the owners for the time being of the estate; and North J held that the persons entitled to the settled estate were entitled to have the money whether or not it was laid out as directed by the testator. He said:

Then, the sole question is where this money is to go to. Of course, it is a perfectly good legacy. There is nothing illegal in the matter, and the direction to plant might easily be carried out; but it is not necessarily capable of being performed, because the owner of the estate might say he would not have any trees planted upon it at all. If that were the line he took, and he did not contend for anything more than that, the legacy would fail; but he says he does not refuse to have trees planted upon it; he is content that trees should be planted upon some part of it; but the legacy has not failed. If it were necessary to uphold it, the trees can be planted upon the whole of it until the fund is exhausted. Therefore, there is nothing illegal in the gift itself; but the owners of the estate now say 'It is a very disadvantageous way of spending this money; the money is to be spent for our benefit, and that of no one else; it was not intended for any purpose other than our benefit and that of the estate. That is no reason why it should be thrown away by doing what is not for our benefit, instead of being given to us, who want to have the enjoyment of it'. I think their contention is right. I think the fund is devoted to improving the estate, and improving the estate for the benefit of the persons who are absolutely entitled to it.

I can see no reason why the same reasoning should not apply in the present case simply because the beneficiary is an unincorporated non-charitable association. I do not think the fact that the testator has directed the application 'solely' for the specified purpose adds any legal force to the direction. The beneficiaries, the members of the association for the time being, are the persons who could enforce the purpose and they must, as it seems to me, be entitled not to enforce it or, indeed, to vary it.

Thus, it seems to me that whether one treats the gifts as a 'purpose' trust or as an absolute gift with a super added direction or, on the analogy of *Re Turkington* [1937] 4 All ER 501, as a gift where the trustees and the beneficiaries are the same persons, all roads lead to the same conclusion.

Question
To what extent may gifts to unincorporated associations be valid?

THE MANDATE OR AGENCY PRINCIPLE

In some cases, a group of persons may join together in order to promote a common objective, without undertaking mutual duties or obligations, or adopting rules which identify where control of the association lies. In these circumstances, the assembly of individuals will not be treated as an unincorporated association and the trust and contract rules mentioned earlier may not be appropriate to such bodies.

In *Conservative and Unionist Central Office v Burrell*, the court decided that the Conservative Party was not an unincorporated association.

Conservative and Unionist Central Office v Burrell [1982] 1 WLR 522, HC

Facts
The issue concerned the legal status of the Conservative Party and whether it was liable to corporation tax on its profits (corporation tax is payable by incorporated and unincorporated associations: see ss 6(1), 8(1) and 832 of the Taxes Act 1988).

Held
The Court of Appeal decided that the party was not an unincorporated association but an amorphous combination of various elements. The nature of gifts to the party involved an accretion to the funds of the body which were to be dealt with in accordance with its rules, on analogy with *Re Recher*. The legal rights created in favour of donors and contributors exist on the basis of a mandate or agency. A contributor gives funds in effect to the treasurer of the party with a mandate to use the same in a particular way. If the moneys are not spent, the donor is entitled to demand the return of his moneys, except if he agreed that his donation was irrevocable. If the officers within the party spend the funds on unauthorised activities, the donor or contributor retains *locus standi* to sue for breach of fiduciary obligations based on general principles of agency law. Thus, apart from the fiduciary relationship inherent in the principal/agent relationship, there

was no trust relationship involved between donors and contributors on the one hand, and treasurer and other officers of the party.

Warburton, J, 'The holding of property by unincorporated associations' [1985] Conv 318
Warburton examines a variety of methods by which unincorporated associations can hold property. An unincorporated association, of course, has no separate legal entity. The association cannot own the legal and equitable interests in property. Accordingly, a person or persons must hold property on its behalf. Warburton considers the various methods of retaining such property and comments on the advantages and disadvantages of each method:

> It has been said that there are three methods by which property can be held by an unincorporated association. First, property can be held by the members of the association as joint tenants. Secondly, property can be held by the members subject to their contractual rights and liabilities to each other as set out in the rules of the association. Thirdly, it can be held on trust for the purposes of the association. To these methods must be added the holding of property on trust for the members . . . [I]t is often not clear which method is being used by an association, either because the rules are silent or because the relevant rule is not properly drafted.

Question
What is an unincorporated association?

FURTHER READING

Emery, C, 'Do we need a rule against perpetuities?' (1994) 57 MLR 602.

Gardner, S, 'A detail in the construction of gifts to unincorporated associations' [1998] Conv 8.

Gravells, N, 'Gifts to unincorporated associations: where there is a will there is a way' (1977) 40 MLR 231.

Lovell, P, 'Non-charitable purpose trusts – further reflection' [1970] 34 Conv 77.

McKay, L, 'Trusts for purposes' [1973] 37 Conv 420.

Rickett, C, 'Unincorporated associations and their dissolution' [1980] CLJ 88.

Wilkinson, W, 'Your money or your life or lives in being' [1994] Conv 92.

CHARITABLE TRUSTS: PRIVILEGES

INTRODUCTION

Charitable trusts are, generally speaking, subject to the same rules as private trusts but, in recognition of the public nature of such trusts, charities enjoy a number of advantages over private trusts:

(a) Certainty of objects. A charitable trust is subject to a unique test for certainty of objects, namely, whether the objects are exclusively charitable. Indeed, it is unnecessary for the settlor or testator to specify the charitable objects, provided that his or her intention was to devote the funds for charitable purposes. The Charity Commissioners and the courts have the jurisdiction to establish a scheme for the application of the funds.

(b) The rule against perpetuities. Charities are not subject to the rule against excessive duration. However, charitable gifts, like private gifts, are subject to the rule against remote vesting.

(c) The *cy-près* rule. When a charitable trust fails to vest in the relevant association, the funds may be applied *cy-près* (to the nearest alternative) instead of being held on resulting trust.

(d) Fiscal privileges. A variety of tax reliefs are enjoyed by both charitable bodies and members of the public (including companies) who donate funds for charitable purposes.

CHARITABLE PRIVILEGES

A charitable trust is a public trust which is enforceable by the Attorney General on behalf of the Crown. The purpose of the trust is to benefit society as a whole, or a sufficiently large section of the community so that it may be considered public. Charitable trusts may be treated as a species of purpose trusts, that is, trusts designed for the benefit of purposes such as the RSPCA, the promotion of cremation of bodies, or the maintenance of the graves in a church-yard. However, in benefiting or furthering a purpose directly, the trust may result in indivi-duals enjoying indirect benefits, such as from the maintenance of schools or places of worship, or the trust may be designed for the benefit of individuals pure and simple, such as the NSPCC, Oxfam, etc.

Private trusts, on the other hand, seek to benefit defined persons or narrower sections of society than charitable trusts and, as we have seen, a private purpose trust is void for lack of a person to enforce the trust.

Basically, charitable trusts are subject to the same rules as private trusts, but as a result of the public nature of charitable trusts, such trusts enjoy a number of advantages over private trusts in respect of:

(a) certainty of objects;

(b) the perpetuity rule;

(c) the *cy-près* rule; and

(d) fiscal privileges.

In *Dingle v Turner*, Lord Cross identified a number of privileges enjoyed by charities.

Dingle v Turner [1972] AC 601, HL

Lord Cross of Chelsea: In answering the question whether any given trust is a charitable trust the courts – as I see it – cannot avoid having regard to the fiscal privileges accorded to charities. As counsel for the Attorney General remarked in the course of argument the law of charity is bedevilled by the fact that charitable trusts enjoy two quite different sorts of privilege. On the one hand, they enjoy immunity from the laws against perpetuity and uncertainty and though individual potential beneficiaries cannot sue to enforce them, the public interest arising is protected by the Attorney General . . . But that is not all. Charities automatically enjoy fiscal privileges which . . . have become more and more important . . .

CERTAINTY OF OBJECTS

Charitable trusts, like private trusts, are subject to a test of certainty of objects. In Chapters 3 and 6, we examined the tests for certainty of objects in respect of private trusts (fixed trusts – *Inland Revenue Commissioners v Broadway Cottages Ltd* [1955] Ch 20; discretionary trusts – *McPhail v Doulton* [1971] AC 424). A charitable trust is subject to a unique test for certainty of objects, namely, whether the objects are exclusively charitable. In other words, if the trust funds may be used solely for charitable purposes, the test will be satisfied. Indeed, it is unnecessary for the settlor or testator to specify the charitable objects which are intended to take the trust property. Provided that the trust instrument manifests a clear intention to devote the funds for 'charitable purposes', the test will be satisfied. In *Morice v Bishop of Durham*, the court decided that the gift failed the test for charitable objects. However, a gift 'on trust for charitable purposes' will satisfy this test. The Charity Commission and the court have the jurisdiction to establish a scheme for application of the funds (that is, the court will make an order indicating the specific charitable objects which will benefit).

Morice v Bishop of Durham (1804) 9 Ves 399, CA

Facts

A fund was given upon trust for such objects of benevolence and liberality as the Bishop of Durham should approve.

Held

The gift was not valid as the objects were not exclusively charitable. A resulting trust was created:

> **Sir William Grant MR:** That it is a trust, unless it be of a charitable nature, too indefinite to be executed by this court, has not been, and cannot be, denied. There can be no trust, over the exercise of which this court will not assume a control; for an uncontrollable power of disposition would be ownership, and not trust. If there be a clear trust, but for uncertain objects, the property, that is the subject of the trust, is undisposed of; and the benefit of such trust must result to those, to whom the law gives the ownership, in default of disposition by the former owner. But this doctrine does not hold good with regard to trusts for charity. Every other trust must have a definite object. There must be somebody, in whose favour the court can decree performance. But it is now settled, upon authority, which it is too late to controvert, that, where a charitable purpose is expressed, however general, the bequest shall not fail on account of the uncertainty of the object: but the particular mode of application will be directed by the King in some cases, in others by this court. I am not aware of any case, in which the bequest has been held to be charitable, where the testator has not either used that word, to denote his general purpose or specified some particular purpose, which this court has determined to be charitable in its nature.

In *Moggridge v Thackwell*, the test for certainty of charitable objects was satisfied in the context of a discretionary trust for solely charitable purposes.

Moggridge v Thackwell (1807) 13 Ves 416

Facts

A testatrix transferred her residuary personalty to a trustee in order to dispose of the same to such charities as he should think fit. The trustee predeceased the testatrix.

Held

It was immaterial that the trustee had predeceased the testatrix. On the death of the testatrix, the gift had vested for charitable purposes. The court approved a scheme for the disposition of the residuary estate.

In *Inland Revenue Commissioners v City of Glasgow Police Athletic Association*, it was decided that, on construction of the instrument and surrounding circumstances, the trust funds were capable of being devoted for both charitable and non-charitable purposes and the gift was invalid for charitable purposes.

Inland Revenue Commissioners v City of Glasgow Police Athletic Association
[1953] 1 All ER 747, HL

Facts

The question in issue was whether the Police Athletic Association was a charitable body.

Held

On construction of the objects of the association, the body was not charitable. Its primary object was the provision of recreation and sport for its members (non charitable purposes), although the body had the incidental effect of promoting a charitable purpose, namely, improving the efficiency of the Police Force:

> **Lord Normand:** The question is what are the purposes for which the association is established, as shown by the rules, its activities and its relation to the police force and the public. And what the respondents must show in the circumstances of this case is that, so viewed objectively, the association is established for a public purpose, and that the private benefits to members are the unsought consequences of the pursuit of the public purpose, and can therefore be disregarded as incidental. That is a view which I cannot take. The private benefits to members are essential. The recreation of the members is an end in itself, and without its attainment the public purposes would never come into view. The private advantage of members is a purpose for which the association is established and it therefore cannot be said that this is an association established for a public charitable purpose only.
>
> In principle, therefore, if an association has two purposes, one charitable and the other not, and if the two purposes are such and so related that the non-charitable purpose cannot be regarded as incidental to the other, the association is not a body established for charitable purpose only.

Charitable or benevolent purposes

Where the draftsman of the objects clause uses words such as 'charitable or benevolent purposes', the court may, on construction of the clause, decide that the word 'or' ought to be interpreted disjunctively, with the effect that benevolent purposes which are not charitable are capable of acquiring a benefit. Accordingly, the gift will fail as a charitable donation. This was the construction adopted in *AG v National Provincial Bank*.

AG v National Provincial and Union Bank of England [1924] AC 262, HL

Facts

A testator, by his will, directed his trustees to apply one fifth of his residuary estate 'for such patriotic purposes or objects and such charitable institution or institutions or charitable object or objects in the British Empire' as they should select in their absolute discretion.

Held

The gift was not a valid charitable donation because the gift was not exclusively for charitable purposes:

> **Viscount Cave LC:** My Lords, it has been pointed out more than once, and particularly by the members of the Court of Appeal in *In re Macduff* [1896] 2 Ch 451, that Lord MacNaghten did not mean that, all trusts for purposes beneficial to the community are charitable, but that there were certain charitable trusts which fell within that category; and accordingly to argue that because a trust is for a purpose beneficial to the community it is therefore a charitable trust is to turn round his sentence and to give it a different meaning. So here it is not enough to say that the trust in question is for public purposes beneficial to the community or for the public welfare; you must also show it to be a charitable trust. My Lords, I am not able to say that this is a charitable trust. The expression 'patriotic purposes' is vague and uncertain. It seems to me therefore that the expression 'patriotic purposes' is one which cannot be said to bring the trust within the category of a charitable trust.

Likewise, in *Chichester Diocesan Fund v Simpson*, the court came to a similar conclusion that the trust was void for uncertainty of charitable objects.

Chichester Diocesan Fund v Simpson [1944] 2 All ER 60, HL

Facts

A testator directed his executors to apply the residue of his estate 'for such charitable or benevolent objects' as they might select. The executors assumed that the clause created a valid charitable gift and distributed most of the funds to charitable bodies.

Held

The clause did not create charitable gifts and therefore the gifts were void. A resulting trust was set up for the testator's estate:

> **Viscount Simon LC:** It is not disputed that the words 'charitable' and 'benevolent' do not ordinarily mean the same thing; they overlap in the sense that each of them, as a matter of legal interpretation, covers some common ground, but also something which is not covered by the other. It appears to me that it inevitably follows that the phrase 'charitable or benevolent' occurring in a will must, in its ordinary context, be regarded as too vague to give the certainty necessary before such a provision can be supported or enforced.
>
> The conjunction 'or' may be sometimes used to join two words whose meaning is the same, but, as the conjunction appears in this will, it seems to me to indicate a variation rather than an identity between the coupled conceptions. Its use is analogous in the present instance to its use in a phrase like 'the House of Lords or the House of Commons', rather than to its use in a phrase like 'the House of Lords or the Upper Chamber'.
>
> I regret that we have to arrive at such a conclusion, but we have no right to set at nought an established principle such as this in the construction of wills, and I, therefore, move the House to dismiss the appeal.

In the modern case of *AG for the Bahamas v Royal Trust*, a wide objects clause declared in a will failed as a charitable trust.

AG of the Bahamas v Royal Trust Co [1986] 1 WLR 1001, PC

Facts

A testator directed that the residue of his estate be held by trustees 'for any purpose for, and/or connected with the education and welfare of Bahamian children and young people . . .'. The question in issue was whether the bequest was valid as a charitable trust.

Held

The expression 'welfare' was a word of wide import and, taken in the context of the expression 'education and welfare', was not restricted to the educational prosperity of the objects. The gift was therefore void for charitable purposes:

> **Lord Oliver of Aylmerton:** The point is not one which is susceptible of a great deal of elaboration and their Lordships need say no more than that they agree with Blake CJ and the Court of Appeal that the phrase 'education and welfare' in this will inevitably falls to be construed disjunctively. It follows that, for the reasons which were fully explored in the judgments in the courts below, and as is now conceded on the footing of a disjunctive construction, the trusts in paragraph (t) do not constitute valid charitable trusts.

Charitable and benevolent purposes

The position would be different if the word 'or' were construed conjunctively or as equivalent to the use of the word 'and' in the phrase 'charitable and benevolent'. In such a case, only benevolent purposes which are charitable are eligible to benefit: see *Re Best*.

Re Best [1904] 2 Ch 354, HC

The facts of the case appear in the judgment:

> **Farwell J:** The words here are upon trust for 'such charitable and benevolent institutions' in the city of Birmingham, and so on, as the lord mayor shall determine, and it appears to me that the institutions, the objects of this gift, must be both charitable and benevolent. Having regard to the curiously technical meaning which has

been given by the English court to the world 'charitable', I am not surprised that the testator should have desired that the institutions should be not only charitable, but should be also benevolent. There are certainly some which I think it would be difficult to say are benevolent, such as the distribution of the works of Joanna Southcote, although that was held to be charitable. I think the testator here intended that the institutions should be both charitable and benevolent; and I see no reason for reading the conjunction 'and' as 'or'.

In the two circumstances stated below, an objects clause that seeks to benefit both charitable and non-charitable purposes will not fail.

Incidental non-charitable purpose

If the non-charitable purpose is construed as being incidental to the main charitable purpose, the gift is treated as valid. This involves a question of construction for the courts to evaluate the importance of each class of objects. This approach is illustrated by *Re Coxen*.

Re Coxen [1948] Ch 747, HC

Facts

A testator bequeathed £200,000 to the Court of Aldermen of the City of London on trust to pay:

(a) £100 per annum to provide a dinner for the trustees when they met on trust business;

(b) one guinea to each trustee who attended the whole of the meeting; and

(c) the balance of the income for the benefit of orthopaedic hospitals.

Held

The gifts as a whole were charitable. The principal aim of the trust was stated in (c) above, but purposes (a) and (b), despite being non-charitable, were designed to promote the principal aim:

> **Jenkins J:** I was referred to a number of cases in which the effect of dispositions of this type has been considered, and the result of the authorities appears to be: (a) that where the amount applicable to the non-charitable purpose can be quantified the trusts fail *quoad* that amount but take effect in favour of the charitable purpose as regards the remainder; (b) that where the amount applicable to the non-charitable purpose cannot be quantified the trusts both charitable and non-charitable wholly fail because it cannot in such a case be held that any ascertainable part of the fund or the income thereof is devoted to charity; (c) that there is an exception to the general rule in what are commonly known as the 'Tomb cases', that is to say, cases in which there is a primary trust to apply the income of a fund in perpetuity in the repair of a tomb not in a church, followed by a charitable trust in terms extending only in cases of this particular class being to ignore the invalid trust for the repair of the tomb and treat the whole income as devoted to the charitable purpose; and (d) that there is an exception of a more general character where as a matter of construction the gift to charity is a gift of the entire fund or income subject to the payments thereout required to give effect to the non-charitable purpose, in which case the amount set free by the failure of the non-charitable gift is caught by and passes under the charitable gift. See (for example) *Chapman v Brown* (1801) 6 Ves 404; *In Re Birkett* (1878) 9 Ch D 576; *In Re Taylor* (1888) 58 LT 538; *In Re Porter* [1925] Ch 746; *In Re Dalziel* [1943] Ch 277; and *In Re Parnell* [1944] Ch 107.
>
> It remains to consider whether the trusts in question are indeed invalid. In my judgment they are not. It is no doubt perfectly true that a trust simply to provide an annual dinner for the Court of Aldermen of the City of London is not charitable, any more than the trust to provide dinners for the Painters Stainers Company in *In Re Barnett* (1908) 24 TLR 788 was charitable. It is also no doubt perfectly true that a trust simply to pay periodical guineas to selected aldermen of the City of London is not charitable. But the trusts here in question are of a different character. The annual dinner is to be provided for the Court of Aldermen as trustees of the charitable trust when they meet on the business of the trust, and the guineas are payable only to aldermen who are members of the committee administering the charity when they meet for that purpose, and subject to the express condition that a member in order to qualify for his guinea must be present during the whole of a given committee meeting. The annual dinner and the guinea attendance fees can therefore fairly be regarded as in the nature of remuneration in kind or in cash to the trustees and committee of management for their services in administering the affairs of the trust, and as I have already said the testator no doubt thought that these concrete expressions of his appreciation of the time and trouble involved would be conducive, in the ways mentioned above, to the attainment of his charitable purpose. In other words, his motive and object in providing for the

annual dinner and the guinea attendance fees was, I think, clearly to benefit the charity and not the members for the time being of the Court of Aldermen or the members for the time being of the committee appointed by them.

Severance

In limited circumstances, the court is entitled to apportion the fund and devote the charitable portion of the fund for charitable purposes. An apportionment will be ordered where part only of the fund is payable for charitable purposes and the other part for non-charitable purposes. In the absence of circumstances requiring a different division, the court will apply the maxim 'equality is equity' and order an equal division of the fund: see *Salusbury v Denton*.

Salusbury v Denton (1857) 3 K & J 529, HC

Facts
The testator's widow was subject to a duty to dispose, by will, of a fund so as to apply part of it for the benefit of 'a charity school or such other charitable endowment for the benefit of the poor [charitable purpose] ... and to dispose of the remainder among the testator's relatives'. The widow died without making the distribution.

Held
The fund was divided into two equal parts and the charitable portion was devoted to charitable purposes:

> **Page Wood VC:** It is one thing to direct a trustee to give a part of a fund to one set of objects, and the remainder to another, and it is a distinct thing to direct him to give 'either' to one set of objects 'or' to another. *Down v Worrall* (1833) 1 My & K 561, was a case of the latter description. There the trustees could give all to either of the objects. This is a case of the former description. Here the trustee was bound to give a part to each.

In *Re Clark*, the court decided that the primary gift by will was allowed to take effect in favour of the charitable objects, in equal shares.

In Re Clarke, Bracey v Royal National Lifeboat Institution [1923] 2 Ch 407, HC

Facts
By his will, the testator disposed of his residuary estate as follows:

> I give and bequeath all the residue and remainder of my estate ...to: (a) such institution, society or nursing home ...as assist or provide for persons of moderate means; (b) the Royal National Lifeboat Institution; (c) the Lister Institute of Preventive Medicine; (d) and such other funds, charities and institutions as my executors in their absolute discretion shall think fit. And I direct that such residue shall be divided amongst the legatees named in paragraphs (a), (b), (c) and (d) in such shares and proportions as my trustees shall determine.

The executors issued a summons to determine whether the gifts within the residuary clause were valid or void.

Held
The gift within class (d) was void for uncertainty and this one-quarter share was taken by the next of kin. Subject to the executors exercising their power of distribution, the fund vested in charitable objects in equal one-third shares:

> **Romer J:** The principle of the matter appears to me to be this. Where a fund is directed to be held upon trust for charitable and non-charitable indefinite purposes indiscriminately, the trust fails by reason of the uncertainty as to the non-charitable objects of the trust and the consequent inability of the court to control its administration. Where on the other hand a fund is to be held upon trust for charitable and for non-charitable definite purposes there is no uncertainty as to the non-charitable objects of the trust and the trust is a valid one. In both these cases the question that has to be considered is whether the objects of the trust can or cannot be ascertained by the court. But in a case where a part of a fund is given for charitable purposes and the other part is given for non-charitable purposes, the first question that has to be considered is whether the court can ascertain what are the two parts. In such a case the court finds no difficulty where the non-charitable purposes

are definite, as appears from *Salusbury v Denton* (1857) 3 K & J 529, and I cannot see that there is any greater difficulty where the non-charitable purposes are indefinite.

The effect of the residuary gift appears to me to be that the testator has given his residue to the four objects or sets of objects (a), (b), (c) and (d), with power to his executors to determine in what shares and proportions the residue is to be divided between the four. There is no express gift in default of the executors so determining, but the rule of the court in such a case has been laid down as follows, 'If the instrument itself gives the property to a class, but gives a power to A to appoint in what shares and in what manner the members of that class shall take, the property vests, until the power is exercised, in all the members of the class, and they will all take in default of appointment': see *Lambert v Thwaites* (1866) LR 2 Eq 151, p 155.

I therefore arrive at the conclusion that each one of the four objects or sets of objects takes a share in residue, and in accordance with the principle that equality is equity (of which *Salusbury v Denton* is an example) they take it in equal shares. The result is that one-fourth of the residue is held upon trust for the charitable objects specified in heading (a), one fourth each for the Royal National Lifeboat Institution and the Lister Institute of Preventive Medicine and the remaining, one fourth in trust for the persons entitled to the testator's estate as upon an intestacy.

The position is different if the trustees are not under a duty to dispose of, at least, part of the fund for charitable purposes, but may legitimately dispose of the entirety for a non-charitable purpose or purposes. In such a case, there is no power vested in the court to apportion the fund and rescue the intended charitable gift. The entire gift will fail as a charitable donation, illustrated by *Re Porter*.

Re Porter [1925] Ch 746, HC

Facts

A testator bequeathed a legacy of £10,000 to the trustees of a masonic temple in memory of his son. The income from the fund was required to be used primarily for the maintenance and upkeep of the temple, and the balance (if any) to be applied in favour of any masonic charity the trustees should select. The question in issue concerned the validity of the gift.

Held

The court held that the gift was void. The intended gift in favour of the private purpose failed as a trust for imperfect obligations and, since there was no duty to transfer a part of the fund for charitable purposes, the court had no power to sever the fund and distribute a part for charitable purposes:

> **Eve J:** The primary purpose of the gift is the maintenance and upkeep of the temple, and the whole income is charged with that trust, and as the expenditure is at the sole discretion of the trustees, they may properly apply the whole. Is the court entitled to control this discretion and to define the limits within which the expenditure ought to be kept? Could it, in fact, ascertain with any certainty whether there would be any surplus or not after providing for this primary object? I do not think it would be possible. The whole income might be properly so applied, and if so there would be no available surplus. It is clear that the testator contemplated that the whole might be required. In my opinion it results from this, that the ultimate gift for the charities is too indefinite and uncertain, and I must hold that the whole gift is void.

Question

What test for certainty of objects is applicable to charitable trusts?

RULE AGAINST PERPETUITIES

Charitable trusts, like private trusts, are subject to the rule against perpetuities (see Chapter 13 above). There are two aspects to the rule against perpetuities:

(a) the rule against remote vesting (that is, the rule against the vesting of a future interest outside the perpetuity period); and

(b) the rule against excessive duration.

Charities are not subject to the rule against excessive duration. Indeed, many charities (schools and universities) continue indefinitely and rely heavily on perpetual donations. But charitable gifts, like private gifts, are subject to the rule against remote vesting, that is, the subject matter of the gift is required to vest in the charity within the perpetuity period. Thus, in *Re Lord Stratheden and Campbell*, the gift was void because a distribution could have been made outside the perpetuity period.

Re Lord Stratheden and Campbell [1894] 3 Ch 265, HC

Facts

An annuity of £100 was bequeathed to the Central London Rangers on the appointment of the next Lieutenant Colonel. The question in issue was the validity of the gift.

Held

Since an appointment might not have been made within the perpetuity period, the condition transgressed the rule and the gift was void:

> **Romer J:** The annuity is not to be paid except on the appointment of the next lieutenant-colonel; and if a lieutenant-colonel is not appointed, the annuity is not to commence or be paid. That being so, it being conditional, can I say that the condition must arise within the time that is prescribed by the rules of law against perpetuities? I am sorry to say I cannot.

Note

The position would be different today, following the introduction of the principle of 'wait and see' under the Perpetuities and Accumulations Act 1964.

Charitable concession

With regard to the perpetuity rule, the courts have introduced a concession for charities, namely, charitable unity. Once a gift has vested in a specific charity then, subject to any express declarations to the contrary, it vests forever for charitable purposes. Accordingly, a gift which vests in one charity (A) with a gift over in favour of another charity (B) on the occurrence of an event, will be valid even if the event occurs outside the perpetuity period. This concessionary rule does not apply to a gift over to a charity after a gift in favour of a non-charity. The normal rules as to vesting apply. Similarly, a gift over from a charity to a non-charity is caught by the rule as to remote vesting: see *Re Bowen*.

Re Bowen [1893] 2 Ch 491, HC

Facts

A testator, who died in 1847, bequeathed a fund to trustees on trust to establish a day school in certain parishes in Wales. He directed that if the Government established 'a general system of education', the trust should cease and the surplus should fall into residue. He appointed his three sisters to be his residuary legatees. Following the Elementary Education Act 1870, the charitable trust terminated and the trustees applied to the court to determine whether the legacies had fallen into residue.

Held

The bequest to the residuary legatees was void as infringing the perpetuity rule and, consequently, the gift was taken by the next of kin:

> **Stirling J:** I think that on the true construction of the will there is an immediate disposition in favour of charity in perpetuity, and not for any shorter period. That is followed by a gift over if at any time the Government should establish a general system of education; and under that gift over the residuary legatees take a future interest conditional on an event which need not necessarily occur within perpetuity limits. It follows that the gift over is bad; and, consequently, the summons must be dismissed.

The concessionary rule in respect of charitable unity is capable of being abused by some drafts-men who seek to benefit non-charitable purposes for a period exceeding the perpetuity period. The technique that has been employed is to provide a fund for a charitable purpose (A) subject to a determining event, to the effect that, if a non-charitable purpose (B) is not fulfilled, a gift over in favour of another charity (C) will take effect. A prudent draftsman would be wise to ensure that the private purpose promoted is incidental to the charitable purpose, and that the stipulation concerning the non-charitable purpose does not impose an obligation on the trustees.

In Re Tyler [1891] 3 Ch 252, CA

Facts

A testator bequeathed £42,000 in stock to the trustees of the London Missionary Society (charity), with a gift over to the Blue Coat School, London (charity) if the society failed to keep a family vault at Highgate Cemetery in good repair. The society failed to maintain the vault. The question in issue was whether the gift over took effect.

Held

The gift over to the School took effect for the testator did not impose an obligation on the trustees to maintain the family vault (private purpose):

Lindley LJ: This property is given to the London Missionary Society for their charitable purposes. Then, there is a condition that, if the tomb is not kept in order, the fund shall go over to another charity. That appears to me, both on principle and authority, to be valid; and I do not think it is a sufficient answer to say that such a conclusion is an inducement to do that which contravenes the law against perpetuities. There is nothing illegal in keeping up a tomb; on the contrary, it is a very laudable thing to do. It is a rule of law that you shall not tie up property in such a way as to infringe what we know as the law against perpetuities; but there is nothing illegal in what the testator has done here.

By way of contrast, in *Re Dalziel*, the stipulation concerning the private purpose imposed an obligation on the trustees. This resulted in the gift failing as a charitable donation.

Re Dalziel [1943] 2 All ER 656, HC

Facts

A testatrix gave the governors of St Bartholomew's Hospital £20,000 'subject to the condition that they shall use the income' for the upkeep and repair of a mausoleum in Highgate Cemetery, with a gift over to another charity 'if they failed to do so'. The question in issue was whether the gift over took effect.

Held

The direction concerning the mausoleum created a trust of imperfect obligations which was void for infringing the perpetuity rule. The gift over was also void for infringing the perpetuity rule:

Cohen J: [the learned judge considered *In Re Tyler* [1891] 3 Ch 252, above, and continued:] The obligation as to rebuilding the tomb is not limited to rebuilding out of income, but would require the hospital, if necessary, to have recourse to capital. The void trust might, therefore, involve not only the whole income, but even the corpus. In my judgment, therefore, the gift fails *in toto*, for it is clear that, on the basis of the conclusion to which I have come, the event in which the gift over was to take effect, namely, the breach of an obligation by the hospital, can never occur.

Question

To what extent is the rule against the remote vesting aspect of the perpetuity rule applicable to charities?

THE *CY-PRÈS* DOCTRINE

The *cy-près* doctrine will be considered in more detail in Chapter 17. The advantage charitable trusts have over private trusts is that when a gift vests in a charity then, subject to express provisions to the contrary, the gift vests for charitable purposes. Accordingly, the settlor (and his estate) is excluded from any implied reversionary interests by way of a resulting trust in the event of a failure of the charitable trust. Thus, the *cy-près* doctrine is an alternative to the resulting trust principle.

FISCAL PRIVILEGES

Donations to charities, as well as charities, enjoy a variety of fiscal privileges. The effect is that the Inland Revenue, or the taypayer, endow significant subsidies for the promotion of charitable purposes. In *Dingle v Turner*, Lord Cross lamented the close correlation between charitable trusts and fiscal privileges.

Dingle v Turner [1972] AC 601, HL

Lord Cross of Chelsea: . . . charities automatically enjoy fiscal privileges which with the increasing burden of taxation have become more and more important in deciding that such and such a trust is a charitable trust, the court is endowing it with a substantial annual subsidy at the expense of the taxpayer. Indeed, claims for trusts to rank as charities are just as often challenged by the Revenue as by those who would take the fund if the trust was invalid. It is, of course, unfortunate that the recognition of any trust as a valid charitable trust should automatically attract fiscal privileges, for the question whether a trust to further some purpose is so little likely to benefit the public that it ought to be declared invalid and the question whether it is likely to confer such great benefits on the public that it should enjoy fiscal immunity are really two quite different questions. The logical solution would be to separate them and to say that only some charities should enjoy fiscal privileges.

A variety of fiscal reliefs are enjoyed by both charitable bodies and members of the public (including companies) who donate funds for charitable purposes.

Tax reliefs available to charities

Under s 505 of the Taxes Act 1988, charities are exempt from income tax and corporation tax in respect of rents, interest, dividends and annual payments, provided that the income is applied for charitable purposes only. In respect of income tax deducted at source by the payer, the recipient charity is entitled to recover the tax from the Inland Revenue.

In addition, income tax is not chargeable in respect of profits of a trade carried on by a charity if its profits are applied solely for the purposes of the charity and either the trade is exercised in the course of the actual carrying out of a primary purpose of the charity (for example, an educational charity running a school), or the work in connection with the trade is mainly carried out by beneficiaries of the charity (such as a charity set up to promote concerts arranged and conducted by its members). Where these conditions are not satisfied, it is common for charities to incorporate a company to carry out the work and for the company either to covenant its profits to the main charity, or to pay its profits to the main charity by way of dividends. The effect is that the company does not pay corporation tax.

Under s 256 of the Taxation of Chargeable Gains Act 1992, charities do not pay capital gains tax on the disposal of assets, provided that the gain accruing to the charity is applicable and applied for charitable purposes.

Charities are also exempt from stamp duty on conveyances, but are required to pay value added tax on goods and services purchased.

Tax reliefs in respect of donations to charities

A variety of reliefs is available in respect of donations to charities. Indeed, with the substantial number of tax reliefs available it is fair to say that the Government subsidises charitable bodies in a major way. Below are some of the tax reliefs that are connected to charities.

Gift aid

Section 25 of the Finance Act 1990 introduced a specific relief, 'gift aid', in respect of single gifts of money to charities. The scheme entitles individuals and companies to make gifts (qualifying donations) which do not exceed the total income of the individual or company for the relevant year. Such sums are paid to the charity after deduction of tax at the basic rate, but the charity is entitled to recover from the Revenue the tax deducted. In order to constitute a qualifying donation, the gift to the charity is required to be made by a UK resident individual and also:

(a) constitutes any sums of money, including chargeable assets; and

(b) is subject to no repayment condition; and

(c) from 6 April 2000 may include a 'covenanted payment to charity'; and

(d) must not fall with the 'payroll deduction scheme' (see below); and

(e) must not be conditional or associated with an arrangement involving the acquisition of property by the charity, otherwise than by way of gift, from the donor or person connected with him or her; and

(f) is subject to a charitable declaration by the donor.

Similar conditions are required to be satisfied by companies. Donors who are higher rate tax-payers are entitled to deduct the gross sum paid to the charity from their taxable income, and companies are entitled to treat gross payments to charities as charges on income.

Deeds of covenant

The separate regime for covenanted payments to charities has been repealed with effect from April 2000. Henceforth, payments under deeds of covenant by both individuals and companies are to be treated as donations under the gift aid scheme.

Payroll deduction scheme: s 202 of the Taxes Act 1988

On the assumption that a recognised scheme is run by an employer, employees are entitled to make tax effective donations to charities of their choice with no maximum limit. The employees who wish to participate in the scheme authorise their employers to deduct the relevant sums from their salary, before calculating PAYE tax due, and pay over the sums to an agent approved by the Inland Revenue. The agent then pays the relevant sums to the appropriate charity. The donations by the employees are treated as deductible expenses. Thus, full relief is enjoyed by the donors even in respect of basic rate taxpayers.

Gifts of shares and securities to charities: s 43 of the Finance Act 2000

A new relief was created for gifts of 'qualifying investments' to charities by individuals or companies that are not themselves charities. Qualifying investments are quoted shares or securities; units in an authorised unit trust; shares in an open-ended investment company or interests in offshore funds. Individual donors are able to claim a deduction against total income of the full market value of the investment at the date of the donation plus incidental costs of the disposal. For corporate donors, the same amount is treated as a charge on income.

Relief from capital gains tax: s 257 of the Taxation of Chargeable Gains Act 1992

A donation of a capital asset to a charity is treated as giving rise to no gain and no loss. Thus, the disposal proceeds are treated as equivalent to the allowable expenditure with the effect that no capital gains tax is payable.

Gifts by businesses to educational establishments: s 84 of the Taxes Act 1988

Businesses (such as trades, professions, vocations conducted by companies or unincorporated associations) are entitled to relief in respect of plant and machinery or other equipment (either manufactured, sold or used in the course of its trade) donated to educational establishments.

The business is allowed a deduction in respect of the full cost of producing or acquiring the subject matter of the gift.

Exemption from inheritance tax: s 23 of the Inheritance Tax Act 1984

Gifts to charities without limit are exempt from inheritance tax.

Question
What priviliges do charities enjoy?

VARIETIES OF FORMS OF CHARITABLE INSTITUTIONS

Charitable bodies may exist in a variety of forms. The choice of charitable medium is determined by the founders of the charity.

Express trusts

An individual may promote a charitable purpose by donating funds *inter vivos* or by will to trustees on trust to fulfil a charitable objective. The purpose need not be specified by the donor for the test here is whether all the purposes are charitable, for example, a trust will be charitable if the donor disposes of property on trust for 'charitable and benevolent purposes'. It may be necessary for the trustees to draw up a scheme with the Charity Commission or with the approval of the court in order to identify the specific charitable purposes which will benefit. It was pointed out earlier that charitable trusts are exempt from the test for certainty of objects applicable to private trusts.

Alternatively, the donor may identify the charitable objectives which he or she had in mind and, if these objectives are contested, the courts will decide whether the purposes are indeed charitable.

Corporations

A great deal of charitable activity is conducted through corporations. Such bodies may be incorporated by royal charter, such as the 'old' universities, or by special statute under which many public institutions, such as hospitals and 'new' universities, have been created. In addition, many charitable bodies have been created under the Companies Act 2006, usually as private companies limited by guarantee. In these circumstances, there is no need for separate trustees; since the corporations are independent persons, the property may vest directly in such bodies.

Charitable incorporated organisations

Section 34 and Schedule 7 of the Charities Act 2006 (Part 8(A) of the Charities Act 1993) introduce provisions creating a new legal form known as a 'charitable incorporated organisation' (CIO). The CIO is the first legal form to be created specifically to meet the needs of charities. A CIO is a body corporate with a constitution with at least one member. The purpose of a CIO is to avoid the need for charities that wish to benefit from incorporation to register as companies and be liable to comply with regulations from Companies House and the Charity Commission. Any one or more persons may apply to the Charity Commission for a CIO to be registered as a charity. The effect of registration is that all the property of the applicant's organisation shall become vested in the CIO. The Minister may make provisions for the winding up, insolvency, dissolution and revival of CIOs. The regulations may provide for the transfer of the property and rights of a CIO to the official custodian or another person or body or *cy-près*.

Unincorporated associations

A group of persons may join together in order to promote a charitable purpose. Such an association, unlike a corporation, has no separate existence. The funds are usually held by a committee in order to benefit the charitable purpose. In the absence of such a committee, the funds may be vested in the members of the association on trust for the charitable activity.

Question
In what forms may charitable institutions exist?

FURTHER READING

Gravells, N, 'Public purpose trusts' [1978] Conv 92.

Norris, D, 'Charitable covenants: a benefit or not?' [1989] Conv 321.

Parry, N, 'Imperfect charitable trust instruments: *AG of Bahamas v Royal Trust Co*' (1987) 131 SJ 1537.

Stopforth, D, 'Charitable covenants by individuals' [1986] BTR 101.

Warburton, J, 'Charitable trusts – unique' [1999] Conv 20.

CHARITABLE TRUSTS: DEFINITION AND PUBLIC BENEFIT

INTRODUCTION

By virtue of the Charities Act 2006 a purpose is treated as charitable if it satisfies two requirements: the purpose must be exclusively charitable and must satisfy the public benefit test, see s 2
of the Charities Act 2006. Prior to the Charities Act 2006, purposes were treated as charitable
were those mentioned in the preamble to the Charitable Uses Act 1601 and those which, by
analogy, were within the 'spirit and intendment' of the preamble. These purposes were classified
under four heads by Lord MacNaghten in *Inland Revenue Commissioners v Pemsel* [1891] AC 531.
These are trusts for: (a) the relief of poverty; (b) the advancement of education; (c) the advancement of religion; and (d) other purposes beneficial to the community. Today, s 2(2) of the Charities
Act 2006 lays down a description of 13 heads of charities which is intended to comprise an all
inclusive definition of charitable purposes. This comprises the first statutory definition of charitable purposes and is heavily reliant on the vast body of case law on the subject. At common law
the public benefit test may be satisfied if the beneficiaries are not numerically negligible and there
is no personal nexus between the donors and the beneficiaries, or indeed between the beneficiaries themselves. This common law principle has been preserved by s 3(3) of the 2006. However, the
common law presumption in favour of public benefit regarding trusts for the relief of poverty,
advancement of education and religion has been repealed: see s 3(2) of the Charities Act 2006. The
Charity Commission has the task of promoting understanding and awareness of the operation of
the public benefit requirement.

REGISTRATION

Most charitable bodies are required, under the new s 3(A) of the Charities Act 1993 (amended by
the Charities Act 2006), to be registered with the Charity Commission. The new s 3(A) of the
Charities Act 1993 deals with the register of charities, which the Charity Commission will continue to maintain. Section 3(A) prescribes the content of the register and the circumstances when
the Commission may remove charities or institutions that are no longer considered to be charities.
Section 3(A) of the 1993 Act lays down the general rule that all charities are required to be
registered with the exception of exempt, excepted and certain small charities.

Charities Act 1993, s 3(A) (1)

Every charity must be registered in the register of charities unless subsection (2) . . . applies to it.

The effect of registration creates a conclusive presumption of charitable status: see s 4(1) of the
Charities Act 1993.

Charities Act 1993, s 4(1)

An institution shall for all purposes other than rectification of the register be conclusively presumed to be or to
have been a charity at any time when it is or was on the register of charities.

Question
What is the effect of registering an institution on the charities register?

DEFINITION

Pre-Charities Act 2006
Ever since the passing of the Charitable Uses Act 1601 (sometimes referred to as the Statute of

Elizabeth I), the courts had developed the practice of referring to the preamble for guidance as to charitable purposes. The preamble contained a catalogue of purposes which at that time was regarded as charitable. It was not intended to constitute a definition of charities. Thus, the list of purposes in the preamble formed the foundation of the modern law of charitable purposes. This was achieved almost entirely through case law. The preamble was expressly preserved by s 38(4) of the Charities Act 1960.

Charitable Uses Act 1601, preamble

The relief of aged, impotent and poor people; the maintenance of sick and maimed soldiers and mariners, schools of learning, free schools and scholars of universities; the repair of bridges, ports, havens, causeways, churches, sea banks and highways; the education and preferment of orphans; the relief, stock or maintenance of houses of correction; the marriages of poor maids; the supportation, aid and help of young tradesmen, handicapped men and persons decayed; the relief or redemption of prisoners or captives; and the aid or care of any poor inhabitants concerning the payments of fifteens, setting out of soldiers and other taxes.

Admittedly, the above-mentioned purposes were of limited effect, but Lord Macnaghten, in *Inland Revenue Commissioners v Pemsel*, classified charitable purposes within four categories as follows:

> . . . charity in its legal sense comprises four principal divisions: trusts for relief of poverty; trusts for the advancement of education; trusts for the advancement of religion; and trusts for other purposes beneficial to the community.

In *McGovern v AG* (see Chapter 16, p 414 below for the facts), Slade J commented on the preamble.

McGovern v AG [1981] 3 All ER 493, HC

Slade J: As a broad proposition, I would thus accept that a trust for the relief of human suffering and distress would *prima facie* be capable of being of a charitable nature, within the spirit and intendment of the preamble to the Statute of Elizabeth, as being what Hoffmann J termed a 'charity of compassion'. It does not, however, follow that a trust established for good compassionate purposes will necessarily qualify as a charity according to English law, any more than it necessarily follows that such a qualification will attach to a trust for the relief of poverty or for the advancement of education or for the advancement of religion. There are other requirements which it must still satisfy if it is to enjoy charitable status.

The approach of the courts concerning novel charitable purposes regarded the examples as stated in the preamble as guidance in deciding on the validity of the relevant purpose. Two judicial approaches may be discerned by the courts, namely, reasoning by analogy and applying the 'spirit and intendment' of the preamble. These approaches are now endorsed in s 2(4) of the Charities Act 2006.

Reasoning by analogy

The approach here is to ascertain whether a purpose has some resemblance to an example as stated in the preamble, or to an earlier decided case which was considered charitable. In *Scottish Burial Reform Society v City of Glasgow Corp*, for example, the provision of a crematorium was considered charitable by analogy with the repair of churches (and the maintenance of burial grounds within churches) as stated in the preamble.

Scottish Burial Reform and Cremation Society v City of Glasgow Corp [1968] AC 138, HL

Facts

A company was formed for the purpose of the disposal of bodies by cremation. The question in issue was whether the objects clause of the company was charitable.

Held

The purposes of the company were charitable. Lord Wilberforce reasoned by reference to an analogy with a purpose stated in the preamble:

Lord Wilberforce: Was the company established for charitable purposes only? I interpret its objects clause as meaning that the company was formed for a general and a particular purpose: the general purpose was to promote methods of disposal of the dead which should be inexpensive and sanitary; the particular purpose (to which the company has in fact confined itself) to promote the method known as cremation. It is this combination of purposes which has to be examined in order to see whether it satisfies the legal test of charitable purposes.

On this subject, the law of England, though no doubt not very satisfactory and in need of rationalisation, is tolerably clear. The purposes in question, to be charitable, must be shown to be for the benefit of the public, or the community, in a sense or manner within the intendment of the preamble to the statute 43 Eliz 1, c 4. The latter requirement does not mean quite what it says; for:

it is now accepted that what must be regarded is not the wording of the preamble itself, but the effect of decisions given by the court as to its scope, decisions which have endeavoured to keep the law as to charities moving according as new social needs arise or old ones become obsolete or satisfied. Lord MacNaghten's grouping of the heads of recognised charity in *Pemsel's* case [1891] AC 531, is one that has proved to be of value and there are many problems which it solves. But three things may be said about it, which its author would surely not have denied: first that, since it is a classification of convenience, there may well be purposes which do not fit neatly into one or other of the headings; secondly, that the words used must not be given the force of a statute to be construed: and thirdly, that the law of charity is a moving subject which may well have evolved ever since 1891 [emphasis added].

With this in mind, approach may be made to the question whether the provision of facilities for the disposal of human remains, whether, generally, in an inexpensive and sanitary manner, or, particularly, by cremation, can be considered as within the spirit of the statute. Decided cases help us, at any rate, to the point of showing that trusts for the repair or maintenance of burial grounds connected with a church are charitable. This was, if not decided, certainly assumed in *In Re Vaughan* (1886) 33 Ch D 187 as it had been earlier assumed in *AG v Blizard* (1855) 21 Beav 233.

I regard, then, the provision of cremation services as falling naturally, and in their own right, within the spirit of the preamble.

One other point requires mention. The company makes charges for its services to enable it, in the words of the joint agreed minute, to fulfil effectively the objects for which it was formed. These charges, though apparently modest, are not shown to be higher or lower than those levied for other burial services. In my opinion, the fact that cremation is provided for a fee rather than gratuitously does not affect the charitable character of the company's activity, for that does not consist in the fact of providing financial relief but in the provision of services. That the charging for services for the achievement of a purpose which is in itself shown to be charitable does not destroy the charitable element was clearly, and, in my opinion, rightly, decided in *IRC v Falkirk Temperance Cafe Trust* [1927] SC 261 as well as in English authorities.

The spirit and intendment of the preamble

This approach is much wider than the previous approach. The courts decide if the purpose of the organisation is 'within the spirit and intendment' or 'within the equity' of the statute unhindered by the specific purposes as stated in the preamble. In other words, the examples enumerated in the preamble are treated as the context or 'flavour' in respect of which the purpose under scrutiny may be determined. In this respect, it has been suggested by Russell LJ in *Incorporated Council of Law Reporting v AG* that a purpose beneficial to the community is *prima facie* charitable, unless it is a purpose which could not have been intended by the draftsman of the Statute of Elizabeth, assuming the draftsman was aware of the changes in society.

Incorporated Council of Law Reporting v AG [1972] Ch 73, CA

Russell LJ: . . . if a purpose is shown to be so beneficial, or of such utility, it is *prima facie* charitable in law, but the courts have left open a line of retreat based on the equity of the statute in case they are faced with a purpose (for example, a political purpose) which could not have been within the contemplation of the statute even if the then legislators had been endowed with the gift of foresight into the circumstances of later centuries.

Facts

The primary object of the council, as stated in its memorandum of association, was 'The preparation and publication ... at a moderate price, of *Reports of Judicial Decisions of the Superior and Appellate Courts in England'*. The council carried on a business and profits, if any, were required to be applied in further pursuit of its objects. The Charity Commissioners refused to register the council as a charity.

Held

The Incorporated Council of Law Reporting was a charitable body on the grounds of advancing education and other purposes beneficial to society. The fact that the reports might be used by members of the legal profession for their 'personal gain' was incidental to the main charitable purposes:

> **Russell LJ:** The Council was established for the purpose of recording in a reliably accurate manner the development and application of judge made law and of disseminating the knowledge of that law, its development and judicial application, in a way which is essential to the study of the law. The primary object of the council is, I think, confined to this purpose exclusively and is charitable. The subsidiary objects, such as printing and publishing statutes, the provision of a noting-up service and so forth, are ancillary to this primary object and do not detract from its exclusively charitable character. Indeed, the publication of statues of the realm is itself, I think, a charitable purpose for reasons analogous to those applicable to reporting judicial decisions.
>
> The fact that the council's publications can be regarded as a necessary part of a practising lawyer's equipment does not prevent the council from being established exclusively for charitable purposes. The practising lawyer and the judge must both be lifelong students in that field of scholarship for the study of which the *Law Reports* provide essential material and a necessary service. The benefit which the council confers upon members of the legal profession in making accurate reports available is that it facilitates the study and ascertainment of the law. It also helps the lawyer to earn his livelihood, but that is incidental to or consequential on the primary scholastic function of advancing and disseminating knowledge of the law, and does not detract from the knowledge of the law, and does not detract from the exclusively charitable character of the council's objects: compare *Royal College of Nursing v St Marylebone Borough Council* [1959] 1 WLR 1077.
>
> The service which publication of the *Law Reports* provides benefits not only those actively engaged in the practice and administration of the law but also those whose business it is to study and teach law academically, and many others who need to study the law for the purposes of their trades, businesses, professions or affairs. In all these fields, however, the nature of the service is the same: it enables the reader to study, and by study to acquaint himself with and instruct himself in the law of this country. There is nothing here which negatives an exclusively charitable purpose.
>
> Although the objects of the council are commercial in the sense that the council exists to publish and sell its publications, they are unselfregarding. The members are prohibited from deriving any profit from the council's activities, and the council itself, although not debarred from making a profit out of its business, can only apply any such profit in the further pursuit of its objects. The council is consequently not prevented from being a charity by reason of any commercial element in its activities.
>
> I therefore reach the conclusion that the council is a body established 'exclusively for charitable purposes and is entitled to be registered under the Act of 1960'.

Section 1 of the Charities Act 2006

Section 1(1) adopts a general definition of a charity which endorses the principle laid down in s 96(1) of the Charities Act 1993. This is that 'charity':

> means a body or trust which –
>
> (a) is established for charitable purposes *only*, and
>
> (b) falls to be subject to the control of the High Court in the exercise of its jurisdiction with respect to charities.
> [emphasis added]

This broad definition preserves the current approach to charities by reference to the identification of the objects as exclusively charitable. In *Inland Revenue Commissioners v City of Glasgow Police*

Athletic Association [1953] 1 All ER 747, the House of Lords decided that a gift to the City of Glasgow Police Athletic Association was not charitable on the ground that the trust funds were capable of being devoted for both charitable and non-charitable purposes. The charitable purpose namely, improving the efficiency of the Police Force, was purely incidental to the non-charitable purpose of providing recreational activities for members of the Force.

Lord Normand declared:

> In principle . . . if an association has two purposes, one charitable and the other not, and if the two purposes are such and so related that the non-charitable purpose cannot be regarded as incidental to the other, the association is not a body established for charitable purpose only.

The policy of s 1(1)(b) of the 2006 Act involves the jurisdictional aspect of the definition. For all practical purposes a charity needs to be under the control of the High Court. In *Gaudiya Mission v Bramachary* [1997] 4 All ER 957, the Court of Appeal decided that an institution registered and established under the laws of a foreign jurisdiction did not satisfy the definition of a charity.

Section 1(2) of the Charities Act 2006 preserves the definition of charity in other enactments and s 1(3) preserves the definition of a charity by reference to the preamble to the Charitable Uses Act 1601. The effect is that the modern law of charities has endorsed the judicial approaches adopted in the past to maintain a degree of flexibility in deciding on charitable purposes.

Question
How have the courts been able to maintain the law of charities by reference to a limited number of purposes listed in the preamble to the Charitable Uses Act 1601 and are these judicial approaches relevant today?

PUBLIC BENEFIT REQUIREMENT

While the requirement of public benefit has not been stated in the preamble to the 1601 statute, it was established by the Court of Chancery that a trust must be of a public character in order to be charitable. It must not be assumed that all trusts for public purposes will be treated as charitable (see *Chichester Diocesan Fund v Simpson* [1944] 2 All ER 60, considered at p 362 above). This is because the meaning of charity has a particular legal significance which is narrower than the ordinary, popular meaning of the word. What is important is that the benefit is something that is beneficial in a way that the law regards as charitable. The nature of the benefit may take a variety of forms including tangible and intangible benefits. The criteria for charitable status are:

(a) the purpose is required to be within one of the 13 descriptions of charity laid down in s 2(2) of the Charities Act 2006; and

(b) compliance with the public benefit test.

Public benefit

The public benefit test is used to distinguish public trusts from private trusts. This is a two-tier test. The first requirement involves the usefulness of the activity to society. Prior to the Charities Act 2006 a presumption of public benefit existed if the purpose was within the first three heads of the *Pemsel* classification (trusts for the relief of poverty and advancement of education and religion see 'Introduction', above). This presumption has been abolished by s 3(2) of the Charities Act 2006. The effect is that all charitable purposes are put on an equal footing with the trustees being required to prove that the activity satisfies the judicial test for charities. The second requirement concerns the identification of the public (the community) or an appreciable section of society, with the exception of trusts for the relief of poverty. The satisfaction of the test is a question of law for the judge to decide on the evidence submitted to him.

The policy that underpins the second aspect of the test was laid down by Lord Simonds in *Inland Revenue Commissioners v Baddeley*.

Inland Revenue Commissioners v Baddeley [1955] AC 572, HL

Lord Simonds: [There is a] distinction between a form of relief accorded to the whole community yet, by its very nature, advantageous only to a few and a form of relief accorded to a selected few out of a larger number equally willing and able to take advantage of it . . . for example, a bridge which is available for all the public may undoubtedly be a charity and it is indifferent how many people use it. But confine its use to a selected number of persons, however numerous and important; it is then clearly not a charity. It is not of general public utility; for it does not serve the public purpose which its nature qualifies it to serve.

In this case, a trust in favour of Methodists in West Ham and Leyton failed the public element test for the beneficiaries comprised a class within a class:

Lord Simonds: In the case under appeal the intended beneficiaries are a class within a class; they are those of the inhabitants of a particular area who are members of a particular church: the area is comparatively large and populous and the members may be numerous. But, if this trust is charitable for them, does it cease to be charitable as the area narrows down and the numbers diminish? Suppose the area is confined to a single street and the beneficiaries to those whose creed commands few adherents: or suppose the class is one that is determined not by religious belief but by membership of a particular profession or by pursuit of a particular trade. These were considerations which influenced the House in the recent case of *Oppenheim* [1950] Ch 633. That was a case of an educational trust, but I think that they have even greater weight in the case of trusts which by their nominal classification depend for their validity upon general public utility.

I should in the present case conclude that a trust cannot qualify as a charity within the fourth class in *Income Tax Commissioners v Pemsel* [1891] AC 531 if the beneficiaries are a class of persons not only confined to a particular area but selected from within it by reference to a particular creed.

Personal nexus

The public benefit test will not be satisfied if there is a personal nexus between the donor and the beneficiaries, or between the beneficiaries themselves. The nexus may take the form of a 'blood' relationship.

In *Re Compton*, the Court of Appeal decided that the test was not satisfied where the gift was on trust for the education of the children of three named relatives.

Re Compton [1945] Ch 123, CA Lord

Greene MR: In the first place it may be laid down as a universal rule that the law recognises no purpose as charitable unless it is of a public character. That is to say, a purpose must, in order to be charitable, be directed to the benefit of the community or a section of the community.

No definition of what is meant by a section of the public had, so far as I am aware, been laid down and I certainly do not propose to be the first to make the attempt to define it. In the case of many charitable gifts it is possible to identify the individuals who are to benefit or who at any given moment constitute the class from which the beneficiaries are to be selected. This circumstance does not, however, deprive the gift of its public character. Thus, if there is a gift to relieve the poor inhabitants of a parish the class to benefit is readily ascertainable. But they do not enjoy the benefit when they receive it by virtue of their character as individuals but by virtue of their membership of the specified class. In such a case the common quality which unites the potential beneficiaries into a class is essentially an impersonal one. It is definable by reference to what each has in common with the others and that is something into which their status as individuals does not enter. *I come to the conclusion, therefore, that on principle a gift under which the beneficiaries are defined by reference to a purely personal relationship to a named* propositus *cannot on principle be a valid charitable gift.* And this, I think, must be the case whether the relationship be near or distant, whether it is limited to one generation or is extended to two or three or in perpetuity. The inherent vice of the personal element is present however long the chain and the claimant cannot avoid basing his claim upon it [emphasis added].

This test was approved and extended to a personal nexus by way of contract in *Oppenheim v Tobacco Securities Trust Co Ltd*.

Oppenheim v Tobacco Securities Trust Co Ltd [1951] AC 297, HL (Lords Simonds, Normand, Oaksey and Morton of Henryton; Lord MacDermott dissenting)

Facts

Trustees were directed to apply moneys in providing for the education of employees or ex-employees of British American Tobacco or any of its subsidiary companies. The employees numbered 110,000. The issue was whether the company was charitable.

Held

In view of the personal nexus between the employees themselves (being employed by the same employer), the public element test was not satisfied.

> **Lord Simonds:** It is a clearly established principle of the law of charity that a trust is not charitable unless it is directed to the public benefit. This is sometimes stated in the proposition that it must benefit the community or a section of the community.
>
> If I may begin at the bottom of the scale, a trust established by a father for the education of his son is not a charity. The public element, as I will call it, is not supplied by the fact that from that son's education all may benefit. At the other end of the scale the establishment of a college or university is beyond doubt a charity. 'Schools of learning and free schools' and 'scholars of universities' are the very words of the preamble to the Statute of Elizabeth. So also the endowment of a college, university or school by the creation of scholarships or bursaries is a charity and none the less because competition may be limited to a particular class of persons.
>
> The difficulty arises where the trust is not for the benefit of any institution either then existing or by the terms of the trust to be brought into existence, but for the benefit of a class of persons at large. Then the question is whether that class of persons can be regarded as such a 'section of the community' as to satisfy the test of public benefit. These words 'section of the community' have no special sanctity, but they conveniently indicate *first, that the possible (I emphasise the word 'possible') beneficiaries must not be numerically negligible, and secondly, that the quality which distinguishes them from other members of the community, so that they form by themselves a section of it, must be a quality which does not depend on their relationship to a particular individual*. It is for this reason that a trust for the education of members of a family or, as in *In re Compton* [1945] Ch 123, p 136, of a number of families cannot be regarded as charitable. A group of persons may be numerous but, if the nexus between them is their personal relationship to a single *propositus* or to several *propositi*, they are neither the community nor a section of the community for charitable purposes [emphasis added].
>
> I come, then, to the present case where the class of beneficiaries is numerous but the difficulty arises in regard to their common and distinguishing quality. That quality is being children of employees of one or other of a group of companies. I can make no distinction between children of employees and the employees themselves. In both cases the common quality is found in employment by particular employers. It appears to me that it would be an extension, for which there is no justification in principle or authority, to regard common employment as a quality which constitutes those employed a section of the community. It must not, I think, be forgotten that charitable institutions enjoy rare and increasing privileges, and that the claim to come within that privileged claim, should be clearly established.

Lord MacDermott dissented and expressed the view that, although the personal 'common link' test was of some value, it should not be an overriding consideration as the majority believed:

> **Lord MacDermott (dissenting):** I see much difficulty in dividing the qualities or attributes, which may serve to bind human beings into classes, into two mutually exclusive groups, the one involving individual status and purely personal, the other disregarding such status and quite impersonal.
>
> But can any really fundamental distinction, as respects the personal or impersonal nature of the common link, be drawn between those employed, for example, by a particular university and those whom the same university has put in a certain category as the result of individual examination and assessment? Again, if the bond between those employed by a particular railway is purely personal, why should the bond between those who are employed as railway men be so essentially different? Is a distinction to be drawn in this respect between those who are employed in a particular industry before it is nationalised and those who are employed therein after

that process has been completed and one employer has taken the place of many? Are miners in the service of the National Coal Board now in one category and miners at a particular pit or of a particular district in another? Is the relationship between those in the service of the Crown to be distinguished from that obtaining between those in the service of some other employer? Or, if not, are the children of, say, soldiers or civil servants to be regarded as not constituting a sufficient section of the public to make a trust for their education charitable?

More recently, in *Dingle v Turner* [1972] AC 601, HL (see p 384 below), Lord Cross of Chelsea gave his support for this view.

Preference for specified individuals

There is some support (albeit, slender) for the view that if the donor sets up a trust for the benefit of the public or a large section of the public, but expresses a preference (not amounting to an obligation) in favour of specified individuals, the gift is capable of satisfying the public element test: see *Re Koettgen*.

Re Koettgen's Will Trust [1954] Ch 252, HC

Facts

A trust was created for the promotion and furtherance of the commercial education of British born subjects, subject to a direction that preference be given to the employees of a company.

Held

On construction of the trust instrument, the preference was intended as permitting, without obliging, the trustees to consider distributing the property in favour of the employees:

Upjohn J: In my judgment, it is at the stage when the primary class of eligible persons is ascertained that the question of the public nature of the trust arises and falls to be decided, and it seems to me that the will satisfies that requirement and that the trust is of a sufficiently public nature.

If, when selecting from that primary class the trustees are directed to give a preference to the employees of the company and members of their families, that cannot affect the validity of the primary trust, it being quite uncertain whether such persons will exhaust in any year 75% of the trust fund. On the true construction of this will, that is not (as to 75%) primarily a trust for persons connected with John Batt & Co and the class of persons to benefit is not 'confined' to them, and in my judgment the trust contained in clauses 7 and 8 of the will of the testatrix is a valid charitable trust.

This decision has been criticised by Lord Radcliffe in the Privy Council in *Caffoor v Commissioners of Income Tax, Colombo* [1961] AC 584 as being in essence an 'employee trust' and 'had edged very near to being inconsistent with the *Oppenheim* case'.

In *Inland Revenue Commissioners v Educational Grants Association Ltd*, the Court of Appeal refused to follow the reasoning in *Re Koettgen*.

Inland Revenue Commissioners v Educational Grants Association Ltd [1967] 3 WLR 41, CA

Facts

The association was established for the advancement of education by, *inter alia*, making grants to individuals. Its principal source of income consisted of annual sums paid to it by Metal Box Ltd. About 85% of the association's income during the relevant years was applied to the children of employees of Metal Box Ltd. The question in issue was whether the association was a charitable body.

Held

The application of the high proportion of the income for the benefit of children connected with Metal Box Ltd was inconsistent with an application for charitable purposes.

The Court of Appeal affirmed the decision of Pennywick J at first instance and refused to follow *Re Koettgen*:

Pennycuick J: I find considerable difficulty in the *Re Koettgen* decision. I should have thought that a trust for the public with reference for a private class comprised in the public might be regarded as a trust for the application of income at the discretion of the trustees between charitable and non-charitable objects.

Lord Denning MR: The greater part of these funds [75%–85%] were applied to advance the education of Metal Box children. The remaining 15% to 25% was applied for children unconnected with Metal Box and for educational institutions. Those are conceded to be for the public benefit. So we have a case where part of the income was applied for private benefit of Metal Box children (which is not charitable) and the other part for the public benefit (which is charitable). In so far as the income was applied for Metal Box children, it was not applied for charitable purposes and does not qualify for exemption. The commissioners took a different view. They seem to have been influenced by the decision of Upjohn J in *In Re Koettgen's Will Trusts* [1954] Ch 252, but that has to be read subject to the doubts thrown out by Lord Radcliffe in *Caffoor v Income Tax Commissioner* [1961] AC 584. In my opinion we are compelled by *Oppenheim*'s case to hold that the application for Metal Box children was not charitable.

Question

To what extent is *Re Koettgen* inconsistent with *Oppenheim v Tobacco Securities Trust Co Ltd*?

In *Inland Revenue Commissioners v Oldham Training and Enterprise Council*, the court decided that the Oldham Training and Enterprise Council, which was set up to promote commerce for the benefit of the public in Oldham, was not a charitable entity. The council lacked a public element.

Inland Revenue Commissioners v Oldham Training and Enterprise Council
(1996) The Times, 10 October, HC

Facts

Oldham TEC was incorporated in 1989 as a company limited by guarantee and not having a share capital. Its activities, as authorised by its memorandum of association, were classified under three categories, namely: (a) enterprise services, including information and advice, diagnostic services and business skills training; (b) business startup services, including a free enterprise training programme for anyone thinking of setting up a new business, and cash payments of up to £2,800 for any individual in lieu of unemployment and social security benefits; and (c) training, both of the young and retraining of the unemployed. These services were generally provided by private sector firms, universities and colleges. The costs were shared by recipient businesses and Oldham TEC. The question in issue was whether the company was established for charitable purposes within s 506 of the Taxes Act 1988 and exempt from corporation tax. The status of some 80 other training and enterprise councils with identical objects clauses was dependent on this decision. It was submitted on behalf of the council that, on construction of the objects clause, the main purpose of the TEC permitted the application of its funds solely for charitable purposes. Any non-charitable purposes were purely incidental to the main charitable purpose.

Held

The court found in favour of the Revenue on the ground that the objects clause of the company promoted primarily the interests of individuals and other entities engaged in trade, commerce or enterprise, as opposed to a public benefit. Accordingly, the TEC was not a charitable company.

In essence, the public element test will be satisfied if:

(a) the beneficiaries are not numerically negligible; and

(b) the beneficiaries have no 'link' in contract or in blood between themselves or with a narrow group of individuals.

These requirements were laid down by Lord Simonds in *Oppenheim*.

Oppenheim v Tobacco Securities Trust Co Ltd [1951] AC 297, HL

Lord Simonds: To constitute a section of the public, the possible beneficiaries must not be numerically negligible and secondly, the quality which distinguishes them from other members of the community so that they form by themselves a section of it must be a quality which does not depend on their relationship to a particular individual . . . A group of persons may be numerous but, if the nexus between them is their personal relationship to a single *propositus* or to several *propositi* they are neither the community nor a section of the community for charitable purposes.

Question of degree

Subject to the absence of a personal nexus between the beneficiaries and/or a limited class of individuals, the issue whether or not the beneficiaries constitute a section of the public in order to satisfy the public element test is a question of degree. There are many decisions which appear to be inconsistent with each other. In *Gilmour v Coats*, a community of 20 cloistered nuns was insufficient to satisfy the public element test.

Gilmour v Coats and Others [1949] 1 All ER 848, HL

Facts

The case concerned a gift to a Carmelite convent which consisted of a community of 20 cloistered nuns, who devoted themselves to prayer and contemplation and engaged in no work outside the convent. The question in issue was whether the gift was charitable.

Held

The gift did not satisfy the public element test for the community of nuns was insufficiently integrated with society:

> **Lord Simonds:** The nuns take vows of perpetual poverty, chastity and obedience and live under rules which impose and regulate the strict enclosure and observance of silence, which are said to be the conditions of the true and fruitful following of the contemplative life. So, too, their rules prescribe the occupations which are to fill their lives. They must assist devoutly and every day at the celebration of the mass and the recital of the Divine Office and other offices and prayers of the Church, must spend all the time that is not occupied in community duties in prayer or spiritual reading or work in their cells. Further, the rules prescribe practices to further the spirit of humility and particular mortifications, as, for example, a monastic fast lasting from 14 September to Easter, and the prohibition throughout their lives of those aids to comfort which by ordinary women are regarded as necessities rather than luxuries of life.
>
> This, then, is the life which it is the purpose of this community to promote in the women who join it. Is it a charitable purpose and is a trust for its furtherance a charitable trust? The community does not engage in – indeed, it is by its rules debarred from – any exterior work, such as teaching, nursing, or tending the poor, which distinguishes the active branches of the same order.
>
> My Lords, I would speak with all respect and reverence of those who spend their lives in cloistered piety, and in this House of Lords Spiritual and Temporal, which daily commences its proceedings with intercessory prayers, how can I deny that the Divine Being may in His wisdom think fit to answer them? But, my Lords, whether I affirm or deny, whether I believe or disbelieve, what has that to do with the proof which the court demands that a particular purpose satisfies the test of benefit to the community? Here is something which is manifestly not susceptible of proof. But, then it is said, this is a matter not of proof but of belief, for the value of intercessory prayer is a tenet of the Catholic faith, therefore, and, in such prayer there is benefit to the community. But it is just at this 'therefore' that I must pause. It is, no doubt, true that the advancement of religion is, generally speaking, one of the heads of charity, but it does not follow from this that the court must accept as proved whatever a particular church believes. The faithful must embrace their faith believing where they cannot prove: the court can act only on proof. A gift to two or ten or a hundred cloistered nuns in the belief that their prayers will benefit the world at large does not from that belief alone derive validity any more than does the belief of any other donor for any other purpose.
>
> Of the decision of Luxmoore J, in *Re Caus* [1934] Ch 162, I would only say that his *ratio decidendi* is expressly stated to be, first, that it (ie, a gift for the saying of masses) enables a ritual act to be performed which is

recognised by a large proportion of Christian people to be the central act of their religion, and, secondly, that it assists in the endowment of priests whose duty it is to perform the ritual act. The decision, therefore, does not assist the prioress' argument in the present case and I make no further comments on it.

On the other hand, in *Neville Estates v Madden*, the members of the Catford Synagogue were treated as an appreciable section of the public and satisfied the public element test because the objects were not numerically negligible and integrated with the rest of society.

Neville Estates Ltd v Madden and Others [1962] 1 Ch 832, HC

Facts

Following an appeal by the Catford Synagogue, money was raised to purchase a house. This was achieved and the house was conveyed to trustees by deed which declared that the purchase moneys were the property of the members of the synagogue. Part of the house was used as a synagogue; the other part was used as the minister's residence. Following another appeal, other land was bought and conveyed to the trustees on the same terms. The synagogue contracted to sell part of the land to the plaintiff for £10,000. After the contract was signed, the synagogue received another offer for £14,300 and wished to accept this offer. The plaintiff brought an action for specific performance. The Charity Commissioners notified the synagogue that they would refuse to consent to the sale to the plaintiff for less than £14,300. The plaintiff commenced proceedings claiming that the consent of the Commissioners was not necessary for the land was not held for charitable purposes.

Held

The purchase moneys following both appeals did not belong to the members beneficially but were held upon trust for the synagogue. The trust was charitable for the purpose of advancing religion and the consent of the Commissioners was a prerequisite to the sale:

Cross J: The decision of the House of Lords in *Gilmour v Coats* [1949] AC 426 has made it clear that a trust for a religious purpose must be shown to have some element of public benefit in order to qualify as a charitable trust. The trust with which I am concerned resembles that in *Gilmour v Coats* in this, that the persons immediately benefited by it are not a section of the public but the members of a private body. All persons of the Jewish faith living in or about Catford might well constitute a section of the public, but the members for the time being of the Catford Synagogue are no more a section of the public than the members for the time being of a Carmelite Priory. The two cases, however, differ from one another in that the members of the Catford Synagogue spend their lives in the world, whereas the members of a Carmelite Priory live secluded from the world. If once one refuses to pay any regard – as the courts refused to pay any regard – to the influence which these nuns living in seclusion might have on the outside world, then it must follow that no public benefit is involved in a trust to support a Carmelite Priory. But the court it, I think, entitled to assume that some benefit accrues to the public from the attendance at places of worship of persons who live in this world and mix with their fellow citizens. As between different religions the law stands neutral, but it assumes that any religion is at least likely to be better than none.

Generally speaking, no doubt, an association which is supported by its members for the purposes of providing benefits for themselves will not be a charity. But I do not think that this principle can apply with full force in the case of trusts for religious purposes. As Lord Simonds pointed out, the law of charity has been built up not logically but empirically, and there is a political background peculiar to religious trusts which may well have influenced the development of the law with regard to them.

In my judgment, this trust with which I am concerned in this case is a charitable trust.

Note

In *Re Lewis* [1954] 3 All ER 257, a gift for the benefit of 10 blind boys and 10 blind girls in Tottenham was charitable.

Question

How may *Gilmour v Coats* be reconciled with *Neville Estates v Madden*?

In *Williams Trustees v Inland Revenue Commissioners,* the gift failed as a charity for it purported to benefit a narrow section of society.

Williams Trustees v Inland Revenue Commissioners [1947] AC 447, HL

Facts

A gift was made in order to create an institute in London for the promotion of Welsh culture. The question in issue was whether the gift was charitable.

Held

The gift was not charitable on the ground that it lacked a public element owing to the fact that it promoted a class within a class:

> **Lord Simonds:** If the purposes are not charitable *per se*, the localisation of them will not make them charitable.
>
> The rule is thus stated by Lord Wrenbury in *Verge v Sommerville* [1924] AC 650:
>
>> To ascertain whether a gift constitutes a valid charitable trust so as to escape being void on the ground of perpetuity, a first inquiry must be whether it is public – whether it is for the benefit of the community or of an appreciably important class of the community. The inhabitants of a parish or town, or any particular class of such inhabitants, may for instance, be the objects of such a gift, but private individuals, or a fluctuating body of private individuals, cannot.
>
> It is, I think, obvious that this rule, necessary as it is, must often be difficult of application and so the courts have found. Each case must be judged on its own facts and the dividing line is not easily drawn. But the difficulty, of finding the community in the present case, when the definition of 'Welsh people' in the first deed is remembered, would not I think be less than that of finding the community of Jews in *Keren*'s case [1932] AC 650.

Note

The same principle was applied in *Inland Revenue Commissioners v Baddeley* (see p 378 above).

In *McGovern v AG,* Slade J stated that the question whether the public benefit test is satisfied or not is a question of law based on the evidence.

McGovern v AG [1981] 3 All ER 493, HC

> **Slade J:** The question whether a purpose will or may operate for the public benefit is to be answered by the court forming an opinion on the evidence before it: see *National Anti-Vivisection Society v IRC* [1948] AC 31, p 44, *per* Lord Wright. No doubt in some cases a purpose may be so manifestly beneficial to the public that it would be absurd to call evidence on this point. In many other instances, however, the element of public benefit may be much more debatable. Indeed, in some cases the court will regard this element of being incapable of proof one way or the other and thus will inevitably decline to recognise the trust as being of a charitable nature.

Question

What is meant by the 'public element' or 'public benefit' test?

Poverty exception

Trusts for the relief of poverty are charitable even though the beneficiaries are linked *inter se* or with an individual or small group of individuals. In short, trusts for the relief of poverty are not subject to the public element test. The practice of the courts (see *Re Compton,* p 378 above) has always been to exclude such trusts from the public element test. Accordingly, in *Gibson v South American Stores Ltd* [1950] Ch 177 and *Dingle v Turner,* the courts reviewed the authorities and decided that gifts in order to relieve poverty amongst employees of a company were charitable.

Dingle v Turner [1972] AC 601, HL

Facts

A testator by his will transferred property to his trustees and directed them to apply the income '... in paying pensions to poor employees of Dingle Ltd'. At the time of the testator's death, there were 705 full-time employees and 189 part-time employees. The question in issue was whether the gift was charitable.

Held

The gift was charitable. Gifts or trusts for the relief of poverty were not subject to the public element test. Accordingly, the contractual connection between the donor and donees did not invalidate the gift:

> **Lord Cross of Chelsea:** The status of some of the 'poor relations' trusts as valid charitable trusts was recognised more than 200 years ago and a few of those then recognised are still being administered as charities today. In *In Re Compton* [1945] Ch 123, Lord Greene MR said, at p 139, that it was 'quite impossible' for the Court of Appeal to overrule such old decisions and in *Oppenheim* [1951] AC 297 Lord Simonds in speaking of them remarked, at p 309, on the unwisdom of casting doubt on 'decisions of respectable antiquity in order to introduce a greater harmony into the law of charity as a whole'. Indeed, counsel for the appellant hardly ventured to suggest that we overrule the 'poor relations' cases. His submission was that which was accepted by the Court of Appeal for Ontario in *In Re Cox* [1951] OR 205 – namely that while the 'poor relations' cases might have to be left as long standing anomalies there was no good reason for sparing the 'poor employees' cases which only date from *In Re Gosling* [1900] 48 WR 300, and which have been under suspicion ever since the decision in *In Re Compton*. But the 'poor members' and the 'poor employees' decisions were a natural development of the 'poor relations' decisions and to draw a distinction between different sorts of 'poverty' trusts would be quite illogical and could certainly not be said to be introducing 'greater harmony' into the law of charity. Moreover, though not as old as the 'poor relations' trusts 'poor employees' trusts have been recognised as charities for many years; there are now a large number of such trusts in existence; and assuming, as one must, that they are properly administered in the sense that benefits under them are only given to people who can fairly be said to be, according to current standards, 'poor persons', to treat such trusts as charities is not open to any practical objection. So as it seems to me it must be accepted that wherever else it may hold sway the *Compton* rule has no application in the field of trusts for there the dividing line between a charitable trust and a private trust lies where the Court of Appeal drew it in *In Re Scarisbrick's Will Trusts* [1951] Ch 622.
>
> In answering the question whether any given trust is a charitable trust the courts – as I see it – cannot avoid having regard to the fiscal privileges accorded to charities. But, as things are, validity and fiscal immunity march hand in hand and the decisions in the *Compton* and *Oppenheim* cases were pretty obviously influenced by the consideration that if such trust as were there in question were held valid they would enjoy an undeserved fiscal immunity.

Question

On what basis is a trust for the relief of poverty exempt from the public element test?

Private trusts compared with public trusts for the relief of poverty

Although trusts for the relief of poverty are exempt from the public element test, the courts have drawn a subtle distinction between private trusts for the relief of poverty and public trusts for the same purpose. For example, a gift for the settlor's poor relations, A, B and C, may not be charitable but may exist as a private trust, whereas a gift for the benefit of the settlor's poor relations without identifying them (even if they happen to be A, B and C) may be charitable. It appears that the distinction between the two types of trusts lies in the degree of precision in which the objects have been identified. The more precise the language used by the settlor in identifying the poor relations, the stronger the risk of failure as a charitable trust. This is a question of degree: see *Re Scarisbrick*.

Re Scarisbrick [1951] Ch 622, CA

Facts

A bequest was made on trust 'for such relations of my said son and daughters as in the opinion of the survivor shall be in needy circumstances'. The issue was whether the bequest was valid as a charitable trust.

Held

The gift was charitable for the relief of poverty.

Jenkins LJ: The following general propositions may be stated:

(i) it is a general rule that a trust or gift in order to be charitable in the legal sense must be for the benefit of the public or some section of the public: see *In Re Compton* [1945] Ch 123; *In Re Hobourn Aero Components Ltd's Air Raid Distress Fund* [1946] Ch 194; and *Gilmour v Coats* [1949] AC 426;

(ii) an aggregate of individuals ascertained by reference to some personal tie (for example, of blood or contract), such as the relations of a particular individual, the members of particular family, the employees of a particular firm, the members of a particular association, does not amount to the public or a section thereof for the purposes of the general rules: see *In Re Drummond* [1914] 2 Ch 90, *In Re Compton, In Re Hobourn Aero Components Ltd's Air Raid Distress Fund*, and *Oppenheim v Tobacco Securities Trust Co Ltd;*

(iii) it follows that according to the general rule above stated a trust or gift under which the beneficiaries or potential beneficiaries are confined to some aggregate of individuals ascertained as above is not legally charitable even though its purposes are such that it would have been legally charitable if the range of potential beneficiaries had extended to the public at large or a section thereof (for example, an educational trust confined as *In re Compton*, to the lawful descendants of three named persons, or, as in *Oppenheim v Tobacco Securities Trust Co Ltd* [1951] AC 297, to the children of employees or former employees of a particular company);

(iv) there is, however, an exception to the general rule, in that trusts or gifts for the relief of poverty have been held to be charitable even though they are limited in their application to some aggregate of individuals ascertained as above, and are therefore not trusts or gifts for the benefit of the public or a section thereof. This exception operated whether the personal tie is one of blood (as in the numerous so called 'poor relations' cases, to some of which I will presently refer) or of contract (for example, the relief of poverty amongst the members of a particular society, as in *Spiller v Maude* (1881) 32 Ch D 158, or amongst employees of a particular company or their dependants, as in *Gibson v South American Stores (Gath & Chaves) Ltd* [1950] Ch 177);

(v) this exception cannot be accounted for by reference to any principle, but is established by a series of authorities of long standing, and must at the present date be accepted as valid, at all events as far as this court is concerned (see *In Re Compton*) though doubtless open to review in the House of Lords (as appears from the observation of Lords Simonds and Morton of Henryton in *Oppenheim v Tobacco Securities Trust Co Ltd*).

'Poverty' is necessarily to some extent a relative matter, a matter of opinion, and it is not to be assumed that the person made the judge of 'needy circumstances' in the present case would have acted otherwise than in accordance with an opinion fairly and honestly formed as to the circumstances, needy or otherwise, of anyone coming into consideration as a potential object of the power. Under a similar trust which did not expressly make the appointor's opinion the test of eligibility, the appointor would in practice have to make the selection according to the best of his or her opinion or judgment. The express reference to the appointor's opinion merely serves to reduce the possibility of dispute as to the eligibility or otherwise of any particular individual on the score of needy circumstances.

It is no doubt true that a gift or trust is not necessarily charitable as being in relief of poverty because the object or objects of it in order to take must be poor. Such a gift or trust may be no more than an ordinary gift to some particular individual or individuals limited to the amount required to relieve his or their necessities if in necessitous circumstances. One can conceive of a testator making a limited provision of this character for a child or children whose conduct in his view had reduced their claims on his bounty to a minimum. A disposition of that sort would obviously not be for the relief of poverty in the charitable sense. The same must be said of gifts to named persons if in needy circumstances, or to a narrow class of near relatives, as for example to such of a testator's statutory next of kin as at his death shall be in needy circumstances.

It is difficult to draw any exact line, but I do not think the trust here in question can fairly be held disqualified as a trust for the relief of poverty in the charitable sense on grounds such as those illustrated above. The class of relations to whom the selective power of appointment here extends is not confined to relations of the testatrix herself but consists of relations of testatrix's son and daughters. 'Relations' in this context cannot, in my opinion, be construed as meaning only the statutory next of kin of the son and daughters.

I am accordingly of opinion that as the law now stands the trust in question should be upheld as a valid charitable trust for the relief of poverty.

Trust purpose restricted to the relief of poverty

Similarly, a gift or trust is not necessarily charitable as being for the relief of poverty because the object(s) is (are) identified as being poor. Such a gift or trust may be no more than an ordinary gift to some particular individual or individuals limited to the amount required to relieve his, her or their necessities in the stated circumstances.

In *Re Segelman*, a charitable trust was created when a testator selected poor members of a class of individuals, which was not closed at the time of his death.

Re Segelman (Decd) [1996] 2 WLR 173, HC

Facts

Two months before his death, Mr Segelman, a 92 year old testator, gave instructions to his solicitor to prepare a will for his signature. His solicitors executed a draft will and in clause 11(a) established a trust fund from the residuary estate to be used for the assistance of 'the poor and needy' from a class of persons set out in the second schedule to the will. On his own initiative, the solicitor drafted a proviso to clause 11(a), which provided that, if any of the persons named in the schedule died during the testator's lifetime or within 21 years from his death, 'such issue shall stand in the place of such person and be eligible to benefit' under the trust. Clause 11(b) gave the trustees a discretion to distribute property in favour of 'the poor and needy' from the class named in the schedule, subject to a gift over in favour of charitable institutions and purposes 'in the event of there being no such persons eligible to benefit'. The testator's secretary subsequently provided the solicitor with the list of persons comprising the second schedule. The list contained six named members of the testator's extended family and the 'issue' (unnamed) of five of them. The solicitor failed to appreciate the need to alter the proviso to clause 11(a) in the light of the wording of the second schedule. The will was duly executed.

After the testator's death and the admission of the will to probate, five of the named persons in the schedule commenced proceedings seeking rectification of the will pursuant to s 20(1) of the Administration of Justice Act 1982, by deletion of the proviso to clause 11(a) on the grounds that, in consequence of 'clerical error' and contrary to the intention of the testator, the proviso had the effect of restricting the class of persons constituted in the second schedule by excluding the issue of the named individuals while their named ancestors were still alive. The executors of the will appealed from a determination of the Inland Revenue to the effect that the dispositions within clause 11 were not charitable and, accordingly, not exempt under s 23 of the Inheritance Tax Act 1984. The court consolidated the claims and considered them together.

Held

(a) Rectification of the will was ordered.

(b) The discretionary trust in favour of the 'poor and needy' was charitable.

(c) The charitable trust was treated as an exempt transfer under s 23 of the Inheritance Tax Act 1984.

Chadwick J: [after deciding that the claim for rectification of the will was successful, continued:] The second main question raised by the construction summons, is whether clause 11(a) of the will creates a valid charitable gift.

Prima facie, a gift for the benefit of poor and needy persons is a gift for the relief of poverty, and so falls squarely within the first of the four divisions of charity identified by Lord MacNaghten in *Income Tax Special Purposes Commissioners v Pemsel* [1891] AC 531, p 583. Further, a gift for the relief of poverty is no less charitable because those whose poverty is to be relieved are confined to a particular class limited by ties of blood or employment: see *In Re Scarisbrick* [1951] Ch 622, pp 648–49; and *Dingle v Turner* [1972] AC 601, pp 622–23.

The conclusion that I draw from the evidence is that the testator selected the members of the second schedule class on the basis that they were persons who might need financial help from time to time in the future – as had been the case, at least in relation to some of them, in the past – and that they were persons who, by reasons of ties of blood or affection, he would wish to help after his death, as he had done from time to time during his lifetime.

The basis for disqualification as a charitable gift must be that the restricted nature of the class leads to the conclusion that the gift is really a gift to the individual members of the class. In my view, the gift in clause 11 of the will is not of that character. The gift with which I am concerned has, in common with the gift which the Court of Appeal had to consider in Re Scarisbrick, the feature that the class of those eligible to benefit was not closed upon the testator's death. It remained open for a further period of 21 years. During that period issue of the named individuals born after the death of the testator will become members of the class. It is, in my view, impossible to attribute to the testator an intention to make a gift to those after-born issue as such. His intention must be taken to have been the relief of poverty amongst the class of which they would become members.

It follows that I am satisfied that the gift to the poor and needy of the class of persons set out in the second schedule to the will falls on the charitable side of the line, wherever that line has to be drawn. I hold that the gift in clause 11(a) of the will for the assistance of the poor and needy of the class, during the period of 21 years from the death of the testator, is a gift for charitable purposes, and that the gift for distribution among the poor and needy of the class, upon the expiration of that 21 year period, is also a gift for charitable purposes.

Question
How would you distinguish a private trust for the relief of poverty from a charitable trust for the same purpose?

FURTHER READING

Atiyah, P, 'Public benefit in charities' (1958) 21 MLR 138.

Bright, S, 'Charity and trusts for the public benefit: time for a rethink' [1981] Conv 28.

Cohen 'Charities – A utilitarian perspective' (1983) 36 Current Legal Problems 241.

Cross, G, 'Some recent developments on the law of charity' (1956) 72 LQR 187.

Dawson, N, 'Equity is not a computer: *Winkworth v Edward Baron Development Co Ltd*' [1987] Conv 14.

Histed, E, 'Rectification of wills – charitable trusts for poor relations – broadening the boundaries: *Re Segelman*' [1996] Conv 379.

Maurice, 'The public element in charitable trusts' (1951) 15 CPL (NS) 328.

Plowright, 'Public benefit in charitable trusts' (1975) 39 Conv 183.

CHARITABLE TRUSTS: CLASSIFICATION OF CHARITABLE PURPOSES

INTRODUCTION

Pre-Charities Act 2006

In *Inland Revenue Commissioners v Pemsel*, Lord MacNaghten analysed the charitable purposes as stated in the preamble to the Charitable Uses Act 1601 (see Chapter 15 above) and classified them into four categories, as follows:

(a) the relief of poverty;

(b) the advancement of education;

(c) the advancement of religion;

(d) other purposes beneficial to the community.

Inland Revenue Commissioners v Pemsel [1891] AC 531, HL

Lord MacNaghten: 'Charity', in its legal sense, comprises four principal divisions: trusts for the relief of poverty; trusts for the advancement of education; trusts for the advancement of religion; and trusts for other purposes beneficial to the community, not falling under any of the preceding heads.

This list of purposes, as stated in the preamble, is construed as charitable purposes by virtue of s 38(4) of the Charities Act 1960.

Charities Act 1960, s 38(4)

. . . a reference to charity within the preamble shall be construed as a reference to charity within the UK law.

Background

The Charities Bill 2006, which mirrors the proposals made in the Charities Bill 2004, received Royal assent on 8th November 2006 and is now known as the Charities Act 2006. The Act provides a modern framework for charities and a clear role for the Charity Commission to ensure compliance with charity rules and accountability.

In 2001, the Prime Minister's Strategy Unit commissioned a review of the law and regulation of charities and not-for-profit organisations. The review was carried out and in September 2002 a document entitled, 'Private Action, Public Benefit' was published. This involved an analysis of the strengths and weaknesses of the current legal framework of charities. In July 2003, the Government published a report entitled 'Charities and Not-for-Profits: a Modern Legal Framework', which summarised the results of the Strategy Unit's recommendations. The Charities Act 2006 reflects the majority of these recommendations.

CHARITIES ACT 2006

The Act is a consolidating statute and contains 80 sections and 10 Schedules. It is divided into four Parts. Part 1 deals with the definition of a charity, including the public benefit test. Part 2 deals with the regulation of charities including the objectives, functions and the constitution of the Charity Commission and an amendment regarding schemes that may be applied *cy près*. Part 3 regulates the fundraising activities of charities and Part 4 deals with miscellaneous, incidental matters. This commentary is in respect of Part 1 of the Act.

Charity – its meaning
Section 1(1) of the 2006 Act adopts a general definition of a charity which means 'a body or trust
which:

(a) is established for charitable purposes *only*, and

(b) falls to be subject to the control of the High Court in the exercise of its jurisdiction with respect
to charities.'

This broad definition was discussed in Chapter 15.

Statutory definition of charitable purposes
There has been a great value in the guidance provided by Lord MacNaghten's classification of
charitable trusts in *Pemsel* and the approach of the courts. Despite the general words of the fourth
category (other purposes beneficial to society) on which the vast majority of disputes have
centred, the four heads of charity have created a degree of certainty and predictability regarding
the main characteristics of charitable status. At the same time, the classification of charitable
purposes and approaches of the courts have provided a degree of flexibility that has allowed the
meaning of charity to adapt to the changing needs and expectations of society. However, the four
heads of charity provide little effective guidance to the public about what is a charitable purpose.
The classification of charitable purposes by Lord MacNaghten is a vague indication of some
charitable activities. Charitable purposes extend beyond education, religion and relief of the poor.
Indeed, but for the creative approach of the courts, as evidenced by the multitude of judicial
decisions, the law of charities would have been in a state of disarray. This state of affairs
prompted Lord Sterndale MR in *Re Tetley* to express his dissatisfaction in being unable to find any
guidance as to what constitutes a charitable purpose.

Re Tetley [1923] 1 Ch 258, CA

Lord Sterndale MR: I am unable to find any principle which will guide one easily and safely, through the tangle
of cases as to what is and what is not a charitable gift. If it is possible I hope sincerely that at some time or other a
principle will be laid down.

Section 2 of the Charities Act 2006 addresses some of these limitations by adopting a statutory
definition of 'charitable purposes'. This is achieved by reference to a two-step approach – the
listing or identification of a variety of charitable purposes and the public benefit test. This is the
first ever statutory definition of a charity. Section 2(2) contains a list of 13 charitable purposes – 12
specific descriptions of charitable purposes and a general provision designed to maintain flexibility in the law of charities. The charitable purposes enacted is intended to be a comprehensive list
of charitable activities. Most of these purposes, in any event, were charitable before the Act was
introduced. These purposes are:

(a) the prevention or relief of poverty;

(b) the advancement of education;

(c) the advancement of religion;

(d) the advancement of health [including the prevention or relief of sickness, disease or human
suffering];

(e) the advancement of citizenship or community development;

(f) the advancement of the arts, heritage or science;

(g) the advancement of amateur sport [games which promote health by involving physical or
mental skill or exertion];

(h) the advancement of human rights, conflict resolution or reconciliation;

(i) the advancement of environmental protection or improvement;

(j) the relief of those in need, by reason of youth, age, ill-health, disability, financial hardship or other disadvantage [including the provision of accommodation and care to the beneficiaries mentioned within this clause];

(k)   the advancement of animal welfare;

(l)   the promotion of the efficiency of the armed forces of the Crown, or of the efficiency of the police, fire and rescue services or ambulance services;

(m)   any other purpose within subsection (4).

With the exception of amateur sport, arguably, all of these purposes were charitable under the law that existed before the 2006 Act, as illustrated by the wealth of case law.

Section 2(5) endorses the common law approach to charitable objects by reference to the purposes declared in paragraphs (a) to (l) above. This is done by determining whether a purpose has some resemblance to an example as stated in the preamble, or to an earlier decided case that was considered charitable; the same meaning will be attributable to the term.

Section 2(4) affirms the pre-2006 broad approach to purposes within the fourth heading of the *Pemsel* classification as summarised by Lord Wilberforce in *Scottish Burial Reform and Cremation Society v City of Glasgow Corporation* [1968] AC 138, thus:

> The purposes in question, to be charitable, must be shown to be for the benefit of the public, or the community, in a sense or manner within the intendment of the preamble to the [Charitable Uses Act 1601] . The latter requirement does not mean quite what it says; for *it is now accepted that what must be regarded is not the wording of the preamble itself, but the effect of decisions given by the court as to its scope, decisions which have endeavoured to keep the law as to charities moving according as new social needs arise or old ones become obsolete or satisfied.*

Public benefit

Section 3 of the 2006 Act lays down the second part of the definition of a charity, namely the 'public benefit' test. Section 3(1) stipulates that each of the listed purposes indicated above is required to satisfy the public benefit test. Section 3(2) declares that 'no presumption' will be made to the effect that a purpose satisfies the public benefit test. This subsection has the effect of abolishing the common law approach of presuming that a purpose within the first three heads of Lord Macnaghten's classification in *IRC v Pemsel* [1891] AC 531, has a real and substantial benefit to society. By virtue of this innovation the trustees of an organisation will be required to demonstrate positively that the activity is beneficial to the public, within the judicial test for charities.

Section 3(3) consolidates the case law meaning of public benefit. This involves a two-step test of demonstrating a benefit to society (as mentioned above) and that those eligible to receive benefits must comprise a large enough group to be considered as the public and without a personal or private relationship being used to limit those who may benefit [see Chapter 15].

In summary, the legal re-definition of a charity in terms of classifying the objects into 13 purposes coupled with the statutory test of public benefit, has done little more than to consolidate the law. The courts will continue to adapt the law to keep abreast with the changing needs of society.

The law as set out in the following pages remains unchanged by the Charities Act 2006.

THE RELIEF OF POVERTY

Section 2(2)(a) of the Charities Act 2006 enacts that the 'prevention or relief of poverty' is capable of being a charitable purpose. As stated earlier this description consolidates the common law.

'Poverty' includes destitution, but is not interpreted that narrowly to mean destitution. It connotes that the beneficiaries are in straitened circumstances and unable to maintain a modest standard of living (determined objectively). This expression was described by Lord Evershed in *Re Coulthurst*.

Re Coulthurst's Will Trust [1951] Ch 661, CA

Facts

A testator transferred a fund of £20,000 to his trustees and directed that the income be paid to the widows and orphans of deceased officers and ex-officers of Coutts & Co as the trustees may decide the most deserving of such assistance having regard to their financial circumstances. The question in issue was whether the gift was charitable.

Held

On construction of the terms of the gift, the donation was charitable for the relief of poverty:

> **Lord Evershed MR:** But as was pointed out by Russell J, in *In Re Lucas* [1922] 2 Ch 52, p 58 (quoting from the judgment of Stirling J in *In Re Dudgeon* (1896) 74 LT 613):
>
> > . . . it appears to me that the cases cited on behalf of the charity do show this, that it is not absolutely necessary to find poverty expressed in so many words, but that the court will look at the whole gift, and, if it comes to the conclusion that the relief or poverty was meant, will give effect to it although the word 'poverty' is not to be found in it.
>
> > It is quite clearly established that poverty does not mean destitution; it is a word of wide and somewhat indefinite import; it may not unfairly be paraphrased for present purposes as meaning persons who have to 'go short' in the ordinary acceptation of that term, due regard being had to their status in life, and so forth.
>
> > The persons selected are persons whose financial circumstances are such that they are not only deserving of assistance, that is to say, wanting help, but, of all such, are those who most want it.

Question

What is meant by the expression, 'poverty', in the law of charities?

In addition to satisfying the test of poverty, the gift is required to relieve the misery of poverty by providing the basic necessities of human existence – food, shelter and clothing. The expression, 'relief', signifies that the beneficiaries have a need attributable to their condition that requires alleviating and which the beneficiaries may find difficulty in alleviating from their own resources. Gibson J, in *Joseph Rowntree Memorial Trust Housing Association Ltd v AG* [1983] 1 All ER 288, stated:

> The word 'relief' implies that the persons in question have a need attributable to their condition . . . as poor persons which requires alleviating, and which those persons could not alleviate, or would find difficulty in alleviating themselves from their own resources. The word 'relief' is not synonymous with 'benefit'.

In *Biscoe v Jackson* (1887) 25 Ch D 460 (see p 435 below), a gift to establish a soup kitchen in Shoreditch was construed as a valid charitable trust for the relief of poverty. Likewise, in *Shaw v Halifax Corp* [1915] 2 KB 170, it was decided that a home for ladies in reduced circumstances was charitable. Similarly, in *Re Clarke* [1923] 2 Ch 407, a gift to provide a nursing home for persons of moderate means was charitable.

In *Re Sanders*, however, it was decided that a gift for the 'working classes' does not connote poverty.

In Re Sanders' Will Trusts [1954] 1 Ch 265, Ch D

Facts

A testator by his will transferred one third of his residuary estate to his trustees 'to provide or assist in providing dwellings for the working classes and their families resident in the area of Pembroke Dock, Pembridgeshire, Wales'. The question in issue was whether the gift was charitable for the relief of poverty.

Held

The gift was not charitable because the expression 'working classes' was not synonymous with poverty:

> **Harman J:** It has been pointed out recently by Denning LJ when sitting at first instance, in *HE Green & Sons v Minister of Health (No 2)* [1948] 1 KB 34, p 38, that the expression 'working classes' is an anachronism and does

not really mean anything in these days. 'Much has been said,' said the judge, 'in this case as to the meaning of "working classes" '. These words, 'working classes', have appeared in a number of Acts for the last 100 years. I have no doubt that in former times it had a meaning which was reasonably well understood. 'Working classes,' 50 years ago, denoted a class which included men working in the fields or the factories, in the docks or the mines, on the railway or the roads, at a weekly wage. The wages of people of that class were lower than those of most of the other members of the community, and they were looked upon as a lower class. That has all now disappeared. The social revolution in the last 50 years has made the words 'working classes' quite inappropriate today. There is no such separate class as the working classes. The bank clerk or the civil servant, the school teacher or the cashier, the tradesman or the clergyman, do not earn wages or salaries higher than the mechanic or the electrician, the fitter of the mine worker, the bricklayer or the dock labourer. Nor is there any social distinction between one or the other. No one of them is of a higher or a lower class. In my opinion the words 'working classes' used in the Acts are quite inappropriate to modern social conditions.

On the other hand, a gift for the construction of a 'working men's hostel' was construed as charitable under this head: see *Re Niyazi's Will Trusts*.

Re Niyazi's Will Trusts [1978] 3 All ER 785, HC

Facts

A testator provided that his residuary estate valued at £15,000 should be paid to the mayor of Famagusta, Cyprus to be used for the 'construction of or contribution towards the construction of a working men's hostel'. The question in issue was whether the gift was charitable.

Held

On construction of the will and in view of the grave housing shortage in the area, the gift was charitable for the relief of poverty:

Megarry VC: Certain points seem reasonably plain. First, 'poverty' is not confined to destitution, but extends to those who have small means and so have to 'go short'. Secondly, a gift which in terms is not confined to the relief of poverty may by inference be thus confined. In *Re Lucas* [1922] 2 Ch 52, there was a gift of 5 s per week to the oldest respectable inhabitants of a village. As the law then stood, Russell J was unable to hold that a gift merely to the aged was charitable; but he held that the limitation to 5 s a per week indicated quite clearly that only those to whom such a sum would be of importance and a benefit were to take, and so the gift was charitable as being for the relief of poverty. I do not think that it can be said that nothing save the smallness of the benefit can restrict an otherwise unrestricted benefit so as to confine it within the bounds of charity. I think that anything in the terms of the gift which by implication prevents it from going outside those bounds will suffice. In *In Re Glyn's Will Trusts* [1950] 2 All ER 1150, Danckwerts J held that a trust for building free cottages for old women of the working classes aged 60 or more provided a sufficient context to show an intention to benefit indigent persons, and so was charitable.

I think that the adjectival expression 'working men' plainly has some flavour of 'lower income' about it, just as 'upper class' has some flavour of comfortable means. Of course there are impoverished members of the 'upper' and 'middle' classes, just as there are some 'working men' who are at least of comfortable means, if not affluence: in construing a will I think that I am concerned with the ordinary or general import of words rather than exceptional cases; and, whatever may be the further meaning of 'working men' or 'working class', I think that by 1967 such phrases had not lost their general connotation of 'lower income'. I may add that nobody has suggested that any difficulty arose from the use of 'working men' as distinct from 'working persons' or 'working women'.

The connotation of 'lower income' is, I think, emphasised by the word 'hostel'. The word 'hostel' has to my mind a strong flavour of a building which provides somewhat modest accommodation for those who have some temporary need for it and are willing to accept accommodation of that standard in order to meet the need. When 'hostel' is prefixed by the expression 'working men's', then the further restriction is introduced of this hostel being intended for those with a relatively low income who work for their living, especially as manual workers. It seems to me that the word 'hostel' in this case is significantly different from the word 'dwellings' in *Re Sanders' Will Trusts* [1954] 1 All ER 667, a word which is appropriate to ordinary houses in which the well-to-do may live, as well as the relatively poor.

Has the expression 'working men's hostel' a sufficient connotation of poverty in it to satisfy the requirement of charity? On any footing the case is desperately near the borderline, and I have hesitated in reaching my conclusion. On the whole, however, for the reasons that I have been discussing, I think that the trust is charitable, though by no great margin. This view is in my judgment supported by two further considerations. First, there is the amount of the trust fund, which in 1969 was a little under £15,000. £15,000 will not go very far in such project, and it seems improbable that contributions from other sources towards constructing a 'working men's hostel' would enable or encourage the construction of any grandiose building.

The other consideration is that of the state of housing in Famagusta. I think that a trust to erect a hostel in a slum or in an area of acute housing need may have to be construed differently from a trust to erect a hostel in an area of housing affluence or plenty. Where there is a grave housing shortage, it is plain that the poor are likely to suffer more than the prosperous, and that the provision of a 'working men's hostel' is likely to help the poor and not the rich.

In the result, then, I hold that the trust is charitable.

Question
How may *Re Niyazi's Will Trusts* be reconciled with *Re Sanders' Will Trusts*?

Under this head, it is essential that all the objects fall within the designation 'poor'. If someone who is not poor is able to benefit from the funds, the gift will fail as not being one for the relief of poverty: see *Re Gwyon*.

In Re Gwyon, Public Trustee v AG [1930] 1 Ch 255, HC

Facts
A testator transferred his residuary estate to his executor upon trust to establish the 'Gwyon's Boys Clothing Foundation'. The details were specified in the will. The income from the fund was required to be used to provide 'knickers' for boys of Farnham aged between 10 and 15, subject to a number of qualifications. No preference was given to boys from poor parents. Indeed, boys maintained by charitable institutions or whose parents were in receipt of poor relief were expressly excluded. The executors applied to the court to consider whether the gift was charitable on the ground of relief of poverty.

Held
The gift was not charitable for there was no element of relief of poverty:

> **Eve J:** None of these conditions necessarily import poverty nor could the recipients be accurately described as a class of aged, impotent or poor persons. I think that according to the true construction of these testamentary documents the benevolence of the testator was intended for all eligible boys other than paupers, and I cannot spell out of them any indication which would justify the Foundation Trustees refusing an applicant otherwise eligible on the ground that his material circumstances were of too affluent a character. In these circumstances I cannot hold this trust to be within the description of a legal charitable trust.

A charitable trust for the relief of poverty may be achieved directly or indirectly. Relief may be provided directly for the intended beneficiaries and includes apprenticing poor children, see *AG v Minshull* (1798) 4 Ves 11; the provision of allotments or buying land to be let to the poor at a low rent, see *Crafton v Firth* (1851) 4 De G & Sm 237; the provision of cheap flats to be let to aged persons of small means at rents that they can afford to pay, *Re Cottam* [1955] 1 WLR 1299; gifts for the establishment or support of institutions for the benefit of particular classes of poor persons such as railway servants, see *Hull v Derby Sanitary Authority* (1885) 16 QBD 163; policemen, see *Re Douglas* (1887) 35 Ch D 472. Relief may be provided indirectly such as providing accommodation for relatives coming from a distance to visit patients critically ill in hospital, see *Re Dean's Will Trust* [1950] 1 All ER 882; a home of rest for nurses at a particular hospital, see *Re White's Will Trust* [1951] 1 All ER 528

THE ADVANCEMENT OF EDUCATION

Section 2(2)(b) of the Charities Act 2006 also describes the advancement of education as a charitable purpose.

This classification originates from the preamble to the Charitable Uses Act 1601, which refers to 'the maintenance of ... schools of learning, free schools and scholars of universities'. The phrase 'advancement of education' has been said to extend to 'the improvement of a useful branch of knowledge and its public dissemination', per Buckley LJ in *ICLR v AG* [1972] 1 Ch 73. Education has been interpreted generously and is not restricted to the classroom mode of disseminating knowledge, but requires some element of instruction or supervision. Thus, research is capable of being construed as the provision of education: see *Re Hopkin's Will Trust*.

Re Hopkin's Will Trust [1964] 3 All ER 46, HC

Facts

Money was bequeathed to the Francis Bacon Society to be used to search for the manuscripts of plays commonly ascribed to Shakespeare but believed by the society to have been written by Bacon.

Held

The gift was for the advancement of education. The discovery of such manuscripts would be of the highest value to history and literature:

> **Wilberforce J:** It would seem to me that a bequest for the purpose of search, or research, for the original manuscripts of England's greatest dramatist (whoever he was) would be well within the law's conception of charitable purposes. The discovery of such manuscript, or of one such manuscripts, would be of the highest value to history and to literature.
>
> I think, therefore, that the word 'education' as used by Harman J, in *Re Shaw* [1957] 1 All ER 745, must be used in a wide sense, certainly extending beyond teaching, and that the requirement is that, in order to be charitable, research must either be of educational value to the researcher or must be so directed as to lead to something which will pass into the store of educational material, or so as to improve the sum of communicable knowledge in an area which education may cover – education in this last context extending to the formation of literary taste and appreciation (compare *Royal Choral Society v IRC* [1943] 2 All ER 101). Whether or not the test is wider than this, it is, as I have stated it, amply wide enough to include the purpose of the gift in this case.

More recently, in *McGovern v AG* [1981] 3 All ER 493 (see p 414 below), Slade J summarised the principles concerning research as a charitable purpose for the advancement of education, thus:

(i) A trust for research will ordinarily qualify as a charitable trust if, but only if (a) the subject matter of the proposed research is a useful object of study; and (b) it is contemplated that the knowledge acquired as a result of the research will be disseminated to others; and (c) the trust is for the benefit of the public, or a sufficiently important section of the public.

(ii) In the absence of a contrary context, however, the court will be readily inclined to construe a trust for research as importing subsequent dissemination of the results thereof.

(iii) Furthermore, if a trust for research is to constitute a valid trust for the advancement of education, it is not necessary either (a) that the teacher/pupil relationship should be in contemplation, or (b) that the persons to benefit from the knowledge to be acquired should be persons who are already in the course of receiving 'education' in the conventional sense.

(iv) In any case where the court has to determine whether a bequest for the purposes of research is or is not of a charitable nature, it must pay due regard to any admissible extrinsic evidence which is available to explain the wording of the will in question or the circumstances in which it was made.

'Education' is not restricted to education in academic subjects in a school or University but includes the promotion of education and the giving of instruction in a wide range of subjects such as Christian knowledge (*AG v Stepney* (1804) 10 Ves 22), psychological healing (*Re Osmund* [1944] Ch 206). On the other hand, the mere acquisition of knowledge without dissemination or advancement will not be charitable: see *Re Shaw*.

Re Shaw, Public Trustee v Day [1957] 1 All ER 745, HC

Facts

The testator, George Bernard Shaw, bequeathed money to be used to develop a 40-letter alphabet and translate his play, *Androcles and the Lion*, into this alphabet.

Held

The gift was not charitable as it was aimed merely at the increase of knowledge. In addition, the gift was political in the sense of attempting to cause a change in the law:

> **Harman J:** The research and propaganda enjoined by the testator seem to me merely to tend to the increase of public knowledge in a certain respect, namely, the saving of time and money by the use of the proposed alphabet. There is no element of teaching or education combined with this, nor does the propaganda element in the trusts tend to more than to persuade the public that the adoption of the new script would be 'a good thing', and that, in my view, is not education. Therefore I reject this element.
>
> There remains the fourth category.
>
> The testator is convinced, and sets out to convince the world, but the fact that he considers the proposed reform to be beneficial does not make it so any more than the fact that he describes the trust as charitable constrains the court to hold that it is.
>
> A case on a parallel subject, spelling reform, came before Rowlatt J, on an income tax point. That is *Trustees of the Sir GB Hunter (1922) 'C' Trust v IRC* (1929) 14 TC 427. The headnote reads:
>
> > The trust deed provided that the net income and, after a period of years, the capital, of the trust should be paid or applied to the benefit of the Simplified Spelling Society or in certain circumstances, as to which the trustees had wide discretionary powers, to the benefit of or to promote the formation of any other society or association having similar objects. The objects of the society were to recommend and to further the general use of simpler spellings of English words than those now in use. It engaged in propaganda to influence public opinion in favour of its objects and to gain for them the approval of education authorities. The appellants claimed that the purposes for which the society was established were charitable either as being educational or as being beneficial to the community. Held that the trust was not established for charitable purposes.
>
> > The objects of this society or any other society which would benefit under this trust is simply to make spelling more simple. Everyone would agree up to a point that it is probably advantageous. Probably, as you go on, you will get differences of opinion; but, right or wrong, the question is whether that is a charitable object. You have people trying to promote the simplification of spelling, or the simplification of grammar, or the uniformity of pronouncing, or the simplification of dress, or the simplification or reform of any of the conveniences of life. But in my judgment they are nowhere near either of the express categories mentioned by Lord MacNaghten in the well known judgment, *Income Tax Special Purposes Commissioners v Pemsel* [1891] AC 531, or within the classes of cases which come within the general classes in the Act. I think that this case is hardly arguable.
>
> Such words of such a judge must have great weight with me. It seems to me that the objects of the alphabet trusts are analogous to trusts for political purposes, which advocate a change in the law. Such objects have never been considered charitable.
>
> I, therefore, do not reach the further inquiry whether the benefit is one within the spirit or intendment (as it is called) of the Statute of Elizabeth (43 Eliz, c 4), but, if I had to decide that point, I should hold that it was not.

Gifts for the advancement of education generally are charitable, e.g. gifts 'for the benefit, advancement and propagation of education and learning in every part of the world' (*Whicker v Hume* (1858) 7 HL Cases 124). Gifts which have been upheld as charitable under this head have included trusts for choral singing in London (*Royal Choral Society v Inland Revenue Commissioners* [1943] 2 All ER 101); the diffusion of knowledge of Egyptology and the training of students in Egyptology (*Re British School of Egyptian Archaeology* [1954] 1 All ER 887); the encouragement of chess playing by boys or young men resident in the city of Portsmouth (*Re Dupree's Trusts* [1944] 2 All ER 443); the furtherance of the Boy Scout Movement by helping to purchase sites for camping (*Re Webber* [1954] 1 WLR 1500); the promotion of the education of the Irish by teaching self-control, elocution, oratory deportment, the arts of personal contact or social intercourse

(*Re Shaw's Will Trust* [1952] 1 All ER 712); the publication of law reports which record the development of judge made law (*Incorporated Council of Law Reporting for England and Wales v AG* [1972] Ch 73); the promotion of the works of a famous composer (*Re Delius' Will Trust* [1957] 1 All ER 854) or celebrated writer (*Re Shakespeare Memorial Trust* [1923] 2 Ch 389); the students' union of a university (*Baldry v Feintuck* [1972] 2 All ER 81); the furtherance of the Wilton Park project, that is, a conference centre for discussion of matters of international importance (*Re Koeppler's Will Trust* [1986] Ch 423); the provision of facilities at schools and universities to play association football or other games (*Inland Revenue Commissioners v McMullen* [1981] AC 1); professional bodies which exist for the promotion of the arts or sciences (*Royal College of Surgeons of England v National Provincial Bank Ltd* [1952] 1 All ER 984).

Evaluation

Before deciding whether the gifts are charitable or not, the courts are required to take into account the usefulness of the gifts to the public. This may be effected by judicial notice of the value of the gift to society. In the event of doubt, the courts may take into account the opinions of experts. The opinions of the donors are inconclusive: see *Re Pinion*.

Re Pinion [1965] 1 Ch 85, CA

Facts

Gifts of a studio and contents, to be maintained as a collection, were made to the National Trust. The National Trust refused to accept the donation as a collection, although it was willing to accept selected items as valuable for display. The question in issue was whether the gifts were valuable as a collection.

Held

After due consideration of the expert evidence, the court decided that the donation failed as a charity. The collection as a whole lacked any artistic merit. Harman LJ could conceive of no useful purpose in 'foisting upon the public this mass of junk':

> **Harman LJ:** Where a museum is concerned and the utility of the gift is brought in question it is, in my opinion, and herein I agree with the judge, essential to know at least something of the quality of the proposed exhibits in order to judge whether they will be conducive to the education of the public. There is a strong body of evidence here that as a means of education this collection is worthless. The testator's own paintings, of which there are over 50, are said by competent persons to be in an academic style and 'atrociously bad' and the other picture without exception worthless. Even the so called 'Lely' turns out to be a 20th century copy.
>
> The most that skilful cross-examination extracted from the expert witnesses was that there were a dozen chairs which might perhaps be acceptable to a minor provincial museum and perhaps another dozen not altogether worthless, but two dozen chairs do not make a museum and they must, to accord with the will, be exhibited stifled by a large number of absolutely worthless pictures and objects.
>
> I can conceive of no useful object to be served in foisting upon the public this mass of junk. It has neither public utility nor educative value. I would hold that the testator's project ought not to be carried into effect and that his next of kin is entitled to the residue of his estate.

The promotion of education of a political nature will be subject to process of construction by the courts to ascertain the primary purpose of the gift. If the main object is political the gift will fail as a charity. But if the political element is subsidiary to the main political objective the gift will be valid.

In *Buxton v Public Trustee* (1962) TC 235, the trust was to promote and aid the improvement of international relations and intercourse by various prescribed methods. The court held that the trust was not charitable because its objects were 'public utility or political'. Whereas, in *Re Koeppler's Will Trust* [1986] Ch 423 the gift created a valid charitable trust. In this case the gift was to create 'Wilton Park', i.e. a conference centre for participants who were capable of influencing opinion in Member States of the Organisation for Economic Co-operation and Development. The court decided that, on construction of the objects of the centre, there was no question of the conferences being intended to further the interests of political parties, or to procure changes in the law or government policy of any country. Even when the conferences touched on political issues they constituted no more than genuine attempts to ascertain and disseminate the truth.

Question

What is meant by the 'advancement of education' in the law of charities?

THE ADVANCEMENT OF RELIGION

This purpose has been endorsed in s 2(2)(c) of the Charities Act 2006 and clarifies the common law with regard to polytheistc religions and religions that do not involve belief in God.

The preamble to the Charitable Uses Act 1601 refers to 'the repair of . . . churches'. English law steers a neutral course between all forms of religions. 'Religion' is defined in the *Oxford Dictionary* as a 'recognition on the part of man of some higher unseen power as having control of his destiny and as being entitled to obedience, reverence and worship' or 'a particular system of faith and worship'. There is not a great deal of judicial authority recognising non-Christian religions (although Judaism has been recognised in *Strauss v Goldsmith* (1857) 8 Sim 614 and *Neville Estates v Madden* [1962] Ch 832 (see p 383 above)), but regulations made under the Charities Act 1993 assume that non-Christian religions are charitable. Section 2(3)(a) of the Charities Act 2006 defines religion as including 'a religion which involves belief in more than one god and a religion which does not involve belief in god'. This would include a polytheistic religion such as Hinduism. Buddhism, which does not involve a belief in God, is universally regarded as a religion and will now be treated as a religion under the English law of charities. On the other hand, in *Re South Place Ethical Society* [1980] 1 WLR 1565, it was decided that the study and dissemination of ethical principles, but which did not involve faith in a deity, could not constitute religion, although the society was charitable on the ground of advancement of education.

Re South Place Ethical Society [1980] 1 WLR 1565, HC

Dillon J: 'Religion,' as I see it, is concerned with man's relations with God and 'ethics' is concerned with man's relation with man. The two are not the same and are not made the same by sincere inquiry into the question: What is God? If reason leads people not to accept Christianity or any known religion, but they do believe in the excellence of qualities such as truth, beauty and love, their beliefs may be to them the equivalent of a religion but viewed objectively they are not religion.

Similarly, a body, such as the Freemason's Society, whose rules demand the highest personal and social standards does not constitute a religion (see *United Grand Lodge of Freemasons in England and Wales v Holborn BC* [1957] 1 WLR 1090). With similar effect in principle, a trust to promote atheism or to demonstrate that religious belief is erroneous will not be charitable under this head.

Unlike trusts for the advancement of education, the courts do not evaluate the merit of one religion as opposed to another, or indeed the benefit to the public of religious instruction. Provided that the religious gift is not subversive of all morality, the gift will be charitable: see *Thornton v Howe*.

Thornton v Howe (1862) 31 Beav 14

Facts

A trust was created for the publication of the writings of Joanna Southcote, who believed that she would miraculously conceive and give birth, at an advanced age, to the second Messiah. The question in issue was whether the publication was charitable for the advancement of religion.

Held

The gift was charitable even though Romilly MR was of the opinion that the tenets of this faith were 'foolish, deluded and confused'.

Similarly, in *Re Watson*, the court decided that a gift to publish the religious works of Hobbs (which had no intrinsic value) was charitable.

Re Watson (Decd), Hobbs v Smith and Others [1973] 3 All ER 678, HC

Plowman J: Now the result of the cases, including the *Anti-Vivisection* case [1948] AC 31 to which counsel for the next of kin referred, in my judgment, is this. First of all, as Romilly MR said in *Thornton v Howe* (1862) 31 Beav 14, the court does not prefer one religion to another and it does not prefer one sect to another. Secondly, where the purposes in question are of a religious nature – and, in my opinion, they clearly are here – then the court assumes a public benefit unless the contrary is shown.

And thirdly, that having regard to the fact that the court does not draw a distinction between one religion and another or one sect and another, the only way of disproving a public benefit is to show, in the words of Romilly MR in *Thornton v Howe*, that the doctrines inculcated are – 'adverse to the very foundations of all religion, and that they are subversive of all morality', and that in my judgment, as I have said already, is clearly not the case here, and I therefore conclude that this case is really on all fours with *Thornton v Howe* and for that reason is a valid charitable trust.

Meaning of advancement of religion

The institution or association concerned is required to promote or advance religion. This was considered by Donovan J in *United Grand Lodge of Freemasons in England and Wales v Holborn BC*.

United Grand Lodge of Freemasons in England and Wales v Holborn BC [1957] 1 WLR 1090, HC

Donovan J: To advance religion means to promote it, to spread its message ever wider among mankind; to take some positive steps to sustain and increase religious belief; and these things are done in a variety of ways which may be comprehensively described as pastoral and missionary. It should include religious instruction, a programme for the persuasion of unbelievers, religious supervision to see that its members remain active and constant in the various religions they may profess.

Religion may be advanced in a variety of ways, such as the maintenance of places of worship, including the upkeep of churchyards, gifts for the clergy, the provision of an organ or maintenance of a choir, and the active spread of religion at home and abroad. However, a gift for 'parish work' will be void as including many objects which are not charitable: see *Farley v Westminster Bank*.

Farley and Others v Westminster Bank Ltd and Others, Re Ashton's Estate, Westminster Bank Ltd v Farley [1939] 3 All ER 491, HL

The facts appear in the judgment of Lord Atkin.

Lord Atkin: The question is, what is the meaning of the words 'the vicar and churchwardens of St Columba's Church, Hoxton (for parish work)'? 'Parish work' seems to me to be of such vague import as to go far beyond the ordinary meaning of charity, in this case in the sense of being a religious purpose. The expression covers the whole of the ordinary activities of the parish, some of which no doubt fall within the definition of religious purposes, and all of which no doubt are religious from the point of view of the person who is responsible for the spiritual care of the parish, in the sense that they are conducive, perhaps, to the moral and spiritual good of his congregation. However, that, I think, quite plainly is not enough, and the words are so wide that I am afraid that on no construction can they be brought within the limited meaning of 'charitable' as used in the law.

A gift to an officer of the church in his official capacity (the vicar) to be applied in his absolute discretion may be construed as imposing an implied limitation on the transferee's discretion, namely, use for ecclesiastical (or official) purposes: see *Re Garrard*.

Re Garrard [1907] I Ch 382, HC

Facts

A testatrix bequeathed £400 'to the vicar and churchwardens for the time being of Kington, to be applied by them in such manner as they in their sole discretion think fit'.

Held

On construction, the gift was charitable for the advancement of religion:

> **Joyce J:** The churchwardens are the officers of the parish in ecclesiastical matters, so that a mere gift or legacy to the vicar and churchwardens for the time being of a parish, without more, is a gift or charitable legacy to them for ecclesiastical purposes in the parish. It was suggested that the words in the latter part of the gift were inconsistent with its being a charitable gift, and that they implied that the vicar and churchwardens were to take beneficially. In my opinion there is no contradiction or inconsistency in the will whatever. The words 'to be applied by them in such manner as they shall in their sole discretion think fit', to my mind merely direct that the particular mode of application within the charitable purposes of the legacy is to be settled by those individuals, or rather that there is power given to them to do it, subject always, of course, to the jurisdiction of the court. Therefore, I declare this to be a good charitable legacy for the benefit of the parish of Kington for ecclesiastical purposes.

Saying of masses

A gift for the saying of masses in public is charitable because the gift promotes an integral part of religion, namely, the saying of prayers. Such prayers, although incapable *per se* of proving beneficial to mankind, are assumed to provide a sufficient element of public benefit. The *prima facie* assumption that is made is that prayers stipulated by a settlor in a will or an *inter vivos* instrument are assumed to be said in public: see *Re Caus*.

Re Caus [1934] Ch 162, HC

Facts

A testator, a Roman Catholic priest, by his will bequeathed £1,000 'for masses to be said for my soul and the souls of my parents and relatives ... with a reversion to the parish of St Peter's Roman Catholic Church'. The question in issue was the validity of this gift as charitable.

Held

The gift was charitable for the advancement of religion on the grounds that:

(a) prayers provided a ritual act central to the religion of a large proportion of Christian people; and

(b) the donation assisted in the upkeep of priests whose duties involved performance of the acts.

Note

However, the court failed to draw a distinction between public and private masses and the predominant nexus between the donor and the purpose of the gift.

In *Re Hetherington*, the High Court found support in *Gilmour v Coats* (see p 382 above) which enabled it to limit the effect of *Re Caus*. Accordingly, the latter decision is no longer good law to the extent that it condoned the saying of masses in private as a charitable purpose.

Re Hetherington [1989] 2 All ER 129, HC

Facts

By her will, a testatrix bequeathed £2,000 to the Roman Catholic Bishop of Westminster for the saying of 'masses for the souls of my husband, parents, sisters and myself'. The issue concerned the validity of the gift.

Held

The legacy was donated for the advancement of religion:

Browne-Wilkinson J: In my judgment *Gilmour v Coats* [1949] AC 426 does not impair the validity of the decision in *In Re Caus* [1934] Ch 162. Certainly, the judgment of Luxmoore J which suggests that public benefit can be shown from the mere celebration of a religious rite is no longer good law. The same in my judgment is true of Luxmoore J's first ground of decision, if it suggests that the performance in private of a religious ritual act is charitable as being for the public benefit. But in my judgment there is nothing in the House of Lords' decision which impugns Luxmoore J's second ground of decision, namely that the public benefit was to be found in the endowment of the priesthood. Therefore, the decision in *In Re Caus* is still good law and I must follow it.

The grounds on which the trust in the present case can be attacked are that there is no express requirement that the Masses for souls which are to be celebrated are to be celebrated in public. The evidence shows that celebration in public is the invariable practice but there is no requirement of Canon law to that effect. Therefore, it is said the money could be applied to saying Masses in private which would not be charitable since there would be no sufficient element of public benefit.

In my judgment the cases establish the following propositions:

(1) A trust for the advancement of education, the relief of poverty or the advancement of religion is *prima facie* charitable and assumed to be for the public benefit. *National Anti-Vivisection Society v IRC* [1948] AC 31, pp 42, 65. This assumption of public benefit can be rebutted by showing that in fact the particular trust in question cannot operate so as to confer a legally recognised benefit on the public, as in *Gilmour v Coats* [1949] AC 426.

(2) The celebration of a religious rite in public does confer a sufficient public benefit because of the edifying and improving effect of such celebration on the members of the public who attend. As Lord Reid said in *Gilmour v Coats ibid*, p 459:

A religion can be regarded as beneficial without it being necessary to assume that all its beliefs are true, and a religious service can be regarded as beneficial to all those who attend it without it being necessary to determine the spiritual efficacy of that service or to accept any particular belief about it.

(3) The celebration of a religious rite in private does not contain the necessary element of public benefit since any benefit by prayer or example is incapable of proof in the legal sense, and any element of edification is limited to a private, not public, class of those present at the celebration: see *Gilmour v Coats; Yeap Cheah Neo v Ong Cheng Neo* (1875) LR 6 PC 381 and *Hoare v Hoare* (1886) 56 LT 147. Where there is a gift for a religious purpose which could be carried out in a way which is beneficial to the public (that is, by public Masses) but could also be carried out in a way which would not have sufficient element of public benefit (that is, by private Masses) the gift is to be construed as a gift to be carried out only by the methods that are charitable, all non-charitable methods being excluded: see *In Re White* [1893] 2 Ch 41, pp 52–53; and *In Re Banfield* [1968] 1 WLR 846.

Applying those principles to the present case, a gift for the saying of Masses is *prima facie* charitable, being for a religious purpose. In practice, those Masses will be celebrated in public which provides a sufficient element of public benefit. The provision of stipends for priests saying the Masses, by relieving the Roman Catholic Church *pro tanto* of the liability to provide such stipends, is a further benefit. The gift is to be construed as a gift for public Masses only on the principle of *In Re White*, private Masses not being permissible since it would not be a charitable application of the fund for a religious purpose.

[Declaration made.]

Question

To what extent is *Re Caus* still good law?

More recently, in *Funnell v Stewart*, the court decided that the promotion of faith healing, within limits, was a charitable activity, either for the advancement of religion, or for purposes beneficial to the community.

Funnell v Stewart [1996] 1 WLR 288, HC

Facts

Prior to her death, the testatrix had been involved with a small religious and healing movement centred at her home at 139 Hoadswood Road, Hastings. The movement had been operating for at least 30 years. The healing process involved the laying on of hands by those with a healing gift and the saying of prayers. The activities of the group fell into two categories: healing sessions and religious services. The spiritual healing sessions were available to the public, but only a quarter of the religious services were open to the public.

The testatrix, by her will, left her residuary estate, including the house in Hoadswood Road, to Mrs Stewart and Mrs Austen, subject to the following declaration, 'and I direct that they shall use the same ... to further the spiritual work carried on by us together ... for so long as the law permits'. The residuary estate was worth £150,000. The executors issued an originating summons against the two trustees and the next of kin, inquiring whether the gift by will created a valid charitable trust or was invalid as being a non-charitable purpose trust.

Held

Judge Hazel Williamson QC decided that a gift to further faith healing was a valid charitable gift for purposes beneficial to the community and also for the advancement of religion. The private element in the religious services was, on the evidence, clearly ancillary to the public faith healing aspect of the group's work and did not disqualify it from being charitable:

> **Williamson QC:** The 'work' to which persons are referring carries the connotation of doing something for others, doing good to others outside the movement. As regards the exclusivity point, the testatrix herself would have regarded the private services as an integral part of this general work. In the light of my view of the essence of the work of the group, I find that this private element was clearly ancillary or subsidiary to the public faith healing part of the group's work, which was its predominant function. If one had asked what was the *raison d'être* of this group, it seems to me that the answer that would have been given was clearly the spiritual healing work it did for members of the community. It follows that, in my judgment, the testatrix's gift for the furtherance of this spiritual work is not prevented from being charitable by reason of the inclusion of the possibility that private services, which could clearly not themselves be charitable, might be held as part of such total activity. The only question left is, therefore, whether this spiritual healing work itself, in the form of the faith healing part of the group's work, which I find to be the substance of the group's work, is indeed charitable. On this point I have again come to the conclusion that Mr Henderson is right. I accept his argument that it is charitable, and I so hold either on the basis that faith healing has, by the present time (although this would not necessarily have been the case when In Re Hummeltenberg, Beatty v London Spiritualistic Alliance Ltd [1923] 1 Ch 237 was decided), become a recognised activity of public benefit or, in any event, on the basis that the religious element in the present case, and the religious nature of the faith healing movement in question, renders this work a charitable purpose within which a sufficient element of public benefit is assumed so as to enable the charity to be recognised by law as being such unless there is contrary evidence. There is no such contrary evidence. Accordingly, I find that this is a charitable trust. It follows that it is unnecessary for me to consider the question whether the evidence of actual public benefit in the form of the demonstrable efficaciousness of the healing work of the group is actually required.

OTHER PURPOSES BENEFICIAL TO THE COMMUNITY

The preamble to the Charitable Uses Act 1601 refers to a list of miscellaneous purposes which are charitable. The approach of the courts to novel purposes capable of being decided under this head has already been mentioned (see Chapter 15). It does not follow that every purpose which is beneficial to the community will be charitable. Thus, a gift for 'charitable or benevolent purposes' is not charitable (see *Chichester Diocesan Fund v Simpson* [1944] AC 341). In order to establish that a purpose is charitable under this head, it must be shown that the purpose is beneficial to the community in a way that the law considers charitable, that is, the purpose is within the spirit and intendment of the preamble (*per* Viscount Cave LC in *AG v National Provincial and Union Bank of England*).

AG v National Provincial and Union Bank of England [1924] AC 262, HL

Viscount Cave LC: Lord Macnaghten did not mean that all trusts for purposes beneficial to the community are charitable, but that there are certain beneficial trusts which fall within that category; and accordingly, to argue that because a trust is for a purpose beneficial to the community, it is therefore a charitable trust, is to turn his sentence round and to give it a different meaning . . . it is not enough to say that the trust in question is for public purposes beneficial to the community, or for the public welfare; you must also show that it is a charitable trust.

Section 2(2) (m) of the Charities Act 2006 creates a general residual class of charitable purposes similar to the miscellaneous charitable purposes recognized by the courts before the Act. In addition, the court has the power to identify new charitable purposes as the need arises, i.e. purposes not listed specifically in s 2(2)(a) to (l).

Charities Act 2006, s 2(2)(m) and s2(4)

Section 2(2) A purpose falls within this subsection if it falls within any of the following descriptions of purposes–

   (m) Any other purpose within subsection (4)

(4) The purposes within this subsection (see subsection (2)(m) are–

   (a) any purposes not within paragraphs (a) to (l) of subsection (2) but recognized as charitable purposes under existing charity law or by virtue of section 1 of the Recreational Charities Act 1958;

   (b) any purposes that may reasonably be regarded as analogous to, or within the spirit of, any purposes falling within any of those paragraphs or paragraph (a) above; and

   (c) any purposes that may reasonably be regarded as analogous to, or within the spirit of, any purposes which have been recognized under charity law as falling within paragraph (b) above or this paragraph.

The effect of this provision is that the wealth of case law that existed before the 2006 Act is relevant in identifying miscellaneous charitable purposes.

Illustrations of charitable purposes under this head

The following illustrations of charitable purposes under the fourth heading of Lord Macnaghten's classification of charities in *Inland Revenue Commissioners v Pemsel* (or s 2(2)(m) of the 2006 Act) indicate how wide-ranging such purposes are.

Animals

A trust that promotes the welfare of animals generally, or even a species of animals (as opposed to benefiting specific animals), is a valid charitable trust because it is calculated to promote public morality by checking an inborn tendency in humans towards cruelty. Today, the advancement of animal welfare is a stated charitable purpose within s 2(2)(k) of the Charities Act 2006. The common law approach to this head contains a useful guide as to the interpretation of this subsection.

In *In Re Wedgwood*, a trust for the protection and benefit of animals was treated as a charitable purpose at common law.

In Re Wedgwood, Allen v Wedgwood [1915] 1 Ch 113, CA

Facts

A testatrix by her will gave the residue of her estate to the defendant, Cecil Wedgwood, on a secret trust. It transpired that Mr Wedgwood had agreed with the testatrix to hold the property upon trust for the protection and benefit of animals.

Held

A charitable trust was created for the benefit of animals on the ground that the gift promoted public morality by checking an inborn tendency towards cruelty:

> **Lord Cozens-Hardy MR:** In my opinion it is not possible for us to hold that this trust for the protection of animals is not a good charitable purpose. Apart from authorities which are binding upon us, I should be prepared to support the trust on the ground that it tends to promote public morality by checking the innate tendency to cruelty. In the language of Holmes LJ in *In Re Cranston* [1898] 1 IR 457:

... gifts the object of which is to prevent cruelty to animals and to ameliorate the position of the brute creation are charitable ... If it is beneficial to the community to promote virtue and to discourage vice, it must be beneficial to teach the duty of justice and fair treatment to the brute creation, and to repress one of the most revolting kinds of cruelty.

I desire also to mention the judgment of Chatterton VC in *Armstrong v Reeves* (1890) 25 LR IR 325, especially the passage at p 341, where he points out that objects of general mercy to animals of all kinds, whether useful to man or not, are charitable.

Note
Similarly, in *University of London v Yarrow* (1857) 1 De G & J 72, a hospital for sick animals was charitable. *In Re Moss* [1949] 1 All ER 495, a home for unwanted or stray cats was charitable.

It is essential to establish that the welfare of the animals provides some benefit to mankind, albeit indirect. Failure to establish such benefit was fatal in *Re Grove-Grady*.

Re Grove-Grady [1929] I Ch 557, CA

Facts
A gift was made to set up an animal sanctuary (game reserve) where all animals were allowed to live free from 'molestation or destruction by man'. The question in issue was whether the gift was charitable or not.

Held
The gift was not charitable because there were no safeguards against the destruction of the weaker animals by the stronger:

Russell LJ: It is merely a trust to secure that all animals within the area shall be free from molestation or destruction by man. It is not a trust directed to ensure absence or diminution of pain or cruelty in the destruction of animal life. If this trust is carried out according to its tenor, no animal within the area may be destroyed by man no matter how necessary that destruction may be in the interests of mankind or in the interests of the other denizens of the area or in the interests of the animal itself; and no matter how painlessly such destruction may be brought about. It seems to be impossible to say that the carrying out of such a trust necessarily involves benefit to the public. Consistently with the trust the public could be excluded from entering the area or even looking into it. All that the public need know about the matter would be that one or more areas existed in which all animals were allowed to live free from any risk of being molested or killed by man, though liable to be molested and killed by other denizens of the area. For myself, I feel quite unable to say that any benefit to the community will necessarily result from applying the trust fund to the purposes indicated in the first object.

If then benefit to the community as a necessary result of the execution of the trust is essential, this trust is not charitable. It is well settled that if consistently with the trust the funds may be applied for a purpose not charitable, the trust will fail for perpetuity notwithstanding that the funds might under the trust have been applied for purposes strictly charitable.

Moreover, when the welfare of animals (anti-vivisection) conflicts with the interests of mankind (scientific research), the latter prevails and the animal welfare body will not be charitable. Such an organisation does not promote a public benefit owing to its detrimental effect on medical science and research: see *National Anti-Vivisection Society v Inland Revenue Commissioners*.

National Anti-Vivisection Society v Inland Revenue Commissioners [1948] AC 31, HL

Facts
The society claimed exemption from income tax on the ground that its purposes (*inter alia*, the total suppression of vivisection) were charitable.

Held
The society's purposes were not charitable for its purposes were detrimental to medical science and research. In addition, one its main objects was political in advocating a change in the law. The House of Lords overruled *Re Foveaux* [1895] 2 Ch 501:

Lord Simonds: Here the finding of the commissioners is itself conclusive. 'We are satisfied,' they say, 'that the main object of the society is the total abolition of vivisection ... and (for that purpose) the repeal of the Cruelty to Animals Act 1876, and the substitution of a new enactment prohibiting vivisection altogether'. This is a finding that the main purpose of the society is the compulsory abolition of vivisection by Act of Parliament. What else can it mean? And how else can it be supposed that vivisection is to be abolished? Abolition and suppression are words that connote some form of compulsion. It can only be by Act of Parliament that that element can be supplied.

Tyssen on Charitable Bequests, 1st edn, 1898: the passage which is at p 176, is worth repeating at length:

> It is a common practice for a number of individuals amongst us to form an association for the purpose of promoting some change in the law, and it is worth our while to consider the effect of a gift to such an association. It is clear that such an association is not of a charitable nature. However desirable the change may really be, the law could not stultify itself by holding that it was for the public benefit that the law is right as it stands. On the other hand, such a gift could not be held void for illegality.

I would rather say that, when a purpose appears broadly to fall within one of the familiar categories of charity, the court will assume it to be for the benefit of the community and, therefore, charitable, unless the contrary is shown, and further that the court will not be astute in such a case to defeat on doubtful evidence the avowed benevolent intention of the donor. But, my Lords, the next step is one that I cannot take. Where on the evidence before it the court concludes that, however well intentioned the donor, the achievement of his object will be greatly to the public disadvantage, there can be no justification for saying that it is a charitable object. If and so far as there is any judicial decision to the contrary, it must, in my opinion, be regarded as inconsistent with principle and be overruled.

The distinction between a political association and a charitable trust has not been defined and I doubt whether it admits of precise definition. The Attorney General however submitted that any association which included among its objects the passing by Parliament any legislation, unless it were an uncontroversial enabling Act, was to be considered a political association, and must be refused the privileges which the law allows to charities. But no authority was cited which would warrant so extreme a proposition.

I conclude upon this part of the case that a main object of the society is not established for charitable purposes only.

The relief of the aged and impotent

The preamble to the 1601 Act specifically refers to 'The relief of aged, impotent and poor people'. The words have been construed disjunctively. Accordingly, the objects need not qualify on all three grounds: see *Joseph Rowntree Memorial Trust v AG*.

Joseph Rowntree Memorial Trust Housing Association v AG [1983] 1 All ER 288, HC

Peter Gibson J: The first set of charitable purposes contained in the preamble is 'the relief of aged, impotent and poor people'. Looking at those words, I would have thought that two inferences were tolerably clear. First, the words must be read disjunctively. It would be absurd to require that the aged must be impotent and poor ... Secondly, the gift should relieve aged, impotent and poor people. The word 'relief' implies that the persons in question have a need attributable to their condition as aged, impotent and poor people requires alleviating and which those persons could not alleviate or would find difficulty in alleviating from their own resources.

Facts

The claimant, a housing trust, designed a scheme to build small, self-contained dwellings for sale to elderly people on long leases in consideration of a capital payment. The applicants were required to attain the age of 65 if male, and 60 if female, to be able to pay the service charge, to lead an independent life and to be in need of the type of accommodation provided. The Charity Commissioners refused to approve the scheme as charitable in law on the ground that the scheme provided benefits by contract and not by bounty and was merely a commercial enterprise. The claimant appealed.

Held

The scheme was charitable for the relief of the aged on the following grounds:

(a) the words in the preamble ('relief of aged, impotent and poor people') were to be construed disjunctively;

(b) the purpose of the proposed scheme by the trustees was designed to provide a benefit for old persons in need;

(c) the absence of bounty in the provision of the benefit did not prevent the activity from being considered charitable.

Peter Gibson J: In *In Re Glyn (Decd)* [1950] 66 TLR 510, Danckwerts J was faced with a bequest for building cottages for old women of the working classes of the age of 60 years or upwards. He said, at p 511:

> I have not the slightest doubt that this is a good charitable bequest. The preamble to the Statute of Elizabeth refers to the relief of aged, impotent and poor people. The words 'aged, impotent and poor' should be read disjunctively. It had never been suggested that poor people must also be aged to be objects of charity, and there is no reason for holding that aged people must also be poor to come within the meaning of the preamble to the Statute. A trust for the relief of aged persons would be charitable unless it was qualified in some way which would clearly render it not charitable.

He then went on to say that there was a sufficient context to show that the testatrix intended to benefit indigent persons.

In *In Re Bradbury (Decd)* [1950] 2 All ER 1150, Vaisey J followed *In Re Glyn (Decd)* in holding that a bequest to pay sums for the maintenance of an aged person in a nursing home was charitable.

In *In Re Robinson (Decd)* [1951] Ch 198, a testator made a gift to the old people over 65 of a specified district to be given as his trustees thought best. Vaisey J held that the words 'aged, impotent and poor' in the preamble should be read disjunctively. He said it was sufficient that a gift should be to the aged, and commented on his decision in *In Re Bradbury* that the aged person in a nursing home might be a person not at all in need of any sort of pecuniary assistance.

In *In Re Cottam* [1955] 1 WLR 1299, a gift to provide flats for persons over 65 to be let at economic rents was said by Danckwerts J to be a trust for the benefit of aged persons and therefore *prima facie* charitable, though he went on to find it was a trust for the aged of small means.

In *In Re Lewis (Decd)* [1955] Ch 104 there was a gift to 10 blind girls, Tottenham residents if possible, of £100 each, and a similar gift to 10 blind boys. Roxburgh J held that the words 'aged, impotent and poor' in the preamble must be read disjunctively and that the trust was therefore charitable.

In *In Re Neal (Decd)* (1966) 110 SJ 549, a testator provided a gift for the founding of a home for old persons. Further directions provided for fees to be charged sufficient to maintain the home with sufficient staff to run it and cover the costs of the trustees. Goff J, in a very briefly reported judgment, said that in order to conclude whether a trust was charitable or not it was not necessary to find in it an element of relief against poverty, but it was sufficient to find an intention to relieve aged persons. The form of the gift and directions were a provision for succouring and supplying such needs of old persons as they had because they were old persons. Therefore, he held it was a charitable bequest.

In *In Re Adams (Decd)* [1968] Ch 80, p 93, Danckwerts J again referred to the necessity of construing disjunctively the words 'impotent and poor' in the preamble. By parity of reasoning he must be taken to have been of the view that 'aged, impotent and poor' should be read disjunctively, too.

Lastly, in *In Re Resch's Will Trusts* [1969] 1 AC 514, the Privy Council had to consider a gift of income to be applied for the general purposes of a named private hospital. The hospital charged substantial fees but was not run for the profit of individuals. Lord Wilberforce, delivering the judgment of the Board, referred to an objection that had been raised that the private hospital was not carried on for purposes beneficial to the community because it provided only for persons of means, capable of paying the fees required as a condition of admission. He said, at p 542:

> In dealing with this objection, it is necessary first to dispose of a misapprehension. It is not a condition of validity of a trust for the relief of the sick that it should be limited to the poor sick. Whether one regards the charitable character of trusts for the relief of the sick as flowing from the word 'impotent' ('aged, impotent

and poor people') in the preamble to 43 Eliz, c 4, or, more broadly, as derived from the conception of benefit to the community, there is no warrant for adding to the condition of sickness that of poverty.

He returned to the question of public benefit and need, at p 544:

> To provide, in response to public need, medical treatment otherwise inaccessible but in its nature expensive, without any profit motive, might well be charitable: on the other hand to limit admission to a nursing home to the rich would not be so. The test is essentially one of public benefit, and indirect as well as direct benefit enters into the account. In the present case, the element of public benefit is strongly present. It is not disputed that a need exists to provide accommodation and medical treatment in conditions of greater privacy and relaxation than would be possible in a general hospital and as a supplement to the facilities of a general hospital. This is what the private hospital does and it does so at, approximately, cost price. The service is needed by all, not only by the well to do. So far as its nature permits it is open to all: the charges are not low, but the evidence shows that it cannot be said that the poor are excluded . . .

These authorities convincingly confirm the correctness of the proposition that the relief of the aged does not have to be relief for the aged poor. In other words the phrase 'aged, impotent and poor people' in the preamble must be read disjunctively. The decisions in *In Re Glyn (Decd); In Re Bradbury (Decd); In Re Robinson (Decd); In Re Cottam;* and *In Re Lewis (Decd),* give support to the view that it is a sufficient charitable purpose to benefit the aged, or the impotent, without more. But these are all decisions at first instance and with great respect to the judges who decided them they appear to me to pay no regard to the word 'relief'. I have no hesitation in preferring the approach adopted in *In Re Neal (Decd)* and *In Re Resch's Will Trusts* that there must be a need which is to be relieved by the charitable gift, such need being attributable to the aged or impotent condition of the person to be benefited. My attention was drawn to Picarda, *The Law and Practice Relating to Charities,* 1977, p 79 where a similar approach is adopted by the author.

In any event in the present case, as I have indicated, the plaintiffs do not submit that the proposed schemes are charitable simply because they are for the benefit of the aged. The plaintiffs have identified a particular need for special housing to be provided for the elderly in the ways proposed and it seems to me that on any view of the matter that is a charitable purpose.

Recreational facilities

The promotion of sport *simpliciter* is not charitable, as such activity is not within the preamble or spirit and intendment of the preamble – see *Re Nottage* [1895] 2 Ch 649 (the provision of a cup annually in order to promote the sport of yacht racing) and *Inland Revenue Commissioners v City of Glasgow Police Athletic Association* [1953] 1 All ER 747 (sport within the police force) (cited in Chapter 15).

However, s 2(2)(g) of the Charities Act 2006 has recognized that the advancement of amateur sport is now to be treated as a charitable activity. 'Sport' for these purposes has been broadly defined 'as sports or games which promote health by involving physical or mental skill or exertion', see s2(3)(d) of the Charities Act 2006. Thus, the charitable status of such activity is dependent on the way the facility is organized.

Independently of the 2006 Act, gifts to promote sport may, in appropriate cases, be included under the heading 'advancement of education'. To achieve this status, the sport is required to be provided within a school or as part of the educational curriculum. It is well recognised that adequate recreational activities (physical and mental development) are an integral part of the educational process – see *Re Mariette* [1915] 2 Ch 284 (the provision of prizes for sport in a school). Similarly, in *Inland Revenue Commissioners v McMullen,* the promotion of football within schools and universities was considered to be charitable for the advancement of education.

Inland Revenue Commissioners v McMullen and Others [1981] AC 1, HL

Facts

By a deed dated 30 October 1972, made between the Football Association and the trustees, the Football Association Youth Trust was established. The main object of the trust was set out in clause 3(a) of the deed as follows:

. . . to organise and provide facilities which will enable and encourage pupils of Schools and Universities in any part of the UK to play football or other games or sports and *thereby* to assist in ensuring that due attention is given to the physical education and development of such pupils as well as to the development and occupation of their minds and with a view to furthering this object . . .

The Charity Commissioners registered the trust as a charity but the Inland Revenue objected and claimed a declaration to de-register the trust. The High Court and the Court of Appeal (by a majority) held in favour of the Revenue. The Football Association appealed to the House of Lords.

Held

On construction of the deed, the trust was charitable for the advancement of education:

> **Lord Hailsham of St Marylebone LC:** I do not think that the courts have as yet explored the extent to which elements of organisation, instruction, or the disciplined inculcation of information, instruction or skill may limit the whole concept of education. I believe that in some ways it will prove more extensive, in others more restrictive than has been thought hitherto. But it is clear at least to me that the decision in *In re Mariette* [1915] 2 Ch 284, is not to be read in a sense which confines its application for ever to gifts for annual treats for schoolchildren in a particular locality (another decision of Eve J); to playgrounds for children (*In Re Chesters* (1934) unreported, 25 July, and possibly not educational, but referred to in *IRC v Baddeley* [1955] AC 572, p 596); to children's outing (*In Re Ward's Estate* (1937) 81 SJ 397); to a prize for chess to boys and young men resident in the city of Portsmouth (*In Re Dupree's Deed Trusts* [1945] Ch 16, a decision of Vaisey J) and for the furthering the Boy Scouts movement by helping to purchase sites for camping, outfits, etc (*In Re Webber* [1954] 1 WLR 1500, another decision of Vaisey J).
>
> It is important to remember that in the instant appeal we are dealing with the concept of physical education and development of the young deliberately associated by the settlor with the status of pupillage in schools or universities (of which, according to the evidence, about 95% are within the age group 17 to 22). We are not dealing with adult education physical or otherwise, as to which some consideration may be different.
>
> I reject any idea which would cramp the education of the young within the school or university syllabus. I can find nothing contrary to the law of charity which prevents a donor providing a trust which is designed to improve the balance between the various elements which go into the education of the young.

Recreational Charities Act 1958

The provision of recreational facilities in limited circumstances has been regarded as charitable purposes and many village and town halls are used in part for recreational purposes. The decision of the House of Lords in *Inland Revenue Commissioners v Baddeley* (see Chapter 15 above) created doubts as to whether a number of bodies created for recreational purposes were charitable. The Recreational Charities Act 1958 was passed in order to clarify the law. Section 1(1) of the Act stipulates that the provision of recreational facilities will be charitable if two criteria are fulfilled, namely: (1) the public benefit test is satisfied; and (2) the facilities are provided in the interests of social welfare.

> **Recreational Charities Act 1958, s 1 (as amended by the Charities Act 2006)**
>
> (1) Subject to the provisions of this Act, it shall be and be deemed always to have been charitable to provide, or assist in the provision of, facilities for recreation or other leisure-time occupation, if the facilities are provided in the interests of social welfare: provided that nothing in this section shall be taken to derogate from the principle that a trust or institution to be charitable must be for the public benefit.
>
> (2) [The requirement] that the facilities are provided in the interests of social welfare cannot be satisfied if the basic conditions are not met.
>
> (2A) The basic conditions are—
>
>   (a) that the facilities are provided with the object of improving the conditions of life for the persons for whom the facilities are primarily intended; and
>
>   (b) that either—

(i) those persons have need for such facilities by reason of their youth, age, infirmity or disablement, poverty or social and economic circumstances; or

(ii) the facilities are available to the members of the public at large or to male or to female members of the public at large.

Note

Under the 1958 Act, the 'social welfare' test will be complied with if two conditions are satisfied as enacted in s 1(2). The first requirement is continuous as stipulated in s 1(2)(a). The second requirement may be satisfied in alternative ways either by proving that the facilities are available to a limited class of objects who have a need for such facilities by virtue of one or more of the factors enumerated within s 1(2)(b)(i) (such as a youth club or an organised outing for orphaned children), or 'the facilities are available to the members of the public at large' or male or female members of the public (such as a public swimming pool or a public park, women's institutes, etc).

Recreational Charities Act 1958

Under s 1(3) of the Recreational Charities Act 1958:

> Section 1(3) [subject to the provision of social welfare,] subsection (1) of this section applies in particular to the provision of facilities at village halls, community centres and women's institutes, and to the provision and maintenance of grounds and buildings to be used for purposes of recreation or leisure-time occupation, and extends to the provision of facilities for those purposes by the organising of any activity.

The House of Lords, in *Guild v Inland Revenue Commissioners*, construed the requirements under s 1(2)(a) liberally and rejected the view that it is necessary to prove that the beneficiaries were deprived of those facilities which are provided in order to alleviate their needs. The test today is whether the facilities are provided with the purpose of improving the conditions of life of the beneficiaries, irrespective of whether the participating members of society are disadvantaged or not. In short, the material issue concerns the nature of the facilities rather than the status of the participants: 'Hyde Park improves the conditions of life for residents in Mayfair and Belgravia as much as those in Pimlico or the Portobello Road, and the village hall may improve the conditions of life for the squire and his family as well as for the cottagers' (*per* Bridge LJ in *Inland Revenue Commissioners v McMullen* [1979] 1 WLR 130, CA, pp 142–43).

Guild v Inland Revenue Commissioners [1992] 2 All ER 10, HL

Facts

A testator by his will disposed of the residue of his estate to the Town Council of North Berwick, '(i) for the use in connection with the Sports Centre in North Berwick; and (ii) some similar purpose in connection with sport'. The Inland Revenue opposed a claim by the executor for exemption from capital transfer tax (now inheritance tax) on the grounds that the gift was not for the promotion of charitable purposes.

Held

The gift was charitable under the Recreational Charities Act 1958 and, adopting a benignant construction of the second part of the residuary clause, the gift was exclusively in favour of charitable purposes:

> **Lord Keith of Kinkel:** In the course of his argument in relation to the first branch of the bequest counsel for the commissioners accepted that it assisted in the provision of facilities for recreation or other leisure time occupation within the meaning of sub-s (1) of s 1 of the Act, and also that the requirement of public benefit in the proviso to the subsection was satisfied. It was further accepted that the facilities of the sports centre were available to the public at large so that the condition of sub-s (2)(b)(ii) was satisfied.

> It was maintained, however, that these facilities were not provided 'in the interests of social welfare' as required by sub-s (1), because they did not meet the condition laid down in sub-s (2)(a), namely, that they should be 'provided with the object of improving the conditions of life for the persons for whom the facilities are primarily intended'. The reason why it was said that this condition was not met was that on a proper construction it

involved that the facilities should be provided with the object of meeting a need for such facilities in people who suffered from a position of relative social disadvantage. Reliance was placed on a passage from the judgment of Walton J in *IRC v McMullen* [1978] 1 WLR 664.

He said, at p 675, in relation to the words 'social welfare' in sub-s (1):

> In my view, however, these words in themselves indicate that there is some kind of deprivation – not, of course, by any means necessarily of money – which falls to be alleviated; and I think that this is made even clearer by the terms of sub-s (2)(a).

> The facilities must be provided with the object of improving the conditions of life for persons for whom the facilities are primarily intended. In other words, they must be to some extent and in some way deprived persons.

When the case went to the Court of Appeal [1979] 1 WLR 130 the majority (Stamp and Orr LJJ) affirmed the judgment of Walton J on both points, but Bridge LJ dissented. As regards the Recreational Charities Act 1958 point he said, at pp 142–43:

> I turn therefore to consider whether the object defined by clause 3(a) is charitable under the express terms of s 1 of the Recreational Charities Act 1958. Are the facilities for recreation contemplated in this clause to be 'provided in the interests of social welfare' under s 1(1)? If this phrase stood without further statutory elaboration, I should not hesitate to decide that sporting facilities for persons undergoing any formal process of education are provided in the interests of social welfare. Save in the sense that the interests of social welfare can only be served by the meeting of some social need, I cannot accept the judge's view [Walton J] that the interests of social welfare can only be served in relation to some 'deprived' class. The judge found this view reinforced by the requirement of sub-s (2)(a) of s 1 that the facilities must be provided 'with the object of improving the conditions of life for the persons for whom the facilities are primarily intended . . .'. Here, again, I can see no reason to conclude that only the deprived can have their conditions of life improved. Hyde Park improves the conditions of life for residents in Mayfair and Belgravia as much as for those in Pimlico or the Portobello Road, and the village hall may improve the conditions of life for the squire and his family as well as for the cottagers. The persons for whom the facilities here are primarily intended are pupils of schools and universities, as defined in the trust deed, and these facilities are in my judgment unquestionably to be provided with the object of improving their conditions of life. Accordingly, the ultimate question on which the application of the statute to this trust depends, is whether the requirements of s 1(2)(b)(i) are satisfied on the ground that such pupils as a class have need of facilities for games or sports which will promote their physical education and development by reason either of their youth or of their social and economic circumstances, or both. The overwhelming majority of pupils within the definition of young persons and the tiny minority of mature students can be ignored as *de minimis*. There cannot surely be any doubt that young persons as part of their education do need facilities for organised games and sports both by reason of their youth and by reason of their social and economic circumstances. They cannot provide such facilities for themselves but are dependent on what is provided for them.

In the House of Lords the case was decided against the Crown upon the ground that the trust was one for the advancement of education, opinion being reserved on the point under the Recreational Charities Act 1958.

The fact is that persons in all walks of life and all kinds of social circumstances may have their conditions of life improved by the provision of recreational facilities of suitable character. The proviso requiring public benefit excludes facilities of an undesirable nature. In my opinion the view expressed by Bridge LJ in *IRC v McMullen* is clearly correct and that of Walton J in the same case is incorrect. I would therefore reject the argument that the facilities are not provided in the interests of social welfare unless they are provided with the object of improving the conditions of life for persons who suffer from some form of social disadvantage. It suffices if they are provided with the object of improving the conditions of life for members of the community generally.

It remains to consider the point upon which the executor was unsuccessful before the First Division, namely whether or not the second branch of the bequest of residue, referring to 'some similar purpose in connection with sport', is so widely expressed as to admit of the funds being applied in some manner which falls outside the requirements of s 1 of the Act of 1958. Counsel for the executor invited your Lordships, in construing this part of the bequest, to adopt the benignant approach which has regularly been favoured in the interpretation of trust deeds capable of being regarded as evincing a charitable intention. That approach is appropriate where the language used is susceptible of two constructions one of which would make it void and the other effectual: *IRC v McMullen* [1981] AC 1, p 14, per Lord Hailsham of St Marylebone LC.

The leading characteristics of the sports centre lie in the nature of the facilities which are provided there and the fact that those facilities are available to the public at large. These are the characteristics which enable it to satisfy s 1 of the Act of 1958. Adopting so far as necessary a benignant construction, I infer that the intention of the testator was that any other purpose to which the town council might apply the bequest or any part of it should also display those characteristics. In the result I am of opinion, the first part of the bequest having been found to be charitable within the meaning of s 1 of the Act of 1958, that the same is true of the second part, so that the funds in question qualify for exemption from capital transfer tax.

Miscellaneous examples

Trusts for the provision of various public facilities in defined areas have been held to be charitable. Thus, the provision of a library (*Abbot v Fraser* (1874) LR 6 PC 96); a museum (*British Trustees Museum v White* (1826) 2 Sim & St 594); a public hall (*Re Spence* [1938] Ch 96); a reading room (*Re Scowcroft* [1898] 2 Ch 638) to which the public has access have all been held to be charitable. Other charitable purposes decided under Lord Macnaghten's fourth heading, but some of these may now be endorsed in one of the listed purposes in s 2 of the Charities Act 2006, include gifts for the production of better organists and better organ music (*Re Levien* [1953] 3 All ER 35) [see now s 2(2)(f) of the Charities Act 2006]; likewise, the encouragement and advancement of choral singing (*Royal Choral Society v Inland Revenue Commissioners* [1943] 2 All ER 101 and the promotion of industry, commerce and art (*Crystal Palace Trustees v Minister of Town and Country Planning* [1950] 2 All ER 857); gifts for the promotion of the defence of the United Kingdom (*Re Good* [1950] 2 All ER 653) and a gift to provide a local fire brigade (*Re Wokingham Fire Brigade Trusts* [1951] 1 All ER 454) [consolidated in s 2(2)(l) of the 2006 Act]; a trust to relieve hardship and suffering by the local people as a result of a disaster (*Re North Devon and West Somerset Relief Fund Trusts* [1953] 2 All ER 1032) (but it is imperative that the size of the class of beneficiaries be sufficiently large to satisfy the public element test) [endorsed by s 2(2)(j) of the 2006 Act]; the publication and dissemination of law reports (*Incorporated Council for Law Reporting v AG* [1972] Ch 73); the general improvement of agriculture (*Inland Revenue Commissioners v Yorkshire Agricultural Society* [1928] 1 KB 611); the promotion of inexpensive and sanitary methods of disposal of the dead, in particular, cremation (*Scottish Burial Reform and Cremation Society Ltd v Glasgow City Corp* [1968] AC 138); the study and dissemination of ethical principles and the cultivation of a national religious sentiment (*Re South Place Ethical Society* [1980] 1 WLR 1565); a gift to the inhabitants of a town or village (*Goodman v Saltash Corp* (1882) 7 App Cas 633).

The promotion of any form of defence (locally and nationally) is a charitable purpose as is the maintenance of law and order, see s 2(2)(l) of the Charities Act 2006. In *Re Driffil* [1950] Ch 92, a gift to trustees to be devoted 'in whatever manner they may consider desirable to promote the defence of the UK against the attack of hostile aircraft' was treated as charitable. In much the same way a patriotic purpose was upheld as charitable in *Re Smith*.

Re Smith [1932] 1 Ch 153, CA

In this case, the Court of Appeal decided that a gift 'unto my country, England' was charitable. The Attorney General was authorised to receive the gift:

Lord Hanworth MR: I then come to the question: Is a bequest to a country, here England, good? Two questions are somewhat mixed up. One has to consider, at the same time, whether it is good as not being uncertain, and whether it is a charitable gift so as to eliminate any danger from the other rules of law. As far back as *West v Knight* (1669) 1 Ch Cas 134, which was decided in 1669, it was decided that a gift by a testator to the parish of Great Creaton, where he was born, without saying to what use, was good.

Then comes *Nightingale v Goulburn* (1849) 5 Hare 484 where there was a bequest 'to the Queen's Chancellor of the Exchequer for the time being, to be by him appropriated to the benefit and advantage of Great Britain'. That bequest was held to be valid so far as related to the personalty.

Now those cases have all been considered from time to time and held good. In *Goodman v Mayor of Saltash* (1882)

7 App Cas 633. Lord Selborne, a master of accurate diction, says: 'A gift subject to a condition or trust for the benefit of the inhabitants of a parish or town, or of any particular class of such inhabitants, is (as I understand the law) a charitable trust: and no charitable trust can be void on the ground of perpetuity.'

It is quite impossible, certainly in this court, to set aside the weighty opinions of two such distinguished lawyers and Lord Chancellors. There seems to be abundant and clear approval of the cases to which I have already referred.

I come to the conclusion that there is a definitive purpose – namely, that the bequest is to be for England. That is good in the same sense that, although general, when the sum bequeathed comes to be used it is to be applied to charitable purposes, as in *AG v Webster* (1875) LR 20 Eq 483. There is no area or purpose of distribution suggested which is not charitable. Why not then give effect to the plain meaning that it is for the advantage, within the meaning of the rule as to the interpretation of the word 'charitable', of the inhabitants of England?

In my opinion, therefore, the Attorney General succeeds upon his appeal. Under these circumstances the right course is to hand this money over to the person designated under the sign manual by the supreme head of the country for the advantage of the country, England. That supreme head, as Lord Eldon said, being the *parens patriae*, will cause it to be distributed in accordance with the law applicable to charitable moneys.

In *Re Harding*, the High Court considered the consequence of the gift being in terms expressly limited to benefit the black community. The court took into account that the law permitted a charitable trust to be made for the benefit of a particular part of the community. The phrase 'the Black community' was not uncertain and is taken to mean in modern usage, black people and a reference to 'the community' does not negative a charitable intention.

Re Harding [2007] EWHC 3 (Ch), (High Court)

Facts

Sister Joseph Harding was born in Liberia and brought up in the West Indies. In the 1970s she became involved in running the Caribbean Community Centre (CCC), a non-charitable unincorporated association, which was designed to provide a spiritual and community centre for Caribbean people in North London. Premises were provided free of charge by the Roman Catholic Diocese of Westminster and Sister Harding provided financial support for the project. By a will written for her in manuscript and executed in March 2003, Sister Harding declared 'it is my wish that everything I possess be taken over by the Roman Catholic Diocese of Westminster to hold in trust for the Black community of Hackney, Haringey, Islington and Tower Hamlet'. The question in issue concerned the validity of the bequest. The court considered the various possible outcomes namely:

- Whether the Diocese took the estate absolutely?
- Whether the Diocese held the deceased's estate on charitable trust?
- Whether the estate should be held on trust for the Caribbean Community Centre?
- Whether the estate should pass to the deceased's next of kin under the intestacy rules?

Held

The court decided that the use of the precatory words, 'it is my wish' on construction of the will as a whole created a trust. Further, the bequest in the deceased's will took effect as a gift to the Roman Catholic Diocese of Westminster on charitable trusts that could be detailed in a scheme. The court rejected arguments in favour of an absolute gift to the Diocese of Westminster or a trust for the CCC as being inconsistent with the intention of the testatrix as expressed in the will.

Lewison J: The principles applicable in order to determine whether a gift such as the one I am considering creates a valid charitable gift are, I think, as follows:

i) The court leans in favour of making a testator's testamentary dispositions effective if possible within the limitations and in accordance with the principles of law: *Re Smith* [1932] 1 Ch 153, 158, 100 LJ Ch 409, [1931] All ER Rep 617;

ii) A gift to the inhabitants of a locality, without specifying a particular purpose for which the gift is to be applied, is a valid charitable gift: *Re Smith* ("my country England");

iii) The same principle applies to a gift to a particular class of inhabitants within a locality: *Mitford v Reynolds* (1842) 1 Ph 185, 12 LJ Ch 40, 7 Jur 3, 41 ER 602 (native inhabitants of Dacca); *Goodman v Mayor of Saltash* (1882) 7 App Cas 633, 47 JP 276, 52 LJQB 193 (freemen of the borough of Saltash); *Re Mellody* [1918] 1 Ch 228, 82 JP 128, 87 LJ Ch 185 (schoolchildren of Turton);

iv) The rationale for this principle is that the court construes the gift as implicitly limited to charitable purposes: *Re Strakosch* [1949] Ch 529, 539, [1949] 2 All ER 6, [1949] LJR 1477. This principle applies unless there is something in the gift to exclude it: *Peggs v Lamb* [1994] Ch 172, 195, [1994] 2 All ER 15, [1994] 2 WLR 1. I suspect that the reason for this principle is, first, that it is a way of saving a gift that would otherwise be invalid; and second, that an absolute gift for the inhabitants of a locality is likely to produce such a small dividend as to be an absurd intention to impute to a testator;

v) However, if an express purpose is stated, that purpose must itself be charitable; and a non-charitable purpose trust cannot be validated by localising the gift: *Williams Trustees v IRC* [1947] AC 447, [1947] 1 All ER 513, 27 TC 409.

Mr Schaw Miller (counsel for the defendants) argued that the reference in the will to the black "community" was itself the specification of an express purpose. The purpose was widely expressed in terms that could embrace non-charitable purposes, with the consequence that the gift fell within the second of Lord Simonds' categories. I do not agree. First, the phrase "the Black community" is no more than another way of saying, in modern usage, black people. Second, judicial usage does not suggest that a reference to "the community" negatives a charitable intention. In *Re Mellody* Eve J, in upholding the gift to the schoolchildren of Turton, described the gift as a gift "for purposes beneficial to a section of the community"; and described the schoolchildren themselves as "a very important section of the community". He did not appear to regard the use of this word as being incompatible with a charitable gift. In *Peggs v Lamb* the Attorney General submitted that:

the trust [in question] was one for the benefit of the community in a particular area without the specification of any particular purpose with the consequence that the permitted purposes are limited to those within the spirit and intendment of the preamble.

Morritt J did not regard this submission as an oxymoron. On the contrary, he accepted it. I therefore reject the submission that the use of the word "community" takes the case outside the principle in *Re Smith*.

The second suggested difficulty was that a gift for the benefit of the black community was contrary to public policy because it was discriminatory on racial grounds. The remedy in cases where charitable benefits are to be provided to a class defined by colour is not to invalidate the gift completely, but to remove the reference to colour. This is the mechanism for which s 34 of the Race Relations Act 1976 provides.

Political purposes

Political purposes include attempts to change the law and gifts to further the objects of political parties. A trust for political purposes is incapable of subsisting as a charity, for the court may not stultify itself by deciding that it is in the public good for the law to be changed (see *National Anti-Vivisection Society v Inland Revenue Commissioners* (see above) *and McGovern v AG* (see below)). In *Bowman v Secular Society*, Lord Parker stated the reason behind the general rule.

Bowman v Secular Society Ltd [1917] AC 406, HL

Lord Parker: A trust for the attainment of political objects has always been held invalid, not because it is illegal, for everyone is at liberty to advocate or promote by any lawful means a change in the law, but because the court has no means of judging whether a proposed change in the law will or will not be for the public benefit, and therefore cannot say that a gift to secure the change is a charitable gift.

Accordingly, an educational trust under the guise of promoting the interests of the Labour Party failed in *Re Hopkinson* [1949] 1 All ER 346. Similarly, prior to the Charities Act 2006, a gift to Amnesty International failed in *McGovern v AG* for the court is incapable of evaluating whether a proposed change in the law is for the public good.

McGovern v AG [1981] 3 All ER 493, HC

Facts

Amnesty International, an unincorporated, non-profit making association, established a trust and sought registration with the Charity Commissioners. This was refused and the trustees appealed to the court.

Held

The organisation was not a charitable body because some of its purposes (for example, procuring the abolition of torture, or inhuman or degrading treatment) were political and did not comply with the definition of charitable purposes. Admittedly, some of its purposes were charitable, such as the promotion of research into the maintenance and observance of human rights. On construction, its main purposes were not exclusively charitable:

Slade J:

The requirement of public benefit

Trusts to promote changes in the law of England are generally regarded as being non-charitable for [lacking a public benefit].

There is now no doubt whatever that a trust of which a principal object is to alter the law of this country cannot be regarded as charitable. In *National Anti-Vivisection Society v IRC* [1948] AC 31. As Lord Wright said, at pp 49–50: 'But there is another and essentially different ground on which in my opinion it must fail; that is, because its object is to secure legislation to give legal effect to it.' It is, in my opinion, a political purpose within the meaning of Lord Parker's pronouncement in *Bowman v Secular Society Ltd* [1917] AC 406.

From the passages from the speeches of Lord Parker and Lord Wright I extract the principle that the court will not regard as charitable a trust of which a main object is to procure an alteration of the law of the United Kingdom for one or both of two reasons: *first, the court will ordinarily have no sufficient means of judging as a matter of evidence whether the proposed change will or will not be for the public benefit. Secondly, even if the evidence suffices to enable it to form a prima facie opinion that a change in the law is desirable, it must still decide the case on the principle that the law is right as it stands, since to do otherwise would usurp the functions of the legislature.* I interpret the point made by Lord Simonds concerning the position of the Attorney General as merely illustrating some of the anomalies and undesirable consequences that might ensue if the courts began to encroach on the functions of the legislature by ascribing charitable status to trusts of which a main object is to procure a change in the law of the United Kingdom, as being for the public benefit [emphasis added].

The point with which I am at present concerned is whether a trust of which the direct and main object is to secure a change in the laws of a foreign country can ever be regarded as charitable under English law. Though I do not think that any authority cited to me precisely covers the point, I have come to the clear conclusion that it cannot.

In my judgment, however, there remain overwhelming reasons why such a trust still cannot be regarded as charitable. All the reasoning of Lord Parker of Waddington in *Bowman v Secular Society Ltd* [1917] AC 406 seems to me to apply *a fortiori* in such a case. *A fortiori* the court will have no adequate means of judging whether a proposed change in the law of a foreign country will or will not be for the public benefit. Sir Raymond Evershed MR in *Camille and Henry Dreyfus Foundation Inc v IRC* [1954] Ch 672, p 684 expressed the *prima facie* view that the community which has to be considered in this context, even in the case of a trust to be executed abroad, is the community of the United Kingdom. Assuming that this is the right test, the court in applying it would still be bound to take account of the probable effects of attempts to procure the proposed legislation, or of its actual enactment, on the inhabitants of the country concerned which would doubtless have a history and social structure quite different from that of the United Kingdom. Whatever might be its view as to the content of the relevant law from the standpoint of an English lawyer, it would, I think, have no satisfactory means of judging such probable effects upon the local community.

Furthermore, before ascribing charitable status to an English trust of which a main object was to secure the alteration of a foreign law, the court would also, I conceive, be bound to consider the consequences for this country as a matter of public policy. In a number of such cases there would arise a substantial *prima facie* risk that such a trust, if enforced could prejudice the relations of this country with the foreign country concerned: compare *Habershon v Vardon* (1851) 4 De G & Sm 467. The court would have no satisfactory means of assessing the extent of such risk, which would not be capable of being readily dealt with by evidence and would be a matter more for political than for legal judgment.

For all these reasons, I conclude that a trust of which a main purpose is to procure a change in the laws of a foreign country is a trust for the attainment of political objects within the spirit of Lord Parker of Waddington's pronouncement and, as such, is non-charitable.

Summary of conclusions relating to trusts for political purposes

Founding them principally on the House of Lords' decisions in the *Bowman* case [1917] AC 406 and the *National Anti-Vivisection Society* case [1948] AC 31, I therefore summarise my conclusions in relation to trusts for political purposes as follows. (1) Even if it otherwise appears to fall within the spirit and intendment of the preamble to the Statute of Elizabeth, a trust for political purposes falling within the spirit of Lord Parker's pronouncement in *Bowman*'s case can never be regarded as being for the public benefit in the manner which the law regards as charitable. (2) Trusts for political purposes falling within the spirit of this pronouncement include, *inter alia*, trusts of which a direct and principal purpose is either: (i) to further the interests of a particular political party; or (ii) to procure changes in the laws of this country; or (iii) to procure changes in the laws of a foreign country; or (iv) to procure a reversal of government policy or of particular decisions of governmental authorities in this country; or (v) to procure a reversal of government policy or of particular decisions of governmental authorities in a foreign country.

This categorisation is not intended to be an exhaustive one, but I think it will suffice for the purposes of this judgment; I would further emphasise that it is directed to trusts of which the purposes are political. As will appear later, the mere fact that trustees may be at liberty to employ political means in furthering the non-political purposes of a trust does not necessarily render it non-charitable.

Conclusion

Indisputably, laws do exist both in this country and in many foreign countries which many reasonable persons consider unjust. No less indisputably, laws themselves will from time to time be administered by governmental authorities in a manner which many reasonable persons consider unjust, inhuman or degrading. Amnesty International, in striving to remedy what it considers to be such injustices, is performing a function which many will regard as being of great value to humanity. Fortunately, the laws of this country place very few restrictions on the rights of philanthropic organisations such as this, or of individuals, to strive for the remedy of what they regard as instances of injustice, whether occurring here or abroad. However, for reasons which I think adequately appear from Lord Parker of Waddington's pronouncement in *Bowman*'s case [1917] AC 406, the elimination of injustice has not as such ever been held to be a trust purpose which qualifies for the privileges afforded to charities by English law. I cannot hold it to be a charitable purpose now.

Note
Section 2(2)(h) of the Charities Act 2006 has enacted that 'the advancement of human rights, conflict resolution or reconciliation or the promotion of religious or racial harmony or equality and diversity' are charitable purposes. It is arguable that the decision in *McGovern v AG* has been reversed as a result of this modification of the law.

Alternatively, a trust may be treated as charitable if its political purpose, on construction, is purely incidental to its main charitable purpose.

A borderline case is *Re Scowcroft*.

Re Scowcroft [1898] 2 Ch 638, HC

Facts
The gift was for the maintenance of a village club and reading room 'to be used for the furtherance of Conservative principles'. The issue was whether the gift was charitable.

Held
The gift was charitable for the advancement of education:

Stirling J: Whether or not a gift for the furtherance of Conservative principles is a good charitable gift is a question upon which I do not think it necessary to express any opinion in this case, because it seems to me that the reading which is suggested is not the true one, but that this is a gift for the furtherance of Conservative principles and religious and mental improvement in combination. It is either a gift for the furtherance of Conservative principles in such a way as to advance religious and mental improvement at the same time, or a gift for the furtherance of religious and mental improvement in accordance with Conservative principles; and in either case the furtherance of religious and mental improvement is, in my judgment, an essential portion of the gift. It is, therefore, a gift in one form or another for religious and mental improvement, no doubt in combination with the advancement of Conservative principles; but that limitation, it appears to me, is not sufficient to prevent it from being a perfectly good charitable gift, as undoubtedly it would be if it were a gift for the furtherance of religious and mental improvement alone. I think that that construction is aided by the direction which follows, which is that the building in question is to be kept free from intoxicants and dancing.

It occurs to me that possibly the whole matter may be viewed in another way, namely, that this is a devise of a building for the public benefit, and that it may be supported on that ground just as the gift of a library or museum would be held to be a good charitable gift. However that may be, I think that all three objects are intended to be advanced simultaneously by this gift, and it seems to me a good charity.

In *Southwood v AG* (1998) *The Times*, 26 October, the High Court decided that, on construction, the purposes of a trust designed to challenge the current policies of Western governments to promote military disarmament were not charitable. The purposes were considered political.

Question
To what extent are trusts to provide recreational facilities treated as charitable?

CHARITABLE ACTIVITIES OUTSIDE THE UNITED KINGDOM

A number of British registered charities carry on their activities abroad. There is little judicial authority on the attitude of the courts to such overseas activities. In 1963, the Charity Commissioners issued guidelines on the way they would approach this problem. Their view is that the activities of trusts within the first three heads of Lord Macnaghten's classification (trusts for the relief of poverty, the advancement of education and religion) are charitable wherever such operations are conducted. In respect of the fourth head, such purposes would be charitable only if carried on for the benefit (directly or reasonably directly) of the UK community, such as medical research. The Commissioners added that it may be easier to establish this benefit in relation to the Commonwealth (although this link has become weaker since this statement was made).

The limited number of authorities in this field seem to make no distinction between activities conducted abroad as opposed to UK activities: see *Keren Kayemeth Le Jisroel Ltd v Inland Revenue Commissioners*.

Keren Kayemeth Le Jisroel Ltd v Inland Revenue Commissioners [1932] AC 650, HL
Facts
A company was formed with the main object of purchasing land in Palestine, Syria and parts of Turkey for the purpose of settling Jews in such lands. Counsel argued that the company was established for charitable purposes, namely, the advancement of religion, the relief of poverty and other purposes beneficial to the community.

Held
The company was not charitable because of the lack of evidence of religion and poverty. In addition, the company was not charitable under the fourth head because of the uncertainty of identifying the community:

Lord Tomlin: We are concerned here only with the language which is employed in this memorandum before us. There is not in it a word which can suggest anything of a religious character. In my view, therefore, the first point, that this is a religious charity, necessarily fails.

Then the next point is that, if it is not religious, it is said to be beneficial to the community. I have great difficulty, as indeed counsel for the appellants had, in identifying the community. They suggest some alternatives. First of all, they suggest that the community is the community of all the Jews throughout the world. That seems to me to be very difficult. They next suggest that it is the Jews in the prescribed region, but I have great difficulty in seeing why they should be the community, because, although the Jews who are to be settled under the objects no doubt include Jews in the prescribed region, there are also included Jews outside the prescribed region, and whether a settling of Jews from outside the prescribed region is for the benefit of Jews within the prescribed region – it may or may not be; I do not see any indication one way or the other I think it is extraordinarily difficult to say that within the meaning of the cases there is really any community to be found in the circumstances before your Lordships' House.

My Lords, that leaves the third point – the poverty point. I confess that this point seems to me very difficult to advance consistently with the argument which has been put before your Lordships on the point that the association is an institution for religious purposes. The two things do not seem to me to be really consistent, but on the merits of the point I confess I am unable to see how, by any straining of the language, this can be limited to poor Jews.

In *Re Jacobs* (1970) 114 SJ 515, a trust for the planting of a clump of trees in Israel was held to be charitable because soil conservation in arid parts of Israel is of essential importance to the Israeli community. The court relied on *Inland Revenue Commissioners v Yorkshire Agricultural Society* (the promotion of agriculture is a charitable purpose).

Inland Revenue Commissioners v Yorkshire Agricultural Society [1928] 1 KB 611, CA

Facts

The Yorkshire Agricultural Society was formed with the object of holding an annual meeting for the exhibition of livestock, implements, etc, and the general promotion of agriculture. Special privileges were open to members, such as free admission to shows, the use of a reading and writing room on the show grounds, special railway facilities, etc. The society was assessed to income tax on the excess of income over expenditure. The society claimed exemption on the ground that it was a charity. The Special Commissioners for income tax found that the society was a charity. On appeal to the High Court, Rowlatt J reversed this decision. The society appealed.

Held

The society was established for charitable purposes notwithstanding the enjoyment of benefits by its members:

> **Atkin LJ:** There is plenty of evidence in this case that the operations of the society are general and extend to the promotion of agriculture generally and not merely to the benefit of the members.

In *Gaudiya Mission v Brahmachary*, the expression, 'charity' did not include an institution registered and established under the laws of a foreign jurisdiction. It would be impractical for the High Court to seek to extend its supervisory jurisdiction to control an overseas registered charity.

Gaudiya Mission and Others v Brahmachary and Others [1997] 4 All ER 957, CA

Facts

The claimants, a registered Indian charity (the Mission), its president and secretary, maintained preaching centres and temples in order to advance the doctrines of the Vaishnava faith throughout India and also Cricklewood, North West London. The Mission was not registered in England. Rival factions within the Mission set up a trust under the name 'Gaudiya Mission Society Trust' (the Society), which was a registered English charity. The defendants were a priest in charge of the charity's London temple and the trustees of the English registered Society. The claimants contended that the assets held by the Society belonged to them and that the Society was passing itself off as the Mission. The question in issue was whether the Mission was an institution established for charitable purposes and thereby subject to the control of the High Court under its supervisory jurisdiction. The judge decided that the Mission was within the control of the High Court and, consequently, that the Attorney General ought to be added as a party to the proceedings. The Attorney General appealed to the Court of Appeal.

Held

The Court of Appeal allowed the appeal on the ground that it was not expressly enacted, nor could it be implied, that the Charities Act 1993 applied to institutions other than those established for charitable purposes in England and Wales. Charities within England and Wales are required to register with the Charity Commissioners. The implied territorial limits of legislation and the practical considerations of enforceability are decisive factors, which indicate that the Act was never intended to extend to an institution registered abroad. Thus, the Mission was not a charity within the Charities Act 1993 and the Attorney General was not a proper party to be joined.

Question

To what extent are British registered charities entitled to conduct activities outside the United Kingdom?

FURTHER READING

Chesterman, M, ' Foundations of charity law in the new Welfare State' (1999) 62 MLR 333.
Farder, C, 'Too political to be charitable' [1984] Conv 263.
Hopkins, J, 'Charity – trusts for the saying of masses' [1989] CLJ 373.
Hopkins, J, 'Trusts for the advancement of sport – Recreational Charities Act 1958' [1992] CLJ 429.
Nobles, R, 'Politics, public benefit and charity' (1982) 45 MLR 704.
Norman, H, 'Sporting charities – social welfare defined: *Guild v IRC*' [1992] Conv 361.
Parry, N, 'Trusts for masses – *Re Hetherington*' [1989] Conv 453.
Watkin, T, 'Casenote – *Re Koeppler*' [1985] Conv 56.
Watkin, T, 'Where there is a will' [1985] Conv 412.

CHARITABLE TRUSTS: THE *CY-PRÈS* DOCTRINE

INTRODUCTION

If the purpose of a charitable gift becomes impossible or impractical to carry out, the fund is not held on an automatic resulting trust, as would be the case with a private trust. A *cy-près* scheme may be drawn up and the fund will continue to be applied for charitable purposes 'as nearly as possible' (*cy-près*) to the original charitable purpose or purposes. This principle requires two conditions to be satisfied, namely: (a) it has become impossible or impractical to carry out the original charitable purpose; and (b) the donor has manifested a general charitable intention.

THE *CY-PRÈS* DOCTRINE

The expression *cy-près* originates from Norman French meaning 'near this'. Over the centuries the expression has been taken to mean 'as nearly as possible'. The *cy-près* doctrine is a principle applicable to gifts for charitable purposes which fail (initially or subsequently) owing to the impossibility or impracticality of giving effect to the donor's intention. Schemes may be approved by the Charity Commissioners and the courts for the application of the funds as nearly as possible to the original purposes as stated by the settlor. When the *cy-près* doctrine is adopted, the donor or his or her estate is excluded from benefiting by way of a resulting trust.

There are only two conditions to be satisfied for a *cy-près* application of funds, namely:

(a) the impossibility or impracticality of carrying out the original charitable purpose, or the existence of a surplus of funds after the charitable purpose has been fulfilled; and

(b) the manifestation of a general charitable intention by the donor as opposed to a specific charitable intention.

IMPOSSIBILITY

Prior to the introduction of the Charities Act 1960 (now the Charities Act 1993), the courts approached this question by considering whether the purposes, as stated by the settlor, were capable of being achieved as distinct from merely being undesirable. In *AG v City of London* (1790) 3 Bro CC 171, trust funds to be used for the advancement and propagation of the Christian religion among the infidels in Virginia were applied *cy-près* when it became clear that there were no longer any 'infidels' in Virginia. Similarly, in *AG v Ironmongers Co* (1844) 10 Cl & Fin 908, funds devoted to the redemption of British slaves in Turkey and Barbary were applied *cy-près* when the purpose subsequently became impossible to achieve.

The test of 'impossibility' was construed broadly in *Re Dominion Students' Hall Trust*.

Re Dominion Students' Hall Trust [1947] 1 Ch 183, HC

Facts

A limited company was formed for charitable purposes. The memorandum of association declared its object to be to maintain a hostel for students 'of European origin' from the overseas dominions of the British Empire. The company proposed a scheme, for approval by the court, whereby the offensive words 'of European origin' would be deleted so that the company would be better equipped to administer the funds for the benefit of all students from the dominions regardless of racial origin.

Held

The scheme was approved because the retention of the colour bar had the effect of defeating the main object of the charity:

> **Evershed J:** The purpose of both the petition and the summons is that a restriction which has hitherto been characteristic of the charity, limiting its objects so as to exclude coloured students of the British Empire, should be removed and that the benefits of the charity should be open to all citizens from the Empire without what is commonly known as the 'colour bar'.

> The word 'impossible' should be given a wide significance: see *In Re Campden Charities* (1881) 18 Ch D 310; *In Re Robinson* [1923] 2 Ch 332. It is not necessary to go to the length of saying that the original scheme is absolutely impracticable. Were that so, it would not be possible to establish in the present case that the charity could not be carried on at all if it continued to be so limited as to exclude coloured members of the Empire.

> I have, however, to consider the primary intention of the charity. At the time when it came into being, the objects of promoting community of citizenship, culture and tradition among all members of the British Commonwealth of Nations might best have been attained by confining the Hall to members of the Empire of European origin. But times have changed, particularly as a result of the war; and it is said that to retain the condition, so far from furthering the charity's main object, might defeat it and would be liable to antagonize those students, both white and coloured, whose support and goodwill it is the purpose of the charity to sustain. The case, therefore, can be said to fall within the broad description of impossibility.

On the other hand, the test of impossibility was not satisfied in *Re Weir Hospital*.

Re Weir Hospital [1910] 2 Ch 124, CA

Facts

The testator devised property to be used as the site for a hospital. Expert evidence was admitted to the effect that the site was not suitable for a hospital and a scheme was proposed for the building of a nurses' home instead.

Held

It was not impossible to carry out the testator's wishes but was simply inadvisable. Accordingly, the court refused to approve the scheme:

> **Cozens-Hardy MR:** Wherever the *cy-près* doctrine has to be applied, it is competent to the court to consider the comparative advantages of various charitable objects and to adopt by the scheme the one which seems most beneficial. But there can be no question of *cy-près* until it is clearly established that the directions of the testator cannot be carried into effect.

> I am of opinion that neither the trustees nor the Commissioners have authority to choose their charity so as to leave a surplus to be applied *cy-près*. They are bound to apply the funds in the named charities unless it be impracticable. It is clearly impossible for the Commissioners or trustees to decline to carry out the trusts of a single named lawful charity because they disapproved of it. It is equally clear that if they have the choice of two or more charities they cannot apply a part of the trusts funds towards one of such charities and refuse to apply the balance to the others because they disapprove of them. A case for the *cy-près* application of trust funds cannot be manufactured, but must arise *ex necessitate rei*. I, of course, give the Commissioners and the trustees full credit for desiring to do their best; but it is of great importance that their conduct should be in accordance with law. It is contrary to principle that a testator's wishes should be set aside, and his bounty administered not according to his wishes but according to the view of the Commissioners.

Question

How has the expression 'impossibility' been interpreted by the courts in the context of the *cy-près* principle?

Section 13 of the Charities Act 1993 (which re-enacts s 13 of the Charities Act 1960) consolidates to some extent and substantially extends the powers of the Charity Commissioners and the courts to apply property *cy-près*. The circumstances when the purposes of the charity will become impractical or impossible are enacted in s 13(1)(a)–(e) of the Charities Act 1993.

Charities Act 1993, s 13(1)

(a) where the original purposes in whole or in part – (i) have been as far as may be fulfilled; or (ii) cannot be carried out or not according to the directions given and to the spirit of the gift . . .

Note

This sub-section gives the court the jurisdiction to decide that the original purposes of the gift have been fulfilled or have become impractical. The only restriction on the discretion of the court is with regard to the construction of the 'spirit of the gift'.

The phrase, 'spirit of the gift', as used in the Charities Act 1993 (originally adopted in the Charities Act 1960) has been interpreted by Pennycuick VC in *Re Lepton's Charity* as meaning 'the basic intention underlying the gift, as ascertained from its terms in the light of admissible evidence'.

Re Lepton's Charity [1972] Ch 276, HC

Facts

A testator who died in 1716 devised specific property to trustees on trust to pay an annual sum of £3 to the Protestant Minister in Pudsey, and the surplus income to the poor and aged people of Pudsey. In 1716, the total income was £5. On the date of the application to the court, that income was £790 per annum. Two questions arose for the determination of the court, namely:

(a) whether on a true construction of the will the minister ought to be paid a fixed sum of £3 or three-fifths of the annual income; and

(b) whether the court would approve a *cy-près* scheme increasing the minister's entitlement to £100 per annum.

Held

On a construction of the will, the minister was not entitled to three-fifths of the annual income but only to a fixed sum of £3 per annum. But having regard to the spirit of the gift, a *cy-près* scheme would be approved entitling the minister to £100 annually.

Pennycuick VC: The occasions for applying property *cy-près* are now set out in s 13 of the Charities Act 1960 [now s 13 of the Charities Act 1993]. It is clear that this section in part restates the principles applied under the existing law, but also extends those principles. The section should be read as a whole, but for the present purpose it will be sufficient to refer specifically only to a few sentences.

[The learned judge then read s 13(1) and continued:] Sub-section (1)(e)(iii) appears to be no more than a final writing out large of para (a)(ii). The expression 'spirit of the gift' may be an echo of words used in the *Campden Charities* case (1880) 18 Ch D 310. *It must, I think, be equivalent in meaning to the basic intention underlying the gift, that intention being ascertainable from the terms of the relevant instrument read in the light of admissible evidence* [emphasis added].

It seems to me that the words 'the original purposes of a charitable gift' are apt to apply to the trusts as a whole in such a case. Where a testator or settlor disposes of the entire income of a fund for charitable purposes, it is natural to speak of the disposition as a single charitable gift, albeit the gift is for more than one charitable purpose. Conversely, it would be rather unnatural to speak of the disposition as constituting two or more several charitable gifts each for a single purpose. In a trust of the present character there is an obvious inter-relation between the two trusts in that changes in the amount of the income and the value of money may completely distort the relative benefits taken under the respective trusts. The point is familiar in other instances of fixed annuity and residual income.

Once it is accepted that the words 'the original purposes of a charitable gift' bear the meaning which I have put upon them it is to my mind clear that in the circumstances of the present case the original purposes of the gift of Dickroyd cannot be carried out according to the spirit of the gift, or to use the words of para (e)(iii) 'have ceased . . . to provide a suitable and effective method of using the property . . . regard being had to the spirit of the gift'. The intention underlying the gift was to divide a sum which, according to the values of 1715, was modest but not negligible, in such a manner that the minister took what was then a clear three fifths of it. This intention is plainly defeated when in the conditions of today the minister takes a derisory £3 out of a total of £791.

It is not suggested that sub-s (2) has any significant bearing upon the present question, for it is precisely the condition requiring the failure of the original purposes that sub-s (1)(a)(ii) and sub-s (1)(e)(iii) are concerned to modify.

If, contrary to my view, the words 'the original purposes of a charitable gift' must be read severally in relation to the trust for payment of the fixed annual sum and to the trust for payment of residuary income, I think it is no less clear that paras (a)(ii) and (e)(iii) would have no application. On this footing it would be impossible to maintain in respect of either trust that the original purposes cannot be carried out in the spirit of the gift. The minister is available to receive £3 a year, for what it is worth, and it is conceded by Mr Browne-Wilkinson that there are sufficient poor, aged and necessitous people in Pudsey to absorb £788 a year.

More recently, in *Oldham BC v AG*, the Court of Appeal was required to construe the original purpose in respect of a devise of land for use as playing fields.

Oldham BC v AG [1993] 2 WLR 224, CA

Facts

The original purpose of a devise of land to the Oldham BC was to hold 'on trust to preserve and manage the same as playing fields known as the "Clayton Playing Fields" for the benefit of inhabitants of Oldham, Chatterton and Royton'. The question in issue was whether an obligation was imposed on the local authority to maintain the land for use only as a playing field.

Held

On construction of the instrument, the original purpose of the devise was not intended to impose an obligation on the council to retain the site in perpetuity, for use only as playing fields for the local community, but to make provision for playing fields for the benefit of the local community. Accordingly, the council was entitled to sell the site to developers and use the proceeds to acquire a new site for playing fields for the local community:

Dillon LJ: Broadly, the effect (of s 13 of the Charities Act 1960) is that an alteration of the 'original purposes' of a charitable gift can only be authorised by a scheme for the *cy-près* application of the trust property and such a scheme can only be made in the circumstances set out in paras (a) to (e) of s 13(1).

[After considering the terms of the deed Dillon LJ continued:] I come to what I regard as the crux of this case, viz, the true construction of the words 'original purposes of a charitable gift' in s 13 of the Act of 1960. Do the 'original purposes' include the intention and purpose of the donor that the land given should be used for ever for the purposes of the charity, or are they limited to the purposes of the charity?

Certain of the authorities cited to us can be put on one side. Thus, in *In Re JW Laing Trust* [1984] Ch 143, p 153, Peter Gibson J said, plainly correctly:

> It cannot be right that any provision, even if only administrative, made applicable by a donor to his gift should be treated as a condition and hence as a purpose.

In that case, however, the provision, which was held to be administrative and was plainly not a 'purpose', was a provision that the capital was to be wholly distributed within the settlor's lifetime or within 10 years of his death.

It is necessary, in my judgment, in order to answer the crucial question of the true construction of s 13, to appreciate the legislative purpose of s 13. Pennycuick VC said in *In Re Lepton's Charity* [1972] Ch 276, p 284 that the section 'in part restates the principles applied under the existing law, but also extends those principles'. That section is concerned with the *cy-près* application of charitable funds, but sales of charitable lands have, in so far as they have been dealt with by Parliament, always been dealt with by other sections not concerned with the *cy-près* doctrine.

There are, of course, some cases where the qualities of the property which is the subject matter of the gift are themselves the factors which make the purposes of the gift charitable, for example, where there is a trust to retain for the public benefit a particular house once owned by a particular historical figure or a particular building for its architectural merit or a particular area of land of outstanding natural beauty. In such cases, sale of the house, building or land would necessitate an alteration of the original charitable purposes and, therefore, a *cy-près* scheme because after a sale the proceeds or any property acquired with the proceeds could not possibly be applied for the original charitable purpose. But that is far away from cases such as the present, where the charitable purpose – playing fields for the benefit and enjoyment of the inhabitants of the districts of the original donees, or it might equally be a museum, school or clinic in a particular town – can be carried on on other land.

Accordingly, I would allow this appeal, set aside the declaration made by the judge, and substitute a declaration to the opposite effect.

In *Re Laing Trust*, the court drew a distinction between the 'original purposes' of the trust under s 13, which may be reviewed by the court on a *cy-près* application, and a direction to distribute within a specific period of time, which is treated as an administrative provision outside of s 13. Under the inherent jurisdiction of the court, a scheme may be approved even though the court has no jurisdiction within s 13.

Re Laing Trust [1984] Ch 143, HC

Facts

In 1922, a settlor transferred shares to the plaintiff company as trustee to hold for charitable purposes. Both capital and income were to be wholly distributed during the lifetime of the settlor or within 10 years of his death. The settlor died in 1978. By 1982, the capital which was undistributed was worth £24 million. The plaintiff company applied to the court to sanction a scheme dispensing with the obligation to distribute the capital within 10 years of the settlor's death.

Held

The court had no jurisdiction to sanction the scheme under s 13, as the 'original purposes' of the charitable gift did not include an administrative provision concerning the date of distribution, but, in the exercise of its inherent jurisdiction, the court would approve the proposed scheme:

> **Peter Gibson J:** For the court to have jurisdiction to make the order sought by the plaintiff under s 13 two questions must be answered affirmatively: (1) Is the requirement to distribute before the expiration of 10 years from the settlor's death included in the 'the original purposes' of the charitable gift? (2) If so, have the original purposes, in whole or in part, since they were laid down, ceased to provide a suitable and effective method of using the property available by virtue of the gift?
>
> To answer the first question it is necessary to identify the original purposes of the gift. I venture to suggest that, as a matter of ordinary language, those purposes in the present case should be identified as general charitable purposes and nothing further. I would regard it as an abuse of language to describe the requirement as to distribution as a purpose of the gift. To my mind the purposes of a charitable gift would ordinarily be understood as meaning those charitable objects on which the property given is to be applied. It is not meaningful to talk of the requirement as to distribution being either charitable or non-charitable.
>
> Both Mr McCall and Mr Picarda advanced a more subtle argument on the following lines: (1) s 13 not merely re-enacted the circumstances in which *cy-près* applications were allowed under the previous law but also extended those circumstances; (2) prior to the Act of 1960 the court had allowed by way of *cy-près* schemes the removal of impracticable conditions attached to charitable gifts; (3) such conditions must be regarded as purposes within the meaning of s 13; (4) the requirement as to distribution is also to be treated as, or as similar to, a condition and so a purpose within s 13. I accept the first and second of these propositions. The first is supported by the remarks of Sir John Pennycuick VC in *In Re Lepton's Charity* [1972] Ch 276. The second is illustrated by cases such as *In Re Robinson* [1923] 2 Ch 332 and *In Re Dominion Students' Hall Trust* [1947] Ch 183.
>
> But I have difficulty with the third and fourth propositions. I baulk at the universality of the third. Take the case of *In Re Robinson* [1923] 2 Ch 332. The testatrix gave money for the endowment of an evangelical church but imposed 'an abiding condition' that a black gown be worn in the pulpit, a condition held by Lawrence J to be impracticable as defeating the main evangelical intention of the gift. It is not clear from the report whether the money that was given could be used for the provision of black gowns. If it could, then I would accept that the condition might accurately be described as a subsidiary purpose, as indeed the judge, at p 336, appears to describe the condition. But if not, to my mind this case is more accurately described as falling within the class of cases where the main charitable purpose is practicable but a subsidiary purpose or direction is impracticable.
>
> In my judgment, therefore, it does not follow that all conditions attached to gifts must be treated as 'purposes' within s 13. It cannot be right that any provision, even if only administrative, made applicable by a donor to his gift should be treated as a condition and hence as a purpose. I confess that from the outset I have found difficulty in

accepting that it is meaningful to talk of a *cy-près* application of property that has from the date of the gift been devoted both as to capital and income to charitable purposes generally, albeit subject to a direction as to the timing of the capital distributions. No case remotely like the present had been drawn to my attention. In the result, despite all the arguments that have been ably advanced, I remain unpersuaded that such a gift is capable of being applied *cy-près* and, in particular, I am not persuaded that the requirement as to distribution is a purpose within the meaning of s 13. Rather, it seems to me to fall on the administrative side of the line, going, as it does, to the mechanics of how the property devoted to charitable purposes is to be distributed. Accordingly, I must refuse the application so far as it is based on s 13. That conclusion renders it unnecessary for me to answer the second question which had to be answered affirmatively if s 13 were to apply. However, many of the submissions made by counsel on that question are of direct relevance to my consideration of the next question for me to answer, that is to say, whether the court, under its inherent jurisdiction, should direct the removal of the requirement as to distribution. To that question I now turn.

On this question Mr Picarda and Mr McCall submit, and I accept, that the court is not fettered by the particular conditions imposed by s 13(1)(e)(iii), but can, and should, take into account all the circumstances of the charity, including how the charity has been distributing its money, in considering whether it is expedient to regulate the administration of the charity by removing the requirement as to distribution within ten years of the settlor's death.

In my judgment, the plaintiff has made out a very powerful case for the removal of the requirement as to distribution, which seems to me to be inexpedient in the very altered circumstances of the charity since that requirement was laid down 60 years ago.

Charities Act 1993, s 13(1)

(b) where the original purposes provide a use for part only of the property available by virtue of the gift . . .

The approval of the court may be granted under this paragraph where a surplus of funds are left over after the original charitable purposes have been carried out. This paragraph merely declares the law that existed before 1960, illustrated by *Re North Devon and West Somerset Relief Fund*.

Re North Devon and West Somerset Relief Fund [1953] 2 All ER 1032, HC

Facts

As a result of the 1952 floods in North Devon and West Somerset, an appeal was launched 'to contribute to a fund for the relief of all those who have suffered . . . We ask the whole country to support this fund'. There was a generous response to this appeal and it was contemplated that a large surplus would remain after providing for all requirements. The questions in issue were whether the collection was charitable and, if so, whether the surplus was applicable *cy-près* or was held on resulting trust for the contributors.

Held

(a) The purpose of the appeal was to relieve hardship and suffering among the victims of the disaster which was a charitable initiative.

(b) Having regard to all the circumstances, the intention of the contributors was to part with their funds out and out. Thus, the surplus fund was applicable *cy-près*:

Wynn-Parry J: Looking at that document as a whole, I extract from it an intention on the part of the authors to apply the money which may be subscribed at their invitation to relieve hardship and suffering which has been experienced both by what are called 'the local people' and others who were within the area at the time of the disaster and to achieve that by the charity of the community. I am unable to dissect this document in such a way as to discover in it, either by looseness of phrasing, and, therefore, by inference, or by express words, any intention to benefit this part of the community in a way which the law would not regard as charitable.

For those reasons, I propose in answer to question (i) of the summons to declare that the trusts affecting the fund are valid charitable trusts.

[On the second question the learned judge continued:] The nearest case to be found in the reports to the present case is *Re Welsh Hospital (Netley) Fund* [1921] 1 Ch 655. That was a decision of Lawrence J. The facts were that on the outbreak of the war in 1914 a hospital was erected at Netley, and equipped and run during the war, for the benefit of sick and wounded Welsh soldiers by means of large voluntary subscriptions raised in Wales. In 1919 the hospital was closed, the staff disbanded, and the property sold to the War Office, and, after winding-up the affairs of the hospital, there was a surplus of some £9,000. It was held, on the evidence, that there was not a resulting trust of the surplus for the subscribers to the hospital, but a general charitable intention for sick and wounded Welshmen which enabled the court to apply the fund *cy-près*.

The appeal, as the learned judge points out, was an appeal to the inhabitants of Wales for subscriptions to a Welsh hospital. In the course of his judgment, PO Lawrence J says *ibid*, p 660:

I am of opinion that the true inference to be drawn is that these subscribers intended to part with their contributions out and out, and that they did not intend that the surplus, if any, of their contributions should be returned to them when the immediate object of the charity should have come to an end. In the result I hold that although all the contributions were in the first instance made for the particular purpose of building, equipping and maintaining the Welsh Hospital at Netley, the main underlying object of the contributors was to provide money for the comfort of sick and wounded Welshmen, and that all the subscribers intended to devote their contributions not only to the particular object, but generally to the benefit of their sick and wounded countrymen.

It appears to me, on careful consideration, that it is impossible to draw a distinction of any substance between the facts of that case and the facts of the present case. It appears to me not in the least decisive that there is a reference in the appeal to persons other than local residents who suffered distress by the disaster.

Charities Act 1993, s 13(1) (as amended by the Charities Act 2006)

(c) where the property available by virtue of the gift and other property applicable for similar purposes can be more effectively used in conjunction, and to that end can suitably, regard being had to the appropriate considerations, be made applicable to common purposes . . .

This provision enables a number of small charities with common purposes to be amalgamated in order to create larger funds. This sub-section merely consolidates the common law.

Re Faraker [1912] 2 Ch 488, CA

Facts

A testatrix, who died in 1911, left a legacy to 'Mrs Bailey's Charity, Rotherhithe'. A charity was founded by Mrs Hannah Bayly in 1756 for poor widows in Rotherhithe. In 1905, the charity was consolidated with a number of local charities under a scheme, approved by the Charity Commissioners, for the benefit of the poor in Rotherhithe.

Held

The legacy was taken by the consolidated charities:

Cozens-Hardy MR: Hannah Bayly's Charity is not extinct, it is not dead, and I go further and say it cannot die. Its objects may be changed, though not otherwise than in accordance with law: they may be changed either by the Court of Chancery in its own jurisdiction over charities or by schemes formed by the Charity Commissioners, to whom Parliament has entrusted that particular duty. Subject to that lawful alteration by competent authority of the objects, Hannah Bayly's Charity is not extinct, it exists just as much as it did when the testatrix died in 1756, as it did when there were changes made in 1814, and as it does today.

Now it is to be remembered, as has been pointed out by Kennedy LJ, that this legacy was not given to Mrs Bayly's Charity for widows; it was simply given to a charity which is identified by name. It was given to an ancient endowed charity, and in my opinion a gift of that kind carries with it the application of it according to the lawful objects of the charity funds for the time being.

Charities Act 1993, s 13(1) [as amended by the Charities Act 2006]

(d) where the original purposes were laid down by reference to an area which there was but has since ceased to be a unit for some other purpose, or by reference to a class of persons or to an area which has for any reasons since ceased to be suitable, regard being had to the appropriate considerationsor to be practical in administering the gift . . .

Under this paragraph, the court is entitled to consider that the original class of beneficiaries has become difficult to identify, owing to local government boundary changes, or the class of beneficiaries has dwindled over the years (see *AG v City of London* and *Ironmongers Co v AG* (see p 419)). *Peggs v Lamb* illustrates the application of this sub-section.

Peggs and Others v Lamb [1994] 2 WLR 1, HC

Facts

In this case, the court considered a *cy-près* scheme under s 13(1)(d) of the Charities Act 1960. Freemen and their widows in the Ancient Borough of Huntingdon were entitled to the income from specific plots of land. In 1992, the number of beneficiaries had dwindled to 15 and the income available for distribution had risen to £550,000. An application was made to adopt a *cy-près* scheme under s 13(1)(d) of the Charities Act 1960 (which has been repealed and replaced by s 13(1)(d) of the 1993 Act).

Held

Under s 13(1)(d), the original purpose of the gift was to benefit the freemen and widows in the Huntingdon Borough, but the class of beneficiaries had dwindled to such an extent that they ceased to be a suitable class for the deployment of the funds (due consideration being paid to the spirit of the gift). Accordingly, a scheme would be approved whereby the class of beneficiaries would be enlarged to include the inhabitants of the borough as a whole:

> **Morritt J:** The real issue is whether in the circumstances there is jurisdiction to order the settlement of a scheme for the *cy-près* application of the income. This depends on s 13 of the Charities Act 1960.
>
> [The learned judge read out s 13 of the Charities Act 1960, and continued:] The effect of the Municipal Corporations Act 1835 was to destroy the political importance of the freemen and thereby to undermine their social and economic importance too. But, of more importance, membership of the class was thereby restricted, in the case of these charities, to those who were the sons of freemen and born in the ancient borough. The inevitable consequence after over 150 years is that the class has dwindled very considerably. There will come a time, if it has not arrived already, when the class of freemen ceases to be a section of the public at all. It is not necessary to decide whether that time has passed so that a case for a scheme can be made out under s 13(1)(e)(ii) of the Act of 1960 because I think it is clear that a sufficient case is made out under para (d).
>
> The original basic intention or 'spirit of the gift' *[this was the original expression in the Act before the amendment to appropriate considerations]* was the benefit of the Borough of Huntingdon. It would, in my judgment, be entirely consistent with that, that in 1993 the class of persons by reference to which the charitable purposes are laid down should be enlarged from the freemen to the inhabitants as a whole. Accordingly I will direct the settlement of a scheme. [amendment added]

Charities Act 1993, s 13(1) [as amended by the Charities Act 2006]

(e) where the original purposes, in whole or in part, have since they were laid down –

    (i) been adequately provided for by other means; or

    (ii) ceased, as being useless or harmful to the community or for other reasons, to be in law charitable; or

    (iii) ceased in any other way to provide a suitable and effective method of using the property available by virtue of the gift, regard being had to the appropriate considerations.

Section 1(A) In subsection (1) above 'the appropriate considerations' means –

(a) (on the one hand) the spirit of the gift concerned, and

(b) the social and economic circumstances prevailing at the time of the proposed alteration of the original purposes.

Section 15 of the Charities Act 2006 amends s 13 (1) (c), (d) and (e)(iii) of the Charities Act 1993 by substituting the expression, 'the appropriate considerations' for 'the spirit of the gift' in that section. Section 1(A) defines the expression, 'appropriate considerations' to include the spirit of the gift and the social and economic circumstances prevailing at the time of the proposed alteration in the purpose. Thus, the Charity Commission is required to take these circumstances into consideration when making a scheme.

Paragraph (e)(i) empowers the court to modify the original purposes as stated by the donor, in view of the charitable purposes being provided for by other bodies such as central and local government. For example, the repair of roads and bridges may not be an appropriate mode of utilising charitable resources.

Paragraph (e)(ii) will rarely be used. It assumes that a purpose was once charitable but, owing to changed circumstances, has ceased to be charitable. For example, antivivisection in the early 19th century was considered a charitable purpose (see *Re Fouveaux* [1895] 2 Ch 501), but with the advance of medical research, anti-vivisection is no longer treated as a charitable purpose. At the time when the Anti-Vivisection Society was removed from the charities' register, its funds could have been applied *cy-près*. Section 13(1)(e)(ii) merely confirms this approach.

Paragraph (e)(iii) enacts a wide-ranging provision giving the courts the power to consider whether the original purposes selected by the donor represent an effective method of using the property. In *Re Lepton's Charity* (see p 421 above), the court assumed jurisdiction, *inter alia*, under s 13(1)(e)(iii), to sanction the scheme.

In *Varsani v Jesani*, the Court of Appeal decided that the jurisdiction of the court under s 13(1) of the Charities Act 1993 is far-reaching and is not restricted to cases where the original purposes have become impossible or impractical.

Varsani v Jesani [1998] 3 All ER 272, CA

Facts

A charitable trust was set up in 1967 to promote the faith of Swaminarayan, a Hindu sect, as practised in accordance with the teachings and tenets of its leader. He was reputed to have a divine status. In 1974 a successor was appointed on the death of the leader. By 1985 the members were split into two groups following allegations of misconduct made against the successor. The majority of the members did not accept the allegations and continued to recognise his authority. The minority of the members believed the allegations and asserted that he had lost his right to succession. An attempt was made to reconcile the differences between both groups of members, but in 1997 such talks broke down. The majority brought proceedings seeking a scheme for the administration of the property of the charity *cy-près* under s 13(1)(e)(iii) of the Charities Act 1993. The judge accepted jurisdiction under the Act. The minority group appealed.

Held

Dismissing the appeal, the Court of Appeal held that the original purpose had 'ceased to be a suitable and effective method of using' the available property, because the adherents were now divided into two irreconcilable groups, each of which believed that they alone continued to profess that faith. The effect was that neither group was able to worship in the same temple as the other; thus, the minority group had been excluded from the facilities of worship which the charity was established to provide. This impasse between the two groups could not be resolved having regard to the original purpose. Accordingly, the original purpose had ceased to be a suitable and effective method of using the available property. The *cy-près* scheme involved dividing the property between the two groups.

Question

To what extent has s 13 of the Charities Act 1993 extended the term 'impossibility'.

GENERAL CHARITABLE INTENTION

This is the second condition that is required to be fulfilled before the charitable funds may be applied *cy-près*.

Subsequent failure

There is one type of event where the courts have dispensed with the need to prove a general charitable intention. These are cases of 'subsequent failure', that is, occasions when the charitable bodies exist at the appropriate date of vesting but cease to exist subsequently. The appropriate date of vesting varies with the nature of the instrument creating the gift. An *inter vivos* transfer by deed takes effect on the date of the execution of the deed, and a transfer by will takes effect on the date of death of the testator. Once the gift vests in the charity, the donor and his or her heirs are excluded from benefiting on a subsequent liquidation of the charity, irrespective of whether the gift was made subject to a general or specific charitable intention: see *Re Wright*.

Re Wright [1954] Ch 347, CA

Facts

A testatrix, who died in 1933, gave her residuary estate to trustees on trust for a tenant for life, Mr Webb (who died in 1942), with remainder to found and maintain a convalescent home for 'impecunious gentlewomen'. On the date of the testatrix's death, the residuary estate was sufficient to implement her wishes, but at the time of Webb's death, the fund was insufficient to carry out the charitable purpose. It was argued that the appropriate date for deciding whether the charitable purpose was practical or not was the date of Webb's death.

Held

The Court of Appeal rejected the above argument and concluded that the date for deciding whether the funds were applicable *cy-près* was the date of vesting, namely, the date of death of the testatrix.

> **Romer LJ:** Once money is effectually dedicated to charity, whether in pursuance of a general or a particular charitable intent, the testator's next-of-kin or residuary legatee are for ever excluded and no question of subsequent lapse, or of anything analogous to lapse, between the date of the testator's death and the time when the money becomes available for actual application to the testator's purpose can affect the matter so far as they are concerned.

The same principle is applicable where the charity existed at the testator's death but was liquidated before the gift was distributed by the executor: see *In Re Slevin*.

In Re Slevin [1891] 2 Ch 236, CA

Facts

The testator left money to St Dominic's orphanage in Newcastle. The orphanage existed at the date of the death but closed down soon afterwards, before it received the legacy.

Held

The fund had vested in the charity and no resulting trust had arisen:

> **Kay LJ:** The orphanage did come to an end before the legacy was paid over. In the case of a legacy to an individual, if he survived the testator it could not be argued that the legacy would fall into the residue. Even if the legatee died intestate and without next of kin, still the money was his, and the residuary legatee would have no right whatever against the Crown. So, if the legatee were a corporation which was dissolved after the testator's death, the residuary legatee would have no claim.

More recently, in *Re ARMS*, the High Court decided that bequests made to a charitable company, which was in existence on the dates of death of the testators but subsequently went into liquidation, took effect *prima facie* as gifts beneficially to the company. Unless there was some indication that the gifts took effect as trusts, the testators' estates were excluded from benefiting from a return of the properties. While it is possible that, had the testators known of the company's insolvent liquidation, they might not have wished to donate their properties to it, the court was reluctant to speculate about the testators' intentions in the face of the plain words of the wills. Accordingly, the gifts were taken by the company beneficially and were available for distribution amongst the company's creditors.

In Re ARMS (Multiple Sclerosis Research) Ltd [1997] 1 WLR 877, HC

Facts

Several testators made testamentary gifts to a named company which had been incorporated to carry out charitable purposes. The principal objects of the company, as stated in its memorandum of association, were the promotion of research into the cause, cure and prevention of multiple sclerosis and the assistance of its victims. Various gifts by wills were made by deceased testators to the company before it was formally liquidated. The liquidator applied to the court for directions as to how the bequests should be dealt with.

Held

The bequests formed part of the company's assets and were available for distribution among its creditors:

> **Neuberger J:** In the present case, at the date of Mr Dove's death, the company was still in existence: indeed, even now it has not been dissolved. Accordingly, Mr Alleyne and the trust contend that Mr Dove has effected a simple 'bequest to a corporate body', namely, the company, which 'takes effect simply as a gift to that body beneficially'. The fact that the body is in liquidation does not alter the fact that it still exists. Furthermore, they contend that there are no circumstances to suggest that the company was intended to take the gift as a trustee.
>
> If, as a matter of construction of the will, the gift is expressed to be for a company then 'unless there are circumstances which show that the recipient is to take the gift as a trustee' (*per* Buckley J in *In Re Vernon's Will Trusts (Note)* [1972] Ch 300, p 303) it takes effect so long as the company is in existence at the date of the testator's death.
>
> In general, one has the very strong suspicion that, where a testator makes a will leaving a gift to a company established for charitable purposes, and that company subsequently goes into insolvent liquidation, prior to his death, the testator would not have intended the gift to go to the company. However, in my judgment that is insufficient to justify a departure from the plain words of a will. If, according to their natural tenor, the words of a will provide that a specific gift is to be given to a specific company, then it is not for the court to speculate as to whether the testator would in fact have intended the gift to take effect had he known of a change in the circumstances of the company between the making of his will and his death.
>
> Accordingly, while I have sympathy for the proposition that the testator would not have intended the gift to the company to take effect had he known that the company was in insolvent liquidation at the date of his death, I reject the Attorney General's argument.

However, as a prerequisite to the *Re Wright* solution, it is essential that an absolute and perpetual gift be made to the charity at the time of vesting. If, alternatively, a limited gift (for a number of years) is made to the charity which existed on the date of vesting, but which has ceased to exist at the time the gift purports to take effect, the court may, on construction, decide that a resulting trust in favour of the settlor's estate may take effect in accordance with the settlor's intention: see *Re Cooper*.

Re Cooper's Conveyance Trusts [1956] 3 All ER 28, HC

Facts

By a deed dated 13 April 1864, a donor conveyed land and buildings to trustees upon trust for the purposes of the Orphan Girls' Home at Kendal, and on failure of the trust, for the benefit of specified beneficiaries, 'and upon or for no other trust or purpose whatsoever'. In June 1954, the orphanage was closed. The trustees applied to the court for directions.

Held

(a) On a true construction of the trust deed, the donor manifested an intention to provide a limited benefit to the charity, namely, so long as the Orphan Girls' Home subsisted.

(b) The gift over in favour of the specified beneficiaries failed for remoteness of vesting.

(c) The trust deed manifested a specific charitable intention. Thus, there was no room for the application of the fund *cy-près*.

Accordingly, the property was held on resulting trust for the estate of the donor:

Upjohn J: The question whether the property, ie, the lands and buildings, ought now to be applied on charitable trusts *cy-près* or results to the estate of the donor depends on the true construction of the deed. A number of authorities have been cited to me. They establish clearly the following proposition: Where in terms an absolute and perpetual gift to charity is made with a gift over on cesser which fails for remoteness or for some other reason, the original perpetual gift to charity remains; but, on the other hand, where there is a gift to charity for a limited period then the undisposed of interest reverts to the grantor . . .

I draw attention to the words 'property given absolutely and perpetually to charity'.

In the present case, if there had been no gift over on the failure of the orphanage, it would hardly have been suggested that on the subsequent failure of it there would have been a resulting trust. Where, however, the donor uses language showing an intention that in some circumstances he contemplates a failure of the purpose or indicates that his gift is only to be for a limited time or purpose, then it becomes a question of construction, whether he has made an out-and-out or perpetual gift to charity or not, and that is not inaptly expressed by asking whether he has evinced a general charitable intention.

Accordingly, in my judgment, I think this is a case where the donor intended a gift to charity only for a limited time and for a limited purpose; the time is limited by the time for which the orphanage could be carried on. That period having come to an end, in my judgment, there is an interest in the donor remaining undisposed of; that is held on trust for her estate by way of resulting trust, and I must declare accordingly.

Question

Is a general charitable intention required to be manifested as a prerequisite prior to the court sanctioning a *cy-près* scheme?

Initial failure

In the event of an initial failure of the charitable institution, it is essential to prove a general charitable intention before the funds are applied *cy-près*. In other words, if, at the time of the vesting of the gift, the charitable body, specified by the donor, did not exist, the fund may be applied *cy-près* only on proof of a general charitable intention as opposed to a specific charitable intention.

The intention of the donor is essentially a question of fact. The courts are required to consider all the circumstances in order to determine whether the donor intended to benefit a charitable 'purpose' *simpliciter*, identified by reference to a charitable institution (paramount charitable intention), or whether the settlor's intention was to benefit a specific charitable body identified by him.

In *Re Roberts* the court adopted a scheme for the application of funds devoted to promote an identified charitable purpose rather than a specific charitable body which ceased to exist on the date the will took effect.

Re Roberts [1963] 1 All ER 674, HC

Facts

By her will dated 12 July 1930, a testatrix gave her residue to her trustees to be divided amongst six named charitable institutions including the Sheffield Boys' Working Home. The testatrix died on 12 March 1960. By a conveyance dated 19 October 1889, premises for the home were conveyed to trustees to be used for the benefit of poor boys. Clause 19 provided that the governors of the home, if they considered it ought to be discontinued, might authorise the trustees to sell the premises or otherwise dispose of them and pay the proceeds for the benefit of charitable institutions or poor inhabitants in Sheffield. In 1945 the home became empty. As a result of a resolution of the governors the trustees sold the property, gave £1,000 to a hostel for boys and transferred the balance to the Sheffield Town Trust requesting that the income be used for the benefit of boys' organisations.

Held

The court directed a *cy-près* scheme for the application of the residuary estate on the ground that the gift of the residuary estate was not so correlated with the physical entity of the institution, namely the premises that were the home. Accordingly,the continued existence of the institution was not a pre-requisite for the vesting of the gift. Clause 19 of the deed only empowered the governors to decide whether the particular machinery of the Boys' Home could not be carried out on particular premises and thus, the charitable trusts as a whole could not be terminated under cl 19.

> **Wilberforce J:** In the circumstances . . . the legacy in the will in favour of the Sheffield Boys' Working Home . . . appears at first sight plainly to lapse by reason of the disappearance of the named charity before the death of the testatrix. This is a case where, on the face of it, the testatrix had given a legacy to an institution with an accurate description and with its correct address, and that undoubtedly has gone. Notwithstanding that, the position is that the courts have gone very far in the decided cases to resist the conclusion that a legacy to a charitable institution lapses, and a number of very refined arguments have been found acceptable with a view to avoiding that conclusion.
>
> The Attorney General puts his case in this way. He says that this was a trust for an unincorporated charity and that it should be treated as a trust for the purposes for which the charity existed. He says that those purposes still exist though the particular premises have gone. At to cl 19 of the trust deed, that clause is only concerned with the physical hereditament where the home was conducted and did not authorise the termination of the charity as a whole or warrant the handing over of anything other than the hereditaments themselves for particular purposes.
>
> . . . I think that the gift of the testatrix in her will was for the purposes of an institution, and that it was not so exclusively tied up with a particular home physically located on the premises used by the home as to enable me to say that, when the trusts of the physical home ceased to exist, the charity ended.

Note

In *Farren v Abbeyfield London Polish Society Ltd* [2006] All ER (D) 108, the High Court adopted the principle in *Re Roberts* and decided that a bequest of funds to a charitable society identified by the testatrix but ceasing to exist on the date of death of the testatrix was taken by a society carrying out similar purposes.

The court adopted a broad approach to the issue of the testatrix's intention in *Re Lysaght* and deleted a clause in her will that imposed a religious bar.

Re Lysaght [1966] Ch 191, HC

Facts

A testatrix bequeathed £5,000 to the Royal College of Surgeons (trustees) on trust to apply the income in establishing studentships with disqualifications in respect of Jews and Roman Catholics. The College declined to accept the gift, but declared that if the religious bar was excised it would be willing to accept the gift. The issue was whether the religious bar could be excluded under a *cy-près* scheme.

Held

In accordance with the paramount charitable intention of the testatrix, the religious bar would be deleted. On construction, the court decided that the paramount charitable intention of the testatrix was to make the College a trustee of the fund and, since this paramount intention was capable of being defeated if the religious bar was upheld, the court was entitled to delete the offending clause in order to give effect to the paramount intention of the settlor:

> **Buckley J:** Let me consider for a moment the meaning of the term 'general charitable intent'. Whether a donor has or has not evinced such an intent is relevant in any case in which the donor has made a charitable gift in terms which cannot be carried out exactly. In such a case the court has to discover whether the donor's true intention can be carried out notwithstanding that it is impracticable to give effect to some part of his particular directions.

A general charitable intention, then, may be said to be a paramount intention on the part of a donor to effect some charitable purpose which the court can find a method of putting into operation, notwithstanding that it is impracticable to give effect to some direction by the donor which is not an essential part of his true intention – not, that is to say, part of his paramount intention.

In contrast, a particular charitable intention exists where the donor means his charitable disposition to take effect if, but only if, it can be carried into effect in a particular specified way, for example, in connection with a particular school to be established at a particular place, *In Re Wilson* [1913] 1 Ch 314, or by establishing a home in a particular house: *In Re Packe* [1918] 1 Ch 437.

In the present case there would be a wide field open to any trustee of the endowment fund for the selection of students who manifestly satisfy the qualification of being neither of the Jewish nor of the Roman Catholic faith. Accordingly, I do not think that this part of the trust is affected by the vice of uncertainty. Nor, in my judgment, is it contrary to public policy, as Mr Balcombe suggests. I accept that racial and religious discrimination is nowadays widely regarded as deplorable in many respects and I am aware that there is a Bill dealing with racial relations at present under consideration by Parliament, but I think that it is going much too far to say that the endowment of a charity, the beneficiaries of which are to be drawn from a particular faith or are to exclude adherents to a particular faith, is contrary to public policy. The testatrix's desire to exclude persons of the Jewish faith or of the Roman Catholic faith from those eligible for the studentship in the present case appears to me to be unamiable, and I would accept Mr Clauson's suggestion that it is undesirable, but it is not, I think, contrary to public policy.

If it is of the essence of a trust that the trustees selected by the settlor and no one else shall act as the trustees of it and those trustees cannot or will not undertake the office, the trust must fail: *In Re Lawton* [1936] 3 All ER 378 and see *Reeve v AG* (1843) 3 Hare 191, p 197, and *Tudor on Charities* 5th edn, 1929, p 128. I have already reached the conclusion that it is an essential part of the testatrix's intention that the college should be the trustee of the endowment fund. The college is, as I have said, unalterably opposed to accepting the trust if any provision for religious discrimination is an effective part of it.

The impracticability of giving effect to some inessential part of the testatrix's intention cannot, in my judgment, be allowed to defeat her paramount charitable intention.

In *In Re Robinson* [1923] 2 Ch 332 Lawrence J had to deal with a fund bequeathed many years earlier for the endowment of a church of an evangelical character to which conditions were attached, including what was called an 'abiding' condition that a black gown should be worn in the pulpit unless this should become illegal. The evidence showed that in 1923 the wearing of a black gown in the pulpit, though not illegal, would be detrimental to the teaching and practice of evangelical doctrines and services in the church in question. Lawrence J had to determine whether a scheme could properly be sanctioned dispensing with the observance of this condition. He said [1923] 2 Ch 332, p 336:

> The contention on behalf of the petitioner is that the condition as to the wearing of a black gown in the pulpit is impracticable, but that it is subsidiary to the main purpose of the bequest, and that the present case falls within that class of cases when the main charitable purpose is practicable, but a subsidiary purpose is impracticable. If that contention be correct, I am satisfied that the court, on assuming the execution of the charitable trusts declared by the testatrix, has ample jurisdiction to execute those trusts *cy-près* and to sanction a scheme, modifying the trusts by dispensing with the subsidiary purpose, so as to carry out, as nearly as possible, the main charitable intentions of the testatrix. In my judgment, the contention that the condition as to the black gown is subsidiary to the main purpose of the bequest is sound.

The judge held on the evidence that the effect of insisting upon the condition would be to defeat the main intention of the testatrix. He held that, although compliance with the condition was not impossible in an absolute sense, it was impracticable and ought to be dispensed with.

If I am right in the view that I have formed, that it was an essential part of the testatrix's intention in the present case that the college should be the trustee of the endowment fund, then I think that the reasoning in *In re Robinson* is precisely applicable to the present case.

Accordingly, in my judgment, the court can and should enable the college to carry the trust into effect without any element of religious discrimination.

The court came to a similar conclusion in *Re Woodhams*.

Re Woodhams (Decd) [1981] 1 All ER 202, HC

Facts

Scholarships were awarded to two music colleges. A limitation was attached to the awards restricting applicants to boys from Dr Barnardo's Homes and the Church of England Children's Society Homes. The colleges refused to accept the gifts subject to these limitations. The question in issue was whether the limitations could be deleted.

Held

A scheme deleting the restrictions was approved by the court because the limitation was impractical:

Vinelott J: The question which I have to decide is whether the fact that each of the London College and the old Tonic Sol-fa College would have refused to accept a reversionary interest in a half share of the residuary estate on terms that they would be bound when the interest fell into possession to found and administer scholarships restricted to absolute orphans from one of the named homes has the consequence that the residuary gifts fail altogether.

A similar question (but without the complication of an intervening life interest) arose in *Re Lysaght (Decd)* [1965] 2 All ER 888.

[The learned judge then considered *Re Lysaght*, and continued:] Returning to the residuary gift in the instant case the testator devoted his whole estate to the furtherance of two charitable objects, namely music and the welfare of orphans cared for by Dr Barnardo's or the Church of England Children's Society homes.

As I see it the intention which can be discerned from the bequest is twofold. The testator wanted to further musical education and to do so by means of founding scholarships at colleges with which he had a long and, as is apparent from paragraphs (c) and (d) of clause 4 of the will, a valued connection. He chose absolute orphans from homes run by well-known charities as those most likely to need assistance. But it was not, as I see it, an essential part of this scheme that the scholarships should be so restricted, whatever needs might present themselves in changed circumstances. That being so, that part of the scheme or mode of achieving a charitable purpose can be modified without frustrating his intention.

In my judgment, therefore, the trusts of residue do not fail. At the date of the testator's will the trusts could have been carried into effect by a modification of the trust of each moiety, deleting the restriction to absolute orphans from the named homes. There have been further changes of circumstances as regards the old Tonic Sol-fa College since the testator's death and a more radical scheme may be required. I will therefore refer to the Charity Commissioners the settlement of a scheme.

The Court of Appeal in *Re Broadbent (Decd)* decided that a gift by a testatrix to a charitable body (a specified church) which ceased to exist on the date of vesting might be construed as a gift for charitable purposes.

Re Broadbent (Decd) [2001] All ER (D) 219, CA

Facts

Mrs Broadbent (B) made her will in 1987 and, after creating specific legacies, directed that the residue of her estate be held upon trust for three charities in equal shares. One of the charities was St Matthews Church, Stalybridge (the church). Its share was to be used for the general purposes of the church, but primarily for the upkeep of the fabric of the church building. The church building was vested in trustees subject to a trust declared in 1913. The condition of the church had deteriorated over the years and in 1990 the trustees decided to close the building and sell it. The proceeds of sale were received and retained by the trustees. In 1992, B executed a codicil revoking some of the legacies but in other respects confirming her will. In 1996, B died and the bulk of her estate fell into residue. The National Westminster Bank, as sole executor of B's will, sought the determination of the court as to whether the gift to the church failed and, if so, upon what trusts the share was held. The two other charities claimed to be equally entitled to the share which would otherwise have been available to the church. They claimed that the gift to the church created a trust for the premises (which ceased to exist) and not for the purposes of the church. The judge held that the gift was for the purposes of the church which continued to exist, and thus the gift did not lapse.

Held

The Court of Appeal dismissed the appeal and decided that, on construction, the gift was for the purposes of the church and not to maintain the fabric of the building, on the following grounds:

(a) The court's objective was to identify the charity which the testatrix sought to benefit.

(b) In identifying the testatrix's intention, the court was entitled to consider all the circumstances of the case, including evidence extrinsic to the will. This was evident by s 21 of the Administration of Justice Act 1982.

(c) The gift did not fail because the selected charitable body ceased to exist. If the purposes of the charity did not come to an end on the closure of the church building then the gift remained valid.

(d) It was not B's primary wish that her residuary estate be shared between two charities equally, but instead that it be divided between three charities equally.

(e) Accordingly, the trustees of St Matthews Church, Stalybridge, were entitled to one-third of the residue of the estate which they were required to hold upon the trusts declared in 1913.

> **Mummery LJ:** The court's task is to identify in each case the charity which the testator really wanted to benefit by the bequest. This involves a careful examination by the court of the scheme and language of the will, the relevant surrounding circumstances and the events which have thrown the continued existence of the charity into doubt.
>
> It appears from *Re Roberts* [1963] 1 WLR 406 and similar cases, such as *Re Rymer* [1894] 1 Ch 19, *Re Faraker* [1912] 2 Ch 488, *Re Withal* [1932] 2 Ch 236, *Re Lucas* [1948] 1 Ch 425 and *Re Slatter's WT* [1964] 1 WLR 512, that the court must ascertain whether the intention of the testator was to benefit a charitable purpose promoted in the work of the named institution, as distinct from an intention to benefit only the named institution in the carrying out of its charitable purpose at or in connection with particular premises. This problem commonly arises in the case of bequests to a named college, school, hospital, or Home which, prior to the death of the testator, has closed down, moved, amalgamated, expanded or undergone some other potentially significant change, such as a scheme altering its objects. If, on examination of the relevant material, the court is satisfied that the gift is for a charitable purpose which the institution existed to promote and there are existing funds dedicated to that purpose (to which the bequest can be added), the gift will not be allowed to fail simply because the particular institution used as a means of attaining the charitable end has ceased to exist.
>
> On that approach ... the share in clause 5 (b) is obviously given in augmentation of the funds already held by present trustees on trusts of clause (ix) in the 1913 deed. The appeal should be dismissed.

Form and substance

The classic statement of the distinction between a general charitable intention and a specific charitable intention was given by Parker J in *Re Wilson*.

Re Wilson [1913] 1 Ch 314, HC

Facts

A testator by will gave his entire property to his three daughters and their children, with a gift over in the event of the daughters dying without issue (which in fact happened). The gift over was to provide the salary of a schoolmaster of a school to be built by subscriptions from local residents. The details of the location of the school to be built, as well as the duties of the schoolmaster, were specified by the testator. There was no prospect of the school being built.

Held

The testator manifested a specific charitable intention:

> **Parker J:** For the purposes of this case I think the authorities must be divided into two classes. First of all, we have a class of cases where, in form, the gift is given for a particular charitable purpose, but it is possible, taking

the will as a whole, to say that, notwithstanding the form of the gift, the paramount intention, according to the true construction of the will, is to give the property in the first instance for a general charitable purpose rather than a particular charitable purpose, and to graft on to the general gift a direction as to the desire or intentions of the testator as to the manner in which the general gift is to be carried into effect. In that case, though it is impossible to carry out the precise directions, on ordinary principles the gift for the general charitable purpose will remain and be perfectly good, and the court, by virtue of its administrative jurisdiction, can direct a scheme as to how it is to be carried out. In fact the will will be read as though the particular direction had not been in the will at all, but there had been simply a general direction as to the application of the fund for the general charitable purpose in question.

Then there is the second class of cases, where, on the true construction of the will, no such paramount general intention can be inferred, and where the gift, being in form a particular gift, a gift for a particular purpose – and it being impossible to carry out that particular purpose, the whole gift is held to fail. In my opinion, the question whether a particular case falls within one of those classes of cases or within the other is simply a question of the construction of a particular instrument.

It appears to be the fact that there is no reasonable chance of any such school being established at or in the neighbourhood of the place where the testator directs the school to be built, and it is, I think, in substance admitted, on behalf of the Attorney General, that no scheme giving effect to any of these directions is practicable, and that, unless I can construe the gift as a gift for the promotion of higher education in the district, the gift must necessarily be incapable of taking effect.

In my opinion, I am not justified in holding that I can disregard all the particular directions and construe the gift as a general gift for the purposes of promoting higher education. It appears to me that what the testator had in mind is, that he is dissatisfied with the provisions for the education in the district in certain respects, and that he desires that subscriptions shall be collected for the building of a school to teach certain other subjects which have not hitherto been taught, and if those subscriptions are made and a school house and a school are built, then he desires to endow or provide a salary for the schoolmaster subject to certain conditions as to certain scholars being admitted free and otherwise. I think that the whole gift is really in the testator's mind dependent upon it being feasible and possible to carry out these particular directions, and that I am not justified in reading into the will from this gift any such general intention of promoting higher education in the district or neighbourhood of the district as is suggested.

The first category of circumstances of a general charitable intention, as laid down by Parker J in *Re Wilson*, is where the gift in form appears to benefit a specific charitable purpose, but, in substance, the court may construe the gift as promoting a general charitable intention. Examples of cases within this first category of circumstances are *Re Lysaght* [1966] Ch 191, *Re Woodhams* [1981] 1 All ER 202 and *Biscoe v Jackson*.

Biscoe v Jackson (1887) 35 Ch D 460, CA

Facts

A legacy was bequeathed for the establishment of a soup kitchen and a cottage hospital in the parish of Shoreditch. A suitable site in Shoreditch could not be found. The issue concerned a *cy-près* application of the funds.

Held

On construction of the will, a general charitable intention to benefit the poor in Shoreditch could be ascertained:

Cotton LJ: Looking at this whole clause, we see an intention on the part of the testator to give £10,000 to the sick and poor of the parish of Shoreditch, pointing out how he desires that to be applied; and that particular mode having failed, as we must for the purposes of this appeal assume to be the case, then the intention to benefit the poor of Shoreditch, being a good charitable object, will have effect given to it according to the general principle laid down long ago by this court, by applying it *cy-près*. If the will had said that the trustees must build the particular building within the parish of Shoreditch there might be some difficulty, but what the testator desires to do is to provide a particular kind of hospital and a soup kitchen for the poor of the parish of Shoreditch. To my mind that shews that he intends not that it is to be located in a particular place, though that would be a proper mode of giving effect to the particular directions contained, if a place in the parish could be found; but that it is for the benefit of the parish, that is of the poor in the parish of Shoreditch.

Within the second category of cases laid down by Parker J in *Re Wilson*, the courts are entitled to draw the inference that the donor has manifested a specific charitable intention if he or she has described the charitable purpose with precision. Indeed, the clearer the description of the charitable objective which the donor has in mind, the stronger the inference that the intention is specific (illustrated by *Re Wilson*, above).

Likewise, in *Re Good*, the court, on construction, decided that the testator intended to promote a specific charitable purpose.

Re Good [1950] 2 All ER 653, HC

Facts

A legacy to provide rest homes in Hull was subject to a detailed scheme as to the types of homes to be provided, the types of inmates to be admitted and the management powers of the trustees. The scheme proved impracticable because the funds were insufficient. On a *cy-près* application, the issue arose as to whether the testator had manifested a general charitable intention.

Held

The testator had not manifested a general charitable intention. Accordingly, the funds resulted to the residuary legatees.

Question

What are the two classes of cases referred to by Parker J in *Re Wilson*?

Non-existent charitable bodies

A factor which may influence the judge in deciding the question of the intention of the donor is the fact that the charitable body selected by the donor has never been in existence. The approach here is that the specification by the donor of a named charitable institution, which has never existed, may be construed as a reference to the purpose to which the donor intended to devote his funds and is evidence of a general charitable intention: see *Re Harwood*.

Re Harwood [1936] Ch 285, HC

Facts

A testatrix bequeathed legacies to: (a) the 'Wisbech Peace Society, Cambridge' (a society which had existed at one time but had ceased to exist before the testatrix's death); and (b) the 'Peace Society of Belfast' (which had never existed).

Held

The gift to the Wisbech Peace Society manifested a specific charitable intention because the object of the testatrix's bounty was carefully selected and identified, and that portion of the estate was held on resulting trust. However, the legacy to the Belfast Society was applicable *cy-près* because her intention must have been to benefit any charitable society which promoted peace in Belfast:

> **Farwell J:** I do not propose to decide that it can never be possible for the court to hold that there is a general charitable intent in a case where the charity named in the will once existed but ceased to exist before the death. Without deciding that, it is enough for me to say that, where the testator selects as the object of his bounty a particular charity and shows in the will itself some care to identify the particular society which he desires to benefit, the difficulty of finding any general charitable intent in such case if the named society once existed, but ceased to exist before the death of the testator, is very great. Here the testatrix has gone out of her way to identify the object of her bounty. In this particular case she has identified it as being 'the Wisbech Peace Society Cambridge (which is a branch of the London Peace Society)'. Under those circumstances, I do not think it is open to me to hold that there is in this case any such general charitable intent as to allow the application of the *cy-près* doctrine.
>
> Accordingly, in my judgment, the legacy of £200 fails and is undisposed of.
>
> Then there is the gift to the 'Peace Society of Belfast'. The claimant for this legacy is the Belfast Branch of the

League of Nations Union. I am quite unable on the evidence to say that that was the society which this lady intended to benefit, and I doubt whether the lady herself knew exactly what society she did mean to benefit. I think she had a desire to benefit any society which was formed for the purpose of promoting peace and was connected with Belfast. Beyond that, I do not think that she had any very clear idea in her mind. That is rather indicated by the pencil note which was found after her death. At any rate I cannot say that by the description, 'the Peace Society of Belfast', the lady meant the Belfast Branch of the League of Nations Union; but there is enough in this case to enable me to say that, although there is no gift to any existing society, the gift does not fail. It is a good charitable gift and must be applied *cy-près*.

A similar approach was adopted by the Court of Appeal in *Re Satterthwaite's Will Trust*.

Re Satterthwaite's Will Trust [1966] 1 WLR 277, CA

Facts

A testatrix, who announced to a bank official that she hated the whole human race and wished to leave her estate to animal charities, made her will in December 1952 and died in 1962 leaving her residuary estate equally to nine animal welfare organisations selected from a telephone directory. Seven of these bodies were animal charities, but the remaining two were an anti-vivisection society and the London Animal Hospital. The question in issue concerned the one-ninth share bequeathed in favour of the London Animal Hospital. This share was claimed, *inter alia*, by a veterinary surgeon who had carried on his profession under that name from 1943 to July 1952 when, following the Veterinary Surgeons Act 1948, the name was withdrawn from the Register of Animal Hospitals. At all material times, this hospital was private and not charitable. There was no evidence that the testatrix had any knowledge of the surgeon's establishment, or that she knew that it was a private hospital.

Held

The one-ninth share of the residuary estate in question was applicable *cy-près*. The evidence suggested that the testatrix meant to benefit a purpose and not an individual. The other bequests taken as a whole (despite the one-ninth share to the Anti-Vivisection Society) showed a general charitable intention to benefit animals:

Harman LJ: If a particular donee were intended which cannot be identified, no general intent would follow. When one looks at the whole of the residuary bequest, however, it seems plain that each share is intended to go to some object connected with the care or cure of animals. That antivivisection has been declared not to be in law a charitable object, *National Anti-Vivisection Society v IRC* [1947] 2 All ER 217, is irrelevant. The society exists to save animals from suffering. The other names make the same sort of suggestion, though it is true that the evidence suggested that the words 'clinic' often indicated a place where the business of animal surgery was carried on rather than a charitable organisation.

The judge has held that there is a general charitable intent sufficient to cause share No (8) to be applied *cy-près*, and it would be inconsistent to come to a different conclusion in the case of share No (4) if, as I have held, the object there too is not identifiable. It follows that a scheme must in this instance also be settled.

Incorporated and unincorporated associations

Another factor, that has found favour with the courts in deciding the intention of the settlor, concerns the distinction between charitable corporations and unincorporated associations. An incorporated association, as distinct from an unincorporated association, has an independent legal existence distinct from its members (see p 150 above).

In *Re Vernon's Will Trust*, Buckley J expressed the view that a gift to a corporate charity is *prima facie* intended to take effect as a beneficial gift to the named body and will lapse if the charity ceases to exist before the testator's death. It will only be possible to apply the funds *cy-près* if the court, on construction, find a general charitable intention. On the other hand, where the gift is to an unincorporated association, the gift *prima facie* takes effect for the purposes of the association. The named unincorporated association is treated as the trustee to carry out the charitable purpose. Accordingly, if the association ceases to exist, the court is entitled to use its inherent jurisdiction to ensure that the trust will not fail for want of a trustee and may appoint new trustees to continue the charitable purposes. (This *prima facie* rule may be rebutted by evidence which shows that the gift was dependent upon the continued existence of the particular trustees.)

Re Vernon's Will Trust [1972] Ch 300, HC

Facts
A testatrix who made her will in 1937 directed that her residuary estate be divided among several charitable institutions equally, including the Coventry Crippled Children's Guild. The testatrix died in 1960 but, on the date of the execution of the will, an institution was in existence called the 'Coventry and District Crippled Children's Guild'. This institution was incorporated under the Companies Act 1919 and provided orthopaedic clinics and convalescent homes for crippled children. In 1948, the assets of the company were vested in the Minister of Health under the National Health Service Act 1946. The company was dissolved in 1952, but a clinic and hospital had been founded by the Guild and was in existence at the date of the testatrix's death. However, in 1949 an unincorporated charitable body was formed known as the 'Coventry and District Cripples' Guild'. This association supported crippled children, but did not carry out any orthopaedic work. The question in issue centred on which institution was entitled to part of the residuary gift.

Held
The testatrix intended to benefit the institution which existed at the time she made her will in 1937. There was therefore a valid gift to this body for the purpose of its work. Since the body had ceased to exist but its work was still carried on by a hospital and clinic under the control of the Minister of Health, the fund was applicable *cy-près*:

> **Buckley J:** Every bequest to an unincorporated charity by name without more must take effect as a gift for a charitable purpose. No individual or aggregate of individuals could claim to take such a bequest beneficially. If the gift is to be permitted to take effect at all, it must be as a bequest for a purpose, ie that charitable purpose which the named charity exists to serve. A bequest which is in terms made for a charitable purpose will not fail for lack of a trustee but will be carried into effect either under the sign manual or by means of a scheme. A bequest to a named unincorporated charity, however, may on its true interpretation show that the testator's intention to make the gift at all was dependent on the named charitable organisation being available at the time when the gift takes effect to serve as the instrument for applying the subject matter of the gift to the charitable purpose for which it is by inference given. If so and the named charity ceases to exist in the lifetime of the testator, the gift fails (*Re Ovey, Broadbent v Barrow*) (1885) 29 Ch D 560.
>
> A bequest to a corporate body, on the other hand, takes effect simply as a gift to that body beneficially, unless there are circumstances which show that the recipient is to take the gift as a trustee. There is no need in such a case to infer a trust for any particular purpose. The objects to which the corporate body can properly apply its funds may be restricted by its constitution, but this does not necessitate inferring as a matter of construction of the testator's will a direction that the bequest is to be held in trust to be applied for those purposes; the natural construction is that the bequest is made to the corporate body as part of its general funds, that is to say, beneficially and without the imposition of any trust. That the testator's motive in making the bequest may have undoubtedly been to assist the work of the incorporated body would be insufficient to create a trust. It was, I think, with considerations of this kind in mind that Harman J decided *Re Meyers (Decd), London Life Association v St George's Hospital* [1951] 1 All ER 538 on the grounds that he did.
>
> The bequest was, in my judgment, a simple bequest to the incorporated guild which that body, had it survived the testatrix, would have been entitled to receive as part of its general funds unfettered by any trust imposed by the testatrix as to the purposes for which it should be used. Had the incorporated guild been other than a charitable body, that would have been the end of the matter, for the bequest would lapse on account of the dissolution of the incorporated guild in the lifetime of the testatrix.
>
> In my judgment, the charity which at the date of the testatrix's will was being carried on by the incorporated guild continued in existence down to and after the date of her death in the form of the orthopaedic clinic and hospital which were conducted by the first defendant at 55 Holyhead Road and the Paybody Hospital. The fact that its continued existence after 5 July 1948 may be said to have been precarious, because those with power

under the National Health Service Act 1946 to decide such things might at any time have decided to discontinue the use of the properties for orthopaedic purposes and might possibly have done so without transferring the orthopaedic activities theretofore carried on in the clinic and the hospital and continuing them elsewhere, is, in my judgment irrelevant. If on the true view the charity existed at the testatrix's death and so became entitled to the bequest, its subsequently ceasing to exist would not cause the bequest to fail (*Re Slevin, Slevin v Hepburn*) [1891] 2 Ch 236.

As in *Re Lucas* [1922] 2 Ch 52, the court held that the bequest to the Crippled Children's Home, Lindley Moor, Huddersfield, was on its true construction a gift simply in augmentation of the funds of the charity so described, so in the present case I think the bequest to the 'Coventry Crippled Children's Guild' was on its true construction a gift simply in augmentation of the funds of the incorporated guild; and as in *Re Lucas* the bequest did not fail by reason of the physical home having been closed but took effect in favour of the charity in the new and different form into which it had been transmuted by an order of the charity commissioners, so by parity of reasoning, in my judgment, in the present case the bequest took effect at the death of the testatrix in favour of the charity then being conducted by the first defendant in unbroken continuance of the charity which at the date of the will was being conducted by the incorporated guild.

I accordingly reach the conclusion that the bequest on the one third share of residue with which I am concerned does not take effect in favour of the new guild, and does not fail through lapse or for uncertainty, nor is it undisposed of by the will for any other reason but that it took effect as a valid charitable gift in favour of the charity consisting of the orthopaedic clinic at 55 Holyhead Road and the orthopaedic hospital carried on in the building known as the Paybody Hospital which the first defendant was engaged in carrying on when the testatrix died. Accordingly I declare that the gift is a valid charitable gift.

This approach appealed to Goff J in *Re Finger's Will Trust*.

Re Finger's Will Trust [1972] Ch 286, HC

Facts

A testatrix, by her will made in 1930 but who died in 1965, transferred her residuary estate on trust in favour of 11 charitable institutions equally. One share was given to the 'National Radium Commission'. No institution by that name existed, although an unincorporated body called the 'Radium Commission' had existed since 1929 but was liquidated in 1947 when the National Health Service was set up. The work previously undertaken by the Commission was carried on by the Minister of Health. The court construed the bequest as intended for the Radium Commission. Another share of the bequest was given to the National Council for Maternity and Child Welfare. This was a corporate body which was in existence at the time of the execution of the will but was wound up in 1948. The bulk of the assets were transferred to the National Association for Maternity and Child Welfare, an association similar to the Council and which continued the Council's activities. The question in issue was whether both shares might be applied *cy-près*.

Held

The testatrix exhibited a general charitable intention in respect of both gifts. The gift to the unincorporated association (Radium Commission) was construed as intended for the purposes of the Commission which were not dependent on the continued existence of the Commission. The gift to the incorporated association which ceased to exist on the date of vesting was treated *prima facie* as a gift to the body (see *Re Harwood*) but was still capable of being construed as a general charitable gift since virtually the whole estate was devoted for charitable purposes, the testatrix regarded herself as having no relatives and the Council merely had a co-ordinating function:

Goff J: The first question which arises is whether as a matter of construction the gift of a share of residue to the National Radium Commission was a gift to the corporate body known as the National Radium Trust or to the unincorporated body defined in the charter as the Radium Commission. The words in the will do not describe either body with complete accuracy, but it seems to me that the word 'Commission' has more significance that 'National', particularly as both bodies operated on a national basis. It is also, I think, significant that the commission was in substance the operative body which organised the supplies. I therefore hold that the first share in question was given to the Radium Commission.

[The learned judge referred to Buckley J's judgment in *Re Vernon's Will Trusts* [1972] Ch 300, and continued:] As I read the *dictum* in *Re Vernon* [1972] Ch 300, Buckley J's view was that in the case of an unincorporated body the gift is *per se* a purpose trust and, provided that the work is still being carried on, will have effect given to it by way of scheme notwithstanding the disappearance of the donee in the lifetime of the testator, unless there is something positive to show that the continued existence of the donee was essential to the gift. Then Buckley J put his *dictum* into practice and decided *Re Morrison, Wakefield v Falmouth* (1967) 111 SJ 758, on that very basis, for there was nothing in that case beyond the bare fact of a gift to a dissolved unincorporated committee. In the case of a corporation, however, *Re Vernon* shows that the position is different as there has to be something positive in the will to create a purpose trust at all.

Accordingly I hold that the bequest to the National Radium Commission being a gift to an unincorporated charity is a purpose trust for the work of the commission which does not fail but is applicable under a scheme, provided (1) there is nothing in the context of the will to show – and I quote from *Re Vernon* – that the testatrix's intention to make the gift at all was dependent on the named charitable organisation being available at the time when the gift took effect to serve as the instrument for applying the subject matter of the gift to the charitable purpose for which it was by inference given; (2) that charitable purpose still survives; but that the gift to the National Council for Maternity and Child Welfare, 117 Piccadilly, London being a gift to a corporate body fails, notwithstanding the work continues, unless there is a context in the will to show that the gift was intended to be on trust for that purpose and not an absolute gift to the corporation.

I take first the National Radium Commission and I find in this will no context whatever to make that body of the essence of the gift . . .

In my judgment, therefore, this is a valid gift for the purposes of the Radium Commission as specified in article 7 of the supplemental charter of 20 July 1939 and I direct that a scheme be settled for the administration of the gift.

I turn to the other gift and here I can find no context from which to imply a purpose trust. In the present case there are at best three different groups of charities not one; they are not in fact grouped in the order in which they appear in the will, and the particular donees within the respective groups are not all of the same type or character. Further, and worse, two do not fit into any grouping at all, and for what it is worth they come first in the list. In my judgment, therefore, this case is not comparable with *Re Meyers (Decd), London Life Association v St George's Hospital* [1951] Ch 534 and I cannot find a context unless I am prepared, which I am not, to say that the mere fact that residue is given to a number of charities, some of which are incorporated and others not, is of itself a sufficient context to fasten a purpose trust on the corporation. In my judgment, therefore, the bequest to the National Council for Maternity and Child Welfare fails.

Finally, I must consider, however whether the share passes on intestacy or whether the will discloses a general charitable intention. Here, of course, I was at once presented with *Re Harwood, Coleman v Innes* [1936] Ch 285, and I feel the force of the argument on behalf of the next-of-kin based on that case, although I confess that I have always felt the decision in that case to be rather remarkable. However, Farwell J did not say that it was impossible to find a general charitable intention where there is a gift to an identifiable body which has ceased to exist but only that it would be very difficult.

In the present case the circumstances are very special. First, of course, apart from the life interest given to the mother and two small personal legacies the whole estate is devoted to charity, and that is, I think, somewhat emphasised by the specific dedication to charity in the preface:

> And after payment of the said legacies my trustees shall hold the balance then remaining of my residuary estate upon trust to divide the same in equal shares between the following charitable institutions and funds.

Again, I am, I think, entitled to take into account the nature of the council, which as I have said was mainly, if not exclusively, a co-ordinating body. I cannot believe that this testatrix meant to benefit that organisation and that alone. Finally, I am entitled to place myself in the armchair of the testatrix and I have evidence that she regarded herself as having no relatives.

Taking all these matters into account, in my judgment I can and ought to distinguish *Re Harwood* and find, as I do, a general charitable intention. Accordingly, this share is applicable *cy-près*.

The method by which Goff J in *Re Finger's Will Trust* was able to distinguish *Re Harwood* was doubted by Megarry VC in *Re Spence*.

Re Spence [1979] Ch 483, HC

Facts

A testatrix who died in 1972, by her will dated 4 December 1968 bequeathed her residuary estate equally between 'The Blind Home, Scott Street, Keighley' and the 'Old Folks Home at Hillworth Lodge, Keighley, for the benefit of the patients'. The Keighley and District Association for the Blind was the only charity connected with the blind in the Keighley area. It ran a home in Scott Street which was often called 'The Blind Home', 'The Keighley and District Home for the Blind', and 'Keighley Home for the Blind'. A similar home was also run by the Association at Bingley. Hillworth Lodge was built as a workhouse in 1858 and was closed in 1939. In 1948, it became an aged person's home under the National Assistance Act 1948, but was closed down in 1971. Since then the building had been used as government offices. The question in issue was whether the testatrix had manifested a general or specific charitable intention.

Held

(a) The testatrix intended to benefit the patients at the Blind Home, Scott Street, Keighley and did not intend to augment the funds of the charity which ran the home.

(b) The gift to the 'Old Folks Home' failed and the fund was not applicable *cy-près*.

The court applied *Re Harwood* and refused to follow *Re Finger's Will Trust*. The testatrix had manifested a specific charitable intention by identifying a particular charitable purpose which on the date of the will was capable of being carried out, but was incapable of being fulfilled at the time of death:

> **Sir Robert Megarry VC:** There is therefore the question whether the moiety should go to the charity as an accretion to its endowment, and so be capable of being employed on any part of its activities, or whether it is to be confined to the particular part of the charity's activities that are carried on at the Blind Home in Scott Street, Keighley.
>
> The testatrix was making provision of the benefit of the patients for the time being at a particular home, namely, the home usually known as the Blind Home at Scott Street, Keighley. She was giving the money not to augment generally the endowment of the charity which runs that home, with the consequence that the money might be used for purposes other than the benefit of the patients at that home, but was giving the money so that it would be used exclusively for the benefit of those patients. The only way in which this can conveniently be done is to give the money to the charity but to confine its use for the benefit of the patients for the time being at the home. That, I think, requires a scheme; but I see no need to direct that a scheme should be settled in chambers. Instead, I think that I can follow the convenient course taken by Goff J in *In Re Finger's Will Trusts* [1972] Ch 286, p 300. I shall, therefore, order by way of scheme (the Attorney General not objecting) that the moiety be paid to the proper officer of the charity to be held on trust to apply it for the benefit of the patients for the time being of the home known as the Blind Home, Scott Street, Keighley.
>
> I now turn to the other moiety of residue, given by the will to 'the Old Folks Home' at Hillworth Lodge, Keighley for the benefit of the patients.
>
> Now without looking at the authorities, I would have said that this was a fairly plain case of a will which made a gift for a particular purpose in fairly specific terms. The gift was for the benefit of the patients at a particular home, namely, the Old Folks Home at Hillworth Lodge, Keighley. At the date of the will there were patients at that home. When the testatrix died, there was no longer any home there, but offices instead; and so there were no longer any patients there, or any possibility of them. The gift was a gift for a charitable purpose which at the date of the will was capable of accomplishment and at the date of death was not. *Prima facie*, therefore the gift fails unless a general charitable intention has been manifested so that the property can be applied *cy-près*.
>
> The case before me is a gift for a purpose, namely, the benefit of the patients at a particular Old Folks Home. It therefore seems to me that I ought to consider the question, of which little or nothing was said in argument, whether the principle in *In Re Harwood* [1936] Ch 285, or a parallel principle, has any application to such case. In other words, is a similar distinction to be made between, on the one hand, a case in which the testator has selected a particular charitable purpose, taking some care to identify it, and before the testator dies that purpose has become impracticable or impossible of accomplishment, and on the other hand, a case where the charitable purpose has never been possible or practicable?

As at present advised I would answer 'Yes' to that question. I do not think that the reasoning of the *In Re Harwood* line of case is directed to any feature of institutions as distinct from purposes. Instead, I think the essence of the distinction is in the difference between particularity and generality. If a particular institution or purpose is specified, then it is that institution or purpose, and no other, that is to be the object of the benefaction. The specific displaces the general. It is otherwise where the testator has been unable to specify any particular charitable institution or practicable purpose, and so, although his intention of charity can be seen, he has failed to provide any way of giving effect to it. There, the absence of the specific leaves the general undisturbed. It follows that in my view in the case before me, where the testatrix has clearly specified a particular charitable purpose which before her death became impossible to carry out, Mr Mummery has to face that level of great difficulty in demonstrating the existence of a general charitable intention which was indicated by *In Re Harwood*.

One way in which Mr Mummery sought to meet that difficulty was by citing *In Re Finger's Will Trusts* [1972] Ch 286. There, Goff J distinguished *In Re Harwood* and held that the will before him displayed a general charitable intention. He did this on the footing that the circumstances of the case were 'very special'. The gift that failed was a gift to an incorporated charity which had ceased to exist before the testatrix died. The 'very special' circumstances were, first, that apart from a life interest and two small legacies, the whole estate was devoted to charity, and that this was emphasised by the direction to hold the residue in trust for division 'between the following charitable institutions and funds'. Second, the charitable donee that had ceased to exist was mainly, if not exclusively, a co-ordinated body, and the judge could not believe that the testatrix meant to benefit that body alone. Third, there was evidence that the testatrix regarded herself as having no relatives.

In the case before me neither of these last two circumstances applies, nor have any substitute special circumstances been suggested. As for the first, the will before me gives 17 pecuniary legacies to relations and friends, amounting in all to well over one third of the net estate. Further, in *In Re Rymer* [1895] 1 Ch 19, which does not appear to have been cited, the will had prefaced the disputed gift by the words 'I give the following charitable legacies to the following institutions and persons respectively'. These words correspond to the direction which in *In Re Finger's Will Trusts* was regarded as providing emphasis, and yet they did not suffice to avoid the conclusion of Chitty J and the Court of Appeal that a gift to an institution which has ceased to exist before the testator's death lapsed and could not be applied *cy-près*. I am not sure that I have been able to appreciate to the full the cogency of the special circumstances that appealed to Goff J; but however that may be, I can see neither those nor any other special circumstances in the present case which would suffice to distinguish *In Re Harwood*.

From what I have said it follows that I have been quite unable to extract from the will, construed in its context, any expression of a general charitable intention which would suffice for the moiety to be applied *cy-près*. Instead, in my judgment, the moiety was given for a specific charitable purpose which, though possible when the will was made, became impossible before the testatrix died. The gift of the moiety accordingly fails, and it passes as on intestacy.

Question
How would you reconcile *Re Finger's Will Trust* with *Re Spence*?

Charities Act 1993, s 14

The general rule, as detailed above, is that property given for a specific charitable purpose which fails from the outset cannot be applied *cy-près* if no general charitable intention can be imputed to the donor. Such property will be held on resulting trust for the donor.

By the way of exception to the general rule, s 14 of the Charities Act 1993 (reenacting s 14 of the Charities Act 1960) states that property given for specific charitable purposes which fail shall be applicable *cy-près* as if given for charitable purposes generally. This is the case where the property belongs to a donor who cannot be identified or found after reasonable inquiries and advertisements have been made, or who disclaims his or her right to the property in writing.

Charities Act 1993, s 14 [as amended by the Charities Act 2006]

(1) Property given for specific charitable purposes which fail shall be applicable *cy-près* as if given for charitable purposes generally, where it belongs –

(a) to a donor who after –

(i) the prescribed advertisements and inquiries have been published and made; and

(ii) he prescribed period beginning with the publication of those advertisements has expired,

cannot be identified or cannot be found; or

(b) to a donor who has executed a disclaimer in the prescribed form of his right to have the property returned.

(2) Where the prescribed advertisements and inquiries have been published and made by or on behalf of trustees with respect to any such property, the trustees shall not be liable to any person in respect of the property if no claim by him to be interested in it is received by them before the expiry of the period mentioned in sub-s (1)(a)(ii) above.

(3) For the purposes of this section property shall be conclusively presumed (without any advertisement or inquiry) to belong to donors who cannot be identified, in so far as it consists:

(a) of the proceeds of cash collections made by means of collecting boxes or by other means not adapted for distinguishing one gift from another; or

(b) of the proceeds of any lottery, competition, entertainment, sale or similar money-raising activity, after allowing for property given to provide prizes or articles for sale or otherwise to enable the activity to be undertaken.

(4) The court [or the Commission] may by order direct that property not falling within sub-s (3) above shall for the purposes of this section be treated (without any advertisement or inquiry) as belonging to donors who cannot be identified where it appears to the court either:

(a) that it would be unreasonable, having regard to the amounts likely to be returned to the donors, to incur expense with a view to returning the property; or

(b) that it would be unreasonable, having regard to the nature, circumstances and amounts of the gifts, and to the lapse of time since the gifts were made, for the donors to expect the property to be returned.

(7) For the purposes of this section, charitable purposes shall be deemed to 'fail' where any difficulty in applying property to those purposes makes that property or the part not applicable *cy-près* available to be returned to the donors.

. . . . . .

(10) In this section, except in so far as the context otherwise requires, references to a donor include persons claiming through or under the original donor, and references to property given include the property for the time being representing the property originally given or property derived from it.

(11) This section shall apply to property given for charitable purposes, notwithstanding that it was so given before the commencement of this Act.

What constitutes 'prescribed advertisements and inquiries' under s 14(1) of the Charities Act 1993 will vary with the circumstances of each case: see *Re Henry Wood National Memorial Trusts*.

Re Henry Wood National Memorial Trusts (1965) 109 SJ 876, HC

Facts

A nationwide appeal was launched to raise funds to build a concert hall to be named after Sir Henry Wood. One of the purposes as stated in the appeal was 'improving and extending knowledge and appreciation of good music'. The fund raised proved insufficient to build the concert hall. The trustees of the appeal sought directions from the court concerning the surplus.

Held

Notices in *The Times*, *The Telegraph* and *The Scotsman* newspapers, and letters to addresses of donors noted in the appeal records constituted reasonable advertisements and inquiries.

Sections 17 and 18 of the Charities Act 2006 modifies s 14 of the Charities Act 1993 by introducing two new subsections, ss 14(A) and (B). The purpose is intended to enlarge the jurisdiction of the court or the Commission to make schemes for the application of the property *cy-près*.

Charities Act 1993 s 14(A)

(1) This section applies to property given –

    (a) for specific charitable purposes, and

    (b) in response to a solicitation within subsection (2) below.

(2) A solicitation is within this subsection if –

    (a) it is made for specific charitable purposes, and

    (b) it is accompanied by a statement to the effect that property given in response to it will, in the event of those purposes failing, be applicable cy pres as if given for charitable purposes generally, unless the donor makes a relevant declaration at the time of making the gift.

(3) A 'relevant declaration' is a declaration in writing by the donor to the effect that, in the event of the specific charitable purposes failing, he wishes the trustees holding the property to give him the opportunity to request the return of the property in question . . .

(4) Subsections (5) and (6) below apply if –

    (a) a person has given property as mentioned in subsection (1) above,

    (b) the specific charitable purposes fail, and

    (c) the donor has made a relevant declaration.

(5) The trustees holding the property must take the prescribed steps for the purpose of –

    (a) informing the donor of the failure of the purposes,

    (b) enquiring whether he wishes to request the return of the property . . . and

    (c) if within the prescribed period he makes such a request, returning the property . . . to him

(6) If those trustees have taken all appropriate prescribed steps but –

    (a) they have failed to find the donor, or

    (b) the donor does not within the prescribed period request the return of the property . . .

    section 14(1) above shall apply to the property as if it belonged to a donor within paragraph (b) of that subsection (application of property where the donor has disclaimed right to return of property).

(7) If –

    (a) a person has given property as mentioned in subsection (1) above,

    (b) the specific charitable purposes fail, and

    (c) the donor has not made a relevant declaration,

    section 14(1) above, shall similarly apply to the property as if it belonged to a donor within paragraph (b) of that subsection.

(8) For the purposes of this section –

    (a) 'solicitation' means a solicitation made in any manner and however communicated to the persons to whom it is addressed,

    (b) it is irrelevant whether any consideration is or is to be given in return for the property in question, and

    (c) where any appeal consists of both solicitations that are accompanied by statements within subsection (2)(b) and solicitations that are not so accompanied, a person giving property as a result of the appeal is to be taken to have responded to the former solicitations and not the latter, unless he proves otherwise.

(9) In this section 'prescribed' means prescribed by regulations made by the Commission, and any such regulations shall be published by the Commission in such manner as it thinks fit.

(10) Subsections (7) and (10) of section 14 shall apply for the purposes of this section as they apply for the purposes of section 14.

The effect of the new s 14(A) of the 1993 Act is to enlarge the jurisdiction of the court or the Commission to apply funds *cy près* where a donor transfers funds for a specific charitable purpose that fails. This is the position where the donation is made in response to a solicitation as defined in s 14(A)(2). This result will be achieved where the appeal by the charity is made subject to an accompanying statement to that effect and may be communicated in any manner to the relevant persons. The funds will be applied *cy près* as if the donor had disclaimed an interest in the property. Alternatively, the donor may prevent the funds being applied *cy près* and thus retain an interest in the property, if he makes a relevant declaration in writing as defined in s 14(3). The effect is that the onus is on the donor to demonstrate that, within a prescribed period, he wishes to have the opportunity to request the return of the property should the gift fail. If, however, the trustees have taken the prescribed steps to inform the donor of the failure of the purposes, but the donor cannot be found or he does not request the return of the property within the prescribed period, the property may be applied *cy près* as if the donor has disclaimed his right to the return of the property.

Charities Act 1993 s14(B)

(1) The power of the court or the Commission to make schemes for the application of property cy pres shall be exercised in accordance with this section.

(2) Where any property given for charitable purposes is applicable cy pres, the court or the Comission may make a scheme providing for the property to be applied –

    (a) for such charitable purposes, and

    (b) (if the scheme provides for the property to be transferred to another charity) by or on trust for such other charity,

as it considers appropriate, having regards to the matters set out in subsection (3).

(3) The matters are –

    (a) the spirit of the original gift,

    (b) the desirability of securing that the property is applied for charitable purposes which are close to the original purposes, and

    (c) the need for the relevant charity to have purposes which are suitable and effective in the light of current social and economic circumstances.

    The 'relevant charity' means the charity by or on behalf of which the property is to be applied under the scheme.

(4) If a scheme provides for the property to be transferred to another charity, the scheme may impose on the charity trustees of that charity a duty to secure that the property is applied for purposes which are, so far as is reasonably practicable, similar in character to the original purposes.

(5) In this section references to property include the property for the time being representing the property originally given or property derived from it.

(6) In this section references to the transfer of property to a charity are references to its transfer –

    (a) to the charity, or

    (b) to the charity trustees, or

    (c) to any trustee for the charity, or

    (d) to a person nominated by the charity trustees to hold it in trust for the charity,

as the scheme may provide.

The purpose of the new s14((B) of the 1993 Act is to clarify the operation of the powers of the court or the Commission when applying property *cy près*. The court or the Commission is required to have regard to the matters set out in s14(B)(3) when making a scheme changing the charitable purposes for which the property was donated. This applies either when the scheme involves the transfer of property from one charity to another or when there is no transfer and the scheme changes the purposes of the charity as the court or the Commission considers appropriate.

Question
What is the policy behind the enactment of s 14 of the Charities Act 1993?

THE CHARITY COMMISSION

The office of the Charity Commissioners was established in 1853 by the Charitable Trusts Act of that year to provide a simple and inexpensive means of dealing with difficulties encountered by charities. The office had no legal existence as a body but carried out a number of important functions on behalf of the Crown. Section 6(1) of the Charities Act 2006 abolishes the office of the Charity Commissioners and sets up a new body corporate in its place, called the Charity Commission. This new body has inherited the functions, property, rights and liabilities of its predecessor. The Commission will be a non-ministerial Government Department and will have a significant degree of independence from Ministers and other Government Departments. The Commission will consist of a chairman and at least four, but not more than eight other members, see Schedule 1 of the 2006 Act. The Commission is subject to the jurisdiction of the High Court in the exercise of their quasi-judicial powers, and appeals from their decisions may be made to the High Court.

Section 7 of the 2006 Act inserts four new sections – sections 1B to 1E into the Charities Act 1993. These provide the Commission with five objectives, six general functions, six general duties and incidental powers.

Charity Tribunal

Section 8 of the Charities Act 2006 introduces four new provisions to the Charities Act 1993 – ss 2(A) to 2(D). These sections create a new tribunal called the charity tribunal to act as 'the court of first instance' for appeals and applications in respect of certain decisions of the new Charity Commission. It also enables the Tribunal to consider matters referred to it by the Attorney-General or, with the Attorney-General's consent, by the Charity Commission. The provisions cover the practice, procedure, membership and appointments to the Tribunal. Appeals from the Tribunal are made to the High Court only on points of law.

Charities' register

Section 9 of the Charities Act 2006 introduces three new sections – 3, 3(A) and 3(B) into the Charities Act 1993. Under the new s 3 of the Charities Act 1993, the Charity Commission will continue to maintain a register of charities which is open to the public. All charities are required to register with the Commissioners save for exempt charities (specified in Sched 2 to the Charities Act 1993, including the British Museum, the Victoria and Albert Museum and registered Friendly Societies) and excepted charities (including the Boy Scouts and Girl Guides Associations, and certain charities connected with the promotion of the efficiency of the armed forces). In addition, religious organisations having places of worship need not register, nor need small charities, that is, any charity which has neither: (a) any permanent endowment; nor (b) the use and occupation of any land, and whose income does not in aggregate amount to more than £5,000 per annum (s 3(A)(2)).

The effect of registration, under s 4(1) of the Charities Act 1993, is that the organisation is conclusively presumed to be charitable.

Legal proceedings

Section 32 of the Charities Act 1993 empowers the Commission to exercise the same powers as are exercisable by the Attorney General in respect of the taking of legal proceedings with reference to charities, or compromising claims with a view to avoiding or ending such proceedings.

Section 33(1) of the Charities Act 1993 lists the persons who may bring proceedings in respect of charitable matters. These are: (a) the charity; (b) any charity trustees; (c) any person interested in the charity; (d) in the case of a local charity, any two or more inhabitants of the area. The sub-section concludes 'but not by any other person'. Thus, no other person may bring proceedings, except the Attorney General in his capacity as *parens patriae*. Owing to the public nature of such trusts, the Attorney General is always required to be included as a party to legal proceedings.

Section 33(2) states that no such proceedings shall be entertained or proceeded with in any court unless authorised by order of the Commissioners. See *Gaudiya Mission v Brahmachary* [1997] 4 All ER 957 (see p 417 above).

The expression 'any person interested in the charity' within s 33(1) of the Charities Act 1993 was considered by the court in *Gunning and Others v Buckfast Abbey Trustees and Another*.

Gunning and Others v Buckfast Abbey Trustees and Another (1994)
The Times, 9 June, HC

Facts
The claimants were the fee-paying parents of children at a school managed by the first defendants (trustees of property applied in the charitable activities of the monks). The school was founded by monks in 1967 as a Roman Catholic preparatory school. On 15 February 1994, the trustees announced that the school was to be closed at the end of the summer term 1994. The decision was taken by the Abbot with the consent of a committee known as the Abbot's council. The claimants challenged this decision. The questions before the court involved two preliminary questions, namely: (a) whether the claimants possessed a sufficient standing to bring the proceedings; and (b) whether, on a true construction of the trust deed, the consent of the Abbot's council was necessary to close the school. The court was not concerned with the reasons leading to the decision to close the school.

Held
Arden J decided in favour of the claimants on the grounds that:

(a) the claimants' children were beneficiaries of the trust. They could become pupils only as a result of their parents making a contract with the trustees. The mere fact that the claimants had such contracts did not mean that they were barred from bringing charity proceedings. They would be so barred if they were seeking to use the charity proceedings to assist them to pursue an adverse claim against the trustees;

(b) on construction of the trust deed, the decision to close the school required the advice but not the consent of the Abbot's council.

Question
Who, under s 33 of the Charities Act 1993, is entitled to bring legal proceedings in respect of matters concerning specific charities?

In *Gaudiya Mission v Brahmachary* (see p 417 above), the Court of Appeal decided that the expression 'charity' in s 33 of the Charities Act 1993, did not include an institution registered and established under the laws of a foreign jurisdiction. It would be impractical for the High Court to seek to extend its supervisory jurisdiction to control an overseas registered charity.

FURTHER READING

Baxter, C, 'Trustees' personal liability and the role of liability insurance' [1996] Conv 12.

Cotterell, R, 'Gifts to charitable institutions: a note on recent developments' [1972] 36 Conv 198.

Duncan, G, 'Re Broadbent: the ultimate destination of a testamentary gift to a non-existent charity' [2002] PCB 243.

Luxton, P, 'In pursuit of "purpose" through s 13 of the Charities Act 1960' [1985] Conv 313.

Morris, D, 'Broadcast advertising by charities' [1990] Conv 106.

Warburton, J, 'Casenote on Re JW Laing Trust' [1984] Conv 319.

APPOINTMENT, RETIREMENT AND REMOVAL OF TRUSTEES

INTRODUCTION

Following the constitution of a trust, new trustees may be appointed by persons nominated in the trust instrument. In the absence of such a clause, the authority to appoint new trustees is specified in s 36(1) of the Trustee Act 1925. As a last resort, the court is entitled to appoint trustees under s 41 of the Trustee Act 1925.

A trustee may retire from the trust in one of five ways:

(a) by taking advantage of a power in the trust instrument;

(b) by taking advantage of a statutory power under:

    (i)   s 36(1) of the Trustee Act 1925 when a replacement trustee is appointed; or

    (ii)   s 39 of the Trustee Act 1925 where no new trustee is appointed;

(c) by obtaining the consent of all the beneficiaries who are *sui juris* and absolutely entitled to the trust property under the rule in *Saunders v Vautier* (1841) 4 Beav 115;

(d) further to a direction from the relevant beneficiaries under s 19 of the Trusts of Land and Appointment of Trustees Act 1996; or

(e) by obtaining the authority of the court.

A trustee may be removed from office in one of the following four ways:

(a) by virtue of a power contained in the trust instrument;

(b) under s 36 of the Trustee Act 1925;

(c) in the circumstances specified in ss 19 and 20 of the Trusts of Land and Appointment of Trustees Act 1996; or

(d) by virtue of a court order under s 41 of the Trustee Act 1925 or the inherent jurisdiction of the court.

APPOINTMENT

There are only two occasions when it may be necessary to appoint trustees:

(a) on the creation of a new trust – whether *inter vivos* or by will; and

(b) during the continuance of an existing trust, either in replacement of a trustee or as an additional trustee.

Creation of a new trust

There are two ways in which a settlor may create an *inter vivos* trust, namely, by way of self-declaration (that is, he declares that he will be a trustee of specific property for the benefit of another or others) or by transferring property to a third party/parties (trustee/trustees) subject to a declaration of trust (see the *Milroy v Lord* rule, in Chapter 3 above). In the latter case, it seems clear that if the document purporting to transfer the property to the intended trustee is a nullity, no trust is created. This may be the case where the document purporting to transfer the property is improperly executed, or where the intended trustees are not identified or are dead or have otherwise ceased to exist. In these circumstances, the property remains vested in the settlor.

On the other hand, if the trust is already completely constituted (that is, the trust property is vested in the trustees subject to the terms of the trust) and circumstances arise where the appointed trustee (or trustees) ceases (or cease) to exist (for example, death or refusal to act as trustee), the trust will not fail for lack of a trustee. If the trust instrument authorises any person to appoint trustees, that power may be utilised. The settlor may have reserved in the instrument the power to appoint trustees. If this is the case, he could then exercise the power to make an appointment not *qua* settlor but as someone entitled to effect an appointment under the instrument. In the absence of such authority, resort may be had to the statutory power enacted in s 36 of the Trustee Act 1925 (see p 451 below) or ss 19–21 of the Trusts of Land and Appointment of Trustees Act 1996 (see p 454 below). As a last resort, the court may make an appointment in the exercise of its inherent jurisdiction. In doing so, it will apply the maxim, 'Equity will not allow a trust to fail for want of a trustee'.

In the case of a trust declared by the testator's will, a legal transfer of the property is effected automatically in favour of the executor(s) when the latter obtains probate. The executor's functions include the collection of assets belonging to the deceased, settling the deceased's debts and distributing the estate in accordance with the will. If the will declares a trust and obliges the executor to distribute the property accordingly, but no trustees were identified by the testator, or they predecease him or they refuse to act as trustees, the trust will still be valid. The personal representatives (ie, the executor or administrator of the deceased's estate) will be deemed to be the trustees until replacement trustees are appointed.

Continuance of the trust

When a trust is created (whether *inter vivos* or by will), the trust property (real or personal) vests in all the trustees as joint tenants (see s 18(1) of the Trustee Act 1925). The effect is that, on the death of a trustee, the property devolves on the survivors.

Trustee Act 1925, s 18(1)

Where a power or trust is given to or imposed on two or more trustees jointly, the same may be exercised or performed by the survivors or survivor of them for the time being.

On the death of the sole or surviving trustee, the property vests in his personal representatives, subject to the trust, until replacement trustees are appointed (see s 18(2) of the Trustee Act 1925).

Trustee Act 1925, s 18(2)

Until the appointment of new trustees, the personal representatives or representative for the time being of a sole trustee, or, where there were two or more trustees of the last surviving or continuing trustee, shall be capable of exercising or performing any power or trust which was given to or capable of being exercised by, the sole or last surviving or continuing trustee, or other trustees or trustee for the time being of the trust.

Question
On what occasions may the need to appoint trustees arise?

The authority to appoint new trustees may be derived from three sources, namely:

(a) an express power;

(b) a statutory power;

(c) the court.

This hierarchical order of authority to appoint trustees is required to be followed strictly. Only when there is no person in one group willing to make an appointment can the power be exercised by a person in a different group: see *Re Higginbottom*.

Re Higginbottom [1892] 3 Ch 132, HC

Facts

Mary Broadbent became the sole executrix of the sole surviving trustee and was entitled to exercise the statutory power to appoint new trustees. Her selection of candidates as trustees was opposed by the majority of the beneficiaries, who petitioned the court to secure the appointment of two other candidates.

Held

The court had no jurisdiction to interfere in the appointment of trustees by Mary, provided that the appointment was made in good faith.

Express power

The trust instrument may confer the authority to appoint a trustee. This is exceptional because the statutory power to appoint is generally regarded as adequate. The express authority may be general or special. A general authority is one which confers an authority to appoint trustees in any circumstances. If the person named in the instrument is willing to exercise the power, this will be decisive as to the authority to appoint trustees provided that the power is exercised in good faith. However, it is doubtful whether the appointor is entitled to appoint himself, for reasons stated by Kay J in *Re Skeat*.

Re Skeat (1889) 42 Ch D 522, HC

Kay J: A man should not be judge in his own case . . . and to appoint himself among other people, or excluding them to appoint himself, would certainly be an improper exercise of any power of selection of a fiduciary character.

If the authority is special (that is, exercisable in limited circumstances), it will be strictly construed by the courts: see *Re Wheeler and De Rochow*.

Re Wheeler and De Rochow [1896] 1 Ch 315, HC

Facts

A marriage settlement gave the husband and wife or the survivor of them the power to appoint new trustees in specified circumstances, including the occasion when a trustee became 'incapable' of acting. One of the trustees became bankrupt. This made him 'unfit' but not incapable of acting as a trustee. The question in issue was whether a new trustee should have been appointed by the husband (as survivor), or by the continuing trustees (under statute).

Held

The continuing trustees had the power to appoint a new trustee. The occasion entitling the express power to be exercised had not arisen.

Note

Similarly, where two or more persons have the power to appoint new trustees, they are required to exercise the authority jointly, unless there are express provisions to the contrary. It follows that such a joint power cannot be exercised where one of the appointors dies, or they cannot agree on the candidate to be appointed as trustee (see *Re Harding* [1923] 1 Ch 182).

Statutory power: s 36 of the Trustee Act 1925

The statutory power to appoint trustees is contained in s 36 of the Trustee Act 1925 (replacing the Trustee Act 1893). The occasions giving rise to the need to appoint trustees are enacted in s 36(1) (replacement trustees) and s 36(6) (additional trustees) of the Trustee Act 1925.

Replacement trustees: s 36(1) of the Trustee Act 1925

There are seven circumstances listed in s 36(1) of the Trustee Act 1925 when a replacement trustee may be appointed. These are:

(1) where a trustee is dead. Under s 36(8) of the Trustee Act 1925, this includes the person nominated as trustee under a will but predeceasing the testator;

(2) where a trustee remains outside the UK for a continuous period of 12 months or more. The UK includes England, Wales, Scotland and Northern Ireland, but does not include the Channel Islands or the Isle of Man. The motive for remaining outside the UK is irrelevant; this condition will be satisfied even if the trustee remains outside the UK against his will;

(3) where a trustee desires to be discharged from all or any of the trusts or powers reposed in or conferred on him. Thus, a trustee may retire from part only of the trust;

(4) where a trustee refuses to act. This includes the occasion when the trustee disclaims his office. It is advisable that the disclaimer be executed by deed;

(5) where a trustee is unfit to act. Unfitness refers to some defect in the character of the trustee which suggests an element of risk in leaving the property in the hands of the individual, for example, a conviction for an offence involving dishonesty or bankruptcy (see *Re Wheeler and De Rochow*, p 451 above);

(6) where a trustee is incapable of acting. Incapacity refers to some physical or mental inability to administer the trust adequately, but does not include bankruptcy (see *Re Wheeler and De Rochow*, p 451 above). Under s 36(3) of the Trustee Act 1925, a corporation becomes incapable of acting on the date of its dissolution;

(7) where the trustee is an infant, that is, a person under the age of 18. Such a person may become a trustee under an implied trust (resulting or constructive). An infant is incapable of becoming an express trustee.

Persons who may exercise the statutory power

Section 36(1) of the Trustee Act 1925 lists, in order of priority, the persons who are entitled to exercise the statutory power of appointing replacement trustees. These are:

(a) the person or persons nominated in the trust instrument for the purpose of appointing new trustees; or

(b) if there is no such person, or no such person able and willing to act, then the surviving or continuing trustee; or

(c) the personal representatives of the last surviving or continuing trustee.

Section 36(1) of the Trustee Act 1925 was enacted to empower a sole retiring trustee to appoint his or her successor. It enables a 'retiring' or 'refusing' trustee to participate with the surviving trustees in appointing a successor (s 36(8) of the Trustee Act 1925). But there is no obligation on such 'retiring' trustee to concur in making the appointment. An appointment by the remaining trustees would be valid if the retiring trustee does not participate in the appointment (see *Re Coates* (1886) 34 Ch D 370).

A trustee who is legitimately removed as a trustee is not a 'continuing', or 'refusing' or 'retiring' trustee for the purposes of s 36(8) of the Trustee Act 1925. He is a removed trustee. Thus, following *Re Stoneham*, a trustee who is removed from his or her office is not entitled to participate in the appointment of new trustees.

Re Stoneham's Settlement Trust [1953] Ch 59, HC

Facts

The two trustees of the settlement were X and Y. Y remained out of the UK for a period exceeding 12 months. X executed a deed retiring from the trust and appointed two others in place of Y and himself. Y challenged the validity of the new appointments on the ground that he was entitled to participate in making the appointments.

Held

The court rejected Y's claim and decided that, since Y was compulsorily removed from the trust, he was not a 'retiring' or 'refusing' trustee within s 36(8) of the Trustee Act 1925:

> **Danckwerts J:** . . . I come to the conclusion quite plainly that a trustee who is removed against his will is not a refusing or retiring trustee, not, at any rate, in the case of a trustee removed because of his absence outside the UK for consecutive periods of more than 12 months.

In order to become a surviving or continuing trustee, the property is required to vest in the individual as a trustee. Accordingly, if all the persons entitled to act as trustees under a will predecease the testator, the personal representative of the last to die would not be empowered to appoint new trustees. The personal representative of the testator will become the trustee and, subject to provisions to the contrary, will be entitled to appoint new trustees.

Section 36(4) of the Trustee Act 1925 provides that the personal representative of the last surviving or continuing trustee includes those who have proved the will of the testator or the administrator of a person dying intestate.

Section 36(5) of the Trustee Act 1925 provides that a sole or last surviving executor intending to renounce probate shall have the power of appointment of trustees at any time before renouncing probate.

Additional trustees: s 36(6) of the Trustee Act 1925

Section 36(6) of the Trustee Act 1925 authorises the appointment of additional trustees although no trustee needs to be replaced.

Trustee Act 1925, s 36(6)

> Where a sole trustee, other than a trust corporation, is or has been originally appointed to act in a trust, or where, in the case of any trust, there are not more than three trustees (none of them being a trust corporation) either original or substituted and whether appointed by the court or otherwise, then and in any such case:
>
> (a) the person or persons nominated for the purpose of appointing new trustees by the instrument, if any, creating the trust; or
>
> (b) if there is no such person, or no such person able and willing to act, then the trustee or trustees for the time being
>
> may, by writing, appoint another person or other persons to be an additional trustee or additional trustees, but it shall not be obligatory to appoint any additional trustee, unless the instrument, if any, creating the trust, or any statutory enactment provides to the contrary, nor shall the number of trustees be increased beyond four by virtue of any appointment.

Note

The sub-section is self-explanatory, but it may be observed that a trust corporation (a corporate professional trustee, such as a bank or an insurance company) has the power of two or more individual trustees. No power exists under s 36(6) of the Trustee Act 1925 to increase the number of trustees beyond four.

Question

Who has the authority to appoint new trustees?

The Trustee Delegation Act 1999 amended s 36 of the Trustee Act 1925 by inserting four new sub-sections – s 36(6A)–(6D). The purpose of the provisions is to authorise the donee of an enduring power of attorney to appoint additional trustees, but subject to a maximum of four trustees (including the attorney). The new provisions only operate where the attorney intends to exercise trustee functions relating to land, or its proceeds of sale, or income from land by virtue of a delegation under s 25 of the Trustee Act 1925, or the trust instrument. This new power may be limited by the trust instrument or the terms of the power of attorney.

Trustee Act 1925, s 36(6A)–(6D)

(6A) A person who is either –

    (a) both a trustee and attorney for the other trustee (if one other), or for both of the other trustees (if two others), under a registered power; or

    (b) attorney under a registered power for the trustee (if one) or for both or each of the trustees (if two or three),

    may, if subsection (6B) of this section is satisfied in relation to him, make an appointment under subsection (6)(b) of this section on behalf of the trustee or trustees.

(6B) This subsection is satisfied in relation to an attorney under a registered power for one or more trustees if (as attorney under the power) –

    (a) he intends to exercise any function of the trustee or trustees by virtue of section 1(1) of the Trustee Delegation Act 1999, or

    (b) he intends to exercise any function of the trustee or trustees in relation to any land, capital proceeds of a conveyance of land or income from land by virtue of its delegation to him under section 25 of this Act or the instrument (if any) creating the trust.

(6C) In subsections (6A) and (6B) of this section 'registered power' means a power of attorney created by an instrument which is for the time being registered under section 6 of the Enduring Powers of Attorney Act 1985.

(6D) Subsection (6A) of this section –

    (a) applies only if and so far as a contrary intention is not expressed in the instrument creating the power of attorney (or, where more than one, any of them) or the instrument (if any) creating the trust; and

    (b) has effect subject to the terms of those instruments.

Direction of the beneficiaries

Sections 19–21 of the Trusts of Land and Appointment of Trustees Act 1996 have invested new powers in the beneficiaries to direct a retirement of trustees and/or appointment of trustees. These provisions relate to trusts of all types of property (whether land or personalty). However, the provisions may be excluded in whole or in part by the trust instrument.

Section 19 applies where there is no person nominated under the trust instrument to appoint new trustees, and all the beneficiaries are of full age and capacity and collectively are absolutely entitled to the trust property. The beneficiaries have either one or both of the following rights: a right to direct in writing that one or more of the trustees shall retire from the trust; and/or that a named person or persons be appointed, in writing, as new trustee or trustees. The direction may be by way of substitution for a trustee or trustees directed to retire, or as an additional trustee or trustees.

If a direction to retire is given, the trustee concerned *shall* execute a deed effecting his retirement if:

(a) reasonable arrangements have been made to protect his rights under the trust;

(b) after retirement, there will be either a trust corporation or at least two persons to act as trustees; and

(c) either a replacement trustee is to be appointed on his retirement, or the continuing trustees, by deed, consent to his retirement.

Section 19 contains no provision compelling the trustees (or the personal representative of the last surviving trustee) to act on a direction to appoint a person as a new trustee. On a practical level, the trustee is unlikely to refuse to make the appointment without good reason.

Section 20 of the Trusts of Land and Appointment of Trustees Act 1996 applies where:

(a) a trustee becomes mentally incapable of exercising his functions as trustee;

(b) no person entitled to appoint new trustees is willing and able to do so; and

(c) the beneficiaries are of full age and capacity and are collectively entitled to the trust property.

The beneficiaries may then give a written direction to the trustee's receiver or his attorney under a registered enduring power, or to a person authorised under the Mental Health Act 1983 to appoint a particular person to be a new trustee. The Act is silent on the consequences of a failure to act on the direction.

Section 21(1) of the Trusts of Land and Appointment of Trustees Act 1996 enacts that a direction for the purposes of ss 19 or 20 of the 1996 Act may take one of two forms:

(a) a single direction collectively executed by all the beneficiaries; or

(b) a number of directions, whether solely or jointly with one or more, but not all, of the beneficiaries,

identifying the same person or persons for retirement or appointment.

Section 21(3) of the 1996 Act declares that the effect of an appointment of a new trustee under ss 19 or 20 of the 1996 Act is the same as if the new trustee were appointed under s 36(7) of the Trustee Act 1925, that is, he shall have the same powers and discretions as if he was appointed under the trust.

Section 36(7) of the Trustee Act 1925 (as amended by the Trusts of Land and Appointment of Trustees Act 1996) provides that the effect of an appointment under s 36 of the Trustee Act 1925 or ss 19 or 20 of the Trusts of Land and Appointment of Trustees Act 1996 shall have the same consequences 'as if he [the new trustee] had been originally appointed a trustee by the instrument, if any, creating the trust'.

Question
When may replacement and additional trustees be appointed? What influence, if any, do beneficiaries have in the appointment of trustees?

The number of trustees

Section 34 of the Trustee Act 1925 (as amended by the Trusts of Land and Appointment of Trustees Act 1996) provides that where land is held on trust, there may not be more than four trustees. If the instrument purports to appoint more than four trustees, only the first four named as trustees will take the property.

On the other hand, while a sole trustee is not forbidden, s 14(2) of the Trustee Act 1925 states that a sole trusteeship (other than a trust corporation) may not give a valid receipt for the proceeds of sale arising under a trust of land or capital money arising under the Settled Land Act 1925.

In theory, there is no restriction on the number of persons who may be appointed trustees of personalty.

In practice, it may be inconvenient and cumbersome to have too many trustees. The office of trusteeship requires unanimous approval of all the trustees (charities are treated as an exception). The law does not recognise a 'sleeping' or inactive trustee. A breach may be committed by a 'sleeping' trustee in failing to oppose a decision taken by his colleagues: see *Bahin v Hughes* (1886) 31 Ch D 390, p 472 below.

There are rarely more than four trustees and, if the appointment is made under s 36 of the Trustee Act 1925, there will not be more than four trustees.

Alternatively, a sole trustee is most unsatisfactory because of the risk of fraud or misconduct in administering the trust.

Vesting of trust property in trustees

On an appointment of a replacement or additional trustee, the trust property is required to be vested in the new trustee to enable him to carry out his duties. Trustees hold the property as joint tenants so that the right of survivorship applies.

The vesting of the property in a new trustee may be effected in one of two ways, namely:

(a) by a conveyance or transfer effective to vest the property in the transferee. The relevant formalities that are required to be complied with vary with the nature of the property involved. The legal title to unregistered land requires a conveyance, whereas registered land requires the new owner to be registered as the proprietor. Shares require registration in the share register of the company; or

(b) s 40(1) of the Trustee Act 1925.

Trustee Act 1925, s 40(1)

Where by a deed a new trustee is appointed, then:

(a) if the deed contains a declaration by the appointor to the effect that any estate or interest in any land, or in any chattel, or the right to recover or receive any debt or thing in action, shall vest in the persons who by virtue of the deed become or are the trustees for performing the trust, the deed shall operate without any conveyance or assignment to vest in those persons as joint tenants . . .; and

(b) if the deed . . . does not contain such a declaration, it shall, subject to any express provision to the contrary, operate as if it had contained such a declaration by the appointor extending to all the estates, interests and rights with respect to which a declaration could have been made.

Similar provisions are enacted in s 40(2) (as amended by the Trusts of Land and Appointment of Trustees Act 1996) in respect of a retiring trustee.

Note
The effect of s 40(1) and (2) is to create a short form and inexpensive method of vesting the trust property in the new trustee or trustees. Under s 40(1)(a), if the deed merely declares that the property vests in the new trustee, this would be sufficient without a conveyance, etc. Section 40(1)(b) enacts that if the deed of appointment omits to include a vesting declaration, it will be treated as if it had contained the same.

Exceptions

Section 40(4) of the Trustee Act 1925 excludes certain types of property from the general provisions in s 40(1) and (2). These include:

(a) land held by trustees on a mortgage as security for a loan of trust money;

(b) leases containing a condition prohibiting dispositions without consent unless the consent has already been obtained;

(c) stocks and shares.

In these circumstances, the property is required to be transferred in accordance with the appropriate formalities for that type of property.

Question

How may the trust property become vested in replacement or additional trustees?

Appointment by the court

Section 41 of the Trustee Act 1925 enacts the sweeping power of the court to appoint new trustees either as replacement or additional trustees.

Trustee Act 1925, s 41(1)

The court may, whenever it is expedient to appoint a new trustee or new trustees, and it is found inexpedient, difficult or impracticable so to do without the assistance of the court, make an order appointing a new trustee or new trustees either in substitution for or in addition to any existing trustee or trustees, or although there is no existing trustee . . .

The most popular occasions when the court's discretion may be exercised are where a sole surviving trustee dies intestate, or where an appointor is incapable of making an appointment because of infancy, or where all the trustees of a testamentary trust predecease the testator or where there is friction between the trustees.

The court will exercise its power to appoint trustees only when all other avenues have been exhausted. Thus, the court will not exercise its power where an express or statutory power can be exercised.

In exercising its discretion under s 41, the court will have regard to the wishes of the settlor, the interests of the beneficiaries and the efficient administration of the trust. In *Re Tempest*, the Court of Appeal issued guidelines concerning appointments of trustees by the court.

Re Tempest (1866) I Ch App 485, CA

Facts

A family settlement was created by will. There were two trustees appointed, one of whom predeceased the testator. Those with the power to appoint new trustees were unable to agree as to the appropriate candidate and an application was made for the appointment of Mr Petre (P). One beneficiary opposed this appointment on the ground that P came from a part of the family with whom the testator had an ongoing dispute.

Held

P was not a suitable person to be appointed a trustee for his appointment might have impeded the proper administration of the trust:

> **Turner LJ:** The following rules and principles may, I think, safely be laid down as applying to all cases of appointments by the court of new trustees. First, the court will have regard to the wishes of the persons by whom the trust has been created, if expressed in the instrument creating the trust, or clearly to be collected from it . . . Another rule which may safely be laid down is this – that the court will not appoint a person to be trustee in opposition to the interests of the beneficiaries . . . it is of the essence of the duty of every trustee to hold an even hand between the parties interested under the trust . . . A third rule is that the court in appointing a trustee will have regard to the question, whether his appointment will promote or impede the execution of the trust, for the very purpose of the appointment is that the trust may by better carried into execution.
>
> These are the principles by which, in my judgment, we ought to be guided in determining whether Mr Petre ought to be appointed to be a trustee of this will, and, in my opinion, there are substantial objections to his appointment on each of the three grounds to which I have referred.
>
> . . . there cannot, I think, be any doubt that the court ought not to appoint a trustee whose appointment will impede the due execution of the trust; but, on the other hand, if the continuing or surviving trustee refuses to act with a trustee who may be proposed to be appointed . . . I think it would be going too far to say that the court ought, on that ground alone, to refuse to appoint the proposed trustee; for this would be to give the continuing or surviving trustee a veto upon the appointment of the new trustee. In such a case, I think it must be the duty of the court to inquire and ascertain whether the objection of the surviving or continuing trustee is well founded

or not, and to act or refuse to act upon it accordingly. If the surviving or continuing trustee has improperly refused to act with the proposed trustee, it must be a ground for removing him from the trust. Upon the facts of this case, however, it seems to me that the objections to the appointment of Mr Petre were and are well founded.

Section 43 of the Trustee Act 1925 enacts that the effect of an appointment by the court will be treated 'as if the appointee had been originally appointed a trustee by the instrument, if any, creating the trust'.

Question
When a court exercises its discretion to appoint trustees, what factors should the judge take into account?

RETIREMENT

A trustee may retire from the trust in one of five ways:

(a) by taking advantage of a power in the trust instrument;

(b) by taking advantage of a statutory power under:

  (i) s 36(1) of the Trustee Act 1925 when a new trustee is appointed, that is, the trustee is 'desirous of being discharged'; or

  (ii) s 39 of the Trustee Act 1925, where no new trustee is appointed;

(c) by obtaining the consent of all the beneficiaries who are *sui juris* and absolutely entitled to the trust property under the *Saunders v Vautier* principle (see p 519 below);

(d) by direction from the relevant beneficiaries under s 19 of the Trusts of Land and Appointment of Trustees Act 1996 (see p 455 above); or

(e) by obtaining the authority of the court.

Trustee Act 1925, s 39(1) (as amended by the Trusts of Land and Appointment of Trustees Act 1996)

Where a trustee is desirous of being discharged from the trust, and after his discharge there will be either a trust corporation or at least two persons to act as trustees to perform the trust, then, if such trustee as aforesaid by deed declares that he is desirous of being discharged from the trust, and if his co-trustees and such other person, if any, as is empowered to appoint trustees, by deed consent to the discharge of the trustee, and to the vesting in the co-trustees alone of the trust property, the trustee desirous of being discharged shall be deemed to have retired from the trust, and shall, by deed, be discharged therefrom under this Act, without any new trustee being appointed in his place.

Unlike a retirement under s 36(1) of the Trustee Act 1925, a trustee is not allowed to retire from part of a trust under s 39 of the Trustee Act 1925. He is required to retire from the trust as a whole or not at all.

The procedure for retirement under s 39 of the Trustee Act 1925 is as follows:

(a) at least two individuals will continue to act as trustees or a trust corporation;

(b) the remaining trustees (or trustee) and other persons empowered to appoint trustees consent to the retirement by deed; and

(c) the retiring trustee makes such a declaration by deed.

It should be noted that a retiring trustee remains liable for breaches of trust committed whilst he was a trustee. He is absolved from liability in respect of subsequent breaches, unless he retired in order to facilitate a breach of trust: see *Head v Gould* [1898] 1 Ch 250, p 559 below.

Retirement under a court order

Generally speaking, the court will not discharge a trustee under its statutory jurisdiction under s 41 of the Trustee Act 1925, unless it appoints a replacement trustee. However, the court has an inherent jurisdiction to discharge a trustee without replacement, in accordance with its responsibility to administer the trust. This will be the position when s 39 of the Trustee Act 1925 is not applicable because the appropriate consent cannot be obtained.

REMOVAL OF TRUSTEES

A trustee may be removed from office in one of the following four ways:

(a) by virtue of a power contained in the trust instrument. This is highly unusual, but if such power exists the court is required to construe the instrument to ascertain whether the circumstances have arisen which give rise to the exercise of the power;

(b) under s 36 of the Trustee Act 1925. This involves the removal of and appointment of a replacement trustee in circumstances laid down in s 36(1) of the 1925 Act (see p 452 above);

(c) in the circumstances specified in ss 19 to 21 of the Trusts of Land and Appointment of Trustees Act 1996; (see p 454)

(d) under a court order under s 41 of the Trustee Act 1925 or the inherent jurisdiction of the court.

Court order

Under s 41 of the Trustee Act 1925, the court has the jurisdiction to remove an existing trustee and appoint a replacement trustee (see p 457 above).

Under its inherent jurisdiction to secure the proper administration of the trust, the court has the power to remove a trustee without appointing a replacement trustee. In *Letterstedt v Broers*, the Privy Council declared that the court had a general duty to ensure that the trusts were properly executed and their main guide was the welfare of the beneficiaries. Accordingly, friction and hostility between the trustees and the beneficiaries which is likely to prejudice the proper administration of the trust may be a ground for the removal of trustees.

Letterstedt v Broers (1884) 9 App Cas 371, PC

Facts

A beneficiary under a trust created by will made allegations of misconduct against a trustee concerning the administration of the trust.

Held

Notwithstanding that the allegations were not substantiated, the court would exercise its jurisdiction to remove the trustees:

> **Lord Blackburn:** . . . the whole case has been argued here, and, as far as their Lordships can perceive, in the court below, as depending on the principles which should guide an English court of equity when called upon to remove old trustees and substitute new ones. It is not disputed that there is a jurisdiction 'in cases requiring such a remedy' as is said in Story's *Equity Jurisprudence*, s 1287, but there is very little to be found to guide us in saying what are the cases requiring such a remedy; so little that their Lordships are compelled to have recourse to general principles.

> Story says, s 1289:

>> But in cases of positive misconduct, courts of equity have no difficulty in interposing to remove trustees who have abused their trust; it is not indeed every mistake or neglect of duty, or inaccuracy of conduct of trustees, which will induce courts of equity to adopt such a course. But the acts or omissions must be such as to endanger the trust property or to show a want of honesty, or a want of proper capacity to execute the duties, or a want of reasonable fidelity.

It seems to their Lordships that the jurisdiction which a court of equity has no difficulty in exercising under the circumstances indicated by Story is merely ancillary to its principal duty, to see that the trusts are properly executed. This duty is constantly being performed by the substitution of new trustees in the place of original trustees for a variety of reasons in noncontentious cases. And therefore, though it should appear that the charges of misconduct were either not made out, or were greatly exaggerated, so that the trustee was justified in resisting them, and the court might consider that in awarding costs, yet if satisfied that the continuance of the trustee would prevent the trusts being properly executed, the trustee might be removed. It must always be borne in mind that trustees exist for the benefit of those to whom the creator of the trust has given the trust estate.

. . . if it appears clear that the continuance of the trustee would be detrimental to the execution of the trusts, even if for no other reason than that human infirmity would prevent those beneficially interested, or those who act for them, from working in harmony with the trustee . . . the trustee is always advised by his own counsel to resign, and does so. If, without any reasonable ground, he refused to do so, it seems that the court might think it proper to remove him.

It is quite true that friction or hostility between trustees and the immediate possessor of the trust estate is not of itself a reason for the removal of the trustees. But where the hostility is grounded on the mode in which the trust has been administered, where it has been caused wholly or partially by substantial overcharges against the trust estate, it is certainly not to be disregarded.

Looking, therefore, at the whole circumstances of this very peculiar case, the complete change of position, the unfortunate hostility that has arisen, and the difficult and delicate duties that may yet have to be performed, their Lordships can come to no other conclusion than that it is necessary, for the welfare of the beneficiaries, that the Board should no longer be trustees.

The guiding principles were also considered by the court in *Re Wrightson*.

Re Wrightson [1908] 1 Ch 789, HC

Facts
The trustees admitted a breach of trust in connection with an advance of a part of the trust funds upon mortgage. The question in issue was whether one of the trustees should be removed. A substantial proportion of the beneficiaries opposed his removal but others supported it.

Held
Having regard to all the circumstances, the court would not make an order for the removal of the trustee. The test was whether the trust property could safely be left in the hands of the trustee. Important factors to be taken into consideration were that a substantial number of the beneficiaries wished the trustee to continue, a change of trustees would involve expense and the court foresaw that there was unlikely to be any future breaches of trust:

Warrington J: Is it necessary here, having regard to the welfare of the beneficiaries and for the protection of this trust to remove the trustee? At the present moment nothing remains for the trustees to do except to wind up the estate; the testator's widow is dead; the whole of the estate is divisible amongst a number of persons who are *sui juris* . . . having regard to the fact that the court has now the power of seeing that the trust is properly executed, to the fact that a large proportion of the beneficiaries do not require the trustees to be removed, and further to the extra expense and loss to the trust estate which must be occasioned by the change of trustees, I think it would not be for the welfare of the beneficiaries generally, or for the protection of the trust estate, that these trustees should be removed.

Note
In *Moore v McGlynn* [1894] 1 IR 74, it was decided that a trustee who started up a business in competition with the trust was placed in such a position of conflict with the trust that his removal was justified.

Question
When may a trustee retire or be removed from a trust?

FURTHER READING

Hopkins, N, 'The Trusts of Land and Appointment of Trustees Act 1996' [1996] Conv 411.

Jones, G, 'Delegation by trustees – a reappraisal' (1959) 22 MLR 381.

Kenny, A, 'Living up to expectations' (1996) 146 NLJ 348.

Parry, N, 'Remuneration of trustees' [1984] Conv 275.

DUTIES AND POWERS OF TRUSTEES

INTRODUCTION

Trustees are subject to a variety of wide-ranging duties in the administration of trusts. The duties imposed on trustees have been developed by the courts and statutory provisions over several centuries. These duties may be modified, within limits, by the trust instrument. The general policy regarding the duties of trustees may be categorised into two broad principles, namely:

(a) an obligation to act honestly and with reasonable diligence in preserving the trust funds; and

(b) an obligation to act fairly and impartially in their dealings with the beneficiaries.

Linked with the duties imposed on trustees is a variety of powers. The sources of these powers are the trust instrument, statutory provisions, the authority of the beneficiaries and directions from the court. The legitimate exercise of these powers varies with the facts of each case.

TRUSTEES' DUTIES

The office of a trustee or fiduciary reflects a variety of onerous duties on the trustee or fiduciary. Far from receiving gratitude from the beneficiaries, the trustees may be subject to claims by beneficiaries for breaches of trust (see *Williams v Barton* [1927] 2 Ch 9, HC, Chapter 9). In performing their duties, the trustees are required to act honestly, diligently and in the best interests of the beneficiaries. Thus, the trustees are not entitled to show favour to a beneficiary or group of beneficiaries, but are required to act impartially and in the best interests of all the beneficiaries. For the application of this rule, see *Lloyds Bank v Duker*.

Lloyds Bank plc v Duker [1987] 3 All ER 193, HC

Facts

An application was made to the court for an order entitling the trustees to transfer to a residuary beneficiary his share (46/80ths or 574 shares) of the residuary estate of 999 shares. This would have entitled him to a majority holding which would have exceeded the value of the rest of the shares subject to the trust.

Held

The court refused the application and instead ordered all the shares to be sold and the proceeds divided between the beneficiaries in accordance with the will:

Mowbray QC: ... the general rule stated in *Snell's Principles of Equity* 28 ed 1982, p 233 is as follows:

The general rule is that in the absence of some good reason to the contrary a person who is indefeasibly entitled to a share in divisible personalty is entitled to have his share transferred to him, even if the property is held on trust for sale with power to postpone sale and the transfer would diminish the value of the other shares.

For that proposition *Snell's Principles of Equity*, and Mr Harrod, cite *In re Marshall* [1914] 1 Ch 192; *In Re Sandeman's Will Trusts* [1937] 1 All ER 368 and *In Re Weiner (Decd)* [1956] 1 WLR 579. Nevertheless, as Snell indicates, the rule is not without exceptions. The general rule requiring a distribution was applied in the first three authorities I have mentioned, but in *In re Marshall* [1914] 1 Ch 192, pp 199, 200, Cozens-Hardy MR recognised that it could be excluded by 'special circumstances', and in *In Re Sandeman's Will Trusts* [1937] 1 All ER 368, p 371, Clauson J said the court would not order a transfer if there was some good ground to the contrary and he said, at p 373:

I can conceive that there might be circumstances – they would have to be very special – which would justify the court in refusing to give effect to the plaintiff's rights ...

Are the circumstances in the present case such as to require the bank to sell all 999 shares, rather than distributing 574 of them to Mr Duker? To answer this question, I need to see what kind of circumstances would exclude his normal right to have this aliquot part of the shares distributed to him. Clauson J ruefully said in *In Re Sandeman's Will Trusts* [1937] 1 All ER 368, p 372: 'The court has, I think, been rather careful never to define in precise terms exactly.'

I accept *In Re Sandeman's Will Trusts* [1937] 1 All ER 368 and *In Re Weiner (Decd)* [1956] 1 WLR 579 as authorities which ought to be followed at first instance that the general rule is not excluded by the fact that the distribution breaks up a controlling interest, and so reduces the value of the whole. I assume that is correct, and if that were the only reason for ordering a sale of the 999 shares as a whole in the present case, the decisions in *In Re Sandeman's Will Trusts* and *In Re Weiner (Decd)* would be against it. But it is not the only reason for a sale in the present case, as I see it. The operative reason is that, if the shares were transferred out in the one 80th fractions, Mr Duker would get a greater value per share than the other beneficiaries and so would get more than his 46/80ths of the total value received by the beneficiaries as a body.

I can, though, get some help from another general principle. I mean the principle that trustees are bound to hold an even hand among their beneficiaries, and not favour one as against another, stated for instance in *Snell's Principles of Equity op cit*, p 225. Of course Mr Duker must have a larger part than the other beneficiaries. But if he takes 46/80ths of the shares he will be favoured beyond what Mr Smith intended, because his shares will each be worth more than the others. The trustees' duty to hold an even hand seems to indicate that they should sell all 999 shares instead. Mr Romer pointed out that it is this duty which imposes a trust for sale under the first branch of the rule in *Howe v Earl of Dartmouth* (1802) 7 Ves Jun 137.

In all the circumstances, to prevent the unfairness which would result from a transfer of 574 of the shares to Mr Duker, and to ensure that he takes 48/80ths of the residuary estate measured by value, I consider that the bank should not transfer any of the shares to him, but should sell all 999 on the general market, Mr Duker being left free to become a buyer.

The duty on the trustees to act impartially or with even-handedness is acute with regard to the exercise of the trustees' discretion. The claimant will undoubtedly bear the legal burden to prove that the trustee has acted in breach of his duty of impartiality, but it is not an easy task to challenge the exercise by a trustee of a discretion. One basis on which the trustee's decision might be challenged would be to establish that it was perverse, in the sense that no reasonable trustee could properly have taken it. Another would be to show that the trustee had proceeded on the basis of some mistake of fact or law which vitiates the decision. That is the principle often referred to as the rule in *Re Hastings Bass* [1975] Ch 25. It is now established that in the case of a discretion which the trustee is not under a duty to exercise a party seeking to challenge the trustee's decision has to show that the trustee would (and not merely might) have taken a different decision had he not made the mistake (see *Sieff v Fox* [2005] 1 WLR 3811 and *Betafence v Veys* [2006] EWHC 999 (Ch)). A third basis would be to show that the trustee exercised his discretion to achieve an unlawful purpose, that is to say a purpose other than that for which the power was given. In *Chirkinian v Arnfield* the court decided that although a beneficial unsecured loan potentially puts the assets of the trust in jeopardy, the risks are taken for the benefit of the beneficiary. Such a loan should not be recalled unless the trustee considered it to be in the interests of the debtor beneficiary, or other beneficiaries to do so. The judge ruled that, on the facts of this case, a decision to call in a beneficial loan and pursue the beneficiary debtor to the point of bankruptcy could not be treated as an instance of the trustee acting neutrally. From the evidence no consideration was given to the interests of the beneficiary and the judgment of the trustee was seriously flawed. In reality the trustee appeared to prefer the interests of the liquidator as opposed to the interests of the beneficiary.

Chirkinian v Arnfield [2006] EWHC 1917 (Ch), (High Court)

Facts

The appellant, Mr Chirkinian, was formerly the sole shareholder and managing director of a private company called Larcom Ltd (the company). The company was initially successful with a turnover of £492m in the year ending January 2002. Subsequently the company ran into financial difficulties and has since been the subject of a winding up order. In December 2002, the company set up an employee benefit trust. The trustee was Charwell Trustees Ltd, which was resident in Jersey. The trusts were governed by Jersey law, subject to a power for the trustees to change that law. The purpose of setting up the employee benefit trust was to secure the most tax efficient way in which the appellant may receive profits from the company. In furtherance of this plan it was intended that capital of the trust fund be loaned to him on an interest free basis. The total amount to the appellant was £5.1m of which £435,000 was repaid. In 2004, the liquidator of the company exercised its power to remove Charwell Trustees Ltd as trustee and appoint the respondent in its place. In June 2005, the respondent as trustee exercised its power to change the proper law of the trust from Jersey law to English law. In July 2005, written demand for the repayment of the loan was made on the appellant. When no payment was received the respondent followed up its demands with a statutory demand in October 2005. This appeal is brought to set aside the statutory demand on the basis that the debt is disputed on grounds which appear to be substantial. The appellant's contention was that the respondent's decision to call in the loans was taken in breach of trust.

Held

Allowing the appeal and setting aside the statutory demand on the ground that the respondent trustee acted in breach of trust in promoting the interests of the liquidator over the interests of the beneficiary.

Michael Furness QC: In my view there substantial grounds for thinking that the Respondent has acted in breach of trust. I hold this view for the following reasons:

(1) It appears from Ms Knight's evidence that the Respondent proceeded on the basis that the duty to preserve trust assets compelled it to seek to recover the loan. But where the loan in question has been made under a power to make beneficial loans to beneficiaries, that is an oversimplification of the position. Any beneficial unsecured loan potentially puts the assets of the trust in jeopardy, but the risk is taken for the benefit of the beneficiary. Such a loan should not, in my view, be recalled unless the trustee considers it to be in the interests of either the debtor beneficiary, or other beneficiaries, to do so. Of course, if the loans had been purportedly made by way of investment of the trust fund then the Respondent would have been under a duty to recover them – indeed the loans should never have been made as investments at all. But where loans are made in the exercise of a beneficial, and not an investment power, different considerations come into play. The evidence shows that in the present case the trustee has no present plans as to how to use the recovered assets for the benefit of any of the other beneficiaries. The decision to call in the loan appears to have been taken simply for the sake of preserving the assets of the trust.

(2) In reality it appears that the interests of the liquidator may lie behind the decision to recall the loans. In my view, even if those interests were matters which the Respondent could have properly taken into account (see below), it was premature for it to do so before any claim had been made by the liquidator. There is no evidence of a claim having been made by the liquidator, and no evidence that a claim has even been intimated. In these circumstances it cannot be right for a trustee to prefer the potential interests of the liquidator over the interests of the beneficiaries of the trust of which it is trustee.

(3) Even if a claim had been made by a liquidator I think it is doubtful whether a trustee would be justified in taking action to prefer the liquidator's interests over those of the beneficiaries of the trust.

For present purposes it suffices to note that even if Mr Beltrami (counsel for the respondent) is right to say that the trustee should exercise its powers in a "neutral" way in these circumstances, it can hardly be said that a decision to call in a beneficial loan and pursue the beneficiary debtor to bankruptcy if payment is not made is acting neutrally. It is clear from the evidence that in calling in this loan no consideration was given the interests of the Appellant as beneficiary at all. Instead the trustee has assumed it was under a duty to prefer the interests of the liquidator, by getting in the assets.

For the above reasons I consider that the trustees decision was seriously flawed.

Note

The effect of this even-handedness rule is that the trustees are required to take positive steps to avoid placing themselves in a position where their duties may conflict with their personal interests. If there is a conflict of the trustees' duties and interest, the trustees are required to hand over any unauthorised benefit to the beneficiaries (see Chapter 9). Thus, it is imperative that the trustees do not deviate from the terms of the trust without the authority of the beneficiaries or the court.

The standard of care and skill

A feature of the fiduciary duties imposed on trustees is that they are required to execute their duties with a degree of care and skill expected from trustees.

At common law

Throughout the administration of the trust, the trustees are required to exhibit an objective standard of skill such as would be expected from an ordinary prudent man of business. In the case of a power of investment, the duty would be exercised so as to yield the best return for all the beneficiaries, judged in relation to the risks inherent in the investments and the prospects of the yield of income and capital appreciation. The classical statement of the rule was laid down by Lord Watson in *Learoyd v Whiteley*.

Learoyd v Whiteley (1887) 12 AC 727, HL

Lord Watson: As a general rule the law requires of a trustee no higher degree of diligence in the execution of his office than a man of ordinary prudence would exercise in the management of his own private affairs. Yet he is not allowed the same discretion in investing the moneys of the trust as if he were a person *sui juris* dealing with his own estate. Businessmen of prudence may, and frequently do, select investments which are more or less of a speculative character but it is the duty of a trustee to confine himself to the class of investments which are permitted by the trust and likewise to avoid all investments of that class which are attended with hazard. As long as he acts in the honest observance of these limitations the general rule already stated will apply.

The courts will have regard to all the circumstances of each case in order to ascertain whether the trustees' conduct fell below the standard imposed on such persons.

In considering the investment policy of the trust, the trustees are required to put on one side their own personal interests and views. They may have strongly held social or political views. They may be firmly opposed to any investments in companies connected with alcohol, tobacco, armaments or many other things. In the conduct of their own affairs, trustees are free to abstain from making any such investments. However, in performance of their fiduciary duties, if investments of the morally reprehensible type would be more beneficial to the beneficiaries than other investments, the trustees must not refrain from making the investments by reason of the views that they hold. Trustees may even act dishonourably (though not illegally) if the interests of their beneficiaries require it, as in *Buttle v Saunders*.

Buttle v Saunders [1950] 2 All ER 193, HC

Facts
Trustees for sale had struck a bargain for the sale of the trust property but had not bound themselves by a legally binding contract. They received a higher offer but the trustees felt morally obliged to accept the earlier offer. The question in issue was whether they were obliged to consider the higher offer.

Held
The trustees were under a duty to consider and explore a better offer received by them and were not required to accept the lesser offer because they felt morally bound.

The court reviewed the law and came to a similar conclusion in *Cowan v Scargill*.

Cowan v Scargill and Others [1984] 3 WLR 501, HC

Facts

The defendants were trustees of the Mineworkers Pension Scheme who raised an objection to a new investment plan of trust funds. The grounds were that the proposed strategy involved investments overseas in competing forms of energy.

Held

The investment plan would yield the best return for the beneficiaries; the court refused the application:

Megarry VC: I turn to the law. The starting point is the duty of trustees to exercise their powers in the best interests of the present and future beneficiaries of the trust, holding the scales impartially between different classes of beneficiaries. This duty of the trustees towards their beneficiaries is paramount. They must, of course, obey the law; but subject to that, they must put the interests of their beneficiaries first. When the purpose of the trust is to provide financial benefits for the beneficiaries, as is usually the case, the best interests of the beneficiaries are normally their best financial interests. In the case of a power of investment, as in the present case, the power must be exercised so as to yield the best return for the beneficiaries, judged in relation to the risks of the investments in question; and the prospects of the yield of income and capital appreciation both have to be considered in judging the return from the investment.

In considering what investments to make trustees must put on one side their own personal interests and views. Trustees may have strongly held social or political views. They may be firmly opposed to any investment in South Africa or other countries, or they may object to any form of investment in companies concerned with alcohol, tobacco, armaments or many other things. In the conduct of their own affairs, of course, they are free to abstain from making any such investments. Yet under a trust, if investments of this type would be more beneficial to the beneficiaries than other investments, the trustees must not refrain from making the investments by reason of the views that they hold. Trustees may even have to act dishonourably (though not illegally) if the interests of their beneficiaries require it. Thus, where trustees for sale had struck a bargain for the sale of trust property but had not bound themselves by a legally enforceable contract, they were held to be under a duty to consider and explore a better offer that they received, and not to carry through the bargain to which they felt in honour bound (*Buttle v Saunders* [1950] 2 All ER 193). In other words, the duty of trustees to their beneficiaries may include a duty to 'gazump,' however honourable the trustees. As Wynn-Parry J said at p 195, trustees 'have an overriding duty to obtain the best price which they can for their beneficiaries'. In applying this to an official receiver in *In Re Wyvern Developments Ltd* [1974] 1 WLR 1097, p 1106, Templeman J said that he 'must do his best by his creditors and contributories. He is in a fiduciary capacity and cannot make moral gestures, nor can the court authorise him to do so'. In the words of Sir James Wigram VC in *Balls v Strutt* (1841) 1 Hare 146, p 149:

> It is a principle in this court, that a trustee shall not be permitted to use the powers which the trust may confer upon him at law, except for the legitimate purposes of his trust . . .

By way of caveat I should say that I am not asserting that the benefit of the beneficiaries which a trustee must make his paramount concern inevitably and solely means their financial benefit, even if the only object of the trust is to provide financial benefits. Thus, if the only actual or potential beneficiaries of a trust are all adults with very strict views on moral and social matters, condemning all forms of alcohol, tobacco and popular entertainment, as well as armaments, I can well understand that it might not be for the 'benefit' of such beneficiaries to know that they are obtaining rather larger financial returns under the trust by reason of investments in those activities than they would have received if the trustees had invested the trust funds in other investments. The beneficiaries might well consider that it was far better to receive less than to receive more money from what they consider to be evil and tainted sources. But I would emphasise that such cases are likely to be very rare, and in any case I think that under a trust for the provision of financial benefits the burden would rest, and rest heavy, on him who asserts that it is for the benefit of the beneficiaries as a whole to receive less by reason of the exclusion of some of the possibly more profitable forms of investment. Plainly the present case is not one of this rare type of cases. Subject to such matters, under a trust for the provision of financial benefits, the paramount duty of the trustees is to provide the greatest financial benefits for the present and future beneficiaries.

Trustees must do the best they can for the benefit of their beneficiaries, and not merely avoid harming them. I find it impossible to see how it will assist trustees to do the best they can for their beneficiaries by prohibiting a wide range of investments that are authorised by the terms of the trust. Whatever the position today, nobody can say that conditions tomorrow cannot possibly make it advantageous to invest in one of the prohibited investments. It is the duty of trustees, in the interests of their beneficiaries, to take advantage of the full range of investments authorised by the terms of the trust, instead of resolving to narrow that range.

Accordingly, on the case as a whole, in my judgment the plaintiffs are right and the defendants are wrong.

Where the investment policy of the trust incorporates the requirement that the trustees take into consideration non-financial considerations, the trustees have the difficult task of balancing such non-financial considerations with the most profitable, authorised return. The approach of the courts was considered in *Harries v Church Commissioners*.

Harries and Others v Church Commissioners for England [1992] 1 WLR 1241, HC

Facts

The Church Commissioners for England, a charitable body corporate, were trustees owning assets worth £2.6 billion upon trust for the advancement of religion. The investment policy of the Commissioners, as set out in their annual report, declared that their primary aim in the management of the assets was to produce the best return and, in so doing, they would take proper account of social, ethical and environmental issues. The plaintiffs instituted proceedings against the Commissioners claiming a declaration that the defendants were guided too rigorously by purely financial considerations and, while not ignoring moral factors, gave insufficient weight to ethical considerations. The plaintiffs alleged, for example, that investments in an additional 24% of UK companies which traded with South Africa ought to have been withheld. The defendants' view was that while they took ethical considerations into account, the restricted investment policy proposed by the plaintiffs was not sufficiently balanced to be adopted.

Held

The declaration sought by the plaintiffs would not be granted on the ground that there was no evidence that the Commissioners had failed to take into account proper ethical considerations in adopting a balanced portfolio of investments:

Nicholls VC: Broadly speaking, property held by charity trustees falls into two categories. First, there is property held by trustees for what may be called functional purposes. The National Trust owns historic houses and open spaces. The Salvation Army owns hostels for the destitute. And many charities need office accommodation in which to carry out essential administrative work. Secondly, there is property held by trustees for the purpose of generating money, whether from income or capital growth, with which to further the work of the trust. In other words, property held by trustees as an investment. Where property is so held, *prima facie*, the purposes of the trust will be best served by the trustees seeking to obtain therefrom the maximum return, whether by way of income or capital growth, which is consistent with commercial prudence. That is the starting point for all charity trustees when considering the exercise of their investment powers. Most charities need money; and the more of it there is available, the more the trustees can seek to accomplish.

In most cases this *prima facie* position will govern the trustees' conduct. In most cases the best interests of the charity require that the trustees' choice of investments should be made solely on the basis of well established investment criteria, having taken expert advice where appropriate and having due regard to such matters as the need to diversify, the need to balance income against capital growth, and the need to balance risk against return.

In a minority of cases the position will not be so straightforward. There will be some cases, I suspect comparatively rare, when the objects of the charity are such that investments of a particular type would conflict with the aims of the charity. Much cited examples are those of cancer research companies and tobacco shares, trustees of temperance charities and brewery and distillery shares, and trustees of charities of the Society of Friends and shares in companies engaged in production of armaments. If, as would be likely in those examples, trustees were satisfied that investing in a company engaged in a particular type of business would conflict with the very objects their charity is seeking to achieve, they should not so invest. Carried to its logical conclusion the trustees should take this course even if it would be likely to result in significant financial detriment to the charity.

There will also be some cases, again I suspect comparatively rare, when trustees' holdings of particular investments might hamper a charity's work either by making potential recipients of aid unwilling to be helped because of the source of the charity's money, or by alienating some of those who support the charity financially. In these cases the trustees will need to balance the difficulties they would encounter, or likely financial loss they would sustain, if they were to hold the investments against the risk of financial detriment if those investments were excluded from their portfolio. The greater the risk of financial detriment, the more certain the trustees should be of countervailing disadvantages to the charity before they incur that risk.

No doubt there will be other cases where trustees are justified in departing from what should always be their starting point. The instances I have given are not comprehensive. But I must emphasise that of their very nature, and by definition, investments are held by trustees to aid the work of the charity in a particular way: by generating money. That is the purpose for which they are held. That is their *raison d'être*. Trustees cannot properly use assets held as an investment for other, viz, non-investment, purposes. To the extent that they do they are not properly exercising their powers of investment.

I should mention one other particular situation. There will be instances today when those who support or benefit from a charity take widely different views on a particular type of investment, some saying that on moral grounds it conflicts with the aims of the charity, others saying the opposite. One example is the holding of arms industry shares by a religious charity. There is a real difficulty here. To many questions raising moral issues there are no certain answers. On moral questions widely differing views are held by well-meaning, responsible people. This is not always so. But frequently, when questions of the morality of conduct are being canvassed, there is no identifiable yardstick which can be applied to a set of facts so as to yield one answer which can be seen to be 'right' and the other 'wrong'. If that situation confronts trustees of a charity, the law does not require them to find an answer to the unanswerable.

The evidence does show that the commissioners have declined to adopt financially disadvantageous policies advocated by, among others, the Bishop of Oxford. I add only this. In bringing these proceedings the Bishop of Oxford and his colleagues are actuated by the highest moral concern. But, as I have sought to show, the approach they wish the commissioners to adopt to investment decisions would involve a departure by the commissioners from their legal obligations. Whether such a departure would or would not be desirable is, of course, not an issue in these proceedings. That is a matter to be pursued, if at all, elsewhere than in this court.

Note
Alternatively, in *Ward v Ward* (1843) 2 HL Cas 777, the House of Lords decided that a trustee had acted reasonably in not suing a debtor (who was also a beneficiary) for the repayment of a loan, for this could have resulted in his (the debtor's) financial ruin and would have put his children (who were also beneficiaries) in precarious circumstances.

In an action for breach of trust, the claimant is required to establish that the trust has suffered a loss which is attributable to the conduct or omission of the trustee. If the trustee's conduct or omission fell below the required standard of care imposed on trustees, he becomes personally liable, irrespective of whether he acted in good faith or not: see *Re Lucking*.

Re Lucking's Will Trust [1968] 1 WLR 866, HC

Facts

A trustee-director of a company allowed the managing director and friend to appropriate £15,000 of the company funds. Blank cheques, which were signed by the trustee, were delivered to the managing director, who then dissipated the funds.

Held

The trustee was liable for breach of trust:

> **Cross J:** . . . trustees holding a controlling interest ought to ensure so far as they can that they have such information as to the progress of the company's affairs as directors would have. If they sit back and allow the company to be run by the minority shareholder and receive no more information than shareholders are entitled to, they do so at their risk if things go wrong . . . The conduct of the defendant trustees is, I think, to be judged by the standard applied in *Speight v Gaunt* (1883) 9 App Cas 1, namely, that a trustee is only bound to conduct the business of the trust in such a way as an ordinary prudent man would conduct a business of his own . . .

With regard to professional trustees such as banks and insurance companies, the standard of care imposed on such bodies is higher than the degree of diligence expected from non-professional trustees. The professional trustee is required to administer the trust with such a degree of expertise as would be expected from a specialist in trust administration. This flexible objective standard is applied by the courts after due consideration of the facts of each case: see *Bartlett v Barclays Bank.*

Bartlett v Barclays Bank [1980] Ch 515, HC

Brightman J: . . . trust corporations, including the bank, hold themselves out as possessing a superior ability for the conduct of trust business . . . a trust corporation holds itself out in its advertising literature as being above ordinary mortals. With a specialist staff of trained trust officers and managers, with ready access to financial information and professional advice, dealing with and solving trust problems day after day, the trust corporation holds itself out, and rightly, as capable of providing an expertise which it would be unrealistic to expect and unjust to demand from the ordinary prudent man or woman who accepts, probably unpaid and sometimes reluctantly from a sense of family duty, the burdens of trusteeship.

Facts

The trust estate was the majority shareholder in a property company and the trustee was a professional trust company. The board of directors, for good commercial reasons, decided to restructure the investment portfolio and invest in land development. The trustee did not actively participate in the company's deliberations, nor was it provided with regular information concerning the company's activities but was content to rely on the annual balance sheet and profit and loss account. One of the schemes pursued by the company proved to be disastrous. An action was brought against the trustee.

Held

The trustee was liable for it (the trust corporation) had not acted with reasonable care in the administration of the trust.

On the other hand, the claimant failed in her action in *Nestle v National Westminster Bank*, on the ground that she failed to prove positively that the defendant's action or inaction resulted in a loss to the trust.

Nestlé v National Westminster Bank [1993] 1 WLR 1260, CA

Facts

The claimant was the remainderman under a trust created by her grandfather at a time when the property was worth £50,000. In 1986, the claimant became absolutely entitled to the trust property which was then worth £269,203. During the trust period, the cost of living index had multiplied by a factor of 20. Had the trust fund increased at the same rate, it would have been worth £1 million. It was apparent that the real value of the fund was reduced during the trust period. The claimant alleged that the trustees had mismanaged the investments without adducing evidence to this effect, but sought to rely on a presumption of a loss to the trust as a result of the actions of the trustees.

Held

The Court of Appeal found in favour of the defendant on the ground that the claimant failed to prove that the trustees made decisions which reasonable trustees would not have made, or failed to make decisions which reasonable trustees would have made:

Staughton LJ: The misunderstanding of the investment clause and the failure to conduct periodic reviews do not by themselves, whether separately or together, afford the plaintiff a remedy. They were symptoms of incompetence or idleness – not on the part of National Westminster Bank but of their predecessors; they were not, without more, breaches of trust. The plaintiff must show that, through one or other or both of those causes, the trustees made decisions which they should not have made or failed to make decisions which they should have made. If that were proved, and if at first sight loss resulted, it would be appropriate to order an inquiry as to the loss suffered by the trust fund.

It may be difficult to discharge that burden, and particularly to show that decisions were not taken when they should have been. But that does not absolve a plaintiff from discharging it, and I cannot find that it was discharged in this case.

That brings me to what I regard as the substance of the case, the failure to invest a higher proportion of the trust fund in ordinary shares. Here one must take care to avoid two errors. First, the trustees' performance must not be judged with hindsight: after the event even a fool is wise, as a poet said nearly 3,000 years ago. Secondly (unless this is the same point), one must bear in mind that investment philosophy was very different in the early years of this trust from what it became later. Inflation was non-existent, overall, from 1921 to 1938. It occurred in modest degree during the war years, and became a more persistent phenomenon from 1947 onwards. Equities were regarded as risky during the 1920s and 1930s, and yielded a higher return then gilt-edged securities. It was only in 1959 that the so called reverse yield gap occurred.

During the period from 1922 until the death of Mrs Barbara Nestlé in 1960, the proportion of ordinary shares in the trust fund as a whole varied between 46 and 82%. Until 1951 it never rose above 57%; there was then quite a sharp rise until 1960, not caused by any change in investment policy but presumably by a general rise in the value of ordinary shares (183%, according to the index, between 1950 and 1960).

In my judgment the trustees are not shown to have failed in their duties at any time up to 1959 in this respect. I cannot say that, in the light of investment conditions then prevailing, they were in breach of trust by not holding a higher proportion of ordinary shares. I see no reason to believe that equities bought in 1959 with the proceeds of the house and contents would have remained exempt from the trustees' general policy, of according some preference to income from tax-exempt gilts, and maintaining roughly speaking proportions of 50:50 overall. So I do not find that there is a *prima facie* case of loss to the trust from the 1959 transaction.

I would dismiss the appeal.

Standard of care under the Trustee Act 2000

Section 1 of the Trustee Act 2000 reformulates the duty of care applicable to powers exercisable by trustees. This provision replaces the common law standard of care as illustrated above. Section 1 provides that a trustee is required to exercise such care and skill as is reasonable in the circumstances:

(a) having regard to any special knowledge or experience he has or holds himself out as having; and

(b) if he acts as a trustee in the course of a business or profession, having regard to any special knowledge or experience that it is reasonable to expect of a person acting in the course of that kind of business or profession.

Thus, the section has created an objective/subjective test of the standard of care required from the trustees. The minimum degree of care and skill expected from a trustee is to be determined objectively by the court. However, this standard of care may be increased by reference to the trustee's special knowledge or experience acquired personally, or held out by him. This provision echoes the view of Brightman J in *Bartlett v Barclays Bank*.

Bartlett v Barclays Bank [1980] Ch 515

Brightman J: . . . trust corporations, including the bank, hold themselves out as possessing a superior ability for the conduct of trust business . . . a trust corporation holds itself out in its advertising literature as being above ordinary mortals.

Schedule 1 to the Trustee Act 2000 lists the occasions when the duty of care arises. The duty of care arises in the *exercise* of the statutory and express powers of investment, which includes the duty to have regard to the standard investment criteria and the duty to obtain and consider proper advice. In addition, the duty applies to the trustees' power to acquire land. Moreover, the duty of care applies when trustees enter into arrangements in order to delegate functions to agents, nominees and custodians, as well as to the review of their actions.

The Lord Chancellor, in introducing the Trustee Bill in the House of Lords (*Hansard*, HL Debs, 14 April 1999), declared: 'The new duty will apply to the way trustees *exercise* discretionary power. It will not apply to a decision by the trustees as to whether to exercise the discretionary power in the first place.' On this view, it would appear that the statutory duty will apply when the trustees actively perform acts concerning the investment of the trust property, but will not apply when the trustees decide not to exercise their power of investment. In the latter event, the common law duty of care will apply to the trustees. This is an unsatisfactory state of affairs in that there are now two duties of care – a statutory duty for the *exercise* of the trustee's discretion, eg, to invest the trust funds, and a common law duty of care in the event of an *omission* to exercise a discretion, eg, to invest the trust funds. It will be interesting to see whether the courts approach this provision in the way suggested by the Lord Chancellor.

Question
To what extent has the Trustee Act 2000 modified the standard of care imposed on trustees?

Unanimity

Subject to provisions to the contrary in the trust instrument, trustees are required to act unanimously. The settlor has given all of his or her trustees the responsibility to act on behalf of the trust. The acts and decisions of some of the trustees (even a majority of trustees) are not binding on others. Thus, once a trust decision is made, the trustees become jointly and severally liable to the beneficiaries in the event of a breach of trust. There is no such thing as an 'active' or 'passive' trustee. Each becomes liable as a representative of the trust. The main issue in this context is whether a trustee who disagrees with the decision or views of his co-trustees ought to hold firm and make an application to the court, or succumb to the views of the co-trustees. This would vary with the circumstances of each case: see *Bahin v Hughes*.

Bahin v Hughes (1886) 31 Ch D 390, CA

Facts
Three trustees, A (Eliza Hughes), B (Mrs Burden) and Mrs C (Mrs Edwards), held property on trust for Mrs Bahin for life with remainder to her children. A invested the funds in unauthorised investments and a loss occurred. Mrs C had died before proceedings had commenced. Mrs Bahin sued A, B and Mr C (Mrs C's husband) for breach of trust. B and Mr C claimed an indemnity from A on the ground that A was an 'active' trustee.

Held
The trustees were all liable. An indemnity would be available only if A was the solicitor to the trust and B and C acted on his advice, or if A had obtained a personal gain from the breach:

> **Cotton LJ:** Where one trustee has got the money into his own hands, and made use of it, he will be liable to his co-trustee to give him an indemnity. Now I think it wrong to lay down any limitation of the circumstances under which one trustee would be held liable to the other for indemnity, both having been held liable to the *cestui que trust*; but so far as cases have gone at present, relief has only been granted against a trustee who has himself got the benefit of the breach of trust, or between whom and his co-trustees there has existed a relation which will justify the court in treating him as solely liable for the breach of trust . . .
>
> Miss Hughes was the active trustee and Mr Edwards did nothing, and in my opinion it would be laying down a wrong rule to hold that where one trustee acts honestly, though erroneously, the other trustee is to be held entitled to indemnity who by doing nothing neglects his duty more than the acting trustee. That Miss Hughes made an improper investment is true, but she acted honestly, and intended to do the best she could, and believed that the property was sufficient security for the money, although she made no inquiries about their being leasehold houses. In my opinion the money was lost just as much by the default of Mr Edwards as by the innocent though erroneous action of his co-trustee, Miss Hughes. All the trustees were in the wrong, and everyone is equally liable to indemnify the beneficiaries.

Note
A claim by one trustee against his or her co-trustee is now subject to the Civil Liability

(Contribution) Act 1978 (see p 554 below). Briefly, a trustee who is sued for breach of trust may claim a contribution from his co-trustee. The court has a discretion to make a contribution order if such 'is just and equitable having regard to the extent of the [co-trustee's] responsibility for the damage in question'.

Question
Are 'sleeping trustees' recognised in equity?

Duty to act personally

Generally speaking, a trustee is appointed by a settlor because of his personal qualities. He may possess a number of attributes which appeal to the settlor – such as honesty and integrity, reliability and business skill. It is expected that the trustee will act personally in the execution of his duties. The general rule is *delegatus non potest delegare* ('the delegate cannot delegate').

However, in the contemporary commercial climate, the functions of and needs for the proper administration of a trust have become increasingly complex, requiring specialised skill and knowledge. Accordingly, it is unrealistic to expect trustees to act personally in all matters relating to the trust. Trustees are entitled to appoint agents to perform acts in respect of the trust.

Collective delegation before the Trustee Act 2000

The courts had recognised the principle that trustees were entitled in limited circumstances to employ agents. In *Speight v Gaunt* (1883) 9 App Cas 1 and *Learoyd v Whiteley* (1887) 12 App Cas 727, the House of Lords decided that trustees might delegate administrative functions to an agent, provided that a reasonable man of business would have done so and the trustees exercised proper care in the selection of the agent. In addition, the trustees were required to exercise proper supervision over the agent. Thus, if the ordinary man of business would not have employed an agent at all, or would not have employed the selected agent, the trustee would be in breach of trust without proof of negligence because he would have been in breach of his primary duty as trustee.

The Trustee Act 1925 widened the circumstances when an agent might be appointed. Under s 23(1) of the Trustee Act 1925, trustees were entitled to delegate any acts of an administrative nature to an agent, and they would not be responsible for the default of the agent if 'employed in good faith'. Section 30 of the Trustee Act 1925 provided that the trustee was responsible for his own acts and not the acts of his co-trustees or agents, unless the trustee was guilty of 'wilful default'. In *Re Vickery* [1931] 1 Ch 572, the court decided that 'wilful default' meant 'consciousness of negligence or breach of duty, or recklessness in the performance of a duty'. This test was severely criticised and, in *Re Lucking* [1968] 1 WLR 866, the court decided that the 1925 Act did not change the law with regard to the duty to supervise the agent. Accordingly, the trustee might be liable for breach of trust if he did not act like a 'prudent man of business' in his supervision of the acts of the agent.

Collective delegation under the Trustee Act 2000

Part IV of the Trustee Act 2000 has reformed the law as to the trustees' powers of delegation. It repeals ss 23 and 30 of the Trustee Act 1925 and introduces provisions with a clearer framework for delegation. Generally, the new provisions deal with the appointment of agents, nominees and custodians, and the liability of the trustees for such persons.

Sections 11–20 of the Trustee Act 2000 deal with the appointment of agents, nominees and custodians. Sections 21–23 deal with the review of acts of the agents, nominees and custodians, and the question of liability for their acts.

Section 11(1) provides that the trustees of a trust 'may authorise any person to exercise any or all of their delegable functions as their agent'. Section 11(2) defines 'delegable functions' as *any function* of the trustee, subject to four exceptions. These are:

(a) functions relating to the distribution of assets in favour of beneficiaries, ie, dispositive functions;

(b) any power to allocate fees and other payments to capital or income;

(c) any power to appoint trustees; and

(d) any power conferred by the trust instrument or any enactment which allows trustees to delegate their administrative functions to another person.

Thus, the trustees cannot delegate their discretion under a discretionary trust to distribute the funds or to select beneficiaries from a group of objects. But they may delegate their investment decision-making power and thereby obtain skilled professional advice from an investment manager.

In the case of charitable trusts, the trustees' *delegable functions* are set out in s 11(3). These are:

(a) any function consisting of carrying out a decision that the trustees have taken;

(b) any function concerning investment of assets subject to the trust;

(c) any function relating to the raising of funds for the trust otherwise than by means of profits of a trade which is an integral part of carrying out the trust's charitable purpose;

(d) any other function prescribed by order of the Secretary of State.

Section 12 provides who may or may not be appointed an agent of the trustees. The trustees may appoint one of their number to act as an agent, but cannot appoint a beneficiary to carry out that function. If more than one person is appointed to exercise the same function, they are required to act jointly. Section 14 authorises the trustees to appoint agents on such terms as to remuneration and other matters as they may determine. But certain terms of the agency contract are subject to a test of reasonableness. These are terms permitting the agent to sub-delegate to another agent, or to restrict his liability to the trustees or the beneficiaries, or to allow the agent to carry out functions that are capable of giving rise to a conflict of interest. Thus, sub delegation to another agent, or the insertion of an exclusion clause in the contract appointing the agent, is subject to a test of reasonableness.

Section 15 imposes special restrictions within certain types of agency contracts. With regard to asset management functions, the agreement is required to be evidenced in writing. In addition, the trustees are required include a 'policy statement' in the agreement giving the agent guidance as to how the functions ought to be exercised, and should seek an undertaking from the agent that he will secure compliance with the policy statement. In the ordinary course of events, the policy statement will refer to the 'standard investment criteria' and, in the case of beneficiaries entitled in succession, require the agent to provide investments with a balance between income and capital. Section 24 provides that a failure to observe these limits does not invalidate the authorisation or appointment.

Power to appoint nominees
Section 16 of the Trustee Act 2000 authorises trustees to appoint nominees in relation to such of the trust assets as they may determine (other than settled land). In addition, the trustees may take steps to ensure the vesting of those assets in the nominee. Such appointment is required to be evidenced in writing.

Power to appoint custodians
Section 17 of the Trustee Act 2000 authorises the trustees to appoint a person to act as custodian in relation to specified assets. A custodian is a person who undertakes the safe custody of the assets,

or of any documents or records concerning the assets. The appointment is required to be evidenced in writing.

Persons who may be appointed as nominees or custodians

Section 19 of the Trustee Act 2000 provides that a person may not be appointed as a nominee or custodian unless he carries on a business which consists of or includes acting as a nominee or custodian, or is a body corporate controlled by the trustees. The trustees may appoint as a nominee or custodian one of their number if that is a trust corporation, or two (or more) of their number if they act jointly.

Review of acts of agents, nominees and custodians

Provided that the agent, nominee or custodian continues to act for the trust, the trustees are required:

(a) to keep under review the arrangements under which they act, and how those arrangements are put into effect;

(b) to *consider* whether to exercise any powers of intervention, if the circumstances are appropriate;

(c) to intervene if they consider a need has arisen for such action.

Liability for the acts of agents, nominees and custodians

Section 23 of the Trustee Act 2000 provides that a trustee will not be liable for the acts of agents, nominees and custodians provided that he complies with the general duty of care laid down in s 1 and Sched 1, both in respect of the initial appointment of the agent, etc and when carrying out his duties under s 22 (review of the acts of agents, etc). The effect of this provision is that it lays to rest the eccentric principles that were applied under the 1925 Act, and introduces one standard objective test concerning the trustees' duty of care.

Other statutory provisions permitting the delegation of discretions

Trustees may delegate their discretions under the following statutory provisions:

(a) Pt IV of the Trustee Act 2000;

(b) s 25 of the Trustee Act 1925 (as amended by the Trustee Delegation Act 1999); and

(c) s 9 of the Trusts of Land and Appointment of Trustees Act 1996.

Individual delegation

Section 25 of the Trustee Act 1925 (as re-enacted by s 5 of the Trustee Delegation Act 1999) enables a trustee to delegate, by a power of attorney, 'the execution or exercise of all or any of the trusts, powers and discretions vested in him either alone or jointly with any other person or persons'. The delegation of the powers commences on the date of execution or such time as stated in the instrument, and continues for a period of 12 months or such shorter period as mentioned in the instrument. Written notice is required to be given by the donor of the power to each nominee under the trust instrument who is entitled to appoint trustees, and to each other trustee within seven days after its creation. The donor of the power remains liable for the acts or defaults of the donee.

Delegation under the Trusts of Land and Appointment of Trustees Act 1996

Section 9 of the Trusts of Land and Appointment of Trustees Act 1996 provides that trustees of land may delegate any of their 'powers in relation to the land' to adult beneficiaries who are currently entitled to 'interests in possession'. The trustees' powers in respect of land and the meaning of 'interests in possession' require some elucidation.

The 'powers of trustees in respect of land' are enacted in s 6 of the 1996 Act, which states that these powers are equivalent to 'all the powers of an absolute owner', in accordance with the rules of law and equity. This includes the power to transfer land included in the trust to an adult beneficiary or beneficiaries who are solely entitled, whether or not they have requested it (s 6(2)). This may effectively terminate the trust. If the land is conveyed to more than one beneficiary, the beneficiaries will, in turn, become trustees of a trust of land. The trustees' powers include the power to purchase land as an investment, or as a home for a beneficiary, or for any other reason (s 6(4)). The trustees have the power to reinvest the proceeds of sale of land or other assets in which the proceeds have been invested in purchasing the legal estate in other land (ss 6(3) and 17(3)).

In exercising their powers, the trustees are required to have regard to the rights of the beneficiaries and are obliged to observe any rules of law and equity. Thus, the trustees may not favour or prejudice the interest of any beneficiary when exercising their powers. The trustees have a general duty to consult, so far as is practicable, adult beneficiaries with interests in possession, and give effect to their wishes (or of the majority of them, according to their combined interests), in so far as this is consistent with the general interest of the trust (s 11(1)). The latter duty is excluded in respect of a power under s 6(2) to convey the trust land to an adult beneficiary absolutely entitled.

The powers included in s 6 relate only to a trust of land and not to any personal property. For example, s 6 is applicable to freehold land (but not shares) held by T1 and T2 upon trust for A for life, remainder to B and C equally. These powers enacted in s 6 may be amended or excluded by the settlement, or made subject to obtaining the consent of any person (s 8). Thus, the settlor may prevent any dealing with the land (although this could be challenged under s 14). In the case of charitable trusts, the trustees' powers may not be amended or excluded, but they may be made subject to obtaining consent.

An 'interest in possession in land' as distinct from 'an interest in remainder', on general principles, involves a present right to present possession of the land or a right to the income from the land, for example, the interest in land of a life tenant, as opposed to the interest of the remainderman. It follows that the interest of an object under a discretionary trust is not a vested interest, and certainly not an interest in possession. Emphasis is placed on the expression 'right'. A beneficiary has a right in possession if he or she is entitled to demand the property subject to the right. If the trustees are entitled to decide whether or not to pay the sum over to the beneficiary, the beneficiary does not have a right to possess (see *Pearson v Inland Revenue Commissioners* [1981] AC 753). But there is no reason why the settlor cannot expressly include the relevant powers of the trustees in respect of land, or some of these powers, in the trust instrument.

Delegation of the powers of trustees under s 9 of the 1996 Act is by power of attorney (which cannot be an enduring power of attorney). All the trustees, jointly, are required to join in the delegation, which may be for an indefinite or fixed time. The trustees are not liable for the acts of the delegate, unless they did not exercise reasonable care in deciding to delegate their powers to a beneficiary or beneficiaries (s 9(8)). Thus, if the trustees failed to exercise reasonable care in deciding to delegate their powers, they will be jointly and severally liable for any act or default of the delegate-beneficiary. But, assuming reasonable care had been taken by the trustees of land in deciding to delegate their powers, there is no duty on the part of the trustees, imposed by the 1996 Act, to supervise the delegate. The delegate is liable for his acts as if he were the trustee, but he is not a trustee in any other sense. The effect is that the delegate, 'pseudo-trustee' cannot, in turn, delegate his functions, and his receipt of capital money will not discharge the purchaser (s 9(7)).

Revocation

A power of attorney (through which the delegation must be made) is required to be executed by all the trustees jointly. Unless the power of attorney is stated to be irrevocable and is to secure a mortgage or similar security, it may be revoked by any one trustee. It may also be revoked by the appointment of a new trustee (s 9(3) of the 1996 Act). The delegation is also revoked in respect of a delegate who ceases to be beneficially entitled to an interest in possession under the trust. Likewise, in respect of a delegation to a number of beneficiaries, if one or more ceases to be entitled beneficially to an interest in possession, the delegation is revoked in respect of each of the delegates whose interest ceases, but the delegation remains valid with respect to the remaining beneficiaries. The position remains the same whether the powers are exercisable jointly or separately (s 9(5)).

Protection of purchasers from the delegate

In respect of land, where a person deals with the delegate in good faith in the belief that the trustees were entitled to delegate to that person, it is presumed that the trustees were entitled to delegate to that person, unless the purchaser had knowledge at the time of the transaction that the trustees were not so entitled (s 9(2) of the 1996 Act). 'Knowledge', for these purposes, has not been defined in the legislation, but it is submitted that since we are concerned here with a proprietary interest, any type of cognisance will suffice for these purposes, even constructive knowledge.

Where further transactions have taken place in relation to a relevant plot of land since the first transaction by the delegate, a subsequent purchaser in good faith is entitled to rely on a statutory declaration made by the first or subsequent purchasers, before, or within three months after, completion of the most recent purchase. Under s 9, such transactions are treated as giving rise to a 'conclusive presumption'. The declaration is required to state that the first or subsequent purchaser dealt in good faith and without notice that the trustees were not entitled to make the delegation.

EXCLUSION CLAUSES

On analogy with the law of contract, exclusion clauses that are validly inserted in trust instruments may have the effect of limiting the liability of trustees. Much depends on the wording of such clauses. *Prima facie*, any ambiguities inherent in such clauses are construed against the trustees. Such clauses are not, without more, void on public policy grounds. Moreover, provided the clause does not purport to exclude the basic minimum duties of the trustees, it may not be construed as being void for repugnancy to the trust. Some of the minimum duties which may not be excluded are the duties of honesty, good faith and acting for the benefit of the beneficiaries: see *Armitage v Nurse*.

Armitage v Nurse and Others [1997] 3 WLR 1046, CA

Facts

By a settlement made on 11 October 1984, the income from a farm was held by trustees upon trust to accumulate until the claimant, Paula (then aged 17), attained the age of 25. Thereafter, the trustees were required to pay the income to Paula until she attained the age of 40. On attaining that age, Paula became entitled to the capital, subject to gifts over in the event of her death under that age. Clause 15 of the settlement (which was properly incorporated) exempted the trustees from liability for any loss or damage to the income or capital of the fund 'unless such loss or damage shall be caused by [their] own actual fraud'. The plaintiff brought an action against the trustees alleging breaches of trust committed by them. The tenor of the claim involved a deliberate or reckless course of conduct on the part of the trustees to disregard the interests of Paula and subordinate them to the interests of family members who were not objects of the trust. The judge decided that the defendants were absolved from liability by virtue of clause 15 and that the claim was not statute-barred. The judge also decided that the trustees would be deprived of 20% of their costs and they were barred from recovering their costs from the trust fund.

The plaintiff appealed to the Court of Appeal to set aside the judge's declaration regarding clause 15, and the defendants cross-appealed from the judge's order as to costs.

Held

The Court of Appeal dismissed the plaintiff's appeal and allowed the trustees' cross-appeal on the following grounds:

(a) on analogy with the law of contract, it was open to the parties to a settlement to exclude or restrict their liability for breach of trust;

(b) on construction of the clause, the expression, 'actual fraud', would be given its literal meaning. 'Actual fraud' involves an intention on the part of the trustee to pursue a course of action, either knowing that it is contrary to the interests of the beneficiaries or being recklessly indifferent whether it is contrary to their interests or not. The word, 'actual', was deliberately selected by the settlor and was clearly distinguishable from 'constructive or equitable fraud'. This expression connotes some dealing by a fiduciary involving a risk that the fiduciary may have exploited his or her position to his or her own advantage. Examples include breach of fiduciary duties, undue influence, abuse of confidence, unconscionable bargains, the self-dealing rule and making unauthorised profits with the aid of trust property;

(c) the exclusion clause was not repugnant to the trust or contrary to public policy;

(d) the plaintiff was allowed to examine the trust documents and investigate the trustees' management;

(e) s 21(1)(a) of the Limitation Act 1980 was applicable to cases of fraudulent breaches of trust without a time limit. This was not evident on the facts of this case;

(f) a cause of action does not accrue in favour of a beneficiary entitled to a future interest in the trust property until the interest falls into possession; see the proviso to s 21(3) of the Limitation Act 1980. Paula enjoyed a future interest until she attained the age of 25. Consequently, her claim was not statute-barred;

(g) the trustees were entitled to a lien on the trust fund for the costs of successfully defending an action for breach of trust. Thus, there was no basis for the judge's order depriving them of this entitlement. Accordingly, the trustees were entitled to recover their costs from the trust fund.

Millett LJ: The main questions which arise in this appeal are concerned with the true construction of a trustee exemption clause in a settlement and the legitimate scope of such clauses in English law.

The expression, 'actual fraud', in clause 15 is not used to describe the common tort of deceit. As the judge appreciated, it simply means dishonesty. I accept the formulation put forward by Mr Hill on behalf of the respondents which (as I have slightly modified it) is that it:

> ... connotes, at the minimum, an intention on the part of the trustee to pursue a particular course of action, either knowing that it is contrary to the interests of the beneficiaries or being recklessly indifferent whether it is contrary to their interests or not.

The permitted scope of trustee exemption clauses

It is submitted on behalf of Paula that a trustee exemption clause which purports to exclude all liability except for actual fraud is void, either for repugnancy or as contrary to public policy. There is some academic support for the submission (notably an article by Professor Matthews, 'The efficacy of trustee exemption clauses in English law' [1989] Conv 42 and *Hanbury and Martin's Modern Equity*, 14th edn, 1993, pp 473–74) that liability for gross negligence cannot be excluded, but this is not the view taken in *Underhill and Hayton's Law of Trusts and Trustees*, 15th edn, 1995, pp 560–61 (where it appears to be taken only because the editor confusingly uses the term 'gross negligence' to mean reckless indifference to the interests of the beneficiaries). In its consultation paper,

Fiduciary Duties and Regulatory Rules: A Summary, 1992, Law Com No 124, London: HMSO, para 3.3.41, the Law Commission states:

> Beyond this, trustees and fiduciaries cannot exempt themselves from liability for fraud, bad faith and wilful default. It is not, however, clear whether the prohibition on exclusion of liability for 'fraud' in this context only prohibits the exclusion of common law fraud or extends to the much broader doctrine of equitable fraud. It is also not altogether clear whether the prohibition on the exclusion of liability for 'wilful default' also prohibits exclusion of liability for gross negligence although we incline to the view that it does.

A trustee who is guilty of such conduct [wilful default] either consciously takes a risk that loss will result, or is recklessly indifferent whether it will or not. If the risk eventuates he is personally liable. But if he consciously takes the risk in good faith and with the best intentions, honestly believing that the risk is one which ought to be taken in the interests of the beneficiaries, there is no reason why he should not be protected by an exemption clause which excludes liability for wilful default.

The Law Commission was considering the position of fiduciaries as well as trustees, and in such a context, it is sensible to consider the exclusion of liability for so called equitable fraud. But it makes no sense in the present context. The nature of equitable fraud may be collected from the speech of Viscount Haldane LC, in *Nocton v Lord Ashburton* [1914] AC 932, p 953, and *Snell's Equity*, 29th edn, 1990, pp 550–51. It covers breach of fiduciary duty, undue influence, abuse of confidence, unconscionable bargains and frauds on powers. With the sole exception of the last, which is a technical doctrine in which the word 'fraud' merely connotes excess of *vires*, it involves some dealing by the fiduciary with his principal and the risk that the fiduciary may have exploited his position to his own advantage. In *Earl of Aylesford v Morris* (1873) LR 8 Ch App 484, pp 490–91, Lord Selborne LC said: 'Fraud does not here mean deceit or circumvention; it means an unconscientious use of the power arising out of these circumstances and conditions . . .' A trustee exemption clause, such as clause 15 of the settlement does not purport to exclude the liability of the fiduciary in such cases. Suppose, for example, that one of the respondents had purchased Paula's land at a proper price from his fellow trustees. The sale would be liable to be set aside. Clause 15 would not prevent this. This is not because the purchasing trustee would have been guilty of equitable fraud, but because by claiming to recover the trust property (or even equitable compensation) Paula would not be suing in respect of any 'loss or damage' to the trust. Her right to recover the land would not depend on proof of loss or damage. Her claim would succeed even if the sale was at an undervalue; the purchasing trustee could never obtain more than a defeasible title from such transaction. But clause 15 would be effective to exempt his fellow trustees from liability for making good any loss which the sale had occasioned to the trust estate, so long as they had acted in good faith and in what they honestly believed was Paula's interests.

It is a bold submission that a clause taken from one standard precedent book and to the same effect as a clause found in another, included in a settlement drawn by chancery counsel and approved by counsel acting for an infant settlor and by the court on her behalf, should be so repugnant to the trusts or contrary to public policy that it is liable to be set aside at her suit. But the submission has been made and we must consider it. In my judgment it is without foundation.

I accept the submission made on behalf of Paula that there is an irreducible core of obligations owed by the trustees to the beneficiaries and enforceable by them which is fundamental to the concept of a trust. If the beneficiaries have no rights enforceable against the trustees there are no trusts. But I do not accept the further submission that these core obligations include the duties of skill and care, prudence and diligence. *The duty of the trustees to perform the trusts honestly and in good faith for the benefit of the beneficiaries is the minimum necessary to give substance to the trusts*, but in my opinion it is sufficient [emphasis added].

It is, of course, far too late to suggest that the exclusion in a contract of liability for ordinary negligence or want of care is contrary to public policy. What is true of a contract must be equally true of a settlement.

The *contra proferentem* rule concerning exclusion clauses

If there is an ambiguity within an exemption clause that cannot be resolved, the court is entitled to construe the provision against the person seeking to rely on the clause, namely the trustee, ie, *contra proferentem*. Thus, where a trust settlement incorporated two conflicting exemption clauses, one protecting all trustees from liability for breach of trust (a general exemption clause), the other applying only to unpaid trustees, the paid trustees could not rely on the general exemption clause: see *Wight v Olswang*.

Wight v Olswang [2001] Lloyd's Rep 269, CA

Facts

The trust fund consisted of a substantial holding of shares in Aegis plc. The defendants were practising solicitors and paid trustees. The trustees took advice from a firm of stockbrokers and decided in principle to sell the shares. However, the sale took place in stages over a period of six years. During this period, the value of the shares had declined dramatically. The claimants brought an action alleging that the defendants, as professional trustees, had failed to carry out their duties and were required to compensate the trust. The defendants denied breaches of trust and relied on exemption clauses contained in clauses 11, 18(A) and 18(B) of the settlement. Clause 11 contained a trustee exemption clause in common form which was expressed to apply to all trustees. Clause 18(B) contained a further exemption clause which covered much the same ground but applied only to unpaid trustees. Clause 18(A) adopted a broad exemption clause and provided thus: 'Every discretion or power hereby or by law conferred on the trustees shall be an absolute and uncontrolled discretion or power and no trustee shall be held liable for any loss or damage accruing as a result of the trustees concurring or failing to concur in the exercise of any such discretion or power.'

The trial judge decided that the defendants, as paid trustees, could not rely on clause 11 because there was a conflict between clause 11 and clause 18(B) and the latter prevailed over the former. But the trustees could rely on clause 18(A) which dealt with powers and discretions and the consequences of such exercise or failure to exercise. By way of contrast, clause 18(B) addressed the exemption from liability of unpaid trustees. The claimants appealed to the Court of Appeal and the defendants cross-appealed.

Held

(a) Affirming the decision of the judge and dismissing the cross-appeal, the court considered the approach adopted in the contract case, *Elderslie Steamship Co v Borthwick* [1905] AC 93 and the guidelines laid down by Millett LJ in *Bogg v Raper* (1998) *The Times*, 22 April. With regard to exemption clauses in wills and settlements, Millett LJ expressed the view that the burden of proof lies on the party seeking to rely on an exemption clause. Accordingly, any ambiguity in the clause will be construed against such party. In the case of a will or settlement, the terms of the document reflect the intention of the testator or settlor. In the present case, there was no inherent improbability that the settlor should intend to absolve his executors or trustees from liability from the consequences of their negligence.

(b) Reversing the decision of the judge and holding in favour of the claimants, the court decided that the judge had misconstrued the effect of clause 18(A). The first part of clause 18(A) was intended to enable the trustees to act without consulting or obtaining the consent of any beneficiary or anyone else. The latter part of clause 18(A) was subject to a very narrow construction, its purpose being to make clear that the trustees would not be liable for exercising or not exercising a discretion or power merely because the court considered the trustees' grounds unreasonable, or merely because the court would not have exercised the discretion or power in the same way. Moreover, the court stated that, while professional trustees are entitled to have professionally drawn exemption clauses inserted into trust settlements, such clauses are construed according to the natural meaning of the words used. Exclusion of liability for breaches of trust or negligence by a trustee is required to be clear and unambiguous. Clause 18(A) did not have that effect:

> **Peter Gibson LJ:** It is in our opinion correct that the first part of sub-clause (A), in making every discretion or power conferred on the trustees an absolute and undoubted discretion or power, must have been intended to enable the trustees to act without consulting or obtaining the consent of any beneficiary or anyone else and to limit the scope for intervention by the court. The second part of the clause, whilst on its face exempting every trustee from liability does so only in relation to loss or damage accruing as a result of the trustees concurring or failing to concur in the exercise of the absolute and uncontrolled discretion or power. It is significant that there is

no reference to, for example, a breach of trust or other impropriety in the exercise or non-exercise of the power and that to our mind suggests that the scope of the second part of the same subclause (A) is limited as [counsel] suggests. The wording of the second part indicates that the loss or damage liability for which is exempted is that which accrues merely as a result of the trustee concurring or failing to concur. Further, as [counsel] pointed out, if the wording is construed as covering any breach of trust committed in the exercise or non-exercise of the power or discretion, that would purportedly exclude a wilful or dishonest breach of trust, which in the light of limb (4) of clause 11 and limb (d) of clause 18(B) cannot have been intended. Moreover, subclause (A) would be inconsistent with sub-clause (B), a construction which should be avoided particularly when both form part of the same clause. The judge's solution of importing words into sub-clause (B) was a bold one, which again should be avoided if possible. Finally, it is to be borne in mind that whilst professional trustees are entitled to have professionally drawn exemption clauses for which they are not responsible fairly construed according to the natural meaning of the words used, the court should not be astute to construe an exemption clause beyond its natural meaning. To exclude liability for breaches of trust or negligence by a trustee there should be clear and unambiguous words in the settlement. We do not find them in clause 18(A) which on the face is limited to exempting a trustee from liability for loss or damage accruing only from the trustee concurring or failing to concur in the exercise of an absolute and uncontrolled discretion or power.

Two types of exclusion clauses

In substance, it would appear that there are two types of exclusion clauses:

(a) a clause which excludes the trustees' *liability* for breach of trust; and

(b) a clause which not only excludes the trustees' liability, but also excludes the *duties*, or some of the duties, of the trustees from a claim for a breach of trust.

In respect of the first type of clause, Millett LJ in *Armitage v Nurse* (above) took the view that the trustees may only exclude their liability for negligence, but they remain liable for dishonest breaches of trust. Regarding the second type of clause, Millett LJ in the same case expressed his opinion that the 'core duties' of trustees cannot be effectively excluded for this may lead to repugnancy with the trust. He stated, 'the duty of the trustees to perform the trusts honestly and in good faith for the benefit of the beneficiaries is the minimum necessary to give substance to the trusts'.

In *Armitage*, Millett LJ equated 'actual fraud' with 'dishonesty' and 'recklessness', but treated these concepts as distinct from the tort of deceit. His definition of actual fraud was that it 'connotes, at the minimum, an intention on the part of the trustee to pursue a particular course of action, either knowing that it is contrary to the interests of the beneficiaries or being recklessly indifferent whether it is contrary to their interests or not'. This is a purely subjective test on the part of the trustee, with negligence and even gross negligence being excluded from the equation. However, the standard that has been adopted for evaluating dishonesty in the context of accessory liability is the combined test involving both elements of objectivity and subjectivity, as laid down by the majority decision of the House of Lords in *Twinsectra v Yardley* [2002] UKHL 12 (see p 293 above). It would be odd if the standard applicable to dishonesty differed with the nature of the claim: a subjective standard in respect of a claim that involves challenging an exclusion clause, and a combined standard for accessory liability.

The difficulties in pursuing a claim for breach of trust in seeking to restrict an exclusion clause in the trust deed by reference to the Unfair Contract Terms Act 1977 (included in Tuckey LJ's judgment below) were considered by the Court of Appeal in *Baker v JE Clark & Co*. The court decided that the notice requirement under the 1977 Act was impractical and the clause did not exclude liability under a 'contract'.

Baker v JE Clark & Co and another [2006] All ER (D) 337 (CA)

Facts

The claimant was the wife of the deceased who was employed by the first defendant (the company). The company sponsored a personal pension plan which included provision for death in service benefits. The rules of the scheme were set out in a supplementary trust deed containing an exemption clause excluding liability unless there was bad faith. The second defendant was appointed scheme administrator (administrator). The deceased received a letter from the administrator informing him of the scheme. The deceased duly joined the scheme. Subsequently, the underwriters refused to renew coverage for the scheme. The effect was that when the deceased passed away from a brain tumour in the service of the company, no death benefits were payable. The claimant brought proceedings against the administrator alleging breaches of his duty of care at common law or equity and under UCTA 1977. The trial judge struck out the claim. The claimant appealed to the Court of Appeal.

Held

Dismissing the appeal on the following grounds:

(1) The administrator was a trustee who accepted the duties of trusteeship. There were no further duties in common law or equity.

(2) There was no requirement of notice of the exemption clause to be given in advance. Indeed, such a requirement would be impractical. Trustees undertook unilateral obligations and their terms of service were not dependent on the consent of the beneficiary.

(3) There were insuperable difficulties in applying UCTA 1977 to trustee exemption clauses. Such clauses did not necessarily arise under contracts with the trustees because trust deeds were not contracts.

Tuckey LJ: it seems to me that the matters relied on by Mr McMeel (counsel for the claimant) show no more than that Mr Clark assumed the usual responsibilities of a trustee of a scheme of this kind and no more. There is therefore no basis for saying that he assumed some super-added common law or equitable duty of care, even if in such circumstances on other facts it was possible to spell out such a duty, which I doubt.

As to Mr McMeel's incorporation argument, the judge's answer was:

> It seeks, in my judgment, to import contractual concepts of the consensual relationship into the relationship which arises between a trustee and a beneficiary of the trust. In a trust relationship there is no such consensus. What cl 13(3) of the trust deed does is to define the ambit of the liability under which the trustees of that trust were prepared to act from the date the deed was executed. That willingness to act on those terms was not dependant on any assent on the part of the beneficiaries or any knowledge on their behalf as to what the trust deed provided.

I agree. As Mr Virgo, counsel for Mr Clark, says trustees undertake unilateral obligations and are entitled to limit the extent of the duties they assume other than the core duties of honesty and good faith. If a beneficiary wishes to take advantage of the terms of a settlement of this kind, he must do so on its terms. The judge went on to point out, in my view correctly, that the potential beneficiaries of a group scheme of this kind would be a shifting class whom it might be difficult to identify and that the trustees would have had an obligation to make a copy of the trust deed available to any beneficiary who asked for it.

I turn finally to the argument about the Unfair Contract Terms Act. The relevant provisions of that act are as follows. Section 1 says that for the purposes of Pt 1 of this act:

> ... negligence means the breach –

> (a) of any obligation, arising from the express or implied terms of a contract, to take reasonable care or exercise reasonable skill in the performance of the contract;

> (b) of any common law duty to take reasonable care or exercise reasonable skill.

Mr McMeel rightly concedes that the obligation he contends for does not arise from a contract because a trust is not a contract so it is s 1(1)(b) which applies if this Act applies at all. That takes one to s 2(1) of the Act which says that:

A person cannot by reference to any contract term or to a notice given to persons generally or to particular persons exclude or restrict his liability for ... loss or damage ... except insofar as the term or notice satisfies the requirement of reasonableness.

Section 14 says that:

'notice' includes an announcement, whether or not in writing, and any other communication ...

It seems to me that there are insuperable difficulties in seeking to apply the 1977 Act to an exemption clause of the kind with which this case is concerned. Assuming that there is a common law duty of care, the question is whether the Cl 13.3 (of the scheme) is a notice of the kind referred to in s 2. I do not think it is.

This point was considered by the Law Commission in their consultation paper 171 published in 2003 on the subject of trustee exemption clauses. After having concluded that a trustee exemption clause is not a contract they say at para 2.62:

While there may be a stronger argument that a trustee exemption clause is a form of 'notice', this may also be somewhat speculative in that it would seem that 'notice' within the 1977 Act is primarily intended to cover attempts to exclude liability by reference to a sign outside the confines of a formal legal document.

It is probably their reference to the argument being somewhat speculative which led them to say in para 4.46 of the report:

We have already made reference to the Unfair Contract Terms Act 1977 where we came to the conclusion that it does not generally apply to trustee exemption clauses.

It is worth noting that although the 1977 Act has been in force for many years and trustee exemption clauses have been a subject of some controversy there is no reported case of any attempt to impugn such a clause by reference to the 1977 Act. The point was not taken in the leading case on such clauses, *Armitage v Nurse* [1998] 2 Ch 241, [1997] 2 All ER 705, [1997] 3 WLR 1046, although it is apparent from the report that a host of other points were. In their report the Law Commission referred to this case and say that it is now settled law in England and Wales that trustee exemption clauses can validly exempt trustees from liability for breaches of trust, except fraud.

Law Commission proposals

On 19 July 2006, the Law Commission published its report on 'Trustee Exemption Clauses' and listed a number of recommendations. Prior to this, a consultation paper on 'Trustee Exemption Clauses', published in 2003, identified a number of responses. Some of these are:

(1) There was a general distaste for wide exclusion clauses especially where the settler is unaware of their existence or meaning.

(2) A distinction ought to be drawn between professional and lay trustees, but it was recognized that this may be difficult to apply and liable to cause unfairness (especially in relation to professionals acting *pro bono*).

(3) The practicality of the proposal that all trustees should have the power to purchase indemnity insurance using trust funds was questioned on the grounds of costs and availability.

(4) There was widespread concern about the likely adverse impact of statutory regulation restricting reliance on trustee exemption clauses. This may result in increased indemnity insurance premiums and the possible unavailability of insurance, a decrease in the flexibility of the management of trust property and the increase in speculative litigation for breach of trust and a possible reluctance to accept trusteeship.

The 2006 Report recommends that the trust industry adopt a non-statutory rule of practice and this should be enforced by the regulatory and professional bodies that govern trustees and drafters of trusts. The rule will be enforced by professional bodies who may discipline its members who fail to comply. The recommended rule of practice requires paid trustees and drafters of trust instruments to take reasonable steps to ensure that settlors understand the meaning and effect of exemption clauses to be included in trusts instruments, before the creation of such trusts. This rule will not apply to pension trusts or trusts already subject to statutory regulation.

Goodhart, W, 'Trustee exemption clauses and the Unfair Contract Terms Act 1977' [1980] Conv 333

Goodhart argues that Unfair Contract Terms Act 1977 is capable of applying to trustee exemption clauses. Assuming that the clause is incorporated under a contract of 'business liability', which Goodhart suggests would apply to corporations and 'professional' trustees, there are a number of limitations envisaged. The 1977 Act has no application to trustees appointed by the court under s 41 of the Trustee Act 1925. In addition, the exemption clause is required to satisfy the test of 'reasonableness' referred to in s 2(3) of the 1977 Act. Goodhart submits that, in the ordinary case, the trustee will be hard pressed to persuade the court that an exemption clause is reasonable. Trustees are adequately protected by s 30 of the Trustee Act 1925 (now s 23 of the Trustee Act 2000) and s 61 of the Trustee Act 1925 affords them some measure of relief.

McCormack, G, 'The liability of trustees for gross negligence' [1998] Conv 100

McCormack examines the English and Scottish authorities on trustee exemption clauses, referred to by Millett LJ in *Armitage v Nurse* [1997] 3 WLR 1046. These are *Wilkins v Hogg* (1861) 31 LJ Ch 41; *Knox v Mackinnon* (1888) 13 App Cas 753; *Pass v Dundas* (1880) 43 LT 665; *Rae v Meek* (1889) 14 App Cas 558; and *Clarke v Clarke's Trustees* [1925] SC 693. Millett LJ, in *Armitage v Nurse*, referred to these authorities as decisions on the true construction of the particular clauses which were in common form at the time. McCormack questions the correctness of Millett LJ's interpretation of these cases and responds thus:

> It may be straining things a little to say that the judicial hostility to clauses exempting trustees from liability for gross negligence manifested therein reflects simply a principle of construction.

McCormack concludes with the following suggestions:

(1) The *contra proferentem* principle of construction ought to be adopted in construing ambiguous exemption clauses. He states:

> The party proferring the clause is purporting to relieve himself from general legal liabilities that would otherwise apply and on this basis alone the clause should be accorded a narrow construction.

(2) Trustee exemption clauses ought to be treated differently from contractual exemption clauses, because trustees are fiduciaries. He states:

> The trustee is placed under an obligation to safeguard the interests of trust beneficiaries. That is the essence of trusteeship. Clauses in a trust instrument which permit the trustee to engage in subjective wrongdoing to the detriment of the beneficiaries are at variance with the key concept of trusteeship and cannot be recognised because of this.

(3) Parliament ought to enact legislation in order to control trustee exemption clauses. McCormack writes:

> Perhaps the clearest path out of the thicket is to follow the lines suggested by Millett LJ in *Armitage v Nurse* and to advocate an extension of the legislative solution. Precisely what sort of legislative solution is envisaged? Should one adopt the approach found in s 33 of the Pensions Act 1995, which subjects all clauses excluding liability for negligent investment decisions to an invalidating taint? A less draconian solution would be to subject trustee exemption clauses to a requirement of reasonableness. It is submitted that this is the best approach.

Question
To what extent may trustees exclude their liability for breach of trust?

Duty to provide accounts and information

Owing to the nature of the fiduciary relationship of trustees, a duty is imposed on them to keep proper accounts for the trust. In pursuance of this objective, the trustees may employ an agent (an accountant) to draw up the trust accounts. The beneficiaries are entitled to inspect the accounts, but if they need copies they are required to pay for these from their own resources. Where there is a succession of beneficial interests, the accounts should differentiate between income and capital. The income beneficiaries would be entitled to inspect the 'full accounts'. The remainderman is only entitled to information relating to the 'capital accounts'.

There is no general requirement that the accounts be audited annually but, by virtue of s 22(4) of the Trustee Act 1925, the trustees in their discretion may have the accounts examined by an independent auditor every three years and may pay the costs out of income or capital.

In addition, the beneficiaries are entitled to be informed about matters concerning the trust. In order to have such information at hand, a prudent trustee would maintain a trust diary in which decisions and other relevant facts are recorded. Documents created in the course of the administration of the trust are trust documents and are *prima facie* the property of the beneficiaries and available for inspection.

Trust documents

Trust documents were described by Salmon LJ in *Re Marquess of Londonderry's Settlement* [1965] Ch 918 as possessing the following characteristics:

(i)   they are documents in the possession of the trustees as trustees; and

(ii) they contain information about the trust, which the beneficiaries are entitled to know; and

(iii) the beneficiaries have a proprietary interest in the documents, and, accordingly, are entitled to see them.

The difficulty faced by trustees concerns the circumstances when they have a discretion and are not required to give reasons for their decisions but *bona fide* record these reasons in a trust document. An aggrieved beneficiary may be entitled to challenge the decisions of the trustees by resorting to his or her right to inspect the documents. If the grounds for trustees' decisions are known, the court will consider them. In *Re Marquess of Londonderry*, the court adopted an approach which to some extent preserved the confidential nature of the trustees' discretion.

Re Marquess of Londonderry's Settlement [1965] Ch 918, CA

Facts

An object under a discretionary trust was dissatisfied with the manner in which trustees exercised their discretions. She sought to obtain copies of the agenda and minutes of meetings, and of correspondence between trustees and between the trustees and solicitors in connection with the administration of the trust. The trustees were reluctant to allow her to see the documents for this would have revealed the reasons for their decisions which they claimed were confidential. The trustees applied to the court for a declaration to determine which, if any, of the following documents they were bound to disclose:

(a) the minutes of trust meetings;

(b) agendas and other documents prepared for the purpose of such meetings;

(c) correspondence concerning the administration of the trust between:

   (i)   the trustees and other fiduciaries (called appointors, that is, named persons who were required to consent to an appointment in special circumstances);

   (ii) the trustees and the solicitors; and

   (iii) the trustees and the beneficiaries.

Held

The trustees' right to exercise their discretion in confidence prevailed over the beneficiary's right to inspect because the disclosure of such documents had the potential to cause 'family strife'.

Indeed, the court went so far as to say that if trust documents contain confidential information which ought not to be disclosed, the relevant portions of the documents may be covered up. On the facts, the correspondence between the trustees were not trust documents and were not available for inspection:

Harman LJ: The court is really required here to resolve two principles that come into conflict, or at least apparent conflict. The first is that . . . trustees exercising a discretionary power are not bound to disclose to the beneficiaries the reasons actuating them in coming to a decision. This is a long standing principle and rests largely, I think, on the view that nobody could be called upon to accept a trusteeship involving the exercise of a discretion unless, in the absence of bad faith, he were not liable to have his motives or his reasons called in question either by the beneficiaries or by the court. To this there is added a rider, namely, that if trustees do give reasons, their soundness can be considered by the court . . .

It would seem on the face of it that there is no reason why this principle should be confined to decisions orally arrived at and should not extend to a case, like the present, where, owing to the complexity of the trust and the large sums involved, the trustees, who act subject to the consent of another body called the appointors, have brought into existence various written documents, including, in particular, agenda for and minutes of their meetings from time to time held in order to consider distributions made of the fund and its income. It is here that the conflicting principle is said to emerge. All these documents, it is argued, came into existence for the purpose of the trust and are in the possession of the trustees as such and are, therefore, trust documents, the property of the beneficiaries, and as such open to them to inspect . . .

Apart from this, the defendant relied on certain observations in *O'Rourke v Darbishire* [1920] AC 581. The decision was that the plaintiff was not entitled to the production of what were called the 'trust documents'.

Lord Wrenbury says:

If the plaintiff is right in saying that he is a beneficiary, and if the documents are documents belonging to the executors as executors, he has a right to access to the documents which he desires to inspect upon what has been called in the judgments in this case a proprietary right. The beneficiary is entitled to see all the trust documents because they are trust documents and because he is a beneficiary. They are in a sense his own. Action or no action, he is entitled to access to them. This has nothing to do with discovery. The right to discovery is a right to see someone else's documents. A proprietary right is a right to access to documents which are your own. No question of professional privilege arises in such a case. Documents containing professional advice taken by the executors as trustees contain advice taken by trustees for their *cestuis que* trust, and the beneficiaries are entitled to see them because they are beneficiaries.

General observations of this sort give very little guidance, for first they beg the question what are trust documents, and secondly their Lordships were not considering the point here that papers are asked for which bear on the question of the exercise of the trustees' discretion. In my judgment category (a) . . . viz, the minutes of the meetings of the trustees . . .; and part of (b) viz, agenda prepared for trustees' meetings, are, in the absence of an action impugning the trustees' good faith, documents which a beneficiary cannot claim the right to inspect. If the defendant is allowed to examine these, she will know at once the very matters which the trustees are not bound to disclose to her, namely, their motives and reasons. Trustees who wish to preserve their rights in this respect must either commit nothing to paper or destroy everything from meeting to meeting. Indeed, if the defendant be right, I doubt if the last course is open, for she must succeed, if at all, on the ground that the papers belong to her, and if so, the trustees have no right to destroy them.

I would hold that even if documents of this type ought properly to be described as trust documents, they are protected for the special reason which protects the trustees' deliberations on a discretionary matter from disclosure. If necessary, I hold that this principle overrides the ordinary rule. This is, in my judgment, no less in the true interest of the beneficiary than of the trustees. Again, if one of the trustees commits to paper his suggestions and circulates them among his co-trustees; or if inquiries are made in writing as to the circumstances of a member of the class; I decline to hold that such documents are trust documents, the property of the beneficiaries . . . On the other hand, if the solicitor advising the trustees commits to paper an *aide memoire* summarising the state of the fund or of the family and reminding the trustees of past distributions and future possibilities, I think that must be a document which any beneficiary must be at liberty to inspect. It seems to me, therefore, that category (b) embraces documents on both sides of the line.

As to (c), I cannot think that communications passing between individual trustees and appointors are documents in which beneficiaries have a proprietary right. On the other hand, as to category (ii), in general the letters of the trustees' solicitors to the trustees do seem to me to be trust documents in which the beneficiaries have a property. As to category (iii) I do not think letters to or from an individual beneficiary ought to be open to inspection by another beneficiary.

In the recent case of *Schmidt v Rosewood Trust Ltd*, the Privy Council reviewed the right to seek disclosure of trust documents and concluded that it is one aspect of the court's inherent jurisdiction to supervise, and if necessary to intervene in, the administration of trusts. Thus, the beneficiary's right to inspect trust documents is founded not on an equitable proprietary right in respect of those documents, but upon the trustee's fiduciary duty to inform the beneficiary and to render accounts. This right to seek the court's intervention is not restricted to beneficiaries with fixed interests in the trust, but also extends to objects under a discretionary trust. However, the power to seek disclosure may be restricted by the court in the exercise of its discretion. The court is required to balance the competing interests of the different beneficiaries, the trustees and third parties.

Schmidt v Rosewood Trust Ltd [2003] 3 All ER 76, PC

Facts

The settlor executed two Isle of Man trust settlements which created discretionary trusts in favour of a group of objects, including the claimant, the son of the settlor. The defendant company became the sole trustee of the two settlements. The settlor died intestate and letters of administration were granted to the claimant. The claimant alleged that he devoted considerable time and resources in an attempt to trace his father's assets and believed that his efforts had been frustrated by the defendant. He applied in his personal capacity as a member of a class of objects, and as administrator of his father's estate for disclosure of trust accounts and information about the trust assets. The defendant contended that a beneficiary's right of disclosure of trust documents is to be treated as a proprietary right and that an object of a discretionary power does not have such a right, but merely a hope of acquiring a benefit. The Isle of Man court held in favour of the defendant and the claimant appealed to the Privy Council.

Held

The claimant was entitled to seek disclosure on the following grounds:

(a) the court has jurisdiction to supervise and, if appropriate, intervene in the administration of a trust, including a discretionary trust;

(b) the right to seek the court's intervention does not depend on entitlement to an interest under the trust. An object of a discretionary trust (including a mere power of appointment) may also be afforded protection by the court, although the circumstances concerning protection and the nature of the protection would depend on the court's discretion;

(c) no beneficiary has an entitlement, as of right, to disclosure of trust documents. Where there are issues of personal and commercial confidentiality, the court will have to balance the competing interests of the beneficiaries, the trustees and third parties, and limitations or safeguards may be imposed:

Lord Walker: [Considered *O'Rourke v Darbishire* [1920] AC 581 and *Re Londonderry's Settlement* [1965] Ch 918, and continued:] . . . the more principled and correct approach is to regard the right to seek disclosure of trust documents as one aspect of the court's inherent jurisdiction to supervise, and if necessary to intervene in, the administration of trusts. The right to seek the court's intervention does not depend on entitlement to a fixed and transmissible beneficial interest. The object of a discretion (including a mere power) may also be entitled to protection from a court of equity, although the circumstances in which he may seek protection, and the nature of the protection he may expect to obtain, will depend on the court's discretion . . . no beneficiary (and least of all a discretionary object) has any entitlement as of right to disclosure of anything which can plausibly be described as a trust document. Especially when there are issues as to personal or commercial confidentiality, the court may have to balance the competing interests of different beneficiaries, the trustees themselves and third parties. Disclosure may have to be limited and safeguards may have to be put in place. Evaluation of the claims of a beneficiary (and especially of a discretionary object) may be an important part of the balancing exercise which the court has to perform on the materials placed before it. In many cases the court may have no difficulty in concluding that an applicant with no more than a theoretical possibility of benefit ought not to be granted any relief.

Question
What are 'trust documents' and what are the consequences of identifying such documents in the administration of trusts?

Duty to distribute to the right beneficiaries

It is an elementary principle of trust law that the trustees are required to distribute the trust property (income and/or capital) to the beneficiaries properly entitled to receive the same. Failure to distribute to the correct beneficiary subjects the trustees to liability for breach of trust, although in appropriate cases they may apply to the court for relief under s 61 of the Trustee Act 1925. Thus, in *Eaves v Hickson* (1861) 30 Beav 136, trustees were liable to make good sums wrongly paid to a beneficiary in reliance on a forged marriage certificate. Likewise, in *Re Hulkes* (1886) 33 Ch D 552, the trustees were liable for sums paid to the wrong beneficiaries based on an honest, but incorrect, construction of the trust instrument.

Where the trustee makes an overpayment of income or instalment of capital, he or she may recover the amount of the overpayment by adjusting the payments subsequently made to the same beneficiary. Where the payment is made to a person who is not entitled to receive the sum, the trustee has the right to recover the amount based on a quasi-contractual claim of money paid under a mistake of fact. Such claim will not succeed if the mistake was one of law (see *Re Diplock* [1947] Ch 716, p 596 below). In *Woolwich Building Society v Inland Revenue Commissioners (No 2)* [1992] 3 All ER 737, the House of Lords decided that money paid by a member of the public to a public authority in the form of taxes paid, pursuant to an *ultra vires* demand by the authority, is *prima facie* recoverable by the member of the public as of right. An aggrieved beneficiary may, in addition to his right to sue the trustee, trace his property in the hands of the wrongly paid person (see Chapter 21).

Where the trustees have a reasonable doubt as to the validity of claims of the beneficiaries, they may apply to the court for directions, and will be protected, provided that they act in accordance with those directions. The court has the power to make a '*Benjamin* order' (derived from the case *Re Benjamin* [1902] 1 Ch 723), authorising the distribution of the trust property without identifying all the beneficiaries and creditors. In addition, where the trustees cannot identify all the beneficiaries, they are entitled to pay the trust funds into court as a last resort (see *Re Gillingham Bus Disaster Fund* [1959] Ch 62, p 148 above). Where there is no good reason for a payment into court, the trustees may personally have to pay the costs of such an application.

Under s 27 of the Trustee Act 1925, a simplified form of distribution is allowed and, at the same time, the trustees or personal representatives are given protection from claims for breach of trust. The section permits the trustees (or personal representatives) to advertise for beneficiaries in an appropriate newspaper or gazette and, after the expiration of a period of time, not being less than two months, they are entitled to distribute the property to the beneficiaries of whom the trustees are aware. If the trustees comply with the requirements of s 27, they will not be liable for breach of trust at the instance of beneficiaries of whom the trustees were unaware. However, the ignored beneficiaries are entitled to trace their property in the hands of the recipient. Lastly, the section is incapable of being excluded or modified by the trust instrument.

Trustee Act 1925, s 27 (as amended by the Trusts of Land and Appointment of Trustees Act 1996)

(1) With a view to the conveyance to or distribution among the persons entitled to any real or personal property, the trustees of a settlement, trustees of land, trustees for sale of personal property or personal representatives, may give notice by advertisement in the Gazette, and in a newspaper circulating in the district in which the land is situated, and such other like notices, including notices elsewhere than in England and Wales, as would, in any special case, have been directed by a court of competent jurisdiction in an action for administration, of their intention to make such conveyance or distribution as aforesaid, and requiring any person interested to send to the trustees or personal representatives within the time, not being less than two months, fixed in the notice or, where more than one notice is given, in the last of the notices, particulars of his claim in respect of the property or any part thereof to which the notice relates.

(2) At the expiration of the time fixed by the notice, the trustees or personal representatives may convey or distribute the property or any part thereof to which the notice relates, to or among the persons entitled thereto, have regard only to claims, whether formal or not, of which the trustees or personal representatives then had notice and shall not, as respects the property so conveyed or distributed, be liable to any person of whose claim the trustees or personal representatives have not had notice at the time of conveyance or distribution; but nothing in this section:

  (a) prejudices the right of any person to follow the property, or any property representing the same, into the hands of any person, other than a purchaser, who may have received it; or

  (b) frees the trustees or personal representatives from any obligation to make searches or obtain official certificates of search similar to those which an intending purchaser would be advised to make or obtain.

(3) This section applies notwithstanding anything to the contrary in the will or other instrument, if any, creating the trust.

Duty to convert

A duty to convert trust assets may arise from the express terms of the trust instrument or by statute. Under s 3 of the Trusts of Land and Appointment of Trustees Act 1996, the doctrine of conversion is abolished in respect of a trust of land. In short, where land is held by trustees subject to a trust for sale, the land is not treated as personal property. Irrespective of the source of the duty, the trustees are required to comply with the duty. In this section we are concerned with the creation of the duty by the courts.

As a corollary to the duty of impartiality imposed on the trustees, where there is a conflict of beneficial interests under the trust, equity presumes that the trustees will hold a balance between them. This is in accordance with the presumed intention of the testator.

For example, a testator by will bequeaths the residue of his estate upon trust for A for life with remainder to B absolutely. Let us assume that the residue estate consists of a car, a computer and paintings. If these assets are retained in their original state, A would derive the greater enjoyment of the depreciating assets (car and computer) which may become virtually worthless at the time of A's death. On the other hand, A may derive no income from the paintings and, if these are appreciating assets, B will derive a disproportionate benefit from the capital. The courts presume that this could not have been the testator's intention. The trustees are required to sell the assets and invest the proceeds in authorised investments but, in the interim period, to apportion the income and pay part of it to the life tenant and capitalise the balance.

Where the trust assets consist of residuary personalty bequeathed under a will and the assets are of a wasting, hazardous, reversionary or unauthorised character, and the beneficiaries enjoy their interests in succession, the trustees are required to convert the trust property into authorised investments in accordance with the rule in *Howe v Lord Dartmouth*.

Howe v Lord Dartmouth (1802) 7 Ves 137

Facts
The residuary clause in the testator's will transferred bank stock and annuities to beneficiaries in succession. The trustees converted these assets and reinvested the same. The question in issue was whether the trustees were in breach of trust.

Held
There was no breach of trust, for the conversion was quite proper in the circumstances.

> **Lord Eldon LC:** ... unless the testator directs the mode so that it is to continue as it was, the court understands that it shall be put in such a state, that the others may enjoy it after the decease of the first; and the thing is quite equal.

In *Hinves v Hinves*, Wigram VC explained the rationale behind the duty to convert.

Hinves v Hinves (1844) 3 Hare 609, HC

> **Wigram VC:** ... where personal estate is given in terms amounting to a general residuary bequest to be enjoyed by persons in succession, the interpretation the court puts upon the bequest is that the persons indicated are to enjoy the same thing in succession; and, in order to effectuate that intention, the court as a general rule converts into permanent investments so much of the personalty as is of a wasting or perishable nature at the death of the testator, and also reversionary interests. The rule did not originally ascribe to testators the intention to effect such conversions, except in so far as a testator may be supposed to intend that which the law will do, but the court, finding the intention of the testator to be that the objects of his bounty shall take successive interests in one and the same thing, converts the property, as the only means of giving effect to that intention.

Exclusion

The rule in *Howe v Lord Dartmouth*, that is, an implied duty to convert, does not operate if the testator has manifested a contrary intention. Such contrary intention may be express, as with an express duty to convert (see *Alcock v Sloper* (1833) 2 My & K 699), or may be implied, with respect to a discretion to convert (*Re Sewell's Estate* (1870) 11 Eq 80), or a direction that the property is to be enjoyed *in specie* (see *McDonald v Irvine* (1878) 8 Ch D 101). Under the Trusts of Land and Appointment of Trustees Act 1996, all trusts where the subject matter includes land are treated as trusts of land. Under such trusts the property is held by the trustees subject to a power to sell the land. The effect of this rule is that the principle in *Howe v Lord Dartmouth* will not apply to such trusts.

The rule is not applicable to *inter vivos* settlements on the basis that the settlor intended the specific assets settled to be enjoyed by the beneficiaries: see *Re Straubenzee* [1901] 2 Ch 779.

Equitable apportionments

The rule in Howe v Lord Dartmouth

Having converted the assets into authorised investments, one of the features of the rule in *Howe v Lord Dartmouth* is that the life tenant is entitled to receive income at the rate of 4% per annum (less income tax) from the date of death to the date of conversion. The value on which the 4% is to be calculated depends on whether the trustees are given the power to postpone conversion of the investment or not. The position is as follows:

(a) where the trustees have no power to postpone conversion, the 4% is based on the value of the investment at the end of the executor's year (one year from the date of death), or the proceeds of sale if earlier: see *Re Fawcett* [1940] Ch 402;

(b) where the trustees are given a power to postpone the conversion, the 4% is based on the value of the investment at the date of death: see *Re Parry* [1947] Ch 23.

Where there is insufficient income to pay the 4%, the shortfall may be made good out of the sale proceeds of unauthorised investments, or out of the income from unauthorised investments.

The rule in Re Earl of Chesterfield's Trusts

The rule in *Re Earl of Chesterfield's Trust* (1833) 24 Ch D 643 applies where there are different interests in a trust which includes a non-income producing asset such as a reversion or a life policy. The proceeds of the non-income producing asset are apportioned between the life tenant and the remainderman. The remainderman receives a sum which, if invested at compound interest at the date of death at 4% per annum (less income tax), would produce the proceeds of sale. The balance is paid over to the life tenant.

The rule in Allhusen v Whittell

Where the residue of an estate is left to a life tenant, the assumption is that the life tenant is to be entitled to income on the 'pure residue' only. Where there is a delay in paying debts, inheritance tax, legacies and other liabilities, the life tenant's income is augmented. But for the rule in *Allhusen v Whittel* (1867) LR 4 Eq 295, the longer the delay in settling debts, the larger the gain to the life tenant. The effect of the rule is to charge the life tenant with interest on the sums used to pay debts and other liabilities in order to maintain equality between the beneficiaries. As the various expenses are paid, they should be apportioned between income and capital. The amount charged to capital should be such capital sum which, if invested at the date of death, would amount exactly to the sum paid. The balance is charged to income. The rate of interest to be used in this calculation is the average rate of interest received during the year.

The rule in Re Atkinson

The rule in *Re Atkinson* [1904] 2 Ch 160 applies where one of the assets of an estate consists of a loan on mortgage and the security is insufficient to repay the principal and interest in full. The proceeds of sale are apportioned between the life tenant and remainderman in the proportion which the arrears bear to the amount due in respect of principal. In short, the proceeds of sale are abated *pro rata* between the life tenant and the remainderman as follows:

(a) the amount due to the remainderman is the principal outstanding plus any interest due to the date of death minus any rent received as mortgagee in possession;

(b) the amount due to the life tenant is the income due from the date of death to the date of realisation minus any rent received as mortgagee in possession or, where a foreclosure order is obtained, the income due to the date of the foreclosure order minus any rent received as mortgagee in possession. Rent received after foreclosure belongs to the life tenant in lieu of interest.

Rent received as mortgagee in possession is to be applied as follows:

(a) interest to the date of death (remainderman);

(b) interest from the date of death to realisation or foreclosure order (life tenant);

(c) repayment of capital (remainderman).

Question
In what circumstances is there an implied duty to convert trust funds?

POWERS OF INVESTMENT

The trustees' primary duty is to achieve the purpose of the trust as declared by the settlor in the trust instrument. As a corollary to this principle, the trustees have a duty to preserve the trust funds in the interests of the beneficiaries. If there is a succession of interests enjoyed by the beneficiaries, the trustees have a duty to maintain evenhandedness between the beneficiaries. Thus, the trustees will be under a duty to invest the trust funds in such a way to ensure a fair balance between income and capital (*per* Megarry VC in *Cowan v Scargill*).

Cowan v Scargill [1984] 2 All ER 750, HC

Megarry VC: The starting point is the duty of trustees to exercise their powers in the best interests of the present and future beneficiaries of the trust, holding the scales impartially between different classes of beneficiaries . . . In the case of a power of investment . . . the power must be exercised so as to yield the best return for the beneficiaries, judged in relation to the risks of the investments in question; and the prospects of the yield of income and capital appreciation both have to be considered in judging the return from the investments.

In exercising their power of investment, the trustees are required to exercise their duty of care. Prior to the passing of the Trustee Act 2000, the common law standard of care was that of a person 'of ordinary prudence . . . in the management of his own private affairs' (*per* Lord Watson in *Learoyd v Whiteley* (1887) 12 AC 727). Lord Watson continued, 'He is not allowed the same discretion in investing the moneys of the trust as if he were a person *sui juris* dealing with his own estate. It is the duty of a trustee to confine himself to the class of investments which are permitted by the trust and likewise to avoid all investments of that class which are attended with hazard'. This standard was applied purely objectively.

The term 'investment' in the law of trusts refers to property which will produce an income yield (see *Re Wragg* [1918–19] All ER 233). The purchase of property for the purpose of pure capital appreciation without producing income has been construed as not being an investment (see *Re Power* [1947] Ch 572). In that case, a power to purchase freehold property did not authorise the purchase of a freehold house for the occupation of the beneficiary.

The statutory provisions that deal with the trustees' powers of investment have consistently failed to offer a definition of the expression.

The power of trustees to invest the trust fund is based on express or implied authority:

(a) by the trust instrument;

(b) under general principles of trust law; or

(c) by statute as default provisions.

Express powers of investment

Authority may be conferred expressly on the trustees by the trust instrument. A professionally drafted contemporary trust deed will often contain a wide investment clause giving the trustees a broad discretion to invest the trust funds as they see fit. The modern approach to such clauses is to construe them liberally: see *Re Harari's Settlement*.

Re Harari's Settlement [1949] 1 All ER 430, HC

Facts
The issue concerned the effect of a clause in the trust instrument, to make such 'investments as the trustees may think fit'.

Held
The clause regarding investment powers should be given its ordinary meaning without restriction:

Jenkins J: The question turns primarily on the meaning to be attached to the words 'in or upon such investments as to them may seem fit'. *Prima facie* those words mean what they say – that the trustees are not to be limited in any way by any statutory range of investments, but can invest in any investment which they may select as seeming to them a fit one for the money subject to the trusts of the settlement.

It seems to me that I am left free to construe this settlement according to what I consider to be the natural and proper meaning of the words used in their context, and, so construing the words 'in or upon such investments as to them may seem fit', I see no justification for implying any restriction. I think the trustees have power, under the plain meaning of these words, to invest in any investments which they honestly think are desirable investments . . . To hold otherwise would really be to read words into the settlement which are not there.

The real ground, however, for my decision is the plain and ordinary meaning of the words 'in or upon such investments as to them may seem fit'. Having found nothing in the authorities to constrain me to construe those words otherwise than in accordance with their plain meaning, that is the meaning I propose to place on them.

Moreover, the settlor may authorise the trustees to purchase a dwelling house for the benefit of a beneficiary, thus overcoming the limitation that existed in *Re Power*. In addition, the settlor may impose an obligation on the trustees to invest exclusively in shares in a specified company or in any other specific investments. In such a case, the trustees will have no choice but to comply with the directions of the settlor.

Statutory powers of investment

There have been occasions when Parliament has introduced default provisions concerning the investment powers of trustees. The current scheme of default provisions is to be found in the Trustee Act 2000, which repeals and replaces the Trustee Investment Act 1961.

Statutory powers under the Trustee Investment Act 1961

If the trust instrument was silent as to the trustees' power of investment, the trustees were authorised to invest by reference to the statutory default provisions enacted in the Trustee Investment Act 1961. This Act permitted trustees to invest in fixed interest investments and equities without abandoning the policy of caution of safe investments. The 1961 Act restricted trust investments in authorised investments. The Act divided investments into 'narrower range' (fixed rate investments) and 'wider range' investments (shares in public companies). Trustees were entitled to invest the entire trust fund in narrower range investments. These were investments which could be made with professional advice (Part II narrower range investments, such as gilts and fixed rate interest) or without advice (Part I narrower range investments, such as government bonds and savings accounts). However, if they wanted to invest in shares, the fund was required to be divided into two parts – narrower range (up to 25%) and wider range (up to 75%) – and the wider range part of the fund could be invested in equities. The 1961 Act was criticised as being unduly restrictive. What was needed was, first, power on the part of trustees to utilise professional advice by delegating the entire process of selecting and acquiring investments to professional persons (see now 'Collective delegation under the Trustee Act 2000', pp 473–74 above); and, secondly, power on the part of trustees to invest the trust fund in more varied and contemporary forms of investments, which would reflect the fundamental changes in the way investment business is transacted today.

Statutory powers of investment under the Trustee Act 2000

The Trustee Act 2000 (which came into force on 1 February 2001) repeals and replaces the Trustee Investment Act 1961. The new statutory power of investment is found in s 3(1) of the Trustee Act 2000. Under s 3, 'a trustee may make any kind of investment that he could make if he were absolutely entitled to the assets of the trust'. The trustee must, of course, comply with the general duty of care as stated in s 1 of the Act (see p 471 above). This new power is required to be considered in the light of the new powers of delegation. As will be seen, trustees will be able to delegate their discretion as well as their duty to invest.

The new power is treated as a *default provision* and will operate only in so far as there is no contrary provision in the trust instrument. It should be noted that restrictions imposed by the trust instrument prior to 3 August 1961 are treated as void (see s 7(2) of the Trustee Act 2000). This new power operates retrospectively in the sense that trusts existing before or after the commencement of the 2000 Act are subject to this default provision. However, the new regime does not apply to occupational pensions schemes, authorised unit trusts and schemes under the Charities Act 1993.

Section 4 of the 2000 Act requires trustees to have regard to the 'standard investment criteria' when investing. This is defined in s 4(3) to mean the suitability of the investment to the trust and the need for diversification as is appropriate in the circumstances. Thus, trustees are no longer restricted as to the type of investments they may make but are restricted by reference to the standard investment criteria. The standard investment criteria are important because the suitability of investments vary from trust to trust. Having exercised the power of investment, the trustees are required to review the trust investments periodically by reference to the standard investment criteria (s 4(2)). The purpose of this provision is to require the trustees to determine whether the trust fund ought to be re-invested or not.

By virtue of s 5 of the Trustee Act 2000, trustees are required to obtain and consider proper advice before investing unless, in the circumstances, they reasonably conclude that it is unnecessary to do so. For example, if funds are paid in to an interest-bearing account pending investment by the trustees, it may be unnecessary to take advice regarding the interim account, or one or more of the trustees may be suitably qualified to give proper advice. Section 5(4) defines 'proper advice' as 'advice of a person who is *reasonably believed* by the trustee to be qualified to give it by his ability in and practical experience of financial and other matters relating to the proposed investment' [emphasis added]. This is an objective issue and the test is not restricted to individuals with paper qualifications but includes those with practical experience. Although the provision does not require the advice to be in writing, a prudent trustee will require advice to be in such form.

Mortgages

Prior to the Trustee Act 2000, the trustees' powers to invest in mortgages was laid down in the Trustee Investment Act 1961 and s 8 of the Trustee Act 1925. The effect of these provisions was that trustees were authorised to invest in mortgages of freehold property, or leasehold property where the lease had at least 60 years to run. Section 8 of the Trustee Act 1925 provided that a trustee was not impeachable for breach of trust if the amount of the loan did not exceed two-thirds of the value of the property, and he acted on the written advice of a suitable and independent valuer.

The Trustee Act 2000 repeals and replaces these provisions. Section 3 of the Act of 2000 authorises the trustees to invest by way of a loan secured on land. Although the point is far from clear, it is generally advisable for the trustees to invest in a legal estate by way of a legal mortgage as under the previous law. In addition, the security is restricted to land in the UK.

Acquisition of land

Before the passing of the Trustee Act 2000, trustees had no general power to purchase land as an investment. There were two exceptions to this rule. First, the trust instrument might authorise trustees to purchase land as an investment. For these purposes, and subject to any contrary provision, the land was required to be bought in order to generate an income. Secondly, s 6(4) of the Trusts of Land and Appointment of Trustees Act 1996 empowered trustees of land to purchase land as an investment, or for the occupation by a beneficiary or for other purposes. The trustees may sell all of the land subject to the trust and purchase further land with the proceeds of sale (s 17 of the 1996 Act). The trustees of land have wide powers to mortgage or lease the land, though not to make a gift of the property or sale at an undervalue (such action will involve a loss to the trust, but may be lawful if all the beneficiaries, being of full age and capacity, consent to such action). The trustees under s 6 are subject to the statutory duty of care under s 1 of the Trustee Act 2000 and will be in breach of trust if they enter into a dealing for less than the full market value of the land. In exercising their powers under s 6, the trustees are required to have regard to the rights of the beneficiaries and any rule of law or equity or statute. The trustees are required to consult the beneficiaries entitled to possession and give effect to the wishes of the majority, measured by reference to the value of their interest (if consistent with the general interests of the trust). Moreover, the trust deed may impose an obligation on the trustees to obtain the consent of any person prior to a dealing. Failure to consult such a person may not necessarily invalidate the transaction, but will give rise to liability for breach of trust, unless the court dispenses with the need to obtain consent by an order under s 14 of the 1996 Act.

Under s 8 of the Trustee Act 2000, trustees are now entitled to purchase freehold or leasehold land in the UK:

(a) as an investment;

(b) for the occupation by a beneficiary; or

(c) for any other purpose.

Thus, the new power mirrors the power of trustees under s 6(4) of the Trusts of Land and Appointment of Trustees Act 1996, which has been repealed and replaced by s 8 of the 2000 Act. Once trustees have acquired the relevant land, they will be vested with the same powers as an absolute owner of land. Accordingly, the trustees will be able to sell, lease and mortgage the land. This new power is a *default* provision which may be excluded by a contrary intention in the trust instrument.

Duty of care

In exercising their new powers of investment the trustees are required to conform to the combined objective/subjective standard of care laid down in s 1 of the Trustee Act 2000 (considered earlier at p 471 above).

Enlargement of investment powers

Trustees are entitled to apply to the court under s 57 of the Trustee Act 1925 or under the Variation of Trusts Act 1958 (see Chapter 20 below) in order to widen their investment powers. After some initial uneasiness (see *Re Kolb's Will Trusts* [1962] Ch 531), the approach of the courts has been encouraging in granting their approval in order to update the investment policy of trusts beyond the scope of the old Trustee Investments Act 1961: see *Mason v Farbrother*.

Mason v Farbrother [1983] 2 All ER 1078, HC

Facts

The court approved a scheme to widen the investment powers of trustees of the employees of the Co-operative Society's pension fund owing to the effects of inflation and the size of the funds (some £127 million).

Held

Blackett-Ord VC: I have indicated that after 1959 a great many applications were made by trustees of trusts under the Variation of Trusts Act 1958 to obtain wider investment powers, but Parliament then passed the 1961 Act extending investment powers of trustees and in two later cases, namely, *Re Cooper's Settlement* [1962] Ch 826, and *Re Kolb's Will Trusts* [1962] Ch 531, Buckley J and Cross J respectively expressed the view that in the light of such recent expression of the views of Parliament, it would not be right for the courts to continue to extend investment clauses with the enthusiasm with which they had done up to date; and for many years few applications, if any, were made.

But the rule was not an absolute one; it was said to apply in the absence of special circumstances, and the special circumstances in the present case are manifest: in a word, inflation since 1961. And also of course the fact that the trust is an unusual one in that it is not a private or family trust but a pension fund with perhaps something of a public element.

In my judgment there is no reason why in a proper case an application such as the present one should not be acceded to under s 57 of the Trustee Act 1925. And it seems to me on the evidence that it is (in the words of the section) 'expedient' that the application should succeed.

In *Trustees of the British Museum v AG* [1984] 1 All ER 337, the trustees' powers were enlarged to include a power to invest abroad. The judge enumerated a number of factors to be taken into account, such as the standing of the trustees, the size of the fund, the object of the trust, the effectiveness of provisions for advice and the exercising of control over investment decisions.

This approach was followed in *Steel v Wellcome Custodian Trustee* [1988] 1 WLR 167. The trustees of the Wellcome Trust, a group of charitable trusts with combined assets worth £3.2 billion, were entitled to have their powers of investment enlarged.

The rights of beneficiaries to occupy land

Section 12 of the Trusts of Land and Appointment of Trustees Act 1996 confers on a beneficiary entitled to an interest in possession under a trust of land the right to occupy the land. The right to occupy exists where the purposes of the trust include making the land available for occupation by him personally, or by beneficiaries of whom he is one, or the terms of the trust make the land available for occupation by him. However, the right to occupy does not apply where the land is not available or is unsuitable for occupation by the beneficiary. Section 13 of the Act allows the trustees to impose reasonable conditions on a beneficiary who is allowed to occupy the land (for example, to pay rates and outgoings or an occupation rent, or to restrict the use of land).

Where a number of beneficiaries are entitled to occupy land under s 12, the trustees are empowered under s 13 to exclude or restrict, on reasonable grounds, the right of some of the beneficiaries to occupy. Moreover, the trustees are entitled to impose reasonable conditions on an occupying beneficiary and, if appropriate, to compensate a beneficiary whose right of occupation has been excluded or restricted. In exercising their s 13 powers, the trustees are required to have regard to the settlor's intentions, the purposes of the trust, and the wishes of the beneficiaries entitled to possession. In addition, the trustees are required to act reasonably when dealing with the claims of competing beneficiaries. The s 12 power cannot be used to evict an existing occupier (whether or not he is a beneficiary) without his consent or a court order.

POWERS OF MAINTENANCE AND ADVANCEMENT

Let us suppose that one of the beneficiaries under a trust is an infant (a person under the age of 18). The settlor, for personal reasons, may not wish to transfer an immediate interest to the child but may postpone the enjoyment of his interest subject to a contingency, such as attaining the age of majority or qualifying as an accountant.

For example, a fund is transferred to trustees on trust for A provided that he attains the age of 18. A is 14 years old and in need of funds for his education. Since A does not have a vested interest in the income or capital, but merely a contingent interest, the trustees, *prima facie*, are not entitled to pay A any part of the income and capital.

Prior to the fulfilment of the contingency, circumstances may arise which indicate the need for the beneficiary to have access to part of the fund. It would be senseless to treat the beneficiary as entitled to a fortune in the future but in the meantime to be deprived of any access to his potential fortune. In this regard, it might be possible for the trustees to pay some or all of the income to or on behalf of an infant beneficiary until his interest becomes vested in possession or fails before achieving the relevant event (power of maintenance), or to pay part of the capital for the benefit of the beneficiary whether or not he is an infant, pending the vesting or failure of his interest (power of advancement).

Maintenance payments are expenditure incurred out of the income of a fund for routine recurring purposes such as food, clothing, rent and education.

Advancements are payments out of capital to cover major non-recurring capital expenses, such as the purchase of a business or a home.

POWERS OF MAINTENANCE

Maintenance

A power of maintenance is a discretion granted to the trustees to pay or apply income for the benefit of an infant beneficiary at a time prior to the beneficiary acquiring a right to the income or capital of the trust.

The issues that are required to be considered by the trustees are:

(a) whether they have a power to maintain an infant beneficiary;

(b) whether there is any income available for maintenance;

(c) whether the trustees are prepared to exercise their discretion to maintain the beneficiary.

Authority to maintain

Express power

A settlor may expressly include a power of maintenance in the trust instrument. Most profession-ally drafted settlements will include this power. If this is the case, the trustees' duties will be encapsulated in the clause.

Inherent power

The court has an inherent power to authorise the trustees to maintain beneficiaries. The under-lying unexpressed intention of the settlor must have been consistent with the maintenance payments in favour of the infant beneficiary or beneficiaries.

Statutory power

Section 31 of the Trustee Act 1925 authorises the trustees in their discretion to pay the whole or part of the income from the trust to the parent or guardian of an infant beneficiary, or otherwise apply the relevant amount towards the maintenance, education or benefit of the infant beneficiary, during his infancy or until his interest fails.

Trustee Act 1925, s 31(1)

Where any property is held by trustees in trust for any person for any interest whatsoever, whether vested or contingent, then, subject to any prior interests or charges affecting that property:

(i) during the infancy of any such person, if his interest so long continues, the trustees may, at their sole discretion, pay to his parent or guardian, if any, or otherwise apply for or towards his maintenance, education or benefit, the whole or such part, if any, of the income of that property as may, in all the circumstances, be reasonable, whether or not there is:

(a) any other fund applicable to the same purpose; or

(b) any person bound by law to provide for his maintenance or education.

But this statutory power may be modified or excluded by the settlor in the trust instrument: see s 69(2) of the 1925 Act.

Trustee Act 1925, s 69(2)

The powers conferred by this Act on trustees are in addition to the powers conferred by the instrument, if any, creating the trust, but those powers, unless otherwise stated, apply if and so far only as a contrary intention is not expressed in the instrument, if any, creating the trust, and have effect subject to the terms of that instrument.

An exclusion of the power may be express or implied in the settlement. Section 31 of the 1925 Act was intended to be implied into every settlement subject to any contrary intention expressed by the terms of the instrument. A contrary intention will be established if the settlor has specifically disposed of the income, for example, a payment of the income to another, or has directed an accumulation of income.

Indeed, the settlor may impliedly exclude s 31 of the Trustee Act 1925, even though the clause in the settlement that has this effect is void. In *Re Erskine's Settlement Trust* [1971] 1 WLR 162, the clause directing the accumulation of income (which expressed a contrary intention) was void for infringing the perpetuity rule. In *Re Delamere*, it was decided that an appointment of capital to infant beneficiaries does not, on its own, manifest a contrary intention under s 69(2) to exclude the power of maintenance under s 31(1) of the Trustee Act 1925.

Re Delamere's Settlement Trust [1984] 1 WLR 813, CA

Facts

The trustees of a settlement executed a revocable deed of appointment in 1971 whereby the income from trust funds was to be held upon trust for six infant beneficiaries 'in equal shares absolutely'. The income was not distributed and, in 1980, the trustees executed a further deed revoking the trusts of the 1971 appointment and appointed new trusts in respect of that capital and its future interest. The trustees applied to the court to determine whether the accumulated income was vested in the beneficiaries between 1971 and 1980.

Held

On construction of the 1971 appointment, the beneficiaries had acquired indefeasible interests in the income during the relevant period. In so far as the terms of the appointment were inconsistent with s 31 of the 1925 Act, the Act was excluded. Accordingly s 31(2) was excluded but not s 31(1):

Waller LJ: Section 31 of the Trustee Act 1925 was enacted in order both to simplify the task of the draftsman of a trust instrument and to fill gaps which he might unwittingly leave in the disposal of the trust income. And in the absence of a contrary intention in the trust instrument s 31(2) provided in effect that income of a beneficiary up to the age of 18, which was not applied for his maintenance, should be accumulated as part of the trust fund so that if he died unmarried before the age of 18 the accumulated income would form part of the trust fund and not vest in his personal representatives. By contrast s 31(4) provided that in the case of a vested annuity accumulations made during his infancy should belong to him or his personal representatives 'absolutely'. There are no doubt good reasons for making this distinction in the absence of a contrary intention but the difference between the two sub-sections does emphasise the necessity of examining the wording of the trust instrument carefully. In this case the deed of appointment is commendably brief in form and I agree with Slade LJ that this circumstance indicates that every word is included for a purpose. Even in the absence of the word 'absolutely' the effect of the 1971 appointment would have been to give the grandchildren a title to all accrued income defeasible only if he or she died before the age of 18 unmarried. Without the word 'absolutely', however, the construction contended for by the seventh defendant would have taken effect and the income would have been held by the trustees in accordance with the provisions of s 31(2). One has to ask therefore why the word 'absolutely' was included.

In my opinion there are two features of the deed of appointment which make it clear that the deed must be construed as having been intended to vary the provisions of s 31(2). These two features are that the deed was expressed to be a settlement of income and that it was expressed to be on trust for the grandchildren in equal shares 'absolutely'. In my opinion that combination leads to the conclusion that the deed was intended to ensure that the income vested in the appointee as and when it became due and in so far as it was not used for maintenance of the appointee was held by the trustees absolutely and indefeasibly for the appointee.

Availability of income

The issue here is whether the income of the trust is available to maintain the infant beneficiary. The effect of complex rules of case law, s 175 of the Law of Property Act 1925 and s 31(3) of the Trustee Act 1925, is that a vested interest carries the intermediate income unless someone else is entitled to it, or the income is required to be accumulated.

Law of Property Act 1925, s 175

A contingent or future specific devise or bequest of property, whether real or personal, and a contingent residuary devise of freehold land, and a specific or residuary devise of freehold land to trustees upon trust for persons whose interests are contingent or executory shall, subject to the statutory provisions relating to accumulations, carry the intermediate income of that property from the death of the testator, except so far as such income, or any part thereof, may be otherwise expressly disposed of.

Trustee Act 1925, s 31(3)

This section applies in the case of a contingent interest only if the limitation or trust carries the intermediate income of the property, but it applies to a future or contingent legacy by the parent of, or a person standing *in loco parentis* to the legatee, if and for such period as, under the general law, the legacy carries interest for the maintenance of the legatee, and in any such case the rate of interest shall (if the income available is sufficient, and subject to any rules of court to the contrary) be 5% per annum.

Thus, if A, an adult, is entitled to the income for life with remainder to B, an infant, absolutely, the income will not be available to maintain B. This is because the income is expressly payable to another beneficiary, A. Another way of expressing the same point is to recognise that the settlor by paying the income to A has expressed a contrary intention in the trust instrument, that is, the power to maintain B during infancy has been excluded: see *Re McGeorge*.

Re McGeorge [1963] Ch 544, HC

Facts

A testator by his will devised land to his daughter, Helen. By clause 4 of the will, he declared that the gift should not take effect 'until after the death of my wife, should she survive me'. This gift was subject to gifts over if Helen did not survive the widow. Helen survived the testator and claimed the income under s 31(1)(ii) of the 1925 Act.

Held

The income was required to be accumulated on the following grounds:

(a) the devise to Helen was a future specific devise within s 175 of the Law of Property Act and thus carried the intermediate income, subject to defeasance if Helen died before the widow;

(b) Helen was not entitled to be maintained from the income because:

   (i) the will expressed a contrary intention by deferring Helen's interest until the widow's death; and

   (ii) Helen did not have a contingent but a vested interest in the land (albeit not in possession but in interest) which was outside s 31(1)(ii). This sub-section applies to those without a vested interest in property.

Cross J: It was argued in this case that the fact that the will contained a residuary gift constituted an express disposition of the income of the land in question which prevented the section from applying. I am afraid that I cannot accept this submission. I have little doubt that the testator expected the income of the land to form part of the income of residue during his widow's lifetime, but he has made no express disposition of it. I agree with what was said in this connection by Eve J in *Re Raine* [1929] 1 Ch 716. As the devise is not vested indefeasibly in the daughter but is subject to defeasance during the mother's lifetime the intermediate income which the gift carries by virtue of s 175 ought *prima facie* to be accumulated to see who eventually becomes entitled to it. It was, however, submitted by counsel for the daughter that she could claim payment of it under s 31(1) of the Trustee Act 1925.

[The learned judge summarised the sub-section, and continued:] There are, as I see it, two answers to the daughter's claim. The first – and narrower – answer is that her interest in the income of the devised land is a vested interest. It is a future interest liable to be divested but it is not contingent. Therefore s 31(1) does not apply to it. The second – and wider – answer is that the whole framework of s 31 shows that it is inapplicable to a future gift of this sort and that a will containing such a gift expresses a contrary intention within s 69(2) which prevents the sub-section from applying. By deferring the enjoyment of the devise until after the widow's death the testator has expressed the intention that the daughter shall not have the immediate income. It is true that as he has not expressly disposed of it in any other way, s 175 of the Law of Property Act 1925 defeats that intention to the extent of making the future devise carry the income, so that the daughter will get it eventually, if she survives her mother or dies before her leaving no children to take by substitution. Even if, however, the words of s 31(1) of the Trustee Act 1925 fitted the case, there would be no warrant for defeating the testator's intention still further by reading s 31(1) into the will and thus giving the daughter an interest in possession in the income during her mother's lifetime. In the result, the income . . . must be accumulated.

Contingent interests created *inter vivos* or by will carry the intermediate income (save in so far as the settlor or testator has otherwise disposed of the income). A contingent pecuniary legacy does not carry the income except where the gift was made by the infant's father or a person standing *in loco parentis*, the contingency is attaining the age of majority and no other fund is set aside for the maintenance of the legatee.

Question

When would income be available to maintain an infant beneficiary?

Exercise of power during infancy

Subject to the above, the trustees have a discretion (to maintain infant beneficiaries) which they are required to exercise responsibly and as objectively as ordinary prudent men of business. Thus, trustees who applied the income automatically to the infant's father without consciously exercising their discretion were liable to the beneficiaries for breach of trust when the father used the sums for his own benefit: see *Wilson v Turner*.

Wilson v Turner (1883) 22 Ch D 521, HC

Facts

A trust settlement was created for Mrs Wilson for life with remainder to her children. The trustees were given express power to pay the income for the maintenance, education or benefit of any infant children. The wife died leaving a nine year old son who was maintained by his father. The trustees, without exercising their discretion, paid the father the income as it arose as though the property belonged to him. Such property was dissipated and after his death an action was brought requiring repayment to the trust.

Held

The trustees were liable to repay the income for the benefit of the son.

Under the proviso to s 31(1) of the Trustee Act 1925, the trustees are required to take a number of factors into account, such as the age and requirements of the infant, whether other income is applicable for the same purpose and, generally, all the surrounding circumstances. The exercise of the power will vary with the facts of each case.

Trustee Act 1925, proviso to s 31(1)

Provided that, in deciding whether the whole or any part of the income of the property is during the minority to be paid or applied for the purposes aforesaid, the trustees shall have regard to the age of the infant and his requirements and generally to the circumstances of the case, and in particular to what other income, if any, is applicable for the same purposes; and where trustees have notice that the income of more than one fund is applicable for those purposes, then, so far as practicable, unless the entire income of the funds is paid or applied as aforesaid or the court otherwise directs, a proportionate part only of the income of each fund shall be so paid or applied.

In *Fuller v Evans*, the High Court decided that a settlement that prohibited the use of trust funds for the benefit of the settlor, did not prevent the trustees from exercising their discretion to pay school fees on behalf of the beneficiaries, even though this provided an incidental benefit to the settlor.

Fuller v Evans and Others [2000] Wills & Trust Law Reports 5, HC

Facts

An accumulation and maintenance trust was created in favour of the settlor's present and future children. On the date of the proceedings, the settlor had two children, aged 14 and 12 years. The settlement conferred on each of the children (present and future) a life interest in a share of the trust fund, and provided that after their deaths their shares would pass to their children and remoter issue. The settlement provided for an accumulation period of 21 years commencing on the date of the settlement. Prior to a beneficiary attaining the age of 21 or until the expiration of the accumulation period (whichever happened earlier), the settlement conferred a discretion on the trustees to apply the whole or part of the income for the maintenance and education of such beneficiary. Clause 12 of the settlement provided, *inter alia*, that no part of the capital or income of the trust fund might be paid, or lent to or applied for the benefit of the settlor, either directly or indirectly. On a divorce between the settlor and his wife, a consent order was made requiring the settlor to pay, *inter alia*, the children's school fees until they reached the age of 17. The trustees wished to exercise their power of maintenance and provide funds for the children's education, but were unclear as to the validity of the proposed exercise of their power. An application was made to the court to clarify the situation.

Held

The exercise of the power of maintenance was not restricted by clause 12 of the settlement. The incidental effect of relieving the settlor from his obligation to provide school fees on behalf of his children did not suspend the trustees' power of maintenance. The exercise of the discretion of the trustees ought to be considered in two stages. The first stage required the trustees to consider their discretion on the assumption that clause 12 was not inserted into the settlement. In this situation, the trustees were required to have regard exclusively to the interests of the beneficiaries. If the trustees were not minded to exercise their discretion, that would be the end of the matter. The second stage in the analysis allowed the trustees to exercise their discretion, even though a by-product of the exercise resulted in an advantage to the settlor. The court interpreted clause 12 as an affirmation of the duty of the trustees to have regard exclusively to the best interests of the beneficiaries and to ignore those of the settlor. This view was in conformity with the approach adopted by Lord Reid in *Oakes v Commissioner of Stamp Duties of New South Wales* [1954] AC 57.

Accumulations

The trustees may accumulate the income instead of maintaining the infant with the fund. Such accumulations (or capitalised income) will produce further income if invested in authorised investments. The additional income as well as accumulations of income become available for maintenance of the infant beneficiary in the future, should the need arise (proviso to s 31(2) of the Trustee Act 1925).

Trustee Act 1925, proviso to s 31(2)

But the trustees may, at any time during the infancy of such person if his interest so long continues, apply those accumulations, or any part thereof, as if they were income arising in the then current year.

If, in accordance with the express terms of the trust instrument, the beneficiary attains a vested interest in the income on attaining the age of majority (18), or marries under that age, he becomes entitled to the accumulated income (s 31(2)(i)(a)).

Trustee Act 1925, s 31(2)

During the infancy of any such person, if his interest so long continues, the trustees shall accumulate all the residue of that income in the way of compound interest by investing the same and the resulting income thereof from time to time in authorised investments, and shall hold those accumulations as follows:

(i)   If such person:

    (a)   attains the age of 18 years, or marries under that age, and his interest in such income during his infancy or until his marriage is a vested interest; or

    (b)   on attaining the age of 18 years or on marriage under that age becomes entitled to the property from which such income arose in fee simple, absolute or determinable, or absolutely, or for an entailed interest;

    the trustees shall hold the accumulations in trust for such person absolutely, but without prejudice to any provision with respect thereto contained in any settlement by him made under any statutory powers during his infancy, and so that the receipt of such person after marriage, and though still an infant, shall be a good discharge; and

(ii) In any other case the trustees shall, notwithstanding that such person had a vested interest in such income, hold the accumulations as an accretion to the capital of the property from which such accumulations arose, and as one fund with such capital for all purposes, and so that, if such property is settled land, such accumulations shall be held upon the same trusts as if the same were capital money arising therefrom.

For example, if trustees hold property 'on trust for A for life provided that he attains the age of 18', on attaining the age of majority, A becomes entitled to the accumulated income. He also becomes entitled to future income (s 31(2)(i)(a)).

Where the beneficiary acquires a vested interest in capital on attaining the age of majority or earlier marriage, he also becomes entitled to the accumulated income (s 31(2)(i)(b)).

For example, if shares are held 'on trust for A provided that he attains the age of 18', on attaining the age of majority, A becomes entitled to the accumulated dividends from the shares in addition to the capital.

Attaining the age of majority

If the beneficiary attains the age of majority without attaining a vested interest under the terms of the trust, the trustees are required to pay the income to the beneficiary until he acquires a vested interest or dies, or his interest fails (s 31(1)(ii)). The payment includes accumulated income. Accordingly, a beneficiary acquires a vested interest in the income of the trust by statute on attaining the age of majority even though under the trust he does not enjoy a vested interest.

Trustee Act 1925, s 31(1)(ii)

If such person on attaining the age of 18 years has not a vested interest in such income, the trustees shall thenceforth pay the income of that property and of any accretion thereto under sub-s (2) of this section to him, until he either attains a vested interest therein or dies, or until failure of his interest.

For example, property is held 'on trust for A provided he attains the age of 25': on attaining the age of 18, the beneficiary becomes entitled to an interest in possession.

However, this provision is subject to any contrary intention stipulated by the settlor. Such contrary intention may be manifested by the settlor directing the income to be accumulated beyond the age of majority: see *Re Turner*.

Re Turner's Will Trust [1937] Ch 15, HC

Facts

A testator gave a share of his residuary estate on trust for such of the children of his late son, Charles, as should attain the age of 28 years. The will contained an express power of maintenance of such children as should attain the age of 21 years and included instructions to the trustees to accumulate the surplus. Two of the testator's grandchildren attained the age of 28 but a third, Geoffrey, died having attained the age of 24. His share of the income had been accumulated. The question in issue was whether estate duty was payable on his death.

Held

Estate duty was not payable because Geoffrey did not have a vested interest in income under s 31(1)(ii). A contrary intention was manifested as evidenced by a direction to accumulate the income.

Question

What is the effect of a beneficiary attaining the age of majority under s 31 of the Trustee Act 1925?

POWERS OF ADVANCEMENT

An advancement is a payment from the capital funds of a trust to or on behalf of a beneficiary in respect of some long-term commitment, such as the purchase of a house or establishment of a business. A potential beneficiary may be in need of capital from the trust fund prior to the beneficiary becoming entitled as of right to the capital from the fund. In such a case, the trustees may be entitled to accelerate the enjoyment of his or her interest by an advance payment of capital to the beneficiary.

For example, S transfers £50,000 to T1 and T2 on trust for B contingently on attaining the age of 25. Assuming that while B is only 14 years old, a legitimate need for capital arises, but for special provisions to the contrary, the trustees would be prevented from making an advancement to B on the grounds that the contingency entitling B to the capital has not taken place and, in any event, B, as a minor, is incapable of giving a valid receipt for the payment of capital. If, on the other hand, the trustees validly exercise their power of advancement, capital may be released in favour of B before the satisfaction of the contingency and B will be prevented from claiming the capital a second time.

Authority to advance

The authority to exercise a power of advancement may originate from a variety of sources, such as the trust instrument, the inherent jurisdiction of the courts or a statutory power. These will be considered in turn.

Trust instrument

A settlor may be prompted to include an express power of advancement in the trust instrument, perhaps in order to widen or vary the statutory power which would otherwise be excluded in the instrument. The trustees are required to obey the express provision, the purport of which will vary with the circumstances of each case.

Inherent jurisdiction

Under the inherent jurisdiction of the court, an order may be made authorising an infant's property to be transferred so that capital may be applied for his advancement or benefit.

Statutory power

Section 32 of the Trustee Act 1925 creates a statutory power of advancement, which is not limited to minors but invests the trustees with a discretion to distribute capital in favour of any beneficiary who may become entitled to the whole or part of the capital in the future.

Trustee Act 1925, s 32

(1) Trustees may at any time or times pay or apply any capital money subject to a trust, for the advancement or benefit, in such manner as they may, in their absolute discretion, think fit, of any person entitled to the capital of the trust property or of any share thereof, whether absolutely or contingently on his attaining any specified age or on the occurrence of any other event, or subject to a gift over on his death under any specified age or on the occurrence of any other event, and whether in possession or in remainder or reversion, and such payment or application may be made notwithstanding that the interest of such person is liable to be defeated by the exercise of a power of appointment or revocation, or to be diminished by the increase of the class to which he belongs:

Provided that:

(a) the money so paid or applied for the advancement or benefit of any person shall not exceed altogether in amount one half of the presumptive or vested share or interest of that person in the trust property; and

(b) if that person is or becomes absolutely and indefeasibly entitled to a share in the trust property the money so paid or applied shall be brought into account as part of such share; and

(c) no such payment or application shall be made so as to prejudice any person entitled to any prior life or other interest, whether vested or contingent, in the money paid or applied unless such person is in existence and of full age and consents in writing to such payment or application.

(2) This section applies only where the trust property consists of money or securities or of property held upon trust for sale . . .

However, this statutory power may be excluded expressly or impliedly by the settlor. An implied exclusion involves any power of advancement which is inconsistent with the statutory power, such as an express power which exceeds the statutory maximum amount which may be used to advance the beneficiaries. In *Inland Revenue Commissioners v Bernstein* [1961] Ch 399, the Court of Appeal decided that a direction to accumulate income during the lifetime of the settlor expressed a contrary intention to exclude s 32 of the 1925 Act. The direction was indicative of the intention of the settlor to build up a large capital sum and to prohibit the advancement of capital.

Advancement or benefit

Under s 32 of the 1925 Act, the trustees are entitled to pay or apply capital in their discretion for the 'advancement or benefit' of a beneficiary. The expression has been considered widely by the courts and 'benefit' has been interpreted as extending the wide ambit of 'advancement'.

Pilkington v Inland Revenue Commissioners [1964] AC 612, HL

Viscount Radcliffe: The word 'advancement' itself meant . . . the establishment in life of the beneficiary who was the object of the power or at any rate some step that would contribute to the furtherance of his establishment . . . Typical instances of expenditure for such purposes under the social conditions of the nineteenth century were an apprenticeship or the purchase of a commission in the Army or of an interest in a business. In the case of a girl there could be an advancement on marriage . . . such words as 'or otherwise for his or her benefit' were often added to the word 'advancement'. It was always recognised that these added words were 'large words' ... The expression means any use of the money which will improve the material situation of the beneficiary.

Thus, the phrase includes the use of money not only for the immediate personal benefit of the beneficiary, but also to promote an indirect 'benefit': see *Re Clore*.

Re Clore's Settlement [1966] 2 All ER 272, HC

Facts

A wealthy beneficiary under a trust who had a future interest in capital felt morally obliged to make charitable donations. The question in issue was whether advancements could be made for such purposes.

Held

The advancements to the charities selected by the beneficiary were valid.

Similarly, the power may be exercised with the intention of benefiting the object under a trust by making a loan to the beneficiary's husband to facilitate him to set up a business in England in order to keep the family together: see *Re Kershaw* (1868) LR 6 Eq 322.

Property subject to s 32 of the Trustee Act 1925

Under s 32(2) of the Trustee Act 1925, the power to advance is available in respect of 'money or securities or property held on trust for sale', provided that such property is not treated as land. The settlor may expressly extend the power that exists under the section by manifesting such an intention in the trust instrument.

Status of the beneficiaries under s 32(1) of the Trustee Act 1925

The widest form of definition of the types of beneficiaries who may benefit under s 32(1) is adopted thus:

... any person entitled to the capital of the trust property or any share thereof, whether absolutely or contingently on his attaining any specified age or on the occurrence of any other event, or subject to a gift over on his death under any specified age or on the occurrence of any other event, and whether in possession or in remainder or reversion ... and notwithstanding that the interest of such person is liable to be defeated by the exercise of a power of appointment or revocation, or to be diminished by the increase of the class to which he belongs.

Scope of s 32 of the Trustee Act 1925

The policy of s 32 is to invest trustees with a discretion to appoint up to one-half of the presumptive share of the capital of the beneficiary for his or her advancement or benefit.

The value of the presumptive share of the beneficiary is measured on the date of the advancement. If the ceiling concerning the statutory power of advancement has been reached (that is, one-quarter of the presumptive share of capital), the statutory power of advancement would be exhausted even if the value of the capital increases subsequently: see *Marquess of Abergavenny v Ram*.

Marquess of Abergavenny v Ram [1981] 2 All ER 643, HC

Facts

Under the Marquess of Abergavenny's Estate Act 1946, a trust was created in favour of the plaintiff for life with remainder in favour of other beneficiaries. The trustees were expressly given a wide discretionary power to pay 'any part or parts not exceeding in all one half in value of the settled fund of which he becomes tenant for life in possession'. In 1965, the trustees exercised their power to its full extent in favour of the plaintiff. Since then, the money value of the retained half share of the fund had considerably appreciated. The question in issue was whether the trustees were entitled to make further advancements based on the appreciation in the value of the trust property.

Held

Since the plaintiff received the maximum amount of property as stated in the trust deed, the trustees had no power to make further payments to him:

> **Goulding J:** I think myself that the reason why there is no direct authority on the question is because the answer has always seemed plain. Any layman, and any lawyer I think . . . would feel that where there is a power to make successive payments to a person up to a limit of a certain fraction of a fund and at a certain date, he, the beneficiary, has received assets then fully reaching the prescribed limit, thereafter no further exercise of the power is possible. All that the settlor authorised has been done. It would be to my mind strange and unexpected if the object of the power as such retained an interest or possibility of interest in the fund still in settlement, so that he could require accounts from the trustees and demand reconsideration of his position whenever there should be an appreciation of assets.

However, the settlor may increase the ceiling of sums which may be advanced, but this may only be done expressly.

The sum advanced is credited to the prospective share of the beneficiary, so that if a beneficiary becomes absolutely entitled to a share as of right, the sum advanced is taken into account (s 32(1)(b)).

For example, shares worth £100,000 are held on trust for B provided that he attains the age of 25. B is currently 22 years of age. The trustees advance up to £50,000 to him. When B attains the relevant age and acquires a vested and indefeasible interest in the capital, the sum advanced is brought into account.

Prior interests

If a beneficiary is entitled to a prior interest (life interest), whether vested or contingent, the consent in writing of such beneficiary is required to be obtained prior to the exercise of the power of advancement. The reason being that an advancement reduces the income available to other beneficiaries (s 32(1)(c)).

For example, in a gift to A for life, remainder to B absolutely, A's consent in writing is required before B receives any part of the capital by way of an advancement.

Resettlements

In *Pilkington v Inland Revenue Commissioners* [1964] AC 612, the question arose as to whether a 'resettlement' of part of the capital of a beneficiary by way of an advancement would be a proper exercise of the discretion of the trustees.

For example, assume that property is held by T1 and T2 on trust for A for life, remainder to B absolutely. The trustees (with the consent of A in writing) for fiscal purposes propose to advance one-quarter of the capital to T3 and T4 on 'protective' trust for B. Would the exercise be valid?

Two objections are capable of being levelled against such exercise, namely:

(a) the resettlement or sub-trust is capable of infringing the rule prohibiting the trustees from delegating their discretions. The House of Lords in *Pilkington v Inland Revenue Commissioners* rejected this objection on the ground that the real issue is one of authority. The rule is not that the trustees cannot delegate their powers *per se*, but that the trustees cannot delegate their discretions without authority. If, therefore, the trustees possess the authority to delegate their discretions then, provided that the exercise of their power to delegate is *bona fide* and in accordance with their duty of care, the delegation is valid;

(b) the resettlement or sub-trust is subject to the rule against perpetuities. The exercise of the power of advancement under the 'head' settlement is analogous to the exercise of a special power of appointment. Accordingly, the perpetuity period is measured by reference to the 'head' settlement. In other words, the perpetuity rule will be construed as if the resettlement was a term of and read into the 'head' settlement. Before the Perpetuities and Accumulations Act 1964, the resettlement was capable of being invalidated on the basis of the possibility of the property not vesting within the perpetuity period. This point was accepted by the House of Lords in *Pilkington v Inland Revenue Commissioners*. Under the Perpetuities and Accumulations Act 1964, the court will 'wait and see' whether or not the property subject to the resettled trust will vest within the relevant period.

Pilkington v Inland Revenue Commissioners [1964] AC 612, HL

Facts

The testator, William, bequeathed the income of his residuary estate on protective trusts for his nephews and nieces. The will authorised the principal beneficiaries to consent to the trustees exercising their power of advancement without causing a forfeiture. The capital was required to be held on trust for the children of the beneficiaries in such shares as the beneficiaries might appoint, and in default of appointment in equal shares. Richard, one of the testator's nephews, had three children, one of whom was Penelope, a two year old. The trustees proposed (subject to Richard's consent) to advance up to one-half of Penelope's expectant share on a new trust for Penelope's benefit. The purpose of the intended advancement was to save estate duty on Richard's death. Under the proposed new trust, Penelope would become entitled to capital at the age of 30, but was entitled to be maintained from the income. The trustees sought directions from the court.

Held

(a) The exercise of the power was within s 32 of the Trustee Act 1925 for the benefit of Penelope, even though the exercise amounted to a resettlement.

(b) However, the proposed exercise would be void for infringing the perpetuity rule as the gift in favour of Penelope was capable of vesting beyond the period of 21 years from the death of Richard:

Viscount Radcliffe: The Commissioners' objections seem to be concentrated upon such propositions as that the proposed transaction is 'nothing less than a resettlement' and that a power of advancement cannot be used so as to alter or vary the trusts created by the settlement from which it is derived. Such a transaction, they say, amounts to using the power of advancement as a way of appointing or declaring new trusts different from those of the settlement. The reason why I do not find that these propositions have any compulsive effect upon my mind is that they seem to me merely vivid ways of describing the substantial effect of that which is proposed to be done and they do not in themselves amount to convincing arguments against doing it. Of course, whenever money is raised for advancement on terms that it is to be settled on the beneficiary, the money only passes from one settlement to be caught up in the other. It is therefore the same thing as a resettlement. But, unless one is to say that such moneys can never be applied by way of settlement, an argument which, as I have shown, has few supporters and is contrary to authority, it merely describes the inevitable effect of such an advancement to say that it is nothing less than a resettlement. Similarly, if it is part of the trusts and powers created by one settlement that the trustees of it should have power to raise money and make it available for a beneficiary upon new trusts approved by them, then they are in substance given power to free the money from one trust and to subject it to another. So be it: but, unless they cannot require a settlement of it at all, the transaction they carry out is the same thing in effect as an appointment of new trusts.

In the same way I am unconvinced by the argument that the trustees would be improperly delegating their trust by allowing the money raised to pass over to new trustees under a settlement conferring new powers on the latter. In fact I think that the whole issue of delegation is here beside the mark. The law is not that trustees cannot delegate: it is that trustees cannot delegate unless they have authority to do so. If the power of advancement which they possess is so read as to allow them to raise money for the purpose of having it settled, then they do have the necessary authority to let the money pass out of the old settlement into the new trusts. No question of delegation of their powers or trusts arises.

It is quite true, as the Commissioners have pointed out, that you might have really extravagant cases of resettlements being forced on beneficiaries in the name of advancement, even a few months before an absolute vesting in possession would have destroyed the power. I have tried to give due weight to such possibilities, but when all is said I do not think that they ought to compel us to introduce a limitation of which no one, with all respect, can produce a satisfactory definition. First, I do not believe that it is wise to try to cut down an admittedly wide and discretionary power, enacted for general use, through fear of its being abused in certain hypothetical instances. And moreover, as regards this fear, I think that it must be remembered that we are speaking of a power intended to be in the hands of trustees chosen by a settlor because of his confidence in their discretion and good sense and subject to the external check that no exercise can take place without the consent of a prior life tenant; and that there does remain at all times a residual power in the court to restrain or correct any purported exercise that can be shown to be merely wanton or capricious and not to be attributable to a genuine discretion. I think, therefore, that, although extravagant possibilities exist, they may be more menacing in argument than in real life.

Trustees' duties

The trustees are required to exercise their power of advancement in a fiduciary manner. The exercise will not be *bona fide* and will be void if the trustees advance funds to a beneficiary on condition that the sum is used to repay a loan made by one of the trustees (see *Molyneux v Fletcher* [1898] 1 QB 648). Moreover, the trustees may transfer the capital to the beneficiary directly if they reasonably believe that he or she may be trusted with the money. If the trustees specify a particular purpose which they reasonably believe the beneficiary is capable of fulfilling, they (the trustees) may pay the fund over to him. However, the trustees are under an obligation to ensure that the beneficiary recipient of the fund expends the sum for the specific purpose.

Re Pauling's Settlement Trust [1964] Ch 303, CA

Willmer LJ: What they [the trustees] cannot do is prescribe a particular purpose and then raise and pay the money over to the advancee leaving him or her entirely free, legally and morally, to apply it for that purpose or to spend it in any way he or she chooses without any responsibility on the trustees even to inquire as to its application.

Facts
The trustees of a marriage settlement held property upon trust for a wife for life with remainder to the children of the marriage. The trustees were given a power to advance up to half of the children's presumptive share to the children. The trustees made advances notionally to the children but the money was used for the benefit of the family generally. The family lived beyond their means. The trustees believed that they were exercising their power validly by paying the sums to the children and leaving them to do what they wished with the sums. A claim was brought against the trustees for breach of trust.

Held
The trustees were liable for breach of trust in that they had improperly exercised their discretion.

Question
What is meant by an advancement of capital to, or on behalf of, a beneficiary?

POWERS OF SALE

Trustees, as controllers of the trust property, are required to manage the trust on behalf of the beneficiaries. Accordingly, trustees may have a power of sale. The source of this power may vary with the circumstances of each case. Thus, trustees may be given express authority in the trust instrument to sell the trust assets, or the power may be implied or may originate by statute. The precise source of the power is required to be identified.

Trust instrument

Whether the instrument authorises the trustees to sell the property is a question of fact. Many professionally drafted trust instruments will include such a clause subject to qualifications or not. Assuming the trustees have such authority, they are still required to exercise the requisite standard of skill and prudence in the exercise of such power.

Implied power

In exceptional circumstances, the court may impose a duty on the trustees to sell trust property and apply the proceeds in a particular manner (see *Howe v Lord Dartmouth*, in respect of residuary personal property, p 490 above).

Statutory power

The power of sale may be created by statute. There are many statutory sources imposing a power of sale on trustees. The following are mentioned by way of illustration.

Trustee Act 1925, s 16

(1) Where trustees are authorised by the trust instrument, if any, creating the trust or by law to pay or apply capital money subject to the trust for any purpose or in any manner, they shall have and shall be deemed always to have had power to raise the money required by sale, conversion, calling in, or mortgage of all or any part of the trust property for the time being in possession.

Settled Land Act 1925, s 38

A tenant for life:

(i) May sell the settled land, or any part thereof, or any easement, right or privilege of any kind over or in relation to the land; and

(ii) ... [repealed]

(iii) may make an exchange of the settled land, or any part thereof, or of any easement, right, or privilege of any kind ... including an exchange in consideration of money paid for equality of exchange.

Note

It should be borne in mind here that the person with the power of sale is not the trustee of the settlement *qua* trustee but the tenant for life who is treated as the 'statutory owner'.

Settled Land Act 1925, s 67(1)

Where personal chattels are settled so as to devolve with settled land, or to devolve therewith as nearly as may be in accordance with the law or practice in force at the date of the settlement, or are settled together with land, or upon trusts declared by reference to the trusts affecting land, a tenant for life of the land may sell the chattels or any of them.

Law of Property Act 1925, s 130(5)

Where personal chattels are settled without reference to settled land on trusts creating entailed interests therein, the trustees, with the consent of the usufructuary [beneficiary with a limited interest in the property] for the time being if of full age, may sell the chattels or any of them, and the net proceeds of any such sale shall be held in trust for and shall go to the same persons successively ...

Under s 6 of the Trusts of Land and Appointment of Trustees Act 1996, the trustees of land have all the 'powers of an absolute owner' in respect of the land. This includes a power to sell the land subject to the trust. In exercising this power, the trustees are required to have regard to the rights of the beneficiaries and any rules of law or equity or statutory provisions. The trust of land may require the consent of any person to any dealing with the land. Moreover, any power of the trustees, including the sale of the land, may be excluded or restricted by the trust deed.

In exceptional circumstances where the trustees have no power of sale within any of the above sources, they may apply to the court under s 57 of the Trustee Act 1925 (see Chapter 20 below).

A power of sale is required to be exercised with the same degree of diligence and care as would be exercised by a prudent man in the conduct of his affairs.

The mode of effecting the sale is stipulated in s 12 of the Trustee Act 1925 (as amended by the Trusts of Land and Appointment of Trustees Act 1996).

Trustee Act 1925, s 12 (as amended by the Trusts of Land and Appointment of Trustees Act 1996)

(1) Where a trustee has a duty or power to sell property, he may sell or concur with any other person in selling all or any part of the property . . . either together or in lots, by public auction or by private contract, subject to any such conditions respecting title or evidence of title or other matter as the trustee thinks fit, with power to vary any contract for sale, and to buy in at any auction, or to rescind any contract for sale and to re-sell, without being answerable for any loss.

(2) A duty or power to sell or dispose of land includes a duty or power to sell or dispose of part thereof, whether the division is horizontal, vertical, or made in any other way.

(3) This section does not enable an express power to sell settled land to be exercised where the power is not vested in the tenant for life or statutory owner.

In order to protect both trustees and third party purchasers who have acted *bona fide* and prudently, relief may be claimed under s 13 of the Trustee Act 1925.

Trustee Act 1925, s 13

(1) No sale made by a trustee shall be impeached by any beneficiary upon the ground that any of the conditions subject to which the sale was made may have been unnecessarily depreciatory, unless it also appears that the consideration for the sale was thereby rendered inadequate.

(2) No sale made by a trustee shall, after the execution of the conveyance, be impeached as against the purchaser upon the ground that any of the conditions subject to which the sale was made may have been unnecessarily depreciatory, unless it appears that the purchaser was acting in collusion with the trustee at the time when the contract for sale was made.

(3) No purchaser, upon any sale made by a trustee, shall be at liberty to make any objection against the title upon any of the grounds aforesaid.

Question
When will trustees have a power to sell the trust property?

POWER TO PARTITION LAND UNDER A TRUST OF LAND

Section 7 of the Trusts of Land and Appointment of Trustees 1996, which repeals s 28 of the Law of Property Act 1925, confers on trustees of land the power to partition the land, or part of it, among adult beneficiaries who are absolutely entitled in undivided shares, subject to their consent. If an infant is absolutely entitled to a share, partition may still take place, but the trustees will hold his share on trust for him. This may end the co-ownership of the whole or part of the land subject to the trust. This section may be excluded or varied by the settlement, except in the case of trusts for ecclesiastical, public or charitable purposes.

The trust settlement may require the trustees to obtain the consent of any person before exercising any of their powers as trustees of land. If the consent of more than two persons is required, and has not been obtained, the purchaser is protected if, at least two consents are obtained (s 10). However, this is without prejudice to the liability of the trustees for breach of trust. In the case of land held on ecclesiastical, charitable or public purposes, the purchaser is required to ensure that all necessary consents have been obtained. The consent of an infant is not required, but in such a case the trustees are duty bound to obtain the consent of the person with parental responsibility for the infant or the infant's guardian.

POWER TO INSURE THE TRUST PROPERTY

Section 34 of the Trustee Act 2000 re-enacts s 19 of the Trustee Act 1925. The new s 19 of the 1925 Act authorises the trustees to insure trust property 'against loss or damage due to any event'. The trustees are entitled to pay the premium out of the trust fund. In the case of property held on a bare trust, the power to insure is subject to any directions given by the beneficiary or each of the beneficiaries.

POWER TO GIVE RECEIPTS

Section 14 of the Trustee Act 1925 introduced a provision to protect third party purchasers of trust property from the trustees:

Trustee Act 1925, s 14

(1) The receipt in writing of a trustee for any money, securities, or other personal property or effects payable, transferable, or deliverable to him under any trust or power shall be a sufficient discharge to the person paying, transferring, or delivering the same and shall effectually exonerate him from seeing to the application or being answerable for any loss or misapplication thereof.

(2) This section does not, except where the trustee is a trust corporation, enable a sole trustee to give a valid receipt for:

    (a) the proceeds of sale or other capital money arising under a . . . trust of land;

    (b) capital money arising under the Settled Land Act 1925.

(3) This section applies notwithstanding anything to the contrary in the instrument, if any, creating the trust.

Note
Subject to provisions to the contrary in the trust instrument, transactions involving the trust are the joint actions of the trustees. Accordingly, only a joint receipt by all the trustees is capable of binding the trust.

POWER TO CLAIM REIMBURSEMENT

Trustees as managers or representatives of the trust property are entitled to claim a refund or reimbursement from the trust funds for expenses properly incurred in the administration of the trust. Prior to the introduction of s 30(2) of the Trustee Act 1925 (now s 31 of the Trustee Act 2000), it was decided that trustees' right of reimbursement was equivalent to a lien or first charge on the trust assets in respect of expenses properly incurred in the administration of the trust. This right of reimbursement took priority over the claims of beneficiaries and third parties: see *Stott v Milne*.

Stott v Milne (1884) 25 Ch D 710, HL

Facts

The defendant trustees used their own resources to institute proceedings against third parties in connection with the trust. The trustees recouped their expenses from part of the income. The plaintiff beneficiary (life tenant) was unaware of such proceedings and brought an action claiming repayment of the income by the trustees.

Held

The trustees were entitled to retain part of the income to reimburse themselves:

> **Lord Selborne LC:** I feel no doubt that the trustees acted *bona fide* and reasonably in bringing the actions. The property was peculiarly circumstanced, it was not large, but was available for building purposes, and anything done by tenants or neighbours which would give any other persons rights over it might cause a material depreciation in its value. The trustees therefore had an anxious duty to perform.
>
> The right of trustees to indemnity against all costs and expenses properly incurred by them in the execution of the trust is a first charge on all the trust property, both income and *corpus*. The trustees, therefore, had a right to retain the costs out of the income until provision could be made for raising them out of the corpus. I am of opinion that their costs of this action ought to be raised and paid out of the estate in the same way as the costs of the former actions.

Prior to the enactment of the Trustee Act 2000, s 30(2) of the Trustee Act 1925 made provision for the reimbursement of trustees out of the trust fund for expenses incurred in the administration of the trust.

In *Armitage v Nurse*, Millett LJ considered the rights of the trustees to a lien on the trust fund for their costs of litigation.

Armitage v Nurse [1997] 3 WLR 1046, CA

Millett LJ:

Costs

Trustees are entitled to a lien on the trust fund for the costs of successfully defending themselves against an action for breach of trust. That was the position in *In Re Spurling's Will Trusts* [1966] 1 WLR 920, as it was in *Walters v Woolbridge* (1878) 7 Ch D 504, which it followed. But on what principle can one justify their right to recoup themselves out of the trust fund for the costs of unsuccessfully defending themselves against such action? It offends all sense of justice. The respondents rely on *Turner v Hancock* (1882) 20 Ch D 303 and submit that that was just such a case; but I do not think that it was. The action was an action for an account. On taking the accounts it was found that a sum was due from the trustee and not to him as he contended. It was, therefore, a case in which the trustee was unsuccessful; but it was not a case in which he was found to be guilty of misconduct or breach of trust. In the course of his judgment Sir George Jessel MR said, at p 305:

> These rights . . . can only be lost or curtailed by such inequitable conduct on the part of a mortgagee or trustee as may amount to a violation or culpable neglect of his duty under the contract . . . It is not the course of the court in modern times to discourage persons from becoming trustees by inflicting costs upon them if they have done their duty, or even if they have committed an innocent breach of trust.

In the present case, the judge deprived the respondents of 20% of their costs because they had put forward arguments on which they had been unsuccessful. That was a proper exercise of his discretion. But he also deprived them of their right to recoup themselves out of the trust fund to the extent of the 20%, on the ground that the claim was a hostile claim against them personally for breach of trust. In my opinion, that was not a sufficient ground for denying them their contractual rights.

It must be stressed that this right of recovery existed only in respect of expenses reasonably incurred. If, therefore, trustees incurred unreasonable expenses, they had no right to recover their loss from the trust assets: see *Holding and Management Ltd v Property Holding Trust*.

Holding and Management Ltd v Property Holding and Investment Trust plc and Others
[1989] 1 WLR 1313, CA

Facts

The plaintiff, a trustee company, was the maintenance trustee of a block of flats. The plaintiff proposed a programme of works which was opposed by the tenants. The plaintiff applied to the court for directions as to whether the scheme was within its powers. A compromise arrangement was reached between the parties during the course of the hearing. The Court of Appeal considered the question of costs.

Held

The plaintiff was not entitled to a refund as it had acted unreasonably and could not be said to have represented the interests of the beneficiaries:

Nicholls LJ: To be entitled to an indemnity the costs and expenses in question must have been properly incurred by the trustee. This is axiomatic. In the present case the plaintiff did not bring proceedings to protect the maintenance fund for the benefit of the beneficiaries. The beneficiaries of that fund, as I have sought to indicate, are the tenants plus the landlord. The proceedings were brought against the tenants to establish whether they were obliged to engage the fund to be applied for their benefit beyond what they and the landlord wished. I do not think that costs so incurred were properly incurred.

Section 31(1) of the Trustee Act 2000 re-enacts s 30(2) of the Trustee Act 1925.

Trustee Act 2000, s 31(1)

A trustee—

(a) is entitled to be reimbursed from the trust funds, or

(b) may pay out of the trust funds,

expenses properly incurred by him when acting on behalf of the trust.

Under s 31(1) of the Trustee Act 2000, trustees are entitled to recover from the trust fund the costs and expenses properly incurred in respect of legal proceedings conducted in the interests of the trust. A prudent trustee will seek a *Beddoe* order (that is, leave from the court to bring or defend an action) before entering into legal proceedings on behalf of the trust. The effect of the order is to protect him against the *cestui que trust* and entitle him to be reimbursed the costs of litigation from the trust fund, irrespective of the result of the litigation in the main proceedings. A trustee who omits to take the precaution of obtaining leave from the court, but nevertheless becomes involved in trust litigation, runs the risk of not recovering his expenses if the court decides that litigation was unnecessary. Lindley LJ explained the nature of the rule in *Re Beddoe* thus:

Lindley LJ in Re Beddoe [1893] 1 Ch 547: . . . a trustee who, without the sanction of the court, commences an action or defends an action unsuccessfully, does so at his own risk as regards the costs, even if he acts on counsel's opinion; and when the trustee seeks to obtain such costs out of the trust estate, he ought not to be allowed to charge them against his *cestui que trust* unless under *very exceptional circumstances*. If, indeed, the judge comes to the conclusion that he would have authorized the action or defence had he been applied to, he might in the exercise of his discretion, allow the costs incurred by the trustees out of the estate; but I cannot imagine any other circumstances under which the costs of an unauthorized and unsuccessful action brought or defended by a trustee could properly be thrown on the estate. [author's emphasis].

In reality there is no inconsistency between the principle involved in a *Beddoe* application and the test applied under s 31(1) of the Trustee Act 2000. At the end of the day the trustee must show that the expenditure in question, or the cost of the litigation, was properly and reasonably incurred. The beneficiaries are required to be joined in the *Beddoe* application for one of the purposes of the application is to inform the court about the strengths and weaknesses of the case, the views of the trustees and beneficiaries about the prospects of success and the course it is proposed to take in the action.

Alternatively, if the trustees omit to apply for a *Beddoe* order they may still be entitled to be reimbursed their costs if the action is considered to have been properly brought or defended on behalf of the trust.

Lightman J in *Alsop Wilkinson v Neary* [1996] 1 WLR 1220 decided that the trustees might be involved in three types of disputes:

(a) a 'trust dispute', namely, a dispute concerning the terms of the trust. This may be friendly, that is, involving the construction of the trust instrument, or hostile, that is, a challenge as to the validity of the trust;

(b) a 'beneficiaries dispute', namely, when one or more beneficiaries question the propriety of any action taken or omitted by the trustees;

(c) a 'third party dispute', namely, proceedings involving a stranger to the trust in respect of rights or liabilities under the trust.

This analysis, of course, does not determine whether the trustees' involvement in the proceedings is necessary. This will depend on the nature and extent of the claim. Lightman J, in *Alsop Wilkinson v Neary*, criticised Kekewich J's decision in *Ideal Bedding Co v Holland*.

Ideal Bedding Co v Holland [1907] 2 Ch 157, HC

Facts
The plaintiffs obtained an order against the trustees declaring the settlement void as against the plaintiffs and other creditors. The question arose whether one of the trustees who had defended the action ought to have his costs paid out of the trust estate.

Held
The trustees had a duty to defend the action brought against the trust.

Lightman J in the *Alsop* case felt that the trustees ought to have remained neutral in such proceedings.

Alsop Wilkinson v Neary and Others [1996] 1 WLR 1220, HC

Facts
The plaintiff applied by summons for an order under s 423 of the Insolvency Act 1986 to set aside a trust. The beneficiaries under the trust threatened proceedings for breach of trust if the trustees failed to defend the action. In the same proceedings, the applicants, trustees, sought leave from the court to determine whether they ought to defend the action (the *Beddoe* application).

Held
The court refused to grant leave to the trustees to defend the action. The dispute was between rival claimants to a beneficial interest in the subject matter of the trust. In such circumstances, the trustees are duty bound to remain neutral and offer to submit to the court's directions, leaving the rival claimants to fight their battle. Moreover, the *Beddoe* application ought to be brought in proceedings separate from the main action: first, because it would involve disclosure of the trustees' case and other confidential information to the other parties to the main action; and, secondly, to ensure that all the relevant parties to the application were before the court:

Lightman J:

A Background

Trustees may be involved in three kinds of dispute:

(1) The first (which I shall call 'a trust dispute') is a dispute as to the trusts on which they hold the subject matter of the settlement. This may be 'friendly' litigation involving, for example, the true construction of the trust instrument or some other question arising in the course of the administration of the trust; or 'hostile' litigation, for example, a challenge in whole or in part to the validity of the settlement by the settlor, on grounds of undue influence, or by a trustee in bankruptcy or a defrauded creditor of the settlor, in which

case the claim is that the trustees hold the trust funds as trustees for the settlor, the trustee in bankruptcy or creditor in place of or in addition to the beneficiaries specified in the settlement. The line between friendly and hostile litigation, which is relevant as to the incidence of costs, is not always easy to draw: see *In Re Buckton, Buckton v Buckton* [1907] 2 Ch 406.

(2) The second (which I shall call 'a beneficiaries dispute') is a dispute with one or more of the beneficiaries as to the propriety of any action which the trustees have taken or omitted to take or may or may not take in the future. This may take the form of proceedings by a beneficiary alleging breach of trust by the trustees and seeking removal of the trustees, and/or damages for breach of trust.

(3) The third (which I shall call 'a third party dispute') is a dispute with persons, otherwise than in the capacity of beneficiaries, in respect of rights and liabilities, for example, in contract or tort assumed by the trustees, as such, in the course of administration of the trust.

Trustees (express and constructive) are entitled to an indemnity against all costs, expenses and liabilities properly incurred in administering the trust and have a lien on the trust assets to secure such indemnity. Trustees have a duty to protect and preserve the trust estate for the benefit of the beneficiaries and accordingly to represent the trust in a third party dispute. Accordingly, their right to an indemnity and lien extends in the case of a third party dispute to the costs of proceedings properly brought or defended for the benefit of the trust estate. Views may vary whether proceedings are properly brought or defended, and to avoid the risk of a challenge to their entitlement to the indemnity (a beneficiary dispute), trustees are well advised to seek court authorisation before they sue or defend. The right to an indemnity and lien will ordinarily extend to the costs of such an application. The form of application is a separate action to which all the beneficiaries are parties (either in person or by a representative defendant). With the benefit of their views, the judge, thereupon exercising his discretion, determines what course the interests of justice require to be taken in the proceedings: see *In Re Evans (Decd)* [1986] 1 WLR 101, considered by Hoffmann LJ in *McDonald v Horn* [1995] ICR 685. So long as the trustees make full disclosure of the strengths and weaknesses of their case, if the trustees act as authorised by the court, their entitlement to an indemnity and lien is secure.

A beneficiaries dispute is regarded as ordinary hostile litigation in which costs follow the event and do not come out of the trust estate: see *per* Hoffmann LJ in *McDonald v Horn* [1995] ICR 685, p 696.

In *Ideal Bedding Co Ltd v Holland* [1907] 2 Ch 157, the plaintiffs, who were judgment creditors, obtained against the trustees of a settlement, an order declaring the settlement void as against the plaintiffs and other creditors under the statute 13 Eliz, c 5 on the ground that it 'delayed, hindered and defrauded' the plaintiffs and other creditors. The question arose whether one of the trustees who had defended the action ought to have his costs out of the trust estate. Kekewich J held that the trustee had had a duty to defend the trust as he did and that in his discretion he should have his costs.

I do not think that the view expressed by Kekewich J in the *Ideal Bedding* case, that in the case of a trust dispute (as was the dispute in that case), a trustee has a duty to defend the trust, is correct or in accordance with modern authority. In a case where the dispute is between rival claimants to a beneficial interest in the subject matter of the trust, rather, the duty of the trustee is to remain neutral and (in the absence of any court direction to the contrary and substantially, as happened in *Merry v Pownall* [1895] 1 Ch 306) offer to submit to the court's directions leaving it to the rivals to fight their battles. If this stance is adopted, in respect of the costs necessarily and properly incurred, for example, in serving a defence agreeing to submit to the courts direction and in making discovery, the trustees will be entitled to an indemnity and lien. If the trustees do actively defend the trust and succeed, for example, in challenging a claim by the settlor to set aside for undue influence, they may be entitled to their costs out of the trust, for they have preserved the interests of the beneficiaries under the trust: consider *In Re Holden ex p Official Receiver* (1887) 20 QBD 43. But if they fail, then, in particular, in the case of hostile litigation, although in an exceptional case the court may consider that the trustees should have their costs (see *Bullock v Lloyds Bank Ltd* [1955] 1 Ch 317), ordinarily, the trustees will not be entitled to any indemnity, for they have incurred expenditure and liabilities in an unsuccessful effort to prefer one class of beneficiaries, for example, the express beneficiaries specified in the trust instrument, over another, for example, the trustees in bankruptcy or creditors, and so have acted unreasonably and otherwise than for the benefit of the trust estate: consider RSC Ord 62 r 6; and see *National Anti-Vivisection Society v Duddington* (1989) *The Times*, 23 November; and *Snell's Equity*, 29th edn, 1990, p 258.

B Present applications

Beddoe [follow on] **application**

The trustees have sought by means of a summons, in this action, to obtain directions whether or not to defend the action. Master Gower held that this course was not appropriate and I agree.

The attempted *Beddoe* application is, I think, fundamentally flawed on at least two grounds. The first is that the application must be made in separate proceedings. This is for good reason. The purpose of the application is to inform the judge as to the strengths and weaknesses of the trustees' case and the course to be taken, for example, in respect of a possible compromise. It would be quite inappropriate for all this to be revealed to the court which has to try the case or the other parties to the litigation. On the other hand, as a matter of principle, each of the parties to the action itself is entitled to know everything that is communicated to the court in that action: see *Smith v Croft* [1986] 1 WLR 580, p 588.

The second is that the necessary parties are not before the court. The parties to the action and the necessary parties to a *Beddoe* application are not the same: in particular, the settlor's wife and their issue are not represented. The justification for the protection afforded to trustees by *Beddoe* order is that the beneficiaries are given the opportunity to make representations to the court before the order is made. (In the case where there are unresolved disputes as to the identity of the beneficiaries, for example, because of a trust dispute, then all possible claimants should be joined.) An order should not be made in proceedings which are so constituted that beneficiaries are precluded from being heard. It is nothing to the point, as suggested by Miss Proudman, that it is obvious what the representations of such beneficiaries would have been and that they may be thought incapable of affecting the decision.

The matter has not been argued whether the *Beddoe* application should be the courts of the forum of administration, that is, Jersey, rather than of England, and I do not have to consider that question.

I therefore take the view that the application for directions must be refused.

In *X v A and Others*, the High Court decided that a trustee's lien over the trust fund for proper costs and expenses extended to an indemnity against future liabilities.

X v A and Others [1999] All ER (D) 946, HC

Facts

The applicant was the sole trustee of the will of the testator. The testator had created a trust of his residuary estate, including land. The estate was held on trust for the testator's children, the defendants, absolutely. The application by the trustee was made out of concerns over the potential effect of the Environmental Protection Act 1990 which, when it was brought into force, would impose a new and far-reaching liability on owners of contaminated land. Although Pt IIA of the 1990 Act was not in force at the time of the application, an abatement notice could be served on the trustee, as owner of the site under the statutory nuisance provisions of the Act. In addition, the owner might be liable at common law for nuisance, or under the *Rylands v Fletcher* principle. The trustee applied for directions as to whether he had a lien over the trust funds for the liabilities to which he potentially could be liable in respect of the land.

Held

A trustee has a lien over the trust fund for his proper costs and expenses (see *Stott v Milne* (1884) 25 Ch D 710, *Re Beddoe* [1893] 1 Ch 547 and *Re Pauling's Settlement (No 2)* [1963] Ch 576). This right extended to an indemnity against future liabilities even though the liabilities were contingent upon a number of issues, including the commencement of Pt IIA of the EPA 1990.

Question

Are trustees allowed to claim reimbursement of expenses properly incurred?

FURTHER READING

Bartlett, R, 'The Law Reform Committee's trust investment recommendations' [1992] Conv 425.

Beatson, J, 'Restitution of taxes, levies and other imports: defining the extent of the *Woolwich* principle' (1993) 109 LQR 401.

Bridge, S, 'Better regulation of trustee exemption clauses' (2006) 156 NLJ 1589.

Clements, L, 'The changing face of trusts: the Trusts of Land and Appointment of Trustees Act 1996' (1998) 61 MLR 56.

Ham, R, 'Third party liability of trustees – contract, tort and tax' (1996) 10 Tru LI 45.

Hochberg, D and Norris, W, 'The rights of beneficiaries to information concerning a trust' [1999] PCB 292.

Hunter, R, 'The Trustee Act 2000 and the Human Rights Act' [2001] PCB 101.

Jaconelli, J, 'Decision taking by private and charitable trustees' [1991] Conv 30.

Kenny, A, 'Are a bank trustee's fees performance related? *Nestlé v National Westminster Bank*' [1993] Conv 63.

Kenny, A, 'Living up to expectations' (1996) 146 NLJ 348.

Lee, N, 'Absolutely entitled – a new meaning?' [1978] Conv 456.

Luxton, P, 'Ethical investments in hard times' (1992) 55 MLR 587.

Matthews, P, 'Trusts of flawed assets: the liability of trustees' (1998) 4 T & T 6.

McCormack, G, 'Liability of trustees for gross negligence' [1998] Conv 100.

Megarry, R, 'The ambit of a trustee's duty of disclosure' (1965) 81 LQR 192.

Milner, P and Holmes, J, 'Trust law reforms: are we nearly there yet' [2000] PCB 114.

Lord Nicholls of Birkenhead, 'Trustees and their broader community: where duty, morality and ethics converge' (1995) 9 Tru LI 71.

Nobles, R, 'The exercise of trustees' discretion under a pension scheme' [1992] JBL 261.

O'Hagan, P, 'Trustees' duty to disclose' (1995) 145 NLJ 1414.

Paling, D, 'The trustees' duty of skill and care' [1973] 37 Conv 48.

Panesar, S, 'The Trustee Act' [2001] ICCLR 151.

Pearce, P and Samuels, A, 'Trustees and beneficiaries and investment politics' [1985] Conv 52.

Riddall, J, '*Re Ransome* revisited or first the good nuns' [1979] Conv 243.

Russell, M, 'Apportioning windfalls' (1998) 142 SJ 284.

Samuels, A, 'Disclosure of trust documents' (1965) 28 MLR 220.

Shindler, G, 'Casenote – *Bartlett v Barclays Bank Trust Co Ltd*' [1980] Conv 155.

Virgo, G, 'Restitution of overpaid tax – justice at the expense of certainty' [1993] CLJ 31.

Watt, G, 'Escaping s 8(1) provisions in "new style" trusts of land' [1997] Conv 263.

VARIATION OF TRUSTS

INTRODUCTION

The trustees are obliged to administer the trust in accordance with its terms, as laid down in the trust instrument and the general law. A failure to do so will render them liable to a claim for breach of trust. However, circumstances may arise that require prudent trustees to depart from the terms of the trust. Indeed, the trustees may be duty bound to explore a departure from the terms of the trust. In such circumstances, the trustees are required to seek authority to deviate from the terms of the trust. There are a variety of sources of authority available to the trustees. A distinctive feature of these sources of authority is a departure from the terms of the trust in the administration of the trust and an alteration of beneficial interests.

VARIATION OF TRUSTS

Trustees are required to administer the trust in accordance with its terms. They have a primary duty to obey the instructions as detailed by the settlor or implied by law. Any deviation from the terms of the trust is a breach, making them personally liable, irrespective of how well intentioned the trustees might have been. However, circumstances might have arisen, since the setting up of the trust, that indicate that the trust might be more advantageously administered if the terms were altered.

For example, prior to the introduction of the Trustee Act 2000, the investment powers of the trustees were extremely limited and out of date. An application to the court to increase the investment powers of the trustees might increase the yield to the trust. Likewise, the impact of a potential liability to taxation might have the effect of depreciating the trust assets if no action were taken. The entire capital might suffer inheritance tax on the death of the life tenant and, a second time, on the death of the remainderman, whereas a partitioning of the trust property between the life tenant and remainderman might have the effect of avoiding inheritance tax if the life tenant survives for seven years or more.

In these circumstances, the trustees require some mechanism whereby authority may be conferred on them to depart from or vary the terms of the trust. Such authority may be conferred in a variety of ways.

In *Saunders v Vautier*, it was held that, where the beneficiaries are of full age and of sound mind and are absolutely entitled to the trust property, they may deal with the equitable interest in any way they wish. They may sell, exchange or gift away their interest. As a corollary to this rule, such beneficiaries acting in unison are entitled to terminate the trust. Equally, such beneficiaries acting in concert are entitled to empower the trustees to perform such acts as they (the beneficiaries) consider appropriate. In short, the beneficiaries, collectively, are entitled to rewrite the terms of the trust.

Saunders v Vautier (1841) Cr & Ph 240, CA

Facts

Stock was bequeathed upon trust to accumulate the dividends until Vautier (V) attained the age of 25. At this age, the trustees were required to transfer the capital and accumulated income to V. V attained the age of majority (21) and claimed the fund at this age. The question in issue was whether the trustees were required to transfer the fund to V.

Held

Since the fund had vested in V, the sole beneficiary, subject to the enjoyment being postponed until he was of full age, he was entitled to claim the entire fund. The beneficiary had a vested interest in the income, and the accumulations were for his sole benefit, which he was entitled to waive:

> **Lord Langdale MR:** I think that principle has been repeatedly acted upon; and where a legacy is directed to accumulate for a certain period, or where the payment is postponed the legatee, if he has an absolute indefeasible interest in the legacy, is not bound to wait until the expiration of that period, but may require payment the moment he is competent to give a valid discharge.

Question

What is the rule in *Saunders v Vautier*?

Where minors, or persons under a disability or persons unborn are beneficiaries (or potential beneficiaries), there cannot be a departure from the terms of the trust without the court's approval.

The courts draw a distinction between:

(a) a variation concerning the management and administration of trusts; and

(b) a variation of the beneficial interests under the trusts.

MANAGEMENT AND ADMINISTRATION

The purpose of the application for authority to alter the terms of the trust under this head is to improve the management and administration of the trust. The beneficiaries' interests remain unaltered.

Inherent jurisdiction of the court

The court has an inherent jurisdiction to depart from the terms of a trust in the case of an 'emergency', that is, an occasion when no provision was made in the trust instrument and the event could not have been foreseen by the settlor. This power is very narrow and arises in order to 'salvage' the trust property, for example, by effecting essential repairs to buildings.

The power was exercised in *Re New*, which was described as the 'high water mark' of the emergency jurisdiction.

Re New [1901] 2 Ch 534, CA

Facts

The trust property consisted of shares in a company divided in £100 units. The issue was whether the court would approve a scheme for splitting the shares into smaller units.

Held

The court approved a scheme of capital reconstruction on behalf of minors and unborn persons by splitting the shares into smaller units so that they could be more easily realised. Romer LJ summarised the court's jurisdiction:

> **Romer LJ:** In the management of a trust it not infrequently happens that some peculiar state of circumstances arises for which provision is not expressly made by the trust instrument, and which renders it most desirable, and it may be even essential, for the benefit of the estate and in the interests of all the *cestuis que* trust, that certain acts should be done by the trustees which in ordinary circumstances they have no power to do. In a case of this kind, which may reasonably be supposed to be one not foreseen or anticipated by the author of the trust, where the trustees are embarrassed by the emergency that has arisen and the duty cast on them to do what is best for the estate, and the consent of all the beneficiaries cannot be obtained by reason of some of them not

being *sui juris* or in existence, then it may be right for the court, to sanction on behalf of all concerned such acts on behalf of the trustees. The jurisdiction is one to be exercised with great caution, and the court will take care not to strain its powers . . . it need scarcely be said that the court will not be justified in sanctioning every act desired by trustees and beneficiaries merely because it may appear beneficial to the estate; and certainly the court will not be disposed to sanction transactions of a speculative or risky character.

In *Re Tollemache* [1903] 1 Ch 955, the court refused to sanction a scheme authorising the mortgage of the life tenant's beneficial interest in order to increase her income. There was no emergency.

Question

How would you describe the inherent jurisdiction of the court to approve schemes that vary the terms of a trust?

Section 57 of the Trustee Act 1925

Section 57 of the Trustee Act 1925 is drafted in fairly wide terms and empowers the court to confer the authority on the trustees to perform functions whenever it is expedient to do so.

Trustee Act 1925, s 57

(1) . . . where in the management or administration of any property . . . any sale, lease, mortgage, surrender, release or other disposition or any purchase, investment, acquisition, expenditure or other transaction is in the opinion of the court expedient, but the same can not be effected by reason of the absence of any power . . . the court may by order confer on the trustees, either generally or in any particular instance the necessary power . . .

(2) The court may from time to time, rescind or vary any order made under this section, or may make any new or further order.

(3) An application to the court . . . may be made by the trustees, or by any of them, or by any person beneficially interested under the trust.

(4) This section does not apply to trustees of a settlement for the purposes of the Settled Land Act 1925.

The policy of s 57 is to secure that the trust property is managed as advantageously as possible in the interests of the beneficiaries and to authorise specific dealings with the trust property outside the scope of the inherent jurisdiction of the court. It may not be possible to establish an emergency or that the settlor could not reasonably have foreseen the circumstances which have arisen. In these circumstances, the court may sanction the scheme presented for its approval (see Lord Evershed MR in *Re Downshire's Settled Estates* [1953] Ch 218, p 525 below).

Limitations on s 57 applications

There are a number of limitations concerning applications under s 57 of the Trustee Act 1925.

First, the scheme proposed by the trustees is required to be for the benefit of the trust as a whole and not only for an individual beneficiary: see *Re Craven (No 2)*.

Re Craven's Estate (No 2) [1937] Ch 431, HC

Facts

The issue was whether the court would approve a scheme authorising an advancement to a beneficiary for the purpose of becoming a Lloyd's underwriter.

Held

The court refused the application because the scheme would not have been expedient for the trust as a whole.

Secondly, additional powers may be conferred on the trustees only with regard to the 'management or administration' of the trust. No power exists under s 57 to alter the beneficial interest or to rewrite the trust administration clause, as opposed to merely authorising specific dispositions or transactions. This distinction is one of degree (see *Re Coates' Trusts* (1886) 34 Ch D 370 and *Re Byng's Will Trusts* [1959] 1 WLR 375).

Under this provision, the courts have sanctioned schemes for the partition of land: *Re Thomas* [1939] 1 Ch 194; a sale of land where the necessary consent could not be obtained: *Re Beale's Settlement Trust* [1932] 2 Ch 15; the sale of a reversionary interest which the trustees had no power to sell until it fell into possession: *Re Heyworth's Contingent Reversionary Interest* [1956] Ch 364; blending two charitable trusts into one: *Re Shipwrecked Fishermen's and Mariners' Benevolent Fund* [1959] Ch 220; the extension of investment powers of pension fund trustees: *Mason v Farbrother* [1983] 2 All ER 1078 (see p 495 above); a power to invest abroad: *Trustees of the British Museum v AG* [1984] 1 All ER 337; and a power to invest as if the trustees were beneficial owners, subject to certain guidelines: *Steel v Wellcome Custodian Trustee*.

Steel v Wellcome Custodian Trustees [1988] 1 WLR 167, HC

Facts

The claimants were professional trustees of a charitable fund established in 1932 by the will of the philanthropist, Sir Henry Solomon Wellcome. The trustees were bequeathed the entire share capital in Wellcome Ltd (W) with limited powers of investment. In 1956, the powers of investment were extended by order of the court so as to allow investment in UK and US fixed interest stocks and equities, but the use of the extended powers was limited to two-thirds of the value of the assets. The claimants applied to the court for approval in order to extend their powers of investment to acquire any property whatever as if they were beneficial owners of the fund, save that they were required to observe certain guidelines in choosing investments.

Held

The court granted its approval to invest in the way sought by the claimants:

> **Hoffmann J:** It seems to me clear that the powers conferred by the will of 1932 and augmented by the order of Upjohn J are hopelessly out of date. The only reason why the present application was not forced on the trustees at a much earlier date is because, until the Wellcome plc flotation, only a relatively tiny part of the value of the fund was subject to those investment powers. The requirement that a third of the fund must be in fixed interest securities is unnecessarily restrictive and the provision for determining the proportions from time to time is both administratively cumbersome and a penalty on success. The prohibition against investing in equities not quoted on the London or New York stock exchanges has prevented the trustees from participating in the boom in Pacific Basin shares, while the need for a five year dividend record means that they cannot buy shares in privatised industries. The Attorney General therefore accepts that the investment powers must be recast.

> Having regard therefore to the size of this fund, the eminence of the trustees, the provisions of the scheme for obtaining and acting on advice and the quality of advice available, as well as the special circumstances pertaining to the large holding in the shares of a single company, I am willing to approve the present scheme without any restriction on the kind of assets in which all or any of the fund may be invested.

Enlarging the trustees' power of investment

Applications to enlarge the trustees' powers of investment may be made under s 57 of the Trustee Act 1925, or under s 1 of the Variation of Trusts Act 1958. Where the application does not involve an alteration of the beneficial interest, it is more convenient for the applicant to use s 57 of the Trustee Act 1925. Under this section, the trustees are the appropriate applicants. The consent of every adult beneficiary is not required. The court does not consent on behalf of each separate category of adult beneficiary but considers the interests collectively, and in practice s 57 applications are heard by the judge in chambers, rather than in open court.

Anker-Petersen v Anker-Petersen (1991) LS Gaz 32, HC

Facts

The trust involved in this application was created by will in 1956. The current trustees were an English solicitor, two Isle of Man accountants and a Danish lawyer. The tenant for life under a trust lived in England, but the other beneficiaries lived in Denmark. The trustees' powers were limited under the Trustee Investments Act 1961. The tenant for life applied to the court under s 57 of the Trustee Act 1925 and s 1 of the Variation of Trusts 1958. The purpose of the application was for the approval of the court to extend the trustees' powers of management to enable the trustees to invest the trust funds for the benefit of the beneficiaries, to delegate the exercise of their powers of investment to an investment manager and to borrow money for any purpose.

Held

The High Court granted the application for the following reasons:

(a) The beneficiaries would be better off by requiring the trustees to obtain and consider advice before investing, as opposed to the trustees being required to invest in particular investments.

(b) The majority of the trustees lived abroad, which could have impeded the day to day running of the trust, whereas the granting of the application facilitated quick decision making by the trustees.

(c) The additional powers to appoint nominees and to enable borrowings were merely ancillary to the powers of investment and were desirable.

Note

Fewer applications will be made to the court as a result of the enlargement of the trustees' powers of investment under the Trustee Act 2000.

VARIATION OF BENEFICIAL INTERESTS

The court has jurisdiction to approve schemes which go beyond an alteration of the management powers of trustees and effect arrangements which vary the beneficial interest under a trust.

Section 53 of the Trustee Act 1925

Where an infant is beneficially entitled to real or personal property and the property does not produce income that may be used for the infant's maintenance, education or benefit, the court may adopt a proposal authorising a 'conveyance' of the infant's interest with a view to the application of the capital or income for the maintenance, education or benefit of the infant.

Section 53 of the Trustee Act 1925 may not be used simply to terminate a settlement without making some new trust provision for the infant. In *Re Meux* [1958] Ch 154, the plaintiff was a life tenant of a trust fund and his infant son was entitled to a contingent reversionary interest. The court sanctioned a scheme on behalf of the infant whereby a person was appointed to convey the infant's interest to the plaintiff in consideration of a purchase price which was paid to the trustees for the benefit of the infant.

Sections 23 and 24 of the Matrimonial Causes Act 1973

The court has wide powers under ss 23 and 24 of the Matrimonial Causes Act 1973 to make orders in favour of a party to a marriage or a child of the family. The court may order one spouse to transfer to (or settle for the benefit of) the other spouse or the children any property to which he or she is entitled in possession or reversion. In addition, the court may vary, for the benefit of the parties to the marriage or the children of the family, any ante-nuptial or post-nuptial settlements made on the parties to the marriage.

The Mental Health Act 1983

Section 96(1) of the Mental Health Act 1983 entitles the Court of Protection to make a settlement of the patient's property.

Section 64 of the Settled Land Act 1925

Settled land is excluded from s 57 of the Trustee Act 1925 (see p 521 above) because of the separate provision enacted for such property.

Settled Land Act 1925, s 64

(1) Any transaction affecting or concerning the settled land, or any part thereof, or any other land (not being a transaction otherwise authorised by this Act, or by the settlement) which in the opinion of the court would be for the benefit of the settled land, or any part thereof, or the persons interested under the settlement, may, under an order of the court, be effected by a tenant for life, if it is one which could have been validly effected by an absolute owner.

(2) In this section 'transaction' includes any sale, exchange, assurance, grant, lease, surrender, reconveyance, release, reservation, or other disposition, and any purchase or other acquisition, and any covenant, contract or option and any application of capital money, and any compromise or other dealing or arrangement; and 'effected' has the meaning appropriate to the particular transaction; and the references to land include references to restrictions and burdens affecting land.

The jurisdiction of the courts under s 64 of the Settled Land Act 1925 is much wider than the jurisdiction under s 57 of the Trustee Act 1925. Section 64 entitles the court to sanction not only schemes connected with the management and administration of the trust, but also the alteration of beneficial interests under the settlement. Moreover, s 64 by implication extends to land held upon trust for sale, because s 28(1) of the Law of Property Act 1925 confers upon trustees of land held upon trust for sale all the powers which the Settled Land Act 1925 confers upon the tenant for life of settled land.

The wide justification conferred on the courts by s 64 of the Settled Land Act 1925 may be illustrated by *Re Simmons*.

Re Simmons [1956] Ch 125, HC

Facts
A protected life tenant, who had a general power of appointment exercisable by will or codicil, wanted to dispose of capital.

Held
The court approved a scheme authorising a part of the capital to be transferred to the life tenant in return for releasing her general power of appointment over part of the fund.

Law of Property Act 1925, s 28(1)

Trustees for sale shall, in relation to land or to manorial incidents and to the proceeds of sale, have all the powers of a tenant for life and the trustees of a settlement under the Settled Land Act 1925, including in relation to the land the powers of management conferred by that Act during a minority; and (subject to any express trust to the contrary) all capital money arising under the said powers shall, unless paid or applied for any purpose authorised by the Settled Land Act 1925, be applicable in the same manner as if the money represented proceeds of sale arising under the trust for sale.

The limitation within s 64 requires the scheme or transaction to be beneficial to the settled land itself, or for the benefit of any person interested under the settlement. Thus, variations of beneficial interests and transactions designed to reduce fiscal liability have been sanctioned by the courts.

Peter Gibson J, in *Raikes v Lygon* [1988] 1 All ER 884, pointed out that s 64(1) of the Settled Land Act 1925 created five prerequisites for the approval of a scheme. These are as follows:

(i)   a 'transaction' as defined in s 64(2) of the Settled Land Act 1925;

(ii)   affecting or concerning the settled land or any part thereof;

(iii) not being a transaction otherwise authorised by the Settled Land Act 1925 or the settlement;

(iv) in the opinion of the court being for the benefit of:

    (a) the settled land or any part of it; or

    (b) the persons interested under the settlement; and

(v)   being one which could have been effected by an absolute owner.

In this case (*Raikes v Lygon*), the High Court authorised the transfer of trust property to a maintenance fund. The transaction was regarded as fiscally advantageous but otherwise an unauthorised investment.

In *Re White-Popham Settled Estates* [1936] 2 All ER 1486, the Court of Appeal approved an arrangement whereby the debts of the life tenant were repaid out of capital because on the facts this arrangement was for the benefit of all the beneficiaries. The capital was to be repaid by an insurance policy on the life of the life tenant, of which all the premiums except the first were to be charged to the income of the trust fund.

In *Re Downshire's Settled Estates*, the Court of Appeal approved a scheme designed to avoid estate duty. Under the scheme, the tenant for life of settled land proposed to surrender his protected life interest in £700,000 of capital money and settled land worth £400,000 in favour of the remainderman. Provision would be made for any possible future beneficiaries under the protective trust by means of insurance policies. The transaction 'affected or concerned' the settled land indirectly.

More recently, in *Hambro v The Duke of Marlborough*, the High Court assumed jurisdiction under s 64 of the Settled Land Act 1925 to permit the trustees of a settled estate, which could in the future devolve to a financially irresponsible heir, to prepare a scheme for the proper running of the estate. This was the position notwithstanding that the heir was of full age and capacity and did not consent to the proposed scheme.

Hambro and Others v The Duke of Marlborough and Others [1994] 3 WLR 341, HC

Facts

By an Act of Parliament in 1704, Queen Anne gave the manor of Woodstock and surrounding lands to the first Duke of Marlborough in fee simple as a reward for his services, particularly his victory at Blenheim. By a further Act of Parliament in 1706, any Duke was prohibited from undertaking any activity which would hinder, bar or disinherit a successor from possessing and enjoying the land ('the entrenching provision'). Under s 20(1)(i) of the Settled Land Act 1925, each successive Duke had the powers of a tenant for life. The first defendant (the 11th Duke), currently the tenant in tail in possession, and the trustees of the settlement (the plaintiffs) became very concerned about the future of the estate. In particular, the irresponsible disposition of the second defendant, the Marquis of Blandford (the eldest son of the Duke and heir apparent) led the plaintiffs and the Duke to conclude, reluctantly, that the Marquis was not capable of managing the estate. The plaintiffs prepared a scheme for the proper running of the estate in the future. Under the scheme, a new settlement was to be created whereby the estate would be subject to a trust for sale and the trust fund was to be held to pay the income to the Duke for life and, subject thereto, on protective trust for the Marquis for his life and, subject thereto, as to both income and capital on the trusts of the existing settlement. The effect of the scheme, if approved, would affect the Marquis in a material way in that he would be deprived of the benefits to be derived from being a tenant for life, with the right to live in and manage Blenheim Palace. The Marquis opposed the scheme. The issue before the court was not concerned with the merits of approving the scheme or not, but with whether the court had the jurisdiction to approve the scheme under s 64 of the Settled Land Act 1925.

The trustees contended that the court had the jurisdiction to approve the scheme without the consent of the Marquis and in alteration of his beneficial interests. The Marquis submitted that s 64 of the 1925 Act did not authorise the beneficial interests of a person who was *sui juris* to be varied without his consent, though it might be used to alter the interests of infant, unborn or unascertained beneficiaries as part of the transaction to be sanctioned by the court. In particular, it was submitted that the word 'transaction' did not cover the unilateral act of imposing on the estate a trust for sale (thereby freeing it and the trustees from the Settled Land Act 1925) and that the concluding words in sub-s (1), 'if it is one which could have been validly effected by an absolute owner', did not cover the case of one person disposing of the property of another. In addition, the entrenching section of the 1706 Act prohibited the alteration of beneficial interests proposed by the scheme.

Held

The court decided in favour of the trustees on the following grounds:

(a) on construction, the expression, 'transaction', was a word of wide import. The proposed new settlement or conveyance was a 'transaction' within s 64(2) of the 1925 Act as it amounted to a transfer of property which was an 'assurance . . . or other disposition';

(b) as far as jurisdiction was concerned, a transaction approved under s 64 of 1925 Act may vary the beneficial interest of an ascertained beneficiary of full age and capacity provided such variation is for the benefit of the settled land or of all the beneficiaries under the settlement;

(c) the proposed conveyance was inconsistent with the entrenched section of the 1706 Act and amounted to a 'hindrance' under this Act. However, s 20(1)(i) of the Settled Land Act 1925 (which repealed and re-enacted s 58(1)(i) of the Settled Land Act 1882) conferred the powers of a tenant for life on a tenant in tail. These powers include powers of sale. The effect, therefore, was that the 1882 Act overrode the entrenching provision.

Compromise

The court has the jurisdiction to approve compromise arrangements governing the rights of beneficiaries, including infants and unborn persons under trusts. Before the House of Lords decision in *Chapman v Chapman* [1954] AC 429, there was some doubt as to whether the jurisdiction existed if there was not a genuine dispute between the beneficiaries. The House of Lords in *Chapman v Chapman* clarified the meaning of the expression, 'compromise', by deciding that its jurisdiction concerned cases of genuine disputes about the existence of rights. In this case, the trustees applied for leave to execute a scheme releasing certain properties from the trust in order to avoid estate duty. Some of the interests were enjoyed by infants and might be enjoyed by unborn persons, so that any rearrangement of interests required the consent of the court. The House of Lords held that the scheme would not be approved because the court had no jurisdiction to sanction a rearrangement of beneficial interests on behalf of infants and unborn persons where there was no real dispute.

In *Allen v Distillers Ltd*, the question in issue was whether the court had jurisdiction to approve a settlement of an action brought on behalf of child victims of the thalidomide drug. The court, in granting its approval to the settlement as a compromise arrangement, decided, as a subsidiary issue, that it did not have an inherent jurisdiction to postpone the vesting of the capital in the children to an age greater than 18.

Allen v Distillers Ltd [1974] 2 All ER 365, HC

Eveleigh J: I do not think that the payment out to the trustees in the first instance gives rise to the kind of trust contemplated by the Act [ie, the Variation of Trusts Act 1958]. The Act contemplates a situation where a beneficial interest is created which did not previously exist and probably one which is related to at least one other beneficial interest. Moreover, the Act is designed to deal with a situation where the original disposition was intended to endure according to its terms but which in the light of changed attitudes and circumstances it is fair and reasonable to vary.

In any event, I do not think that the so called variation would be a variation at all. It would be a new trust made on behalf of an absolute owner.

If the court were to attempt to participate in the device suggested it would be making use of the Variation of Trusts Act 1958 to give it a jurisdiction not previously possessed and for a purpose not contemplated by the Act.

There is no doubt that the court could sanction a postponement of the infant's entitlement as part of a compromise where that is made a term of the compromise: see *Warren v King* [1964] 1 WLR 122. There, at the suggestion of the Court of Appeal, a clause was inserted in a trust deed deferring the infant's entitlement. The parties themselves, however, reached agreement upon the matter and it came before the court for approval as a term of the compromise. What ultimately happened, is not reported. No one in argument before me has cast any doubt upon the court's power to approve such a compromise where an infant is concerned. The court must clearly possess the power to do so. A son might sue his father in a property dispute and the father might well be prepared to give way on terms including one which postpones the vesting of the absolute interest. Clearly such an agreement could be made an order of the court.

I can see no reason why there should not be a compromise which, instead of specifying the period for postponement of entitlement, agrees to such a period as the court may decide is beneficial to the infant.

In *D (a child) v O*, the High Court decided that it had the power to lift the statutory limitation that exists under s 32 of the Trustee Act 1925 (power of advancement). This power was exercisable under the Variation of Trusts Act 1958. In *Allen v Distillers* the court ruled that it did not have jurisdiction to modify an interest under the VTA 1958. In the present case the court distinguished *Allen v Distillers* on the ground that Eveleigh J was not considering the sort of case of absolute entitlement that was before the court on this occasion. In *D v O*, what was proposed would have the effect of accelerating the benefit of the claimant by allowing the whole of the claimant's fund to be used for her benefit while she was still under age. It could not have been for the claimant's benefit to divert any part of the fund from her.

D (a child) v O [2004] 3 All ER 780 (H.C.)

Facts

The proceedings concerned part of the proceeds of two life insurance policies. Under the trust the trustees held certain powers of appointment (which were not exercised) and in default of any such appointment the fund was held on trust for three minors equally. Although the proceeds of the policy were not divided separately between the beneficiaries, in practice the proceeds were treated as if they were separate funds. The claimant was one of the beneficiaries and a minor. The income from the policy had been applied to meet the school fees of the claimant under s 31 of the Trustee Act 1925. This section authorises the trustees in their discretion, to pay the whole or part of the income from the trust to the parent or guardian of an infant beneficiary, or otherwise apply the relevant amount towards the maintenance, education or benefit of the infant beneficiary, during his infancy or until his interest fails. Part of the capital was also advanced under s 32 of the Trustee Act 1925 for the same purpose. Section 32 of the Trustee Act 1925 authorises the trustees in their discretion to distribute the capital fund in favour of any beneficiary who may become entitled to the whole or part of the capital in the future. However, proviso (a) of s 32 restricts the amount of funds available for distribution to 50% of the beneficiary's presumptive or vested interest. The application in this case was intended to secure the *whole* of the capital for the purpose of paying the child's school fees.

The application to the court raised two issues. First, whether the court had the jurisdiction to vary the trust terms in the way proposed. Secondly, whether it was in the claimant's interest to empower the trustees, in their discretion, to apply more than 50% of the capital for the claimant's education.

Held

The court decided both issues in favour of the claimant. The court had the jurisdiction under the Variation of Trusts Act 1958 to modify the statutory power of advancement and was satisfied that it was for the claimant's benefit that the limit imposed by s 32 of the Trustee Act 1925 ought to be lifted.

> **Lloyd J :** Eveleigh J in *Allen v Distillers Ltd* [1974] 2 All ER 365, was not considering the sort of case of absolute entitlement with which I am concerned. In the case before him there was no prior trust of any kind. Despite the potential width of the word 'disposition', it would be difficult to conclude that money paid by an alleged tortfeasor by way of compensation for injury to a minor was 'property . . . held on trusts arising . . . under any will, settlement or other disposition'. Accordingly I would not venture to disagree with his conclusion that the 1958 Act did not apply to the fund that he was concerned with.
>
> His observation that the 1958 Act is concerned with a trust where there is more than one beneficial interest was not necessary to his decision. If it were right the 1958 Act could not apply to C's fund, at any rate once it is split off from the rest of the fund. In my judgment it is not correct. Whether it could be appropriate in any circumstances to exercise the power conferred by the 1958 Act in relation to a fund held for a minor absolutely so as to reduce his or her entitlement in any respect, for example as was sought in *Allen* by deferring the date when the person in question can call for the fund, I do not need to decide. What is proposed in the present case would have the effect, in a sense, of accelerating the benefit for C, by allowing the whole of the fund to be used for her benefit while she is still under age. In other circumstances it may be possible to use the power under s 32 of the 1925 Act in such a way that the trust property does not become vested in the beneficiary (see *Pilkington v IRC* [1964] AC 612, [1962] 3 All ER 622). On the present and foreseeable facts of this case this is no more than theoretical. It could not be for C's benefit to divert any part of the fund from her.
>
> In my judgment both the whole trust fund, and C's fund separately, are 'property . . . held on trusts arising . . . under any will, settlement or other disposition'. It is therefore open to the court to exercise the powers conferred by the 1958 Act in relation to the funds, so long as it is satisfied that the proposed variation of the trusts is for the benefit of the relevant beneficiary. I am satisfied that it is for C's benefit to vary the trusts applying to her fund so that the whole fund, not merely one-half, may be applied pursuant to s 32 of the 1925 Act. I have therefore approved on her behalf a variation of the trusts applying to C's fund so as to permit the powers under s 32 to be exercised in relation to the whole, not only half, of the fund.

Question

In what circumstances may the court exercise its jurisdiction to approve compromise arrangements concerning the rights of beneficiaries?

THE VARIATION OF TRUSTS ACT 1958

The Variation of Trusts Act 1958 was passed in order to reverse the decision of the House of Lords in *Chapman v Chapman* and to introduce sweeping changes in the law. The jurisdiction of the courts was extended in order to approve variations of trusts (in respect of both administrative matters and beneficial interests) on behalf of infants, unborn persons and others. The court is entitled to sanction 'any arrangement varying or revoking all or any trusts or enlarging the powers of the trustees of managing or administering any of the property subject to the trusts'.

The court in its discretion may make an order approving a scheme, provided that the following four conditions are satisfied:

(1) property, whether real or personal, is held on trust;

(2) the trust was created by will, or *inter vivos* settlement or other disposition;

(3) the beneficiary (or beneficiaries), actual or potential, falls within at least one of the four categories as enumerated in s 1(1) of the Variation of Trusts Act 1958, that is:

(a) any person having directly or indirectly, an interest, whether vested or contingent under the trusts, who by reason of infancy or other incapacity is incapable of assenting; or

(b) any person (whether ascertained or not) who may become entitled, directly or indirectly, to an interest at a future date or on the happening of a future event, a person of any specified description or a member of any specified class of persons, but not including any person who would be of that description or a member of that class if the said date had fallen or the said event had happened at the date of the application to the court; or

(c) any person unborn; or

(d) any person in respect of any discretionary interest of his under protective trusts where the interest of the principal beneficiary has not failed or determined;

(4) provided that, with the exception of para (d) above, the arrangement was carried out for the benefit of that person.

The purpose of the Act is to permit the court to approve arrangements on behalf of beneficiaries who cannot give their consent by virtue of infancy or other incapacity, or because their identity is unascertained, such as a future spouse. It follows, therefore, that the court has no jurisdiction to approve arrangements on behalf of beneficiaries who are *sui juris*, adult and ascertained. Thus, the consent of all adult ascertained beneficiaries must be obtained before the court grants its approval to a scheme.

For example, T1 and T2 hold property on trust for A (adult) for life, remainder to B (an infant) for life with remainder to C (adult) absolutely. A scheme of equal division is proposed. The court may approve the scheme on behalf of B (the infant) but not in respect of A and C. Their consent must be obtained.

The only exception to the above rule is to be found in s 1(1)(d) of the Act, namely, that the court may consent on behalf of an adult 'beneficiary' who may become entitled to an interest on the failure of the principal beneficiary's interest under a protective trust.

For example, trustees hold property on protective trust for M for life. A scheme is submitted for the approval of the court to grant M's wife, W, a one-fifth share of the capital. The court may approve the arrangement on behalf of W, but M is required to consent to the scheme.

The nature of the jurisdiction of the court under the Variation of Trusts Act 1958 was described by Lord Reid in *Re Holmden's Settlement Trusts*:

Re Holmden's Settlement Trusts [1968] AC 685, HL

Lord Reid: Under the Variation of Trusts Act 1958, the court does not itself amend or vary the trusts of the original settlement. The beneficiaries are not bound by variations because the court has made the variation. Each beneficiary is bound because he has consented to the variation. If he was not of full age when the arrangement was made, he is bound because the court was authorised by the Act of 1958 to approve of it on his behalf and did so by making an order. If he was of full age and did not in fact consent, he is not affected by the order of the court and he is not bound. So the arrangement must be regarded as an arrangement made by the beneficiaries themselves. The court merely acted on behalf of or as representing those beneficiaries who were not in a position to give their own consent and approval.

Section 1(1)(b) of the Variation of Trusts Act 1958

Generally, the court may consent on behalf of potential beneficiaries who have a contingent interest in the trust (see s 1(1)(b) of the 1958 Act). However, the proviso to s 1(1)(b) prevents the court from approving on behalf of adult beneficiaries who stand only one step removed from entitlement under the trust. It was the intention of Parliament that such persons should be allowed to consent for themselves.

For example, trustees hold property on trust for A for life with an ultimate remainder for his next of kin. A is a widower with one son, B (adult). A scheme is proposed in order to divide the fund equally between A and B. In such a case, B is required to consent to the arrangement under the proviso to s 1(1)(b) on the ground that B is only one step removed (namely, the death of A) from acquiring a vested interest: see *Re Suffert*.

Re Suffert's Settlement [1961] Ch 1, HC

Facts

Under a settlement, B was granted a protected life interest with a power to appoint the capital and income on trust for her children. The settlement provided that if B had no children, the property was to be transferred to anyone whom B might appoint (that is, a general power), with a gift over in default of appointment in favour of B's statutory next of kin. B was 61 years of age, unmarried and without issue. She had three first cousins (next of kin), all of whom had attained the age of majority. B and one of her cousins sought to vary the settlement. The other two cousins had not consented and were not joined as parties. The court was asked to approve the arrangement on behalf of any unborn or unascertained persons and the two adult cousins.

Held

The court approved the arrangement on behalf of unborn and unascertained persons but could not grant its approval on behalf of the two cousins. Their consent was required:

> **Buckley J:** What the sub-section required was that the applicant should be treated as having died at the date of the issue of the summons, to find out who in that event would have been her statutory next of kin, and any persons who are within that class are persons whose interest the section provides that the court cannot bind. It is impossible to say who are the statutory next of kin of somebody who is alive, but it is not impossible to say who are the persons who would fill that description on the hypothesis that the *propositus* is already dead.

In *Knocker v Youle* the court decided that it could not grant its approval on behalf of beneficiaries with contingent interests in the trust property.

Knocker v Youle [1986] 1 WLR 934, HC

Facts

Under a settlement created in 1937, property was settled on trust for the settlor's daughter for life, and on her death (her share including accumulated income) was to be held on trust for such persons as she might appoint by her will. In default of appointment, the property was to be acquired by the settlor's son upon a similar trust. It was provided in the trust instrument that in the event of the trusts failing, the property was to be held on trust for the settlor's wife for life, and subject thereto for the settlor's four married sisters or their children *per stirpes*. The settlor's wife and sisters were all dead. There were numerous children from the four sisters. The settlor's daughter and son sought a variation of the trust under s 1(1)(b) of the 1958 Act which would have affected the interests of the children of the settlor's four sisters.

Held

The court had no jurisdiction in the circumstances. Section 1(1)(b) of the Act was not applicable to a person who had an interest under the trust. The children of the settlor's four sisters had a contingent interest under the trust, however remote, thus depriving the court of jurisdiction:

> **Warner J:** It is not strictly accurate to describe the cousins as persons 'who may become entitled . . . to an interest under the trusts'. There is no doubt of course that they are members of a 'specified class'. Each of them is, however, entitled now to an interest under the trusts, albeit a contingent one (in the case of those who are under 21, a doubly contingent one) and albeit also that it is an interest that is defeasible on the exercise of the general testamentary powers of appointment vested in Mrs Youle and Mr Knocker. Nonetheless, it is properly described in legal language as an interest, and the word 'interest' is used in its technical, legal sense. Otherwise, the words 'whether vested or contingent' in s 1(1)(a) would be out of place. It seems to me, however, that a person who has an actual interest directly conferred upon him or her by a settlement, albeit a remote interest, cannot properly be described as one who 'may become' entitled to an interest.

Variation or resettlement?

Although the Act gives the court a wide discretion to approve a scheme varying the terms of a trust, there appears to be a limitation on this discretion. The courts have adopted the policy of not 'rewriting' the trust. Accordingly, a distinction is drawn between a 'variation' and a 'resettlement'. A 'variation' retains the basic fundamental purpose of the trust but alters some important characteristic of the trust, whereas a 'resettlement' destroys the foundation or substance of the original design or purpose of the trust. Whether a scheme amounts to a variation or a resettlement will vary with the facts of each case: see *Re Ball*.

Re Ball's Settlement [1968] I WLR 899, HC

Facts

A settlement conferred a life interest on the settlor with remainder, subject to a power of appointment, in favour of his sons and grandchildren. In default of appointment, the fund was to be divided between the two sons of the settlor or their issue *per stirpes* (that is, the son's issue if either predeceased the settlor). A scheme was proposed for approval by the court, whereby the original settlement would be revoked and replaced by new provisions in which the fund would be split into two equal portions each held on trust for each of the sons for life and, subject thereto, for such of each son's children equally as were born before 1 October 1977.

Held

The court approved the scheme because the variation proposed did not involve a resettlement:

> **Megarry J:** The test is if the arrangement changes the whole substratum of the trust, then it may well be that it cannot be regarded merely as varying that trust. But if an arrangement, while leaving the substratum, effectuates the purpose of the original trusts by other means, it may still be possible to regard that arrangement as merely varying the original trusts, even though the means employed are wholly different and even though the form is completely changed . . . In this case, it seems to me that the substratum of the original trust remains. True, the settlor's life interest disappears; but the remaining trusts are still in essence trusts of half the fund for each of the two named sons and their families . . . The differences between the old and new provisions lie in detail rather than substance.

Question

Under the Variation of Trusts Act 1958, is there a distinction between 'variation' and 'resettlement'?

Settlor's intention

In exercising its discretion whether to approve an arrangement or not, the function of the court is to determine, by reference to all the circumstances, whether the arrangement as a whole is beneficial to the stipulated class of beneficiaries. Under the proviso to s 1(1) of the Variation of Trusts Act 1958, the court is prohibited from approving a scheme unless it is designed for the *benefit* of the classes of persons within s 1(1)(a), (b) or (c) of the 1958 Act. The court acts on behalf of the specified classes of persons and, in appropriate cases, supplies consent for persons incapable of consenting. The requirement of benefit to the relevant classes of persons is mandatory.

On the other hand, the court may or may not approve a scheme under the 1958 Act, irrespective of whether the arrangement is or is not for the benefit of persons classified within s 1(1)(d) of the Act. In short, benefit is not a requirement under the Act for this category of persons: see *Re Steed's Will Trust*, below.

Although the 1958 Act makes no mention of the settlor or testator, rules of court have been made requiring the joinder of the settlor, if living, as a defendant to an application under the Act.

Schedule 1, RSC Ord 93, r 6(2)

In addition to any other persons who are necessary and proper defendants to the originating summons by which an application under the said s 1 is made, the settlor and any other person who provided property for the purposes of the trust to which the application relates must, if still alive and not the plaintiff, be made a defendant unless the court for some special reason otherwise directs.

However, in the context of deciding whether to approve an arrangement or not, the intention of the settlor or testator is only a factor (if relevant) to be taken into consideration by the court; it is certainly not an overriding factor, nor even a weighty consideration, in determining how the discretion of the court is to be exercised. The role of the court is not to act as a representative of the settlor or testator in varying the trust.

Re Steed's Will Trust [1960] Ch 407, CA

Facts

A testator devised a farm to trustees on protective trust for his housekeeper, Gladys, for life, and after her death for such persons as she might by deed or will appoint, and in default of appointment on trust for her next of kin. The will declared the testator's 'wish that she shall have the use and enjoyment of the capital value if she needs it during her life and if and when the property is sold the trustees may apply the proceeds to or for her benefit provided that they shall consider the necessity for retaining sufficient capital to prevent her from being without adequate means at any time during her life'. Gladys exercised the power of appointment in her favour. The farm was let to her brother, but he failed to pay any rent. The trustees decided to sell the farm, but Gladys opposed the sale and brought a summons under the Variation of Trusts Act 1958, asking the court to approve an arrangement under which the trustees would hold the property on trust for her absolutely.

Held

Having regard to all the circumstances, including the intention of the settlor, the scheme would not be approved:

Lord Evershed: The court must, in performing its duty under the Variation of Trusts Act 1958, regard the proposal in the light of the purpose of the trust as shown by the evidence of the will or settlement itself and any other relevant evidence available . . . It was part of the testator's scheme, made manifest in the will, that it was his intention and desire that this trust should be available for Gladys so that she would have proper provision made for her throughout her life, and would not be exposed to the risk that she might, if she had been handed the money, part with it in favour of another individual about whom the testator felt apprehension, which apprehension is plainly shared by the trustees.

In *Re Remnant's Settlement Trust* [1970] Ch 560 (see p 537 below), the High Court decided on the special facts of that case that a forfeiture clause, promoting a religious bar, would be deleted from a trust, despite defeating the intention of the settlor. The settlor's wishes were regarded as warranting serious consideration, but were not conclusive. In any event, *Re Steed's Will Trust* was not considered in *Re Remnant*.

In *Goulding v James*, Mummery LJ reviewed *Re Steed's Will Trust* and decided that the latter case did not lay down 'any rule, principle or guideline of general application on the importance of the intentions and wishes of the settlor or testator to applications to approve arrangements under the 1958 Act'. In other words, the settlor's wishes coincided with, but were not a cause for, the court's refusal to vary the trust.

Goulding v James [1997] 2 All ER 239, CA

Mummery LJ: A close examination of the facts and reasoning in *Re Steed's Will Trusts* [1960] Ch 407 reveals two significant features of that case: (a) The applicant in that case, unlike Mrs Jane Goulding [who had a life interest under the settlement], had only a protected life interest, held on protective trusts in s 33 of the Trustee Act 1925. (b) Very different considerations affected the court's discretion in *Re Steed's Will Trusts*. The court was asked to approve the arrangement proposed by the protected life tenant on behalf of the person or persons specified in s 1(1)(d) of the 1958 Act ... The proviso as regards benefit does not apply to that paragraph, so that the court may approve an arrangement, the carrying out of which would not be for the benefit of that person. The court may consider whether or not there is benefit as a discretionary factor, but lack of benefit for such a person is no barrier to the approval of the court.

[In *Re Steed's Will Trust*] the Court of Appeal was satisfied that the testator's purpose, evidenced in the will, was still justified at the time of the application to vary. That was a view shared by the trustees, who opposed the application by the protected life tenant. In those circumstances there was an overwhelming reason for the continuation of the protective trusts and in the continuance of the interest of the para (d) class of person. That explained and justified the court's refusal to approve. The court in that case was not engaged in the exercise demanded in this case of deciding whether a mandatory benefit, bargained on behalf of a specified class, is outweighed by some other countervailing discretionary factor, such as the purpose of the trust or the intention of the testatrix in making it.

The court decided that, in the exercise of its discretion, it would approve a scheme of variation of a trust, despite the contradiction of the clear intention of a testatrix concerning adult, ascertained beneficiaries.

Goulding v James [1997] 2 All ER 239, CA

Facts

The testatrix (Mrs Froud) made a will in 1992 and, *inter alia*, left her estate equally to her daughter (June) and son-in-law (Kenneth). In 1994, the testatrix revoked her will and executed a new will, under which she gave a life interest in her residuary estate to June with remainder to her grandson, Marcus, provided that he attained the age of 40. This contingent remainder interest was subject to gifts over in favour of any of Marcus' children who were alive at the time of Marcus' death. One effect of this new will was that June did not have an interest in the capital of the trust. The testatrix died in December 1994. June and Marcus (who had no children) applied to the court for the approval of a scheme under s 1(1)(c) of the Variation of Trusts Act 1958. Under the proposed variation, the will trust would be varied from the date of the testatrix's death in order to transfer 90% of the residuary estate to June and Marcus equally. The remaining 10% of the estate would be invested in a fund for the benefit of any children of Marcus.

The plaintiffs adduced actuarial evidence to the effect that the proposed scheme was capable of being eight times more beneficial to Marcus' unborn children than the existing arrangement. The defendants, trustees of the testatrix's will trusts, did not oppose the plaintiffs' proposals, but felt obliged to put a number of relevant issues before the court. These were that the testatrix made it abundantly clear to her solicitors and accountants that she did not want her daughter to have an interest in the capital of her estate. She also felt that Marcus would, with time, adopt a more financially responsible attitude to life. The proposed scheme was contrary to the views expressed by the testatrix. The trial judge decided against the scheme. In his discretion, he felt that he was not entitled to disregard the clear views of the testatrix. The plaintiffs appealed.

Held

Reversing the decision of the trial judge and approving the scheme of variation, the Court of Appeal decided that the testatrix's views concerning the adult beneficiaries were irrelevant in deciding whether the court might exercise its jurisdiction under s 1(1)(c) of the Variation of Trusts Act 1958. The court's discretion is exercisable with regard to all the relevant considerations in the statutory context. The flaw in the trial judge's reasoning was that he allowed extrinsic evidence of the testatrix's intention to outweigh the benefit to the class of adult, consenting beneficiaries. The court also issued a caution to trustees and their advisers to take special care in considering the relevance, quality and cogency of extrinsic evidence of the settlor's or testator's intentions and wishes in making applications under the 1958 Act so as to avoid the risk of irrelevant evidence being admitted and to reduce the costs of such applications:

Mummery LJ: I leave consideration of the evidence with this comment. Trustees and those advising them should, before filing extrinsic evidence of a testator's or settlor's intentions, wishes and motives in relation to an application under the 1958 Act, take particular care to consider its relevance, quality and cogency. If in doubt, trustees can outline the nature of such evidence to the court and seek directions as to whether more detailed evidence should be filed. Unless special care is taken with such evidence there is a risk that irrelevant, and possibly inflammatory, collateral issues will be raised, thereby adding unnecessarily to the costs of the case.

In my judgment, the legal position is as follows:

(1) The court has a discretion whether or not to approve a proposed arrangement.

(2) That discretion is fettered by only one express restriction. The proviso to s 1 prohibits the court from approving an arrangement which is not for the benefit of the classes referred to in (a), (b) or (c). The approval of this arrangement is not prevented by that proviso, since it is plainly the case that it is greatly for the benefit of the class specified in s 1(1)(c).

(3) It does not follow from the fact of benefit to unborns that the arrangement must be approved.

In *Re Van Gruisen's Will Trusts, Bagger v Dean* [1964] 1 WLR 449, p 450, Ungoed-Thomas J said: It is shown that, actuarially, the provisions for the infants and unborn persons are more beneficial for them under the arrangement than under the present trusts of the will. That, however, does not conclude the case. The court is not merely concerned with this actuarial calculation, even assuming that it satisfies the statutory requirement that the arrangement must be for the benefit of the infants and unborn persons. The court is also concerned whether the arrangement as a whole, in all the circumstances, is such that it is proper to approve it. The court's concern involves, *inter alia*, a practical and business-like consideration of the arrangement, including the total amounts of the advantages which the various parties obtain, and their bargaining strength.

(4) That overall discretion described by Ungoed-Thomas J is to be exercised with regard to all relevant factors properly considered in the statutory context. The context is that the court is empowered to approve an arrangement 'on behalf of' the members of the specified class. As Lord Denning MR said in *Re Weston's Settlements* [1969] 1 Ch 223, p 245, 'in exercising its discretion, the function of the court is to protect those who cannot protect themselves'.

In relation to the members of the specified class who cannot act for themselves, the court is almost in the position of a 'statutory attorney', a striking expression used by Mr Goulding QC in his illuminating submissions to the Court of Appeal in *Re Weston's Settlement*. The court is not in the position of a statutory attorney for the settlor or for the adult beneficiaries and the court is not, as was made clear in *Re Holmden's Settlement* [1968] AC 685, in the position of a statutory settlor.

(5) Viewed in that context, an important factor in this case is that Mrs June Goulding and Mr Marcus Goulding are *sui juris* and Mrs Froud's intentions and wishes related to their beneficial interests under the testamentary trusts rather than to the contingent interests of her unborn great grandchildren whom the court is concerned to protect. Mrs Froud's contrary non-testamentary wishes could not inhibit Mrs June Goulding's proprietary rights, as a person beneficially entitled to the life interest in residue.

(6) In these circumstances, the critical question is: what relevance, if any, can Mrs Froud's intentions and wishes with regard to the interests in residue taken under the will by her daughter and grandson and with regard to the exclusion of her son in law from direct or indirect benefit, have to the exercise of the court's jurisdiction on behalf of unborn great-grandchildren of Mrs Froud?

(7) [The judge reviewed the principle in *Re Steed's Will Trusts*, distinguished that case and continued:] . . .

(8) The fact that the rules of court require a living settlor to be joined as a party to proceedings under the 1958 Act does not mean that the court attaches any overbearing or special significance to the wishes of the settlor. The court has a discretion to approve an arrangement under the Act, even though the settlement or will may make it crystal clear that the settlor or testator does not want any departure from any of the strict terms of the trust.

In *Re Remnant's Settlement Trusts, Hooper v Wenhasten* [1970] Ch 560, the forfeiture provision plainly expressed a strongly held wish on the part of the testator as to who should not benefit under his will. The court nevertheless approved an arrangement deleting that forfeiture provision and thereby defeated the testator's clear intentions. The court did so because Pennycuick J was of the view that it was for the benefit of all concerned to delete that provision; he was satisfied that the arrangement was a fair and proper one.

It may also be worthy of note that in *Re Weston's Settlement*, it was the settlor himself who applied for the approval of an arrangement for the export of his trust to Jersey, where he had gone to live. But he was unable to persuade either Stamp J or the Court of Appeal to approve the arrangement. They held that it was not for the benefit of the specified class and refused to approve it.

To sum up, the flaw in the judge's refusal to approve the arrangement is that, in reliance on the supposed scope of the decision in *Re Steed's Will Trusts*, he allowed extrinsic evidence of the subjective wishes of Mrs Froud as regards her daughter, son in law and grandson to outweigh considerations of objective and substantial benefit to the class on whose behalf the court is empowered to act. If the judge had adopted the correct approach to the exercise of his discretion, he could only have come to the conclusion that the intentions and wishes of Mrs Froud, expressed externally to her will in relation to the adult beneficiaries and an adult non-beneficiary, had little, if any, relevance or weight to the issue of approval on behalf of the future unborn great-grandchildren, whose interest in residue was multiplied five-fold under the proposed arrangement.

Benefit (proviso to s 1(1))

The scheme of variation is required to display some benefit for the persons as stated in s 1(1)(a)–(c) of the Variation of Trusts Act 1958. No such requirement exists for persons in category (d) of s 1(1) of the Act. The statute does not list the factors which the court is required to take into account in deciding the issue. It seems that all the circumstances are required to be considered, and the court must weigh up the possible advantages against the disadvantages of adopting a scheme of variation of the trust and decide accordingly. A wide variety of factors has been prominent in either the approval or rejection of schemes of variation.

Tax avoidance

The majority of applications have been made with a view to reducing the tax which would otherwise have been payable if the variation were not made.

For example, if property was settled on trust for A for life with remainder to B absolutely, inheritance tax would be payable on the entire estate on A's death and a second time on B's death. If the settlement was varied so that the fund was divided between A and B equally, inheritance tax would be payable on only half of the trust fund on the death of each of the beneficiaries.

The courts are required to be satisfied that the scheme as a whole is advantageous to the objects. It follows that the court will not approve a scheme if the overall effect is detrimental to the objects, even though there may be financial rewards inherent in the scheme. Tax avoidance is merely one factor to be taken into account by the courts. In *Re Weston*, the court decided that a tax avoidance scheme requiring the beneficiaries to emigrate to a tax haven might not be treated as beneficial to the trust.

Re Weston's Settlement [1969] 1 Ch 223, CA

Facts

The settlor created two settlements in 1964 for the benefit of his two sons. A total of 500,000 shares was transferred to the trustees. In 1965, capital gains tax was introduced. The shares rose in value and at the time of hearing the tax due on a disposal of the shares was £163,000. The settlor lived in England until 1967. He made three short visits to Jersey in 1967 and then purchased a house there in August 1967 in which he intended to live. An application was made to the court under the Variation of Trusts Act 1958, in November 1967, to appoint two trustees in Jersey as trustees of the two English settlements. In addition, the plaintiff sought the court's sanction to 'export' the trust to Jersey on identical terms. The motive was to save capital gains tax and estate duty.

Held

The scheme would not be approved because it would have been morally and socially detrimental to the beneficiaries despite being financially advantageous:

Lord Denning: The court should not consider merely the financial benefit to the infants and unborn children but also their educational and social benefit. There are many things in life more worthwhile than money. One of these things is to be brought up in this our England, which is still the envy of less happier lands. I do not believe it is for the benefit of children to be uprooted from England and transported to another country simply to avoid tax. I should imagine that even if they had stayed in this country they would have had a very considerable fortune at their disposal even after paying tax. The only thing that Jersey can do for them is to give them a greater fortune. Many a child has been ruined by being given too much. The avoidance of tax may be lawful, but it is not yet a virtue. The children may well change their minds and come back to this country to enjoy their untaxed gains. Are they to be wanderers over the face of the earth moving from this country to that according to where they can best avoid tax? Children are like trees, they grow stronger with firm roots.

On the other hand, where the applicants have a long-standing connection with the foreign country concerned in the proposed scheme, the court may grant its approval: see *Re Windeatt*.

Re Windeatt's Will Trust [1969] 1 WLR 692, HC

Facts

The settlor, who was domiciled in England, created a trust for the benefit of his children who had lived in Jersey for 19 years prior to the application to transfer the trust to Jersey. The question in issue was whether the court would approve the transfer of the trust to the foreign jurisdiction.

Held

The court approved the scheme because the beneficiaries were permanently resident in Jersey.

Moral benefit

The court may have regard to evidence which establishes the financial instability of infant beneficiaries and may adopt a scheme which has the effect of postponing the vesting of such beneficiary's interest in capital: see *Re T's Settlement Trusts*.

Re T's Settlement Trusts [1964] Ch 158, HC

Facts

An infant was entitled absolutely to a quarter of a trust fund on attaining the age of 21 years (the age of majority at that time) and a further quarter on the death of her mother. Eighteen days before she reached the age of majority, her mother asked the court to approve a transfer to new trustees of the infant's share to be held either:

(a) on protective trust for her for life; or

(b) postponing the vesting of capital until she reached the age of 25, but in the meantime on protective trust.

The court accepted that the infant was alarmingly immature and irresponsible in respect of financial matters.

Held

(a) The protective trust for life would have amounted to a 'resettlement' of property which was outside the jurisdiction of the court, and in any event would not be beneficial to the child.

(b) However, the postponement of the capital until a later date and the interim protective trust were approved:

Wilberforce J: . . . it appears to me to be a definite benefit for this infant for a period during which it is to be hoped that independence may bring her to maturity and responsibility to be protected against creditors . . . And this is the kind of benefit which seems to be within the spirit of the Act.

In *Re Holt*, the court approved the principle in *Re T's Settlement Trusts*, but postponed the vesting of an infant's benefit without evidence of financial immaturity.

Re Holt's Settlement [1969] 1 Ch 100, HC

Facts

Personal property was settled on Mrs Wilson for life with remainder to such of her children as would reach the age of 21 years and, if more than one, in equal shares. She wanted to surrender her life interest in half of the income for the benefit of the children (in order to reduce the impact of income tax on her husband and her) and to rearrange the trusts so that the interest of the children would vest at the age of 30 years.

Held

The court approved the scheme because on the whole it was for the benefit of the children:

> **Megarry J:** It seems to me that the arrangement proposed is for the benefit of each of the beneficiaries contemplated by s 1(1) of the 1958 Act. The financial detriment to the children is that the absolute vesting of their interests will be postponed from age 21 to 30. As against this, they will obtain very substantial financial benefits, both in the acceleration of their interests in a moiety of the trust fund and in the savings of estate duty . . . it is also most important that young children should be reasonably advanced in a career and settled in life before they are in receipt of an income sufficient to make them independent of the need to work. The word 'benefit' in the proviso to s 1(1) is plainly not confined to financial benefit, but may extend to moral and social benefit as is shown in *Re T's Settlement*.

Avoidance of family dissension

The court may approve an arrangement if its effect would be to prevent real or potential conflict within a family. In this respect, although the intention of the settlor carries a great deal of weight, it is not conclusive: see *Re Remnant*.

Re Remnant's Settlement Trust [1970] Ch 560, HC

Facts

A trust created contingent interests in favour of the children of two sisters, Dawn and Merrial, and contained a forfeiture clause if they practised Roman Catholicism, or married or lived with a Roman Catholic. The children of Dawn were Protestants, whereas the children of Merrial were Roman Catholics. The sisters sought the court's approval of a scheme which deleted the forfeiture clause.

Held

The court approved the scheme in order to prevent family conflict. Although Dawn's children did not benefit financially from the deletion of the clause, the court decided that, on the whole, they would be better off because the religious bar could have deterred them from selecting a spouse:

> **Pennycuick J:** Obviously a forfeiture provision of this kind might well cause very serious dissension between the families of two sisters . . . I am entitled to take a broad view of what is meant by 'benefit', and so taking it, I think this arrangement can fairly be said to be for their 'benefit' . . . It remains to be considered whether the arrangement is a fair and proper one. As far as I can see, there is no reason for saying otherwise, except that the arrangement defeats this testator's intention. That is a serious but by no means conclusive consideration. I have reached the clear conclusion that these forfeiture provisions are undesirable in the circumstances of this case and that an arrangement involving their deletion is a fair and proper one.

Question

When may the court approve schemes varying beneficial interests under trusts?

FURTHER READING

Cooke, E, 'What to do with an unbarrable entail – *Hambro v The Duke of Marlborough*' [1994] Conv 492.

Cotterell, R, 'The requirement of "benefit" under the Variation of Trusts Act 1958' (1971) 34 MLR 96.

Evans, D, 'The Variation of Trusts Act in practice' (1963) 27 Conv 6.

Harris, J, 'Ten years of variation of trusts' (1969) 33 Conv 113 and 183.

Hayes, M, 'Breaking and varying trusts painlessly' (1998) 4 MLR 17.

Luxton, P, 'An unascertainable problem in variation of trusts' (1986) 136 NLJ 1057.

Riddall, J, 'Does it or doesn't it? Contingent interests and Variation of Trusts Act 1958' [1987] Conv 144.

INTRODUCTION

Trustees are liable for breach of trust if they fail to observe their duties. The claimant may bring proceedings *in personam* against the trustees for breach of trust. Such a claim is required to be brought within the time periods as declared in the Limitation Act 1980. The policy of measuring the damages payable to the trust is to place the trust estate in the position it would have been but for the breach. The strict common law rules of remoteness of damage are not applicable, but a link must be established between the trustees' breach of trust and the loss to the trust. In addition, a claim *in rem* may be instituted against the trustees to recover (or trace) the trust property. This claim is not subject to the Limitation Act 1980 but is subject to the doctrine of laches.

BREACH OF TRUST

A trustee is liable for a breach of trust if he fails to perform his duties either by omitting to do any act which he ought to do, or doing an act which he ought not to do. Such duties may be created by the settlor in the trust instrument (such as the duty to distribute both income and capital), or may be imposed generally, in accordance with trusts law (for example, duties of care and impartiality). A breach of trust may range from a fraudulent disposal of trust property to an innocent dereliction of duties by investing trust moneys in unauthorised investments. The beneficiary is required to establish a causal connection between the breach of trust and the loss suffered either directly or indirectly by the trust. Indeed, even if the trust suffers no loss, the beneficiary is entitled to claim any profit accruing to the trustees as a result of a breach.

Measure of liability for damages

Trustees' liability for breach of trust is based on principles of restitution to the trust estate. The trustee in default is required to restore the trust property, or its equivalent, to the trust estate. In respect of a breach of trust claim, the basic right of the beneficiary is to have the trust duly administered in accordance with the trust instrument and the general law. In respect of a monetary claim, the equitable rules of compensation are based on the restoration to the trust fund of property that ought to be there. Thus, the trustees responsible for the breach are required to pay, to the trust estate, assets or compensation for loss suffered by the trust as a result of their breach. In this respect, the common law rules of remoteness of damage and causation are not applied strictly, but there still has to be some causal link between the breach of trust and loss to the estate. Once the trust fund is 'reconstituted', the defaulting trustee becomes a bare trustee for the claimant and will have no answer to a claim by the claimant for the payment over of the moneys in the 'reconstituted' fund. In *Bartlett v Barclays Bank*, Brightman J declared the general policy regarding claims for compensation for breach of trust.

Bartlett v Barclays Bank Trust Co Ltd (No 2) [1980] 2 All ER 92, HC

Brightman J: The obligation of a trustee who is held liable for breach of trust is fundamentally different from the obligation of a contractual or tortious wrongdoer. The trustee's obligation is to restore to the trust estate the assets of which he has deprived it.

If the trust property cannot be restored to the trust, compensation may be payable to the trust in order to maintain the value of the trust assets. The trust is required to be compensated fully for any loss caused by the breach. The extent of this liability is not restricted by the strict common law principles governing remoteness of damage in claims in tort or breach of contract. Once a breach of trust has been committed, the trustees become liable to place the trust estate in the same position as it would have been in if no breach had been committed. Although liability is not unlimited, the time of assessment of the loss is at the time of the trial: see *Caffrey v Darby*.

Caffrey v Darby (1801) 6 Ves 488

Facts

Trustees, owing to their negligence, failed to recover possession of part of the trust assets and, later still, the assets became lost. The trustees argued that the subsequent loss was not attributable to their neglect.

Held

Once the trustees committed a breach of trust, they were responsible for compensating the estate in respect of the resulting loss:

> **Lord Eldon:** if they have already been guilty of negligence, they must be responsible for any loss, in any way, to that property, for whatever may be the immediate cause, the property would not have been in a situation to sustain that loss if it had not been for their negligence. If the loss had happened by fire, lightning, or any other accident, that would not be an excuse for them if guilty of previous negligence.

At common law, there are two principles that are fundamental to the award of damages:

(a) the breach must cause the loss claimed by the claimant; and

(b) the claimant must be put in the same position as he would have been in had he not suffered a breach.

In equity, although the starting point to a compensation claim is different, the award of damages is, to a large extent, governed by the same two principles. The strict test of foreseeability is not a concern in assessing compensation, but it is essential that the losses claimed are the losses which are caused by the breach. This broader approach to the issue of causation was referred to by Lord Browne-Wilkinson in *Target Holdings v Redferns*.

Target Holdings v Redferns [1995] 3 All ER 785, HL

> **Lord Browne-Wilkinson:** In both systems the defendant is not responsible for damage not caused by his wrong or to pay more compensation than the loss suffered by the plaintiff. Under both systems liability is fault-based. The defendant is only liable for the consequences of the legal wrong he has done to the plaintiff and to make good the damage caused by such wrong. The detailed rules of equity as to causation and the quantification of loss differ, at least ostensibly, from those applicable at common law.

However, if at the time of the claim the trust is at an end, so that the trustees hold the trust property as *bare* trustees, the beneficiary has the right to have the trust assets retained by the trustees until they have fully accounted for the assets to him. For example, under a trust for A for life with remainder to B absolutely, after A's death, B becomes absolutely entitled to the trust property. If the trustees commit a breach of trust, there is no reason for compensating the breach by way of compensation to the trust fund as opposed to the beneficiary himself or herself. The beneficiary's right, in these circumstances, is no longer to have the trust duly administered, for he is the sole owner of the trust estate. The measure of compensation is the difference between what the beneficiary would have received and what he has in fact received.

A trustee who wrongly pays away trust money, such as a trustee who makes an unauthorised investment, commits a breach of trust and comes under an immediate duty to remedy such breach. If proceedings are brought promptly, the court will make an immediate order requiring restoration to the trust fund, and will order a sale of the unauthorised investments and payment of compensation for any loss suffered. But the fact that there is an accrued cause of action as soon as the breach is committed does not mean that the quantum of the compensation payable is ultimately fixed as at the date when the breach occurred. The quantum is fixed at the date of judgment, according to circumstances which would put the beneficiary back into the position he would have been in but for the breach. The claimant's actual loss is assessed with the full benefit of hindsight. In *Target Holdings v Redferns*, the court rejected the allegation of the plaintiffs that the loss was to be measured at the time of the breach. This would have entitled the plaintiffs to obtain compensation of an amount which exceeded their loss and would not have reflected the basic principles of equitable compensation.

Target Holdings Ltd v Redferns [1995] 3 All ER 785, HL

Facts

A company, Crowngate Ltd (C Ltd), agreed to purchase a property for £775,000 and then approached the mortgagee, Target Holdings Ltd (T Ltd), for a loan of £1.525 million to be secured by way of a mortgage on the property. The purchase price of the property was stated as £2 million, having been valued negligently by a firm of estate agents. T Ltd was not informed that the property was not being purchased for £775,000. A scheme was arranged by C Ltd to obtain a mortgage for £1.525m from T Ltd in order to purchase a property for £775,000. C Ltd instructed one of the defendants, a firm of solicitors, to incorporate another company, Panther Ltd (P Ltd), in order to purchase the property from the vendors for £775,000. P Ltd would sell the property to Kohli Ltd (K Ltd, owned by C Ltd) for £1.25 million and K Ltd would sell the property to C Ltd for £2 million. The defendant firm of solicitors acted for the three companies and T Ltd. T Ltd approved the loan and paid the defendant £1.525 million. Prior to the completion of the sale, the defendant notified T Ltd that the sale of the property and mortgage charge had been completed. Some days later, C Ltd arranged for £775,000 to be paid to the vendor of the property, and the various transfers and T Ltd's charge were completed. C Ltd became insolvent and T Ltd repossessed the property. The property was sold for £500,000. T Ltd brought an action against the defendant firm of solicitors and the valuer. The firm of solicitors conceded that it acted in breach of trust by paying out the mortgage funds to the three companies without authority, but argued that it was not liable to compensate T Ltd for the loss suffered because its breach did not cause the loss sustained by the company.

Held

The loss suffered by T Ltd was not directly attributable to the defendant firm of solicitors but was wholly caused by the fraud of third parties. T Ltd would have advanced the same amount of money, obtained the same security and received the same amount on the realisation of that security, with or without the breach of trust committed by Redferns:

> **Lord Browne-Wilkinson:** My Lords, this appeal raises a novel point on the liability of a trustee who commits a breach of trust to compensate beneficiaries for such breach. Is the trustee liable to compensate the beneficiary not only for losses caused by the breach but also for losses which the beneficiary would, in any event, have suffered even if there had been no such breach?
>
> *[Fault based liability for damages at common law and equity]*
> At common law, there are two principles fundamental to the award of damages. First, that the defendant's wrongful act must cause the damage complained of. Second, that the plaintiff is to be put 'in the same position as he would have been in if he had not sustained the wrong for which he is now getting his compensation or reparation': *Livingstone v Rawyards Coal Co* (1880) 5 App Cas 25, p 39, per Lord Blackburn. Although, as will appear, in many ways equity approaches liability for making good a breach of trust from a different starting point, in my judgment those two principles are applicable as much in equity as at common law. Under both systems liability is fault-based: the defendant is only liable for the consequences of the legal wrong he has done to the plaintiff and to make good the damage caused by such wrong. He is not responsible for damage not caused by his wrong or to pay by way of compensation more than the loss suffered from such wrong. The detailed rules of equity as to causation and the quantification of loss differ, at least ostensibly, from those applicable at common law. But the principles underlying both systems are the same.
>
> *[Beneficiary's right to due administration of the trust]*
> The basic right of a beneficiary is to have the trust duly administered in accordance with the provisions of the trust instrument, if any, and the general law. Thus, in relation to a traditional trust, where the fund is held in trust

for a number of beneficiaries having different, usually successive, equitable interests (for example, A for life with remainder to B), the right of each beneficiary is to have the whole fund vested in the trustees so as to be available to satisfy his equitable interest when, and if, it falls into possession. Accordingly, in the case of a breach of such a trust involving the wrongful paying away of trust assets, the liability of the trustee is to restore to the trust fund, often called 'the trust estate', what ought to have been there.

[Subsisting trust]

The equitable rules of compensation for breach of trust have been largely developed in relation to such traditional trusts, where the only way in which all the beneficiaries' rights can be protected, is to restore to the trust fund what ought to be there. In such a case the basic rule is that a trustee in breach of trust must restore or pay to the trust estate either the assets which have been lost to the estate by reason of the breach, or compensation for such loss. Courts of equity did not award damages but, acting *in personam*, ordered the defaulting trustee to restore the trust estate: see *Nocton v Ashburton (Lord)* [1914] AC 932, pp 952, 958, per Viscount Haldane LC. Thus, the common law rules of remoteness of damage and causation do not apply. However, there does have to be some causal connection between the breach of trust and the loss to the trust estate for which compensation is recoverable, viz, the fact that the loss would not have occurred but for the breach: see also *In Re Miller's Deed Trusts* (1978) 75 LSG 454; *Nestlé v National Westminster Bank plc* [1993] 1 WLR 1260.

[Discontinuance of the trust]

What if at the time of the action claiming compensation for breach of trust those trusts have come to an end? Take as an example again the trust for A for life with remainder to B. During A's lifetime B's only right is to have the trust duly administered and, in the event of a breach, to have the trust fund restored. After A's death, B becomes absolutely entitled. He, of course, has the right to have the trust assets retained by the trustees until they have fully accounted for them to him. But if the trustees commit a breach of trust, there is no reason for compensating the breach of trust by way of an order for restitution and compensation to the trust fund as opposed to the beneficiary himself. The beneficiary's right is no longer simply to have the trust duly administered: he is, in equity, the sole owner of the trust estate. Nor, for the same reason, is restitution to the trust fund necessary to protect other beneficiaries. Therefore, although I do not wholly rule out the possibility that even in those circumstances an order to reconstitute the fund may be appropriate, in the ordinary case, where a beneficiary becomes absolutely entitled to the trust fund, the court orders, not restitution to the trust estate, but the payment of compensation directly to the beneficiary. The measure of such compensation is the same, that is, the difference between what the beneficiary has in fact received and the amount he would have received but for the breach of trust.

[Commercial trusts]

Even applying the strict rules so developed in relation to traditional trusts, it seems to me very doubtful whether Target is now entitled to have the trust fund reconstituted. But in my judgment it is in any event wrong to lift wholesale the detailed rules developed in the context of traditional trusts and then seek to apply them to trusts of quite a different kind [such as commercial and financial trusts].

The obligation to reconstitute the trust fund applicable in the case of traditional trusts reflects the fact that no one beneficiary is entitled to the trust property and the need to compensate all beneficiaries for the breach. That rationale has no application to a case such as the present. To impose such an obligation in order to enable the beneficiary solely entitled (that is, the client) to recover from the solicitor more than the client has in fact lost, flies in the face of common sense and is in direct conflict with the basic principles of equitable compensation. In my judgment, once a conveyancing transaction has been completed, the client has no right to have the solicitor's client account reconstituted as a 'trust fund'.

[Compensation measured at the date of judgment]

A trustee who wrongly pays away trust money, like a trustee who makes an unauthorised investment, commits a breach of trust and comes under an immediate duty to remedy such breach. If immediate proceedings are brought, the court will make an immediate order requiring restoration to the trust fund of the assets wrongly distributed or, in the case of an unauthorised investment, will order the sale of the unauthorised investment and the payment of compensation for any loss suffered. But the fact that there is an accrued cause of action as soon as the breach is committed does not, in my judgment, mean that the quantum of the compensation payable is ultimately fixed as at the date when the breach occurred.

[His Lordship considered the decisions of *Re Dawson (Decd)* [1966] 2 NSWR 211 and *Canson Enterprises Ltd v Boughton & Co* (1991) 85 DLR 129, and continued:] The equitable compensation for breach of trust has to be assessed as at the date of judgment and not at an earlier date. Equitable compensation for breach of trust is designed to achieve exactly what the word compensation suggests: to make good a loss in fact suffered by the beneficiaries and which, using hindsight and common sense, can be seen to have been caused by the breach.

The Court of Appeal relied on two authorities in support of the 'stop the clock' approach: *Alliance & Leicester Building Society v Edgestop Ltd* (1991) unreported, 18 January (Hoffmann J), was another case of mortgage fraud very similar to the present. The plaintiff building society had paid moneys to solicitors in circumstances similar to the present case and the solicitors had wrongly paid them away in breach of their instructions. The building society obtained orders for interim payment against the solicitors on the grounds that they were liable for breach of trust. The case however is distinguishable because of one crucial difference, viz, the judge found that if the building society had known the true facts it would not have made the advance, that is, one of the facts that has to be assumed to the contrary in the present case. In that case, therefore, at the date of judgment, a certain loss had been demonstrated in that the breach of trust had caused the building society to enter into a transaction in which they would not have participated had there been no breach of trust.

In *Bishopsgate Investment Management Ltd v Maxwell (No 2)* [1994] 1 All ER 261, the plaintiff company was a trustee of a pension fund. It brought proceedings for breach of fiduciary duty against a director who had improperly transferred to a stranger shares held by the plaintiff company as such trustee. The Court of Appeal held that the judge had properly given summary judgment for an assessment of damages for breach of fiduciary duty and ordered an interim payment of £500,000. In that case, apart from one possibility, there was no doubt the shares were irretrievably lost and that the value of the shares so lost was in excess of £500,000. The only possibility of reducing that loss was that the plaintiff might have a claim to recover the shares from the transferee on the grounds that the transferee had notice of the impropriety. In the context of the claim for an interim payment, Hoffmann LJ said, at p 267:

> Secondly, [counsel] says it does not follow that the company's loss would be the full value of the shares. It might be able to get something back from Credit Suisse. But the company held the shares as trustee for the pension fund and its liability as trustee was to restore the fund. *Prima facie*, therefore, its loss was its liability to make good the value of the shares. Credit Suisse appears to have taken the shares on the basis that they were registered in the name of Robert Maxwell Group plc and claim to be *bona fide* pledgees. I do not think that the judge was required to speculate on the possibility that the company might be able to defeat this plea. It has no duty to engage in doubtful litigation for the purpose of minimising the loss for which Mr Ian Maxwell is liable. In my judgment, therefore, the judge was acting within his discretion in deciding that £500,000 was a reasonable proportion of the damages which the company was likely to recover.

In my judgment, these remarks provide no basis for holding that final judgment can be given when, on the facts known at the date of judgment, the plaintiff has eventually suffered no loss. First, Hoffmann LJ was only considering the amount of the interim payment: the order for final judgment was for damages to be assessed. Secondly, it is sound law that a plaintiff is not required to engage in hazardous litigation in order to mitigate his loss. The only way in which the plaintiff company's loss could be less than the value of the shares wrongly transferred was if such hazardous litigation should be successfully pursued to judgment. It did not lie in the mouth of the wrong-doing director to seek to reduce the quantum of his liability by relying on the plaintiff company to take steps it was under no legal duty to take. The position is wholly different in the instant case where, on the facts to be assumed, it is demonstrated that no loss has in fact been incurred by reason of the breach of trust.

For these reasons I reach the conclusion that, on the facts which must currently be assumed, Target has not demonstrated that it is entitled to any compensation for breach of trust. Assuming that moneys would have been forthcoming from some other source to complete the purchase from Mirage if the moneys had not been wrongly provided by Redferns in breach of trust, Target obtained exactly what it would have obtained had no breach occurred, that is, a valid security for the sum advanced. Therefore, on the assumption made, Target has suffered no compensatable loss.

Note

In *Templeton Insurance Ltd v Penningtons* [2006] All ER (D) 191, the High Court decided that a firm of solicitors who received a fund subject to a *Quistclose* trust, but disposed of a part of the fund for an unauthorised purpose in breach of trust, was liable to compensate the claimant by way of damages.

Breach of fiduciary duty

In *Nationwide Building Society v Various Solicitors (No 3)*, the High Court applied the principles laid down by Lord Browne-Wilkinson in the *Target* case in assessing damages for breach of fiduciary duty.

Nationwide Building Society v Various Solicitors (No 3) [1999] PNLR 52, HC

Facts

The claimant issued 12 claims against 12 firms of solicitors retained by it. The claims arose out of the consequences of Nationwide making secured advances to borrowers between May 1988 and May 1993. The defendants were retained by the claimant to act for it. In each case, the defendants also acted for the borrowers. The claimant sued the solicitors alleging that in breach of their duties they failed to disclose such facts which, if disclosed, would have led to the claimant withdrawing its offer of advance. Typical examples of breaches, which the defendants were aware of, or ought to have been aware of, concerned a contract price which was less than that specified by the borrower in the mortgage application form; a purchase by way of sub-sale, or even sub-sub sale, with a marked uplift in the contract prices between sale and sub-sale; a borrower who had no intention of residing in the property; and a failure of a borrower to disclose other borrowings.

Held

The correct approach is to put the beneficiary in the position he would have been if the fiduciary had performed his duty. The court reduced the damages awarded to the claimant owing to its contributory negligence:

(a) The court relied on the approach adopted in *Target Holdings Ltd v Redferns*, to the effect that the sensible approach to quantifying the loss suffered as a result of breach of a fiduciary duty was to consider what would have happened if the fiduciary had performed his or her duty. The court could have regard to any inferences which could properly be drawn as to the consequences had the fiduciary performed his or her duties.

(b) Failing any such evidence, the claimant was entitled to be placed in the position he or she was in before the breach occurred.

(c) As a partial defence, it was open to the fiduciary, on whom the onus lay, to establish, if he or she could, what the claimant would have done if there had been no breach of fiduciary duty.

(d) In this case, the court decided that the levels of contributory negligence by the claimant in many cases reduced the damages by between 20% and 90% of the sums claimed.

(e) Factors which were relevant to such findings of contributory negligence included: failure to heed warnings issued by the industry regulator concerning the need to be prudent about lending; placing too much emphasis on the value of the underlying security and too little on the borrower's covenant; lending at excessively high loan-to-value percentages; and failing to spell out its reporting needs in its printed instructions to solicitors.

In a claim based on constructive fraud, the aggrieved party is required to establish a causal connection between the breach of fiduciary duty and the loss. A claim for equitable compensation based on constructive fraud (that is, an abuse or breach of a fiduciary relationship: see *Nocton v Ashburton (Lord)* [1914] AC 932), as distinct from deceit or actual fraud, is not dependent on proof of dishonesty or deception. The equitable remedies available for breach of fiduciary duty are more varied than the common law remedy of damages for fraud or deceit. Equitable remedies include rescission, where restitution is possible; accounting for profits and benefits acquired in breach of duty; and payment of compensation to put the aggrieved party in a pecuniarily similar position to that he was in before the breach. The measure of compensation may not always be the same as damages. In considering equitable compensation in respect of breach of fiduciary obligation, foreseeability and remoteness of damage are, in general, irrelevant. The focus of attention is restitution, but it is still necessary to address the question of causation: see *Swindle v Harrison*.

Swindle and Others v Harrison and Others [1997] 4 All ER 705, CA

Facts

Mrs Harrison owned a house known as 13 Warwick Place, Leamington Spa, where she lived. In June 1991, she mortgaged the house to the National Home Loans Corp (NHL) in order to finance, in part, the purchase of a hotel, Aylesford Hotel. This mortgage raised £180,000. The plaintiffs, Alsters, a firm of solicitors, were instructed to act on behalf of Mrs Harrison. A further £100,000 was proposed to be raised by a loan from Banks' Brewery. In July 1991, contracts for the purchase of Aylesford Hotel for £220,000 were exchanged and completion was fixed for 8 August 1991. Time was of the essence. Access to the hotel was given to Mrs Harrison in order to carry out alterations and repairs. A further loan had failed to materialise. On 7 August 1991, Alsters offered a bridging loan to Mrs Harrison for £75,000 secured by a first charge on Aylesford Hotel. Alsters borrowed this sum from the Royal Bank of Scotland. Mrs Harrison was unaware that the firm would make a profit of £625 as an arrangement fee. Mrs Harrison was advised by Alsters of her right to take independent legal advice, but there was no time for this to be done. Completion took place on 8 August 1991. Aylesford Hotel failed. NHL obtained a possession order on 15 December 1992 on 13 Warwick Place. The plaintiffs started proceedings for possession of Aylesford Hotel. The defendants counterclaimed, on the ground that the plaintiffs were in breach of their fiduciary obligations and were liable to pay the defendants equitable compensation. The judge decided in favour of the plaintiffs and dismissed the counterclaim. The defendants appealed.

Held

The plaintiffs received unauthorised profits for which they were accountable, but the defendants failed to establish a causal connection between the plaintiffs' actions and their loss:

(a) There is no doubt that the solicitor/client relationship is a confidential relationship. Accordingly, Mr Swindle, the defendants' solicitor, was a fiduciary. The firm made an unauthorised 'profit' from its client as a result of this relationship. The profit was part of the arrangement fee as well as the differential in the rate of interest payable on the loan. These material facts were not disclosed to Mrs Harrison. These omissions evidently amounted to breaches of the fiduciary relationship. Mrs Harrison would have been entitled to recover the unauthorised profit made by the firm from the bridging loan.

(b) The particulars of the breaches in respect of the bridging loan were that the plaintiffs failed to disclose to Mrs Harrison:

   (i)   the split of the arrangement fee with the bank;

   (ii) the differential in the rate of interest which they were charging Mrs Harrison; and

   (iii) information that the brewery was unlikely to make the loan.

(c) However, Mrs Harrison's claim was drafted so as to recover compensation for the alleged 'loss' that she suffered. But the 'loss' suffered by Mrs Harrison, namely, her home and a substantial debt to NHL, did not flow from the plaintiffs' breach of fiduciary duty. Mrs Harrison would have accepted the bridging loan and completed the purchase of the hotel, even if full disclosure had been made. Since she would have lost the value of the equity in her home in any event, her claim was not sustainable.

Mummery LJ: A wrongdoer is only liable for the consequences of his being wrong and not for all the consequences of a course of action. In the present case, there was no fiduciary duty on Alsters to abstain from lending money to Mrs Harrison in all circumstances or to prevent her from completing the purchase of Aylesford Hotel in accordance with the contract of purchase. Alsters' duty was to make full disclosure of material facts relevant to the bridging loan to enable her to make a fully informed decision about it. They were in breach of that duty; but, as found by the judge, the probabilities are that Mrs Harrison would still have entered into the bridging loan, even if that breach of duty had not occurred, because she was intent on completing the purchase of the Aylesford Hotel, whatever independent legal advice she received. *The loss which she suffered did not flow from that breach of fiduciary duty. It flowed from her own decision to take the risk involved in mortgaging her own home to finance her son's restaurant business at the hotel.* Alsters were not under a duty to decline to act for Mrs Harrison on the purchase or to stop her from going ahead with the purchase, if that is what she wanted to do [emphasis added].

In brief, the loss of the equity in 13 Warwick Place was not a result of Alsters' breach of fiduciary duty in relation to the bridging loan which enabled Mrs Harrison to complete the contract for the acquisition of the Aylesford Hotel. It would be contrary to common sense and fairness to put on Alsters the whole risk of the purchase transaction on the basis that they had failed to make full disclosure in a related loan transaction, when disclosure would not have affected the client's decision to proceed with the purchase. Mrs Harrison's position would have been the same even if there had been no breach of duty.

Question
What principles are applied by the court in order to measure the damages the claimant is entitled to recover on a claim for breach of trust?

The following examples illustrate the principles that are applied by the courts:

(1) Where the trustees make an unauthorised investment, they are liable for any loss incurred on the sale of the unauthorised assets. The position remains the same even if the sale is ordered by the courts and, but for the order of sale within a specified time, the investments would have produced a profit had they been retained for a longer period. The loss is measured by deducting the proceeds of sale of the unauthorised investment (accruing to the trust) from the amount improperly invested: see *Knott v Cottee*.

Knott v Cottee (1852) 16 Beav 77, CA

Facts
A testator who died in 1844 directed his trustee to invest in government stocks and land in England and Wales. In 1845 and 1846, the executor-trustee invested part of the estate in Exchequer bills, which in 1846 were ordered into court and sold at a loss. In 1848, the court declared that the investment was improper. If, however, the investment had been retained, its realisation at the time of the declaration in 1848 would have resulted in a profit.

Held
The trustee was liable to compensate the estate for the difference in the value of the assets between 1848 and the sale proceeds in 1846:

Romilly MR: The case must either be treated as if these investments had not been made, or had been made for his own benefit out of his own monies, and that he had at the same time retained monies of the testator in his hands.

(2) Where the trustees, in breach of their duties, fail to dispose of unauthorised investments and improperly retain the assets, they will be liable for the difference between the current value of the assets and the value at the time when they should have been sold: see *Fry v Fry*.

Fry v Fry (1859) 28 LJ Ch 591

Facts
A testator who died in March 1834 directed his trustees to sell a house 'as soon as convenient after his death . . . for the most money that could be normally obtained'. In April 1836, the trustees advertised the house for £1,000. In 1837, they refused an offer of £900. A railway was built near the property in 1843 which caused it to depreciate in value. The property remained unsold in 1856, by which time both the original trustees had died.

Held
The court decided that the trustees' estates were liable for the difference between £900 and the sum receivable for the house when it was eventually sold.

(3) Where the trustees retain an authorised investment they will not be liable for breach of trust unless their conduct falls short of the ordinary prudence required of trustees (see *Re Chapman*

[1896] 2 Ch 763). In accordance with the standard investment criteria provided by s 4 of the Trustee Act 2000, the trustees, from time to time, are required to obtain and consider advice on whether the retention of the investment is satisfactory, having regard to the need for diversification and suitability of the investment.

(4) Where the trustees improperly sell authorised investments and re-invest the proceeds in unauthorised investments, they will be liable to replace the authorised investments if these have risen in value, or the proceeds of sale of the authorised investments.

Re Massingberd's Settlement (1890) 63 LT 296, HC

Facts

The trustees of a settlement had power to invest in government securities. In 1875, they sold consols (authorised investments) and re-invested in unauthorised mortgages. The mortgages were called in and the whole of the money invested was recovered. At this time, the consols had risen in value. A claim was brought against the trustees for an account:

Held

The trustees were required to replace the stock sold or its money equivalent.

(5) Where the trustees are directed by the settlor to invest in an identified or specific investment (for example, shares in British Telecom plc) and the trustees fail to acquire the stipulated investments, they will be required to purchase the same at the proper time. If the specified investments have fallen in value, the trustees may be ordered to pay compensation to the trust, equivalent to the difference between the value of the investments at the time the investments should have been made, and the value of the investments at the time of the judgment.

On the other hand, where the trustees retain a discretion to invest in a specified range of investments and they fail to invest, they are chargeable with the trust fund itself and not with the amount of one or other of the investments which might have been purchased. In short, there is no one specific investment which may be used to measure the loss suffered by the trust: see *Shepherd v Mouls* (1845) 4 Hare 500.

(6) Where the trustees, in breach of trust, make a profit in one transaction and a loss in another separate venture, they are not allowed to set off the loss incurred in one scheme against the profit made in a different transaction. However, a set-off is allowed when the profit and loss are made as part of one transaction. This may occur if the trustees adopt a consistent commercial strategy in respect of two or more business ventures with varying success: see *Bartlett v Barclays Bank*.

Bartlett v Barclays Bank Trust Co (No 2) [1980] Ch 515, HC

Facts

The trust estate consisted of a majority shareholding in a property company and the trustees were a professional trust company. For a number of years, the property company maintained traditional investments and these were sufficient to maintain large dividends. As a result of inflation, the board resolved to restructure the investment portfolio into land developments. The new investments, known as the 'Old Bailey' project and the 'Guildford' project, were not completely successful and resulted in a loss to the trust. The court found that the new investments were in breach of trust and, *inter alia*, the trustees attempted to set off a loss made in the 'Old Bailey' project against a gain made in the 'Guildford' scheme.

Held

The court allowed the set-off by the trustees as the mixed fortunes of the commercial arrangement originated from the same transaction:

Brightman J: The general rule as stated in all the textbooks, with some reservations, is that where a trustee is liable in respect of distinct breaches of trust, one of which has resulted in a loss and the other a gain, he is not entitled to set off the gain against the loss unless they arise in the same transaction. The relevant cases are not, however, altogether easy to reconcile. All are centenarians and none is quite like the present. The 'Guildford' development stemmed from exactly the same policy and exemplified the same folly as the 'Old Bailey' project. Part of the profit was in fact used to finance the 'Old Bailey' disaster. By sheer luck the gamble paid off handsomely on capital account. I think it would be unjust to deprive the bank of this element of salvage in the course of assessing the cost of the shipwreck. My order will therefore reflect the bank's right to an appropriate set off.

(7) The principles of restitution that govern the computation of the loss to the trust are concerned with the gross loss suffered by the estate. The tax position of the beneficiaries is irrelevant in the assessment of the loss to the estate. Accordingly, compensation to the trust will not be reduced by an equivalent amount of tax which the beneficiaries would have paid had the trustees not committed a breach of trust (see *BTC v Gourley* [1956] AC 185). In *Bartlett* the court excluded the *Gourley* principle.

Bartlett v Barclays Bank Trust Co Ltd (No 2) [1980] Ch 515, HC

Brightman J: I have reached the conclusion that tax ought not to be taken into account . . . but I do not feel that the established principles on which equitable relief is granted enable me to apply the *Gourley* [1956] AC 185 principles to this case.

(8) As a general rule, the court is entitled to award simple interest under s 35A of the Supreme Court Act 1981 on monetary sums payable by the trustees. There is no consistent view as to the rate of interest. In recent years, some courts have taken the view that the rate of interest is 1% above the minimum lending rate (see *Belmont Finance Corp v Williams Furniture Ltd (No 2)* [1980] 1 All ER 393). Other courts have suggested that the appropriate rate is that allowed from time to time on the court's short-term investment account (see *Bartlett v Barclays Bank (No 2)* [1980] 2 WLR 448).

The court has a discretion to award compound interest against the trustees. The purpose of such an order is not designed to punish the trustees but to require them to disgorge the benefit of the use of the trust funds. The principle here stems from the policy of preventing the trustees profiting from their breach. The Law Lords in the *Westdeutsche* case considered that the jurisdiction to award compound interest originated exclusively in equity. In the absence of fraud, this jurisdiction is exercised against a defendant who is a trustee or otherwise stands in a fiduciary position, and who makes an unauthorised profit or is assumed to have made an unauthorised profit. The majority of the Law Lords decided that, since the defendant did not owe fiduciary duties to the bank in relation to the payment made in June 1987, compound interest would not be awarded. To award compound interest in the circumstances of this case would be tantamount to the courts usurping the function of Parliament. However, simple interest would be awarded on the balance of the fund remaining outstanding, calculated from the date of the original payment by the bank to the local authority.

The two dissenting Law Lords, Lords Goff and Woolf, adopted a more robust view concerning the award of compound interest. They took the view that since the council had the use of the bank's money, which it would otherwise have had to borrow at compound interest, it had, to that extent, profited from the use of the bank's money. Moreover, if the bank had not advanced the money to the council, it would have employed the money in its business. The award of compound interest should be based on the principle of promoting justice or to prevent unjust enrichment. If the defendant has wrongfully profited, or may be presumed to have so profited from having the use of the plaintiff's money, justice demands that the sum be repayable with compound interest. This would be the position irrespective of whether the plaintiff's claim arises *in personam* or *in rem*.

The court decided unanimously that the facts of the case did not reveal a resulting trust in favour of the bank. The circumstances of the transfer of money under the agreement did not fit any of the recognisable categories of resulting trust. Moreover, the parties had entered into a commercial transaction which proved to be void. The plaintiff bank ought not to be given any additional benefits which flow from a proprietary claim, such as priority over the defendant's creditors in the event of insolvency. After all, the bank had entered into a commercial transaction, just like the defendant's other creditors who had contracted with it. The bank's claim to restitution at common law arose from the fact that the payment made by the bank to the council was effected under a purported contract which, unknown to both parties, was *ultra vires* and void *ab initio*. Accordingly, no consideration had been given for the making of the payment.

Westdeutsche Landesbank Girozentrale v Islington BC [1996] 2 All ER 961, HL

Facts

On 16 June 1987, an interest rate swap agreement was made between the council and the bank. The arrangement was intended to run for 10 years, starting on 18 June 1987. The interest sums were to be calculated on a notional principal sum of £25 million. The bank was the fixed rate payer at a rate of 7.5% per annum and the council was the floating rate payer at the domestic London Interbank Offered Rate (LIBOR). In addition, on 18 June 1987, the bank made an 'upfront payment' of £2.5 million to the council. The council made four payments totalling approximately £1.35 million. Further to the decision in *Hazell v Hammersmith and Fulham BC* [1992] 2 AC 1 (where the House of Lords decided that such arrangements were *ultra vires* and void), the council discontinued making payments to the bank. The bank brought an action against the local authority, claiming repayments of approximately £1.15 million, representing the difference between the initial lump sum payment and the payments made by the local authority, with interest as from 18 June 1987. The judge decided that the bank was entitled to recover the principal sum plus compound interest awarded as from April 1990. The Court of Appeal dismissed the local authority's appeal, but allowed a cross-appeal from the bank to award compound interest as from June 1987. The local authority conceded that it was personally liable to repay the balance of the capital, but appealed to the House of Lords against the award of compound interest.

Held

(a) The House of Lords, by a majority, decided that it had no jurisdiction to award compound interest on these facts. Accordingly, only simple interest was payable under s 35A of the Supreme Court Act 1981, as from the date of the accrual of the cause of action, namely, 18 June 1987.

(b) The House of Lords unanimously considered, *obiter*, that the right to recover the balance of the capital of £1.15 million was not based on the notion of a trust but a personal action at law on the ground of a total failure of consideration:

Lord Browne-Wilkinson: My Lords, in the last decade many local authorities entered into interest rate swap agreements with banks and other finance houses. In *Hazell v Hammersmith and Fulham BC* [1992] 2 AC 1, your Lordships held that such contracts were *ultra vires* local authorities and therefore void. Your Lordships left open the question whether payments made pursuant to such swap agreements were recoverable or not. The action which is the subject matter of this appeal is one of a number in which the court has had to consider the extent to which moneys paid under such an agreement are recoverable.

An interest rate swap agreement is an agreement between two parties, by which each agrees to pay the other on a specified date or dates, an amount calculated by reference to the interest which would have accrued over a given period, on a notional principal sum. The rate of interest payable by each party (on the same notional sum) is different. One rate of interest is usually fixed and does not change (and the payer is called 'the fixed rate payer'); the other rate is a variable or floating rate based on a fluctuating interest rate such as the six month London Interbank Offered Rate ('LIBOR') and the payer is known as 'the floating rate payer'. Normally, the parties do not make the actual payments they have contracted for, but the party owing the higher amount pays to the other party the difference between the two amounts.

Compound interest in equity

In the absence of fraud, courts of equity have never awarded compound interest, except against a trustee or other person owing fiduciary duties, who is accountable for profits made from his position. Equity awarded simple interest at a time when courts of law had no right under common law or statute to award any interest. The award of compound interest was restricted to cases where the award was in lieu of an account of profits improperly made by the trustee. We were not referred to any case where compound interest had been awarded in the absence of fiduciary accountability for a profit. The principle is clearly stated by Lord Hatherley LC in *Burdick v Garrick* (1870) LR 5 Ch App 233, p 241:

> ... the court does not proceed against an accounting party by way of punishing him for making use of the plaintiff's money by directing rests, or payment of compound interest, but proceeds upon this principle: either that he has made, or has put himself into such a position as that he is to be presumed to have made 5%, or compound interest, as the case may be.

The principle was more fully stated by Buckley LJ in *Wallersteiner v Moir (No 2)* [1975] QB 373, p 397:

> Where a trustee has retained trust money in his own hands, he will be accountable for the profit which he has made or which he is assumed to have made from the use of the money.

In *AG v Alford* (1855) De GM & G 843, p 851, Lord Cranworth LC said:

> What the court ought to do, I think, is to charge him only with the interest which he has received, or which it is justly entitled to say he ought to have received, or which it is so fairly to be presumed that he did receive that he is estopped from saying that he did not receive it.

These authorities establish that, in the absence of fraud, equity only awards compound (as opposed to simple) interest against a defendant who is a trustee or otherwise in a fiduciary position, by way of recouping from such a defendant an improper profit made by him. It is unnecessary to decide whether in such a case compound interest can only be paid where the defendant has used trust moneys in his own trade or (as I tend to think) extends to all cases where a fiduciary has improperly profited from his trust. Unless the local authority owed fiduciary duties to the bank in relation to the upfront payment, compound interest cannot be awarded.

Although the actual question in issue on the appeal is a narrow one, on the arguments presented, it is necessary to consider fundamental principles of trust law. Does the recipient of money under a contract subsequently found to be void for mistake or as being *ultra vires* hold the moneys received on trust even where he had no knowledge at any relevant time that the contract was void? If he does hold on trust, such trust must arise at the date of receipt or, at the latest, at the date the legal title of the payer is extinguished by mixing moneys in a bank account: in the present case, it does not matter at which of those dates the legal title was extinguished. If there is a trust, two consequences follow: (a) the recipient will be personally liable, regardless of fault, for any subsequent payment away of the moneys to third parties, even though, at the date of such payment, the 'trustee' was still ignorant of the existence of any trust: see Burrows, A, 'Swaps and the friction between common law and equity' [1995] RLR 15; (b) as from the date of the establishment of the trust (ie, receipt or mixing of the moneys by the 'trustee') the original payer will have an equitable proprietary interest in the moneys, so long as they are traceable into whomsoever's hands they come, other than a purchaser, for value of the legal interest without notice. Therefore, although in the present case the only question directly in issue is the personal liability of the local authority as a trustee, it is not possible to hold the local authority liable without imposing a trust which, in other cases will create property rights affecting third parties, because moneys received under a void contract are 'trust property'.

The relevant principles of trust law

[Lord Browne-Wilkinson outlined the core principles concerning a trust (see above) and continued:] Those basic principles are inconsistent with the case being advanced by the bank. The latest time at which there was any possibility of identifying the 'trust property' was the date on which the moneys in the mixed bank account of the local authority ceased to be traceable when the local authority's account went into overdraft in June 1987. At that date, the local authority had no knowledge of the invalidity of the contract but regarded the moneys as its own to spend as it thought fit. There was, therefore, never a time at which both (a) there was defined trust property, and (b) the conscience of the local authority in relation to such defined trust property was affected. The basic requirements of a trust were never satisfied.

Resulting trust

[Lord Browne-Wilkinson classified resulting trusts into two categories: (a) presumed resulting trusts; and (b) express trusts which do not exhaust the whole beneficial interest (see above), and continued:] Applying these conventional principles of resulting trust to the present case, the bank's claim must fail. There was no transfer of money to the local authority on express trusts: therefore a resulting trust of type (b), above could not arise. As to type (a), above, any presumption of resulting trust is rebutted since it is demonstrated that the bank paid, and the local authority received, the upfront payment with the intention that the moneys so paid should become the absolute property of the local authority.

[His Lordship reviewed the decision of *Sinclair v Brougham* [1914] AC 398, and continued:] As has been pointed out frequently over the 80 years since it was decided, *Sinclair v Brougham* is a bewildering authority: no single *ratio decidendi* can be detected; all the reasoning is open to serious objection; it was only intended to deal with cases where there were no trade creditors in competition and the reasoning is incapable of application where there are such creditors. In my view the decision as to rights *in rem* in *Sinclair v Brougham* should also be overruled. Although the case is one where property rights are involved, such overruling should not in practice disturb long settled titles. However, your Lordships should not be taken to be casting any doubt on the principles of tracing as established in *In Re Diplock*.

If *Sinclair v Brougham*, in both its aspects, is overruled the law can be established in accordance with principle and commercial common sense: a claimant for restitution of moneys paid under an *ultra vires*, and therefore void, contract has a personal action at law to recover the moneys paid as on a total failure of consideration; he will not have an equitable proprietary claim which gives him either rights against third parties or priority in an insolvency; nor will he have a personal claim in equity, since the recipient is not a trustee.

[His Lordship expressed his views on the decision of Goulding J in *Chase Manhattan Bank NA v Israel-British Bank (London) Ltd* [1981] Ch 105 and continued:] However, although I do not accept the reasoning of Goulding J, *Chase Manhattan* may well have been rightly decided. The defendant bank knew of the mistake made by the paying bank within two days of the receipt of the moneys: see p 115A. The judge treated this fact as irrelevant (p 114F) but in my judgment it may well provide a proper foundation for the decision. Although the mere receipt of the moneys, in ignorance of the mistake, gives rise to no trust, the retention of the moneys after the recipient bank learned of the mistake may well have given rise to a constructive trust: see *Snell's Equity*, 29th edn, 1990, p 193; Pettit, *Equity and the Law of Trusts*, 7th edn, 1993, p 168; *Metall und Rohstoff AG v Donaldson Lufkin & Jenrette Inc* [1990] 1 QB 391, pp 473–74.

Restitution and equitable rights

Although the resulting trust is an unsuitable basis for developing proprietary restitutionary remedies, the remedial constructive trust, if introduced into English law, may provide a more satisfactory road forward. The court, by way of remedy, might impose a constructive trust on a defendant who knowingly retains property of which the plaintiff has been unjustly deprived. Since the remedy can be tailored to the circumstances of the particular case, innocent third parties would not be prejudiced and restitutionary defences, such as change of position, are capable of being given effect. However, whether English law should follow the United States and Canada by adopting the remedial constructive trust will have to be decided in some future case when the point is directly in issue.

The date from which interest is payable

I fully appreciate the strength of the moral claim of the bank in this case to receive full restitution, including compound interest. But I am unable to accept that it would be right in the circumstances of this case for your Lordships to develop the law in the manner proposed. I take this view for two reasons.

First, Parliament has twice since 1934 considered what interest should be awarded on claims at common law. Both s 3(1) of the [Supreme Court] Act of 1934 and its successor, s 35A of the [Supreme Court] Act of 1981, make it clear that the Act does not authorise the award of compound interest. However, both Acts equally make it clear that they do not impinge on the award of interest in equity. At the time those Acts were passed, and indeed at all times down to the present day, equity has only awarded compound interest in the limited circumstances which I have mentioned. In my judgment, your Lordships would be usurping the function of Parliament if, by expanding the equitable rules for the award of compound interest, this House were now to hold that the court exercising its equitable jurisdiction in aid of the common law can award compound interest which the statutes have expressly not authorised the court to award in exercise of its common law jurisdiction.

Secondly, the arguments relied upon by my noble and learned friends were not advanced by the bank at the hearing. The local authority would have a legitimate ground to feel aggrieved if the case were decided against them on a point which they had had no opportunity to address. Moreover, in my view it would be imprudent to introduce such an important change in the law without this House first having heard full argument upon it.

For these reasons, which are in substance the same as those advanced by my noble and learned friend, Lord Lloyd of Berwick, I am unable to agree with the views of Lord Goff of Chieveley and Lord Woolf.

The question of the jurisdiction of the court to award compound interest arose in *Sempra Metals Ltd v HM Commissioners of Inland Revenue*; the House of Lords decided that the courts have a common law jurisdiction to award interest, simple and compound, as damages on claims for non-payment of debts as well as on other claims for breach of contract and in tort. A cause of action was available at common law for money paid under a mistake of law. The court had jurisdiction at common law to award compound interest where the claimant sought a restitutionary remedy for the time value of money paid under a mistake. The remedy of restitution differed from that of damages. In restitution claims it was the gain that needed to be measured, not the loss to the claimant. The gain is required to be reversed if the claimant was to make good his remedy. The process was one of subtraction, not compensation. As in cases of property other than money where the claim included restitution for the value of the use of the asset that had been transferred, subtraction of the enrichment from the defendant included more than the return of the money that was transferred at its nominal or face value.

Sempra Metals Ltd v HM Commissioners of Inland Revenue [2007] UKHL 34 (House of Lords)

Facts

The claimant company paid Advance Corporation Tax (ACT) on its dividends paid to a member of a group of companies. This was a form of advance payment of mainstream corporation tax. The claimant company sought group relief on the ACT paid. Section 247 of the Income and Corporation Taxes Act 1988 enabled parent companies and subsidiary companies jointly to make an election, having the effect of excluding dividends paid by a subsidiary to its parent from the obligation to pay ACT and the Revenue refused its claim on the ground that group relief was available only when the parent company and its subsidiary were resident in the UK. A group income election was not available if the parent company was resident outside the UK. The European Court of Justice rejected the contention put forward by the Revenue on the ground that that provision contravened parent companies' freedom of establishment, contrary to art 52 (now art 43) of the EC Treaty. In the instant claim by the taxpayer company for compensation in respect of the UK's breach of art 52, the judge held that the compensation should be calculated on a compound basis. The Revenue's appeal was dismissed by the Court of Appeal, which held that ordinary commercial rates on interest would be used. The Revenue appealed.

Held

Dismissing the appeal on the ground of unjust enrichment by the Revenue. The claimant was entitled to an award for restitution of the value of money that was to be measured by compound interest. The subject matter of the taxpayer's claim was the time value of the enrichment, and restitution required that the entirety of that time value be transferred from the Revenue back to the taxpayer. Accordingly, the principal sum to be awarded in the instant case should be calculated on the basis of compound interest.

Lord Hope: The claim that is made in this case, however, is for restitution. It is presented as a claim for the time value of money by which the Defendant was enriched unjustly. The Claimant submits that the common law requires that it be paid a sum which represents the value of the money over the period of that enrichment, and that this sum falls to be calculated by compounding interest over that period.

Simple interest is available under the statute on a sum for which judgment is given for the recovery of a debt or damages or where a sum of that kind is paid before judgment: see s 35A(1) of the Supreme Court Act 1981, inserted by the Administration of Justice Act 1982, s 15(1) and Sch 1, Pt 1. Interest is available in equity in cases that lie within equity's exclusive jurisdiction, especially in cases of fraud or against a trustee or other person in a fiduciary position in respect of profits improperly made. It is also available in the exercise of equity's jurisdiction in aid of rights that are enforceable at common law. In cases that lie within equity's exclusive jurisdiction compound as well as simple interest is available. As Steven Elliott, 'Rethinking interest on withheld and misapplied trust money' [2001] 65 Conv 313 puts it, when applying the inherent jurisdiction the courts have been able to craft interest awards that meet economic realities. But where equity is invoked in aid of the common law the reverse is true. In *Westdeutsche Landesbank Girozentrale v Islington London Borough Council* [1996] 2 All ER 961, the House held, by a majority, that it would be usurping the function of Parliament if it were in equity to award compound interest in aid of the bank's common law claim for repayment of the principal sum, as the court was not authorised to award compound interest in the exercise of its common law jurisdiction under the statute.

I wish to concentrate on the approach that should be taken to the restitutionary cause of action on which Sempra prefers and is entitled to rely, which is its claim that the money was paid under a mistake. The conclusion that the court has jurisdiction to award compound interest as damages at common law is, however, a valuable one. It provides us with a building block which was missing when the House rejected the use of compound interest as a possible solution in equity in *Westdeutsche Landesbank Girozentrale v Islington London Borough Council* [1996] AC 669. Ancillary interest was sought on a sum for which the court was to give judgment in satisfaction of the council's restitutionary claim against the bank. It was common ground that there was no jurisdiction to award compound interest in such a case at common law or by statute: per Lord Goff of Chieveley, p 690H.

In *Kleinwort Benson Ltd v Lincoln City Council* [1999] 2 AC 349, [1998] 4 All ER 513, Lord Goff of Chieveley referred to the development of a coherent law of restitution, a doctrine first recognised by this House in *Lipkin Gorman v Karpnale Ltd* [1992] 4 All ER 512. He said there was a general right of recovery of money paid under a mistake and that it was founded upon the principle of unjust enrichment. At p 373C he said that a blanket rule of non-recovery on the ground of a mistake of law could not survive in a rubric of the law based on that principle. This led him to conclude that there was 'a general right' to recover money paid under a mistake, whether of fact or law, subject to the defences available in the law of restitution: p 375H. At p 377C he said that the common law should now recognise that restitution may be granted in respect of money paid under a mistake of law. At p 379H he said that, subject to any applicable defences, the payer was "entitled" to recover the money paid under a mistake. Throughout his speech he was addressing a common law remedy, not one that was available in equity. I think that it can now be taken as settled that, under the *Kleinwort Benson* principle, a cause of action at common law is available for money paid under a mistake of law: *Deutsche Morgan Grenfell Group plc v IRC* [2007] 1 AC 558, para 62. I also think that the time has come to recognise that the court has jurisdiction at common law to award compound interest where the Claimant seeks a restitutionary remedy for the time value of money paid under a mistake.

The question then is whether the Claimant in unjust enrichment must nevertheless have suffered a loss corresponding to the Defendant's enrichment. In *Unjust Enrichment* 2nd ed, pp 167–168, Professor Birks said that there was no need for this to be the measure of the enrichment:

> By insisting, artificially but firmly, on an enlargement of the everyday sense of 'restitution' we avoid being accidentally trapped by the choice of a word into believing that the answer must be yes. If 'restitution' meant 'giving back', no other answer would be possible. The larger meaning leaves the matter open. An alternative strategy to the same effect would be to switch from 'restitution' to 'disgorgement', which has no restrictive overtone.

I would apply the reasoning in these passages to the claim for interest in this case. A remedy in unjust enrichment is not claim of damages. Nor is it a contractual remedy, so there is no need to search for an express or an implied term as the basis for recovery. The old rules which inhibited awards of interest to ancillary interest on sums due on contractual debts or on claims for money had and received do not apply. The essence of the claim is that the Revenue was unjustly enriched because Sempra paid the tax when it did in the mistaken belief that it was obliged to do so when in fact it was being levied prematurely. So the Revenue must give back to Sempra the whole of the benefit of the enrichment which it obtained. The process is one of subtraction, not compensation.

. . . money has a value, and in my opinion the measure of the right to subtraction of the enrichment that resulted from its receipt does not depend on proof by Sempra of what the Revenue actually did with it. It was the opportunity to turn the money to account during the period of the enrichment that passed from Sempra to the Revenue. This is the benefit which the Defendant is presumed to have derived from money in its hands.

The proposition that a conventional rate should be used leaves open for further discussion questions of detail such as how that rate is to be arrived at and what rests should be adopted. The enrichment principle indicates that these questions should be resolved by looking at the circumstances of the enrichee. The use of ordinary commercial rates of interest, at ordinary rests, would be appropriate if those rates were relevant to the enrichee's circumstances. But I would hold that it is open to the enrichee to show that it would have been able to borrow money at rates or on terms more favourable to it than those available in the ordinary commercial market. If it can do that, then ordinary rates and other terms must give way to those that are relevant to the circumstances of the enrichee. The unusual position of the Revenue has been sufficiently demonstrated. It seems to me that Mr Glick's suggestion is in accordance with principle, and I would adopt it.

Conclusion

For these reasons I agree with Lord Nicholls and Lord Walker that Sempra's claim for restitution ought to be measured by an award of compound interest at conventional rates calculated by reference to the rates of interest and other terms applicable to borrowing by the Government in the market during the relevant period. I would vary para 3 of the judge's order to that effect. I would delete para 2 of the Court of Appeal's order because the assumption on which it was based, that ordinary commercial rates of interest would be used, is being departed from. Otherwise I would dismiss the appeal.

Question
Is simple or compound interest payable on damages awarded against a defendant for breach of trust?

Capper, D, 'Compensation for breach of trust' [1997] Conv 14
Capper reviewed the decision in *Target Holdings Ltd v Redferns* and commented:

> The specific test applied in *Target* [1995] 3 All ER 785 was whether the loss would have happened 'but for' the breach. There seems to be no need to enquire whether the breach is a predominant cause or to compare its importance to other operative causes. But where the loss would have occurred regardless of the breach, the causation requirement is not satisfied.

> Their Lordships' decision that there can be no liability for breach of trust absent causation is to be welcomed. It resolves a difficult problem on which there was no authority and little expression of view from commentators. The contrary view would be an affront to common sense and productive of much injustice . . . the approach to calculating equitable compensation is to look back to the breach and see if the loss can be traced to it. This contrasts with contract and tort where one looks forward from the acceptance of contractual risks or the breach of duty and asks whether the loss occurring was foreseeable.

CONTRIBUTION AND INDEMNITY BETWEEN TRUSTEES

Trustees are under a duty to act jointly and unanimously. In principle, each trustee has an equal role and standing in the administration of the trust. Accordingly, if a breach of trust has occurred, each trustee is equally liable or the trustees are collectively liable to the beneficiary. Thus, the liability of the trustees is joint and several. The innocent beneficiary may sue one or more or all of the trustees.

If a successful claim is brought against one trustee, he has a right of contribution against his co-trustees, with the effect that each trustee will contribute equally to the damages awarded in favour of the claimant, unless the court decides otherwise. The position today is that the right of contribution is governed by the Civil Liability (Contribution) Act 1978. The court has a discretion concerning the amount of the contribution which may be recoverable from any other person liable in respect of the same damage. The discretion is enacted in s 2 of the Act.

Civil Liability (Contribution) Act 1978
S 1(1) . . . any person liable in respect of any damage suffered by another person may recover contribution from any other person liable in respect of the same damage (whether jointly with him or otherwise).

S 2 . . . in any proceedings . . . the amount of contribution shall be such as may be found by the court to be just and equitable having regard to the extent of that person's responsibility for the damage in question.

Section 6(1) A person is liable in respect of any damage . . . if the person who suffered it . . . is entitled to recover compensation from him in respect of that *damage* (whatever the legal basis of his liability, whether tort, breach of contract, breach of trust or otherwise).

In the recent decision, *Charter plc v City Index Ltd*, the High Court considered whether a knowing receipt claim is one to 'recover compensation or damage' within the 1978 Act. The court decided that the effect of the authorities concerning a knowing receipt claim, involves a disposal of the assets of the claimant in breach of trust or fiduciary duty. In other words, a claim for knowing receipt is parasitic on a claim for breach of trust in the sense that it cannot exist in the absence of the breach of trust from which the receipt originated. Such an unauthorised disposal must give rise to a loss to the trust and a liability on the part of the trustee to make good that which he wrongly took or transferred. Accordingly, the legal basis of liability is a breach of trust within the express terms of s 6(1) of the 1978 Act. The loss to the trust constitutes 'damage' in the wide sense of the word. In these circumstances the right of the beneficiary is to recover, on behalf of the trust, compensation in respect of that loss within the 1978 Act. The court concluded that a disposition in breach of trust gives rise to damage, loss or harm to the trust and consequently a liability on the part of both the defaulting trustee and a knowing recipient based on that breach of trust. The effect is that they are required to compensate the trust for that damage, loss or harm by restoring to the trust the equivalent of that loss.

The Pt 20 defendants or third parties contended that a claim for contribution within the 1978 Act was one for compensation for damage suffered whereas the legal basis of a knowing receipt claim was restitutionary and not within the Act. The court considered that the wealth of authorities found such distinction is immaterial for a claim to contribution. In the Court of Appeal decision in *Friends' Provident Life Office v Hillier, Parker, May & Rowden* [1997] QB 85, Auld LJ said:

In my judgment, despite the distinction between a claim for restitution and one for damages, each may be a claim for compensation for damage under sections 1(1) and 6(1) of the Act of 1978. The difference between asking for a particular sum of money back or for an equivalent sum of money for the damage suffered because of the withholding of it is immaterial in this statutory context, which is concerned with "compensation" for "damage".

This decision was followed by the Court of Appeal decisions in *Hurstwood Developments Ltd v Motor and General & Andersley Insurance Services Ltd* [2001] EWCA 1785 and *Niru Battery v Milestone Trading Ltd* [2004] 2 LILR 319. In contrast, in *Royal Brompton NHS Trust v Hammond* [2002] 1 WLR 1397, the House of Lords decided that the phrase 'the same damage' is required to be interpreted and applied on a correct evaluation and comparison of claims to qualify for contribution under s 1(1). Lord Steyn quoted with approval a passage from Goff & Jones, The Law of Restitution, 5th edn, p 396:

To conclude that a restitutionary claim is one for "damage suffered" cannot be justified in principle; nor is it, in our view, consistent with the natural meaning of the statutory language. A claim for restitution cannot be said to be a claim to recover compensation within the meaning of section 1(1).

In *Charter v City Index* the court decided that the *Friends Provident* decision was not overruled expressly or impliedly by the House of Lords decision in *Royal Brompton*. Further, even if the cause of action can be described as restitutionary it does not necessarily follow that it is not also for the recovery of compensation and so within s 6(1), per Morritt J. 'A claim for knowing receipt is a claim for compesation for damage sustained in consequence of a breach of trust notwithstanding that it may also be described as restitutionary.'

Charter plc v City Index Ltd [2006] EWHC 2509 (Ch)

Facts

Charter plc, (Charter) was the holding company of a multinational group of engineering companies. Mr Chu (C) was employed by Charter Central Services Ltd (Central), one of the subsidiary companies within the Charter group, as the treasury manager with particular responsibility for sterling and dollar cash requirements and foreign exchange. City Index Ltd, (Index) the defendant, carried on business of spread betting primarily in relation to financial markets. Between February 2000 and his summary dismissal on 23rd August 2004 C procured that funds of Charter, to a value of over £9m, were transferred to an account of Index in order to finance his personal spread betting transactions with Index. On 10th December 2004 C was convicted of theft in relation to the transfers. In 2005 Charter brought a claim against Index for the recovery of over £9m of its funds, but this claim was settled on terms that Index paid the claimant £5.5m on or before 20th February 2006, which it did. Meanwhile, in 2005 Index commenced Pt 20 proceedings (third party proceedings) against some of the past and current directors of Charter and the group auditors claiming a contribution or indemnity under the Civil Liability (Contribution) Act 1978. None of the sums transferred by C into Index account was retained by Index. Further, the sum of £5.5m which Index paid to Charter by way of settlement was substantially more than Index made on C's account, which was approximately £3m in total. The Pt. 20 defendants contended that:

- Index's claim to contribution was not authorised under the 1978 Act,
- in the alternative, Index's claim to contribution had no real prospect of success for Index used the sums transferred to it for its own purposes.

Held

(1) A claim for knowing receipt was a claim for compensation for damage sustained in consequence of a breach of trust notwithstanding that it also may be described as restitutionary. Accordingly, a disposition in breach of trust gave rise to damage, loss or harm to the trust and the beneficiaries within the Act. Index's claim therefore satisfied the provisions in ss 1 and 6 of the 1978 Act.

(2) There was no real prospect of Index obtaining an order against any of the Pt 20 defendants for contribution towards the sum of £5.5 m. Accordingly, the court would summarily dismiss the Pt 20 proceedings brought by Index.

Morritt J: [on the issue of whether a knowing receipt claim is restitutionary or compensatory, the learned judge declared] I can express my view quite shortly . . . the passages in the speech of Lord Steyn [in the *Royal Brompton* case [2002] 2 All ER 801] dealing with the meaning and application of the phrase 'the same damage' in s 1(1) of the 1978 Act are a necessary part of the decision of the House of Lords in *Royal Brompton Hospital NHS Trust v Hammond (Taylor Woodrow Construction (Holdings) Ltd, Pt 20 defendant)* [2002] 2 All ER 801, [2002] 1 WLR 1397. But in that case no question of restitution arose as all relevant liabilities arose in contract or tort. By contrast, in the *Friends' Provident* case questions of restitution and knowing receipt did arise. The passage in the judgment of Auld LJ ([1995] 4 All ER 260 at 272–273, [1997] QB 85 at 102–103) to which the criticism of *Goff and Jones* and Lord Steyn was directed related to the claim in restitution not that dealing with knowing receipt. It is true that in dealing with the latter claim (see [1995] 4 All ER 260 at 277–278, [1997] QB 85 at 108), Auld LJ referred back to his earlier construction of ss 1(1) and 6(1) of the 1978 Act but his conclusion that the claim in knowing receipt came within the Act was not criticised. Accordingly I share the views of counsel in *Niru Battery Manufacturing Co v Milestone Trading Ltd (No 2)*, supported by the *prima facie* opinions of the members of the Court of Appeal in that case, that the statement of Lord Steyn ([2002] 2 All ER 801 at [33], [2002] 1 WLR 1397) is *obiter dictum*. It follows that the decision of the Court of Appeal in *Friends' Provident Life Office v Hillier Parker May & Rowden (a firm) (Estates and General plc and ors, third parties)* [1995] 4 All ER 260 at 275–278, [1997] QB 85 at 106–108 is binding on me for the proposition that a claim in knowing receipt is one 'to recover compensation . . . in respect of damage'.

However, given the weight to be attached to the obiter dicta in the *Royal Brompton NHS Trust* case, I should consider the position if I am wrong in concluding that I am bound by the decision on knowing receipt in the *Friends' Provident* case. Counsel for the directors and for the auditors rely on a number of judicial statements as to the nature of the liability for knowing receipt in contexts other than the 1978 Act. Thus, in *Royal Brunei Airlines Sdn Bhd v Tan* [1995] 3 All ER 97 at 103, [1995] 2 AC 378 at 386, [1995] 3 WLR 64 Lord Nicholls of Birkenhead stated in relation to the two heads of liability established in *Barnes v Addy* (1874) LR 9 Ch App 244 that 'recipient liability is restitution-based; accessory liability is not'. In *Twinsectra Ltd v Yardley* [2002] UKHL 12 at [105], [2002]

2 All ER 377 at [105], [2002] 2 AC 164, Lord Millett described the cause of action for knowing receipt as 'restitutionary'. In *Grupo Torras v Al-Sabah* [1999] All ER (D) 698 (at para V.4) Mance J considered that liability based on knowing receipt did not 'depend on the commission of any wrong or give rise to any obligation to make good any loss other than by way of restitution'. In *Bank of Credit and Commerce International (Overseas) Ltd (in liq) v Akindele* [2000] 4 All ER 221 at 235–236, [2001] Ch 437 at 455, Nourse LJ recognised liability for knowing receipt as part of our law of restitution. Similarly in *Niru Battery Manufacturing Co v Milestone Trading Ltd* [2004] 1 All ER (Comm) 193 at [149]–[162], [2004] QB 985 Clarke LJ treated the claim for knowing receipt as a species of restitution.

. . . if a cause of action can be described as restitutionary it does not necessarily follow that it is not also for the recovery of compensation and so within s 6(1) of the 1978 Act. The question is whether a claim based on knowing receipt is a claim to recover compensation for damage sustained by virtue of the initial breach of trust. . . . I consider that it is even if it also may be described as restitutionary. Accordingly even if I am bound by the dictum of Lord Steyn I must consider whether the remedy of knowing receipt is only restitutionary or whether it is also compensatory. In my view it is compensatory within the provisions of s 6(1) even if it may also be described as restitutionary.

In summary therefore I conclude that the Pt 20 claim of City Index does satisfy the provisions of ss 1 and 6 of the 1978 Act because (a) the decision of the Court of Appeal in respect of knowing receipt in *Friends' Provident Life Office v Hillier Parker May & Rowden (a firm) (Estates and General plc and ors, third parties)* [1995] 4 All ER 260 at 275–278, [1997] QB 85 at 106–108 was not overruled expressly or by implication by the House of Lords in *Royal Brompton Hospital NHS Trust v Hammond (Taylor Woodrow Construction (Holdings) Ltd, Pt 20 defendant)* [2002] 2 All ER 801, [2002] 1 WLR 1397; and (b) a claim for knowing receipt is a claim for compensation for damage sustained in consequence of a breach of trust notwithstanding that it may also be described as restitutionary. I derive comfort for those views from the fact that if I am wrong it would seem that all the counsel and all the judges concerned with *Dubai Aluminium Co Ltd v Salaam (Livingstone and ors, third parties)* [2002] UKHL 48, [2003] 1 All ER 97, [2003] 2 AC 366 failed to appreciate that the 1978 Act did not apply to any of the contribution claims made and considered by Rix J, the Court of Appeal and the House of Lords notwithstanding that the *Royal Brompton NHS Trust* case was referred to in argument in the House of Lords. Accordingly, in my judgment, the Pt 20 claim is not liable to be struck out or summarily dismissed on this ground.

The question what, if any, contribution should be ordered to be paid by the directors or the auditors is one for the discretion of the court to be exercised in the light of all the relevant facts and circumstances. At this stage I must assume that City Index will be successful in establishing the negligence of the directors and auditors on which it relies. It will follow that their acts and omissions were a cause of the loss suffered by Charter. But it does not follow that if their conduct is a cause then they should be ordered to pay some contribution. The submission of counsel for City Index to that effect is contrary to the conclusions of the Court of Appeal and House of Lords in each of *Dubai Aluminium Co Ltd v Salaam (Livingstone and ors, third parties)* [2003] 1 All ER 97, [2003] 2 AC 366, *Cressman v Coys of Kensington (Sales) Ltd (McDonald, Pt 20 defendant)* [2004] 1 WLR 2775 and the *Niru Battery* case.

Each of those cases shows the importance to be attached to the receipt and retention of the relevant property by one of those found liable to the claimant. In this case City Index admits to having made a profit of £3m from the spread betting activities of Mr Chu financed by the £9m he stole from Charter. In my judgment it is inconceivable that City Index would get contribution from the directors or auditors such as to restore to them any part of that profit. This much I understood counsel for City Index to accept.

Accordingly the issue is whether there is a real prospect of City Index obtaining contribution in respect of the balance of £2·5m it paid to Charter to settle the claim. In my view there is not.

The general rule in equity, as exemplified in *Bahin v Hughes* (1886) 31 Ch D390 and *Wynne v Tempest* [1897] Ch 110 cannot be dismissed on the grounds that the 1978 Act provides for a new regime. They are clear instances of what, in common circumstances, is to be regarded as just and equitable. In each case the overriding consideration is the fact that one of the two trustees received the trust money and made use of it. It is not necessary that he should have retained it. The overriding cause of the loss in all such cases is that the recipient, having received the money, instead of paying it back paid it to someone else. It would be unwise to suggest that the recipient, with the requisite knowledge, of money wrongly applied by a fiduciary can never obtain contribution from the fiduciary. But no facts were relied on by counsel for City Index as taking this case out of the normal rule. Nor, in my judgment, is there any reason of justice or equity why, in the general run of cases, negligent directors and auditors should contribute to the liability of the knowing recipient who has either retained the money so received or paid it away for his own purposes, use and benefit.

The 1978 Act does not apply to an indemnity which is governed entirely by case law. There are three circumstances when a trustee is required to indemnify his co-trustees in respect of their liability to the beneficiaries:

(1) Where one trustee has fraudulently obtained a benefit from a breach of trust. Such a claim for indemnity failed in *Bahin v Hughes*.

Bahin v Hughes (1886) 31 Ch D 390, CA

Facts

A testator bequeathed a legacy of £2,000 to his three daughters, Miss Hughes, Mrs Edwards and Mrs Burden, on specified trusts. Miss Hughes did all the administration of the trust. The trust money was invested in unauthorised investments resulting in a loss. Miss Hughes and Mrs Burden (in whose name the money was entered) selected the investment and by letter told Mrs Edwards, who failed to give her consent. The trustees were liable to the beneficiaries for breach of trust. Mr Edwards (whose wife had died) claimed that Miss Hughes, as an active trustee, ought to indemnify him against his late wife's liability.

Held

The defendants were jointly and severally liable to replace the £2,000 and Edwards had no right of indemnity against Miss Hughes:

> **Cotton LJ:** . . . where one trustee has got the money into his own hands, and made use of it, he will be liable to his co-trustee to give him an indemnity . . . relief has only been granted against a trustee who has himself got the benefit of the breach of trust, or between whom and his co-trustees there has existed a relation which will justify the court in treating him solely liable for the breach of trust . . . Miss Hughes was the active trustee and Mr Edwards did nothing, and in my opinion it would be laying down a wrong rule that where one trustee acts honestly, though erroneously, the other trustee is to be held entitled to an indemnity who by doing nothing neglects his duty more than the acting trustee . . . In my opinion the money was lost just as much by the default of Mr Edwards as by the innocent though erroneous action of his co-trustee, Miss Hughes.

(2) Where the breach of trust was committed on the advice of a solicitor-trustee. In addition to a breach of trust, the requirements here are:

(a) the co-trustee is a solicitor; and

(b) the breach of trust was committed in respect of his advice; and

(c) the co-trustees had relied solely on his advice and did not exercise an independent judgment.

This principle is illustrated by *Re Partington*.

Re Partington (1887) 57 LT 654, HC

Facts

Mrs Partington and Mr Allen, a solicitor, were trustees who were liable for a breach of trust. The trust fund was invested in an improper mortgage which resulted in a loss. Mr Allen had assured Mrs Partington that he would find a good investment on behalf of the trust. He failed in his duties to verify statements by the borrower, he failed to give proper instructions to the valuers and he did not give sufficient information to Mrs Partington to enable her to exercise an independent judgment.

Held

Mrs Partington was entitled to claim an indemnity from Mr Allen.

In *Head v Gould*, the claim for an indemnity against a solicitor-trustee failed because the co-trustee actively encouraged the solicitor-trustee to commit the breach of trust. The mere fact that the co-trustee is a solicitor is insufficient to establish the claim.

Head v Gould [1898] 2 Ch 250, HC

Kekewich J: I do not think that a man is bound to indemnify his co-trustee against any loss merely because he was a solicitor, when that co-trustee was an active participator in the breach of trust complained of, and is not proved to have participated merely in consequence of the advice and control of the solicitor.

(3) According to the rule in *Chillingworth v Chambers* [1896] 1 Ch 385, where a trustee is also a beneficiary (whether he receives a benefit or not is immaterial) and the trustees are liable for breach of trust, the beneficiary/trustee is required to indemnify his co-trustee, to the extent of his beneficial interest. If the loss exceeds the beneficial interest, the trustees will share the surplus loss equally.

Question

When is a trustee entitled to claim a contribution or indemnity from his co-trustees for breach of trust?

DEFENCES TO A CLAIM FOR BREACH OF TRUST

In pursuance of a claim against trustees for breach of trust, there are a number of defences which the trustees are entitled to raise.

Knowledge and consent of the beneficiaries

A beneficiary who has freely consented to or concurred in a breach of trust is not entitled to renege on his promise and bring a claim against the trustees.

In order to be estopped from bringing a claim against the trustees, the beneficiary is required to be of full age and sound mind, with full knowledge of all the relevant facts, and to exercise an independent judgment. The burden of proof will be on the trustees to establish these elements: see *Nail v Punter*.

Nail v Punter (1832) 5 Sim 555

Facts

The husband of a life tenant under a trust encouraged the trustees to pay him money from the trust fund in breach of trust. The life tenant commenced proceedings against the trustees, but died shortly afterwards. The husband became a beneficiary and continued the action against the trustees for breach of trust.

Held

The action could not succeed because the husband was a party to the breach.

The trustees are required to prove that the consent was not obtained as a result of undue influence. In *Re Pauling's Settlement Trust* (see p 507 above for the facts), the trustees claimed that the children were not entitled to bring an action because they had consented to the advancements. The court rejected this argument and decided that the consent was not freely obtained from the children because they were under the influence of their parents who benefited from the advancements. The statement of the principle by Wilberforce J was approved by the Court of Appeal.

Re Pauling's Settlement Trust [1964] Ch 303, HC

Wilberforce J: The court has to consider all the circumstances in which the concurrence of the beneficiary was given with a view to seeing whether it is fair and equitable that, having given his concurrence, he should afterwards turn around and sue the trustees ... subject to this, it is not necessary that he should know that what he is concurring in is a breach of trust, provided that he fully understands what he is concurring in, and ... it is not necessary that he should himself have directly benefited by the breach of trust.

Impounding the interest of a beneficiary

In the above section, the beneficiary who concurs or acquiesces in a breach of trust will not be allowed to bring a claim against the trustees. However, this principle does not prevent other beneficiaries from bringing an action against the trustees. In these circumstances, the court has a power to impound the interest of the beneficiary who instigated the breach for the purpose of indemnifying the trustees.

Under the inherent jurisdiction of the court, a beneficiary who instigated the breach of trust may be required to indemnify the trustees. The rule was extended in s 62 of the Trustee Act 1925.

Trustee Act 1925, s 62

Where a trustee commits a breach of trust at the instigation or request or with the consent in writing of a beneficiary, the court may if it thinks fit make such order as the court seems just for impounding all or any part of the interest of the beneficiary in the trust estate by way of indemnity to the trustee or persons claiming through him.

It is clear from s 62 that the court has a discretion which it will not exercise if the beneficiary was not aware of the full facts. Section 62 is applicable irrespective of an intention, on the part of the beneficiary, to receive a personal benefit or not, provided that the beneficiary was fully appraised of the facts. The beneficiary's consent is required to be in writing as stipulated by s 62 of the 1925 Act.

Relief under s 61 of the Trustee Act 1925

Trustee Act 1925, s 61

If it appears to the court that a trustee . . . is or may be personally liable for any breach of trust . . . but has acted honestly and reasonably, and ought fairly to be excused for the breach of trust and for omitting to obtain the directions of the court in the matter in which he committed such breach, then the court may relieve him either wholly or partly from personal liability for the same.

This section re-enacted, with slight modifications, s 3 of the Judicial Trustees Act 1896.

The section provides three main ingredients for granting relief, namely:

(a) the trustee acted honestly;

(b) the trustee acted reasonably; and

(c) the trustee ought fairly to be excused in respect of the breach and omitting to obtain directions of the court.

These ingredients are cumulative and the trustee has the burden of proof.

The expression 'honestly' means that the trustee acted in good faith. This is a question of fact. The word 'reasonably' indicates that the trustee acted prudently. If these two criteria are satisfied, the court has a discretion whether to excuse the trustee or not. The test in exercising the discretion is to have regard to both the interests of the trustees and the beneficiaries, and to decide whether the breach of trust ought to be forgiven in whole or in part. In the absence of special circumstances, a trustee who has acted honestly and reasonably ought to be relieved. In *Perrins v Bellamy*, the trustees were able to discharge this burden of proof.

Perrins v Bellamy [1899] 1 Ch 797, HC

Facts

The trustees of a settlement were erroneously advised by their solicitor that they had a power of sale. They sold the leaseholds comprised in the settlement, thereby diminishing the income of the plaintiff, the tenant for life. The plaintiff commenced an action against the trustees for breach of trust. The lay trustees claimed relief under the predecessor to s 61 of the Trustee Act 1925.

Held

The court in its discretion granted relief to the trustees for they acted in good faith in reliance on the advice of their solicitors:

> **Kekewich J:** I venture, however, to think that, in general and in the absence of special circumstances, a trustee who has acted 'reasonably' ought to be relieved, and it is not incumbent on the court to consider whether he ought 'fairly' to be excused, unless there is evidence of a special character showing that the provisions of the section ought not to be applied in his favour.

Each case is decided on its own facts. A factor that is capable of influencing the court is whether the trustee is an expert, professional trustee or not.

In *National Trustee Co of Australia Ltd v General Finance Co* [1905] AC 373, the court refused relief to professional trustees who had acted honestly and reasonably and on the advice of a solicitor in committing a breach of trust.

A similar view was echoed by Brightman J in *Bartlett v Barclays Bank* (for the facts, see p 471 above). The professional trustee company was refused relief under s 61 of the Trustee Act 1925 because it acted unreasonably in failing to keep abreast or informed of the changes in the activities of the investment company.

Bartlett v Barclays Bank Trust Co Ltd (No 2) [1980] Ch 515, HC

> **Brightman J:** A trust corporation holds itself out in its advertising literature as being above ordinary mortals. With a specialist staff of trained trust officers and managers, with ready access to financial information and professional advice, dealing with and solving trust problems day after day, the trust corporation holds itself out, and rightly, as capable of providing an expertise which it would be unrealistic to expect and unjust to demand from the ordinary prudent man or woman who accepts, probably unpaid and sometimes reluctantly from a sense of family duty, the burden of trusteeship. Just as, under the law of contract, a professional person possessed a particular skill is liable for breach of contract if he neglects to use the skill and experience which he professes, so I think that a professional corporate trustee is liable for breach of trust if loss is caused to the trust fund, because it neglects to exercise the special care and skill which it professes to have.

Other factors that have been taken into account by the courts are the status of the adviser to the trust and the size of the trust estate. It has been suggested that nothing less than the advice of a Queen's Counsel should be taken by the trustees in respect of a large estate. Other considerations that are relevant include whether the breach of trust originated from a complicated rule of law, and whether the trustees acted on an erroneous belief that the beneficiaries had consented.

Question

When a trustee is liable for breach of trust, what reliefs are available to him or her in respect of the beneficiaries, their interests and concerning the trustee's conduct?

Limitation

The limitation periods concern the time limits during which a beneficiary is entitled to pursue a cause of action in respect of trust property. The remarks of Kekewich J in *Re Timmins* [1902] 1 Ch 176 refer to the rationale concerning an earlier limitation statute:

> **Kekewich J:** The intention of the statute was to give a trustee the benefit of the lapse of time when, although he had done something legally or technically wrong, he had done nothing morally wrong or dishonest, but it was not intended to protect him where, if he pleaded the statute, he would come off with something he ought not to have, ie, money of the trust received by him and converted to his own use.

Six-year limitation period

Under s 21(3) of the Limitation Act 1980, the general rule concerning the limitation period for claims for breach of trust is six years from the date on which the cause of action accrued. A cause of action does not accrue in respect of future interests (remainders and reversions) until the interest falls into possession. Thus, a life tenant under a trust is required to bring a claim within six years of the breach of trust but a remainderman has up to six years from the death of the life tenant before his cause of action becomes time-barred. In addition, time does not begin to run against a beneficiary suffering from a disability (infancy or mental incapacity) at the time of the breach until the disability ends. For these purposes, a trustee includes a personal representative and no distinction is drawn between express, implied or constructive trustees.

Limitation Act 1980, s 21(3)

Subject to the preceding provisions of this section, an action by a beneficiary to recover trust property or in respect of any breach of trust, not being an action for which a period of limitation is prescribed by any other provision of this Act, shall not be brought after the expiration of six years from the date on which the right of action accrued.

For the purposes of this sub-section, the right of action shall not be treated as having accrued to any beneficiary entitled to a future interest in the trust property until the interest falls into possession.

In *Armitage v Nurse* (for the facts, see p 512 above), Millett LJ considered the scope of s 21 of the Limitation Act 1980.

Armitage v Nurse [1997] 3 WLR 1046, CA

Millett LJ:

Limitation

[His Lordship referred to s 21 of the Limitation Act 1980, and continued:] Two questions have been argued. The first is whether s 21(1)(a) is limited to cases of fraud or fraudulent breach of trust property so called, that is to say to cases involving dishonesty. The judge held that it is. In my judgment, he was plainly right. I have explained the meaning of the word 'fraud' in a trustee exemption clause, and there is no reason to ascribe a different meaning to the word where it appears in s 21(1)(a) of the Limitation Act 1980.

The second question is whether Paula had a present interest while she was under the age of 25 or whether she had only a future interest which fell into possession when she attained that age. The judge held that she had merely a future interest. In my judgment, he was right. Until Paula attained 25 the trustees held the trust fund upon trust to accumulate the income with power instead to pay it to Paula or to apply it for her benefit. She had no present right to capital or income but only the right to require the trustees to consider from time to time whether to accumulate the income or to exercise their power to pay or apply it for her benefit. That, in my judgment, is not an interest in possession.

The rationale of s 21(3) of the Limitation Act 1980 appears to me to be not that a beneficiary with a future interest has not the means of discovery, but that he should not be compelled to litigate (at considerable personal expense) in respect of an injury to an interest which he may never live to enjoy.

Section 21(3) of the Limitation Act 1980 is drafted by reference to claims brought by beneficiaries. If the trustees bring such a claim the courts will consider, in substance, who are the real litigants. In this respect the real litigants are required to be those who have a real interest in the outcome. Accordingly, trustees who do not have a personal interest may bring claims exclusively on behalf of beneficiaries with a personal interest, albeit in the future, outside the six-year limitation period.

Cattley v Pollard [2006] EWHC 3130 (High Court)

Facts

A solicitor/trustee misappropriated a substantial amount of assets belonging to the estate of a deceased. New trustees were appointed and brought claims against the fraudulent former trustee. These proceedings were settled. Further proceedings were brought outside the six-year period against the former trustee's accomplices but on behalf of nine life beneficiaries and 17 residual beneficiaries whose interests were yet to fall into possession.

Held

The claim was not statute barred as regards the beneficiaries with future interests.

> **Richard Sheldon QC:** I find that s 21(3) applies in the present case, at least by analogy to the present claim brought by the trustees. The claimants as trustees have no personal interest in the outcome. The real litigants – those with a real interest in the outcome – are the beneficiaries. I consider that when s 21(3) refers to an action by beneficiaries, it includes, at least by analogy, actions brought exclusively on their behalf by trustees who do not have any personal interest in the outcome. This approach echoes that followed in *St Mary Magdalen, Oxford (President, etc) v A-G* (1857) 6 HL Cas 189 and the argument considered by Harman J in *A-G v Cocke* [1988] 2 All ER 391, [1988] Ch 414. It follows that the last subparagraph of s 21(3) applies to the second proceedings. Time has not begun to run as regards the beneficiaries with a future interest in the estate and the second proceedings are therefore not time-barred.

Limitation periods for claims for accounts

Section 23 of the Limitation Act 1980 declares that in an action for an account the same limitation period will apply as is applicable to the claim which underlies the duty to account.

Limitation Act 1980, s 23

An action for an account shall not be brought after the expiration of any time limit under this Act which is applicable to the claim which is the basis of the duty to account.

The application of s 23 of the Limitation Act 1980 was considered in *Paragon Finance v Thakerar*.

Paragon Finance v Thakerar [1999] I All ER 400, CA

Facts

The defendant solicitor acted in breach of his contractual duties to the claimant. The action for breach of contract and negligence was brought more than six years after the cause of action had accrued. The claimant applied to the court for leave to amend its claim in order to allege fraud and intentional breach of fiduciary duty.

Held

The facts did not reveal a new cause of action and the claim was statute barred:

> **Millett LJ:** Actions founded on tort are barred after six years, and there is no exception for actions founded on fraud, though the start of the limitation period may be deferred in such cases. There is no logical basis for distinguishing between an action for damages for fraud at common law and the corresponding claim in equity for 'an account as constructive trustee' founded on the same fraud. Section 21 of the 1980 Act can sensibly be limited to wrongs cognisable by equity in the exercise of its exclusive jurisdiction. It makes no sense to extend it to the exercise of its concurrent jurisdiction. Any principled system of limitation should be based on the cause of action and not the remedy. There is a case for treating fraudulent breach of trust differently from other frauds, but only if what is involved really is a breach of trust. There is no case for distinguishing between an action for damages for fraud at common law and its counterpart in equity based on the same facts merely because equity employs the formula of constructive trust to justify the exercise of the equitable jurisdiction.

In *Nelson v Rye* [1996] 2 All ER 186, a musician sued his manager for an account of fees and royalties extending back for a period in excess of six years before the action. The High Court allowed the claim on the ground that the action was in respect of a breach of fiduciary duty. This decision was doubted and the case overruled by Millett LJ in *Paragon Finance*.

> **Millett LJ:** Whether he [Mr Rye] was in fact a trustee of the money may be open to doubt. Unless I have misunderstood the facts or they were very unusual it would appear that the defendant was entitled to pay receipts into his own account, mix them with his own money, use them for his own cash flow, deduct his own commission, and account for the balance to the plaintiff only at the end of the year. It is fundamental to the existence of a trust that the trustee is bound to keep the trust property separate from his own and apply it exclusively for the benefit of his beneficiary. Any right on the part of the defendant to mix the money which he received with his own and use it for his own cash flow would be inconsistent with the existence of a trust. So

would a liability to account annually, for a trustee is obliged to account to his beneficiary and pay over the trust property on demand. The fact that the defendant was a fiduciary was irrelevant if he had no fiduciary or trust obligations in regard to the money. If this was the position, then the defendant was a fiduciary and subject to an equitable duty to account, but he was not a constructive trustee. His liability arose from his failure to account, not from his retention and use of the money for his own benefit, for this was something which he was entitled to do.

Unless the defendant was a trustee of the money which he received, however, the claim for an account was barred after six years. The fact that the defendant was a fiduciary did not make his failure to account a breach of fiduciary duty or make him liable to pay equitable compensation. His liability to account arose from his receipt of money in circumstances which made him an accounting party. It did not arise from any breach of duty, fiduciary or otherwise. The defendant was merely an accounting party who had failed to render an account.

Accordingly, in so far as it decided that the defendant was liable to account without limit of time even if the money was not trust money, *Nelson v Rye* was in my opinion wrongly decided.

An action for an account, in the absence of a trust, is based on legal, not equitable, rights. There is therefore no equitable content in such an action. Thus, an action for an account for breach of contract remains a contractual claim and the limitation period at common law applies.

In *Coulthard v Disco Mix Club and Others*, the High Court decided that the six-year period was applicable to an action for an account arising out of a contractual claim. The court decided that the 1980 Act could not be sidestepped by framing a contractual claim as a claim for breach of fiduciary duty.

Coulthard v Disco Mix Club and Others [2000] 1 WLR 707, HC

Facts

The claimant, a barrister, had previously worked as a disc jockey. He claimed that the defendants had under-accounted for moneys due to him under various management and agency agreements concerning disco beat-mixing recordings. The claim was brought outside the six-year period of limitation, but the claimant framed his action for an account arising from breach of fiduciary duties, relying on *Nelson v Rye*.

Held

The claim was struck out as being vexatious and frivolous. The court adopted the principles stated by Millett LJ in *Paragon* and refused to follow *Nelson v Rye* on the ground that the facts in that case did not give rise to a trust:

> **Mr Jules Sher QC:** The best description of the circumstances in which a Court of Equity acted by analogy to the statute is, I think, contained in the speech of Lord Westbury in *Knox v Gye* (1872) 5 App Cas 656:
>
> > The general principle [is that] where a Court of Equity assumes a concurrent jurisdiction with Courts of Law no account will be given after the legal limit of six years, if the statute is pleaded. Where the remedy in Equity is correspondent to the remedy at Law, and the latter is subject to a limit in point of time by the Statute of Limitations, a Court of Equity acts by analogy to the statute, and imposes on the remedy it affords the same limitation. This is the meaning of the common phrase, that a Court of Equity acts by analogy to the Statute of Limitations, the meaning being, that where the suit in Equity corresponds with an action at Law which is included in the words of the statute, a Court of Equity adopts the enactment of the statute as its own rule or procedure.
>
> Two things emerge from this passage. First, where the Court of Equity was simply exercising a concurrent jurisdiction giving the same relief as was available in a court of law the statute of limitation would be applied. But secondly, even if the relief afforded by the Court of Equity was wider than that available at law, the Court of Equity would apply the statute by analogy where there was 'correspondence' between the remedies available at law or in equity.
>
> Now, in my judgment, the true breaches of fiduciary duty (ie the allegations of deliberate and dishonest under-accounting) are based on the same factual allegations as the common law claims for fraud. The breaches of fiduciary duty are thus no more than the equitable counterparts of the claims at common law. The Court of

Equity, in granting relief for such breaches would be exercising a concurrent jurisdiction with that of the common law. I have little doubt but that to such a claim the statute would have been applied.

One could scarcely imagine a more correspondent set of remedies as damages for fraudulent breach of contract and equitable compensation for breach of fiduciary duty in relation to the same factual situation, namely, the deliberate withholding of money due by a manager to his artist. It would have been a blot on our jurisprudence if those self same facts gave rise to a time bar in the common law courts but none in the Court of Equity.

Exceptions to the six-year limitation period

Under s 21(1) of the Limitation Act 1980, where a beneficiary brings a claim in respect of any fraud by the trustee, or to recover trust property or the proceeds of sale from trust property (that is, claims *in rem* (see below)), the limitation period fixed shall not apply. A transferee from a trustee is in the same position as the trustee unless he or she is a *bona fide* transferee of the legal estate for value without notice.

Limitation Act 1980, s 21(1)

No period of limitation prescribed by this Act shall apply to an action by a beneficiary under a trust, being an action:

(a) in respect of any fraud or fraudulent breach of trust to which the trustee was a party or privy; or

(b) to recover from the trustee trust property or the proceeds of trust property in the possession of the trustee, or previously received by the trustee and converted to his use.

The reason for this exception is that the possession of the property by a trustee is never by virtue of any right of his own, but is acquired initially for and on behalf of the beneficiaries. The trustee's ownership or possession is representative of the beneficiary's interest. The effect is that time does not run in the trustee's favour and against the beneficiary.

Section 38 of the Limitation Act 1980 provides that the expressions 'trust' and 'trustee' have the same meanings respectively as in the Trustee Act 1925. This extends the meaning of those expressions to 'implied and constructive trusts': see s 68(17) of the Trustee Act 1925.

The relaxation of the limitation period laid down in s 21(1) of the 1980 Act is not restricted to express trustees but extends to those in an analogous position who have abused the trust and confidence reposed in them.

In *Halton International Inc and another v Guernroy Ltd* the Court of Appeal decided that the exception enacted in s 21(1) of the Limitation Act 1980 was not applicable to a disputed transaction that did not involve proprietary rights. Carnwath LJ remarked that the exception is required to be clearly justified by reference to the statutory language and the policy behind it. The policy 'is not about culpability as such' but about 'deemed possession – the fiction that the possession of property by a trustee is treated from the outset as that of the beneficiary'.

Halton International Inc and another v Guernroy Ltd [2006] EWCA Civ 801 (CA)

Facts

The parties were all shareholders in an airline business, British Mediterranean Airways Ltd (BMed). The claimants were two of the original founders of BMed. The defendant was also a shareholder in BMed, its shares were held as nominee for various trusts connected with Wafic Said, a wealthy businessman. BMed 's initial performance was poor and in 1996 it needed substantial fresh capital. In August 1996 BMed reached a franchise agreement with British Airways (BA) but this was conditional on BMed being able to raise £5.5 million of new equity. There were insuperable difficulties raising this capital until October 1996; an arrangement was reached between the shareholders to enable Mr Said to raise the necessary finance. This involved the principal shareholders of BMed giving full authority to Guernroy Ltd to use its votes to facilitate negotiations with BA and take action and execute documents in the absolute discretion of Guernroy Ltd ('voting agreement'). In November 1996, the claimants were given notice that investment in BMed's shares was being invited but they chose not to participate. By February 1997 the necessary finance was raised and a reconstruction of the company implemented. The shares were reallocated with the effect that the defendant increased its holdings from 20% to 51% and the claimants' holding was reduced from 41% to 9%. The claimants did not become aware of the dilution of their shares until September 2001, when they were invited to participate in a further issue of shares in proportion to the amount of their diluted shares. They decided not to participate because they did not wish to prejudice their case that the dilution of their interest was wrongful.

The claimants commenced proceedings in October 2003. They asserted that Guernroy had used the voting agreement to obtain a profit for itself in that it obtained shares in 1997 and 2001 that had greatly increased in value. They contended that Guernroy owed a fiduciary duty to them not to use the voting agreement to obtain a profit for itself without the claimants' informed consent. The trial judge rejected the claim that Guernroy owed such a duty on the ground that 'it failed to recognise the commercial realities involved'. In addition, he held that the claim was time-barred in that the proceedings had commenced more than six years after the dispute arose in February 1997. It was common ground that the claim was time-barred unless it fell within the exception enacted in s 21(1) of the Limitation Act 1980. The claimants appealed against the rulings of the judge and permission was granted in respect of the limitation issue.

Held

The Court of Appeal dismissed the appeal and decided that the exception within s 21(1) of the Limitation Act 1980 would apply only if there had been a trust (or trust-like responsibility) regarding specific property, and not merely the means to obtain the property in the future. The alleged breach involved the 'voting rights' but these were part of the means by which the defendants acquired the new shares. Thus, the exception was not applicable.

> **Carnwath LJ:** By section 38, applying the Trustee Act 1925 s 68(17), trusts for these purposes include 'implied and constructive trusts'. For these purposes, as was explained by Millett LJ in *Paragon Finance plc v DB Thakerar & Co* [1999] 1 AER 400, 408, it is necessary to distinguish between two possible uses of the term 'constructive trust':
>
>> . . . the expressions "constructive trust" and "constructive trustee" have been used by equity lawyers to describe two entirely different situations. The first covers those cases . . . where the defendant, though not expressly appointed as trustee, has assumed the duties of a trustee by a lawful transaction which was independent of and preceded the breach of trust and is not impeached by the plaintiff. The second covers those cases where the trust obligation arises as a direct consequence of the unlawful transaction which is impeached by the plaintiff. . . .
>
> Only the first category ('class 1') is treated as a 'trust' for the purposes of the section 21 exception to the ordinary limitation rules.
>
> Section 21(1) provides an exception to the ordinary limitation rule that civil actions are barred after six years. Such an exception needs to be clearly justified by reference to the statutory language and the policy behind it. It is important therefore to keep in mind the reasoning behind the exception. It is not about culpability as such; fraud may not be sufficient to avoid the ordinary rule. It is about deemed possession: the fiction that the possession of a property by a trustee is treated from the outset as that of the beneficiary. In the words of Millett LJ, the possession of the trustee is 'taken from the first for and on behalf of the beneficiaries' and is 'consequently treated as the possession of the beneficiaries'. An action by the beneficiary to recover that property is not time-barred, because in legal theory it has been in his possession throughout.
>
> Turning to the present case, to treat the voting rights as class 1 trust property, even if justified on the facts, does not assist the claim. That is not the property which the claimants are seeking to recover. The most that can be said is that the voting rights were part of the means by which the defendants acquired the new shares.

Likewise in *Cattley v Pollard* [2006] EWHC 3130 (Ch) (see earlier), the High Court decided that the limitation period for dishonest assistance claims ('class 2 actions') is the normal period of six years from the date of the accrual of the cause of action.

In *James v Williams*, the Court of Appeal decided that where a beneficiary acted as if he were the sole owner of trust property, he would be treated as a constructive trustee and a claim against him would be exempt from the limitation period.

James v Williams [2000] Ch 1, CA

Facts

The defendant's predecessor in title assumed ownership of her parents' house after their deaths. The claimant brought a claim to recover the property some 24 years after the cause of action accrued.

Held

The defendant had acquired title from a constructive trustee and the claim was not time barred.

In *Gwembe Valley Development Co Ltd v Koshy*, the Court of Appeal clarified the law with regard to the limitation periods for claims for an account. In an action for an account based on breaches of fiduciary duties the existence or non-existence of a limitation period depended on:

(i) the nature and classification of the fiduciary relationship, as laid down by Millett LJ in the *Paragon Finance plc v Thakerar* [1999] 1 All ER 400 (see p 282 above). The first covers 'genuine' cases of constructive trusts concerning a pre-existing fiduciary relationship (proprietary claims) and the second use involves those cases where the breach of duties creates the fiduciary obligation (personal claims);

(ii) the nature of the conduct which gave rise to the duty to account. At one end of the spectrum would be a case in which a director has acted innocently, by failing to disclose an interest of which he was unaware, but is nonetheless liable to account for any profits. At the other end would be a case in which the non-disclosure of interest was deliberate and fraudulent. In the former, the limitation period of six years will apply but in the latter s 21(1)(a) of the 1980 Act will operate, and no limitation periods will apply to the claim.

Gwembe Valley Development Co Ltd v Koshy and Others [2003] EWCA 1048, CA

Facts

In 1986, a joint business venture was formed to develop a cotton and wheat farm of 2,500 hectares in Zambia. A group of investors founded the project. Each investor was allowed representation on the board of Gwembe Valley Development Co Ltd (GVDC) as the corporate vehicle for the project. Representation on the board was proportionate to the size of the investment. By far the largest investment in GVDC was made by a UK company, Lasco, controlled by Mr Koshy (Mr K). In 1987 Lasco made a loan of $5.8 million (US) to GVDC, repayable to Lasco on demand. Mr K was a director and in de facto control of Lasco. At the same time he was the managing director of GVDC. Lasco stood to make a massive profit of $4.8 million (US) on the deal. By 1993 the venture failed. The investors fell out. GVDC became insolvent and was put into receivership. In 1996 GVDC, through its receiver, commenced proceedings against Mr K and Lasco for an account of the profits made from the business transaction, equitable compensation for breaches of fiduciary duty and a declaration that Mr K and Lasco were liable as constructive trustees for all of GVDC monies received by them. The trial judge found that Mr K was dishonest and in breach of his fiduciary duties in procuring GVDC to enter into the loan transaction with Lasco without making proper disclosure to the other directors of GVDC of the extent of his personal interest in Lasco. The judge limited the account to the value of property, belonging in equity to GVDC, that Mr K had received, and refused a more general account of profits. The defendant appealed against these findings and alleged that the claims were statute-barred under the Limitation Act 1980. GVDC contended that the judge should have ordered an account of *all* of the unauthorised profits made by Mr K as a result of his breaches of fiduciary duties.

Held

The Court of Appeal dismissed the appeal by Mr K and allowed GVDC's appeal on the following grounds:

(1) Mr K acted in breach of his fiduciary duties as a director of GVDC in deliberately and dishonestly concealing from the other directors the nature and extent of the profits made by him in the loan transaction.

(2) A claim by GVDC for an account of profits against Mr K is a claim for, or is treated for limitation purposes as analogous to an action for, 'fraud or fraudulent breach of trust' under s 21(1)(a) of the Limitation Act 1980.

(3) The claim for an account of profits against Mr K was not a claim 'to recover from the trustee trust property . . . in the possession of the trustee' within s 21(1)(b) of the Limitation Act 1980.

(4) No limitation period applied to the claim by GDVC against Mr K.

(5) The claim by GDVC was not barred by laches or acquiescence.

(6) The judge was wrong to confine the scope of the account of profits. A general account of the profits was ordered:

Mummery LJ: The fiduciary relationship has developed by analogy from the trust relationship to cover cases in which a person has assumed responsibilities for the management of another person's assets. There is a distinction between – 'those whose fiduciary obligations preceded the acts complained of and those whose liability in equity was occasioned by the acts of which complaint was made.' (See Millett LJ in *Paragon Finanance v Thakerar* [1999] 1 All ER 400 at 414.)

For limitation purposes the two classes of trust and/or fiduciary duty are treated differently. The first class of case arising from the breach of a pre-existing duty is, or is treated by analogy as, an action by a beneficiary for breach of trust falling within s 21(1) of the 1980 Act. This means that there is no limitation period for the cases falling within s 21(1)(a) or (b); but that there is a six-year limitation period for cases falling within s 21(3).

In the second class of case s 21 would not apply, but a limitation defence to a claim might be available by analogy with common law claims, such as tort (for example, deceit) or breach of contract, even though the liability is exclusively equitable, as may be the case with breaches of fiduciary duty in the absence of a contract.

. . . in our view it is possible to simplify the court's task when considering the application of the 1980 Act to claims against fiduciaries. The starting assumption should be that a six year limitation period will apply – under one or other provision of the Act, applied directly or by analogy – unless it is specifically excluded by the Act or established case law. Personal claims against fiduciaries will normally be subject to limits by analogy with claims in tort or contract (1980 Act, ss 2, 5); see *Cia De Seguros Imperio v Heath* [2001] 1 WLR 112. By contrast, claims for breach of fiduciary duty, in the special sense explained in *Bristol and West Building Society v Mothew* [1998] Ch 1 (see p 186), will normally be covered by s 21. The six-year time limit under s 21(3), will apply, directly or by analogy, unless excluded by sub-s 21(1)(a) (fraud) or (b) (Class 1 trusts).

In the present case, it is clear that these principles were applicable to a director in Mr Koshy's position. He had 'trustee-like responsibilities' in the exercise of the powers of management of the property of GVDC and in dealing with the application of its property for the purposes, and in the interests, of the company and of all its members. In our view, accordingly, the claim for an account, if it was based on a failure in the exercise of those responsibilities, was within the scope of s 21. It was in principle subject to a six-year time limit under s 21(3). The question is whether it was excluded under either of the two statutory exceptions in s 21(1)(a) and (b).

Limitation Act 1980, s 21(2)

Where a trustee who is also a beneficiary under the trust receives or retains trust property or its proceeds as his share on a distribution of trust property under the trust, his liability in any action brought by virtue of sub-s (1)(b) above to recover that property or its proceeds after the expiration of the period of limitation prescribed by this Act for bringing an action to recover trust property shall be limited to the excess over his proper share.

This sub-section only applies if the trustee acted honestly and reasonably in making the distribution.

Where the right of action has been concealed by fraud, or where the claim is for relief from the consequences of a mistake, time does not begin to run until the claimant discovers the fraud or mistake, or ought with reasonable diligence to have discovered it (see s 32 of the Limitation Act 1980).

Limitation Act 1980, s 32(1); 32(2)

(1) ... where in the case of any action for which a period of limitation is prescribed by this Act, either:

    (a) the action is based upon the fraud of the defendant; or

    (b) any fact relevant to the plaintiff's right of action has been deliberately concealed from him by the defendant (defined in s 32(2)); or

    (c) the action is for relief from the consequences of a mistake,

    the period of limitation shall not begin to run until the plaintiff has discovered the fraud, concealment or mistake (as the case may be) or could with reasonable diligence have discovered it.

    References in this sub-section to the defendant include references to the defendant's agent and to any person through whom the defendant claims and his agent.

(2) ... deliberate commission of a breach of trust in circumstances in which it is unlikely to be discovered for some time amounts to deliberate concealment of the facts ...

There are two limbs to that part of s 32. The first requires deliberate concealment in the ordinary sense of the words. The concealment may take place at any time during what would otherwise have been the running of the period of limitation. In such a case time does not begin to run until the concealment has been discovered, see *Sheldon v RHM Outhwaite (Underwriting Agencies) Ltd* [1995] 2 All ER 558, per Lord Browne-Wilkinson. The second limb deals with deliberate breach of duty. This has been the subject of authoritative consideration by the House of Lords in *Cave v Robinson Jarvis & Rolfe* [2002] 2 All ER 641. The House decided that s 32(2) applied to cases where the breach of duty was deliberately committed, in the sense that there was intentional wrong-doing: see Lord Millett. The other ingredient needed to bring s 32(2) into play is that the breach is committed in circumstances where it is unlikely to be discovered 'for some time'. Although the quoted phrase is imprecise, the better view is that the implicit contrast that it is setting up is one between a breach of duty that would be immediately discovered (e.g. the infliction of a physical injury) and one that would not. Section 32(1) then poses the question: when could the Claimant have discovered the concealment with reasonable diligence? On this issue Millett LJ in *Paragon* stated:

> The question is not whether the Plaintiffs should have discovered the fraud sooner; but whether they could with reasonable diligence have done so. The burden of proof is on them. They must establish that they could not have discovered the fraud without exceptional measures which they could not reasonably have been expected to take. In this context the length of the applicable period of limitation is irrelevant. In the course of argument May LJ observed that reasonable diligence must be measured against some standard, but that the six-year limitation period did not provide the relevant standard. He suggested that the test was how a person carrying on a business of the relevant kind would act if he had adequate but not unlimited staff and resources and were motivated by a reasonable but not excessive sense of urgency. I respectfully agree.

Under s 22 of the Limitation Act 1980, the limitation period in respect of any claim to the estate of a deceased person is 12 years.

Limitation Act 1980, s 22

Subject to s 21(1) and (2) of this Act:

(a) no action in respect of any claim to the personal estate of a deceased person or to any share or interest in any such estate (whether under a will or on intestacy) shall be brought after the expiration of 12 years from the date on which the right to receive the share or interest accrued; and

(b) no action to recover arrears of interest in respect of any legacy, or damages in respect of such arrears, shall be brought after the expiration of six years from the date on which the interest became due.

Furthermore, the limitation periods do not apply to a claim for an account brought by the Attorney General against a charitable trust, because charitable trusts do not have beneficiaries in a way similar to private trusts (see *AG v Cocke* [1988] Ch 414).

Where no limitation period specified

Section 36 of the Limitation Act 1980 provides that the traditional specified time limits as laid down in the Act (six years or 12 years, depending on the cause of action):

> shall not apply to any claim for specific performance of a contract or for an injunction or for other equitable relief, except in so far as any such time limit may be applied by the court by analogy in like manner as the corresponding time limit under any enactment repealed by the Limitation Act 1939 was applied before 1st July 1940.

As a result of this section, a limitation period is applied where a court of equity exercised a concurrent jurisdiction giving the same relief as was available in a court of law, or where there was 'correspondence' between the remedies available at law or in equity. This principle was enacted to avoid the law being brought into disrepute, that is, to prevent a plaintiff succeeding in an action in equity when, on the same facts, he would be subject to a time bar in the common law courts.

This section was considered in *Companhia de Seguros Imperio v Heath Ltd*, where the court decided that the claim in equity for breach of fiduciary duty was statute-barred on analogy with the common law.

Companhia de Seguros Imperio v Heath Ltd [2001] 1 WLR 112, CA

Facts
The claimant was a Portuguese insurance company. The defendants acted as brokers and accepted the reinsurance of various long-term risks. The claimant alleged that the defendants were in breach of contract and commenced proceedings for breach of contract, tort and breach of fiduciary duty. These claims were based on identical facts. The defendants pleaded that the claims were statute barred. The judge decided in favour of the defendants and the claimant appealed.

Held
The claim was statute-barred. The claim for equitable damages for breach of fiduciary duty fell within s 36 of the 1980 Act. The test to be applied was not whether equity was exercising its 'exclusive' jurisdiction, but whether a court of equity sitting prior to 1 July 1940 would have applied a limitation on analogy with the claim. Since the claims were based on the same facts, the court was entitled to apply the same limitation period:

> **Waller LJ: 'Construction of section 36'** A claim to 'equitable damages' or 'equitable compensation' is a claim to equitable relief as Mr Flaux accepted. Thus section 36 applies to it. Furthermore, in my view, the court is not looking to see whether a limitation period was actually applied to a dishonest breach of fiduciary duty by analogy before 1 July 1940, but looking to see whether it would have been applied. It might, for example, have been so obvious that in a claim for 'equitable damages' equity would follow the law and apply the statutes of limitation by analogy that one could not in fact find an authority precisely in point. What the court must do is act 'in like manner' to a court sitting prior to 1 July 1940.

> **Would a court of equity have applied statutes of limitation by analogy?** The question seems to me to be this. Would a court of equity have applied limitation by analogy to a claim for equitable compensation or damages for a dishonest breach of fiduciary duty?

> [Waller LJ referred to Lord Westbury's judgment in *Knox v Gye* (1872) LR 5 HL 656, and continued:] *Spry Equitable Remedies* 5th edition p 419 says:

>> ... a statute of limitations may be raised by analogy in defence to a claim that is brought in the exclusive jurisdiction of a court of equity, such as in proceedings for the enforcement of a trust, rather than in its auxiliary or concurrent jurisdictions. Here there is no question of merely recognising and giving effect to an

abrogation of a right at law or of acting in obedience to a statute that relates to rights at law. Hence it must be seen first whether there is a special statutory provision that affects directly, whether expressly or by implication, the particular equitable right that is in question. But if there is no such provision, the court may decide that the material equitable right is so similar to legal rights to which a limitation period is applicable that that limitation period should be applied to it also. In this latter case the limitation period is said to be applied by analogy, and the principles that govern cases of this kind are that if there is a sufficiently close similarity between the exclusive equitable right in question and legal rights to which the statutory provision applies a court of equity will ordinarily act upon it by analogy but that it will so act only if there is nothing in the particular circumstances of the case that renders it unjust to do so. What is regarded by courts of equity as a sufficiently close similarity for this purpose involves a question of degree. and reference must be made to the relevant authorities. The basis of these principles is that, in the absence of special circumstances rendering this position unjust, the relevant equitable rules should accord with comparable legal rules.

Mr Gross referred us to various authorities in which equity had applied the statutes by analogy and some where it had not. The authorities included *Hovenden v Lord Annesley* (1806) 2 Sch & Lef 607; *Burdick v Garrick* (1870) LR 5 Ch 233; *Friend v Young* [1897] 2 Ch 421 and *North American Land v Watkins* [1904] 1 Ch 242 (where many other authorities were reviewed). In my view the authorities cited by Mr Gross and the broad principles set out in the above quotations support the submission that equity would have taken the view that it should apply the statute by analogy to a claim for damages or compensation for a dishonest breach of fiduciary duty. I say that because what is alleged against Heaths as giving rise to the dishonest breach of fiduciary duty are precisely those facts which are also relied on for alleging breach of contract or breach of duty in tort. It is true that there is an extra allegation of 'intention' but that does not detract from the fact that the essential factual allegations are the same. Furthermore, the claim is one for 'damages'. The prayer for relief has now been amended with our leave to add a claim for 'equitable compensation', but the reality of the claim is that it is one for damages, the assessment of which would be no different whether the claim was maintained as a breach of contract claim or continued simply as a dishonest breach of fiduciary duty claim.

[The learned judge applied the principles laid down by Millett LJ in *Paragon Finance v Thakerar* [1999] 1 All ER 400, and continued:] It is true that *Nelson v Rye* [1996] 2 All ER 186, might have been said to have supported Mr Flaux but that decision has been comprehensively demolished by Millett LJ in *Paragon* and in any event was a decision in which section 36 was not referred to. The decision of Ebsworth J in *Kershaw v Whelan (No 2)* unreported, January 23 1997, was also a decision in Mr Flaux's favour but he did not feel able to rely on its reasoning to support his argument. In my view the reasoning of the judge in this case and that of Mr Jules Sher QC in *Coulthard* demonstrate that *Kershaw v Whelan (No 2)* was wrongly decided and should be overruled.

In my view the appeal should be dismissed.

Staughton LJ, in the same case, lamented the fact that in certain circumstances the approach involving the limitation period applicable to claims is still dependent on considering whether the claim is within the 'concurrent' or 'exclusive' jurisdiction of equity:

Staughton LJ: It is not obvious to me why it is still necessary to have special rules for the limitation of claims for specific performance, or an injunction, or other equitable relief. And if it is still necessary to do so, I do not see any merit in continuing to define the circumstances where a particular claim will be time-barred by reference to what happened, or might have happened, more than sixty years ago. If a distinction still has to be drawn between common law and equitable claims for limitation purposes, I would hope that a revised statute will enact with some precision where that distinction should be drawn, rather than leave it to the product of researches into cases decided long ago.

Question

What limitation periods, if any, exist in respect of the following:

(a) A claim for damages for breach of trust?

(b) A claim against the trustee for an account?

(c) A claim to trace the trust assets or their proceeds in the hands of the trustees?

Laches

Where no period of limitation has been specified under the Limitation Act 1980 (see s 21(1)), the doctrine of laches will apply to equitable claims. Section 36(2) of the 1980 Act confers this jurisdiction

Limitation Act 1980, s 36(2)

Nothing in the Act shall affect any equitable jurisdiction to refuse relief on the grounds of acquiescence or otherwise.

The doctrine of laches consists of a substantial lapse of time coupled with the existence of circumstances which make it inequitable to enforce the claim of the claimant. Factors that are taken into account are hardship on the defendant as a result of the delay by the claimant and the adverse effects on third parties.

The doctrine is summarised in the maxim, 'equity aids the vigilant and not the indolent'. The rationale behind the doctrine was stated by Lord Camden LC in *Smith v Clay*.

Smith v Clay (1767) 3 Bro CC 639, HL

Lord Camden LC: A court of equity has always refused its aid to stale demands, where a party has slept upon his rights and acquiesced for a great length of time. Nothing can call forth this court into activity, but conscience, good faith and reasonable diligence; where these are wanting, the court is passive and does nothing.

It may be treated as inequitable to enforce the claimant's cause of action where the delay has led the defendant to change his position to his detriment in the reasonable belief that the claimant's action has been abandoned, or the delay has led to the loss of evidence which might assist the defence, or if the claim is to a business (for the claimant should not be allowed to wait and see if it prospers).

The jurisdiction of the court in respect of laches was summarised by Lord Selborne in *Lindsay Petroleum Co v Hurd*.

Lindsay Petroleum Co v Hurd (1874) LR 5 PC 221

Lord Selborne: Now the doctrine of laches in courts of equity is not an arbitrary or technical doctrine. Where it could be practically unjust to give a remedy either because the party has, by his conduct, done that which might fairly be regarded as equivalent to a waiver of it or where by his conduct and neglect he has, though perhaps not waiving that remedy, yet put the other party in a situation in which it would not be reasonable to place him if the remedy were afterwards to be asserted, in either of these cases lapse of time and delay are most material.

The applicability of the equitable doctrines of laches and acquiescence depends on the facts of each case. Unreasonable delay by the claimant, substantial prejudice and manifest injustice to the defendant are significant factors to be taken into consideration by the court. In order to raise a successful defence, the defendant is required to establish the following three elements:

(1) that there has been unreasonable delay in bringing the claim by the claimant;

(2) that there has been consequent substantial prejudice or detriment to the defendant;

(3) the balance of justice requires the claimant's cause of action to be withheld.

In *Nelson v Rye*, the judge considered the nature of the doctrine of laches.

Nelson v Rye [1996] 2 All ER 186, HC

Laddie J:

The equitable defence

[This aspect of the case was not overruled by the Court of Appeal in *Paragon Finance v Thakerar*: see p 563 above.]

For Mr Nelson it was argued that, to succeed on this issue, Mr Rye must show: (a) that there was an express or implied representation by the plaintiff that he intended not to compel performance *in specie* by the defendant of the obligation in question; (b) that the plaintiff was aware, or ought to have been aware, of the possibility that the defendant would act to his prejudice in reliance on the representation; and (c) that, in consequence of that representation, it becomes unjust to grant the equitable relief sought as the defendant has been prejudiced by reliance on it (in the sense of being in a 'substantially worse position' than he would otherwise have been). For these propositions Mr Anderson relied on *Spry on Equitable Remedies*, 4th edn, 1990, London: Sweet & Maxwell, pp 236–38. In relation to laches, he said that in order to raise a *prima facie* case, a defendant must establish two facts: (a) that there has been unreasonable delay by the plaintiff; and (b) that there has been consequent substantial prejudice or detriment to the defendant which justifies the refusal of the equitable relief sought. He said that mere delay *per se* is not sufficient. A defendant must show a causal link between the delay and the preju-dice/detriment: see *Lindsay Petroleum Co v Hurd* (1874) LR 5 PC 221, pp 239–40; *Lazard Bros & Co v Fairfield Properties Co (Mayfair) Ltd* (1977) *The Times*, 12 October; and Spry, 4th edn, pp 227–28. At least at one stage in his argument, Mr Anderson suggested that the defendant needs to prove that the prejudice was substantially caused by the delay.

So, here, these defences are not technical or arbitrary. The courts have indicated over the years some of the factors which must be taken into consideration in deciding whether the defence runs. Those factors include the period of the delay, the extent to which the defendant's position has been prejudiced by the delay and the extent to which that prejudice was caused by the actions of the plaintiff. I accept that mere delay alone will almost never suffice, but the court has to look at all the circumstances, including in particular those factors set out above, and then decide whether the balance of justice or injustice is in favour of granting the remedy or withholding it. If substantial prejudice will be suffered by the defendant, it is not necessary for the defendant to prove that it was caused by the delay. On the other hand, the plaintiff's knowledge that the delay will cause such prejudice is a factor to be taken into account. With these considerations in mind, I turn to the facts.

[Laddie J reviewed the facts and continued:] In my view there was a wilful refusal by Mr Nelson to involve himself in his financial affairs. He deliberately ignored advice both from Mr Rye and Mr Thomas to get round the table to see how the figures worked out. I find as a fact that he declined to attend two meetings with Mr Rye and Mr Thomas for no good reason. He was happy to drive his Rolls Royce, live in a mansion and take far more out of Happytronics than could be justified on the basis of its receipts, but he did not want to know the details of how the sums added up – or failed to add up. He rejected all advice. He was not interested in the account as between him and Mr Rye. He knew or suspected that working out any of the figures would merely confirm that he was living beyond his means. This was something which he preferred to ignore. He would leave his manager and Mr Thomas to sort out the problems. His only concerns arose when Mr Rye sought to put a brake on his wages. I accept that then he would demand to know why he could not have more and, from time to time, asked to see the figures. But this was simply part and parcel of trying to place the blame for his financial problems on others and, in particular, Mr Rye.

I have come to the conclusion that there was unreasonable delay in commencing these proceedings.

I turn to consider whether Mr Rye has suffered prejudice as a result of that delay. Mr Oppenheim relied on two matters. First, he says that documents relevant to the account which did exist in the past now no longer exist. Secondly, he says that it is inevitable that matters more than six years ago will be poorly remembered. In other words, Mr Rye's ability to give evidence has been prejudiced by the delay.

I have considered all of the above matters. In my view Mr Rye will suffer substantial prejudice for both of the reasons advanced by Mr Oppenheim and this is a case where it would be unreasonable and unjust to allow Mr Nelson to assert his right to an account against Mr Rye in the period prior to 24 December 1985. The defence of laches or acquiescence is made out.

In *Patel v Shah*, Mummery LJ referred to the modern approach to the defence of laches. He referred to the judgment of Adous LJ in the unreported case, *Frawley v Neill*.

Frawley v Neill [2000] CP Reports 20 (CA)

Aldous LJ: In my view, the more modern approach should not require an inquiry as to whether the circum-stances can be fitted within the confines of a preconceived formula derived from earlier cases. The inquiry should require a broad approach, directed to ascertaining whether it would in all the circumstances be unconscionable for a party to be permitted to assert his beneficial right. No doubt the circumstances which gave rise to a particular result in decided cases are relevant to the question whether or not it would be conscionable or unconscionable for the relief to be asserted, but each case has to be decided on its facts applying the broad approach.

In *Patel v Shah* the Court of Appeal endorsed the modern 'broad approach' and decided that the defence would be available to a defendant who could establish that it would be unconscionable for the claimant to assert his right to the property in question.

Patel v Shah [2005] EWCA Civ 157

Facts

The defendants purchased a number of commercial properties between February 1989 and March 1990. They bought the properties as a joint venture. All the properties, save two, were subject to substantial mortgages. At the time the property market was rising and it was intended that the properties should be sold fairly quickly to realise a profit. In the early 1990s the property market declined and, rather than sell the properties at a loss, the defendants decided to keep them for the long term in the hope of a rise in the market. The defendants bore the shortfall when the rental income did not meet the mortgage repayments and funded the properties from their own pockets. One of the investment companies, Greetflow Ltd, had suffered financial difficulty and was unable to contribute to the shortfall. The claimants, as successor in title to Greetflow Ltd, claimed a beneficial interest in the properties when in 2002 the property market had recovered. Their purpose was to benefit from the income and capital gains that accrued to the properties. As the claim involved an assertion of beneficial ownership in the properties the limitation periods were not applicable. The defendants resisted the claim on the ground of laches. The judge decided in favour of the defendants on the ground that the latter shouldered the costs of maintaining the properties and the mortgages during the property slump, whereas the claimants appeared on the scene only when the market had recovered. It was thus unconscionable for the claimants to regain the value of the properties. The claimants appealed to the Court of Appeal on the ground that the defence of laches was not available to an action brought by a beneficiary against trustees.

Held

The appeal would be dismissed. The aim of the venture was not to create a trust, but for the parties to work together in order to sell the properties for a profit. The trust that existed on the facts could be distinguished from the traditional trust whereby trustees held property on trust for beneficiaries. The defendants had been released from their equitable obligations to the claimants when their predecessors opted out of the arrangement. It would have been unconscionable for the claimants to claim the profits from the properties.

Mummery LJ: The effect of conduct by the Claimants, which may properly be described as unconscionable, is to release a Defendant trustee from the equitable trust obligation, which binds his conscience as the holder of the legal title for the benefit of others. In the case of an ordinary trust by way of gift to trustees for the benefit of the beneficiaries, where the beneficiary is not required or expected to do more than receive what has been given for his benefit, it will obviously be extremely rare for laches and delay on the part of the beneficiary to make it unconscionable for that beneficiary to assert his claim to the beneficial interest, or for the trustee to claim that he has been released from the equitable obligations that bind his conscience.

The general commercial setting of the particular facts of this case make it, in my view, a different kind of case from that of a beneficiary under a gift trust. As Keene LJ pointed out in the course of argument, the persons investing in the purchase of the various properties held from time to time by the Defendants were in substance trading in land. They were buying and selling properties with a view to making a quick profit. It was a collaborative commercial venture, in which those participating in it were expected to work together in making their contributions to achieve the aim of the joint ventures, the aim in the case of each acquisition being the same. The creation of resulting trusts arising on the purchases by the Defendants of properties in their name, with contributions made by predecessors of the Claimants and others, was, as Sullivan J pointed out in oral argument, not the aim of the joint ventures. The trusts were a by-product or incidental equitable consequence, a vehicle for accomplishing the commercial aim.

What of the conduct of the Claimants and their predecessor in title? Until the risk had passed away, the

Claimants had been lying low. They did not inform the Defendant trustees of the assignments of the interests in August 1992. They did not alert the Defendants to any claim made by them until 2000, when they discovered that the funds had produced income and capital gains.

In my judgment, the deputy judge was right to regard the conduct of the Claimants as conduct on which he was entitled to dismiss the claim as unconscionable and barred by laches. The fact that the Claimants were seeking to recover capital beneficial interest from the Defendants as trustees does not, in my view, make it any the less unconscionable.

... the venture ceased to be joint, as it was originally intended, when, as a result of Greetflow assigning its interest to the Claimants and then being struck off and dissolved, no further contributions were made to the joint venture. Everything was left for the Defendants to deal with, including financing shortfalls from their own pockets. The Claimants and their predecessors had departed from the commercial arrangements. They had ceased to bear any of the risk or the expense. Such conduct on their part falls within the principle stated in *Frawley v Neil*.

Note:
The modern approach adopted in *Patel v Shah* was applied in *Re Loftus* [2006] EWCA 1124.

Question
When will the equitable doctrine of laches be available to a defendant?

PROPRIETARY REMEDIES (TRACING OR CLAIMS *IN REM*)

The claimant beneficiary who suffers a loss as a result of a breach of trust is entitled to claim restitution of the trust estate in an action for an account against the wrongdoer trustees. Such an action is a claim against the trustees and is referred to as a claim *in personam*, that is, the claim is against the trustees personally who are required to satisfy the claim from their personal assets. Provided that the trustees are solvent and have sufficient assets to satisfy the claim of the innocent beneficiary, the claimant will not be out of pocket. But if the trustees are insolvent, the claimant's cause of action will rank with the claims of the trustees' other unsecured creditors. This may result in the order of the court remaining unsatisfied. An alternative remedy available to the beneficiary is to 'follow' or 'trace' the trust assets in the hands of the trustees or third parties, not being *bona fide* transferees of the legal estate for value without notice, and recover such property or obtain a charging order in priority over the trustees' creditors. This is known as a proprietary remedy, or a claim *in rem* or a tracing order.

'Following' the assets in the hands of the defendant involves the process of identifying the same asset (but not in any substituted form, such as the proceeds of sale of the asset) as it moves from hand to hand with the effect that the claimant may attach an order on the property. On the other hand, 'tracing' is a much broader process than following. 'Tracing' is a process whereby the claimant establishes and protects his title to assets in the hands of another. Both remedies are 'proprietary' in the sense that the order is attached to specific property under the control of another, or may take the form of a charging order thereby treating the claimant as a secured creditor. The remedies at common law and equity are mainly 'personal' in the sense that they are remedies which force the defendant to do or refrain from doing something in order to compensate the claimant for the wrong suffered. The proprietary remedy exists as a right to proceed against a particular asset in the hands of the defendant.

In *Boscawen v Bajwa*, Millett LJ commented on the process of tracing.

Boscawen v Bajwa [1996] 1 WLR 328, CA

Millett LJ: Equity lawyers habitually use the expressions 'the tracing claim' and 'the tracing remedy' to describe the proprietary claim and the proprietary remedy which equity makes available to the beneficial owner who seeks to recover his property *in specie* from those into whose hands it has come. Tracing properly so called, however, is neither a claim nor a remedy but a process. Moreover, it is not confined to the case where the plaintiff seeks a proprietary remedy; it is equally necessary where he seeks a personal remedy against the knowing recipient or knowing assistant. It is the process by which the plaintiff traces what has happened to his property, identifies the persons who have handled or received it, and justifies his claim that the money which they handled or received (and, if necessary, which they still retain) can properly be regarded as representing his property. He needs to do this because his claim is based on the retention by him of a beneficial interest in the property which the defendant handled or received. Unless he can prove this he cannot (in the traditional language of equity) raise an equity against the defendant or (in the modern language of restitution) show that the defendant's unjust enrichment was at his expense.

In such a case, the defendant will either challenge the plaintiff's claim that the property in question represents his property (that is, he will challenge the validity of the tracing exercise) or he will raise a priority dispute (for example, by claiming to be a *bona fide* purchaser without notice). If all else fails, he will raise the defence of innocent change of position. This was not a defence which was recognised in England before 1991 but it was widely accepted throughout the common law world. In *Lipkin Gorman v Karpnale Ltd* [1991] 2 AC 548, the House of Lords acknowledged it to be part of English law also. The introduction of this defence not only provides the court with a means of doing justice in future, but allows a re-examination of many decisions of the past in which the absence of the defence may have led judges to distort basic principles in order to avoid injustice to the defendant.

If the plaintiff succeeds in tracing his property, whether in its original or in some changed form, into the hands of the defendant, and overcomes any defences which are put forward on the defendant's behalf, he is entitled to a remedy. The remedy will be fashioned to the circumstances. The plaintiff will generally be entitled to a personal remedy; if he seeks a proprietary remedy he must usually prove that the property to which he lays claim is still in the ownership of the defendant. If he succeeds in doing this the court will treat the defendant as holding the property on a constructive trust for the plaintiff and will order the defendant to transfer it *in specie*, to the plaintiff. But this is only one of the proprietary remedies which are available to a court of equity. If the plaintiff's money has been applied by the defendant, for example, not in the acquisition of a landed property but in its improvement, then the court may treat the land as charged with the payment to the plaintiff of a sum representing the amount by which the value of the defendant's land has been enhanced by the use of the plaintiff's money. And if the plaintiff's money has been used to discharge a mortgage on the defendant's land, then the court may achieve a similar result by treating the land as subject to a charge by way of subrogation in favour of the plaintiff.

A personal claim for 'money had and received', on the other hand, is distinct from a proprietary claim. Such personal claims are based on the notion that the defendant, without authority, has received the claimant's money. It is immaterial whether or not the defendant has retained the claimant's money. The claim is complete when the defendant receives the money, subject to the defence of change of position. But this personal action will be of no benefit to the claimant if the defendant becomes bankrupt. The claim is essentially a quasi-contractual remedy based on the principle of reversing the unjust enrichment of the defendant at the expense of the claimant. With this rationale in mind, Nourse LJ, in *FC Jones v Jones* [1996] 3 WLR 703 (see p 579 below), decided that the plaintiff was entitled to recover any profit made by the defendant through the use of the funds.

Advantages of the proprietary remedy over personal remedies

The proprietary remedy has a number of advantages over the personal remedy, namely:

(a) the claim is not dependent on the solvency of the defendant. Indeed, the claimant's action is based on an assertion of ownership of the asset in question;

(b) the claimant may be able to take advantage of increases in the value of the property in appropriate cases;

(c) on a proprietary claim, interest accrues from the date the property was acquired by the defendant, while claims *in personam* carry interest only from the date of the judgment;

(d) the limitation periods for commencing claims are not applicable to claimants who seek to trace their property in the hands of the defendant.

Question

What are the advantages of a proprietary claim over a personal remedy?

Tracing at common law

To a limited extent, the right to trace exists at common law. The approach here is that, provided the claimant's property is 'identifiable', the process of tracing may continue through any number of transformations. The form in which the property exists is irrelevant, provided that the claimant shows a direct connection between his or her property in its original form and the property in its altered form in the hands of the defendant.

The main restriction in the common law right to trace is that the property ceases to be 'identifiable' when it becomes comprised in a mixed fund, or when the asset ceases to be wholly owned by the claimant: see *Taylor v Plumer*.

Taylor v Plumer (1815) 3 M & S 562

Facts

The defendant, Sir Thomas Plumer (later Master of the Rolls), had given money to Walsh, his stockbroker, in order to purchase Exchequer bills. Walsh without authority purchased American investments and bullion and attempted to abscond to America. There was a dramatic chase by the defendant's attorney and a police officer caught up with Walsh at Falmouth where he was waiting for a boat bound for Lisbon. Walsh handed the property over to the defendant's agents and was later adjudicated bankrupt. His assignee in bankruptcy claimed to recover the property from the defendant.

Held

The defendant was entitled to retain the property, for it had belonged to him:

> **Lord Ellenborough CJ:** It makes no difference in reason or in law into what other form, different from the original, the change may have been made . . . for the product of or substitute for the original thing still follows the nature of the thing itself, as long as it can be ascertained to be such and the right only ceases when the means of ascertainment fail which is the case when the subject is turned into money and mixed and compounded in a general mass of the same description.

Note

The modern view is that *Taylor v Plumer* was not concerned with the common law rule of tracing but with the equitable rule. See Smith, 'Tracing in *Taylor v Plumer*: equity in the Court of King's Bench' (1995) LMCLQ 240.

In *Lipkin Gorman*, the plaintiff had not sought a tracing order (proprietary claim), but Lord Goff considered that such a claim might have had a reasonable chance of success. The relationship of banker and customer (debtor and creditor) created a chose in action in favour of the plaintiff. The customer was entitled to trace his property (chose) in its unconverted form or in its substituted form, such as the cash drawn by Cass from the client's account. Since the club had conceded that it had retained some of the solicitor's cash, namely, £154,695, the firm would have been entitled at common law to trace this sum into the hands of the defendant: see *Taylor v Plumer*.

Lipkin Gorman (A Firm) v Karpnale Ltd [1991] 3 WLR 10, HL

Facts

Mr Cass, a partner in the plaintiff's firm of solicitors, was a compulsive gambler, unbeknown to the other partners. He drew cheques on the firm's client account by making out cheques for cash and sending the firm's cashier to cash them. He withdrew a total of £323,222 from the account. From this amount, £100,313 was replaced, accounted for or recovered. The balance of £222,909 represented money which Cass stole from the firm and was irrecoverable from him. Cass used the relevant funds at the gaming tables of the Playboy Club, owned by the defendant. It was conceded that the club was still in possession of £154,695 which was derived from the firm's account. On one occasion, Cass procured a banker's draft for £3,735 drawn in favour of the firm which was paid for by a cheque drawn on the firm's account. He endorsed the draft on behalf of the firm (without authority) and proferred it to the club for 'chips' which Cass used for gambling. Within the club, 'chips' were treated as the currency, and Cass would redeem these for money whenever he chose to do so. The 'chips' were worthless outside the casino and at all times remained the property of the club. Cass was convicted of theft. The club at all times had acted in good faith and had no knowledge that Cass was using unauthorised funds.

The questions in issue were, first, whether the plaintiff was entitled to maintain an action against the defendant in quasi-contract for money had and received and, secondly, whether the defendant was entitled to retain the proceeds of the draft of £3,735.

Held

The House of Lords decided as follows:

(a) The club, as the recipient in good faith of stolen money, was under an obligation to pay the equivalent to the plaintiff. The club had provided no valuable consideration to Cass and had been unjustly enriched at the expense of the plaintiff.

(b) The 'purchase' and use of 'chips' were convenient mechanisms for facilitating gambling. Gamblers did not make separate contracts to 'purchase' or acquire 'chips'. The property in the 'chips' remained in the club. No valuable consideration was provided by the club in exchanging cash for 'chips' or vice versa.

(c) Each bet placed by a gambler and accepted by the club created a separate contract, which was void by virtue of s 18 of the Gaming Act 1845. The club was under no legal obligation to honour bets. If it paid out funds in respect of winning bets, these payments were construed as gifts. Equally, gamblers who lost bets were treated as making gifts of their stakes to the club. Accordingly, the club did not provide any valuable consideration, despite running the risk of voluntarily paying out sums in respect of winning bets.

(d) The firm of solicitors was entitled to recover the amount as stated in the banker's draft (£3,735). The club did not become a holder in due course under s 29(1) of the Bills of Exchange Act 1882. The draft was made payable to the firm and the unauthorised indorsement by Cass, in favour of the club, was done on behalf of the firm of solicitors:

Lord Goff: It is well established that a legal owner is entitled to trace his property into its product, provided that the latter is indeed identifiable as the product of his property ... Of course, 'tracing' or 'following' property into its product involves a decision by the owner of the original property to assert his title to the product in place of his original property ... the bank was the debtor and the solicitors were its creditors. Such a debt constitutes a chose in action, which is a species of property; and since the debt was enforceable at common law, the chose in action was legal property belonging to the solicitors at common law. There is in my opinion no reason why the solicitors should not be able to trace their property at common law in that chose in action, or in any part of it, into its product, ie, cash drawn by loss from their client account at the bank. Such a claim is consistent with their assertion that the money so obtained by loss was their property at common law.

Note

Had Cass mixed his money with the firm's property, the right to trace would have been governed by equitable rules. The plaintiff would be entitled to trace its property in the hands of Cass, who would be considered a constructive trustee. The firm would then have a first charge on the mixed fund in the hands of Cass (see *Re Hallett's Estate* (1880) 13 Ch D 696, below). The onus would then be on Cass to establish the amount of the mixed fund which belonged to him (see Ungoed-Thomas J in *Re Tilley* [1967] Ch 1179, p 590 below). The firm of solicitors would then be entitled to trace its property in the hands of the club, an innocent volunteer, and effect a charge ranking in 'pari passu' (see *Sinclair v Brougham* [1914] AC 398, p 596 below).

The common law right to trace property belonging to the claimant extends to profits accruing to such property. The justification for allowing the claimant to seek the profits made by the defendant lies in restitution, to prevent the defendant being unjustly enriched at the expense of the claimant: see Millett LJ's judgment in *FC Jones v Jones* below. However, Nourse LJ, in the same decision, extended the basis of the claim for money had and received to include the recovery of profits made by the defendant's use of the claimant's money. The justification here is based on the defendant's conscience.

Trustee of the Property of FC Jones and Sons (A Firm) v Jones [1996] 3 WLR 703, CA

Facts

In 1984, the partners of FC Jones and Sons, potato growers, committed an act of bankruptcy and in due course were adjudicated bankrupt. Following the act of bankruptcy, but before the adjudication, the defendant, the wife of one of the partners, paid in £11,700 of partnership money to the account of commodity brokers. The defendant subsequently dealt in potato futures which proved to be a success. She received cheques totalling £50,760 from the brokers and paid these sums into an account she had opened with R Raphael and Sons plc. The Official Receiver informed Raphaels of his claim to the money and, thereupon, the defendant demanded the release of it. On an interpleader summons, the sum was ordered to be paid into court. The defendant conceded to the trustee's claim to the original £11,700, but argued that his claim could not extend to the profits generated by the original sum. The trial judge held in favour of the claimant on the ground that the defendant had received the money in a fiduciary capacity and was a constructive trustee of the money, including the profit element. The defendant appealed to the Court of Appeal.

Held

The Court of Appeal dismissed the appeal but decided the case on different grounds from the High Court. The case was treated as involving tracing at common law. The defendant had clearly not received the money as a fiduciary and was not a constructive trustee. She had no title to the money at law or in equity but was merely in possession of it. This was due to the bankruptcy doctrine of relation back. The effect of this doctrine was to vest the legal title in the trustee in bankruptcy. The trustee's claim to trace the money was not made in equity. There was no mixture of the funds and, as such, the trustee was required to bring his claim at common law. He was entitled to trace his funds (including the profits) by applying common law principles because the money and profits belonged to him at law:

> **Millett LJ:** It is, however, in my view plain that the defendant did not receive the money in a fiduciary capacity and that she did not become a constructive trustee. The deputy judge's conclusion presupposes that A, who in this case is the bankrupt, had a legal title to transfer. In the present case, however, the bankrupt had been divested of all title by statute. Mr FWJ Jones had no title at all at law or in equity to the money in the joint account at Midland Bank, and could confer no title on the defendant. While, however, I accept the submissions of counsel for the defendant that she did not become a constructive trustee, I do not accept the proposition that the trustee in bankruptcy is unable to recover the profits which the defendant made by the use of his money unless she can be shown to have received it in one or other of the two capacities mentioned; nor do I consider it necessary for him to invoke the assistance of equity in order to maintain his claim. In short, I do not accept the main submission of counsel that the only action at law which was available to the trustee was an action against the defendant for money had and received.
>
> Accordingly, as from the date of the act of bankruptcy the money in the bankrupts' joint account at Midland Bank belonged to the trustee. The account holders had no title to it at law or in equity. The cheques which they drew in favour of the defendant were not 'void' or 'voidable' but, in the events which happened, they were incapable of passing any legal or equitable title. They were not, however, without legal effect, for the bank honoured them. The result was to affect the identity of the debtor but not the creditor and to put the defendant in possession of funds to which she had no title. A debt formally owed by Midland Bank, apparently to Mr FWJ Jones and Mr AC

Jones, but in reality, to their trustee, ultimately became a debt owed by Raphaels, apparently to the defendant, but in reality to the trustee.

The defendant had no title at all, at law or in equity. If she became bankrupt, the money would not vest in her trustee. But this would not be because it was trust property; it would be because it was not her property at all. If she made a profit, how could she have any claim to the profit made by the use of someone else's money? In my judgment she could not. If she were to retain the profit made by the use of the trustee's money, then, in the language of the modern law of restitution, she would be unjustly enriched at the expense of the trustee.

Given that the trustee can trace his money at Midland Bank into the money in the defendant's account with the commodity brokers, can he successfully assert a claim to that part of the money which represents the profit made by the use of his money? I have no doubt that, in the particular circumstances of this case, he can. There is no need to trace through the dealings on the London potato futures market.

Given, then, that the trustee has established his legal claim to the £11,700 and the profits earned by the use of his money, and has located the money, first, in the defendant's account with the commodity brokers and, later, in the defendant's account at Raphaels, I am satisfied that the common law has adequate remedies to enable him to recover his property. He did not need to sue the defendant; and he did not do so. He was entitled to bring an action for debt against Raphaels and obtain an order for payment. When he threatened to do so, Raphaels interpleaded, and the issue between the trustee and the defendant was which of them could give a good receipt to Raphaels. That depended upon which of them had the legal title to the chose in action. The money now being in court, the court can grant an appropriate declaration and make an order for payment.

In my judgment the trustee was entitled at law to the money in the joint account of the bankrupts at Midland Bank, which had vested in him by statute. He was, similarly, entitled to the balance of the money in the defendant's account with the commodity brokers, and the fact that it included profits made by the use of that money is immaterial. He was similarly entitled to the money in the defendant's account at Raphaels and able to give them a good receipt for the money. The defendant never had any interest, legal or equitable, in any of those moneys.

Nourse LJ: I also agree that the appeal must be dismissed. I recognise that our decision goes further than that of the House of Lords in *Lipkin Gorman v Karpnale Ltd* [1991] 2 AC 548, in that it holds that the action for money had and received entitles the legal owner to trace his property into its product, not only in the sense of property for which it is exchanged, but also in the sense of property representing the original and the profit made by the defendant's use of it.

Chu, W and Todd, P, 'Profits recoverable in common law tracing claim: *FC Jones v Jones*' [1996] 5 Web JCLI

The authors, after examining Millett and Nourse LJJ's views in *FC Jones v Jones*, conclude:

At first Millett LJ's view is limited to the unusual situation where the money is not mixed with any of the recipient's own, but closer examination shows that he is merely removing an anomaly. Had the money become mixed, legal title would have passed to Mrs Jones, and she would have been liable as a constructive trustee. Clearly, there is no reason why she should be better off merely because the money never became mixed. It is, however, more difficult to justify the result where the recipient's conscience is unaffected, since, in that event, the outcome will depend on whether or not the money is mixed.

Nourse LJ's view is far more radical than that of Millett LJ, but seems to confuse personal and proprietary claims. It is also unclear when the broad brush principles derived from Lord Mansfield CJ's judgment will apply. It is therefore to be hoped that the views of Millett LJ, rather than those of Nourse LJ, will be developed in future cases.

In *Box v Barclays Bank plc* (for facts, p 199 above), Ferris J reviewed the principles laid down in the *Lipkin Gorman* case concerning the right to trace at common law.

Box v Barclays Bank plc [1998] 1 All ER 108, HC

Ferris J: A number of points arise from this decision [*Lipkin Gorman*]. First, a claim made on the basis upheld in that case is exclusively a common law claim. It is essential, therefore, that the plaintiff shall be able to show that the property which has come into the hands of the defendant is, or represents, by the application of common law rules of tracing, property to which the plaintiff had a legal title. It will not suffice for the plaintiff to claim that he had an equitable title to the property, or that he can trace his property into that which has come into the hands of the defendant by the application of equitable rules of tracing. Secondly, although the right to recover depends upon the plaintiff showing the requisite proprietary interest at the outset of the transaction, that right will not be defeated by showing that the defendant no longer has the plaintiff's property (unless he has parted with it in circumstances enabling him to take advantage of the defence of change of position) or that he has mixed it with other property in such a way that it can no longer be identified. Thirdly, the defendant must have received the plaintiff's property for its own benefit. Fourthly, it will be a defence if the defendant can show that it was a *bona fide* purchaser for value.

Where the plaintiffs' claim [in *Box v Barclays Bank plc*] based on a common law right to recover money had and received breaks down, is, in my judgment, that the plaintiffs cannot show that what came in to Sylcon's No 1 account was their money at the time when it reached that account. This can be illustrated by reference to the first deposit made by Mrs Jacobs. This was the cash sum of £10,000 which Mrs Jacobs withdrew from her building society account. There is no doubt that Mrs Jacobs had a legal title to this cash. But she then paid it over to Mr Reuben who received it on behalf of Sylcon on the terms of what I have held to be a contractual deposit. The cash then became Sylcon's property. Mrs Jacobs obtained in return for it contractual rights against Sylcon. No doubt these rights constituted a legal, not an equitable, chose in action vested in the Mrs Jacobs, but it was not this item of property which reached the hands of the bank. What the bank received was the cash. But when the bank received it the cash was Sylcon's property, not Mrs Jacobs'. The facts of her case are thus distinguishable in a vital respect from those of *Lipkin Gorman* [1991] 3 WLR 10, where, on the facts, the House of Lords accepted that the solicitors had a legal right to the cash which Cass paid to the gambling club at the time when it was paid over.

Question
What are the limits to the process of tracing at common law?

Tracing in equity

Equity has developed a more realistic approach to tracing than the common law. Equity has conceived the notion that once property is identifiable, recognition of the claimant's right can be given by:

(a) attaching the order to specific property; or

(b) charging the asset for the amount of the claim.

Unmixed fund

Equity follows the common law and declares that where the trust property has been transformed into property of a different form by the trustees and has been kept separate and distinct from the trustees' resources, the beneficiary may take the proceeds. If the proceeds of sale have been used to acquire further property, the beneficiary may elect:

(a) to take the property which has been acquired wholly with the trust property; or

(b) to charge the property for the amount belonging to the trust.

This principle was stated in an *obiter* pronouncement by Jessel MR in *Re Hallett*.

Re Hallett's Estate (1880) 13 Ch D 696, CA

Sir George Jessel MR: The modern doctrine of equity as regards property disposed of by persons in a fiduciary position is a very clear and well established doctrine. There is no distinction between a rightful or wrongful disposition of the property so far as the right of the beneficial owner to follow the 'proceeds'. You can take the proceeds of sale if you can identify them. But it very often happens that you cannot identify the proceeds. The proceeds may have been invested together with money belonging to the person standing in a fiduciary position, in a purchase. He may have bought land with it. In that case, according to the now well established doctrine of equity, the beneficial owner has a right to elect either to take the property purchased, or to hold it as security for the amount of the purchase money, or, as we generally express it, he is entitled at his election either to take the property or to have a charge on the property for the amount of the trust money . . .

In *Banque Belge pour l'Etranger v Hambrouck*, the court applied this principle to funds in a bank account.

Banque Belge pour l'Etranger v Hambrouck [1921] 1 KB 321, CA

Facts

Hambrouck was an accounts clerk at the Pelabon works. By fraud, he procured more than £6,000 by drawing cheques on his employer's bank account at Banque Belge. Hambrouck paid the cheques into his own account at Farrow's bank. Hambrouck voluntarily paid various sums to his Belgian mistress, Mlle Spanoghe, and she in turn paid sums into the Twickenham branch of her bank, the London Joint City and Midland Bank. After Hambrouck was convicted and sentenced for fraud, Banque Belge sought restitution of some £315 which remained in Mlle Spanoghe's account. The bank paid that sum into court. The judge awarded restitution and Mlle Spanoghe appealed.

Held

The claimant's fund was traceable into the bank account:

Atkin LJ: If the question be the right of the plaintiffs in equity to follow their property, I apprehend that no difficulty arises. The case of *Re Hallett's Estate* (1880) 13 Ch D 696 makes it plain that the court will investigate a banking account into which another person's money has been wrongfully paid, and will impute all drawings out of the account in the first instance to the wrongdoer's own moneys, leaving the plaintiff's money intact so far as it remains in the account at all. There can be no difficulty in this case in following every change of form of the money in question, whether in the hands of Hambrouck or of the appellant, and it appears to me that the plaintiffs were entitled to a specific order for the return of the money in question.

The question whether they are entitled to a common law judgment for money had and received may involve other considerations. If, following the principles laid down in *Re Hallett*, it can be ascertained either that the money in the bank, or the commodity which it has bought, is 'the product of, or substitute for, the original thing', then it still follows 'the nature of the thing itself'. On these principles, it would follow that, as the money paid into the bank can be identified as the product of the original money, the plaintiffs have the common law right to claim it, and can sue for money had and received. In the present case less difficulty than usual is experienced in tracing the descent of the money, for substantially no other money has ever been mixed with the proceeds of the fraud.

Mixed fund

Where the trustee or fiduciary has mixed his funds with that of the beneficiary, or has purchased further property with the mixed fund, the beneficiary loses his right to elect to take the property acquired because the property would not have been bought with the beneficiary's money pure and simple but with the mixed fund. However, in the exercise of the exclusive jurisdiction of equity, the beneficiary would be entitled to have the property charged for the amount of the trust money: see *Re Hallett*.

Re Hallett's Estate (1880) 13 Ch D 696, CA

Sir George Jessel MR: But where the trustee has mixed the money with his own the beneficiary can no longer elect to take the property, because it is no longer bought with the trust money but with a mixed fund. He is, however, still entitled to a charge on the property purchased for the amount of the trust money laid out in the purchase . . . That is the modern doctrine of equity.

Facts

Mr Hallett was a solicitor and a trustee of his own marriage settlement in favour of his wife for life and subject thereto for himself for life with remainder to the issue of the marriage. He paid the trust moneys into his bank account. As a solicitor, he acted on behalf of Mrs Cotterill and paid a sum of money received on her behalf into his account. He made various payments into and out of the account. At the time of his death, the account had sufficient funds to meet the claims of the trust and Mrs Cotterill but not, in addition, the claims of the general creditors.

The personal representatives of Hallett sued to ascertain whether or not the trustees and Mrs Cotterill (collectively) had priority in satisfaction of their claim over the general creditors.

Held

The trustees and Mrs Cotterill had priority over the general creditors and were entitled to a charge on the bank account.

In *Re Hallett*, the personal representatives had argued that the amounts withdrawn from the account were primarily trust moneys so that the balance remaining in the account belonged to the personal representatives. This argument was rejected by the Court of Appeal on the ground that an individual who controls funds belonging to an innocent person which have been mixed with his own, and withdraws part of the fund which is dissipated, is assumed to have withdrawn his own funds before depleting the innocent person's balance in the account.

Re Hallett's Estate (1880) 13 Ch D 696, CA

Sir George Jessel MR: Where a man does an act which may be rightfully performed, he cannot say that that act was intentionally and in fact done wrongly. When we come to apply that principle to the case of a trustee who has blended trust monies with his own, it seems to me perfectly plain that he cannot be heard to say that he took away the trust money when he had a right to take away his own money. The simplest case put is the mingling of trust monies in a bag with money of the trustee's own. Suppose he had 100 sovereigns in a bag and he adds to them another 100 sovereigns of his own, so that they are co-mingled in such a way that they cannot be distinguished and the next day he draws out for his own purposes £100, is it tolerable for anybody to allege that what he drew out was the first £100 of trust monies and that he misappropriated it and left his own £100 in the bag? It is obvious he must have taken away that which he had a right to take away, his own £100.

The rule in *Re Hallett's Estate* seems 'to be that if a trustee or fiduciary mixes trust moneys with his own:

(a) the beneficiary is entitled, in the first place, to a charge on the amalgam of the fund in order to satisfy his claim;

(b) if the trustee or fiduciary withdraws moneys for his own purposes, he is deemed to draw out his own moneys, so that the beneficiary may claim the balance of the fund as against the trustee's general creditors.

In *Space Investments Ltd v Canadian Imperial Bank of Commerce Trust Co*, the Privy Council decided that a customer who deposits funds into a bank account acquires a chose in action which he is entitled to trace into the assets of the bank in the event of a liquidation of the bank. But where a bank trustee lawfully mixes the trust funds with its own funds and goes into liquidation, the funds becomes the bank's (including the trust funds) and the beneficiaries' proprietary right to trace is lost because the trust funds are no longer identifiable.

Space Investments Ltd v Canadian Imperial Bank of Commerce Trust Co
[1986] 1 WLR 1072, PC

Facts

The defendant bank was trustee of a variety of settlements and had deposited the funds in deposit accounts at its bank. The bank went into liquidation. The beneficiaries of the trusts attempted to trace the trust funds into the bank's assets and recover in priority over the unsecured creditors.

Held

The claims failed because the bank was expressly authorised to deposit the funds into its account for the general purposes of the bank. The beneficiaries therefore were not entitled to identify their assets:

Lord Templeman: A customer who deposits money with a bank authorises the bank to use that money for the benefit of the bank in any manner the bank pleases. The customer does not acquire any interest in or charge over any asset of the bank or over all the assets of the bank. The deposit account is an acknowledgement and record by the bank of the amount from time to time deposited and withdrawn and of the interest earned. The customer acquires a chose in action, namely the right on request to payment by the bank of the whole or any part of the aggregate amount of principal and interest which has been credited or ought to be credited to the account. If the bank becomes insolvent the customer can only prove in the liquidation of the bank as unsecured creditor for the amount which was, or ought to have been, credited to the account at the date when the bank went into liquidation.

On the other hand, a trustee has no power to use trust money for his own benefit unless the trust instrument expressly authorises him to do so. A bank trustee, like any other trustee, may only apply trust money in the manner authorised by the trust instrument, or by law, for the sole benefit of the beneficiaries and to the exclusion of any benefit to the bank trustee unless the trust instrument otherwise provides. A bank trustee misappropriating trust money for its own use and benefit without authority commits a breach of trust and cannot justify that breach of trust by maintaining a trust deposit account which records the amount which the bank has misappropriated and credits interest which the bank considers appropriate. The beneficiaries have a chose in action, namely, an action against the trustee bank for damages for breach of trust and in addition they possess the equitable remedy of tracing the trust money to any property into which it has been converted directly or indirectly.

A bank in fact uses all deposit moneys for the general purposes of the bank. Whether a bank trustee lawfully receives deposits or wrongly treats trust money as on deposit from trusts, all the moneys are in fact dealt with and expended by the bank for the general purposes of the bank. In these circumstances it is impossible for the beneficiaries interested in trust money misappropriated from their trust to trace their money to any particular asset belonging to the trustee bank. But equity allows the beneficiaries . . . to trace the trust money to all the assets of the bank and to recover the trust money by the exercise of an equitable charge over all the assets of the bank. Where an insolvent bank goes into liquidation that equitable charge secures for the beneficiaries and the trust priority over the claims of the customers in respect of their deposits and over the claims of all other unsecured creditors. This priority is conferred because the customers and other unsecured creditors voluntarily accept the risk that the trustee bank might become insolvent and unable to discharge its obligations in full. On the other hand, the settlor of the trust and the beneficiaries interested under the trust, never accept any risks involved in the possible insolvency of the trustee bank . . . Where a bank trustee is insolvent, trust money wrongfully treated as being on deposit with the bank must be repaid in full so far as may be out of the assets of the bank in priority to any payment of customers' deposits and other unsecured creditors.

Note

Lord Templeman's view of the termination of the proprietary right to trace is highly controversial. It is based on the assumption that if the bank trustee is entitled to mix trust funds with its own, it is entitled to treat the amalgamated fund as its own. This is clearly in direct contradiction of the principle in *Re Hallett* and has not generally been supported. In addition, Lord Templeman declared that where the beneficiaries are entitled to trace as against the bank trustee, but no specific asset is identifiable, the beneficiaries may be entitled to a charging order over all the assets of the bank. This is clearly an over-simplification of the tracing rules.

If the trustee uses trust money to improve the asset of another, such as an innocent third party, *prima facie* the beneficiaries will be entitled to a charge over the asset in order to recover their funds. This is not a transaction that attracts the notion of a constructive trust, because the trustee has no beneficial interest in the asset. The application of this charge is subject to the limitation of not producing unfairness to the innocent third party (or *bona fide* change of position) (see Lord Greene MR in *Re Diplock* [1948] Ch 465, p 596 below).

However, where a trustee misappropriates trust funds in order to fund premiums on a life assurance policy, the beneficiaries (under the trust) become part owners of a chose in action, and thus the policy proceeds, and are entitled to a *pro rata* share of the sum assured: see *Foskett v McKeown*.

Foskett v McKeown [2001] 1 AC 102, HL

Facts

Messrs Murphy and Deasy held sums totalling £2.7 million as trustees for various investors in an Algarve property development scheme. Although land in the Algarve was purchased, it was never developed. The funds of the investors, which existed in two accounts, were dissipated. In November 1986, which was prior to the Algarve land development scheme, Mr Murphy effected a whole life insurance policy in the sum of £1 million. A premium of £10,220 was payable annually throughout Mr Murphy's life. The first two annual premiums (November 1986 and 1987) were paid out of Mr Murphy's funds. The source of the third premium (November 1988) was unclear, but it was conceded that the fourth and fifth premiums (November 1989 and 1990) were paid out of the investors' funds. Mr Murphy committed suicide in March 1991. The insurance company duly paid the proceeds to the trustees of the policy. Mr Foskett, the claimant, sued as a representative of the investors. Mrs McKeown and another, the defendants, were the surviving trustees of the policy.

The claimants contended that a trust was created in their favour when Mr Murphy received their money in pursuance of the Algarve land development scheme. In fraudulent breach of trust, Mr Murphy used their money to pay the 1989 and 1990 (and in part the 1988) premiums. These payments gave them an equitable proprietary interest in the policy and its proceeds. Accordingly, they claimed a *pro rata* share of the proceeds of the policy. Alternatively, they contended that they were entitled to an equitable charge upon the policy and its proceeds to ensure the repayment of the premiums.

The defendants asserted that although the investors' moneys could be traced into the premiums, they could not be traced into the policy proceeds. The policy conferred a contractual right to payment of £1 million on the death of Mr Murphy. This contractual right was acquired when the contract was made and the first premium was paid. Mr Murphy financed all the premiums from his own funds, save for the 1989 and 1990 premiums. Since the premiums paid after the inception of the policy had not contributed to the creation of the contractual right, those persons whose moneys were used to pay the premiums could not claim an interest in the proceeds.

Held

The majority of the Law Lords decided in favour of the claimants on the basis that the investors were entitled to a *pro rata* share of the proceeds of the policy. They treated the policy and its proceeds as if they were assets standing in the name of Mr Murphy beneficially. The majority of the Law Lords reasoned that, immediately before the payment of the fourth premium, the property, held in trust for the defendants, was a chose in action (ie, the bundle of rights enforceable under the policy against the insurers). Mr Murphy, the trustee, by paying the fourth premium out of the moneys of the claimants' trust fund, wrongly mixed the value of the premium with the value of the policy. Thereafter, the trustee for the defendants held the same chose in action (ie, the policy) but with the enhanced value of both contributions. The court drew an analogy with the situation where a trustee mixes the funds of two groups of innocent beneficiaries in a bank account. On this basis, the majority of the Law Lords decided that the proceeds of the policy were held in proportion to the contributions which the parties made to the five premiums:

Lord Millett: [He outlined the distinction between 'following' and 'tracing' property, and continued:]

The tracing rules

The simplest case is where a trustee wrongfully misappropriates trust property and uses it exclusively to acquire other property for his own benefit. In such a case the beneficiary is entitled at his option either to assert his beneficial ownership of the proceeds or to bring a personal claim against the trustee for breach of trust and enforce an equitable lien or charge on the proceeds to secure restoration of the trust fund. He will normally exercise the option in the way most advantageous to himself. If the traceable proceeds have increased in value and are worth more than the original asset, he will assert his beneficial ownership and obtain the profit for himself. There is nothing unfair in this. The trustee cannot be permitted to keep any profit resulting from his misappropriation for himself, and his donees cannot obtain a better title than their donor. If the traceable proceeds are worth less than the original asset, it does not usually matter how the beneficiary exercises his option. He will take the whole of the proceeds on either basis. This is why it is not possible to identify the basis on which the claim succeeded in some of the cases.

[Mixed funds]

A more complicated case is where there is a mixed substitution. This occurs where the trust money represents only part of the cost of acquiring the new asset. I would state the basic rule as follows. Where a trustee wrongfully uses trust money to provide part of the cost of acquiring an asset, the beneficiary is entitled at his option either to claim a proportionate share of the asset or to enforce a lien upon it to secure his personal claim against the trustee for the amount of the misapplied money. It does not matter whether the trustee mixed the trust money with his own in a single fund before using it to acquire the asset, or made separate payments (whether simultaneously or sequentially) out of the differently owned funds to acquire a single asset.

Two observations are necessary at this point. First, there is a mixed substitution (with the results already described) whenever the claimant's property has contributed in part only towards the acquisition of the new asset. It is not necessary for the claimant to show in addition that his property has contributed to any increase in the value of the new asset. This is because this branch of the law is concerned with vindicating rights of property and not with reversing unjust enrichment. Secondly, the beneficiary's right to claim a lien is available only against a wrongdoer and those deriving title under him otherwise than for value. It is not available against competing contributors who are innocent of any wrongdoing. The tracing rules are not the result of any presumption or principle peculiar to equity. They correspond to the common law rules for following into physical mixtures (though the consequences may not be identical). Common to both is the principle that the interests of the wrongdoer who was responsible for the mixing and those who derive title under him otherwise than for value are subordinated to those of innocent contributors. As against the wrongdoer and his successors, the bene-ficiary is entitled to locate his contribution in any part of the mixture and to subordinate their claims to share in the mixture until his own contribution has been satisfied. This has the effect of giving the beneficiary a lien for his contribution if the mixture is deficient.

Innocent contributors, however, must be treated equally inter se. Where the beneficiary's claim is in competition with the claims of other innocent contributors, there is no basis upon which any of the claims can be subordin-ated to any of the others. Where the fund is deficient, the beneficiary is not entitled to enforce a lien for his contributions; all must share rateably in the fund.

The primary rule in regard to a mixed fund, therefore, is that gains and losses are borne by the contributors rateably. The beneficiary's right to elect instead to enforce a lien to obtain repayment is an exception to the primary rule, exercisable where the fund is deficient and the claim is made against the wrongdoer and those claiming through him. It is not necessary to consider whether there are any circumstances in which the bene-ficiary is confined to a lien in cases where the fund is more than sufficient to repay the contributions of all parties. It is sufficient to say that he is not so confined in a case like the present. It is not enough that those defending the claim are innocent of any wrongdoing if they are not themselves contributors but, like the trustees and Mr Murphy's children in the present case, are volunteers who derive title under the wrongdoer otherwise than for value. On ordinary principles such persons are in no better position than the wrongdoer, and are liable to suffer the same subordination of their interests to those of the claimant as the wrongdoer would have been. They certainly cannot do better than the claimant by confining him to a lien and keeping any profit for themselves.

Insurance policies

In the case of an ordinary whole life policy the insurance company undertakes to pay a stated sum on the death of the assured in return for fixed annual premiums payable throughout his life. Such a policy is an entire contract, not a contract for a year with a right of renewal. It is not a series of single premium policies for one year term assurance. It is not like an indemnity policy where each premium buys cover for a year after which the policy-holder must renew or the cover expires. The fact that the policy will lapse if the premiums are not paid makes no difference. The amounts of the annual premiums and of the sum assured are fixed in advance at the outset and assume the payment of annual premiums throughout the term of the policy. The relationship between them is based on the life expectancy of the assured and the rates of interest available on long term government securities at the inception of the policy.

It is, however, of critical importance in the present case to appreciate that the plaintiffs do not trace the premiums directly into the insurance money. They trace them first into the policy and thence into the proceeds of the policy. It is essential not to elide the two steps. In this context, of course, the word 'policy' does not mean the contract of insurance. You do not trace the payment of a premium into the insurance contract any more than you trace a payment into a bank account into the banking contract. The word 'policy' is here used to describe the bundle of rights to which the policyholder is entitled in return for the premiums. These rights, which may be very complex, together constitute a chose in action, viz the right to payment of a debt payable on a future event and contingent upon the continued payment of further premiums until the happening of the event. That chose in action represents the traceable proceeds of the premiums; its current value fluctuates from time to time. When the policy matures, the insurance money represents the traceable proceeds of the policy and hence indirectly of the premiums.

It follows that, if a claimant can show that premiums were paid with his money, he can claim a proportionate share of the policy. His interest arises by reason of and immediately upon the payment of the premiums, and the extent of his share is ascertainable at once. He does not have to wait until the policy matures in order to claim his property. His share in the policy and its proceeds may increase or decrease as further premiums are paid; but it is not affected by the realisation of the policy. His share remains the same whether the policy is sold or surrendered or held until maturity; these are merely different methods of realising the policy. They may affect the amount of the proceeds received on realisation but they cannot affect the extent of his share in the proceeds. In principle the plaintiffs are entitled to the insurance money which was paid on Mr Murphy's death in the same shares and proportions as they were entitled in the policy immediately before his death.

The application of these principles ought not to depend on the nature of the chose in action. They should apply to a policy of life assurance as they apply to a bank account or a lottery ticket.

[Lord Millett reviewed the reasoning in the Court of Appeal, and continued:]

The relevant proportions
A mixed fund, like a physical mixture, is divisible between the parties who contributed to it rateably in proportion to the value of their respective contributions, and this must be ascertained at the time they are added to the mixture. Where the mixed fund consists of sterling or a sterling account or where both parties make their contributions to the mixture at the same time, there is no difference between the cost of the contributions and their sterling value. But where there is a physical mixture or the mixture consists of an account maintained in other units of account and the parties make their contributions at different times, it is essential to value the contributions of both parties at the same time. If this is not done, the resulting proportions will not reflect a comparison of like with like. The appropriate time for valuing the parties' respective contributions is when successive contributions are added to the mixture.

This is certainly what happens with physical mixtures. If 20 gallons of A's oil are mixed with 40 gallons of B's oil to produce a uniform mixture of 60 gallons, A and B are entitled to share in the mixture in the proportions of 1 to 2. It makes no difference if A's oil, being purchased later, cost £2 a gallon and B's oil cost only £1 a gallon, so that they each paid out £40. This is because the mixture is divisible between the parties rateably in proportion to the value of their respective contributions and not in proportion to their respective cost. B's contribution to the mixture was made when A's oil was added to his, and both parties' contributions should be valued at that date. Should a further 20 gallons of A's oil be added to the mixture to produce a uniform mixture of 80 gallons at a time when the oil was worth £3 a gallon, the oil would be divisible equally between them. (A's further 20 gallons are worth £3 a gallon – but so are the 60 gallons belonging to both of them to which they have been added.) It is not of course necessary to go through the laborious task of valuing every successive contribution separately in sterling. It is simpler to take the account by measuring the contributions in gallons rather than sterling. This is merely a short cut which produces the same result.

In my opinion the same principle operates whenever the mixture consists of fungibles, whether these be physical assets like oil, grain or wine or intangibles like money in an account. Take the case where a trustee misappropriates trust money in a sterling bank account and pays it into his personal dollar account which also contains funds of his own. The dollars are, of course, merely units of account; the account holder has no proprietary interest in them. But no one, I think, would doubt that the beneficiary could claim the dollar value of the contributions made with trust money. Most people would explain this by saying that it is because the account is kept in dollars. But the correct explanation is that it is because the contributions are made in dollars. In order to allocate the fund between the parties rateably in proportion to the value of their respective contributions, it is necessary to identify the point at which the trust money becomes mixed with the trustee's own money. This does not occur when the trustee pays in a sterling cheque drawn on the trust account. At that stage the trust money is still identifiable. It occurs when the bank credits the dollar equivalent of the sterling cheque to the trustee's personal account. Those dollars represent the contribution made by the trust. The sterling value of the trust's contribution must be valued at that time; and it follows that the trustee's contributions, which were also made in dollars, must be valued at the same time. Otherwise one or other party will suffer the injustice of having his contributions undervalued.

Calculating the plaintiff's share

Where money belonging to different parties is used to pay the premiums under a policy of this kind, it cannot be right to divide the proceeds of the policy crudely according to the number of premiums paid by each of them. The only sensible way of apportioning the proceeds of such a policy is by reference to the number of units allocated to the policy in return for each premium. This is readily ascertainable, since policyholders are normally issued with an annual statement showing the number of units held before receipt of the latest premium, the number allocated in respect of the premium, and the total number currently held. But in any case these numbers can easily be calculated from published material.

This would obviously be the right method to adopt if the policyholder acquired a proprietary interest in the units. These would fall to be dealt with in the same way as grain, oil or wine. There would of course still be a mixed substitution, since after the mixture neither party's contributions can be identified. Neither can recover his own property, but only a proportion of the whole. Unlike Roman law, the common law applied the same principles whenever there is no means of identifying the specific assets owned by either party. In the United States they have been applied to logs, pork, turkeys, sheep and straw hats: see *Dr Lionel Smith, The Law of Tracing*, at p.70. In fact unit-linked policies normally provide that the policyholder has no proprietary interest in the units allocated to the policy. They are merely units of account. The absence of a proprietary interest in the units would be highly material in the event of the insolvency of the insurance company. But it should have no effect on the method of calculating the shares in which competing claimants are entitled to the proceeds of the policy.

The policy in the present case is only a variant of the unit-linked policy of the kind I have described. It is also primarily a savings medium but it offers an additional element of life assurance. This protects the assured against the risk of death before the value of the units allocated to the policy reaches a predetermined amount. On receipt of each premium, the insurance company allocates accumulation units in the designated fund to the policy ('the investment element'), and immediately thereafter cancels sufficient of the units to provide 'the insurance element'.

In my opinion the correct method of apportioning the sum assured between the parties is to deal separately with its two components. The investment element (which amounted to £39,347 at the date of death in the present case) should be divided between the parties by reference to the value at maturity of the units allocated in respect of each premium and not cancelled. The balance of the sum assured should be divided between the parties rateably in the proportions in which they contributed to the internal premiums. This is not to treat the allocated units as a real investment separate from the life cover when it was not. Nor is it to treat the method by which the benefits payable under the policy is calculated as determinative or even relevant. It is to recognise the true nature of the policy, and to give effect to the fact that the sum assured had two components, to one of which the parties made their contributions in units and to the other of which they made their contributions in the sterling proceeds of realised units.

These calculations require the policyholder's account to be redrawn as two accounts, one for each party. The number of units allocated to the policy on the receipt of each premium should be credited to the account of the party whose money was used to pay the premium. The number of units so allocated should be readily ascertainable from the records of the insurance company, but if not it can easily be worked out. The number of units which were cancelled to provide the internal premium should then be ascertained in similar fashion and debited to the appropriate account. In the case of the earlier premiums paid with Mr Murphy's own money this will be the trustees' account. In the case of the later premiums paid with the plaintiffs' money, the cancelled units should not be debited wholly to the plaintiffs' account, but rateably to the two accounts. The amount of the internal premiums should then be credited to the two accounts in the same proportions as those in which the cancelled units were debited to provide them.

Assets purchased

Since the beneficiaries are entitled to trace their property (including a charge) into a mixed fund, it follows that that right (to trace) may extend to property (assets) acquired with the mixed fund.

Accordingly, if a part of the fund is used to purchase an asset which is identifiable and the remainder of the fund has been exhausted (the right to trace against the fund becoming otiose), the beneficiary may claim to trace against the asset acquired by the trustees.

In short, from the point of view of the beneficiary, the trustee and his successors in title are prevented from denying the interest deemed to be acquired with the mixed fund: see *Re Oatway*.

Re Oatway [1903] 2 Ch 356, HC

Facts

O, a trustee, paid trust moneys of £3,000 into his private bank account containing his own moneys. He later purchased shares in Oceana Ltd for £2,137. After this drawing out, there was still more in the account than the amount of trust moneys paid in. O paid further sums into the account, but his subsequent drawings for his own purposes exhausted the entire amount standing to his credit. The shares were later sold for £2,474. O died insolvent. The beneficiaries claimed that the proceeds of sale of the shares represented their moneys. The personal representatives claimed that, as O had sufficient moneys in his account to satisfy the claim of the beneficiaries at the time of the purchase of the shares, that purchase was met by the trustee's own funds.

Held

The court found in favour of the beneficiaries on the ground that the personal representatives were not entitled to allege that the dissipated funds from the account belonged to the beneficiaries:

> **Joyce J:** It is clear that when any of the money drawn out has been invested and the investment remains in the name or under the control of the trustee, the balance having been dissipated by him, he cannot maintain that the investment which remains represents his own money and that what was spent and can no longer be recovered was the money belonging to the trust. In other words, when private money of the trustee and that which he held in a fiduciary capacity have been mixed in the same banking account from which various payments have been made, then, in order to determine to whom any remaining balance or any investment paid for out of the account ought to be deemed to belong, the trustee must be debited with all the sums that have been withdrawn and applied to his own use so as to be no longer recoverable, and the trust money in like manner debited with any sums taken out and duly invested in the names of the proper trustees. The personal representatives have contended that the trustee was entitled to withdraw from the account and rightly applied the fund for his own purposes; and accordingly the shares belong to his estate. To this I answer that he never was entitled to withdraw the £2,137 from the account or, at all events, that he could not be entitled to take that sum from the account and hold it or the investments made therewith, freed from the charge in favour of the trust, unless and until the trust money paid into the account had been first restored and the trust fund reinstated by due investment of the money in the joint names of the proper trustees, which was never done.

Scope of the charge

After some hesitation, it appears that a beneficiary who has a right to trace into an asset bought by the trustees will be permitted to claim any increase in the asset purchased. It makes no difference whether the asset was bought with an unmixed or a mixed fund. No difficulty arises if the asset was bought with an unmixed fund, for the claimant is the sole owner of such asset; the difficulty surrounds the claim to any increase in the value of the asset bought with a mixed fund. One argument which has been put forward is that the charge on the asset ought to be limited to the amount of the trust moneys and no more, for the claimant is only seeking to recover his money and not claiming the asset bought with his funds. Supporters of this view refer to Jessel MR's judgment in *Re Hallett's Estate* as advancing this argument. However, Ungoed-Thomas J in *Re Tilley's Will Trust* distinguished the statement by Jessel MR in *Re Hallett* on the ground that the judge was not considering the question of the 'proportion' of the property that would have been subject to the charge, but was only dealing with whether the charge existed or not. Furthermore, Ungoed-Thomas J in *Re Tilley* declared, *obiter*, that the beneficiary's charge on the asset would be in respect of a proportionate part of the increase in value because, otherwise, the trustee (and his successors in title who ought to be in no better position) might profit from the breach of trust.

Re Tilley's Will Trust [1967] Ch 1179, HC

Facts

A testator, who died in 1932, left property to his widow, as sole trustee, on trust to her for life, remainder to Charles and Mabel (his children by a former marriage) in equal shares. The trust properties were realised between 1933 and 1952 for a total of £2,237 (trust moneys). This amount was paid into the widow's bank account and was blended with her own moneys. Until 1951, the widow's bank account was at various times substantially overdrawn (in 1945, she had an overdraft of £23,536). Investments were purchased by the widow financed by overdraft facilities at the bank. From 1951, her account was sufficiently in credit from her own personal contributions, that is, without regard to any trust moneys. In 1959, the widow died with an estate valued at £94,000. Mabel had predeceased the widow and her administrators sued the widow's personal representatives claiming that Mabel's estate was entitled to one-half of the proportion of the profits made by the widow, that is, on the assumption that the widow's personal representatives failed to show that Mrs Tilley's investments were made out of her personal moneys, the claimant was entitled to a *pro rata* amount of the profits from the investments.

Held

The trust moneys were not used to purchase the investments made by Mrs Tilley (the trustee) but were used only to reduce her overdraft which was the source of the purchase moneys. In short, there was a *causa sine qua non* between the trust moneys and the investments, but the trust moneys were not the *causa causans* of the profit:

> **Ungoed-Thomas J:** . . . it seems to me, on a proper appraisal of all the facts of this case, that Mrs Tilley's breach halted at the mixing of the funds in her bank account. Although properties bought out of those funds would, like the bank account itself (at any rate if the monies in the bank account were inadequate) be charged with repayment of the trust monies which then would stand in the same position as the bank account, yet the trust monies were not invested in properties at all but merely went in reduction of Mrs Tilley's overdraft which was in reality the source of the purchase monies. The plaintiff's claim therefore failed and he was entitled to no more than repayment of half of £2,237 . . .
>
> [However, Ungoed-Thomas J considered, *obiter*, the scope of the charge on the assets bought had the claimant been entitled to trace into the investments and reasoned thus:]
>
> In *Re Hallett* (1880) 13 Ch D 696, the claim was against a bank balance of mixed fiduciary and personal funds, and it is in the context of such a claim that it was held that the person in a fiduciary character drawing out money from the bank account must be taken to have drawn out his own money in preference to the trust money, so that the claim of the beneficiaries prevailed against the balance of the account.
>
> *Re Oatway* [1903] 2 Ch 356, was the converse of the decision in *Re Hallett*. In that case the claim was not against the balance left in the bank of such mixed monies, but against the proceeds of sale of shares which the trustee had purchased with monies which, as in *Re Hallett*, he had drawn from the bank account. But unlike the situation in *Re Hallett*, his later drawings had exhausted the account so that it was useless to proceed against the account. It was held that the beneficiary was entitled to the proceeds of sale of the shares which were more than their purchase price but less than the trust monies paid into the account. Further, *Re Oatway* did not raise the question whether the beneficiary is entitled to any profit made out of the purchase of property by the trustee out of a fund consisting of his personal monies which he mixed with the trust monies and so the judgment was not directed to, and did not deal with that question . . . Lord Parker in *Sinclair v Brougham* [1914] AC 398 had considered *Re Hallett* but he did not address his mind to the question of whether the beneficiary could claim a proportion of the property corresponding to his own contribution to the purchase. In *Snell's Principles of Equity* 26th ed, 1966, p 315, the law is thus stated:
>
> > Where the trustee purchases shares with part of a mixed fund and then dissipates the balance, the beneficiary's charge binds the shares; for although the trustee is presumed to have bought the shares out of his own money, the charge attaches to the entire fund and could be discharged only be restoring the trust monies.

Where the property purchased has increased in value, the charge will not be merely for the amount of the trust monies but for a proportionate part of increased value.

Lowest intermediate balance

The rule in *Re Hallett's Estate* (vis à vis the 'balance' in a blended bank account) is to the effect that withdrawals from a mixed fund are deemed to take the order of the trustee's moneys before the beneficiary's funds. Accordingly, if the funds in the account fall below the amount of the trust funds originally paid in, that part of the trust fund (the depreciation) is presumed to have been spent. The right to trace into the balance held in the bank account will be depreciated to the extent of the lowest balance in the account. The lowest intermediate balance is presumed to be the trust property. Subsequent payments in are not *prima facie* treated as repayments to the trust fund in order to repair the breach, unless the trustee earmarks such repayments as having that effect: see *Roscoe v Winder*.

Roscoe v Winder [1915] 1 Ch 62, HC

Facts

In accordance with an agreement for the sale of the goodwill of a business, the purchaser, Wigham, had agreed to collect the debt and pay it over to the company. He collected the debt (£623, 8s, 5d) and paid £455, 18s, 1d into his personal bank account. The remainder of the debt was unaccounted for. He drew out funds which were dissipated until the credit balance in his account was only £25, 18s. Later, he paid in more of his own moneys and died leaving a balance in the account of £358, 5s, 5d. The question in issue was the extent to which the plaintiff could claim a charge under the rule in *Re Hallett's Estate*.

Held

Although Wigham had held the money as trustee, the charge was limited to £25, 18s – the lowest intermediate balance subsequent to the appropriation:

Sargant J: It appears that after the payment in by the debtor of a portion of the book debts which he had received, the balance at the bank was reduced by his drawings to a sum of £25, 18s. So that, although the ultimate balance at the debtor's death was about £358, there had been an intermediate balance of only £25, 18s. The result of that seems to me to be that the trust monies cannot possibly be traced into this common fund which was standing to the debtor's credit at his death to an extent of more than £25, 18s because although *prima facie* under the second rule in *Re Hallett* any drawings out by the debtor ought to be attributed to the private monies which he had at the bank and not to the trust monies, yet, when the drawings out had revealed such an amount that the whole of his private money part had been exhausted, it necessarily followed that the rest of the drawings must have been against trust monies. Counsel for the plaintiff contended that the account ought to be treated as a whole and the balance from time to time standing to the credit of that account was subject to one continual charge or trust ... you must for the purpose of tracing put your finger on some definite fund which either remains in its original state or can be found in another shape. That is tracing and tracing seems to be excluded except as to £25, 18s.

Certainly, after having heard *Re Hallett's Estate* (1880) 13 Ch D 616, stated over and over again, I should have thought that the general view of that decision was that it only applied to such an amount of the balance ultimately standing to the credit of the trustee as did not exceed the lowest balance of the account during the intervening period.

This decision was approved and the principles adopted by the Privy Council in *Re Goldcorp Exchange Ltd* in respect of gold bullion.

Re Goldcorp Exchange Ltd [1994] 3 WLR 199, PC

Facts

Goldcorp Exchange Ltd (the company), a dealer in gold and other precious metals, was put into receivership by the Bank of New Zealand under the terms of a debenture issued by the company. The company in its promotional literature had made excessive claims and attracted a great deal of interest from members of the public. Amongst its assets was a stock of gold, platinum and silver bullion. This stock was insufficient to satisfy the claims of members of the public who had purchased precious metals for future delivery. The debts secured by the debentures and floating charges were in excess of the entire assets of the company, so that if the secured interest of the bank was satisfied in preference to the claims of the purchasers, the latter were entitled to nothing. The private investors asserted proprietary claims in respect of the bullion. They were classified into three categories. The first and largest category comprised those customers who were referred to as 'non-allocated claimants'. These were customers who had purchased bullion for future delivery. The second category of claimant was Mr Liggett, who purchased specific gold coins from the company and agreed to buy a further 1,000 coins on a non-allocated basis and to store all the coins with the company. The company subsequently acquired a substantial quantity of gold coins, but not expressly for him. The third category of claimants consisted of those who had made contracts for the purchase of bullion from Walker & Hall Commodities Ltd (W Ltd) before the business of that company was acquired by Goldcorp Ltd. The receivers applied to the court for directions concerning the disposal. The High Court rejected the claims of the first two categories of claimants but allowed the claims of W Ltd's customers. The Court of Appeal of New Zealand allowed the appeals of the first and second categories of claimants, on the ground that these claimants had retained beneficial interests in the purchase moneys paid under the contracts of sale. Such interests entitled the claimants to trace into the general assets of the company in priority to the bank's charges. The Court of Appeal also declared that customers of W Ltd were in the same position. The receivers and bank appealed to the Privy Council.

Held

(a) The first and second category of claimants had contracted to purchase unascertained goods in which no property passed to them in law or in equity immediately on making the purchases.

(b) The collateral promises made in the company's brochures and by its employees did not constitute declarations of trust by the company in favour of the customers.

(c) The company did not become a fiduciary towards its customers.

(d) The company did not become a trustee of the purchase moneys for each customer and, as such, was entitled to spend such sums as it wished.

(e) The bullion belonging to W Ltd's claimants comprised the lowest balance thereof held by the company at any time.

Lord Mustill: On the facts found by the judge, the company as bailee held bullion belonging to the individual Walker & Hall claimants, intermingled the bullion of all such claimants, mixed that bullion with bullion belonging to the company, withdrew bullion from the mixed fund and then purchased more bullion, which was added to the mixed fund, without the intention of replacing the bullion of the Walker & Hall claimants. In these circumstances, the bullion belonging to the Walker & Hall claimants which became held by the company's receivers consisted of bullion equal to the lowest balance of metal held by the company at any time: see *James Roscoe (Bolton) Ltd v Winder* [1915] 1 Ch 62 . . .

The Walker & Hall claimants now seek to go further and ask the court to impose an equitable lien on all the property of the company at the date of the receivership to recover the value of their bullion unlawfully misappropriated by the company. Such a lien was considered by the Board in *Space Investments Ltd v Canadian Imperial Bank of Commerce Trust Co (Bahamas) Ltd* [1986] 1 WLR 1072. In that case the Board held that beneficiaries could not claim trust moneys lawfully deposited by a bank trustee with itself as banker in priority to other depositors and unsecured creditors. But Lord Templeman considered the position which would arise if a bank trustee unlawfully borrowed trust moneys. He said, at p 1074:

> A bank in fact uses all deposit moneys for the general purposes of the bank. Whether a bank trustee lawfully receives deposits or wrongly treats trust money as on deposit from trusts, all the moneys are in fact dealt with and expended by the bank for the general purposes of the bank. In these circumstances, it is impossible for the beneficiaries interested in trust money misappropriated from their trust to trace their money to any particular asset belonging to the trustee bank. But equity allows the beneficiaries, or a new trustee

appointed in place of an insolvent bank trustee, to protect the interests of the beneficiaries, to trace the trust money to all the assets of the bank and to recover the trust money by the exercise of an equitable charge over all the assets of the bank.

These observations were criticised by Professor Goode in his 'Mary Oliver Memorial Address' (1987) 103 LQR 433, pp 445–47, as being inconsistent with the observations of the Court of Appeal in *In Re Diplock* [1948] Ch 465, p 521, where it was said:

> The equitable remedies presuppose the continued existence of the money either as a separate fund or as part of a mixed fund or as latent in property acquired by means of such a fund. If, on the facts of any individual case, such continued existence is not established, equity is as helpless as the common law itself. If the fund, mixed or unmixed, is spent upon a dinner, equity, which dealt only in specific relief and not in damages, could do nothing. If the case was one which at common law involved breach of contract the common law could, of course, award damages but specific relief would be out of the question. It is, therefore, a necessary matter for consideration in each case where it is sought to trace money in equity, whether it has such a continued existence, actual or notional, as will enable equity to grant specific relief.

In the present case it is not necessary or appropriate to consider the scope and ambit of the observations in the *Space Investments* case [1986] 1 WLR 1072 or their application to trustees other than bank trustees, because all members of this Board are agreed that it would be inequitable to impose a lien in favour of the Walker & Hall claimants. Those claimants received the same certificates and trusted the company in a manner no different from other bullion customers. There is no evidence that the debenture holders and the unsecured creditors at the date of the receivership benefited directly or indirectly from the breaches of trust committed by the company or that Walker & Hall bullion continued to exist as a fund latent in property vested in the receivers.

In these circumstances, the Walker & Hall claimants must be restored to the remedies granted to them by the trial judge.

The same principle was applied in *Bishopsgate Investment v Homan* concerning an attempt to trace into a bank account which was overdrawn at one point in its history.

Bishopsgate Investment Management Ltd v Homan [1994] 3 WLR 1270, CA

Facts

BIM Ltd was trustee of certain assets of pensio schemes, held on trust for the benefit of employees and ex-employees of Maxwell Communication Corporation plc (MCC). MCC fraudulently paid these assets into its overdrawn account. The liquidator of BIM claimed to be entitled to an equitable charge in priority to all of the other unsecured creditors of MCC. The judge refused to make the order. The plaintiff appealed.

Held

Equitable tracing did not extend to tracing through an overdrawn account, whether overdrawn at the time the money was paid into the account or subsequently. The court applied the principle in *Roscoe v Winder* and distinguished the *Space Investments* case:

Dillon LJ: [Counsel for BIM] claims (as it has been explained to us) to be entitled to an equitable charge as security for its claims against MCC: (i) over any moneys standing to the credit at the time of the appointment of the administrators of MCC of any banking account maintained by MCC into which any moneys of BIM or the proceeds of any assets of BIM misappropriated from it were paid; and (ii) over any assets acquired out of any such bank account, whether or not in credit as at the date such assets were acquired.

So far as (i) is concerned, the point is that the National Westminster Bank account into which the misappropriated BIM trust moneys were paid, happened to be in credit when the administrators were appointed. BIM therefore claims a lien on that credit balance in the National Westminster Bank account for the amount of the misappropriated trust moneys. It is difficult to suppose, however, in the circumstances of Robert Maxwell's last days – and I know no evidence – that Robert Maxwell intended to make good the misappropriation of the BIM pension moneys by the cryptic expedient of arranging to put MCC's account with National Westminster Bank into credit – but without repaying the credit balance this created to BIM. But in the absence of clear evidence of intention to make good the depredations on BIM, it is not possible to assume that the credit balance has been clothed with a trust in favour of BIM and its beneficiaries: see *James Roscoe (Bolton) Ltd v Winder* [1915] 1 Ch 62. As to (ii), this seems to be going back to the original wide interpretation of what Lord Templeman said in the

Space Investments case [1986] 1 WLR 1072 and applying it to an overdrawn account because the misappropriated moneys that went into the account were trust moneys and thus different from other moneys that may have gone into that account. But the moneys in the *Space Investments* case were also trust moneys, and so, if argument (ii) is valid in the present case, it would also have been valid, as a matter of law, in the *Space Investments* case. But that was rejected in *In re Goldcorp Exchange Ltd* [1994] 3 WLR 199, because equitable tracing, though devised for the protection of trust moneys misapplied, cannot be pursued through an overdrawn and therefore non-existent fund. Acceptance of argument (ii) would, in my judgment, require the rejection of *In Re Diplock* [1948] Ch 465, which is binding on us, and of Lord Mustill's explanation of Lord Templeman's statement in the *Space Investments* case in *In Re Goldcorp Exchange Ltd* [1994] 3 WLR 199, p 222.

It is not open to us to say that because the moneys were trust moneys the fact that they were paid into an overdrawn account or have otherwise been dissipated presents no difficulty to raising an equitable charge on assets of MCC for their amount in favour of BIM. The difficulty Lord Mustill referred to is not displaced.

Note
The logical effect of this rule is that, *prima facie*, if the mixed account is left without funds after the appropriation by the trustee, the claimant will not be entitled to a charge under *Re Hallett*. This is the position whether subsequent funds are paid in or not.

Question
What is meant by the 'lowest intermediate balance' in respect of a tracing claim?

If the trustees, after the appropriation, deliberately earmark a repayment or purchase as belonging to the trust, the beneficiaries will be entitled to trace into that fund or asset: see *Robertson v Morrice*.

Robertson v Morrice (1845) 4 LT OS 430

Facts
A trustee, who held stock subject to a trust and additionally similar stock of his own, mixed both sets of properties and treated them as one holding. He sold parts of the mixed stock from time to time so that shortly before his death the amount left was less than what he should have been holding on trust. On his deathbed, he instructed the clerk to buy more stock of a similar nature in order to replace that which he had misappropriated from the trust. This was done by the clerk. The beneficiaries claimed to be entitled to the stock as trust property.

Held
The entire portfolio of stock was subject to the trust on the following grounds:

(a) the balance of the original mixed holding was subject to the charge that attached on the mixing;

(b) the newly acquired holding was trust property owing to the declaration by the trustee that such purchase was designed to replace the trust property.

The rule in *Clayton's Case*

The rule in *Clayton's Case* is a rule of banking law and one of convenience that had been adopted in the early part of the 19th century to ascertain the respective interests in a bank account of two innocent parties *inter se*. Where a trustee mixes trust funds subsisting in an active current bank account belonging to two beneficiaries, the amount of the balance in the account is determined by attributing withdrawals in the order of sums paid in to the account: first in, first out (FIFO).

The rule is applied as between beneficiaries (or innocent parties) *inter se* in order to:

(a) ascertain ownership of the balance of the fund; and

(b) ascertain ownership of specific items bought from funds withdrawn from the account.

The basis of the rule lies in the fact that as between the beneficiaries (or innocent parties) the 'equities are equal', that is, there is no need to give one beneficiary any special treatment over the other. It is worth noting, however, that as between the trustee and beneficiary, the rule in *Re Hallett* and not *Clayton* applies. The wrongdoer may never take advantage of the FIFO rule.

Clayton's Case, Devaynes v Noble (1816) 1 Mer 529, CA

Facts

Mr Clayton, a customer at a bank, had a balance of £1,713 in his favour at the time of the death of Devaynes, a partner in a bank. Clayton drew out more than £1,713 (thus creating an overdraft) and then paid in further sums totalling more than the overdraft. Later, the firm of bankers went bankrupt. Clayton sought to recover from Devaynes' estate.

Held

The sums withdrawn by Clayton, after Devaynes died, must have been appropriated to the earlier debt of £1,713 so that Devaynes' estate was free from liability. The sums which Clayton subsequently paid in constituted a 'new debt' for which the surviving partners alone were liable:

> **Grant MR:** This is a case of a banking account, where all the sums paid in form one blended fund, the parts of which have no longer any distinct existence. Neither banker nor customer ever thinks of saying, this draft is to be placed to the account of the £500 paid in on Monday, and this other to the account of the £500 paid in on Tuesday. There is a fund of £1,000 to draw upon, and that is enough. In such a case, there is no room for any other appropriation than that which arises from the order in which the receipts and payments take place and are carried into the account. Presumably, it is the sum first paid in, that is first drawn out. It is the first item on the debit side of the account that is discharged, or reduced, by the first item on the credit side. The appropriation is made by the very act of setting the two items against each other. Upon that principle, all accounts current are settled, and particularly cash accounts.

The rule in *Clayton's Case*, as originally formulated, was a rule in banking law applicable in determining ownership of funds in an account. However, the rule has been extended to ascertain the interests of:

(a) beneficiaries *inter se* under two or more separate trusts; and

(b) competing claimants or beneficiaries under the same trust.

Question
What is the rule in *Clayton's Case*?

In *Re Stenning*, the court in an *obiter* pronouncement considered the application of the rule in *Clayton's Case*.

Re Stenning [1895] 2 Ch 433, HC

Facts

A solicitor paid moneys belonging to a number of clients into his personal bank account. This money included £448, 18s, 6d which was due to Mrs Smith. There was often more than this amount in the account, but there was often less than the total of the clients' moneys paid in. Mrs Smith brought a claim against the solicitor alleging that she was a beneficiary under a trust.

Held

No trust had been created on the facts, but only a loan was made by agreement. But if the £448, 18s, 6d had been trust moneys, *Clayton's Case* would have applied as between Mrs Smith and the other clients.

Note

One criticism that has been levelled against the rule in *Clayton's Case* is that it lacks justice as between claimants of equal standing. The rule exists as a rough and ready solution, the outcome to which depends on a matter of chance, that is, the application of the rule depends on the precise time when money from two trusts (or moneys from the same trust but belonging to two or more beneficiaries) was paid into a current account.

A more equitable solution, as compared with *Clayton's Case*, would have been to allow the two groups of beneficiaries to share the balance in the account, rateably, in proportion to the sums originally placed in the account from the two trusts, that is, the beneficiaries ought to be entitled to an order ranking in *pari passu*. The House of Lords adopted this equitable solution in respect of the claims of two innocent parties *inter se* to a fund, not being a current account, which had been mixed by a fiduciary: see *Sinclair v Brougham*.

Sinclair v Brougham [1914] AC 398, HL

Facts

The litigation arose when the Birkbeck Building Society, having borrowing power, established and developed, in addition to the legitimate business of a building society, a banking business which was admittedly *ultra vires*. In connection with this banking business, customers deposited sums of money. In 1911, the society was wound up. The assets were claimed, *inter alia*, by the ordinary shareholders and the depositors. Each group claimed priority over the other.

Held

The two classes of claimants were entitled to the assets rateably, following the rule in *Re Hallett*, that is, an order was made entitling both groups of claimants to a charge ranking in *pari passu* reflecting the proportions of their respective contributions:

> **Lord Sumner:** My Lords, I agree that the principle on which *Hallett's* case is founded justifies an order allowing the appellants to follow the assets, not merely to the verge of actual identification, but even somewhat further in a case like the present, where after a process of exclusion only two classes or groups of persons, having equal claims, are left in and all superior classes have been eliminated. Tracing in a sense it is not, for we know that the money coming from A went into one security and that coming from B into another and that the two securities did not probably depreciate exactly in the same percentage and we know further that no one will ever know anymore. Still I think this well within the 'tracing' equity, and that among persons making up these two groups the principle of rateable division of the assets is sound . . .

Note

This case was overruled in *Westdeutsche Landesbank v Islington BC* (see Lord Browne-Wilkinson's judgment, p 549 above) on the ground that no single *ratio* could be detected. However, *Sinclair v Brougham* is mentioned here in order to demonstrate the application of the *Re Hallett* principle and the court's reluctance to follow *Clayton*.

Re Hallett extended in Sinclair v Brougham

The litigation in *Re Hallett* was between persons of unequal standing, namely, the innocent claimant and the wrongdoer (or successor). The wrongdoer is prevented from denying the interest acquired by the innocent claimant to the mixed fund.

The litigation in *Sinclair v Brougham*, however, was between two groups of innocent claimants (of equal standing) whose moneys had been represented in assets available for distribution. Accordingly, the House of Lords extended the principle in *Re Hallett* in concluding that the claimants were entitled to the assets rateably. This view was expressed by Lord Greene HR in *Re Diplock*.

Re Diplock [1948] Ch 465, CA

Lord Greene MR: [Analysing the *Sinclair v Brougham* decision:] Each of the two classes of contributors claimed priority over the other. Until the case reached the House of Lords, the possibility that they might rank *pari passu* does not appear to have been considered . . . The House of Lords held that on the principle on which *Hallett's* case (1880) 13 Ch D 696, was founded, the two classes shared rateably. In one respect, no doubt, this application of the principle is an extension of it since, although the right of individuals to trace their own money (if they could) was preserved in the order of the House, the order provided for tracing the aggregate contributions of the two classes as classes . . . the extension of the principle in *Sinclair v Brougham* [1914] AC 398, was the obvious and, indeed on the facts, the only practical method of securing a first distribution of the assets . . .

Similarly, in *Barlow Clowes v Vaughan*, the Court of Appeal favoured the *pari passu* charge where the claimants were investors in a common fund, as opposed to the 'rough and ready' solution in *Clayton's Case*.

Barlow Clowes International Ltd (In Liquidation) and Others v Vaughan and Others [1992] 4 All ER 22, CA

Facts

The companies promoted and managed certain investment plans in gilt-edged stock. Funds had been misapplied and the companies went into liquidation, and receivers were appointed. At the time of the collapse, the companies had a total liability of £115 million owed to around 11,000 investors. The amount available was far less than the amount of the investors' claims. The moneys and assets available for distribution to investors were contributed by three classes of claimants, namely:

(a) moneys paid by investors for investments in gilts which were acquired by the companies;

(b) moneys in bank accounts awaiting investment in gilts at the time the receivers were appointed;

(c) the net proceeds of sale of additional assets, including a yacht, *Boukephalos*.

The receivers brought proceedings for directions as to the basis on which the assets and moneys ought to be distributed. The judge (Peter Gibson J) decided that the distribution should be made in accordance with the rule in *Clayton's Case* ('first in, first out'). Thus, the investors were to be paid in the reverse order to that in which they had made deposits, so that later investors were more likely to be repaid. The second defendant appealed.

Held

The moneys and assets were intended to form a common investment pool and the claimants ranked in *pari passu*. Thus, they were entitled to a charge on the common investment pool shared rateably, in proportion to their contributions, in accordance with the principle in *Sinclair v Brougham*. Where the rule in *Clayton* is impractical, or may cause injustice, or is contrary to the intention of the investors, the court is entitled to refuse to apply it, provided that an alternative method of distribution is available. *Clayton's* rule was considered to be time-consuming and expensive. In addition, the rule would cause injustice, because a relatively small number of investors would become entitled to most of the fund and the rule was, in any event, not applicable to tracing claims. An alternative method, known as the 'rolling charge', was rejected by the court. This solution regards a mixture of funds from different sources as a 'blend or cocktail'. The effect is that a withdrawal is treated as a depletion of an interest in the account in the same proportion as the interest bears to the fund immediately before the withdrawal is made. Thus, losses are borne proportionately, but later payments in the account are unaffected by earlier withdrawals. The court rejected this solution as complex, expensive and impractical:

> **Dillon LJ:** The question is, in relation to the balances in the bank accounts specified in schedule A to the judge's order: which were moneys contributed by investors for investment, which had not been invested by the time BCI went into liquidation and the receivers were appointed, whether these moneys became part of the common funds as soon as they were received into the bank accounts of BCI from the investors?
>
> There are attractions in the view that if moneys are paid for investment in a common fund of gilt-edged investments they only become part of the common fund when invested in gilts, and are, in the meantime, held on resulting trust for the payers. On the other hand, the terms of application, in general, expressly authorise the placing of any uninvested funds with any bank, etc, on such terms as BCI thinks fit, whether bearing interest or not.

What troubles me at this stage, on the particular facts of the present case, is the contrast between the large amounts held in the accounts specified in schedule A to the judge's order and the much smaller amount of the gilts, above-mentioned, which came into the control of the receivers. There is also the consideration of the very large amounts of investors' moneys which have been lost to the investors without ever having been invested as envisaged in the documents relating to the portfolios. In one sense, it is unreal to treat the moneys in the bank accounts in schedule A as the uninvested part of a common investment fund. But the question posed by Lord Halsbury LC in *Mecca* [1897] AC 286, p 290 ['... the circumstances of a case may afford ground for inferring that transactions of the parties were not so intended as to come under the rule in *Clayton*'], must, I apprehend, be answered by considering the nature of the transaction as the investors intended it to be at the outset, when they paid their moneys to BCI, not the very different circumstances of the actual outcome, of which, when they contributed, they knew nothing. Therefore, after considerable hesitation, I conclude that the moneys in the bank accounts in schedule A ought to be treated, for the purposes of distribution, as the uninvested part of the common investment fund.

As for the proceeds of sale of the yacht, *Boukephalos*, on the material before this court the yacht was never an authorised investment for funds paid to BCI for investment in gilt-edged securities, and its purchase was a misapplication of trust moneys. Nonetheless, the moneys applied in the purchase of the yacht were part of the the common investment fund – for the same reasons as the moneys in the accounts specified in schedule A to the judge's order. Accordingly, the proceeds of the yacht must also be treated as part of the common fund.

I would allow this appeal and set aside the order of the judge and I would declare that the rule in *Clayton's Case* (1816) 1 Mer 529, is not to be applied on the distribution of the moneys in the bank accounts specified in schedules A and B to the judge's order or of the proceeds of sale of the additional assets. Instead, these were held on trust for all unpaid investors *pari passu* rateably, in proportion to the amounts due to them.

Woolf LJ: The approach, in summary, which I would adopt to resolving the issues raised by this appeal are as follows:

(i) While the rule in *Clayton's Case* (1816) 1 Mer 529, is, *prima facie*, available to determine the interests of investors in a fund into which their investments have been paid, the use of the rule is a matter of convenience and if its application in particular circumstances would be impracticable or result in injustice between the investors it will not be applied if there is a preferable alternative.

(ii) Here, the rule will not be applied because this would be contrary to either the express or inferred or presumed intention of the investors. If the investments were required by the terms of the investment contract to be paid into a common pool, this indicates that the investors did not intend to apply the rule. If the investments were intended to be separately invested, as a result of the investments being collectively misapplied by BCI, a common pool of the investments was created. Because of their shared misfortune, the investors will be presumed to have intended the rule not to apply.

(iii) As the rule is inapplicable, the approach which should be adopted by the court depends on which of the possible alternative solutions is the most satisfactory in the circumstances. If the North American solution [rolling charge] is practical, this would probably have advantages over the *pari passu* solution. However, the complications of applying the North American solution in this case make the third solution the most satisfactory.

(iv) It must, however, be remembered that any solution depends on the ability to trace and if the fund had been exhausted (that is, the account became overdrawn) the investors whose moneys were in the fund prior to the fund being exhausted will not be able to claim against moneys which were subsequently paid into the fund.

Their claims will be limited to following, if this is possible, any of the moneys paid out of the fund into other assets before it was exhausted.

For these reasons I would allow the appeal and substitute the orders proposed by Dillon J.

Leggatt LJ: All the moneys which were provided by the investors were treated by BCI as a common pool to which they could have resort for their own purposes. Since all the investors have equitable charges, and their equities are equal, and they presumably intended their money to be dealt with collectively, they should share rateably what is left in the pool, as did the claimants in *Sinclair v Brougham* [1914] AC 398.

In *Commerzbank Aktiengesellschaft v IMB Morgan plc*, the High Court, in reliance on the decision in *Barlow Clowes v Vaughan*, concluded that the rule in *Clayton's* case ought to be resisted in the interest of fairness and justice.

Commerzbank Aktiengesellschaft v IMB Morgan plc and others **[2004] EWHC 2771**

Facts

The applicant was a major German bank with a London branch, Commerzbank, London. In December 2000, two accounts were opened in the London branch by its original customer (IMBM), a stockbroker based in Nigeria. The accounts were a US dollar and a sterling account. These accounts were corresponding bank accounts, i.e. accounts established to receive deposits from, make payments on behalf of, or handle other financial transactions related to a foreign institution (generally a foreign bank). The features of such accounts were that all the receipts into the accounts became mingled. It was not possible to identify any part of the funds as relating to a particular client of the foreign institution. The funds were held on behalf of the foreign institution with whom the correspondent relationship existed and not individual clients. In other words, the bank would generally have received funds from third parties to be credited to the accounts of IMBM without knowing the identity of IMBM's clients to whom the funds would eventually be credited by IMBM.

In May 2002 the accounts were frozen and the relationship between the applicant and IMBM terminated as a result of a number of incidents and a subsequent police investigation that concluded that there was strong evidence that the accounts were being used for money laundering. The applicant was left in the position of having to determine what to do with the funds in the accounts and how to deal with the potential competing claims to the funds by various parties.

In addition to IMBM the parties with potential claims to the funds were:

(i) victims of possible fraud who attempted to make payments via the accounts to an IMBM client that has been identified as possibly being connected with fraudulent activity;

(ii) third parties who attempted to make payments via the accounts to an IMBM client in respect of whom no complaint of fraud had been made. In addition these third parties requested refunds, generally because the intended beneficiary had alleged not to have received the funds;

(iii) apparently innocent IMBM clients in whose favour funds were transferred as part of an ostensibly legitimate business transaction.

In February 2003 Commerzbank filed an interpleader application for payments to be made to claimants who were identified after the service of notice inviting claims to the funds. The amount of valid claims exceeded the amount available for distribution. IMBM made no claims to the funds.

The question in issue arose as to the method of distribution and in particular, whether the rule in *Clayton's* case was applicable – 'first in first out' (FIFO).

Held

(1) IMBM became a constructive trustee for the innocent claimants and thus the claimants had a proprietary right to trace their monies in the accounts.

(2) There were payments in and out of the accounts, by or on behalf of the claimants, and thus the funds became mixed.

(3) The rule in *Clayton's* case that attributes payments in to an account with payments out of the account on the basis of 'first in first out' (FIFO) would not apply where this process would be onerous.

(4) Where, as in this case, the claimants have an equal right to be paid it would be appropriate for the parties to be entitled to the mixed fund *pari passu*, i.e. the fund would be shared rateably amongst the beneficiaries according to their contributions.

Collins J: In order to establish a claim to a share in the fund, claimants must show that they have a proprietary right, i.e. a right in property and not simply a debt due from IMB. There are three relevant bases for such a claim, and most of the claimants have a claim (if any) under the first basis, which is that a person who has been defrauded may trace property into the hands of the recipient. ". . . [W]hen property is obtained by fraud equity imposes a constructive trust on the fraudulent recipient: the property is recoverable and traceable in equity": *Westdeutsche Landesbank Girozentrale v Islington London Borough Council* [1996] AC 669, 716. The victims of fraud can follow their money in equity through bank accounts where it has been mixed with other money because equity treats the money in such accounts as charged with the repayment of their money: *El Ajou v Dollar Land Holdings plc (No. 1)* [1993] 3 All ER 717 (revd on other grounds [1994] 1 All ER 685). See also *Bristol and West Building Society v Mothew* [1998] Ch 1; *Bankers Trust Co. v Shapira* [1980] 1 WLR 1274, 1282. In *Bank of Credit and Commerce International (Overseas) Ltd (in liquidation) and another v Akindele* [2001] Ch 437 it was held that the recipient's state of knowledge should be such as to make it unconscionable for him to retain the benefit of the receipt. Consequently, even if IMB Morgan was not a party to the frauds, the defrauded claimants have a tracing remedy. The second basis for a claim is that a payment was made by mistake. Whether a person who has made a payment by mistake has a proprietary claim is by no means clear. But I am satisfied that in a case of this kind, where (as in the case of the payment by Citizens Union Bank) double payment was made at the request of the recipient (IMB Morgan), where there is an identifiable fund, and where the recipient has notice of the claim, it would be unconscionable for IMB Morgan (and in effect the other claimants to the fund) to retain the benefit of that payment: *Chase Manhattan Bank v Israel-British Bank* [1981] Ch. 10, as explained in *Westdeutsche Landesbank Girozentrale v Islington London Borough Council* [1996] AC 669, 714–715; Virgo, *Principles of the Law of Restitution* (1999), pp 630–632; and see also *Papamichael v National Westminster Bank plc* [2003] EWHC 164 (Comm), [2003] 1 Lloyd's Rep 341 (Judge Chambers QC). Third, where money is paid for a purpose which is not fulfilled, the recipient holds the money on trust for the payer: *Barclays Bank Ltd v Quistclose Investments Ltd* [1970] AC 567; *Carreras Rothmans Ltd v Freeman Matthews Treasure Ltd* [1985] 1 All ER 155. The third head applies to the claims by Mr Vine/Hawick Plant Auctions, and Mr Baker.

The result of my findings is that the amount of valid claims far exceeds the amount available for distribution. Because the claims exceed the amount held by the Court the question arises as to the method of distribution, and in particular whether the rule in *Clayton's Case* (*Devaynes v. Noble: Clayton's Case* (1816) 1 Mer. 572) applies.

According to the rule in *Clayton's Case* payments out of an account are attributed to payments into the account in the order in which payments were made in. *Clayton's Case* was a case about appropriation of payments and not about tracing. The first payment out is attributed to the first payment in, and so on. But it can cause injustice when applied to tracing claims. The result can be 'capricious and arbitrary' (Goff and Jones, *Restitution*, 6th ed Jones, 2002, para 2-039). As *Lewin on Trusts*, 17th ed Mowbray et al, 2000, paras 41–53, points out, the effect of the rule, where withdrawals have been made and spent, is to establish a reverse order of priority. The later the payment into the account the greater the prospect of that payment not being attributed to payments out and hence of still being represented in the remaining credit balance.

Where the rule in *Clayton's Case* does not apply, then (at least where the claimants have an equal right to be paid) it will normally be appropriate for the parties to be entitled to the mixed fund *pari passu*, i.e. the fund will be shared rateably amongst the beneficiaries according to the amount of their contributions.

This is a case where the claimants are entitled to trace monies in the Accounts, or where IMB Morgan is an actual or constructive trustee of payments by innocent claimants. Part of the funds have been withdrawn on the instructions of IMB Morgan and replaced with other funds supplied by innocent claimants. Accordingly, there has been mixing (and payment away) of the money held on trust for the claimants. But it would be an extremely onerous (and perhaps impossible task) to determine what sums IMB Morgan has paid away. That is because the nature of a correspondent bank account is such that debits to the account may not necessarily be equated with payments out by IMB Morgan. Some of the debits may be payments to another account held by IMB Morgan, or payments to persons who hold on behalf of IMB Morgan. For example, there are in August 2001 debits of $100,000 (transfer to Bank Nigeria), $250,000 and £25,000 (transfers to Platinum Bank Ltd), $500,000 (Citizens International Bank Ltd).

I am satisfied that the rule in *Clayton's Case* should not apply here, because it would be both impracticable and unjust to apply it. The only fair way to share the balances on each of the Accounts would be in proportion to the claims on the respective Accounts.

Innocent volunteers

In *Sinclair v Brougham*, the mixing of the funds of the two innocent claimants was effected by a fiduciary, namely, the directors of the building society. This was consistent with the *Hallett* principle.

However, a controversial issue was whether the tracing remedy would be available to a claimant when the mixing was effected by an innocent volunteer and not by the fiduciary. The Court of Appeal, in *Re Diplock*, stated (*obiter*) that the remedy would be available.

For example, trustees hold property on trust for A for life, remainder to B absolutely. The trustees, without authority, distribute £2,000 of the trust income to remainderman B, who pays the same into a bank account containing £3,000 of his personal moneys. The trust is later terminated (see *Saunders v Vautier* (1841) Cr & Ph 240, CA, in Chapter 20) and B becomes bankrupt. A may be entitled to a charge on B's bank account ranking in *pari passu*.

Re Diplock [1948] Ch 465, CA

Greene MR: Where an innocent volunteer (as distinct from a purchaser for value without notice) mixes 'money' of his own with 'money' which in equity belongs to another person, or is found in possession of such a mixture, although that other person cannot claim a charge on the mass superior to the claim of the volunteer . . . it appears to us to be wrong to treat the principle which underlies *Hallett*'s case as coming into operation only where the person who does the mixing is not only in a fiduciary position but is also a party to the tracing action. If he is a party to the action he is, of course, precluded from setting up a case inconsistent with the obligations of his fiduciary position. But supposing he is not a party? The result cannot surely depend on what equity would or would not have allowed him to say if he had been a party.

Facts

Caleb Diplock, by his will, directed his executors to apply the residue of his estate 'for such charitable institutions or other charitable or benevolent objects in England as they may select in their absolute discretion'. The executors assumed that the will created a valid charitable trust and distributed £203,000 among 139 different charities before the validity of the distribution was challenged by the next of kin. In the earlier litigation in *Chichester Diocesan Fund v Simpson* [1944] AC 341, the House of Lords decided that the clause in Caleb Diplock's will failed to create a charitable trust for uncertainty of charitable objects. The next of kin sued the executors and charities. The claim against the executors was eventually compromised. But the claimants persisted in their action against the wrongly paid charities on two grounds, namely:

(a) claims *in personam* against the recipient institutions (see *Ministry of Health v Simpson* [1951] AC 251, affirming the decision of the Court of Appeal); and

(b) claims *in rem* against the assets held by the institutions.

Held

The action *in rem* would not succeed because the next of kin's moneys were no longer identifiable. In any event, had a claim *in rem* existed, the charge ranking in *pari passu* would have inflicted an injustice on the institutions in causing the institutions to sell such assets.

Limitations

The Court of Appeal, in *Re Diplock*, enunciated the limits surrounding the right to trace:

(a) *Bona fide purchaser:* The equitable remedy does not affect rights obtained by a *bona fide* transferee of the legal estate for value without notice. All equitable claims are extinguished against such persons.

(b) *Change of position:* Tracing will not be permitted if the result will produce inequity, for 'he who comes to equity must do equity'. Accordingly, if an innocent volunteer spends money improving his land, there can be no declaration of charge because the method of enforcing the charge would be by way of sale, thus forcing the volunteer to convert his property. The modern expression for this concept is 'change of position'.

In English law, there is no general recognition of the defence of change of position in the context of restitutionary claims. The usual approach adopted by the courts is based on estoppel, which has limitations that makes it unsuitable to restitutionary claims. The estoppel is based upon a representation by the claimant, whether express or implied, that the defendant is entitled to treat the money as his own. The mere payment of money under a mistake cannot, by itself, constitute a representation which will estop the payer from asserting his right to receive his payment.

The defence of change of position has been recognised throughout the common law world. It has gained statutory recognition in the United States of America.

Restatement of the Law on Restitution, s 142

(1) The right of a person to restitution from another, because of a benefit received, is terminated or diminished if, after the receipt of the benefit, circumstances have so changed that it would be inequitable to require the other to make full restitution.

(2) Change of circumstances may be a defence or a partial defence if the conduct of the recipient was not tortious and he was no more at fault for his receipt, retention or dealing with the subject matter than was the claimant.

(3) Change of circumstances is not a defence if:

    (a) the conduct of the recipient in obtaining, retaining or dealing with the subject matter was tortious; or

    (b) the change occurred after the recipient had knowledge of the facts entitling the other to restitution, and had an opportunity to make restitution.

In New Zealand, see s 94B of the Judicature Act 1908; in Western Australia, see s 24 of the Western Australia Law Reform (Property, Perpetuities and Succession) Act 1962 and s 65(B) of the Western Australia Trustee Act 1962. In addition, the defence has been judicially recognised by the Supreme Court of Canada: see *Rural Municipality of Storthooks v Mobil Oil of Canada Ltd* (1975) 55 DLR (3ed) 1.

In the *Lipkin Gorman* case, Lord Goff of Chieveley advocated that a general defence of change of position ought to be adopted in the UK. The defence ought to be developed on a case by case basis. It would be available to an innocent volunteer who, after receiving the claimant's money, has altered his position to such an extent that, having regard to all the circumstances, it would be inequitable to require him to make full restitution to the claimant, see *Abou-Ramah v Abacha* [2006] All ER (D) 80 (Chapter 11). The defence ought not to be available to a defendant who has changed his position in bad faith, that is, a defendant who spends the claimant's money after knowledge of facts entitling the claimant to restitution. Likewise, in *Cressman v Coys of Kensington* [2004] EWCA Civ 47, the Court of Appeal decided that the defence was not available to the defendant who acquired a personalised, cherised number plate by mistake and consciously disposed of it in order to avoid the claimant's action.

On the issue of good faith the Court of Appeal in *Niru Battery Manufacturing Ltd v Milestone Trading Ltd*, [2004] QB 985 approved passages from Harrison J, in the court below, as follows: (at p 1004, paragraph 165):

> I do not think that it is desirable to attempt to define the limits of good faith. It is a broad concept, the definition of which, in so far as it is capable of definition at all will have to be worked out through the cases. In my view it is capable of embracing a failure to act in a commercially acceptable way and sharp practice of a kind that falls short of outright dishonesty as well as dishonesty itself. The factors which will determine whether it is inequitable to allow the claimant to obtain restitution in a case of mistaken payment will vary from case to case, but where the payee has voluntarily parted with the money much is likely to depend on the circumstances in which he did so and the extent of his knowledge about how payment came to be made. Where he knows that the payment he has received was made by mistake the position is quite straightforward: he must return it. This applies as much to

a banker who receives a payment for the account of his customer as to any other person . . . Greater difficulty may arise, however, in cases where the payee has grounds for believing that the payment may have been made by mistake, but cannot be sure. In such cases good faith may well dictate that an inquiry be made of the payer. The nature and extent of the inquiry called for will, of course, depend on the circumstances of the case, but I do not think that a person who has or thinks he has, good reason to believe that the payment was made by mistake will often be found to have acted in good faith if he pays the money away without first making inquiries of the person from whom he received it . . .

Similarly, the defence will not be available to a wrongdoer. In any event, the defendant is required to establish that there is a causal link between the mistaken receipt of the overpayment and the recipient's change of position, which makes it inequitable for the recipient to be required to make restitution, see *Scottish Equitable plc v Derby* [2001] 3 All ER 818. The mere fact that the defendant has spent the money in whole or in part, in the ordinary course of things, does not, of itself, render it inequitable that he should be called upon to repay the claimant. But if the defendant has spent the claimant's money on a venture which would not have been undertaken but for the gift, such conduct would be capable of being construed as a change of position. In the *Lipkin Gorman* case, the defence was not available to the club, for it did not provide consideration for the bets placed by Cass and had agreed that it had retained £154,695 of the claimant's money.

Lipkin Gorman (A Firm) v Karpnale [1991] 3 WLR 10, HL

Lord Goff: Whether change of position is, or should be, recognised as a defence to claims in restitution is a subject which has been much debated in the books. It is, however, a matter on which there is a remarkable unanimity of view, the consensus being to the effect that such a defence should be recognised in English law. I myself am under no doubt that this is right . . . At present I do not wish to state the principle any less broadly than this: that the defence is available to a person whose position has so changed that it would be inequitable in all the circumstances to require him to make restitution or alternatively to make restitution in full.

In *Credit Suisse (Monaco) SA v Attar*, the court decided that dishonesty on the part of the defendant would deprive him of the defence of change of position. Likewise, the repayment of a debt that was required to be repaid sooner or later would not afford a defence to the defendant, for in such a case there is no causal connection between the mistaken receipt and the expenditure.

Credit Suisse (Monaco) SA v Attar and Others [2004] EWHC 374 (Comm)

Facts

The claimant was a bank incorporated under the laws of Monaco. The first defendant, Mr Attar, had been a customer of the claimant bank and the second defendant was his wife. Mr Attar presented a cheque to the claimant for FF8,510,490 made payable to APGIS (translated the Salaried Professionals Provident Society) but fraudulently endorsed by a person calling himself Mr Apgis in favour of Mr Attar. This was the position despite the cheque being non-endorseable. Subsequently, the claimant transferred £525,000, part of the proceeds of the cheque, into an HSBC account in London in the joint names of the defendants.

The claimant subsequently realised the true position and commenced proceedings against the defendants. As against Mr Attar, it sought to recover the proceeds of the cheque in a claim for restitution on the ground of Mr Attar's bad faith amounting to dishonesty. The claim against Mrs Attar was brought in restitution for repayment of £525,000 plus interest. No allegations of bad faith were made against her. Mr Attar denied dishonesty, alleged that he did not realise that the endorsement was a forgery and gave an explanation as to the circumstances concerning the payment to him of the amount stated in the cheque. Mrs Attar alleged that she knew nothing regarding the source of the cheque and claimed a defence of change of position on the ground that she had used part of the funds to repay the mortgage on her house in Surrey and credit card debts.

Held

The claim succeeded against both defendants. It was not disputed that Mr Attar received the proceeds of the cheque when the sum was credited to his account. The cheque had been misappropriated and Mr Attar was not entitled to retain the proceeds. Liability was strict in accordance with Monegasque law. Further, negligence, if any, on the part of the claimant would not afford Mr Attar a defence. Thus, Mr Attar did not have a defence. In any event the judge rejected Mr Attar's explanation of the circumstances leading up to the payment of the sum to himself. His story was described by the judge as 'incredible and defies belief'. He concluded that Mr Attar was dishonest. The same principles applied to Mrs Attar. However, on the facts, even if English law was applicable Mrs Attar would have no defence of change of position. There was no causal link between the mistaken receipt of the cheque and any change of position on her part.

> **Gross J:** [Having analysed Mr Attar's evidence the learned judge continued] it follows that when Mr. Attar presented the cheque to Credit Suisse he knew that the cheque had been the subject of a fraud and was one to which he was not entitled, or he had equivalent blind-eye knowledge thereof. Plainly he should not have presented it to Credit Suisse for payment. Doing so, involved a breach of his duty of good faith. The matter does not however end there. In a variety of other respects, I conclude that Mr. Attar's evidence has been untruthful; such conclusions serve to reinforce those to which I have already come.

'Blind-eye knowledge' or 'wilful blindness' was described by Lord Clyde in *Manifest Shipping Co v Uni-Polaris Shipping Co* [2001] UKHL 1, as involving 'a conscious reason for blinding the eye. There must be at least a suspicion of a truth about which you do not want to know and which you refuse to investigate.' Lord Scott in the same case elaborated on the circumstances that will give rise to such 'knowledge'. He said:

> In summary, blind-eye knowledge requires . . . a suspicion that the relevant facts do exist and a deliberate decision to avoid confirming that they exist. But a warning should be sounded. Suspicion is a word that can be used to describe a state-of-mind that may, at one extreme, be no more than a vague feeling of unease and, at the other extreme, reflect a firm belief in the existence of the relevant facts. . . . in order for there to be blind-eye knowledge, the suspicion must be firmly grounded and targeted on specific facts. The deliberate decision must be a decision to avoid obtaining confirmation of facts in whose existence the individual has good reason to believe. To allow blind-eye knowledge to be constituted by a decision not to enquire into untargeted or speculative suspicion would be to allow negligence, albeit gross, to be the basis of a finding of privity.

Wilful blindness with regard to a windfall amount received by the defendant followed by a payment out of his account will be insufficient to support the defence, see *Fea v Roberts*.

Fea v Roberts [2005] All ER (D) 69, (High Court)

Facts

The claimants were the executors of the will of Basil Prichard who died in June 1976. By his will, the testator gave his widow a life interest in his estate and divided the remainder between such of his nephew, niece and four godsons who should survive him. One such godson was Edward Roberts of Bridgnorth, Shropshire. The executors were solicitors in the firm, Martineau Johnson of Birmingham. The life tenant died in March 1995. Owing to a genuine mistake by the executors, the net value of Edward Roberts's share of the estate, worth £100,000, was paid, between August 1995 and February 1997, to the wrong beneficiary, namely William Edward Roberts of the West Midlands. At all material times the written correspondence from the solicitors were headed with the name of the deceased. In October 2003 the wife of Edward Roberts telephoned the firm of solicitors to enquire about his inheritance under the will of Basil Prichard and it emerged that it was this Mr Roberts who was the testator's godson, and entitled to property under the will. The executor conceded that he had made no checks about the identity of the Roberts with whom his firm was in contact, or whether he was the godson of Basil Prichard, or whether he lived in Bridgnorth. After some correspondence with William Edward Roberts (the wrongly paid recipient of the funds) between November 2003 and February 2004, proceedings commenced in 2004 against the defendant for the recovery of the monies paid to him. The defendant spent a substantial portion of the monies on hobbies (shooting), entertainment (holidays), improvements to his home and donated generous sums to his children. He argued that it was as a result of the windfall that he spent so lavishly. The defendant raised the defences of limitation, estoppel and change of position.

The judge found that Mr Roberts knew full well that he was not the truly intended beneficiary under the will and chose not to raise this point but to close his eyes to the obvious and accept the monies in the hope that it would never be queried.

Held

The court allowed the claim and rejected the defences put forward by the defendant.

> **Williamson QC:** The purpose of the [Limitation] Act [1980] is to provide appropriate time limits during which people must assert their claims or rights, or lose them. The purpose of s 32 is to ensure that such a time limit does not operate unfairly against people who are as yet unaware that have a claim which they ought to assert. Since a cause of action for money paid under a mistake accrues regardless of whether the mistake was made carelessly, it would be illogical for that fact then to affect the limitation period otherwise available to the maker of the mistake, in which to commence an action.
>
> The effect of Mrs Preston's argument would actually be that the running of time would never be postponed in the case of a claim to recover money paid under a careless mistake. However, the Act does not suggest that there is any such distinction.
>
> In short, s 32(2)(c) [of the Limitation Act 1980] applies a general principle as to the postponement of time running, until the maker of the mistake actually does know of his mistake, with an exception where he ought, with due diligence, to have discovered it earlier – not where he ought, with due diligence, to have avoided making it in the first place.
>
> For these reasons, I reject Mrs Preston's defence of limitation.
>
> *Estoppel and 'change of position'*
> The other two defences advanced by Mrs Preston on Mr Roberts' behalf are those of estoppel, and of change of position.
>
> These two defences are quite similar, and indeed, the latter may be in the course of superseding the former, as the law in this area develops. Mr Halpern accepts, however, that they currently remain, and are recognised, as separate and distinct defences, and I should consider each separately. It is convenient, however, to consider them in parallel.
>
> The elements of the defence of estoppel, raised against a claim for repayment of money paid under a mistake, are (i) the making of a sufficiently clear representation by the payer to the payee that the payee has the right, as against the payer, to the money (or assets), (ii) reliance by the payee in good faith on such representation, which (iii) causes him to act to his detriment, and (iv) that the original mistake should not have been caused by the payee. If those elements are made out, then the payer is estopped from asserting the falsity of the representation which he has made, and therefore, in principle, cannot recover the money or assets.
>
> This defence is procedural in its origins, arising out of rules of evidence. As such, it has been something of a blunt instrument, with an 'all or nothing' effect on the outcome. Once detrimental reliance had been proved, none of the money or assets could be recovered.
>
> This result could obviously work unreasonably. If a significant sum of money had been paid and a small, but not negligible sum of money had been dissipated out of it, proof of the elements of the estoppel would prevent the payer from recovering even the balance. Judicial discomfort at this was obvious, and produced strained findings in earlier cases as to whether or not a representation had been made, or whether reliance had been placed on it, in order to enable the court to come to whichever conclusion, (recovery or no recovery) came closer to the view of justice in the particular situation.
>
> The essential question [regarding the change of position defence] boils down to whether it would be unjust in all the circumstances for the recipient to retain the benefit. Apart from the circumstances of the payment/receipt itself, the only other aspect which is relevant is therefore what has happened in the intervening period since the payment. This gives rise to the defence conveniently labelled 'change of position': *Lipkin Gorman v Karpnale* [1992] AC 548.
>
> The similarities to estoppel are obvious, but this remedy has always been intrinsically far more flexible. The test of 'unconscionability' is easily adapted to allow a partial recovery only, if appropriate. The very generality of the

defence which provides its flexibility has, however, made it necessary to emphasise aspects of it, so as to keep the defence in bounds and prevent the outcome, in this kind of case, degenerating into a discretionary analysis of 'justice' on a case by case basis, without clear application of principle: see, e.g. Robert Walker J in *Scottish Equitable v Derby* [2001] 3 All ER 818 at page 828 : "the court must proceed on the basis of principle, not sympathy."

Having considered his written and oral evidence, I am unable to find that Mr Roberts did act in good faith as required to make out the defence of 'change of position'. The only important point for present purposes is that I am perfectly satisfied that in August/September 1995 Mr Roberts knew full well that there were aspects of the legacy which was being given to him which suggested very strongly that he was not the truly intended recipient, and he chose not to raise these points but to close his eyes to them, and to accept the money and the shares in the hope that it would never be queried.

Acting in such a manner is not, in my judgment, acting 'in good faith' for the purposes of a defence of change of position. Likewise, if the matter were analysed in estoppel terms, acting in such a manner is not, in my judgment, acting in *reasonable* reliance on the representations which have been made.

Question
What is the scope of the defence of *bona fide* change of position?

(c) *Identification:* The right to trace is extinguished if the claimant's property is no longer identifiable, for example, the trust moneys have been spent on a dinner or a cruise, or in paying off a loan: see Greene MR's pronouncement in *Re Diplock.*

Re Diplock [1948] Ch 465, CA

Greene MR: The equitable remedies presuppose the continued existence of the money either as a separate fund or as part of a mixed fund or as latent in property acquired by means of such a fund. If, on the facts of any individual case, such continued existence is not established, equity is as helpless as the common law itself . . .

(d) *Fiduciary relationship*: It is essential that the claimant proves that the property was held by another on his or her behalf in a fiduciary or quasi-fiduciary capacity in order to attract the jurisdiction of equity. This fiduciary need not be the person who mixes the funds or the assets. The mixture may be effected by an innocent volunteer, as in *Re Diplock.*

In *Agip (Africa) Ltd v Jackson and Others* (see Chapter 11), the Court of Appeal decided that the plaintiff company was entitled to trace in equity a fraudulent payment of £518,822, which was received by the defendants.

Agip (Africa) Ltd v Jackson and Others [1991] Ch 547, CA

Fox LJ: . . . in the present case, there is no difficulty about the mechanics of tracing in equity. The money can be traced through the various bank accounts to Baker Oil and onwards. It is, however, a prerequisite to the operation of the remedy in equity that there must be a fiduciary relationship which calls the equitable jurisdiction into being. There is no difficulty about that in the present case since Mr Zdiri must have been in a fiduciary relationship with Agip. He was the chief accountant of Agip and was entrusted with the signed drafts or orders . . .

In *Chase Manhattan Bank v Israel-British Bank*, the court decided that a payment of funds, by mistake, from the plaintiff bank to the defendant bank affected the conscience of the latter to such an extent that the defendant bank became subject to a fiduciary duty to repay the fund to the plaintiff.

Chase Manhattan Bank v Israel-British Bank [1979] 3 All ER 1025, HC

Facts
The plaintiff, Chase, a New York bank, acting on instructions, paid $2,000,687 to another New York bank, via the New York clearing house system, for the defendant's account. Later on the same day, owing to a clerical error on the part of an employee of Chase, a second payment of the same amount was made. The defendant, another bank based in London, received the funds and

discovered the mistake two days later. Subsequently, the defendant company was wound up and was found to be insolvent. The plaintiff brought an action in equity to trace its funds in the hands of the defendant.

Held

The plaintiff had retained a proprietary right in the funds and was entitled to a charging order against the defendant:

> **Goulding J:** The plaintiff's claim, viewed in the first place without reference to any system of positive law, raises problems to which the answers, if not always difficult, are at any rate not obvious. If one party P pays money to another party D by reason of a factual mistake, either common to both parties or made by P alone, few conscientious persons would doubt that D ought to return it. But suppose that D is, or becomes, insolvent before repayment is made, so that P comes into competition with D's general creditors, what then? If the money can still be traced, either in its original form or through successive conversions, and is found among D's remaining assets, ought not P to be able to claim it, or what represents it, as his own? If he ought, and if in a particular case the money has been blended with other assets and is represented by a mixed fund, no longer as valuable as the sum total of its original constituents, what priorities or equalities should govern the distribution of the mixed fund? If the money can no longer be traced, either separate or in mixture, should P have any priority over ordinary creditors of D? In any of these cases, does it make any difference whether the mistake was inevitable, or was caused by P's carelessness, or was contributed to by some fault, short of dishonesty, on the part of D?
>
> At this stage I am asked to take only one step forward, and to answer the initial question of principle, whether the plaintiff is entitled in equity to trace the mistaken payment and to recover what now properly represents the money . . .
>
> The facts and decisions in *Sinclair v Brougham* [1914] AC 398 and in *Re Diplock* [1948] Ch 465 are well known and I shall not take time to recite them. I summarise my view of the *Diplock* judgment as follows: (1) The Court of Appeal's interpretation of *Sinclair v Brougham* was an essential part of their decision and is binding on me. (2) The court thought that the majority of the House of Lords in *Sinclair v Brougham* had not accepted Lord Dunedin's opinion in that case, and themselves rejected it. (3) The court held that an initial fiduciary relationship is a necessary foundation of the equitable right of tracing. (4) They also held that the relationship between the building society directors and depositors in *Sinclair v Brougham* was a sufficient fiduciary relationship for the purpose: [1948] Ch 465, 529, 540 . . .
>
> The fourth point shows that the fund to be traced need not (as was the case in *Re Diplock* itself) have been the subject of fiduciary obligations before it got into the wrong hands. It is enough that, as in *Sinclair v Brougham* [1914] AC 398, the payment into the wrong hands itself gave rise to a fiduciary relationship . . . *In the same way, I would suppose, a person who pays money to another under a factual mistake retains an equitable property in it and the conscience of that other is subjected to a fiduciary duty to respect his proprietary right* [emphasis added] . . .
>
> Thus, in the belief that the point is not expressly covered by English authority and that *Re Diplock* does not conclude it by necessary implication, I hold that the equitable remedy of tracing is in principle available, on the ground of continuing proprietary interest, to a party who has paid money under a mistake of fact . . .

Questions

(1) On what basis was a fiduciary relationship founded in the *Chase Manhattan* case?

(2) What limits exist in respect of the right to trace in equity?

Tracing/subrogation

Subrogation is the process whereby the claimant (A) steps in to the shoes of another (B) and thereby claims, as against the defendant (C) the rights and remedies to which the other (B) is entitled. For example, if A Co Ltd insures B's car under a comprehensive insurance policy and C, another motorist, negligently causes damage to B's car, A Co Ltd may compensate B for the damage, but is entitled to bring proceedings against C (albeit in B's name). The underlying basis of subrogation is the reversal of unjust enrichment. The remedy is available in a wide variety of different circumstances. Some of these are contracts of guarantee, contracts of indemnity insurance and the trust relationship.

In *Boscawen v Bajwa*, Millett LJ clarified the relationship between 'tracing' and 'subrogation'. The issue concerned the rights of a bank (Abbey National) to be subrogated to the rights of the mortgagee. The bank's fund intended for its customer for the purchase of property was released prematurely, through an error of judgment on the part of the purchaser's solicitor, to the vendor. This fund was then used to discharge the vendor's mortgage. The intended purchase by Abbey's customer fell through and the vendor became bankrupt.

Boscawen and Others v Bajwa and Others, Abbey National plc v Boscawen and Others
[1995] All ER 769, CA

Facts

At all material times, the property was registered in the name of Mr Bajwa. In 1989, he charged the property to the Halifax Building Society and the charge was duly registered. In 1990, Mr Bajwa exchanged contracts for the sale of the property for £165,000. The balance of the purchase price payable on completion was £140,000. The intended purchasers had obtained a mortgage offer from Abbey National for £140,000, which was to be secured by a first legal charge on the property. On 9 August 1990, Abbey National sent £140,000 by telegraphic transfer to the purchaser's solicitors, Dave and Co, who were acting as solicitors for both the purchaser and Abbey National. Dave and Co received the sum from Abbey National on terms which obliged them to use the amount for completion of the purchase or return it if, for any reason, completion did not take place. On 16 August, following discussions between Hill Lawson (Mr Bajwa's solicitors) and Dave and Co, Dave and Co issued instructions to their bank for the transmission of £137,405 to Hill Lawson. Dave and Co sent a cheque to Hill Lawson for £2,595 in respect of the balance of the purchase moneys. On 23 August 1990, Hill Lawson remitted £140,000 to the Halifax by telegraphic transfer. In October 1990, Dave and Co ceased to exist and Mr Dave, the sole equity partner, was made the subject of a bankruptcy order. The sale fell through and the purchasers never acquired the legal title to the property. The plaintiffs were judgment creditors of Mr Bajwa and had obtained a charging order on the property. They commenced proceedings against Mr Bajwa and Abbey National for enforcement of the charging order. An order for the sale of the property was made and the property was sold for £105,311. Abbey National counterclaimed, claiming an interest in the proceeds of sale.

The judge held that £137,405 of Abbey National's money could be traced into the payment to the Halifax which was used to discharge the Halifax's legal charge. Abbey National was entitled to a charge on the property by way of subrogation to the rights of the Halifax. The plaintiffs appealed on the grounds that Abbey National's tracing claim failed because its (Abbey National's) money was used to pay off a debt and no traceable assets were received in exchange for Abbey National's money. In addition, the judge erred by invoking the doctrine of subrogation, which had the effect of giving Abbey National an interest in priority over the plaintiff's charging order.

Held

(a) It was a prerequisite of the right to trace in equity that there was a fiduciary relationship which attracted the equitable jurisdiction (see *Agip (Africa) Ltd v Jackson* [1991] Ch 547). That requirement was satisfied in the present case by the fact that, from the first moment of its receipt by Dave and Co, the £140,000 was money held in trust for Abbey National.

(b) Abbey National had not intended to be an unsecured creditor of anyone. It had intended to retain the beneficial interest in its money, unless and until that interest was replaced by a first legal mortgage on the property. Abbey National's equitable right to subrogation arose from the conduct of the parties at the moment that the building society's charge was discharged in whole or in part with its (Abbey National's) money:

Millett LJ: Subrogation is a remedy, not a cause of action: see Goff and Jones, *Law of Restitution*, 4th edn, 1993, pp 589 *et seq*; *Orakpo v Manson Investments Ltd* [1978] AC 95, p 104, *per* Lord Diplock; and *In Re TH Knitwear (Wholesale) Ltd* [1988] Ch 275, p 284. It is available in a wide variety of different factual situations in which it is required in order to reverse the defendant's unjust enrichment. Equity lawyers speak of a right of subrogation, or of an equity of subrogation, but this merely reflects the fact that it is not a remedy which the court has a general discretion to impose whenever it thinks it just to do so. The equity arises from the conduct of the parties on well settled principles and in defined circumstances, which make it unconscionable for the defendant to deny the proprietary interest claimed by the plaintiff. A constructive trust arises in the same way. Once the equity is established, the court satisfies it by declaring that the property in question is subject to a charge, by way of subrogation in the one case, or a constructive trust in the other.

It is still a prerequisite of the right to trace in equity that there must be a fiduciary relationship which calls the equitable jurisdiction into being: see *Agip (Africa) Ltd v Jackson* [1991] Ch 547, p 566, *per* Fox LJ. That requirement is satisfied in the present case by the fact that, from the first moment of its receipt by Dave and Co in their general client account, the £140,000 was trust money held in trust for the Abbey National.

Subrogation

In the present case, the payment was made by Hill Lawson, and it is their intention which matters. As fiduciaries, they could not be heard to say that they had paid out their principal's money otherwise than for the benefit of their principal. Accordingly, their intention must be taken to have been to keep the Halifax's charge alive for the benefit of the Abbey National pending completion. In my judgment, this is sufficient to bring the doctrine of subrogation into play.

The application of the doctrine in the present case does not create the problem which confronted Oliver J in *Paul v Speirway Ltd* [1976] Ch 220. The Abbey National did not intend to be an unsecured creditor of anyone. It intended to retain the beneficial interest in its money unless and until that interest was replaced by a first legal mortgage on the property. The factual context in which the claim to subrogation arises is a novel one which does not appear to have arisen before, but the justice of its claim cannot be denied. The Abbey National's beneficial interest in the money can no longer be restored to it. If it is subrogated to the Halifax's charge its position will not be improved, nor will Mr Bajwa's position be adversely affected. Both parties will be restored as nearly as may be to the positions which they were respectively intended to occupy.

In the *Banque Financière* case, the House of Lords decided that, as a restitutionary remedy, subrogation is dependent on the following four principles:

(a) whether the defendant would be enriched;

(b) whether the enrichment was at the expense of the claimant;

(c) whether the enrichment would be unjust; and

(d) whether there are any policy reasons for denying the remedy.

Banque Financière de la Cité v Parc (Battersea) Ltd and Others [1998] 2 WLR 475, HL

Facts

Parc was a company registered in the UK, owning land for development in Battersea. Omnicorp Overseas Ltd (OOL) was registered in the British Virgin Islands. They belonged to the Omni Group, based in Switzerland, where the ultimate holding company, Omni Holding AG, was incorporated. The principal officers of Holding were its founder and principal shareholder, Mr Rey, and its chief financial officer, Mr Herzig. Parc acquired the Battersea property in 1988 with the aid of a £30 million bridging loan from Royal Trust Bank (Switzerland) (RTB), secured by a first charge. Additional finance was obtained from OOL in return for a second charge. The RTB loan was partially repaid in 1989, but £20 million was extended until 28 September 1990. Parc was unable to refinance its borrowing on the London market and turned to Mr Herzig for help. He approached Banque Financière (BFC), which had previously lent to the Omni Group. On 14 September 1990, it agreed, in principle, to advance DM30 million for two months. A difficulty was that a further loan to a member of the Omni Group would have had to have been reported to the Swiss banking authorities. To avoid this, BFC agreed to make the loan to Mr Herzig personally, on the basis that he would pass it on to Parc. In return, Parc would issue him with a promissory note which he would assign to BFC as security. The principal security was to be the pledge of 35,000 bearer shares in Holding, which BFC valued at DM40 million, and BFC required an undertaking from the Omni Group to postpone any claims by the group for repayment of loans until full repayment of the loan of DM30m to Mr Herzig was made (a postponement letter). Completion took place on 28 September 1990, when Mr Herzig handed over the pledged shares and post-ponement letter and BFC paid DM30 million to RTB for the account of Parc. On 1 October 1990, Parc issued a promissory note for the relevant sum and Mr Herzig assigned the note to BFC.

Mr Herzig defaulted on repayment of the loan. In April 1991, the Omni Group collapsed. Parc was insolvent. BFC obtained a judgment order for £12 million against Parc, representing the sum due on the note with interest. BFC had realised some of the pledged shares before they became worthless. Parc still owned the Battersea land. BFC brought a claim against Parc and OOL con-tending that, by reason of the letter of postponement and its utilisation to obtain the refinancing package, the rights of BFC took priority over the rights of OOL (in short, BFC stepped into the shoes of RTB and was claiming a first charge on the assets of the defendants). Parc and OOL had been unaware of the letter of postponement, and contended that the debt owed to OOL took priority over the debt owed to BFC.

Held

The House of Lords found in favour of the plaintiffs, BFC, on the following grounds:

(a) there was no difficulty in tracing the plaintiffs' money into the discharge of the debt owed to RTB;

(b) there was no conceptual difficulty about the plaintiffs and RTB appearing to share the same security. The plaintiffs were not seeking to obtain priority over RTB's security, but relied on it only for the purpose of obtaining priority over OOL;

(c) RTB's security was 'kept alive' for the benefit of the plaintiffs to prevent OOL from being unjustly enriched at the plaintiffs' expense. The plaintiffs' money was used to pay off RTB's charge and, thus, the plaintiffs did not obtain rights for which they had not bargained;

(d) the plaintiffs were entitled to be treated, as against OOL, as if they had the benefit of RTB's charge.

Lord Hoffmann: It is a mistake to regard the availability of subrogation as a remedy to prevent unjust enrichment as turning entirely upon the question of intention, whether common or unilateral. Such an analysis has inevitably to be propped up by presumptions which can verge upon fictions more appropriate to a less developed legal system than we now have. I would venture to suggest that the reason why intention has played so prominent a part in the earlier cases is because of the influence of cases on contractual subrogation. But I think it should be recognised that one is here concerned with a restitutionary remedy.

In this case, I think that, in the absence of subrogation, OOL would be enriched at BFC's expense and that, *prima facie*, such enrichment would be unjust. The bank advanced the DM30 m upon the mistaken assumption that it was obtaining a postponement letter which would be effective to give it priority over any intra-group indebted-ness. It would not otherwise have done so. On the construction of the letter adopted by Robert Walker J (at first instance), namely that Holdings was purporting to contract on behalf of all companies in the Omni Group, the payment was made under a mistake as to Holdings' authority. On the construction adopted by the Court of Appeal, the mistake was as to the power of Holdings to ensure that other group companies would postpone their claims. For my part, I prefer the construction adopted by the judge. But I do not think that, for present purposes, it matters which view one takes. In either case, BFC failed to obtain that priority over intra-group indebtedness which was an essential part of the transaction under which it paid money. It may have attached more importance to the pledge of the shares but the provision of the postponement letter was a condition of completion. The result of the transaction is that BFC's DM30 m has been used to reduce the debt secured by RTB's first charge and that this reduction will, by reason of OOL's second charge, enure wholly to the latter's advantage.

His Lordship examined and rejected the grounds on which the Court of Appeal decided that the enrichment of

OOL would not be unjust, and continued:] It follows that subrogation as against OOL, which is all that BFC claims in the action, would not give it greater rights than it bargained for. All that would happen is that OOL would be prevented from being able to enrich itself to the extent that BFC's money paid off the RTB charge. This is fully within the scope of the equitable remedy.

Millett, PJ, 'Tracing the proceeds of fraud' (1991) 107 LQR 71

Millett (currently Lord Millett) advocated that the requirement for a breach of trust or some other fiduciary obligation in order to initiate the tracing process in equity is indefensible and should be discarded:

> The doctrine can be reconsidered only by the House of Lords. It assumes that tracing is a product of equity's exclusive rather than its auxiliary jurisdiction; but it is far from clear that this is so. It has been suggested (Jacobs, *Law of Trusts in Australia*, 4th edn, 1977, p 570) that it rests upon a misreading of the decision of the House of Lords in *Sinclair v Brougham* [1914] AC 398, a case which, it has been justly observed, 'is largely what one chooses to make of it'.

> The requirement is, in fact, less restrictive of equity's ability to intervene than is often supposed. In the first place, it is not necessary that the fund to be traced should have been the subject of fiduciary obligations before it got into the wrong hands; it is sufficient that the payment to the defendant itself gave rise to a fiduciary relationship: *Chase Manhattan Bank NA v Israel-British Bank Ltd* [1979] 3 All ER 1025.

> In the second place, the requirement is readily satisfied in most cases of commercial fraud, since the embezzlement of a company's funds almost inevitably involves a breach of fiduciary duty on the part of one of the company's employees or agents. The question has been asked: 'What sort of fiduciary is relevant for tracing purposes and why?' An answer was suggested in *Agip (Africa) Ltd v Jackson* [1990] Ch 265, p 290. He need not be a director or a signatory on the company's bank account. It is sufficient that he was a person whose fiduciary position gave him control of the company's funds or provided him with the opportunity to misdirect them.

> The only situation, in practice, in which it may be impossible to invoke the assistance of equity is where the money has been stolen by a thief. In England, at least, it would be heretical to regard a thief as a fiduciary or a simple theft as giving rise to a constructive trust ... There is no reason, in principle, why equity should not intervene in such a case on the basis of a resulting trust. Theft does not deprive the true owner of his legal title; *a fortiori*, it does not deprive him of his equitable title. It has never been a requirement of the equitable tracing claim that the legal and equitable titles should be divided. The requirement that the loss must have arisen from a breach of fiduciary duty is difficult to understand and impossible to defend.

In *Box v Barclays Bank plc* (for facts, see p 199 above), Ferris J considered the claimant's right to trace in equity.

Box v Barclays Bank plc [1998] 1 All ER 108, HC

Ferris J: Mr Browne-Wilkinson (counsel for the plaintiffs) argued that, even if the plaintiffs cannot succeed in a common law claim for money had and received, they can trace their money in equity into Sylcon's No 1 account and are entitled to recover it from the bank unless the bank is able to show that it had no knowledge of the plaintiffs' rights. He referred me to the succinct statement of Millett J in *Agip (Africa) Ltd v Jackson* [1990] Ch 265, p 290:

> The tracing claim in equity gives rise to a proprietary remedy which depends on the continued existence of the trust property in the hands of the defendant. Unless he is a *bona fide* purchaser for value without notice, he must restore the trust property to its rightful owner if he still has it. But even a volunteer who has received trust property cannot be made subject to a personal liability to account for it as a constructive trustee, if he has parted with it without having previously acquired some knowledge of the existence of the trust.

The bank cannot, he contended, claim that it has parted with the plaintiffs' property because, in accordance with the rule in *Re Hallett's Estate* [1880] 13 Ch D 696, it is to be deemed to have used its own money, not the plaintiffs' in making whatever payments have been made and debited to Sylcon's account.

This argument cannot prevail in the light of my earlier conclusion that the relationship between the plaintiffs and Sylcon was purely contractual, not that of trustee and beneficiary. Equitable tracing is only available where there is an equity to trace, which requires that there must be an initial fiduciary relationship between the person claiming to trace and the party who is said to have misapplied that person's money (see *Snell's Equity*, 29th edn, 1991, London: Sweet & Maxwell, p 302 and *Agip*, p 290).

That, by itself, is a complete answer to the claim to trace in equity. But there is another equally complete answer, namely, that it is impossible to trace in equity through an overdrawn account (see *Re Goldcorp Exchange Ltd* [1995] AC 74, pp 104–05; the *Westdeutsche* case [1996] AC 669, p 105G–H; and – most explicitly – *Bishopsgate Investment Management Ltd v Homan* [1995] Ch 211 particularly pp 220F–20H and 222D–22F). It is not necessary in these circumstances to consider whether or not the bank had notice of the plaintiffs' rights. There were no relevant rights for the bank to have notice of.

FURTHER READING

Andrews, N, 'Tracing and subrogation' (1996) 55 CLJ 199.

Barker, K, 'Theorising unjust enrichment law' (2006) 26 OJLS 609.

Beatson, J and Prentice, D, 'Restitutionary claims by company directors' (1990) 106 LQR 365.

Birks, P, 'Proprietary restitution: an intelligible approach' (1995) 9 Tru LI 43.

Birks, P, 'Tracing misused – *Bank Tejarat v Hong Kong and Shanghai Banking Corp*' (1995) 9 Tru LI 91.

Birks, P, 'Tracing, subrogation and change of position' (1996) 9 Tru LI 124.

Chambers, R, 'Tracing, trusts and liens' (1997) 11 Tru LI 86.

Elliott, S, 'Rethinking interest on witheld and misapplied trust money' [2001] 65 Conv 313.

Goldsworth, J and Andre, R, ' Exculpation: a trustee's last hope' (1997) 3 T & T 22.

Goode, R, 'The right to trace and its impact on commercial transactions' (1976) 92 LQR 360.

Grantham, R and Rickett, C, 'Tracing and property rights: the categorical truth' (2000) MLR 905.

Halliwell, M, 'Restitutionary claims: a change of position defence?' [1992] Conv 124.

Halliwell, M, 'The relationship between unjust enrichment and subrogation: *Banque Financière de la Cité v Parc*' [1999] IL 57.

Ham, R, 'Trustees' liability' (1995) 9 Tru LI 21

Hayton, D, 'Rights of creditors against trustees and trust funds' (1997) 11 Tru LI 58.

Jones, A, 'Identification of improperly appropriated trust money – mixing and *Maxwell*' [1996] Conv 129.

Jones, G, '*Ultra vires* swaps: the common law and equitable fall out' (1996) 55 CLJ 432.

Kenny, A, 'Living up to expectations' (1996) 146 NLJ 348.

Maudsley, R, 'Proprietary remedies for the recovery of money' (1959) 75 LQR 234.

McBride, N, 'Trustees' exemption clauses' (1998) 57 CLJ 33.

Mitchell, C, 'Subrogation, tracing and the *Quistclose* principle' [1995] LMCLQ 45.

Oakley, AJ, 'Proprietary claims and their priority in insolvency' (1995) 54 CLJ 377.

Oliver, P, 'The extent of equitable tracing' (1995) 9 Tru LI 78.

Panesar, S, 'Actual fraud and gross negligence: the scope of trustee exemption clauses' (1998) 19 BLR 8.

Pavlowski, M, 'The demise of the rule in *Clayton's Case*' [2003] Conv 339.

Rickett, C, 'Equitable compensation: the giant stirs' (1996) 112 LQR 521.

Sealy, L, 'Contract to sell unascertained goods – no passing of property, no equitable or restitutionary relief' (1994) 53 CLJ 443.

Smith, L, 'Tracing into the payment of a debt' (1995) 54 CLJ 290.

Smith, L, 'Tracing in *Taylor v Plumer*: equity in the Court of King's Bench' (1995) LMCLQ 240.

Stevens, J, 'Vindicating the proprietary nature of tracing' [2001] Conv 94.

Ulph, J, 'Harmony in the law: hitting the target? *Target Holdings v Redferns*' (1995) 9 Tru LI 86.

Ulph, J, 'Retaining proprietary rights at common law through mixtures and changes' (2001) LMCLQ 449.

INTRODUCTION

Courts of equity have had the power to grant injunctions for a considerable period of time. Injunctions, like all equitable remedies, are discretionary, but the court will exercise its discretion according to well-established equitable principles. Originally, injunctions were unavailable in the common law courts, but s 79 of the Common Law Procedure Act 1854 gave such courts the power to issue an injunction instead of awarding damages. Likewise, the Chancery Procedure Amendment Act 1858, known as Lord Cairns' Act, gave the courts of equity the power to award damages instead of granting an injunction. This power, entitling a court of equity to award damages, does not mean that the court will be more reluctant to issue an injunction when the circumstances warrant such a remedy.

In *Shelfer v City of London Electric Lighting Co* [1895] 1 Ch 287, Lord Lindley said:

> . . . ever since *Lord Cairns*' Act was passed the Court of Chancery has repudiated the notion that the Legislature intended to turn that Court into a tribunal for legalizing wrongful acts; or in other words, the Court has always protested against the notion that it ought to allow a wrong to continue simply because the wrongdoer is able and willing to pay for the injury he may inflict. Neither has the circumstance that the wrongdoer is in some sense a public benefactor (e.g., a gas or water company or a sewer authority) ever been considered a sufficient reason for refusing to protect by injunction an individual whose rights are being persistently infringed.

In *Leeds Industrial Co-Op v Slack* [1924] AC 851, Lord Sumner, indicated when damages may be awarded in substitution for an injunction. He said:

> . . . no money awarded in substitution can be justly awarded, unless it is at any rate designed to be a preferable equivalent for an injunction and therefore an adequate substitute for it, and this involves the necessity for taking the future as well as the past and the present into account so as to end matters once for all, instead of awarding damages only *toties quoties*, as was done in common law actions, leaving the injured party to bring as many further actions as there might be further separate torts . . .

Since the Judicature Acts 1873–75 both legal and equitable remedies have been available in the same court, but it seems that the template governing the principles that are applicable to injunctions remains the same.

PROCEDURE

There are several different types of injunctions. An injunction may be 'prohibitory', i.e. forbidding the performance of a particular act; or 'mandatory', i.e. ordering the defendant to do a particular act. Injunctions could also be classified as 'perpetual', i.e. following the final determination of the rights of the parties or, until recently, as 'interlocutory', i.e. pending the determination of rights at the trial. In addition, a *'quia timet'* (literally, 'because he fears') injunction could be obtained where the claimant fears that damage may occur in the future. However, changes were introduced by the Civil Procedure Rules 1998. The stated objective of the Rules is to provide a comprehensive and self-contained procedural code for both the County and High Courts. Some of the modifications by the Rules involve a change in terminology – an interlocutory injunction is now known as an 'interim' injunction. A 'Mareva' injunction is now known as a 'freezing' injunction and an 'Anton Piller' order is now referred to as a 'search order'. These important changes are contained in Rule 25 of the CPR. The pre-CPR cases, of course, used the old terminology, but in the remainder of this chapter we will use the new expressions in the text.

Another important Rule affecting injunctions is Rule 1 of the CPR. This states that the overriding objective of the Rules is to enable the court to deal with cases justly. It explains that the phrase 'dealing with a case justly' includes in so far as it is possible:

- ensuring that the parties are on an equal footing;
- saving expense;
- dealing with the case in ways that are proportionate:
  - to the amount of money involved,
  - to the importance of the case,
  - to the complexity of the issues, and
  - to the financial position of each party;
- ensuring that it is dealt with expeditiously and fairly; and
- allotting an appropriate share of the court's resources, while taking into account the need to allot resources to other cases.

The question is whether the new procedural rules will alter the factors that the court will take into account when deciding whether to grant an application for an interim injunction. The weight of academic opinion is that previous case law on this particular subject will continue to apply, save that, the court will now have to take into account the overriding objective in Rule 1.

ESTABLISHED PRINCIPLES

In general, the court will take similar principles into account when considering applications for each type of injunction. These principles are:

- The claimant is required to prove the infringement or potential infringement (in the case of a *quia timet* injunction) of a right that is recognised either in equity or at common law as a precondition for the grant of an injunction, see *Day v Brownrigg*.

Day v Brownrigg (1878) 10 Ch D 294, (CA)

Facts
The claimants sought an injunction to prevent the defendant from naming his house, 'Ashford Lodge', a name used by the claimant for sixty years. The claimants alleged that the defendant's conduct caused them a great deal of inconvenience and annoyance, and had materially diminished the value of their property.

Held
The act of defendant was not a violation of any legal right of the claimant and therefore the claim was dismissed.

Thesiger LJ: . . . it appears to me that there is no legal right which has been invaded in this case. It is not contended now that the right which has been invaded is the title. In other words, it is not contended that the injury is one which comes within the definition of slander of title. On the other hand, it cannot reasonably be contended that this case stands upon the same footing as the cases of trade-marks, which undoubtedly stand upon a very peculiar footing. Therefore the only right which can be alleged is this, namely, that there is a right to the exclusive appropriation of the name here adopted in respect of any particular property. It seems to me there is neither principle nor authority in support of that contention.

James LJ: This Court can only interfere where there is an invasion of a legal or equitable right. No such legal or equitable right exists . . . I think it right to add that the power given to the Court by sect. 25, sub-sect. 8, of the *Judicature Act*, 1873, to grant an injunction in all cases in which it shall appear to the Court to by 'just or convenient' to do so, does not in the least alter the principles on which the Court should act.

- The injunction will not be granted where damages are an appropriate remedy, e.g. where the damage had already occurred and could be rectified by a monetary payment and was not likely to be repeated.

But once the claimant has shown that the defendant has infringed his (claimant's) rights and intends to continue with such course of conduct, then the claimant will *prima facie* be entitled to an injunction. In *Pride of Derby and Derbyshire Angling Association v British Celanese* [1953] Ch 149, an injunction was granted on behalf of the claimants in order to restrain the defendants from causing or permitting the pollution of the rivers Trent and Derwent, owing to their business activities.

> **Harman J:** . . . the question arises whether there should be any injunction in the circumstances or whether the plaintiffs, should content themselves with some less relief? *Prima facie*, a plaintiff, whose rights have been invaded . . . is entitled to relief from this court by way of injunction.

A similar approach was taken in *Shelfer v City of London Electric Lighting Co* [1895] 1 Ch 287. In this case the operations of the defendant electricity company caused structural damage to a house and nuisance to its occupier. The owner and occupier sought relief by way of injunction. The trial judge refused injunctive relief and awarded damages. His decision was reversed by the Court of Appeal, which roundly rejected the view that wrongs should be permitted to continue simply because the wrongdoer was able and willing to pay damages. The court gave guidance as to the circumstances in which damages may properly be awarded in lieu of an injunction.

> **Smith LJ:** Many judges have stated, and I emphatically agree with them, that a person by committing a wrongful act (whether it be a public company for public purposes or a private individual) is not thereby entitled to ask the Court to sanction his doing so by purchasing his neighbour's rights, by assessing damages in that behalf, leaving his neighbour with the nuisance, or his lights dimmed, as the case may be. In such cases the well-known rule is not to accede to the application, but to grant the injunction sought, for the plaintiff's legal right has been invaded, and he is *primâ facie* entitled to an injunction. There are, however, cases in which this rule may be relaxed, and in which damages may be awarded in substitution for an injunction as authorized by this section. In any instance in which a case for an injunction has been made out, if the plaintiff by his acts or laches has disentitled himself to an injunction the Court may award damages in its place. So again, whether the case be for a mandatory injunction or to restrain a continuing nuisance, the appropriate remedy may be damages in lieu of an injunction, assuming a case for an injunction to be made out. In my opinion, it may be stated as a good working rule that—(1.) If the injury to the plaintiff's legal rights is small, (2.) And is one which is capable of being estimated in money, (3.) And is one which can be adequately compensated by a small money payment, (4.) And the case is one in which it would be oppressive to the defendant to grant an injunction:—then damages in substitution for an injunction may be given. There may also be cases in which, though the four above-mentioned requirements exist, the defendant by his conduct, as, for instance, hurrying up his buildings so as if possible to avoid an injunction, or otherwise acting with reckless disregard to the plaintiff's rights, has disentitled himself from asking that damages may be assessed in substitution for an injunction. It is impossible to lay down any rule as to what, under the differing circumstances of each case, constitutes either a small injury, or one that can be estimated in money, or what is a small money payment, or an adequate compensation, or what would be oppressive to the defendant. This must be left to the good sense of the tribunal which deals with each case as it comes up for adjudication. For instance, an injury to the plaintiff's legal right to light to a window in a cottage represented by £15 might well be held to be not small but considerable; whereas a similar injury to a warehouse or other large building represented by ten times that amount might be held to be inconsiderable. Each case must be decided upon its own facts; but to escape the rule it must be brought within the exception. In the present case it appears to me that the injury to the Plaintiff is certainly not small, nor is it in my judgment capable of being estimated in money, or of being adequately compensated by a small money payment.

In *Leeds Industrial Co-Op v Slack* [1924] AC 851, Lord Sumner, in colourful language, explained why damages may not be an appropriate remedy:

> **Lord Sumner:** I doubt . . . whether it is complete justice to allow the big man, with his big building and his enhanced rateable value and his improvement of the neighbourhood, to have his way, and to solace the little man for his darkened and stuffy little house by giving him a cheque which he does not ask for.

See also *Kennaway v Thompson* [1980] 3 WLR 361, where the claimant was granted an injunction to restrain a motorboat racing club from committing a nuisance by excessive noise.

- An injunction will not be granted where the injury to the claimant's rights is trivial and an alternative remedy is available.

Thus, in *Llandudno UDC v Woods* [1899] 2 Ch 705, Cozens-Hardy J refused to grant the claimants an injunction restraining the defendant from preaching on a beach at Lladudno as the matter was 'too trivial' for the injunction. However, the claimants were entitled to a declaration that the defendant was a trespasser.

> **Cozens – Hardy J:** The plaintiffs have *prima facie* a right to treat every bather, every nursemaid with a perambulator, every boy riding a donkey, and every preacher, on the shore at Llandudno as a trespasser . . . The defendant seems to imagine that his position as a clergyman of the Established Church, bound to preach the Gospel both in season and out of season, gives him some special and peculiar rights. It is needless for me to say that this contention cannot for one moment be maintained . . . It is no part of the duty of the council, as lessees from the Crown for an unexpired term of two years, to prevent a harmless user of the shore. There are persons who derive satisfaction from listening to the addresses of the defendant, and the defendant derives satisfaction from delivering these addresses. I cannot conceive why they should be deprived of this innocent pleasure. Nobody is obliged to listen. Nobody is molested . . . I cannot refuse to make a declaration that the defendant is not entitled, without the consent of the plaintiffs, to hold meetings or deliver addresses, lectures, or sermons on any part of the foreshore in lease from the Crown. But I decline to go further. I decline to grant an injunction. That is a formidable legal weapon which ought to be reserved for less trivial occasions.

- The court will take into account the general equitable principles such as hardship to the parties, inordinate delay on the part of the claimant in initiating proceedings and whether the claimant comes to court 'with clean hands'.

The relative importance of these factors may vary depending on the type of injunction sought by the claimant. In *Jaggard v Sawyer* [1995] 1 WLR 269, the court refused to grant an injunction to prevent trespass over the claimant's property in breach of a restrictive covenant that prohibited building on the plot. The claimant delayed by about two years in seeking an injunction against the defendant from building a house on the plot. At this time the building was at an advanced stage. The court concluded that the grant of an injunction would have been unduly oppressive to the defendant. In reaching that conclusion, the court took into account the conduct of the claimant and defendants, the nature of the trespass and the relevant land. The court decided that it had jurisdiction to award damages instead of granting an injunction to restrain continuing acts of trespass or breach of covenant where (i) the injury to the claimant's rights was small, (ii) its value was capable of being estimated in money, (iii) of being adequately compensated by a small money payment, and (iv) it would be oppressive to the defendant to grant an injunction. When considering the question of oppression the court should not slide into application of a general balance of convenience test. Oppression has to be judged as at the date the court is asked to grant an injunction, and the court could not ignore the reality with which it is then confronted – the fact that the claimant could at an early stage have sought interim relief is clearly relevant, as is the fact that the defendant could have sought a declaration as of right. Those considerations are not however decisive; for example, it would weigh against a finding of oppression if the defendant had acted in blatant and calculated disregard of the claimant's rights. On the facts, the trial judge had been correct in finding that conditions (i), (ii) and (iii) above were satisfied. He had also been entitled to conclude on the basis of the material before him at the trial, in particular the defendants' conduct, the claimant's failure to seek interim relief at an early stage and the fact that restrictive covenants were not absolute or perpetually inviolable, that the grant of an injunction would have been oppressive, and awarded the claimant damages in lieu of an injunction.

> **Millett LJ:** When the plaintiff claims an injunction and the defendant asks the court to award damages instead, the proper approach for the court to adopt cannot be in doubt. Clearly the plaintiff must first establish a case for equitable relief, not only by proving his legal right and an actual or threatened infringement by the defendant, but also by overcoming all equitable defences such as laches, acquiescence or estoppel. If he succeeds in doing this, he is *prima facie* entitled to an injunction. The court may nevertheless in its discretion withhold injunctive relief and award damages instead. How is this discretion to be exercised? In a well-known passage in *Shelfer v City of London Electric Lighting Co* [1895] 1 Ch 287 [see above]. Laid down just 100 years ago, AL Smith LJ's checklist has stood

the test of time; but it needs to be remembered that it is only a working rule and does not purport to be an exhaustive statement of the circumstances in which damages may be awarded instead of an injunction.

Reported cases are merely illustrations of circumstances in which particular judges have exercised their discretion, in some cases by granting an injunction, and in others by awarding damages instead. Since they are all cases on the exercise of a discretion, none of them is a binding authority on how the discretion should be exercised. The most that any of them can demonstrate is that in similar circumstances it would not be wrong to exercise the discretion in the same way. But it does not follow that it would be wrong to exercise it differently.

The outcome of any particular case usually turns on the question: would it in all the circumstances be oppressive to the defendant to grant the injunction to which the plaintiff is prima facie entitled? Most of the cases in which the injunction has been refused are cases where the plaintiff has sought a mandatory injunction to pull down a building which infringes his right to light or which has been built in breach of a restrictive covenant. In such cases the court is faced with a fait accompli. The jurisdiction to grant a mandatory injunction in those circumstances cannot be doubted, but to grant it would subject the defendant to a loss out of all proportion to that which would be suffered by the plaintiff if it were refused, and would indeed deliver him to the plaintiff bound hand and foot to be subjected to any extortionate demands the plaintiff might make. In the present case, as in the closely similar case of *Bracewell v Appleby* [1975] 1 All ER 993, the plaintiff sought a prohibitory injunction to restrain the use of a road giving access to the defendants' house. The result of granting the injunction would be much the same: the house would not have to be pulled down, but it would be rendered landlocked and incapable of beneficial enjoyment.

In the cases of oversailing cranes and other trespasses to the plaintiff's air space, on the other hand, the court has not been faced with a similar fait accompli. The grant of an injunction would merely restore the parties to the same position, with each of them enjoying the same bargaining strength, that they had enjoyed before the trespass began. *Goodson v Richardson* (1874) LR 9 Ch App 221 was a case of this character. The defendant, being desirous of laying pipes for the supply of water to some houses which he had built, applied to the local highways board for permission to lay the pipes in the soil under the highway. Permission was granted, but he was expressly told that this was subject to the rights of the adjoining owners. He made no approach to the adjoining owners, of whom the plaintiff was one, but began to lay pipes in the soil of their land, whereupon the plaintiff brought prompt action for an injunction. The court granted an injunction, regarding the case as a deliberate and unlawful invasion by one man of another man's land for the purpose of a continuing trespass, to the gain and profit of the trespasser, without the consent of the owner of the land. The injunction required the pipes to be removed, but this involved relatively little cost and could hardly be considered oppressive. The defendant had acted with his eyes open, and the injunction merely restored him, after a little expenditure on his part, to the position he was in at the start.

In considering whether the grant of an injunction would be oppressive to the defendant, all the circumstances of the case have to be considered. At one extreme, the defendant may have acted openly and in good faith and in ignorance of the plaintiff's rights, and thereby inadvertently placed himself in a position where the grant of an injunction would either force him to yield to the plaintiff's extortionate demands or expose him to substantial loss. At the other extreme, the defendant may have acted with his eyes open and in full knowledge that he was invading the plaintiff's rights, and hurried on his work in the hope that by presenting the court with a fait accompli he could compel the plaintiff to accept monetary compensation. Most cases, like the present, fall somewhere in between.

In the present case, the defendants acted openly and in good faith and in the not unreasonable belief that they were entitled to make use of Ashleigh Avenue for access to the house that they were building. At the same time, they had been warned by the plaintiff and her solicitors that Ashleigh Avenue was a private road, that they were not entitled to use it for access to the new house and that it would be a breach of covenant for them to use the garden of No 5 to gain access to No 5A. They went ahead, not with their eyes open, but at their own risk. On the other hand, the plaintiff did not seek interlocutory relief at a time when she would almost certainly have obtained it. She should not be criticised for that, but it follows that she also took a risk, viz that by the time her case came for trial the court would be presented with a fait accompli. The case was a difficult one, but in an exemplary judgment the judge took into account all the relevant considerations, both those which told in favour of granting an injunction and those which told against, and in the exercise of his discretion he decided to refuse it. In my judgment his conclusion cannot be faulted.

Question
To what extent is it posible to discern settled principles applied by the courts in granting injunctions?

TYPES OF INJUNCTIONS

As indicated earlier, there are various types of injunctions – prohibitory, mandatory, *quia timet*, interim, freezing and search orders. Another classification of injunctions is into perpetual or interim. This section will consider the various types of injunction.

Perpetual injunctions

A perpetual or final injunction is one that is granted at the trial of the claim or other hearing in which final judgment is given, whereas an interim injunction is one made prior to the trial and which is intended to last only until the trial at the latest. A perpetual injunction may be prohibitory, mandatory or *quia timet*.

Prohibitory injunctions

A prohibitory injunction is generally said to be easier to obtain than a mandatory one and is available to restrain the defendant from acting in a particular way, as in *Shelfer's case* and *Pride of Derby v British Celanese*, see above.

A prohibitory injunction would also be available to restrain the breach of a negative term of a contract, see *Lumley v Wagner* (1852) 1 De GM & G 604. In such a case it has been said that the court must grant the injunction once it is satisfied that there has been a breach of the term. In *Doherty v Allman* (1878) 3 App Cas 709. Lord Cairns explained that in such a case it was not necessary to consider factors like the balance of convenience, as the parties had themselves freely contracted not to do a particular thing. The court has a discretion as to whether the injunction will be granted. In exercising that discretion the court will consider, among other things, whether the performance of the act sought to be restrained will produce an injury to the party seeking the injunction, whether that injury can be remedied or atoned for, and, if capable of being atoned for by damages, whether those damages must be sought in successive suits, or could be obtained once for all. In this case two leases of land were granted subject to positive covenants to maintain the premises in good order, but without a reservation of a power of re-entry for breaches of the covenants. The defendants were proposing to act in breach of the covenant and the claimants sought an injunction. The court refused the application in the exercise of its discretion.

> **Lord Cairns LC:** . . . there is here no negative covenant – not to turn these buildings to any other use. My Lords, if there had been a negative covenant, I apprehend, according to well-settled practice, a Court of Equity would have had no discretion to exercise. If parties, for valuable consideration, with their eyes open, contract that a particular thing shall not be done, all that a Court of Equity has to do is to say, by way of injunction, that which the parties have already said by way of covenant, that the thing shall not be done; and in such case the injunction does nothing more than give the sanction of the process of the Court to that which already is the contract between the parties. It is not then a question of the balance of convenience or inconvenience, or of the amount of damage or of injury – it is the specific performance, by the Court, of that negative bargain which the parties have made, with their eyes open, between themselves. But, my Lords, if there be not a negative covenant but only an affirmative covenant, it appears to me that the case admits of a very different construction. I entirely admit that an affirmative covenant may be of such a character that a Court of Equity, although it cannot enforce affirmatively the performance of the covenant, may, in special cases, interpose to prevent that being done which would be a departure from, and a violation of, the covenant. That is a well-settled and well-known jurisdiction of the Court of Equity. But in that case, my Lords, there appear to me to come in considerations which do not occur in the case of a negative covenant. It may be that a Court of Equity will see that, by

interposing in a case of that kind, in place of leaving the parties to their remedy in damages, it would be doing more harm than it could possibly do good, and there are, as we well know, different matters which the Court of Equity will, under those circumstances, take into its view. It will consider for example whether the injury which it is asked to restrain is an injury which if done cannot be remedied. It will consider whether, if done, it can or cannot be sufficiently atoned for by the payment of a sum of money in damages. It will ask also this question, – Suppose the act to be done, would the right to damages for it be decided exhaustively, once and for all, by one action, or would there necessarily be a repetition of actions for the purpose of recovering damages from time to time? Those are matters which a Court of Equity would well look to, and on the other hand a Court of Equity would look to this: If we interfere and say, in aid of this affirmative covenant, that something shall not be done which would be a departure from it, no doubt we shall succour and help the Plaintiff who comes for our assistance. But shall we do that? Will the effect of our doing that be to cause possible damage to the Defendant, very much greater than any possible advantage we can give to the Plaintiff? Now, in a case of that kind, where there is an amount of discretion which the Court must exercise, those are all considerations which the Court will carefully entertain before it decides how it will exercise its discretion.

Now, my Lords, ... I do not think it is denied at the Bar that on a covenant of this kind the Court of Chancery before it interferes to prevent what was said to be a departure from the terms of the covenant must exercise its discretion with regard to the whole of the circumstances of the case – it appears to me that what I have said will probably convince your Lordships that there is every reason against the exercise, by the Court of Chancery, of its power of giving an injunction, and everything in favour of its leaving this matter to be the subject of damages, for any person who thinks it worth while to bring an action for damages. My Lords, I therefore think that the case, so far as it is founded on the covenant, is one which, looking upon it as an application for an injunction, entirely fails.

The Attorney-General may apply for a prohibitory injunction to restrain the continued commission of a criminal offence if he considers that such a course of action will be in the public interest. This procedure may be used where a statutory penalty is inadequate, see *AG v Sharp* [1931] 1 Ch 121. In *Gouriet v Union of Post Office Workers* [1977] 3 WLR 300, the House of Lords stressed that this procedure is restricted to the Attorney-General in order to enforce public rights and is not available to individuals. In *Gouriet*, the Union of Post Office Workers had resolved to call on its members not to handle mail in the course of transmission between England and Wales and apartheid South Africa during the week starting on Sunday, 16 January 1977. The claimant applied to the Attorney-General for his permission to seek an injunction to restrain the union from taking the proposed action. The AG refused to grant his permission. The claimant brought the action and the House of Lords rejected his application.

Lord Wilberforce: ... in my opinion, there is no support in authority for the proposition that declaratory relief can be granted unless the plaintiff, in proper proceedings, in which there is a dispute between the plaintiff and the defendant concerning their legal respective rights or liabilities, either asserts a legal right which is denied or threatened, or claims immunity from some claim of the defendant against him, or claims that the defendant is infringing or threatens to infringe some public right so as to inflict special damage on the plaintiff. The present proceedings do not possess the required characteristics. In my opinion the law is clear, and rightly so, that only the Attorney General, either ex officio or ex relatione, can apply to the civil courts for injunctive relief against threatened breaches of the law. The present proceedings are misconceived and should have been struck out.

Mandatory injunctions

In its early jurisdiction it used to be the case that the courts would refuse to grant mandatory injunctions but would, instead, phrase the injunction in a negative form, e.g. a defendant would be ordered 'not to allow a wall to remain' rather than simply be instructed to pull down the offending wall. Fortunately, this practice has now been discontinued, but a mandatory injunction may still be difficult to obtain.

The question of hardship to the defendant is of particular importance. Moreover, the defendant must know exactly what it is that he has to do as disobedience to an injunction is a contempt of court. In *Wrotham Park Estates Ltd v Parkside Homes Ltd* [1974] 3 All ER 321, Brightman J refused to grant a mandatory injunction ordering the defendants to demolish houses that had been built in breach of a restrictive covenant. The grant of an injunction is always discretionary and in this case the court took the view that it would have been 'an unpardonable waste of much needed houses' to order their demolition. A just substitute for mandatory injunctions would be damages, i.e. a sum of money as might reasonably have been demanded by the claimants from defendants as a quid pro quo for relaxing the covenants, per Brightman J below.

> **Brightman J:** it is no answer to a claim for a mandatory injunction that the plaintiffs, having issued proceedings, deliberately held their hand and did not seek the assistance of the court for the purpose of preserving the status quo. On the other hand, it is, in my view, equally true that a plaintiff is not entitled 'as of course' to have everything pulled down that was built after the issue of the writ. The erection of the houses, whether one likes it or not, is a fait accompli and the houses are now the homes of people. I accept that this particular fait accompli is reversible and could be undone. But I cannot close my eyes to the fact that the houses now exist. It would, in my opinion, be an unpardonable waste of much needed houses to direct that they now be pulled down and I have never had a moment's doubt during the hearing of this case that such an order ought to be refused. No damage of a financial nature has been done to the plaintiffs by the breach of the layout stipulation. The plaintiffs' use of the Wrotham Park estate has not been and will not be impeded. It is totally unnecessary to demolish the houses in order to preserve the integrity of the restrictive covenants imposed . . . Without hesitation I decline to grant a mandatory injunction.

However, in *Charrington v Simons Co Ltd* [1971] 1 WLR 598, the Court of Appeal took a different view and granted a mandatory injunction requiring the defendant company to remedy its breach of a covenant contained in a deed of conveyance made between the parties. There had been a plain breach of covenant, which resulted in interference with the claimant's business. The trial judge suspended the injunction for up to three years to enable the defendant to carry out works on the claimant's land, with a strong indication that if the claimant did not consent to this the injunction would be discharged. On appeal the court modified the order and deleted the suspension contained in the order.

> **Russell LJ:** In our judgment the learned judge, in adopting the course which he did, travelled beyond the bounds within which discretion may be judicially exercised; for in effect he sought to force on a reluctant plaintiff something very like a settlement involving operations by the defendant company on the plaintiff's land which must lead to greatly increased harm to his business, as a condition or term of his obtaining a mandatory injunction should the works not prove a satisfactory solution. If the learned judge, in his judgment, had said to the plaintiff that he would not grant the injunction unless the plaintiff consented to submit to these works, and the plaintiff refused so to give consent, it would not in our judgment have been a proper ground on which to withhold the injunction to which the plaintiff was otherwise entitled. The course taken by the judge was, it seems to us, no different in substance. We accordingly allow the appeal on this point, with the result, we think, that so much of the order as suspends the operation of the injunction and is dependent on such suspension should be deleted.

Quia timet injunctions

It was stated earlier that this expression literally means 'because he fears'. A *quia timet* injunction is available to the claimant before the occurrence of an apprehended injury or damage to person or property, e.g. where the defendant threatened to demolish a building and the claimant alleged a right of support. To some extent, this type of injunction conflicted with the general principle that the claimant must show injury to a recognised right. Hence, a *quia timet* injunction was difficult to obtain. Lord Upjohn in *Redland Bricks v Morris* [1970] AC 652, explained the nature of a *quia timet* injunction thus:

> **Lord Upjohn:** My Lords, quia timet actions are broadly applicable to two types of cases: first, where the defendant has as yet done no hurt to the plaintiff but is threatening and intending (so the plaintiff alleges) to do works which will render irreparable harm to him or his property if carried to completion. Your Lordships are not concerned with that and those cases are normally, though not exclusively, concerned with negative injunctions. Secondly, the type of case where the plaintiff has been fully recompensed both at law and in equity for the

damage he has suffered but where he alleges that the earlier actions of the defendant may lead to future causes of action. In practice this means the case of which that which is before your Lordships' House is typical, where the defendant has withdrawn support from his neighbour's land or where he has so acted in depositing his soil from his mining operations as to constitute a menace to the plaintiff's land. It is in this field that the undoubted jurisdiction of equity to grant a mandatory injunction, that is an injunction ordering the defendant to carry out positive works, finds its main expression, though of course it is equally applicable to many other cases. Thus, to take the simplest example, if the defendant, the owner of land, including a metalled road over which the plaintiff has a right of way, ploughs up that land so that it is no longer usable, no doubt a mandatory injunction will go to restore it; damages are not a sufficient remedy, for the plaintiff has no right to go upon the defendant's land to remake his right of way.

It is particularly difficult to obtain a mandatory *quia timet* injunction. In *Redland Bricks v Morris*, the claimants sought an injunction against the defendants to order the latter to restore support to their market garden. The House of Lords refused the injunction and reviewed the principles applicable to mandatory *quia timet* injunctions. Lord Upjohn stated that such injunctions would normally only be granted:

- where the claimant showed a strong possibility of damage occurring;
- where the remedy of damages would not be appropriate if such damage did occur;
- where the cost to the defendant was not disproportionate (as the claimant would retain his normal remedies if damage did occur).

The defendant's conduct might also be relevant and, if the injunction was granted, it would have to tell the defendant exactly what it was that he had to do. In *Redland Bricks* the injunction against the brick company was discharged as the defendants had not behaved unreasonably. It was not clear that further damage would occur and the cost of restoring support to the building was out of all proportion to the value of the respondent's land. Lord Upjohn laid down the following guidelines.

Lord Upjohn: The grant of a mandatory injunction is, of course, entirely discretionary and unlike a negative injunction can never be 'as of course'. Every case must depend essentially upon its own particular circumstances. Any general principles for its application can only be laid down in the most general terms:

1. A mandatory injunction can only be granted where the plaintiff shows a very strong probability upon the facts that grave damage will accrue to him in the future. As Lord Dunedin said in 1919 it is not sufficient to say 'timeo'. [*Attorney-General for the Dominion of Canada v. Ritchie Contracting and Supply Co.* [1919] A.C. 999. It is a jurisdiction to be exercised sparingly and with caution but in the proper case unhesitatingly.

2. Damages will not be a sufficient or adequate remedy if such damage does happen. This is only the application of a general principle of equity; it has nothing to do with Lord Cairns' Act or *Shelfer's case* [1895] 1 Ch. 287.

3. Unlike the case where a negative injunction is granted to prevent the continuance or recurrence of a wrongful act the question of the cost to the defendant to do works to prevent or lessen the likelihood of a future apprehended wrong must be an element to be taken into account:

   (a) where the defendant has acted without regard to his neighbour's rights, or has tried to steal a march on him or has tried to evade the jurisdiction of the court or, to sum it up, has acted wantonly and quite unreasonably in relation to his neighbour he may be ordered to repair his wanton and unreasonable acts by doing positive work to restore the status quo even if the expense to him is out of all proportion to the advantage thereby accruing to the plaintiff. As illustrative of this see *Woodhouse v. Newry Navigation Co.* [1898] 1 I.R. 161;

   (b) but where the defendant has acted reasonably, though in the event wrongly, the cost of remedying by positive action his earlier activities is most important for two reasons. First, because no legal wrong has yet occurred (for which he has not been recompensed at law and in equity) and, in spite of gloomy expert opinion, may never occur or possibly only upon a much smaller scale than anticipated. Secondly. because if ultimately heavy damage does occur the plaintiff is in no way prejudiced for he has his action at law and all his consequential remedies in equity. So the amount to be expended under a mandatory order by the defendant must be balanced with these considerations in mind against the anticipated possible damage to the plaintiff and if, on such balance, it seems unreasonable to inflict such expenditure upon one who for this purpose is no more than a potential wrongdoer then the court must exercise its jurisdiction accordingly. Of course, the court does not have to order such works as upon the evidence before it will remedy the wrong but may think it proper to impose upon the defendant the obligation of doing certain works which may upon expert opinion merely lessen the likelihood of any further injury to the plaintiff's land. Sargant J. pointed this out in effect in the celebrated 'Moving Mountain' case, *Kennard v. Cory Bros. & Co. Ltd.* [1922] 1 Ch. 265 at the foot of p. 274 (his judgment was affirmed in the Court of Appeal [1922] 2 Ch. 1).

4.   If in the exercise of its discretion the court decides that it is a proper case to grant a mandatory injunction, then the court must be careful to see that the defendant knows exactly in fact what he has to do and this means not as a matter of law but as a matter of fact, so that in carrying out an order he can give his contractors the proper instructions.

However, Lord Upjohn's judgment in this case has been criticised as it is considered inappropriate for a court to lay down rigid guidelines when granting injunctions. Despite this, most of the principles will be relevant to the granting of any injunction.

Interim injunctions

An interim injunction is one made after the commencement of the proceedings but prior to the final determination of the court. As there is often some delay between the issue of the summons and the trial of the action, a claimant may apply for an interim injunction in order to ensure that the defendant does not continue in his injurious conduct during the period before the trial. Normally the claimant will be required to give an undertaking in damages, i.e. the claimant will undertake to reimburse the defendant for any losses that he may have suffered consequent upon the granting of the injunction if it is decided at the trial that he (defendant) did not act unlawfully.

The court's jurisdiction to grant an interim injunction is now governed by s 37 of Supreme Court Act 1981 (now referred to as the Senior Courts Act 1981, introduced by the Constitutional Reform Act 2005). The claim to an interim injunction under s 37 is required to be incidental to, and dependent upon, the enforcement of a substantive right in the main proceedings. In *Newport Association Football Club Ltd v Football Association of Wales Ltd* [1995] 2 All ER 87, the court held that it had jurisdiction to grant an interim injunction even where the cause of action was a claim for a declaration.

The claimant applies for the interim injunction by filing an application notice. This must state the order sought, the date, time and place of the hearing. The application is required to be accompanied by evidence in support. This can be in the form of witness statements, statements of the case or application, verified by a statement of truth. These documents must be served on the defendant three days before the court hears the application. In the case of a freezing injunction or search order, there must be affidavit evidence. In the event of extremely urgent applications the application may be dealt with by telephone.

The principles applicable to the granting of interim injunctions have been the source of much judicial dispute. At one time the court would refuse to grant an interim injunction unless the claimant could show a strong probability of success at the trial of the action. This was the approach taken by the House of Lords in *Stratford v Lindley* [1965] AC 269. However, in *Hubbard v Vosper* [1972] 2 QB 84, Lord Denning stated that the remedy of an injunction should remain flexible and that the court should take into account all the circumstances of the case.

The principles governing the granting of interim injunctions were reviewed by the House of Lords in *American Cyanamid Co v Ethicon Ltd* [1975] 2 WLR 316. The claimants, an American company, owned a patent covering certain sterile absorbable surgical sutures. The defendants, also an American company, manufactured in the United States and were about to launch on the British market a suture that the claimants alleged infringed their patent. The claimants applied for an interim injunction (originally called an interlocutory injunction) to restrain the defendants' conduct. The injunction was granted by the judge at first instance with the usual undertaking in damages by the claimants. The Court of Appeal reversed his decision on the ground that no *prima facie* case of infringement had been made out. On the claimant's appeal:

The House of Lords allowed the appeal on the following grounds:

(1) that in all cases, including patent cases, the court must determine the matter on a balance of convenience, there being no rule that it could not do so unless first satisfied that, if the case went to trial on no other evidence than that available at the hearing of the application, the claimant would be entitled to a permanent injunction in the terms of the interlocutory injunction sought; where there was a doubt as to the parties' respective remedies in damages being adequate to compensate them for loss occasioned by any restraint imposed on them, it would be prudent to preserve the status quo.

(2) That there was no ground for interfering with the judge's assessment of the balance of convenience or his exercise of discretion and the injunction should be granted accordingly.

In this case, Lord Diplock took the opportunity to modify the principles on which an interim injunction may be granted. The relevant principles, and the order in which they should be considered, are as follows:

- Is there a serious question to be tried? This means that the claim must not be frivolous or vexatious. If the answer is no, then the injunction should be refused. If the answer is yes, then the next question should be considered.

- Which way does the balance of convenience lie?

  - Are damages an adequate remedy for the claimant and is the defendant able to pay such sum? If the answer is yes, then the injunction should be refused. If the answer is no, then the next question should be considered.

  - Does the undertaking as to damages provided by the claimant constitute adequate protection for the defendant and will the claimant be able to honour it? If the answer is yes, then the injunction will be granted. If the answer is no, then the next question should be considered.

  - The maintenance of the status quo. Where the other factors are evenly balanced, the court will prefer to maintain the status quo. The status quo is that state of affairs that existed before the last change of circumstances occurred. Normally this will work in the claimant's favour but it is not by itself conclusive. Where it is not, the court will go on to consider:

    - Other factors. Where the court, having considered the circumstances as stated above and in that order, is still unable to arrive at a decision, it can then go on to consider other factors, including social and economic factors. In *American Cyanamid* the court took into account the fact that no jobs would be lost and no factories would be closed if the injunction was granted, see *Hubbard v Pitt* [1976] QB 142.

    - The relative strength of the parties' cases. As a last resort, where the court, having considered all of the above, is still unable to arrive at a decision it can take into account the relative strength of the parties' cases.

Lord Diplock: My Lords, when an application for an interlocutory injunction to restrain a defendant from doing acts alleged to be in violation of the plaintiff's legal right is made upon contested facts, the decision whether or not to grant an interlocutory injunction has to be taken at a time when ex hypothesi the existence of the right or the violation of it, or both, is uncertain and will remain uncertain until final judgment is given in the action. It was to mitigate the risk of injustice to the plaintiff during the period before that uncertainty could be resolved that the practice arose of granting him relief by way of interlocutory injunction; but since the middle of the 19th century this has been made subject to his undertaking to pay damages to the defendant for any loss sustained by reason of the injunction if it should be held at the trial that the plaintiff had not been entitled to restrain the defendant from doing what he was threatening to do. The object of the interlocutory injunction is to protect the plaintiff against injury by violation of his right for which he could not be adequately compensated in damages recoverable in the action if the uncertainty were resolved in his favour at the trial; but the plaintiff's need for such protection must be weighed against the corresponding need of the defendant to be protected against injury resulting from his having been prevented from exercising his own legal rights for which he could not be adequately compensated under the plaintiff's undertaking in damages if the uncertainty were resolved in the defendant's favour at the trial. The court must weigh one need against another and determine where "the balance of convenience" lies.

In those cases where the legal rights of the parties depend upon facts that are in dispute between them, the evidence available to the court at the hearing of the application for an interlocutory injunction is incomplete. It is given on affidavit and has not been tested by oral cross-examination. The purpose sought to be achieved by giving to the court discretion to grant such injunctions would be stultified if the discretion were clogged by a technical rule forbidding its exercise if upon that incomplete untested evidence the court evaluated the chances of the plaintiff's ultimate success in the action at 50 per cent. or less, but permitting its exercise if the court evaluated his chances at more than 50 per cent.

The notion that it is incumbent upon the court to undertake what is in effect a preliminary trial of the action upon evidential material different from that upon which the actual trial will be conducted, is, I think, of comparatively recent origin, though it can be supported by references in earlier cases to the need to show "a probability that the plaintiffs are entitled to relief" (*Preston v. Luck* (1884) 27 Ch.D. 497, 506, *per* Cotton L.J.) or "a strong prima facie case that the right which he seeks to protect in fact exists" (*Smith v. Grigg Ltd.* [1924] I K.B. 655, 659, *per* Atkin L.J.). These are to be contrasted with expressions in other cases indicating a much less onerous criterion, such as the need to show that there is "certainly a case to be tried" (*Jones v. Pacaya Rubber and Produce Co. Ltd.* [1911] I K.B. 455, 457, *per* Buckley L.J.) which corresponds more closely with what judges generally treated as sufficient to justify their considering the balance of convenience upon applications for interlocutory injunctions, at any rate up to the time when I became a member of your Lordships' House.

An attempt had been made to reconcile these apparently differing approaches to the exercise of the discretion by holding that the need to show a probability or a strong prima facie case applied only to the establishment by the plaintiff of his right, and that the lesser burden of showing an arguable case to be tried applied to the alleged violation of that right by the defendant (*Donmar Productions Ltd. v. Bart (Note)* [1967] I W.L.R. 740, 742, *per* Ungoed-Thomas J., *Harman Pictures N.V. v. Osborne* [1967] I W.L.R. 723, 738, *per* Goff J.). The suggested distinction between what the plaintiff must establish as respects his right and what he must show as respects its violation did not long survive. It was rejected by the Court of Appeal in *Hubbard v. Vosper* [1972] 2 Q.B. 84 – a case in which the plaintiff's entitlement to copyright was undisputed but an injunction was refused despite the apparent weakness of the suggested defence. The court, however, expressly deprecated any attempt to fetter the discretion of the court by laying down any rules which would have the effect of limiting the flexibility of the remedy as a means of achieving the objects that I have indicated above. Nevertheless this authority was treated by Graham J. and the Court of Appeal in the instant appeal as leaving intact the supposed rule that the court is not entitled to take any account of the balance of convenience unless it has first been satisfied that if the case went to trial upon no other evidence than is before the court at the hearing of the application the plaintiff would be entitled to judgment for a permanent injunction in the same terms as the interlocutory injunction sought.

Your Lordships should in my view take this opportunity of declaring that there is no such rule. The use of such expressions as 'a probability,' 'a *prima facie* case,' or 'a strong *prima facie* case' in the context of the exercise of a discretionary power to grant an interlocutory injunction leads to confusion as to the object sought to be achieved by this form of temporary relief. The court no doubt must be satisfied that the claim is not frivolous or vexatious, in other words, that there is a serious question to be tried.

It is no part of the court's function at this stage of the litigation to try to resolve conflicts of evidence on affidavit as to facts on which the claims of either party may ultimately depend nor to decide difficult questions of law which call for detailed argument and mature considerations. These are matters to be dealt with at the trial. One of the reasons for the introduction of the practice of requiring an undertaking as to damages upon the grant of an interlocutory injunction was that 'it aided the court in doing that which was its great object, viz. abstaining from expressing any opinion upon the merits of the case until the hearing': *Wakefield v. Duke of Buccleugh* (1865) 12 L.T. 628, 629. So unless the material available to the court at the hearing of the application for an interlocutory injunction fails to disclose that the plaintiff has any real prospect of succeeding in his claim for a permanent injunction at the trial, the court should go on to consider whether the balance of convenience lies in favour of granting or refusing the interlocutory relief that is sought.

As to that, the governing principle is that the court should first consider whether, if the plaintiff were to succeed at the trial in establishing his right to a permanent injunction, he would be adequately compensated by an award of damages for the the loss he would have sustained as a result of the defendant's continuing to do what was sought to be en joined between the time of the application and the time of the trial. If damages in the measure recoverable at common law would be adequate remedy and the defendant would be in a financial position to pay them, no interlocutory injunction should normally be granted, however strong the plaintiff's claim appeared to be at that stage. If, on the other hand, damages would not provide an adequate remedy for the plaintiff in the event of his succeeding at the trial, the court should then consider whether, on the contrary hypothesis that the defendant were to succeed at the trial in establishing his right to do that which was sought to be enjoined, he would be adequately compensated under the plaintiff's undertaking as to damages for the loss he would have sustained by being prevented from doing so between the time of the application and the time of the trial. If damages in the measure recoverable under such an undertaking would be an adequate remedy and the plaintiff would be in a financial position to pay them, there would be no reason upon this ground to refuse an interlocutory injunction.

It is where there is doubt as to the adequacy of the respective remedies in damages available to either party or to both, that the question of balance of convenience arises. It would be unwise to attempt even to list all the various matters which may need to be taken into consideration in deciding where the balance lies, let alone to suggest the relative weight to be attached to them. These will vary from case to case.

Where other factors appear to be evenly balanced it is a counsel of prudence to take such measures as are calculated to preserve the status quo. If the defendant is enjoined temporarily from doing something that he has not done before, the only effect of the interlocutory injunction in the event of his succeeding at the trial is to postpone the date at which he is able to embark upon a course of action which he has not previously found it necessary to undertake; whereas to interrupt him in the conduct of an established enterprise would cause much greater inconvenience to him since he would have to start again to establish it in the event of his succeeding at the trial.

Save in the simplest cases, the decision to grant or to refuse an interlocutory injunction will cause to whichever party is unsuccessful on the application some disadvantages which his ultimate success at the trial may show he ought to have been spared and the disadvantages may be such that the recovery of damages to which he would then be entitled either in the action or under the plaintiff's undertaking would not be sufficient to compensate him fully for all of them. The extent to which the disadvantages to each party would be incapable of being compensated in damages in the event of his succeeding at the trial is always a significant factor in assessing where the balance of convenience lies, and if the extent of the uncompensatable disadvantage to each party would not differ widely, it may not be improper to take into account in tipping the balance the relative strength of each party's case as revealed by the affidavit evidence adduced on the hearing of the application. This, however, should be done only where it is apparent upon the facts disclosed by evidence as to which there is no credible dispute that the strength of one party's case is disproportionate to that of the other party. The court is not justified in embarking upon anything resembling a trial of the action upon conflicting affidavits in order to evaluate the strength of either party's case.

I would reiterate that, in addition to those to which I have referred, there may be many other special factors to be taken into consideration in the particular circumstances of individual cases.

Lord Diplock did not refer to *Stratford v Lindley* [1965] AC 269; in his judgment, accordingly, it is arguable that the two cases conflict. However, subsequent cases have suggested that the principles set out in *American Cyanamid* are only guidelines and that the point about not considering the relative strength of the parties cases relate to those cases in which there are difficult issues of fact and law to decide. In *Series 5 Software Ltd v Clarke* [1996] 1 All ER 853, Laddie J suggested that Lord Diplock in *American Cyanamid* did not intend to exclude consideration of the relative strength of the parties' cases in most applications for interim injunctions. He suggested that what was intended was to avoid having to resolve difficult issues of fact or law on an interim application. The consideration of the relative strength of the parties' cases is thus not a matter of last resort but should be avoided in cases involving difficult disputes of fact or law. In this case the claimant company sought an interim injunction to restrain use of commercial information and company equipment by ex-employees. The High Court refused the application on the following grounds: the claimant's case, while arguable in the sense that the facts at trial could possibly support the allegations made, was weak in relation to some claims, and in relation to others it was impossible at an interlocutory stage to come to a conclusion as to whether there was substance in the claim or the defence. As far as the balance of convenience was concerned, while it was clear that the injunctions sought could effectively deprive the defendants of their means of earning a living, the claimant's assertion of substantial and immediate damage was unsubstantiated. The court also added that it was not precluded from considering the strength of each party's case when deciding whether to grant an application for interlocutory relief, but should rarely attempt to resolve difficult issues of fact or law, and any view as to the strength of the parties' cases should be reached only where it was apparent from the affidavit evidence and any exhibited contemporary documents that one party's case was much stronger than the other's. It followed that the major factors relevant to the court's discretion were:

(a) the extent to which damages were likely to be an adequate remedy for each party, and the ability of the other party to pay;

(b) the balance of convenience;

(c) the maintenance of the status quo; and

(d) any clear view the court was able to reach as to the relative strength of the parties' cases.

> **Laddie J:** In my view Lord Diplock did not intend . . . [in *American Cyanamid*] to exclude consideration of the strength of the cases in most applications for interlocutory relief. It appears to me that what is intended is that the court should not attempt to resolve difficult issues of fact or law on an application for interlocutory relief. If, on the other hand, the court is able to come to a view as to the strength of the parties' cases on the credible evidence, then it can do so. In fact, as any lawyer who has experience of interlocutory proceedings will know, it is frequently the case that it is easy to determine who is most likely to win the trial on the basis of the affidavit evidence and any exhibited contemporaneous documents. If it is apparent from that material that one party's case is much stronger than the other's then that is a matter the court should not ignore. To suggest otherwise would be to exclude from consideration an important factor and such exclusion would fly in the face of the flexibility advocated earlier earlier in *American Cyanamid*.
>
> Accordingly, it appears to me that in deciding whether to grant interlocutory relief, the court should bear the following matters in mind. (1) The grant of an interlocutory injunction is a matter of discretion and depends on all the facts of the case. (2) There are no fixed rules as to when an injunction should or should not be granted. The relief must be kept flexible. (3) Because of the practice adopted on the hearing of applications for interlocutory relief, the court should rarely attempt to resolve complex issues of disputed fact or law. (4) Major factors the court can bear in mind are (a) the extent to which damages are likely to be an adequate remedy for each party and the ability of the other party to pay, (b) the balance of convenience, (c) the maintenance of the status quo, and (d) any clear view the court may reach as to the relative strength of the parties' cases.

Exceptions to American Cyanamid

American Cyanamid was a commercial case involving breach of copyright. In other types of cases it may be difficult to apply the same principles. Accordingly, the court will take the strength of the parties' case into account in certain exceptional circumstances (rather than apply the guidelines suggested in *American Cyanamid*), for example:

• Where there is a likelihood of a defence (in respect of those acts that are done in contemplation or furtherance of a trade dispute) under s 221 of the Trade Union and Labour Relations (Consolidation) Act 1992.

This statutory defence requires the court to consider the likelihood of the defendant establishing a defence under the Act when deciding whether to grant an injunction. The scope of this defence has, however, been considerably narrowed in recent years.

• Where the injunction will finally dispose of the matter.

To obtain interim relief in such cases the claimant must show a strong *prima facie* case, or at least more than an arguable case, otherwise the court will permit the defendant's right to a trial. In

Cayne v Global Natural Resources plc [1984] 1 All ER 225, the Court of Appeal decided that in the case of an application for an interlocutory injunction, containing a triable issue between the parties and amounts to a serious question to be tried (i.e. one for which there is some supporting material) of which the outcome is uncertain. In these circumstances, where the claimant's case relies solely on inference and the defendant has sworn a positive affidavit which, if true and accepted, destroys that inference, the court should not necessarily conclude that the claimant has failed to establish a triable issue, because on such an application it is not necessary for the parties to establish firmly the outcome of the case, and the mere fact that a party's case is contested does not make it incontrovertible. In addition, where the grant or refusal of an interlocutory injunction will have the practical effect of putting an end to the action, the court should approach the case on the broad principle of what it can do in its best endeavour to avoid injustice, and to balance the risk of doing an injustice to either party. In such a case the court should bear in mind that to grant the injunction sought by the claimant would mean giving him judgment in the case against the defendant without permitting the defendant the right of trial. Accordingly, the established guidelines requiring the court to look at the balance of convenience when deciding whether to grant or refuse an interlocutory injunction do not apply in such a case, since, whatever the strengths of either side, the defendant should not be precluded by the grant of an interlocutory injunction from disputing the claimant's claim at a trial. In this case the claimant appealed against a refusal of an injunction to restrain the defendant until trial of the action or until further order from doing certain acts without first obtaining the approval of Global in general meeting. The Court of Appeal dismissed the appeal.

> **Eveleigh LJ:** In the present case, if this is to be approached as one in which a triable issue has to be established, I myself would come to the conclusion that there was here a triable case. The plaintiffs' evidence, as I have said, clearly pointed to the inference which they asked the court to draw. Global's evidence, if true and accepted, of course clearly destroyed that inference. But the great question that has to be determined is whether the defendants' case is accepted or not. The mere fact it is deposed to does not make it incontrovertible. Therefore, when the evidence is not accepted by the plaintiffs, I am left in doubt as to the outcome of the trial on that issue. If I am in doubt and if the issue seems to be one that is not frivolous, in other words is one for which there is supporting material, then I would conclude that there is a triable issue.
>
> Counsel for the plaintiffs has submitted, however, that *NWL Ltd v Woods* does not govern the present case and we ought not to have regard to it. Largely, as I understand it, he bases that submission on the contention that Global can adequately be compensated in damages and that *NWL Ltd v Woods* was dealing with a case where the loss caused could not be met by an award of damages.
>
> In *NWL Ltd v Woods* [1979] 1 WLR 1294 at 1307 Lord Diplock said:
>
>> Where, however, the grant or refusal of the interlocutory injunction will have the practical effect of putting an end to the action because the harm that will have been already caused to the losing party by its grant or its refusal is complete and of a kind for which money cannot constitute any worthwhile recompense, the degree of likelihood that the plaintiff would have succeeded in establishing his right to an injunction if the action had gone to trial is a factor to be brought into the balance by the judge in weighing the risks that injustice may result from his deciding the application one way rather than the other.
>
> It was that passage which Sir Robert Megarry V-C [at first instance] relied on.
>
> In my view, whether this is a complete *NWL* case or not, it is not one which lends itself to the convenience test. The fact that there may be some further collateral matter to be tried and the fact that there cannot subsequently be a claim by Global for damages arising from the grant of an injunction does not mean that the case must be one which is suitable for the application of the balance of convenience guidelines laid down in the *Cyanamid* case. Having asked myself the various questions referred to in *Cyanamid*, I have reached the conclusion that this case is one that the court has to approach on a broad principle: what can the court do in its best endeavour to avoid injustice?

- Where the defendant has no arguable defence.

In such cases the court does not consider the principles in *American Cyanamid*, but it will consider the relative strengths of the parties' cases, see *Patel v WH Smith* [1987] 1 WLR 853.

- Cases involving public as opposed to private rights.

Where an interim injunction affects public rights, the court will take into account the public interest when determining the balance of convenience. Hence, the principles in *American Cyanamid* will not be strictly adhered to, see *Lewis v Heffer* [1978] 1 WLR 1061. In this case involving factional fighting between two rival candidates in a safe Labour seat, the National Executive Committee of the Labour party (NEC) resolved to suspend the general committee, the executive committee and the officers of the constituency party pending the results of the enquiry and to authorise the party's national agent to conduct the day-to-day affairs of the constituency party and to take the necessary steps to convene the next general committee meeting. The claimant sought an injunction that was refused on the ground that it was impossible to find that the NEC had acted from any ulterior motive and the balance of convenience was in favour of refusing the injunction. If it were granted the chaos that existed in the constituency before the suspension of the officers and committees would only be reinstated.

> **Lord Denning MR:** The one remaining question is: what is the balance of convenience? It seems to me that, if an injunction is granted, saying that the officers and committees are not to be suspended, it will not do anything to remove the chaos. There would then be these questions to be answered: how is the local general meeting to be convened? How are the delegates to it to be ascertained? Are the rules to be regarded as amended or not? All these questions are controversial and may not be able to be solved without further applications to the court. Whereas, if an injunction is refused, the officers and committees will remain suspended, and it should be possible, under the direction of Mr Underhill, for order to be restored. The rules will have been amended at the meeting on 16 January. The local general meeting on 23 February can be convened. Whatever the result of that meeting, the party should be in proper shape to go forward for the future. So, on the balance of convenience, in order to restore order, the right thing would be to refuse the injunction.

- Interim mandatory injunctions.

A mandatory injunction is concerned with undoing what has been done. Granting such an injunction might prove to be a waste of time and money if it transpires that the defendant's conduct was justified. Accordingly, the court is reluctant to grant such interim injunctions. In *Shepherd Homes Ltd v Sandham* [1971] 1 Ch 340, Megarry J refused to grant an interim mandatory injunction where the defendant had erected a fence in breach of a restrictive covenant. He went on to say that the case has to be unusually strong and clear before the mandatory injunction will be granted.

> **Megarry J:** I may summarise my conclusions as follows. First, Lord Cairns LC's statement of principle *prima facie* applies to mandatory injunctions; but it does not apply in its full width. The matter is tempered by a judicial discretion which will be exercised so as to withhold an injunction more readily if it is mandatory than if it is prohibitory. Even a blameless plaintiff cannot as of right claim at the trial to enforce a negative covenant by a mandatory injunction. Second, although it may not be possible to state in any comprehensive way the grounds on which the court will refuse to grant a mandatory injunction in such cases at the trial, they at least include the triviality of the damage to the plaintiff and the existence of a disproportion between the detriment that the injunction would inflict on the defendant and the benefit that it would confer on the plaintiff. The basic concept is that of producing a 'fair result', and this involves the exercise of a judicial discretion.
>
> Third, on motion, as contrasted with the trial, the court is far more reluctant to grant a mandatory injunction than it would be to grant a comparable prohibitory injunction. In a normal case the court must, *inter alia*, feel a high degree of assurance that at the trial it will appear that the injunction was rightly granted; and this is a higher standard than is required for a prohibitory injunction. Fourth, it follows that the statement in 21 *Halsbury's Laws* (3rd edn) p 369, para 774, founded on *Morris v Grant* (1875) 24 WR 55, namely:
>
> > . . . if the defendant, after express notice, has committed a clear violation of an express contract . . . a mandatory injunction will be granted on an interlocutory application,
>
> is too wide. Both the case itself and the statement founded on it have to be qualified in the light of the other authorities.

American Cyanamid does not appear to have altered this position, see also *Locobail International Finance v Agroexport* [1986] 1 WLR 657 where the Court of Appeal decided that a mandatory injunction ought not to be granted on an interlocutory application in the absence of special circumstances, and then only in clear cases either where the court thought that the matter ought to be decided at once or where the injunction was directed at a simple and summary act which could be easily remedied or where the defendant had attempted to steal a march on the claimant. Moreover, before granting a mandatory interlocutory injunction the court had to feel a high degree of assurance that at the trial it would appear that the injunction had rightly been granted, that being a different and higher standard than was required for a prohibitory injunction.

Moreover, there would be no question of further relief at the trial as the claimants would have already obtained their remedy. A mandatory injunction will therefore be granted only very rarely at the interim stage and even then only if the claimant can show that there is a high probability that his claim will succeed at trial.

The traditional reluctance of the court to grant a mandatory injunction at an interim stage can be seen in *Moran v University College Salford (No 2)* [1994] ELR 187. Here, as a result of clerical error, the claimant was given an unconditional offer in the prescribed manner by notifying the Central Admissions System and the University. By accepting this offer he was no longer eligible to seek an alternative place through the clearing system and this in itself was capable of providing good consideration for the agreement between himself and UCS. The Court of Appeal decided that the claimant had a strong and clear case and therefore a good chance of succeeding in establishing that there was an agreement, for good consideration between UCS and himself. However, it would be wrong to grant a mandatory injunction at an interim stage. The appeal was dismissed.

Another illustration of the court's reluctance to grant interim mandatory injunctions is the case of *Zockoll Group Ltd v Mercury Communications Ltd* [1998] 1 CL 50. Here, Z acquired 3,000 telephone numbers from M, which corresponded by alphanumeric code to the names of trades or businesses. Z was a franchising company and had intended to advertise franchised businesses for sale using those names. M withdrew one of the numbers, which spelled the word, 'flights'. Z applied for an interim mandatory injunction restraining M from withdrawing that particular number. The court refused Z's application at first instance and M issued the number to another company. Z appealed. The Court of Appeal held that in deciding whether to grant such an injunction, the principles that the court would apply were: which course of action was likely to produce the least risk of injustice should it turn out that the injunction was wrongly granted, and, the strength of the degree of assurance held by the court that the applicant could prove its case. In the present case, it was more risky to grant a mandatory injunction than a prohibitory one and, as such, no injunction would be granted, but an order would be made for the trial to be expedited. The court provided useful guidance on the principles that it would apply when granting such injunctions. In essence, the court would look at the strength of the applicant's case and, unless it was clear and unequivocal, the court would be unlikely to grant such an order.

Question
What factors ought to be considered by the court when deciding whether or not to grant an order for a mandatory interim injunction?

Freezing injunctions

In recent years the courts have developed new forms of interim injunctions which can be regarded as formidable weapons in the litigation armoury. One of these is the 'Mareva' injunction, which is now known as a freezing injunction.

This type of injunction is designed to prevent a defendant from removing assets from the jurisdiction of the British courts (or dissipating assets within the jurisdiction) which, if not prohibited, would defeat the whole purpose of litigation. Lord Denning described this injunction as '. . . the greatest piece of judicial law reform in (his) time.'

The title of the injunction originally took its name from the case, *Mareva Compania Naviera SA v International Bulkcarriers SA* [1975] 2 Lloyds Rep 509. In this case, the claimants, Mareva Compania Naviera SA ('the shipowners), issued a writ on 25 June 1975 claiming against the defendants, International Bulkcarriers SA ('the charterers'), unpaid hire and damages for repudiation of a charterparty. On an *ex parte* application Donaldson J granted an injunction until 17.00 hours on 23 June restraining the charterers from removing or disposing out of the jurisdiction moneys standing to the credit of the charterers' account at a London bank. The shipowners appealed against Donaldson J's refusal to extend the injunction beyond 17.00 hours on 23 June. The Court of Appeal dismissed the appeal and extended the injunction until the date of the judgment at the trial.

> **Lord Denning MR:** In my opinion the principle [concerning a freezing order] applies to a creditor who has a right to be paid the debt owing to him, even before he has established his right by getting judgment for it. If it appears that the debt is due and owing, and there is a danger that the debtor may dispose of his assets so as to defeat it before judgment, the court has jurisdiction in a proper case to grant an interlocutory judgment so as to prevent him disposing of those assets. It seems to me that this is a proper case for the exercise of this jurisdiction. There is money in a bank in London which stands in the name of these charterers. The charterers have control of it. They may at any time dispose of it or remove it out of this country. If they do so, the shipowners may never get their charter hire. The ship is now on the high seas. It has passed Cape Town on its way to India. It will complete the voyage and the cargo will be discharged. And the shipowners may not get their charter hire at all. In face of this danger, I think this court ought to grant an injunction to restrain the charterers from disposing of these moneys now in the bank in London until the trial or judgment in this action. If the charterers have any grievance about it when they hear of it, they can apply to discharge it. But meanwhile the shipowners should be protected. It is only just and right that this court should grant an injunction. I would therefore continue the injunction.

The earliest example of this injunction occurred in *Nippon Kaisha v Karageorgis* [1975] 3 All ER 282. Here, the claimants, shipowners, chartered three ships to the defendants who, in breach of their contracts, failed to pay the claimants. The claimants believed that the defendants had funds in London and feared that the defendants would transmit the funds out of the jurisdiction. Thus, the claimants applied for an interim injunction against the defendants to restrain them from disposing of or removing any of their assets outside the jurisdiction. The High Court judge refused the application and the claimants appealed to the Court of Appeal.

The Court of Appeal held that the injunction ought to be granted.

> **Lord Denning MR:** It seems to me that the time has come when we should revise our practice. There is no reason why the High Court or this court should not make an order such as is asked for here. It is warranted by s 45 of the Supreme Court of Judicature (Consolidation) Act 1925 which says the High Court may grant a mandamus or injunction or appoint a receiver by an interlocutory order in all cases in which it appears to the court to be just or convenient so to do. It seems to me that this is just such a case. There is a strong *prima facie* case that the hire is owing and unpaid. If an injunction is not granted, these moneys may be removed out of the jurisdiction and the shipowners will have the greatest difficulty in recovering anything.
>
> It seems to me plain that the injunction should be continued on this ex parte application and should be continued until after judgment in these proceedings, to restrain the defendants from disposing of their assets here. On notice being given, the banks, of course, will not part with the money. If the defendants wish to challenge this order, they can, of course, apply to discharge it, if they have grounds for doing so.

The practice of issuing such an injunction was approved and explained by the House of Lords in *The Siskina* [1977] 3 WLR 818, where Lord Diplock stated that the purpose of a Mareva (freezing) injunction was to ensure that a fund was available if the English court eventually adjudicated in the claimant's favour.

An interim injunction is ancillary to an existing cause of action. Thus, the court cannot grant a freezing injunction unless the claimant has a legal or equitable right that can be enforced by final judgment, see *Veracruz Transportation Inc v VC Shipping Co Inc* (1991) *The Times*, 14 November. In *Re Q's Estate* (1999) 1 Lloyds Rep 931, the court reiterated that it had no jurisdiction to grant a *quia timet*-type freezing injunction. Applying the *Siskina* the court stated that there must be an accrued cause of action. In *Q's Estate* the High Court decided that it had jurisdiction to issue an injunction despite the parties agreeing to exclusive arbitration but applying the *Siskina* the court stated that there must be an accrued cause of action.

> **Rix J:** In my judgment, therefore, the word 'exclusive' in the present clause [of the agreement] is merely intended to underline the general rule, which is that substantive proceedings must be by way of arbitration, rather than to introduce the exceptional situation where the parties are barred from ancillary proceedings in court. The emphasis makes perfectly good sense in the light of the exclusion of any right of appeal. It seems to me that if the parties wanted to exclude the right to resort to the court under section 44 [Arbitration Act 1996] for assistance in ancillary matters, they could and should have done so by more specific wording. In conclusion, therefore, this court did not lack jurisdiction to make the Mareva order that it was asked to make by reason of the terms of the arbitration clause in this case. The Mareva order was discharged on the merits and not on the ground of any lack of jurisdiction.

> In *The Veracruz I* (1991) the Court of Appeal decided that without an accrued cause of action a plaintiff could not obtain a Mareva injunction. They considered that their decision was forced on them by *The Siskina* [1979] AC 210. The 'sensible and desirable approach' (per Sir John Megaw at 361) adopted by Saville J in *A v. B* [1989] 2 Lloyd's Rep 423, whereby an injunction was granted prior to the falling in of the anticipated cause of action but its operation was suspended until the cause of action arose, was therefore not open. *The Veracruz I* was a case, not in principle unlike the present case, where a cause of action for the defective condition of a ship subject to a sale contract was expected to accrue upon its imminent delivery to the buyer, in circumstances where it was to be supposed that the purchase price would be removed from the jurisdiction as soon as it was paid.

The exception to the rule that the court has no jurisdiction to grant a freezing injunction, unless it is ancillary to a cause of action within the jurisdiction of the court occurred in cases where s 25 of the Civil Jurisdiction and Judgments Act 1982 applies. The High Court will have jurisdiction to grant a freezing injunction even though there is no cause of action in the UK, provided a court in one of the contracting states to the Brussels or Lugano Convention has jurisdiction. Where the cause of action arises in a non-contracting state, the rule used to be that the court could not grant a freezing injunction. In *Mercedes Benz AG v Leiduck* [1996] 1 AC 284, the Privy Council took the view that the Hong Kong court did not have jurisdiction to order a freezing injunction in support of an action outside the jurisdiction. However, if such facts were to come before the English courts today, the court could grant such an injunction. This is due to the Civil Jurisdiction and Judgments Act 1982 (Interim Relief) Order 1997, which extended s 25 to cover non-contracting states.

The court's power to grant freezing injunctions was confirmed by s 37 of the Supreme Court Act 1981 (now the Senior Courts Act 1981, introduced by the Constitutional Reform Act 2005). This section gives the court power to grant a freezing injunction whenever it is 'just and convenient'.

As the freezing injunction is a form of interim injunction the guidelines laid down in *American Cyamamid* would first have to be satisfied. Kerr LJ in *Ninemia Maritime Corporation v Trave S. GMBH* [1984] 1 All ER 398, made clear that, despite the wide wording of s 37, certain material criteria had already been established by the cases.

The criteria to be satisfied before the court can grant a freezing injunction are as follows:

- that the claimant has a good arguable case;
- that the claimant has satisfied the court that there are assets within the jurisdiction and, where an extra territorial order is sought, assets exist outside the jurisdiction;
- that there is a real risk of dissipation or secretion of assets which would render nugatory any judgment which the claimant might obtain; and
- that the applicant who seeks a freezing injunction *ex parte* must make full disclosure of all material facts, including any facts that he might reasonably discover.

> **Kerr LJ:** . . . the issue on this appeal is whether or not this court should interfere with the exercise of the judge's discretion when he decided to discharge the injunctions. As to this, we are clearly of the view, for the reasons discussed below, that no case has been made out on behalf of the buyers which would justify us taking this

course. Recent decisions of the House of Lords have emphasised the importance of appellate courts resisting the temptation to interfere with the exercise of judicial discretions other than in limited circumstances which do not apply here.

Since the origin of this jurisdiction, the authorities clearly show that in order to obtain a Mareva injunction, a plaintiff must show that he would suffer some prejudice as a result of what the judge referred to in his second question as a 'dissipation of assets' in the event of the injunction being refused. The issue is as to the test which the plaintiff must satisfy . . . In our view the test is whether, on the assumption that the plaintiff has shown at least 'a good arguable case'. the court concludes, on the whole of the evidence then before it, that the refusal of a Mareva injunction would involve a real risk that a judgment or award in favour of the plaintiff would remain unsatisfied.

It has also been made clear in the case of *Third Chandris Shipping Corporation v Unimarine SA* [1979] 2 All ER 972, that the claimant should make full and frank disclosure of all relevant material and be required to give particulars of his claim against the defendant, stating the grounds of his claim and the amount, and fairly stating the points made against him by the defendant. If he does not comply with this duty he will normally be deprived of the benefits of the order without consideration of the merits and irrespective of whether the non-disclosure was innocent or deliberate or whether he would have obtained the order if he had made full disclosure. However, if the injunction is discharged because of material non-disclosure the court has a discretion to grant a second injunction when all the facts are placed before it and a second injunction may well be granted if the non-disclosure was innocent and an injunction could properly have been granted on the disclosed facts. In *Third Chandris* case, the claimants chartered three vessels to Panamanian charterers who became liable to the claimants for breach of contract. The claimants requested prompt payment of sums due to the claimants but received no reply. The claimants had learned that the charterers (defendants) had a bank account in London and obtained a *Mareva* injunction *ex parte* restraining the charterers from removing assets out of the jurisdiction, save as to sums in excess of that claimed. The defendants applied to discharge the injunction. The High Court refused to discharge the injunction and the defendants appealed.

The Court of Appeal dismissed the appeal on the following grounds: that the High Court had jurisdiction under section 45 (1) of the Supreme Court of Judicature (Consolidation) Act 1925 to grant a *Mareva* injunction as an interlocutory order in appropriate cases where it appeared that a debt, which was or was likely to be the subject of proceedings in England, was owing and there was a real risk of the debtor removing assets from within the jurisdiction so as to defeat the claim regarding the debt.

Lord Denning MR: It is just four years ago now since we introduced here the procedure known as *Mareva* injunctions. All the other legal systems of the world have a similar procedure. It is called in the civil law saisie conservatoire. It has been welcomed in the City of London and has proved extremely beneficial. It enables a creditor in a proper case to stop his debtor from parting with his assets pending trial. Two years ago, the House of Lords had this procedure under their close consideration. It was in *Siskina (Owners of Cargo lately laden on board) v. Distos Compania Naviera S.A.* [1979] A.C. 210. If the House had any doubts about our jurisdiction in the matter, I should have expected them to give voice to them, rather than let the legal profession continue in error. But none of their Lordships did cast any doubt on it. Impressed with the unanimity of his colleagues, Lord Hailsham of St. Marylebone said, at p. 261:

> Since the House is no way casting doubt on the validity of the new practice by its decision in the instant appeal, I do not wish in any way to do so myself.

In the *Siskina case* [1979] A.C. 210 the House placed this restriction upon the procedure. It applies only in the case of an 'interlocutory order'. In order to obtain a *Mareva* injunction there has to be in existence a substantive cause of action on which the plaintiff is suing or about to sue in the High Court in England or is enforcing or about to enforce by arbitration in England. The procedure was, therefore, not available in the *Siskina case*. In that case the bills of lading contained a clause giving exclusive jurisdiction to the courts of Genoa. The cargo was arrested *in rem* in Cyprus. There was no jurisdiction in England at all over the substantive claim.

The House left open the position of a plaintiff making a claim against an English-based defendant. Lord Hailsham of St. Marylebone said significantly, at p. 261:

Either the position of a plaintiff making a claim against an English-based defendant will have to be altered or the principle of the *Mareva cases* will have to be modified.

In the recent case of *Chartered Bank v. Daklouche* (unreported), March 16, 1979; Court of Appeal (Civil Division) Transcript No. 308 of 1979, we did apply the *Mareva* injunction to an English-based defendant. wife came from Abu Dhabi in the Persian Gulf to England. She bought a large house in Hampshire, and had £70,000 in a bank in England in her own name. Mocatta J. granted a *Mareva* injunction, and this court affirmed it. I said:

The law should be that there is jurisdiction to grant a *Mareva* injunction even though the defendant may be served here. If he makes a fleeting visit, or if there is a danger that he may abscond, or that the assets or moneys may disappear and be taken out of the reach of the creditors, a *Mareva* injunction can be granted. Here is this £70,000 lying in a bank in England, which can be removed at the stroke of a pen from England outside the reach of the creditors.

Much as I am in favour of the *Mareva* injunction, it must not be stretched too far lest it be endangered. In endeavouring to set out some guidelines, I have had recourse to the practice of many other countries which have been put before us. They have been most helpful. These are the points which those who apply for it should bear in mind:

(i) The plaintiff should make full and frank disclosure of all matters in his knowledge which are material for the judge to know: see *Negocios Del Mar S.A. v. Doric Shipping Corporation S.A. (The Assios)* [1979] 1 Lloyd's Rep. 331.

(ii) The plaintiff should give particulars of his claim against the defendant, stating the ground of his claim and the amount thereof, and fairly stating the points made against it by the defendant.

(iii) The plaintiff should give some grounds for believing that the defendant has assets here. I think that this requirement was put too high in *MBPXL Corporation v. Intercontinental Banking Corporation Ltd.* August 28, 1975; Court of Appeal (Civil Division) Transcript No. 411 of 1975. In most cases the plaintiff will not know the extent of the assets. He will only have indications of them. The existence of a bank account in England is enough, whether it is in overdraft or not.

(iv) The plaintiff should give some grounds for believing that there is a risk of the assets being removed before the judgment or award is satisfied. The mere fact that the defendant is abroad is not by itself sufficient. No one would wish any reputable foreign company to be plagued with a *Mareva* injunction simply because it has agreed to London arbitration. But there are some foreign companies whose structure invites comment. We often see in this court a corporation which is registered in a country where the company law is so loose that nothing is known about it – where it does no work and has no officers and no assets. Nothing can be found out about the membership, or its control, or its assets, or the charges on them. Judgment cannot be enforced against it. There is no reciprocal enforcement of judgments. It is nothing more than a name grasped from the air, as elusive as the Cheshire Cat. In such cases the very fact of incorporation there gives some ground for believing there is a risk that, if judgment or an award is obtained, it may go unsatisfied. Such registration of such companies may carry many advantages to the individuals who control them, but they may suffer the disadvantage of having a *Mareva* injunction granted against them. The giving of security for a debt is a small price to pay for the convenience of such a registration. Security would certainly be required in New York. So also it may be in London. Other grounds may be shown for believing there is a risk. But some such should be shown.

(v) The plaintiff must, of course, give an undertaking in damages – in case he fails in his claim or the injunction turns out to be unjustified. In a suitable case this should be supported by a bond or security: and the injunction only granted on it being given, or undertaken to be given.

In setting out those guidelines, I hope we shall do nothing to reduce the efficacy of the present practice. In it speed is of the essence. Ex parte is of the essence. If there is delay, or if advance warning is given, the assets may well be removed before the injunction can bite. It is rather like the new injunction in Chancery, the *Anton Piller* injunction *(Anton Piller KG v. Manufacturing Processes Ltd.* [1976] Ch. 55), which has proved equally beneficial. That must be done speedily ex parte before the incriminating material is removed. So here in *Mareva* injunctions before the assets are removed. The solicitors of the City of London can, I believe, continue their present practice so long as they do it with due regard to their responsibilities: and so long as the judges exercise a wise discretion so as to see that the procedure is not abused.

Further guidelines issued by the courts, from time to time, include:

(1) the claimant must establish a good arguable case, see *Ninemia Maritime Corp v Trave Schiffahrts Gmbh* [1984] 1 All ER 398;

(2) the difference between a good arguable case and a serious question to be tried (which is incapable of definition), does not affect the applicability of the general principle that it is no part of the court's function at the interim stage to try to resolve factual disputes on which the claims of either party may ultimately depend, nor to decide difficult questions of law that call for detailed argument and mature consideration, see *Derby v Weldon* [1990] Ch 48;

(3) the defendant should not be prevented from using his assets for a purpose that does not conflict with the purpose of a freezing injunction, for example the making of payments that the defendant in good faith considers he should make in the ordinary course of business, see *Garvin v Domus Publishing Ltd* [1989] 2 All ER 344;

(4) the order should normally specify a maximum sum, that is to say it should restrain removal or dissipation of assets save in so far as such assets exceed a specified sum, see *Z Ltd v A* [1982] 1 All ER 556;

(5) the order should not be used to prevent a defendant from living as he has always lived, or from paying legal costs to defend the proceedings, see *United Mizrahi Bank Ltd v Doherty* [1998] 2 All ER 230;

(6) the order should make reasonable provision for the protection of third parties and should include notice of their right to seek variation of the order, see *Guinness Peat Aviation (Belgium) v Hispania Lineas Aereas SA* [1992] 1 Lloyds Rep 190.

Some of these guidelines have been applied in *Gulf Interstate Oil v Ant Trade & Transport Ltd of Malta* (1999) 1 Lloyds Rep 867.

As with all injunctions the claimant has to give an undertaking in damages in case his claim fails or the injunction is subsequently shown not to be justified.

According to *Derby & Co v Weldon* [1989] 2 WLR 279, these criteria can be satisfied with comparatively little evidence. See also *Re BCCI (No 9)* [1994] 3 All ER 764, where these criteria were applied. In this case an application was made by the English liquidators of Bank of Credit and Commerce International SA (BCCI) for directions as to whether, before transferring funds to the Luxembourg liquidators of BCCI, the English liquidators should make provision for various matters. The issue before the High Court was whether the English liquidators, who wished to transfer the funds at their disposal to the foreign liquidators to facilitate a worldwide distribution among creditors *pari passu*, but where the two jurisdictions had contrary rules as to insolvency set-off, were required to retain sufficient funds to satisfy those creditors proving in the English liquidation who would be entitled to enjoy the benefit of set-off. Sir Richard Scott V.C. had come to the clear conclusion that provision should be made by the English liquidators for the dividend that net creditors would receive in an English winding-up but that no provision should be made for net debtors who would be unable to prove in an English winding-up and to whom the English liquidators had no liability.

A further criterion would appear to be that the court will generally be reluctant to grant a freezing injunction that would interfere with the defendant's business, see *Commissioners of Customs & Excise v Anchor Foods Ltd* [1999] 3 All ER 268. In the case of *Polly Peck International v Nadir (No 2)* [1992] 4 All ER 769, the Court of Appeal held that it would not grant a freezing injunction before any liability had been established if the grant of the injunction would interfere with the normal course of the defendant's business. This would particularly be the case if the cause of action is no more than merely speculative. The court would also be reluctant to grant a freezing injunction against a bank except in unusual circumstances. It is unclear whether this is a rule of general application. It is suggested that the principle is restricted to the facts of the case. It is pertinent that the relevant bank was the Central Bank of Northern Cyprus. If a freezing injunction had been granted it may have had disastrous consequences for the banking system of that country.

Scott LJ: As a general principle, a Mareva injunction ought not to interfere with the ordinary course of business of the defendant. It is not intended to give the plaintiff security in advance of judgment but merely to prevent the defendant from defeating the plaintiff's chances of recovery by dissipating or secreting away assets. This principle makes the grant of a Mareva injunction against a bank, at any rate a bank carrying on a normal banking business, very difficult. A Mareva injunction ought never to prevent a defendant from paying his creditors their due debts. A bank must repay its depositors in accordance with the terms on which the deposits are held.

[Having outlined the nature and evidence of the defendants' banking business, he continued] In my opinion, the evidence before this court impels the conclusion that the Mareva injunction granted on 7 November 1991 has already seriously interfered with the Central Bank's normal manner of carrying on its banking business. A trial in such a mammoth and complex action as the present must be a long way ahead. To maintain the Mareva injunction in the meantime would, in my opinion, be likely to inflict irreparable harm on the Central Bank.

The other side of the coin must also be taken into account. If the injunction is lifted, is it likely that any funds will be left in England against which judgment can be executed if, in the event, the action against the Central Bank succeeds?

. . . If PPI's action against the Central Bank succeeds to the extent of the full £44m that is claimed, the Central Bank would be hopelessly insolvent. Well before judgment, if there were any likelihood of its being an adverse one, I think it likely that the Central Bank would have looked for a safer place than London for its foreign currency reserves.

In these circumstances I think the administrators are entitled to be of the opinion that there may not be much in the way of funds left in England when they come to execute their judgment. It does not follow, however, that the absence of funds in England will necessarily prevent PPI from enforcing its judgment (if it obtains one) against the Central Bank. The Central Bank must keep its foreign currency funds somewhere. Funds kept in any of the Brussels Convention countries will be vulnerable to enforcement procedure by PPI.

In summary, therefore, it comes to this. PPI has a claim against the Central Bank that, though a possible one, is at present based on little more than speculation. A Mareva injunction will, inevitably, seriously interfere with the Central Bank's normal course of business and will, quite possibly, destroy the Central Bank; if the Mareva injunction is lifted, it is possible that a judgment obtained by PPI will be worthless.

In my judgment, for two reasons the balance comes down against the continuance of the Mareva injunction.

First, I regard PPI's present case against the Central Bank as no more than speculative. Second, it is, in my opinion, wrong in principle to grant a Mareva injunction so as, before any liability has been established, to interfere with the normal course of business of the defendant. To impose a Mareva injunction that will have that effect in order to protect a cause of action that is no more than speculative is not simply wrong in principle but positively unfair.

A similar approach was taken by the court in *Camdex International Ltd v Bank of Zambia (No 2)* [1997] 1 WLR 632. In this case, the claimant obtained a freezing injunction to prevent the removal of the defendant's assets from the jurisdiction. The defendant was the Central Bank of Zambia and had considerable external debts and obligations to international financial institutions. It was also responsible for the management and issue of the Zambian currency and, as part of this, had arranged for the printing of a quantity of high denomination Zambian banknotes in England. The defendant applied for a discharge from the freezing injunction and the consequent release of the unissued bank notes on the ground that this was of importance to the Zambian economy. The Court of Appeal varied the injunction and decided that the purpose of the freezing injunction is to prevent the dissipation or removal of assets from the jurisdiction. Such an injunction was not intended to pressurize the defendant into paying the judgment debt. As the unissued banknotes had no value on the open market, they (the notes) could not be regarded as assets to which a freezing injunction could attach. Further, substantial national hardship would result if the banknotes were not issued in Zambia.

In *Camdex*, public policy played an important part. The consequences to the economy of Zambia if the court refused to vary the injunction would have been very serious indeed. The court also made it clear that the defendant, bearing in mind its role in the Zambian economy, could not be blamed for wanting to pay off its debts to the international financial institutions and to pay creditors on a pro rata basis.

When proceedings have been compromised and judgment obtained against one defendant, the court has jurisdiction to grant a freezing injunction and a disclosure order against another defendant (against whom all causes of action have been discontinued) as an aid to enforcement of the judgment against the former. This is especially so where the latter has been involved in the affairs of the former in order to defeat the claimant's attempts to execute the judgment, see *Mercantile Group (Europe) AG v Aiyela* (1993) *The Times*, 4 August.

Foreign defendants

Freezing injunctions are available against defendants who are resident in the jurisdiction as well as against foreign defendants. In *Chartered Bank v Daklouche* [1980] 1 WLR 107, a freezing injunction was granted where the defendant was present and had assets within the jurisdiction as there was a danger that he might remove them. A similar approach was taken in *Barclay – Johnson v Yuill* [1980] 1 WLR 1259. In this case the claimant and defendant were jointly engaged in the purchase, renovation and resale of a flat. The proceeds of the resale, amounting to some £3,300, were paid into a bank account in the defendant's name. A dispute arose between the parties over a sum of £2,000, which the claimant alleged the defendant owed her. The claimant discovered that the defendant had sold his own flat, had gone abroad and was cruising in an ocean-going yacht of which he was a part-owner. The defendant, who was an English national with an English domicile, had previously lived abroad when in financial difficulties, and the claimant, fearing that he would again do so and transfer his assets out of the jurisdiction, obtained a Mareva injunction restraining the defendant from removing the proceeds of the resale of the flat out of the jurisdiction. When the injunction came up for extension the defendant submitted that it should not be continued because the Mareva jurisdiction was restricted to preventing foreign nationals from removing assets out of the jurisdiction and the court ought not to grant a Mareva injunction against an English national domiciled in England. The court held that the grant of a Mareva injunction was not barred merely because the defendant was not a foreigner or a foreign-based person, although the defendant's nationality, domicile and place of residence could be material to a greater or lesser degree in determining whether there was a real risk that the assets would be removed from the jurisdiction. The essence of the jurisdiction was the existence of a real risk that the defendant would remove his assets from the jurisdiction and thereby stultify the judgment sought by the claimant. On the facts, the claimant had, on balance, established that there was a real risk of removal of the fund in the bank account and the injunction would accordingly be continued.

> **Megarry VC:** It seems to me that the heart and core of the Mareva injunction is the risk of the defendant removing his assets from the jurisdiction and so stultifying any judgment given by the courts in the action. If there is no real risk of this, such an injunction should be refused; if there is a real risk, then if the other requirements are satisfied the injunction ought to be granted. If the assets are likely to remain in the jurisdiction, then the plaintiff, like all others with claims against the defendant, must run the risk, common to all, that the defendant may dissipate his assets, or consume them in discharging other liabilities, and so leave nothing with which to satisfy any judgment. On the other hand, if there is a real risk of the assets being removed from the jurisdiction, a Mareva injunction will prevent their removal. It is not enough for such an injunction merely to forbid the defendant to remove them from the jurisdiction, for otherwise he might transfer them to some collaborator who would then remove them; accordingly, the injunction will restrain the defendant from disposing of them even within the jurisdiction. But that does not mean that the assets will remain sterilised for the benefit of the plaintiff, for the court will permit the defendant to use them for paying debts as they fall due: see *Iraqi Ministry of Defence v Arcepey Shipping Co SA* [1980] 1 All ER 480 at 486, [1980] 1 WLR 488 at 494 per Robert Goff J.
>
> If, then, the essence of the jurisdiction is the risk of the assets being removed from the jurisdiction, I cannot see why it should be confined to 'foreigners', in any sense of that term.

Why should it make all the difference if instead he had been a foreign national with a foreign domicile who, after living and working here for a while, was preparing to leave with his assets? Is it really to be said that in relation to Mareva injunctions, there is one law for the foreigner and another for the English, and that this flows from a statutory power to grant an injunction if it appears to the court to be 'just or convenient' to do so? I cannot see any sensible ground for holding that in this respect there is some privilege or immunity for the English and Welsh.

In saying this, I do not intend to suggest that matters of nationality, domicile, residence and so on are irrelevant in Mareva applications. Any or all of them may be of considerable importance in so far as they bear on the risk of removal. If the defendant has not even come to this country, the risk of his assets here being removed abroad will normally be high. If a foreign national is here, his nationality will often make it easier for him at short notice to go abroad with his assets, and remain there, easier than for a citizen of the United Kingdom; and his foreign domicile would render it more probable that he would do this. At the same time, it must be remembered that since the first Mareva injunction was granted, there has been a significant change, in that within the last year the abolition of exchange control has made it easier for everybody to transfer assets abroad.

I would hold (1) that it is no bar to the grant of a Mareva injunction that the defendant is not a foreigner, or is not foreign-based, in any sense of those terms, (2) that it is essential that there should be a real risk of the defendant's assets being removed from the jurisdiction in such a way as to stultify any judgment that the plaintiff may obtain, and (3) that, in determining whether there is such a risk, questions of the defendant's nationality, domicile, place of residence and many other matters may be material to a greater or a lesser degree.

Nature of assets

The nature of the defendant's assets is apparently immaterial. In *Allen v Jambo Holdings* [1980] 1 WLR 1252, the defendant's only asset within the jurisdiction was an aeroplane, but an injunction was granted to prevent its removal. Moreover, in *TDK Tape Distributors v Videochoice Ltd* [1986] 1 WLR 141, the court expressed the view that even 'after-acquired' assets (i.e. assets acquired after the issue of the court order and before its execution) could fall within the ambit of a freezing injunction. In this case the claimants obtained a Mareva injunction, subject to the usual undertakings, restraining the defendant until further order from disposing of, or dealing with, any of his assets or any interest in assets within the jurisdiction, save in so far as they exceeded some £600,000 and save for £100 per week ordinary living expenses. Subsequent to a disclosure order by the court the defendant failed to disclose in his affidavit of assets, the proceeds of an insurance policy that matured on the death of his wife. This sum was paid to the defendant's solicitor who used the amount to pay counsel for defending the defendant in criminal proceedings. The claimants applied to have the defendant and his firm of solicitors punished for contempt of court because (i) the defendant had breached the order for discovery and the Mareva injunction by failing to disclose the policy in his affidavit and in paying the proceeds to his solicitors, and (ii) the solicitors had procured or allowed the proceeds of the policy to be paid to them in breach of the court's orders. The defendant and his solicitors contended (i) that the life policy, or its proceeds, was not an asset or an interest in an asset at the material time since the proceeds of the policy were acquired after the injunction had been obtained, and (ii) that the payment of legal fees did not fall within the scope of the injunction since it was not a dissipation of assets of the kind at which the injunction was aimed.

Skinner J held: (1) The defendant's and his wife's interest in the insurance policy existed at the time the Mareva injunction was made because they could at any time have redeemed the mortgage and retrieved their rights in the policy. Accordingly, the policy, or the proceeds thereof, was an asset or an interest in an asset at the material time and was not an after-acquired asset; (2) The terms of a Mareva injunction may include the usual undertakings restraining the defendant from disposing of or dealing with any of his assets save for a specified amount 'for ordinary living expenses'. The term 'ordinary living expenses' meant the ordinary, recurrent expenses involved in maintaining the defendant in the style to which he was reasonably accustomed and did not include exceptional expenses, such as legal expenses incurred by the defendant in employing Queen's Counsel to defend him against serious criminal charges; (3) Although the defendant was at fault in failing to disclose the policy in his affidavit of assets, the real responsibility for his failure and for anything that he did in relation to the proceeds of the policy rested with his solicitor. Accordingly, the defendant and the individual solicitor who dealt with the defendant's affairs were guilty of contempt of court.

> **Skinner J:** Counsel for the fourth defendant argues, however, that there was no breach and no contempt. His first argument is that the insurance policy in question, or its proceeds, was not an asset or an interest in an asset at any material time. He says that it was an asset or an interest acquired after the order was made and that this particular injunction, and Mareva injunctions in general, unless they spell it out specifically, do not apply to what he calls 'after-acquired' assets. That argument, of course, depends on whether the asset here was 'after-acquired'. Counsel for the plaintiffs says it plainly was not; it was an asset, or at the very least an interest in an asset, which was in existence at the time of the order. He stresses the fact that this was money which by the exercise of certain rights the fourth defendant could have regained possession of and power over. Counsel for the fourth defendant says: 'Well, he never had any right over this money until his wife died and the insurance moneys became due under the policy.' Counsel for the plaintiffs replies: 'No, it had a value; at the time the order was made, it had a value in that it had the potential of reducing the indebtedness of the fourth defendant and his wife to the building society from which they acquired the mortgage funds.' If the fourth defendant or his wife had redeemed the mortgage and paid it off, then the policy would have been reassignable to the mortgagors, the fourth defendant and his wife. They would then have the right to surrender that policy for full value under the terms of the general conditions of the policy. In my judgment on that ground alone this was an asset which was in existence at the time of the Mareva injunction and would be caught by it. Putting it at its very lowest the fourth defendant and his wife had an interest in that particular asset at the material time in the shape of their right, which could not be given away, to redeem the mortgage and therefore retrieve their rights in the insurance policy.
>
> I only say this. *In this particular case the asset in question was not an after-acquired asset. Second, even if it was, on the arguments presented to me, I would have found that it was caught by this particular injunction. It seems to me that it would be a negation of the purpose of that injunction if, every time the defendant acquired some new asset or property, it was up to the plaintiffs to discover it and make an application to the court that the existing injunction be extended to deal with it. It seems to me that a Mareva injunction is looking to the future and is dealing with the situation between the obtaining of the judgment and its eventual execution, and it will cover any assets which are acquired between the granting of the order and the eventual execution of any judgment obtained in the action in question.* [emphasis added]

Assessment of damages

Where the freezing injunction has been discharged, the appropriate time for the assessment of damages to be carried out is at the trial of the action. This is because it is only then that the court can be in a position to make a decision having regard to all the circumstances of the case, see *Cheltenham & Gloucester Building Society v Ricketts* [1993] 3 All ER 276.

Where the claimant has discontinued, as opposed to the abandonment of a claim that involved a freezing injunction, the court will take into consideration the circumstances in which the action was discontinued before enforcing an undertaking as to damages, see *Goldman Sachs International v Lyons* (1995) *The Times*, 28 February. In this case the action was discontinued because the claimant came to the conclusion that, in the light of the defendant's financial position, it was unlikely to recover any more monies from the defendant. In the circumstances, the court decided that it would be inequitable to enforce the claimant's undertaking in damages.

World-wide freezing injunctions

The rationale for this aspect of the rule was summarized by Jessel MR in *Beddow v Beddow* (1878) 9 Ch D 89 thus:

> . . . I have unlimited power to grant an injunction in any case where it would be right or just to do so: and what is right or just must be decided, not by the caprice of the Judge, but according to sufficient legal reasons or on settled legal principles.

This remains the position to this day, the only issue being whether in particular circumstances the grant is 'right or just'. What changes is not the power or the principles but the circumstances, both special and general, in which courts are asked to exercise this jurisdiction. Practicality or effectiveness of the court order that includes a foreign element is the main concern. A development in this area is the extension of the freezing injunction to cover foreign assets as well. In *Ashtiani v Kashi* [1986] 3 WLR 647, the Court of Appeal held that in general this type of injunction should be restricted to assets within the jurisdiction, so that it was not proper to order a defendant to disclose particulars of assets abroad.

However, an application for a pre-judgment freezing injunction was made in *Republic of Haiti v Duvalier* (1988) *The Times*, 28 July. In this case the court granted a freezing injunction in respect of worldwide assets, although it recognised that this was a most unusual measure and should rarely be taken. Factors which have been held sufficient to justify such an injunction include: (1) the admitted intention of the defendant to move its assets out of reach of the English courts; (2) the resources and skills the defendants have shown in removing the assets; and (3) the magnitude of the funds involved. The injunction itself was granted subject to the proviso that it should not affect third parties save to the extent that the order was enforced by the courts of the country in which the assets were based.

Stricter safeguards were required in *Derby Co Ltd v Weldon* [1989] 2 WLR 279, where a similar worldwide freezing injunction was granted. The Court of Appeal stated that, apart from the normal requirements of a freezing injunction the claimant must also show that any English assets are insufficient, that there are foreign assets and that there is real risk of the disposal of the latter. The court must also be satisfied either by undertaking or proviso, that:

- the defendant will not be oppressed by the exposure to a multiplicity of proceedings;
- the defendant will be protected against the misuse of any information gained; and
- that third parties will be protected.

Lord Donaldson MR stated the general policy concerning the issue of a freezing injunction thus:

> **Lord Donaldson MR:** In my judgment, the key requirement for any Mareva injunction, whether or not it extends to foreign assets, is that it shall accord with the rationale on which Mareva relief has been based in the past. That rationale, legitimate purpose and fundamental principle . . . [is that] that no court should permit a defendant to take action designed to frustrate subsequent orders of the court. If for the achievement of this purpose it is necessary to make orders concerning foreign assets, such orders should be made, subject, of course, to ordinary principles of international law.

The safeguards and restrictions imposed by *Derby Co v Weldon* were applied in *Re BCCI (No 9)* [1994] 3 All ER 764. The Court of Appeal had to consider, *inter alia*, whether the form of order granted at first instance provided the necessary safeguards against the multiplicity of proceedings in other jurisdictions. It should be noted that this requirement is usually satisfied by the claimant giving an undertaking to the court that it would not seek to enforce the freezing injunction out of England and Wales without the leave of the court. It was argued that this was not sufficient protection and that the order should include an undertaking not to commence fresh proceedings in other jurisdictions which arise out of the same matter. The Court of Appeal held that, in the circumstances of the case, it was reasonable to require the claimant to undertake that it would not commence fresh civil proceedings in other jurisdictions.

Further, in *Derby Co Ltd v Weldon (No 3 and 4)* (1989) 139 NLJ 11, the court made clear that the order will not be made if there is no effective sanction. In most cases sanctions exist because of the possibility of being debarred from defending the substantive action. This was re-emphasised in *Canada Trust v Stolzenberg*, (1997) *The Times*, 10 November. In this case the court stated that, where a foreign defendant with no assets within the jurisdiction fails to comply with a discovery order made pursuant to a freezing injunction and provided there was a strong case against the defendant, the appropriate sanction against the defendant would be to debar him from taking any further action in the proceedings and from defending the case. However, the defendant must have been given reasonable time to comply with the order.

In *Cala Cristal SA v Al–Borno (Emran)* (1994) *The Times*, 6 May, the Court of Appeal decided that it would allow the defendant to use funds frozen under a worldwide freezing injunction to pay his legal fees. This was because the purpose of the freezing injunction was to prevent dissipation of assets by the defendant. Payment of legal fees did not amount to such dissipation.

It should be noted that, even where the court is not prepared to grant a worldwide freezing injunction against the defendant, the court could nonetheless make a disclosure order in respect of the worldwide assets of the defendant, see *Gidrxslme Shipping Ltd v Tantomartranportes Maritimos* [1995] 1 WLR 299.

It should be borne in mind that a post-judgment freezing injunction should normally be of limited duration. The claimant should be encouraged to proceed with proper methods of execution.

Recently the Court of Appeal in *Dadourian Group International Inc v Simms* [2006] EWCA 399, issued the following guidelines with regard to the issue of a worldwide freezing injunction:

(1) The principle applying to the grant of permission to enforce a WFO abroad is that the grant of that permission should be just and convenient for the purpose of ensuring the effectiveness of the WFO, and in addition that it is not oppressive to the parties to the English proceedings or to third parties who may be joined to the foreign proceedings.

(2) All the relevant circumstances and options need to be considered. In particular, consideration should be given to granting relief on terms, for example terms as to the extension to third parties of the undertaking to compensate for costs incurred as a result of the WFO and as to the type of proceedings that may be commenced abroad. Consideration should also be given to the proportionality of the steps proposed to be taken abroad, and in addition to the form of any order.

(3) The interests of the applicant should be balanced against the interests of the other parties to the proceedings and any new party likely to be joined to the foreign proceedings.

(4) Permission should not normally be given in terms that would enable the applicant to obtain relief in the foreign proceedings which is superior to the relief given by the WFO.

(5) The evidence in support of the application for permission should contain all the information (so far as it can reasonably be obtained in the time available) necessary to enable the judge to reach an informed decision, including evidence as to the applicable law and practice in the foreign court, evidence as to the nature of the proposed proceedings to be commenced and evidence as to the assets believed to be located in the jurisdiction of the foreign court and the names of the parties by whom such assets are held.

(6) The standard of proof as to the existence of assets that are both within the WFO and within the jurisdiction of the foreign court is a real prospect, that is the applicant must show that there is a real prospect that such assets are located within the jurisdiction of the foreign court in question.

(7) There must be evidence of a risk of dissipation of the assets in question.

(8) Normally the application should be made on notice to the respondent, but in cases of urgency, where it is just to do so, the permission may be given without notice to the party against whom relief will be sought in the foreign proceedings, but that the party should have the earliest practicable opportunity of having the matter reconsidered by the court at a hearing of which he is given notice.

The position of third parties

The court is required to bear in mind not only the balance of convenience and justice between the claimant and defendant, but also as between the claimant and third parties. Where assets of a defendant are held by a third party in accordance with the general business of the third party, such as funds of a defendant held by a bank or goods held by a bailee as custodian in a warehouse. An effective indemnity in favour of the third party may adequately hold this balance in order to avoid major interference with the third party's business. Where the balance is in favour of the grant of an injunction, the claimant will normally be required to give such undertakings as the court considers reasonably necessary to protect third party interests. However, with respect to the performance of a contract between the third party and the defendant concerning the asset that is the subject of a freezing injunction, the right of the third party in relation to his contract prevails over the claimant's wish to secure the defendant's assets.

The question has arisen as to the effect of a freezing injunction on third parties. In *Z Ltd v AA-LL* [1982] 2 WLR 280, the Court of Appeal stressed that a freezing injunction operated '*in rem*', i.e. against the property of the defendant. Accordingly, everyone with knowledge of the injunction is required to do all that is reasonably necessary to preserve the assets affected. Failure in this regard would constitute a contempt of court. Therefore, once a bank had notice of a freezing injunction it might be unlawful for it to honour a customer's cheques. Where an injunction was obtained against a third party, it was particularly important that the injunction specified exactly what the third party was entitled to do. If the third party was put to expense, he would be entitled to reimbursement by the claimant. If the claimant could not specify the defendant's bank account, he could require the bank or other third party to conduct searches provided he paid the costs of such searches. In *Galaxia Maritime SA v Mineral Import-Export* [1982] 1 WLR 539, the Court of Appeal refused to grant a freezing injunction as it would have seriously disrupted the activities of a third party. The court decided that where the effect of granting a freezing injunction would be to interfere substantially with an innocent third party's freedom of action generally or freedom to trade (for example, by interfering with his performance of a contract made between him and the defendant relating to the assets in question), the third party's right to freedom of action and freedom to trade should prevail over the claimant's wish to secure the defendant's assets for himself. Accordingly, in this case, it was an abuse of the freezing injunction jurisdiction to allow a claimant to serve a shipowner with a freezing injunction relating to cargo owned, or alleged to be owned, by the defendant, which was on board the shipowner's vessel in order to prevent the vessel sailing out of the jurisdiction with the cargo. The fact that the claimant had undertaken to indemnify the shipowner against loss or damage suffered in consequence of the grant of the injunction was not a sufficient reason to allow the injunction to be served on the shipowner if he objected to the injunction, since the mere proffering of an indemnity did not entitle the claimant to interfere with the shipowner's business activities and to obtain the advantage of a freezing injunction at the shipowner's expense. Since the effect of granting the injunction would be to prevent the shipowner sending its ship on a voyage out of the jurisdiction under a previously concluded contract with the defendants, it would be an abuse of the freezing injunction jurisdiction to allow the injunction to continue. Accordingly, the application to discharge the injunction would be granted. Similarly, a claimant could not, merely to secure a benefit for himself under a Mareva injunction, coerce a third party into serious risk of litigation or arbitration with the defendant, through compliance with the injunction, merely by offering the third party an indemnity against the risk

Eveleigh LJ: The effect of this present injunction, in so far as the owners of the *Eleftherios* are concerned, is to interfere with their trading assets. Counsel for the plaintiffs has submitted to this court that that is a matter which should not affect the final outcome because, as he says, his clients have given a guarantee. For myself I do not believe that when the third party protests, the fact that a guarantee has been given should be decisive in the matter at all. A third party is entitled to freedom of action and he is entitled to trade freely. I do not think that a plaintiff has the right to a 'compulsory purchase' of the rights of a third party and that is what it amounts to in this case.

Extension of the freezing injunction

The freezing injunction has facilitated the development of other similar orders. The court has the power to make all such ancillary orders as appear to it to be just and convenient to ensure that the freezing injunction achieves its purpose. The court has the power to grant an order of disclosure directing a party to provide information about the location of relevant property or assets or to provide information about relevant property or assets that are or may be the subject of an application for a freezing injunction. An order of disclosure may require the defendant to disclose the nature, location and value of all his assets within and, in some cases, outside the jurisdiction, including the identity of any bank accounts, but excluding any asset that exceeds the value of the claim.

In *Astro Exito Navegacion SA v Southland Enterprise Ltd (No 2)* [1982] 3 WLR 296, the claimants sought an order that required the defendants to authorize their bank to release a sum of money into a London bank in order to provide security for their claim. The bank argued that the effect of this was to grant a freezing injunction, but in mandatory form, and that the court had no jurisdiction to make such an order at an interim stage. The Court of Appeal rejected this argument and held that it could grant an interim mandatory order in an appropriate case such as this. This case was followed in *Bayer AG v Winter* [1986] 1 WLR 497, where the Court of Appeal granted orders restraining the defendant from leaving the country and requiring him to deliver up his passport. The court stressed that it had a wide discretion when granting interim injunctions and should not shrink from granting relief of a novel character if it was of the opinion that it was necessary for the proper protection of a party to the action. In this case the claimants, a pharmaceutical company, began an action against the defendants, claiming damages in respect of the alleged wrongful worldwide distribution and sale of counterfeit insecticide purporting to be a product of the claimants. Pending the hearing of the action the claimants applied to the High Court for *inter alia* a Mareva injunction, which was granted. Fearing that the defendant would evade the effects of the court orders by leaving the jurisdiction, the claimants sought further injunctive relief, namely (i) that the first defendant deliver up his passports and (ii) that he be restrained from leaving the jurisdiction until the Anton Piller (search) order had been executed. The trial judge refused further relief and the claimants appealed. The Court of Appeal held that it had jurisdiction to grant the further relief sought. However, since the further relief would constitute an interference with the liberty of the subject, it would not be granted for any longer than was necessary to enable the claimants to execute the Mareva and Anton Piller (search) orders.

> **Fox LJ:** The court has to exercise that discretion according to established principles, and the particular matter with which we are concerned at the moment, namely of an injunctive restraint on a person leaving the jurisdiction, is not one on which there appears to be previous authority. It is clear, however, that the law in relation to the grant of injunctive relief for the protection of a litigant's rights pending the hearing of an action has been transformed over the past ten years by the Anton Piller and Mareva relief which has greatly extended the law on this topic as previously understood so as to meet the needs of justice.
>
> Bearing in mind we are exercising a jurisdiction which is statutory, and which is expressed in terms of considerable width, it seems to me that the court should not shrink, if it is of opinion that an injunction is necessary for the proper protection of a party to the action, from granting relief, notwithstanding it may, in its terms, be of a novel character.
>
> The position here appears to be this: first, so far as the first defendant is concerned, one asks what harm will this order do him? If he says it will cause him some embarrassment or hardship, he can apply to the High Court forthwith, on evidence, to ask that it be varied or, if necessary, discharged. He has therefore an opportunity, if it imposes hardship on him, of establishing that very quickly before a court.
>
> I turn next to the position from the point of view of the plaintiffs. If the first defendant, on the service of Walton

J's order requiring disclosure of the information to which I have referred, declines to give that information, or is not frank in the answers which he gives, then if he leaves the United Kingdom, the plaintiffs are at risk that they will be unable to obtain that information. It appears to be doubtful, at any rate, whether the first defendant has in fact a permanent residence in this country.

In the circumstances which I have mentioned of the first defendant failing to provide answers to the matters referred to in the order of Walton J, or on his failure to be frank in the answers which he gaves, it is open to the plaintiffs to seek an order for cross-examination; and the first defendant, if he remains within the jurisdiction, could be compelled to attend for that purpose. If, however, he has left the jurisdiction, then in those circumstances the order would be frustrated.

Therefore it seems to me that the court is faced with a situation in which there is a risk to the plaintiffs that they may not obtain the information ordered to be disclosed, unless the order which is now sought is granted; while, at the same time, any risk of hardship to the first defendant is dealt with by his capacity to apply to a judge to vary or discharge the order.

Moreover, in *Standard Chartered Bank v Walker*, (1991) *Financial Times*, 7 August, the court held that it could use a freezing injunction to restrain a defendant shareholder from wilfully dissipating the assets of the company by exercising his voting rights in such a way as would eventually lead to the company's collapse.

In the *Department of Social Security v Butler* [1995] 1 WLR 1528, the Court of Appeal decided that the High Court did not have jurisdiction to grant a freezing injunction (or any other interim injunction) in aid of, or ancillary to, prospective proceedings in inferior courts for the enforcement and collection of maintenance assessments under the Child Support Act 1991.

An injunction similar to a freezing injunction has also been used to freeze a defendant's assets in a criminal case, see *Chief Constable of Kent v V* [1982] 3 WLR 462. However, in *Chief Constable of Hampshire v A Ltd* [1984] 2 WLR 954, the Court of Appeal cast some doubt on the previous decision and refused to extend it to a case where slightly different orders were sought.

Questions

1. What factors will the court take into account in deciding whether or not to grant a freezing order?

2. What difference, if any, would it make if the claimant applied for a worldwide freezing order?

Search orders (originally known as Anton Piller orders)

There has been another relatively recent development derived from the court's power to grant interim injunctions *ex parte*. This type of order is known as a 'search order'. In *Anton Piller KG v Manufacturing Processes Ltd* [1976] 1 All ER 779, the Court of Appeal granted an order that authorized the claimants to enter the defendant's premises and view documents and make copies that were relevant to the claimant's case because the latter feared that the documents may be destroyed. Ormrod LJ laid down three conditions for the granting of such an order:

- the claimant must have a strong *prima facie* case;
- the claimant must show actual or potential damage of a very serious nature;
- there is clear evidence that the defendant has incriminating documents or things and that there is a real possibility of these documents or things being destroyed before an *inter partes* application could be made.

A further condition appears to be that the search order is not to be used as a fishing expedition. Moreover, the claimant is required to give an undertaking to the court as to damages at the time of making the application.

In *Universal Thermosensors Ltd v Hibben*, [992] 3 All ER 257, the Vice Chancellor suggested that the claimants could be asked to give the following undertakings before a search order would be granted:

- that the order be served and supervised by a solicitor from a different firm to that acting for the claimant;
- that the solicitor supervising the search should be experienced and knowledgeable about the workings of search orders;
- that the solicitor should prepare a written report on the execution of the order;
- that a copy of the report should be served on the defendant and that the report should be presented to the court at an *inter partes* hearing;
- that the orders should be served on weekdays during office hours in order to give the defendants the opportunity to obtain legal advice;
- that the party serving the order should include a woman if it is likely that a woman might be alone at the premises.

In *Universal Thermosensors*, the court decided that, despite the claimant being entitled at the time it applied for the interlocutory injunction to be protected by an injunction against any further misuse by the defendants of the claimants' confidential information in the future, it was not entitled at that time to an injunction in respect of misuse that had already occurred. Albeit it was entitled, to damages or restitutionary relief such as an account of profits for such misuse. If, by misuse of confidential information, Thermo Probes Ltd (TPL) had already made contact with a customer and had received an order, the misuse occurred when the claimant's customer was approached and an injunction to restrain TPL from fulfilling that order or any future order would go too far as it would not be aimed at preventing further misuse of confidential information. The effect of the injunction restraining TPL from dealing with customers it had already approached was to put TPL out of business and the claimant in a better position for the future than if there had been no misuse of information and, in those circumstances, the protection given to the claimant by the injunction went beyond that required for the proper protection of its legitimate rights. Accordingly, the defendants were entitled to damages under the claimant's undertaking but, having regard to TPL's tenuous market and financial position and the fact that the defendants ought to pay compensation to the claimant for the benefits they had derived from the wrongful use of the claimant's confidential information, only modest damages of £20,000 would be awarded.

> **Sir Donald Nicholls V.C. :** In my view . . . the plaintiff was entitled to be protected, by means of an injunction, against any *further* misuse by the defendants of the plaintiff's confidential information. For instance, they must no longer use the item 3 list. An injunction in those terms would be without limit in point of time. For the *future* TPL must obtain from independent sources any information it needed about potential customers and contacts. It must search through directories, and it must then make sustained efforts over the telephone to reach the appropriate personnel. In aid of this injunction the plaintiff was entitled to have documents such as the item 3 list delivered up.
>
> The matter stands quite differently regarding misuse which had *already* occurred before July 1990. By this date TPL had already made contact with many of the plaintiff's customers. In respect of such past misuse the clock could not be put back. The plaintiff was entitled to appropriate financial recompense, by way of damages or restitutionary relief such as an account of profits. In my view, however, in respect of misuse which had already occurred the plaintiff was not entitled to more. In particular, if by misuse of confidential information TPL had already made contact with a customer and had received an order from him, an injunction to restrain TPL from fulfilling that order or any future order would go too far. An injunction in such a form would not be aimed at preventing further misuse of confidential information. The misuse occurred when the plaintiff's customer and contact were approached. Fulfilling outstanding or future orders would not be a further misuse of confidential information by TPL.
>
> What, then, would be the justification for such an injunction here from July 1990? . . . it could not be justified, even for a limited period of time, as affording the means for putting the parties back into the position they would have occupied had there been no misuse. In some cases that will be so, but not in the instant case.

Prior to *Universal Thermosensors*, certain safeguards did exist. In *ITC Film Distributors Ltd v Video Exchange Ltd* [1982] Ch 431, the court made it clear that the solicitor serving the search order should avoid arriving simultaneously with the police so as to give the impression that the order had the same effect as a search warrant. Moreover, in *Columbia Picture Industries Inc v Robinson* [1987] Ch 38, the court ruled that the claimant, having obtained the search order, should not act oppressively nor abuse its power in the execution of the order. In addition the court stated that the draconian and essentially unfair nature of a search order in its effect on a defendant requires that it be drawn so as to extend no further than the minimum extent necessary to achieve the purpose for which it was granted, namely the preservation of documents or articles which might otherwise be destroyed or concealed; anything beyond that is impossible to justify. Thus, an order that allows the claimant's solicitors to take and retain all relevant documentary material and correspondence cannot be justified. Once the claimant's solicitors have satisfied themselves what material exists and have had an opportunity to take copies thereof, the material ought to be returned to the owner, and should only be retained for a relatively short period for such purpose. It is inappropriate for seized material, the ownership of which is in dispute, such as alleged pirate tapes, to be retained by the claimant's solicitor pending trial. Although the solicitor is an officer of the court, the main role of the solicitor for the claimant is to act for the claimant. As soon as a solicitor for the defendant is on the record, the claimant's solicitor ought to deliver the material to the defendant's solicitor on his undertaking to keep it in safe custody and produce it, if required, in court.

There is also the requirement that full and frank disclosure of all relevant materials must be made to the court, see *Tate Access Floors Inc v Boswell* [1991] 2 WLR 304.

Where these safeguards have been breached by either the claimant or his solicitor, the court may set aside the order. In the event of the order not being set aside, the court can award exemplary damages and the solicitor may be liable for contempt of court.

This type of order has been used in a number of cases and is now authorised by the Supreme Court Act 1981 (now the Senior Courts Act 1981 introduced by the Constitutional Reform Act 2005). A further development of the search order occurred in *Bankers Trust v Shapira* [1980] 1 WLR 1280. The claimants brought an action to trace funds into various banks accounts. They subsequently applied for further orders requiring the banks to disclose details both of cheques drawn on the accounts and also correspondence relating thereto. The trial judge refused to grant the order as it was at odds with the confidential relationship between a banker and his client. However, the Court of Appeal reversed this decision on the grounds that the court had the power to grant the order as part of its 'new and developing jurisdiction against third parties', but the claimants were required to undertake to use the information only for the purposes of the tracing claim.

In *Emanuel v Emanuel* [1982] 1 WLR 669, a search order was granted in a divorce case in order to enable the claimant to inspect documents relating to properties that should have been transferred to her.

The effectiveness of the search order has been restricted by the application of the defendant's privilege against self-incrimination. In *Rank Film Distributors Ltd v Video Information Centre* [1982] AC 380, the court upheld the defendant's claim to the privilege against self-incrimination in a case that involved breach of copyright. It should be noted that s 72 of the Supreme Court Act 1981 now prohibits the defendant from relying on this privilege in cases involving passing off and/or cases relating to the infringement of intellectual property rights. However, where the case falls outside the ambit of s 72, the defendant can rely on the privilege against self-incrimination. This would appear to be clear from the case of *Tate Access Floors Inc v Boswell* (1990) *The Times*, 14 June, where the court stated that, in civil proceedings involving an allegation that could give rise to a criminal charge of conspiracy, the court could not make a search order since this would infringe the defendant's privilege against self-incrimination.

In *IBM (UK) Ltd v Prime Data International Ltd* [1994] 4 All ER 248, the court made it clear that a search order that would expose a defendant to a real risk of criminal prosecution for conspiracy could only properly be made and served on the defendant if it contained a proviso that adequately protected the defendant's right to claim privilege against self-incrimination. The order would not, however, be executed until the defendant had been informed, in layman's terms, that he properly understood his right to claim the privilege and that he expressly declined to claim the right.

Another case illustrating the application of s 72 of the Supreme Court Act 1981 is *Coca Cola Co v Gilbey* (1995) *The Times*, 28 November. Here, G made an application for the discharge of a search order allowing the search of his premises in an action for infringement of C's rights against a large scale criminal organization that produced and sold counterfeit Coca Cola. G alleged that, if he provided the information sought by C, he would be incriminating himself and would expose himself to the risk of violence. The court held that G's application should be dismissed as it was clear from s 72 that, in the case of an order made in proceedings for the infringement of a trademark or passing off, the risk of self-incrimination did not excuse the person from being required to comply with the order. The risk of violence to G was not a ground upon which the search order could be discharged.

The court's jurisdiction to grant search orders was reviewed generally in *Digital Equipment Corp v Darkcrest Ltd* [1984] 3 WLR 617. In *Distributori Automaci Italia v Holford General Trading Ltd* [1985] 1 WLR 1006, the claimants had obtained judgment against the defendants and garnishee orders had been issued but remained unsatisfied. The claimants subsequently applied for an order requiring the defendants to allow them access to their premises and to view and copy relevant documents. This raised the question of whether a search order was available after judgment. Leggatt J granted the order on the grounds that the court had a wide discretion when granting such orders and would exercise the same where there was 'a risk of justice being thwarted by a defendant intent upon rendering any judgment nugatory'.

The court also has jurisdiction to grant a search order allowing inspection of premises outside the UK. In *Cook Industries v Galliher* [1979] Ch 439, the court allowed the inspection of a flat in Paris and to take an inventory of the furniture in the flat. The foreign defendant had been properly served in England, had entered an appearance and, indeed, was represented by counsel at the hearing. The question involved whether the English court had jurisdiction to entertain the action involving title to the flat in Paris and to the furniture in that flat. The judge held that the court did have jurisdiction since the claimant's action was based on an equity and sought in personam relief against the defendants.

However, if the defendant is foreign then the search order will be less useful. In *Altertext v Advanced Data Communications Ltd* [1985] 1 All ER 395, the court held that a search order should not be granted without giving the foreign defendant the opportunity to object; it was immaterial that this would obviously render the order useless. Here, the claimant applied *ex parte* for a variety of interlocutory orders, including search orders against all of the six defendants. The sixth defendant, Advanced Data Communications (Europe) SA, was a Belgian company and with business premises in Belgium, but did not carry on business in England. A search order was sought by the claimant requiring the sixth defendant to allow the claimant and its solicitors to enter on the sixth defendant's premises in Belgium and to photograph or remove therefrom documentary and other material relevant to the action. It was implicit in the order that the documents and material removed from the premises would be taken by the claimant's solicitors out of Belgium and brought to England.

The court refused the application for the search order for the requirement was one of discretion to be exercised once the claimant has validly served the claim on the foreign defendant. In the present case no such service was made.

Scott J: . . . a foreign defendant is, *prima facie*, not subject to the jurisdiction of the court. Such a defendant may become subject to the jurisdiction of the court if service of process can be effected on the defendant in England, or if the defendant submits to the jurisdiction (as, for instance, by instructing solicitors to accept service), or if the court assumes jurisdiction by authorising service under Ord 11. But until service has been effected the foreign defendant does not become subject to the jurisdiction of the court. The remedy of a foreign defendant against whom an order under Ord 11 for service abroad has been made is to apply to set aside that order. It is well established that such an application is not a submission to the jurisdiction. If the application succeeds, and the order is set aside, the court is, in effect, declining to assume jurisdiction over that foreign defendant.

An Anton Piller order is an in personam order. It is an order which it is within the power of the court to make in an action in which the court has jurisdiction. It ought not, however, in my view, to be made except against a party over whom the court does have jurisdiction. If the order is sought ex parte, before service of the writ, and against a foreign defendant in respect of foreign premises, an essential requirement must be that the case is one in which leave under Ord 11 for service outside the jurisdiction ought to be given. Otherwise the court has no jurisdiction over that defendant. But since the initial application is ex parte, and since the foreign defendant may seek to have the leave under Ord 11 set aside, the assumption by the court of jurisdiction is, in a sense, provisional only. In my view, where an Anton Piller order against a foreign defendant has to be accompanied by leave under Ord 11 for service abroad, the Anton Piller order ought not to be executed until the foreign defendant has been given the opportunity to apply to set aside the Ord 11 leave. The assumption by the court of jurisdiction over foreign defendants is, under Ord 11, strictly controlled. It would be wrong, in my view, for the court to assume jurisdiction over a foreign defendant on an ex parte application, and then require a mandatory order of an Anton Piller character to be executed on the foreign defendant before he has had an opportunity to challenge the court's assumption of jurisdiction over him.

Accordingly, I indicated to counsel for the plaintiff that, having granted leave for service on the sixth defendant outside the jurisdiction, I was prepared to grant an Anton Piller order against that defendant in respect of its premises in Belgium but with a proviso that execution of the Anton Piller order was to be suspended for a short period sufficient to enable the sixth defendant to apply to set aside the Ord 11 leave. Counsel for the plaintiff took the view that that proviso would render the Anton Piller order valueless against the sixth defendant and pressed his application for that order without any such proviso. For the reasons I have given I declined to make it. I indicated to counsel for the plaintiff that I doubted my jurisdiction to do so. On reflection I am not sure that, strictly, the point is one of jurisdiction. The court has, I think, jurisdiction arising out of the leave given under Ord 11 and the service abroad of the writ pursuant to that leave. As I have said, the plaintiff's intention was to serve the writ and the Anton Piller order together. The point is rather, I think, one of discretion. The court is not, in my view, justified in acting on an assumed jurisdiction in order to make against a foreign defendant in respect of foreign premises a mandatory order required to be executed before the foreign defendant has had a chance of contesting the jurisdiction.

Question
What is the procedure for obtaining a search order?

FURTHER READING

Andoh, B, 'The search order and the privilege against self-incrimination' (2006) 26 BLR 6.

Anthony, W, 'Trace the assets' (2003) 153 NLJ 868.

Brooks, O, Tickner, J, 'Freezing orders – cold comfort for defendants' In House Lawyer, Nov 2004, 32.

Collins, L, Howell, A, 'Fast freeze' (2006) 150 SJ Issue 30, p1006.

Devonshire, P, 'Freezing orders, disappearing assets and the problem of enjoining' (2002) 118 LQR 124.

Douglas, M, Charlton, A, Drew, J, 'Mandatory injunctions in IT disputes' (2006) ITLT Vol 13, Issue 4, p 2.

Howell, A, Smith, D, 'Walking on thin ice' (2006) 156 NLJ 1865.

Lewis, M, 'Indeterminate liability' (2006) 156 NLJ 1236.

Molyneux, B, 'The privilege against self-incrimination in ancillary relief proceedings' (2001) 31 Fam Law 603.

Reyes, E, 'Money troubles' In House Lawyer, Feb 2005, 26.

Rutherford, T, 'Frozen over' (2006) 156 NLJ 837.

Sim, G, 'Asset tracing – a practical guide' (2004) 154 NLJ 1774.

Smith, P, 'Freezing suspicious bank accounts' (2005) 155 NLJ 1286.

Tinkler, N, 'The bank, the thief, the freezing order' (2005) 155 NLJ 82.

Tromans, C, 'Asset control – securing claimants' interests' (2002) LS Gaz, 35.

INTRODUCTION

The remedy at common law for breach of contract is damages. But in some cases an award of damages would be inappropriate, e.g. where there is a contract for the sale of land or shares in a private company the claimant might want the land or shares for their unique value and would regard damages as a poor substitute. The equitable remedy of specific performance supplements the common law remedy and, in some circumstances, the court will order the defendant to perform his duties under the contract.

VALIDITY OF THE CONTRACT

In an action for specific performance the claimant is required to show that there is a contract that is enforceable at law. Hence, all the essential elements of a contract, such as agreement and consideration must be present. Similarly, specific performance will not be granted where for some reason the contract is void at common law – for example where it is illegal, or where the contract is for the sale of land and the formalities have not been complied with under s 2 of the Law of Property (Miscellaneous Provisions) Act 1989. However, the defendant may not be allowed to raise the defences that would have been relevant at common law.

It seems that the court will be particularly willing to grant specific performance where the claimant has performed his part of the contract – thus, in *Hart v Hart* (1881) 18 Ch D 670, the court ordered specific performance of the terms of a separation deed under which the claimant had performed her duties, Kay J stated:

> When an agreement for valuable consideration between two parties has been partially performed, the court ought to do its utmost to carry out that agreement by a decree of specific performance. It is the duty of the Court, as far as it is possible to do so, to ascertain the terms of the agreement, and to give effect to it. That is, as I understand, the rule of equity, that although there may be considerable vagueness in the terms, and although it may be such an agreement as the Court would hesitate to decree specific performance of, if there had not been part performance, yet when there has been part performance the Court is bound to struggle against the difficulty arising from the vagueness.

It has often been said that specific performance will not be available unless the contract is 'mutual' (see *Flight v Boland* (1882) 4 Russ 298) or specifically enforceable by either party. However, it seems that this may be an over-simplification. In fact one party may be disentitled to specific performance because he has either delayed in bringing the action or he does not come to the court with 'clean hands', e.g. he may have breached a term of the contract. However, the other party may still be entitled to specific performance if he so desires. Thus, the contract may be enforced despite an apparent lack of mutuality. In *Price v Strange* [1977] 3 All ER 371, it was held that mutuality was merely a factor to be considered in the exercise of the court's discretion. The relevant time for considering the defence of want of mutuality was not the date of the contract but the date of the trial. If at that date the court could not ensure that any unperformed obligations of the claimant would be specifically performed, it would not, as a general rule, compel the defendant to perform his obligations specifically. The issue was whether the court would grant an order of specific performance of a lease where the defendant stood by and allowed the claimant to effect repairs to premises. The Court of Appeal reversed the decision of the trial judge and granted an order of specific performance. The court also decided that if the relevant date at which mutuality must be ascertained was the date of the contract, lack of mutuality at that date does not result in the court being without 'jurisdiction to entertain an application . . . for the specific performance of [a] contract', within s 2 of Lord Cairns Act of 1858, for considerations of mutuality go to discretion and not to jurisdiction. Furthermore, the court is not deprived of jurisdiction where the contract is one for the execution of building repairs. Although it does not often order specific performance of a contract to do repairs, either because of the difficulty in ascertaining precisely what is to be done or because of the difficulty of supervising performance, it has the power to do so. Accordingly the court had at all relevant times jurisdiction to entertain the claimant's action for specific performance and consequently it had a discretion under s 2 of the 1858 Act to award damages in addition to, or in substitution for, specific performance.

> **Goff LJ:** The true principle is that one judges the defence of want of mutuality on the facts and circumstances as they exist at the hearing, albeit in the light of the whole conduct of the parties in relation to the subject-matter, and in the absence of any other disqualifying circumstances, the court will grant specific performance if it can be done without injustice or unfairness to the defendant.
>
> . . . the defendant by standing by and allowing the plaintiff to spend time and money in carrying out an appreciable part of the work, created an equity against herself. This is supported first by *Hart v Hart* ((1881) 18 Ch D 670 at 685) and *Parker v Taswell* ((1858) 2 De G & J 559 at 571), which shows that where there has been part performance the court will struggle against difficulties to secure total performance, but much more strongly, by the principles laid down in *Chalmers v Pardoe* ([1963] 3 All ER 552, at 555, [1963] 1 WLR 677 at 681, 682). That case shows that where A encourages or permits B to build on or improve A's land on the faith of an understanding or assurance, short of a binding contract, that he will permit him to have it or use it for B's own benefit, equity will in a proper case not merely give B a lien for recovering his expenditure but compel A to implement the understanding. A fortiori must it be so where, as here, the plaintiff was allowed to start work on the defendant's property on the faith of an actual contract which, notwithstanding the want of writing, was by the very act of part performance made enforceable in equity.

PRINCIPLES UNDERPINNING SPECIFIC PERFORMANCE

Damages must not be an adequate remedy

Courts of equity were originally prepared to grant decrees of specific performance because it was recognised that in some cases the common law remedy of damages would be inadequate, particularly in the case of contracts for the sale of land. Provided such contracts comply with requirements of s 2 of the Law of Property (Miscellaneous Provisions) Act 1989 the court will grant a decree of specific performance readily as it is recognised that land is a commodity that might have a particular non-monetary value to a particular buyer, see *Sudbrook Trading Estate Ltd v Eggleton* [1983] 1 AC 444. In this case, the claimants, lessees, were granted options to purchase the freehold reversions in several plots of land at a price to be determined by two valuers, one selected by the defendants and the other selected by the claimants. The defendants refused to select a valuer and the claimants brought an action for specific performance of the agreement. The House of Lords granted specific performance of the agreement on the ground that the machinery by which the value of a property was to be ascertained was subsidiary and non-essential to the main part of an agreement for the sale and purchase of the property at a fair and reasonable price. In these circumstances the court could, if the machinery for ascertaining the value broke down, substitute other machinery to ascertain the price in order to ensure that the agreement was carried out. Since the contract between the parties provided that the price was to be determined by valuers, it necessarily followed that the contract was a contract for sale at a fair and reasonable price assessed by applying objective standards, and on the exercise of the option clauses a complete contract for the sale and purchase of the freehold reversion was constituted; it was unrealistic to treat the machinery provided by the option clauses for ascertaining the price as an essential term of the contract when it merely consisted of provision for the appointment of valuers and an umpire, none of whom was named or identified. The only reason the machinery had not been implemented was the lessors' own breach of contract in refusing to appoint their valuer. It followed that, since such machinery was not essential, there was no reason why the court should not substitute its own machinery.

> **Lord Diplock :** ... the real issue is whether the court has jurisdiction to enforce the lessors' primary obligation under the contract to convey the fee simple by decreeing specific performance of that primary obligation, or whether its jurisdiction is limited to enforcing the secondary obligation arising on failure to fulfil that primary obligation, by awarding the lessees damages to an amount equivalent to the monetary loss they have sustained by their inability to acquire the fee simple at a fair and reasonable price, ie for what the fee simple was worth. Since if they do not acquire the fee simple they will not have to pay that price, the damages for loss of such a bargain would be negligible and, as in most cases of breach of contract for the sale of land at a market price by refusal to convey it, would constitute a wholly inadequate and unjust remedy for the breach. That is why the normal remedy is by a decree for specific performance by the vendor of his primary obligation to convey, on the purchaser's performing or being willing to perform his own primary obligations under the contract.
>
> Why should the presence in the option clause of a convenient and sensible machinery for ascertaining what is a fair and reasonable price, which the lessors, in breach of their contractual duty, prevent from operating, deprive the lessees of the only remedy which would result in justice being done to them? It may be that where on the true construction of the contract the price to be paid is not to be a fair and reasonable one assessed by applying objective standards used by valuers in the exercise of their professional task but a price fixed by a named individual applying such subjective standards as he personally thinks fit, and that individual, without being insti-gated by either party to the contract of sale, refuses to fix the price or is unable through death or disability to do so, the contract of sale is thereupon determined by frustration. But such is not the present case. In the first place the contract on its true construction is in my view a contract for sale at a fair and reasonable price assessed by applying objective standards. In the second place the only thing that has prevented the machinery provided by the option clause for ascertaining the fair and reasonable price from operating is the lessors' own breach of contract in refusing to appoint their valuer. So if the synallagmatic contract created by the exercise of the option were allowed to be treated by the lessors as frustrated the frustration would be self-induced, a circumstance which English law does not allow a party to a contract to rely on to his own advantage. So I see no reason why, because they have broken one contractual obligation, the lessors should not be ordered by the court to perform another contractual obligation on their part, namely to convey the fee simple in the premises to the lessees against payment of a fair and reasonable price assessed by applying the objective standards to which I have referred.
>
> The machinery by which the value of a property was to be ascertained was subsidiary and non-essential to the main part of an agreement for the sale and purchase of the property at a fair and reasonable price, the court could, if the machinery for ascertaining the value broke down, substitute other machinery to ascertain the price in order to ensure that the agreement was carried out. Since the contract between the parties provided that the price was to be determined by valuers, it necessarily followed that the contract was a contract for sale at a fair and reasonable price assessed by applying objective standards, and on the exercise of the option clauses a complete contract for the sale and purchase of the freehold reversion was constituted; it was unrealistic to treat the machinery provided by the option clauses for ascertaining the price as an essential term of the contract when it merely consisted of provision for the appointment of valuers and an umpire, none of whom was named or identified. The only reason the machinery had not been implemented was the lessors' own breach of contract in refusing to appoint their valuer. It followed that, since such machinery was not essential, there was no reason why the court should not substitute its own machinery.
>
> As regards the assessment of the fair and reasonable price to be paid by the lessees on specific performance of the contract to convey, the lessors have clearly waived their contractual right to have that price assessed by the machinery for which the option clause provides. The lessees in their turn are content also to waive their corresponding right to use that machinery. This will leave it to the court itself to determine on the expert evidence of valuers what is the fair and reasonable price. In these circumstances I do not find it necessary to decide whether in the absence of such waiver by the lessees the court would have jurisdiction to compel the lessors to appoint a valuer; but it must not be taken that I am accepting that it would not.

At the same time the grant of the remedy of specific performance is ultimately discretionary in nature. The court has also granted specific performance of a contractual licence to occupy land. In *Verrall v Great Yarmouth B.C.* [1981] QB 202, specific performance of a contractual licence to occupy the council's premises was granted to the National Front for its annual conference. See also *Winter Garden Theatre (London) Ltd v Millenium Productions Ltd* [1948] AC 173.

Where damages would adequately compensate the claimant, a decree of specific performance will not be ordered. This is especially so in the case of a contract for the sale of unascertained goods or goods that are freely available on the open market. In such a situation, the claimant would be left with his common law remedy of damages as this would enable him to purchase the goods elsewhere. But where the goods are unique or possess a particular intrinsic value, specific performance will be available, see *Falcke v Gray* (1859) 4 Drew 65. This has been reaffirmed in s 52 of the Sale of Goods Act 1979 (which re-enacted a similar provision in the Sale of Goods Act 1893). This section provides that the court has the power to grant specific performance where the goods are specific or ascertained.

The purpose of the statutory provision was to widen the ambit of specific performance but its application has not always been consistent. In *Cohen v Roche* [1927] 1 KB 169, specific performance of a contract for the sale of eight Hepplewhite chairs was refused. By contrast, in *Behnke v Bede Shipping Co* [1927] 1 KB 649, specific performance of a contract for the sale of a ship was granted, the court recognized that the ship was of a unique value to the purchaser, per Wright J.

> **Wright J:** It is curious how little guidance there is on the question whether specific performance should be granted of a contract for the sale of a ship. Sect. 52 of the Sale of Goods Act gives the Court a discretion, if it thinks fit, in any action for breach of contract to deliver specific or ascertained goods, to direct that the contract shall be performed specifically. I think a ship is a specific chattel within the Act.
>
> In the present case there is evidence that the *City* was of peculiar and practically unique value to the plaintiff. She was a cheap vessel, being old, having been built in 1892, but her engines and boilers were practically new and such as to satisfy the German regulations, and hence the plaintiff could, as a German shipowner, have her at once put on the German register. A very experienced ship valuer has said that he knew of only one other comparable ship, but that may now have been sold. The plaintiff wants the ship for immediate use, and I do not think damages would be an adequate compensation. I think he is entitled to the ship and a decree of specific performance in order that justice may be done. What is the position between the defendants and the other buyers, whose contract was later in time than that of the plaintiff, is irrelevant in this action.

In the case of *Sky Petroleum Ltd v V.I. P. Petroleum Ltd* [1974] 1 WLR 576, the court extended its jurisdiction to grant specific performance. In this case the claimant had entered into a contract whereby the defendant had agreed to supply to the claimant all the petrol it needed. The defendant purported to terminate the contract during a period of limited petrol supplies. The court granted an interim injunction restraining the defendant from refusing to supply the petrol. The court acknowledged that this amounted to specific performance of the contract, but stated that it did have the jurisdiction to grant specific performance of a contract for the sale of chattels even though they were unascertained goods, per Goulding J.

> **Goulding J:** There is trade evidence that the plaintiff company has no great prospect of finding any alternative source of supply for the filling stations which constitute its business. The defendant company has indicated its willingness to continue to supply the plaintiff company, but only at prices which, according to the plaintiff company's evidence, would not be serious prices from a commercial point of view. There is, in my judgment, so far as I can make out on the evidence before me, a serious danger that unless the court interferes at this stage the plaintiff company will be forced out of business. In those circumstances, unless there is some specific reason which debars me from doing so, I should be disposed to grant an injunction to restore the former position under the contract until the rights and wrongs of the parties can be fully tried out.
>
> Now I come to the most serious hurdle in the way of the plaintiff company which is the well-known doctrine that the court refuses specific performance of a contract to sell and purchase chattels not specific or ascertained. That is a well-established and salutary rule and I am entirely unconvinced by counsel for the plaintiff company when he tells me that an injunction in the form sought by him would not be specific enforcement at all. The matter is one of substance and not of form and it is, in my judgment, quite plain that I am for the time being specifically enforcing the contract if I grant an injunction. However the ratio behind the rule is, as I believe, that under the ordinary contract for the sale of non-specific goods, damages are a sufficient remedy. That, to my mind,

is lacking in the circumstances of the present case. The evidence suggests, and indeed it is common knowledge, that the petroleum market is in an unusual state in which a would-be buyer cannot go out into the market and contract with another seller, possibly at some sacrifice as to price. Here, the defendant company appears for practical purposes to be the plaintiff company's sole means of keeping its business going, and I am prepared so far to depart from the general rule as to try to preserve the position under the contract until a later date. I therefore propose to grant an injunction.

A similar approach appears to have been taken in *Howard Perry v British Railway Board* [1980] 1 WLR 1375. Here, Megarry VC decided that specific performance would be ordered for the delivery of 500 tons of steel. This was on the basis that damages would be an inadequate remedy as it was at that time difficult to obtain substitute steel and the claimant's business might have been seriously disrupted. However, in contrast with this, in *Société Des Industries Metallurgious v Bronx Engineering Co* [1975] 1 Lloyds Rep 465, the court took the approach that an interlocutory injunction restraining the sellers from removing certain machinery from the jurisdiction would not be granted. This was on the basis that the claimants, who were buyers of the machinery, would not obtain specific performance of the contract at the trial of the action. This decision was made notwithstanding that the court recognised that the delay in getting alternative machinery would disrupt the claimant's business. Thus it would appear that the current state of the law on this issue remains unsettled.

It was also said that specific performance would not be granted in relation to a contract to pay money as in such a case damages would always be an adequate remedy. But in appropriate cases, as in *Beswick v Beswick* [1968] AC 58, the court may be prepared to grant a decree of specific performance.

DISCRETIONARY NATURE OF THE REMEDY

Like all equitable remedies, specific performance is discretionary. Accordingly, the courts will take many factors into account when considering whether or not to grant a decree, including laches, the conduct of the claimant and the question of hardship to the defendant. In *Patel v Ali* [1984] 1 All ER 978, it was held that, in considering the issue of hardship to the defendant, the court could take into account events which had occurred after the contract had been entered into, although this would be rare. In this case there was an unforeseen change in the defendant's circumstances subsequent to the date of the contract for the sale of a house. The defendant, a young married woman with three young children contracted bone cancer resulting in amputation of a leg subsequent to the date of contract. The defendant became dependent on assistance from family and friends living in the neighbourhood of the house contracted to be sold. Goulding J decided that it would have inflicted hardship amounting to injustice on the defendant to order specific performance of the contract since that would have the effect of asking her to do what she had never bargained for, viz. to complete the sale after more than four years and after all the unforeseeable changes that had taken place during that period. Moreover, after the long period of delay (for which neither party was to blame) it would have been just to leave the claimants to their remedy in damages. The court said that it could, in the exercise of its discretion in a proper case, refuse specific performance of such a contract on the ground of hardship suffered by the defendant subsequent to the date of the contract, even if the hardship was not caused by the claimant and did not relate to the subject matter of the contract.

Goulding J: It is not in dispute that, like other equitable relief, the specific performance of contracts is a discretionary remedy, but, in the ordinary case of a sale of land or buildings, the court normally grants it as of course and withholds it only on proof of special facts. The textbooks and reported decisions have long recognised hardship as one ground on which, in a proper case, a purchaser or vendor may be refused specific performance and be left to his right to damages for breach of contract at law. The difficulty is to determine within what limits hardship to a defendant can properly be said to justify this exercise of judicial discretion. There is no doubt that, in the majority of cases, the hardship which moves the court to refuse specific performance is either a hardship existing at the date of the contract or a hardship due in some way to the plaintiff. In the present case, neither of those conditions being satisfied, the plaintiffs, rely strongly on that principle or practice, which is stated in varying terms in all the well-known textbooks. It is sufficient for me to cite a passage from *Fry on Specific Performance* (6th edn, 1921) p 199, paras 417–418:

> It is a well-established doctrine that the Court will not enforce the specific performance of a contract, the result of which would be to impose great hardship on either of the parties to it; and this although the party seeking specific performance may be free from the least impropriety of conduct. The question of the hardship of a contract is generally to be judged of at the time at which it is entered into: if it be then fair and just and not productive of hardship, it will be immaterial that it may, by the force of subsequent circumstances or change of events, have become less beneficial to one party, except where these subsequent events have been in some way due to the party who seeks the performance of the contract. For whatever contingencies may attach to a contract, or be involved in the performance of either part, have been taken upon themselves by the parties to it. It has been determined that the reasonableness of a contract is to be judged of at the time it is entered into, and not by the light of subsequent events, and we have already seen that the same principle applies in considering the fairness of a contract.

However, the principle so stated cannot be erected into a fixed limitation of the court's equitable jurisdiction. It is recognised, both by Fry LJ's book and in the argument of counsel for the plaintiffs in the present action, that the court has sometimes refused specific performance because of a change of circumstances supervening after the making of the contract and not in any way attributable to the plaintiff.

The important and true principle, in my view, is that only in extraordinary and persuasive circumstances can hardship supply an excuse for resisting performance of a contract for the sale of immovable property. A person of full capacity who sells or buys a house takes the risk of hardship to himself and his dependants, whether arising from existing facts or unexpectedly supervening in the interval before completion. This is where, to my mind, great importance attaches to the immense delay in the present case, not attributable to the defendant's conduct. Even after issue of the writ, she could not complete, if she had wanted to, without the concurrence of the absent Mr Ahmed. Thus, in a sense, she can say she is being asked to do what she never bargained for, namely to complete the sale after more than four years, after all the unforeseeable changes that such a period entails. I think that in this way she can fairly assert that specific performance would inflict on her 'a hardship amounting to injustice' to use the phrase employed by James LJ, in a different but comparable context, in *Tamplin v James* (1880) 15 ChD 215 at 221, [1874–80] All ER Rep 560 at 562. Equitable relief may, in my view, be refused because of an unforeseen change of circumstances not amounting to legal frustration, just as it may on the ground of mistake insufficient to avoid a contract at law.

In the end, I am satisfied that it is within the court's discretion to accede to the defendant's prayer if satisfied that it is just to do so. And, on the whole, looking at the position of both sides after the long unpredictable delay for which neither seeks to make the other responsible, I am of opinion that it is just to leave the plaintiffs to their remedy in damages if that can indeed be effective.

I have come to this conclusion without taking into account the welfare of the defendant's children except as involved in her own personal hardship. I much doubt whether, even in the present atmosphere of opinion on which her counsel dwelt in his address, the interests of the children are material in their own right, though he did derive some support from the obiter observations of Isaacs J in the High Court of Australia in *Gall v Mitchell* (1924) 35 CLR 222 at 230, where he said:

> Hardships of third persons entirely unconnected with the property are immaterial. But I do not think that rule excludes the case of third persons so connected with the defendant that, by reason of some legal or moral duty which he owes them, it would be "highly unreasonable" for the Court actively to prevent the defendant from discharging his duty. The circumstances of such a case might, in my opinion, be properly weighed for the purpose of determining the discretion of the Court.

The court may also take into account the hardship that would be suffered by a third party in deciding whether to grant the decree of specific performance, see *Thames Guaranty Ltd v Campbell* [1984] 2 All ER 585.

The discretionary nature of the remedy of specific performance was considered by the Court of Appeal in *Quadrant Visual Communications v Hutchinson Telephone (UK)* [1993] BCLC 442. In this case, the defendant agreed to acquire from the claimant its mobile and car telephone business.

Part of the consideration for the sale was deferred and was to be calculated based on the number of subscribers obtained by the defendant after the sale. One of the terms of the agreement provided that the consideration was to be paid free from 'any equity cross-claim . . . whatsoever'. At the completion of the agreement, the claimant did not disclose to the defendant the fact that the claimant had entered into a contract with a marketing company for a campaign that provided for the issuing of vouchers to provide free mobile telephones. The claimant later applied for summary judgment and an order for specific performance of the agreement, namely for the payment of the deferred consideration. The Master granted an order for specific performance, but Roch J decided that as the claimant had not come to the court with 'clean hands', in that it failed to disclose this agreement with the marketing company to the defendant, specific performance would be refused. The claimant appealed. The Court of Appeal, in dismissing the appeal, held that the claimant did not come before the court with 'clean hands', since the non-disclosure of the other agreement to the defendant was reprehensible. The words, 'any equity' in the agreement did not cover the concept of coming to court with 'clean hands' and even if it did attempt to do so, the court's discretion to refuse to grant an order for specific performance could not be fettered by a term in the agreement. This decision makes it clear that the discretion of the court cannot be excluded or fettered by any agreement between the parties.

> **Stocker LJ :** I would not consider the words 'any equity' [in the agreement between the parties] apt to embrace the clean hands concept. Even if it was, and could bind the parties, it could not have the effect of fettering the discretion of the court. Once the court is asked for the equitable remedy of specific performance, its discretion cannot be fettered. Once the assistance of the court is involved by one of the parties in a discretionary matter, that party is bound by the general discretion of the court to grant or refuse the remedy sought. If Mr Tabachnik's submission that the court is bound by the terms of the contract and therefore has no discretion to exercise is correct, the function of the court would be reduced to that of a rubber stamp. In my opinion, this could not be and is not the situation.
>
> As a factual matter, I find the passage in *Snell's Equity* (29th edn, 1990) p 611 in point. Under the general topic of specific performance and under the specific heading of 'Trickiness', the learned authors of *Snell* state:
>
>> But even if there is no fraud or misrepresentation sufficient to justify the rescission of the contract, the court may still refuse the equitable remedy of specific performance if the conduct of the plaintiff has been tricky or unfair, for 'he who comes into equity must come with clean hands', and the court is not bound to decree specific performance in every case in which it would not set aside the contract.
>
> I have no doubt at all that the conduct of Mr Guttridge, in disclosing only one of the consumer promotion agreements and suppressing the other, amounted at the very least to trickery. The consequence of this trick exposed the defendants to the risk of very serious losses without giving them any proper opportunity to consider the matter, and in particular to consider whether or not they wanted to complete.

If the claimant has defaulted in some way, for example, if he has failed to perform his part of the contract by the time specified, then the defendant may use the fact of the claimant's default in his defence. Except in specific circumstances, equity will not consider time to be of the essence of a contract. The exceptions have been clearly set out by Browne-Wilkinson VC in *British and Commonwealth Holdings v Quadrex Holdings* [1989] 3 All ER 492, where he stated:

> However, in three types of case time is of the essence in equity: first, where the contract expressly so stipulates; second, where the circumstances of the case or the subject matter of the contract indicate that the time for completion is of the essence; thirdly, where a valid notice to complete has been given.

Even though time is not of the essence, the claimant may still not be entitled to specific performance if he has delayed in bringing his action, see *Mills v Haywood* (1877) 6 Ch D 196.

An example of delay not being a bar to a claim for specific performance can be seen in the case of *Eagleview Ltd v Worthgate Ltd* [1998] EGCS 119. In this case, the first defendant bought a property from a mortgagee sale in 1993. It contracted to sell the property to the claimant for £320,000. Completion of this sale was due on 15 April 1993, but on or about 8 April, it was discovered that there were squatters on the property. Further, a purported agent of the first defendant granted a one-year lease of the property to a Mr Parkin. On 19 April 1993, the first defendant served a completion notice on the claimant, which he objected to in view of the squatters. The notice was then withdrawn. A second completion notice was served on 23 April 1993, which the claimant ignored and the first defendant took no action. A third completion notice was served on 6 May 1993, requiring completion a week later. The first defendant purported to rescind the contract on the expiry of the notice and forfeited the deposit. The first defendant then entered into a new contract with the second defendant for the sale of the property. The claimant registered a caution on the property and commenced an action claiming, firstly, that the rescission was void and, secondly, specific performance of the contract. At the same time the second defendant paid the purchase monies and took possession of the property. It was decided that the rescission of the contract was ineffective because it was unclear whether the first defendant could give vacant possession in view of the squatters and the one year lease. The claimant was not prevented from claiming specific performance as a result of the delay because the claimant had never abandoned the contract nor had it caused any prejudice to the first defendant or any third party.

Question
What factors do the courts take into consideration in deciding whether to exercise its discretion concering an award of specific performance?

CONTRACTS REQUIRING SUPERVISION

In particular cases, such as those involving contracts that require supervision, other considerations may be relevant. It seems that the courts will view as one of degree the question of whether or not a contract requires continuous supervision. Even if continuous supervision of a contract should prove to be necessary, specific performance could still be granted provided that it is quite clear what the defendant is required to do. Thus, in *Beswick v Beswick* all the Law Lords thought it unimportant that the obligation under the contract was a continuing one.

The question of supervision in the context of specific performance was considered in *Co-operative Insurance Society Ltd v Argyll Stores (Holdings) Ltd* [1997] 3 All ER 294. The House of Lords reversed the Court of Appeal's decision and decided that the defendant would not be compelled to keep its supermarket open pursuant to a 'keep open' clause in the lease. One reason for this was because the court would not order specific performance of a contract requiring constant supervision.

Lord Hoffman: The practice of not ordering a defendant to carry on a business is not entirely dependent upon damages being an adequate remedy. In *Dowty Boulton Paul Ltd v Wolverhampton Corp* [1971] 2 All ER 277 at 284, [1971] 1 WLR 204 at 211, 212

Pennycuick V-C refused to order the corporation to maintain an airfield as a going concern because:

It is very well established that the court will not order specific performance of an obligation to carry on a business ... It is unnecessary in the circumstances to discuss whether damages would be an adequate remedy to the company.

Thus the reasons which underlie the established practice may justify a refusal of specific performance even when damages are not an adequate remedy.

The most frequent reason given in the cases for declining to order someone to carry on a business is that it would require constant supervision by the court. In *J C Williamson Ltd v Lukey* (1931) 45 CLR 282 at 297–298 Dixon J said flatly: 'Specific performance is inapplicable when the continued supervision of the Court is necessary in order to ensure the fulfilment of the contract.'

There has, I think, been some misunderstanding about what is meant by continued superintendence. It may at first sight suggest that the judge (or some other officer of the court) would literally have to supervise the execution of the order. In *C H Giles & Co Ltd v Morris* [1972] 1 All ER 960 at 969, [1972] 1 WLR 307 at 318 Megarry J said that 'difficulties of constant superintendence' were a 'narrow consideration' because—

there is normally no question of the court having to send its officers to supervise the performance of the order ... Performance ... is normally secured by the realisation of the person enjoined that he is liable to be punished for contempt if evidence of his disobedience to the order is put before the court ...

This is, of course, true but does not really meet the point. The judges who have said that the need for constant supervision was an objection to such orders were no doubt well aware that supervision would in practice take the form of rulings by the court, on applications made by the parties, as to whether there had been a breach of the order. It is the possibility of the court having to give an indefinite series of such rulings in order to ensure the execution of the order which has been regarded as undesirable.

Why should this be so? A principal reason is that, as Megarry J pointed out in the passage to which I have referred, the only means available to the court to enforce its order is the quasi-criminal procedure of punishment for contempt. This is a powerful weapon; so powerful, in fact, as often to be unsuitable as an instrument for adjudicating upon the disputes which may arise over whether a business is being run in accordance with the terms of the court's order. The heavy-handed nature of the enforcement mechanism is a consideration which may go to the exercise of the court's discretion in other cases as well.

This is a convenient point at which to distinguish between orders which require a defendant to carry on an activity, such as running a business over a more or less extended period of time, and orders which require him to achieve a result. The possibility of repeated applications for rulings on compliance with the order which arises in the former case does not exist to anything like the same extent in the latter. Even if the achievement of the result is a complicated matter which will take some time, the court, if called upon to rule, only has to examine the finished work and say whether it complies with the order. This point was made in the context of relief against forfeiture in *Shiloh Spinners Ltd v Harding* [1973] 1 All ER 90, [1973] AC 691. If it is a condition of relief that the tenant should have complied with a repairing covenant, difficulty of supervision need not be an objection. As Lord Wilberforce said ([1973] 1 All ER 90 at 102, [1973] AC 691 at 724):

... what the court has to do is to satisfy itself, ex post facto, that the covenanted work has been done, and it has ample machinery, through certificates, or by enquiry, to do precisely this.

This distinction between orders to carry on activities and to achieve results explains why the courts have in appropriate circumstances ordered specific performance of building contracts and repairing covenants (see *Wolverhampton Corp v Emmons* [1901] 1 KB 515 (building contract) and *Jeune v Queens Cross Properties Ltd* [1973] 3 All ER 97, [1974] Ch 97 (repairing covenant)). It by no means follows, however, that even obligations to achieve a result will always be enforced by specific performance.

Contracts for personal services

It used to be suggested that the difficulties which the court would encounter in supervising performance would prevent it from enforcing contracts for personal services. In *Wolverhampton and Walsall Railway Co v London and North Western Railway* (1873) LR 16 Eq 433, Lord Selborne stated:

It is obvious that if the notion of specific performance were applied to ordinary contracts for work or labour, or hiring or service, it would require a series of orders and a general superintendence which could not conveniently be undertaken by any court of justice.

In addition, it was thought to be contrary to public policy to compel the parties to continue a working relationship where one of them was unwilling to do so. To grant an order for specific performance in such circumstances could be tantamount to turning the contracts of employment into contracts of slavery, see *Francesco v Barnum* (1890) 45 Ch D 430. In *Lumley v Wagner* (1852) 1 De G M &g 604, the court refused to grant specific performance of a contract to sing at a theatre. In *Giles & Co v Morris* [1972] 1 All ER 960, Megarry J stated the rationale for the general rule thus:

Megarry J: The reasons why the court is reluctant to decree specific performance of a contract for personal services (and I would regard it as a strong reluctance rather than the rule) are, I think, more complex, and more firmly bottomed on human nature. If a singer contracts to sing, there could no doubt be proceedings for committal if, ordered to sing, the singer remained obstinately dumb. But instead the singer sang sharp, or flat, or too fast or too slowly ... the threat of committal would reveal itself as a most unsatisfactory weapon.

Not all contracts for personal services present such difficulties. In *Hill v CA Parsons Ltd* [1971] 3 All ER 1345, an employee was dismissed after having refused to join the trade union at his place of employment where a closed shop was in operation. The court granted an interim injunction restraining the termination of his employment on the grounds that the Industrial Relations Act 1971 (since repealed) would have come into force within a few weeks and would have given the employee protection in any event. Furthermore, the employer and employee retained mutual confidence in each other. Lord Denning noted that the decision in fact had the effect of granting specific performance of a contract of employment.

In *Erskine McDonald Ltd v Eyles* [1921] 1 Ch 631, the court decided that a breach of a copyright agreement offering the defendant, an authoress, a publishing contract to write her next three books subject to certain royalty terms, was specifically enforceable. In breach of this agreement the defendant attempted to sell her manuscripts to a rival publisher. The court decided that such agreements were not contracts to render personal services, but contracts to sell the products of the labour or industry of the contracting party.

> **Peterson J:** . . . it was said that the plaintiffs' attempt to enforce the provisions of clause 10 was an endeavour to obtain indirectly specific performance of a contract of personal service. This is not, in my opinion, a contract of personal service. It is a contract by Mrs. Eyles to hand over to the plaintiffs for a consideration the product of her labour; and I can see no difference in principle between this contract and a contract to transfer all future patents or improvements on an invention or a contract by a farmer for the sale of a future crop: see *Ward, Lock & Co v Long* [1906] 2 Ch 550. They are not contracts to render personal service, but contracts to sell the products of the labour or industry of the contracting party. In my opinion the plaintiffs are entitled as against Mrs. Eyles to require Mrs. Eyles to hand to them the manuscript of 'Captivity' in order that they may determine whether they will undertake the publication of it, and are entitled to an injunction restraining her from disposing of the book without regard to the provisions of clause 10.

It should be noted that the courts are prepared to grant specific performance of restraint of trade covenants contained in contracts of employment. In *Awnayday & Co v D'Alphen* (1997) *The Times*, 24 June, the Court of Appeal enforced anti-solicitation and anti-competition covenants contained in an agreement against the defendants.

Building contracts

For similar reasons the courts used to be reluctant to grant specific performance of a contract for building work or repairs. In *Wolverhampton Corp v Emmons* [1901] KB 514, Romer LJ specified three conditions that had to be fulfilled before a contract for building work could be enforced:

1. the work must be sufficiently defined in the contract;

2. the claimant must have a substantial interest in the performance of the contract of such a nature that damages would not be sufficient to compensate him for the defendant's failure to build; and

3. the defendant must have entered on to the claimant's land in pursuance of the contract.

The first two conditions are simply general principles that the court would consider when granting specific performance in any event and it seems that the third condition may be waived. Collins LJ in the same case expressed his opinion with an element of uncertainty.

> **COLLINS LJ:** I am of the same opinion. I must confess that I cannot altogether understand the principle upon which Courts of Equity have acted in sometimes granting orders for specific performance in these cases, and sometimes not. I think that possibly the explanation is that the Courts have not uniformly adhered to one principle in such cases. It looks to me as if the views of the Courts of Equity have gone through a process of development with regard to the subject. In early times they seem to have granted decrees for specific performance in such cases. Then came a period in which they would not grant such decrees on the ground that the Court could not undertake to supervise the performance of the contract. Later on again they seem to have attached less importance to this consideration, and returned to some extent to the more ancient practice,

holding that they could order specific performance in certain cases in which the works were specified by the contract in a sufficiently definite manner.

In *Jeune v Queen's Cross Properties* [1973] 3 All ER 97, specific performance was granted of a landlord's covenant to repair since it was quite clear from the lease and the circumstances of the case what it was the landlord had to do, per Pennycuick VC.

> **Pennycuick VC:** Now, on the face of it, in common sense and justice, it seems perfectly clear that this is the appropriate relief. The defendant's repairing covenants require it to maintain, repair and renew the structure, including the external walls. A mandatory order on the defendant to reinstate the balcony is a much more convenient order than an award of damages leaving it to the individual plaintiffs to do the work. There is nothing burdensome or unfair in the order sought.

The courts have generally been reluctant to grant orders for specific performance of covenants to repair contained in leases. In *Rainbow Estates Ltd v Tokenhold Ltd* [1998] 2 All ER 860, the court was prepared to make such an order. The court had to decide whether the remedy of specific performance was available to enforce a tenant's obligation to repair contained in a lease. The court decided that the facts of the case were unusual in that damages would not be an appropriate remedy given that there was neither a proviso for re-entry nor a forfeiture clause. There was also no covenant in the lease allowing the lessor the right to enter upon the premises to undertake the repairs to the property and recover the cost from the lessees. The lease merely allowed the lessor to enter upon the premises to inspect the condition of the property. It would be appropriate to grant an order for the specific performance of the tenant's obligations. The court made it clear that there was no modern authority on the issue of specific performance of the tenant's repairing obligations, although there was a Law Commission report in 1996 recommending that the courts be given the power to make such orders. The judge considered the general principles relating to an agreement to build and emphasised that the court could grant such an order where there was no injustice or oppression to the defendant. It also stressed that such an order would be refused where the application was made in order to avoid the effect of the Leasehold Property (Repairs) Act 1938. In view of the unusual circumstances in this case, the court was prepared to grant an order for the specific performance of the lessee's repairing obligations.

> **Collins QC:** In my judgment, a modern law of remedies requires specific performance of a tenant's repairing covenant to be available in appropriate circumstances, and there are no constraints of principle or binding authority against the availability of the remedy. First, even if want of mutuality were any longer a decisive factor (which it is not) the availability of the remedy against the tenant would restore mutuality as against the landlord. Second, the problems of defining the work and the need for supervision can be overcome by ensuring that there is sufficient definition of what has to be done in order to comply with the order of the court. Third, the court should not be constrained by the supposed rule that the court will not enforce the defendant's obligation in part: this is a problem raised by paras 9.10 and 9.13 of the Law Commission Report *Landlord and Tenant: Responsibility for State and Condition of Property*, but it is not raised elsewhere as an objection; it is by no means clear that there is such a principle, and in any event if there is such a principle, it applies where the contract is in part unenforceable (*Jones and Goodhart* pp 57–61); it does not mean that the court cannot in an appropriate case enforce compliance with a particular obligation such as a repairing covenant.
>
> Subject to the overriding need to avoid injustice or oppression, the remedy should be available when damages are not an adequate remedy or, in the more modern formulation, when specific performance is the appropriate remedy. This will be particularly important if there is substantial difficulty in the way of the landlord effecting repairs: the landlord may not have a right of access to the property to effect necessary repairs, since (in the absence of contrary agreement) a landlord has no right to enter the premises, and the condition of the premises may be deteriorating.
>
> In all cases the court must be astute to prevent oppression, even if tenants are no longer (as they were said to be in *Rayner v Stone* (1762) 2 Eden 128 at 130, 28 ER 845) for the most part of 'mean and low circumstances'.

The conditions were further considered in *Tito v Waddell (Ocean island No 2)* [1977] 2 WLR 496, where Megarry J held that on the facts of the case the difficulties of supervising performance would not be insurmountable, but that for other reasons the remedy of damages would be more appropriate.

Agreements that are futile

As a general principle, specific performance will not be granted where it would be futile or impossible as 'equity does nothing in vain'. Thus, specific performance will not be ordered of a partnership agreement which is not for a fixed term as the partnership could be terminated anyway at will, see *Hercy v Birch* (1804) 9 Ves 357.

Mistake and misrepresentation

Both mistake and misrepresentation may give one party the right to rescind the contract. They may also be used as a 'defence' to an action for specific performance as it seems that the court may be more willing to refuse a decree of specific performance than to grant rescission. Thus, in *Denny v Hancock* (1870) Ch App 1, the defendant bid for property at an auction, believing that it included, 'three fine elm trees', whereas in fact it did not. His mistake was attributable to a plan provided by the claimant which the court found to be misleading. The defendant subsequently wished to withdraw from the contract and the claimant sued for specific performance. The claimant's application was refused as it was felt that to grant it would be inequitable. The court also remarked that a unilateral mistake not induced by the claimant might be a ground for refusing specific performance, although it would not entitle the defendant to rescind the contract. See also *Malins v Freeman* (1837) 2 Keen 25 and *Tamplin v James* (1880) 15 Ch D 215.

DAMAGES IN LIEU OF SPECIFIC PERFORMANCE

As was stated in Chapter 22, Lord Cairns' Act 1858 gave courts of equity the power to award damages instead of equitable remedies such as specific performance. Although this Act has been repealed the jurisdiction conferred by it remains and it seems that damages in equity may be computed on a basis that differs from that used at common law. In *Wroth v Tyler* [1973] 1 All ER 897, the defendant was unable to complete the sale of his house to the claimant as his wife had registered a right of occupation under the Matrimonial Homes Act 1967. The claimant sued for breach of contract and claimed specific performance of the contract of sale. On the date fixed for completion, the value of the house was £7,500 but, because of a very rapid increase in house prices, by the time of the trial it was worth £11,500. Megarry J held that this was not a suitable case for specific performance (even though it was a contract for the sale of land) because such a decree would compel the defendant to litigate against his wife in order to remove her entry from the Land Charges register. The court should therefore award damages instead. This, in turn, raised the question of how damages should be computed. At common law, damages for breach of contract of this type would be the difference between the contract price and the market value of the property at the time fixed for completion. Here, house prices had risen so rapidly that this basis of computation would not be a true substitute for specific performance as it would not enable the claimant to buy another similar house. Megarry J held that if damages were awarded in equity it must be a true substitute for specific performance and so should be based on the difference in value of the property between the date of the contract and the date of the trial.

> **Megarry J:** As the evidence stands, I think that the defendant has sufficiently attempted to obtain her consent, short of litigation. The mere fact that he sought to withdraw from the contract before he had made all his attempts does not seem to me to make much difference; if a later attempt had succeeded, he could still have completed at the date fixed for completion.
>
> Persuasion having failed, I think that the court should be slow to grant a decree of specific performance that

would require an unwilling husband to make an application to the court under s 1(2) of the 1967 Act [Matrimonial Homes Act], particularly as the decision of the court depends on the application of phrases such as 'just and reasonable' under s 1(3). In any case, the court would be reluctant to make an order which requires a husband to take legal proceedings against his wife, especially while they are still living together. Accordingly, although this is a contract of a type which the court is normally ready to enforce by a decree of specific performance, in my judgment it would . . . be 'highly unreasonable' to make such a decree if there is any other form of order that could do justice.

In my judgment . . . if under Lord Cairns' Act damages are awarded in substitution for specific performance, the court has jurisdiction to award such damages as will put the plaintiffs into as good a position as if the contract had been performed, even if to do so means awarding damages assessed by reference to a period subsequent to the date of the breach. This seems to me to be consonant with the nature of specific performance, which is a continuing remedy, designed to secure, inter alia, that the purchaser receives in fact what is his in equity as soon as the contract is made, subject to the vendor's right to the money, and so on. On the one hand, a decree may be sought before any breach of contract has occurred, and so before any action lies for common law damages; and on the other hand the right to a decree may continue long after the breach has occurred. On the facts of this case, the damages that may be awarded are not limited to the £1,500 that is appropriate to the date of the breach, but extend to the £5,500 that is appropriate at the present day, when they are being awarded in substitution for specific performance. I should add that no contention has been advanced (in my judgment, quite rightly) that the case does not fall within Lord Cairns' Act. The sale of a house is a case par excellence in which the court 'has jurisdiction to entertain an application . . . for the specific performance' of a contract, and the plaintiffs have done nothing to disentitle themselves to a decree. The undesirability of granting the decree if any suitable alternative exists springs from the position of the defendant and his wife.

Wroth v Tyler was followed by the Court of Appeal in *Malhotra v Choudhury* [1978] 3 WLR 825, although in the latter case it was found that, as the claimant had delayed in bringing his action, the date of assessment would be put back by one year.

Cumming-Bruce LJ: . . . it is unfair to the defendant that the deliberation with which the plaintiff moved from the middle of 1975 until he issued the present proceedings in January 1977 should be allowed to enhance the damage which the defendant has to pay the plaintiff if the price level of real property has risen during that period. For my part I would think that justice is done between them by holding that the plaintiff did not sufficiently mitigate his damage by proceeding with greater celerity in the various and difficult legal convolutions that he has been forced to undergo. The right order is that, for purposes of valuation of Novar, and the loss sustained by the plaintiff by the failure of the defendant to honour the contract for sale, the terminal date by reason of delay should be moved back from 20 October 1977 to 20 October 1976. Therefore the task of the assessment of damages is to arrive at the value on 4 June 1974 and the value in October 1976 and to award the plaintiff as one of the items in his damages the difference between these two sums.

In *Tito v Waddell*, Megarry J stated that in some cases damages under Lord Cairns' Act would be the same as that available at common law. The House of Lords in *Johnson v Agnew* [1978] 2 WLR 806, doubted whether the Act did allow a departure from the common law.

The jurisdiction to award damages under Lord Cairns Act may be useful where for some reason damages would not be available at common law. In *Johnson v Agnew* the claimants contracted to sell a plot of land to the defendant. The land had previously been mortgaged to the claimant's bank. The defendant failed to complete and the claimants sued for specific performance. A decree of specific performance was granted but meanwhile the mortgagees had taken possession and sold the property for a price substantially less than that which the defendant had agreed to pay. The claimants were then unable to pursue their remedy of specific performance, but subsequently brought an action claiming the balance of the purchase price with interest, but with a reduction for the amount realised by the sale, or, alternatively, a declaration that they could treat the contract as repudiated and sue for damages at common law. The House of Lords held that it was unable to grant the first form of relief as the claimants were unable to convey the property. Accordingly, it was unreasonable to require the defendant to pay the balance of the purchase price. As regards the second claim, the normal rule was that a claimant who had chosen to affirm the contract and sue for specific performance could not change his mind and sue for damages for breach instead. In the normal case, this would be fair; if specific performance subsequently became impossible the claimant would be relieved of his obligations under the contract but would retain the property which would usually have appreciated in value. If the property had depreciated in value or if the claimant no longer owned the property then he must seek another remedy. In such a case the court could use its power to award damages under Lord Cairns' Act. This jurisdiction was available in any case where the court could grant specific performance and continued even though specific performance had subsequently become impossible.

> **Lord Wilberforce:** In cases where a breach of a contract for sale has occurred, and the innocent party reasonably continues to try to have the contract completed, it would to me appear more logical and just rather than tie him to the date of the original breach, to assess damages as at the date when (otherwise than by his default) the contract is lost. Support for this approach is to be found in the cases. In *Ogle v Earl Vane* (1868) LR 3 QB 272, the date was fixed by reference to the time when the innocent party, acting reasonably, went into the market; in *Hickman v Haynes* (1875) LR 10 CP 598, at a reasonable time after the last request of the defendants (the buyers) to withhold delivery. In *Radford v De Froberville* [1978] 1 All ER 33, where the defendant had covenanted to build a wall, damages were held measurable as at the date of the hearing rather than at the date of the defendant's breach, unless the plaintiff ought reasonably to have mitigated the breach at an earlier date.
>
> In the present case if it is accepted, as I would accept, that the vendors acted reasonably in pursuing the remedy of specific performance, the date on which that remedy became aborted (not by the vendors' fault) should logically be fixed as the date on which damages should be assessed. Choice of this date would be in accordance both with common law principle, as indicated in the authorities I have mentioned, and with the wording of the Act 'in substitution for . . . specific performance'. The date which emerges from this is 3 April 1975, the first date on which mortgagees contracted to sell a portion of the property. I would vary the order of the Court of Appeal by substituting this date for that fixed by them, viz 26 November 1974. The same date (3 April 1975) should be used for the purpose of limiting the respondents' right to interest on damages.

Question

To what extent is it true to say that there must be mutuality between the parties before the court will grant an order for specific performance?

FURTHER READING

Burrows, A, 'Specific performance at the crossroads' (1984) 4 Legal Studies 102.

Burrows, A, 'We do this at common law but that in equity' (2002) 22 OJLS 1.

Chen, M, 'Unjust factors and the restitutionary response' (2000) 20 OJLS 557.

Kronman, A, 'Specific performance' (1978) 45 University of Chicago Law Review 351.

McKendrick, E, Specific implement and specific performance – a comparison' (1986) Scots Law Times 249.

Schwartz, G, 'The case for specific performance' (1979) 89 Yale Law Journal 271.

Smith, S, 'Performance, punishment and the nature of contractual obligations' (1997) 60 MLR 360.

Wilkinson, H, 'Specific performance of a tenant's covenant' (1998) 148 NLJ 1475.

INTRODUCTION

The remedy of rectification is yet another equitable remedy devised by the Court of Chancery in the exercise of its concurrent jurisdiction. The general equitable principles already referred to in the context of equitable remedies are equally applicable here. Rectification is not ancillary to other remedies such as specific performance, but is independent. The basis of the relief is that the claimant is not put at risk or prejudiced by the existence of a document which would be unconscionable, but for the remedy of rectification.

JURISDICTION

The jurisdiction of courts of equity in respect of the rectification of documents is to bring the written document executed in pursuance of an antecedent agreement into conformity with that agreement. The conditions of its exercise are that there must be an antecedent contract and the common intention of embodying or giving effect to the whole of that contract by the writing, and there must be clear evidence that the document by common mistake failed to embody such contract and either contained provisions not agreed on, or omitted something which was agreed on, or otherwise departed from its terms. In other words, the remedy operates where the parties have reached agreement, but owing to some error made during the process of reducing the agreement into writng, the document does not accord with the intentions of the parties. If these conditions are fulfilled, on principle, the instrument so rectified should have the same force as if the mistake had not been made. The principles to be applied by a court determining a claim to rectification on the ground of mutual mistake were set out in the judgment of Peter Gibson LJ in *Swainland Builders Ltd v. Freehold Properties Ltd* [2002] EWCA 560:

> The party seeking rectification must show that:
>
> 1 the parties had a common continuing intention, whether or not amounting to an agreement, in respect of a particular matter in the instrument to be rectified;
>
> 2 there was an outward expression of accord;
>
> 3 the intention continued at the time of the execution of the instrument sought to be rectified;
>
> 4 by mistake, the instrument did not reflect that common intention.

Where the parties agree that there has been an error, they will usually correct the written document themselves without recourse to the courts. Accordingly, in most cases of dispute only one party objects to the terms of the written agreement, the other party claims that it accurately records the intentions of the parties. In such cases difficult questions of proof may arise and for some time there was some doubt as to whether it was necessary to show a concluded agreement before rectification was available or whether it was enough to show a continuous common intention. This difficulty was considered in *Joscelyne v Nissen*, where the Court of Appeal decided that it was enough to show a continuous common intention, provided that there was 'some outward expression of accord' that would furnish convincing proof of the parties' intentions.

Joscelyne v Nissen [1970] 1 All ER 1213, (CA)

Facts

The father and mother lived in a house called Martindale from where he carried on a car hire business. In 1960, the father received a notice to quit. The daughter, in order to help her parents, bought Martindale with the help of a mortgage and let her husband's house furnished to pay off the mortgage instalments and moved to Martindale. The parents occupied the ground floor and the daughter and her husband the first floor. In 1963, the daughter's mother became very ill with two successive strokes and was unable to look after herself. The father had to devote a good deal of his time to looking after her with the result that his business was adversely affected. The father and the daughter discussed a scheme, which culminated in the signing by them of a written contract, dated 18 June 1964. By this contract the father agreed to transfer his motor car hire business to the daughter on certain terms and conditions, one of which was that in consideration of the transfer, the daughter would permit the father during his life to have the uncontrolled right to occupy and reside in the ground floor of Martindale 'free of all rent and outgoings of every kind in any event'. In pursuance of this term in the contract the daughter for a time paid the gas, electricity and coal bills and the cost of home help for the father. Trouble then arose between the daughter and her parents, and the father commenced proceedings in the county court against the daughter. The daughter contended that the wording of the contract did not require her to pay for the items previously mentioned and she accordingly stopped further payments of those items. The father amended his particulars of claim to raise the point either as a matter of construction or by way of rectification.

Held

Dismissing the appeal on the ground that both parties were in agreement up to the moment when they executed the written contract that the daughter should pay all outgoings on Martindale, and the written contract did not conform with that agreement. Accordingly, the court had jurisdiction to rectify the written contract.

Russell LJ: [Having reviewed the leading authorities said] In *Crane v Hegeman-Harris Co Inc* Simonds J said ([1939] 1 All ER at 664, 665):

> . . . it is necessary to say a few words upon the principles which must guide me in this matter. I am clear that I must follow the decision of CLAUSON, J., as he then was, in *Shipley Urban District Council v. Bradford Corpn.* [1936] Ch 375, the point of which is that, in order that this court may exercise its jurisdiction to rectify a written instrument, it is not necessary to find a concluded and binding contract between the parties antecedent to the agreement which it is sought to rectify. The judge held, and I respectfully concur with his reasoning and his conclusion, that it is sufficient to find a common continuing intention in regard to a particular provision or aspect of the agreement. If one finds that, in regard to a particular point, the parties were in agreement up to the moment when they executed their formal instrument, and the formal instrument does not conform with that common agreement, then this court has jurisdiction to rectify, although it may be that there was, until the formal instrument was executed, no concluded and binding contract between the parties. That is what the judge decided, and, as I say, with his reasoning I wholly concur, and I can add nothing to his authority in the matter, except that I would say that, if it were not so, it would be a strange thing, for the result would be that two parties binding themselves by a mistake to which each had equally contributed, by an instrument which did not express their real intention, would yet be bound by it. That is a state of affairs which I hold is not the law, and, until a higher court tells me it is the law, I shall continue to exercise the jurisdiction which CLAUSON, J., as I think rightly, held might be entertained by this court. Secondly, I want to say this upon the principle of the jurisdiction. It is a jurisdiction which is to be exercised only upon convincing proof that the concluded instrument does not represent the common intention of the parties. That is particularly the case where one finds prolonged negotiations between the parties eventually assuming the shape of a formal instrument in which they have been advised by their respective skilled legal advisers. The assumption is very strong in such a case that the instrument does represent their real intention, and it must be only upon proof which LORD ELDON, I think, in a somewhat picturesque phrase described as "irrefragable" that the court can act. I would rather, I think, say that the court can only act if it is satisfied beyond all reasonable doubt that the instrument does not represent their common intention, and is further satisfied as to what their common intention was. For let it be clear that it is not sufficient to show that the written instrument does not represent their common intention unless positively also one can show what their common intention was. It is the light of those principles that I must examine the facts of this somewhat complicated case.

In our judgment the law is as expounded by Simonds J in *Crane's* case [1939] 1 All ER 662, with the qualification that some outward expression of accord is required. We do not wish to attempt to state in any different phrases that with which we entirely agree, except to say that it is in our view better to use only the phrase 'convincing proof' without echoing an old fashioned word such as 'irrefragable' and without importing from the criminal law the phrase 'beyond all reasonable doubt.' Remembering always the strong burden of proof that lies on the shoulders of those seeking rectification, and that the requisite accord and continuance of accord of intention may be the more difficult to establish if a complete antecedent concluded contract be not shown, it would be a sorry state of affairs if when that burden is discharged a party to a written contract could, on discovery that the written language chosen for the document did not on its true construction reflect the accord of the parties on a particular point, take advantage of the fact.

We wish to stress that this is a case of rectification based on antecedent expressed accord on a point adhered to in intention by the parties to the subsequent written contract: we were in no way concerned with arguments as to collateral terms of a contract.

Formalities

In many cases the only evidence of the mistake will be in a prior oral agreement. Where the contract is required by statute to be in writing, the question arises as to whether the oral contract is admissible in evidence. Rectification can be granted of a written agreement on parol evidence of mutual mistake, although that agreement is complete in itself and has been carried out by a more formal document based on it, e.g. a conveyance in the case of a contract for the sale of land. After rectification the written agreement does not continue to exist with a parol variation. It is to be read as if it had been originally drawn in its rectified form, and it is of that document alone of which specific performance can be decreed. This is so in the case of a contract for the sale of land. Normally the parol evidence rule precludes the admissibility of such evidence, but in *Thompson v Hickman* [1907] 1 Ch 550, Neville J criticised the reluctance to admit oral evidence and the Court of Appeal in *Cradock Bros. v Hunt* [1923] 2 Ch 136, eventually held that oral evidence would be admissible.

Unilateral mistake

In the ordinary course of events rectification is not available unless the mistake is common to both parties, but the court may order rectification where one party knows that the other is mistaken, but allows him to proceed and complete the contract. In these circumstances, the remedy of rectification for unilateral mistake is a drastic remedy, for it involves imposing on the defendant, a contract that he did not intend to make. In *Riverlate Properties Ltd v Paul* [1974] 3 All ER 656, the court decided that a unilateral mistake in a lease was not a ground for rescission. Since the lessee had neither directly nor through her solicitors known of the lessor's mistake and since the mistake was in no way attributable to anything said or done by her, the lessor was not entitled to rescission of the lease, either with or without the option to the lessee to accept rectification to cure the mistake. For the court of equity to intervene there must be additional circumstances that render reliance on the document unconscionable.

The conditions for the grant of relief on the ground of unilateral mistake were set out in the judgment of Buckley LJ in *Thomas Bates Ltd v. Wyndhams (Lingerie) Ltd* [1981] 1 WLR 505, thus:

. . . it must be shown: first, that one party A erroneously believed that the document sought to be rectified contained a particular term or provision . . .; secondly, that the other party B was aware of the omission or the inclusion and that it was due to a mistake on the part of A; thirdly, that B has omitted to draw the mistake to the notice of A. And I think there must be a fourth element involved, namely, that the mistake must be one calculated to benefit B. If these requirements are satisfied, the court may regard it as inequitable to allow B to resist rectification to give effect to A's intention on the ground that the mistake was not, at the time of execution of the document, a mutual mistake.

These conditions for the grant of relief by way of rectification must be strictly satisfied, see

Rowallan Group Ltd v. Edgehill Portfolio No. 1 Ltd [2007] EWHC (Ch) 32. The issue in this case was whether the claimant, the vendor under a contract for sale of a lease to the defendant was liable under the agreement to pay an instalment of £65,000 of the premium charged on the grant by the landlord of the lease due in April 2006. The provisions of the agreement clearly so provided, but the claimant in its particulars of claim contended that it was entitled to rectification of the agreement transferring the liability to the defendant. The question between the parties on this application was the availability of the remedy of rectification on grounds of unilateral mistake made by the claimant. The High Court rejected the application of the claimant on the ground that there was no evidence to prove that the defendant was aware of the claimant's misapprehension.

> **Lightman J:** There have been a series of cases on the legal requirements for rectification on the ground of unilateral mistake culminating in the decision of the Court of Appeal in *George Wimpey v. V I Construction Ltd* [2005] EWCA 77. These cases underline that the remedy of rectification for unilateral mistake is a drastic remedy, for it has the result of imposing on the defendant to the claim a contract which he did not, and did not intend to, make. Accordingly the conditions for the grant of such relief must be strictly satisfied.
>
> To establish its claim to rectification of the Agreement the Claimant is required to plead and establish that the Defendant had actual knowledge of the mistake on the part of the Claimant that under the terms of the Agreement the Defendant would be liable to pay the Instalment. There are two qualifications to this requirement. The first is that actual knowledge includes wilfully shutting one's eyes to the obvious and wilfully and recklessly failing to make such inquiries as an honest or reasonable man would make. The second is that if the Defendant intended that the Claimant should be mistaken in this regard and deliberately set about diverting the Claimant's attention from discovering the mistake, it is unnecessary that the Defendant actually knew that the Claimant was mistaken: it is sufficient that the Defendant merely suspected that it was so.
>
> There was no sharp practice on the Defendant's part in not stating explicitly that the Defendant wanted a reduction in the previously agreed price and that the payment of the Instalment by the Claimant achieved this objective. This was the plain and obvious effect of the amendment requiring the Claimant to produce a receipt for that payment. Likewise there was no reason why the Defendant could or should have known or even suspected the pleaded mistake on the part of the Claimant. The insuperable hurdles facing the Claimant's claim are highlighted by the form of rectification sought. In place of the clause requiring the Claimant to deliver a receipt for payment of the capital payment due on the 24th April 2006, the Claimant seeks substitution of a clause requiring delivery of a receipt for the Premium due on the 23rd April 2006. I can see no basis for the suggestion that the Defendant knew or suspected that the Claimant believed that the 24th April 2006 was a mistake for the 23rd April 2006. The 24th April 2006 was clearly on its face the date on which the Instalment fell due and the Defendant had no reason to believe that this was not appreciated by Mr Montlake.

The court will not grant rectification where the parties appear to be in agreement but are acting under a misapprehension. In *Frederick Rose Ltd v William Pym* [1953] 2 QB 450, the claimants were asked by third parties to acquire some 'horsebeans, described as feveroles'. They contacted the defendants, suppliers of beans, who said that feveroles were 'just horsebeans'. Subsequently a written contract was drawn up for the sale of horsebeans. The third parties complained that the wrong type of beans had been delivered and sued the claimants. The claimants sued for rectification of the contract with the defendants. The claim failed for rectification was only available where the parties were in complete agreement as to the terms of the contract but wrote them down incorrectly. Here the parties had orally agreed to buy and sell horsebeans and this was what the contract stated. Accordingly rectification was not possible.

Wills

Originally, rectification of wills was not possible except in cases of fraud. Today, s 20 of the Administration of Justice Act 1982 allows rectification in cases of clerical errors or failure to understand instructions in drafting a will. The application for rectification is required to be brought within a period of six months following the grant of probate, except where the court grants leave to extend this period. For a recent application of this provision see *Re Craig* [2006] EWHC 2561 (Ch).

Discretion

Rectification is an equitable remedy that may be withheld at the discretion of the court in accordance with general equitable principles. The discretion of the court commonly involves different considerations from those that arise in cases of specific performance where the claimant is entitled to alternative relief in damages. If, on the other hand, rectification is refused and the document remains in existence in an unamended form, as a general rule the claimant will not be entitled to an alternative remedy and may suffer greater hardship or prejudice than those claiming specific performance. Thus, relief by way of rectification may be refused by reference to the discretion of the courts only on exceptional grounds such as laches and acquiescence and absence of 'clean hands'.

Question
To what extent is it true that there must be common mistake between the parties before the court will grant an order for rectification of a written instrument?

FURTHER READING

George, M and Penny, P, 'Rectification of deeds of variation' [2004] PCB 369.
Lacey, S, 'Rectification and the need for specific intent' (1996) 146 NLJ 1589.
O'Dell, E, 'Restitution, rectification and mitigation : negligent solicitors and wills, again' (2002) 65 MLR 360.
Saunders, I and Pincher, R, 'Rectification and reconstruction' (1997) Tax Journal, Issue 343, p 16.
Skovron, J, 'Rectification versus alteration', 23 August 2003, Estates Gazette, 23.
Swerling, L, 'Attempting to avoid probate claims' (2007) 5 EMIS Prop Service 1, 31.

INTRODUCTION

Rescission is a process whereby the parties to a contract are relieved from their obligations under the contract. The party making a successful application for rescission will be entitled to set aside the contract and to be restored to his former position prior to the contract. The contract is not void from the beginning but may be terminated at the option of one or both of the parties.

This remedy was possible to a limited extent at common law, but equitable rescission is more flexible as the court may be able to impose terms or make orders for financial adjustments. The aim of rescission is to return the parties to the position in which they would have been had the contract not been made. Thus, rescission will not be available where 'restitutio in integrum' (restoration to the original position) would be impossible, see *Erlanger v New Sombrero Phosphate Co* [1878] 3 App Cas 1218, or where the property has come into the hands of an innocent third party.

Normally, a party may rescind a contract without applying to the court. Strictly speaking, in one sense rescission is not a legal 'remedy'. Rescission will be effective when one party makes it clear to the other that he no longer intends to be bound by the contract, *Abram SS Co v Westville Shipping Co Ltd* [1923] AC 773. The normal rule is that rescission will not be effective until it is communicated to the other party although a limited exception was formulated in *Car and Universal Finance Co v Caldwell* [1965] 1 QB 525. Communication will not be necessary where the other party to the contract has been fraudulent and disappeared.

GROUNDS FOR RESCISSION

Misrepresentation

At common law a fraudulent misrepresentation which was material and induced the contract might give the representee the right to avoid the contract. There could be no remedy at common law for innocent misrepresentation unless the representation had become a term of the contract, in which case it might be possible to sue for contract.

Equity exercised a concurrent jurisdiction in cases of fraud but would also grant rescission for innocent misrepresentations if the misrepresentation was material and the representee entered the contract in reliance thereon, see *Redgrave v Hurd* [1881] 20 Ch D 1.

Until 1967 there was some doubt as to whether there was a right to rescind in equity where the representation had become a term of the contract. Section 1 of the Misrepresentation Act 1967 gave the right to rescind for innocent misrepresentation even though the representation had become a term of the contract and even though the contract had been performed. But it was not clear how this related to the common law rights to repudiate a contract for breach of an important term or to sue for damages for breach of a lesser term. Could the claimant rescind the contract under s 1 of the Misrepresentation Act 1967 and also sue for damages at common law? It is arguable that rescission has the effect of destroying all liabilities and rights under the contract including the right to damages.

Section 2 (2) of the Misrepresentation Act 1967 gave the court a discretionary power to declare the contract subsisting and to award damages as a substitute for rescission in cases where rescission would otherwise be available. It is not clear whether this power to award damages will survive if rescission is no longer available, as where 'restitutio in integrum' would be impossible.

A literal interpretation of the section would suggest that in such a case the court no longer has the power to award damages, but it seems an undesirable result.

Contracts *uberrimae fidei*

In some cases equity may designate the relationship between the parties as being *'uberrimae fidei'* (or of the utmost good faith). In such a case the parties are under a duty to disclose all material facts when negotiating an agreement and the failure to do so will give the other party the right to rescind the contract. In equity this will occur where there is a fiduciary relationship between the parties and by statute contracts of insurance are contracts where full disclosure is required.

Mistake

At common law mistake might operate to render a contract void in limited circumstances, see *Cooper v Phibbs* (1867) LR 2 HL 149 and *Cundy v Lindsay* [1878] 3 AC 459. The consequences of declaring a contract void from the beginning may be far reaching, especially when third parties have become involved. Any subsequent dealings relying on the contract will also be void. Thus, the courts have taken a restrictive approach in cases of mistake. In *Bell v Lever Bros* [1932] AC 161, Lord Atkin stated that a contract would only be void for mistake if there was a mistake as to a quality which made the thing without the quality 'essentially different from the thing it was believed to be'.

Equity follows the law in cases where the contract would be void at common law, but it seems that equity may also grant rescission of a contract for mistake in cases where the contract would be valid at law. In *Solle v Butcher* [1950] 1 KB 671, Lord Denning MR said, 'A contract is liable in equity to be set aside if the parties were under a common misapprehension either as to facts or as to their relative and respective rights, provided that the misapprehension was fundamental and that the party seeking to set it aside was not himself at fault.' *Solle v Butcher* was followed in *Grist v Bailey* [1967] Ch 532 and in *Magee v Pennine Insurance Co* [1969] 2 QB 507, though there is some doubt about the equitable jurisdiction in such cases as it had never apparently been used until *Solle v Butcher*. In *Amalgamated Investment and Property Co v John Walker* [1977] 1 WLR 164, the Court of Appeal held that on the facts there had been no common mistake so that there was no need to discuss the interesting question as to whether *Solle v Butcher* could stand with *Bell v Lever Bros*. This indicates that the basis of the equitable jurisdiction is in some doubt.

It is clear that rescission will not be available where only one party is mistaken and his mistake was not induced by the other party. In *Riverlate Properties v Paul* [1974] 3 All ER 656, the claimant sought to rescind a lease on the grounds of unilateral mistake. The Court of Appeal held that there was nothing in principle or authority to suggest that rescission was available in such a case. Russell LJ commented:

> If reference be made to principles of equity, it operates on conscience. If conscience is clear at the time of the transaction, why should equity disrupt it? If a man may be said to have been fortunate in obtaining a property at a bargain price . . . because the other party, unknown to him, has made a miscalculation or mistake, some high-minded men might consider it appropriate that he should consent to a fresh bargain . . . But if equity were to enforce the views of those high- minded men, we have no doubt that it would run counter to the attitudes of the greater part of mankind, and would be venturing on the field of moral philosophy where it would soon be in difficulties.

Duress and undue influence

The common law recognised the doctrine of duress, whereby a contract might be avoided if one of the parties had been forced to enter it under pressure. It was also possible to set a contract aside in equity for undue influence if a party seeking to avoid it could show that he was so influenced by the other party that he did not exercise his free will. In effect, duress and undue influence overlap and it may be appropriate to plead both, though the elements of each are different. The effect of the plea of duress or undue inluence makes the contract voidable at the instance of the aggrieved party.

Duress

Duress to person may consist of actual or threatened violence to the claimant or members of his family. In *Barton v Armstrong* [1975] 2 All ER 465 PC, during a company boardroom battle, the chairman of the board offered to resign in return for a substantial 'golden handshake'. In order to get his rival director to agree, he made death threats to him. The rival director accepted the terms, although he would probably have done so even without the threats. Nevertheless, the Privy Council set aside the agreements, stating that if duress had been one factor leading to the execution of a document, it was irrelevant that other factors had also been operative. The burden of disproving that it did not have an effect on the contract lies on the party alleged to have used duress.

The same principle is applicable to duress of goods, i.e. an unlawful threat of damage to the claimant's goods as opposed to his person, see *The Siboen and The Sibotre* [1976] 1 Lloyd's Rep 293.

It should be noted that a related issue that has been developed by the courts concerns economic duress. This type of duress arises where one party uses his superior economic power in an 'illegitimate' way so as to coerce the other contracting party to agree to a particular set of terms. Lord Scarman in *Universe Tankships Inc of Monrovia v International Transport Workers' Federation* [1982] 2 All ER 67, laid down three ingredients of the claim. There must be pressure:

(a) whose practical effect is compulsion on, or a lack of practical choice for the victim;

(b) that is illegitimate;

(c) that is a significant cause inducing the claimant to enter the contract.

Subsequent cases have clarified these requirements. At the same time there is a distinction between economic duress and the pressures of the commercial world. The distinction is one of degree.

Undue influence

Equity developed a more sophisticated principle of undue influence. Equity provided relief in the case of transactions induced by other forms of improper pressure or influence on the part of a person on whom reliance had been placed. In *R v Attorney General for England and Wales* [2003] UKPC 22, Lord Hoffman stated:

> Like duress at common law, undue influence is based upon the principle that a transaction to which consent has been obtained by unacceptable means should not be allowed to stand. Undue influence has concentrated in particular upon the unfair exploitation by one party of a relationship which gives him ascendancy or influence over the other

Where undue influence is established the contract is voidable and can be rescinded. The bars to rescission are the same as those that apply to rescission for misrepresentation.

In two definitive House of Lords decisions in 1994, the Law Lords restated the basis of liability for undue influence or misrepresentation where a mortgage had been secured as a result of the impropriety of the borrower. These decisions were *Barclays Bank v O'Brien* [1994] AC 180 and *CIBC v Pitt* [1994] 1 AC 200. The issue concerned the extent to which a mortgagor (e.g. a wife) may set aside a mortgage if she had been induced to enter into the transaction as a result of the undue influence or misrepresentation of the debtor (e.g. her husband), whose liability had been secured by the mortgage. In *O'Brien*, the matrimonial home, which was in the joint names of Mr and Mrs O'Brien, was mortgaged to secure an overdraft for the husband's business. Mr O'Brien was told by the bank that his wife's signature was needed to secure the overdraft. Mrs O'Brien signed the mortgage and a side letter without reading the documents. The effect of signing the side letter was that she falsely acknowledged that the mortgage had been fully explained to her. Her perception, encouraged by her husband, was that the mortgage was limited to £60,000. Instead, the mortgage contained an all monies clause. On the date of the mortgage, the indebtedness had increased from £60,000 to £135,000. Mr O'Brien defaulted on repayments and the bank sought to enforce the mortgage. At this time the debt had increased to £154,000. She resisted the claim on the ground that her husband had exercised undue influence in procuring her signature to the document and/or misrepresented the nature and scope of the transaction to the knowledge of the bank, and accordingly the transaction ought to be set aside. The House of Lords held in her favour.

In *Pitt*, the matrimonial home was in the joint names of the husband and wife. In 1986, the house was valued at £270,000 and was subject to a mortgage of £16,700. Mr Pitt wished to borrow £150,000, secured on the house, to invest in the stock market. His wife was extremely reluctant to do this, but was persuaded by her husband to go along with the plan. The finance company was told that the purpose of the loan was to pay off the existing mortgage and to buy a holiday home. Some time later, the investments became worthless as a result of the stock market crash and the value of the house plummeted in value. The finance company claimed repossession of the house. Mrs Pitt defended on the ground of undue influence of her husband. The House of Lords rejected her claim and decided that the mortgage was enforceable.

In these cases, the Law Lords clarified the law regarding undue influence held out by a principal debtor as against a mortgagor, which affects the conscience of the mortgagee to such an extent that the mortgage may be set aside. Undue influence may be either 'actual' or 'presumed'.

Actual undue influence may be established by the mortgagor proving the following:

(1) the principal debtor who induced the transaction had the capacity to influence the mortgagor;

(2) the principal debtor exercised influence on the mortgagor;

(3) such influence was undue in the sense that it exceeded the bounds of reasonable persuasion; and

(4) there is a causal connection between the influence and the mortgage transaction.

The circumstances concerning actual undue influence are akin to duress. These vary enormously in degree and range from occasions where a husband threatens to strangle his wife, to a threat to leave the family home, unless she signs the mortgage document.

Presumed undue influence exists where the relationship between the principal debtor and the mortgagor is one of trust and confidence and the transaction is of such a nature that it is fair to presume that the principal debtor abused that relationship. The claimant is not required to establish that actual undue influence was exerted. Such confidential relationships may be established in two ways:

Class (A)

Certain relationships are treated as a matter of law as confidential *per se*, without a need to establish reliance on the judgment of the fiduciary. This category includes the following relationships: solicitor/client, medical advisor/patient, parent/child, priest/parishioner, etc. It is not surprising that mortgage cases within this category are rare.

Class (B)

The claimant (mortgagor) is required to prove the existence of a de facto relationship under which he or she reposed confidence and trust in the principal debtor.

In addition to a presumed fiduciary relationship (within category A or B), the claimant is required to establish that the transaction is to his or her 'manifest disadvantage'. For these purposes, it is enough that the mortgagor has been wrongly induced to enter a transaction that he or she would not otherwise have entered. Surprisingly, this principle is not applicable in cases of actual undue influence.

Moreover, the claimant is required to establish that the mortgagee is responsible for the undue influence exercised by the principal debtor. In the unusual case of the mortgagee directly exercising undue influence, this requirement may not cause a great deal of difficulty. In the normal course of events, the allegation that is frequently made is that a person, other than the mortgagee (e.g. the husband), has directly exercised undue influence and that the mortgagee is responsible for such impropriety. This may be established through either of the following:

(i) the agency principle, i.e. the principal debtor was acting as agent for the mortgagee to secure the signature of the mortgagor. Such cases are likely to be extremely rare for the principal debtor, more likely than not, will be acting on his own behalf in persuading the mortgagor to sign the document.

(ii) (a) Notice gained by the mortgagee that the principal debtor acted with impropriety in securing the mortgagor's signature, and (b) the mortgagee has taken no reasonable steps to ensure that the mortgagor was independently advised. 'Notice' in this context refers to actual or constructive knowledge on the part of the mortgagee. Very little needs to be said about actual notice, which is a subjective inquiry. Constructive notice refers to knowledge of facts which reasonable inquiries would have revealed. This is an objective standard.

In *O'Brien*, Lord Browne-Wilkinson explained this concept thus:

> A creditor is put on inquiry when a wife offers to stand surety for her husband's debts by the combination of two factors: (a) the transaction is on its face not to the financial advantage of the wife; and (b) there is a substantial risk in transactions of that kind that, in procuring the wife to act as surety, the husband has committed a legal or equitable wrong that entitles the wife to set aside the transaction.

Where the mortgage appears to be regular and for the joint benefit of the mortgagor and principal debtor, the mortgagee is unlikely to be saddled with notice of undue influence, see *CIBC v Pitt* (ante). In *Bank of Scotland v Bennett* [1999] 1 FLR 1115, the family income was created by the business and the loan appeared both reasonable and necessary for the business. In these circumstances the bank was not put on inquiry, see also *Leggatt v National Westminster Bank* [2000] All ER (D) 1458.

An issue that has attracted the attention of the courts is the extent of steps that the mortgagee is required to take in order to negate notice, which would otherwise be imputed to him. The action that the mortgagee is required to take is to ensure that independent legal advice is offered to the mortgagor. The latter is required to be informed as to the nature and extent of the liability undertaken. Where it appears probable that undue influence has taken place, the mortgagee may be required to insist that the mortgagor take independent legal advice. It appears that the advice has two functions. First it may rebut the presumption of undue influence. Secondly, the mortgagee may be freed from constructive notice,

In *O'Brien*, the House of Lords declared that the principles as stated above 'are applicable to cases where there is an emotional relationship between cohabitees'. The reason being 'the underlying risk of one cohabitee exploiting the emotional involvement and trust of the other'. However, in subsequent authorities, the principles have been applied to relationships where there was no cohabitation, but were based on trust and confidence. These cases include the following relationships:

(i) where a woman charged her house as surety for loans made to a close male friend, see *Banco Exterior Internacional S.A. v Thomas* [1997] 1 WLR 221;

(ii) where a junior employee mortgaged her house as security for her employer's indebtedness, see *Credit Lyonnais Bank Nederland N.V. v Burch* [1997] 1 All ER 144;

(iii) where a father charged his property to secure a loan to his son, see *UCB Bank Plc v Sharif* [1997] EGCS 52;

(iv) where a sister mortgaged her home to secure a loan for her brother, see *Northern Rock BS v Archer* (1998) 78 P & C.R. 65.

In *Royal Bank of Scotland v Etridge (No 2)* [2001] UKHL44, the House of Lords reviewed the law concerning undue influence. This decision built on the *O'Brien* and *Pitt* decisions. The categorisation of classes 2A and 2B are now thought to be unnecessary (see the opinions of Lords Hobhouse and Scott).

What is required for a case of presumed undue influence is:

- a relationship of trust and confidence between the parties;
- there must be something about the transaction in question which 'calls for an explanation', e.g. too large a sum of money to be accounted for on the basis of a relationship, charity, or other ordinary motives on which ordinary men act, per Lindley LJ *Allcard v Skinner* (1887) 36 Ch D 145.

Once these two requirements have been found the court will examine whether the presumption has been rebutted. It would be rebutted if it could be shown that the claimant had competent, independent legal advice before entering the transaction. Unlike the case of *Hammond v Osborn* [2002] EWCA Civ 885, where a 74-year-old man gave over 90% of his assets to Mrs Osborn, his 'carer'. It was decided that, although there was nothing sinister in the gift, this was not sufficient to answer the claim regarding undue influence.

Actual undue influence

In *Etridge* the Law Lords affirmed the distinction between actual and presumed undue influence. Equity will set aside an agreement obtained by improper pressure short of duress, such as a promise to pay money obtained by a threat to prosecute the promisor, see *Williams v Bayley* (1866) LR 1 HL 200. The burden of proving that the agreement was obtained by improper pressure lies on the party making the allegation. In *Pitt* (above), Mrs Pitt established that as against her husband she was entitled to set aside the mortgage on the jointly owned family home because of her husband's actual undue influence. However, she was not able to set aside the mortgage as against the claimant creditor. This was because Mr Pitt was not acting as the claimant's agent nor did the claimant have actual or constructive notice of the undue influence. It was a joint loan to the husband and wife to discharge an existing mortgage and to buy a holiday home. There was nothing to indicate to the claimant that this was anything other than a normal advance for their joint benefit.

Presumption of undue influence

Lord Browne-Wilkinson in *O'Brien* acknowledged that certain relationships were recognised by the law as raising the presumption of undue influence. It is then a question of fact whether the presumption can be rebutted. It is certain that cases under the old Class 2A undue influence exist in such relationships as:

- solicitor and client;
- doctor and patient;
- religious leader and disciple;
- parent and child.

Lord Nicholls in *Etridge* stated that in certain relationships the law presumes irrebuttably that one party had influence over the other. It was further confirmed that the relationship of husband and wife does not give rise to a presumption of undue influence. Where a wife alleges presumed undue influence, she would have to prove that a relationship of trust and confidence exists between the parties and that the transaction is one that is not explicable by ordinary motives of ordinary people.

The claimant is required to prove that the transaction was 'manifestly disadvantageous' to her. This phrase was coined by Lord Scarman in *National Westminster Bank plc v Morgan* [1985] AC 686. However, Lord Nicholls in *Etridge* observed that 'experience has . . . shown that this expression can give rise to misunderstanding' and has been 'causing difficulty'. Lord Nicholls in *Etridge* said:

> It would be absurd for the law to presume that every gift by a child to a parent, or every transaction between a client and his solicitor or between a patient and his doctor, was brought about by undue influence unless the contrary is affirmatively proved. Such a presumption would be too far-reaching. The law would be out of touch with everyday life if the presumption were to apply to every Christmas or birthday gift by a child to a parent, or to an agreement whereby a client or patient agrees to be responsible for the reasonable fees of his legal or medical adviser. The law would be rightly open to ridicule, for transactions such as these are unexceptionable. They do not suggest that something may be amiss. So something more is needed before the law reverses the burden of proof, something which calls for an explanation. When that something more is present, the greater the disadvantage to the vulnerable person, the more cogent must be the explanation before the presumption will be regarded as rebutted.

He returned to the test originally laid down by Lindley LJ's in *Allcard v Skinner* (1887) 36 Ch D 145, i.e. that the gift must have been so large that it cannot be accounted for on the basis of friendship, etc. In *Allcard*, the claimant gave all her property to a convent she had joined and as was expected when obeying the vow of poverty. When she left the convent she sought to recover certain items. The Court of Appeal held that although the claimant was under the undue influence of the lady superior, she had lost her right to avoid the transaction by delaying in instituting proceedings after leaving the convent.

Setting aside the transaction

In *Cheese v Thomas* [1994] 1 All ER 35, the Court of Appeal held that the basic objective of the court in setting aside a contract for undue influence was, so far as possible, to restore the parties to their original position. In this case the claimant had contributed £43,000 to the purchase of a house. The house had been purchased in 1990 at a cost of £83,000 and sold in 1993 for £55,400. The claimant sought to recover £43,000. The court held that in fairness the defendant, an innocent fiduciary, should not bear all the losses resulting from the fall in the property market. The transaction had not been the loan of a sum of money but a contribution to the purchase of property. Therefore, the claimant should not recover £43,000 from the defendant, but could recover the same proportion of the sale price as was his contribution to the original purchase price (i.e. 43/83rds of £55,400 = £28,701 approx.).

Although a transaction obtained by undue influence is voidable, as in a claim for misrepresentation, the right to rescind may be lost by affirmation (e.g. *Allcard v Skinner*), lapse of time, or where an innocent third party has acquired rights in the subject-matter of the contract.

However, third party rights may be defeated where the third party has constructive notice of the undue influence or the misrepresentation. In *Etridge* the House of Lords declared that a lender will always be put on inquiry if a person stands surety for another's debts if that surety is not offered as a commercial service (i.e. the wife or other is not being paid to act as surety). It is the nature of the transaction which puts the lender on notice, so this would apply to unmarried couples of different or the same sex. Once the lender is put on notice he is given practical advice to avoid tainting the transaction. Lord Nicholls gave clear guidelines for the effective protection of wives such as seeking reliable, independent legal advice before deciding to act as guarantors of their husband's debts.

The primary remedy for undue influence is to have the contract set aside and, where appropriate, for the defendant to account for any profits. Other cases have considered the position of 'surety wives'. In *National Westminster Bank plc v Leggatt* [2001] 1 FLR 563 (2000) *The Times*, November 16 CA, a wife, had signed as surety for 1972 and 1976 charges over the family home that were not vulnerable to attack under *O'Brien* (above). Later, however, she signed as surety for a 1990 recharge that replaced the two previous charges. In all cases, the charges were to support borrowings of her husband's business, a partnership. In respect of the 1990 charge, the wife was advised by an independent solicitor but there were mistakes in the bank's instructions to that solicitor. They referred to the fund as 'to be advanced', whereas some of the funds had already been advanced. In addition, the instructions stated that the bank had been offered the guarantee by the wife. In fact, the bank had insisted upon it. The wife claimed that these inaccuracies disabled the bank from defending itself from her claim that it had constructive notice of the undue influence of her husband which she alleged persuaded her to sign the further 1990 charge. The Court of Appeal held that the inaccuracies were not material and that the wife had not been able to show a manifest disadvantage caused by the 1990 charge. When signing it, she must have known that, if she did not sign it, the bank could claim against her on the basis of her signing as surety for the two previous charges that the 1990 charge was to replace. Effectively, the wife's position had not been altered, merely updated.

In *Barclays Bank plc v Coleman* [2000] 1 All ER 385, the Court of Appeal considered the nature of the requirement that a party to a 'Class 2B' relationship who claims undue influence must, in order to raise a presumption of undue influence, show the manifest disadvantage of the transaction, all of which is subject to *Etridge*, but a second issue concerned the nature of 'independent legal advice'; whether the bank could rely upon a certificate prepared and signed by a legal executive to the effect that the surety wife had voluntarily signed a charge over the matrimonial home. Mr Coleman obtained a loan from the bank to purchase a property for investment purposes. The loan was secured by a legal 'all monies' charge over the jointly owned matrimonial home. Mrs Coleman and Mr Coleman executed the charge together at a solicitor's office that was local to them and where they were attended by a legal executive, who prepared and attested to a certificate stating that Mrs Coleman had voluntarily signed the legal charge after having it explained to her by him and having understood it. The husband returned the charge and the certificate to the bank. Subsequently, he defaulted on the loan, the bank sought to enforce its charge over the matrimonial home, and Mrs Coleman claimed that her consent to the charge was the product of her husband's undue influence of which the bank had constructive notice. The county court held that, although the bank was not entitled to rely upon the legal executive's certificate, Mrs Coleman's claim failed because the transaction was not manifestly disadvantageous to her. The Court of Appeal reversed both grounds. The Court of Appeal noted that the authorities were in an unsatisfactory state and that requirement of manifest disadvantage originated in an unusual case involving a banker and customer (*National Westminster Bank v Morgan*), not a husband and wife. Nonetheless, the court was bound to hold that manifest disadvantage was a necessary ingredient of the presumption of undue influence. It was incumbent on a party to the transaction to show that it is manifestly disadvantageous before he can invoke the presumption. The court was less concerned with the fact that the certificate was attested by a legal executive rather than by a solicitor. What was required was legal advice independent of the mortgagee. Provided that the legal advice of a legal executive is given with the authority of the principal, there is a proper delegation, and the advice is sufficient. The court did not, perhaps surprisingly, discuss the fact that Mr and Mrs Coleman attended the meeting with the solicitor 'together'.

Question
To what extent have the courts clarified the law regarding undue influence?

BARS TO RESCISSION

The courts have implemented a number of principles that have the effect of restricting a claim for rescission. These are referred to as 'bars' to rescission. They are:

(1) Where the property has come into the hands of an innocent third party who is a bona fide purchaser for value without notice, see *Lewis v Avery* [1971] 3 All ER 90. Where the third party is a volunteer, the right to rescind will not usually be affected though the court may use its power to award damages in lieu of rescission.

(2) Rescission will not be granted where *restitutio in integrum* is impossible. This follows as a matter of course because as was stated earlier the effect of rescission is to put the parties in the position they were before the breach of contract, see *Erlanger v New Sombrero Phosphate Co* [1878] 3 App Cas 1218.

(3) As with other equitable remedies, rescission will not be granted where the claimant does not come to court with 'clean hands' or where he has unreasonably delayed in bringing the claim or has shown signs of acquiescence once he became aware of the true state of affairs. In *Leaf v International Galleries* [1950] 2 KB 86, the defendants sold the claimants a painting allegedly by Constable. Five years later, the claimant was told that it was not a Constable painting and sought rescission of the contract. The Court of Appeal held that since five years had elapsed during which time he had made no attempt to check the authenticity of the painting the claimant was no longer entitled to rescission.

> **Jenkins J:** Clearly if, before he had taken delivery of the picture, he had obtained other advice and come to the conclusion that the picture was not a Constable, it would have been open to him to rescind. It may be that if, having taken delivery of the picture on the faith of the representation and having taken it home, he had, within a reasonable time, taken other advice and satisfied himself that it was not a Constable, he might have been able to make good his claim to rescission notwithstanding the delivery . . . What in fact happened was that he took delivery of the picture, kept it for some five years, and took no steps to obtain any further evidence as to its authorship; and that, finally, when he was minded to sell the picture at the end of a matter of five years, the untruth of the representation was brought to light.
>
> In those circumstances, it seems to me to be quite out of the question that a court of equity should grant relief by way of rescission.

(4) The right to rescind will be lost if the party seeking rescission has already affirmed the contract, see *Scholey v Central Railway Co of Venezeula* [1868] LR 9 Eq 266.

FURTHER READING

Birks, P, 'The travails of duress' [1990] LMCLQ 342.
Cleaver, K and Twomey, M, 'Damages in lieu of rescission' (1996) 140 SJ 772.
Dobbs, D, 'The risk of mistake in contract' (2002) 152 NLJ 1654.
Giglio, F, 'A systematic approach to "unjust" and "unjustified" enrichment' (2003) 23 OJLS 455.
Hansell, M, 'Under the influence' (2005) 155 NLJ 1579.
Levy, J, 'Under duress' (2006) 156 NLJ 936.
O'Sullivan, D, 'Developing O'Brien' (2002) 118 LQR 337.
Pawlowski, M, 'Late completion: equitable relief' (1997) 141 SJ 774.

Smith, S, 'Contracting under pressure: a theory of duress' [1997] CLJ 343.

Swadling, W, 'Rescission, property and the common law' (2005) 121 LQR 123.

Thompson, M, 'Wives, sureties and banks' [2002] Conv and Property Lawyer 174.

Withers, B, 'Property: Remedies – errors and omissions' (2004) 2 EMIS Property Service Issue 3, p 3.

Vann, V, 'Equitable compensation when rescission is impossible – a response' (2003) 17 TLI 66.

INTRODUCTION

Account is a remedy that enables the claimant to investigate the amount of funds owed to him by the defendant. A similar remedy was available at common law but the common law procedure was quite lengthy and cumbersome and became obsolete, so eventually the equitable remedy prevailed.

By the early nineteenth century equitable account was commonly used to assist in the enforcement of legal rights, as between principal and agent, (see *Beaumont v Boultbee* (1802) 7 Ves 599) or where matters were too complex for the common law to investigate (*Taff Railway Co v Nixon* (1847) 1 HLC 111). Equity allowed a claimant to annex a claim to account to a claim for an injunction and this facility proved extremely useful, especially in cases that involved infringements of patents or trademarks.

Equitable account was also used to assist the enforcement of equitable rights, as where there existed a fiduciary relationship between the parties and the fiduciary profited from his position, see *Regal (Hastings) Ltd v Gulliver* [1967] AC 134. The equitable remedy was also available where one co-owner of property had profited from the property more than the other owners, see *Strelly v Winson* (1684) 1 Vern 297.

In *London, Chatham and Dover Railway Co v South Eastern Railway Co* [1892] 1 Ch 120, Lindley LJ provided a summary of the jurisdiction of the court of equity to order an account, thus:

> **Lindley LJ:** Before the Judicature Acts a suit for an account could be maintained in equity in the following cases – (1) Where the plaintiff had a legal right to have money payable to him ascertained and paid, but which right, owing to defective legal machinery, he could not practically enforce at law. Suits for an account between principal and agent and between partners are familiar instances of this class of case. (2) Where the plaintiff would have had a legal right to have money ascertained and paid to him by the defendant if the defendant had not wrongfully prevented such right from accruing to the plaintiff. In such a case a Court of Law could only give unliquidated damages for the defendant's wrongful act: and there was often no machinery for satisfactorily ascertaining what would have been due and payable if the defendant had acted properly. In such a case, however, a Court of Equity decreed an account, ascertained what would have been payable if the defendant had acted as he ought to have done and ordered him to pay the amount . . . (3) Where the plaintiff had no legal but only equitable rights against the defendant, and where an account was necessary to give effect to those equitable rights. Ordinary suits by *cestui que trust* against their trustees and suits for equitable waste fell within this class. (4) Combination of the above cases.

ACCOUNT ON THE BASIS OF WILFUL DEFAULT

There are two possible bases for an action for account:

(a) Common account, where the claim is for money actually received by the defendant.

(b) Account on the basis of wilful default, where the claimant may claim not only what the defendant received but also what he would have received but for his wilful default, *Re Tebbs* [1976] 2 All ER 858. An account on the basis of wilful default is available where the defendant is in legal or physical possession of property and the claimant has an equitable interest therein, as where there is a trust or where there is the relationship of mortgagor and mortgagee. In the latter case, account on the basis of wilful default is always possible. In other cases the claimant must prove one example of wilful default by the defendant, *Job v Job* (1877) 6 Ch D 562.

DEFENCES TO AN ACTION FOR ACCOUNT

(1) Lapse of time: Section 23 of the Limitation Act 1980 provides that an action for account cannot be brought after the expiration of any time limit under the Act which bars the claim that forms the basis of the action. Thus, an action for account owing to the wilful default of the trustee is required to be brought within six years from the date of the breach of trust. In equity it may, however, be possible to reopen accounts unless the claimant's delay would make this inequitable.

(2) Agreement by the parties: 'Settled accounts' and 'accounts stated'. Where the parties have both agreed to a written statement of accounts this will normally be final. Before this allegation may be pleaded as a defence, there is required to be an agreement for valuable consideration between the parties stating what one owes to the other. There must be 'mutuality' and the settlement must deal with all matters between the parties. The equitable defence of 'settled accounts' has now apparently been merged with the common law plea of 'accounts stated' and both rest on a very similar principle. In both cases the defence will be defeated by evidence of fraud, and in equity the claimant would be allowed to 'surcharge on falsify' if he could show that items had been omitted or wrongly included. The effect of the liberty to surcharge and falsify is to leave the account in full force as a settled account except in so far as it can be impugned by the claimant by proving errors or mistakes.

FURTHER READING

Watterson, S, 'An account of profits or damages? The history of orthodoxy' (2004) 24 OJLS 471.

INDEX